Foreign Relations
of the
United States
1947

Volume VIII

The American Republics

United States
Government Printing Office
Washington : 1972

DEPARTMENT OF STATE PUBLICATION 8587

HISTORICAL OFFICE
BUREAU OF PUBLIC AFFAIRS

For sale by the
Superintendent of Documents, U.S. Government Printing Office
Washington, D.C. 20402 - Price $5.75 (Buckram)
Stock Number 4400-1408

PREFACE

This volume was prepared under the direct supervision of S. Everett Gleason, Chief of the Foreign Relations Division, assisted by Fredrick Aandahl and David H. Stauffer.

The documentation on United States relations with the republics of the South American continent and Panama was compiled by former staff member Almon R. Wright.

Documentation on United States relations with the Central American republics and those of the Caribbean area was compiled by former staff member Velma Hastings Cassidy.

The compilations on United States policy with respect to inter-American regional problems were the work of both Mr. Wright and Mrs. Cassidy.

The Publishing and Reproduction Services Division (Jerome H. Perlmutter, Chief) was responsible for the technical editing of this volume.

William M. Franklin
Director, Historical Office,
Bureau of Public Affairs

July 15, 1971

Principles for the Compilation and Editing of
"Foreign Relations"

The principles which guide the compilation and editing of *Foreign Relations* are stated in Department of State Regulation 2 FAM 1350 of June 15, 1961, a revision of the order approved on March 26, 1925, by Mr. Frank B. Kellogg, then Secretary of State. The text of the regulation, as further amended, is printed below:

1350 Documentary Record of American Diplomacy

1351 *Scope of Documentation*

The publication *Foreign Relations of the United States* constitutes the official record of the foreign policy of the United States. These volumes include, subject to necessary security considerations, all documents needed to give a comprehensive record of the major foreign policy decisions within the range of the Department of State's responsibilities, together with appropriate materials concerning the facts which contributed to the formulation of policies. When further material is needed to supplement the documentation in the Department's files for a proper understanding of the relevant policies of the United States, such papers should be obtained from other Government agencies.

1352 *Editorial Preparation*

The basic documentary diplomatic record to be printed in *Foreign Relations of the United States* is edited by the Historical Office, Bureau of Public Affairs of the Department of State. The editing of the record is guided by the principles of historical objectivity. There may be no alteration of the text, no deletions without indicating where in the text the deletion is made, and no omission of facts which were of major importance in reaching a decision. Nothing may be omitted for the purpose of concealing or glossing over what might be regarded by some as a defect of policy. However, certain omissions of documents are permissible for the following reasons:

   a. To avoid publication of matters which would tend to impede current diplomatic negotiations or other business.
   b. To condense the record and avoid repetition of needless details.
   c. To preserve the confidence reposed in the Department by individuals and by foreign governments.
   d. To avoid giving needless offense to other nationalities or individuals.
   e. To eliminate personal opinions presented in despatches and not acted upon by the Department. To this consideration there is one qualification—in connection with major decisions it is desirable, where possible, to show the alternatives presented to the Department before the decision was made.

1353 *Clearance*

To obtain appropriate clearances of material to be published in *Foreign Relations of the United States*, the Historical Office:

   a. Refers to the appropriate policy offices of the Department and of other agencies of the Government such papers as appear to require policy clearance.
   b. Refers to the appropriate foreign governments requests for permission to print as part of the diplomatic correspondence of the United States those previously unpublished documents which were originated by the foreign governments.

CONTENTS

	Page
Preface	III
List of Abbreviations and Symbols	IX

General:

The Inter-American Conference for the maintenance of continental peace and security held at Rio de Janeiro, August 15–September 2, 1947	1
Preliminary discussions concerning the Ninth International Conference of American States to meet in Bogotá	94
The Emergency Advisory Committee for Political Defense	95
United States policy with respect to the provision of military assistance and armaments to the other American Republics	101
Position of the United States with respect to the sale of arms by Brazil to the Dominican Republic	131
Cooperation of the United States with other governments in the construction of the Inter-American Highway and Rama Road	145
The Inter-American coffee agreement	155
Boundary dispute: Ecuador and Peru	162

Argentina:

United States interest in the political situation in Argentina: efforts to extirpate Nazi influences	163
Policy of the United States with respect to the provision of arms to Argentina	215
Problems of air transit between the United States and Argentina	238
Discrimination by Argentina against American and other foreign shipping and trade	251
Concern of the United States with the petroleum problems of Argentina and the American petroleum companies	278
Efforts of the United States to make Argentine grains available to countries in need	304
Position of the United States with respect to the opposition press in Argentina	317

Bolivia:

Problems involved in the procurement of Bolivian tin by the United States	326
Financial and technical aid by the United States for the economic development of Bolivia	342
Negotiations for an air transport agreement between the United States and Bolivia	363
Continuing efforts to eliminate Axis economic interests in Bolivia	378
Efforts to liquidate the lend-lease account with Bolivia	384

CONTENTS

Brazil:
	Page
The position of the United States with respect to the breach in relations between Brazil and the Soviet Union	391
Questions concerning the disposal of United States military equipment to Brazil under the lend-lease and surplus property arrangements	406
Discussions with Brazil concerning trade and shipping questions	421
Efforts of the United States to provide financial assistance for Brazilian economic development	441
The United States interest in proposed Brazilian legislation on petroleum and in current requirements	458
The response of the United States to the Brazilian requests for wheat	467
Problems in the liquidation of the rubber development corporation	480
Interest of the United States in Brazilian problems involving former enemy property and persons	486

Chile:
Attitude of the United States toward labor violence in Chile and the ensuing breach of relations between Chile and the Soviet Union, Czechoslovakia, and Yugoslavia	497
United States policy in providing arms to Chile	518
Position of the United States on the provision of economic assistance to Chile	527
Chile's reluctance to enter into an agreement with the United States regarding trade	549

Colombia:
Discriminatory treatment of American shipping interests by Colombia	554
Agreement between the United States and Colombia respecting a civil aviation mission	569
Discussions concerning Colombia's debt and need for capital	570

Costa Rica:
United States policy of nonintervention in the internal affairs of Costa Rica	578
Financial and military assistance by the United States to Costa Rica	591
United States interest in Costa Rican fisheries legislation	598

Cuba:
Efforts to settle outstanding problems between the United States and Cuba	604
Agreement between the United States and Cuba amending and extending the agreement of July 17 and August 2, 1944, respecting a cooperative program for weather stations in Cuba	628

Dominican Republic:
United States policy of nonintervention in Dominican political affairs	629
Termination of United States-Dominican Customs Convention of 1940	663

CONTENTS

ECUADOR:

	Page
The question of recognizing the Mancheno, the Suarez, and the Arosemena regimes in Ecuador	664
United States military assistance to Ecuador; the Galápagos bases	676
Financing Ecuadoran highway development and other economic proposals	690

EL SALVADOR:

Agreement between the United States and El Salvador respecting a military aviation mission	699
Agreement between the United States and El Salvador for the one-year renewal of the agreement of May 21, 1943, providing for the detail of an officer of the United States Army to serve as director of the Military School and of the Military Academy of El Salvador	699

GUATEMALA:

Agreement between the United States and Guatemala respecting United States armed forces in Guatemala	700
Settlement of the remaining obligation of the United States under its mutual aid agreement with Guatemala	700
United States concern over provisions of new Guatemalan labor code appearing to discriminate against American companies	705

HAITI:

United States efforts to assist Haiti in solving financial and other problems	720

HONDURAS:

The question of military cooperation with the Honduran regime	738
Agreement between the United States and Honduras respecting a cooperative health and sanitation program in Honduras, further amending and extending the agreement of May 8, 1942	745

MEXICO:

Discussions of the problem of lend-lease obligations of Mexico to the United States	746
Breakdown of United States-Mexican negotiations on a proposed bilateral air transport agreement	751
Export-Import Bank loans to Mexico for purchase of United States equipment, materials and services for public works and industrialization projects	764
Discussions between the United States and Mexico regarding Mexican import restrictions and trade agreement revision	772
United States policy regarding the participation of foreign oil companies in the Mexican oil industry	787
Conflicts in United States-Mexican fisheries relations and exchange of views on a proposed fisheries treaty	802
Joint United States-Mexican campaign against foot-and-mouth disease	811
Arrangements by the United States and Mexico regarding temporary migration of agricultural and other workers into the United States	823
United States efforts to eliminate illicit traffic in narcotic drugs between Mexico and the United States	836

Nicaragua:

Political upheaval in Nicaragua: United States policies of nonintervention and nonrecognition 841

Panama:

Rejection by the Panamanian assembly of the defense sites agreement . . 881
Discussions of alleged discriminatory treatment of certain labor classes in the Canal Zone 948
The regulation of radio communications in Panama and the Canal Zone . 967

Paraguay:

The position of the United States toward the insurrection in Paraguay . 972
Air transport agreement between the United States and Paraguay . . . 997
Agreement between the United States and Paraguay on reciprocal trade 997
Agreement between the United States and Paraguay renewing the agreement of December 10, 1943, providing for a military mission from the United States to Paraguay 997
Agreement between the United States and Paraguay renewing the agreement of October 27, 1943, which constituted the United States military aviation mission to Paraguay 997

Peru:

Conversations concerning a Peruvian debt settlement and Peru's need for loans 998
Conflict between Peruvian trade regulations and the United States–Peru trade agreement 1015
Efforts of the United States to meet Peruvian food requirements . . . 1031

Uruguay:

The position of the United States with respect to Uruguay's defense needs and the lend-lease account 1045
The end of the campaign against Axis influence in Uruguay 1051

Venezuela:

The position of the United States with respect to revolutionary activity in Venezuela 1054

Index 1065

LIST OF ABBREVIATIONS AND SYMBOLS

EDITOR'S NOTE.—This list does not include standard abbreviations in common usage; unusual abbreviations of rare occurrence which are clarified at appropriate points; and those abbreviations and contractions which, although uncommon, are understandable from the context.

A–A, Assistant Secretary of State: Acheson
A–A, Assistant Secretary of State for Political Affairs: Armour
A–Br, Assistant Secretary of State for American Republic Affairs: Braden
ABWEHR, Foreign Intelligence Service of the High Command of the German Armed Forces
ACEDE, Administrative Commission for Economic Defense (in Brazil)
ActSecy, Acting Secretary
AD, *Acción Democrática* (Democratic Action Party in Venezuela)
AFTOSA Commission, Mexican-United States Commission for the Eradication of Foot and Mouth Disease
Agri, Dept. of Agriculture
A–H, Assistant Secretary of State for Occupied Areas: Hilldring
a.i. ad interim
Amb, Ambassador
ammo, ammunition
AmReps, American Republics
AP, Associated Press
ARA, Office of American Republic Affairs
Arg, Argentina
AT, Assistant Secretary of State for Economic Affairs, Thorpe
AT–6, transport plane
AT–11, light transport plane
AV, Aviation Division
AWS, Air Warning Station
B, Balboas
B–17, Flying Fortress
B–25, horizontal bomber
BA, Buenos Aires
BA, Division of Brazilian Affairs, Department of State
BBC, British Broadcasting Corporation
BC, Division of British Commonwealth Affairs
BCB, Banco de Credito da Borracha
BDC, Bolivian Development Corporation
BDC, British Disposals Commission
Bol, Bolivia
Braz, Brazil
Brit, British
C–47, transport plane
CAA, Civil Aeronautics Administration
CAB, Civil Aeronautics Board, Dept. of Commerce
CBF, *Corporación Boliviano Fomento*
CCC, Commodity Credit Corporation
CDC, Caribbean Defense Command
Chil, Chilean
ChilGov, Chilean Government
Cia, *compañia*
C.i.f., Commission, Insurance, Freight
CIO, Congress of Industrial Organizations
CMA, Mexican air carrier (*Compañia Mexicana de Aviación*)
Col, Colombia
ComGenCarib, Commanding General, Caribbean Defense Command
Conf, Conference
conf, confidential
Cong, Congress
COPEI, *Comite de Organizatión Politica Electoral Independiente* of Venezuela
Cos, companies
CP, Division of Commercial Policy
CPA, Division of Central America and Panama Affairs

IX

LIST OF ABBREVIATIONS AND SYMBOLS

CPD, Committee for Political Defense
CPH, Communist Party of Haiti
Cr, cruzeiros
CRB, Division of Caribbean Affairs
CSGID, CSAF, US War Department, transmission code symbols
CTC, Confederación de Trabajadores de Colombia
CTCh, Confederación de Trabajadores de Chile
DE, destroyer escort
DelSec, Delegation Secretariat
Depcirins, Department circular instruction
Depcirtel, Department circular telegram
Depgam, Department airgram
Deptel, Department telegram
Des, despatch
DNC, National Coffee Department of Brazil
ECOSOC, Economic and Social Council of the United Nations
ED, Division of Investment and Economic Development
Emb, Embassy
Embdesp, Embassy despatch
Embtel, Embassy telegram
EO, Executive Order
ERP, European Recovery Program
ES, Division of Economic Security
EUR, Office of European Affairs
Eximbank, Export-Import Bank of Washington
FAMA, *Flota Aérea Mercante Argentina* (Argentine Mercantile Air Fleet, joint governmental and private company)
FAO, Food and Agricultural Organization
fas, free along side ship
FBI, Federal Bureau of Investigation
FBO, Division of Foreign Buildings Operations
FBPC, Foreign Bondholders Protective Council
FE, Office of Far Eastern Affairs
FLC, Foreign Liquidation Commissioner
Fld Comm, Field Commissioner, Foreign Liquidation Commissioner's Office

FN, Division of Financial Affairs
FonMin, Foreign Minister
FonOff, Foreign Office
ForOffs, Foreign Offices
FPL, Guatemalan political party (*Frente Popular Libertador*)
FRITO, From International Trade Organization
GAO, General Accounting Office, United States Government
GA, Division of German and Austrian Economic Affairs
GATT, General Agreement on Tariffs and Trade
GA UN, General Assembly, United Nations
Gov Bd PAU, Governing Board of the Pan American Union
HQ, Headquarters
IA, Division of Special Inter-American Affairs
IARA, Inter-Allied Reparation Agency
ICAO, International Civil Aviation Organization
IEF, *see* **IEFC**
IEFC, Internal Emergency Food Council
IIAA, Institute of Inter-American Affairs
ILO, International Labor Office
info, information
IR, International Resources Division
IS, Division of International Security Affairs
ITO, International Trade Organization, United Nations
I T & T, International Telephone and Telegraph Corporation
JBUSDC, Joint Brazil-US Defense Commission
JBUSMC, Joint Brazil-US Military Commission
JCS, Joint Chiefs of Staff
LA, Latin America
LAB, *Lloyd Aéreo Boliviano*
LAMSA, Mexican air carrier (*Lineas Aéreas Mexicanas*)
LCI, landing craft; infantry
LCT, landing craft; tank
LCVP, landing craft; vehicles, personnel
Le, Legal Adviser

LIST OF ABBREVIATIONS AND SYMBOLS

LL, Lend Lease
LP, Division of Lend Lease and Surplus War Property Affairs
LST, landing ship; tank
LT, long ton
MA, Division of Mexican Affairs
Marit Comm, Maritime Commission
MD, Munitions Division
Mex, Inter-American Conference at Mexico City, 1945
Min, Ministry
mitel, my telegram
ML, Naval vessel; launch
MOS, Ministry of Supply of the United Kingdom
mytel, my telegram
mygam, my airgram
NAC, National Advisory Council
NEA, Office of Near Eastern and African Affairs
NSDAP, *National Sozialistische Deutsche Arbeiter Partei*
NWC, Division of North and West Coast Affairs
OA, Division of International Organization Affairs
OA or PBY, Navy patrol-bomber
OFD, Office of Financial and Development Policy
OFLC, Office of the Foreign Liquidation Commissioner
OIT, Office of International Trade
OMA, Office of Mutual Aid of Belgium
ONI, Office of Naval Intelligence
OPA, Office of Price Administration
ourtel, our telegram
P-38, pursuit plane
PAA, Pan American Airways
Panagra, Pan American Grace Airways
Pan Am, Pan American
PanAir, Pan American Airways
Par, Paraguayan, Paraguay
PAR, Guatemalan political party (*Partido Acción Revolucionaria*)
Para, Paraguay
Parag, Paraguay
PAU, Pan American Union
PCA, Policy Committee on Arms and Armaments
PED, Petroleum Division

PEMEX, Mexican Government agency responsible for management of the Mexican petroleum industry (*Petroleos Mexicanos*)
PICAO, Provisional International Civil Aviation Organization
PR, Public Resolution
PRA, Public Roads Administration, Federal Works Agency
Pres, President
PRN, National Republican Party (Costa Rica)
PSP, Popular Socialist Party (Haiti)
PT, trainer plane
PT-, motor torpedo boat
PUN, National Union Party (Costa Rica)
RDC, Rubber Development Corporation
reDeptel, regarding Department telegram
reEmbdesp, regarding Embassy despatch
reEmbgram, regarding Embassy airgram
reEmbtel, regarding Embassy telegram
refEmtel, reference, Embassy telegram
remytel, regarding my telegram
res, resolution
re tel, regarding telegram
reurlet, regarding your letter
reurtel, regarding your telegram
RFC, Reconstruction Finance Corporation
RPA, Division of River Plate Affairs
SA, South America
SD, Shipping Division of the Department of State
SD, *Sicherheitsdienst* (Security Service of the National Socialist Elite Guard in Germany)
SHADA, Haitian-American Society for Agricultural Development (*Société Haitiano-Américaine de Développement Agricole*)
SPA, Office of Special Political Affairs
SOP, Standard Operating Procedure
S/S-PR, Protocol Staff
SWNCC, State–War–Navy Coordinating Committee

TACA, Central American Air Transport Company (*Transportes Aéreos Centroamericanos, S.A.*)
U, Under Secretary of State
UE, Under Secretary of State for Economic Affairs
UK, United Kingdom
UN, United Nations
UNGA, United Nations General Assembly
UP, United Press
ur, your
URD, *Union Republicana Democratica* of Venezuela
urinfo, your information
urtel, your telegram
USDA, United States Department of Agriculture
USDel, United States Delegation
U.S.S.R., Union of Soviet Socialist Republics
V-E Day, Allied victory in Europe
Ven, Venezuela
YNG, gate vessel
YPF, *Yacimientos Petroliferos Fiscale* of Argentina
YPFB, *Yacimientos Petroliferos Fiscales Bolivianos* (Bolivian Petroleum Company, a government monopoly)

THE INTER-AMERICAN CONFERENCE FOR THE MAINTENANCE OF CONTINENTAL PEACE AND SECURITY, HELD AT RIO DE JANEIRO, AUGUST 15–SEPTEMBER 2, 1947 [1]

I. PREPARATIONS

710 Consultation 4/5–2947

The Assistant Secretary of State for American Republic Affairs (Braden) to the Under Secretary of State (Acheson)

SECRET [WASHINGTON,] May 29, 1947.

Subject: Status of Preparations on Substantive Matters for Rio Conference.

. . . .

Three main subjects have been considered in connection with the Rio Conference: the text of a treaty based upon the Act of Chapultepec;[2] a resolution establishing a permanent inter-American military agency; and the question of a possible treaty of pacific settlement. The status of work is indicated below with respect to each of these items.

Text of Treaty

The United States draft for the proposed treaty of Rio was approved by the President and by the Congressional leaders at the end of 1945 and was distributed to the other American governments, except Argentina, on December 21, 1945. A copy of this draft is attached.[3]

In addition to the United States, the following governments also have submitted draft texts for the treaty: Bolivia, Brazil, Chile, Ecuador, Mexico, Panama and Uruguay. All texts, including the United States draft, were analyzed by a committee of the Governing Board of the Pan American Union in which the United States representative took a leading part. A copy of the report issued by the Governing Board of the Union containing the analysis of main problems pre-

---

[1] For documentation on discussions concerning the proposed Conference, see *Foreign Relations*, 1946, vol. XI, p. 1 ff. For a narrative account of the Conference, its resolutions, and the final Conference documents, see Department of State, *Inter-American Conference for the Maintenance of Continental Peace and Security, Quitandinha, Brazil, August 15–September 2, 1947: Report of the Delegation of the United States of America* (Washington, Government Printing Office, 1948).

[2] Approved March 8, 1945, at Mexico City; for text, see Department of State, Treaties and Other International Acts Series No. 1543, or 60 Stat. (pt. 2) 1831.

[3] Enclosures mentioned in this document not printed.

sented by the various drafts, and the text of all drafts, is also attached.

The working group in the Department has started to make comments on every provision of every draft with a view to determining exactly how much language the United States might accept from the drafts of other countries, but this work has not been completed.

The main problems in concluding the treaty may be expected to arise in connection with the following: (1) Obtaining a firm commitment from all countries (as provided for in the United States draft) to "assist" any American republic on which an armed attack is made. The Act of Chapultepec, and practically all of the Latin American draft treaties, contain the legal obligation merely to "consult" in case of such an attack, although a moral commitment to assist is implied. (The troublesome problem created by attempts to define "armed attack" and "act of aggression" may be anticipated.) (2) Providing adequately for steps to be taken in connection with acts of aggression other than armed attack. (It is believed that the United States draft treaty should be reviewed in this respect.) (3) Specifying satisfactory procedures for reaching majority decisions in the consultations called for under the treaty that will not bind the United States without its consent. (4) Concluding provisions which will adequately cover acts or threats of aggression executed through subversive activities, but which will not take the form of an alliance directed against the Soviet Union nor provide grounds for repression of democratic political opposition by dictatorial governments. (5) Insuring concordance of the treaty with the spirit and letter of the Charter of the United Nations.[4]

Military Agency

Some representatives of the War Department wished to have the draft treaty include provisions for the establishment of an Inter-American Military Staff Organization and for granting of military rights, facilities, etc. whenever military enforcement action was necessary. It was finally decided, however, not to include such matters in the treaty but to cover the establishment of a military agency in a separate resolution.

General agreement on a working level was reached with the War and Navy Departments on a draft resolution for the establishment of an inter-American military agency, but this document never received the approval of the respective Secretaries, nor was it discussed with the Congressional leaders. A copy of this draft resolution is attached.[5]

---

[4] Treaties and Other International Acts Series No. 993, or 59 Stat. (pt. 2) 1031.
[5] Not printed. In letters to the Secretary of War and the Secretary of the Navy, July 21, 1947, the Secretary of State indicated that the three Departments were in agreement that the United States should favor the creation of an Inter-American military agency but that discussions toward that end should be carried on not at Rio de Janeiro but at the forthcoming conference at Bogotá. (710 Consultation 4/7–1747)

In the meantime, the Inter-American Defense Board has also produced a draft resolution for the establishment of an inter-American military council which follows in general, but differs in detail from, the paper drafted in the three Departments.

The Resolution will therefore have to be reviewed by the three Departments and be finally approved as representative of the United States position on this subject.

. . . .

Pacific Settlement Procedures

There is some question whether the subject of pacific settlement of inter-American disputes should be taken up at the Rio Conference. The Mexico City Conference suggested an Inter-American Conference of Jurists be called to conclude a consolidated treaty of pacific settlement procedures,[6] and a draft treaty has already been prepared by the Inter-American Juridical Committee. However, some Latin American countries, notably Mexico, have recommended, in their draft treaties for Rio de Janeiro, provisions for pacific settlement of disputes. The Department was considering a year ago, when work on the Rio Conference ceased, whether or not to recommend that the Rio Conference undertake the conclusion of a treaty of pacific settlement as a companion document to the treaty based on the Act of Chapultepec. No final decision on this point was reached, although the Brazilian Government had indicated it was not favorable to such an idea. It will therefore have to be decided whether the United States will press for such a treaty at Rio, bearing in mind such factors as: (*a*) the desirability of complementing the military assistance treaty with a treaty for pacific settlement which is in the tradition of inter-American efforts to prevent war, and mitigating such undesirable psychological reactions as the exclusive emphasis on a military assistance treaty might produce; (*b*) the attitude of other participating states as to whether a peaceful settlement treaty should be concluded at Rio de Janeiro or at another conference; and (*c*) the time available for perfecting a draft treaty, already under consideration, to make it satisfactory to the United States.

General

In addition to the decisions called for above, and the necessity for reviewing and giving final approval to the actual draft documents to be presented to the Conference, there remains the task of preparing more detailed instructions for the American delegation outlining the policies and decisions expressed in the draft treaty and resolution.

SPRUILLE BRADEN

---

[6] For resolutions of the Conference, see Pan American Union, *Final Act of the Inter-American Conference on Problems of War and Peace, Mexico City, February–March, 1945* (Washington, 1945).

710 Consultation 4/6–2047

Memorandum of Conversation, by the Chief of the Division of Brazilian Affairs (Allan Dawson)

CONFIDENTIAL [WASHINGTON,] June 20, 1947.

Participants: Mr. Carlos Martins, Ambassador of Brazil
A–Br—Mr. Braden
ARA—Mr. Briggs [7]
BA—Mr. Dawson

The Brazilian Ambassador called and left a memorandum of which the following is a translation:

"The Brazilian Government has taken cognizance of the fact that the American Government insists on prior agreement on the principles of the treaty which is the object of the Rio de Janeiro Conference and consequently prefers the date of October for the calling of the Conference.

"In this regard the Brazilian Government desires to point out that there is no guarantee whatever that the date of October would not interfere with the General Assembly of the United Nations, which is to meet on September 15 with a very heavy agenda and presumably a duration of more than six weeks.

"The Brazilian Government considers more advisable that the Rio de Janeiro Conference be convened at the end of November.

"The Brazilian Government is of the opinion that whatever the time for prior consultation any agreement through separate consultations on the eight drafts or proposals now in existence is impossible.

"The Brazilian Government therefore suggests that the agreement in question be attempted through the delegates to the Pan American Union as the sole means of eliminating fundamental differences."

The Ambassador then stated that he had just come from the White House where he had extended an invitation to President Truman from President Dutra to visit Brazil. He said that the President indicated that he would be glad to accept the invitation and that he hoped to make his trip at the time of the Rio de Janeiro Conference, mentioning the possibility of making the voyage on the USS *Missouri*.

Mr. Martins pointed out that these developments made the November date most recently suggested by his Government for the Conference a difficult one since the President would presumably not wish to be away for a protracted spell while Congress was in session. The Ambassador thought that, under the circumstances, perhaps an August date would be the most practicable.

---

[7] Ellis O. Briggs, Director of the Office of American Republic Affairs.

Following press reports, based on a statement by Ambassador Martins as he left the White House, that the President had accepted the invitation, the following was released to the press at the White House:

"The President told the Ambassador he was happy to receive the invitation and hoped he would be able to come."

Mr. Stanley Woodward of S/S–PR, who was present at Ambassador Martins' meeting with the President, confirms that the latter indicated that he would like to visit Rio de Janeiro at the time of the Conference on the USS *Missouri* but said that his movements were necessarily somewhat limited by whether Congress were in session. The Ambassador pointed out that no date had yet been set for the Conference which was under discussion with the Department. The President then said that he would be glad to consider the question of the date of his trip after that of the date of the Conference had been decided. Mr. Woodward states that nothing was said by the President which would definitely make the visit coincide with the Conference.

---

710. Consultation 4/6–2547

Memorandum by the Chief of the Division of Special Inter-American Affairs (Dreier)[8]

CONFIDENTIAL [WASHINGTON,] June 25, 1947.

In submitting the attached draft telegrams [9] concerning steps taken to assure agreement in advance on the principles to be contained in the Rio Treaty, I should like to caution against any great optimism that these exchanges of views will in fact provide much assurance as to the easy conclusion of the conference.

First, some of the main problems to be expected at the conference are not touched upon: i.e. an anti-Communist pact, which may very likely be proposed by Argentina or another Latin American country; or military provisions, such as establishment of a permanent military agency, which has already been suggested by General Von der Becke.[10]

Second, in regard to the principles which are referred to in these telegrams, what is needed at this stage of negotiations is agreement on words, not principles. Agreement "in principle" to the inclusion in the treaty of a provision for concrete action in event of armed attack does not make the difficult problem of wording such a provision much easier. You may recall that the wording of the United States draft

---

[8] Addressed to the Director of the Office of American Republic Affairs (Briggs); the Assistant Secretaries of State for American Republic Affairs and for Political Affairs (Braden and Armour); and the Under Secretary of State (Acheson).
[9] Not printed.
[10] Gen. Carlos Von der Becke, Adviser to the Argentine delegation.

was finally fixed only after lengthy discussions by representatives of the State, War and Navy Departments.

Finally, this virtual insistence upon acceptance of the United States draft can be expected to arouse no enthusiasm in some Latin American quarters.

JOHN C. DREIER

---

710. Consultation 4/6–2647 : Telegram

The Secretary of State to the Embassy in Brazil

CONFIDENTIAL
US URGENT

WASHINGTON, June 26, 1947—8 p.m.

684. Brazilian Ambassador was informed today that on further consideration this Government would be glad to have Rio Conference on Maintenance of Peace and Security called for August 15 if this were agreeable to Brazil and the other American countries. The Ambassador was also advised that, while this Government will not insist on agreement on general principles of treaty as prerequisite to holding of meeting, it does feel that consultation through Governing Board of Pan American Union should in intervening time try to reach as wide an area of agreement as possible in keeping with Brazilian suggestion conveyed by Ambassador on June 20 (Deptel 659 June 20 [11]). Consultation will be suggested at special meeting of Governing Board tomorrow but representative of this Government will not raise question of date since Brazil will presumably now extend consultations on this point and make announcement when concurrence of other countries received.

Brazilian Ambassador stated that in his Government's opinion agenda for Conference has been approved by Governing Board PAU and consisted of only one point, the preparation of a treaty as called for in Act of Chapultepec. He added that his Government felt the agenda should not be expanded and that the only point connected with the agenda remaining to be resolved was the date of the Conference. He was informed that the Department fully shared these views.

MARSHALL

---

710 Consultation/6–2747

Statement by Mr. William Dawson, United States Representative at the Meeting of the Governing Board of the Pan American Union

[WASHINGTON,] June 27, 1947.

1. My Government shares the desire of the Representative from Colombia and of all of us that the forthcoming Rio Conference be a

---

[11] Not printed.

significant one and that it complete its labors without lengthy and unproductive debate. To that end my Government is in full agreement that it would be helpful to have a further preliminary exchange of views to help crystallize our agreement on the basic principles which the proposed treaty should contain.

2. My Government likewise feels that the Governing Board is the most adequate forum through which this procedure can be carried out. The work already performed through the Board by the Special Committee appointed to analyze the proposals submitted for the treaty, and embodied in its Report approved by the Board on May 22, 1946,[12] not only proves the effectiveness of the Board in performing this function, but provides a convenient point of departure for our future labors.

3. I feel sure that we shall encounter no great difficulties in our discussions. The basic framework for the treaty is contained in two great international instruments to which all our governments have adhered: the Act of Chapultepec and the Charter of the UN. Our task is the comparatively simple one of converting the war time and temporary Act of Chapultepec into a permanent treaty—a treaty consistent with the subsequently adopted Charter of the UN. The negotiation of such a treaty is the sole item on the Rio de Janeiro agenda.

Within these terms of reference, and with the spirit of friendly and frank cooperation which characterizes our meetings, I am confident we can assure a successful Conference.

---

710 Consultation 4/7-347 : Circular telegram

The Secretary of State to the Diplomatic Representatives in the American Republics

WASHINGTON, July 3, 1947.

Depcirtel June 27.[13] At meeting July 2 Pan American Union Governing Board agreed upon following points of consultation:

"POINT I

Commentary

Armed attack against an American state places the victim of the aggression in situation in which it can exercise the right of individual self-defense, under the terms of Article 51 of the Charter of the United Nations. The pact of solidarity among the twenty-one American Republics places all of these States in a situation in which they can exercise the right of collective self-defense, under the terms of the same Article 51. The American states have consequently the right to repel aggression, individually or collectively, until the Security Council has

---

[12] For text, see *Report of the Delegation of the United States of America*, Appendix 3, pt. 3, p. 172.
[13] Not printed.

taken the necessary measures to maintain or reestablish peace. The proposal of the United States contemplates that there shall be two categories of obligation in the event of an armed attack:

(*a*) Each one of the contracting parties agrees to assist in meeting the attack; and (*b*) each of the parties agrees to consult with respect to the collective measures that should be taken.

Questions

1. In the event of an armed attack against an American state are the high contracting parties obligated by the principles of inter-American solidarity and in the exercise of the right of self-defense recognized in Article 51 of the Charter of the United Nations to assist the state which is the immediate victim of the aggression?

2. Is it understood that each one of the high contracting parties shall determine the nature, extent and timing of the immediate measures which it should take?

POINT II

Commentary

All the drafts propose consultation as the means by which the collective measures which may be adopted to prevent or repel aggression shall be determined.

Only three drafts (Ecuador, Panama, the United States) contain provisions with respect to voting in the consultative meetings for the determination of the measures. The Act of Chapultepec does not contemplate voting procedures nor does it indicate whether the parties who do not concur in the decisions of the consultations are or are not bound by the measures agreed upon.

Questions

1. Shall the collective measures be agreed upon by:

    (*a*) unanimous vote?
    (*b*) two-thirds of the parties (proposals of Ecuador, Panama and United States)?
    (*c*) a simple or absolute majority?

2. Are the collective measures agreed upon in consultation obligatory:

    (*a*) for all of the contracting parties?
    (*b*) only for those who in the consultation have concurred in them (proposals of Panama and the United States)?

POINT III

Commentary

Various projects (Bolivia, Chile, Mexico and Uruguay) contemplate the creation of a permanent military organization. In the resolution approved by the Governing Board of the Pan American Union on September 13, 1945 [14] the agenda of the Conference of Rio de Janeiro was limited to 'the preparation of an inter-American treaty of reciprocal assistance to give permanent form to the principles embodied in the "Act of Chapultepec".' Resolution IX of the Mexico City Conference [15] and the proposed agenda of the Ninth International

---

[14] See *Report of the Delegation of the United States of America*, Appendix 3, pt. 2, p. 156.

[15] *Final Act of the Inter-American Conference on Problems of War and Peace*, p. 44.

Conference of American States contemplate that the creation of a permanent military organization should be considered at the Bogotá Conference.[16]

Question

Do the Governments desire to maintain the decisions already taken to consider the creation of a permanent military organization at the Ninth International Conference of American States at Bogotá?"

MARSHALL

---

710 Consultation 4/7–347 : Circular telegram

The Secretary of State to the Diplomatic Representatives in the American Republics Except Nicaragua

RESTRICTED WASHINGTON, July 3, 1947—4 p. m.

ReDepcirtel June 27.[17] Separate telegram transmits contents resolution Pan American Union Governing Board at July 2 meeting presenting three general questions on which agreement should be sought through Governing Board prior Rio Conference. All govts requested present their views on three questions to Board by July 9.

Dept anxious eliminate evident widespread confusion on program Rio Conference and nature of treaty to be concluded there, especially since confusion associated with exaggerated expectations. Conference is special *ad hoc* meeting with only purpose that of converting temporary Act of Chapultepec into permanent treaty in accordance Part II, Resolution VIII, Mex City Conference.[18] Such treaty must be consistent with provisions UN Charter concluded after Mex City. Such treaty is essentially political rather than military agreement, establishing terms of inter-American political solidarity for the maintenance of peace and security.

With respect US position on first two points presented by Governing Board resolution consult US draft treaty enclosed circular instruction Dec 13, 1945.[19]

On point I, in US view principle that armed attack on one is aggression against all imposes common obligation immediately assist in meeting such attack. Measures of immediate assistance not specified or in any way defined and parties consequently left free determine nature immediate assistance, whether military or otherwise. Such assistance would be in accordance right of individual and collective self-defense set forth Article 51 UN Charter. Hence contingency limited to case of "armed attack" referred to in Article 51. Occurrence of

---

[16] Relative to this Conference, see bracketed note, p. 94.
[17] Not printed.
[18] *Final Act of the Inter-American Conference on Problems of War and Peace*, p. 40.
[19] See "Proposals by the United States for the Provisions of an Inter-American Treaty of Mutual Assistance" and footnote 26, *Foreign Relations*, 1945, vol IX, p. 168.

armed attack also imposes obligation consult to agree on common measures to meet attack but individual assistance need not await such consultation. In any case, individual and collective self-defense may be continued only until Security Council has taken necessary measures to maintain international peace and security.

On point II US position favors two-thirds majority for decisions of consultations, such decisions binding only on states that concur. Less than two-thirds agreement would not be adequate for solidary inter-American action. Unanimity requirement, on other hand, would enable a single state to frustrate solidary purpose of all other parties to consultation and prevent collective measures of self-defense. In this sense it would introduce principle of veto into Inter-American System. It would not be practicable to attempt to require participation in collective measures by states not concurring.

Unless you perceive objection pls orally explain this Govt's position and its thinking along above lines to authorities of govt to which accredited, requesting any info they may care to give in return on that govt's views. US recognizes that each govt should reach position that accords with own best judgment.

US views on point III Governing Board resolution will be sent shortly, but approach to authorities on first two points shld not await their receipt.[20]

Telegraph any indications local views.

MARSHALL

---

710 Consultation 4/7–347 : Telegram

The Secretary of State to the Embassy in Brazil

CONFIDENTIAL   WASHINGTON, July 3, 1947—7 p. m.
US URGENT

720. At meeting of Governing Board PAU yesterday acting Brazilian representative presented communication that his Government was inviting all other American Governments with which it maintains diplomatic relations to attend Rio Conference opening August 15. Long and fruitless debate ensued on question of whether right of any member of PAU to participate in Inter-American Conferences could be subject to question of recognition of its Government. Nicaragua was not mentioned directly but entire debate of course concerned it.[21] Brazilian acting representative withdrew communication as result of developments.

[20] In circular telegram of July 8, 8 p. m., the Secretary indicated that the U.S. position on point III was to defer to the Bogotá Conference the subject of establishing a permanent inter-American military agency (710-Consultation 4/7–847).

[21] For documentation on the Nicaraguan problem, see pp. 841 ff.

Department today discussed problem with Brazilian Minister-Counselor and acting representative, in absence of Ambassadors Martins [22] and Muniz,[23] making it clear that its only interest was to avoid difficulties and ascertain Brazil's position in hope of being able to support it effectively. It was suggested that, at same time as Brazil notified other American Governments except Nicaragua of date now selected, it consult other Governments as to whether they feel that Nicaragua should participate in Conference in view of fact that Lacayo Sacasa regime is recognized by no other American Government and of unsettled situation in Nicaragua. When Brazilians suggested that this consultation could be carried out in effect in Governing Board it was pointed out that this would bring danger of continued unavailing debate with possibility of issue becoming involved and cause delay since presumably members of Governing Board would have to request instructions from their Governments. Direct consultation would have virtue of quickly establishing consensus of Governments. After some discussion, Brazilians agreed that Department's suggestion was only practical solution and offered to present it to their Government.

In event that consensus is that Nicaragua should be represented further question would arise as to which Nicaraguan, Lacayo Sacasa or Argüello, should be notified of date. This could properly be subject of further consultation. Presumably, if Lacayo Sacasa regime were to be represented, notification would have to be made by PAU since neither Brazil nor any other American Government now recognizes it. However, at this stage such possibilities are purely speculative and Department hopes that Brazil will see its way clear to following suggestion outlined in second paragraph as best approach to solving present stage of Nicaraguan participation problem.

Please explain Department's position to Foreign Minister and report his reaction promptly.

MARSHALL

---

710 Consultation 4/7–547 : Telegram

The Chargé in Brazil (Brooks) to the Secretary of State

RIO DE JANEIRO, July 5, 1947.

834. Embtel 829, 3d.[24] Foreign Office released following to press afternoon 4th:

"The *de facto* government installed in the capital of Nicaragua in consequence of the deposition of President Argüello, which occurred

---

[22] Carlos Martins, Brazilian Ambassador to the United States.
[23] João Carlos Muniz, Brazilian Representative on the Governing Board of the Pan American Union.
[24] Not printed.

a few weeks after his investiture, protested against the suggestion of the Brazilian Government to the Pan American Union that an invitation to the next Inter-American Conference not be extended to that Republic.

That subject is being discussed by the Council of Directors of the Pan American Union where the attitude of the Brazilian Government was criticized by several representatives.

It should be explained, in these circumstances, that the Brazilian suggestion is based on the circumstance that the *de facto* government of Nicaragua is not recognized by any American Government, the Itamarati [25] having been notified by several governments that that recognition was not admissible.

On the other hand, President Argüello, deposed, took asylum in the Mexican Embassy in Managua, and still is there deprived of means of exercising any kind of governmental authority.

This being the case, there being precedents of Inter-American Conferences at which, for circumstances of a transitory nature, one of the member states failed to appear, because of the lack of an invitation, or through voluntary abstinence, and it being inconvenient to postpone the Conference until the situation in Nicaragua is regularized, one of the solutions for the resulting emergency was not to extend the invitation to that Republic, to which adherence to agreements which resulted from the Conference would always remain open.

Another solution would be to invite one of the two pretenders to the Government of Nicaragua. But, the scruples of the Brazilian Government, as organizer of the Conference, against imposing a unilateral choice on the other Republics are understood.

In consequence the subject was left by the Itamarati for the judgment of the Pan-American Union, whose decisions it will accept, without prejudice to its own point of view in that which concerns its direct relations with the Government of Nicaragua."

BROOKS

---

710 Consultation 4/7–747 : Telegram

The Chargé in Ecuador (Shaw) to the Secretary of State

RESTRICTED　　　　　　　　　　　　　　QUITO, July 7, 1947—7 p. m.

277. Ecuador's reply to questions contained Department's two circular telegrams July 3 received in memorandum July 7 received this evening.

Point of view Ecuador Rio Conference should be special *ad hoc* meeting to convert Act Chapultepec into permanent treaty in accordance part 2, Resolution VIII, Mexico City Conference; also that such treaty is essentially political rather than military.

Treaty should be consistent with UN Charter and is suggested that points of treaty should be included in joint charter of Americas that will come out of Conference at Bogotá so that it will form part of an old statute with its American regional correlation.

---

[25] The Brazilian Foreign Office.

That attack against one is aggression against all with obligation of immediate assistance is agreeable, the measures of immediate assistance and nature thereof with the right of self-defense set forth in article 51 of UN Charter all as stated in Department's telegrams coincides with Ecuadoran point of view.

As regards question No. 2, Ecuador decidedly in favor of two-thirds majority vote for decisions on consultations. It is against a system which would permit of an effective veto.

The only point of difference is the matter of obliging participation in collective measures by state not concurring. Ecuador believes that as a matter of principle and order not to destroy democratic system it should be stated at least that the states not concurring are obliged to participate. The last sentence in Foreign Office memo under reference reads. "It is believed that the same principle of effective American solidarity demands, at least in principle, the obligatory participation in the collective measures by those states that may not concur with their favorable vote in the decision of the two-thirds."

Ecuadoran Ambassador Washington being advised in above sense by cable tonight.

Answer to question on creation of permanent military organization at Bogotá follows later.

Following given orally and informally: "Rio Conference should be held without Nicaraguan participation (Dept's circular telegram July 1 [26]) if situation remains as at present. Accepting representatives of Argüello government really dealing with a government in exile which Ecuador considers dangerous and unnecessary as Nicaragua would be bound by two-thirds vote if Ecuadoran proposal accepted.["]

SHAW

---

710. Consultation 4/7-747

Memorandum of Conversation, by the Chief of the Division of Special Inter-American Affairs (Dreier)

RESTRICTED [WASHINGTON,] July 7, 1947.

Participants: Ambassador Antonio Rocha—Chairman of the Governing Board, Pan American Union
Dr. Alberto Lleras Camargo—Director General, Pan American Union
Messrs. Briggs, Wright,[27] Dawson, Dreier.

Mr. Briggs expressed his appreciation for the willingness of Ambassador Rocha and Dr. Lleras to come to his office, explaining that he thought it would be desirable to plan in advance how to handle the

---

[26] Not printed.
[27] James H. Wright, Special Assistant to Assistant Secretary of State Braden.

question of Nicaraguan participation in the Rio Conference, which the Brazilian Government had now placed in the hands of the Governing Board and would probably come up at the next meeting. Mr. Briggs expressed the hope that the matter could be settled without provoking long and fruitless debate in the Governing Board.

Various aspects of the Brazilian note, as reported in the press, were discussed. It was generally agreed that the best thing would be for the Governing Board to propose to the various governments, through the representatives on the Board, some questions concerning Nicaraguan participation, the answers to which would settle the issue. At the same time, however, the Brazilian note should be transmitted by the Union to the other governments.

Ambassador Rocha first suggested that a theoretical question be posed on whether at inter-American conferences all American republics should be represented, to be followed by a specific question namely, which faction should be invited to represent Nicaragua.

Further discussion led to the desirability of approaching the subject entirely on a theoretical basis and it was finally agreed, largely on the initiative of Dr. Lleras, that the questions should be framed as follows:

What procedures should be followed in regard to invitations to inter-American conferences when:

    1. a government of one republic is not recognized by any other republics?;
    2. a government of one republic is recognized by a minority of the other republics?;
    3. a government of one republic is recognized by a majority of the other republics but not by the host government?

It was indicated by Dr. Lleras and Ambassador Rocha that the answers to these questions should provide a formula with which the present Nicaraguan case could be settled.

Those present agreed to talk with various members of the Governing Board before the meeting on Wednesday, July 9, in order to get general agreement to approach the subject on a basis of principle as outlined above.

---

710. Consultation 4/7–847 : Telegram

The Chargé in Uruguay (Sparks) to the Secretary of State

CONFIDENTIAL   MONTEVIDEO, July 8, 1947—7 p. m.
US URGENT

297. Depcirtel July 3. Uruguayan general attitude reported Embtel 276, June 27.[28] Foreign Minister [29] states Uruguayan desires Rio treaty

[28] Not printed.
[29] Mateo Marques Castro.

to represent advance in efficacy of Inter-American system. He considers draft treaty fails to satisfy Uruguayan aspirations for immediate effective assistance in case of armed attack and that contemplated consultations do not afford desired assurances. He points out decisions are binding only on those concurring and with two-thirds vote seven states could be free to abstain from implementing. He is concerned that if those not concurring included US, Brazil, Mexico, Argentina, decisions would be inoperative. He also mentioned long time required for consultations and remarked Uruguay could be completely overrun in 15 days.

In discussion Foreign Minister recognized majority of states probably would be reluctant to make prior specific commitments for military assistance but should not be opposed to requirements for breaking relations, suspension of communications and severance of economic relations. Nevertheless, he holds categorical opinion that treaty should specify definitely military and other measures to be invoked automatically in case armed attack and that without such specific commitments treaty will be viewed as postponement if not step backward in evolution of practical meaning of American solidarity.

I mentioned declared opposition by Herreristas to Rio treaty. Foreign Minister remarked that government could anticipate less internal opposition to present draft than what he proposes but Uruguay adheres to its traditional foreign policy and aspires that treaty represent real contribution to Inter-American system.

SPARKS

---

710 Consultation 4/7–947 : Telegram

The Chargé in Argentina (O'Donoghue) to the Secretary of State

RESTRICTED BUENOS AIRES, July 9, 1947—10 a. m.

842. In Tucumán press conference Foreign Minister,[30] referring to Rio Conference, said Argentine delegation will have no special plan but on contrary its actuation will follow agenda which may be presented. Said according his information first point of agenda, mutual defense treaty, will be only one treated; in any event Argentina believes this should be first point for discussion. Questioned as to voting procedure in conference Bramuglia stated Argentine supports its "traditional point of view which is unanimity".

Re President Perón's radio address July 6 Foreign Minister said President had outlined aid which Argentina can extend Europe; "we are awaiting the word of the nations".

O'DONOGHUE

---

[30] Juan Atilio Bramuglia.

710. Consultation 4/7–947 : Telegram

The Ambassador in Cuba (*Norweb*) to the Secretary of State

CONFIDENTIAL   HABANA, July 9, 1947—2 p. m.

338. During hour long conversation with Minister State [31] today I discussed with him substance of Department's circular telegrams July 3 and July 3, 4 p. m. re Rio Conference, US views, and questions for Governing Board PAU July 9 meeting.

Re Cuban position with respect to the questions he early remarked Government's views had been placed in hands Ambassador Belt.[32] He had apparently not been acquainted with matter under discussion and was thinking on his feet. After some time he expressed definite view that permanent military organization should be left to Bogotá Conference. With regard to voting in consultation procedures he said Cuba traditionally favored "unanimity and solidarity" among American states but conceded that in case of consultation to determine collective measures in such emergency as armed attack on American state by non-American state less inclusive agreement might become more practical. He agreed with our thesis that collective measures accepted in consultation should be obligatory only for those who in consultation had concurred in them and on both questions under point I.

He suggested though without apparent vexation that Rio Conference after being many times postponed had now been called on rather short notice. He did not know who would attend for Cuba but conceded that "Minister State" (himself) and "four or five advisors" would possibly compose delegation. I mentioned rumored desire of General Pérez [33] to attend but he offered no comment. He was curious re size and composition of American delegation and "spirit by which it would be guided". I impressed upon him our feeling conference should be limited to conversion into treaty of temporary Act of Chapultepec. I should like to repeat that I came away with impression our initiative caught him quite unprepared but that after long cogitation he found himself substantially in agreement with us.

Although I gave him several opportunities he did not bring up subject of sugar bill [34] nor mention whether Belt's recent visit here was in any way connected with it.

NORWEB

---

[31] Rafael P. González Muñoz.
[32] Guillermo Belt, Cuban Ambassador in the United States.
[33] Presumably Gen. Genovevo Pérez y Damera, Cuban Chief of Staff.
[34] See circular airgram, August 1, 3:40 p.m., p. 30.

710 Consultation 4/7–947

Memorandum by the Assistant Chief of the Division of Special Inter-American Affairs (Halle) to the Director of the Office of American Republic Affairs (Briggs)

[WASHINGTON,] July 9, 1947.

We have now heard from our embassies in Bolivia, Chile, Ecuador, Guatemala, Haiti, Mexico, Panama, Paraguay, Peru and Uruguay on the preliminary consultations for the Rio Conference. The information from Chile, Haiti, Paraguay* and Peru does not bear directly on the specific points of the consultation.

In *Chile*, the absence of the President and Foreign Minister has prevented the Government from formulating its views. A minor official said Chile has an eye on the problem of "aggression against its Antarctic Territory."

Paraguay is actively studying the proposals in spite of other preoccupations.

The *Peruvian* Foreign Minister implied that the Peruvian attitude would be favorable to the US position.

The *Haitian* Foreign Minister was glad to have, from the Embassy, a correction of his previous belief that the Conference would be occupied principally with military matters.

The positions of the other governments on the points of consultation are as follows:

Point I, Question 1: Should the treaty state an obligation to assist? No dissent from US position.

Point I, Question 2: Should assistance remain undefined? Bolivia, Ecuador, Guatemala and Panama agree with US. Mexico thinks measures of assistance should be defined. Uruguay thinks treaty should specify definitely military and other measures of assistance.

Point II, Question 1: Voting in consultation? Bolivia, Ecuador, Mexico and Panama favor two-thirds. Guatemala is reluctant to abandon principle of unanimity but feels two-thirds may be only workable solution. Uruguay is silent.

Point II, Question 2: Shall the minority be bound? Bolivia, Ecuador, Paraguay and Uruguay believe the minority should be bound. Guatemala would like to see it bound but feels this may not be practicable. Mexico feels it should be bound with respect to other than military measures (those not taking military measures agreed upon by majority would be reported to the Security Council). Uruguay seems to share Mexico's general view. Panama agrees with US position that minority should not be bound.

---

*Except for Point II, Question 2. [Footnote in the original.]

Point III: Establishment of military agency at Rio? Bolivia favors some action at Rio. Panama opposes such action.

LOUIS J. HALLE, JR.

---

710 Consultation 4/7–1047

The Director General of the Pan American Union (*Lleras*) to the Secretary of State

WASHINGTON, July 10, 1947.

MY DEAR MR. SECRETARY: The Government of Brazil has requested the Pan American Union to extend, on its behalf, to the Government of the United States of America a cordial invitation to be represented at the Inter-American Conference for the Maintenance of Continental Peace and Security, which will meet at Rio de Janeiro beginning August 15, for the purpose of giving permanent form to the principles incorporated in the Act of Chapultepec.

In the name of the Government of Brazil, therefore, the Pan American Union has the honor to invite the Government of the United States of America to send delegates to the said Conference.

I beg to remain, my dear Mr. Secretary,

Very sincerely yours, ALBERTO LLERAS

---

710. Consultation 4/7–1147: Circular telegram

The Secretary of State to the Diplomatic Representatives in the American Republics

RESTRICTED WASHINGTON, July 11, 1947—8 a. m.

At Governing Board consultation July 9 Nicaragua absent and representatives of Chile, Paraguay, Venezuela had not received instructions. Consultation among other countries revealed following:

1. Substantial agreement with US position on Point I.
2. Unanimous agreement on Point III.
3. On Point II, Question 1, all except Argentina, which favored unanimity, and Uruguay, which favored simple majority, came out for two-thirds vote.
4. On Point II, Question 2, majority favored making consultative decisions binding on all parties. Only Brazil, Cuba, Panama agreed with US position. Mexico proposed that decisions not implying use of military forces binding on all, but decisions implying use of such forces binding only on those concurring.

MARSHALL

710 Consultation 4/7–1447

Memorandum by the Assistant Chief of the Division of Special Inter-American Affairs (Halle) to the Director of the Office of American Republic Affairs (Briggs) [35]

[WASHINGTON,] July 14, 1947.

Brazil, having received formal requests from "two or three" unspecified non-American governments that they be represented by observers at the forthcoming Rio Conference, has asked the Governing Board of the Pan American Union what kind of reply it should make. I attended, on Saturday, July 12, a meeting of a committee of the Board to report on this question. The members of the Committee were: The Ambassador of Haiti (Chairman), the Ambassador of Honduras, the Representative of Brazil and the Representative of the United States. The Director General and Assistant Director were present.

The meeting opened with the distribution of the attached memorandum [36] citing the results of previous considerations in the Inter-American System of the question whether observers should be admitted to inter-American conferences. As this memorandum shows, the Lima Conference of 1938 came to the conclusion that there was no need to raise the question of official observers since the meetings were public, while the Governing Board in 1944 decided that, for special reasons, a non-member state might be allowed to send an observer to a particular inter-American conference if the Governing Board decided so on the basis of a proposal to that effect by one of the members. Since Brazil was not making such a proposal, it appeared that the conclusion reached at Lima applied to this case and there was no problem.

The Brazilian was not at all satisfied, however, to accept the Lima decision as a basis for reply, considering that the Lima decision was unsatisfactory, that the world had changed since Lima, and that it would seem "very strange" to tell these non-American governments that they would not be permitted to send official observers. He made it quite plain that he, personally, hoped to see the Governing Board make a new decision that would permit observers to attend the Rio Conference. At one point, however, he said he had no instructions to this respect from his government but that he supposed his government would not be referring the question to the Governing Board if the Lima decision were considered satisfactory.

---

[35] Marginal notation reads as follows: "ARA/Mr. Wright. Another profitless red herring. Since Rio sessions will be open, the whole problem is futile. B[riggs]."
[36] Not printed.

Other members of the Committee expressed the view that the question of admitting observers had implications of such fundamental importance that it should not be decided off the cuff by the Governing Board but should be dealt with, if at all, at the Bogotá Conference. The Brazilian was obviously not of this mind.

The Ambassador of Honduras [37] then enthusiastically proposed and wrote out a resolution whereby each request from a non-member government to be represented by observers at the Rio Conference should be referred to the Conference itself for decision. The Representative of the United States was finally constrained to point out the danger that the Conference would devote its first week or ten days to an extended and bitter discussion of which non-American governments might or might not have official observers, with attendant newspaper publicity, confusion and bad feeling.

After these matters had been debated for a full 2 hours, the Director General saved the day with a proposal that in order that the members of the United Nations might be fully and officially informed of the developments and conclusions at the Conference, the United Nations Organization, i.e., Trygve Lie,[38] should be invited to have an observer present. This would obviate any need for the appointment by individual United Nations of observers.

This solution, being acceptable to all (though accepted without enthusiasm by the Brazilian), the Director General immediately drafted a resolution calling for consideration at an International Conference of American States of a permanent decision with respect to observers of inter-American conferences and calling, in addition, for a formal invitation to the United Nations Organization to have an observer at Rio.

This draft resolution will be submitted to the Governing Board at the next meeting on July 16.

LOUIS J. HALLE, JR.

---

710 Consultation 4/7–1247 : Telegram

The Secretary of State to the Embassy in Paraguay

CONFIDENTIAL   WASHINGTON, July 15, 1947—8 p. m.

190. Urtel 377, July 12.[39] US draft treaty does not attempt to define "aggression" since determination whether aggression is being prepared or threat of aggression exists would be made in each case through consultation of all parties on initiative any one of them. Aggression can take so many forms in modern world that definition not practi-

---

[37] Julián R. Cáceres.
[38] Secretary General of the United Nations.
[39] Not printed.

cable and any attempt to define would limit free determination of parties in above consultations. Language of US draft would allow subversion or political attack aimed at subversion by any state against any American state to be regarded as threat of aggression if consultation so determines. Enforcement measures to meet threat of aggression could be taken only with authority Security Council in accordance Art. 53 UN Charter.

MARSHALL

---

710. Consultation 4/7–1647 : Airgram

The Chargé in Argentina (Ray) to the Secretary of State

BUENOS AIRES, July 16, 1947.

A-449. RefEmtel No. 868 July 15 [40] regarding Foreign Minister Bramuglia's statement to press. Full extent of his remarks are indicated below.

Argentina has formally accepted invitation to Rio Conference through its Ambassador in Washington.[41] Bramuglia will head Mission which will be composed of representatives of Ministries of War, Marine, Aeronautics and Foreign Affairs. Bramuglia declined to give names of other members of Mission but stated that it has already been formed and is now studying the problems which might arise at Conference.

He was asked if Conference would treat matters other than those of Continental defence. He replied: "In view of the fact that the invitation (says that the Conference) is in order to give form to the principles incorporated in the Act of Chapultepec, I understand that other matters will not be touched upon."

Referring to Nicaragua, Bramuglia stated that "Argentina considers that all the American nations should be invited and that the credentials of each one should be discussed later at Conference."

Bramuglia was asked if Canada would be invited to the Conference. He replied that "Executive Power has formed its opinion in this regard but has not taken any initiative."

The press of the last few days has carried a number of stories regarding the possible visit of President Perón to Bolivia, Chile and Uruguay. Foreign Minister in his press conference confirmed that the President had received invitations to visit each of these countries but added that, because of the pressure of work, he would not be able to go for the present although he might do so later.

RAY

---

[40] Not printed.
[41] Oscar Ivanissevich.

710 Consultation (4)/7–1647 : Telegram

The Ambassador in Chile (Bowers) to the Secretary of State

RESTRICTED SANTIAGO, July 16, 1947—5 p. m.

584. Depcirtels July 3, 9:30 a. m. and July 8, 8 p. m.[42] Last night Chile sent following reply to Pan American Union on Rio Conference consultation:

Point I. Question 1—affirmative answer.

Point I. Question 2—affirmative reply, although possibility might be considered of reaching prior agreements on nature, scope and desirability of immediate help in event of armed attack.

Point II. Questions 1 and 2—the two-thirds principle accepted. Govt of Chile considers it advisable distinguish between obligations of American states in accordance with nature of measures adopted (political, financial, military). In any case, it believes there should be agreement on part of signatory states which have not agreed to measures taken not to do anything that might jeopardize their fulfillment.

Point III. It is accepted that creation of a military organization should be referred to Bogotá Conference.

BOWERS

---

710 Consultation 4/7–1747

Memorandum by the Chief of the Division of Brazilian Affairs (Dawson) to the Director of the Office of American Republic Affairs (Briggs)

CONFIDENTIAL [WASHINGTON,] July 17, 1947.

Mr. Wells[43] informs me that he had conversations today with Ambassador Prado of Peru and Ambassador Ponce of Ecuador in which both indicated the positions of their Governments regarding Nicaraguan participation in the Rio Conference. Ambassador Prado stated that the Peruvian representative on the Governing Board of the Pan American Union had instructions from his Government to follow this Government's lead on the consultation concerning Nicaraguan participation. Consequently, the Peruvians would appreciate it if we would let them know what our reply to the *consulta* would be when we had reached a decision.

The Ecuadoran Ambassador stated that the position of his Government was that no government should be invited to participate in an inter-American conference unless recognized by a majority of the other American republics.

In view of the statement of July 15 by Ambassador Cáceres to Assistant Secretary Armour that he had received instructions from the Honduran Government to cooperate with the Department's position

---

[42] Latter not printed.
[43] Milton K. Wells, Chief, Division of North and West Coast Affairs.

on the Nicaraguan question, it would seem that there is a considerable bloc of countries which will vote against participation by the Lacayo Sacasa régime should the Department decide on such an attitude for itself. The representatives of Guatemala, Panama, Bolivia and Venezuela have indicated in one form or another that their governments are opposed to Lacayo Sacasa participation. Mexico, while equally unfriendly to the Lacayo Sacasa régime, is in a special position because of the intricacies of trying to maintain the Estrada Doctrine.[44]

The Argentine opposition to a *consulta* of any nature, indicated by Ambassador Ivanissevitch's [44a] refusal to sign the report to the Governing Board of its committee considering the Nicaraguan question, may become "contraproducente". If Argentina carries its opposition to the *consulta* to the point of not replying to it, only ten votes will be necessary to form a majority against inviting the Lacayo Sacasa régime.

ALLAN DAWSON

---

710 Consultation 4/7–1847

Memorandum of Telephone Conversation, by Mr. Gordon S. Reid of the Division of Central America and Panama Affairs

[WASHINGTON,] July 18, 1947.

Mr. Rogers [45] called me this morning to discuss the Nicaraguan situation and at the end of our talk stated that the Canadian Government understood that it was being invited to the Rio Conference in the role of observer. He then amended that so [*and said?*] that he understood the Brazilians were attempting to have Canada invite them. He said he thought I would be interested to know that the Canadian Government was hoping that they would not be invited either as an observer or in any other way. He ended by saying that it would certainly look funny to have the invitation issued to "the United Nations and Canada". When he finished the conversation he was still wondering whether that was an insult or compliment.

---

710 Consultation 4/7–1847 : Telegram

The Secretary of State to the Embassy in Chile

CONFIDENTIAL   WASHINGTON, July 18, 1947—8 p. m.

765. Brazilian Emb here has had in succession four telegrams from FonOff giving changing instructions re observers at Rio Conference.

---

[44] Doctrine concerning recognition of states, set forth by the Mexican Minister for Foreign Affairs in 1930. See Instituto Americano de Derecho y Legislación Comparada, *La Opinión Universal Sobre la Doctrina Estrada* (Mexico, 1931).
[44a] Dr. Oscar Ivanissevich, Argentine Ambassador to the United States.
[45] R. L. Rogers, Third Secretary of the Canadian Embassy.

First told representative on Governing Board of Pan American Union that Great Britain and France had asked Brazil to be allowed to have observers at Conference and that he should submit matter to Director General PAU. Second said that Brazil was inclined to disapprove of suggestion since it would create precedent for similar requests on part of other Govts which might not be welcome. Third gave Brazilian Govt's position as being opposed to observers of non-American countries in general but favoring Canada being represented by an observer if it desired and inviting Secretary General of United Nations to be present. Special committee of Governing Board to consider problem understood to be presenting report to Governing Board at next meeting July 21 along lines of third suggestion.

Today Brazilian Emb informed Dept it had recd tel suggesting formula to invite all countries having territorial interests in western hemisphere to have observers at Conference, thus allowing Canada, Great Britain, France and Netherlands to be represented, and stating that if US representative on Governing Board would introduce resolution to this effect it would have support of Brazil.

Brazilian Emb has been informed that, while Dept would be prepared to go along with idea of Secretariat General and Canadian observers, it is definitely opposed to any extension. This is in keeping with precedent established at previous inter-American conferences. Dept feels strongly that attendance even in observation capacity by any non-American countries under whatever pretext would tend to open door to further, perhaps undesirable requests. Meeting is regional one and general interest in it would seem to be adequately covered by invitation to Secretary General.

Brazilian Emb stated it would immediately inform FonOff of Dept's position but foregoing is transmitted for your guidance in any conversations with FonOff.

MARSHALL

---

710 Consultation 4/7–2447 : Circular telegram

The Secretary of State to the Diplomatic Representatives in the American Republics

RESTRICTED   WASHINGTON, July 24, 1947—1 a. m.

On July 7 Brazilian Govt asked Governing Board Pan American Union to decide whether invitation to Rio Conference should be extended to *de facto* regime in Nicaragua in view of fact that it was not recognized by 19 of the American Republics, Brazil feeling that it could not take unilateral decision on matter since it is fulfilling collective mandate in acting as host to Conference.

On July 21 Governing Board passed resolution recommending that its members consult their Govts on questions of to whom Nicaraguan invitation should be addressed and whether invitation should be made with reservation that it does not affect bilateral relations of any Govt with Nicaragua. Preamble of resolution points out that Statutes of PAU provide that the various American Govts enjoy the inherent right of representation at inter-American conferences but that they contain no provisions covering Govts which do not have normal diplomatic relations with a majority of the other American Govts. Decision on Nicaraguan participation scheduled to be taken at Governing Board meeting of July 28.

Position which US representative on Governing Board will take is that, while Nicaragua as a state has right to be represented at Rio Conference, there is no Govt at present which can properly represent it. Deposed Argüello regime does not have the generally accepted attributes of sovereignty. Fact that overwhelming majority of American Republics do not recognize Lacayo regime would make its participation in Conference anomalous. This Govt hopes that steps may be taken in Nicaragua to normalize situation before Rio Conference so that basis for recognition of a Govt by a majority of the American Republics may exist in which case it feels that an invitation should then be extended. In the unfortunate event of this not occurring this Govt would favor leaving treaty to be elaborated at Rio open to adherence by Nicaragua once normal relations between it and a majority of the other American Republics are restored. In any event this Govt feels that question of Nicaraguan participation should be decided by majority vote of Governing Board of PAU and it will of course support the decision of the majority.

You should not bring the subject up on your own initiative in conversations with FonOff. If FonOff broaches matter to you, you should explain US position as outlined above, endeavor to ascertain its position and telegraph Dept.

Sent to Managua for info only.

MARSHALL

---

710 Consultation 4/7-2447: Telegram

The Ambassador in Ecuador (Simmons) to the Secretary of State

QUITO, July 24, 1947—1 p. m.

296. Principal newspapers Quito last night and this morning carried identical articles evidently originating Foreign Office outlining items Ecuador intends to present for agenda at Rio Conference.

Points of view agreed upon by President and Minister Foreign Affairs [46] follow:

1. Constitution of the American regional organization and its connection with United Nations;
2. Ratification of all treaties, agreements and resolutions of various Pan American conferences relative to security of continent and maintenance of peace;
3. Definition of aggressor and authority that declares it, which will be board (*consejo directivo*) of Pan American Union;
4. Efficacious means for avoiding continental or extra-continental aggression;
5. Political, economic and military means for sanctioning aggression; [47]
6. All resolutions must be decided by two-thirds vote and all of 21 American Republics being obliged thereby.

Press also confirms that Ecuadoran Delegation will depart for Rio August 8. Minister Foreign Affairs will accept invitation Argentine Government spend 2 days in Buenos Aires en route. Press notices purporting to have originated in Foreign Office state Ecuadoran Government is considering sending a number of recently elected Senators and deputies as delegates to Rio Conference. These probably in addition to names previously reported. Idea seems to be this would facilitate ratification of Rio resolutions in next Ecuadoran Congress.

While not mentioned in press I feel it might be that this maneuver is contemplated with a view to avoiding calling extraordinary session of Congress in Ecuador for present.

SIMMONS

---

710 Consultation 4/7–2547

The Secretary of State to the Secretary of the Navy (Forrestal)

WASHINGTON, July 25, 1947.

DEAR MR. SECRETARY: In order to assure a concerted United States position on the issues in connection with the inter-American treaty of mutual assistance to be concluded at the forthcoming Conference in Rio de Janeiro, there are certain matters I should like to take up with you.

As you know, the United States proposals for the treaty (copy attached) [48] were originally developed in consultation with the War and Navy Departments and approved by them, by Congressional leaders and by the President in December, 1945. In the past few weeks

---

[46] José María Velasco Ibarra and José Vicente Trujillo, respectively.
[47] Presumably "Political, economic and military sanctions against aggression".
[48] *Foreign Relations,* 1945, vol. IX, p. 168.

representatives of the three Departments have been reexamining these proposals and have reached the conclusion that, except for the point mentioned below, the previously approved draft remains satisfactory.

With respect to the voting provisions and the binding effect of decisions to take action under the treaty, the original draft provides that decisions to take action to meet an armed attack or other aggression should be by two-thirds vote and should bind only those concurring. In the light of the recently expressed views of a majority of the other American Republics that all parties should be bound and in view of our own desire to make the treaty as effective as possible, these provisions have been reexamined and we have concluded that a two-thirds decision to take action, including action of a military character under the treaty, should bind all parties, but that no state should be required to provide armed forces without its consent. It accordingly seems necessary that the treaty enumerate the various types of measures to be taken. I attach a proposed revision [49] to this effect, which I understand meets with the informal approval of representatives of your Department.

I likewise refer to a communication of July 21, 1947 from the Assistant Secretary of State, Mr. Armour, to the Under Secretary of the Navy, Mr. Sullivan,[50] setting forth the agreed position of the three departments on the problem of the establishment of a permanent inter-American military agency.

In view of the short time available for discussion of the matter with Congressional leaders whom I will wish to consult, I am informing them of these matters with the explanation that the above views have only the informal concurrence of the three departments. I would, therefore, appreciate at your earliest convenience your confirmation of my understanding that the views stated above represent the approved position of the three departments. I am transmitting a similar communication to the Secretary of War.

Faithfully yours, G. C. MARSHALL

710 Consultation 4/7–2947 : Circular telegram

The Secretary of State to the Diplomatic Representatives in the American Republics

RESTRICTED WASHINGTON, July 29, 1947—2 a. m.

Depcirtel July 24. At meeting Governing Board PAU yesterday positions of Govts on participation Nicaragua in Rio Conference

---

[49] Not printed, but see *Report of the Delegation of the United States of America*, Appendix 2, pt. 1, pp. 102–104.
[50] Not printed.

were recorded. Thirteen countries opposed extension invitation to Lacayo regime and five favored it.[51] Consequently no invitation to Nicaragua will be issued by PAU. It was held by Chairman that question Nicaraguan participation could again be broached if conditions should be altered in Nicaragua before end Rio Conference, e.g., if Govt recognized by majority American Republics should be established there.

MARSHALL

710 Consultation 4/7-2947 : Telegram

The Ambassador in Brazil (Pawley) to the Secretary of State

RESTRICTED   RIO DE JANEIRO, July 29, 1947—6 p. m.

984. Department's circular telegrams July 3; July 3, 4 p. m.; July 8, 8 p. m.[52] The following is a translation of a memo from the Brazilian Ministry of Foreign Affairs dated July 19 and received by the Embassy July 25, in response to Embassy's request for views on three general questions on which agreement should be sought through Governing Board Pan American Union prior to Rio Conference. Embassy understands these views already transmitted Brazilian representatives Washington.

"With reference to the memorandum from the Embassy of the United States of America, delivered on July 8, 1947, the Ministry of Foreign Affairs desires to express its agreement with the opinion of the Department of State with respect to the purpose of the Conference of Rio de Janeiro and the nature of the treaty which it is called to consider.

The Conference will take place, in effect, pursuant to the express mandate of Resolution VIII of the Conference of Chapultepec, for the special purpose of discussing and eventually concluding a pact for continental defense. There should be added further that the Governing Board of the Pan American Union, at its extraordinary session of September 26, 1945 approved, unanimously, a recommendation expressing its full agreement with the suggestion of the Brazilian Government, aiming to limit the program of the Conference to the drafting of a treaty of reciprocal assistance designed to give permanent form to the principles incorporated in the Act of Chapultepec.

And since such a treaty is intended to fix the general rules which will regulate the procedure of the American Republics in the matter of mutual assistance, the Ministry of Foreign Affairs understands that its content is essentially of a political nature.

With regard to the items of the questionnaire presented to the Amer-

---

[51] According to airgram A-101, August 4, 1947, to Tegucigalpa, the five countries were: Argentina, Colombia, Costa Rica, Dominican Republic, and Paraguay (710 Consultation 4/7-3147).

[52] Circular telegram dated July 8, 8 p. m., not printed.

ican Republics by the Governing Board of the Pan American Union, the Ministry of Foreign Affairs adopts the following position:

Item I. The various drafts of the treaty, with the exception of that proposed by the US, speak of collective defense against acts of aggression, an expression the meaning of which they immediately go on to define. The American proposal meanwhile speaks specifically of armed attack, which is the expression used in article 51 of the United Nations Charter. Article 51 of the Charter only authorizes legitimate defense when an 'armed attack' is directed against one of the members of the United Nations.

The 'act of aggression' spoken of in the drafts of the Inter-American Defense Treaty should, then, be understood, in accordance with Article 51 of the Charter, in the sense of 'armed attack'.

And in this case, in which the legitimate right of defense is inherent to the sovereignty of the state, it is understood that, within the principle of inter-American solidarity, the contracting states bind themselves to assist the victim of the attack.

As to knowing if it falls to each of the high contracting parties to determine the nature, extent and timing of the immediate measure which it should take, the Ministry of Foreign Affairs has already issued the opinion that such measures should be coordinated by means of consultations and, if possible, determined, beforehand, through agreements, by the inter-American military organization, to be created.

It appears that there should not be denied to any of the American Republics the right to determine, itself, the nature and manner of its aid to the state attacked. But this assistance should not be measured hastily, in the case of each conflict, but should be defined, beforehand, through negotiated agreements. In these agreements there will be regulated also the question of the timeliness of the assistance.

Item II. The Brazilian Government also expressed itself with reference to the case of the consultations for application of sanctions against the aggressor state. In its opinion, the application of such measures should be voted by a qualified majority of two-thirds.

But in this case, what cooperation should be required from the countries whose vote is defeated? The Brazilian Government understands that there should be required of them at least a strict neutrality. Nevertheless, within the principle of American solidarity, the Brazilian Government will be disposed to agree that there should be required of them the application of all the measures of sanctions, with the exception of the military measures.

This last opinion seems more in conformity with the principle of Item I, in accordance with which, in the opinion of the Brazilian Government, all the American Republics would oblige themselves to lend assistance to the American state directly attacked.

Item III. Concerning the creation of a permanent military organization, the Ministry of Foreign Affairs is in agreement that the matter be discussed at the forthcoming Pan American Conference at Bogotá.

The Brazilian Military authorities are currently studying the draft of the Inter-American Defense Committee, on which document the Ministry of Foreign Affairs will express its point of view at the opportune time, trusting that in this matter, as in other topics of the

Conference of Bogotá, it will be given the opportunity to compare its ideas with those of the Department of State."

PAWLEY

710 Consultation 4/8–147 : Circular airgram

The Secretary of State to the Diplomatic Representatives in the American Republics

RESTRICTED WASHINGTON, August 1, 1947—3:40 p. m.

At Governing Board PAU July 28, Cuban Ambassador presented motion member Governments be consulted on inclusion clause Rio defense treaty that Section 202(e) Sugar Act 1948 [53] would be considered as threat within meaning of treaty. In public session threatened Cuban non-participation Rio Conference if consultation not made. Motion rejected but minutes contain statement that "the Delegate of Cuba on the Governing Board of the Pan American Union states, so that the delegates may bring it to the knowledge of their respective Governments, that it deems it to be indispensable that, at the Conference of Rio de Janeiro, there be included a clause taking into consideration measures of an economic nature which, on being put into effect unilaterally by any American country, would constitute a threat to the economic stability of another American country or countries."

If question raised you are authorized to make the following statement to appropriate officials:

1. Section 202(e) of the Sugar Act of 1948, when signed, will provide that the Secretary of Agriculture shall have authority to withhold or withdraw any increase in the quota provided for by the new Act as compared to the Sugar Act of 1937, if the Secretary of State finds that any foreign country denies fair and equitable treatment to the nationals of the United States, its commerce, navigation or industry.

2. This section does not constitute an economic threat to any country. It provides only for the right to withdraw the increase in the quota allowed under the Act if any country denies fair and equitable treatment to American citizens or enterprises. It does not apply to basic quotas.

3. It is permissive and not mandatory; it applies to all foreign countries and not to any country in particular. It represents no change in the economic policy of this country toward other countries in this Hemisphere. The section has ample precedent in the legislation of the United States.

4. The matter of claims in connection with this section has been greatly over-emphasized. This Government is, as it always has been, ready to submit claims of its citizens against foreign countries to

---

[53] Public Law No. 388, signed by President Truman August 8, 1947, Sugar Act of 1948, 61 Stat. 922. See telegram 62, August 23, from Petrópolis, p. 59; see also pp. 604 ff. *passim*.

international arbitration or adjudication. No country which is similarly prepared to submit claims to arbitration or judicial processes need ever expect that this section will be brought into operation with respect to such matters.

MARSHALL

---

710 Consultation 4/8–147 : Telegram

The Chargé in Argentina (Ray) to the Secretary of State

SECRET   BUENOS AIRES, August 1, 1947—8 p. m.

948. I had lunch today with Ambassador Enrique Corominas who will be one of principal Argentine Delegates to Rio Conference. The theme of his extensive and seemingly authoritative remarks was that Argentina wishes to cooperate with the US to make Conference a success, and that all other considerations must be subordinated to achieving harmoniously a completely united front against extra-hemispheric aggression, particularly against Russia. When pressed it was clear that he wished to avoid question of aggression within hemisphere by American nations. He said Argentina will bring up no controversial matters. He envisages that Nicaragua will not be admitted, that discussion of Nicaraguan problem will be postponed till end of conference when she will be told that when she sets her house in order she may adhere to treaty. He expects that Paraguay will offer no problem. He hinted that Argentina might wish to obtain general adherence to its July 7 proposed peace resolution.[54] He intimated that Argentina might agree to proposed two-thirds majority rule. He emphasized that these are all small problems which must not be permitted interfere success Conference. The foregoing accords completely previous info Embtel 918 July 26.[55]

Corominas had considerable to say about the need of US not imposing its will or direction upon other countries; about the desire for parity (presumably in arms with Brazil) and the need of US help in industrialization. He intimated strongly that Marshall Plan should be extended to Latin America, particularly Argentina.

Corominas also referred repeatedly and directly to Russian activities in trying to play off Argentina against US and Brazilian attempts to create antagonisms between US and Argentina; he did not actually name those countries. In his expressed opinion however the only nation which counts besides US is Argentina and an Argentine–US understanding will eliminate all difficulties.

---

[54] The proposed resolution called upon governments to seek internal and international pacification, to subscribe to the doctrine that peace rests upon respect for human rights, and to support ideals of juridical equality, compulsory arbitration, and economic cooperation.
[55] Not printed.

In the most specific way he indicated that this understanding could be achieved by pre-Conference conversations, either in Buenos Aires or Rio or both. He was also specific that we should take intiative in frank talk with Bramuglia. At beginning he said Rio would be success if US and Argentina have pre-conference understanding.

He finally proposed arrange conversation with Bramuglia Monday, Aug. 4 at which he also would be present. I said such interview would be very useful. I have impression approach for conversations was inspired by Bramuglia himself.

If meeting develops I shall immediately inform Dept.

Repeated Rio.

RAY

710 Consultation 4/8–447 : Telegram

The Ambasador in Brazil (Pawley) to the Secretary of State

SECRET   RIO DE JANEIRO, August 4, 1947—9 p. m.

1037. Department's telegram 849, August 1, 9 : 55 a. m., sent Habana as 371; Department's telegram 850, August 1, 7 p. m.[56] The injection of question of operation of Section 202(e) Sugar Act 1948 into considerations of Rio Conference several weeks after passage of measure and in spite of assurances by the Department that Act does not constitute economic threat against any country is probably conscious effort on part Cuban Ambassador to create confusion and misunderstandings which might prejudice outcome Conference.

It is important to remember that Ambassador Belt was member of Left-Wing group which supported electoral campaign of President Grau San Martin and that since going to Washington as Ambassador has, I am reliably informed, adopted policy of steady opposition to hemisphere defense pact and Rio Conference.

Department may find that in several countries of this hemisphere small difficulties and problems which might cause suspicion and lack of confidence have been and are still being created by Left-Wing groups, with strong support from local Communist organizations, hoping that they might endanger success of Conference which is so sincerely and anxiously desired by majority countries this hemisphere. It is significant that local Communist organ *Tribuna Popular* has been only publication to seize upon Belt's protest and use it along with their other propaganda against hemispheric understanding. If this particular act had not been available as disruptive weapon another could have been fabricated.

---

[56] Neither printed.

I have transmitted to Foreign Minister the contents of Department's telegrams under reference and also Department's telegram 855, August 2, 4 p. m.[57] I believe that ulterior motives behind this controversy are becoming apparent to Brazilian Government and that their support may be expected in preventing this question from hindering successful conclusion of Conference. Foreign Minister indicated he no longer fears Cuban problem will present formidable obstacle and added that he would do anything he could to counteract any misinformation on this subject brought to him by other Chiefs of Mission.

PAWLEY

---

710 Consultation 4/8-547 : Telegram

The Ambassador in Brazil (Pawley) to the Secretary of State

CONFIDENTIAL   RIO DE JANEIRO, August 5, 1947—7 p. m.

1046. In view number telephone calls received by Foreign Minister on subject I held luncheon today at Embassy, attended by Chiefs all Latin American Missions and Secretary General FonOff Accioly at which I discussed 1948 Sugar Act and endeavored to impress on them that its provisions with respect to allocation increased quotas would not constitute, in any way, an economic threat to any country. At same time I presented each one present a memorandum embodying substance of Deptel 850, August 1 and Under-Secretary's press interview, Deptel 849, August 1.[58] In discussion that ensued, I gained impression that all present were personally satisfied that the law did not constitute an economic threat but the point was raised by Uruguayan Ambassador Buero, who had some support from Mexican Ambassador,[59] that the law was not clearly drawn in that it did not specifically state that the right to withdraw increase in quota could be submitted to international arbitration only after it had been determined that American citizens or enterprises had exhausted all legal recourse in local courts.

I feel reasonably certain as result of today's meeting that an attempt will be made to bring this point up for discussion at Conference and that it will have some support by Mexican and Uruguayan delegations and possibly those of Colombia and Bolivia.

Cuban Ambassador [60] stated that he was uninstructed with respect to Sugar Act but expressed himself as being satisfied with it. He stressed

---

[57] Not printed.
[58] Neither printed.
[59] Antonio Villalobos.
[60] Gabriel Landa.

sacrifices made by Americans in achievement of Cuba's liberation, the traditional friendship that has always existed between Cuba and United States. He remarked that there never had been and he was sure there never would be any questions between the two countries that could not be settled amicably.

Secretary General Accioly, who is outstanding international jurist, expressed opinion, after the discussion, that the law was unobjectionable and should controversy arise at Conference that Brazil would support United States.

Emphasized several times during the luncheon was the fact that the adoption by US of any measure that might constitute a threat to the economy of any American nation would be completely inconsistent with United States economic policy.

PAWLEY

---

710. Consultation 4/8–1547 : Telegham

The Chairman of the United States Delegation (Marshall) to the Acting Secretary of State

PETRÓPOLIS, August 15, 1947.

8. For Lincoln White from McDermott.[61] Secretary of State and Chairman of the United States Delegation made the following stmt on Aug 15.

In their replies to the recent consultations concerning the treaty to be signed at Rio de Janeiro a majority of the American Republics expressed the opinion that decisions for collective measures should be obligatory on all parties to the treaty.

The United States is anxious to contribute in every possible way to the formulation of a treaty of maximum effectiveness, and has been encouraged by the results of the consultation to review its position regarding obligatory decisions.

It is now the intention of the United States Delegation to submit a revised draft in which it will propose that those collective measures specifically mentioned in the Act of Chapultepec shall be obligatory on all contracting parties when agreed upon in consultation by a vote of two-thirds of the parties, with the sole exception that no state shall be required to furnish armed forces without its consent.

[McDermott]
MARSHALL

---

[61] Michael J. McDermott, Special Assistant to the Secretary of State for Press Relations, and Press Relations Officer at the Conference. Lincoln White was Executive Assistant to Mr. McDermott in the Department.

II. DELIBERATIONS AND DECISIONS

710 Consultation 4/8–1647 : Telegram

The Chairman of the United States Delegation (Marshall) to the Acting Secretary of State

RESTRICTED   PETRÓPOLIS, August 16, 1947—4 p. m.

11–12. Following is first daily summary Conference developments: Preliminary session heads of delegations held Friday morning at which following matters decided, subject confirmation first plenary session to be held Saturday, August 16: (1) Brazilian Foreign Minister [62] unanimously chosen president Conference. (2) Bolivia, Ecuador and Venezuela elected Credentials Committee. (3) Brazil, Colombia, Haiti and US elected language drafting committee. (4) Following working committees established: First Committee, principles, preamble and protocolary articles; Second Committee, action in case of threats or acts of aggression; Third Committee, procedures and agencies for execution treaty. (5) Order precedence determined by lot, with US and Argentina last. (6) Date closing Conference still undecided. (7) Following Uruguayan resolution approved: "Conference declares that, without any desire to intervene in internal affairs of Paraguay,[62a] it urges contending parties to lay down arms and accept generous offer mediation, made by Brazil along with Argentina and Bolivia and with support of other governments".

Inaugural session Friday p. m. opened by President Dutra in essentially formal speech. Mexican Foreign Minister [63] made reply laying great stress on necessity increased economic cooperation and help to less fortunate republics as the one way to provide only sound basis for hemisphere peace. Also stressed Mexican proposal incorporating principles adopted this Conference together with concrete economic provisions in overall organic pact of inter-American system to be adopted Bogotá Conference.[64]

Part 2 first daily summary: At US delegation meeting Friday a. m., all delegates agreed revised US position that decisions of two-thirds parties to take any of measures enumerated in Act Chapultepec [65]

---

[62] Raúl Fernandes.
[62a] For documentation on the situation in Paraguay, see pp. 972 ff.
[63] Jaime Torres Bodet.
[64] Relative to this Conference, see bracketed note, p. 94.
[65] For text, see Department of State, Treaties and Other International Acts Series (TIAS) No. 1543, or 60 Stat. (pt. 2) 1831; the Act of Chapultepec was Resolution VIII of the Inter-American Conference on Problems of War and Peace; for the resolutions of this Conference, see Pan American Union, *Final Act of the Inter-American Conference on Problems of War and Peace, Mexico City, February–March, 1945* (Washington, 1945).

should bind all parties except that no state required provide armed forces without its consent. Vandenberg [66] and Bloom [67] originally suggested through prepared statement on US position include reference to necessity "constitutional consent" for furnishing Armed Forces in order make clear that effect of treaty would not be to broaden powers of Executive. It was finally agreed omit reference constitution in statement and that Secretary would make point clear to US press. This was done unobtrusively at press conference Friday evening.

MARSHALL

---

710 Consultation 4/8–1847 : Telegram

The Chairman of the United States Delegation (Marshall) to the Acting Secretary of State

RESTRICTED   PETRÓPOLIS, August 18, 1947—1 a. m.

20. Conference summary 2. First plenary session August 16 approved decisions Preliminary Meeting report Summary 1 plus resolutions appreciation to Brazil, homage to memory Roosevelt, Berreta (Uruguay) [68] and welcome to Lie.[69] Speeches by Bramuglia (Argentina) Vergara (Chile) Marques Castro (Uruguay) and Cáceres (Honduras). Vergara stressed need economic cooperation. Marques Castro emphasized necessity social and economic development as basis democracy and peace, in effect restating Rodríguez Larreta [70] doctrine but making clear that before community can act against violation human rights, must have juridical foundation based on prior agreement. Although reference unclear, he suggested distinction in treaty between procedures applicable to American attack and those to non-American attack. He stressed deep concern re armaments race and emphasized need give "juridical" basis to Rio agreement. In subsequent conversations Uruguayan delegates indicated this means Uruguay will seek as irreducible minimum adoption resolution favoring unlimited arbitration or judicial settlement on ground Rio treaty would be meaningless without this foundation.

Bramuglia repeated Perón [71] thesis re dangers capitalism and imperialism of either right or left. He mentioned economic cooperation only in passing and made no proposals.

MARSHALL

---

[66] Arthur H. Vandenberg, member of the Senate Foreign Relations Committee.
[67] Sol Bloom, member of the House Foreign Affairs Committee.
[68] Tomás Berreta, the President of Uruguay, whose death occurred on August 2, 1947.
[69] Trygve Lie, Secretary General of the United Nations.
[70] Former Minister for Foreign Affairs in Uruguay.
[71] Juan Perón, President of Argentina.

710 Consultation 4/8–1847

Memorandum of Conversation, by the Assistant Secretary of State for Political Affairs (Armour)[72]

SECRET   PETRÓPOLIS, August 18, 1947.

Today I lunched with the Peruvian Minister for Foreign Affairs, Dr. Enrique García Sayán. He brought up the economic question and indicated that his country would favor the Mexican plan to have the question referred to the Inter-American Social and Economic Council.[73] In such case, he felt that the Council should be strengthened by the designation of special representation. In the meantime he realized that certain of the more immediate problems affecting Peru could be taken up with us on a bilateral basis and in this connection expressed appreciation of the helpful attitude shown by the President of the Exim Bank and others during his recent visit to the United States.

He then referred to the matter of aggression and said that while he was in agreement that there should be no modification in the language of the Act of Chapultepec to the extent of making a distinction between aggression from abroad and within the continent, nevertheless he felt that in practice there would be a difference in approach in the two cases. He said that certain members of his delegation were frankly worried as to how armed force would be used in the case of aggression by one American country against another and cited as a hypothetical case an attack by Chile against Bolivia. If such an event, it might be that Peru and Argentina would be the only countries ready to use their armed forces and Chile might then try to turn the tables by charging aggression against these two countries and we might find ourselves faced with a very difficult situation. However, he said that this was an extreme case which he did not anticipate would ever arise but it did show the need for careful examination as to how the proposed plan would work out in practice should we ever have to resort to extreme measures. The point he wished to make was, he said, that in the case of aggression or a threat of aggression within the continent, all the procedures of pacific settlement should be exhausted before resort should be had to more extreme measures.

Referring to the consultative body he thought this should be the Pan American Union and suggested that perhaps the charter of the Union could be changed by which the Foreign Ministers of the various countries could be made the representatives and they in turn could designate their representatives. This would have the advantage that

---

[72] Mr. Armour was also Political Adviser to the U.S. delegation to the Conference.
[73] For documentation concerning the economic question in Peru, see pp. 998 ff.

in the event of an urgent call there would be a body ready to act: when the Ministers could not come themselves their representatives would be there and prepared to handle the case promptly. I suggested that his proposal might affect the standing of the representation. In other words, where the various governments are now represented by ambassadors or special representatives, under his plan they would be merely deputies for the Foreign Ministers. He agreed that this was perhaps not a practical suggestion but he had been merely thinking out loud.

The Minister then referred to the Peruvian-Ecuadorian Boundary question. He said that he had dined with the Ecuadorian Foreign Minister Señor Trujillo at the latter's invitation and that they had reached an agreement to settle the latest boundary incident between themselves. The larger issue still, of course, remained in the competence of the four Guarantor Powers.

N. A[RMOUR]

710 Consultation 4/8–1947 : Telegram

The Chairman of the United States Delegation (Marshall) to the Acting Secretary of State

RESTRICTED   PETRÓPOLIS, August 19, 1947—1 a. m.

23. Daily Conference summary No. 3. Working committees met and installed Monday without controversy. Following officers elected: Committee I, chairman Uruguay, vice chairman Mexico, *rapporteur* Ecuador; Committee II, chairman Panama, vice-chairman Chile, *rapporteur* Bolivia; Committee III, chairman Costa Rica, vice-chairman Peru, *rapporteur* Colombia. US delegates seconded nominations. Informal agreement working plan for Committees follows PAU report 1946.

Speeches afternoon plenary session Lleras Camargo (PA Union), Guachalla (Bolivia), Belt (Cuba), Morales (Venezuela), Nuñez (Salvador).

Lleras made extensive comparison between inter-American system and UN pointing out that UN is only experiment and weak, experiencing "continuous friction with reality, very similar in appearance to failure". He added, however, Charter is last hope peace and security and should be supported. He stated San Francisco Conference showed "almost brutal contrast between our inter-national democratic world and old world of alliances, balance power, zones influence and insatiable imperialistic ambition". Stated no question of compatibility between Charter and Inter-American system because American Representatives saw to it that Charter fully recognized latter. Otherwise,

UN would not have been born. Gave US high praise for having accepted equality with other Republics and having proposed that in treaty US be bound decisions two-thirds, thus assuring veto no place Inter-American system.

Guachalla stressed importance economic problems and desirability some action regarding them either before or in preparation Bogotá Conference.

Belt speech very aggressive and mostly devoted attack economic aggression. Stated President instructed him propose treaty provision against any form economic threats or intervention and that Cuba would fight for this. Said economic sanctions as dangerous as military action and impossible conclude treaty that does not outlaw all forms economic aggression.

Morales stated indispensable differentiate in treaty between aggression by American state and by non-American state and establish different procedures for former particularly pacific settlement. General support increasing for some such distinction.

MARSHALL

---

710 Consultation 4/8–1947 : Telegram

The Acting Secretary of State to the United States Delegation

CONFIDENTIAL WASHINGTON, August 19, 1947—8 p. m.

41. For Armour. It has been our consistent position, both in Pan Am Union debate prior to Rio and in our informal conversations with Sevilla Sacasa [74] and members of diplomatic corps here, that we would "follow the majority" in so far as possible in connection with question of Nicaraguan attendance at Rio and, for that matter, eventual recognition. We have expressed hope both in circular telegram to our missions in field [75] and in Wright's statement before Pan Am Union [76] that there would exist in Nicaragua a Govt recognized by majority of American republics in sufficient time to permit Nicaragua's attendance at Rio. We continue to feel that this is wise policy and that our present attitude should be very judicious one waiting for substantial body of Govts to act without our giving impression of taking lead in manner which might be interpreted as pressure or tutelage. Our information here is that Honduras should be added to list of countries you mention urtel 26, Aug. 19,[76] as ones not likely to recognize new Govt. Honduras will of course go along with majority but we have definite information that Cáceres' instructions are to follow our lead.

---

[74] Guillermo Sevilla Sacasa, Nicaraguan Ambassador in the United States.
[75] July 24, p. 24.
[76] Not printed.

Telegram went forward today giving you composition of "Argüello" delegation which is going solely as observers. Also Dept has been informed that Argüello Vargas, who, as you know, is Vice Pres in new regime, will attempt to present credentials tomorrow in Rio as representative of newly elected Govt. We are told that if he is not accepted, he will present credentials as representative of "Nicaragua" and credentials will state that acceptance does not imply recognition of regime but rather recognition only of right of Nicaragua to have a delegation seated.

In all honesty we must take into account fact that, like it or not, present regime in Nicaragua has all attributes and qualities of stable *de facto* Govt. It is maintaining public order. It is so far as can be ascertained meeting its international commitments, et cetera. Given the situation in Nicaragua and admitting that the regime is certainly a puppet one and a creature of Somoza [78] (using oppressive measures such as recent detention of leading members of opposition), one of questions for us to decide is whether it is likely that in foreseeable future there will be any other stable regime in Nicaragua composed of other than these same or similar elements. Without condoning methods by which regime has placed itself in power, it is our view that likelihood of strictly constitutional and more representative Govt in near future is slight.

LOVETT

---

710 Consultation 4/8–1947 : Telegram

The Chairman of the United States Delegation (Marshall) to the Acting Secretary of State

SECRET   PETRÓPOLIS, August 19, 1947—11 p. m.

29. Daily Conference summary No. 4. Meetings Committees II and III further outlined work plan but made no substantial progress substantive matters.

Proposed Mexican resolution economic matters formally submitted (retel 27 [79]) under which Conference would instruct inter-American ECOSOC prepare draft agreement of agreements on economic cooperation to submit Bogotá Conference and urge American representative augment ECOSOC staffs on economic and budgetary matters for this purpose. Colombia presented resolution same effect.

Owing impossibility adequate definition, US delegation decided on initiative Vandenberg to drop reference in US revised proposal to

---

[78] Gen. Anastasio Somoza, President of Nicaragua, 1937–1947.
[79] Not printed.

"military measures" other than armed force in listing types measures to which two-thirds vote would bind non-concurring parties. Instead will adhere language Act Chapultepec. Delegation also decided introduce article permitting adherence treaty by nonsignatory states in order permit later Canadian and Nicaraguan adherence.

Eva Perón [80] scheduled arrive Petrópolis August 20 for 1 day's stay.

MARSHALL

---

710 Consultation 4/9–847

Memorandum of Conversation, by the Chairman of the United States Delegation (Marshall)

CONFIDENTIAL PETRÓPOLIS, August 20, 1947.

Participants: Secretary Marshall
Mexican Foreign Minister, Jaime Torres Bodet
Assistant Secretary Armour
Ambassador Dawson [81]

In the apartment of Sr. Torres Bodet, Hotel Quitandinha, August 18, 1947, 6:00 p. m.

I asked the Minister if there were any particular questions concerning the treaty which he would like to discuss.

He referred to the matter of economic cooperation, stating that he believed that a majority of the countries would go along with the Mexican proposal that the subject be referred to the Inter-American Economic and Social Council, which would be requested to prepare one or more draft conventions for submission to the Bogotá Conference. He said that he understood that this would be acceptable to the Bolivian Foreign Minister (Guachalla), although the latter had perhaps not made this quite clear in his speech this afternoon.

Touching on Ambassador Belt's proposal,[82] Sr. Torres Bodet said that he considered it wholly impractical, although, owing to the great interest in economic problems, it might find some support and lead to further discussion of such problems. He remarked that it was difficult enough to define political aggression; that it would be impossible to define satisfactorily economic aggression; and that, if we got into that field, the question of ideological aggression would also be raised. In this connection, he referred to the inclusion in the Brazil-

---

[80] Wife of President Perón of Argentina.
[81] William Dawson, Representative on the Governing Board of the Pan American Union; Political Adviser to the U.S. delegation to the Conference.
[82] See circular airgram of August 1, to the diplomatic representatives in the American Republics, p. 30.

ian draft of a reference to "subversive activities". He said that he viewed this with concern since if subversive activities were to be dealt with in the treaty this might well lead to attempts to restrict fundamental liberties.

I asked Dr. Torres Bodet if he had any comment concerning the Nicaraguan situation. He said this was a delicate matter for Mexico because of proximity and the circumstance that the deposed President was still in asylum in the Mexican Embassy. He expressed the opinion that a majority of countries would probably prefer to recognize the new Nicaraguan regime and then seat its delegates. He thought, however, that the Central American countries might agitate against this with the possible result that such a proposal might be defeated. He said that the argument was being advanced that under certain Central American treaties of 1923 a relative of the author of a revolution was ineligible for the presidency when a new government was set up. He understands that the newly elected President [83] is a relative of Somoza.

With reference to Paraguay, Sr. Torres Bodet expressed the opinion that the alacrity with which the Paraguayan Delegate accepted the Uruguayan resolution (calling on both sides to accept mediation) indicated that the Paraguayan Government was probably in a rather weak position. Sr. Torres Bodet believes that in any case no further action is necessary on the part of the Conference.

---

710 Consultation 4/9–847

Memorandum of Conversation, by the Chairman of the United States Delegation (Marshall)

SECRET   PETRÓPOLIS, August 20, 1947.

Participants: Secretary Marshall
Argentine Foreign Minister, Dr. Juan Atilio Bramuglia
Argentine Ambassador, Dr. Oscar Ivanissevich
Assistant Secretary Armour
Ambassador Dawson

In the apartment of Dr. Bramuglia, Hotel Quitandinha, August 19, 1947, 10:30 a. m.

Dr. Bramuglia touched first upon the Communist danger saying that Argentina views Communist infiltration with great concern and is prepared to join us in combatting it, even to the point of concluding

---

[83] Victor Manuel Román y Reyes.

a secret anti-Communist pact and going to the length of breaking diplomatic relations with the Slav group.

He then passed on to the treaty to be concluded at Rio, stating that he wished to discuss four fundamental and two subsidiary points (the latter he subsequently omitted as too unimportant). The four fundamental points were: (1) A distinction between an extra-continental aggression and one within the continent. He feels that such a distinction should be made and that in the case of an intra-continental conflict the emphasis should be placed on peaceful settlement. He believes that this could be effected by the inclusion of an appropriate clause in the treaty. (2) Economic sanctions. Argentina believes that economic sanctions should be excluded from those collective measures which would be made obligatory on all parties. (3) Provisions for consultation. Although he had this on his list of fundamental points, he did not discuss it, he and Ambassador Ivanissevich agreeing that on further consideration they had found the point satisfactorily covered in our draft. (4) Provisions for denunciation. Argentina considers that, unlike the Charter of the United Nations for example, the instrument to be negotiated at Rio is the sort of treaty which the parties should be permitted to denounce in the usual manner.

I said that before replying, I should like to ask one or two questions.

First, I asked Dr. Bramuglia to comment in greater detail with regard to his position on economic measures. He recalled Argentina's position during the recent war, stating that certain economic sanctions had been taken against it. He said that in the circumstances it would be extremely difficult to induce Argentine public opinion and the Argentine Congress to accept a treaty in which collective economic measures would be obligatory on all parties. He remarked that this would be combatted not only by the opposition but also within the group supporting the Administration.

I told Dr. Bramuglia that we were faced with a somewhat similar problem and that in fact in considering the treaty we were less concerned with the world situation than with problems arising out of our own Governmental structure, and the jealousy of the several powers as respects their prerogatives. I explained to him the restrictions placed on the President by the Congress in legislation dealing with armed forces to be made available to the United Nations.

With regard to the Argentine suggestion that economic measures not be made obligatory, I pointed out that our proposal contemplated an exception with regard to the furnishing of armed forces and that if a further exception as respects economic measures were proposed, this might start a "chain reaction".

I then asked Dr. Bramuglia if he would comment in greater detail on his views concerning the Communist danger. He referred to the political, economic, social, and spiritual aspects of Communist infiltration, stating that in all fields the Communists had the advantage of unity in their dealings with the diversified systems prevailing among the Western countries. In the political field, he suggested among measures which might be taken (*a*) those to combat propaganda, (*b*) outlawing of Communist parties, and (*c*) breaking of diplomatic relations with the Slav countries. He expressed the opinion that, as things now stand and in the absence of war, Communism will win out. He stressed the desirability of establishing against Communism a united front in the economic and social fields. He concluded by saying that in any case Argentina would be definitely on the side of the U.S. in fighting Communism.

I told Dr. Bramuglia that I had been aware before leaving Washington that he would discuss this matter with me (in view of his conversation with our Chargé d'Affaires). I said that at the time our thought was that measures against Communism could best be left to the individual countries; that Communist activities varied from one country to another and each country had its own problems; and that Brazil had taken certain measures, we certain measures, and Argentina also no doubt. I said that we were fully alive to the dangers of Communism which I compared to a fire from which we of the Western Hemisphere were already receiving the sparks. I said that it was necessary to stamp out the fire at its source, to remedy the economic chaos in Western Europe, and to maintain our own countries in a healthy condition.

Dr. Bramuglia said that Argentina realized this and had had it in mind in offering its economic cooperation.

I thanked Dr. Bramuglia for the frankness with which he had spoken, with particular regard to Argentina's domestic political situation. I told him that I had endeavored to use and would continue to use equal frankness in our conversations. I said that I wished to give serious consideration to all that he had said.

In concluding the interview, I asked Dr. Bramuglia if he intended to say anything to the press. He suggested a joint communiqué to which I replied that this seemed rather too formal and might make it necessary to issue communiqués after conversations with other Foreign Ministers. It was agreed that each of us would tell the press merely that we had had an exchange of views regarding the various points of the treaty.

710 Consultation 4/8–847

Memorandum of Conversation, by the Chairman of the United States Delegation (Marshall)

CONFIDENTIAL PETRÓPOLIS, August 20, 1947.

Participants: Secretary Marshall
Chilean Foreign Minister, Dr. Germán Vergara
Assistant Secretary Armour
Ambassador Dawson

In the apartment of Dr. Vergara, Hotel Quitandinha, August 19, 1947, 11:30 a.m.

Dr. Vergara assured me of his desire to cooperate wholeheartedly with the U.S. Delegation.

Referring to his speech of August 16, he stated that he had stressed economic problems largely because of Chile's difficult economic situation [84] and not because he had any intention of pressing for a discussion of economic questions at the present Conference. He indicated that the Mexican and Colombian proposal for referring the subject of economic cooperation to the Inter-American Economic and Social Council and subsequently to the Bogotá Conference would be acceptable.

In response to my inquiries as to the causes underlying Chile's economic difficulties, Dr. Vergara emphasized the following points: The cost of living has tripled since 1938. During the war, the prices of Chile's principal exports (nitrates, copper, iron) remained virtually stabilized, whereas those of its such vital imports as sugar, wheat and cotton rose appreciably. Since the war, there have been further increases in the price of imports with the result that, while the value of its imports is about what it was, in quantity it is receiving only half of what it received before the war. Chile needs in particular machinery (including agricultural implements) and railway rolling stock. As respects industrial development, the country is handicapped by its limited domestic market and to remedy this it has sought agreements with its neighbors (Argentina, Bolivia, and Peru) which would assure its industries wider consuming markets.

Dr. Vergara said that he had come to Rio with the intention of discussing with Assistant Secretary Armour certain specific problems with which he did not wish to bother me. Mr. Armour said that some of these matters had already been taken up by the Chilean Ambassador in Washington and that he (Mr. Armour) would be glad to conduct further conversations with Dr. Vergara here.

---

[84] For documentation on Chile's position with regard to loans and debts, see pp. 527 ff.

Dr. Vergara remarked that, as respects nitrates, it is not Chile's policy to raise prices but rather to increase production and exports. He said with regard to copper that there had been some rise in prices but that consumers had banded together to put a stop to this.

I assured Dr. Vergara of our interest in the economic problems of Chile and other countries. I emphasized the tremendous strain on our economy resulting from our efforts to assist Europe. At this point, he expressed apprehension lest European industries be rehabilitated and re-enter the market before Chilean industries could develop to the point where they could compete. I told him that I felt that European industrial rehabilitation would be a long and slow process. I explained to him in some detail how completely the European business structure had been disrupted, and pointed out that there had been no such disruption in Latin America and that, with good planning and good cooperation, these countries should be able to progress in an orderly manner. I called attention to the example of Henry Ford in developing a large domestic market by producing an article which well paid workers could afford to buy.

---

710 Consultation 4/9–847

Memorandum of Conversation, by the Chairman of the United States Delegation (Marshall)

SECRET   PETRÓPOLIS, August 20, 1947.

Participants: Secretary Marshall
Ecuadoran Foreign Minister Dr. José Vicente Trujillo
Assistant Secretary Armour
Ambassador Dawson

In apartment of Dr. Trujillo, Hotel Quitandinha, August 20, 1947, 10:30 a. m.

After the customary exchanges, I inquired whether Dr. Trujillo had any comments or suggestions with regard to the treaty to be negotiated. He said that Ecuador had submitted its draft to the Pan American Union two years ago and was making no new proposals at this time. With reference to this draft, he commented briefly on one or two points and particularly on provisions regarding conciliation and the more important functions which Ecuador would entrust to the Governing Board of the Pan American Union.

Dr. Trujillo then referred to Ecuador's boundary controversy with Peru and said that it had been his intention to request the good offices of the guarantors of the 1942 boundary treaty (the United States, Argentina, Brazil and Chile) in settling a pending dispute over a small tract (less than 100 square kilometers) which a Brazilian arbiter had at first awarded to Ecuador only to reverse his decision a few months later. Dr. Trujillo produced maps showing the tract in dispute and said that his request would be that the original award of the Brazilian arbiter be complied with.

Dr. Trujillo said that in addition he was interested in obtaining U.S. financial assistance particularly for highway development but that he did not wish to bother me with such matters. Mr. Armour remarked that the question had already been taken up by the Ecuadoran Embassy in Washington.[85]

There followed a brief discussion of Ecuador's economic situation. The following information was brought out in response to various questions which I put to Dr. Trujillo:

The cost of living in Ecuador has increased by about 60 percent as compared with 1938. Since Ecuador produces most of its food requirements and most of the clothing worn by the common people, this increase in the cost of living is due principally to the rise in the international price level and the higher cost of imports. There are certain minor, not serious shortages particularly in clothing and housing. Ecuador's principal exports are rice (about 60,000 tons this year), cacao, bananas, balsa wood, and Panama hats. Ecuador is the principal source of supply for balsa wood and the fact that production was greatly increased during the war and has now declined is a disturbing factor. The same is true of quinine. Ecuador's railways need rolling stock but the road-beds (particularly that of the Guayaquil and Quito railway) are in good condition.

---

710 Consultation 4/9–847

Memorandum of Conversation, by the Chairman of the United States Delegation (Marshall)

SECRET   PETRÓPOLIS, August 20, 1947.

Participants: Secretary Marshall
Venezuelan Foreign Minister Dr. Carlos Morales
Venezuelan Chargé d'Affaires Falcón-Briceño
Assistant Secretary Armour
Ambassador Dawson

In apartment of Dr. Morales, Hotel Quitandinha, August 20, 1947, 11:15 a. m.

After the customary preliminary exchanges, I told Dr. Morales that I was aware of his Government's views concerning a distinction between extra-continental aggression and aggression from within and

---

[85] For documentation concerning this subject, see pp. 690 ff.

that I should be glad to have the benefit of any comments he might wish to make.

Dr. Morales said that Venezuela had given up any intention of proposing the negotiation of two separate treaties but felt strongly that in the single treaty to be negotiated the distinction in question should be clearly drawn. He said that, as respects an extra-continental aggression, it must be presumed that the foreign country would be the aggressor and that all American republics should give immediate assistance. In the case of an intra-continental conflict, he feels that it might be difficult to determine who is the aggressor, that this should be left to the Governing Board of the Pan American Union or to some other organ to be established for the purpose, that it would be the duty of the appropriate organ to order the immediate suspension of hostilities and to examine the situation, and that sanctions would be applied against a party found to be an aggressor, provided efforts for peaceful settlement should fail. Dr. Morales referred to the Leticia incident between Colombia and Peru [86] to illustrate his point, saying that although Colombia had invaded Peru it claimed that it had done so in view of Peruvian preparations to attack Colombia. He said that in such a case the danger existed that some states might side with one party and others with the other.

I told Dr. Morales that we felt that no distinction should be made in the treaty for reasons set forth in an informal document (based on Mr. Dreier's memorandum of August 19—USRio/Gen/15 [87]), the text of which I handed him in English and Spanish. He put his finger immediately on point 2 of this document (distinction unnecessary since under Article 3 of our draft provisions for sanctions in no way impede prior resort to pacific settlement). He contended that in view of Article 51 of the United Nations Charter the distinction *is* necessary since under Article 51 the victim of aggression could call on its sister republics for immediate assistance as a matter of legitimate self-defense.

I told Dr. Morales that he had cited a specific case within his experience, that I had thought of something concrete within my own experience, and that, although I was thinking aloud without knowing the views of my associates, I had in mind the possible case of a revolution in an American republic inspired and abetted by a non-American state. I said that in reality this would constitute an extra-continental aggression and that in dealing with it considerable confusion might result if the distinction advocated by Venezuela were introduced in the treaty. Continuing, I said that after all the value

---

[86] For the position of the United States on this boundary dispute, see *Foreign Relations*, 1935, vol. IV, pp. 199–217.
[87] Not printed.

of a treaty depends less on its terms than on the good faith of the parties (as evidenced by the Russo-German pact); and that even if we allowed for two or three exceptions we could count on the good faith and influence of the vast majority of the American republics to make our treaty work.

In taking leave of Dr. Morales, I thanked him for having set forth his ideas and told him that they had generated some new ideas in my own mind.

At one point in the interview, Dr. Falcón-Briceño explained that the Venezuelan views had been filed with the Secretariat of the Conference as "observations" and not as a formal proposal.

710 Consultation 4/9–847

Memorandum of Conversation, by the Chairman of the United States Delegation (Marshall)

SECRET   PETRÓPOLIS, August 20, 1947.

Participants: Secretary Marshall
              Panamanian Foreign Minister Dr. Ricardo J. Alfaro
              Other members of the Panamanian Delegation present but not participating
              Assistant Secretary Armour
              Ambassador Dawson

In apartment of Dr. Alfaro, Hotel Quitandinha, August 20, 1947, 12 p. m.

I asked the Minister if he would comment on his impressions of the Conference. He replied that he felt that things were proceeding satisfactorily but was somewhat apprehensive lest matters be complicated by the introduction of extraneous questions such as the Ecuadoran-Peruvian boundary controversy, the Belt proposal, et cetera.

After some general conversation, Dr. Alfaro brought up the defense sites question [88] by saying that two or three weeks ago an opposition group in Panama had recommended that Panama place the matter on the Rio agenda and decline to attend the Conference if this were not done. Dr. Alfaro said that his government rejected such a proposal as preposterous and that the Rio Conference was not a "court of justice" for the consideration of such matters.

He then said that Panamanian public opinion was perturbed over the delay in bringing the defense sites negotiations to a conclusion. He said that late in 1945 Panama had made clear its contention that the agreement required the return of the sites one year after the cessation

---

[88] For documentation on the defense sites question, see pp. 881 ff.

of hostilities, that in the Panamanian view the sites not already returned were being held illegally since September, 1946, that Panamanian opposition groups were talking of organizing public demonstrations of protest, that there was much agitation in student circles, and that a difficult and unpleasant political situation existed. He referred to conversations held in May in Panama, in which Murray Wise of the Department of State participated. He said that certain proposals had been made at the time and that the Panamanian Government had heard nothing further from our Government since May 14. Dr. Alfaro stated that he had heard that the delay was due to discussions between the State and War Departments.

I told Dr. Alfaro that, while I was not informed as to the details of the present negotiations, I knew a good deal about the general problem since I had been on both sides of the fence. I said that, having accompanied General Pershing to Panama in 1920 when the Taboga incident [89] was being agitated, I could appreciate his political problem. I reminded him of the great responsibility I had borne for the defense of the Canal and said that in my discussions with Sumner Welles [90] I had found at the time that we necessarily approached the matter from different angles and did not speak the same language. I said that it was my understanding that a reply was being prepared about the time of my departure for Rio and might already have been sent to Panama; that we were looking into this; and that in any case I could assure him of my desire to expedite the negotiations and work out a mutually satisfactory solution.

Dr. Alfaro remarked that the U.S. authorities were inclined perhaps to overlook the psychological factor. He referred to the Taboga incident as an example and with respect to the current negotiations said that the United States was asking for permanent occupation of the defense sites. He said that no Panamanian Government could agree to permanent occupation and remain in office. He suggested that the agreement might provide for a three or four year term, adding that at the expiration of this period it should be possible to determine whether the international situation required further occupation or had so improved as to permit gradual disarmament. I told Dr. Alfaro that in my opinion he was unduly optimistic and that even in the improbable event that peace treaties could be concluded within six months their implementation would be a long process. I said that disarmament would have to come slowly and step by step and that, as

---

[89] Taboga Island, known at one time as a favorite playground of Panamanians, was temporarily occupied by United States military forces. Panamanian protests resulted in the return of the Island, with the exception of a small part, to Panama.
[90] Former Under Secretary of State.

long as I was Secretary of State, I should use every effort to prevent a repetition of the mistake made after the first World War—a mistake which had cost us 1,200,000 casualties and $350,000,000,000. I said that a short-term agreement—three years or five as Dr. Alfaro suggested subsequently—would create a difficult situation if on its expiration world conditions required its extension.

In addition to stressing his desire for expeditious conclusion of the negotiations and for a short-term agreement, Dr. Alfaro mentioned incidentally the possibility of reducing the number of defense sites.

(In recognizing Panama's domestic political problem, I referred confidentially—stating that it was of course understood that my remarks would not be repeated—to Greenland and the very similar and more serious problem confronting the Danish Government).

---

710 Consultation 4/9–847

Memorandum of Conversation, by the Chairman of the United States Delegation (Marshall)

SECRET   PETRÓPOLIS, August 20, 1947.

Participants: Secretary Marshall
                  Peruvian Foreign Minister Dr. Enrique García Sayán
                  Assistant Secretary Armour
                  Ambassador Dawson

In apartment of Dr. García Sayán, Hotel Quitandinha, August 20, 1947, 1:00 p. m.

After the customary preliminary exchanges, I asked Dr. García Sayán if he had any comments or suggestions with regard to the Conference. He said that things seemed to be going satisfactorily and that in particular he believed that our proposal for making collective measures obligatory for all parties was gaining ground.

I told him that I had been discussing with another Foreign Minister the question of drawing a distinction between extra-continental and intra-continental aggression, that we do not favor such a distinction, and that in the course of the discussion I had advanced an argument which I had not yet considered with my associates. I referred to the possible case of a revolution in an American republic inspired and abetted by a non-American state.* I said that in reality this would

---

*Note: In explaining what I had in mind I cited the case of the Japanese Ambassador's plotting in Panama during the war—fifth column activities not only directed against the security of the Canal but even extending to attempts to stir up trouble among the Negroes in the U.S. I also mentioned the case of German and Italian fifth column activities in Brazil early in the war connected with attempts to sink Allied troop ships stopping off in Rio for water. [Footnote in the original.]

constitute an extra-continental aggression and that in dealing with it considerable confusion might result if a distinction between aggression from without and aggression from within were introduced in the treaty. Dr. García Sayán seemed impressed by this argument and in general he gave no indication of favoring the distinction advocated by Venezuela. In departing, Mr. Armour handed him the text of the informal document setting forth our arguments against the distinction (based on Mr. Dreier's memorandum of August 19—US Rio/Gen/15 [91]).

710 Consultation 4/8–2147 : Telegram

The Chairman of the United States Delegation (Marshall) to the Acting Secretary of State

SECRET   PETRÓPOLIS, August 21, 1947—1 a. m.

39. Daily summary No. 5. Accordance prearranged plan Eva Perón arrived Plenary Session today 10 minutes before Secretary's speech.[92] Adroit handling by Brazilians resulted formal reception and recognition her presence following Secretary's speech.

Secretary's speech very well received, followed by Acevedo (Guatemala) Despradel (Dominican Republic) García Sayán (Peru). Acevedo in strong defense democratic principles obliquely attacked present regimes Nicaragua and Dominican Republic. Also urged Conference consideration economic problems.

Despradel in obvious reference Cuba urged broadest definition in treaty to encompass all forms aggression.

García praised US willingness accept two-thirds decision, urged action on economic problems and supported distinction between American and non-American attack.

Brazilian FonMin told Secretary Brazil expects propose tomorrow that all problems inter-American economic cooperation be handled at special conference called not earlier than second half next year, and that American representatives submit any economic proposals inter-American ECOSOC for study in preparation conference. This would represent compromise Argentine, Mexican proposals. Secretary indicated US agreeable.

Plenary Session set 10 p. m. August 21 as deadline for new proposals.

MARSHALL

---

[91] Not printed.
[92] For extracts from the Secretary's speech, see *Report of the Delegation of the United States of America*, pp. 8–9.

710 Consultation 4/8–2247: Telegram

The Chairman of the United States Delegation (Marshall) to the Acting Secretary of State

SECRET   PETRÓPOLIS, August 22, 1947—1 a. m.

51. Daily Conference summary 6. Central Committee approved plan work Conference and fixed August 28 termination work committees. Brazil proposed September 5 closing session but Committee decided leave open, in view possibility earlier termination.

Committee I established two subcommittees begin substantive work. Discussion and proposals. Committee II show considerable support inclusion comprehensive definition aggression. Subcommittee Committee III decided organ consultation under treaty should be meetings Foreign Ministers but that PAU governing board could act on interim basis. Possibility left open use other methods by agreement parties.

Following Mexican proposal economic cooperation now supported fourteen other countries, including US, Brazil, Argentina:

That inter-American ECOSOC prepare draft agreement economic cooperation submission Bogotá; that staffs members be augmented for purpose; and that special economic conference be called second half next year, time to be set by Bogotá Conference, to study procedures carry out agreement and make economic cooperation more effective.

Prearranged plan, which called for presentation above resolution Central Committee today, stalled because Belt (Cuba), pretending cooperation, said he wanted obtain approval government drop Cuban economic resolution in favor Mexican proposal.

Now learn Belt will insist presentation tomorrow proposal economic aggression, notwithstanding pledge cooperation to members US delegation. Therefore present plan is that Mexican proposal will be presented tomorrow and US will second.

Plenary session speeches Trujillo (Ecuador) and Zuleta Angel (Colombia). Trujillo stated hemisphere must close ranks and prepare eventualities in view two opposing forces world today. Stated that after individualistic fight last century for separate sovereignties and period romantic Pan-Americanism, American representatives now see necessary articulate individual sovereignties giving up part in interest sovereignty hemisphere. In discussing Ecuadorian proposals, he stated principle inviolability treaties must be modified prevent perpetuation injustice, insisted must define aggression in treaty; and supported Mexican proposal basic charter Bogotá.

Zuleta placed great emphasis Latin American unity although giving US high praise, and referred brave fight Latin American delegations

San Francisco for autonomy inter-American system. Insisted system should have complete liberty in pacific settlement, full right self-defense and full choice of taking necessary preventive steps in event aggression, limiting rigor of principle of article 53, UN charter by distinguishing between coercive and preventive measures, latter not requiring S[ecurity] C[ouncil] authorization.

MARSHALL

---

710 Consultation 4/9-847

Memorandum of Conversation, by the Chairman of the United States Delegation (Marshall)

SECRET PETRÓPOLIS, August 22, 1947.

Participants: Secretary Marshall
Lt. Gen. Pedro Aurelio de Góes Monteiro, Senator of Brazil
Ambassador William D. Pawley [93]
Major Vernon A. Walters

In apartment of Lt. Gen. Góes Monteiro, Hotel Quitandinha, August 21, 1947, at 11:30 a. m.

After the customary preliminary exchanges, I asked General Góes Monteiro his views concerning the treaty to be negotiated. He briefly reviewed the personality of the members of the Brazilian Delegation. He stated that he felt that no distinction should be made between extra-continental and intra-continental aggression, stating that extra-continental aggression could begin through internal aggression. He further stated that economic questions were well handled in my speech and could not be included at this conference, which is meeting to fix collective responsibility. If the conference were to handle all problems concerning the American republics, it would have to sit for two years. He suggested economic matters could be handled at another conference.

General Góes Monteiro stated that he felt the treaty should include compulsory and automatic measures to be taken in case of aggression, as there will be no time to hold consultations. He felt that such measures should include the right of passage through, and use of bases on the territory of American republics, to other American States coming to the aid of the attacked State. He felt that military organization could be mentioned in the treaty but should be regulated at Bogotá. He stated that he had discussed with the Brazilian Delegation the necessity for including in the protocolary articles a time limit for the ratification of the treaty. He felt that the defense of the South Atlantic

---

[93] Ambassador in Brazil; Delegate to the Conference.

would be the responsibility of U.S., Brazil, Uruguay, Argentina, and because of the Strait of Magellan, Chile.

General Góes Monteiro then spoke of the communist danger which he felt was more serious than the Fifth Column had been during World War II. He stated that in May Brazil had outlawed the Communist Party,[94] and that further measures would soon be taken to cancel the seats of the Communist Party Congressional representatives. He stated that this matter was a little dangerous to bring up at the conference as there would probably be opposition to any anti-Communist action by Mexico, Uruguay, Ecuador, and Chile. I asked General Góes Monteiro whether he felt that the military details of which he had spoken should be handled by bilateral agreements, and he stated that this would be the best way. I then told General Góes Monteiro I would welcome the opportunity to discuss his views at greater length with him. He stated this would be entirely agreeable to him.

On taking leave of General Góes Monteiro he stated that if there were any matters I wished brought to the immediate attention of the President of Brazil, he would be glad to do so, as he had a direct channel of access to the President.

---

710 Consultation 4/9–847

Memorandum of Conversation, by the Chairman of the United States Delegation (Marshall)

SECRET   PETRÓPOLIS, August 22, 1947.

Participants: Secretary Marshall
Dr. Domingo Esguerra, Chairman of the Colombian Delegation and Minister of Foreign Affairs for Colombia
Ambassador Donnelly [95]

I called today on His Excellency Dr. Domingo Esguerra, Chairman of the Colombian Delegation and Colombian Foreign Minister.

I thanked the Minister for the kind references to our country and to me in the speech made by Ambassador Zuleta Angel.[95a]

I requested the Minister's views on the progress of the Conference and he replied that while he was optimistic as to the outcome of it there still remained a few controversial problems to settle. He referred in particular to a resolution submitted by the Ecuadoran Dele-

---

[94] For documentation on relations between Brazil and the Soviet Union, see pp. 391 ff.
[95] Walter J. Donnelly, Ambassador in Costa Rica; Political Adviser to the U.S. delegation to the Conference.
[95a] Eduardo Zuleta Angel, Colombian Minister of Education.

gation calling for revision of boundary treaties of the American republics. He expressed the belief that adoption of the resolution would be a matter of grave concern to his country and to other American republics and that wars might follow. He referred to Colombia's boundary treaties with Venezuela, Ecuador and Peru and said that a revision of the treaties at this time would create a very unfavorable reaction in his country. He expressed the hope I would find it possible to suggest to His Excellency Dr. Raul Fernandes, President of the Conference, that the Ecuadoran Delegate withdraw the resolution. I told him that I would be willing to suggest to Dr. Fernandes that in my opinion the proposed resolution does not come within the province of this Conference. *Note:* This has been done and the resolution has not yet been discussed at the Conference.

The Minister also expressed concern over a report that the Chairman of the Ecuadorian Delegation [96] had said that Senator Vandenberg had indicated his approval of the Ecuadoran resolution. I expressed surprise at this remark and said that I was reasonably certain that Senator Vandenberg had made no such statement. (*Note:* Senator Vandenberg subsequently denied the report and later informed the Colombian Foreign Minister that he had never heard of the resolution.)

The Colombian Minister also expressed concern over the Mexican proposal providing for a defense zone for the Americas and added that while the motives for the resolution were not clear it appeared Mexico hoped, among other things, to create spheres of influence in Central and South America, with Mexico's sphere consisting of Central America and the Caribbean areas. The Minister said that he had not read the resolution and suggested that no action be taken on it until all the Delegates had an opportunity to study it carefully.

The Minister said that he had intended to call in the Colombian Ambassador to the United States [97] for the purpose of discussing certain aspects of the economic situation in Colombia and the possibility of obtaining loans from the United States, but that in view of the shortage of time before the next meeting and the complexity of the problems it might be preferable to arrange a separate meeting. Ambassador Donnelly suggested that instead of a separate meeting that the Minister furnish me with a memorandum covering the points which our Delegation would study here and would forward to the Department for further examination and comment. The Minister agreed with this suggestion.

---

[96] José Vicente Trujillo.
[97] Gonzalo Restrepo Jaramillo.

710 Consultation 4/9–847

Memorandum of Conversation, by the Chairman of the United States Delegation (Marshall)

SECRET   PETRÓPOLIS, August 22, 1947.

Participants: Secretary Marshall
 Dr. Carlos Leonidas Acevedo, Guatemalan Minister of Finance and Chairman of Delegation
 Dr. Ismael Gonzáles Arévalo, Guatemalan Minister to Peru
 Ambassador William D. Pawley
 Major Vernon A. Walters

In the Apartment of Dr. Acevedo, Hotel Quitandinha, August 21, 1947, at 12:15 p. m.

After the customary preliminary exchanges, I inquired of Dr. Acevedo whether he had any comments or suggestions concerning the treaty to be negotiated. He replied that as he had stated in his speech his Government felt that any Government that denied the rights of man and constitutional guarantees was a menace to security, and that the treaty should contain provisions to that effect. I stated that I felt the real force of the treaty would lie in a strong majority rather than in one or two governments which might stray from the path. Dr. Acevedo then stated that he felt some difference existed between external and internal aggression. I pointed out that in my opinion an external action could very well start from within and that it would be difficult to draw such distinction. I added that many thought of aggression in terms of a fleet of planes coming over and ships landing on beaches but that a future aggression could begin by the internal overthrow of one of the governments. After this presentation of my point of view he felt much less inclined to defend such a distinction between internal and external aggression.

Dr. Acevedo stated that he would like a provision in the treaty defining non-recognition of territorial acquisitions to support that such acquisitions must be by violence so that Guatemala's claim of Belize (British Honduras) would not be prejudiced in their discussions with the British [sic]. I asked Dr. Acevedo whether he had any further suggestion and he stated that he had expressed his views fully in his speech which had coincided with mine. I stated that I had noticed the coincidence. Dr. Arévalo then stated that he felt there would be no serious difficulty in drafting the treaty and that there merely remained to harmonize the points of view of the various delegations.

As I was taking my leave, he stated that the Guatemalan Government had asked for *agrément* for Dr. Ismael Gonzáles Arévalo from the U.S. State Department and if such *agrément* were obtained this gentleman would be named next Guatemalan Ambassador to the United States. I replied that I had not yet seen the request but that he could consider the matter settled.

---

710 Consultation 4/9–847

Memorandum of Conversation, by the Chairman of the United States Delegation (Marshall)

SECRET   PETRÓPOLIS, August 22, 1947.

Participants: Secretary Marshall
              Dr. Luiz Anderson, Chairman of the Costa Rican Delegation
              Ambassador Donnelly

I called today on Dr. Luiz Anderson, Chairman of the Costa Rican Delegation and Chairman of Committee III of the Conference.

In reply to my question as to his views on the progress of the Conference, Dr. Anderson said that while he was optimistic as to the final result of it he was preoccupied at the moment with the Argentine, Mexican and Venezuelan draft resolutions providing for more conciliatory measures in cases of aggression within the hemisphere. I remarked in this connection that it is difficult in modern warfare to differentiate between aggression from without and aggression from within the hemisphere because an aggressor nation outside of the hemisphere could by intrigue and espionage create serious internal unrest in a country and conflicts between the American nations thereby breaking down the unity of the Americas preparatory to an attack on this hemisphere. Dr. Anderson expressed complete agreement with my views and said that he was firmly of the opinion that the Conference should not make any difference in the procedures and sanctions to be applied in cases of aggression from without or from within the hemisphere.

He said that the work of his Committee was progressing satisfactorily and that if necessary the Committee could complete its assignment by August 25. I remarked that it was of the utmost importance that the Conference be brought to a successful conclusion as expeditiously as possible and he expressed similar views.

Dr. Anderson made no reference during the meeting to the internal problems of Costa Rica or to the relations between Costa Rica and the United States.

710 Consultation 4/8–2347 : Telegram

The Chairman of the United States Delegation (Marshall) to the Acting Secretary of State

CONFIDENTIAL   PETRÓPOLIS, August 23, 1947—3 p. m.

62. Speaking at meeting Central Committee Friday, Belt (Cuba) insisted idea that Cuba came Conference promote sugar interests absolutely false. Stated incident 202 *e* [98] settled bi-laterally and letter Marshall to Truman [99] when bill signed clarified matter and Marshall's word worth as much as any treaty article. Quoting at length recent statement Truman regarding economic aggression, Belt concluded Truman and Grau [1] complete agreement necessity avoiding economic aggression.

Belt referred several times express instructions Government do all possible obtain treaty provisions proscribing economic aggression but stated knew majority delegates opposed and desired conform majority will. Therefore asked vote on question whether moment opportune deal with subject.

Resulting vote 15 to 5 against Belt who then repeated would adhere will majority.

Believe frank talks with Belt, with Vandenberg and other members United States delegation plus failure win general support other delegations led him use above method save face. With subsequent adoption Mexican resolution directing Inter-American ECOSOC prepare economic agreements for submission Bogotá and calling for economic conference second half 1948, believe economic questions disposed of this Conference.

Department please repeat Habana for information.

MARSHALL

---

710 Consultation 4/8–2547 : Telegram

The United States Military Adviser to the United States Delegation to the Conference (Ridgway) [2] to the Joint Chiefs of Staff

SECRET   RIO DE JANEIRO, August 25, 1947.
PRIORITY

Unnumbered. Mexico has proposed that the signatory states agree that for the purposes of the treaty an armed attack shall be understood

---

[98] Reference is to section 202(*e*) of the Sugar Act of 1948; see footnote 53, p. 30.
[99] Department of State *Bulletin*, August 10, 1947, p. 341.
[1] Ramón Grau San Martín, President of Cuba.
[2] Lt. Gen. M. B. Ridgway, U.S.A., who was also United States Delegate to the Inter-American Defense Board, sent this message to the Department of State for the JCS.

to be any military operation which a state undertakes against the territory or against the land, air or naval forces of an American state, whenever these forces are located within the geographical zone delimited by the "Declaration of Panama" of October 3, 1939 [3] or in any place which, though outside said zone, is an integral part of the territory of an American state. Because of this issue and of world-wide US commitments, Senator Vandenberg has raised the question as to whether we should, within the terms of this treaty and a spirit of reciprocal fairness, seek to bind all Latin American countries to assist US immediately regardless of the locale in which we are attacked, and whether if we did seek such a commitment, from Latin American countries, there is any reasonable expectation of securing their agreement to so obligate themselves.

Under the premise that a decision should be taken to delineate a region, the US Military Advisers are recommending that the zone delimited by the Panama Declaration of October 3, 1939 be modified and roughly extended to ensure the inclusion of the remainder of the North American continent, Greenland, Iceland and the area from approximately 15 degrees west longitude west to 170 degrees west longitude and north to the pole. Opposition to inclusion of Iceland may be anticipated, in which event its exclusion may be necessary.[3a] Under this arrangement all Latin American countries would be bound by those provisions of the treaty relating to armed attack, in case such an attack were to occur within above delineated region, but would assume only the lesser obligation to consult immediately as to measures to be taken in case our forces should be attacked or other act or threat of aggression, as provided in the treaty, were to occur outside the delineated region. Acceptance by US of Mexican concept of the region being definitely limited by boundaries would be dependent upon Mexico accepting new text of draft substituting for the Mexican proposal to define armed attack, our idea to describe the region.

Senator Austin of opinion such substitution would remove implications inconsistent with United Nations Charter. Situation developing rapidly and decision may be reached momentarily. Further reports will be made as circumstances warrant and time permits.

US Delegation familiar with this message.

RIDGWAY

---

[3] Department of State, *Report of the Delegate of the United States of America to the Meeting of the Foreign Ministers of the American Republics, Held at Panama, September 23–October 3, 1939* (Washington, 1940), p. 62.

[3a] In telegram 112, August 27, 6 p.m., the Department commented on possible complications if Iceland were to be included (710 Consultation 4/8–2747).

710 Consultation 4/8–2647 : Telegram

The Chairman of the United States Delegation (Marshall) to the Acting Secretary of State

RESTRICTED   PETRÓPOLIS, August 26, 1947—2 a. m.

76. Conference summary 7. Following are essential points preamble and first two articles tentatively approved Subcommittee Committee I:

"High Contracting Parties, representing their peoples, inspired by desire consolidating and strengthening their relations of friendship and good neighborliness, and considering that Resolution VIII Mexico City recommended conclusion treaty prevent repel threats or acts aggression against any of countries America;

That parties reaffirm existence of regional arrangement or agency defined in Act Chapultepec, contemplated in Charter and compatible with purposes and principles of Charter for dealing with such matters relating to maintenance international peace and security appropriate for regional action;

That parties reaffirm adherence fundamental principles inter-American solidarity and cooperation, and especially those enumerated in whereases and declarations Act Chapultepec, all of which should be understood as accepted as standards mutual relations and juridical basis inter-American system;

That American states propose conclude treaty concerning peace system envisaged Resolution XXXIX Mexico City:

Have resolved conclude treaty accordance foregoing principles in order assure peace, provide effective reciprocal assistance to meet armed attacks against any American State and deal threats aggression against any.

Article 1. Parties formally condemn war and undertake in international relations not resort threat or use force in any manner inconsistent with charter and treaty.

Article 2. As consequence preceding principle, parties undertake submit every controversy whatever nature which may arise between them to methods peaceful settlement and endeavor settle such controversies means procedures inter-American system before referring them to General Assembly or Security Council."

Following is text substantive portion treaty agreed drafting group Subcommittee Committee III consisting representatives US, Brazil, Bolivia, Mexico, Panama, Peru:

"Article A. 1. Armed attack by any state against American State considered attack against all and each undertakes assist in meeting attack in exercise right self-defense recognized article 51 Charter.

2. On request state attacked and until decision of security organ of system, parties may determine immediate measures they may individually adopt in accordance principle continental solidarity and in exercise right collective self-defense. Parties shall consult without delay to examine those measures and agree upon collective measures which should be adopted.

3. Provisions this article shall be applied in case of any armed attack which takes place within region described article B or within territory American State. When attack takes place outside said areas, provisions article D shall be applied.

4. Measures self-defense provided for this article may be taken until Security Council taken measures necessary maintain international peace security.

Article B. Region to which treaty refers comprises geographic area defined declaration Panama 1939, North American Continent, Alaska, Greenland, and area between.

Article C. Parties shall send Security Council complete information, in accordance articles 51, 54 Charter.

Article D. If inviolability or integrity of territory or sovereignty or political independence any American state affected by aggression not armed attack or by threat aggression or by intracontinental or extra-continental conflict, or by any other fact or situation that might endanger peace America, parties shall consult in order agree on measures which should be taken for common defense and maintenance peace and security continent.

Article E. In case conflict between two or more American States, without prejudice exercise of right self-defense and right of aiding country directly attacked conformity article A, parties shall call upon contending states suspend hostilities and shall take all other measures necessary reestablish or maintain peace security and for solution conflict peaceful means.

Article F. For purposes treaty measures on which parties may agree may comprise: Recall chiefs' missions; breaking diplomatic relations; breaking consular relations; complete or partial interruption economic relations or rail, sea, air, postal, telegraphic, telephonic, and radio telephonic or radio telegraphic relations; or use military force.

Article G. In addition other acts which may be characterized aggression, following shall be so considered:

　a. Unprovoked armed attack by state against territory, people, land, sea, or air forces another state;

　b. Invasion territory state by armed forces another state, even without declaration war, by trespassing boundaries, established by treaty or arbitral award and demarcated in accordance therewith, or by means occupation by force of territory subject to effective jurisdiction said state.

Article H. Nothing in treaty shall be construed as impairing rights and obligations of parties in accordance Charter."

MARSHALL

---

710 Consultation 4/8–2747 : Telegram

The Chairman of the United States Delegation (Marshall) to the Acting Secretary of State

RESTRICTED   PETRÓPOLIS, August 27, 1947—2 a. m.

83. Conference summary 8. Action Central Committee re Trujillo as delegate Ecuador reported our telegram 82.[4] Committee I ap-

---

[4] Not printed.

proved articles A, B, C, D as reported Conference summary 7 with following changes:

Article A, paragraph 1, no change. Paragraph 2. "On request state attacked and until decision security organ of system, parties may determine immediate measures they may individually adopt in fulfillment obligation paragraph 1 and in accordance principle, et cetera."

Article A, paragraph 3 and article B approved provisionally as reported our telegram 81.[5] USDel agreed these articles in view insistence several delegations, particularly Mexican, that otherwise obligation to assist would arouse public opposition on ground Latin American Republics would be called upon automatically to underwrite US world-wide commitments not of their making and in view our belief inclusion reference zone would make easier defeat attempts make further distinction between intra- and extra-continental attacks.

Article C, no change.

Article D. "If inviolability or integrity of territory or sovereignty or political independence of American state affected by aggression not armed attack or by intra-continental or extra-continental conflict or by any other fact or situation that might endanger peace America, parties shall consult in order agree on measures which must be taken in case of aggression to assist injured state and in any case on measures which should be taken for common defense and maintenance peace and security continent."

Guatemala proposed inclusion following words: Article D after "peace America" "or the democratic structure of American governments". Immediately Argentina, Dominican Republic and Honduras opposed on plea unanimity, necessity for speed and contravention principle non-intervention. Uruguay supported general ideas in consonance with so-called "Uruguayan initiative" of last year.[6] Vandenberg opposed Guatemalan language as outside proper scope treaty. Brazil supported US position but indicated willingness accept idea that violation human rights is aggression [since?] these rights are guaranteed by treaty or convention. Guatemalan proposal defeated receiving votes only Guatemala and Cuba.

Remaining articles our telegram 76 not yet approved full committee.

Following articles approved Committee III today:

"Article A. Consultations to which treaty refers shall be carried out by meetings FoMins of Republics which have ratified treaty, or in manner or by organ which may be established in future.

---

[5] Not printed.
[6] Presumably the Uruguayan proposal for multilateral intervention in the affairs of states in cases of flagrant violation of human rights or nonfulfillment of freely contracted obligations; see *Foreign Relations*, 1945, vol. IX, pp. 185 ff.

Article B. PAU Governing Board may act provisionally as organ consultation until meeting takes place.

Article C. Consultations shall be initiated on request addressed to Governing Board by any party.

Article D. In voting referred to in treaty only representatives of parties may take part.

Article E. Governing Board shall act in all matters concerning this treaty as an organ of liaison among parties and between them and UN.

Article F. Decisions of Governing Board referred to in Articles C and B shall be adopted by an absolute majority of members entitled to vote.

Article G. Organ of consultation shall adopt its decisions by vote of two-thirds of parties.

Article H. In determining quorum and in voting referred to two preceding articles, votes of parties directly interested in situation or dispute between American states which gave rise to consultation shall be excepted.

Article I. To constitute quorum in meetings referred to previous articles it shall be necessary that number of states represented equal number of valid votes necessary for adoption decision."

MARSHALL

710 Consultation 4/9–847

Memorandum of Conversation, by the Chairman of the United States Delegation (Marshall)

SECRET PETRÓPOLIS, August 27, 1947.

Participants: Dr. Arturo Despradel, Dominican Foreign Minister
Secretary Marshall
Major Vernon A. Walters

At Hotel Quitandinha, August 26, at 10:30 a. m.

After the customary exchange of greetings, Dr. Despradel stated that he wished to reiterate to me what he had stated on the very first day of the Conference, i.e., that he had received instructions from his President[7] to cooperate with the U.S. Delegation in every way possible for the success of the Conference. He stated that the Dominicans would do nothing that would in any way obstruct the work of the Conference and that for this reason, although they had had differences with Cuba, of which he presumed I was aware, they would not bring this matter up at the Conference, as it would only invite controversies and cause difficulties. He stated that perhaps in due time this might be taken up with some of the Pan American organizations. He stated that he wanted me to have a copy of the conciliatory telegram sent by his President to President Grau San Martín of Cuba and handed me a

---

[7] Rafael Leonidas Trujillo.

copy of this telegram. He stated that if the Conference would discuss matters not on the agenda it would last indefinitely.

I asked him if he had any comments to make on the work of the Conference, and he stated that the Mexican suggestion of regional security zones had some advantages but might invite controversy, and if this were the case, the Dominicans would not do anything to stimulate such controversy.

I inquired of Dr. Despradel when he thought the Conference would be able to conclude its work. He stated that two of the committees had almost concluded their work, and that the third committee would conclude its work by the 28th of August. I asked if he believed it would take that long. He felt it would be possible for all committees to conclude their work by the 27th but he felt that the 28th was a more probable date.

I inquired concerning the economic situation of the Dominican Republic with special regard to crops. He stated that their crops were exceedingly good. The coffee crop was larger than the previous year's, and the tobacco crop was also excellent, and the same was true of the cacao crop. Dr. Despradel stated that at the time he left the Dominican Republic an eight million dollar budget surplus was foreseen for this fiscal year. He stated that they intended to pay off the foreign debt this year. This was being handled by the Guarantee Trust Company, and that even after such foreign debt were paid off there would still remain a budget surplus.

I inquired concerning the situation in Haiti and Dr. Despradel informed me that the present administration was doing a very fine job in the line of developing Haitian agriculture.

---

710 Consultation 4/9–847

Memorandum of Conversation, by the Chairman of the United States Delegation (Marshall)

SECRET   PETRÓPOLIS, August 27, 1947.

Participants: Dr. Federico Chaves, Minister of Foreign Relations of Paraguay
Secretary Marshall
Major Vernon A. Walters

At Hotel Quitandinha, August 26, at 12 noon.

After the customary exchange of greetings, Dr. Chaves speaking vehemently, stated to me that the Paraguayan civil war had been won by President Morínigo supported by the National Republican or "Colorado" party, of which he was a member. He stated that this was a democratic party and that for 43 years it had opposed all forms of dictatorship, both as an opposition party and now as a member of the Government. This party had always been a close friend and supporter of the United States even in the dark days of Pearl Harbor and had published many manifestos and declarations to that effect. He stated that the recent civil war had been due to the corruption of the military and their desire to interfere in politics. He added that this was the cancer of South America and that his Government was thinking of closing the military academy and sending some 40 cadets a year to the United States for military training, as this would imbue them with democratic ideas. I replied, speaking of the relations between civil and military authorities in the U.S., explaining how the military are subordinate to civil authority and interference in politics is out of the question. I pointed out that in the U.S. the military are completely dependent on the Congress for the appropriations of funds for the armed forces. I spoke of several occasions during the war when I had to go before Congress and justify expenditures. I stated that I felt that merely sending the 40 cadets to the United States would not solve his problem alone, as upon graduation a cadet sometimes feels he is a great man but that when he goes to a unit where he is the junior officer and has the most obnoxious tasks to perform, this tends to normalize his perspective, and that in the case of the Paraguayan cadets this would not occur and they would not get a correct picture of civil-military relationship in the United States where the military were unquestionably subordinate to the civil authority, as is very much the case in Great Britain. I stated that the subordination of military to civil power depended upon legislative determination of funds, salaries, numbers and rank, coupled with requirement for military leaders to personally justify their proposals before committees of legislature. I suggested that they undertake an educational program within the army by requiring officers to teach every soldier to read and write, by giving them some technical knowledge which would make them valuable citizens and would also avoid the army's being a dead weight on the public economy.

Dr. Chaves replied thanking me and stated that the last two ambassadors could testify to his friendship to the U.S. He was a close friend of Mr. Trueblood, the present Chargé d'Affaires, who had been an eye witness to the recent civil war. He stated that he understood that Mr. Trueblood was shortly to be transferred upon the arrival of the new Ambassador.[8] Without wishing to interfere, he stated that it would be unfortunate especially if Mr. Trueblood were to leave before he had time to thoroughly orient the new Ambassador. He expressed

---

[8] Fletcher Warren.

the hope that the United States would continue to help them in the fields of public health, economy, and military training. He stated that they were considering turning over the National University and their secondary schools, which he said were infiltrated with Communism, to Americans for reorganization.

Dr. Chaves spoke at length concerning the danger which he felt the Communist Party presented in South America. He felt that if it were authorized to continue as a political organization it would provide a nucleus of traitors in each country far more dangerous than the Fifth Column which was largely composed of foreign elements, whereas this nucleus would consist of nationals of the country, and that such nuclei would be extremely dangerous should hostilities occur between the "totalitarian East" and "democratic West". He stated that in any such contingencies Paraguay would unreservedly stand by the U.S. and added a final remark, "100,000 Paraguayans could do a great deal".

---

710 Consultation 4/9–847

Memorandum of Conversation, by the Chairman of the United States Delegation (Marshall)

SECRET PETRÓPOLIS, August 27, 1947—10: 30 a. m.

Participants: Sr. Ernesto Nuñez, Under Secretary for Foreign Affairs, El Salvador
Secretary Marshall
Counsellor of Embassy Dr. Carlos Adalberto Alfaro
Major Vernon Walters

After the customary exchange of greetings we discussed at some length the Parliamentary form of government. I spoke of the high quality and dignity of the debates in the British Parliament at the time of Dunkirk. He replied stating that he felt that that was perhaps the greatest crisis through which the parliamentary form of government had ever passed, but he added that crises had the opposite effect in Latin America where they seemed to bring about an authoritarian form of government. I traced briefly the historical development of the United States constitutional form of government.

I then asked Dr. Nuñez how he viewed the progress of the Conference and he replied that he felt that it was going ahead very well and that he anticipated no obstacles to a speedy conclusion of the treaty. He added that he thought the Committees might be able to conclude their work today (August 27). I mentioned the desirability of arriving at a speedy agreement because of the favorable impression that such an agreement on an important matter would have on the rest of the world.

Dr. Nuñez then mentioned that his President [9] had asked him to express his admiration for my work as Chief of Staff and now on behalf of peace. I thanked him for this expression and took my leave of him.

---

710 Consultation 4/9–847

Memorandum of Conversation, by the Chairman of the United States Delegation (Marshall)

SECRET   PETRÓPOLIS, August 27, 1947—11 a. m.

Participants: Sr. Dr. Luis Fernando Guachalla, Bolivian Foreign Minister
Secretary Marshall
Major Vernon A. Walters

After the customary exchange of greetings I asked Mr. Guachalla how he felt that the work of the Conference was progressing. He replied that he felt that it was progressing very well. He added that he thought that all the Committees would have completed their work by the 28th of August and that it would take three or four days beyond that to translate the drafts into four languages, print the texts etc. Mr. Guachalla thought that everything was going very smoothly.

I spoke of the desirability of reaching a speedy agreement because of the effect that it would have on the rest of the world. He agreed and complimented me on my speech, stating that he was especially gratified by the fact that I had expressed the willingness to take up with other governments economic collaboration, as he felt that such economic collaboration was very important and a necessary adjunct of defensive collaboration.

He hoped that when Latin American countries asked for technical assistance that I would grant such requests as many of the Latin American countries did not have the engineers etc. that they required to develop their countries. He spoke of the desire of his government to build a railroad to the El Beni area, but the serious lack of technicians was slowing down the work on this railroad, as well as the development of the whole country. He said that he believed that up to now the United States had only been able to send military missions but that he hoped that it would soon be possible to send technical missions also.

I then expressed the hope that some way would be found for the

---

[9] Gen. Salvador Castañeda Castro.

Latin American countries to take advantage of U.S. technical assistance and to open up their countries to U.S. capital, without in any way sacrificing their economic sovereignty. I then spoke of the possibilities of Brazil in the petroleum field,[10] and we spoke briefly of the constitutional structure of the United States.

---

710 Consultation 4/8–2747 : Telegram

The Chairman of the United States Delegation (Marshall) to the Acting Secretary of State

RESTRICTED   PETRÓPOLIS, August 27, 1947—6 p. m.

88. Upon receipt of communication from Central Committee reported our telegram 82,[11] Trujillo sent letter president Conference officially informing change of government,[12] stating his appointment as new Foreign Minister and asking official pronouncement on whether he can sign treaty.

Central Committee unanimously decided make following answer:

"Conference of opinion that in view subsequent events in Ecuador set forth communication from Trujillo, powers previously conferred on him expired and he does not have capacity sign treaty."

Central Committee set September 2 date closing session Quitandinha and signature treaty in Rio same day.

Please repeat American Embassy Quito for information.

MARSHALL

---

710 Consultation 4/9–847

Memorandum of Conversation, by the Chairman of the United States Delegation (Marshall)

SECRET   PETRÓPOLIS, August 28, 1947.

Participants: Ambassador Guillermo Belt (Cuba)
                Secretary Marshall
                Major Vernon A. Walters

At Hotel Quitandinha, August 26, at 11 : 00 a. m.

After the customary exchange of greetings, I inquired of Ambassador Belt how he felt that the work of the Conference was progressing. He replied that it was progressing very well, and that we had given a democratic example to Europe. He felt that there would be no further

---

[10] For documentation on the position of the United States with respect to Brazilian petroleum requirements and legislation, see pp. 458 ff.
[11] Not printed.
[12] For documentation on the position of the United States toward this change, see pp. 664 ff.

serious obstacles, and that the last important difference, namely, that concerning unanimity as desired by the Argentines, had been solved in committee the previous night when the Argentines had withdrawn their insistence on unanimity. I expressed the belief that they had abandoned their insistence on unanimity earlier in the Conference, but Ambassador Belt stated that the final smoothing off had occurred the previous night. I then inquired concerning his opinion of the Mexican proposal of a regional security zone. He stated that he believed the Mexicans wanted regional security zones extending out three hundred miles and that he thought this proposal was in large part for home consumption; that they wanted to give their people some assurance that if the United States were to become entangled in Europe or Asia that they would not necessarily also become entangled, but, added Ambassador Belt, "of course, war for the United States would be war for us also."

I then inquired of what was being done in Cuba to get away from the single crop economy. Ambassador Belt stated that it would be impossible to get away from the single crop economy as sugar was so profitable. I inquired concerning other crops. He then spoke at length about tobacco and the manufacture of cigars in Cuba. He also touched on the Cuban colonies in Key West and Tampa. He added that the standard of living in Cuba has risen greatly, and that where a cutter earned 80 cents a day some years ago, today he earns five dollars a day. He stated that a large number of Cubans were home owners and that this was a valuable bulwark against communism. He asked if I had visited Cuba. I replied that although I had flown over Cuba many times, I had not stopped there. He extended an invitation for me to stop there with Mrs. Marshall on the way back, which I declined stating that time would not permit me to do so.

---

710 Consultation 4/9–847

Memorandum of Conversation, by the Chairman of the United States Delegation (Marshall)

SECRET   PETRÓPOLIS, August 28, 1947.

Participants: Ambassador Julian R. Cáceres, Chairman of Honduran Delegation
Secretary Marshall
Major Vernon A. Walters

At Hotel Quitandinha, August 26, 11:30 a. m.

After the customary greetings, I asked Ambassador Cáceres how he felt the Conference was progressing. He replied that he felt that there would be no further obstacles to the success of the Conference and that he felt the Committees would solve all problems without any serious dissension arising between any of the Delegates. I asked him when he felt the Committees would conclude their work, and he stated that he believed such work would be undoubtedly concluded by the 28th. We then spoke concerning the world situation generally and I emphasized the necessity of understanding the point of view of other peoples. We discussed the development of the American West and its relation to Brazil's present problems as well as the constitutional structure of the United States.

---

710 Consultation 4/9-847

Memorandum of Conversation, by the Chairman of the United States Delegation (Marshall)

SECRET   PETRÓPOLIS, August 28, 1947.

Participants: Dr. Mateo Marques Castro, Uruguayan Foreign Minister
Secretary Marshall
Major Vernon A. Walters

At Hotel Quitandinha, August 27, 11:30 a. m.

After the customary greetings, I explained to Dr. Marques Castro that Foreign Minister Raul Fernandes was waiting in my suite for me and that I hoped he would understand. He replied that besides being delighted at the opportunity of being able to speak to me, his purpose was to reaffirm the desire of his Government to cooperate most closely with the United States Government in political, economic and social fields. He stated that Uruguay was well aware of the very great sacrifices made by the United States during the war and subsequently and that his country had no intention of asking for greater sacrifices by the United States other than those which that country is already making in defense of liberty and democracy, which are the ideals which Uruguayans also hold dear. He said Uruguay wished to contribute insofar as she could.

I spoke to the Uruguayan Foreign Minister concerning the desirability and importance of reaching a speedy agreement, not only for the agreement itself but for the effect that such speedy agreement would have upon the rest of the world. I stated that though our purposes might be misrepresented, the fact of a speedy agreement on an important matter could not be disregarded. I mentioned that we have been thwarted so often in our efforts toward peace that such an agreement would be exceedingly well received. I mentioned my surprise at the frequent misrepresentation of my purposes and thoughts, mentioning China and the relative success of such misrepresentation among university students and professors without considering the grossly false character of such propaganda. Dr. Marques Castro stated he felt the First Committee would complete its work tonight and that he felt that such a speedy agreement would be reached.

As I was taking my leave of him, he spoke of the desirability of maintaining the office of the U.S. Naval Attaché at Montevideo. I replied that I was already aware of the situation and would study it immediately upon my return.

710 Consultation 4/9–847

Memorandum of Conversation, by the Chairman of the United States Delegation (Marshall)

SECRET   PETRÓPOLIS, August 28, 1947.

Participants: Dr. Lleras Camargo, Director General of the Pan American Union
Secretary Marshall
Mr. Norman Armour

At my request Dr. Lleras Camargo, Director General of the Pan American Union, called to see me at 12:30 p. m., August 28. I endeavored to call on him but his apartment was in disorder.

Mr. Armour was present during the call.

I asked Dr. Camargo what his reaction was to the progress of the conference and he expressed great satisfaction in what had been done. I then questioned him as to whether or not there was any particular point regarding which he was a little dubious. He brought up the matter of handling the preliminary phases of a military break between two American states. He felt that in its present draft form the treaty did not sufficiently take care of the situation which could easily result in a long debate while the troops of one country occupied a position in the other. He felt that the first enforcement under the treaty should be that the belligerents withdraw their forces within their own boundaries.

It developed that an informal agreement had been reached that this would be the procedure but its inclusion in the treaty had been opposed (Mr. Armour and I understood) by Peru. We told Dr. Camargo that we would talk the matter over with Senator Vandenberg who of course was intimately familiar with the discussions and the drafting regarding this matter. No other points were brought up.

Later it developed that the expression "the troops of belligerents should withdraw to their own boundaries" had actually by mistake been included in the draft.

710 Consultation 4/8–2847 : Telegram

The Chairman of the United States Delegation (Marshall) to the Acting Secretary of State

RESTRICTED   PETRÓPOLIS, August 28, 1947—5 p. m.

104. Conference summary 9. All committees substantially finished work. Coordinating Committee preparing final text.

Committee I approved preamble substantially as reported ourtel 76 [13] substituting following language for second whereas clause "parties reiterate their will to remain united in inter-American system, compatible with purposes and principles of UN, within terms of Charter, and reaffirm existence of the agreement they concluded for dealing with such matters relating to maintenance international peace and security as are appropriate for regional action".

In addition Articles A, B, C, D as reported ourtels 81 [14] and 83,[15] Committee II approved following:

"Article E. In case conflict between two or more American States, without prejudice to right of self-defense in conformity with article 51 of Charter, contracting parties meeting in consultation, shall call upon contending states to suspend hostilities and shall take all other necessary measures to reestablish or maintain inter-American peace and security and for solution of conflict by peaceful means. The refusal to adopt pacific action will be considered in determination of the aggressor and in decision to apply immediately the measures which the consultative meeting may agree upon.

Article F. For purposes treaty measures on which parties may agree collectively will comprise one or more of following: Recall chiefs of missions; breaking of diplomatic relations; breaking of consular relations; complete or partial interruption of economic relations or of rail, sea, air, postal, telegraphic, telephonic and radio telephonic or radio telegraphic relations; and use of armed force.

Article G. In addition to other acts which in consultative meeting may be characterized as aggression, there shall be considered as such:

   a. Unprovoked armed attack by state against territory, people, or land, sea or air forces of another state;
   b. Invasion by armed forces of a state, of the territory of another state, through trespassing of boundaries demarcated in accordance with treaty, judicial decision, or arbitral award, or, in absence of frontiers thus demarcated, invasion affecting a region which is under effective jurisdiction of other state.

Article H. None of provisions this treaty shall be construed as impairing rights and obligations of contracting parties under UN Charter."

---

[13] August 26, p. 61.
[14] Not printed.
[15] August 27, p. 62.

Subcommittee of Argentina, Chile and US has prepared technical description geographic region being reported separate telegram which will be proposed as definitive text Paragraph B ourtel 83 (part 1).

Committee III approved following articles in addition to those reported Conference summary 8, part 2:

"Article J. Decisions to use measures specified in article F (of Committee II draft) shall bind all parties except that no state shall be required to use armed force without its consent.

Article K. Measures agreed upon by the consultative agency shall be executed through procedures and agencies now existing or those which may in future be established."

Following approval article J extensive debate arose as to whether "use armed force" included bases and facilities. Definite interpretation avoided.

Committee I approved following protocolary articles:

"Treaty will enter into effect as soon as the ratifications of two-thirds of signatories have been deposited.

This treaty shall be open to signature by the American states in Rio de Janeiro and shall be ratified as soon as possible in accordance their respective constitutional processes. Ratifications deposited PAU, which will notify all signatories. Such notification shall be considered exchange of ratifications and treaty will be registered in UN Secretariat through PAU, when two-thirds of signatories have deposited ratifications.

This treaty shall remain in force indefinitely, but may be denounced by any party by notification in writing to PAU, which shall inform all other parties. After expiration of two years from date of receipt by PAU of notification of denunciation by any party, treaty shall cease to be in force with respect to such state, but shall remain in full force and effect with respect to all other parties.

When organic pact of inter-American system is drafted, the principles and fundamental provisions of this treaty shall be incorporated in it."

Committee also approved following resolution on armaments and compulsory arbitration:

"Conference recommends that Bogotá Conference study with a view to approving creation of institutions which may give effectiveness to pacific system of security, among them, compulsory arbitration for any dispute which may endanger peace and which is not of juridical nature.

Conference declares that its primary purpose and primary purpose of treaty it has concluded is to assure peace and security of continent and that no provision of treaty and none of obligations created under it should be interpreted as justifying excessive armaments or may be invoked as reason for creation or maintenance of armaments or armed forces beyond those required for common defense in interest maintaining peace and security."

MARSHALL

710 Consultation 4/8–2947 : Telegram

The Chairman of the United States Delegation (Marshall) to the Acting Secretary of State

US URGENT   PETRÓPOLIS, August 29, 1947—7 p. m.

110. Committee II this morning unanimously approved text of article B defining geographic region as quoted our telegram 102, August 28.[16]

Argentina promptly stated it did not recognize existence of any European colonies and possessions in Argentine territories and waters contained within zone and expressly reaffirmed its sovereignty over Falkland Islands.[17]

Vandenberg stated "The Argentine delegation is entitled to enter on the record any unilateral statement it desires. But the basic fact will remain that this treaty does not touch or involve or change any sovereignty in the regional zone here defined. These are questions of fact and this treaty does not directly or indirectly affect these questions of fact."

Further reservations were made by Guatemala and Mexico regarding Belize,[18] Chile regarding areas claimed by her in Antarctica, and Honduras regarding Honduras-Nicaragua frontier. Mexican Foreign Minister stated he agreed fully with US view and made reservation regarding Belize only because Guatemala had raised the question.

After each of these reservations, Vandenberg repeated substance of statement quoted above and emphasized that his statement was to be made part of the record of the Committee with respect to all the above declarations by Latin American countries.

Final approval of text expected in plenary session Saturday.

· · · · · · · ·

MARSHALL

---

710 Consultation 4/8–3947 : Telegram

The Chairman of the United States Delegation (Marshall) to the Acting Secretary of State

RESTRICTED   PETRÓPOLIS, August 29, 1947—8 p. m.

112. Reference our number 111, August 29,[16] text paragraphs 1 and 2, article A, as approved Committee II:

"1. The contracting parties agree that an armed attack by any state against an American state shall be considered as an attack against all

---

[16] Not printed.
[17] Spain and Great Britain claimed sovereignty in a dispute that originated in colonial times.
[18] Settled by British colonists, but British title was never conceded by Spain.

of them, and each one undertakes to assist in meeting the attack in the exercise of the inherent right of individual or collective self-defense recognized by article 51 of the Charter of the United Nations.

"2. On the request of the state or states directly attacked and until the decision of the security organ of the inter-American system, the contracting parties may determine the immediate measures which they may individually adopt in fulfillment of the obligation contained in the preceding paragraph and in accordance with the principle of continental solidarity. The contracting parties shall meet in consultation without delay for the purpose of examining those measures and agreeing upon the measures of collective character that should be adopted."

MARSHALL

---

710 Consultation 4/9–847

Memorandum of Conversation, by the Chairman of the United States Delegation (Marshall), Held August 22, 1947, 11:45 a. m.

SECRET   PETRÓPOLIS, August 30, 1947.

Participants: Sr. Edmé Manigat, Foreign Minister of Haiti
Secretary Marshall
Colonel Antoine Levelt [20]
Major Vernon A. Walters

After the customary exchange of greetings, Dr. Manigat stated that he wished to compliment me on my speech.[21] I thanked him and asked if he had any new points of view to express. He asked whether I was referring to Haiti or to the Conference and I indicated that I was referring to the latter. He stated that Haiti did not have any special point to bring up and was confident that there would be no serious obstacles to the conclusion of the treaty.

I spoke of the difficulty of drawing a line between aggression from within the continent and from without. I cited Hungary as a case in point where a minority of some 10% of the population had taken over the government, and that such an occurrence might be repeated on the American continent and it was almost impossible to differentiate between this type of aggression and open aggression from an extra-continental source. Dr. Manigat replied that they had been inclined to consider some difference because Haiti felt that an extra-continental aggression might be less likely to disrupt the solidarity of the hemisphere than an intra-continental attack. For this reason they had been weighing the Venezuelan proposal,[22] but he added that in view of the

---

[20] Haitian Delegate to the Conference.
[21] On August 21; see telegram 39, August 21, 1 a. m., from Petrópolis, p. 52.
[22] See memorandum of conversation of August 20, between Secretary Marshall, Venezuelan Foreign Minister Morales, and others, p. 47.

thoughts I had expressed the Haitian delegation was prepared to abandon support for the Venezuelan proposal, and that he was in complete agreement that no distinction should be made. He expressed confidence in the success of the Conference in drafting the treaty.

I asked Dr. Manigat whether he had any other views he would like to express and he stated that he did not. He thanked me for my visit as I was taking my leave.

---

710 Consultation 4/8–3047 : Telegram

The Chairman of the United States Delegation (Marshall) to the Acting Secretary of State

RESTRICTED PETRÓPOLIS, August 30, 1947—1 a. m.

114. Conference summary No. 10. Argentina proposed two following amendments today in Committee II : 1. Addition to article E (our telegram 104 [23]) requiring consultation to ask contending parties in inter-American conflict to reestablish *status quo ante bellum;* 2. Addition of following sentence to article G, paragraph *b* "principle of effective jurisdiction shall not be applied except within security zone".

First amendment approved unanimously notwithstanding that yesterday committee had rejected Colombian-sponsored-US-supported amendment in same sense. Through prior arrangement engineered by Argentina and Peru (Belaunde) those who previously opposed inclusion amendment supported both it and second Argentine proposal.

Vandenberg, after unsuccessfully seeking clarification from Argentina of meaning of second amendment, opposed it strongly as applying limitation of obligation to consult to cases aggression inside zone and as placing geographic limitations on concept of aggression.

Committee adjourned a. m. session with question unresolved. On initiative Alfaro and Torres Bodet matter resolved informal conversation by substituting "an American state" for "another state" in paragraph *b* and eliminating proposed amendment. Paragraph as approved evening session reads "Invasion, by armed forces of a state, of territory of an American state, by crossing frontiers established in conformity with treaty, judicial decision, or arbitral award, or, in absence of any established frontiers invasion which affects region under effective jurisdiction of another state." Committee completed work with friendly exchange remarks Argentine–US delegations.

Matter recognizably not basic but expanded beyond real importance by manner Argentine presentation, attitude certain other delegations and press.

---

[23] Dated August 28, 5, p.m., p. 73.

Other developments Committee II reported our telegrams 110 and 112.[24]

MARSHALL

---

710 Consultation 4/9–347

Memorandum by Mr. Edgar L. McGinnis of the Division of North and West Coast Affairs [25]

[WASHINGTON,] September 3, 1947.

In his address September 2 at the closing session of the Inter-American Defense Conference, President Truman made significant reference to the inter-relationship of the economic problems of Europe and the Americas, and indicated the broad outlines of our policy toward Latin American countries in economic matters.[26]

The President made it clear that European economic recovery is fundamental and that while the United States would "do our best to provide economic help for those who are prepared to help themselves and each other," he made it plain that our resources are not unlimited.

He referred to the fact that our own troubles "are small in contrast with the struggle for life itself that engrosses the people of Europe." He stated the hope that the nations of America would be prepared, according to their abilities, to contribute toward the economic needs of Europe. Later in the speech he again emphasized "our collective responsibility for economic assistance" and pointedly referred to the fact that the economies of the Americas were intact with productive powers undiminished and resources not even fully explored.

Significantly he differentiated between the urgent need for rehabilitation of war torn areas and the problems of development elsewhere. The President stated that the problems of the countries in this hemisphere are different from those in Europe and can not be relieved by the same means that are in contemplation for Europe. As he pointed out "here the need is for long-term economic collaboration. This is a type of collaboration in which a much greater role falls to private citizens and groups than is the case in a program designed to aid European countries to recover from the destruction of war."

The President made it clear, however, that the United States was not oblivious to the need of increased economic collaboration within the family of American nations and assured his hearers that these

---

[24] Dated August 29, 7 p. m., and 8 p. m., p. 75.
[25] Addressed to officers of the Division of North and West Coast Affairs.
[26] For text of the address, see Department of State *Bulletin*, September 14, 1947, p. 498.

economic problems "will be approached by us with the utmost good faith and with increased vigor in the coming period."

To sum up, the President put the economic rehabilitation of Europe on a priority basis and sought the aid of the other American Republics in solving this problem. He promised that increasing attention would be given to the economic problems of the Americas, but indicated that these problems were of a long-range character and could be resolved in great measure by private citizens and groups (i.e. by private capital).[27]

III. APPRAISALS

710. Consultation 4/9–947

The Ambassador in Chile (Bowers) to the Secretary of State

No. 15,612   SANTIAGO, September 9, 1947.

SIR: I have the honor to report that upon the return to Santiago of the Chilean delegation to the Rio Conference on September 6 an official declaration was released to the press. It said a general statement was being issued to the public even before the full report was presented to the President of the Republic [28] in view of the fact the President had been in close touch with the delegation throughout the Conference. The exclusive purpose of the Conference, it declared, was to sign a treaty giving the Act of Chapultepec [29] permanent form. This treaty, however, is not a treaty of alliance, but an agreement of mutual defense against war and aggression. The Chilean delegation was particularly careful that this treaty should not prejudice the United Nations Organization, and has the satisfaction of declaring that its provisions "strengthened to the utmost the world organization."

After giving a brief outline of the treaty, the declaration states that, "the features of our constitutional system on the employment of armed force, right of passage, etc., have been fully protected and are in no way affected." At the same time, it had been clearly established that "none of the obligations implied in the treaty should be interpreted in the sense of justifying an armament policy, but, on the contrary, the objective sought was maintenance of peace and security." It likewise pointed out that the final act of the Conference [30] contained

---

[27] A marginal notation in the original reads: "The comments from Bogotá on President Truman's address thus far have been sour. A H G[erberich?]."

[28] Gabriel González Videla.

[29] Department of State, Treaties and Other International Acts Series No. 1543, or 60 Stat. (pt. 2) 1831.

[30] *Report of the Delegation of the United States of America*, Appendix 1, pt. 1, p. 45.

a special reservation of the Chilean delegation in the sense that the security zone along the "coasts corresponding to our country do not recognize the existence of colonies or possessions of European countries, and that the legitimate rights of Chile over the Antarctic territories of the Republic are maintained intact."

The Chilean delegation, it said, was the first to express the connection between economic and political solidarity, insisting on the necessity of establishing this additional system. It felt, however, that the Rio Conference was not the appropriate time to discuss economic problems, but that they should be considered in the immediate future. The Chilean delegation had the satisfaction of being supported in this point of view by all Latin American countries, and the United States delegation, through President Truman and Secretary Marshall, agreed on the desirability of establishing continental economic collaboration. Through the initiative of Chile, Mexico, and Colombia it was resolved to call a special conference during the second semester of next year to discuss inter-American economic cooperation without prejudicing what may be accomplished at the Bogotá Conference.[31]

It concluded that the Chilean delegation, one of the smallest in size, had the great satisfaction of having contributed towards the success of the Conference by acting as a mediator of conflicting opinions. The President of the Republic's instructions had thus been fulfilled in a spirit of collaboration and good faith.

Respectfully yours, CLAUDE G. BOWERS

---

710. Consultation 4/9–1047

The Ambassador in Bolivia (Flack) to the Secretary of State

No. 1706   LA PAZ, September 10, 1947.

SIR: I have the honor to enclose a single copy of a clipping of a press interview of Foreign Minister Luís Fernando Guachalla, head of the Bolivian delegation to the Rio Conference, upon his return to La Paz. Pertinent parts of the interview are quoted below in translation.

Regarding the Conference as a whole, Foreign Minister Guachalla made the following statement:

"It is paradoxical that America has had to resort to a treaty of this nature to preserve its peaceful relations with the rest of the world and between the peoples of the hemisphere. To attain this result there has been signed a political instrument of collective defense based on solidarity against aggression. In reality this result should have been attained by means of a solid juridical structure within which, as some-

---

[31] Relative to this Conference, see bracketed note, p. 94.

thing adjective [*sic*], should figure the defense chapter. I believe that the Bogotá Conference should have preceded, for the reasons noted above, that of Rio de Janeiro."

Regarding the coming Bogotá Conference, Foreign Minister Guachalla had the following to say:

"In Bogotá an effort will be made to coordinate in a principal juridical body, subject to submission for approval by the parliaments of the various nations, the many declarations, recommendations, and resolutions that make up the American international tradition. Within this, which is already known as the Constituent Charter of America, the results which were arrived at in Rio de Janeiro will form only one chapter and not necessarily the most important."

Regarding the subject of economic aggression fostered by Cuba, Foreign Minister Guachalla stated:

"The Cuban delegation made reference to this subject in the speech of its representative, Sr. Guillermo Belt. It did not reach the point of making a concrete proposal, limiting itself to asking whether it was opportune to refer to this subject. Bolivia, with four other nations, voted in favor since it considered that the Conference could not avoid taking cognizance of a subject the importance of which will become evident in Bogotá and in all international meetings."

Regarding the proposed convocation of a special economic conference, Foreign Minister Guachalla's comment was the following:

"Bolivia was one of the first nations that in prior consultations indicated the necessity for studying the economic problems of the defense of the continent. I remember press declarations of mine and even favorable comments made in some newspapers here. All this much before the trip.

"Upon arriving at Rio de Janeiro we Foreign Ministers of Mexico, Colombia and Bolivia got together on the subject and agreed on the advisability of making a proposal in that respect. The Argentine delegate touched on the subject in his speech, after the Foreign Minister of Mexico already had done so. Argentina did not make any proposal in the matter. The only ones (proposals) which were presented were those of Mexico, Bolivia and Colombia to which eleven countries later adhered, among them Argentina. The United States, in spite of having turned down the question in principle, ended by accepting it. This result cannot be attributed personally to any of the delegations, it is a product of a unanimous worry of all the countries of the continent; a preoccupation for urgent and preemptory problems."

The subject of the Rio Conference has received scant press attention since urgent domestic problems, including economic and political developments culminating in a cabinet crisis immediately following the termination of the Rio Conference, have occupied fully public attention.

Respectfully yours,   JOSEPH FLACK

710 Consultation (4)/9–1247: Airgram

The Chargé in Haiti (McBride) to the Secretary of State

CONFIDENTIAL   PORT-AU-PRINCE, September 12, 1947.

A–394. Foreign Minister Manigat on his return from Rio Conference called me in to see him and informed Embassy regarding Haitian view on Rio meeting. He assured me Haiti considered meeting had succeeded although he emphasized this might well be minority view. He said that while he personally would have been happy to see economic subjects discussed, it was fully understood that Conference had only single item on its agenda, namely, implementation provisions of Chapultepec Agreement. Since single item of agenda had been brought to what he termed successful conclusion, Foreign Minister concluded meeting had not failed.

McBRIDE

---

710 Consultation 4/9–1247

The Chargé in Uruguay (Brown) to the Secretary of State

No. 1036   MONTEVIDEO, September 12, 1947.

SIR: With reference to the recent Inter-American Conference of Rio de Janeiro, I have the honor to report that Dr. Dardo Regules, a member of the Uruguayan Delegation, gave a talk over CX8, Radio Sarandí, on September 11 in which he discussed the Conference and the treaty of mutual defense.

Dr. Regules, who is a member of the Uruguayan Senate, is the leader of the Catholic Party Unión Cívica and one of the Catholic lay leaders behind the "Christian-Democrat" movement reported in the Embassy's despatches no. 599 of May 7 and no. 652 of May 19, 1947.[32] His radio talk was of an hour's duration. In it, he made a very clear analysis of the mutual defense treaty, pointing out its significance, explaining in simple terms the nature and extent of Uruguay's obligations under the treaty and the advantages which would accrue to Uruguay thereunder. He gave particular attention to the correction of certain misconceptions of the obligations which the treaty entails, misconceptions which he stated certain political factions in Uruguay are trying to foster in the public mind. He indicated that he was referring to the Communists and Herreristas.

Another important part of his talk was devoted to an attack on the so-called "third position" under which Latin America would disassociate itself from the United States and act as an independent

---

[32] Neither printed.

group. He pointed out that the economic and military weakness of Latin America make such a position impossible and that its best interests lie in hemispheric unity. He stated that the treaty of mutual defense, instead of being a tool for United States imperialistic aggression as the totalitarians of the Left and Right allege, provides a certain control over the United States by the vote of two-thirds of the American Republics, and further subjects it to the weight of continental public opinion.

There is enclosed a clipping from the Independent Blanco *El Plata* of September 10, containing an interview of Dr. Regules, which is a résumé of his radio talk.[33]

Respectfully yours, JAMES E. BROWN, JR.

---

710. Consultation 4/9–1247

The Ambassador in Peru (Cooper) to the Secretary of State

RESTRICTED LIMA, September 12, 1947.
No. 2003

SIR: I have the honor to report that the Peruvian Minister for Foreign Affairs, Dr. Enrique García Sayán, returned to Lima yesterday morning, September 11, from the Rio de Janeiro Conference on the Maintenance of Continental Peace and Security, which he attended as head of the Peruvian delegation.

In a press conference held yesterday evening Dr. García Sayán expressed his satisfaction with the results of the Conference, noting that they were accomplished in a short time and in an atmosphere of complete harmony. He stated that there were no "hegemonic" intentions on the part of any country and that at no time did the delegations adopt irreconcilable positions. According to one press account, the Minister then remarked that the United States desired unanimity.

Referring to the Peruvian delegation, the Foreign Minister declared that the delegates worked as a team and with a spirit of understanding. He praised Dr. Victor Andrés Belaunde for his work in the Second Commission and Dr. Manuel C. Gallagher, who participated in the discussions of the Third Commission and presided over one of the sub-commissions. He declared that the Peruvian proposal which Dr. Belaunde defended in the Second Commission contributed to the success of the Conference. This proposal, he disclosed, called for peaceful consultation before the use of coercive measures.

---

[33] Not reprinted.

In speaking of the address delivered by President Truman [34] at the closing session, Dr. García Sayán characterized it as an expression of interest in the economic problems confronting the continent. He made mention of the President's statement that after the economic reconstruction of Europe, efforts will be made to achieve Inter-American collaboration in the solution of the economic problems of the Western Hemisphere.

When questioned concerning the affair with Ecuador, the Foreign Minister quickly replied that there was no boundary question pending between Ecuador and Peru. He went on to say that he had issued a statement in Rio de Janeiro clarifying this matter, explaining that what had happened was that Ecuador had simply made an observation with respect to the decision of the Brazilian arbiter. (A gist of this statement was reported in the Embassy's despatch No. 1953 of August 27.[35]) He explained that no pronouncement with respect to this matter had been made during the course of the Conference at Quitandinha.

. . . . . .

Respectfully yours, PRENTICE COOPER

710 Consultation 4/9–1647

The Ambassador in Argentina (Bruce) to the Secretary of State

CONFIDENTIAL BUENOS AIRES, September 16, 1947.
No. 2999

SIR: I have the honor to refer to a recent series of despatches from the Embassy concerning the Rio Conference and to report that public and private statements made by Foreign Minister Bramuglia and by Ambassadors De la Rosa and Corominas upon their return from Rio also indicate Argentine satisfaction with the treaty signed there.

Ambassadors Corominas and De la Rosa made public addresses as well as press statements giving some details of the work of the Argentine Delegation at Rio. Foreign Minister Bramuglia made a long statement to the press on the same subject. In private conversations with the Ambassador and other Embassy officers all three delegates expressed great satisfaction with the results of the Conference. Since their remarks were either of a general nature or entered only into details well-known to the Department, the Embassy will not comment at greater length except to say that it believes the expressions of satisfaction to be entirely sincere.

---

[34] For text of the address, see Department of State *Bulletin*, September 14, 1947, p. 498; see also memorandum dated September 3, p. 78.
[35] Not printed.

Ambassador La Rosa has told an Embassy officer that the President very soon will send a special message to Congress requesting ratification of the treaty. He professed to believe that the treaty will be ratified without difficulty before the end of the congressional session on September 30. The Embassy, however, cannot share Ambassador La Rosa's optimism concerning prompt action on ratification since the Congress has many important matters to consider in its few remaining days of session.

Of passing interest in this connection is a suit brought in a Federal Court by one Alejandro Olmos against Foreign Minister Bramuglia for "crimes against the security, peace and dignity of the nation" alleged to have been committed by signing the Inter-American Treaty of Rio. The charges are based on Article XXIX of the Argentine Constitution. Needless to say it is expected that the charges promptly will be dropped by the court. This is but another example of the propaganda efforts made by the nationalists against the treaty. The Alianza Libertadora Nacionalista recently held a public demonstration against the treaty and in its official publication *Alianza* prepared what must have been a long diatribe on the same subject. The newspaper failed to appear in that issue and a statement by its directors indicates that the Government forbade its publication. This would be in line with recent Government action closing a number of opposition newspapers as has already been reported to the Department in several communications from the Embassy.[36]

Respectfully yours,

For the Ambassador:
R. KENNETH OAKLEY
Second Secretary of Embassy

---

710 Consultation (4)/9-1747 : Airgram

The Ambassador in the Soviet Union (Smith) to the Secretary of State

Moscow, September 17, 1947.

A-940. *Red Fleet* of September 11, "On Results of Inter-American Conference in Rio de Janeiro" by A. Osipov, states although everything was done to give appearance of real conference, end of meeting showed diplomats had assembled merely to sign treaty prepared in advance in Washington. US government attributed considerable importance to Conference. Department displayed furious activity before meeting and US press waged unrestrained war of nerves. Solidarity, as Americans understand it, signifies more or less subordination of na-

---

[36] For documentation on this subject, see pp. 317 ff.

tional interests to those of Wall Street. However, attempts to stifle disagreements failed at Rio. Only decision was to appeal to Paraguayan parties to cease civil war. Main contradiction—between USA and Argentina—was apparent at Conference in struggle around issues only remotely connected with defence questions. USA insisted on two-thirds majority, Argentina on unanimity. Raising of question of discussion of economic problems was due to serious difficulties resulting from US domination and military penetration and colonial policy toward Latin America. Extremely favorable moment has arrived for further US economic expansion. Hence US reluctance to discuss economic issues. Militaristic nature of conference was apparent. Under pretext of defense Latin American states now openly at service of US capital. "Security Zone" traced at Conference virtually embraces half world. USA attaches great importance to clause calling for immediate consultation in event of attack, since USA is now turning its attention to Europe, Near and Far East.

SMITH

---

710 Consultation 4/9–2647

The Chargé in Venezuela (Maleady) to the Secretary of State

No. 10486　　　　　　　　　　　　　　　CARACAS, September 26, 1947.

SIR: I have the honor to refer to Despatch No. 10456 dated September 18, 1947 [37] regarding statements made by certain Venezuelan delegates to the Rio Conference and to report that Dr. Carlos Morales, Minister of Foreign Relations, has now returned to this country and granted interviews to local press representatives. In general, Dr. Morales' remarks indicate complete satisfaction with the accomplishments of the Conference.

The Foreign Minister did not arrive in Caracas until September 22, having spent the time since the Conference closed as the guest of honor of the Argentine and Uruguayan Governments. He was accompanied on his travels by Dr. Santiago Perez, Director of International Policy in the Foreign Office and his most influential adviser on policy matters, and also it is believed, by Dr. Aureliano Otañez, Director of Economic Policy.

Referring to the Treaty of Rio de Janeiro, the Minister is quoted as saying, ". . . It is always good to remember that (the treaty) was a triumph for all the Americas because it demonstrates the value of a spirit of conciliation and a desire to maintain the peace in solving political and ideological differences between men and peoples". He then spoke briefly regarding Venezuela's partially successful attempts to

---

[37] Not printed.

have included in the treaty a clause differentiating between extra-continental aggressions and disputes between American States. In this connection one reporter inquired whether he considered extra-continental aggression likely, to which Dr. Morales replied that, although the situation looked bad, he could not imagine that another war could break out so soon after the end of the last one. In answer to another question, the Minister said that at the next inter-American conference, he hoped an agreement could be reached on economic cooperation which would raise the living standards of the people.

. . . .

Respectfully yours, THOMAS J. MALEADY

---

710. Consultation 4/9–3047: Airgram

The Chargé in Honduras (Montamat) to the Secretary of State

RESTRICTED TEGUCIGALPA, September 30, 1947.

A–208. Following reaction has been noted locally to Rio Conference for Maintenance of Continental Peace and Security:

1. Foreign Minister Lainez September 23 mentioned to me that he considered the Rio Conference "had been a great success, providing the juridical basis for inter-American cooperation against any aggressor as well as sanctions and the employment of force to repel such aggression". Mentioning that the Act of Chapultepec "had laid the basic foundation, that the Rio Conference provided the next story, and that the Bogotá Conference would complete the structure", he suggested that while the written agreement between the American Republics was of great importance, of even greater importance was the attitude of the various countries toward the subject. It was his feeling, he said, that no contract or agreement was necessarily worth much if the contracting powers were not "spiritually" disposed to cooperate; in his view the contracting powers this time were "spiritually" so disposed.

2. Minister of Public Education, Professor Angel Hernández, one of the three Honduran delegates to the Conference, in an interview published in the September 25 issue of *Diario Comercial* of San Pedro Sula (practically the only newspaper in the country worthy of the name), referred in most favorable terms to the accomplishments of the Conference. He stated that the drafting of paragraph (*b*) of Article IX of the Treaty "constituted a triumph of the Honduran delegation" since at its insistence the phrase "or arbitral award" (*laudo arbitral*) was added. Despite this triumph, Hernández said, the Honduran delegation signed the Treaty with the "respective reservation".

When questioned concerning Russia, Professor Hernández is reported as stating that he had nothing to say officially since Russia was not dealt with at the Conference. He could add personally, however, that he thought the attitude of Russia, as revealed by recent developments, "does not accord with the spirit of almost all the agreements and declarations signed by Russia during the war nor with many of the provisions of the United Nations Charter". Respecting his own draft American Educational Charter for Peace, which was apparently approved unanimously, Dr. Hernández revealed delight, as he has on other occasions, over its success.

(The other delegates, Ambassador Cáceres and Minister Batres, both now in Tegucigalpa, have also on occasion signified their high satisfaction with the results of the Conference.)

3. The Honduran press has invariably referred favorably to the accomplishments of the Conference on such few occasions when it has been mentioned.

MONTAMAT

710. Consultation 4/10–147

The Chargé in the Dominican Republic (Burrows) to the Secretary of State

No. 1185　　　　　　　　　　　CIUDAD TRUJILLO, October 1, 1947.

SIR: I have the honor to report that on October 1, 1947 *La Nación* of Ciudad Trujillo carried the text of President Trujillo's note to the President of the Dominican Senate submitting to the Senate for its approval and ratification the Inter-American Agreement signed at Rio de Janeiro on September 2, 1947; a clipping is enclosed.

Although a full translation of the President's note has not been made, the following few paragraphs in free translation may be of some interest to the Department:

"At the Rio de Janeiro Conference, the Dominican delegation devoted all of its efforts, in accordance with the instructions which I gave it, and with the traditional policy of my government of collaborating with the others of the continent in everything that might tend to perfect the juridicial system of peace of the peoples of America, to the end that the treaty might correspond to the high objectives contemplated at Chapultepec and to the realistic proposal of making the treaty as effective as possible as an instrument of security and peace.

．　　．　　．　　．　　．　　．　　．

"From the preceding, it may be observed that the treaty in question gives positive expression to the principles of Inter-American solidarity and cooperation repeatedly proclaimed in Inter-American conferences and meetings; it is in agreement in all particulars with the Constitution of the Republic and in harmony with the traditional policy of the Dominican Government, characterized always by the desire for an intimate and balanced cooperation in the field of international relations, as much in times of peace as in those when there has been aggression against a country of the Americas.

"The treaty in all of its articles and in its preamble is in accord finally with the proposals and principles of the United Nations.

"On the basis of all that I have said I have the firm conviction that the Honorable Congress will find it convenient to approve the transcendental document which I am submitting for its high consideration and that the Dominican Republic will not hesitate to accept the responsibilities which may derive from its contents, in accordance with the spirit of cooperation and peace which has always characterized its foreign policy."

Respectfully yours, CHARLES R. BURROWS

---

710. Consultation 4/10-647

The Chargé in Brazil (Key) to the Secretary of State

No. 2872   RIO DE JANEIRO, October 6, 1947.

The Chargé d'Affaires ad interim has the honor to report that the *Jornal do Commercio* of Rio de Janeiro under date of October 5, 1947, carried an article signed by Hildebrando Accioly regarding the treaty recently signed at the conference held at Petrópolis, Brazil. The article is considered of interest as Accioly was one of the outstanding Brazilian delegates to the conference and holds a high position in the Brazilian Foreign Office. Five copies of the article are enclosed.

In general the article regards most favorably the agreement reached at Petrópolis and the author concludes that although it may contain some faults this is only the natural result of the consensus of nineteen different wills and sovereignties. Two matters were singled out for criticism. The limitation by Article Three of immediate defense measures to those attacks which occur within a definite zone is characterized as illogical, Accioly adding that an act of aggression does not depend on its geographical location for its nature. The other matter wherein he felt the agreement was lacking, was in the restrictions contained in Article Seven relating to the action to be taken when one American state suffered aggression at the hands of another American power. Accioly feels these provisions to be impracticable both by their nature and because of the delay they might involve. He contends that this decision was a backward step from the Act of Chapultepec. The body of the article, aside from these criticisms, consists of a historical review of the Pan-American movement and a close examination of the provisions of the treaty, after which Accioly concludes:

"It (the Treaty) constitutes a great step along the road of Pan-American solidarity and represents a document of high importance in international life. . . . In it are represented principles of elevated political achievement, such as the proscription of war among the contracting parties and the obligation of reciprocal assistance to prevent or repel aggression against any of them. It equally constitutes a great conquest for juridical order, i.e. the abandonment of the doctrine of absolute State sovereignty, such abandonment being verified by the repudiation of the right of veto and the admission that sanctions adopted by a two-thirds majority of the signatory states that have ratified the treaty will be binding on all, reserving only the case of employment of armed force . . . In our view, not its smallest benefit will be the influence it may exercise on the organization of the United Nations in the sense of making it into a truly efficient instrument for the preservation of peace and justice in the world."

710 Consultation 4/11–2947

The Acting Secretary of State to President Truman

WASHINGTON, December 1, 1947.

THE PRESIDENT: The undersigned, the Acting Secretary of State, has the honor to lay before the President, with a view to its transmission to the Senate to receive the advice and consent of that body to ratification, if his judgment approve thereof, a certified copy of the inter-American treaty of reciprocal assistance, formulated at the Inter-American Conference for the Maintenance of Continental Peace and Security and signed at Rio de Janeiro in the English, French, Portuguese, and Spanish languages on September 2, 1947, by the plenipotentiaries of the United States of America and by the plenipotentiaries of other American republics.[38]

. . . .

The inter-American treaty of reciprocal assistance was drawn up in accordance with the recommendation in the Act of Chapultepec and within the framework of the United Nations Charter. As stated in the preamble, the treaty deals with "those matters relating to the maintenance of international peace and security which are appropriate for regional action". This regional arrangement is thus of a type contemplated in chapter VIII of the United Nations Charter. It is entirely consistent with the purposes and principles of the United Nations and will facilitate and supplement the effective functioning of the United Nations. The authority of the Security Council with regard to the application of enforcement measures, and its general powers with respect to maintenance of international peace and security are fully recognized in the treaty, and Article 10 contains the stipulation that none of the provisions of the treaty "shall be construed as impairing

---

[38] For text of treaty, see Treaties and Other International Acts Series No. 1838, or 62 Stat. (pt. 2) 1681.

the rights and obligations of the High Contracting Parties under the Charter of the United Nations".

The principal features of the treaty include (a) references to certain basic considerations and precedents (preamble); (b) a reaffirmation of basic principles with respect to the pacific settlement of disputes (Articles 1 and 2); (c) the stipulation of specific obligations in the event of an armed attack against an American State, with a definition of the areas within which an armed attack would invoke the maximum obligations of the treaty (Articles 3 and 4); (d) provisions for consultation and collective measures in the event of certain other dangers to continental peace (Article 6); (e) provisions specifying the types of measures which may be taken in either event and specifying certain acts of aggression (Articles 7, 8, and 9); (f) provisions assuring consistency with and fulfillment of the obligations under the United Nations Charter (Article 3, paragraphs 3 and 4, and Articles 5, 10, and 24); and (g) procedural matters affecting consultation regarding, and execution of, measures, voting and the binding effect of decisions (Articles 11 to 21, inclusive).

The basic principle underlying the Act of Chapultepec is restated and extended in the treaty and concomitant obligations set forth in Article 3 as follows:

"1. The High Contracting Parties agree that an armed attack by any State against an American State shall be considered as an attack against all the American States and, consequently, each one of the said Contracting Parties undertakes to assist in meeting the attack in the exercise of the inherent right of individual or collective self-defense recognized by Article 51 of the Charter of the United Nations.

"2. On the request of the State or States directly attacked and until the decision of the Organ of Consultation of the Inter-American System, each one of the Contracting Parties may determine the immediate measures which it may individually take in fulfillment of the obligation contained in the preceding paragraph and in accordance with the principle of continental solidarity. The Organ of Consultation shall meet without delay for the purpose of examining those measures and agreeing upon the measures of a collective character that should be taken."

Thus, apart from such collective measures as may be agreed upon in consultation, each of the parties obligates itself to take affirmative action to assist in meeting an armed attack. This important provision converts the *right* of individual and collective self-defense, as recognized in the United Nations Charter, into an *obligation* under this treaty. The provision for immediate assistance is applicable to all cases of armed attack taking place within the territory of an American State or anywhere within the region delimited in Article 4. This region embraces the American Continents and Greenland, adjacent waters, and polar regions immediately to the north and south of the American continents.

Regardless of where the armed attack may take place, the parties are obligated to consult immediately with one another to agree upon appropriate collective measures.

The Conference decided that no attempt should be made to define aggression in general terms, but two recognized types of aggression are specified in Article 9.

In the event of an aggression which is not an armed attack or in the event of the occurrence of other possible dangers to the peace, the parties similarly obligate themselves in Article 6 to consult to determine the measures to be taken to aid the victim of the aggression or to restore peace and security.

The recommendation in the Act of Chapultepec with respect to the measures which might be taken to meet threats to inter-American peace and security or acts of aggression against any American State is restated in Article 8 of the treaty as follows:

"For the purposes of this Treaty, the measures on which the Organ of Consultation may agree will comprise one or more of the following: recall of chiefs of diplomatic missions; breaking of diplomatic relations; breaking of consular relations; partial or complete interruption of economic relations or of rail, sea, air, postal, telegraphic, telephonic, and radio-telephonic or radiotelegraphic communications; and use of armed force."

Article 7 provides that in the event of a conflict between two or more American States, the initial collective action to be taken by the parties shall be to call upon the contending States to suspend hostilities and restore the situation to the *status quo ante bellum*.

It is provided in Article 20 that decisions which require the application of the measures specified in Article 8 shall be binding upon all the signatory States which have ratified the treaty, with the sole exception that no State shall be required to use armed force without its consent. In Article 17 it is provided that the Organ of Consultation shall take its decisions by a vote of two-thirds of the signatory States which have ratified the treaty. This arrangement, whereby the measures specified in Article 8, with the one exception, become obligatory for all parties upon a two-thirds vote of the States parties to the treaty, represents a significant advance in international relations.

Article 22 provides that the treaty shall come into effect between the States which ratify it as soon as the ratifications of two-thirds of the signatory States have been deposited. Article 23 contains additional protocolary provisions relating to signature and ratification.

Article 24 determines the procedure for the registration of the treaty, when it has entered into force, with the Secretariat of the United Nations. Such registration is to be effected through the Pan American Union.

Article 25 provides that the treaty shall remain in force indefinitely but that any State party thereto may denounce it by a notification in writing to the Pan American Union, such denunciation to become effective for that State two years from the date of the receipt of such notification by the Pan American Union.

Article 26, the final article, provides that the principles and fundamental provisions of the treaty shall be incorporated in the Organic Pact of the Inter-American System. This has reference to an instrument in the nature of a basic constitution or charter for the reorganization of the System which it is contemplated will be considered and adopted at the forthcoming Ninth International Conference of American States to be held at Bogotá, Colombia, early in 1948.

This treaty represents a significant advance in international cooperation for the maintenance of peace and security. Its provisions commit the other parties promptly to assist the United States in the event of an armed attack by any country on our territory or anywhere in the region defined by the treaty, and the United States similarly pledges its assistance to the other parties in case any of them is subjected to such an attack. In determining collective measures, the parties guarantee in advance to observe important decisions reached by two-thirds of them, reserving for their individual consent among the listed measures only the vital decision as to their participation in the use of armed force. The obligatory character of decisions by a two-thirds majority assures that the general collective will of the community can be made effective, and avoids the possibility that the operation of the treaty might be paralyzed through the nonconcurrence of a small minority.

The vital spirit of Pan American solidarity is implicit in the provisions of the treaty and there is every reason to believe that the treaty affords an adequate guarantee of the peace and security of this Hemisphere, thereby assuring so far as possible a necessary condition to the continued advancement of the economic, political, and social ideals of the peoples of the American States.

Respectfully submitted,   ROBERT A. LOVETT

PRELIMINARY DISCUSSIONS CONCERNING THE NINTH INTERNATIONAL CONFERENCE OF AMERICAN STATES TO MEET IN BOGOTA [1]

[Information on various aspects of preliminary arrangements for the meeting at Bogotá may be found in the following selected publications:

A. *Official documents and analytical and summary accounts:*

(1) *Novena Conferencia Internacional Americana, Bogotá, marzo 30 de 1948: Actas y Documentos*, volumes I–VII (Bogotá, Ministerio de Relaciones Exteriores, 1954);

(2) *Ninth International Conference of American States, Bogotá, Colombia, March 30–May 2, 1948: Report of the Delegation of the United States of America with Related Documents* (Washington, Government Printing Office, 1948);

(3) "Report on the Ninth International Conference of American States", by Alberto Lleras, Secretary General of the Organization of American States, with related documents, in *Annals of the Organization of American States*, volume I, page 1 (Washington, Pan American Union, 1949).

B. *Addresses and articles:*

(1) "The Inter-American System: A Solid Foundation for the Challenge of the Future", by Ellis O. Briggs, Director, Office of American Republic Affairs, in Department of State *Bulletin*, April 27, 1947, page 769;

(2) "Economic Aspects of the Bogotá Conference", by Norman Armour, Assistant Secretary of State for Political Affairs, *ibid.*, December 21, 1947, page 1214;

(3) "Sovereignty and Interdependence in the New World: Comments on Inter-American System", by William Sanders, Associate Chief, Division of International Organization Affairs, *ibid.*, February 8, 1948, page 158.]

---

[1] For 1946 documentation on this subject, see *Foreign Relations*, 1946, vol. XI, pp. 1 ff.

THE EMERGENCY ADVISORY COMMITTEE FOR POLITICAL DEFENSE [1]

710. Consultation 3A/2–747

Memorandum by the Acting Chief of the Division of Special Inter-American Affairs (Dreier) to the Director of the Office of American Republic Affairs (Briggs)

WASHINGTON, February 7, 1947.

In the event you are interested, I attach a copy of the final draft of the Report of the Committee of Political Defense concerning "Conditions Necessary to Assure Political Defense".[2] You may recall that the idea of having the Committee include in its final report a positive statement on the importance of strengthening democracy was agreed to here . . .

. . . . . .

The shortcomings of democracy, the report says, in the American republics is due principally to the following factors:

1. Violation of popular sovereignty and the advocacy of the theory that the individual exists for the state rather than the state for the individual.
2. *Personalismo*.
3. Military intervention in politics (a good attack on the anti-democratic influences of military forces in Latin America).
4. Exercise of political pressure by capitalists and labor organizations.
5. Appeals to religious belief to prevent free expression of opinion.
6. Arbitrary and despotic violations of the rights and individual dignity of citizens.
7. Abuse of the "state of emergency".
8. Racial or religious discrimination.
9. Lack of economic opportunity and decent living conditions.
10. Exaltation of nationalistic philosophies.

The report also calls for economic cooperation as important to the maintenance of democracy and suggests that a consultative inter-American committee be formed to report on the progress of democracy in the continent and offer constructive suggestions for its advancement.

---

[1] For previous documentation on this subject, see *Foreign Relations*, 1946, vol. XI, pp. 76 ff.
[2] Not printed.

Although the report is necessarily couched in general terms, I think it is all to the good.

JOHN C. DREIER

---

710 Consultation 3A/2-2047 : Telegram

The Ambassador in Uruguay (McGurk) to the Secretary of State

MONTEVIDEO, February 20, 1947.

78. For Dreier from Boal.[4] Following is text of press statement accompanying text of resolutions which Committee will release here in Spanish February 25.

"Committee for Political Defense in plenary session has approved and transmitted to all governments of American Republics three recommendations relative to:

1. Expediting the proceedings and simplifying and liberalizing the requirements for travel within continent of nationals of Amercan Republics; 2. to applying to these nationals a common designation such as will reflect the spirit of continental unity instead of classifying them as (aliens); and 3. to the lifting of censorship over all means of communication and of expression of thought.

1. As a practical measure to facilitate travel for nationals of American countries, Committee recommends to governments of these countries that they eliminate general emergency travel restrictions established because of state of war. It further recommends that through bilateral agreements they adopt measures tending to reduce to necessary minimum the requirements for entry, residence and departure of nationals of American Republics and that they facilitate their travel within continent as much as possible.

In view of importance to continental unity of Committee's resolution it is hoped that governments of American Republics will take initiative in making reciprocal agreements with each other with a view to simplifying these travels of nationals of American Republics since this travel, developing mutual understanding, will strengthen fraternal bonds between all peoples of this continent.

2. Recognizing that nationals of countries of this continent are all in broadest sense of term Americans which should prevent their considering one another as aliens Committee further recommends that instead of referring to such nationals as 'aliens' governments of each of countries of continent classify nationals of others as 'Pan Americans'.

3. Finally Committee, on ground that one of fundamental principles of democratic system of government is that which secures and guarantees freedom of expression, recommends to governments of American Republics that if they have not already done so they proceed to abolish censorship over internal and international communica-

---

[4] Pierre de Lagarde Boal, United States representative on the Emergency Advisory Committee for Political Defense.

tions transmitted or disseminated by mail, telegraph, press, radio or over any other means of expression of thought.["]

[Boal]
McGurk

710 Consultation 3A/3–2147 : Telegram

The Ambassador in Uruguay (McGurk) to the Secretary of State

SECRET MONTEVIDEO, March 21, 1947—7 p. m.

121. For Dreier from Boal. As anticipated Carbajal[5] interprets CPD terms of reference to include political defense against all totalitarian infiltration including Soviet. He briefs his conclusion with reference to PCD rules approved by Governing Board PAU February 25, 1942, res 17 Rio,[6] res 42 Mexico City[7] (because of change in wording made in original Uruguayan proposal from "axis" to "groups of aliens which might become a danger to independence, integrity or institutions" of American Republics. See page 70, Spanish minutes of Conference February 21, 1945[8]).

He has sounded President and Foreign Minister on possibility of Uruguayan consultation with other governments on terms of reference and reports acquiescence by President, reluctance by Foreign Minister without final decision.

He suggested to some CPD members public statement by CPD asserting terms of reference include political defense against all totalitarian infiltration into hemisphere. I think I have talked him out of this. He now proposes CPD inquiry PAU on terms of reference and to renew his effort for intergovernmental consultation via Uruguayan Government. I have been discouraging former as tantamount to latter but with disadvantages. I assume any consultation begun would probably result in abeyance at least until after Moscow[9] probably until Rio or Bogotá.[10]

Matter will come up in CPD March 28. I would like to have De-

---

[5] Juan José Carbajal Victorica, Chairman of the Emergency Advisory Committee for Political Defense.
[6] Pan American Union, *Report on the Third Meeting of the Ministers of Foreign Affairs of the American Republics, Rio de Janeiro, January 15–28, 1942* (Washington, 1942), p. 44.
[7] Pan American Union, *Final Act of the Inter-American Conference on Problems of War and Peace, Mexico City, February–March, 1945* (Washington, 1945), p. 80.
[8] Not printed.
[9] The Fourth Session of the Council of Foreign Ministers which met in Moscow, March 10–April 24, 1947.
[10] The Inter-American Conference for the Maintenance of Continental Peace and Security, which met at Quitandinha, Brazil, August 15–September 2, 1947, and the Ninth International Conference of American States, which met at Bogotá, March 30–May 2, 1948.

partment's views as long before that as possible. Carbajal view CPD's scope shared by Peruvian, probably Venezuelan and Brazilian. Opposed by Chilean, probably Mexican, latter absent for month.

Carbajal also said Bramuglia [11] receptive to Argentine return to CPD and his view on anti-totalitarian scope CPD's functions. I have suggested caution on going any further on this pending determination Argentine participation military defense in Rio. Would appreciate Department's views on this also.

Foregoing summarizes letter [12] today's courier. [Boal.]

McGURK

---

710 Consultation 3A/4–247 : Telegram

The Ambassador in Uruguay (McGurk) to the Secretary of State

SECRET MONTEVIDEO, April 2, 1947—noon.

134. For Dreier from Boal. My 121, March 21; 129, March 26.[13] Carbajal still plans at April 7 meeting to present analysis of CPD terms of reference concluding CPD now has powers to recommend defenses against international Communism. Carabajal says this is at Uruguayan FonMin's suggestion and that Uruguay Govt does not wish to undertake direct intergovernmental consultation as FonMin thinks this would imply doubt re scope of terms of reference. At same session Carbajal plans to move that CPD send analysis without publicity to govts and possibly PAU with indication it is proceeding to study any recommendations on subject.

I would like to have as soon before April 7 as possible following information:

(1) Does Dept consider this move should be allowed to proceed or does it wish me to continue to oppose it and suggest other alternatives? (Majority of CPD members present favor Carbajal's suggestion.)

(2) What are Dept's views re possible return of Argentina to CPD at this time?

[Boal]
McGURK

---

710 Consultation 3A/3–2147 : Telegram

The Acting Secretary of State to the Embassy in Uruguay

SECRET WASHINGTON, April 2, 1947—7 p. m.

105. For Boal. Urtel 121 Mar 21. You shld maintain following positions re Carbajal interpretation CPD Charter.

---

[11] Juan Atilio Bramuglia, Argentine Minister for Foreign Affairs and Worship.
[12] Not printed.
[13] Latter not printed.

1. Dept firmly of opinion CPD lacks legal competence to enter broader field of activity. Governing reference is Rio Res 17. While this res is sprinkled with broad terminology sufficient, when taken from context, to include other than Axis ideologies, its historical background and concrete control measures expressed in memorandum attached thereto can leave no doubt that CPD was given emergency mandate corresponding to Axis aggression confronting Amreps at Rio as described whereas clauses. Carbajal view would necessarily imply Rio Conf contemplated CPD as permanent agency with extremely vague substantive jurisdiction and operating directives. Mex Res 7 and 9 [14] confirm this view untenable. Mex Res 42 has no bearing on CPD jurisdiction.

2. Assumption of jurisdiction by CPD itself would be resented by govts as anticipating their decision, and would prejudice standing of CPD. Res 9 Mex Conf indicates subject CPD to be considered by govts at Bogotá.

3. In view proper construction Res 17, no basis exists for reference question to PAU, which cannot enlarge substance Res.

You will also recall discussions in Dept last summer re danger misuse of any CPD recommendations by some govts against any opposition groups. Carbajal shld appreciate this danger.

This Govt is fully alive to Communist problem everywhere. With specific reference Latin America we believe on basis present estimate situation that Bogotá Conf shld offer logical opportunity for Amer govts to consider problem and determine what steps shld be taken.

Arg's return to CPD impossible since no vacancy exists. For your confidential info Dept would have strong reservations re adoption any multilateral policy on basis support Perón [15] govt thus giving Arg possible further opportunity avoid or obscure its attitude toward anti-Nazi commitments.

ACHESON

710 Consultation 3A/4–847 : Telegram

The Ambassador in Uruguay (McGurk) to the Secretary of State

SECRET   MONTEVIDEO, April 8, 1947—5 p. m.

138. For Dreier from Boal. After talking with Carbajal, Góes,[16] Peruvian and Venezuelan members, in general sense of that part of your 105, April 3, [2] dealing with scope of CPD's functions, Carbajal tells me he agrees it is best to delay any suggestion for CPD action

---

[14] *Final Act of the Inter-American Conference on Problems of War and Peace*, pp. 38 and 44, respectively.
[15] Juan D. Perón, President of Argentina.
[16] Gen. Pedro A. Góes Monteiro, Brazilian member on the Emergency Advisory Committee for Political Defense.

in order to leave question open for Government's confidential examination at Rio or Bogotá. This matter was not mentioned at today's meeting. [Boal.]

McGURK

---

710 Consultation 3A/4–847 : Telegram

The Acting Secretary of State to the Embassy in Uruguay

CONFIDENTIAL WASHINGTON, April 24, 1947—4 p. m.

131. For Boal. Recapitulating CPD projects considered current discussions here and with you last August Dept views situation as follows:

(1) Protection democracy human rights and recommendation advisory body thereon amply covered in part of Com report already published. No further consideration by Com required.

(2) Regarding further Com study problem recognition *de facto* governments or recommendations tending to peacetime extension principle Res 22,[17] Dept feels consideration and publicity inopportune at this time in view Paraguay situation [18] and other factors.

(3) In view CPD Res 26, 27, 28 and note Oct. 4, 1946, further implementation Res 7 Mex not called for.

(4) Reduction barriers inter-American travel covered by CPD Res 28 and 29. No objection referring to this subject in final report, calling topic to attention Bogotá Conf.

(5) In view Res 27 and 28 Dept does not deem further recommendations necessary re unwinding wartime controls.

Above review, together with substance urtel 138 Apr 8, indicate no further substantive problems before CPD, except for possible preparation final sections of report summarizing work on some of resolutions mentioned above. Pls confirm or comment on Dept's conclusion.

ACHESON

---

[17] See the *Second Annual Report of the Emergency Advisory Committee for Political Defense* (Montevideo, 1944).
[18] For documentation on this situation, see pp. 972 ff.

UNITED STATES POLICY WITH RESPECT TO THE PROVISION OF MILITARY ASSISTANCE AND ARMAMENTS TO THE OTHER AMERICAN REPUBLICS [1]

810.7962/11-146

The Secretary of State to the Secretary of War (Patterson)

SECRET   WASHINGTON, February 21, 1947.

MY DEAR MR. SECRETARY: The Department has received your letter of November 1, 1946 [2] and has reviewed the enclosed recommendations [3] of the District Engineer, United States Engineer Office, Miami, Florida, for the disposition of the United States interest in:

Airport	Locality	Country
Soledad Airport	Barranquilla	Colombia
La Aurora Airport	Guatemala City	Guatemala
Puerto Barrios Airport	Puerto Barrios	Guatemala
Bowen Field	Port-au-Prince	Haiti
Carmen Airfield	Carmen	Mexico
Chetumal Airport	Chetumal	Mexico
Cozumel Airport	Isla de Cozumel	Mexico
Campo Juanes Airport	Mérida	Mexico
Rihl Field	Tampico	Mexico
Chiapas Field	Tapachula	Mexico
Tehuantepec Airport	Ixtepec–Oaxaca	Mexico
Las Bajadas Airfield	Vera Cruz	Mexico
Las Mercedes Airport	Managua	Nicaragua
Asunción Airport	Asunción	Paraguay

The recommendation for disposition of General Andrews Airport, Ciudad Trujillo, Dominican Republic, has been considered separately, in accordance with your letter of December 26, 1946 [4] and is discussed in another letter.

---

[1] Continued from *Foreign Relations*, 1946, vol. XI, pp. 86–110. For additional 1947 documentation on this subject, see pertinent entries in index under individual countries.

[2] *Ibid.*, p. 105.

[3] Not printed.

[4] Not printed; in it Secretary Patterson submitted a proposal from Pan American Airways System as follows: "We would like to submit a proposal under which our existing agreement would be cancelled and the entire airport turned over to the Dominican Government for maintenance and operation. We would propose that the Dominican Government reimburse us for the value of our investment, plus such additional amount as our Government suggested by way of reim-

Footnote continued on following page.

Your letter states that there is no further War Department requirement for these airports, which were improved under the provisions of the Airport Development Program by Pan American Airways, Inc.

It is a matter of national interest that aviation facilities developed during the war be disposed of in a manner which will promote the world-wide air commerce of the United States. While the Department recognizes that the settlement of the contract is a matter for determination between War Department and the contractor, it believes that in connection therewith it is important that the War Department take such action as may be appropriate to be sure that the beneficial use of facilities constructed or improved through the use of public funds should be available to all United States aircraft authorized to be operated by the United States and the foreign government concerned.

In the event all of the property is not transferred under the obligations and commitments of the contract in the course of the settlement with the airline, the Office of the Foreign Liquidation Commissioner could undoubtedly arrange to delegate authority to the War Department to dispose of such of the property as may be surplus.

You suggest in your letter that the Department advise the Kilgore Committee [5] regarding steps being taken to dispose of the United States interest in these airports. Since these steps are being taken by the War Department, it seems to the Department that the War Department might more conveniently and appropriately advise the Kilgore Committee concerning them.

The recommendations of the Miami District Engineer and returned herewith in accordance with the request in your letter of November 1.[6]

Sincerely yours, For the Secretary of State:
WILLARD L. THORP
Assistant Secretary

---

bursement for the improvements installed under the contract." Secretary Patterson indicated that the value of United States Government constructed facilities at this airport was estimated $1,316,350 with a sale value of $1,000,000. (839.7962/12–2646)

Secretary Patterson was informed of the Department's views in a letter of February 21, as follows: ". . . it is the primary responsibility of a government to provide within its territory the facilities and services required for international civil aviation. The foregoing proposal is in accord with this view and the Department therefore perceives no objection to it." (839.7962/12–2646)

The State Department was informed in a War Department memorandum of May 21, that the War Department was concurrently directing the Chief of Engineers to dispose of General Andrews Field at Ciudad Trujillo, as concurred in by the State Department (839.7962/5–2147).

[5] U.S. Senate Armed Services Committee.

[6] In a memorandum of March 21, the War Department indicated that the Department of State would be advised at the time disposal instructions were issued (810.7962/3–2147).

810.24/2–2747

The Director of the Office of Financial and Development Policy (Ness) to the Chief of the Lend-Lease Fiscal Operations, Treasury Department (Cavanaugh)

WASHINGTON, February 27, 1947.

MY DEAR MR. CAVANAUGH: This is in reference to your letter, dated August 21, 1946,[7] to Mr. Cardozo, Director of the Legal Division, Office of the Foreign Liquidation Commissioner, a copy of which has been referred to this office.

In your letter it is noted that the lend-lease agreements with five of the American republics (Cuba, the Dominican Republic, Haiti, Nicaragua, and Paraguay)[8] provide for payment of definite amounts, with no provision that payments should not be larger than proportional to deliveries.

It is the policy of this Department, however, and has been from the time of the initial billings, that calculations of sums due and requests for payment in every case are to be based on the ratio of specified total payments to specified transfer ceilings and the application of this ratio to the value of actual deliveries, i.e., that payments shall be proportional to deliveries. Consequently, we regard only sums proportional to actual deliveries as being due.

The Office of American Republics Affairs and the Office of the Foreign Liquidation Commissioner have seen this letter and concur in the position set forth above.

Sincerely yours, NORMAN T. NESS

810.34/2–2847

The Secretary of the Navy (Forrestal) to the Secretary of State

WASHINGTON, February 28, 1947.

MY DEAR MR. SECRETARY: The Navy has been holding a number of excess combatant ships, including four (4) Light Cruisers and thirty-three (33) Destroyer Escorts, for eventual transfer to certain South American countries after enabling legislation is passed.

HR 6326, known as the Inter-American Military Cooperation Act,

---

[7] Not printed.
[8] For texts of agreements with Cuba, November 7, 1941; Dominican Republic, August 2 and August 6, 1941; Haiti, September 16, 1941; Nicaragua, October 16, 1941; and Paraguay, September 20, 1941; see *Foreign Relations*, 1941, vol. VII, pp. 122, 253, 319, 410, and 480. respectively.

was presented to Congress last year;[9] but due to the fact that it was presented late in the session (June 7, 1946), Congress adjourned without taking action on it. This Bill was sponsored by the State, War and Navy Departments. The Secretary of State supported the bill before the House Foreign Affairs Committee.

If such legislation is to pass this year, it should be introduced shortly. If it is not desired to transfer the ships concerned to the Latin American Republics, the Navy should terminate the expense involved in the maintenance of the ships. An early decision as to future policy in this regard is, therefore, highly desirable.

In this connection, it appears probable that if it should be decided that the United States will not transfer such ships to the Latin American Republics, they will in many cases be obtained from other sources.

Sincerely yours,   FORRESTAL

810.20 Defense/3–1247

Memorandum by the Chief of the Division of Special Inter-American Affairs (*Dreier*) *to the Assistant Secretary of State for American Republic Affairs* (*Braden*)

CONFIDENTIAL   WASHINGTON, March 12, 1947.

Mr. Gange[10] informs me that the Inter-American Military Cooperation Bill was again discussed by the Secretaries of State, War, and Navy this morning.

The initiative was taken by Secretary Forrestal who reported that the President, while in Mexico,[11] had been asked by the Mexicans when the United States would make available some cruisers and destroyers. The President is reported to have replied that we would be very glad to do this and, when tipped off by an aide that there was no legislation authorizing such transfers, said that if legislation was needed, it would be sought.

Mr. Acheson[12] said that the economic study being made of the program revealed that very few countries could afford to take on a program such as the War and Navy Departments have in mind. He said he

---

[9] See *Inter-American Military Cooperation Act:* Hearings Before the Committee on Foreign Affairs, House of Representatives, 79th Cong., 2d sess., on H.R. 6326, May 28, 29, 1946. For a letter from President Truman with which he submitted to the Congress the bill entitled "The Inter-American Military Cooperation Act", May 6 (H. Doc. 548, 79th Cong.), and statement by the Secretary of State at Hearings before the House Foreign Affairs Committee, May 29, see Department of State *Bulletin*, May 19, 1946, p. 859, and *ibid.*, June 9, 1946, p. 1001.

[10] John F. Gange, Acting Executive Secretary, Central Secretariat.

[11] For an address by President Truman, delivered in Mexico March 3, 1947, see Department of State *Bulletin*, March 16, 1947, p. 498.

[12] Dean Acheson, Under Secretary of State.

would see that copies of this report [13] were made available to the Secretaries of War and Navy for their study.

The economic report referred to was shown to me in draft form this morning. It concludes that only Cuba, Dominican Republic, El Salvador, Panama and Venezuela could afford the program without serious difficulties. A second group of countries which includes Brazil, Colombia and Mexico could afford it only with difficulty, and for a third group of countries including Chile, Ecuador, Peru and Bolivia, the program was economically out of the question. This report is being given to Mr. Acheson tomorrow via Mr. Thorp. Mr. Gerald Smith [14] and I recommended a few changes to point up the undesirable economic consequences on the other countries.

JOHN C. DREIER

810.20 Defense/3-1247

The Acting Secretary of State to the Secretary of War (Patterson) [15]

WASHINGTON, March 19, 1947.

MY DEAR MR. SECRETARY: In accordance with our conversation on March 12, I enclose herewith a copy of an interim report [13] on financial aspects of participation by Latin American countries in the Inter-American Arms Program. This analysis considers the estimates of cost to the Latin American countries, given in your letter of January 2 [13] and in Secretary Forrestal's letter of February 28, in relation to the internal and international financial position of the respective countries included in your estimates.

The report consists of a summary, based on a general survey of the financial position of all the countries under consideration, and some detailed analyses of the financial position of a few selected countries. I should like to take the liberty of emphasizing a few of the most significant conclusions that should be drawn from this financial analysis:

1. Only five countries—Cuba, the Dominican Republic, El Salvador, Panama and Venezuela—are found to have financial resources capable of enabling them to participate without major difficulty in the program proposed by the War and Navy Departments.
2. All the other American republics in the War and Navy Departments' plan referred to above, including Brazil and Mexico, would face major economic problems if they attempted to spend on armaments over the next ten years the amounts which the War and Navy Departments have estimated for the procurement of material only. The economic conditions of Bolivia, Chile, Costa Rica, Ecuador, Nica-

---

[13] Not printed.
[14] H. Gerald Smith, Special Assistant to Assistant Secretary of State Braden.
[15] Similar letter was sent on the same date to Secretary of the Navy Forrestal.

ragua and Peru are such as to make participation in the program virtually impossible for them.

3. The general economic outlook for many of these countries is unfortunately poor, so that the difficulties incident to their meeting the cost of the arms program may be expected to become more severe during the next few years.

4. The capacity of the Latin American countries to service public and private debts already owed to the United States would be seriously jeopardized by the expenditures required under the arms program.

5. Encouragement of expenditures on arms by the Latin American countries runs directly counter to our basic economic and political policies which aim to encourage an improvement in the living standards and economic welfare in those countries. The sacrifices which all of the Latin American countries would be required to make under the proposed program would drastically limit or defer their effectuation of plans for industrialization, improvement of transportation, production of strategic materials needed by the United States, and correction of presently poor conditions of public health, education and social welfare.

The economic handicaps imposed by the proposed arms program would perpetuate and aggravate conditions of economic and political instability which already constitute a serious security problem for this Government in Latin America, and which this Government now proposes to spend large amounts of money to overcome in other parts of the world. Those conditions are the soil in which the seeds of totalitarian regimes are nurtured.

Passage of a bill such as HR 6326, with its widely recognized objective of standardizing the armaments of the American republics by the transfer of United States equipment, cannot fail, in view of the above, to face this Government with two wholly undesirable consequences: we shall encourage expenditures for armaments by the other American republics which will weaken their economies and therefore their political stability, and we shall be called upon by poorer countries to subsidize the program at great cost to this Government. These consequences, in addition to other political factors previously discussed, would, I am convinced, impose a serious risk on some of our most important interests and objectives in the other American republics.

Sincerely yours,

DEAN ACHESON

810.20 Defense/3–2747

The Secretary of War (Patterson) to the Acting Secretary of State

SECRET WASHINGTON, March 27, 1947

DEAR MR. SECRETARY: I have read with great interest your letter of 19 March and the interim report on the financial implications of participation by Latin American countries in the Inter-American Military Cooperation Program. As I understand it, the major points of your study are, first, that passage of the Inter-American Military Cooperation Act is economically hazardous because you imply it would require the Latin American countries to expend greater sums than they can afford for the purchase of United States arms and equipment, and, second, that denial by the United States of such assistance to Latin American countries would thereby prevent large expenditures on their part for military purposes.

As to your first point, I have no thought of questioning the estimate of the economic capabilities of the various South American countries, which is contained in the report accompanying your letter. On the other hand, I am convinced that the conclusions drawn from the report are not necessarily germane to the problem. I am in complete agreement with the United States position on regulation and reduction of armaments and armed forces throughout the world, Latin America and the United States included, a position which affirms the desirability of reducing the economic burdens borne by all peoples in their efforts to maintain armed forces by reducing the scale of armaments and armed forces. There can be no objection to such a principle. However, I am certain you will agree that implementing such a principle will be a long-term, difficult procedure and that the ceilings on armaments likely to be achieved in the foreseeable future would be above any actually implemented program of Western Hemisphere cooperation and standardization.

I am certainly no more desirous than you are of adding to the economic burdens of Latin American countries, but I simply cannot believe that enactment of the proposed legislation will have such a tendency. To me the problem of controlling the cost of military cooperation is entirely one of good judgment on the part of the United States in implementing the program and bears no relation whatever to whether we should obtain authority to engage therein. Even after passage of the Act, the State Department will continue to control the implementation of the program and may, in its discretion, reduce or altogether deny United States military assistance to any American Republic. Nevertheless, I submit that however much the State Department may subsequently reduce the amount and scope of United States assistance, we should be far better off to have authority to carry out that part of the program which appears practicable to the Secretary of State, than to have no legislative authority whatever.

Nor can I agree with the second point set forth in your letter that if the United States declines to provide military equipment to the Latin American Republics, these nations will forego the purchase of military equipment and thereby eliminate substantial expenses now included in their budgets. On the contrary, I am of the opinion that, subject to any future agreements which may limit or regulate armaments, the majority of the sovereign states of the Western Hemisphere will insist upon maintaining such military establishments as *they*, not *we*, feel they require and which *they*, not *we*, feel they can support financially.

Thus, the question we face in Latin America is not, "Shall they have arms?" The basic question which is the vital crux of the whole subject is, "Shall they have United States or foreign arms?"

In connection with this serious question, I feel obliged to re-emphasize the advantage to hemisphere security of standardizing the military establishments of the American Republics as to equipment, training and organization. Of these, the provision of United States equipment is the keystone since United States methods of training and organization must inevitably follow its adoption along with the far-reaching concomitant benefits of permanent United States military missions and the continued flow of Latin American officers through our service schools. Thus will our ideals and ways of life be nurtured in Latin America, to the eventual exclusion of totalitarianism and other foreign ideologies. Thus only can we maintain the security of our southern flank.

Your letter made no mention of Canada. I should point out that the provisions of the Inter-American Military Cooperation Act apply to Canada as well as to any other American state. In the absence of separate legislation to the same end, passage of this Act is essential to achieve the objective sought in the recent United States–Canadian agreement on standardization of arms, training and organization.[17] With respect to Canada, these matters are considered to be vital to the security of the United States.

In the final analysis, I feel very strongly that this legislation is a preventive measure of the highest importance. It is designed to prevent the very type of crisis which has arisen in Turkey and Greece where we are now desperately attempting to lock the stable door while the horse is almost in process of being stolen. In Latin America, we must lock the stable door before the danger ever arises. Prevention is relatively cheap; crises are exorbitantly expensive in money, in time, and often in blood.

Last year, despite the eloquent supporting testimony of Secretary of State Byrnes, the Inter-American Military Cooperation Act died in the last-minute jam of legislation of the 79th Congress. In accordance

---

[17] For a Department press release on this agreement dated February 12, 1947, entitled "U.S.–Canadian Permanent Joint Board on Defense To Continue Collaboration for Security Purposes", see Department of State *Bulletin*, February 23, 1947, p. 361; for documentation on this subject, see volume III.

with our discussion of 12 March 1947,[18] I urge that the Secretary be approached without delay for a decision as to whether or not the Act will be reintroduced in the 80th Congress. Strongly as I favor the enactment of this legislation, I am even stronger in my conviction that an early decision is required.

Sincerely yours,

ROBERT P. PATTERSON

810.20 Defense/3–3147

The Secretary of the Navy (Forrestal) to the Acting Secretary of State

SECRET   WASHINGTON, March 31, 1947.

MY DEAR MR. SECRETARY: I am in receipt of your two letters of March 19, 1947, on the subject of inter-American military cooperation. The letters and the interim report [19] on the financial aspects of participation have received close study in the Department.

The financial position of the Latin American countries is appreciated and the possible adverse effect on the economy of certain countries if an extensive program were initiated is understood. However, the Navy plans do not contemplate an appreciable increase in the overall size of those navies. Except for the supply of some small patrol vessels to be used in coastal work, it is planned to substitute larger units for an approximately equal tonnage of old and obsolete types with a resultant modernization and standardization. The net result should through the economies effected in operation actually produce a year to year saving. In any case the rate of flow of equipment can be controlled to take into account the ability of any particular country to meet its financial obligations. Furthermore, it is believed that some participation in the program may prevent the acceptance of attractive offers reportedly now being made by European countries.

You will recall that extensive staff discussions were held not long ago between military representatives of the United States and various Latin American countries. As a result of these talks a firm opinion exists in Latin America that it is the intention of the United States Government to assist in the modernization of their armed forces and to provide a source of munitions within the Western Hemisphere. Failure on our part to take further steps toward this end may cause the United States to suffer not only a considerable loss of confidence in the eyes of the Latin Americans, but also a loss of the close military

---

[18] See memorandum dated March 12, p. 104.
[19] Letters and report not printed; see letter of March 19 to Secretary Patterson, p. 105.

collaboration gained through the expenditure of large sums of money during the past war.

Again, failure to enact appropriate legislation will restrict our ability to fulfill the commitments of the United States implied in the Act of Chapultepec [20] and the U.S.–Canadian Defense Agreement of 12 February 1947, which envision the consolidation of the Western Hemisphere and the standardization in United States methods of training and equipment. The common defense of the hemisphere will be retarded unless the United States takes the initiative in this matter.

In view of the above, I recommend the introduction into Congress of the proposed legislation, which, I assure you, will receive my full support. In the event decision is made not to introduce this legislation, it is requested that you so inform the President, who, I understand, discussed the question of aid to Mexico with President Alemán.[21]

Sincerely yours,

FORRESTAL

810.20 Defense/4–1747

The Secretary of War (Patterson) to the Acting Secretary of State

SECRET   WASHINGTON, April 17, 1947.

DEAR MR. SECRETARY: In my letter of March 27th on the subject of military assistance to other American states I set forth certain factors in support of our conclusion that prompt action should be taken in sponsoring legislation.

I am taking this opportunity to outline, as briefly as I can, the basic reasons why no further time should be lost, as we see the situation, in introducing legislation along the same lines as the bill offered in the last session of Congress.

1. The first and foremost factor is that the furnishing of training and the transfer of military equipment to other American states will promote the national security of the United States.

In the case of Canada, on the northern flank, there cannot be the slightest doubt as to the value of the proposed legislation. We already have a program underway with Canada for standardization of equipment, training and organization, and the proposed bill will implement and facilitate this program.

In the case of states to the south, the advantages in providing train-

---

[20] For text, see Department of State, Treaties and Other International Acts Series No. 1543; 60 Stat. (pt. 2) 1831.
[21] Miguel Alemán Valdés, President of Mexico. With regard to his visit to the United States April 29–May 7, 1947, see Department of State *Bulletin*, May 25, 1947, p. 1043.

ing and equipment of our type and design, as contrasted with the situation in which European nations would be furnishing such training and equipment, would seem to be manifest. The advantages on the affirmative side are substantial. On the negative side, in the exclusion of training and equipment derived from non-American sources, the strengthening of our national security would be very considerable.

2. One of the chief objectives of communistic propaganda in the Latin American states is to prevent the extension of military assistance by the United States to those states. It would seem that we are playing into the hands of the Communists if by our own decision we disable ourselves from the tender of military assistance.

3. We have, as you know, military missions in a number of other American states. The effectiveness of these missions will be seriously impaired if those countries look to European sources for arms and ammunition. The types and designs of the weapons would be unfamiliar to our military personnel, and there is every probability that military missions from other countries would follow the introduction of their equipment.

4. We are already committed, as we see it, to the support of this legislation. The conferences with the military staffs of the other American states, which were held in 1945 under the auspices of the State Department, and the Act of Chapultepec were definite steps along this line. Over and above that, we have the fact that a similar bill was introduced last year, supported by the State, War, and Navy Departments. The President urged its passage, and Secretary Byrnes testified in favor of it. In our contacts with military representatives of other American states we are at a loss to explain why legislation of the same character is no longer being supported.

The arguments on the other side, advanced as reasons for changing our policy have been thoroughly considered.

There is the argument that passage of the bill will build up armaments. The bill provides otherwise, for the recipient nations are to turn in their existing equipment. It is also to be noted that the bill takes into account any international arrangement for reduction of armaments.

The other point in opposition to the measure is the one stressed in your letter of March 19th, that some of the countries cannot afford to buy weapons.

This factor, it seems to us, overlooks the probability that the poorer countries will acquire weapons in any event; if they cannot get the weapons from us, they will get them elsewhere, and to our disadvantage. The argument on the economic side also overlooks the fact that the bill does not require the President to furnish arms to any and all countries. It simply gives him authority to furnish training and equipment, the decision being his as to the extent of the training and equipment to be given in any case.

This point of economic disadvantage, it is to be noted, was as valid a year ago as it is today. It was not considered controlling a year ago, when the former bill, H.R. 6326, was introduced.

Nearly four months of the present session of Congress have already been lost. If further time is lost in coming to a decision, the matter will be moot, so far as prospect of action at the present session is concerned.

The Secretary of the Navy authorizes me to say that he is in general accord with the views in this letter.

Sincerely yours,
ROBERT P. PATTERSON

810.7962/4–2247

The Acting Secretary of State to the Secretary of War (Patterson)

SECRET　　　　　　　　　　　　　　WASHINGTON, April 22, 1947.

MY DEAR MR. SECRETARY: Reference is made to your letter of November 1, 1946,[22] enclosing recommendations of the District Engineer, United States Engineer Office, Miami, Florida, for the disposition of certain airports constructed or improved under the Airport Development Program.

In its reply of February 21, 1947, this Department interposed no objection to the recommended plan for the disposal of Puerto Barrios and La Aurora Airports at Puerto Barrios and Guatemala City, Guatemala, respectively. The Department now wishes to point out, however, that objection must be raised to such portion of the recommended plan for the disposal of these Airport Development Program airfields in Guatemala as may be found to conflict with the following paragraph of a note, No. 337, which the United States Legation at Guatemala City addressed to the Guatemalan Government on November 16, 1942:[23]

"4. All of the works carried out on Guatemalan territory on the initiative and at the cost of the Government of the United States of America, pursuant to the provisions of the Memorandum of Agreement attached hereto, shall, upon the termination of that agreement, become the exclusive property of the Government of Guatemala, with the exception of the organic armament and equipment of the United States forces, the clothing of the troops, the manual instruments, and everything that constitutes the equipment of such forces."

---

[22] *Foreign Relations*, 1946, vol. XI, p. 105.
[23] *Ibid.*, 1942, vol. VI, p. 443.

The foregoing note is an integral part of this Government's Lend-Lease Agreement with Guatemala.[24]

Sincerely yours, For the Acting Secretary of State:
GARRISON NORTON
Assistant Secretary

810.20 Defense/5-147

Minutes of Meeting of the Secretaries of State, War, and Navy

SECRET   WASHINGTON, May 1, 1947—10:30 a.m.

PRESENT

STATE	WAR	NAVY
Secretary Marshall	Secretary Patterson	Secretary Forrestal
Under Secretary Acheson	Assistant Secretary Petersen	Under Secretary Sullivan
General Hilldring [25]		Rear Admiral Woodridge [*Wooldridge*]
Mr. Allen		
Mr. Moseley (SWNCC),[26] Recorder		

I. *Latin American Arms Program (Inter-American Military Cooperation Act).*

Decision:

It was agreed that the three Departments would support the reintroduction into Congress of the Inter-American Military Cooperation Act.

Implementing Action:

Necessary action to be undertaken to reintroduce the Bill. (No mention was made at the Meeting as to which Department would assume this responsibility.)

Discussion:

SECRETARY PATTERSON reviewed the War Department position with respect to this legislation. He said that the program outlined in this Bill was in line with the purposes of the Act of Chapultepec and our policy of defense of the Western Hemisphere. He pointed out that the President should be given the necessary discretion to aid the Latin American countries and Canada by providing them with American equipment and training their military forces according to American methods. He said that the success of our military missions in those countries depended upon our making available equipment of United

---

[24] The Secretary of War replied in a memorandum of May 29 that the War Department would abide by the objections raised by the Department of State in the above letter (810.7962/5-2947).

[25] Gen. John H. Hilldring, Assistant Secretary of State for Occupied Areas.

[26] H. Wilcox Moseley, Special Assistant to General Hilldring.

States design. He added that if we did not provide the equipment that these nations would obtain it somewhere else. He said that it was very difficult to explain our vacillation in this arms program to our Latin American neighbors. Furthermore, our program to standardize Canadian equipment with ours will be aided by the passage of this Bill.

SECRETARY FORRESTAL said that the Navy Department supported the Bill wholeheartedly and was anxious to see early action on it.

MR. ACHESON said that he had over-ruled objections within his department against the Bill and that the State Department would now support it. He stated that there was one aspect, however, of the arms program which yet had to be resolved. This was the question of finding the dollars to pay for the cost of crating and transferring the equipment to the other American Republics. He said that it was estimated that it would take about 23 million dollars to package and ship the equipment which would be transferred under this Act. He pointed out that some of the countries could not raise the necessary funds, and furthermore there undoubtedly would be arguments as to whether we or they must meet these expenses. He pointed out that under the existing interim program it is still being argued as to who will meet these particular expenses.

SECRETARY PATTERSON said that the War Department is very anxious to get rid of its surplus equipment as it is very expensive to maintain it in condition. He added that it might be to our advantage to pay the costs of crating and delivery as it might be less than the maintenance cost. SECRETARY FORRESTAL said that the Navy Department was confronted with the same conditions—that the upkeep and overhead in keeping vessels in condition was extremely great.

GENERAL HILLDRING said that it was his opinion that unless means were provided to furnish the necessary money to implement the Act, there would not be much accomplished in passing it. He said that he did not necessarily mean that the Act should be amended to provide funds for implementing it, but that he thought that there should be some agreement in the Committee that ways and means would be found to meet the necessary costs. Mr. Acheson said that Congress will certainly ask what costs will be involved in this legislation. He stated that we should be prepared to tell them that there will be probable cost to the U.S. in connection with transferring the equipment. On the other hand, it should be pointed out to Congress the costs involved in maintaining this equipment in condition within the U.S. SECRETARY MARSHALL said that he believed that he should make a frank statement to Congress of the costs involved in this program calling attention to the maintenance costs to the U.S. He said that it is possible that Congress will appropriate some of the funds necessary to carry out the proposed arms program.

Secretary Forrestal stated that passage of the Act was necessary to show our good faith toward our Western Hemisphere neighbors even though no specific commitment to them in this connection was involved. Secretary Patterson said that prompt action was necessary to introduce the bill in order to get consideration in this session of Congress.

There was general agreement that the legislation should be introduced.[27]

II. *Construction of Naval Vessels in Argentina.*

Decision:

It was agreed that consideration of the Argentine request should be deferred until reports have been received from Ambassador Messersmith that the Argentine Government has taken satisfactory action to get rid of Nazi agents remaining in Argentina.

810.20 Defense/6–1347

The Secretary of War (Patterson) to the Secretary of State

CONFIDENTIAL   WASHINGTON, 13 June, 1947.

Dear Mr. Secretary: You have no doubt been informed, both by State and War Department advisors, that the equipment earmarked for the Interim Allocation of the Western Hemisphere Defense Program has been made available to the Field Commissioner for Military Programs, Office of the Foreign Liquidation Commissioner, Department of State. This, of course, is less the amount of equipment that cannot be made available due to the Veterans' Preference Act.[28]

To date, the War Department has received shipping instructions from the State Department (Office of the Foreign Liquidation Commissioner, Field Commissioner for Military Programs) for approximately 40 per cent of the countries authorized to receive equipment under this program.

Due to the decrease of War Department personnel ceilings, the necessity for consolidation of storage space within the Zone of Interior, and the possibility of utilizing portions of equipment earmarked for this program for other War Department commitments, the War De-

---

[27] President Truman transmitted the bill with covering message to the Congress on May 26, 1947. For text of the President's message and the draft bill, see Department of State *Bulletin*, June 8, 1947. Hearings were held on the proposed bill (H.R. 3836, 80th Congress, 1st session) on June 23, 25, 26, and July 2, and it was approved by the House Committee on Foreign Affairs on July 17 after considerable amendment and modification; no further action was taken during 1947. For a statement by the Secretary of State before the House Committee on June 23, see the *Bulletin*, July 6, 1947, p. 5051.

[28] For Veterans' Preference Act of June 27, 1944, see 58 Stat. 387.

partment is most anxious to complete shipment of all Interim Program equipment at the earliest practicable date.

The present War Department policy is that the Interim equipment will not be held beyond 31 December 1947.

Due to the above personnel restrictions, and limited storage space, I recommend that a suspense date of 15 August 1947 be established for all equipment other than aircraft. This would require that all countries which have not yet placed a firm order with the Field Commissioner for Military Programs for Interim Program equipment, do so by this date. All equipment not firmly ordered by this date will revert to War Department stocks for utilization for other approved programs.

In line with the above proposed suspense date of 15 August 1947 for firm orders, the War Department will expect the countries concerned to take complete delivery on or before 31 December 1947. This is in accordance with presently established War Department policy.

I further recommend, that if you are in accord with the above proposed suspense date, that the Foreign Liquidation Commission Field Commissioner for Military Programs be directed to notify the countries concerned without delay, of this decision, and further, that I be notified as soon as practicable of your concurrence or recommendation.[29]

Sincerely yours,

ROBERT L. PATTERSON

810.24/8-447

Memorandum by the Secretary of the Policy Committee on Arms and Armaments (Sohm)

SECRET   WASHINGTON, August 4, 1947.

There is circulated herewith for the information of the Committee the policy on commercial sales and transfers of munitions to the other American republics approved by the Committee at its meeting of August 1, 1947 (see M-54, p. 1, #2 [30]). Also attached is the covering memorandum to the Under Secretary prepared for the signature of General Hilldring as Chairman of the Committee.

EARL D. SOHM

---

[29] In a letter of November 19, Kenneth C. Royall, Secretary of the Army, recommended extension of the retention date of available equipment for the Western Hemisphere Defense Program from December 31, 1947, to June 30, 1948 (810.20 Defense/11–1947). The Department's acceptance of these recommendations was indicated in letters of June 27 and December 12, 1947, to Mr. Patterson and Mr. Royall, respectively (810.20 Defense/6–1347 and /11–1947).

[30] Not printed; the Policy Committee on Arms and Armaments (PCA) was established May 20, 1946, by authority of the Secretary of State to coordinate the Department's policy regarding all matters of arms and armaments.

PROVISION OF MILITARY ASSISTANCE 117

[Annex]

Memorandum by the Chairman of the Policy Committee on Arms and Armaments (Hilldring) to the Under Secretary of State (Acheson)

SECRET   WASHINGTON, August 4, 1947.

Subject: Arms Policy Regarding Argentina and Other American Republics.

As Chairman, and through the Deputy Chairman of the Policy Committee on Arms and Armaments, I reported to that Committee that you had enunciated the policy that commercial purchases of arms, ammunition and implements of war in the United States by the Argentine Government are not to be limited.[31]

The Committee is composed of representatives of A–H, ARA, EUR, NEA, FE, SPA and MD.

The Committee unanimously decided to request further consideration by you of the implications arising from a complete relaxation of all controls of commercial sales of arms to the republics of the Western Hemisphere. The Committee directed me as its Chairman to submit to you their position with respect to this problem.

In accordance with the Committee's decision, I submit for your consideration the action of the Policy Committee. Their recommendations, as given on pages 3 and 4 of the attached brief, were unanimously adopted by the Committee. It will be noted that the Office of American Republic Affairs concurs in these recommendations.

[Subannex]

Memorandum by the Chairman of the Policy Committee on Arms and Armaments (Hilldring) to the Under Secretary of State (Acheson)

SECRET

Subject: Policy Regarding Commercial Transfers or Sales of Munitions to Argentina and the Other American Republics.

Discussion:

At the meeting of the Policy Committee on Arms and Armaments on July 25, 1947, the Deputy Chairman of the Committee, informed

---

[31] A change of policy toward Argentina was announced at the Under Secretary's meeting held July 11, 1947. On July 25, the following statement was made in the minutes of the PCA: "In accordance with the policy enunciated by the Under Secretary (that commercial purchases of arms, ammunition, and implements of war from the United States by the Argentine Government should no longer be limited), the Committee directed MD to approve the licenses for export of arms, ammunition, and implements of war to Argentina now pending in that division." The Committee recommended at this time that the Under Secretary consider further his decision that Argentina receive unlimited commercial arms and the effect of this policy on the other American Republics.

264–330—72——9

the Committee that the Under-Secretary had enunciated the policy that commercial purchases of arms, ammunition, and implements of war in the U.S. by the Argentine Government are not to be limited.

Discussion by the members indicated that it was not clear whether or not this policy toward Argentina necessarily implied the application of a similar policy to commercial sales of munitions to the other American Republics. It was pointed out that, whereas prior to the enunciation of the said policy toward Argentina, that nation was in a more restricted position than the other American Republics (with the exception of the Dominican Republic, Nicaragua, and Honduras) insofar as the purchase of U.S. arms was concerned, under this new policy Argentina would be in a preferential position vis-à-vis the purchase of U.S. arms if a similar policy were not applied to the other American Republics.

Paragraph 8 of SWNCC 202/2, dated March 21, 1946, "Policy Concerning Provision of U.S. Government Military Supplies for Post-War Armed Forces of Foreign Nations", states that:

"It is consistent with United States policy to support with U.S. military supplies the armed forces of the other American Republics to the extent necessary to effect collaboration for the defense of the Hemisphere."

However, in view of the position of this Government concerning the non-compliance of Argentina with certain provisions of the Act of Chapultepec, it has been the policy of this Government to prevent the shipment of munitions to Argentina from the U.S. either from surpluses or commercial sources.

Thus, on June 13, 1946, the Policy Committee on Arms and Armaments recorded the following statement of policy on this subject:

"It is the present policy to withhold from the Argentine Government all arms, ammunition and implements of war as defined by the President's Proclamation 2549,[32] except for certain training and cargo aircraft."

Subsequently, at its meeting on October 8, 1946, the Committee agreed that there should be no change at that time in the existing policy prohibiting shipments of arms, ammunition and implements of war to Argentina. The view was expressed that when Argentina fulfilled its obligations under the Inter-American agreements, there might be a change in policy.

Further, at the meeting of the Policy Committee on Arms and Arm-

---

[32] Dated April 9, 1942; for this proclamation on the enumeration of arms, ammunition, and implements of war, see Department of State *Bulletin*, April 11, 1942, p. 323. For the proclamation effective February 20, 1947, superseding proclamation 2549, see *ibid.*, February 23, 1947, p. 327.

aments on December 13, 1946 and at the meeting of the Secretary's Staff Committee on December 20, 1946, the following was approved:

". . . it is the policy of the U.S. not to authorize transfers to foreign countries, by sale or otherwise, of military supplies of U.S. origin unless such transfers:

a. Fall within one of the following categories: . . .

    4. The interim program for the sale of specified amounts of military, naval and air equipment to other American Republics . . ." (No interim program has been established for Argentina to date.)

b. meet one of the following conditions:

"1. if the transfer is determined to be reasonable and necessary to enable a country to maintain internal order in the reasonable and legitimate exercise of constituted authority, or

2. if the transfer is determined to be reasonable and necessary to enable a country to provide for and to exercise its right of self-defense against armed attack, a right recognized in Article 51 of the Charter of the United Nations,[33] or

3. if the transfer is determined to be reasonable and necessary to assist a country to discharge its international responsibilities for (*a*) furnishing contingents to the Security Council pursuant to Article 43 of the Charter of the United Nations and (*b*) carrying out military occupation in enemy or ex-enemy territory."

In view of the above the Policy Committee on Arms and Armaments concluded at its August 1 meeting that the solution to the present problem lies either in:

a. According to Argentina the same treatment as is presently accorded the other American Republics; i.e., participation in the interim and long-range arms standardization programs plus a careful review of all other proposed munitions sales in order to determine whether or not one or more of the above conditions is met: *or*

b. Applying to the other American Republics a policy similar to that enunciated by the Under-Secretary with respect to Argentina; i.e., lifting all restrictions on commercial sales of munitions.

Recommendations:

Accordingly, the Policy Committee on Arms and Armaments recommends that:

1. Argentina be accorded the same treatment as the other American Republics with respect to transfers or sales of arms, ammunition and implements of war.

2. With respect to all of the Latin American Republics, all transfers or sales of arms, ammunition and implements of war be acted upon in accordance with the criteria indicated below and in line with the U.S. arms standardization policy in Latin America.

---

[33] Department of State Treaty Series No. 993; 59 Stat. (pt. 2) 1031.

a. If the transfer is determined to be reasonable and necessary to enable a country to maintain internal order in the reasonable and legitimate exercise of constituted authority, or

b. If the transfer is determined to be reasonable and necessary to enable a country to provide for and to exercise its right of self-defense against armed attack, a right recognized in Article 51 of the Charter of the United Nations, or

c. If the transfer is determined to be reasonable and necessary to assist a country to discharge its international responsibilities for (1) furnishing contingents to the Security Council pursuant to Article 43 of the Charter of the United Nations and (2) carrying out military occupation in enemy or ex-enemy territory.

Concurrences:

The Office of American Republic Affairs through its representative on the Committee concurs in the above conclusions and recommendations,[34] as well as the other members of the Committee representing A–H, EUR, NEA, FE, SPA and MD.

810.24/8–2247

The Acting Secretary of State to the Secretary of War (Royall)[35]

SECRET WASHINGTON, August 22, 1947.

MY DEAR MR. SECRETARY: I attach herewith, for your information, a copy of a statement of policy of the Department of State in respect to the sale, transfer and export of arms, ammunition and implements of war to the republics of the Western Hemisphere.

You will note that this policy places all these nations upon the same basis with respect to the procurement in the United States of arms, ammunition, and implements of war, subject to certain criteria and to the United States arms standardization policy in Latin America.

Sincerely yours, ROBERT A. LOVETT

[Enclosure]

POLICY WITH RESPECT TO TRANSFERS OR SALES OF ARMS, AMMUNITION, AND IMPLEMENTS OF WAR TO THE REPUBLICS OF THE WESTERN HEMISPHERE

1. Argentina will be accorded the same treatment as the other American Republics with respect to transfers or sales of arms, ammunition, and implements of war.

---

[34] This policy, initiated in the PCA, and later approved by the Under Secretary, was the policy of the Department through the remainder of the year 1947.

[35] The same letter was sent on the same date to the Secretary of the Navy (Forrestal).

2. With respect to all the Latin American Republics, all transfers or sales of arms, ammunition, and implements of war will be acted upon in accordance with the criteria indicated below and in line with the United States arms standardization policy in Latin America.

   a. If the transfer is determined to be reasonable and necessary to enable a country to maintain internal order in the reasonable and legitimate exercise of constituted authority, or

   b. If the transfer is determined to be reasonable and necessary to enable a country to provide for and to exercise its right of self-defense against armed attack, a right recognized in Article 51 of the Charter of the United Nations, or

   c. If the transfer is determined to be reasonable and necessary to assist a country to discharge its international responsibilities for (1) furnishing contingents to the Security Council pursuant to Article 43 of the Charter of the United Nations, and (2) carrying out military occupation in enemy or ex-enemy territory.

800.24/9–347

The Acting Secretary of State to the Secretary of War (Royall)

WASHINGTON, September 3, 1947.

DEAR MR. SECRETARY: In enacting Public Law 271, approved July 30, 1947, the 80th Congress indicated its acquiescence in the carrying to completion of the lend-lease pipeline agreements with the ten countries named therein.[36] It also indicated its intention that the Agreement of October 15, 1945 with the Government of the Union of Soviet Socialist Republics [37] should not be carried out further. It is believed that your Department has on hand certain lend-lease material to be delivered under the agreements with the ten authorized governments, and also a number of articles, including railroad locomotives, intended for the Union of Soviet Socialist Republics.

In view of the intent reflected by the enactment of Public Law 271 this Department hopes that delivery of all material for the ten named countries can be effected promptly. Please advise if there is any assistance that this Department can render in carrying out this purpose.

In view of the intention of Congress expressed by the omission of

---

[36] For an act making supplemental appropriations for the fiscal year ending June 30, 1948, and for other purposes, July 30, 1947, see 61 Stat. 613; Guatemala, Brazil, and Peru were the only three Latin American countries among the ten countries named. For background information on "pipeline" contracts for sale of lend-lease supplies, see letters of January 17 and February 13, 1947, from Under Secretary Clayton and Lend-Lease Administrator Lane, respectively, to Senator Styles Bridges, in Department of State *Bulletin*, February 23, 1947, p. 343.

[37] For text of agreement, see Department of State Treaties and Other International Acts Series No. 3662; for documentation, see *Foreign Relations*, 1945, vol. v, pp. 937 ff.

the Union of Soviet Socialist Republics from the list of authorized countries, lend-lease material held, or under contract, for that Government should not be transferred or shipped under the Agreement of October 15, 1945. All such articles should be disposed of in a manner that will best serve the interests of the United States, either as surplus or in fulfillment of some other requirement of this Government.

If any questions arise in connection with this subject, please do not hesitate to call on this Department for assistance.[38]

Faithfully yours, ROBERT A. LOVETT

810.248/10–1647

Memorandum by the Secretary of the Policy Committee on Arms and Armaments (Sohm)

SECRET WASHINGTON, October 20, 1947.

There is circulated herewith for the consideration of the Committee a letter from the Secretary of the Air Force regarding the Air Force program of military assistance to the other American Republics.

The Air Force believes that the other American Republics should be allowed to purchase aircraft and equipment on the open United States market and the quantities should not be limited to equipment levels established by the over-all Western Hemisphere Defense Program.

EARL D. SOHM

[Annex]

The Secretary of the Air Force (Symington) to the Secretary of State

SECRET WASHINGTON, 16 October 1947.

DEAR MR. SECRETARY: The Department of the Air Force has had under study for some time the Air Force program of military assistance to the other American Republics. As you know, because of the lack of implementing legislation, provisions of the Surplus Property Act of 1944 have been utilized for the transfer, under the "Interim Allocations Program," of certain aircraft and equipment included

---

[38] In reply, Secretary Royall informed the Secretary of State in a letter of September 16 that necessary action would be taken within the War Department to effect prompt delivery of lend-lease pipeline materials to the authorized governments, and all lend-lease material held or under contract for the USSR would be disposed of in such a manner as to best serve the interests of the United States (800.24/9–1647).

in the "Over-all Western Hemisphere Defense Program." Prior to transfer, these aircraft were overhauled and put in excellent mechanical condition and were accompanied by as complete a level of one year's maintenance spares as was available. This was done at considerable expense to the Department of the Air Force in the interest of assuring that the success of this program would not be jeopardized as a result of unsatisfactory equipment being transferred to the Latin American Republics.

Because of budgetary limitations and shortages of aircraft and maintenance spares, it is not now feasible for the Department of the Air Force to offer aircraft for transfer to the other American Republics, except on an "as is where is" basis, and on the understanding that there is a limited availability of spare parts. Moreover, because of higher priority requirements, sufficient aircraft will not be available to implement fully the "Over-all Western Hemisphere Defense Program."

However, there is available ground maintenance, communications and weather equipment, included in this program, and excess to United States Air Force requirements, which could be transferred at little cost to the United States Air Force. Further allocations of this type of equipment can be continued by the Department of the Air Force. It is felt that the purchase of this type of equipment should be encouraged in order to build up technically sound and balanced Air Forces in Latin America.

In order that the Department of the Air Force will not be placed in the position of dictating what air force equipment the other American Republics should have, especially when we are not in a position to furnish such equipment, it is felt that the other American Republics should be allowed to purchase aircraft and equipment on the open United States market. In addition, they should not be limited to equipment levels established by the "Over-all Western Hemisphere Defense Program."

In view of the above and pending passage of authorizing legislation and establishment of a long term program of military collaboration, the Department of the Air Force has no objection, from the military point of view, and without consideration of the political aspects, to the purchase by the other American Republics of new or surplus aircraft and equipment of authorized security classification, from any source on the open United States market. However, it is desired that the approval of export licenses for such equipment be coordinated in each instance with the Department of the Air Force in order to preclude approval of purchases which interfere with United States

Air Force procurement or which are inimical to hemispheric solidarity from the military point of view.

Sincerely yours,
W. STUART SYMINGTON

810.113/10–2747

The Secretary of State to the Secretary of the Army (Royall)

CONFIDENTIAL WASHINGTON, October 27, 1947.

MY DEAR MR. SECRETARY: The question of the position to be taken with respect to requests which may be made by the other American Republics for assistance in establishing arms manufacturing plants has been considered in the Department of State. There is enclosed for your information policy and procedure which has been approved with respect to this subject.

You will note that the wording of this policy and procedure prescribes that each request for assistance will be handled separately.

Sincerely yours, For the Secretary of State:
CHARLES E. SALTZMAN
Assistant Secretary

[Enclosure]

Statement by the Policy Committee on Arms and Armaments

CONFIDENTIAL WASHINGTON, October 9, 1947.

Subject: U.S. Policy in the Establishment of Arms Manufacturing Plants in Latin America

The Department of State is in favor of cooperation with the other American Republics for the purpose of assuring that any facilities established in Latin America for the manufacture of arms be equipped to produce arms of United States type. This cooperation should be limited to technical assistance by this Government and its consent to procurement of manufacturing equipment from the United States. Each request, however, should be forwarded to the Munitions Division of the Department of State, which will obtain clearance with the Departments of the Army, Navy or Air Force, whichever is appropriate. In the State Department the Munitions Division will clear with the Division of Commercial Policy and the Office of American Republic Affairs. The Policy Committee on Arms and Armaments shall be kept informed of the extent of such cooperation and where deemed advisable by the Munitions Division requests will be referred to the Policy Committee on Arms and Armaments for decision.

810.24/11–447

Memorandum by the Chief of the Division of Special Inter-American Affairs (Dreier)[39]

SECRET   [WASHINGTON,] November 4, 1947.

ARMS POLICY FOR OTHER AMERICAN REPUBLICS

The following is presented as a basis for discussion:

1. *Present Policy Questions*

The Department's Arms Policy Committee has before it two important questions regarding the other American republics raised by two letters received from the Departments of the Army and the Air Force:

  a. Should any ceilings be placed on the acquisition of arms by other American republics from commercial sources in the U.S.?
  b. Should the U.S. Government now offer to the other American republics a second and larger "interim program" of surplus equipment without waiting for Congressional action on the Inter-American Military Bill?

Closely associated with these questions is the practical problem presented by a request from the Dominican Republic for permission to purchase 20 B–25's (medium bombers), 4 B–17's (Flying Fortresses), and 18 P–38's (pursuit planes), none of which have been considered suitable or necessary for the Dominican army by our armed services on the basis of the bilateral staff conversations held in 1945.

2. *Background*

The Department of the Army has a considerable amount of surplus armament which is reserved for disposal to Latin America under the standardization program. Because passage of the Inter-American Military Cooperation Bill has been so delayed, and because demands for arms in Greece, Turkey and elsewhere have threatened to make inroads on this reserve supply, the Army wishes to sell much of the remaining equipment to Latin America as soon as possible and to limit commercial purchases of similar types of arms by the other American republics until the Government surplus has been disposed of. The Army furthermore favors an over-all ceiling on all arms purchases by the other American republics consisting of the amounts stipulated in the studies based upon the bilateral staff conversations (except for small arms).

On the other hand, the Air Force has only ground equipment for airfields available in surplus, plus some surplus aircraft in poor con-

---

[39] Addressed to the Director (Daniels) and the Deputy Director (Woodward) of the Office of American Republic Affairs.

dition. The Air Force therefore recommends that the other American republics be allowed to purchase any airplanes in any amount from U.S. manufacturers except when such purchases might interfere with the U.S. Air Force's own procurement or plans for military defense.

Prior to June of this year, ARA and the Department followed a policy of restricting, insofar as possible, the transfers of arms to Latin America. An "interim" program of surplus arms sales was authorized, and additional purchases from commercial sources were discouraged. When the policy of permitting no arms transfers to Argentina was changed, a new policy towards all the other American republics was adopted: all Latin American countries were to receive equal treatment in respect to arms; commercial sales were not to be prohibited if they appeared to be "reasonable and necessary" for the legitimate requirements of the purchasing government. The Arms Policy Committee adopted the practice of using the Army's plans, based on the staff conversations, as the ceiling for judging the "reasonableness" and "necessity". Sales of government surplus arms have not been increased beyond the approved interim program which is still being consummated.

Generally ARA has, in recent months, taken a position of "no political objection" to any arms sales to Latin America, leaving final decision to the Arms Policy Committee.

3. *Main Considerations*

In taking a position on the current and long range issues, the following considerations are important:

a. This Government favors as a general objective the regulation of armaments and, with special reference to Latin America, the prevention of an armaments race.

b. The U.S. also seeks to achieve a standardization of the military organization and equipment of the Latin American forces with those of this country. This objective has a two-fold purpose: primarily to keep out non-American missions in Latin America, and secondarily to facilitate coordination of supply and tactical operations in the Americas in the event of war.

c. International control of arms traffic is not an immediate possibility. In the absence thereof, unless some self-denying regulation is adopted by the Latin American states, there is no way for the U.S. effectively to limit acquisition of arms by the other American republics. If they cannot buy arms here at satisfactory prices, they will buy from Britain, Belgium, Czechoslovakia, Sweden or others.

d. Any increases in cost of maintaining Latin American armed forces cannot fail in most countries to impose added handicaps on the national economies and make more difficult the solution of Latin American economic problems with which the U.S. is faced.

e. Any substantial increase in the strength and influence of military forces in Latin America presents political implications of considerable importance.

f. U.S. manufacturers, especially in the aviation industry, wish to take full advantage of the Latin American market.

g. The British have suggested conversations with us on supplying armaments to Latin America, and the U.S. has so far not replied. The British are actively in the Latin American market.

4. *Conclusions*

a. Unilateral efforts of the U.S. to limit acquisition of arms by other American republics will, so long as other sources of arms are open, jeopardize the objective of standardization. If, for political and economic reasons, we wish to achieve some sort of limitation on armaments in Latin America, and also prevent the introduction of non-standardized arms, the cooperation of the Latin American countries is essential. This cooperation might be sought in the following ways:

Emphasis, in economic discussions, on the importance of holding down military expenditures;

Increasing the effectiveness of military and naval missions in counseling against unwise expenditures supporting the standardization policy, and in developing effective training programs within the economic capacity of the host countries;

Consideration of the possibility of negotiating through political channels some kind of arms agreement which would provide for the publicizing, and possibly review, of all armaments traffic by an inter-American agency.

b. Pending the development of such a program, we should continue to judge individual requests for export licenses on their merits, granting them if the amounts involved are considered "reasonable and necessary". The staff conversation studies should be used as a general but flexible guide.

c. Agree to have the Army make its surplus available for sale, in response to requests, but not to promote its sale in any way. The limits of the staff conversation studies should be applied to these sales.

817.24/9-2547

The Director of the Office of Financial and Development Policy (Ness) to the Commissioner of Accounts of the Treasury Department (Maxwell)

CONFIDENTIAL   WASHINGTON, November 10, 1947.

MY DEAR MR. MAXWELL: This letter is in reference to your three letters, LL-81-JJR, to Mr. Shenefield, dated September 22, 1947 concerning the Dominican Republic lend-lease account, dated September

25, 1947 concerning the Nicaragua account, and dated September 22, 1947 concerning the Paraguay account.[40]

It is noted that the net charges to date (total sums to be paid the United States on lend-lease account) indicated in the subject letters are based on the language of the lend-lease agreements with the respective countries, which provides for payment of a definite amount of dollars for an authorized maximum value of deliveries in dollars. In the agreements with the Dominican Republic, Nicaragua, Paraguay, Haiti, and Cuba no specific provision was made for receiving payment for actual deliveries in the proportion of the maximum dollar obligations to the maximum authorized deliveries.

It is the policy of the Department of State, as expressed in my letter to Mr. Cavanaugh of February 27, 1947, that payment for actual deliveries shall be requested from the Dominican Republic, Nicaragua, Paraguay, and Cuba, as in the case of all of the other Latin American countries except Haiti, in the ratio of total obligations specified by the agreements to delivery ceilings specified by the agreements. In the case of Haiti, where actual deliveries exceeded the specified ceiling, this Department considers the total payment specified by the agreement to be due, and expects to negotiate with the Government of Haiti concerning additional payment for excess transfers.

According to our calculations on the above basis, the balance now due from the Dominican Republic is $91,000 rather than $458,000; the balance due from Nicaragua is $509,000 rather than $779,578.60; and the balance due from Paraguay is $12,000 rather than $267,000. This Department is considering appropriate means of pressing for payment of the sums due from these countries as well as from other American republics which are in arrears on their obligations.

. . . .

Sincerely yours,

NORMAN T. NESS

810.20 Defense/11-147

The Acting Secretary of State to the Secretary of Defense (Forrestal)

WASHINGTON, December 1, 1947.

MY DEAR MR. SECRETARY: I refer to your letter of November 1, 1947 to the Secretary of State [41] concerning draft legislation of particular interest to the National Military Establishment, namely, the Military and Naval Missions Bill (H. R. 2313 and S. 759, 80th Congress) the

---

[40] None printed.
[41] Not printed.

Inter-American Military Cooperation Act (H. R. 3836, 80th Congress) and the bill to provide military advice and assistance to the Republic of China (H. R. 6795 and S. 2337, 79th Congress).

The Military and Naval Missions Bill which was reported out of the Committee on Armed Services of the House of Representatives and which the Secretary supported in an appearance before both Committees will be supported as urgent legislation by the Department of State. As you know, existing legislation authorizes the retention of military missions in certain countries "during war or a declared national emergency". Since this is a tenuous ground upon which to rest important military missions abroad, I am most anxious that the Military and Naval Missions Bill be acted upon favorably at this session of the Congress. Mr. Satterthwaite of the Office of Near Eastern and African Affairs of the Department [42] will be glad to discuss with representatives of your Departments the minor revisions that may be necessary to make the legislation consistent with the terms of the National Security Act of 1947.

The Department of State will urge the enactment of the Inter-American Military Cooperation Act during the forthcoming session of the Congress. This legislation as you know is consistent with the agreements reached at Rio during the past summer. The amendments to which you refer should be discussed with Mr. Swett [43] in the Office of Assistant Secretary Saltzman or with Mr. Marcy in the Office of the Counselor in the Department of State.[44]

[Here follows information on legislation for military aid to China.]

Sincerely yours,
ROBERT A. LOVETT

810.248/10–1647

Memorandum by the Secretary of the Policy Committee on Arms and Armaments (Sohm)

SECRET   WASHINGTON, December 12, 1947.

Subject: Air Force Program of Military Assistance to the Other American Republics

There is circulated herewith for the information of the Committee the State Department reply to the Air Force letter [45] contained in D–11/15. This letter was prepared in accordance with the Committee's action on November 14, 1947 (see M–69, p. 9, #18 [46]).

EARL D. SOHM

---

[42] Joseph C. Satterthwaite, Deputy Director, Office of Near Eastern and African Affairs.
[43] Trevor W. Swett, Deputy Chairman, Committee on Arms and Armaments.
[44] Charles E. Bohlen; Carl M. Marcy was Legislative Assistant.
[45] Dated October 16, p. 122.
[46] Not printed.

[Annex]

The Acting Secretary of State to the Secretary of the Air Force (Symington)[47]

SECRET

My Dear Mr. Secretary: I refer to your letter of October 16, 1947 in which you submit, for the consideration of the State Department, the views of the Air Force with respect to the sale to the other American republics of military aircraft.

The State Department has given careful consideration to the proposals made in your letter, as well as to the political aspects of the problem. In view of the testimony given, in connection with the Inter-American Military Cooperation Bill, to the House Foreign Affairs Committee regarding the control of all exports of arms under the export license system, the Department is of the opinion that some measure of control should be retained over sales of military aircraft in order to assure that they are obtained for a legitimate purpose only. Accordingly, it is believed that, as a general but flexible rule, aircraft procured from commercial sources should be limited to the number and types which each country needs in the over-all hemisphere defense program. The State Department is prepared to consult with the Air Force regarding any future requests for export licenses or government-owned surplus aircraft and to approve them whenever the aircraft requested are considered reasonable and necessary.

With respect to the sale to the other American republics of those aircraft which the Air Force has reserved for the hemisphere defense program, it is believed that no further sales should be promoted until Congress has taken action on the Inter-American Military Cooperation Bill. However, the State Department is prepared to review any requests initiated by the Latin American republics and to approve the sales, if the aircraft requested are considered reasonable and necessary, provided such action is not considered to affect adversely the position of the Executive vis-à-vis the Congress with respect to the requested enactment of the Inter-American Military Cooperation Bill.

The policy set forth herein is subject, of course, to any modifications which the State Department may find it necessary to make, in view of specific and temporary political disturbances arising in any of the Latin American republics.

Sincerely yours, [Robert A. Lovett]

---

[47] Letter transmitted on December 18, 1947; copies transmitted on the same date to the Navy Department and Department of the Army.

POSITION OF THE UNITED STATES WITH RESPECT TO THE SALE OF ARMS BY BRAZIL TO THE DOMINICAN REPUBLIC

839.113/11–3047 : Telegram

The Chargé in Venezuela (Maleady) to the Secretary of State

CONFIDENTIAL   CARACAS, November 30, 1947—noon.

466. Betancourt [1] called in heads Creole,[2] Shell Oil [3] companies last night. Told them has unimpeachable evidence Brazil sold 5,000 automatic rifles, 2,000,000 shells therefor to Dominican Government. Said Trujillo [4] yacht with Dominican Ministry War official aboard touched Trinidad day or two ago presumably en route Brazil pick up arms. Also said Venezuelan Government much concerned since convinced arms destined attempt oust it.

Betancourt went on to say he has told Brazil if arms deal not cancelled he will stop all shipments crude oil refined products there. Inasmuch as we principal supplier oil and latter cannot be obtained elsewhere, Brazil is expected capitulate. If not, he told oil heads, he will ask them cooperate by stopping shipments.

El País reported today Trujillo's yacht en route Brazil pick up arms. Sent Department 466, repeated Rio de Janeiro and Ciudad Trujillo.

MALEADY

839.113/12–347 : Telegram

The Ambassador in Venezuela (Donnelly) to the Secretary of State

SECRET   CARACAS, December 3, 1947—3 p. m.

477. I called on President Betancourt and FonMin [5] last night at their request to discuss procurement of armaments by Dominican Republic from Brazil. President said he had made no progress with Brazilian Embassy here in stopping shipment of armaments; he intervened successfully with Venezuelan labor syndicates prevent public

---

[1] Romulo Betancourt, President of the Revolutionary Junta of Government.
[2] Creole Petroleum Corporation, Holding Company for the Interests of Standard Oil Company of New Jersey in Venezuela.
[3] Royal Dutch Shell Company.
[4] Rafael Leonidas Trujillo, President of the Dominican Republic.
[5] Gonzalo Barrios.

demonstrations against Dominican Republic and Brazil; he had refused embargo shipments petroleum Brazil but he would do so if Brazil permitted exportation armaments and that embargo would include Brazilian tanker enroute Venezuela load Royalty petroleum for Ypiranga plant; he had contemplated referring case Pan American Union or accepting Cuban and Guatemalan proposals intervene with Brazilian Govt. Instead he has decided send representative to Brazil discuss matter with President Dutra and with FonMin [6] and possibly Góes Monteiro.[7] He hopes that once these officials are informed of situation then [they?] will prevent shipment but added that if they refuse to do so his representative, as last resort, will inform Brazil that Venezuela will embargo exportation petroleum Brazil. He did not indicate whom he would send but said that representative would leave shortly arrive Brazil before Trujillo vessels.

President Betancourt suggested that it would be of invaluable assistance to his Govt if our Govt would use its good offices with Brazilian Govt prevent shipment armaments to Dominican Republic. I hope Dept will find it feasible meet President Betancourt's suggestion.

He said his Govt is not apprehensive of successful invasion from Dominican Republic, that it could suppress any attack, but that it feared consequences public reaction here against Dominican Republic and Brazil and added that Communists would welcome this or any other opportunity embarrass Brazil. He stated categorically his govt is not financing movement or engaging in any hostile activities against Trujillo's govt.

It is possible that unless matter is settled soon it may become important issue during closing days of election campaign which is progressing in orderly manner considering that this is first really general and democratic election in history of Venezuela.

Sent Dept 477, repeated to Rio and Ciudad Trujillo.

DONNELLY

839.113/12-447 : Telegram

The Chargé in Brazil (Key) to the Secretary of State

CONFIDENTIAL   RIO DE JANEIRO, December 4, 1947—4 p. m.

1671. Deptel 458 November 24.[8] Foreign Minister confirmed to me last night that Brazil had recently sold arms to Dominican Republic. These consisted of about 10,000 old German rifles and a few other

---

[6] Raul Fernandes.
[7] Gen. Pedro Aurelio de Góes Monteiro, former Minister of War and Chief of Staff of the Brazilian Army.
[8] Not printed.

items. He explained that at first Brazil had hesitated to sell these weapons but it had been decided that since US had furnished Trujillo with modern arms there was no valid reason why Brazil should refrain from disposing of a limited amount of obsolete German equipment for which it had no further use in view of modern equipment procured from US during world war. An unexpected development however had been that Cuban Ambassador [9] had intervened with request that contracts be cancelled on grounds that Trujillo's true purpose in acquiring arms was in order to smuggle them into Cuba for purpose of fomenting trouble against present regime. Fernandes commented that Cuban Ambassador's intervention was too late; contracts had been entered into sometime past, payments had been made and some deliveries effected. It was not feasible to cancel transaction at this late date especially as Trujillo's yacht was on its way here to pick up remaining arms. Furthermore he doubted whether Trujillo's purpose was that portrayed by Cuban Ambassador; Trujillo had a certain number of enemies and it was only logical, especially after abortive attempted Cuban filibustering expedition, that he should wish to be in a position to defend himself. Anyhow the transportation and smuggling into Cuba of this equipment with possible exception of the rifles would present certain difficulties. Fernandes made no mention of Venezuelan objections to arms sales.

Immediately preceding my talk with Foreign Minister Cuban Ambassador discussed same matter with me. He estimated transaction involved between 10,000 and 12,000 rifles, 350 machine guns, 75 mortars and other equipment. He was convinced Trujillo's purpose was to smuggle these weapons into the eastern areas of Cuba in order to foment a revolution. In reply to my query whether arms might constitute threat against some other country, say Venezuela, Ambassador emphatically declared that because of distances involved and Dominican Republic's lack of transport only Cuba was threatened. Smuggling of arms into Cuba could easily be accomplished by small craft in 6 or 7 hours of darkness. Ambassador claimed sale had been consummated by Brazilian general, unnamed, who had personally greatly profited thereby.

Comment: This may explain general lack of knowledge of transaction by those who would ordinarily be informed. (See Embtel 1642 November 28 and Embtel 1653 December 2.[10]) Ambassador anticipated arrival of Trujillo's yacht at any moment.

Sent Department as 1671; repeated Habana, Caracas, Ciudad Trujillo.

KEY

---

[9] Gabriel Landa.
[10] Neither printed.

264–330—72——10

839.113/12-547 : Telegram

The Ambassador in Cuba (Norweb) to the Secretary of State

CONFIDENTIAL   HABANA, December 5, 1947—3 p. m.

713. Reference Brazil's sale of arms to Trujillo see A 1133 December 1 [11] and Rio's telegram 1671 December 4. Brazilian Ambassador [12] informs me Foreign Minister [13] called him December 1 complaining reported arms shipment. Ambassador wired Rio receiving reply 5,000 used Mauser rifles sold, a small and unimportant transaction. Ambassador so informed Foreign Minister December 4 who urged immediate cancellation and stated "situation between Dominican Republic and Cuba is very bad indeed and will not be improved by arrival such arms". Foreign Minister requested Ambassador inform Rio Cuba could not understand Brazil supplying arms to bloody despot like Trujillo.

Foreign Minister told Ambassador he did not expect Trujillo bring up squabble either PAU or elsewhere.

Ambassador informed Rio his opinion arms sale unwise and would not be understood by American nations.

Significant to note that while Ambassador played down to Foreign Office this transaction Rio also minimized importance to its Ambassador if figure of 10,000 rifles proves correct.

As interesting sidelight Embassy officer informed in strict confidence today General Pérez, Cuban Chief Staff requested Juan Arevalo, Cuban labor leader visit Dominican Republic, call on Trujillo to placate him re abortive invasion and sound him out on plans respecting Cuba.

Pérez reported concerned over purchase material by Trujillo and possible aggressive intentions towards Cuba.

Pérez may be acting on own initiate [*initiative?*] and he reportedly told Arevalo point out to Trujillo that he responsible for breaking up invasion and no further such acts possible in Cuba.

Sent Department 713, repeated Ciudad Trujillo.

                                                                        NORWEB

839.113/12-947 : Telegram

The Chargé in the Dominican Republic (Burrows) to the Secretary of State

SECRET   CIUDAD TRUJILLO, December 9, 1947—4 p. m.

339. Reliable information received Dominican LCM *San Rafael* left Calderas naval base some days ago en route Rio to aid in transport-

---

[11] Not printed.
[12] Carlos Alves de Sousa Filho.
[13] Rafael González Muñoz.

ing armaments. Transfer of funds reported Embtel 329, December 1 [14] amounted to 240,000 American dollars. Since 10,000 obsolete rifles and 2 million shells (most recent estimates received here of quantities involved) would account for only small fraction this expenditure the few other items of which Brazilian Foreign Minister spoke (Rio's telegram 1671, December 4) must be more significant part of purchase than has appeared probable. Embassy considers much artillery may be included since this country short this type equipment. Caracas telegram 458 November 24 [14] may furnish more accurate estimate purchases.

Consensus in this Embassy as in Caracas (Caracas telegram 271 December 8 [14]) that armed invasion attack can be completely discounted. No evidence has come to light here of any such preparations and in any event Dominican Republic in no position offer military threat either Cuba or Venezuela. Also more that nature would not serve Trujillo's purposes; believed his feints toward Cuba merely effort embarrass Grau [15] government in return Cuban implication Dominican revolution threat.

If Venezuela or Cuba ripe for revolution, however, certainly conceivable Trujillo would lend moral support and even material aid in terms air force coverage. He is not prepared by any stretch imagination launch open attack any other kind.

· · · · · · · ·

BURROWS

839.113/12–947 : Telegram

The Ambassador in Cuba (Norweb) to the Secretary of State

CONFIDENTIAL   HABANA, December 9, 1947—5 p. m.

724. Embtels 713 Dec 5 and 717 Dec 6.[16] Brazilian Ambassador informed me today he just received telegram that acting apparently on his suggestion Foreign Minister took Cuban Ambassador see President Brazil where satisfactory conversation was held. Ambassador said it appeared to him President intended intervene. He also said this second telegram doubled amount of arms involved which would explain discrepancy pointed out my 713. He added Foreign Minister advised President in addition to broader aspects involved Brazil should not be mixed up in Caribbean affairs.

Sent Dept as 724; repeated Ciudad Trujillo.

NORWEB

---

[14] Not printed.
[15] Ramón Grau San Martín, President of Cuba.
[16] Latter not printed.

839.113/12-947

Memorandum of Conversation, by the Chief of the Division of North and West Coast Affairs (Mills)

CONFIDENTIAL [WASHINGTON,] December 9, 1947.

Participants: Dr. Gonzalo Carnevali, Venezuelan Ambassador
Dr. Falcón-Briceño, Minister-Counselor of the Venezuelan Embassy
Mr. Paul C. Daniels, Director for American Republic Affairs
Mr. Sheldon T. Mills, NWC

Dr. Falcón-Briceño stated that he had told the Ambassador of his conversations with Mr. Daniels on December 5. The Ambassador thereupon spoke with great feeling regarding the "calumnies" of his country by the Dominicans and of threat to Venezuela of the Dominican armament program. He stated all efforts by Venezuela to induce Brazil to cancel the projected sale of armaments to the Dominican Republic had failed.

In reply to a question, he stated that the former Foreign Minister of Venezuela, Dr. Morales, arrived in Rio on Monday, December 8, and he did not have a report of the results of Dr. Morales' representations to Brazilian Foreign Minister Fernandes. Dr. Carnevali added he would send an urgent telegram requesting that he be kept currently posted on the results of these negotiations. He expressed great pessimism as to the outcome.

The Venezuelan Ambassador then stated he had proof the Dominican government was transferring or had transferred $6,000,000 to Brazil to pay for the armament purchases and arming on such a scale could only be because of designs on some foreign country, probably Venezuela. He also said the private yacht of President Trujillo was already in Rio and probably loading arms at the moment.

(A telegram from the American Consul in Trinidad, dated December 6, reported the Trujillo yacht cleared Port-of-Spain on November 29).

The Venezuelan Ambassador then referred to the circular sent to diplomatic and consular officers in 1945 by the private secretary of the President instructing them to offer the hospitality of the Dominican Republic to political exiles from Venezuela. Dr. Carnevali stated that in Trinidad Venezuelan exiles had flocked aboard the Trujillo yacht.

(The December 6 telegram from Trinidad reports advice from the Colonial Government that there are no dangerous Venezuelan political exiles there).

Mr. Daniels expressed a hope that the tense relations between Venezuela and the Dominican Republic could be eased. He referred to a new departure in Inter-American procedure created by the circular letter which the Venezuelan Ambassador sent to colleagues on the Governing Board of the Pan American Union last Friday.[17] Mr. Daniels urged that no precipitate action be taken at the present time which would prejudice pacifying action which might be taken as a consequence of the Ambassador's initiative.

Dr. Carnevali pleaded for support by the American Embassy in Rio of Dr. Morales' efforts with the Brazilian Foreign Minister. He suggested the American Embassy ask the Brazilian Foreign Minister for precise information on the armaments covered by the sale. Mr. Daniels was sympathetic but noncommital although he indicated some such approach might be possible.

(Later in the day the Department sent to Rio a telegraphic instruction calling for discreet inquiry and report on the progress being made by Dr. Morales in his negotiations, and information on the precise armaments covered by the Brazilian-Dominican arrangement.)

With respect to the scope of the arrangement, Mr. Daniels suggested that the Venezuelan Ambassador approach his Brazilian colleague, Mr. Carlos Martíns, and request data on the armaments covered by the sale. During such an approach it would also be possible to impress Martins with the serious view which Venezuela took of the sale.

839.113/12–1347 : Telegram

The Chargé in Brazil (Key) to the Secretary of State

SECRET RIO DE JANEIRO, December 13, 1947—11 a. m.

1707. Embtel 1700, December 11.[18] Cuban Ambassador informed me last night that up to that point neither he nor Morales had met with any success in their efforts to persuade Brazilian Government to cancel arms sale.

Dutra and other Brazilian officials had taken stand that, in view of Trujillo's explicit assurances that arms would be used solely for defense, there was no basis for argument that latter would be used to create disorders or revolution in Cuba and/or Venezuela. Ambassador felt, however, that real reason deal was not being cancelled was that

---

[17] A copy of the letter of December 4, 1947, which was sent on December 5 by the Venezuelan Representative on the Governing Board of the Pan American Union, not printed, was transmitted in circular instruction of December 23 to Diplomatic Representatives in the American Republics (731.39/12–2347).
[18] Not printed.

high officers Brazilian Army (two major generals, brigadier general and several colonels all unnamed) were involved who would not willingly forego the big profits they had pocketed.

Accordingly he was informing his Government that Brazilian Government had apparently made up its mind to consummate the deal and he felt it was useless for him to attempt to do anything further at this end although there was a bare chance that Morales who was still negotiating might at last minute succeed.

Sent Department as 1707, repeated Caracas, Habana and Ciudad Trujillo.

KEY

839.113/12-1447 : Telegram

The Ambassador in Venezuela (Donnelly) to the Secretary of State

SECRET   CARACAS, December 14, 1947—8 p. m.

504. I am disappointed developments reported Rio's telegram 1707, December 13, 11 a. m. to Dept. repeated Caracas.

In spite allegations Brazilian arms destined exclusively defense Dominican Republic, I am convinced Venezuelan Govt genuinely fears at least part of arms will find their way into hands Venezuelan exiles thus increasing danger another attempted coup in cooperation dissident groups here. Venezuelans will probably regard sale as Brazilian favoritism toward Trujillo.

As I have reported, if Morales' mission fails, there is strong possibility anti-Brazilian press campaign and labor demonstrations here as well as legal and informal embargo on shipments Venezuelan oil to Brazil. If these or similar reprisals should be adopted by Venezuela impossible anticipate all consequences. For example, American and British oil companies would be in difficult position if they were informally requested stop direct and indirect shipments to Brazil Venezuelan crude refined Aruba and Curaçao since they need Govt good will in important forthcoming negotiations for new labor contract and wish to get off on right foot with new Govt.

Venezuelan President and Foreign Minister have stated on two occasions that if US Govt would indicate its desire that Brazilians stop ship such action would be effective. I hope Dept will see way clear immediately inform Brazilian Govt unwisdom shipping arms Dominicans at this time.

Sent Dept 504, repeated Rio.

DONNELLY

839.113/12–1447

Memorandum of Conversation, by Mr. Richard H. Post of the Division of North and West Coast Affairs

SECRET [WASHINGTON,] December 15, 1947.

Subject: Venezuelan Government's Request that the United States Should Petition Brazil to Cancel Recent Arms Sales to the Dominican Republic. (Ref. Caracas T–504 Dec. 14).

Participants: ARA: Mr. Daniels
CRB: Mr. Hauch
BA: Mr. Clark
IA: Mr. Spencer
NWC: Mr. Espy, Mr. Post

Careful consideration was given the Venezuelan request, with particular reference to Ambassador Donnelly's telegram 504 of December 14. Mr. Post quoted from Ambasador Donnelly's telegram No. 488 of December 6 [19] regarding the possibility of arms being furnished clandestinely by Dominicans to dissident groups within Venezuela for use in another revolutionary attempt. Post pointed out the possibility of such an attempt growing into a civil war with consequent threat to American oil production and installations.

The following points were then made, each of which points against the making of representations to Brazil:

(1) Since the Dominicans seem determined to buy arms, they would not be deterred by Brazil's refusal to sell. Arms can be acquired from many sources today.

(2) Such a request would constitute United States' intervention in the affairs of Brazil and the Dominican Republic. It might be publicly resented by both these nations. It would be contrary to the spirit and the letter (probably) of the protocol on intervention signed at Buenos Aires in 1936.[20]

(3) Since the United States is currently selling surplus arms and war planes to various nations it would be inconsistent to make this request.

(4) Since there is no definite proof that the arms will be used against Venezuela, in whole or in part, the United States could offer no reasons for objecting to the present sale.

(5) Such a request might jeopardize the United States' position in

---

[19] Not printed.
[20] For text, see *Report of the Delegation of the United States of America to the Inter-American Conference for the Maintenance of Peace, Buenos Aires, December, 1936* (Washington, 1937), p. 116.

the present negotiations to sell surplus arms to Argentina. It would provide the Brazilians with a precedent for objecting to these sales.

(6) The request would weaken the position of the Brazilian Foreign Minister (Fernandes) vis-à-vis the military, which would be most unfortunate, since he has been very helpful to Embassy Rio but could hardly afford to shatter a lance for us in such an unpopular cause.

(7) The Brazilian army officers who have profited from the sale would be quite loath to disgorge now—even if they could be made to by their Government, which is not certain—and they would ever more be resentful of the United States.

(8) It is quite doubtful whether Brazil would accede to such a request. If Brazil refused, the United States would be in an awkward position.[21]

839.113/12–1547 : Telegram

The Chargé in Brazil (Key) to the Secretary of State

SECRET   US URGENT   RIO DE JANEIRO, December 15, 1947—7 p. m.
NIACT

1709. Morales and Venezuelan Ambassador [22] called on me this afternoon. Morales first reviewed his negotiations with Fernandes which however had accomplished nothing tangible and had failed to bring to light any new points of importance except that he stated Brazilian Foreign Minister had eventually admitted that on basis more recent information obtained from War Minister the transaction was "considerably larger" than he had first been led to believe. Morales insists that war material totalling in value $6 million is involved and that this includes rifles, machine guns, artillery, mortars and ammunition but did not claim that this had been corroborated by Foreign Minister.

Morales stated his appointment with President Dutra originally scheduled December 12 had been postponed until 4: 30 tomorrow afternoon December 16. He fears President will take line that since contracts have been entered into and sales made it will be impossible to cancel deliveries at this late date and that furthermore there will be no necessity to do so in view of explicit assurances received from Dominican Republic that arms will be used for defensive purposes only. In view of anticipated unsatisfactory outcome his interview with Dutra tomorrow Morales asked me if I would not at once intercede

---

[21] In telegram 474, December 15, 11 p. m., the Department advised the Embassy in Venezuela that the United States would not intercede (839.113/12–1447).

[22] Estaban Chalbaud Cardona.

at least to extent of pointing out to Foreign Minister the anxiety which this arms deal was creating in various countries including Venezuela and express hope therefore that the transaction would be cancelled. I replied that I felt sure he would appreciate, having once been a Foreign Minister, that I could not interfere in so delicate a matter without explicit instructions from my Government and furthermore that I felt it would be premature for Embassy to raise such a matter before he had had opportunity to present his Government's views to Dutra.

Morales stated he appreciated foregoing but that the reason for urgency was that according to information received from his "agents" a Dominican Republic corvette had arrived here night of December 13, was now loading arms and would probably depart tomorrow. He felt it would be in order therefore for me at least to suggest to Brazilian Foreign Minister that departure of this vessel be delayed. I contented myself with merely asking whether he had himself mentioned this to Fernandes to which he replied in negative. As a matter of fact we have been definitely assured by official of Ministry of Marine that no Dominican vessel is in port and that none is expected for another 48 hours.

I asked Morales whether he had mentioned to Brazilian Foreign Minister possibility of Venezuelan embargo on petroleum shipments to Brazil if latter fails cancel arms sale. He stated he had not done so lest this should be interpreted as a "threat" but that he had referred to this possibility in recent conversation with Brazilian head of Ipiranga Oil Company who said that he in turn would mention it to the head of Conselho Nacional de Petroleo. Morales evaded any direct answer to my query whether he proposed mention oil embargo possibility to Dutra tomorrow but left impression that Dutra would be apprised of this possibility through head of Conselho. Embassy does not share opinion expressed by Venezuelan President and Foreign Minister last paragraph Caracas' 504 December 14 that Brazilians would cancel deal if US Government indicated such was its wish. On contrary we believe intervention would not only be resented but would most probably be ineffective: on legal grounds Brazilian Government has a strong case in view of assurances received from Dominican Republic; as a practical matter involvement high army officers renders it politically inexpedient for Dutra to cancel the deal without running the risk of possible serious domestic political repercussions. Furthermore, sight should not be lost of fact that the support of influential Brazilian Army officers will probably be essential to the enactment of a satisfactory petroleum law. I can think of no better way of antagonizing this group than by interfering in this deal which to all practical purposes appears to be a *fait accompli*.

Please instruct urgently as Morales plans to call on me tomorrow after his interview with Dutra.[23]

Department please repeat to Caracas and Ciudad Trujillo such portions this telegram as is deemed advisable.

KEY

839.113/12–1647

The Ambassador in Cuba (Norweb) to the Secretary of State

CONFIDENTIAL HABANA, December 16, 1947.
No. 4601

SIR: I have the honor to refer to a sale of arms reportedly being made by certain authorities in Brazil to the Dominican Republic. In this connection, I wish to refer to this Embassy's telegram No. 713 of December 5, 1947, and more especially to the telegram from our Embassy in Rio de Janeiro to the Department, No. 1700 of December 13, 1947.[24] As I have reported, the Minister of State of Cuba, Rafael González Muñoz, inquired as to what the United States might do in preventing such a sale of arms, indicating that it might be a threat to Cuba. He asked the Brazilian Ambassador to inform his Government of Cuba's perturbation and to request the authorities in Rio de Janeiro to stop the sale.

In a conversation with the Brazilian Ambassador yesterday, he informed me of his impressions of recent discussions with the Cuban Minister of State. He said that it was becoming apparent that Cuba was not so much afraid that the arms in question might be used against it, but rather that Cuba was more interested in making a villain of President Trujillo. He indicated to me that the Cuban actuation was one of taking the offensive in an effort to strengthen its own defensive position. This I have also found to be true. As late as today the Minister said he had hoped it might be possible for the Brazilian Government to be influenced and call off this sale of arms through the good offices of some other Government such as the United States. I observed that the United States was interested in the maintenance of peaceful conditions and that we disliked to see a questionable sale of arms almost as much as we deplored the illicit traffic in arms. Of all this he was well aware through my continuing conversations with him in connection with the abortive attempt of last summer.[25] While Cuba has not admitted any implication, the Minister of State today said that the Brazilian Ambassador in Habana had also spoken to him along the same lines. However, it appears likely that Cuba will endeavor to em-

---

[23] In telegram 1372, December 16, the Department approved the position taken by the Chargé (839.00/12–1547).
[24] Latter not printed.
[25] For documentation on this subject, see pp. 629 ff.

ploy every device to minimize its culpability or to shift the blame to other quarters.

[Here follows information that a senior Cuban military official, though not anticipating a direct attack on Cuba from the Dominican Republic, felt that the quantities and types of arms sought by the Dominican Republic from Brazil could at some future date be useful to a revolutionary movement seeking to overthrow the Government of Cuba.]

Respectfully yours, R. HENRY NORWEB

839.113/12–1747 : Telegram

The Chargé in Brazil (Key) to the Secretary of State

SECRET RIO DE JANEIRO, December 17, 1947—6 p. m.

1724. Reference mytel 1715.[26] Morales informed me this afternoon that Brazilian Foreign Minister had delivered to him late yesterday a memorandum outlining final Brazilian position on arms transaction as follows: Brazil had decided to complete deal in view of written assurances received from Dominican Republic that arms would be used for defensive purposes only. Memorandum also explained that factor influencing Brazilian decision was that contracts could not effectively be cancelled at this late date.

In his call on Foreign Minister this afternoon, Morales advised Brazilian Foreign Minister that in his opinion Brazilian position outlined in memorandum was unsatisfactory; since object of purchase was illicit, i.e. to arm Venezuelan exiles Brazil would unilaterally cancel transaction. Foreign Minister replied that if arms were used for illegal purposes, Brazil would be the first to protest. Foreign Minister then stated he had heard there existed possibility that Venezuela might retaliate by placing embargo on petroleum shipments to Brazil. He expressed hope that Morales would use his influence to prevent any such development. Morales replied that Venezuelan Government could not foresee what effect Brazilian decision would have in Venezuela but that he would convey Foreign Minister's message to Venezuelan authorities although quite possibly petroleum workers and other labor elements might attempt prevent petroleum exports to Brazil.

Morales stated he was planning leave Rio by plane early tomorrow morning but that before he leaves he will send a communication to Foreign Minister confirming above reported oral statements which he made to Foreign Minister.

Sent Dept; repeated Caracas, Ciudad Trujillo, Habana.

KEY

---

[26] Not printed.

839.113/12–2347 : Telegram

The Ambassador in Venezuela (Donnelly) to the Secretary of State

SECRET   CARACAS, December 23, 1947—6 p. m.

531. Dr. Morales called today inform me results his mission Brazil. He confirmed information repeated Embtel 525, December 21 [27] and indicated Venezuelan Government would request cooperation oil companies embargo oil shipments Dominican Republic, including shipments from Curaçao and Aruba. He said he had no knowledge other measures Venezuelan Government might adopt but that had strongly recommended that Venezuela not embargo oil shipments to Brazil including loading Ypiranga tanker scheduled arrive Venezuela shortly. He repeated he had informed President Betancourt Brazilian Government had acted in good faith but had been misled by small group army officers who received substantial cuts from sales. He said "there is nothing to be gained by our retaliating against Brazil; our real enemy is Dominican Republic and whatever we do should be directed against that country".

Dr. Morales said Brazilian Government had finally confirmed to him in writing that armament contract with Dominican Republic consists following material: 12 75-millimeter cannons; 50,000 shells; 10,000 rifles with 30 million shells; 40,000 mortar shells but denied 800 machine guns which Morales believes are included.

Suggested to Morales time had come for serious consideration of steps to be taken for improvement of relations between Venezuela and Dominican Republic and while he agreed that this matter merits prompt considerations he said several times that it could not result in resumption diplomatic relations between the two countries.

A very reliable contact called today tell me he had received information emanating from Inspector General Venezuelan Army Venezuela might attempt bomb Trujillo's ships carrying arms from Rio to Dominican Republic. Embassy finds it difficult to believe this statement represents view Venezuelan Government.

El País and *El Nacional* continue feature Brazilian–Dominican arms deal and latter attempting involve United States by charging Dominican ship *San Rafael* was given by United States to Dominican Republic during war.

Sent Department 531; repeated Ciudad Trujillo and Rio.

DONNELLY

---

[27] Not printed.

COOPERATION OF THE UNITED STATES WITH OTHER GOVERNMENTS IN THE CONSTRUCTION OF THE INTER-AMERICAN HIGHWAY AND RAMA ROAD [1]

810.154/4-2247

The Administrator of the Federal Works Agency (Fleming) to the Secretary of State

WASHINGTON, April 22, 1947.

SIR: The Independent Offices Appropriation Act for the fiscal year 1946, approved May 3, 1945 (59 Stat. 117), appropriated for the Inter-American Highway $1,000,000 of the $20,000,000 authorized by the Act of December 26, 1941 (Public Law 375).[2] This appropriation, however, was made subject to the condition imposed by the following proviso:

"Provided, That no part of the appropriation made in this paragraph for use in any cooperating country shall be available for obligation or expenditure unless said cooperating country executes a written agreement that it will impose no restrictions on the use of the highway, nor levy directly or indirectly any tax or charge for such use, by traffic or vehicles from any other country that do not apply with equal force to the like use of the highway by traffic or vehicles of the cooperating country."

Three previous acts already had appropriated a total of $14,000,000 of the $20,000,000 authorization, and the act for the fiscal year 1947 appropriated the final $5,000,000. None of these latter four acts carried the above quoted proviso. The proviso, therefore, might reasonably be construed to apply only to the one million dollar appropriation for the fiscal year 1946.

As of March 18, 1947, we had expended a total of $12,078,632 of the $20,000,000 appropriated. We, therefore, have not expended any of the one million dollars appropriated for the fiscal year 1946. Before reaching a point where disbursements against this latter appropriation may be made it appears necessary to bring to the attention of the Governments of Panama and of each of the Central American countries the condition attached by the statute to its expenditure and to secure their assent to a modification of our original agreements with

---

[1] Continued from *Foreign Relations*, 1946, vol. XI, pp. 162–181.
[2] 55 Stat. 860.

them so as to include an appropriate paragraph, or by otherwise securing an agreement, that will meet such condition.

As this is a new requirement of legislation it appears to be within the purview of the State Department to bring the statute and its implications to the attention of the Governments concerned. It, therefore, is requested that you take such action in the matter as appears to you desirable.

For your information, you have previously been furnished with copies of Project Statements and Memoranda of Understanding executed with each of the countries referred to and you may conclude that an amendment of each to incorporate therein the substance of the legal requirement quoted above may adequately accomplish the purpose of the law, or you may consider some other method for meeting the requirement by securing a new agreement through diplomatic correspondence.

In any case, your attention is especially invited to the phrase "from any other country" which appears in the above quoted proviso. There may be a question whether a written understanding between any one of the above governments mentioned and the United States may create such an obligation as that contemplated with respect to other such governments. We can undoubtedly enter into an understanding with any such government with respect to traffic or vehicles from the United States but whether such agreement could have any application to traffic or vehicles from any other country is a matter which we think should have your careful consideration.

It is requested that you advise the Public Roads Administration of the form of action you believe should be taken in this matter.

Sincerely yours, PHILIP B. FLEMING
Major General, U.S.A.

810.154/3–3147

President Truman to the Public Roads Commissioner, Federal Works Agency (MacDonald) [3]

[WASHINGTON,] May 26, 1947.

MY DEAR MR. MACDONALD: I understand construction work by the Public Roads Administration on the Inter-American Highway through Central America and Panama has already been suspended in certain countries due to the lack of funds. I understand also that work is practically at a standstill elsewhere along the route of the Inter-American Highway and on the Rama Road in Nicaragua for

---

[3] Draft letter transmitted to President Truman by Under Secretary Acheson on May 23, and signed by the President on May 26.

the same reason. I am informed that work was suspended some time ago on the Matagalpa–Jinotega spur in Nicaragua although the balance of available funds already appropriated is said to be sufficient to complete this spur.

The successful and prompt completion of the above-mentioned roads has an important bearing upon our relations with the governments of Central America and Panama. Our commitments to them make it advisable that we take steps immediately to complete these roads.

You are accordingly directed to resume work at the earliest possible date on the Matagalpa–Jinotega spur in Nicaragua,[4] and to submit immediately to the Bureau of the Budget [5] for presentation to the Congress legislation providing for necessary additional appropriations to complete the Rama Road in Nicaragua and the Inter-American Highway through Central America and Panama.[6]

Sincerely yours, HARRY S. TRUMAN

810.154/4–2247

The Secretary of State to the Administrator of the Federal Works Agency (Fleming)

WASHINGTON, May 31, 1947.

MY DEAR GENERAL FLEMING: Reference is made to your letter of April 22, 1947, calling this Department's attention to the Independent Offices Appropriation Act for the fiscal year 1946 which appropriated $1,000,000 for use on the Inter-American Highway on the cooperative construction program outlined in the provisions of Public Law 375. It has been noted that under this appropriation act the appropriation shall be available only after the cooperating country in which the money is to be expended executes a written agreement concerning the use of the highway.

---

[4] In a memorandum of June 6 the Chief of the Division of Caribbean and Panama Affairs (Newbegin) reported on a conversation with the Chief of the Inter-American Regional Office, Public Roads Administration (James). Mr. James said that he had just returned from a visit to Central America; while in Nicaragua he had seen President Leonardo Argüello who had assured him that Nicaragua would continue to make its payments of $30,000 monthly for the Rama Road (810.154/6–647).

[5] A memorandum of July 10 by Fred G. Heins, of the Division of Central America and Panama Affairs, indicated that the proposed legislation had been submitted by the PRA to the Budget Bureau, but the Director (Webb) had some doubt as to whether a request to Congress for an appropriation for the Rama Road should be made at that time in view of the United States current refusal to recognize the *de facto* regime in Nicaragua (817.154/7–1047).

[6] In a conversation with Mr. Newbegin on July 18, Mr. James stated that no action was then being taken with regard to new appropriations for the Inter-American Highway and the Rama Road; that Secretary Marshall had decided that that was an inopportune time to submit any bills to Congress authorizing further expenditures on either of the two roads (810.154/7–1847).

In view of previous information received by the Department from the Public Roads Administration to the effect that construction on the highway had been suspended in certain cooperating countries and that funds were not available for the resumption of such work (notwithstanding the fact that, according to your letter under acknowledgment, on March 18, 1947 more than $7,900,000 were still available from the original authorization of $20,000,000), the Department desires more definite information concerning your plans for the expenditure of the present balance.

If there is no immediate prospect for obtaining additional funds so that construction may be resumed in all the cooperating countries, it is believed that the present is not an appropriate time to undertake negotiations for the execution of the proposed new agreements with the countries in which construction has been suspended. However, the Department is prepared to take the necessary action, in compliance with this new legal requirement, with the respective country in which the Public Roads Administration plans to expend the funds obtained under the above-mentioned appropriation act.

It is requested, therefore, that the Department be informed more specifically in which country the above-mentioned appropriation will be used.[7]

Sincerely yours, For the Secretary of State:
SPRUILLE BRADEN

810.154/7-347

The Secretary of State to the Ambassador in Guatemala (Kyle)

No. 826 WASHINGTON, July 29, 1947.

SIR: Reference is made to the Embassy's note No. 120 of May 19, 1943, which is in reply to note No. 6756 693(73-0) of the same date from the Guatemalan Minister of Foreign Affairs (Executive Agreement Series 345), concerning the cooperation between the United States and Guatemala in the improvement of the Inter-American Highway in Guatemala within the provisions of Public Law 375 of December 26, 1941 and subject to the appropriation of the necessary funds by the Congress of the United States.

There are now enclosed for the Embassy's information in connection with this matter copies of letters of April 22 and July 3, 1947 from

---

[7] General Fleming replied in a letter of July 3, as follows:

"We find that the entire appropriation of one million dollars referred to can be included in the allotment made to Guatemala and we have prepared an amendment to the Memorandum of Understanding with that country which will specifically include as a part of the allotment the entire sum appropriated by the said Independent Offices Appropriation Act for the fiscal year 1946." (810.154/7-347)

the Federal Works Agency,[8] and of the Department's letter of May 31, 1947 to the Federal Works Agency, concerning the following proviso with reference to an appropriation of $1,000,000 for the Inter-American Highway in the Independent Offices Appropriation Act for the fiscal year 1946 (59 Stat. 117):

[Here follows text of proviso quoted in second paragraph of letter of April 22 from General Fleming, page 145.]

In view of the intention of the Federal Works Agency, as indicated in its letter of July 3, 1947, to allot the above-mentioned appropriation of $1,000,000 for expenditure in Guatemala, you are requested to undertake the negotiation of a supplementary agreement with the appropriate Guatemalan officials[9] in accordance with the conditions imposed by the above quoted proviso of the 1946 Appropriation Act.

There are enclosed for your guidance suggested drafts of notes to be exchanged in effecting such a supplementary agreement.[10] In the event any changes in those draft notes are desired by you or the Guatemalan Government, you are requested to consult the Department prior to making such changes.

It is further requested that if notes are exchanged, the Embassy transmit to the Department a certified copy of its note, indicating letterhead and signature, and the signed original of the Guatemalan note.

You are also requested to discuss this matter with the Resident Engineer in Guatemala of the Public Roads Administration, and to inform the Department as soon as possible of the results of the proposed negotiations.

Very truly yours,   For the Secretary of State:
NORMAN ARMOUR

810.154/8-1847 : Circular airgram

The Acting Secretary of State to Certain Diplomatic Representatives in the American Republics [11]

RESTRICTED   WASHINGTON, August 18, 1947—8:55 a. m.

The Department is informed that the Public Roads Administration prepared a proposed amendment to Public Law 375, approved December 26, 1941, which would provide an additional authorization of $60,000,000 to be appropriated for the construction of the Inter-American Highway, and would also provide that $26,000,000 of the total

---

[8] Letter of July 3 not printed, but see footnote 7, p. 148.
[9] The Secretary of State informed General Fleming of this request to the Embassy in a letter of July 29 (810.154/7-347).
[10] Not printed.
[11] At Managua, San Jose, Tegucigalpa, San Salvador, Guatemala, and Panama.

additional amount authorized may be expended without requiring the cooperating country to match such funds as provided in the original law. The proposed legislation was not introduced before the adjournment of the first session of the Eightieth Congress but presumably will be presented to second session. The Department is prepared because of existing commitments to give appropriate support to the proposal.

PRA proposes to include in this amendment a provision that the additional funds to be authorized shall not be available for work in any cooperating country until after such country enters into an agreement with the United States which shall provide: (1) that no highway toll or payment having the effect of toll shall be levied or assessed for the use of the highway by vehicles or persons, (2) that no requirements will be established or imposed, nor any tax, charge, or fee levied directly or indirectly upon vehicles or persons from any other country using the highway that do not apply equally to the like use of the highway by vehicles or persons of the cooperating country, (3) that reciprocal recognition of vehicle registration and drivers' licenses will continue to be granted in accordance with the provisions of the Convention For The Regulation Of Inter-American Automotive Traffic [12] now in effect or that hereafter may be in effect and to which such country and the United States are signatories and, (4) for the adequate maintenance at all times of the Inter-American Highway within its borders in condition to serve the needs of national and international traffic.

Although no assurance can be given as to the exact details of any legislation to be introduced at the next session of Congress nor as to the prospects for the enactment of such legislation, the Department would appreciate such comments as the Embassy may wish to make in connection with the provisions of the proposed legislation prepared by PRA. The above should, of course, not be discussed with the local authorities.

LOVETT

810.154/9–947

The Secretary of State to the Ambassador in Honduras (Daniels)

No. 2420 WASHINGTON, September 20, 1947.

SIR: The Department refers to the Embassy's despatch No. 2914 of September 9, 1947,[13] requesting instructions as to whether the Em-

---

[12] Department of State, Treaties and Other International Acts Series No. 1567; 61 Stat. (pt. 2) 1129.
[13] Not printed.

bassy may properly support a request from Mr. E. W. James of the Public Roads Administration for additional funds from Honduras for further work on the Inter-American Highway. Reference is made in this connection to the Department's instruction No. 996 of November 14, 1942 [14] transmitting copies of a note dated September 9, 1942, from the Honduran Legation and the Department's reply of October 26, 1942, regarding the proposed cooperation of the United States in the construction of the Inter-American Highway in Honduras,[15] in accordance with Public Law No. 375 of December 26, 1941.

Pursuant to the Department's above-mentioned note of October 26, 1942, to the Honduran Legation, the Department in a letter of November 14, 1942, copy of which is enclosed [14] for the Embassy's information, authorized the Public Roads Administration to conclude with the appropriate Honduran authorities such subsidiary agreements of a technical nature as may be necessary to carry out the purpose of the above-mentioned Law. In accordance with this authorization, the Public Roads Administration agreed on December 21 and December 22, 1942 to set aside $2,000,000 and Honduras agreed to make available $1,000,000 for the construction on a cooperative basis of the Inter-American Highway in Honduras.

The Department is now informed by the Public Roads Administration that that agency is prepared to conclude a supplementary agreement with Honduras under which the Public Roads Administration would set aside for work on the Inter-American Highway in that country an additional sum of $50,000, already appropriated in accordance with the authorization contained in the above-mentioned Law, provided, Honduras agrees to contribute an additional amount of $25,000 for this cooperative project.

The Embassy is accordingly hereby authorized to cooperate in every practicable way with the Public Roads Administration in its efforts to conclude such a supplementary agreement with the appropriate Honduran authorities.[17]

Very truly yours,

For the Secretary of State:
NORMAN ARMOUR

---

[14] Not printed.
[15] For texts of notes of September 9 and October 26, 1942, see Department of State Executive Agreement Series No. 296, or 56 Stat. (pt. 2) 1848.
[17] Such an agreement was signed by representatives of the Public Roads Administration and the Honduran Government on September 18, 1947.

810.154/10–747

The Ambassador in Guatemala (Kyle) to the Secretary of State

RESTRICTED   GUATEMALA, October 7, 1947.
No. 2658

SIR: I have the honor to refer to the Department's instructions Nos. 826 of July 29, 1947 and 853 of September 11, 1947 [18] requesting the negotiation of a supplemental agreement concerning the cooperation between the United States and Guatemala in the improvement of the Inter-American Highway in this country within the provisions of Public Law 375 of December 26, 1941.

Copies of the proposed exchange of notes enclosed with the Department's instruction No. 826 were submitted by note to the Ministry for Foreign Affairs on August 7, 1947; and the Embassy followed up with a note dated September 16, 1947, inquiring as to the present status of this matter. Subsequently, Mr. Donovan [19] on two or three occasions discussed the matter informally with the Under Secretary for Foreign Affairs, Lic. Arturo Herbruger Asturias, in an effort to expedite Guatemalan consideration of the proposed modification to cover the limitation on the use of the $1,000,000 appropriated by the United States Congress for the Inter-American Highway in the Independent Offices Appropriation Act for the fiscal year 1946. Subsequently, a meeting was held in the Under Secretary's office on October 2 with the attendance of the Under Secretary of Communications, Lic. Ponciano España Rodas, two technical advisors of the latter's Ministry, and Messrs. Donovan and Wells of this Embassy.[20] As an outcome of this meeting, the Guatemalans suggested the addition of a paragraph in the Embassy's proposed note in substantially the following language:

"Except as amended herein, there remain in full power and effect the agreement effected by the exchange of notes of May 19, 1943 [21] and the memorandum of understanding [22] signed September 1, 1944 by the Director General of Roads for the Republic of Guatemala and on September 8, 1944 by the Commissioner of Public Roads, Public Roads Administration, Federal Works Agency for the Public Roads Administration, as modified on June 6, 1947, fixing the total amount to be set aside for the project by the Public Roads Administration at $6,300,000."

The foregoing additional paragraph was believed necessary by the Under Secretary for Communications and the Under Secretary for Foreign Affairs since they said that the proposed supplemental agree-

---
[18] Latter not printed.
[19] Andrew E. Donovan, 2d, former First Secretary of Embassy and Consul at Guatemala, who left that post on October 8, 1947, for another assignment.
[20] Milton K. Wells, First Secretary of Embassy and Consul at Guatemala.
[21] For text, see Executive Agreement Series No. 345, or 57 Stat. (pt. 2) 1111.
[22] Not printed.

ment would have to be submitted to the Guatemalan Congress for ratification. For this reason, officials of the Ministry of Communications felt that the supplemental agreement should stipulate that it would not affect the financial obligations already undertaken by the United States Government in the basic agreement. The officials mentioned expressed the opinion that with this clarification of language there will be no difficulty in obtaining the final approval of the Guatemalan Congress, particularly since present Guatemalan laws do not impose any restrictions of this nature on the use of highways.

While it was made perfectly clear in conversations with the aforementioned officials that the proposed supplementary agreement involves no additional financial commitment on the part of the United States Government and that the new agreement is intended only to facilitate use in Guatemala of the $1,000,000 already appropriated by Congress in the Independent Offices Appropriation Act for the fiscal year 1946, it is important that there should be no ambiguity on this point in the proposed supplemental agreement. While it is believed that, with the suggested additional paragraph, there should be no future misunderstanding, the Department may wish to suggest some improvement in language.

Attention is invited to the Department's restricted circular airgram of August 18, 1947, advising that the Public Roads Administration has prepared a proposed amendment to Public Law 375, approved December 26, 1941, which would provide an additional authorization of $60,000,000 to be appropriated for the construction of the Inter-American Highway, the proposed amendment to include a provision that such additional funds authorized shall not be available for work in any cooperating country until such country enters into an agreement that it will not impose certain restrictions on the use of the highway. Since the language in this proposed amendment to Public Law 375 states more specifically the required guarantees on the part of the cooperating countries than the language used in the Independent Offices Appropriation Act for 1946, the question arises whether the guarantees now sought in a supplemental agreement would be sufficient also for the purposes of the proposed amendment. If not, the Embassy believes that consideration should be given to drafting the proposed exchange of notes in such language as will cover the requirements of the proposed legislation mentioned in the Department's airgram of August 18.

The Embassy will await the Department's **further instructions before** reopening the matter with the appropriate Guatemalan authorities.

Respectfully yours,

For the Ambassador:
MILTON K. WELLS
First Secretary of Embassy

810.154/10-747 : Airgram

The Acting Secretary of State to the Embassy in Guatemala

RESTRICTED   WASHINGTON, November 3, 1947.

A-239. The Embassy's despatch No. 2658 of October 7, 1947 has been discussed with the PRA. No objection is perceived in principle to adding the suggested paragraph to the Embassy's proposed note transmitted with the Department's instruction No. 826 of July 29, 1947. However, it is felt this addition to the proposed Agreement may necessitate a further Agreement if at any time in the future it should become necessary to modify the memorandum of understanding signed September 1, 1944. In order to eliminate that possibility, if the Guatemalans insist that the currently proposed Agreement should provide that it will not affect the present financial obligations, it is suggested that this provision be covered in an additional paragraph in the following language:

"Except as amended herein, there shall remain in full force and effect the Agreement effected by the exchange of notes of May 19, 1943, and any memorandum of understanding related thereto concluded subsequently between the Director General of Roads on behalf of the Republic of Guatemala and the Commissioner of Public Roads on behalf of the Government of the United States of America."

Referring to the penultimate paragraph of the Embassy's despatch, it is believed that no attempt should be made at this time to have the currently proposed Agreement with Guatemala conform with the anticipated provisions of possible legislation that as yet has not been introduced in the Congress.

LOVETT

[The additional paragraph suggested in airgram A-239, printed *supra*, was communicated orally and in memorandum form to the Guatemalan Foreign Office on November 14, 1947, according to airgram A-78, March 24, 1948, from Guatemala, and the subject was twice followed up by personal discussions with the Under Secretary for Foreign Affairs, without progress (810.154/3-2448).]

THE INTER-AMERICAN COFFEE AGREEMENT [1]

561.333D3/3–1347

Memorandum of Conversation, by Mr. Albert H. Gerberich of the Division of North and West Coast Affairs

[WASHINGTON,] March 13, 1947.

Participants: IR —Mr. Edward G. Cale [2]
                Mr. William H. Bray
           CPA —Mr. Fred G. Heins
           BA —Mr. Harold N. Midkiff
           NWC—Mr. Albert H. Gerberich

SUMMARY

Mr. Cale gave a review of the coffee situation since 1939 and explained that the Inter-American Coffee Agreement (of Nov. 28, 1940) [3] will come up for renewal again on Sept. 30, 1947, and he wanted to hear what the feeling is regarding it.

After Mr. Cale's introductory remarks, Mr. Midkiff stated that he could see little purpose in continuing the agreement, as there are no serious problems affecting coffee at the moment.

Mr. Cale said that this is correct, that prices are now extremely high (26¢ per lb. for Santos as compared with 6.38¢ in 1940, for example), and there seems to be no likelihood of a coffee surplus for some time to come, especially since Brazilian exports are down from 22 million bags per year to between 12 and 14 million. Furthermore, there are no quotas to be adjusted, since all OPA controls are off.

He added confidentially that Paul Daniels [4] favors permitting the Agreement to lapse, but Mr. Cale fears that there will be some objection to this from the smaller producing countries, especially Guatemala. Mr. Daniels will be in the Department toward the end of March. The Inter-American Coffee Board will meet again in April,

---

[1] For documentation on the operation of the agreement in 1946, see *Foreign Relations*, 1946, vol. XI, pp. 154 ff.

[2] Associate Chief of the International Resources Division, and Chairman of the Inter-American Coffee Board.

[3] For text, see Department of State Treaty Series No. 970, or 55 Stat. (pt. 2) 1143. For documentation on the Third Pan American Coffee Conference, see *Foreign Relations*, 1940, vol. V, pp. 380 ff.

[4] Counselor of Embassy in Brazil and former Chairman of the Inter-American Coffee Board.

and perhaps Mr. Daniels can be present for another discussion before then.

The report on the world coffee situation called for under Article 3 of the Extension of the Agreement (of Jan. 6, 1947), has been completed, but Mr. Cale expressed himself as somewhat disappointed with it despite its length and detail.

(With regard to the improved conditions in the Colombian coffee industry this recent statement of Roberto Marulanda, Minister of National Economy, is of interest: "In 1946 the *campesinos* had to pay 4 arrobas of coffee for one machete; today they can get four machetes for one arroba.")

561.333D3/4-2547

The Acting Secretary of State to the Embassy in Brazil

CONFIDENTIAL WASHINGTON, April 25, 1947.
No. 656

The Acting Secretary of State refers to the Minutes of the Interdepartmental Technical Committee on Coffee No. M1/47 dated March 25, 1947, the Minutes of the Inter-American Coffee Board Meeting No. 101 dated April 1, 1947, and a Working Outline, Draft Policy Recommendations of the Inter-American Coffee Board dated March 28, 1947,[5] which have been forwarded to the Embassy under cover of transmittal slips from the International Resources Division.

It will be noted from the above referenced documents that discussions are proceeding both within this Government and in the Inter-American Coffee Board concerning the future of the Inter-American Coffee Agreement.

On April 16, 1947, the Inter-American Coffee Board's Committee of Review, which was formed by the Board to review the Technical Coffee Study and make recommendations to the Board with respect to the future of the Agreement, met with the United States Trade Advisory Committee to the Board. The results of this meeting were: (1) The Committee of Review would not recommend the continuation of the Agreement with any quota provisions therein. (2) The Committee would make a complete study of all the aspects involved in continuing the present Agreement after deleting the quota provisions or formulating a new agreement along the lines suggested in alternative 3 of the Working Outline dated March 28, 1947.

This Government recognizes the importance which the American coffee producing countries attach to the Coffee Agreement but prefers to permit the Agreement to lapse on its expiration date, September 30, 1947. However, this Government is prepared to compromise

---

[5] None printed.

its position and continue with an arrangement whereby this Government would indicate that it still maintains its interest in the coffee problems of the American coffee producing countries. This compromise, if necessary, must not include quotas. Any agreement reached should contain definite and worthwhile functions and create an effective organization with which to carry out these functions.

The Department requests that the Embassy transmit, if information can be obtained discreetly, any official or reliable information concerning the Brazilian Government's attitude toward the future of the Inter-American Coffee Agreement. In addition, the Embassy's comments would be appreciated with respect to the proposed positions of the United States regarding the future of the Agreement.

561.333D3/6-1347 : Airgram

The Ambassador in Brazil (Pawley) to the Secretary of State

CONFIDENTIAL   RIO DE JANEIRO, June 13, 1947.

A-499. Re: Department's Despatch No. 656 dated April 25 to American Embassy, Rio de Janeiro. According to Bishop of American Consulate, São Paulo, leaders in coffee industry in State of São Paulo have shown no interest in the continuation of the coffee agreement. Several newspaper editorials have appeared recently expressing the opinion that since Brazil has received little if any benefit from the agreement in the past, there would be nothing to gain from its extension. Inasmuch as the Brazilian Government's policy in regard to coffee matters is generally established by the attitude of the coffee industry of São Paulo State, it seems doubtful that there will be any official opposition from Brazil toward permitting the agreement to lapse.

PAWLEY

561.333D3/8-747

Minutes of a Meeting of the Inter-American Coffee Board by Mr. J. K. Havemeyer of the International Resources Division

Meeting No. 103   WASHINGTON, August 7, 1947.

The Inter-American Coffee Board met at its offices at 2400 Sixteenth Street, N.W., at 11:00 A. M., August 7, 1947 and considered the following matters:

1. *New Delegates*

The Chairman welcomed Mr. Carlos Alzamora, Delegate of Peru and Mr. Miguel A. Herrera, Delegate of the Dominican Republic.

2. *Absentee Representation*

For this meeting, the delegate of Venezuela presented his credentials to represent the Guatemalan delegate and the delegate of Colombia presented his credentials to represent the delegate of Costa Rica.

3. *Approval of Minutes*

Approval of the minutes for meeting No. 102 of July 1, 1947 was postponed until the next meeting of the Board.

4. *Report of Special Committee of Review of the Coffee Study.*

Dr. Casas-Briceño, Chairman of the Special Committee advised the Board that the Committee had met on August 7, 1947 immediately prior to this meeting of the Board. The Committee had received the text of the formal document addressed to the United States Delegate dated August 4, 1947 and signed by the Secretary of State.* He stated that the Special Committee had not reviewed the document, and had agreed to recommend that the formal views of the United States Government on future possible inter-governmental coffee consultative arrangements should be read and discussed in the meeting of the Board.

The Chairman, Mr. E. G. Cale, the United States Delegate, said that pursuant to the Board's resolution on July 1, 1947 the Secretary Manager had written him a letter dated July 2, 1947 requesting a formal statement from the United States Government which would indicate what decision would be acceptable to the United States Government with reference to possible inter-governmental arrangements on coffee, with particular consideration given to the continuation of the Inter-American Coffee Agreement and the Inter-American Coffee Board.

The Chairman read the communication sent him by the United States Secretary of State dated August 4, 1947. In brief, this communication outlines three types of international coffee arrangements in which the United States is prepared to participate:

1. Immediate formation of an international coffee study group with terms of reference in line with general principles of commodity policy embodied in Chapter VII of the draft charter for an International Trade Organization.

2. Immediate formation of an inter-American coffee consultative committee within the framework of the Pan American Union. The United States, moreover, would participate in both an international and an inter-American arrangement provided each accorded with ITO principles.

3. Finally, in view of short time between this date and expiration of Inter-American Coffee Agreement on October 1, 1947 this Government would be prepared to extend Coffee Agreement by protocol for one additional year provided quotas are completely inoperative and the Board determines during that year to follow some line of action indicated in proposals one and two, or to terminate the Agreement.

Mr. Cale stated that the United States had subscribed to the principles governing international commodity arrangements outlined in

---

*Copies of this letter of Instructions from the Secretary to Mr. E. G. Cale were transmitted to all United States Embassies located in countries signatory to the Inter-American Coffee Agreement by transmittal slip bearing reference to the Department's unnumbered circular airgram dated August 11, 1947, 9: 05 A. M. [Footnote in the original; letter and airgram not printed.]

Chapter VII of the proposed International Trade Charter and that the policy with respect to commodity arrangements was being followed with respect to all commodities, with the possible exception of coffee.

The Mexican delegate said that the position taken by the United States led him to believe that it was not necessary to wait another year for the Board to recommend a course of action with respect to the future of the Coffee Agreement.

The alternate delegate of Colombia suggested that it would be better to wait a year to determine whether or not the ITO Charter would come into force. Perhaps in 1948 the Board could determine what arrangements could be made on coffee. Furthermore, he believed that the Board should follow the third proposed coffee arrangement as given in the United States document without discussion of the first two. In addition, he felt that some other alternative might develop during the next year.

The Chairman pointed out that international and inter-American coffee consultative arrangements could be adopted simultaneously. Since 85 percent of world coffee production is in this hemisphere, Western Hemisphere producers would have the dominant voice in an international coffee study group. With both arrangements in force it was most likely that the delegates from American coffee producing countries would be the same on both the inter-American and international groups.

The Brazilian delegate said that he was not in a position to vote one way or the other on any of the proposals because he must obtain instructions from his government. He moved that the Board should make its recommendations on the future of the Coffee Agreement at a meeting to be held in September. The Colombian delegate seconded this motion and it was unanimously approved. It was decided that delegates should confer with their respective governments regarding the United States proposals and be prepared to take action at a special meeting of the Board on September 11, 1947 at 10:30 A.M.

. . . .

J. K. HAVEMEYER

561.333D3/9-1247 : Airgram

The Secretary of State to Certain Diplomatic Representatives in the American Republics [6]

WASHINGTON, September 12, 1947.

On September 11, 1947, the Inter-American Coffee Board passed a motion recommending the continuation of the Inter-American Coffee

[6] At Rio de Janeiro, Bogotá, Tegucigalpa, Mexico City, Guatemala, Caracas, Lima, Habana, Port-au-Prince, San José, Ciudad Trujillo, Managua, Quito, and San Salvador.

Agreement for one year beginning October 1, 1947.[7] Protocol for continuation is the same as Enclosure No. 3 to Instruction to United States Delegate to the Inter-American Coffee Board[8] with minor changes. Copies of this instruction were sent by transmittal slips in August to Embassies receiving this airgram.

MARSHALL

561.333D3/11–1747 : Airgram

The Secretary of State to the Embassy in Brazil

RESTRICTED   WASHINGTON, November 17, 1947.

A–603. For the Embassy's comment and files the Department reports below a telephone conversation on November 5 between an officer of the Department and Mr. George Robbins, President of the National Coffee Association. Mr. Estockler Queiros, DNC, and Mr. Prado of the Brazilian coffee trade have been visiting this country on the invitation of the National Coffee Association. Before these gentlemen left for Brazil on November 3 they summarized to Mr. Robbins the conclusions which were reached during their visit in this country which are listed below:

With respect to the Inter-American Coffee Agreement and Board, the Brazilians wish that the United States would support their request to delay approval of the revised coffee study for sixty days.

With respect to the future of the Agreement they wish to keep the essence of the Coffee Board as an inter-American entity and favor the alternative proposal in the instructions from the Secretary of State to the United States delegate to the Board dated August 4, 1947[9] to establish an inter-American coffee consultative committee within the framework of the Pan American Union. They desire that the operation of such an entity be principally concerned with the collection and publications of coffee statistics.

The Brazilians wish to recommend the reorganization of the Pan American Coffee Bureau by a new commercial agreement with the other countries now represented on the Bureau. In addition, they wish to have cooperation with the National Coffee Association written into the new terms of reference for the Bureau. Mr. Robbins stated that the Brazilians wish to continue the cooperation with Colombia in the leadership of this Bureau.

In order to investigate the Brazilian coffee growers' attitude toward

---

[7] Department of State Treaties and Other International Acts Series No. 1768; 62 Stat. (pt. 2) 1658.
[8] Dated August 4, not printed.
[9] Not printed.

the promotional fund to be used for propaganda purposes in the United States, Mr. Prado is to take a trip in Brazil among the growers to ascertain the feeling of the growers with respect to placing a tax on the export of coffee from Brazil to support the promotional fund. Mr. Queiros is to recommend to President Dutra and to the Minister of Fazenda that a tax be imposed for the promotion of coffee in the United States. After this action has been taken the Brazilians intend to hold a meeting of the seven coffee growing states in order to formalize the request to their government for an export tax for coffee promotion.

The National Coffee Association has agreed to correct or withhold misleading statements which may emanate from this country with respect to conversations which are to be held in Brazil concerning the imposition of a new tax for coffee promotion.

Mr. Queiros is convinced that a tax is required to maintain the fund needed for the promotion of coffee in the United States. He believes that ten cents a bag exported should be collected.

MARSHALL

561.333D3/12-847

Memorandum of Telephone Conversation, by Mr. J. K. Havemeyer of the International Resources Division

WASHINGTON, December 8, 1947.

In the course of a telephone conversation with Mr. George Robbins, Mr. Havemeyer inquired if the protocol for the extension of the Inter-American Coffee Agreement for one year beginning October 1, 1947 is acceptable to the National Coffee Association and to the trade as it is now written. Mr. Robbins replied that the Association and trade agree that the protocol should be presented to the Senate for ratification as it is now written, but he pointed out it is generally agreed that upon the expiration of the year under reference, e.g., as of October 1, 1948, the functions of the Inter-American Coffee Board may advantageously be taken over by the Pan American Union. In addition, Mr. Robbins said that all quotas and references thereto should be eliminated from any future international coffee arrangement.

BOUNDARY DISPUTE: ECUADOR AND PERU

[For protocol between Ecuador and Peru regarding peace, friendship, and boundaries (signed also by representatives of the United States, Argentina, Brazil, and Chile) signed at Rio de Janeiro, January 29, 1942, see Department of State Executive Agreement Series No. 288, or 56 Stat. (pt. 2) 1818. Documentation for 1947 is not published.]

ARGENTINA

UNITED STATES INTEREST IN THE POLITICAL SITUATION IN ARGENTINA: EFFORTS TO EXTIRPATE NAZI INFLUENCES [1]

711.35/1-1547

Statement to the Press by the Argentine Minister for Foreign Affairs and Worship (*Bramuglia*) [2]

[Translation]

[BUENOS AIRES,] January 13, 1947.

The Minister for Foreign Affairs and Worship, Dr. Juan Atilio Bramuglia, delivered last night to the journalists in the Foreign Office the following statements with reference to the remarks made by the ex-Secretary of State of the United States, Mr. James F. Byrnes.[3]

"During the public discussion of foreign affairs held in Cleveland, Mr. James F. Byrnes, the outgoing Secretary of State of the United States, made statements concerning the Argentine Nation, which filled us with surprise because of their intolerance and unfairness.

"Although the remarks in question may be the result of a personal reaction, I believe that they could never be a reflection of the political position of the State of which Mr. Byrnes is a citizen, to whom I reply as such.

"The Argentine Government, faithful to its international pledges, has made every possible effort—and it has succeeded in the appropriate measure, as the Department of State of the United States of America undoubtedly knows—to meet the demands, the resolutions and the advice of the Mexico Conference as contained in the Final Act of Chapultepec.[4] Mr. Messersmith,[5] a gentleman in whom the Argentine people see a gallant exponent of the spirit of a great nation as is that of the United States, can bear witness to our endeavors in this respect.

---

[1] For documentation on the Argentine attitude toward Nazi influences in 1946, see *Foreign Relations*, 1946, vol. XI, pp. 182 ff.

[2] Copy transmitted to the Department in despatch 1651, January 15, 1947, from Buenos Aires; not printed.

[3] In a speech before the 21st Annual Institute of the Cleveland Council of World Affairs; for text, see Department of State *Bulletin*, January 19, 1947. President Truman accepted the resignation of Secretary Byrnes on January 10, but the effective date of resignation was January 21 when Gen. George C. Marshall took the oath of office as his successor.

[4] Pan American Union, *Final Act of the Inter-American Conference on Problems of War and Peace, Mexico City, February–March, 1945* (Washington, 1945).

[5] George S. Messersmith, Ambassador to Argentina, in Washington for consultation until February 1.

"I therefore declare that Argentina has fulfilled, in the same measure and proportion as all the other countries, the obligations deriving from all the juridical instruments that have been signed.

"On the other hand, I refuse to acknowledge the right of having a supreme judge on international matters; much less do I admit the right that such a one-sided and partial judge be the one to condemn, and particularly if it is a matter of one or several men and not a nation.

"In this matter I believe that, were it necessary, the decision should come from the nations of the world that participated in the establishment of cordial relations and maintain that position, for mankind unquestionably stands in need of peace and work.

"It is a well known fact that Argentina maintains fraternal bonds of friendship and concord with all the peoples of the globe, principally with those that bore the heaviest burden of war. Since those nations and their respective governments find nothing in Argentina's conduct to justify an expression of displeasure, we cannot believe in the justice of the purpose that prompts this relentless insistence, which is becoming tedious, on the part of certain officials of a government to which we are linked by common objectives.

"The belief that the consideration of situations such as that discussed at the Cleveland forum, is incumbent on nations and not particularly on individuals, is also expressed by a prominent American personality, the Honorable Senator Vandenberg,[6] when he says: 'I entirely sympathize with the anxiety to purge the Americas of their last vestiges of nazism, but I think that under half a dozen solemn Pan-American treaties to which we are a party, the multilateral decision to summon the Rio de Janeiro Conference [7] should be adopted by all of us jointly,'—he refers to the American nations—, 'and not dictated or influenced by us alone'—he refers to the United States of America.

"Senator Vandenberg goes on to say that 'in a certain sense, it may be said that we have been acting jointly, but I believe it is already past the time to hold the Pan-American Conference which we promised in 1945, in order to resume there the new world authority that constitutes the spirit of the unity of our new world.'

"It is regrettable that truth, which should be the supreme law, has not penetrated the mind and the intelligence of some of the officials to whom Mr. Byrnes refers, just as it failed to penetrate his own intelligence and mind, even though he affirms as a contribution to the definition of peace, 'that a just peace can be achieved by coöpera-

---

[6] Arthur H. Vandenberg, member of the Senate Foreign Relations Committee.
[7] For documentation on this Conference, see pp. 1 ff.

tive effort if we persist with firmness in right as God gives us power to see the right.'

"Under present circumstances and with regard to Argentina, I sincerely think that Mr. Byrnes is not inspired by God in seeing right and assuring peace."

740.35112 RP/1–1547 : Telegram

The Secretary of State to the Embassy in Argentina

CONFIDENTIAL WASHINGTON, January 16, 1947—7 p. m.

35. Text proposed *note verbale*, urtel 42, Jan 15,[8] has been revised with concurrence Amb. Messersmith in following form which you are authorized transmit FonOff : [9]

"The Embassy of the United States of America in Buenos Aires presents its compliments to the Minister of Foreign Relations and, as orally requested, has the honor to suggest that the Argentine Government may wish to consider, as a means of finally eliminating enemy interests in spearhead enterprises, the feasibility of effecting the final and complete acquisition *en bloc* by the Argentine Government of all enemy rights, titles and interests in such concerns; this acquisition could be accompanied by the provisional payment of a specified sum, to be deposited in an appropriate agency of the Argentine Government.

"If such procedure is feasible, it should be the equivalent of vesting and it would be possible to eliminate all enemy interest in the properties in question, leaving for later determination by the Arg Govt the most appropriate means of making final inventories and appraisements, and final disposition."

Dept understands that *note verbale* was requested by **FonOff** and will not be permitted by FonOff to be misinterpreted as "intervention" in Arg internal affairs. It is noted that the *note verbale* is limited to the property question.

Principal changes in draft copied in urtel 42 are:

1. Elimination of suggestion that FonOff would be able to make public announcement which would undoubtedly be received favorably by press and public opinion since it was thought that this might be inappropriate in a note of ours.

2. Changing your language regarding purchase *en bloc* of enemy property to acquisition *en bloc* of enemy interests in spearhead enterprises. This is more restrictive.

3. The reference to subsequent disposition by Argentine Govt is

---

[8] Not printed.
[9] A marginal note reads: "According to report from O'Donoghue at Buenos Aires, action was taken. A minor change was made in note, 2nd paragraph, & this change was cleared with T. C. Mann. 1–22–47." Sidney E. O'Donoghue was Chargé in Argentina; Thomas C. Mann was Chief of the Division of River Plate Affairs.

intended to avoid possible implication that we are requesting permanent Govt ownership and operation.

4. The words "if feasible" and similar expressions are intended to avoid interpretation that we presume to pass on legal and other questions within province of Argentine Govt.

BYRNES

862.20235/1-1747 : Airgram

The Chargé in Argentina (O'Donoghue) to the Secretary of State

SECRET   BUENOS AIRES, January 17, 1947.

A-73. Reference Embdes 1557, December 27, 1946 [10] and previous correspondence regarding deportation German agents.

Foreign Office press release of January 14 states that more of German agents whose deportation has been decreed, have been arrested.

Foreign Ministry orally and confidentially advised me January 16 that six of these agents are in custody. Their identity not known to Embassy. Minister stated that further transportation arrangements will be made for these deportees as soon as the number in custody totals about 12 to 15.

O'DONOGHUE

711.35/1-2147

Memorandum of Conversation, by the Chief of the Division of River Plate Affairs (Mann)

RESTRICTED   [WASHINGTON,] January 21, 1947.

Participants: Ambassador Messersmith
Mr. Braden—A-Br [11]
Mr. Wright—A-Br [12]
Mr. Briggs—ARA [13]
Mr. Mann—RPA [14]

Ambassador Messersmith called on Mr. Braden at the Ambassador's request and the following matters were discussed:

1. Ambassador Messersmith inquired whether Argentine performance in the field of schools and institutions was considered by the Department to be adequate. Mr. Braden stated that on the basis of the Embassy's reports there appears to have been substantial performance

---

[10] Not printed.
[11] Spruille Braden, Assistant Secretary of State for American Republic Affairs.
[12] James H. Wright, Special Assistant to Assistant Secretary of State Braden.
[13] Ellis O. Briggs, Director of the Office of American Republic Affairs.
[14] Thomas C. Mann, Chief of the Division of River Plate Affairs.

in this field with the possible exception that there were some propagators of Nazi ideology who ought to be repatriated. Ambassador Messersmith said that there were none. Mr. Braden stated that the matter of schools and institutions was raised in June 1946 principally for the purpose of ascertaining precisely what had been done by the Argentine Government in this field; and that it had been clear for several months that the principal compliance questions related to the persons and property fields.

2. The Ambassador inquired whether the Department would consider Argentine performance adequate in the field of property if that Government should proceed with its plans to acquire title to enemy interests in a total of about 75 spearhead firms. Mr. Braden replied that it would be necessary to study whatever decrees might be issued by the Argentine Government and to determine whether full and complete title of the enemy owners was in the Argentine Government—whether the proposed Argentine decree would have substantially the same effect as our own vesting laws; and to determine also whether there were any firms in addition to the 75 which ought to be dealt with. Mr. Wright added that the Department did not expect the Argentines to do any more than our own Alien Property Custodian had done in the United States. The Ambassador referred to the Staudt case [15] and said that while the plan was to eliminate the interests owned from Germany, there was no evidence of any activities on the part of Staudt himself subsequent to our entrance in the War. The Ambassador expressed the opinion that no further action should be expected in the Staudt case. There was also some discussion about an instruction which had been prepared in the Division of Economic Security Controls concerning Staudt which none of those present except Ambassador Messersmith had yet seen. The Ambassador expressed the opinion that this instruction was inconclusive since it suggested the submission of certain data to the Argentine Government which that Government already had and did not decide the question of whether Staudt himself should be regarded by this Government as undesirable.

3. With regard to persons, the Ambassador inquired whether we would regard the punishment or repatriation of persons such as Becker and Harnisch [16] as essential to compliance, in view of the efforts which were being made by the Argentine Government to locate

---

[15] Staudt and Company, headed by Ricardo W. Staudt, dealt in wool and other commodities, through numerous branches and subsidiaries. The Company was on the Proclaimed List.

[16] For data on these and other individuals implicated in the German espionage system, see Department of State, *Consultation Among the American Republics With Respect to the Argentine Situation* (Washington, 1946), pp. 13 ff.

these and others in the original group of 52 which had gone into hiding. The Ambassador stated that these agents presumably were warned that a Government roundup was eminent [imminent], in spite of elaborate secrecy precautions, because of the venality of some minor police official. Ambassador Messersmith also referred to the reports that some of the agents in hiding had been caught. Mr. Braden said that it was not possible to pass final judgment on this question until we knew definitely what the Argentine Government had finally accomplished in this field. He said that the Department did not wish to lay down a blueprint of what the minimum requirements were.

4. The Ambassador referred to Mandl's case and said he thought a visa should be granted. It was explained that, at Mr. Acheson's [17] suggestion, this case had been sent to the Visa Division for action and, more recently a memorandum had been sent to the Secretary on the subject but that no reply had been received. The Ambassador said that a strong recommendation on the part of the geographic office in favor of the issuance of a visa would probably resolve the matter and he thought this recommendation should be made.

5. The Ambassador referred to the case of the four frigates [18] and said that the failure to allow their export to Argentina had very unfavorable repercussions in Buenos Aires; that he thought the frigates should be allowed to go to Buenos Aires in view of the fact that the Argentine Government intended to put them to a legitimate use. It was explained that the vessels had been classified as vessels of war by the Arms Committee which brought the vessels within the policy of prohibiting the export of arms, war vessels and implements of war to the Argentine prior to settlement of the compliance question. It was also explained that the Secretary's memorandum asked for the facts and that a summary of the case had been sent to him but that no reply had been received.

At several places in the conversation the Ambassador referred to conversations that he had had with the Secretary on the points referred to above and he expressed the opinion that unless the Argentine situation was resolved very soon—particularly with reference to the matters listed above—Argentine-United States relations would deteriorate.

Thomas C. Mann

---

[17] Dean Acheson, Under Secretary of State.
[18] See memorandum by the Assistant Secretary for American Republic Affairs (Braden), January 8, p. 215.

ARGENTINA

740.35112 RP/1–2447 : Telegram

The Chargé in Argentina (O'Donoghue) to the Secretary of State

CONFIDENTIAL   BUENOS AIRES, January 24, 1947—6 p. m.
US URGENT

87. ReDeptel 35, January 16. Foreign Minister this afternoon gave me copy decree which he said was signed yesterday by President Perón and all Cabinet members reading in translation as follows, and which he said would be published tonight or at latest tomorrow:

In view of:
Resolutions Nos. XVIII and XIX of the Inter-American Conference on Problems of War and Peace,[20] held in Mexico in 1945, or Act of Chapultepec, whereas:
By virtue of the aforementioned Conference the Republic has contracted obligations relating to the liquidation of enemy property;
In order to proceed promptly to liquidate the property in question, it is necessary that the state acquire that property, without this preventing it from subsequently offering the same in sale to private individuals, or from forming mixed corporations, etc.;
The purchase of the property by the state would offer the advantage that the liquidation of such enemy property would thus instantaneously be effected, since it would be transferred from the hands of the enemy into those of the state;
Contrarily, if the property were sold to private individuals, pertinent operations would delay the liquidation of the property in question, inasmuch as it would be necessary to prove balances, inventories, etc.; the measure intended to fulfill the obligation under reference, has its origin in the state of war and is a consequence of the act signed by the country (Act of Chapultepec), which is a supreme law of the nation (article 31 of the national constitution).
Therefore, and in accordance with the provisions of article 9, second part, of the decree No. 11.599/46, the President of the Argentine nation at a general Cabinet meeting decrees:
    Article 1, the acquisition *en bloc*, thru the Central Bank of the Argentine Republic, or thru the entities that are part of the system thereof, all the assets of companies and entities of commercial, industrial or financial character, which may be found to be in a state of liquidation by resolution of the board for vigilance and final liquidation of enemy properties.
    Article 2, the price of the present purchase shall be determined in due course thru inventories, balances and expert appraisals that are made to that end.
    Article 3, the Central Bank of the Argentine Republic will advance, an advance payment on the price, the sum of 100 million pesos Argentina currency.

---

[20] These resolutions concerned the control of enemy property; for text, see *Final Act of the Inter-American Conference on Problems of War and Peace*, pp. 55–59.

Article 4, the aforementioned sum shall be deposited to the order of the President of the Board for vigilance and final liquidation of enemy properties in the said Central Bank of the Argentine Republic.

Article 5, let this be communicated, published, forwarded to the national registry and filed.

Comments follow separate telegram.[21]

O'DONOGHUE

740.35112 RP/1–2447 : Telegram

The Chargé in Argentina (O'Donoghue) to the Secretary of State

SECRET   BUENOS AIRES, January 24, 1947—7 p. m.

88. ReEmbtel 87, January 24. In handing me copy decree Minister stated that he had told President this must be done, and that now if State Dept did not recognize Argentina's goodwill, in compliance Argentina could do nothing more than sit back "tranquilly" and see what happens.

Decree covers principal enemy spearhead firms in Argentina less 10 now in courts. Embassy was advised by competent Foreign Office official that decree will be applicable to such other firms as may later be determined to be enemy firms, as well as partial enemy interests identified in other firms.

In opinion Embassy, the action provided for in this decree constitutes reasonable and substantial compliance with the Act of Chapultepec insofar as enemy property is concerned.

O'DONOGHUE

740.35112A/1–2747 : Telegram

The Chargé in Argentina (O'Donoghue) to the Secretary of State

RESTRICTED   BUENOS AIRES, January 27, 1947—7 p. m.

95. Item appearing *Prensa* today states that Foreign Office circles report Government determined resolve soonest possible expulsion enemy agents still here.

Foreign Minister informed me that location those presently evading police difficult but Government is determined to expel all. Added that another 10 or so have been detained since recent deportation 13 and these will be deported as soon as their number is increased and shipping available.

Foreign Minister repeated his and President's determination to rid country enemy agents.

---

[21] *Infra.*

Minister also said that in few days definitive action would be taken regarding Axis schools now "partially Argentinized". Foreign Office explains unofficially that Minister referred to plans for establishment of purely Argentine schools in quarters of former German schools closed by Government and inoperative for over year.

O'Donoghue

711.35/1-2747

Memorandum of Conversation, by the Under Secretary of State (Acheson)

SECRET [Washington,] January 27, 1947.

The British Ambassador [22] called at his request. He handed me the attached *Aide-Mémoire*. After reading it, I said to him that I regretted very much that the British Government had to take any action at all at just this time as it seemed to me that our policy was producing results in Argentina. I asked him (1) precisely what the British Government had in mind doing, (2) whether the British Government proposed to issue a public statement, and (3) whether it proposed to address any communication to the Argentine Government. As to the first, the Ambassador said that this *Aide-Mémoire* related to the gentleman's agreement [23] not to sell arms to Argentina, that no action would be taken for ten days, and that thereafter the British had no ambitious ideas but only, as Mr. Hadow [24] had informed Mr. Braden, a "trivial program of naval replacement, i.e. parts and equipment, et cetera". As to the public or private statements, he would undertake to find out from his Government. I urged very strongly that no statement be made either to the press or to the Argentine Government.

Dean Acheson

[Annex]

Aide-Mémoire

His Majesty's Government in the United Kingdom have carefully considered the recent actions of the Argentine Government and have come to the conclusion that it is now fulfilling its obligations in respect of enemy aliens, property and interests at least as well as the majority of Latin-American Governments.

---

[22] Lord Inverchapel.
[23] For a reference to an informal agreement between the United States and the United Kingdom not to supply arms and munitions to Argentina, see *Foreign Relations*, 1946, vol. xi, p. 279.
[24] Robert H. Hadow, British Counsellor of Embassy.

His Majesty's Government have therefore requested me to inform the United States Government that they propose henceforth to treat Argentina in all respects on the same footing as other Latin American countries.

740.35112 RP/1-3147

The Chargé in Argentina (O'Donoghue) to the Secretary of State

CONFIDENTIAL   BUENOS AIRES, January 31, 1947.
No. 1779–A

Subject: Final Disposition of Enemy Property in Argentina.

SIR: Reference is made to the Embassy's telegram no. 87 of 6:00 p.m. January 24, 1947 and Embassy's despatch no. 1741 of January 28, 1947,[25] both respecting Argentine Decree no. 1921 of January 24, 1947 whereby enemy property in Argentina is acquired by the State by virtue of purchase through the Banco Central from the Junta de Vigilancia y Disposición Final de la Propiedad Enemiga. In this connection the Embassy now has the honor to offer the following observations:

Due to varying lists of firms which have appeared in the press as coming under the provision of this Decree, and for the purpose of obtaining a clear understanding of the application thereof, officers of the Embassy have conferred with an official of the Ministry of Foreign Affairs who, under the supervision of the Minister, is primarily concerned with the preparation and operation of the Decree, and received from him the interpretation of that Ministry.

According to the aforementioned official, this Decree is applicable to all enemy property in Argentina. It includes those firms previously determined by the Junta as enemy, many of which had been transferred to the Banco Central for disposition; it includes all firms which may, in the future, be so determined; it includes the enemy pharmaceutical firms for which a project of law is now before the Congress providing for their nationalization*; and it includes all fractional participations, credits, or obligations officially determined as enemy-owned. From the foregoing it would therefore appear that technically there now exists no identified enemy-owned property in Argentina and that henceforth the administration, determination, and valuation of this property becomes solely an internal Argentine matter. The Em-

---

[25] Latter not printed.

*Embassy Despatch no. 1024 of October 16, 1946; Subject: Nationalization of Former Axis Pharmaceutical Manufacturers in Argentina. [Footnote in the original.]

bassy will of course continue to supply to the Argentine authorities such proof of enemy ownership as becomes available.

[Here follows a list of firms in which enemy interests had been identified.]

Respectfully yours, For the Chargé d'Affaires ad interim:
HOWARD H. TEWKSBURY
Counselor of Embassy for Economic Affairs

835.00/2–747 : Telegram

The Ambassador in Argentina (Messersmith) to the Secretary of State

TOP SECRET   BUENOS AIRES, February 7, 1947—4 p. m.

134. For the Secretary, Under Secretaries Acheson and Clayton and Assistant Secretary Braden. On return to Buenos Aires I discussed with appropriate officers Embassy all aspects Argentine compliance and progress during my absence. Subsequently on Feb 4, I discussed the matter with FonMin and on Feb 6 with the President, FonMin and Miranda of the Central Bank.[26] As a result of these talks I desire to offer following observations:

1. With respect to schools and institutions and propaganda, there is no question that the Argentine Govt has fully compiled with its obligations under the acts of Mexico City in this field. The Embassy has already in despatches expressed this opinion and the Dept has indicated that it considers there has been satisfactory compliance in this respect. I find that the Argentine Govt continues its vigilance actively with respect to schools and institutions and propaganda and there are to our knowledge no known persons in Argentine schools propagating Nazi or Fascist doctrine.

2. With regard to enemy property, the recent decree of the Argentine Govt through which it takes possession of all enemy interests in any firms in the Argentine definitely cleans up this point of compliance which I understand is also the attitude of the Dept. We are forwarding a despatch listing 109 firms in which such enemy interest thus far has been definitely established. The Junta is investigating some further firms to determine whether enemy interests exist, but the action of the Govt has been so thoroughgoing that in our opinion only in rare instances will enemy interests be discovered by the Govt in firms not included in the list. The list transmitted covers all firms of any importance in which the British and we found any reason to believe there was any enemy interest.

---

[26] Miguel Miranda, President of the Central Bank of Argentina.

In this connection Miranda informed me that the Central Bank has deposited to the credit of the Junta an initial payment of 100,000,000 pesos as required by the decree in order finally and definitely to place ownership in the Govt. Miranda told the President in my presence that he expected to have the whole matter cleaned up in a relatively short time but that it would involve restitution by the Govt to the Junta of certain assets of the companies dissipated by interventors. In this respect that this has happened here is by no means an exclusive Argentine phenomenon because similar situations undoubtedly exist in connection with the action taken by other American govts in regard to enemy property. All this is now a matter for internal action by the Argentine Govt which has assumed in connection with enemy property complete responsibility and so far as we are concerned, the Argentine has complied with its Chapultepec obligations respecting such property. Undoubtedly there will be many suits instituted against the Govt but this is to be expected for we have the same kind of suits growing out of our procedure with respect to enemy property at home. It is my considered opinion that the action taken by the Argentine Govt is as definitive and complete action as that of any American country.

3. Regarding enemy aliens which is the only item of compliance on which action has not been altogether completed, this Embassy is of the opinion that with the action taken prior to the decree which has already been reported in detail to the Dept in despatches, and with the action which it has already taken and is taking under this decree with respect to deportation of 52 additional persons, the Argentine Govt will have adequately met its commitments under the acts of Mexico City in this respect.

Thirteen of these 52 have already been deported to Germany; three others are reliably reported to be outside the Argentine, two in Spain and one in Chile. A number of others are already under detention ready for deportation but no statement is presently being made by the govt with respect thereto to avoid writs of habeas corpus being secured for them. During the Feb 6 conversations with the President and the FonMin, I was informed of the extraordinary steps which the Govt is taking to apprehend the remainder. At the appropriate moment those whom it has been possible to locate and detain will be deported to Germany on an Argentine vessel which it is expected will leave within a maximum of several weeks, by which time it is hoped the principal persons now being sought will have been detained. There is no doubt whatsoever as to the extraordinary efforts the Govt is making in this respect or its complete good faith in endeavoring to find and deport these individuals.

It is my opinion that with the deportation to Germany of this further group, even though it may not have been possible by that time to localize and deport all, our Govt must recognize the good faith of the Argentine Govt in continuing its efforts in this regard, and the moment will have arrived for US to recognize that the Argentine has substantially and reasonably complied with its obligations respecting enemy aliens as we already have with respect to schools and institutions and property; and we should, referring to the Byrnes' statement of April 8, 1946 [27] state that we recognize that the Argentine Govt has met its obligations under the acts of Mexico City and that the way is open to the holding of the Rio meeting.

As I stated in the Dept during my recent visit the question of performance in my opinion must rest upon the good faith of the Argentine Govt in this matter and not upon whether every single one of those persons under deportation orders may have been apprehended. There is now sufficient evidence that the Argentine Govt is proceeding in this matter with all good faith and that it is determined to continue its efforts until the last one of these persons is found if in Argentine territory. We could not therefore delay the liquidation of the situation pending the deportation of the last of these persons as to do this would be unreasonable and completely out of accord with the attitude which we have taken respecting the other American Republics.

It is recognized that with the program already carried through, the Argentine Govt has shown as definite performance and good faith as most of the other American Republics.

British Ambassador Leeper called on me on Feb 4 and stated that under instructions of the British Govt the British Ambassador in Washington had informed the Dept that in the opinion of his Govt the Argentine Govt has taken appropriate action with respect to aliens, property and schools and institutions in which matters the British Govt has been collaborating with US.

The FonMin also told me that Leeper had called on him and advised him of the foregoing attitude of the British Govt.

The FonMin also stated that it was his understanding that the Colombian Govt and several other of the American Republics have informed our Govt that they consider the Argentine has with the steps taken met its obligations under the acts of Mexico City. Of this I have no further knowledge than the statement of the FonMin.

In a memo which I left with the Secretary prior to my return to the Argentine, I set forth fully the reasons why, in my opinion, it is desirable to liquidate this situation and to make a formal statement

---

[27] *Foreign Relations*, 1946, vol. XI, p. 10.

through the Dept by the end of this month to the effect that we are now prepared to attend the Rio meeting with Argentine participating. I have emphasized the importance of this in view of the fact that the other American countries are increasingly more restive under the continuance of the present status feeling that the Argentine has and is meeting its obligations under the acts of Mexico City. In that memo, I brought out some of the consequences which might result from further delay.

The continued statements in the press at home to the effect that the Argentine Govt is taking these compliance measures only in order to be able to secure arms from the US are not only seriously misinforming public opinion in the US but are disturbing factors in others of the American Republics where it is known that if this were the Argentine incentive, it could secure now arms from several sources.[28] It is, I believe, time that we recognize that there is a friendly Govt in the Argentine which is definitely desirous of putting its relations with US in order and in collaborating with US fully and sincerely in the American and international picture; and that its interest in the Rio meeting is not in the securing of arms but because it is convinced of the desirability and necessity of the defense pact and uniformity of training, equipment, and organization in the interest of all of the American Republics.

MESSERSMITH

835.00/2–747

Memorandum by the Assistant Secretary of State for American Republic Affairs (Braden) to the Under Secretary of State (Acheson)

SECRET [WASHINGTON,] February 10, 1947.

No purpose is to be served by a lengthy telegraphic confirmation of the Department's policy which was made clear to Ambassador Messersmith during his recent visit here:[29]

1. In respect of elimination of Axis schools and institutions, the Ambassador knows that some months ago the Department accepted Argentine performance in this field. Why labor the point further?

2. The recent decree purporting to place in the Argentine Government the full enemy titles to a large number of spearhead firms is progress toward compliance in the field of enemy property and we

---

[28] For documentation on the position of the United States with respect to supplying arms to Argentina, see pp. 215 ff.
[29] This memorandum was written as a result of the receipt of Ambassador Messersmith's telegram 134, February 7, *supra*.

so stated in our January 25 release.³⁰ At the appropriate time we will have to be assured that the action consists of something more than a mere paper decree—that all of the steps under such decree have been taken which are essential to a settlement of the decisive title and control question. We should also have a full and complete list of the spearhead firms falling under that decree (The Embassy has not sent this in.). No purpose is to be served in deciding the compliance question piecemeal and we should not finally and irrevocably commit ourselves on this point until we come to decide the question as a whole.

3. No final decision can be made in respect of enemy agents until the names and number actually deported are known.

On the question of good faith, it should be remembered that in his despatch No. 230 of June 25 1946 ³¹ Ambassador Messersmith reported that he was told by the Foreign Minister, when some 40 of the most important and dangerous German espionage agents were released, that the Argentine Government was "employing over 200 people to watch these (40) people and they were taking good care that nobody got beyond the jurisdiction of the court." It will also be remembered that, according to . . . reports, all of the Axis agents were warned in advance that their roundup by the police was eminent [*imminent*]; and Ambassador Messersmith reported that the leak was through the Police Department which was in charge of the roundup.

4. The British Government, which is not party to the Mexico City agreements, has merely said that Argentina "*is now fulfilling* its obligations in respect of enemy aliens, property and interests at least as well as the majority of Latin-American Governments". The British do not say—to use the language of the April 8 statement—that Argentina *has* performed with deeds and not promises.

5. Although there are doubtless American republics which for one reason or another would be willing to proceed with the Rio Conference irrespective of actual compliance, no official representation has been made to this Government by any American republic that Argentina has already complied, nor has this Government been under any pressure to proceed with the Rio Conference without compliance.

6. The basic issue of whether Argentina "is definitely desirous of . . . collaborating with US fully and sincerely in the American and international picture" is treated in a separate memorandum on Argentine policy now in the course of preparation. This issue is, of course, irrelevant to the immediate question since the Embassy and the Department are apparently still in agreement that there has as yet been no satisfactory compliance.

---

³⁰ Department of State *Bulletin*, February 2, 1947, p. 214.
³¹ *Foreign Relations*, vol. XI, p. 265.

7. There was no need whatever for the Embassy's lengthy message [32] which added nothing to our knowledge of the problem.

SPRUILLE BRADEN

835.00/2–2147

The Ambassador in Argentina (Messersmith) to the Secretary of State

[Extracts]

SECRET
No. 1883
SIR: . . .

BUENOS AIRES, February 21, 1947.

. . . .

I am sure that the Department will agree that in view of the character of the January 1947 decree, the manner in which the Argentine Government handles this matter of enemy property now becomes a purely internal concern of the Argentine just as the way in which we handle property under the Alien Property Custodian in the United States is a matter solely of our concern. The Argentine Government has made itself responsible. In this connection, I am sure that the Department will not assume an attitude that we can expect more rapid progress in so difficult a matter as final disposition of some of these firms than we can take at home through the Alien Property Custodian. I will not enter into any details but I am sure the Department is aware that the Alien Property Custodian while having taken possession in the name of our Government of certain German-owned firms has not yet proceeded with the liquidation of some of them. This does not mean that the Alien Property Custodian will not eventually proceed with the liquidation or adequate reorganization of such firms.

. . . .

There remains, therefore, only the completion of the program with respect to enemy aliens on which program the Argentine Government is energetically engaged. The Embassy will keep the Department fully informed of further concrete action of the Argentine Government in this matter.

It is not clear to me what it is desired to convey by the sentence in the Department's telegram no. 112 of February 12, 8 p. m., 1947, to the effect that "we do not understand that Argentina has yet met the

---

[32] The Department replied in telegram 112, February 12, 8 p. m., as follows: "We do not understand that Argentina has yet met the test (urtel 134, Feb. 7). We shall accordingly await developments. In the meantime please report on names of firms actually taken over under January decree and steps taken to assume full control thereof." (835.00/2–747)

test".[33] I thoroughly appreciate that so far as the program of enemy aliens is concerned, there are further steps which the Argentine Government should and must take. I do not know whether the sentence quoted refers to the completion of the program of enemy aliens. I would appreciate any clarification which the Department can give me as it is desirable for my guidance here.

Respectfully yours, GEORGE S. MESSERSMITH

840.35112 RP/1-3147

The Acting Secretary of State to the Ambassador in Argentina (Messersmith)

CONFIDENTIAL   WASHINGTON, March 6, 1947.
No. 600

SIR: Reference is made to your despatch no. 1779-A of January 31, 1947 entitled "Final Disposition of Enemy Property in Argentina". In view of the terms of the April 8 statement of policy, the Department wishes to be absolutely certain that the act of promulgating decree no. 1921 of January 24 amounts to something more than a written promise to purchase Axis property at sometime in the future—that all of the steps necessary to convert the decree into reality have actually been taken.

The Department understands from your reports that the enemy property decree contemplates:

(a) that the full and complete enemy titles to the spearhead firms will first be firmly and unconditionally placed in the Argentine Government which undertakes that the interests purchased will not be returned or sold to the former enemy owners; and

(b) that the Argentine Government, as the full owner of the enemy interests, will then establish procedures for dealing with questions of evaluation, compensation, operation and sale.

Please advise the Department promptly if this understanding of the decree and its operation and effect are incorrect in any particular.

In respect of foregoing paragraph (a), the Department would be pleased to receive a report on the precise steps which must be taken before the decree is implemented in the sense that the full and complete enemy titles to spearhead firms are firmly and unconditionally placed in the State. Presumably, the actual deposits of the purchase money are required and there may be other legal requirements such as registration which may be regarded as conditions precedent to the unconditional passing of title.

---

[33] See footnote 32, p. 178.

Further in respect of foregoing paragraph (*a*), the Department is conducting a study of the lists of business enterprises listed in your despatch [34] which are to be brought under the terms of the new Argentine Enemy Property Decree in order to determine whether there is adequate coverage of spearhead firms.

To the extent that the steps outlined in paragraph (*b*) above are carried out in a manner which is consistent with Argentina's Inter-American commitments, the Department agrees that these steps are internal Argentine matters.

Very truly yours, For the Acting Secretary of State:
WILLARD L. THORP

740.35112 RP/1-3147

The Acting Secretary of State to the Ambassador in Argentina (Messersmith)

SECRET   WASHINGTON, March 13, 1947.
No. 619

SIR: Reference is made to your despatch No. 1883 of February 21, 1947 concerning compliance.

There is no longer any question concerning the matter of enemy schools and institutions.

It is not possible for the Department to say definitely at this time whether there has been compliance in respect of property. It will be necessary to know what steps are required to be taken under the recent property decree in order to place the enemy titles firmly in the State; and whether the necessary legal steps have been taken in the cases of the 109 firms listed in your despatch No. 1779–A of January 31, 1947. In this connection reference is made to the Department's instruction No. 600 of March 6, 1947 which is consistent with the January 21, 1947 memorandum of conversation with Mr. Braden:

"The Ambassador inquired whether the Department would consider Argentine performance adequate in the field of property if that Government should proceed with its plans to acquire title to enemy interests in a total of about 75 spearhead firms. Mr. Braden replied that it would be necessary to study whatever decrees might be issued by the Argentine Government and to determine whether full and complete title of the enemy owners was in the Argentine Government—whether the proposed Argentine decree would have substantially the same effect as our own vesting laws; and to determine also whether there were any firms in addition to the 75 which ought to be dealt with."

---

[34] Despatch 1779–A, January 31, p. 172; lists omitted from despatch as printed.

Since the names and number of the Axis agents now being held for deportation as well as the names and number of those which presumably will soon be apprehended and deported are not known, the Department is unable to form any opinion on the question of compliance with respect of persons.

It is hoped that the Argentine Government will soon give reasonable and substantial compliance. The sentence in the Department's telegram No. 112 of February 12, 1947, to which you refer, was only intended to mean that until there has been reasonable and substantial compliance the Department does not understand that Argentina has met the test laid down in the April 8 statement on Argentine policy.

Very truly yours, For the Acting Secretary of State:
SPRUILLE BRADEN

740.35112 RP/3–1847

The Ambassador in Argentina (Messersmith) to the Secretary of State

[Extracts]

CONFIDENTIAL BUENOS AIRES, March 18, 1947.
No. 2092

SIR: . . .

. . . .

The text of Decree No. 1921 of January 24, 1947, was forwarded with the Embassy's Despatch No. 1741 of January 28, 1947.[35] Subsequently with the Embassy's Despatch No. 1985 of March 5 [35] above referred to there was transmitted to the Department the text of a *Note Verbale* received from the Foreign Ministry discussing the decree and setting forth its broad application. It is the opinion of this Embassy that, through the decree in question, the Argentine acquired, as of the date thereof, *en bloc*, all rights, titles and interests theretofore belonging to enemy nationals; and this view is confirmed by the statements of the Ministry of Foreign Affairs in its note referred to above. The down payment of 100 million Argentine pesos effected by the Argentine Government through the medium of the Banco Central was provided to meet the legal difficulties impeding acquisition under the Argentine Constitution and law by the State, without compensatory value. As reported in the Embassy's Despatch No. 2049 of March 13, 1947,[35] also referred to above, public announcement has been made through an official statement of the Argentine Government of the payment of the

---

[35] Not printed.

amount in question, which actual payment and transfer is believed to have actually taken place some days earlier as it is not unusual for statements of the Bank to follow the act by some days.

The Argentine Government has informed this Embassy orally during the discussions of this matter that, should the value of the property taken over, or to be taken over later as the result of further investigation, exceed in value the amount of 100 million pesos, such further sums will be paid by the Argentine Government as the facts indicate.

There is, therefore, no question under Argentine law and procedure and therefore no question which we could raise with reference to the acquisition by the Argentine Government of the right, title and interests of such property belonging to enemy nationals. It is not improbable that certain suits may be entered against the Argentine Government by enemy nationals for the restitution, in whole or in part, of their property, but there is no reason to believe that, in view of the laws and decrees of the Argentine, such property would be restored to such aliens unless it were conclusively proved that there had been a mistake of identity or an improper seizure. So far as this is concerned, the situation is the same as that which prevails and will prevail in any of the United Nations which have taken such equally definite and complete action with respect to enemy property.

In the Department's Instruction No. 600 [37] under reference, it is stated that the Department understands that the "Argentine Government . . . undertakes that the interest purchased will not be returned or sold to the former enemy owners." As it appears that the Department has some concern in this respect, it will be noted that the preamble to Decree No. 1921 specifically recites the obligations in virtue of Resolutions 18 and 19 of the Inter-American Conference on Problems of War and Peace and, to whatever extent such Resolutions govern the ultimate disposition of enemy property there would seem to be no reason to assume or to believe that they will not be strictly observed.

It will be further observed that Decree No. 1921 refers specifically to the Decree No. 11599/46 on which it heavily depends, and which latter decree was reported in the Embassy's despatch No. 2713 of May 8, 1946.[38] In said Decree No. 11599/46, specific provision is made in [*and*] reference is made to the eligibility of prospective purchasers to acquire former enemy property, as follows:

"Article 10. Properties offered for sale may be acquired only:
"*a*) By the State, provinces, municipalities, or self-governing subdivisions.

---

[37] Dated March 6, p. 179.
[38] Not printed.

"*b*) By native Argentine citizens or citizens naturalized prior to September 3, 1939, who have not belonged to the directorates or high technical or administrative personnel of an enterprise subject to this Decree.

"*c*) By legal entities organized in the Republic in which persons falling within sub-section *b*) predominate. In the case of corporations, they must be organized in the Republic and a majority of their capital stock must be locally subscribed and must belong to persons falling within sub-section *b*)."

To the extent indicated above, provision has been made to prevent the reacquisition by former enemy owners. The Embassy is not, however, aware of any "undertaking", either unilateral or on the international level, on this point, nor is the Embassy so far informed of the Department's views of the matter as to understand that the April 8 Statement of Policy has been extended to envisage or to require such undertaking. It is not believed that the Department has any such specific undertaking in mind, for it would be something required by us from another country and not covered by international or Inter-American Agreements and, therefore, a procedure which would be obnoxious if applied to any specific country other than an enemy country.

. . . .

Respectfully yours, GEORGE S. MESSERSMITH

711.35/3–3147

The Ambassador in Argentina (Messersmith) to the Secretary of State

[Extracts]

SECRET BUENOS AIRES, March 31, 1947.
No. 2119

SIR: I have the honor to make the following report on a conversation which I had some days ago with the Foreign Minister, Dr. Bramuglia, on Wednesday evening, March 19, 1947, in the Foreign Office. I had asked for a conversation with the Minister in order to receive from him the latest information with regard to the activities of the Argentine Government in the matter of enemy aliens. . . .

. . . .

The Minister then went on to say that they had taken action in the field of schools and institutions not on the basis of what other countries had done in this hemisphere but on the basis of what should be done for safety and security. They had carried through this action in the fields of Axis schools and institutions as adequately as that taken in any of the American republics if not more adequately than in most of them. Whatever step had been necessary in this field, they had already taken and carried through and as I knew they were watchful of any activity which anyone might attempt in this field.

In the field of enemy property, the Minister said that they had taken the appropriate and adequate action. I knew of the difficulties which had been in the way and with which the Government had had to deal and that I had been and was in a position, as were the other Chiefs of Mission of the American republics, to see the action which the Argentine Government was taking with respect to enemy property. To resolve the problem and to clear away certain difficulties, the Government had accelerated the solution of enemy property through the decree of January 1947 through which the Government took over all enemy property in the Argentine. He said that his Government was familiar with what had been done elsewhere in the matter of enemy property and there was not a question of making any comparisons because each state was responsible for its action but that there was no doubt that the Argentine Government had carried through completely adequate action in the field of enemy property, had met its commitments under the Mexico City agreements and that he believed that any objective study of the situation would show that the Argentine had presently gone further than any of the American countries except the United States and Canada and that in many respects under similar programs had gone as far in the actual liquidation or reorganization, or elimination as we.

There remained only this matter of enemy aliens, and I must be familiar from my own observation and from the constant contact which I had had with the President and him and high officials of the Argentine Government and which the officers of this Embassy and of the British Embassy had had with the appropriate officials of the Argentine Government that they had been and were doing everything they could in this field since the present administration took office in June 1946. I was familiar with what the Argentine Government had done prior to the last decree of 1946 covering 52 enemy aliens. He was sure that my Government was familiar with what had been done in this field up to the time of the issuance of that decree, and he thought that the record was more impressive than they had been given credit for by the press. He said that the Argentine Government had carefully examined all the lists of names submitted by this Embassy and the British Embassy which included over 600 names. These lists had been submitted by this Embassy and by the British Embassy as covering the names of those persons concerning whom we had any information whatever, and the Argentine Government appreciated this collaboration as on the basis of it they had been able to make further investigations of their own. He stated that the Argentine Government had not been content with merely basing its investigation on the information given by the British Embassy and ourselves but had engaged in its own independent investigations which had covered many persons not on our lists.

In order to clear this matter up definitely, appropriate officials of the Argentine Government, as I knew, had examined all the names covered by our lists and the British and their own, and they had found that of all the persons against whom any information could be established as having committed acts against the state or the United Nations, there remained only 52 against whom appropriate action had not been taken. He observed that in examining these lists they had erred on the side of being too exigent rather than otherwise and that the last list of 52 included all remaining persons against whom there was any information in any way adequate to justify deportation.

He said that they had, therefore, issued deportation decrees against these 52 persons, and he recalled to me that he had in confidence informed me of the extraordinary steps which were taken by the police to make sure that all of these 52 were apprehended. Special squads had been organized in order to take immediate action against all 52. In spite of these extraordinary steps, information had undoubtedly leaked out and it was only possible to apprehend at the outset a certain number of them. They had prepared an Argentine ship to take them out of the country immediately to Germany in order to avoid possibility of writs of habeas corpus being granted by unfriendly courts but in spite of this of the number that they had secured a certain number were able to secure writs of habeas corpus before the S.S. *Pampa* left so that only 13 of the 52 were actually deported and were now in Germany.

He said that since the departure of the *Pampa*, the activities of the police had been redoubled and every possible effort had been and was being made to find these men. He said that in addition to the activities of the police in the capital and throughout the country, the facilities of the Army were being used where there were posts and special squads had been organized to go to parts of the country where it was felt that the most complete collaboration of the local police might not be given. He said that he could inform me in confidence that they now had eight whom they were ready to send out. Among them was Harnisch and several other really important ones. They were making every conceivable effort to get the rest. They were spending thousands of pesos every day in this search. They were somewhat discouraged because in spite of their best efforts, they had not yet been able to get all of these people.

He went on to say that there was no doubt in his opinion and that of high Argentine officials that some of these men had been able to get to the south of Chile where they were being harbored among the thousands of Germans there. He said that others may have got to Bolivia or Paraguay and probably some others to the south of Brazil where there are so many Germans among whom they could merge their identity. They were carrying on their efforts in spite of their discouragement because they realized that the Government must make every effort to get these people but that there were such, what now appeared to be, insuperable difficulties.

. . . .

Respectfully yours, GEORGE S. MESSERSMITH

711.35/4–247 : Telegram

The Acting Secretary of State to the Embassy in Argentina

SECRET WASHINGTON, April 2, 1947—6 p. m.

252. For the secret information of the Ambassador. The President requested Amb Ivanissevich [39] to call at White House at 5:30 P.M. on Mar 31, at which time he was received by the President, Senators Vandenberg and Connally [40] and the ActSecy of State.

Indicating that he had always been desirous of most friendly relations with Arg people and Govt and that he regarded it important that relations be on firm foundations, the President regretted that there had been difficulties between two countries which had taken some time to work out. Progress had been made in solving most of problems and there remained now only matter of deporting some 20 to 30 dangerous Nazi agents who remained in Arg. The President heard Amb Ivanissevich was returning to Arg for a month and wanted him to stress to President Perón the earnest desire that this action be taken promptly.

The Arg Amb then asserted that there were no Nazis in Arg and that it was calumny to say there were; the President must be referring to some Arg citizens whose cases were in the courts. President Truman immediately replied that this was not his information and that he was referring to German agents. Mr. Acheson then said that the Amb was perhaps uninformed of fact that there were German agents

---

[39] Argentine Ambassador in the United States.
[40] Senator Tom Connally, member of the Senate Foreign Relations Committee.

still undeported and that the President had reference to perhaps 20 or 30 of most important of these.

The President said that he had endeavored to make his position fully clear and he hoped that the Amb would in turn make it clear to President Perón. He was speaking for entire Amer Govt. Senators Connally and Vandenberg and ActSecy of State were present so that there would be no doubt on this score. Both Connally and Vandenberg stated they supported the President's position.[41]

The President terminated interview and the two Senators and ActSecy of State accompanied the Amb to White House door. At this time the ActSecy again stressed fact that there were some 20 to 30 dangerous Nazi agents in Arg, that their presence was well known to Arg Govt, and that it was these people about whom the President had spoken so seriously.

It was made clear and understood by all present that interview was entirely off the record and was not to be mentioned except to President Perón.

The Dept wanted you to have this important information coincidentally with arrival in Buenos Aires of Amb Ivanissevich. If you are approached by the responsible Arg authorities in this matter, you should confirm this Govt's position as outlined above.

ACHESON

711.35/4–1147

The Ambassador in Argentina (Messersmith) to the Acting Secretary of State

[Extracts]

SECRET   BUENOS AIRES, April 11, 1947.

DEAR DEAN: . . .

. . . .

The Minister then said that Ivanissevich had seen the President on Sunday, April 6, before the President's departure for his visit to Mendoza where he presently is. He said that Ivanissevich had communicated to President Perón a message from President Truman and then went on to give me the substance of the message. The Minister said that under instructions of the President, Ivanissevich had conveyed the substance of the message to him the night before.

Last night Ivanissevich came in to see me at the Embassy and told me about the conversation with President Truman and you all at the

---

[41] Senator Connally represented the Democratic Party and Senator Vandenberg the Republican Party.

White House and of his conversation with the President here when he communicated the message of President Truman and also with the Foreign Minister.

I have not seen President Perón since he received this message through Ivanissevich from President Truman as the President has been at Mendoza for almost a week and will not return until tomorrow. I do not, therefore, have his direct personal reactions or observations, but he will undoubtedly ask me to come to see him early next week.

The Foreign Minister informs me that the President is very much pleased with this initiative on the part of our Government and with the message conveyed by Ivanissevich from President Truman. He is particularly appreciative of the interest shown by the President and you all and of the fact that the President in his conversation with Ivanissevich indicated that for the composition of the situation there remains only this action with regard to enemy aliens. The President is very much gratified that our Government recognizes that in the matter of schools and institutions and property, the Argentine Government has carried through loyally and effectively and so far as enemy aliens are concerned, the Foreign Minister said that the President is quite understanding of what President Truman said concerning these of the list of 52 with respect to which action still has to be taken.

· · · · · · · ·

He said that I would appreciate that no matter what their concern over this matter was and their desire to get these people immediately and no matter how much they appreciated President Truman's message, he did not see how they could augment their efforts to get these people because they had for some months been doing all they could to get them and that I must know this because I had information from them and undoubtedly through my own sources as to what they were doing. He said he did not know how many they would be able to get, but that one thing our Government could be assured of and that was that no one was more interested in getting every one of these people than they were.

I remarked to the Minister that it was unfortunate that Dr. Ivanissevich had not been better informed concerning this matter of enemy aliens as the statement which he made to President Truman showed that he had not been adequately informed concerning this matter. The Minister said that this was unfortunate but that he had been under the impression that Ivanissevich was being currently informed and that in any event, it was unfortunate that Ivanissevich should have said to President Truman that there were no more of these Nazi agents in the Argentine when the Argentine Government knew that some of them were still here and was making these strenuous efforts to get them. It was unfortunate that Ivanissevich had not been better informed and he could not understand that. He said that Ivanissevich was a very honest and sincere man and so thoroughly interested in the most friendly relations between the two countries that he would not make any misstatements and that he was, therefore, resting under a misapprehension when he made this observation about there being no Nazis left in the country.

. . . .

Believe me, with all good wishes,
    Cordially and faithfully yours,   GEORGE S. MESSERSMITH

862.20235/4–1847

Mr. Donald R. Heath, Chargé in the Office of the United States Political Adviser on German Affairs, to the Secretary of State

SECRET   BERLIN, April 18, 1947.
No. 9610

SIR: With reference to the Department's telegram no. 3055 of December 28, 1946,[42] and to subsequent correspondence regarding the thirteen deportees from Buenos Aires who arrived aboard the Argentine naval transport *Pampa*, I have the honor to report that the interrogation of the thirteen has been finished. . . .

The prisoners were fairly cooperative after some initial resistance in certain cases—notably in that of Harmeyer—and by the end of the questioning the interrogator had the impression that they had not withheld salient facts. All resented the treatment they had received from the Argentines and considered they had been made scapegoats for the bigger men who escaped deportation; but they knew few concrete facts regarding the true relationships between the latter and Argentine officialdom. The SD people were especially resentful, also, of the special treatment accorded in jail to Johannes Siegfried Becker and Gustav Utzinger.[43]

There follows an advance summary, in abbreviated form, of such information as could be gathered concerning the seven topics outlined in the Department's telegraphic instruction under reference. The interrogator was somewhat handicapped by a lack of background information regarding recent happenings in Argentina—notably con-

---

[42] Not printed.
[43] For details concerning these persons, see Department of State, *Consultation Among the American Republics With Respect to the Argentine Situation* (Washington, 1946).

cerning the habeas corpus proceedings of June, 1946, and the events leading up to the deportation in December.

. . . .

2. *Reasons why important agents were not deported; possibility that Argentines warned them in advance; degree of police interrogation on the whereabouts of the fugitives:*
Considerable time was spent on this subject. The deportees' resentment lent a favorable psychological clime for revelations, but they themselves were *ipso facto* those who were warned too late or not at all, wherefore their knowledge of what transpired among the higher-ups could only be from hearsay. It could be established that the person chiefly responsible for the mechanics of warning the SD group was Dr. Octavio Rivarola, the lawyer who represented them in the habeas corpus proceedings. Becker, Rivarola and Vilches were in regular contact from June, 1946, until Becker's flight to avoid deportation. Prieto asserted that he was in Rivarola's office at least ten days before his (Prieto's) arrest on November 17, and that Rivarola's secretary warned him then to go into hiding. Interrogation disclosed that the first public announcements were made on November 14–15, wherefore Rivarola definitely had advance notice and was advising his clients to flee. From him the word was apparently spread in chain form: Harmeyer was told by Szeraws; Manfrini by Seraphin; Amorín was to have been told by Ilvento, but had moved and learned only by chance at Maubach's place of business; Frank Langer also knew of the projected measures before the decree was signed, according to Amorín; Ullrich learned only by calling at Utzinger's house to find the latter had fled, having been advised by Treutler.

The consensus of opinion among the prisoners had it that Rivarola's information came either from Rodriguez or from young Freude, or from both: but none had concrete information to this effect. Schwaiger asserted that Becker and Utzinger boasted the Argentines would not dare deport them because they knew too much—not necessarily about Perón himself but about those around him.

Upon being picked up for deportation, only Harmeyer of the whole group was subject to anything more than a superficial interrogation regarding the whereabouts of the others.

3. *Assurances that the deportees might avoid repatriation or later return to Argentina:*
All prisoners were emphatically negative on this point—in fact, most of them had been arrested in an unnecessarily inconsiderate manner and many were shipped without money or clothing. Schwaiger, however, told of certain assurances to Chantrain by the Honorary Consul of Luxemburg (Tornquist?) that he would not be repatriated.

Chantrain apparently managed to keep most of the money he had brought to Argentina for espionage purposes in June 1944, and used some of it for bribery and some to set himself up in business.

4. *Assistance furnished by members of the German colony:*
Direct aid comprised only the regular food, cigarettes and pin-money gifts sent into the jail regularly by the community, which aid tapered to nothing by early 1946. When this ended, the prisoners earned expense-money by making leather goods, which they sold through their relatives outside. Mueller, in a different category, received about 6,000 pesos in aid from the German Welfare Society, but upon his release he was informed he owed the society that money and could have no more.

No evidence was found of aid by individuals of the colony. However, there was a certain contact between Becker and Ludwig Freude after the former's release in June 1946, according to Amorín and Harmeyer. The former stated that Becker was extremely annoyed when Amorín repeated the story of the Freude meeting, saying it might cause trouble if the story got around.

5. *Source of funds for lawyers, court fees, et cetera:*
Excepting for Amorín, who was defended gratis by his friend Arrego Tassoni, all the SD group was included in a group-defense by Rivarola, arranged by Becker. Schwaiger said Becker paid Rivarola 60,000 pesos, or one-third of the 180,000 pesos impounded at Becker's arrest and returned upon his release. Werner Koennecke also paid Rivarola from 2,000 to 2,500 pesos for Schwaiger's defense, while Leitner's wife sent the lawyer 500 pesos.

Mueller, of the Abwehr, and tried in another connection, was represented by a Dr. Bustamante at the instance of German Consulate, which paid the latter some 10,000 pesos for the defense of Mueller, Schneider, Napp, and Freiwald and entrusted him with 8,000 pesos for their bail. The Consulate also contributed 2,000 pesos for the support of Mueller's family while he was in jail.

6. *Means of livelihood during former and recent liberty:*
These are given in some detail in each man's statement, but nothing suspicious is evident. The regular SD workers were paid by SD funds; the rest had regular occupations. Ullrich, after his release, joined Utzinger and Leeb to form a small radio-parts company in the suburb of Punta Chica: through Utzinger's close connections with Captain Rodriguez they were half-promised government contracts, which hope, however, eventually came to naught.

Rolland's ample funds, mentioned by the Department, came from his multifarious business deals, for which the original capital was furnished by the Abwehr but which he carried out on his own after 1942.

7. *Specific assistance by Axis firms:*

None of the prisoners was important enough in his business firm to know of any but obvious help such as the Winterhilfswerk; excepting for Voelckers, who insisted he knew of no other than this regular help in the case of Clarfeld. Ullrich's position was purely technical, although relatively high: his orders to help Utzinger came from Berlin.

The individual affidavits and interrogation reports will follow in the order of their importance.

Respectfully yours,

DONALD R. HEATH

711.35/3–3147 : Telegram

The Acting Secretary of State to the Embassy in Argentina

SECRET   WASHINGTON, April 23, 1947—11 a. m.
US URGENT

332. Reurlet Apr 3 [44] to Acheson and Desp 2119, Mar 31. Dept considers that issuance of Arg Govt statement would seriously prejudice the chances of a satisfactory solution of this problem by freezing the Arg position and agitating press debate here.

Purpose of White House meeting was to impress on Arg Govt importance of expulsion of most important Nazi agents. While we realistically expect only "reasonable and substantial" compliance we do expect that performance will be genuine on its face and meet the test of deeds and not merely promises set out in Byrnes' Apr 8 statement.[45]

Whether Arg assertion that agents in hiding are actually beyond reach of Arg police is true is a question concerning which we have considerable doubt. Pertinent to this question is fact that, according to Arg FonMin, at the time the approximately 40 dangerous agents were released from custody they were put under strictest kind of surveillance, about 200 persons having been assigned to assure their availability at all times. Not only were Nazi agents apparently able to escape this surveillance but they were warned in advance—probably through leak from Police Dept itself—that their arrest was imminent.

ACHESON

---

[44] Not printed.
[45] A marginal note initialed by Acting Secretary Acheson reads: "A good performance on deporting the more important individuals in the list of 52 would do this."

862.20235/5-747 : Telegram

The Secretary of State to the Embassy in Argentina

SECRET WASHINGTON, May 7, 1947—8 p. m.

395. For the Ambassador from the Secretary. Since my return I have discussed with the President White House meeting with Ivanissevich. I have read your communications and Mr. Acheson's telegram to you (Deptel 332 of Apr 23). Our approach to President Perón through Argentine Ambassador was highly conciliatory and I am therefore disturbed that Argentine Govt has not quickly cleaned up this matter by deporting the 20 to 30 dangerous agents mentioned by the President.

It is necessary that the highest Argentine officials understand importance of apprehending and actually deporting these agents so that our Govt will be in a position to state that there has been substantial compliance with agreements. You are instructed to make this unmistakably clear to Argentine Govt.

Telegraph immediately the names of the enemy agents Argentine Govt has already apprehended but has not yet deported and submit regular telegraphic reports.

MARSHALL

862.20235/5-747

The Ambassador in Argentina (Messersmith) to the Secretary of State

[Extracts]

SECRET BUENOS AIRES, May 7, 1947.
No. 2462

Subject: Action of the Argentine Government in the Matter of Compliance with Its Obligations Undertaken Through Adherence to the Acts of Mexico City, and with Specific Reference to the Statement of Former Secretary Byrnes of April 8, 1946.

SIR: . . .

. . . .

I am addressing the Department on this matter at this time for two reasons.

First, it is the opinion of this Embassy that as the Argentine Government has carried through and is loyally continuing to carry through its obligations with respect to schools, institutions, and propaganda and enemy property, and has done so in a very effective manner and one which does it credit, and as in the matter of enemy aliens who have committed acts against the state and the United Nations it has shown its complete good faith since the constitutional government came into office in June, 1946 in endeavoring to find and deport such aliens and has with this second lot included in the list of 52 sent out of the country all those on which it can lay hands, the time has come when as a matter of equity alone and recognition of the performance of the Argentine Government for our Government to make an appropriate statement removing the reserves expressed by former Secretary Byrnes in his statement of April 8, 1946. The Department is aware from the reports of this Embassy that the British Embassy, which has been following this matter with this Embassy so closely during the war and until recently, is in complete accord and has already indicated that so far as it and the British Government are concerned, it is considered that the Argentine has carried through its obligations.

I will not in this despatch recite the measures which the Argentine Government has taken in the matter of endeavoring to apprehend and deport all of these enemy aliens against whom anything like adequate information has been determined. I can only repeat what I have said in my previous despatches and letters, that I and my associates who have been following this matter in every aspect so closely are convinced that the Argentine Government has used all of the effective means at its disposal in order to apprehend the remainder of these aliens and that its failure up to this time to apprehend all of them in the list of 52 is not due to any negligence on its part or to lack of any zeal or efficiency. Under these circumstances, this Embassy is of the opinion and is of the hope that the President and the Department will be of the opinion that upon the deportation of those whom it has been able to apprehend our Government will be in a position to completely normalize the relations with the Argentine by removing the reserves which we have had with respect to sitting down in the Rio meeting to formulate a defense pact with the Argentine present. There is, in the opinion of this Embassy, no doubt whatever that the Argentine Government will continue its efforts to find those of these remaining aliens in the list.

. . . .

The second reason I am transmitting this despatch at this time is because yesterday the Foreign Minister in a conversation in the Foreign Office informed me that Ambassador Ivanissevich is leaving for Washington to resume his duties there on May 9 and that he will carry a message to President Truman in reply to the communication which President Truman sent to President Perón. The Minister said that Ambassador Ivanissevich would be instructed to express to

President Truman President Perón's appreciation and understanding of President Truman's constructive action. He would carry with him a list of the additional aliens included in the list of 52 whom it has been possible with the best efforts of the Government to apprehend and who will be deported in the relatively near future on an Argentine vessel to Germany. He will be instructed to say that with the best efforts and the use of all the means at its disposal the Argentine Government has not been able to apprehend all of these aliens but that it will continue these efforts and that in the meantime such persons are completely sterilized for if they would show their heads or engage in any activities in the Argentine, their presence would become immediately known and they would be apprehended and deported.

The Foreign Minister said yesterday that a ship was ready to take those whom they had been able to apprehend and that the day after its departure he would make a statement to the press merely to the effect that the ship had left with these additional aliens on board which the Government had been able to apprehend and that it was continuing its efforts to secure the remainder.

. . . .

Respectfully yours, GEORGE S. MESSERSMITH

362.20235/5–847

The Ambassador in Argentina (Messersmith) to the Secretary of State

[Extracts]

SECRET BUENOS AIRES, May 8, 1947.

MY DEAR MR. SECRETARY: Anticipating that shortly after your return from Moscow you would be able to give consideration to this matter of the Argentine and our problems in this hemisphere, and to the Rio meeting, and as the Argentine has really with the steps she has taken and is taking completed her compliance under the Acts of México City, I wrote a despatch yesterday making recommendations to the Department for your consideration of which I enclose a copy (no. 2462 of May 7, 1947).[46] I had dictated a letter to you in which I sent you some observations I thought would be of interest to you, but this morning when the letter was given me for signature there arrived your telegram no. 395 of May 7, 8 p. m., 1947, stating that since your return to Washington you have discussed with President Truman his meeting with the Argentine Ambassador, Dr. Ivanissevich, at the White House. In view of this telegram, I am writing you this letter

---

[46] *Supra.*

instead of the one I had dictated yesterday, as we have a confidential pouch leaving tomorrow.

. . . .

I do not recall in all my service for our Government any situation in a country which has been so misrepresented before our public opinion. This is due to a variety of factors. I cannot in this letter enter into any details, but I have endeavored, and my associates have endeavored, to keep the Department fully informed concerning all that is happening in this country. What we must recognize is that the Argentine Government today is the first government of the Argentine for years to concern itself with some of the fundamental social, economic, and financial problems which previous governments had neglected. We have to recognize that the present Government was constitutionally elected in as fair an election as has been held in the Argentine. We have to recognize that whatever inefficiency, corruption, and inadequacies exist here do not differ from the situation which prevailed under previous Argentine governments and which unfortunately prevails in others of the American republics. Great changes are taking place in the country, but they are long over-due in most respects, and they fit into the times. The Argentine Government has in the political and economic fields as well as in the social field taken some measures which have gone too far, but the pendulum is already swinging back. . . .

. . . .

But what is more important than this is that the Argentine has not and cannot have any aggressive intentions against any of its neighbors. As President Perón has well put it, if the Argentine had any such aggressive intentions it has the money to buy arms in Europe and can get them, and that if it had such aggressive intentions it would certainly not be so eager for the defense pact, for the defense pact will mean not only common action of the American republics against an extra-hemisphere aggressor but against one in this hemisphere. He has frequently remarked to me that if the Argentine had these aggressive intentions it would certainly do everything it could against the defense pact instead of being for it.

I do not know why we are continuing to stress in some quarters that the Argentine has this aim towards a southern bloc and has aggressive intentions against neighbors. As a matter of fact, the present Argentine Government is the first one which has not had in the back of its mind a southern bloc, and one of the principal difficulties which President Perón has is with the extreme nationalists who have removed their support from him because they know he considers this southern bloc idea politically and economically unwise and infeasible.

. . . .

Cordially and faithfully yours,　　　　　George S. Messersmith

862.20235/5–847 : Telegram

The Ambassador in Argentina (Messersmith) to the Secretary of State

SECRET　　　　　　　　　　Buenos Aires, May 8, 1947—1 p. m.

552. Foreign Minister informed me May 6 Ivanissevich leaving by air May 9. Ivanissevich called this morning to say good-bye stating leaving morning May 9, spending 2 days Lima with family, arriving Washington May 14 or 15.

Ivanissevich stated will lunch President today to receive final instructions, and sees Bramuglia tonight same purpose. Foreign Minister has informed me Ivanissevich will carry message from President Perón to President Truman and will ask to see you soon as possible after arrival.

Argentine Government, as stated my letters April 3, 11, 18, 25 to Acheson,[47] is deeply appreciative and understanding of important message from President Truman. It has wished to convey reply through Ivanissevich on his return and in meantime has been continuing its all-out efforts to apprehend remaining aliens. President Perón and highest officials Argentine Government have constantly reiterated their desire to deport all these people whom they wish to get rid of as much as we. They also understand how important it is from our point of view that they get all possible. Concerning this there is no doubt for I should reiterate we are familiar with broad measures Government has been taking and with their concern that efforts last few weeks have not brought greater results.

Foreign Minister informed me May 6 they have delayed actual deportation those apprehended since last deportation of 13 in order to get as many as possible before sending out ship, departure of which is imminent. With reference to concern over delay which you express, I can assure you that delay is due only to Argentine Government's desire to get every one possible as it considers this most important.

For reasons mentioned my letters and reports have not asked for names of 10 or 11 ready deportation but understand include Harnisch and other major individuals. Will secure list those actually arrested and awaiting deportation today and will telegraph.

---

[47] None printed, except extracts from the letter of April 11, p. 187.

I prepared full despatch on this matter yesterday before receipt Deptel 395, May 7, under reply which goes forward confidential pouch Friday night (despatch No. 2462 [48]).

MESSERSMITH

862.20235/5-847 : Telegram

The Secretary of State to the Embassy in Argentina

SECRET   WASHINGTON, May 9, 1947—3 p. m.

404. For Ambassador from Secretary. Re your 552 and 395, your next to last paragraph evidently refers to 10 or 11 individuals who were already in a state of arrest at the time of the President's conciliatory statement to Ivanissevich. The instructions to you in my 395 referred to additional individuals and I desire you to proceed immediately on that basis as directed in next to last paragraph of my message. Acknowledge and report when this is done.

If the Argentine Ambassador's report to the President indicates as appears evident that there has been little or no actual change in the situation then the chances for a conciliatory adjustment will have been seriously diminished.

MARSHALL

862.20235/5-947 : Telegram

The Ambassador in Argentina (Messersmith) to the Secretary of State

SECRET   BUENOS AIRES, May 9, 1947—8 p. m.

567. Foreign Minister informed me today that following aliens included deportation decree November 15, 1946, are under detention and will be deported shortly:

1. Juan Harnisch, German, considered one of the two most important German agents who operated Latin America.
2. Alfonso Chantrain, Luxemburger, considered important.
3. Gustavo Utzinger, German, considered important.
4. Enrique Richter, German, considered important.
5. Juan Lieberth, probably possessing German-Chilean dual citizenship.
6. Ana Sommermeyer, Polish.
7. Alberto Treusch, German.
8. Erico Rath, German.
9. Juan Napp, German.

---

[48] Dated May 7, p. 193.

Foregoing [49] will be deported on Argentine steamers *Teuco* and *Gualeguay* scheduled sail May 18 and 21 respectively for Antwerp and Rotterdam. These vessels being used to avoid heavy expenditure special vessel. Sailings may be a few days earlier or later than dates indicated depending upon cargo loading vessels. No announcement being made by Argentine Government foregoing action until after departure steamers to avoid possibility appeals writs habeas corpus. Department will be duly notified date sailing and persons aboard each vessel so that arrangements may be made with Belgian and/or Dutch authorities to hand over these aliens to our officials from Germany there to receive them. Accommodations these steamers limited which makes necessary use these two vessels.

Any further aliens included decree who may be apprehended before sailing will be deported these vessels.

Foreign Minister informs me that Argentine police have definitely determined that following included decree November 15 are in Chile:

1. Hans Blume, German.
2. Heribarto Schlosser, Austrian.
3. Gertrudis Schlosser, Chilean.
4. Johannes Szeraws, German.
5. Fernando Baulenas Salas, Spanish.

The police have determined the following are in Spain:

1. Manuel de Miguel Arrastia, Spanish.
2. Nicolas Quintana Moreno, Spanish.

The police have information that Frederico Scheu, German, is in Paraguay.

Foreign Minister states that Chilean police have been notified some time ago presence in Chile of above-mentioned as being in Chile but Argentine police have received no reply.

In addition to 13 included list November 15 deported on *Pampa*, Argentine Government has, therefore, detained and is deporting 9 others and 8 above-mentioned established as being outside country.

This makes total 30 accounted for out of list 52. Of remaining 22 fugitives only ones considered important are Juan Becker, who is one of two most important who operated in Latin America and Guillermo Seidlitz of only relative importance. Others are not considered important as Department can determine by statements accompanying my letter Under Secretary Acheson, April 25.[50]

---

[49] In the margin appear numbers indicative of the importance of each individual as appraised by the office of American Republic Affairs and in contrast to the evaluation of the Ambassador.

[50] Not printed.

Foreign Minister states that same active efforts being continued to arrest remaining 22 and while they have hope of arresting some they are not in a position to state whether they are in the Argentine or have escaped to other countries of which in opinion this Embassy there is considerable probability.

Foreign Minister has emphasized that these 22 are fugitives whose description is in possession police and special agents throughout country so that if they show themselves they will be immediately apprehended. As example of difficulties, he cited case of one of more important aliens now detained and said that chief Buenos Aires police has records showing no less than some 20 persons who were detained on information they were this person and had to be released on establishing true identity.

Department will please consider all foregoing information secret until announcement is made by Argentine Government as possibility exists writs habeas corpus being requested and granted by courts in case detention known.

In this connection, I respectfully suggest Embassy's secret despatch 2462, May 7 and my secret letter May 8 to you leaving by courier pouch this evening will be of particular interest as background in reaching any conclusion.

Complete data furnished by Foreign Minister showing deportations and action Argentine Government under decree of November 7, 1945, January 18, 1946, February 8, 1946, February 13, 1946, and February 14, 1946 follows by mail [51] and will show degree effective performance deportations prior to decree November 15, 1946.

MESSERSMITH

711.35/5-1347

Memorandum by the Chief of the Division of River Plate Affairs (Mann) to the Assistant Secretary of State for American Republic Affairs (Braden)

SECRET [WASHINGTON,] May 13, 1947.

Subject: The Present Status of Argentine Performance in Respect of the Deportation of Axis Agents.

Because of the extraordinary influence of the German colony, the pro-Axis sympathies of the extreme nationalist groups and segments of the Army, and the Government's policy of "neutrality", Argentina was the hemisphere center of Axis activities. There were more people in Argentina than in any other American State who genuinely merited

---

[51] Not printed.

deportation or criminal prosecution for their pro-Axis activities. Notwithstanding, Argentina has failed

a) to make good-faith efforts to deport, prosecute criminally or vest the spearhead business interests of key Nazi agents (such as Freude and Martens) who are naturalized Argentine citizens;
b) to deport, prosecute criminally or vest the spearhead property interests of aliens who contributed materially to Axis activities in Argentina of a non-espionage character.

The deportation program which we now have in mind is therefore limited and relates only to proven Nazi espionage agents.

Taking as a basis a list of candidates for deportation prepared in the Department in January 1946 and assuming the deportation of the 9 persons referred to in Buenos Aires telegram No. 567 of May 9, Argentina has deported approximately half of the Axis agents whom we have regarded as the most important. There are 13 agents presumably still in Argentina whom we regard as important and 8 others who are alleged to have escaped from the country. A fuller summary of the situation is given in the attached memorandum.[52]

The Argentine position appears to be that it has now substantially complied since it is unable to locate additional agents in Argentina. In view of the peculiar circumstances surrounding the disappearance of the agents, I find it difficult to believe that important agents such as Becker are really beyond the reach of the Argentine police.

T. C. M[ANN]

---

123 [Messersmith, George S.] : Telegram

The Ambassador in Argentina (Messersmith) to the Secretary of State

[Extract]

CONFIDENTIAL   US URGENT   BUENOS AIRES, June 5, 1947—11 a. m.
NIACT

677. Personal for Secretary Marshall. I received at 9:30 this morning urtel 478, June 4,[52] stating that President has instructed you to inform me that my mission having been completed as announced in press on June 3 my resignation is accepted and that it is desired that I return to the US. You state that in reaching this decision, the President has been moved by the over-riding interests of the country and is not unmindful, as he will tell me on my return, of the years of distinguished service, which he states, I have given to our Govt.

---

[52] Not printed.

You request me to inform FonOff immediately of my recall inasmuch as the President may be compelled to announced this change at his press conference this morning of June 5.[54]

.   .   .   .

MESSERSMITH

862.20235/7–2547

The United States Political Adviser for Germany (Murphy) to the Secretary of State

SECRET   BERLIN, July 25, 1947.
No. 10549

The Political Adviser for Germany refers to his telegram no. 1683, dated July 15, 1947 [55]—in which was announced the conclusion of the interrogation of five of the eight Germans recently deported from Argentina aboard the SS *Rio Teuco*—and has the honor to enclose herewith the sworn statement [55] of one of the repatriates, Hans Lieberth, or Juan Antonio Lieberth Mueller: owing to the subject's dual German-Chilean nationality, there are alternative versions of his name.

Lieberth's case presents a typical example of the way in which the Argentine police built up their story of German espionage in an entirely arbitrary manner to suit the necessities of Argentine policy, using as a means to that end intimidation, torture, and wilful falsification of facts. As will eventually be seen in the interrogation reports of Wolf Franczok (alias Gustav Utzinger) and of Hans Harnisch, the object of the Perón-Farrell regime was to construct an all-over "spy story" which would satisfy Allied demands for a clean-up of German espionage and would at the same time suppress all references which might be embarrassing to members of the Argentine Government. To this end it was necessary for the police to fabricate almost at will in building up a version that would fit governmental specifications; and little people such as Lieberth were forced to assume the roles assigned them by the invention of Comisario Amarante, who was apparently the chief author of the official version. This prisoner claimed to have been made almost impotent by applications of the so-called "picana eléctrica" (electric goad).

---

[54] By direction of the President, the following statement was issued to the press on the evening of June 5: "It is now possible for the State Department to announce that Ambassador Messersmith's mission having been completed, his resignation has been accepted and he will return to the United States." (123 Messersmith, George S.)
[55] Not printed.

According to Wolf Franczok, who was specifically questioned on the point, Lieberth did not in reality know of the trial transmissions being made on the Tandil property of which he was overseer: Franczok's experiments were carried out in great secrecy in a separate building. His affidavit clearing Lieberth of intentional collusion is included herewith as enclosure no. 3.[56] Franczok added, moreover, that the Argentine police, for "window-dressing" purposes, included in their various press releases many more farm properties than were in fact used by his organization for transmitting bases. One such apocryphal addition was Lieberth's later farm, "Mi Capricho."

Although the interrogator was inclined to be skeptical of Lieberth's claims to absolute and innocent ignorance of what was going on, it was sufficiently evident from the known facts and from an appraisal of the prisoner himself that Lieberth did not possess any knowledge of real worth to the ends of the present investigation. He was one more sacrificial goat to the requirements of Argentina's international policy. The internment authorities have therefore been informed that he may be transferred to the Repatriation Center at Ludwigsburg and processed for release, pending ultimate clearance from the Office of the Political Adviser.

862.20235/7–3147

The United States Political Adviser for Germany (Murphy) to the Secretary of State

SECRET   BERLIN, July 31, 1947.
No. 10577

The Political Adviser for Germany refers to his telegram no. 1683, dated July 15, 1947 [56]—in which he announced the conclusion of the interrogation of five of the eight Germans recently deported from Argentina aboard the SS *Río Teuco*—and has the honor to enclose herewith the sworn statement of one of the repatriates, Albert Treusch.[56]

Treusch was without doubt the individual least implicated in espionage of any of the components of the two 1947 deportation groups on the *Pampa* and the *Río Teuco*, with the possible exception of Alfred Voelckers. His fourteen-months' imprisonment rested on the flimsy basis of his having unwittingly aided Melita Tietz and Johannes Siegfried Becker to find a Buenos Aires apartment, without at the time

---

[56] Not printed.

knowing their real identity. There was nothing in the brief background material on this prisoner to indicate that his involvement went further. Probably the only case comparable to Treusch's is that of Heinz Beckedahl, a young Alsatian who was deported on the *Highland Monarch* in 1946 because in 1938 he had lived in the same boarding house with Siegfried Becker; this circumstance led the Argentine police to arrest and torture Beckedahl in 1945 in the conviction that he must then, seven years later, know of Becker's whereabouts.

While Treusch's resentment at the complete disruption of his life conduced to a favorable clime for revelation concerning the mass of collusion, fact-juggling and false witness which went to make up the Argentine handling of the espionage cases, it appears that this very resentment led the prisoner, while in jail, to maintain himself as far as possible removed from the rest of the group. Treusch refused to have anything to do with the habeas corpus defense offered by the lawyer Octavio Rivarola, as he had no desire to be further involved with the people who had been responsible for ruining his career. Since his tenuous connection with the organization did not take place until well after the others had been arrested, he was not required to make false declarations nor to alter his testimony in the interests of a "rounded-out picture" and a dovetailing, if largely fabricated whole. (See the interrogations of Hans Lieberth and Anna Assmann, Berlin despatches nos. 10549 and 10588, dated July 25 and July 31, 1947, respectively.[59])

Once he was released from prison in June, 1946, Treusch was taken back at his old job, and remained working in Buenos Aires until he heard from Willi Lindenstruth, at the end of October, 1946, that new arrests were in the air. When he had confirmed this rumor through Gustav Utzinger—who was also preparing to go into hiding—Treusch fled to the Argentine interior and remained there inconspicuously until he was arrested by the Federal Police in Córdoba on March 13, 1947. The prisoner was unable to say whether the police had just then discovered his presence in the Córdoba hills or whether they had previously known he was there.

In view of the Department's concurrence with Treusch's release (Department's telegram no. 1556, dated July 28, 1947 [60]) he has been transferred from Berlin to the Repatriation Center at Ludwigsburg, where he will be processed and set at liberty.

---

[59] Despatch 10588 not printed.
[60] Not printed.

835.00/8–1447

The Chargé in Argentina (Ray) to the Secretary of State

CONFIDENTIAL   BUENOS AIRES, August 14, 1947.

SIR: I have the honor to submit the following comment on the general political and economic situation in Argentina:

GENERAL

Perón's success in the elimination of Chief of Police Velazco and some other strong nationalists from the Government has created a general impression of strength for Perón's administration. This is strengthened by the fact that such action was accomplished quietly and was not followed by any disturbances. Although the Government appears to have consolidated its position politically, the financial and economic situation is causing it considerable worry and has created wide-spread dissatisfaction. All indications are that the financial and economic situation is becoming worse rather than better. Inflation is becoming more and more evident and is being accentuated by shortages of certain foodstuffs, especially potatoes, and also by the current gasoline shortage. The President and at least some of his high officials realize that the Five-Year Plan is not going in accordance with their high hopes, and that if it is to succeed at all, closer cooperation with the United States must be established. Both Perón and Bramuglia have taken great pains during the past two weeks or so to impress upon me their desire to reach a friendly agreement with the United States at Rio de Janeiro and to establish a basis of general cooperation with the United States. During the first conversation that I had with the President, he placed great emphasis on Argentina's need for industrialization and his realization that such industralization could not take place without the assistance of the United States. He referred to such assistance specifically as the furnishing of technical help and knowledge and shipping machinery from the United States to the Argentine.

At the beginning of my first conversation with the Foreign Minister, he showed considerable reserve and among one of the first questions he asked me was whether his understanding was correct that Ambassador Messersmith's withdrawal did not constitute an unfriendly act towards the Argentine. I remarked that the withdrawal of Mr. Messersmith was a matter of United States internal politics and Foreign Service administration and that it had no significance whatsoever so far as our policy towards Argentina was concerned. I told the Foreign Minister that I hoped our relations would be on an absolutely friendly basis and that we would all have to be realistic about things. I said we would not go on the basis that the Argentine Government was always wrong nor that it was always right but that we would believe what we saw and try to handle every problem on its own merits. During the first conversation I had with the President, he told me that the Foreign Minister had repeated my remarks to him regarding our policy of dealing with the Argentine. I told the President that I could see where we would probably have many differences of opinion, but I thought the only way to handle the situation was to discuss all problems on a friendly basis and work them out to best possible interests of both countries.

It could be argued at length whether Perón is a complete dictator; in any event, his Government has many characteristics of a dictatorship, it does not permit complete freedom of the press, and the tendency of Perón and his closest supporters is intensely nationalistic and towards government control of business. At this time, we must choose between a policy of being completely friendly to Perón, obtaining what advantages and concessions we can from him, and using our influence to prevent him from extreme actions prejudicial to our interests and solidarity in the hemisphere; or turning a cold shoulder to him with the result that we would succeed in making him aware of our moral disapproval of him and his Government and failing to accomplish anything useful. It is true that if we cooperate fully with the Perón government, we will contribute considerably to building up an administration which does not meet with our wholehearted approval. However, unless we make up our minds to be friendly to Perón, our business and commercial relations with the Argentine will become increasingly difficult and agreements at Rio and subsequently at Bogotá will be impossible.

Taken as a whole, the level of ability and integrity in the Perón administration is distressingly low. While in many respects, Perón could be described as a Fascist or at least dangerously near it, he and Bramuglia are the two men in the Government with relative outstanding ability and with whom it is possible to deal on a frank and completely friendly basis.

It is practically impossible to have a conversation with Perón or any of his higher officials without their bringing up the subject of Russia and the threat of Communism. Both Perón and Bramuglia have insisted at length to me that there was no possible question of Argentina taking a neutral position and much less a position favorable to Russia. They emphasized strongly their desire to cooperate with the United States. There is no doubt that they wish to use the threat of Communism to impress upon us the necessity of cooperation between the United States and Argentina, but they have been most careful to avoid any intimation of a threat that they might be neutral or side with Russia.

There is no doubt that the Argentine Government at the present time is deeply concerned with the overmounting inflation and the financial and economic crisis which has developed with comparative suddenness.

Financial and Economic Crisis

Since the beginning of the year, a feeling of uncertainty has been evident in the business atmosphere. It is generally felt that labor is getting somewhat out of control and in addition to the inflation caused by increases in wages, production has fallen at an alarming rate. Recently, the President called in several hundred labor leaders and appealed to them to increase production in order to save the economy of the country. The economy of the country is being handicapped by labor troubles and by restrictive forces including shortages of fuel, replacement materials, and transportation equipment. The Argentine Government recently became suddenly aware of its dwindling dollar balance and has placed restrictions on remittance abroad in foreign currency. Port congestion, decreasing production, the gasoline shortage, precipitate prices, restrictions on importations and on foreign exchange are factors which have contributed greatly to a general undermining of confidence in the Perón government and constitute the principal source of worry for the administration at the present time.

Most American and British businessmen as well as probably most of the Argentine businessmen and property owners are bitterly opposed to the Government and confidentially predict its downfall in the near future. Such predictions have been made regularly since Perón came to power and may be based more on hope than on actual belief. There is no doubt that the serious financial and economic situation is becoming a real threat to the Government although it does not as yet appear sufficiently acute to be an immediate threat to the present regime. There seems to exist at this time no real threat from any source to the existence of the Perón administration.

[Here follow sections on the Trade Promotion Institute (*Instituto Argentino de Promoción del Intercambio*), the Five-Year Plan (*Plan Quinquenal*) for economic development, the employment of technical experts in connection with the Plan, freedom of the press (see pages 317 ff.), Señora Perón, and discrimination against American vessels (see pages 251 ff.)]

Rio Conference

As reported to the Department in several telegrams, the President and Bramuglia have insisted in several conversations on Argentina's sincere desire to have a successful conference at Rio.[61] Argentina's performance in past inter-American conferences makes it difficut to believe that they can go through the Rio-Bogotá conferences without bringing up questions and assuming attitudes calculated to enhance Argentina's prestige and call the attention of the world to Argentina's dominant position at the southern end of the Western Hemisphere. Even high Argentine officials refer to the powerful countries of the world today and glibly mention the United States, Russia, and the Argentine. There are some indications that the Argentines feel that the Rio conference will be purely political and will not definitely settle the fundamental questions in which they are most interested.

Armaments and the Bogotá Conference

Argentine officials discuss the Rio conference with optimism and confidence, but when the question of armaments is mentioned the atmosphere immediately changes. The Argentines make it fairly clear that they resent the idea that the United States' plan for standardization of arms might set a quota for Argentina. Their feeling is that Argentina must be free to arm to whatever extent it sees fit and that it should be the arsenal of at least the southern part of South America. They may be expected to place great emphasis on industrialization in Argentina and the manufacture of armaments in this country. They feel that in the case of war, Argentina should be able to take care of most of its own needs and of the requirements of its neighbors. It would not require an astute observer to reach the conclusion that Argentina is as determined as ever to have a dominant position in its part of the hemisphere. . . .

Communism

Several high officials have remarked to me recently in discussing the Bogotá conference [62] and defense against Communism that the United States needs Argentina much more than Argentina needs the United States. They admit that Argentina needs technical and material assistance from the United States for its industrialization but argue that the fight, when it comes, will be between the United States and Russia and that Argentina will be helping the United States. The logic of all this is not too clear; but it boils down to the fact that while the Argentines who are so preoccupied with the Communist problem are no doubt sincere in their opposition to Communism, they want at the same time to derive every possible advantage

---

[61] For documentation, see pp. 1 ff.
[62] Documentation relating to the Ninth International Conference of American States, held at Bogotá, March 30–May 2, 1948, is scheduled for publication in a subsequent volume of *Foreign Relations*.

from their promise to help us out. In future discussions and especially in the Bogotá conference, they will no doubt harp on the need for industrializing the Argentine and enabling it to manufacture armaments and munitions so that it will not be dependent on the United States in case of an outbreak of war.

As reported to the Department, the Foreign Minister and the President have suggested that we enter into an anti-Communist pact which would not only include an exchange of information but the taking of precautionary measures and defense against Communism. One of these precautionary measures would be the military strengthening of the Argentine. They also suggest a series of bilateral agreements among American countries to combat Communism.

CONCLUSION

Whatever the defects of the Perón administration may be—and they are plentiful—we should realize that both in the Government and outside, the prevailing tendency is one of strong nationalism and an almost exalted feeling of . . . importance. The problem of our relations with the Argentine should not be insoluble; but in dealing with the present administration or any other, we should take into account . . . the general prevailing spirit of nationalism, and the ever-existing Argentine determination to be kingpin in the southern part of the Western Hemisphere.

Respectfully yours,　　　　　　　　　　　　　　　　　　GUY W. RAY

862.20235/8–3047

The United States Political Adviser for Germany (Murphy) to the Secretary of State

SECRET　　　　　　　　　　　　　　　　　　　　BERLIN, August 30, 1947.
No. 10826

SIR: I have the honor to refer to the Department's telegraphic instruction no. 1556, dated July 28, 1947,[63] and to the series of previous communications recently exchanged on the subject of eight Germans deported aboard the SS *Río Teuco* in June of this year from Argentina. Signed affidavits from five of the deportees who were deemed of little importance—namely Georg Heinrich Richter, Hans Lieberth, Hans Napp, Albert Treusch, and Anna Assmann—have already been obtained and forwarded to the Department (cf. despatches nos. 10523, 10549, 10576, 10577, and 10588, dated July 23, 25, 30, 31, 31, respec-

---

[63] Not printed.

tively [65]). The questioning of the remaining three, Hans Harnisch, Wolf Franczok alias Gustav Utzinger, and Josef Schröll alias Alfonso Chantrain, is still going on; and these interrogations have now reached a sufficiently advanced stage to warrant the present interim report of progress.

The five "quota-fillers" named above, Georg Heinrich Richter, Hans Lieberth, Hans Napp, Albert Treusch, and Anna Assmann, have been moved to Ludwigsburg following the Department's approval indicated in telegram no. 1556 of July 28. It is probable that they will soon have been released from the Repatriation Center. Their interrogation was based principally on the directives outlined in the Department's telegraphic instruction no. 3055 of December 28, 1946, and reaffirmed in telegram no. 1244 of June 12, 1947.[66] While nothing of basic importance was gleaned from these five their statements brought out several details which may serve to bolster and corroborate certain aspects of the declarations of Harnisch and Utzinger. The testimony of the five will, of course, be in the Department's hands before reception of the present despatch.

Harnisch and Utzinger, and to a lesser extent Chantrain, are by far the most interesting and fertile subjects made available to date for interrogation on the subject of the Farrell and Perón régimes. Nevertheless, many misunderstandings regarding the real nature and extent of their activities must be corrected, since any information which originated from Argentine sources should now be regarded *a priori* as highly colored and in many instances outright false. All in all, a synthesis of the current testimony presents a very sorry picture of wilful deception and plain double dealing . . . . The latter had one purpose in their investigations: to suppress all evidence of political collusion between Argentine officialdom and the German agents and to present the espionage cases in a purely technical context. There is overwhelming evidence that with the exception of a favored group oriented around the Freudes, father and son, and Werner Koennecke, the large majority of the German prisoners were cajoled or forced—with empty promises that they would go free and/or avoid deportation—into putting their signatures to a specious tissue of half-truths and lies. That this whole fabrication obeyed a basic design laid out by Ludwig Freude—abetted by Juan D. Perón—appears to the interrogator to have been established beyond a reasonable doubt.

The whole handling of the espionage cases by the Argentine government was, in the words of Gustav Utzinger, a juridical farce. Dossiers of favored individuals disappeared from the police files, dates

---
[65] Despatches 10523, 10576, and 10588 not printed.
[66] Neither printed.

were altered and names suppressed, deals were made between the police and the prisoners, confiscated funds disappeared into the pockets of the Coordinación Federal. Shortly after the Utzinger group was broken up and its members arrested in August 1944, Perón, then Minister of War, came to the Coordinación and explicitly instructed Major Oscar Contal as to the line which must be followed in the prisoners' statements. All reference to collusion was to be suppressed, and only the technical aspects of espionage allowed to remain; and even many of the latter were made taboo. Contal thereupon concluded a "gentleman's agreement" with Utzinger, who instructed his group to eliminate from their declarations all reference to the following points: contact with Argentine or other South American political and military personalities; contact with other intelligence groups; money matters; contact with German firms; landing of agents; chemicals and microphotographs; contents of radio messages transmitting experiments, wave lengths, and coding messages. As a *quid pro quo*, the Argentines engaged to spare to the best of their ability the German commercial and financial interests vested in the country. After all the resultant statements had been shoehorned into a pattern which satisfied the requirements of Argentine policy, the prisoners were made to sign them. Then, when Johannes Siegfried Becker had been caught, many prisoners had to revise whole pages of their testimony in order that the allover story might dovetail with Becker's statement. The latter had to be entirely refabricated and cut from 300 to about 50 pages in order to eliminate the many embarrassing declarations the SD chief had made in the first flush of his anger at having been apprehended.

A first brief factual statement made by Hans Harnisch following his arrest in early 1944 was immediately destroyed, even the carbons being burned, and a second and third were later prepared along lines laid down by the Coordinación Federal. As Harnisch pointed out, the police went into excruciatingly minute detail in such irrelevant matters as when and under what circumstances he had met and dealt with a host of unimportant people, but at the same time they dismissed with a vague phrase or two such subjects as his implication in the Hellmuth affair and his intimate associations with high-ranking Argentine and Paraguayan officials.

For the rest, the Argentine Government has evidently played a captious and legalistic game with the lists of German agents demanded by the United States for deportation. By using these specific lists as a basis for bargaining over their "international obligations" and by eventually surrendering a limited number of the "wanted" individuals, the Argentines were able at the end to get what they wanted—participation in the Rio Conference—without being seriously challenged on the score of the potentially far more dangerous Nazi nucleus of former NSDAP leaders. Harnisch and Utzinger were, after all, cogs in a wartime organization the reason for which has now ceased to exist; and, although these two have naturally tried to minimize their individual importance under interrogation, to view them and their kind as the most likely focal point for a resurgence of Nazism in Argentina would be a disorienting mistake.

Owing to the extreme length which the current interrogations are expected to reach by the time they are finished, it is planned to incorporate the results into a series of affidavits, arranged by subjects, with accompanying third-person interrogation reports to cover less controversial matters (biographical sketches, et cetera). Some of these affidavits have already been drawn up and signed, but it is believed that to submit them before the completion of the series would disturb the pattern of the all-over picture. In the meanwhile, excerpts have been made dealing with the two groups of specific topics suggested in the Department's telegraphic instructions nos. 3055 of December 28, 1946, and 1556 of July 28, 1947 (enclosures nos. 1 and 2, herewith).[67]

Respectfully yours, ROBERT MURPHY

862.20235/10–2447

The United States Political Adviser for Germany (Murphy) to the Secretary of State

SECRET   BERLIN, October 24, 1947.
No. 11158

SIR: I have the honor to refer to my despatch no. 10826, dated August 30, 1947, which enclosed an interim report on the interrogation of the three principal deportees who were brought from Argentina aboard the SS *Río Teuco:* Hans Harnisch, Josef Schröll alias Alfonso Chantrain, and Wolf Emil Franczok alias Gustav Utzinger. A final report on the interrogation of the last-named is submitted herewith, in various enclosures.[68] In accordance with the Department's wishes the alias Gustav Utzinger has been used throughout, since practically all records to date so refer to him.

Utzinger's interrogation was a lengthy one, and in matters involving

---

[67] Neither printed.
[68] None printed; enclosure No. 1 indicated that Utzinger denied being in the pay of German intelligence but admitted aiding Becker who was in charge of SD activity in all of Latin America. He agreed to aid in establishing a communication system to serve all intelligence groups but denied transmitting reports of ship movements. He testified that Perón suppressed information on the contact of military and political personalities in the investigation of the Utzinger ring, and required the retouching of testimony, etc.

possibly controversial statements he was required to sign a series of affidavits. These sworn declarations are in most cases rather long and detailed, wherefore in the interests of clarity there subject matter has first been condensed into one all-over report (enclosure no. 1).

The high points of German-Argentine collaboration, as brought out in this and the concomitant interrogations, have already been treated in despatch no. 10826 of August 30. Utzinger was in an advantageous position to observe the many irregularities in Argentina's handling of the espionage cases, and his resentment at having been deported made him a willing witness. Owing to the basic integrity and the high degree of intelligence of this prisoner, his testimony is probably more reliable than that of any of the other repatriates, either on the *Rio Teuco* or the *Pampa*. There were subjects on which he was unable or unwilling to be of help, but in most cases he was cooperative and informative. In spite of certain inconsistencies in the account of his personal motives it is believed that his statements regarding German-Argentine relations are in most cases dependable.

It is not within the province of this Mission to decide whether or not Utzinger will be subject to automatic arrest, although it appears that he may fall within one of the more recent amnesty categories. Nevertheless, he will be held in the Repatriation Center at Ludwigsburg (together with Hans Harnisch, whose interrogation has also been finished and will be reported presently) until it is ascertained that there are no more questions for him. It would therefore be appreciated if the Department would indicate as soon as is convenient whether the results of the interrogation are sufficient.

Respectfully yours, ROBERT MURPHY

862.20235/10–3147

The United States Political Adviser for Germany (Murphy) to the Secretary of State

SECRET BERLIN, October 31, 1947.
No. 11208

SIR: I have the honor to refer to my despatch no. 10826, dated August 30, 1947, which enclosed an interim report on the interrogation of the three principal deportees who were brought from Argentina aboard the SS *Rio Teuco:* Hans Harnisch, Josef Schroell alias Alfonso Chantrain, and Wolf Emil Franczok alias Gustav Utzinger. A final report on the interrogation of Hans Harnisch is submitted herewith, in various enclosures.[69] His testimony was lengthy, and in matters involving possibly controversial statements he was required

---

[69] None printed.

264–330—72——15

to sign a series of affidavits. In view of the rather detailed nature of these sworn declarations, the subject matter has first been summarized in a single all-over report (enclosure no. 1).

At the outset the interrogator was rather taken aback when the prisoner refused to admit what had until then been considered an established premise—that Harnisch was a ranking operative of the Abwehr and the Sicherheitsdienst. He did not deny his dealings with Johannes Siegfried Becker nor with highly placed members of the Argentine government, but he denied any regular affiliation with German intelligence other than his 1941–1942 relations with the Cologne office of the Abwehr (Abwehrstelle-Köln). As the matter was gone into and explanations made, it began to appear that Harnisch might be telling the truth: that he was involved in the Argentine rather than the German side. There were fairly strong indications that the information which was being sent to Berlin under Harnisch's name was being transmitted by Becker and Werner Könnecke on their own initiative. (It is possibly pertinent to note that at the same time Becker and Könnecke were gulling their respective principals in Germany with the cock-and-bull story of their radio "network," which in reality was no more than a single transmitter operated by Gustav Utzinger—*vide* the latter's interrogation, my despatch no. 11158 of October 24, 1947.)

When Argentina's ill-founded plans to solicit German aid in furnishing replacements for her industry were nipped in the bud by the arrest of Osmar Alberto Hellmuth in Trinidad, Harnisch was made a scapegoat and thrown into jail. At first this move was manifestly no more than a measure to save the very red face of the regime; but when General Pedro P. Ramírez and Colonel Enrique P. González took the further step of breaking diplomatic relations with Germany, the element led by Colonel Juan D. Perón promptly intervened and ousted Ramirez. Harnisch's expectations of preferential treatment thus dwindled to almost nil, since his patron had been González; and when his arch enemy Ludwig Freude gained the current ascendancy over Perón, the prisoner realized that his eventual sacrifice to deportation was merely a matter of time and political expediency.

Gustav Utzinger further pointed out that from the time of Harnisch's first arrest in January 1944 until his deportation in May 1947 he was regularly referred to in official Argentine press releases as a "master spy" and a "chief Nazi agent," and that this circumstance was taken advantage of by Könnecke and others to shift onto Harnisch a number of the counts against themselves; and the police were privy to this arrangement. Utzinger asserted, however, that it was absurd to speak of Harnisch's having played a leading role in German espionage—he became implicated through his Argentine connections on the latter's behalf, but he was practically unknown to Germany.

Becker himself confirmed to Utzinger that in Buenos Aires Harnisch was in bad odor with both the Party and the German Embassy, adding that he "was more an Argentine than a Hamburger."

The prisoner's experiences with Argentine police interrogation followed the classic pattern observed in most deportation cases to date. When first summoned to declare he told the bald truth concerning his relations with the régime, and this resulted in his being thrown into solitary confinement, in the immediate suppression of his testimony, and in the summary disciplining of the police officials responsible for allowing him so to declare. A year later he was persuaded to subscribe to two further statements, tailored to fit the exigencies of governmental policy, on the solemn "word of honor" of the Foreign Minister Peluffo that if he signed he would be released. Harnisch was, of course, not released until the espionage agents were freed en masse following the habeas corpus proceedings of June 1946.

Harnisch's retailing of Eduardo Bravo Casares' first-hand account of the ruse by which Perón obtained Argentine citizenship for Ludwig Freude may be of interest as corroboration of what was already known or suspected. It will be recalled that Argentina had "committed herself" not to naturalize any Germans during the war, for which reason it was necessary to manufacture evidence that Freude had applied for naturalization ten years ago.

Since he is not subject to automatic arrest it is proposed to release Harnisch from internment conditionally and to put him under "town arrest" (obligation to remain in a certain city) in case the Department desires a follow-up interrogation. It would therefore be appreciated if the Department would indicate as soon as is convenient whether the present report is sufficient.

Respectfully yours, ROBERT MURPHY

POLICY OF THE UNITED STATES WITH RESPECT TO THE PROVISION OF ARMS TO ARGENTINA [70]

835.34/1-847

The Assistant Secretary of State for American Republic Affairs (Braden) to the Secretary of State

CONFIDENTIAL [WASHINGTON,] January 8, 1947.

Subject: Your Request for Information Concerning the Argentine Navy's Purchase of Four Frigates

These four frigates were sold as surplus to a private United States concern which made an application for an export license. This appli-

---

[70] For documentation on the general policy of the United States in providing military assistance and arms to the American Republics, see pp. 101 ff. For documentation on the embargo of arms to Argentina in 1946, see *Foreign Relations*, 1946, vol. XI, pp. 182 ff.

cation was denied and the Argentines then made a similar application which was also denied. Thereafter, and with full knowledge of the fact that export licenses would not be granted, the Argentine Government purchased the four frigates in question and then informally requested that they be transferred to Argentine registry, a request which, had it been granted, would have nullified the previous actions on the export applications by placing the vessels outside of United States jurisdiction.

The principal basis for denying export of the frigates is that the Policy Committee on Arms and Armaments has classified them as vessels of war; and, under the procedure established by that Committee, they could be exported only on the express recommendation of the geographic office concerned. I have not considered it wise to make such a recommendation, particularly in view of the fact that the frigates could be re-militarized and made capable of tactical use by merely replacing the 3-inch guns and other armament which have been removed therefrom.

Borderline cases inevitably arise in administering our policy of withholding arms and vessels of war from Argentina. In administering this policy we are guided by whether the item for export is in fact an implement or vessel of war rather than by the alleged use to which the equipment will be put.

SPRUILLE BRADEN

835.34/4–3047

The Secretary of State to Mr. W. H. Collins, Vice President of the Shipbuilding Division, Bethlehem Steel Company

WASHINGTON, January 9, 1947.

DEAR MR. COLLINS: I refer to your letter of December 20, 1946 [71] relative to an invitation your company has received from the Argentine Naval Commission to submit bids for the construction of the following types of ships for the Argentine Navy: 1 Escort Aircraft Carrier, 1 Light Cruiser, 4 Destroyers, 3 Submarines, 1 Repair Ship, 1 Tanker, and 1 Troop Ship.

This matter has been given careful consideration and at the present time the United States policy is not to furnish arms, armaments or vessels of war to a number of foreign governments, including that of Argentina.

In view of the above policy, the State Department would not approve an export license should these vessels be constructed in the United

---

[71] Not printed.

States.[72] The Department is also adverse to the request that the Navy Department make available to your company, and the Argentine Government, the necessary design for these ships and the arms and armaments required.

Very truly yours,

For the Secretary of State:
E. T. CUMMINS
Chief, Munitions Division

835.348/1-847 : Airgram

The Secretary of State to the Embassy in Argentina

RESTRICTED WASHINGTON, January 30, 1947.

A-60. The PBY-5A [73] referred to in Embassy A-20 dated January 8, 1947 [74] was not licensed for export from the United States. It is noted that such an airplane was purchased by the Argentine Navy from S. A. Richards, Box 725, Burlington, Vermont (Embassy A-1005, October 10, 1946 [74]), and it is presumed that this is the same airplane and that Mr. Richards shipped the airplane from Canada to Argentina by a different route from the one passing through the United States.

The Department has authorized the exportation of the following aircraft to Argentina:

A. For the Argentine Naval Air Forces:

14 Consolidated PBY-5A, license 3611, October 25, 1946
3 Grumman J2F, license 4017, November 20, 1946
3 Grumman J2F-6, license 4455, November 20, 1946
1 Beechcraft D-18S, license 19, January 6, 1947
3 Grumman JRF-6, license 20, January 6, 1947

B. For the Argentine Secretariat of Aeronautics:

8 Douglas C-47, license 146, January 14, 1947
9 Douglas C-54, license 147, January 14, 1947
20 Beechcraft C-18S (AT-11), license 186, January 14, 1947
10 Beechcraft C-18S (AT-11), license 187, January 14, 1947
2 Beechcraft C-18S (AT-11), license 188, January 14, 1947

An application by the Argentine Naval Commission for license to export 30 North American AT-6 aircraft for the Naval Air Forces was rejected on January 16, 1947. No such application has been received as yet for the 20 AT-6 aircraft which, according to the Embassy's information, were purchased by the Argentine Army.

The C-18S (converted from AT-11) and the D-18S Beech airplanes

---

[72] In a letter of January 17 to the Electric Boat Company this policy was extended to submarines (835.34/12-3046).
[73] Navy patrol bomber.
[74] Not printed.

are considered to be commercial airplanes and therefore exportable. Demilitarization has been required in connection with the Grumman JRF-6 and J2F models. None of the 14 PBY's licensed for export under license no. 3611 has yet been exported from Canada. These PBY aircraft will be shipped intransit from Canada through the United States to Argentina. All except two are required to be converted by the removal of bubbles, gun mountings, and plexiglass noses, the reinforcement of floors, and the installation of hatchways. The two which are not required to be converted will be cannibalized upon their arrival in Argentina.

With respect to the Department's current policy regarding the exportation of these and other aircraft, reference is made to the Department's A-20 dated January 8, 1947.[76]

MARSHALL

835.34/1-3147

Memorandum by Mr. M. S. Carter of the Office of the Secretary of State to the Assistant Secretary of State for American Republic Affairs (Braden)

SECRET WASHINGTON, January 31, 1947.

Quoted below is an extract from the Secretary's notes at the Cabinet meeting today:

"President states that Argentine Government is endeavoring to have certain naval construction carried out in this country, for which they have the cash to pay. Admiral Flannagan,[77] I understand, conveys this information. The President would like this question examined into—what the actual situation is, what our attitude should be."

The Secretary requests that you submit coordinated Department views on this subject for the Secretary's information and guidance.

M. S. CARTER

835.34/4-3047

Memorandum by the Assistant Secretary of State for American Republic Affairs (Braden) to the Secretary of State

SECRET [WASHINGTON,] February 4, 1947.

Subject. Your Memorandum of January 31 Concerning Naval Construction in this Country for the Argentine Government.

Argentina has sought to purchase or to have constructed in this country several frigates, destroyers and submarines, a light cruiser and

---

[76] Not printed.
[77] Presumably Rear Adm. Howard A. Flanigan, Chairman of the Board of Directors of Inter-American Shipping Services, Inc.

an escort carrier and other naval vessels. The requests to obtain these vessels have been denied in accordance with the policy approved by the President that Argentina must give substantial performance under existing inter-American agreements before we will sign a military defense pact with that country or furnish it with arms. Under this policy we would not permit the construction or exportation of ships which have been classified as "vessels of War" by the Arms Policy Committee; but we would allow the construction and exportation of vessels not so classified.

The British have recently terminated an agreement with us to follow a parallel policy; but they have stated they have in mind only a "trivial program" of furnishing Argentina with "parts and equipment, etc." I recommend that representations be made to the British to induce them to continue their agreement with us to limit exports of implements of war to replacement parts; this matter will be made the subject of a separate memorandum. Irrespective of the ultimate British attitude, however, we should adhere to our policy in respect of the exportation of vessels of war to Argentina.

Spruille Braden

835.34/3–2447 : Telegram

The Ambassador in Argentina (Messersmith) to the Secretary of State

SECRET　　　　　　　　　Buenos Aires, March 24, 1947—5 p. m.

308. Re my top secret letter March 14 [78] to Under Secretary Acheson concerning desire Vickers-Armstrong to sell cruiser to Argentine Govt, and also to my top secret letter March 21 [78] to Under Secretary Acheson concerning desire British airplane manufacturers to sell military planes, I am informed by . . . that Vickers-Armstrong is submitting bids on one cruiser, two or three destroyers and several other vessels the total order amounting to approximately 20 million pounds sterling.

Information is that the bids have not yet been accepted, but . . . source is of opinion that Vickers bids would be lower than any bid of competitors. Same source states that Miranda, President Central Bank,[79] strongly opposed placing orders.

Embassy is of opinion there is no doubt that Vickers is offering

---

[78] Not printed.
[79] Miguel Miranda, also President of the Argentine Economic Council.

these vessels Argentine Govt, and that officials Argentine Navy may be interested, but that no action will be taken by Argentine Govt at this time with regards purchase as amount involved is so great and Argentine Govt still wishes to defer purchases of any military material until composition situation between us and Argentina. No doubt of increasing pressures on Govt to purchase certain equipment at this time from available sources.

Will keep Dept informed any developments.

MESSERSMITH

835.24/5-247

Memorandum by the Assistant Secretary of State for American Republic Affairs (Braden) to the Secretary of State

SECRET [WASHINGTON,] May 2, 1947.

MR. SECRETARY: An officer of the Department has learned informally from the British Embassy that Lord Inverchapel intends to discuss the following two problems with you when he calls early next week:

1) Negotiations for the Sale of British-made Arms to Argentina:

On January 27, 1947 the British Ambassador handed Mr. Acheson an *Aide-Mémoire* [82] which had the effect of terminating a "gentlemen's agreement" which the UK and the US previously had made not to sell arms to Argentina. Simultaneously the British Ambassador stated verbally to Mr. Acheson that the British had in mind only "a trivial program of naval replacements, i.e., parts and equipment, etc."

Thereafter, various unconfirmed reports from reliable sources have reached the Department concerning negotiations for the supply by British companies of naval combat vessels and jet fighter planes. Mr. Acheson called these reports to the attention of the British Ambassador on April 7 and the latter replied that he would look into the matter and inform us. To date no reply has been received.

It is recommended that the Secretary refer to the British Ambassador's two previous conversations with Mr. Acheson on the subject; express his concern regarding these reports; and express the hope that the British Government will limit the exportation of arms to "naval replacements, i.e., parts and equipment". A clarification of the British attitude would be desirable.

---

[82] *Ante*, p. 171.

835.34/5–2047

Memorandum by the Director of the Office of American Republic Affairs (Briggs)

TOP SECRET [WASHINGTON,] May 20, 1947.

Discussion:

The British Embassy informed the Department on May 16 of the conclusion of a contract between Argentina and Hawker Siddeley [83] to sell Argentina 100 Meteor jet fighter planes, deliveries beginning this month and ending by September, 1948. The amount of the order is over four million pounds.

For the past two years until this sale, the British and Canadians pursuant to a "Gentleman's Agreement" with the United States did not sell arms to Argentina.[84] In recent months the British have indicated their desire to us to withdraw from the agreement and to regain their freedom of action. They have been impelled by:

a) Need for Argentine foodstuffs. (Argentina is blackmailing the world with food. For example, Canada in order to obtain 26,000 tons of fats and oils was recently forced by Argentina to ration further her own and the U.S. press on news print in order to supply Argentina with larger quantities thereof. Canada nevertheless did refuse to sell Argentina fighter planes).

b) Need for hard currencies to bolster the British economy.

c) Desire of British armament manufacturers to resume their lucrative Latin American arms business.

The British Government in an *aide-mémoire* of April 30 [85] (delivered to the Secretary by Lord Inverchapel on May 6) served notice that it would no longer abide by the Gentleman's Agreement, but at the same time declared that contemplated arms sales would neither embarrass the plans of the American Chiefs of Staff, nor re-arm Latin America unduly. (The jet plane sale would do both. As indicated in the proposed statement to the British Ambassador this transaction cannot be reconciled with the British assurances set forth in the *aide-mémoire*).

The *aide-mémoire* repeats an earlier British suggestion (to which we made no reply) that the British and American Governments jointly examine Latin American arms requirements with a view to seeing how best to meet them in the light of 1) basic U.S. plans, i.e. our standard-

---

[83] Hawker Siddeley Aircraft Company of London.

[84] According to a memorandum of conversation of April 8, by the Chief of the Division of Special Inter-American Affairs (Dreier), the Canadians were considering the sale of 100 to 150 Mosquito bombers to Argentina to improve the Canadian exchange position and fats and oils supply. The Department spokesman indicated such a breach of standing policy would be viewed with great disappointment. (835.248/4–847)

[85] Not printed.

ization program, 2) requirements of other countries concerned, and 3) need to keep British shipyards and factories employed, now and in the future.

The *aide-mémoire* also discussed British dependence on Argentina for food supplies, suggested that Argentina should be treated in respect of arms in the same manner as other Latin American governments (i.e. regardless of the character, record and aims of the Argentine Government), and mentioned pending contracts with Argentina for military aircraft, for war vessels, and for "insignificant" amounts of matériel desired by the Argentine army.

Finally, the *aide-mémoire* suggested that there be excluded from the proposed Anglo-American discussion of the over-all Latin American arms situation, pending sales by Great Britain of naval vessels and military aircraft (for example, it now appears, the jet plane order in question).

In replying orally to the British Ambassador on May 6, the Secretary stated that the British *aide-mémoire* would receive further study, and that the Department hoped that U.S.–Argentine relations would shortly be on a more satisfactory basis.

Facts Bearing on the Situation:

1) Argentina tends toward an authoritarian state and should accordingly be treated with reserve. There is a danger that Argentina aspires to organize a "southern bloc" under Argentine political and economic domination.

The U.S. seeks hemisphere unity, which would be endangered by the formation of a "southern bloc". The policy of the U.S. should therefore be to oppose any development (and in particular any substantial increase in the Argentine military potential) which would facilitate the formation of such a bloc.

2) Jet fighter planes are weapons of aggression. They are not only unnecessary for hemisphere defense, but their acquisition would vastly increase the Argentine military potential, greatly alarm the other American republics . . ., and threaten an arms race disastrous alike to hemisphere unity and to the Latin American economy.

3) The developments mentioned in 2 would make for confusion and power politics and thus facilitate Communist penetration of Latin America as well as the establishment of military dictatorships. Both are inimical to democratic institutions.

4) Acquisition by Argentina of 100 British jet fighter planes would dislocate U.S. standardization plans. (It should be noted however that Argentina has not thus far indicated any enthusiasm for standardization; in the event of the adoption of such a program, Argentina may be expected to acquire U.S. arms to the limit thereof, and then to seek additional arms from whatever source available. It is President

Perón's publicly stated intention to establish an Argentine arms industry which will make that country independent of other sources).

Alternative Courses of Action:

1) Induce Great Britain either to cancel or substantially reduce the jet plane sale. (Whether we wish to accept the British suggestion for a joint Anglo-American examination of Latin American armament requirements would doubtless be a matter for preliminary discussion with War and Navy).

2) Inform the other American republics that we propose to arm them (with the attendant dangers of an arms race, of dislocating their economies, and of facilitating Communist penetration). It is doubtful whether the U.S. public would support such a program. Furthermore Brazil and all the small states bordering on Argentina, lack funds; they can compete with Argentina only if the U.S. underwrites the program.

3) Call the Rio Conference [86] and negotiate a hemisphere defense pact. But the hemisphere is already protected from aggression from overseas by the Declaration of Habana,[87] which does not expire with the end of war powers. The Act of Chapultepec,[88] which expires with the end of war powers, merely adds aggression from within the continent to aggression from overseas. However, there is no assurance that Argentina will accept permanent obligations along the lines of Chapultepec. Although a signatory of the Declaration of Habana, Argentina did not comply therewith after Pearl Harbor; the Argentine record with respect to the Mexico City agreements needs no comment.

4) Seek to add the hemisphere defense pact to the agenda of the Bogotá Conference (January, 1948),[89] where it will be only one of three or four important questions under consideration. (Neither Brazil nor any other Latin American Government is pressing for holding the Rio Conference).

Recommendations:

1) Persuade the British to cancel the jet plane contract. If this proves impossible, induce the British greatly to reduce the size of the order and to make only "token deliveries" pending the Bogotá Conference.

---

[86] For documentation on this Conference, see pp. 1 ff.

[87] See resolution XV in *Second Meeting of the Ministers of Foreign Affairs of the American Republics, Havana, July 21–30, 1940, Report of the Secretary of State* (Washington, Government Printing Office, 1941), p. 71.

[88] Resolution VIII of the Inter-American Conference on Problems of War and Peace; for text, see Department of State, Treaties and Other International Acts Series No. 1543, or 60 Stat. (pt. 2) 1831.

[89] For information on the preliminaries of this Conference, see bracketed note, p. 94.

2) Should War and Navy so desire, agree to the suggestion contained in the British *aide-mémoire* that a joint Anglo-American study of Latin American arms requirements be undertaken.

3) Transfer the hemisphere defense project to the agenda of the Bogotá Conference (abandoning the idea of holding a conference at Rio de Janeiro). At Bogotá we should strive to obtain a politico-juridical defense pact, without armaments commitments.

810.20 Defense/5–2147

The British Ambassador (Inverchapel) to the Secretary of State

TOP SECRET   WASHINGTON, May 21, 1947.
PERSONAL AND IMMEDIATE

DEAR MR. SECRETARY: In continuation of my letter of the 19th May [90] I am asked to give you the following personal message from Mr. Bevin [91]:—

"I have now considered carefully with my colleagues your letter of the 18th May [90] about British aircraft sales to Argentina.

2. I have certainly never had any wish to put difficulties in the way of your relations with Argentina nor to contribute to an arms race in South America. As long ago as July 1946 our Embassy in Washington asked the State Department [92] for information regarding the Inter-American Military Cooperation Bill and regarding press reports of plans under consideration by the Inter-American Defence Board for Western Hemisphere Defence. From the *Aide-Mémoire* which Mr. Acheson sent in reply on August 26th [93] I learned that full standardisation of training organisation and equipment was intended. But we have had no further communication from your Government on this subject.

3. The Gentlemen's Agreement not to supply Argentina was then being enforced by both our Governments but in January last I made it clear to you that (in the light of the degree to which Argentina had then fulfilled her obligations as regards enemy persons and interests) we no longer regarded it as appropriate to maintain this Agreement and that we proposed to treat Argentina henceforward in all respects on the same footing as other Latin American countries.[94]

4. I cannot feel therefore that we have in any way misled you as to our intentions. In the *Aide-Mémoire* which Lord Inverchapel handed you on May 6th [95] it was clearly stated that we had given firm promises of export licences to British firms in respect of important current

---

[90] Not printed.
[91] Ernest Bevin, British Secretary of State for Foreign Affairs.
[92] *Aide-Mémoire* dated July 16, handed to the Under Secretary of State by the British Ambassador on July 18, 1946; for text, see *Foreign Relations*, 1946, vol. XI, p. 278.
[93] *Ibid.*, p. 307.
[94] See memorandum of January 27 and annex, p. 171.
[95] Not printed, but see the memorandum of May 20, *supra*.

tenders for military aircraft. I am sorry that the fact of their being jet aircraft should come as a surprise to you. These aircraft are on the open list and are available for any country to buy and indeed we have already sold manufacturing rights of a later engine to your country; and I am assured that any country wishing to equip its airforce today would want jet types. Representatives of the British Manufacturers of Jet Aircraft have been in Buenos Aires for a considerable time and there has been press speculation regarding possible sale of such types. It had not occurred to us therefore that your people would think we were confining ourselves to Airscrew Types.

5. This contract for 100 Meteors (of which 20 are non-combat dual-control trainers) has been signed and we cannot possibly go back on it. Moreover, I must tell you that a contract for 30 Lincoln bombers is likely to be signed at any moment with our approval, export licences having been promised. In this case also we cannot go back on legitimate undertakings to supply.

6. I need not repeat to you the reasons for our vital need of pesos and why we cannot allow ourselves to be excluded from this market which is quite indispensable to us. I have mentioned to your predecessor our necessity for purchasing essential foods from Argentina and the need to trade in order to purchase. But I pointed out we could not abstain from trading forever. I held to the Gentlemen's Agreement for as long as I felt justified in doing so. But on the 27th January for the reasons already given I felt bound to instruct Lord Inverchapel to inform your Government that we considered ourselves free to sell arms to Argentina. And therefore the main object of our previous approaches to your Government and to you on May 6th was to suggest a general examination of the arms requirements of Latin America and I trust that such discussions will be possible and will take place without delay because we do not wish to be in conflict with you over this matter. I ought to advise you that this is all the more necessary now in that our firms have had other enquiries for aircraft etc. (including an enquiry for Spitfires from Argentina) which we are most anxious to fill."

I shall be happy, when you have considered this message, to discuss it fully and frankly with you; from the angle more especially of re-armament of Latin America, on which we readily recognize that no one is better qualified to speak than yourself.

May I therefore hold myself in readiness for such a personal talk, as soon as it may suit you to indicate a convenient time?

Yours sincerely INVERCHAPEL

835.34/6–2647

Memorandum by the Secretary of State to President Truman

[WASHINGTON,] June 26, 1947.

You will recall the discussion at a recent Cabinet Meeting in respect to the Argentine request for the construction of certain naval vessels in this country.

The Secretaries of State, War and Navy have considered the Argentine request in the light of your statement of June 3 [97] regarding the United States–Argentine relations. It is the opinion of the three Secretaries that the United States should permit the Argentine Government to negotiate for the construction of these vessels with shipbuilding firms in this country.

As a basis for this recommendation, the following points are paramount:

1. The shipbuilding industry in this country is badly in need of work in order to maintain its existence.
2. Should the United States refuse the Argentine request, the Argentines will undoubtedly contract for the ships elsewhere.

I should appreciate it if you will inform me if this recommendation meets with your approval.[98]

G. C. MARSHALL

835.24/6–3047

The Chargé in Argentina (O'Donoghue) to the Secretary of State

RESTRICTED   BUENOS AIRES, June 30, 1947.
No. 2745

SIR: With reference to previous correspondence in connection with the receipt in Buenos Aires of military equipment coming from Belgium, I have the honor to report that under date of June 25, 1947 . . . the War Department [was informed] that a recent visit to the dock area in Buenos Aires revealed that Argentina has just received approximately two hundred (200) Bren Gun Carriers (demilitarized). These vehicles arrived in crates and those seen uncrated appeared to be brand new and in excellent condition. In addition to the above equipment, about forty (40) three-quarter (¾) ton weapons carriers and a few light armored cars (approximately 2 ton) similar to the Canadian model were observed. These latter vehicles were not new but seemed to be in fair condition.

In commenting on the above the . . . [source] stated that in his opinion every effort would be made to get as much of this equipment as possible ready for show in the 19th of July military parade to be held here. This celebration ordinarily takes place on the 9th of July but has been postponed this year to the 19th.

Respectfully yours,   SIDNEY E. O'DONOGHUE

---

[97] Joint statement following discussions with Ambassador Ivanissevich of Argentina, June 3, indicating a readiness to renew conversations concerning a treaty of mutual assistance. For text, see *Public Papers of the Presidents, Harry S. Truman* (Washington, 1963), Document 105.

[98] Notation on the original below the signature of the Secretary: "Approved Harry S Truman".

835.248/8-2247 : Telegram

The Ambassador in Argentina (Bruce) to the Secretary of State

CONFIDENTIAL   BUENOS AIRES, August 22, 1947—6 p. m.

1044. For Lovett. Although outstanding instructions prohibit sale US tactical aircraft Argentina, British, Italian, Canadian tactical aircraft being sold here. Representative North American Aviation states Argentina interested purchase 66 overhauled surplus B-25 bombers. Our unilateral action is ineffective and believe prejudicial US interest. My understanding in Washington was ban had been lifted subject limitations military regulations governing sale aircraft. Please advise.

BRUCE

835.248/8-2247 : Telegram

The Secretary of State to the Embassy in Argentina

CONFIDENTIAL   WASHINGTON, September 9, 1947—5 p. m.

839. Urtel 1044 Aug 22. Dept's policy is to approve export of commercial arms requested by Arg and other Amreps provided amounts and types requested are determined reasonable and necessary for (1) maintaining internal order, (2) providing for self-defense, (3) fulfilling international obligations. Specific requests should be referred to Dept for approval before contracts of sale negotiated.

MARSHALL

835.24/9-947 : Telegram

The Ambassador in Belgium (Kirk) to the Secretary of State

SECRET   BRUSSELS, September 9, 1947—1 p. m.
US URGENT

1371. Saturday, September 6, . . . [an Embassy officer] observed 14 American medium tanks mounting 76 millimetre guns in good condition being loaded at Antwerp on SS *Rio Diamante*. Inquiries Antwerp reveal vessel belongs to Flota Mercantile [*Mercante?*] Estado Argentina [99] Agent Eiffe carrying cargo described general merchandise for individuals Buenos Aires and Montevideo sailing night September 9 for Buenos Aires. Embassy immediately contacted Jacqmin, head Belgian Office mutual aid dealing disposal surplus property, who totally unaware any such shipment. Foreign Office and Minister Exterior Commerce, through whom arms exports licensed, likewise unaware. All making appropriate investigations as

---

[99] Argentine Government shipping corporation.

to source, destination, shipper.[3] Jacqmin suggested possibility British sale to Belgian exporter as scrap or direct British Government sale to Argentina.

. . . [Member British Embassy] contacted this morning denies any knowledge and discussing matter British Ambassador.[4] If fraudulent obtention export license determined, shipment may be stopped.

Please inform War Department.

Sent Department 1371, repeated unnumbered Buenos Aires for transmittal Montevideo information Military Attachés.

KIRK

835.24/9–2647 : Telegram

The Ambassador in Belgium (Kirk) to the Secretary of State

SECRET BRUSSELS, September 26, 1947—8 p. m.

1496. 1. Embassy's telegram 1451, September 21; despatch 1507, September 10.[5] Called on De Gruben [6] re shipment tanks and informed him intended take matter up with Acting Foreign Minister at appointment set tomorrow.

Meantime requested De Gruben furnish names of ships, dates departure, destination and number tanks to which he agreed.[7] Did not disguise my concern lest these might reach Russia. He asked whether we objected to shipment to Argentina. Replied no instructions on this point except as to demilitarization.

2. De Gruben had seen photostats contract between British Disposals and Overseas Trading Corporation which contained one line requiring material to be "demilitarized". He suggested this word might have been subject to "elastic interpretation". Overseas Trading had informed him that distributor caps and sights were removed. I pointed out that these were trifling alterations which could be easily replaced and that "demilitarization" meant rendering them unfit for military use. He said Overseas Trading informed him that they pur-

---

[3] Ambassador Kirk in telegram 1381, September 10, 5 p. m., advised that the *Rio Diamante* had departed, that the depot from which the tanks came contained 1000 American-made medium tanks, and that 84 had already been shipped (835.24/9–1047).

[4] Sir Hughe Montgomery Knatchbull-Hugessen.

[5] Neither printed.

[6] Baron de Gruben, Secretary General of the Belgian Foreign Office.

[7] In telegram 1613, October 17, 3 p. m., Ambassador Kirk reported the following shipments of tanks and tank chassis to Argentina: *Formosa*, sailed June 22 with 40 vehicles; *Rio Gualeguay*, July 13, with 85 vehicles; *Rio Diamante*, September 10, 87 vehicles. All of the Argentina Flota Mercante sailed from Antwerp for Buenos Aires. Other sailings on the same route were *Rio Diamante*, May 10; *Rio Teuco*, June 28; *Formosa*, August 30; and *Rio Secundo*, October 10. (835.24/10–1747)

chased 1,587 tanks. I replied Van Loo [8] had informed . . . [us] that he has purchased 3,000 tanks. I mentioned that some shipments had been described as general merchandise. He seemed obviously unhappy.

3. British . . . [have transmitted report to] London stating 87 tanks were shipped on *Rio Diamante* (see my despatch 1507 under reference) and 13 more will be shipped near future. Another 85 also to be shipped all to Argentina and that 60 or 70 tanks were shipped about a month ago direct to Argentina believed on *Rio Gualeguay*. British state understand some shipments were as "agricultural machinery." British . . . report states tanks were disposed by British distributing 116 RVP northwestern Europe, and documents signed by officer whose signature appears to be Perkins. Van Loo says this deal occurred 2 years ago.

4. Am informed by Hyssong [9] all United States disposed material distributed OFLC was fully demilitarized so matter appears purely British lapse though it may be discovered later Canadian and Dutch materials in Belgium also have been carelessly handled.

5. It occurs to me British may have made similar sales elsewhere in Belgium and in other countries including those where Communists have great influence. Accordingly Department may wish request urgent information from British regarding all such sales and precise steps taken re demilitarization coupled with request that they undertake see all remaining stocks in Belgium and elsewhere are rendered unfit for military use. In this connection Embassy received report that Overseas Trading has branch in Rome and that they were sending military supplies to Bulgaria.

6. Also informed Overseas Trading Corporation purchased large amount radar and radio equipment. Stock held at Namur. My Military Attaché informs me that American radar and radio equipment can be freely purchased so these stocks may not have significance. . . .

7. Even assuming shipments went to Argentina and not reshipped Russia, am concerned that foregoing and future investigations may reveal disguised Russian general plan obtain available Allied military supplies from European dumps. In this connection am informed that Marcel Tralbaut, a well-known Belgian Communist who has recently made trips to Russia, has been in contact with Van Loo.

8. Reference your telegram 1353, September 25, 7 p.m.[10] just received.

According to present information tanks were sold by British Disposals Commission directly to private Belgian company Overseas Trading Corporation prior to date when responsibility such transfers

---

[8] Victor F. Van Loo, head of the Belgian Overseas Trading Corporation.
[9] Maj. Gen. Clyde L. Hyssong, Office of the Foreign Liquidation Commissioner.
[10] Not printed.

became centralized in OMA. There British not Belgian responsibility involved. Tank evidently sold as scrap and should have been demilitarized but BDC evidently lax in matter.

9. As indicated above we have made firm but informal request of Foreign Office for further information which has been promised. British Embassy also disturbed and attempting secure information from Ministry of Supply under which BDC operated.

10. Since evidence here indicated responsibility primarily British recommend our Embassy London be instructed to ask for immediate and full explanation.

Sent Department 1496; repeated London 105, Paris 122, Buenos Aires unnumbered.

KIRK

835.24/9–2647 : Telegram

The Under Secretary of State (Lovett) to the Embassy in the United Kingdom

SECRET WASHINGTON, October 6, 1947—5 p. m.

4298. Brussels Embtel Sep 26 repeated London 105.[12] Please secure complete explanation acquisition American tanks from UK Govt by Belgian Overseas Trading Corp. Especially wish information lend-lease or other origin tanks; identity UK selling and custodial agencies; UK authority under which sale made; whether tanks sold as such or as scrap; date of sale; and contractual conditions of sale with special reference to demilitarization, resale, and re-export. Determine if possible why tanks were not rendered unfit for military use before sale and whether UK sale contract would permit enforcement of any demilitarization clause. Embassy's opinion requested regarding paragraphs 5 and 6 of above referenced cable. See also Dept tel 4010 Sep 16, Brussels Embtel 101 Sep 21.[13]

LOVETT

835.24/10–1047 : Telegram

The Ambassador in Argentina (Bruce) to the Secretary of State

RESTRICTED BUENOS AIRES, October 10, 1947—7 p. m.

1235. Ray[14] and I had long talk President Perón this morning. Argentina is contemplating contract with Skoda[15] in Czechoslovakia for manufacture and delivery for period of 2½ years, 50 batteries 4

---

[12] Telegram 1496, *supra*.
[13] Neither printed.
[14] Guy W. Ray, Counselor of Embassy in Argentina.
[15] Skoda Works, Czechoslovakian munitions producers.

guns each of 88 mm. anti-aircraft equipment and munitions to go with them and total price of 13,081,000 US dollars making price each battery $91,600 and corresponding munitions—time explosive projectiles $63.40, and $61.40 for percussion projectiles. This price includes all equipment for aiming and fire control for each battery. President said that material absolutely necessary for Argentina which has no actually similar material. He would much rather buy this material in US and that this was particularly important in view recommendations President Truman and Secretary Marshall standardization arms. It would make it more complicated for the Argentines if they had to use shells of different types and as they were in agreement with regard to standardization arms they would like begin standardize now. He would very much like purchase this equipment US. We thoroughly endorse this view as they seem to be in accord policy our Government. We would appreciate very much if this cable transmitted proper authorities who before going into detail would let us know in general way whether same has elements practicability.[16]

Military Attaché General Caldwell due Washington about October 15 and will consult appropriate Army officials.

BRUCE

835.24/10–3047

Mr. Thomas S. Strong of the Munitions Division to the Chief of That Division (Cummins)

SECRET [WASHINGTON,] October 30, 1947.

The Department of the Army proposes for Argentina under its overall Latin American Military Program

    (1) Regular Army—210 Medium Tanks
    (2) Reserve Forces—210 Medium Tanks
    (3) Regular Army—560 Light Tanks

Total—980 Tanks

The Army informs (Colonel Skeldon) that the 880 [*980*] figure has not been discussed with the Argentine Government and it is the opinion that this figure would be increased, should the receiving Government set forth sufficient justification for an increase. In addition to a possible increase in the number of units, there would be no breakdown between light and medium tanks, and Argentina would have the approval to purchase, against the total figure, the type tanks (light or medium) most adaptable to her requirements.

---

[16] In his reply, telegram 999, October 21, 2 p. m., the Acting Secretary indicated the practicability of furnishing 12 batteries, 90 mm AA guns, 4 guns to a battery, with fire control equipment, ample ammunition, and 2 spare guns (835.24/10–1947).

835.24/11-347 : Airgram

The Secretary of State to the Embassy in Argentina

SECRET　　　　　　　　　　　　WASHINGTON, November 3, 1947.

A-505. With reference to the Department's telegram no. 851 dated September 12, 1947,[17] and to subsequent communications from Brussels and Frankfort concerning shipments of tanks from Belgium to Argentina, there is quoted below for your information telegram no. 1659 dated October 24 from Brussels:

"De Gruben asked Embassy officer call this afternoon and stated following:

"1. Belgium desperately seeking cereals and has encountered difficulties with hard bargaining Argentines. Nevertheless by Licensing export of 226 tanks has received following at price reductions indicated: 20,000 tons wheat at 45 pesos instead 60, 70 tons barley at 35 instead 45 plus small amount of rye. De Gruben did not know price units. Transactions give Belgium 100,000 tons cereal saving many hundred million francs.

"2. Belgium now negotiating for 200,000 tons corn at 25 instead 35 pesos but negotiations difficult and at one time broken off due Argentine complaints of quality of tanks.

"3. Belgian policy re arms export is freely issue licenses all and any legitimate and friendly governments.

"4. Belgian Government was not a party to the purchases of the tanks by the Overseas Trading Company from British surplus. While not concerned with sale and not wishing to offend US he asks USA consider great importance wheat importation to Belgium. Belgium won't change its policy followed until now unless faced with strong and definite US objection plus some assurance US will supply *quid pro quo* now received from Argentina.

"5. Belgian Government not fostering tank exports but merely issuing export licenses in driblets when absolutely required to obtain Argentine cereals. De Gruben states Spaak [18] aware foregoing and approves."

　　　　　　　　　　　　　　　　　　　　　　　　　MARSHALL

835.24/11-647 : Airgram

The Ambassador in Argentina (Bruce) to the Secretary of State

RESTRICTED　　　　　　　　　　BUENOS AIRES, November 6, 1947.

A-678. With reference to Department's airgram No. A-403 dated July 31, 1947 and instruction No. 49 dated October 13, 1947,[19] the Embassy had not found any evidence to substantiate the report that the equipment involved in certain shipments to Argentina have been or

---

[17] Not printed.
[18] Paul-Henri Spaak, Belgian Minister for Foreign Affairs.
[19] Neither printed.

are destined for transshipment to Russia.[20] On the contrary, some of the half-tracks have been assigned to the Ministry of Public Works, and are in actual use on various projects.

BRUCE

835.24/10–2447 : Telegram

The Secretary of State to the Embassy in Belgium

SECRET   WASHINGTON, November 7, 1947—7 p. m.

1615. Reurtel 1659 Oct 24.[21] For your confidential info current shipments tanks from Belg to Argentina are within requirements, which Army expects to recognize for Argentina under Western Hemisphere Defense Program. For this reason and because Belg's urgent need grain Dept does not wish raise any objection continued exchange tanks and cereals. Please arrange however give us notice all tank shipments as far in advance as possible.

Sent Brussels, repeated Buenos Aires.

MARSHALL

835.34/11–2847

Memorandum by the Chief of the Division of Special Inter-American Affairs (Dreier) to the Chief of the Division of River Plate Affairs (Tewksbury)

TOP SECRET   [WASHINGTON,] November 28, 1947.

From some top secret telegrams in BC, concerning British arms sales, I learned the following:

1. As of November 14, 1947, the British had contracted to sell 100 Meteor 4's (jet fighters) to Argentina, of which 12 had been delivered, 38 more were scheduled for delivery in March, and the balance in September, 1948. They had also sold 3 Derwent–5 aircraft engines and a license for the manufacture thereof.

2. On November 8, Ambassador Douglas[22] reported that Bevin had said he had stopped all further arms sales to Argentina and would do nothing more until he had had a personal talk on the subject with Secretary Marshall.

JOHN C. DREIER

---

[20] According to telegram 1937, December 9, 4 p. m., from Brussels, all shipments of arms were cleared by the Foreign Office and no tank shipments were authorized to any destination except Buenos Aires (835.24/12–947).

[21] For text, see A–505, November 3, to Buenos Aires, p. 232.

[22] Lewis W. Douglas, Ambassador in the United Kingdom.

810.20 Defense/5-2847

Memorandum of Conversation, by the British Ambassador to the Soviet Union (Roberts)[23]

TOP SECRET [LONDON,] 18 December, 1947.

ANGLO-UNITED STATES CONVERSATIONS

The Secretary of State [24] saw Mr. Marshall at 14 Prince's Gate at 12 midday on December 18th to hear from General Robertson [25] and General Clay [26] their ideas for future developments in Germany. The U.S. Ambassador, Mr. Douglas, Mr. Murphy,[27] and Mr. F. K. Roberts were also present. The party stayed to lunch and were joined just before lunch by the U.S. Ambassador to Poland, Mr. Griffis.

Arms for Latin America

Mr. Marshall began the conversation by saying that he would like to refer to his conversation of the previous evening with the Secretary of State about arms for Latin America. He had looked into the matter and feared that it would be quite impracticable at the present time to agree to our proposal to send jet aircraft to Argentine. He wished, however, to be helpful and he had an alternative suggestion, that so far as possible British manufacturing capacity might perhaps be accommodated to produce the type of arms for Latin America which would fit in with the American standardization program. He reminded the Secretary of State of the great difficulties which had arisen between us and the Americans at the time of Dunkirk because even our small arms ammunition was not standardized. The U.S. Government were, however, firmly opposed to our delivering jet planes or heavy bombers to Argentina. In reply to a question from the Secretary of State he said he was not worried so much about delivering warships, although, if they were ships as big as a cruiser, there would be the point about standardization of guns and ammunition. He emphasized that he was not concerned with commercial competition but entirely with the defence requirements of the western hemisphere. In his own case he had to decide, when issuing arms export licenses, how to maintain the balance between different Latin American countries so that one did not get more powerful than another. He would like us to let him know in each individual case and to give the State Department a chance of

---

[23] There is no indication in the Department of State files as to how this memorandum was transmitted to Washington.
[24] The British Secretary of State for Foreign Affairs, Ernest Bevin.
[25] Lt. Gen. Brian H. Robertson, Deputy Military Governor, British Zone of Occupation, Germany.
[26] Lt. Gen. Lucius D. Clay, Deputy Military Governor, American Zone of Occupation, Germany.
[27] Robert D. Murphy, U.S. Political Adviser in Germany.

bringing our needs into harmony with their general defence policy. He hoped that we could arrange to coordinate our manufacture of arms on the lines he had suggested. In reply to a further question from the Secretary of State about the effect of the recent Rio agreement [28] he said he was not quite sure about the details, but general agreement including the Argentine had been reached in regard to cooperation over defence, and the U.S. policy was firmly set towards standardization.

The Secretary of State explained that we had to think about our aircraft design and production. In regard to jet planes we were, he thought, well equipped although all our goods were not in the shop window. We had, however, to keep our works going by finding orders. We could not afford to take the risk of not having our production going in case there was trouble in Europe. Unlike America with its mass production, with which we could not compete, we had to rely upon our higher grade production.

Mr. Marshall repeated that the only thing to which he was absolutely opposed was the export to Latin America of jet planes and heavy bombers. Even as regards this, he would take a different view when jet planes became more common.

The Secretary of State said that he understood that as regards the commercial aspects jet planes were three to four years behind combat planes. His object was to try to keep the commercial side going. He thought we ought to consider with the Americans whether it was wise to have frequent contests which would reveal our speeds. He understood the technicians wished to compete with one another, but we might only encourage others to copy our inventions.

Mr. Marshall said he was less concerned with that aspect of the matter than with the problem of maintaining an aircraft industry producing planes which might have no value whatsoever. Since we and the Americans were maintaining our air forces not like Hitler with a definite date in view for a war, but merely in order to keep the peace, the expense was tremendous. Aircraft were so short-lived and it was difficult to get the necessary appropriations.

Some discussion then took place on the difference between Navies and Air Forces as regards length of life of aircraft and battleships.

Mr. Marshall concluded this part of the conversation by saying that the issue between the United States and the United Kingdom with regard to the Argentine was a relatively small issue as compared with the larger issue of how to keep our respective air forces up to date.

F. K. ROBERTS

---

[28] For text, see Department of State, Treaties and Other International Acts Series No. 1838 or 62 Stat. (pt. 2) 1681; for documentation on the Conference held at Rio de Janeiro, see pp. 1 ff.

835.24/12–1947 : Telegram

The Chargé in Belgium (Millard) to the Secretary of State

SECRET BRUSSELS, December 19, 1947—6 p. m.

2014. Redeptel 1758 [29] and Embtel 1937, December 9. Embdesp 1689, December 11,[29] forwards detailed information from ConsGen Antwerp indicating 583 tanks and 797 jeeps and trucks shipped Antwerp to Argentina from March 5 until November 17, 1947. Have received today FonOff note from De Gruben indicating 361 tanks left Antwerp between June 24 and November 17. These shipments occurred during period when arms transit shipment required license (see Embdesp 1283, May 29 [29]) FonOff adds *Rio Diamante* and *Rio Secundo* schedule load 90 tanks each toward mid-January but license refused. States Lloyd register announced arrival all vessels La Plata. FonOff, therefore, feels tanks not rerouted.

Embassy official last evening saw official Ministry Food and Exportation who stated categorically reports shipment tanks Russia completely unfounded (Embtel 1919, December 6 [29]). Extensive inquiries Brussels and Antwerp have revealed nothing collaborating [*corroborating?*] *Daily Express* story which I consider groundless. Brussels daily *Soir* yesterday and today carries factual obviously inspired article of tanks shipments Argentina in refutation story their shipment USSR which many papers have reprinted. Airmail despatch follows.[29]

Sent Department, repeated Buenos Aires unnumbered.

MILLARD

835.24/12–3147 : Airgram

The Chargé in the United Kingdom (Gallman) to the Secretary of State

SECRET LONDON, December 31, 1947.

A–2652. US–UK: Sale by UK of American tanks in Belgium; export to Argentina.

Question of sale of US tanks in Belgium by UK (Emtel 6477 to Dept, 126 to Brussels, Dec. 15 [29]) has been discussed on several occasions with officials of American and Western Division London FonOff. FonOff has made extensive examination of subject with Min. of Supply in London and Brit. Emb. in Brussels. Following views were communicated orally by Head of Western Dept (Belgium affairs) to Emb. officer:

---

[29] Not printed.

1) Tanks were sold as scrap to Belgian Overseas Trading Corporation by Brit. Min. of Supply. Large number of tanks of both Brit. and Amer. (presumably lend-lease) origin were sold and, according to FonOff info., a total of around 250 only have been exported to Argentina.

2) Brit. selling and custodial agent was the No. 3 Brit. Disposals Commission in Brussels.

3) Sale was made under the general authority of Min. of Supply to dispose of scrap materials.

4) Sale was as "scrap".

5) Sales were made between beginning of May 1946 and end of Aug. 1946.

6) Conditions of sale included "effective demilitarization by the purchasers, and part payment to UK in high carbon steel to be receivered [sic] from the break-down". The contract "did not contain any clause prohibiting resale or re-export" because sales of scrap were not regarded as subject to any such restrictions.

7) Tanks were not demilitarized before sale. Reason that demilitarization was to be carried out by purchaser was "lack of personnel by Min. of Supply in Belgium to carry out any such work." Until March 1947 "a member of staff of Commission was charged with the duty of supervising the carrying into effect of the terms of the contract. He was then withdrawn owing to general shortage of manpower."

8) Sales contract calls for demilitarization and would permit enforcement thereof. Min. of Supply is in contact with Company on carrying out of contract. FonOff is prepared to instruct UK Emb. at Brussels to concert with US Emb. there in any measures thought to be desirable. Company has been asked by UK Emb. to explain "why tanks were not demilitarized."

During these conversations, FonOff officials were distinctly embarrassed and, while endeavoring to make out as good a case as possible, frankly stated that there might have been some laxity on the part of Min. of Supply personnel. This laxity was ascribed to large-scale disposal activities by the Min. in many areas, lack of adequate personnel, constant demands that MOS personnel be reduced abroad, and belief materials sold were only of scrap value. It was insisted that "UK Govt did not make any exceptional profits on deal as tanks were sold for scrap and scrap prices", thus "their hands were clean of any profiteering."

An interesting statement volunteered by the FonOff was to effect that "The Belgium Govt looked benevolently upon the sale of the tanks and tractors to the Argentine", as a part of the "battle for wheat". This was further explained by the statement that, while the Company itself must have made a very good profit on the sale, the

Belgian Govt was interested in using the delivery of such goods to Argentina in its negotiations for the importation of Argentine foodstuffs. The opinion was also expressed that UK Emb. in Brussels would not get much cooperation out of the Belgians in running down the affair, due to element of the transaction with the Argentine.

Finally, both the FonOff and the Min. of Supply appear to be very embarrassed by this matter and to hope that above explanation will be accepted by US, particularly since none of the exported materials have gone elsewhere than the Argentine and the further exports thereto appear to have been stopped either by Belgian action in requisitioning tanks from Company or by the inquiries made by U.S. Govt.

GALLMAN

PROBLEMS OF AIR TRANSIT BETWEEN THE UNITED STATES AND ARGENTINA [33]

835.796/3-2647

Memorandum by Mr. John L. Ohmans of the Division of River Plate Affairs [34]

[WASHINGTON,] March 26, 1947.

SUMMARY OF AVIATION DEVELOPMENTS IN ARGENTINA

Buenos Aires Report 270 of March 20 [35] gives the text of a U.S. Chamber of Commerce Argentina article on FAMA's [36] organization, plans, and problems. The details in it are familiar to RPA, though news of some of the operating and personnel deficiencies it endures is illuminating. Crocker [37] comments that "FAMA's president [38] recently stated that the airline is a political instrument and not a business proposition and the present situation of the airline reflects this status perfectly. The organization is crippled by differences on policies and the consequent restrictions imposed on the delegation of authority to certain capable subordinates, mostly foreign. . . . Its future success largely depends on the organization of an experienced and intelligent body of technicians and managers with the necessary authority to make their knowledge effective."

---

[33] For information on negotiations in 1946 for an air transit agreement, see bracketed note, *Foreign Relations*, 1946, vol. XI, p. 339.

[34] Addressed to Mr. Eugene A. Gilmore, Jr., and Mr. Henry A. Hoyt of the Division of River Plate Affairs, and to Mr. Thomas C. Mann, Chief of that Division.

[35] Not printed.

[36] Flota Aérea Mercante Argentina, a mixed public-private air transport company.

[37] Carson O. Crocker, Civil Air Attaché.

[38] Díaz Bialet.

Ambassador Messersmith on March 14 commented on the negotiation of an aviation agreement with Argentina. He pointed out that he agreed with our pressure on the British to urge them to reopen the negotiations with Argentina. However, he is skeptical as to whether the British Government at this time will on its own initiative take up this matter with Argentina and felt that the British Embassy in Buenos Aires is not inclined to take up the matter with the Argentine Government. His conversations with Perón [39] have made him feel confident that the Argentine Air Ministry and FAMA's stand on the division of traffic cannot and will not be maintained. He said Perón expressed his dissatisfaction with the competence and understanding of some of the air officials. He intended to resume discussions on the matter with the President in several weeks. He also pointed out the difficulties Braniff International is experiencing in inaugurating its U.S.-Argentine services. He advised the Braniff representatives that their personal representations before the Argentines would not be helpful at this time.

Meanwhile, Emb Paris reports that the Argentine-French air negotiations have broken down and Ferreira, Director of Commercial Aviation returned to Buenos Aires. Also yesterday's telegram from Buenos Aires reported Diaz Bialet was to be removed from his position as head of FAMA. AV has cabled Embassy London to urge the British to point out to Argentina that the Anglo-Argentine agreement is regarded as provisional. This chain of events therefore: FAMA's operating difficulties, negotiation failures with the French, Diaz Bialet's probable removal, and probable British renegotiations of their restrictive agreement leads one forcibly to the opinion that prospects for another U.S. attempt to reach an air agreement with Argentina are near at hand. In view of past statements from our Embassy in Buenos Aires, it is likely that negotiations, if they are held, will take place in Buenos Aires.

J. L. OHMANS

735.4127/4–347 : Telegram

The Acting Secretary of State to the Embassy in the United Kingdom

CONFIDENTIAL WASHINGTON, April 7, 1947—7 p. m.

1536. Embtel 2062 Apr 3.[40] Brit procrastination in confirming to Arg their avowed position respect air agreement is not satisfactory to US. Soonest possible Brit expression their intentions to revise bi-

---

[39] Juan D. Perón, President of Argentina.
[40] Not printed.

lateral in accordance Bermuda provisions [41] Dept considers most desirable to provide Emb Buenos Aires much needed support in converting Arg thinking to non-restrictive type agreement. If Brit defer action until Montreal [42] valuable time will be lost since no assurance effect of Brit representation to Arg delegation will be felt in Buenos Aires for some time thereafter, particularly if conference drags out. Direct approach to Arg Govt via Brit Emb preferable and at earliest opportunity.

Sent London; rptd Paris as 1249, Buenos Aires as 272.

ACHESON

711.3527/4–1047 : Telegram

The Ambassador in Argentina (Messersmith) to the Secretary of State

CONFIDENTIAL   BUENOS AIRES, April 10, 1947—7 p. m.

401. ReDept's 272, April 7 [43] and 281, April 8.[44] I have had number of talks with FonMin [45] and during last few weeks, and more particularly yesterday and today, with regard to desirability of a bilateral commercial Air Agreement. These conversations have followed those I have been having over period of some months with President and FonMin on same matter.

I have not been holding conversations recently with Argentina air officials, as I have not believed they serve any purpose; but President and FonMin have been carrying on conversations with them.

During conversation with FonMin yesterday and today he informed me he was convinced an agreement must be reached without delay and that it should be reached before the Montreal meeting, so there will be no divergencies in this matter in the Americas when that meeting takes place. He has now informed me that Argentine air officials realize they must modify their position to meet ours and from his statements I am convinced that it is ready to make an agreement without division of traffic provision on which air officials have been so far insistent.

I believe therefore time is opportune for negotiations and that highest and most competent our officials should be sent immediately

---

[41] Provisions of an agreement resulting from the Bermuda Conference, January–February, 1946, between the United States and the United Kingdom; for text, see Department of State, Treaties and Other International Acts Series No. 1507, or 60 Stat. (pt. 2) 1499.
[42] Site of the International Civil Aviation Organization, the First Assembly of which met May 6–28, 1947.
[43] Same as telegram 1536, *supra*.
[44] Not printed.
[45] Juan Atilio Bramuglia.

to Buenos Aires to negotiate agreement. I told FonMin that I thought conversations should take place here, although I had previously been of opinion they could be held best in Washington. The Minister said that it was important that they be held here, for if the Argentine air officials were too technical and too unyielding, it would be easier for the officials of the Government to assure an agreement if the conversations were held here than in Washington. I am very much in accord with this opinion.

The situation here is such that I believe the time is now very opportune for the conclusion of an agreement, and as there is so little time between now and Montreal, I strongly advise departure Washington as soon as possible our delegation. I will be glad to assist and believe I have laid the necessary background during past months; but I am not competent, nor are my associates adequately informed to carry on negotiation agreement, and for this reason believe it important not only that our negotiators arrive soonest possible but also that they be the best we can send. I hope very much Landis [46] can come.

I discussed with FonMin suspension by Panagra certain services without this suspension being construed as abandonment of frequencies; and FonMin stated that in his opinion the time had come to inform the Argentine aviation officials that their attitude regarding this was arbitrary, and he hoped to bring about in the next few days appropriate approval of Panagra plans without this being construed as abandonment of frequencies. I stressed this latter as I think it would be unwise for us to give the impression we are abandoning these frequencies.

I have put my best into this matter of the air negotiations and it has come to a head rather more quickly than I anticipated, and it is in my opinion important that we seize this moment to negotiate and for this reason cannot stress too strongly immediate arrival delegation. Minister assures me Argentine officials will be ready to begin conversations on arrival our negotiators.

MESSERSMITH

711.3527/4–1147

Memorandum to President Truman by the Assistant Secretary of State for Transport and Communications Affairs (Norton)

[WASHINGTON,] April 11, 1947.

Ambassador Messersmith has just cabled that he has had unexpected success through direct action by President Perón in setting the stage for an Air Transport Agreement on the principles established and

---

[46] James H. Landis, Chairman, Civil Aeronautics Board.

maintained by the United States since Bermuda. This apparently amounts to a reversal of the previous Argentine policy which prevented conclusion of an agreement with an Argentine delegation sent to Washington last fall. President Perón is anxious that agreement be reached before the Montreal Assembly of the International Civil Aviation Organization beginning early in May. Ambassador Messersmith urges that Mr. Landis be sent as head of the delegation.

I not only strongly concur with the Ambassador's request for the services of Mr. Landis but feel that he should go as your Personal Representative and with the personal rank of Minister. The consummation of such an Air Transport Agreement with the Argentines would break the present log jam in Latin America as the Bermuda Agreement did in Europe and the Near East. I believe that following the signing of such an agreement, Chile, Bolivia, Colombia, Venezuela and Mexico would almost certainly fall in line. Mr. Landis' services would not be required except at Buenos Aires. It might then be possible to sign a number of these countries before the Montreal Assembly, in which event our pattern of bilateral agreements along Bermuda lines would be of such an extensive nature and would be so greatly strengthened that many of the difficult problems involved in the multilateral approach now under consideration at Montreal would be solved.

I would, therefore, greatly appreciate it if you would urge Mr. Landis to accept the leadership of this very important mission. We would, of course, staff him with representatives of the Department and would make all arrangements for immediate departure.

711.3527/4–1047 : Telegram

The Acting Secretary of State to the Embassy in Argentina

CONFIDENTIAL WASHINGTON, April 14, 1947—6 p. m.
US URGENT

299. Embtel 401 Apr 10. Highly gratified important and welcome advice you have set stage for negotiation air agreement Argentines on terms consistent US principles. Personal congratulations success your persistent efforts bring both sides together on basis promising conclusions desired.

US delegation will be headed by James M. Landis, travelling as personal representative of the President, with rank of Minister. Accompanying him will be John O. Bell, Associate Chief, Aviation Division, and Thomas T. Carter, also of Aviation Division. Party plans depart New York Apr 17 via Flight 201 Pan American schedule arrive 4:45 p. m. Apr 19. Desire Emb's assistance in reserving rooms at Plaza Hotel if possible. This contemplates commencement negotiations Monday 21st.

Landis has suggested inclusion in delegation of Cloyce K. Tippett, CAA employee formerly stationed in Brazil, stating he was useful in obtaining information direct from aviation sources. Dept doubtful whether he is needed but desires your opinion urgently.

ACHESON

711.3527/4–2247 : Telegram

The Ambassador in Argentina (Messersmith) to the Secretary of State

CONFIDENTIAL   BUENOS AIRES, April 22, 1947—6 p. m.

454. For Merchant [47] from Landis. What policy have you evolved regarding Sixth Freedom? [48] Argentines worried by Peruvian potential acquisition of route to Buenos Aires, putting Peru into Argentina–New York traffic. Same problem presented by Brazil, which, incidentally, now does Sixth Freedom traffic as witness operations Panair Buenos Aires to Paris. We have potentially same problem Montreal–Bermuda, as agreement today specifically grants it, but would you be willing to object to it by, for example, supplementary exchange of notes. [Landis.]

MESSERSMITH

711.3527/4–2347

The Ambassador in Argentina (Messersmith) to the Assistant Secretary of State for Transport and Communications Affairs (Norton)

CONFIDENTIAL   BUENOS AIRES, April 23, 1947.

DEAR NORTON: I have your confidential letter of April 17 in reply to mine of February 28 to Mr. Clayton [49] in which I covered my conversations with Mr. Braniff [50] during his visit to Buenos Aires. I have noted with interest your statements.

In the meantime a good deal of water has run under the bridge, and you have taken note of the despatches and telegrams which I have sent. As a result of the later conversations here, the way seemed to be more propitious for conversations for an agreement on civil aviation and Mr. Landis and his associates arrived last Saturday evening. On Sun-

---

[47] Livingston T. Merchant, Chief of the Aviation Division.
[48] See telegram 338, April 24, 4 p. m., to Buenos Aires, p. 245.
[49] William L. Clayton, Assistant Secretary of State for Economic Affairs; neither letter printed.
[50] Thomas E. Braniff, founder and president of Braniff International Airways.

day morning we had a long session at the Embassy residence together with officials of the Embassy, and the conversations started on the following Monday afternoon.

It is too early to state what the result of the conversations will be, but it is my hope that a satisfactory agreement will be arrived at. I will not go into detail in this letter as Mr. Landis will be in touch with you by telegraph.

After having so carefully arranged the atmosphere for the negotiation of an agreement, we had two unhappy occurrences which I brought to your attention. The one had reference to the shipments of linseed oil but this has, in the meantime, been taken care of satisfactorily through the conversations which we have had with the Commodity Credit Corporation.

The other was the unhappy refusal, in my opinion, of the Maritime Commission to sell three converted C–3s by the Newport News Shipbuilding Company to the Dodero Company.[51] I have exchanged several telegrams with you and am preparing another this afternoon or tomorrow. The refusal of the Maritime Commission has definitely created the feeling among high officials of the Argentine Government that while we are standing for freedom of the air, we are through the refusal of the sale of these vessels endeavoring to restrict the development of the Argentine merchant marine. No matter what may be the real basis of the action of the Maritime Commission, it will be impossible to overcome this feeling. I will not enter into the reasons why this Embassy believes these vessels should be sold to the Dodero interests because I shall cover this in another letter. I believe, however, very definitely, as I conveyed to you over the telephone and in my telegrams to the Department, that if we do not get an air agreement on a satisfactory basis during the present conversations, it will be due basically to the situation created among high officials of the Argentine Government that in one form of navigation we take one position and in another form, we take another position.

I am, in spite of this situation, going to do everything I can to make these conversations a success, because I think it is of the utmost importance not only that we arrive at such an agreement with the Argentine now, and before Montreal, but that it is in the interest of our air service in all of the Americas that such an agreement should be arrived at now.

Believe me, with all good wishes,

  Cordially and sincerely yours,   GEORGE S. MESSERSMITH

---

[51] For documentation on ship sales, see pp. 251 ff.

711.3527/4-2247 : Telegram

The Acting Secretary of State to the Embassy in Argentina

CONFIDENTIAL WASHINGTON, April 24, 1947—4 p. m.
US URGENT

338. For Landis and Bell from Merchant and CAB. Embtel 454 Apr 22. Re sixth freedom. Dept believes strict Bermuda capacity language includes so-called sixth freedom in definition of fifth freedom.[52] Thus additional capacity entitlement cannot be secured for sixth freedom traffic. Discussion 1946 PICAO Assembly indicated fifth freedom language might cover sixth freedom and that special language raised many problems both of draftsmanship and enforcement. See Doc. 2089 Report Commission No. 3 First Interim Assembly[53] which, although not completely indicative position to which US wishes to be bound, is indicative of general thinking. Therefore, Dept and CAB do not favor special agreement in any form with Argentina re sixth freedom. Any such action would raise question construction earlier agreements. Position should be sixth freedom included in fifth freedom and legitimate to extent fifth freedom is proper but no further. Enforcement against double ticketing would lie under general disputes clause as would provision against extra capacity for sixth freedom traffic, with deliberate double ticketing being considered unfair practice as attempt to indirectly do that which is forbidden to be done directly. See Montreal Doc. 2866 page 24. Crocker should have copy.

Dept anxiously awaits word re use new arbitration clause. As interim agreement no longer effective Council ICAO has no express or implied authority act as arbitral body. Approval new clause urgently needed use in other pending agreements. [Merchant and CAB.]

ACHESON

711.3527/4-3047 : Telegram

The Ambassador in Argentina (Messersmith) to the Secretary of State

CONFIDENTIAL BUENOS AIRES, April 30, 1947—5 p. m.

511. For Merchant from Bell. Substitute following for lines 501 through 539 of draft agreements.

"A. Airlines of the United States of America authorized under the present agreement, are accorded rights of transit and nontraffic stop

---

[52] For definitions of air transport freedoms, see the multilateral agreement of December 4, 1944, Department of State Executive Agreement Series No. 488.
[53] Of the Provisional International Civil Aviation Organization.

in the territory of the Argentine Republic, as well as the right to pick up and discharge international traffic in passengers, cargo, and mail at Buenos Aires, Mendoza, Córdoba, Salta, and Tucumán, on the following routes via intermediate points in both directions:

1. The United States via intermediate points on the east coast of South American to Rio de Janeiro and beyond to Buenos Aires (*a*) via intermediate points in Brazil and Paraguay and (*b*) via intermediate points in Brazil and Uruguay.
2. The United States and/or an airport serving the Canal Zone via intermediate points in the Caribbean and South America to Salta, Tucumán, Córdoba, Mendoza, Buenos Aires and beyond.
3. The United States and/or an airport serving the Canal Zone via intermediate points in the Caribbean and South American to Asunción, Paraguay and beyond to Buenos Aires. On each of the above routes the airline or airlines authorized to operate such route may operate nonstop flights between any of the points on such route omitting stops at one or more of the other points on such route.

B. Airlines of the Argentine Republic, authorized under the present agreement, are accorded rights of transit and nontraffic stop in the territory of the United States of America as well as the right to pick up and discharge international traffic in passengers, cargo and mail at (blank) on the following routes."

Argentine route proposals will be communicated when received. [Bell.]

MESSERSMITH

711.3527/5–747

Memorandum by the Chairman of the Civil Aeronautics Board (Landis) to the Secretary of State

WASHINGTON, May 7, 1947.

MY DEAR MR. SECRETARY: I am submitting herewith a brief report of my activities in connection with my recent mission to Argentina to conclude a bilateral air agreement between that country and the United States.

I was very fortunate in the assistance that was provided for me. Messrs. John Bell and Thomas Carter of the Aviation Division of the State Department were not only thoroughly competent in their field but also in their efforts to bring about the desired end of the mission. Mr. Cloyce J. Tippett of the Civil Aeronautics Administration, whom I was fortunate enough to enlist in this enterprise, because of his earlier experience in the Argentine and his knowledge of all the important men in the field of aviation, was an invaluable aide.

The Argentine Negotiating Committee of private individuals

headed by Dr. Ferreira, Director of Civil Aviation, met with us several times during the first week. We made no progress with this committee. They remained insistent upon their formulas for undue limitation of fifth freedom rights and division of traffic—formulas which we could not accept under any circumstances. It will be remembered that this eventuality was anticipated by Ambassador Messersmith and that he had informed the Department at the beginning that resort would have to be made to higher levels in order to reach an agreement. The Ambassador thereupon proceeded to deal with the Foreign Minister and through the Foreign Minister with the President of the Argentine Republic. On my side I made the approach primarily through Mr. Alberto Dodero, head of the Dodero Shipping Company, and a person with very great personal influence with the President. The combination of these two approaches proved successful, for when we finally called upon the President there was a clear indication that the Argentine negotiators had been told to reach an agreement with us along the lines that we had consistently advocated. Within an hour after this visit we met again with these negotiators and in a fourteen-hour session lasting from six P.M. to eight-thirty A.M. we hammered out the agreement.[54] The agreement does not cover routes as the Argentines claimed to be unready to present us with a route proposal. It is anticipated, however, that we shall come to an agreement shortly on the matter of the routes. President Perón also exhibited interest in the possibility of a Technical Mission being sent to the Argentine. This mission would consist of Civil Aeronautics Administration experts and of course would be paid for by the Argentine Government so that no expense would rest upon this government. The Civil Aeronautics Administration, according to my understanding, is anxious to give the Argentines this kind of technical assistance.

. . . .

Sincerely yours, JAMES M. LANDIS

810.79611 PAA/7–1747 : Telegram

The Chargé in Argentina (Ray) to the Secretary of State

CONFIDENTIAL BUENOS AIRES, July 17, 1947—7 p. m.

880. Ferreira interviewed today re route patterns of bilateral stated:
During his absences Diaz Bialet's uncontrolled activities increased FAMA disorganization. New board will be elected August 18, route patterns will be ready then. Delay due entirely FAMA disorganization. Considers it advisable and hopes we not press decision till August

---

[54] Announced May 1, 1947; see Department of State *Bulletin*, May 11, 1947, p. 938.

18. Alternative is govt to govt negotiation since basis Argentine reply not ready immediate result unlikely. Agreed meantime problems will be solved in "spirit of agreement signed by both countries".

Embassy believes necessary await August 18 for route decision and in view "spirit of agreement" statement agrees procedure suggested Deptel 650, July 14 [55] when Panagra plans approved by board.

RAY

811.79635/8–1947 : Telegram

The Acting Secretary of State to the Embassy in Argentina

CONFIDENTIAL   WASHINGTON, August 27, 1947—11 a. m.

797. Embtel 1023, Aug 19.[55] US air transport routes under consideration. Dept expects advice of CAB this week and will then cable route pattern. Dept suggests Emb inform Args US will be ready submit proposed routes by diplomatic notes at early date and suggest Args concurrently present their proposed routes by note. Altho Dept prefers simultaneous exchange, such not prerequisite for submitting US desired routes.

Dept prefers exchange notes for study by both Govts prior entering into actual route negotiations, as such will permit best opportunity further study, and should facilitate and expedite final negotiations when commenced.

Dept will, after studying Arg route proposal, notify Emb of desires re time and place negotiation.

LOVETT

811.79635/9–247 : Telegram

The Secretary of State to the Embassy in Argentina

CONFIDENTIAL   WASHINGTON, September 9, 1947—5 p. m.

840. Embtel 1066, Sept 2.[55] Following are US desired routes:

"A. Airlines of the US of America, authorized under the present agreement, are accorded rights of transit and non-traffic stop in the territory of the Argentine Republic, as well as the right to pick up and discharge international traffic in passengers, cargo, and mail at Buenos Aires, Córdoba, Salta, and Tucumán, on the following routes via intermediate points in both directions:

    1. The United States via intermediate points on the east coast of South America to Rio de Janeiro and beyond to Buenos Aires

---

[55] Not printed.

(a) via intermediate points in Brazil and Paraguay and (b) via intermediate points in Brazil and Uruguay.

2. From the United States and/or an airport serving the Canal Zone (provided that if such airport be located not in the Canal Zone, but in the Republic of Panama, the consent of Panama be obtained) via intermediate points in the Caribbean, Central America, and South America, via Lima, Peru, and/or La Paz, Bolivia, and/or Antofagasta, Chile, and/or Santiago, Chile, to Salta, Tucumán, Córdoba and Buenos Aires, and beyond.

3. The United States and/or an airport serving the Canal Zone (provided that if such airport be located not in the Canal Zone, but in the Republic of Panama, the consent of Panama be obtained) via intermediate points in the Caribbean and the west coast of South America to Asunción, Paraguay, and beyond to Buenos Aires.

"On each of the above routes the airline or airlines authorized to operate such route may operate nonstop flights between any of the points on such route omitting stops at one or more of the other points on such route."

Emb should note BA–Montevideo is included as a US request, and, should Args express ire thereat, statement should be made Arg position is respected but such is nevertheless among US desiderata.

For your info only, Tucumán and Salta may possibly be yielded by US for bargaining, but position in regard thereto not yet firm.

Request Emb indicate to Arg desire for info re Arg route requests soonest.

MARSHALL

810.79611 PAA/10–1047 : Telegram

The Acting Secretary of State to the Embassy in Argentina

CONFIDENTIAL   WASHINGTON, October 10, 1947—3 p. m.

960. Panagra has advised Dept they have dispatched air mail letter to their representatives BA authorizing, if not instructing, them to inform Arg Govt, of company's future operating plans in Arg. Briefly, these plans include inauguration about Nov 1 non-stop services Lima–BA and eventual elimination all Arg stops except BA.

It is suggested Emb contact local Panagra and discuss advisability (pro and con) divulging such info to Arg until really necessary, or route negotiations settled, whichever sooner. Dept unable cite any specific reasons withhold carrier's plans at this time but believes question should be weighed by Emb in light possible effect upon current Arg consideration route patterns.

LOVETT

711.3527/12-1747

Memorandum by Mr. Joseph J. Wolf of the Aviation Division

CONFIDENTIAL [WASHINGTON,] December 17, 1947.

I spoke yesterday at length with Tom Carter and John Bell, and reviewed the Argentine file, in an attempt to clarify Section VII of the Annex of the U.S.–Argentine agreement in my own mind. This search was occasioned by the situation presented by the request for a statement of our position as to what this section means, which came from the Scandinavian countries which are at present negotiating with Argentina.

The following is the information which I received from Messrs. Bell and Carter. It is substantiated by the information in the files.

Up to and including April 24, conferences with the Argentineans had been more or less on general principles, with general discussions concerning division of capacity and traffic as opposed to the U.S. philosophy. As established by Mr. Messersmith's memoranda, the Foreign Minister was approached on Monday, April 28, and given a draft containing the standard U.S. Bermuda language. This was studied by the Argentineans until Wednesday, the 30th. On Wednesday afternoon Messers. Messersmith and Landis saw Perón in the company of the Foreign Minister. At this meeting, Perón indicated that agreement would be reached on the U.S. terms. This is substantiated by Mr. Landis' letter to the Secretary, reporting on his efforts in Argentina.

On Wednesday the Argentines transmitted to the U.S. delegation, without comment or discussion, a new proposed Section VII. This was considered by the U.S. delegation in private and certain amendments thereto were made. A study of this proposal and its amendments indicated that it was not in substance a departure from Bermuda.

The evening of the 30th saw the 14-hour conference which finally produced the agreement. At about three o'clock in the morning Ferreira again started to expound on his theory of division of traffic. This enraged Mr. Landis, who openly expressed his violent displeasure at going back over this old ground. Dr. Ferreira appeared to be deflated by the force exhibited by Mr. Landis, and a short interlude occurred. During this interlude Dr. Ares of the Foreign Office spoke at length with his colleagues and placed a note in writing on the table in front of Dr. Ferreira, who looked at the note, made a despairing gesture, and thereafter proceded to accept the proposal of the U.S. which was thereafter incorporated as Section VII of the Annex.

I believe it to be conclusive evidence that Dr. Ferreira's position was overruled and that he was instructed to abandon his philosophies and accept the proposals of the U.S. delegation.

[The agreement signed on May 1, 1947, was not completed and was not put in force. Differences over route specifications and later over capacity control prevented the consummation of the agreement. The air lines operated under an Argentine system of unilateral permits.]

DISCRIMINATION BY ARGENTINA AGAINST AMERICAN AND OTHER FOREIGN SHIPPING AND TRADE

835.1561/4–147

The Chief of the Shipping Division (Saugstad) to the Ambassador in Argentina (Messersmith)

WASHINGTON, April 1, 1947.

MY DEAR MR. MESSERSMITH: I was very glad to receive your letter of March 5 [58] with your helpful comments on the present port situation in Argentina, and your assurance of personal interest in the matter which is giving us great concern in many directions. I hope through your able handling of this situation that it may be cleared up without too much official disturbance.

For some time the United States Maritime Commission, the National Federation of American Shipping, representatives of European shipping establishments, both official and private, have been piling up charges and allegations on the inconsistent position of the Argentine Government in some of their own undertakings as related to our indirect assistance in selling them tonnage. Two days ago the representative of an important admiralty firm asked me whether the Department would give support to organized opposition on the part of the interested shipping companies, both American and foreign, to Argentine discrimination. This plan contemplates coordinated pressure and representations through industry and diplomatic channels. I told him that such a program would undoubtedly be helpful at the right time, that you were giving personal attention to the matter and that we would want your advice as to procedure in order to make effective representations in a matter which can have a world-wide effect. He agreed to await developments and expressed his confidence in the procedure you propose.

You asked whether any of our ports give preference to American flag vessels over those of foreign registry. In response I believe we can say without fear of contradiction that no American port favors

---

[58] Not printed.

American ships with regard to berthing or to other port facilities. To make a formal statement to this effect on the part of the Government would mean that we would have to contact and question every port authority in the United States, since, as you know, our port system is not under Federal control. I think it is sufficient however to say that neither I nor any other officer in the Shipping Division know of any case of such discrimination against a foreign vessel. I can attest to the fact that during the past ten years I know of no case in which a foreign government has found it necessary to make representations on the subject. During the war, of course, some discrimination did take place under the Ship Warrant scheme, a necessary war device to make shipping effective in a major military operation. This control no longer exists, however, and assignments of berths, et cetera, rests with municipal, state or private owners of port facilities.

You may be interested to note that within the past few days Moore-McCormack has raised with us discrimination questions in regard to preferential treatment of Argentine vessels in Buenos Aires under a decree published March 13. The company has brought to our attention an old United States statute which so far as I know has never been used. This statute is a section of the Shipping Act of 1886 (46 U.S.C. 142)[59] under which the President by proclamation may deny commercial privileges to foreign vessels as a retaliatory measure. While the use of this and possibly other statutes would not be in conformity with our general policy of liberal reciprocity and national treatment of shipping, the fact remains that if discriminations continue to increase there may be sufficient pressure on the part of the shipping companies to force us to take undesirable retaliatory measures. I am sure you will agree that such action should be used only as a last resort since retaliation merely leads to more discrimination, to more retaliation—a vicious circle—to the detriment of all concerned.

There is another matter which has been giving us concern. Article 22 of the Agreement on Economic and Financial Cooperation between the Republics of Chile and Argentina and similar provisions in agreements between Argentina and other countries contemplate preferential treatment. If carried to its logical conclusion this would result in restricting the carriage between the countries concerned to national ships, on a fifty-fifty basis. It is well-known that many of the South American Republics, notably Brazil and Chile, have long advocated such arrangements. As you well know, such an arrangement would be contrary to our navigation treaties and would run counter to our policy of freeing trade from artificial restrictions.

---

[59] 24 Stat. 79.

With reference to this the Argentine Government is not proceeding in a consistent manner. The Argentine Government has on occasion supported the principle that the American nations adhere to the liberal principles of international trade conducted for peaceful motives and based upon equality of treatment and fair and equitable practices. The division of trade such as contemplated by the provisions of treaties either already negotiated or now being negotiated by Argentina with Brazil, Chile, France, Peru, Spain and Switzerland could not be said to be a liberal principle of international trade nor based upon equality of treatment or fair and equitable practices. Moreover, these treaties if concluded would be inconsistent with Resolution X of the Inter-American Maritime Conference of 1940 [60] in which Argentina participated. Resolution X recommended to the Inter-American Financial and Economic Advisory Committee that it request each of the twenty-one governments of the American Republics give sympathetic consideration to the modification of any laws and regulations which restrict the transportation of cargo to vessels of its own registry except in the coastwise trade.

A wave of protest is arising in connection with the income tax on outward ocean freights provided by Decree No. 14338 of the Argentine Government. For your information, I am enclosing a separate memorandum [61] on the subject. You will be interested to note in this connection that we have been approached informally by several governments in regard to our action in selling ships to Argentina. The record shows that Argentina has received proportionately the greatest share of the highest class tonnage sold. This is so serious that it appears to me that we are forced to give consideration to the possibility of holding up ship sales to Argentina in direct opposition to your recommendations. While we want to avoid tying the ship sales program in with other matters, we cannot lose sight of the fact that such sales might prove embarrassing if Argentina continues on a policy of discrimination.

In connection with this and in any discussion you may have with officials of the Argentine Government, you may want to emphasize that Argentine shipping interests which have applied for the purchase of surplus war-built vessels from the United States Maritime Commission have received very expeditious and favorable actions on the applications as compared with applications received from other nationalities. The following Argentine applications for purchase of

---

[60] Department of State, *Inter-American Maritime Conference, Report of the Delegates of the United States* (Washington, 1941.)
[61] Not printed.

vessels are still pending before the United States Maritime Commission for action:

(1) Compañía Argentina de Navegación Dodero for eight Liberty vessels, four Victories of the troop type class.
(2) YPF (Yacimientos Petrolíferos Fiscales) for the purchase of two tankers and one C1–MAV1 type vessel.
(3) Compañía Argentina de Navegación de Ultramar for the purchase of four Liberty vessels.

The possible purchase by Dodero of three Aircraft Carriers (Escort) from the Newport News Shipbuilding and Dry Dock Company, which are now being reconverted to C–3 type cargo vessels is also under consideration.

In view of the language set forth in Article 22 of the Agreement on Economic and Financial Cooperation by the Republic of Argentina and Chile, above referred to, agencies of this government may be criticized for permitting any more sales of American vessels to Argentine shipping companies which vessels may be used as a means of implementing the agreement which is distinctly out of line with the broad economic policy of this government.

Sincerely yours,
J. E. SAUGSTAD

800.85/4–747

The Acting Secretary of State to the Diplomatic Representatives in the American Republics

WASHINGTON, April 7, 1947.

SIRS: It has been brought to the Department's attention that Argentina is attempting to build up its merchant marine through a system of preferences and discriminations. In this regard pressure is being brought upon other countries by Argentina to include a provision in treaties or agreements under negotiation whereby each country shall take necessary measures to assure that the transportation of merchandise shall take place in vessels of the two contracting countries on an equal tonnage basis.

In Washington, D.C., October 24–30, 1946 during its Second and Final Session the United Maritime Consultative Council representing eighteen maritime nations, was unanimously of the opinion that an Inter-Governmental Maritime Consultative Organization be established through the machinery of the United Nations as a permanent agency in the shipping field. Delegations from the following countries participated: Australia, Brazil, Belgium, Canada, Chile, Denmark, France, Greece, India, Netherlands, New Zealand, Norway, Poland, Sweden, Union of South Africa, United Kingdom, United States, and

Yugoslavia (represented at the meetings by an observer). It is expected that the Economic and Social Council of the United Nations will shortly request the Secretary General to convene a diplomatic conference of interested governments to meet in the autumn of 1947 if practicable, to further consider the Draft Convention approved by the Council. Article I of the Draft Convention describing the scope and purposes of the Organization proposes "to encourage the removal of all forms of discriminatory action and unnecessary restrictions by Governments affecting shipping engaged in international trade so as to promote the availability of shipping services to the commerce of the world without discrimination."

The maritime history of the United States of America indicates that nations indulging in policies of discrimination inevitably reap the dubitable rewards of retaliation.

I enclose a memorandum prepared within the Department under date of March 24, 1947 entitled "Shipping Discriminations" [62] for your appropriate use.

The Department is concerned about the current trend in some countries, as evidenced by treaty provisions and by local legislation, towards the adoption of policies of flag discrimination. Accordingly, any comments, statements, or proposed laws, regulations, or treaty provisions, coming to your attention and bearing upon this general situation should be reported to the Department.

Very truly yours, For the Acting Secretary of State:
WALTER A. RADIUS

835.852/4-1147

The Ambassador in Argentina (Messersmith) to the Secretary of State

[Extracts]

CONFIDENTIAL BUENOS AIRES, April 11, 1947.
No. 2264

SIR: I have the honor to refer to the correspondence which I have had with the Department concerning the sale of merchant vessels to Argentine interests. This Embassy has consistently recommended that the sale of merchant vessels which responsible Argentine interests desire to purchase in the United States should be approved, and this attitude of the Embassy has been based on what it believes to be a full consideration of all the factors involved in the matter and on what is our near-range and long-range national interest.

A number of vessels of various types have been sold by our Govern-

---

[62] Not printed.

ment to Argentine interests and a number of applications for further purchases by Argentine interests are before our competent authorities, and there is reason to believe they may be disapproved. The Department's telegram No. 215 of March 25, 1947, 7:00 P.M., in reply to this Embassy's telegram No. 274 of March 14, 1947,[63] states that the Department views with apprehension the program of the Argentine of commercial agreements such as those entered into with Chile and Spain, and probably some other countries, looking forward to division by Government action of traffic between the ships of the countries concerned. The Department feels that there may be difficulty in explaining ship sales to a country which is following a policy contrary to the shipping policy of our Government and which if carried to a logical conclusion would prevent United States participation in certain trade. The telegram states that further detailed information will be forwarded by mail, and I assume that in this connection reference is made to Mr. Saugstad's letter to me of April 1, 1947 to which is attached a drafted instruction which the Department is considering sending to establishments abroad requesting information on possible discrimination against American shipping.

This Embassy is fully understanding of the considerations set forth in the Department's telegram No. 215 of March 25, 7:00 P.M., and is of the opinion that if the Argentine Government were to persist in the inclusion of a clause in commercial agreements providing for division of traffic and if the Argentine Government were to carry through a practice of discriminating in favor of its own flag in Argentine ports and in the carrying of cargo, it would lead to a discriminatory situation which we could not disregard and it would undoubtedly influence public opinion with respect to ship sales.

This Embassy, however, remains of the opinion that in spite of certain present Argentine practices, it would be unwise not to approve further ship sales to responsible Argentine purchasers, and while it is not possible before the departure of the pouch to go into all the many factors involved in this problem, I wish at this time to transmit the following considerations which I think are of basic interest and bear on this problem.

It is correct that in the commercial agreement recently entered into with Chile and with a number of other countries, as set forth in a memorandum hereto attached (enclosure 1),[64] the Argentine Government has included a clause providing for division of traffic between the ships of the two countries, or at least preferential treatment for the flags of the two countries. This provision is opposed to long stand-

---

[63] Neither printed.
[64] Not printed.

ing maritime practice and is a new provision so far as the Argentine procedure is concerned. In this connection it may be stated that the present Argentine Government contains certain highly nationalistic elements. It also contains in the Congress a considerable number of elements who, while they may not be considered as belonging to the extreme nationalist group in the country, are extremely Argentine and who have no understanding of international practice and of maritime rules of long standing. As a rule in the Argentine treaties of commerce and navigation and commercial agreements have been made primarily through the Ministry of Foreign Relations, but since the present administration has come into office, a very considerable amount of authority and initiative in the commercial field has been shifted to the Central Bank. During the last ten months the commercial agreements entered into by the Argentine have increasingly been prepared in the Central Bank under the direction of Mr. Miranda, the President thereof,[65] and his staff and the Ministry of Foreign Affairs has had less part than before in the making of such agreements. The consequence has been that a group of inexperienced persons in international relationships, otherwise in many respects competent, have been drafting these commercial agreements and this accounts in a large measure for the presence in these agreements of this shipping clause providing for division of traffic, or at least discrimination in favor of the flags of the countries covered by the agreement.

. . . .

It is the considered opinion of this Embassy that the Argentine Government can best be brought into line with liberal economic policies which we advocate in an atmosphere of friendly collaboration instead of one of discrimination. I think we must view the problem from the long-rang point of view rather than from the immediate situation which has every indication of being temporary so far as certain economic policies are concerned. On the other hand, in certain countries of Europe some of these economic policies which are directly opposed to those for which we stand and which must prevail if there is to be peace and security, are much more likely to persist longer.

While this temporary aspect of the Argentine situation could be expanded on to advantage, time does not permit me at this writing to go further into the matter.

In this same connection we have taken note of certain discrimination which is allegedly being shown in the port of Buenos Aires in favor of Argentine flag vessels. There have undoubtedly been cases of such discrimination by the port authorities in favor of Argentine vessels, and there is an official order of an agency of the Argentine

---

[65] Miguel Miranda was also President of the Economic Council.

Government which would extend such privileges to Argentine flag vessels. In practice, however, examination shows that the cases of discrimination so far have been few and that our vessels have not suffered. I think in this connection we must bear in mind the whole problem before we think of taking any discriminatory action or retaliatory action. There are more United States flag vessels coming to Argentine ports today than those of any other country. This is an entirely new development so far as Argentine trade is concerned. We have to bear this preponderance which we have in mind when other countries ask us to take discriminatory or retaliatory measures. There is no doubt that such discrimination in favor of the national flag by the Argentine is contrary to the treaty which we have with the Argentine as well as against accepted international practice, but for the present the most important factor is whether we are being hurt by such discrimination and whether it is going to be permanent. A careful examination of the facts shows that American vessels have not seriously suffered by any discrimination in Argentine ports as yet, and any full examination of the situation in all its aspects brings out clearly the probability that such discrimination will soon be recognized to be unwise by the Argentine Government and be abandoned. It is not believed that any discriminatory or retaliatory measures are necessary to bring about a correction of the situation, and to even talk of them is unwise.

. . . .

In Mr. Saugstad's letter he refers to decrees of the Argentine Government with respect to taxation, and these too are unquestionably unwise, but the shipping companies, American and others, are not particularly concerned about these taxation measures as they feel they can pass the cost on to the freights. Even though this may be so, the measures of the Argentine Government in this respect for that reason are not more sound, and there is reason to believe that these taxation measures also are the result of excess of zeal and inexperience and are of a temporary character.

I will not in this despatch endeavor to go fully into some of the considerations raised in Mr. Saugstad's letter of April 1 as time does not permit and I wish this despatch to go forward by the courier pouch which leaves today. I believe that supplementing this despatch the memorandum [66] hereto appended will be found of interest.

. . . .

Respectfully yours,   George S. Messersmith

---

[66] Not printed.

835.852/4–1847

The Ambassador in Argentina (*Messersmith*) to the Assistant Secretary of State for Transportation and Communication (*Norton*)

[Extracts]

CONFIDENTIAL   BUENOS AIRES, April 18, 1947.

DEAR NORTON: I wish to refer to our telephone conversation this morning with regard to ships for the Argentine and the question of linseed oil shipments, and I wish to supplement the conversation with the following:

. . . .

So far as this shipping clause [67] is concerned which has been put into certain treaties by the Argentine, for example with Chile and others, it has no present significance for us because we are not engaged in the trades covered and would not likely be for years, and so far as the clause itself is concerned, it is a clause which will not stand because it is contrary to established maritime practice as well as against international practice, and I know in the Foreign Office here they realize that this clause cannot stand. We have to remember that these treaties have been made recently by people in the Central Bank and not in the Foreign Office, and that they represent certain arbitrary thinking on the part of certain people here who do not know the world. These clauses in these treaties will not stand, and we should not make the mistake of basing any action of ours on such clauses.

So far as discrimination in Argentine ports in favor of Argentine ships is concerned, of which so much has been said recently by Moore-McCormack in particular, there is really nothing to this. There has been some preference shown to Argentine vessels carrying passengers and there has been some preference shown to certain vessels carrying crude oil for the Argentine oil monopoly, but the difficulties caused to American and foreign flag ships in the port of Buenos Aires is due to the tremendous congestion for the most part and to the heavy shipments here and to the large number of ships of our flag and other foreign flags which are coming here. The situation is one which has been chronic in the port of Buenos Aires for years and is now exaggerated by virtue of the heavy shipments. It is a situation which has really little to do with flag discrimination, and so far as flag discrimination is concerned, the Argentine Government knows it is unsound and it will not be carried through.

So far as the tax legislation is concerned concerning which objection has been made, it is covered by a memorandum which is attached

---

[67] Pertaining to the "division by government action of traffic between ships of the countries concerned," i. e., parties to a maritime agreement.

to my despatch No. 2264,[68] and the shipping companies are really not concerned about this because it is not discriminatory in character and they intend to pass any taxes on to freights.

. . . .

We have reached a serious situation with respect to shipping here. Various Argentine interests have bought some ships from us recently and have paid for them. The Dodero Company is the principal purchaser, and it is a private company and for that reason it is all the more important that its ship purchases should be facilitated. No matter how many ships the Argentine Government wants to buy or Argentine interests want to buy for its merchant marine, the number will be small for they have only limited capacity to purchase or to operate. If we were to sell to the Argentine or if she were to buy or have constructed all the ships she wants and can presently absorb, she would still only be able to carry a very small portion of her trade in her bottoms—I should say not more than 10 percent, and I think much less than that. That is certainly reasonable even if it were 10 percent, which it will not be.

A serious crisis has been caused here by the refusal recently of the Maritime Commission to approve the sale of three ships to the Dodero Company which it purchased from the Newport News Shipbuilding Company. These are three of the Navy flat-tops which the Navy did not want and sold for scrap to the Newport News Company. Dodero bought them from the Newport News Company at a cost of $1,750,000.00 each and it was very good business for the Newport News Company because it keeps their shipyard going, and God knows, we need to keep it going. This refusal of this sale has caused consternation here, not only among the Dodero Company and other shipping circles, but in the Government, and rightly or wrongly, the feeling is that we do not want the Argentine to build up her merchant marine. Rightly or wrongly, the feeling here is that the Moore-McCormack interests have been very active with the Maritime Commission, etc. and are responsible for this refusal of the Maritime Commission to approve the sale, although, of course, these other reasons would be advanced for the refusal such as Argentine discriminations, etc.

This is a serious situation and has had its repercussions already.

When I was home in January, our Government asked me to buy 40,000 tons of linseed oil for delivery by the end of May as we needed this as imperatively and urgently as we needed any item. I took it up on my return, and within a few days the Argentine Government sold us these 40,000 tons at the price they had sold 100,000 tons to the British and in spite of the fact that immediate delivery was very

---

[68] Dated April 11, p. 255; memorandum not printed.

difficult, they agreed to give it to us for shipment by the end of May so as to meet our needs. I will not go into details about this sale, but Commodity Credit and I am sure Secretary Anderson [69] will tell you the Argentines were most forthcoming in this whole matter for they did not hold us to certain conditions which others had to meet.

The Argentine Government did not make it a condition of the sale that half should be carried in Argentine bottoms, but they asked us that this should be done, and naturally I agreed with the approval of the Department that this should be done. It is not written into the contract, but it is just as important that we carry through as if it were in the contract.

We tried here in the Embassy and in Commodity Credit to carry this through, but through negligence of some employees in Dodero, we were informed they would not have a ship available which would carry about 10,000 tons when they really had a ship, and as a result Commodity Credit made arrangements for Moore-McCormack to carry most of the oil. I think it probable that while the people here would have been sore about this they would have let it go by if it had not been that the sale of these three vessels to Dodero was not approved by the Maritime Commission. That started things going, and this morning we were told that export licenses would not be issued for more than 20,000 tons of this oil to be carried in U.S. bottoms. It is a silly action and I am sure it will not be carried through when it is brought to the attention of the higher authorities here, but it indicates the state of feeling, and the feeling is that we are trying to keep Argentine ships out of the River Plate–New York trade so as to keep it for Moore-McCormack.

. . . .

I hope from this letter you will see my great preoccupation and why I think it imperative that we do certain things immediately. The first is to see that the Maritime Commission approves immediately the sale of these three vessels to Dodero for if they don't, I have little hope for the air agreement,[70] and if we get the right kind of an air agreement with the Argentine, we will get this whole situation with regard to air agreements with the other American Republics definitely cleared up, and if we don't get the right kind of an agreement with the Argentine, we will have all sorts of trouble even for the existing trades.

The second thing is to see that Commodity Credit obliges Moore-McCormack to cancel some of the space we had taken from them without compensation so that we can let the *Quilmes* of Dodero carry 10,000 tons.

---

[69] Secretary of Agriculture Clinton P. Anderson.
[70] For documentation on this subject, see pp. 238 ff.

I am tremendously concerned about this whole matter because there is a state of tension in the relationships between the two countries and things like this unnecessarily and unhappily complicate the situation.

I have written frankly about this matter because it is necessary to deal with it in the baldest form, and I have had to dictate this very hurriedly to catch the confidential pouch this evening. I think I can handle the oil question with the Commodity Credit, but the question of the sale of three ships is something which will have to be handled by the Department.

Unfortunately, I may say that I think the circular instruction of April 7 to diplomatic officers starting with the sentence "It has been brought to the Department's attention that the Argentine is attempting to build up its merchant marine through a system of preferences and discriminations" is not going to be any too helpful. There are some discrepancies and contradictions in this instruction, and there is no need of bringing this Argentine situation into the foreground before all of our people because the system of preferences is bound not to last, and so far as discriminations are concerned, they are not established. I will make a separate reply to this instruction, but I did want to say I think it is unfortunate we should start a circular instruction to our officers in the field by pointing the finger at the Argentine. It has made mistakes, and there is no doubt about that, but what it is doing is endeavoring to bring about a merchant marine just as we did.

Respectfully yours, GEORGE S. MESSERSMITH

835.852/4–2347

Memorandum by the Economic Analyst of the Division of River Plate Affairs (Gilmore) to the Chief of That Division (Lyon)

[WASHINGTON,] April 23, 1947.

As requested, I discussed with Mr. Falck, SD,[71] today the suggestion that in any future ship sales we include a reservation on the title to combat the present Argentine policy of including discriminatory division of traffic clauses in its trade agreements with Chile, Spain, and other countries. I also raised with him the question of discrimination against the Moore-McCormack ships in the port of Buenos Aires.[72]

Mr. Falck said that he would have to study the question of attempt-

---

[71] L. James Falck, Assistant Chief, Shipping Division.
[72] In a memorandum transmitted with a letter of April 8, by a representative of Moore-McCormack Lines, evidence was presented to show that while an Argentine ship was berthed immediately, 5 of the Line's ships had been waiting from 7 to 19 days (835.1561/4–1547).

ing to place reservations on the title of vessels sold by the Maritime Commission. He stated that for the present the Maritime Commission will not sell any C-3's to any foreign purchasers and that pending applications for Victories [73] will be referred to us before action is taken.

With respect to port discrimination in Buenos Aires, he said that SD will prepare an instruction to the Embassy asking for detailed information before instructing them to make any further representations to the Foreign Office. He pointed out that in view of a congressional resolution which requires American exports financed by the Export Import Bank to be carried in American bottoms our own record regarding discrimination is not particularly clear.

E. A. GILMORE

835.852/4-2447

The Ambassador in Argentina (Messersmith) to the Secretary of State

[Extracts]

CONFIDENTIAL
No. 2365

BUENOS AIRES, April 24, 1947.

SIR: . . .

. . . .

In the Department's telegram no. 322 of April 19, 11 a. m., 1947,[74] I am informed that my despatch no. 2264 of April 11, 1947 had not yet been received in the Department. The telegram further states that the rejection by the Maritime Commission of the transfer of registry of the three C-V's to the Dodero Company was motivated by the Commission's policy that no vessels of this type be sold foreign and that requests for similar transfer of five vessels to Sweden had recently been rejected. The telegram further states that the present position of the Commission is that of the approximately 18 vessels of this category, none will be sold abroad since when reconverted they would be C-3's which are in short supply for American operators.

I am pleased to note from this telegram that the Department of State formally has taken the position that it has no objection to the sale of these vessels. The telegram further states, however, that our statutes give full authority to the Maritime Commission to withhold the sale of vessels to foreigners if this may be in the interest of United States shipping. It is also stated that no evidence of discrimination as between foreign applicants exists and that should any of these ves-

---

[73] Wartime cargo ships.
[74] Not printed.

sels be made available for sale to foreigners, the Department will request that the application of the Dodero Company be reconsidered. The telegram further states that the Ship Sales Act provides that in considering preferences between non-citizens, the Commission should consider the extent to which the countries seeking vessels incurred losses during the war effort. The observation is made that the Argentine fleet is now far above the pre-war level and it has received proportionately a greater share of desirable types of tonnage than any other country. It is further observed that the representatives of several governments have informally called the attention of the Department to the fact that the Argentine has received favorable treatment.

. . . .

In the case of these particular vessels, it is my understanding that the Navy has indicated that it does not need them and that the three vessels in question in which the Dodero Company is interested were sold by the Navy to the Newport News Shipbuilding Company to be scrapped for, I believe, around $170,000.00 each. The Newport News Shipbuilding Company, the maintenance of the facilities of which is of importance to our Navy and defense, considered the possibility of reconverting these vessels for merchant marine purposes and offered them to American shipping firms. According to the information which I have, which seems to be correct, no American firm expressed an interest in these vessels and it was after this expression of lack of interest by American firms that the Newport News Shipbuilding Company sold them to the Dodero Company at a price of $1,750,000.00 each, which the Dodero Company is prepared to pay in cash. It would seem, therefore, if the foregoing facts are correct, that the vessels were offered to United States shipping companies which were not interested.

. . . .

From the standpoint of ocean-going traffic, therefore, the Argentine has some 39 vessels of over 1,500 tons, not including tankers, and it would not seem that such a merchant fleet is out of proportion with the legitimate aspirations of the Argentine economy. It is not believed that it would be the policy of our Government to endeavor to limit the Argentine merchant marine to its pre-war tonnage and even if there should be such a desire on our part, there would be no way in which we could control this, for orders can be placed freely by her in shipyards in the United States or abroad, and unfortunately most of the orders would be placed in foreign shipyards as the cost of construction in our own yards is relatively so high.

. . . .

It is a very real hope of this Embassy that the Department will be able to secure the reconsideration by the Maritime Commission of this refusal to sell three vessels to the Dodero firm, and it is very desirable that this be done in the very near future.

Respectfully yours, GEORGE S. MESSERSMITH

835.852/4–2547 : Telegram

The Ambassador in Argentina (Messersmith) to the Secretary of State

CONFIDENTIAL   BUENOS AIRES, April 25, 1947—11 a. m.

470. For Assistant Secretary Norton. President Central Bank in statement to British correspondent several days ago said that Argentina was prepared to place orders for 250,000 tons merchant shipping in British yards and could pay for ships. This statement probably one of expressions of resentment officials circles here over refusal Maritime Commission authorize sale three vessels (Embtel 437, April 18 and Deptel 322, April 19 [75]). UP dispatch from Washington in morning's papers here today states that Maritime Commission is considering regulation sale surplus US ships to foreign countries and "the regulation will also prevent foreign countries building merchant fleets larger than they had before the war by the purchase of US ships".

It is my hope that the consideration set forth Embdes 2264, April 11, letter to Assistant Secretary Norton dated April 18 and Embdes 2365, April 24 leaving by pouch today will be given consideration by Department and Maritime Commission before any policy decisions respecting sale vessels to Argentina or other American countries are made.

MESSERSMITH

835.852/4–1847

Memorandum by the Director of the Division of Transportation and Communications (Radius) to the Assistant Secretary of State for Transportation and Communications (Norton)

[WASHINGTON,] April 25, 1947.

My conversation with Truitt [76] did not alter the picture in any material way. As I see it, Truitt's basic complaint is against the Maritime Commission for preventing the sale of flattops foreign. While he has some legal points which indicate the Maritime Commission is using questionable technicalities to achieve its objective of not selling any flattops abroad, I do not feel that there is a case for discrimination against Argentina on the matter of sale of flattops. It is true that the Commission's policy contains many inconsistencies and is not

---

[75] Neither printed.
[76] Max Truitt, Legal Counsel of the Dodero Lines.

very logical, nevertheless, since it does apply equally to all countries with respect to this type of ship, it cannot be held to be discriminatory.

There is in course of preparation an analysis of the whole problem of Argentine shipping discriminations and its relationship to ship sales in order to bring to a focus the Department's policy line on this. We should be ready to discuss this with you shortly.

ARA is up to date on this and I assume they are keeping Mr. Braden [77] informed as they feel necessary.

835.1561/4-1547 : Telegram

The Secretary of State to the Embassy in Argentina

CONFIDENTIAL WASHINGTON, May 2, 1947—8 p.m.

383. Department desires more specific information concerning port discrimination referred to page 5 Embassay's despatch 2264, April 11. In view representations by Moore-McCormack implying greater delays of their ships than those of Flota Mercante,[78] has decree March 13 giving Flota exclusive use of certain berthing space resulted in their vessels incurring less delay? If this is case, Department of opinion this action, taken during period of port congestion, is discriminatory and gives Flota unfair competitive advantage unless other lines accorded opportunity acquiring exclusive berthing space. Suggest this matter be taken up officially with Argentine Government if Argentine vessels accorded any competitive advantage.

MARSHALL

835.1561/5-2947

Memorandum by Mr. John L. Ohmans of the Division of River Plate Affairs [79]

[WASHINGTON,] June 12, 1947.

AMBASSADOR MESSERSMITH'S DESPATCH 2612 OF MAY 29 REGARDING ARGENTINE SHIPPING DISCRIMINATIONS [80]

The Embassy has been informed that as of May 27 shipping berth discrimination in favor of Argentine vessels was abolished by order of the Port Administrator. This evidently was the result of several

---

[77] Spruille Braden, Assistant Secretary of State for American Republic Affairs.
[78] A memorandum of conversation by the Chief of the Division of River Plate Affairs (Lyon) April 30, indicated that on April 22, 14 Moore-McCormack ships were awaiting berths while a vessel of the Flota Mercante was berthed immediately upon arrival (835.1561/4-3047).
[79] Addressed to Mr. Cecil B. Lyon and Mr. Rollin S. Atwood of the Division of River Plate Affairs.
[80] Not printed.

conversations the Ambassador had with the Foreign Minister.[81] The Ambassador emphasizes that one of the principal difficulties in the port situation has been the lack of adequate and wise administration. Despite the fact that a commission has been appointed to study the ship handling the Embassy does not anticipate too great immediate results.

The berth discrimination feature was discussed with Mr. Dodero who agreed that the Argentine measures were unfair but pointed out that Argentine shipping in ports like New York is in a disadvantageous position. Dodero was told it was up to him to make appropriate arrangements with New York port authorities. The Ambassador believes that the bulk of the American shipping complaints has been made by the Moore-McCormack Line which is anxious to maintain its dominant position in the U.S.–River Plate trade.

At the Ambassador's suggestion a meeting of the American shipping companies was held in the Embassy to discuss the various problems affecting American shipping interests. It was evident that the companies themselves have been inactive in bringing their various complaints to the attention of Argentine authorities. The Ambassador pointed out to the company representatives that he, as well as his British and Swedish colleagues, feels that the companies must make more adequate approaches to Argentine authorities before formal steps can be taken.

The Embassy is of the opinion that flag discrimination and other shipping discriminations such as the income tax on foreign freight profits are objectionable and undesirable. However, the Ambassador feels that before we can make any formal protest to the other Governments with respect to alleged discriminations or proved discriminations we must be able to come with clean hands. In this respect he cites the provisions of Public Law 17 which require merchandise purchased with Export Import Bank funds to be carried in American bottoms.

The Ambassador emphasizes that other major countries interested in shipping are not disturbed about the situation in the same measure as Moore-McCormack has pressed in on our Government. He suggests that the justification of the 35% surcharge on freight rates might be a useful subject of study.

A memorandum [82] attached to the despatch presents the position of the American shipping companies in the River Plate trade in some detail. It shows that Moore-McCormack has 50 ships in the trade.

It asserts that the Centro de Navigación Transatlántica is a shipping organization representing local as well as foreign shipping interests,

---

[81] Juan Atilio Bramuglia.
[82] Not printed.

although there are actually very few local companies represented. All American companies are members.

With regard to the new income tax affecting shipping profits, Mr. Clarendon, the local Moore-McCormack representative stated that the tax if applied would amount to 1 million pesos for 1946 for his company.

J. L. OHMANS

835.852/6–1747 : Telegram

The Secretary of State to the Embassy in Argentina

US URGENT WASHINGTON, June 17, 1947—7 p. m.
RESTRICTED

531. Deptel 322 Apr 19.[83] Marit Com June 13 approved application Newport News Shipbuilding Co to enter into contract with Dodero to convert 2 CVEs–51 and 52 to commercial cargo vessels. Formal transfer order to be issued when conversion completed.

MARSHALL

835.1561/5–2947

The Secretary of State to the Chargé in Argentina (Ray)

CONFIDENTIAL WASHINGTON, August 2, 1947.
No. 869

SIR: Reference is made to the Embassy's despatch No. 2612 of May 29, 1947,[84] concerning preferential treatment being given to Argentine flag vessels by the Argentine Government, in which it was stated that the Argentine Government had removed any cause or basis for official representations with respect to the preferential berthing of vessels in the port of Buenos Aires.

The Department now has been informed by Moore-McCormack Lines, Inc. that the preferential berthing arrangements were resumed a few days later and that recently this preference was extended to a vessel of the Dodero Company. For the information of the Embassy, there are attached copies of correspondence exchanged recently with Moore-McCormack Lines.[85]

Moore-McCormack Lines recently have instituted a complaint with the United States Maritime Commission under Section 26 of the Shipping Act of 1916 [86] which requires the Maritime Commission to inves-

---

[83] Not printed.
[84] Summarized in Mr. Ohmans' memorandum of June 12, p. 266.
[85] Enclosures not printed.
[86] 39 Stat. 728.

tigate discriminatory actions of this nature. A copy of the Maritime Commission's letter of July 9, 1947 to Moore-McCormack Lines is enclosed.

As stated in the Department's telegram No. 383 of May 2, 1947, the Department is of the opinion that the preferential berthing arrangement in the port of Buenos Aires is discriminatory and gives Argentine shipping an unfair competitive advantage over American shipping. In this connection officers of the Department have been informed by officers of Moore-McCormack that Argentine shipping interests are using this discrimination to obtain cargoes from the United States on the basis that shipments on their vessels are delivered more promptly. Obviously, if this discrimination continues, shippers will use Argentine vessels in preference to American vessels to avoid delays of their shipments.

It is realized that the Embassy has investigated this matter thoroughly and that the matter has been discussed with the Argentine Government. However, it appears that the Argentine Government persists in its discrimination. If the Embassy is able to confirm that the Argentine Government has continued to discriminate against United States shipping, the Embassy is requested to review again this situation with the Argentine Government with a view to eliminating this discrimination against American shipping. It should be pointed out that Argentine shipping is not discriminated against in United States ports.

Since the Maritime Commission is most concerned, it is hoped that the Argentine Government will be able to afford early relief in the matter. The Embassy will recall that this Government has been most generous in its sales of ships to Argentina so that Argentina has been able to build up a merchant fleet far in excess of that operated before the war, which few, if any, other countries have been able to do.

It is requested also that the Embassy submit a complete report on this matter which can be transmitted to the Maritime Commission for use in connection with its investigation.

Very truly yours, For the Secretary of State:
GARRISON NORTON

835.1561/9–447

The Ambassador in Argentina (Bruce) to the Secretary of State

RESTRICTED BUENOS AIRES, September 4, 1947.
No. 2943

SIR: I have the honor to refer to the Department's Confidential Instruction No 869 of August 2, 1947, regarding the preferential berthing of vessels in the Port of Buenos Aires.

Further discussion of the subject matter with the governmental authorities and others named below [87] indicates that preferential treatment has been and continues to be accorded, as a rule, only to ships owned or chartered by the Argentine government.

The authorities referred to felt that this practice was not discriminatory. An interest was expressed in being informed of the practice of the United States government in berthing its own and its chartered merchant vessels engaged in carrying government and/or civilian cargo. Consequently, the Embassy would, before making representations on a higher level, appreciate receiving such information on this subject as the Department and the Maritime Commission may be able to provide, as well as comment on the overall situation as described in the enclosure.

Respectfully yours,

For the Ambassador:
JULIAN C. GREENUP
*Counselor of Embassy
for Economic Affairs*

611.3531/9-2247

The Secretary of State to the Embassy in Argentina

CONFIDENTIAL WASHINGTON, October 22, 1947.
No. 63

The Secretary of State refers to the Embassy's airgram no. A-583 of September 19, 1947 and despatch no. 3016 of September 22, 1947,[88] both relating to the new exchange regulations issued on September 17th by the Argentine Central Bank.

In the despatch under reference the Embassy calls the attention of the Department to the apparent violation by these new controls of Article IV of the United States-Argentine trade agreement,[89] but adds that no action will be taken regarding the matter pending receipt of instructions from the Department.

The Department deems it desirable that the Embassy not make separate representations to the Argentine Government in each case where the exchange controls might be in conflict with some provision of the trade agreement. It is considered preferable that such representations as may be later made should cover thoroughly the entire situation arising from the controls.

Moreover, in the particular case in question, which involves advantages accorded to certain countries in the granting of exchange

---

[87] In enclosure to this despatch; not printed.
[88] Neither printed.
[89] Department of State Executive Agreement Series No. 277.

permits, the Department, after careful study, is of the opinion that this alone does not constitute any violation of the trade agreement, and, accordingly, the Embassy is instructed to take no action in the premises. (See notes annexed to Agreement.)

635.4131/10-1647 : Airgram

The Acting Secretary of State to the Embassy in the United Kingdom

CONFIDENTIAL WASHINGTON, November 4, 1947.

A-998. Reference Embtel 5554, October 16.[90] Regarding possible discrimination by Argentina against US in purchases from UK, Department has following comments:

(1) Argentina now has considerable latitude under Argentine note dated October 14, 1941 appended to US-Argentine trade agreement (Exec. Agreement Series 277). Paragraph 3 of this note is as follows:

"The representatives of the Argentine Government have also pointed out that the ability of Argentina to give full effect to these principles [of non-discrimination][91] is dependent on circumstances beyond the control of Argentina. Recently, the Argentine trade-and-payments position has been aggravated to a very important extent by the trade and financial controls which have been adopted by the belligerents in the present European conflict, notably the United Kingdom, one of the principal markets for Argentine export products. In particular, the inability of Argentina to convert freely into dollars the proceeds of sales to the United Kingdom makes it impossible for the Argentine Government to extend full non-discriminatory treatment to the trade of the United States of America".

(2) As for other countries, consideration would have to be given to any commitments which might be applicable in specific cases. Embassy will note that paragraph 1(*b*) of Article XIV of General Agreement on Trade and Tariffs [92] provides exception similar in purpose to paragraph 5(*b*) of Swedish *aide-mémoire*. While the General Agreement provisions on non-discrimination and exceptions thereto are not effective until January 1, 1949, the Department would seek to persuade foreign countries to keep any discrimination exercised within the limits of these provisions.

LOVETT

---

[90] Not printed.
[91] Brackets appear in the original airgram.
[92] Department of State, Treaties and Other International Acts Series No. 1700; 61 Stat. (pts. 5 and 6).

835.1561/11–1047

The Ambassador in Argentina (Bruce) to the Secretary of State

No. 3193   BUENOS AIRES, November 10, 1947.

SIR: Referring to the Department's Confidential Instruction No. 869 of August 2, 1947, I have the honor to enclose herewith a copy of the Embassy's *Note Verbale* No. 20 of October 9, 1947, to the Argentine Ministry of Foreign Affairs, regarding the preferential treatment said to be accorded in the ports of Argentina to vessels of the Argentine government which are engaged in commercial traffic, and to the unfair competitive advantage which this situation provides.

The Embassy has not yet received a reply to this *Note Verbale*.

Respectfully yours,   For the Ambassador:
                                                     JULIAN GREENUP
                                                     *Counselor of Embassy
                                                     for Economic Affairs*

[Enclosure]

The American Ambassador in Argentina (Bruce) to the Argentine Minister for Foreign Affairs and Worship (Bramuglia)

No. 20   BUENOS AIRES, October 9, 1947.

EXCELLENCY: For such favorable action as Your Excellency may in cooperation accord, I have the honor to call attention to the preferential treatment said to be accorded in the ports of Argentina to vessels of the Argentine government which are engaged in commercial traffic; and to the unfair competitive advantage which this situation provides.

This preferential treatment quite naturally encourages exporters and importers to patronize the Argentine vessels which deliver and receive cargo rapidly, in preference to shipping on vessels which, not enjoying such benefits, have to await long periods in port. Merchants who receive their goods with great delay are handicapped as compared with competitors who receive their merchandise promptly; and the shipping companies which have to defray the expenses of long idleness of vessels are forced to bear an unequal financial burden as compared with the Argentine government ships which turn around quickly.

Before bringing this matter to Your Excellency's attention, it was deemed appropriate to request a complete investigation in the United States pertaining to the handling of vessels of the United States government engaged in commercial traffic. The Embassy has now received an official reply stating that no preference is given to vessels of the

United States or any other nation, apart from the usual international procedure pertaining to considerations of health, perishable cargo, passenger vessels, et cetera.

The communication from Washington indicated that American as well as foreign steamship operators are, however, permitted to own privately or to lease port facilities for their exclusive or preferential use.

In view of this unequal treatment in providing port facilities, and since it so far appears impossible for vessels carrying the United States flag to obtain facilities for their exclusive or preferential use in the ports of Argentina, my government has requested me to discuss this matter with Your Excellency in the usual spirit of friendship and collaboration with the object of determining if a more advantageous arrangement for American vessels in the ports of Argentina may be arranged.

I avail myself [etc.] [JAMES BRUCE]

611.3531/11–1847

The Ambassador in Argentina (Bruce) to the Secretary of State

CONFIDENTIAL BUENOS AIRES, November 18, 1947.
No. 3211

SIR: The Embassy has the honor to acknowledge the Department's unclassified instruction of October 14, 1947,[93] transmitting request from the Office of International Trade of the Department of Commerce, dated October 8, 1947 (Reference: IT–1010–CFC), that the Embassy comment on the exchange aspects of trade and financial relations between the United States and Argentina during the next year.

. . . .

The first report cited above [94] indicates the confusion created by the Central Bank's rulings on capital investments and remittance of profits. Apparently the Bank itself did not realize the many problems that would arise by reason of the vagueness and incompleteness of the regulations and is somewhat overwhelmed with the deluge of questions to which it must give answers. It is now accumulating information in order to make decisions on the points of major interest to business men, and private entities are assembling data with the view to being of assistance.

Until the uncertainties concerning foreign investments already in the country are clarified and/or more definite assurances are received

---

[93] Not printed.
[94] The Ambassador cited his despatches 3116, October 22, and 3099, October 21, and report 989, October 30 (none printed).

from the Central Bank covering new investments, the objectives of the measures on the inflow of funds appear to be nullified. On the other hand, the President of the National Economic Council, Sr. Miguel Miranda, recently explained to the Commercial Attaché [95] of the Embassy that he is the author of the Central Bank Circulars on the subject, that he considers them crystal clear and expressive of a most generous attitude toward foreign capital and its profits, and cannot understand the reported confusion of business men on the subject, and that he will personally be glad to answer any questions addressed to him directly. He characterized the measures as "transitory", "Temporary" and designed to meet "emergency conditions" and not as representing long-range policy. These measures were designed, without doubt, to attract much needed foreign capital; as previously reported, the President has indicated his desire to encourage the investment of American capital in Argentina. It is believed that any liberal attitude on the part of the Argentine Government concerning transfers of capital or remittances of profits derived therefrom will depend on the improvement in the exchange position through trade channels, or upon the realization of the necessity of attracting a growing volume of foreign funds to the country.

The complete suspension of imports in August was followed by the publication in September of a list of permissible imports which was later expanded, and the division of the countries of the world into two groups, with preferential treatment for one group. The Central Bank indicated that in the favored countries Argentina has heavy surpluses of foreign exchange by reason of recently concluded agreements or as the natural results of trading. The channelizing of trade by means of these regulations is already in practice. For example, it has been reported that exchange permits for the importation of galvanized wire from the United States have been refused, and that they will be granted only for imports from Europe, at least until the situation of dollar availability improves or a solution is found to the question of the inconvertibility of the pound. Applications for exchange permits to cover round, flat and square steel bars from the United States have also been rejected, except for that material already having an import license from the Secretary of Industry and Commerce. According to reliable sources, the possibility of lifting the import prohibition against these items would be contemplated in order to facilitate imports from Europe. It may be asserted that the trend is to reject applications for dollar exchange for products that may be imported from Europe, even though the price is much higher, and even though the supply is inadequate.

---

[95] Joseph Louis Apodaca.

The curtailment of exchange for essential U.S. imports may be relieved, at least slightly, by the agreement just concluded by the U.S. Army Grain Mission covering the purchase of grain to be shipped to Europe, and to a greater extent if more purchases are made in the future. Sr. Miranda has stated that Argentina is willing to sell its available production, including meat, at export prices prevailing in the United States, provided his country is guaranteed the delivery of much needed equipment at prices prevailing in the United States for such equipment. This observation was made by Sr. Miranda in view of his recent discussions with the Ambassador on the subject, and apparently the Argentine Government has some hope that this can be arranged.

During a recent interview between officials of the General Motors Corporation, who were escorted by the Commercial Attaché of the Embassy, and Sr. Miranda, the latter categorically refused to grant further exchange permits desired by General Motors for the importation of chassis, refrigeration equipment, and a long list of other materials required for continued operations of General Motors plants in Argentina. Sr. Miranda explained his refusal on the ground that Argentina has no dollar exchange, and that even if it had sufficient exchange for the purpose, it would hesitate to use it for anything that would promote the production of automotive equipment, since such equipment requires the use of gasoline. The country, Sr. Miranda added, is desperately in need of gasoline and must use dollar exchange for its purchase. Sr. Miranda further remarked that so long as Argentina continues to deliver its exports to countries that cannot pay in dollars, as she has been forced to do in recent months, it will be impossible for her to build up the necessary dollar reserves to carry out her much needed industrialization. He spoke of credits having been made to France, Italy, Spain and other countries calling for the delivery of Argentine agricultural products, but he emphasized that payment cannot be foreseen and that none of the countries is in a position to offer dollar payment. The solution to the whole problem, he repeated over and over again, lies with the United States.

Of great importance, also, in the shaping of Argentina's future foreign trade policy will be the arrangements reached with Great Britain. The accentuation of the principle of bilateralism referred to above might also imply that on the conclusion of a satisfactory agreement with Great Britain, British imports will be in a favored position. As indicated in the second report cited above, whether the United Kingdom will be able to manufacture and export to Argentina in quantities sufficient to achieve a balancing of accounts and to supply some of the sorely needed goods here is a moot question. A concerted effort, no doubt, will be made to do this; the morning press, for example, carries a UP despatch date-lined London in which it is reported that British locomotive firms have promised the Trade Mission coming to Buenos Aires that if it gets an order for 300 steam locomotives that are needed for the Five-Year Plan, "delivery will be on time". It is also reported that the British will seek the order as soon as the railway deal [96] is signed and that despite American competitors, will have a good chance because "the British companies are the traditional builders of Argentina's rolling stock and know the railways there inside out". It might be added in this connection that in recent weeks local representatives of American railway equipment manufactures have called on the Embassy several times for assistance in closing orders with the Government. Their difficulty stems from the fact that although they can offer the equipment preferred by Government officials and can guarantee earlier delivery than European competitors, the question of scarcity of dollar exchange weighs heavily in prompting Argentine officials to give serious consideration to European firms.

To summarize, the prospects for United States imports into Argentina at present are not bright, and it is believed that this situation will obtain for some months to come. The most likely improvement in dollar availabilities would result from United States purchases of Argentine foodstuffs for the needy countries of Europe. Rumors of a loan or credits from the United States continue, but these are denied by the authorities.

Respectfully yours,

For the Ambassador:
JULIAN GREENUP
*Counselor of Embassy
for Economic Affairs*

835.1561/12-447

The Ambassador in Argentina (Bruce) to the Secretary of State

RESTRICTED BUENOS AIRES, December 4, 1947.
No. 3288

SIR: I have the honor to refer to this Embassy's despatch No. 2348 of November 26, 1947 on the subject of "Port Facilities in Buenos Aires—Provisions for Equality of Treatment" [97] and to report that we took up with Foreign Minister Bramuglia on December 2 the question of treatment accorded vessels of the Moore-McCormack Lines and

---

[96] Reference is to the transfer of Argentine railroads owned by British interests to the Argentine Government. According to airgram A-307, February 13, from London, the purchase price was said to be 150 million pounds sterling. Management of the railroads was to remain in British hands. (835.51/2-1347)
[97] Not printed.

requested in particular that immediate attention be given the application made by Moore-McCormack for wharfage space. There is enclosed a copy of a letter from Mr. E. P. Clarendon, the local manager of Moore-McCormack [98] in which reference is made to the need for prompt wharfage space and berthing facilities for the S. S. *Argentina*, the S. S. *Uruguay* and the S. S. *Brasil*.

Foreign Minister Bramuglia made notes on the subject and sent for a copy of his note no. 694 of November 20, 1947, a translation of which was transmitted with this Embassy's despatch no. 2348. Bramuglia said that he would take the matter up immediately with the President and would endeavor to obtain prompt action.

We told Bramuglia that we had verified that there was no discrimination against Argentine vessels in the United States and that there seemed to be no doubt left that discrimination is carried out here against American vessels. We added that the only solution seemed to be for the Argentine Government to make it possible for Moore-McCormack to buy or lease wharfage space. We pointed out that otherwise the three vessels comprising the "Good Neighbor Fleet" would probably have to terminate their southern voyages at Montevideo, and while this might not be a serious matter for Argentina from a commercial and financial viewpoint it would cause a lot of criticism and arouse the resentment of tourists who would like to visit Buenos Aires. Bramuglia said that he was sure President Perón would want to do everything in his power to prevent such a development. Bramuglia reiterated that he and the President would give this matter their immediate attention.

Respectfully yours,

For the Ambassador:
Guy W. Ray
Counselor of Embassy

835.1561/1–1248

The Secretary of State to the Embassy in Argentina

No. 47
Washington, February 14, 1948.

Sir: I enclose for the Embassy's information a copy of a letter dated December 24, 1947 addressed to the President of the United States [98] by the Chairman of the United States Maritime Commission with further reference to the action of the Argentine Government in assigning exclusive rights to certain piers and warehouses in the port of Buenos Aires to the Flota Mercante del Estado, a government-owned corporation operating vessels. The letter was referred to the Secretary of State for appropriate action. Although the Department appreciates

---

[98] Not printed.

that the decree mentioned in the letter from the Maritime Commission has been rescinded by the Argentine Government, and will so inform the Maritime Commission when the further information requested below has been received, the letter reflects the concern with which the Maritime Commission, as well as the Department, views discrimination against American shipping.

In the above relation reference is made to the Embassy's despatches no. 27 of January 12, 1948 and no. 3248 of November 26, 1947 enclosing a copy of note no. 694 dated November 20, 1947, and a translation of the same,[1] from the Argentine Ministry of Foreign Affairs. In its closing paragraph the Ministry's note states that the American shipping firms are on a basis of absolute equality with national organizations as concerns the *obtaining of concessions* within the port zone of Buenos Aires, and that it is only necessary that those interested submit their applications to the appropriate authorities. While there undoubtedly has been a great improvement in the port situation at Buenos Aires, it is not clear to the Department that a preferential discrimination does not still exist in favor of vessels of the Flota Mercante del Estado in making berthing space available. The Embassy is requested to make a further investigation of this matter and report to the Department whether or not in the present circumstances there is any actual discrimination against American shipping in Argentine ports.[2]

For the information of the Embassy, the Department has been informed by the American Embassy at Rio de Janeiro that the discriminating berthing priority accorded to Lloyd Brasileiro has been terminated.

Very truly yours,   For the Secretary of State:
WILLARD L. THORP

CONCERN OF THE UNITED STATES WITH THE PETROLEUM PROBLEMS OF ARGENTINA AND THE AMERICAN PETROLEUM COMPANIES

835.6363/3–1347 : Telegram

The Acting Secretary of State to the Embassy in Argentina

CONFIDENTIAL   WASHINGTON, March 26, 1947—7 p. m.

226. *La Prensa* Mar 6 reports five bills introduced Chamber Deputies recommending ban on mixed companies,[3] expropriation private oil

---

[1] None printed.

[2] In despatch 232, March 15, 1948, the Ambassador indicated that the rescinding of objectionable decrees had not been published, that the Argentine Flota Mercante and Dodero continued to enjoy exclusive privileges, but that all ships were berthing with little delay by reason of waning ocean traffic and improvement in port administration (835.1561/3–1548).

[3] Companies jointly operated or regulated by private firms and by the state.

companies, and other restrictive measures. What in opinion Embassy are motives, likelihood action and possible result.

ACHESON

835.6363/3-2747 : Telegram

The Ambassador in Argentina (Messersmith) to the Secretary of State

CONFIDENTIAL   BUENOS AIRES, March 27, 1947— 8 p. m.

334. Some time ago Govt Petroleum Company, YPF,[4] showed some interest in a mixed company and some Deputies opposed such action insisting that YPF should make full report on its operations. Bills referred to in Deptel 226, March 26, all grew out of these rumors concerning YPF and opposition certain deputies to proposed plans of govt to augment petroleum production, possibly through greater use of foreign companies. The bills are under discussion in Chamber, and it is not likely that any of them will be approved. Subject being covered in monthly petroleum report shortly due pursuant Depcirins April 26, 1946.[5]

MESSERSMITH

835.6363/5-947

The Ambassador in Argentina (Messersmith) to the Secretary of State

SECRET   BUENOS AIRES, May 9, 1947.
No. 2482

SIR: I have the honor to refer to the Department's telegram no. 398 of May 8, 6:00 P. M.[6] stating that the Standard Oil Company has informed the Department that the Argentine Government is insisting that wage increases be granted to the workers in the industry before consideration is given to price increases which would be compensatory; that the Standard Oil Company fears noncompliance with the demands of the workers would mean expropriation of the companies under the guise of national emergency; that the Department is inclined to protest to the Argentine Government that continuing forced increases in costs without compensatory price increases is in effect confiscation of the company assets without compensation therefor. The Department states that it is awaiting the Embassy's report and recommendations before recommending such step.

Immediately upon receipt of this telegram I have sent a telegram to the Department, no. 561 of May 9, 1:00 P.M.,[6] in which I state that

---

[4] Yacimientos Petrolíferos Fiscales, a government instrumentality.
[5] Neither printed.
[6] Not printed.

I do not believe it would be desirable to make any formal protest at this time.

In this connection I may inform the Department that shortly after I assumed charge of this Mission I had contact with the heads of the American oil interests in the Argentine. Our interests in the Argentine in this field are covered, I believe, entirely by the Standard of New Jersey which has, I believe, six or seven subsidiaries here, and by the "Ultramar" which is owned jointly by the Texas Company and Socony. The American companies are engaged in production and distribution. The Department is aware that the situation of the American and foreign companies in the Argentine has not been on a very satisfactory basis for some years, and it was for this reason that from the beginning of my stay here I have been in touch with them constantly with regard to their current problems.

Although the situation of the companies has been on this unsatisfactory and somewhat uncertain basis for a number of years, in fact for many years, the immediate position of the companies seemed to be improving in some respects when the present constitutional Government took office in June, 1946. In view of the importance of fuel, and particularly petroleum, in the Argentine economy, there were definite indications that the Argentine Government was viewing the problems of the foreign oil companies with greater understanding, and particularly in view of the fact that the Government was much dissatisfied with the operations of the Government company Yacimientos Petrolíferos Fiscales (YPF).

About three weeks ago the workers in the oil industry outside of the YPF began a slow-down strike. The companies were already losing money because of the inadequate price and these losses were being suffered by the YPF as well as by the private companies, among which there are a number of purely Argentine-owned private companies. The companies began discussions with the Government concerning a price increase, and these had started before the slow-down strike in the private industry. The Government had shown a recognition of the fact that a price increase was necessary if the companies were to operate without loss. The Government apparently had no doubt that the companies were operating at a loss as the Government itself was obliged to make up the considerable deficit of YPF.

When the slow-down strike in the private industry started, the companies entered into conversations with the workers but these made slow progress because of the intransigence of the workers and because the companies were uncertain as to what price increase they could depend upon from the Government. The activity in the refineries under the slow-down strike reached the point where the refineries could not, according to the statement of the companies, be continued without danger. About a week ago, therefore, the companies felt themselves under the necessity of closing down the refineries. This immediately caused a serious gasoline and fuel shortage which has had serious repercussions and great inconvenience for the public.

When this point was raised, I informed the heads of the American companies that I thought every effort should be made by them to reach a solution as public opinion which would ordinarily be with the companies would, through this aggravated shortage, turn against them. The companies were fully aware of this situation, and I believe that their attitude in the conversations with the workers have on the whole been reasonable.

I cannot in this despatch, as the pouch is leaving in a few hours, go into details with regard to the negotiations, but I shall do so in a further despatch to follow in the next confidential pouch. It is sufficient to say that the companies have felt ready to grant the wage increases asked for by the workers even though they did this before the price increases were granted as they felt the Government realizes the present losses of the companies and would grant an adequate price increase. The companies, however, have objected to the demands of the union for a single union to include workers and employees as they are of the opinion, which seems in many respects justified, that this will make proper operations for them practically impossible and as they believe the Government, in imposing such a solution of a single union in this important industry, will create a very difficult precedent for itself and for Argentine industry.

The companies, however, have felt that arbitrary action might be taken and therefore have agreed two days ago to the increases which the workers up to that time had asked and have also agreed to the single union, much as they believe this contrary to the best interests of the industry. There was reason to believe that the Government supported the agreement which was signed two days ago in the Ministry of Labor.

To the surprise of the Government and of the companies, the workers yesterday refused to accept the settlement which the heads of the syndicates and the companies had signed, and the workers are now demanding further wage increases which seem extravagant.

Day before yesterday the Ministry of Labor issued a statement to the press with respect to the shortage of gasoline and the conversations between the workers and the companies, which statement was tendentious and which placed the responsibility for the gasoline shortage on the intransigence of the private companies. If the information which I have from the companies and which the Embassy has from other sources is correct, which it has every reason to believe, then this statement of the Ministry of Labor was not only tendentious but incorrect.

I have during the last week been in touch with the Foreign Minister [8] informally with regard to this matter. I have informed him that the attitude of the companies is reasonable and that they are willing to give any wage increases which the Government may determine just. I informed the Minister that while the companies did not believe it desirable that there should be this single union, they would, if the Government imposed this solution, accept it.

The Foreign Minister stated to me yesterday that he had discussed the matter with the President [9] and that it was recognized that appropriate price increases were necessary in order to meet the costs of the industry. He further stated that expropriation was in his opinion not in question.

. . . .

I have informed the Department in the telegram above mentioned that I do not consider intervention desirable at this time through formal representations. The head of the Standard Oil Company here [10] has informed me this morning that he has not recommended such formal protest by our Government to his principals in New York and that he is deeply appreciative of what the Embassy has done up to now through its interest and informal representations. My own opinion is that to make formal representations at this time would not be justified and could aggravate the situation. The matter up to now is purely an internal one, and up to now is a labor question in which it would be improper for us to intervene. The Government has informed the companies that price increases will be granted. The companies are willing to grant increased wages before the price increase is announced and becomes effective. There has been no formal threat of expropriation or arbitrary action of this kind to take the plants over even temporarily. That there has been thought of such action in certain quarters in the Government there is no doubt. It is not believed, however, that the Argentine Government would proceed with expropriation unless there are developments which presently are not in the offing.

I am following this matter closely with the heads of the American companies, and will keep the Department informed. In case there should be danger of expropriation being undertaken by the Argentine Government, I will inform the Department and request its instructions authorizing me to make a formal protest.

---

[8] Juan Atilio Bramuglia.
[9] Juan D. Perón.
[10] Eugene Holman.

The Embassy considers this whole matter of extreme importance in view of the fact that the American petroleum interests in this country are important and should become more important in the interests of the Argentine Government and economy as well as of the companies. It is to be hoped that the present situation which has developed will not result in arbitrary action or attitudes by the Government which could endanger the favorable developments which have been in the offing so far as this industry is concerned.

Respectfully yours, GEORGE S. MESSERSMITH

711.35/8-2747

Memorandum of Conversation, by the Counselor of Embassy (Ray) [11]

[Extracts]

BUENOS AIRES, August 23, 1947.

Participants: President Perón
Ambassador James Bruce
Acting Minister for Foreign Affairs and Minister of Marine Anadon
Guy Ray, Counselor of Embassy

Following the brief ceremony of presentation of credentials, President Perón invited the Ambassador [12] and the Counselor together with the Acting Foreign Minister, Sr. Anadon, to a separate room for a conversation. The Acting Minister for Foreign Affairs was present but took no part in the conversation. Ambassador Bruce expressed his pleasure at being appointed as American Ambassador in Buenos Aires and his confidence that President Perón and he would be able to establish very friendly personal relations and that they would be able to accomplish much in the interest of the two countries.

President Perón emphasized his desire to cooperate with the United States and remarked that to his mind it was not so much a question of friendship between the two countries as a matter of self-interest. He added that there was really no such thing as lasting friendship between two countries and that friendship usually lasted only as long as there was no direct conflict of interests. The point he wanted to make, he said, was that it was in the interest of Argentina and the United

---

[11] Transmitted to the Department in despatch 2924, August 27, Buenos Aires; received September 5.
[12] Ambassador James Bruce, who succeeded Ambassador George S. Messersmith, assumed his duties in Buenos Aires on August 21, 1947.

States to work together. Perón said that he had been accused of favoring government ownership of business but that such was far from being the case. It was true that he believed in government ownership of public utilities, but he was a great believer in private enterprise which should have control of commerce, industry, and manufacturing. . . .

Perón referred in particular to oil production in Argentina and the current gasoline shortage. He said that he believed Standard of New Jersey and the other American companies now understood the situation and were willing to deal fairly with the Argentine. He added, however, that Standard had taken such an attitude several years ago that there was still a bad taste in the mouths of many Argentines and conversations with congressional leaders had convinced him that it would be impossible for him to get the Argentine Congress to adopt a law which would permit foreign companies (i.e. American companies) to carry out explorations dealings and the development of Argentina's petroleum resources. Ambassador Bruce pointed out that it is very important to increase petroleum resources in the Western Hemisphere and said he hoped an agreement could be reached whereby we could assist in the further development of Argentina's petroleum resources and furnish machinery as well as lending technical assistance. Perón said this was very necessary, expressing the opinion that it would be feasible for Argentina to produce at least ten times as much petroleum as it is producing at the present. He said that petroleum exists in the Argentine from Tierra del Fuego northwards to Neuquen and then on through Mendoza and up as far as Salta. He indicated that he had had recent conversations with the leading American oil companies here, and that while some progress had been made, they had not reached a satisfactory arrangement as yet. Ambassador Bruce said that he would be glad to study this question and as soon as possible discuss it frankly with the President and render any possible assistance. Perón said that he hoped the Ambassador would do so and that he believed with good will on both sides, which he knew to exist, it would be possible to work out a satisfactory solution. Perón referred to the possibility of armed hostilities in the future and said that in such an event, the present petroleum supply in the Western Hemisphere would not be adequate and that it is imperative that oil production be substantially increased, not only in Argentina but in some of the other countries.

GUY W. RAY

835.6363/8-447

Memorandum by the Assistant Chief of the Division of River Plate Affairs (Atwood) to the Director of the Office of American Republic Affairs (Wright)

[WASHINGTON,] September 24, 1947.

SUMMARY OF STANDARD OIL'S REPORT TO AMBASSADOR BRUCE

Present Situation:

A. *Production and Consumption*

1) In July it was estimated Argentina had only a two weeks' reserve supply of gasoline.

2) World shortage of petroleum and refined products exists and will probably continue for several years.

3) Argentina must import 57% of consumption.

4) Refining capacity in Argentina not sufficient to handle all imported crude.

5) Production of YPF decreasing steadily since 1943. Production of private companies about the same 1935–43, with a decrease since 1943. Annual decline in total production the last three years approximately 8%.

B. *Discriminations*

1) Discrimination started in 1935 when YPF was given expansion and producing monopoly.

2) Standard offered to sell in 1936 but Argentine Congress did not ratify.

3) YPF consistently given greater and greater competitive advantage by various means—taxes, regulations, exemptions, number of street pumps, etc.

4) Recent forced increase in wages (20%) has aggravated situation and increased Standard's operating losses. Private companies only get 25% of the recent 10 cent increase in gasoline prices (represents about a 6¼% increase in price).

Remedies Suggested by Standard to Miranda [13]

1. *Immediate Remedy*

Reorganization of industry to permit normal development of YPF activities without interfering with legitimate activities of private companies. If assurances could be given for period of fifteen years, companies could contract advantageously for normal and constant supply for Argentina.

---

[13] Miguel Miranda, President of the Argentine Economic Council and of the Central Bank.

2. *Permanent Remedy*

Argentina would have to encourage and stimulate exploration and exploitation by private capital duly controlled by the State which could cooperate with YPF to increase national production.

Standard's Suggestions to Bruce Regarding What Is Necessary To Provide Incentive To Continue the Oil Business In Argentina

A. *Immediate*

1) Abolition of import-export controls.
2) Abolition of the quota and price fixing systems.
3) Establishment of a reasonable competitive basis for refining and marketing.

B. *Permanent*

1) The elimination of the State's exclusive veto power and all present discriminatory legislation.
2) The establishment of a sound legal basis on which private capital (foreign and domestic) can produce, transport, refine and market on fair, competive terms.

ROLLIN S. ATWOOD

810.6363/9-2547

The Ambassador in Argentina (Bruce) to the Secretary of State

CONFIDENTIAL BUENOS AIRES, September 25, 1947.
No. 3033

SIR: I have the honor to refer to the Department's confidential Circular Airgram of July 9, 8:50 a.m. and the Embassy's Telegram No. 937 of July 30 and its Despatch No. 2844 of July 30 [14] and to report that on September 24, Mr. Ray, Counselor of Embassy, and I had a conversation with President Perón, Foreign Minister Bramuglia and the President of the National Economic Council, Miranda, during which the question of petroleum in Argentina was discussed at length.

The first point which we brought up was the situation of the two important American companies operating in Argentina, that is to say, the Standard group and Ultramar. We dealt with the following points in the order given below:

(1) *Increase in Prices.* We pointed out that since the end of the war there has been an increase in prices of approximately 50 percent in the petroleum world market along with an increase in official freight rates with the result that the American companies here were losing money steadily. In view of this situation and the cost of operation for YPF the Argentine Government issued Decree No. 16,837 on June 14,

---

[14] None printed.

1947 providing for an increase in the retail price of gasoline, kerosene and tractor fuel. In spite of this decree the American companies have been given no relief for the following reasons:

(*a*) Although more than three months have gone by since the June 14th Decree, no decision has been taken as yet concerning the proportion of the increase in price by which the American companies will be allowed to benefit. A commission was appointed to carry out a study to determine what portion of the increase of ten centavos per liter should be granted the companies. This amounts to an increase of ten cents (U.S.) per gallon. The Government has given the companies assurances that they will participate in the increase and that such participation will be made retroactive to June 14, but it has so far been impossible to obtain a decision as to what percentage of the increase will be allowed the company.

(*b*) The Decree in question did not raise the price of lubricating oils in spite of the opinion of YPF and the American companies that such an increase was urgent. This is more serious because while there is still some hope for relief with regard to the price of gasoline since June 14, any increase in the price of lubricating oils now could not be retroactive and there is no way to recover losses which are being incurred daily.

(*c*) The situation has become gradually worse with regard to fuel oil, diesel oil and gas-oil. At the present time Standard is losing probably in excess of $12,000 daily on its operations in Argentina.

The President and Mr. Miranda said that this matter had been brought to their attention but that the Committee appointed had not acted promptly. The President remarked that he was appointing a new Board of Directors of YPF and was giving them orders to follow a policy which would be fairer to the American companies. He said that he thought he could offer relief from this situation within a week. He said he would take action immediately and in a few days would help Mr. Miranda get in touch with the heads of American companies here and that it should be possible to reach a satisfactory solution of this pressing problem.

Mr. Miranda brought up the question of the actual petroleum shortage in Argentina and intimated that the American companies were somewhat to blame because they had not made a sufficiently strong effort to bring additional petroleum to the Argentine. We pointed out that in view of the fact that the companies, especially Standard, are losing important sums of money daily, it is difficult if not impossible for the local representatives of these companies to convince their principals in the United States that it is good business to send more petroleum products to the Argentine simply to lose more money. Mr. Miranda stated repeatedly that the companies had personal assurances from him and the President that a portion of the increase in the price of gasoline would be allocated to them. We stated repeatedly that we had implicit faith in these assurances but the fact remained that the companies were losing money and that no assurance had been given as to the portion of the increase which would fall to the companies. We pointed out to Miranda that the President and he could carry out their promise by granting such a small proportion of the increase to the companies that it would have little useful effect. The President agreed with our argument and said it was important to inform the companies immediately how much of the ten-centavo increase would accrue to their benefit.

We told them that neither this Embassy nor the local representatives of the American companies could make any commitments regarding the delivery of crude petroleum or of refined products to the Argentine, but we could promise that if a satisfactory solution were made both the Embassy and the companies would exert every possible effort to help Argentina over the present acute gasoline shortage. Miranda said that he had endeavored to buy gasoline on the "Black Market" from other companies, but had had relatively little success so far. He inquired why the Embassy could not help him get gasoline this way. We replied that it hardly seemed good business or fair to the local companies for the Embassy to lend its assistance to an operation which would be questionable in the first place and which would also be unfair to the companies which are carrying on established business in Argentina.

(2) *Guarantee of Long-Term Operation of Refinery and Distribution.* We pointed out that the companies could not expand their refinery and distribution facilities because they have no assurance of being able to operate over a long period and because they are assigned a fixed quota and thus would not be able to participate proportionately in any increased refining and distribution. The President, Miranda, and the Foreign Minister all agreed that if the companies were expected to expand they should be granted a percentage of the market rather than being confined to a fixed quota.

The President and the two other officials mentioned stated that with regard to points (1) and (2) the Argentine Government would take immediate steps to satisfy the desires of the companies which they described as just and legitimate.

(3) *Participation in Exploration and Exploitation of Petroleum in Argentina.* We pointed out that during the period 1931–1938 private companies in Argentina produced more petroleum than YPF. In 1934 Standard reached a maximum production of 1140 cubic meters daily. The production of Standard has now fallen to approximately 333 cubic meters daily, due to the enactment of successive Laws and

Decrees restricting more and more the possibility of obtaining new concessions. The President said that the petroleum question in Argentina is political dynamite and that it might even cause the fall of any government which endeavored to change the law to permit foreign companies to obtain new concessions. We pointed out to him that it would probably be many years before Argentina could produce enough petroleum to satisfy its own needs and that the question of depleting Argentine petroleum reserves for exportation would not arise for a long time and that in any event the American companies accept the principle that if the point should be reached where there would be an exportable surplus the Argentine Government would have the full right to determine whether exportation should be made or not. We remarked that if handled on this basis it should be possible to convince the Argentine people and the Congress that the action to be taken was in the interest of Argentine economy and that it should be possible to overcome any political objections. The President was impressed by this argument and said that he and his associates would study the matter immediately. We pointed out to them that Argentina is spending well over 75,000,000 dollars a year for the importation of petroleum and that if the needs of the country could be produced locally this would result in an enormous saving in dollar exchange for Argentina. They all agreed on the importance of this and the desirability of making it possible for the American companies to participate in the further development of the petroleum industry in Argentina. They agreed that the operations of YPF are not sufficiently efficient to guarantee proper development of the industry without foreign help.

Miranda remarked that the United States had refused at one time to furnish machinery and equipment to Argentina and that there was a widespread objection in the United States to the industrialization of Argentina. We pointed out that during the recent war it had been impossible for the United States to supply the needs of the world for machinery and equipment. We told him that the policy of the United States Government is to assist in every possible way in the sound industrial development of Argentina. We pointed out that history has demonstrated that our best customers have always been the most highly industrialized nations and that it was to our own interest to see Argentina industrialized as rapidly as possible.

The President said that he and his associates would study this problem immediately and get in touch with the local representatives of the American companies to see what could be worked out.

We plan to follow this question closely and have further conversations with the President and various Cabinet Ministers on the subject of petroleum in Argentina. We shall keep the Department fully and promptly informed.

Respectfully yours,

For the Ambassador:
Guy W. Ray
Counselor of Embassy

835.6363/10-947

The Ambassador in Argentina (Bruce) to the Secretary of State

CONFIDENTIAL
No. 3069

Buenos Aires, October 9, 1947.

Sir: I have the honor to transmit free translations of two Argentine Government decrees [15] which have been signed but not published textually. The first of these decrees establishes a scale for retention by the private petroleum companies operating in the Argentine of fixed shares of the general increases on sales price of gasoline and kerosene recently authorized. The second of these decrees, which is being jealously guarded by Y.P.F. and the existence of which is not generally known, authorizes an even larger retention of the increase for that entity than is provided for the private companies.

The Embassy, in its report no. 581 of June 26, 1947,[15] reported the signing of a decree whereby increases of ten centavos and three centavos a liter respectively were authorized for sales within the Republic of gasoline and kerosene. It was explained at that time that only 25% of the increase could be retained by the producers, and that the balance would have to be deposited in a special account of the Central Bank pending final government decision as to the amount of the total increase to be retained by the producers.

The first of the two decrees which constitute enclosures to this despatch stipulates that the private companies may retain nine centavos of the total increase of ten centavos a liter when the gasoline is imported from abroad; that they may retain seven centavos a liter when the gasoline is produced from imported crude; and that they may retain five and one half centavos a liter when the gasoline is produced from domestic crude.

In all cases listed immediately above, the producers shall pay, out of their respective shares, an additional commission of one centavo a liter to the retail distributors, thereby reducing their own share by that amount in each category.

The entire three centavo increase on kerosene, as stipulated in the earlier decree, may also now be retained by the private companies,

---

[15] Not printed.

In addition to the increased benefits to the private companies cited above, it will be noted that a further concession has been made in Article 5. In the earlier decree mentioned in paragraph 2, black oils refined within the country, whether from domestic or imported crude, were taxed 23 pesos per ton, while the companies importing black oils were permitted to retain "a reasonable profit" above cost, depositing the excess in sales price to the account of the government in lieu of direct taxation. In actual practice, they were able to retain a considerable portion of the sales price. At the same time, they were losing heavily on their refining of imported crude while the important local producers of crude were still making money. In the Article alluded to above, it will be seen that black oils refined from imported crude are to be treated in the same manner as imported black oils, representing a distinct improvement in the private companies' positions.

In contrast to the terms of the decree described above, those of the decree which constitutes the second enclosure to this despatch will be of especial interest. As previously mentioned, this decree has not been made public. . . .

This decree authorizes the retention by Y.P.F. of the total increase of ten centavos a liter on all gasoline sales without reference to source of origin. It further authorizes the retention of the total increase of three centavos a liter on kerosene. It does not stipulate that Y.P.F. shall pay an additional commission of one centavo a liter to its distributors.

This secret decree, which clearly discriminates against the private oil companies, appears to be the more iniquitous in that Y.P.F. was recently granted a blanket exemption from customs duties on all products other than crude oil. The private companies, of course, are required to pay duties on all products.

On September 30, as was widely announced in the press, Y.P.F. officially denounced the market agreements which had been in force between that entity and the private companies since 1936 and 1937. Under these agreements, the private companies were restricted to a fixed marketing gallonage for gasoline while Y.P.F. was permitted to monopolize any expansion of the market. In exchange, the private companies were permitted to carry on the importation of crude oil and petroleum products with Y.P.F. abstaining from these latter activities.

Although the denouncement of this agreement is described in press releases as having been dictated by "the new revolutionary concepts", the aim appears to be that of legalizing Y.P.F.'s position as an importer of petroleum products. The immediate effect is to throw the market wide open, permitting all segments of the industry to import at will and, conversely, allowing the private companies to expand their internal marketing operations. Although the private companies, through their international ramifications, might be considered as enjoying a preferential position for the acquisition of petroleum abroad, they are placed in an unfavorable competitive position due to the fact that importations effected by Y.P.F. have been exempted from duties.

Officials of the private companies state that the denouncement actually means little at this time since the country needs all the petroleum products it can acquire abroad, and that as long as the present acute shortage exists there is no particular cause for concern on the part of the private companies. The lack of any specific agreement between them and the government entity, however, might prove extremely prejudicial at such time in the future as the world petroleum market may return to normalcy. The exact effect, of course, cannot be foreseen at this time.

Respectfully yours,

For the Ambassador:
JULIAN GREENUP
*Counselor of Embassy
for Economic Affairs*

835.6363/10–1147

Memorandum of Conversation, by the Acting Secretary of State

[WASHINGTON,] October 11, 1947.

Participants: Dr. Oscar Ivanissevich—Argentine Ambassador
Señor Luis Drago—Counselor, Argentine Embassy
Mr. Zaneta—Representative in US of YPF
Mr. Lovett—Acting Secretary
Mr. Tewksbury—RPA

The Argentine Ambassador presented me with a memorandum, dated October 11, stating that an order for 130,000 barrels of gasoline has been placed by the YPF (Government Petroleum Company) in Argentina and requesting the assistance of the Department in obtaining an export license. I explained to Ambassador Ivanissevich that, although I realized that Argentina is faced with a serious gasoline shortage, we in the United States have a similar problem and that there is a virtual embargo at present on the exportation of gasoline. I explained that, in view of Argentina's problem, I should be glad to act as a "friend at court" and do what I could to assist them in this matter and made it perfectly clear that I could not guarantee or even hold out hope of success. I assured the group that I would, however, discuss the matter with Mr. Bruce, Assistant Secretary of Commerce,[17]

---

[17] David K. E. Bruce.

under whose jurisdiction the allocation of gasoline and other commodities in short supply comes, and indicated that, if there is evidence that the supply of gasoline would facilitate the movement of foodstuffs for shipment to Europe, this might prove to be a favorable factor.

Señor Drago, as well as the Ambassador, indicated that they fully understood the problem and expressed their appreciation for such help as I might be able to give.

ROBERT A. LOVETT

835.6363/12-147

The Ambassador in Argentina (Bruce) to the Secretary of State

CONFIDENTIAL
No. 3265

BUENOS AIRES, December 1, 1947.

SIR: I have the honor to inform the Department of certain recent developments in the Argentine petroleum situation which have been the subject of conversations between Embassy officials and representatives of the private petroleum companies. The latter complain that the recent changes in the directorate of Y.P.F. have resulted in a further hampering of their activities and that the formation of an inimical bloc of high officials has once again raised the specter of expropriatory action on the part of the Government.

In the Embassy's report No. 871 of September 3, 1947,[18] the departure of General Albarino, President of Y.P.F., for a four months' leave of absence for reasons of health was reported, together with the appointment to the Board of Directors of that organization of Ing. Julio V. Canessa, a former official of Y.P.F. who was recently serving as President of the Dirección General del Gas del Estado. Captain Alberto Job had been named as acting President of Y.P.F.

Subsequently, Ing. Canessa was elevated to the presidency pro-tem and shortly thereafter, on November 14, a decree was signed which granted Y.P.F. the authority to intervene in the operations of the private companies. A critical shortage of petroleum products and slow down strikes on the part of the company personnel were cited as the justification for this move, and though the latter allegation was denied by the private companies, the immediate result was the placing of interventors in their organizations and the issuance of numerous directives which were a source of embarrassment to the companies. These, for the most part, took the form of charges of failure to maintain normal deliveries of gasoline to gasoline stations and though unfounded, gave Ing. Canessa the opportunity to threaten "appropriate measures" if the companies did not comply promptly and fully with

[18] Not printed.

his directives. The presence of the government interventors throughout the private organizations has been another annoyance.

The concern of the companies was further heightened by an announcement of policy made to company representatives by Sr. José Constantino Barros, Minister of Industry and Commerce and a close collaborator in policy matters with Ing. Canessa, who stated flatly that his idea of future petroleum policy for Argentina envisioned the government as sole producer with the private companies relegated to the roles of importers and refiners. When asked point blank whether such a policy meant "nationalization" of the private producing properties and equipment, he answered that it did, and when asked whether it meant "expropriation", he again replied in the affirmative.

This conversation took place in the office of Miguel Miranda, and although the latter was not present at the moment he was aware of the remarks made by Sr. Barros and later informed the company representatives that the Minister spoke only for himself and that his views were not shared by Miranda, himself. He did not elaborate on this point, however, so his own views are not yet known.

The trend of thinking on the part of Sr. Barros and Ing. Canessa, whose views evidently coincide, has aroused considerable anxiety among the private companies since it has been officially announced that a public pronouncement of future petroleum policy will be made on National Petroleum Day, December 13, and the companies maintain that if the ideas of the Minister and Ing. Canessa should find acceptance among other higher officials it might be found on December 13 that the Government had committed itself to a course of action most prejudicial to company interests.

The Embassy considers that undue panic is evident in the attitude of the company officials, for although Barros and Canessa are unquestionably strongly nationalistic in their attitudes and in a position to cause petty annoyances to the private operators, it seems apparent that their idea of future policy differs from that of President Perón, Miguel Miranda, and other high officials. There may be some significance in the fact that General Albariño has just returned to his duties as President of Y.P.F., a development which may result in a modification of policy in the higher level of that organization.

The rumors of expropriatory action have been discussed by the Ambassador with President Perón and with the Foreign Minister. The former has stated emphatically that his government would not expropriate the petroleum properties or any other American property in Argentina, and that although he would like to see increased production on the part of the private companies, he saw no way of bringing this about under existing laws. He added that the Government was disposed to give the companies long-term contracts, say for 15 years, which would justify increases in their refinery capacity.

Foreign Minister Bramuglia has also given assurances that rumors of expropriatory action are unfounded. He stated on December 2 that President Perón had not, in their conversations, so much as hinted at any such course and that it was evident that if any action of such international ramifications were under consideration, he, the Foreign Minister, would certainly have been apprised.

In the face of these two categorical assertions, the Embassy is forced to the belief that the private company fears of a drastic policy pronouncement on December 13 are immoderate. Although it is conceded that some statement of petroleum policy may be made on that date, it appears highly unlikely that the Argentine Government would irrevocably commit itself to a course of action which would cause such grave international complications as would a policy of outright expropriation, particularly at this time when the President is soliciting the participation of American capital in the expansion of Argentine industrial activity.

Respectfully yours,

For the Ambassador:
JULIAN GREENUP
*Counselor of Embassy
for Economic Affairs*

835.6363/12–547 : Telegram

The Ambassador in Argentina (Bruce) to the Secretary of State

RESTRICTED   NIACT   BUENOS AIRES, December 5, 1947—noon.
US Urgent

1416. President Economic Council Miranda, Acting Secretary Commerce Barros, and No. 2 YPF man Canessa met in Miranda's office yesterday with local representatives Standard, Shell and Ultramar. Companies were told it was highly desirable political reasons announce on December 13 anniversary discovery petroleum in Argentina, that Argentina had taken over all the oil properties. Proposal apparently is that government would buy oil rights owned by Shell and Standard. Companies offered long-term refining marketing contract probably 15 or 18 years stating guarantee would be given for "generous profits". Local representatives inquired whether failure to make affirmative reply by December 9 would mean expropriation and Argentine officials replied they were not prepared to answer for present. Miranda stated three times plan was not his idea but apparently entire motivation was political.

My action pending instructions will be: 1. Inquire whether this plan has full approval President, and 2. Point to obvious unfairness presenting plan on complied basis ultimatum with such short notice. I shall point out to Bramuglia today and ask him inform President immediately that local representatives have no authority make commitment and 4 days in which weekend included is assuredly short time expect representatives obtain decision on such an important question. Argentine officials emphasized necessity foreign companies continuing imports and desire not to prejudice interests of foreign companies. Argentines said continuation of imports would make it possible for Argentina to develop its oil resources "without unnecessary haste". Argentine proposal presented in form of "request" by practical demand for reply by December 9 places it somewhat in the category of an ultimatum.

My conviction is if companies agreed sell oil properties and continue operating contract for refinery and sales, the latter contract would be unsatisfactory over period of years, especially if YPF succeeded in increasing local production. I assume Dept's attitude will be based at least some extent on whether Standard desires sell properties. Ultramar owns no oil properties but operations are confined to importing, refining and selling.

Shell representative was informed his answer would have bearing on negotiations of British Commercial Mission now in Buenos Aires. Such tactics come close to blackmail.

I feel that regardless whether companies wish sell or not, we should make it clear to Perón that presenting such far-reaching demands with so little notice constitutes sharp tactics which will make our relations extremely difficult.

I expect see Bramuglia today and also discuss this with British Ambassador.[19]

More later.

BRUCE

835.6363/12-1547 : Telegram

The Ambassador in Argentina (Bruce) to the Secretary of State

RESTRICTED NIACT BUENOS AIRES, December 5, 1947—1 p. m.
US URGENT

1417. Saw British Ambassador this morning early regarding subject mytel 1416, December 5. Leeper and Bailleu [20] annoyed developments and implications connection oil question with negotiations

---

[19] Sir Reginald Leeper.
[20] Clive Baillieu, head of the British Trade Mission to Argentina.

British Mission. Leeper said giving such short notice absurd. Said would speak Bramuglia or President today along lines explained mytel under reference.

Have just seen Bramuglia who says has discussed matter with President and authorized me inform Department definitely no action will be taken. Added I could assure Department Perón has no intention whatsoever expropriating oil or any other American properties. Bramuglia asked me not inform local oil representatives but emphasized I could give Department definite assurances no cause alarm.

Bramuglia remarked with regard treatment American capital President had instructed him order Molinari [21] return immediately Buenos Aires explain speech and statements Habana. Said President and he were annoyed Molinari's speech and wanted first-hand information. Molinari will probably return Habana after reporting and obtaining new instructions from Perón which Bramuglia said would be categoric and of nature he was sure would not be objectionable to US. In view Bramuglia's emphatic assurance from himself and President that no cause for alarm, am taking no further action pending instructions. Bramuglia said he would guarantee me oil companies would not be required make any reply by December 9 or any other date.

BRUCE

835.6363/12–547 : Telegram

The Acting Secretary of State to the Embassy in Argentina

CONFIDENTIAL
US URGENT
WASHINGTON, December 5, 1947—8 p. m.

1147. Dept concerned at implications contained urtel 1416 Dec 5 re demands on oil companies and agrees your approach. Despite Bramuglia's assurances your 1417 Dec 5 we feel prompt interview shd be had with Perón in order to obtain his personal confirmation Bramulia's statements. In past Bramuglia with complete sincerity has indicated that drastic action wd not be taken insurance legislation example and has been unable prevent final action sponsored by Miranda.

Drastic action proposed wd have far reaching repercussions in economic relations with Arg. For your conf info serious criticisms in foreign relations committees Cong re Arg grain policies. Action of character outlined wd merely aggravate situation and present new obstacles to obtaining Cong authorization for off shore purchases in dollars for ERP.

---

[21] Senator Diego Luis Molinari.

You shd explain to Perón that while US cannot object to principle of nationalizing petroleum industry, if due compensation provided, the proposed precipitate action does not afford reasonable opportunity petroleum companies make adequate studies their problems and present plan to Govt for negotiation mutually agreeable settlement. Action this character wd completely offset Perón's previous statements to you re encouragement foreign investments Arg.

LOVETT

835.6363/12–1047 : Telegram

The Ambassador in Argentina (Bruce) to the Secretary of State

CONFIDENTIAL   BUENOS AIRES, December 10, 1947—7 p. m.

1435. Representatives from oil companies received by Miranda alone noon today. Standard and Shell both replied negative, answering proposal sale Argentine producing properties. Miranda said reply exactly what he expected and, in fact, could not have expected different answer. Miranda then urged foreign companies give prompt consideration long-term marketing and refining problems. Local representative Standard believes this disposes at least for present question sale producing properties.

Reliable information is Barros, Canessa, and extreme Nationalist group brought pressure have President buy or expropriate foreign properties and declare on December 13 Argentine policy is have all petroleum resources nationalized. Appears this group has lost out so far as sale or expropriation concerned, although question has caused bitter battle within government. Perón, Bramuglia, and Miranda realize widespread repercussions expropriation or forced sale would have. Nationalist group will now press President for declaration 13th that no further concessions or contracts be given foreign companies and no mixed societies with foreign capital be approved.

BRUCE

835.6363/12–1147 : Telegram

The Ambassador in Argentina (Bruce) to the Secretary of State

CONFIDENTIAL   BUENOS AIRES, December 11, 1947—8 p. m.

1438. President and Bramuglia assured us today absolutely no thought expropriation or forced sale foreign oil producing properties; companies have replied in negative and Government accepts their reply, thereby closing matter. President stated had been under strong pressure from Nationalists but assured us would make no statement December 13 which could be interpreted as against foreign companies. We have urged against any statement that further development petroleum properties reserved for national Government. Bramuglia has promised make final effort persuade President omit any statement which would exclude foreign companies from participation in further exploration and development. We presented President memorandum which he said he would study carefully.

BRUCE

835.6363/12–1447 : Telegram

The Ambassador in Argentina (Bruce) to the Secretary of State

RESTRICTED BUENOS AIRES, December 14, 1947—2 p. m.

1442. President's Petroleum Day speech yesterday contained only general commitment indefinite to time:

"Since I took office I have struggled to rescue our national economy from strange hands and from international monopolies, (a struggle) which is not incompatible with respect and even with encouragement to as many persons other nationalities as may wish come weld their force [and?] money with ours." President promised increase national production petroleum and hydroelectric power and make possible utilization now wasted gas; continued "Argentina's petroleum policy must be based on same principles on which all its economic policy rests: Absolute conservation Argentine sovereignty over riches our subsoil and rational scientific exploitation by state; making clear that when state retrieves immediate direct control properties which nation possesses, it must not relinquish privilege continuing administer them, without sharing functions with other interests other than those belonging all Argentines." [22]

BRUCE

835.6363/12–1747 : Telegram

The Ambassador in Argentina (Bruce) to the Secretary of State

CONFIDENTIAL BUENOS AIRES, December 17, 1947—6 p. m.

1462. Please advise Holman, president Standard Oil New Jersey, in conference this morning with President Perón and Señor Bramuglia, Perón stated that he was ready to make long term agreement with private oil companies which would enable them increase their refining capacity, keep their proportionate share of the market, and do necessary drilling on their properties. Upon return office, I immediately informed Barbour of Standard and suggested he begin detailed negotiations immediately. If things work out in accordance

---

[22] For a different translation, see fifth paragraph of Argentine News Bulletin of December 26, p. 302.

Perón statement, oil business for private companies will be in best shape it has been in years.

BRUCE

835.6363/12–1747

The Manager of Operations of the Standard Oil Company of New Jersey in Argentina (Metzger) to the Assistant Secretary of State for Political Affairs (Armour)

NEW YORK, December 17, 1947.

DEAR MR. ARMOUR: Enclosed are copies of a memorandum and covering letter [23] being forwarded to the Argentine Ambassador in Washington, Dr. Oscar Ivanissevich. Although somewhat lengthy, the memorandum gives the details of our principal problems in the Argentine. Our first problem is that of prices and, as pointed out during the meeting which you kindly arranged for Mr. Parker [24] and me a week ago, we are still not able to import gasoline into Argentina without losing 2½¢ per gallon, despite the fact that our suppliers bill us at the lowest prevailing market price.

We brought a cargo of gasoline into Argentina on December 2, and have another four cargoes ready for delivery as quickly as ships are available. We have four more cargoes laid out for delivery during 1948. Our loss of 2½¢ per gallon amounts to approximately $125,000. on each cargo, after paying import duties of 5¢ per gallon, or a total of $250,000. per cargo. We are, therefore, extremely anxious that the price adjustments promised to us weeks ago materialize at an early date. It is also still impossible to import kerosene, gas oil or diesel oil without entailing correspondingly high losses, despite the fact that Argentina needs these products badly.

As pointed out in the memorandum for the Argentine Ambassador our affiliates in Argentina have failed to show a profit in 1945 or 1946 and will likewise show a loss in 1947. During the period, March 15 to June 15, our losses on the importation of crude oil amounted to $1,000,-000. U.S., or slightly over $11,000. per day. Although this unsatisfactory situation was remedied by the new price structure, effective June 16, price adjustments have not kept apace of subsequent increases in world market quotations on crude oil, and we are again approaching a precarious position in connection with current crude oil supplies. The price of crude oil was increased by 20¢ per barrel on November 15, which requires an increase of at least 1¼¢ per gallon in the price of gasoline. More recent increases of 50¢ per barrel in current crude oil

---

[23] Neither printed.
[24] George Parker of the Standard Oil Company of New Jersey.

prices will demand a further increase of over 3¢ per gallon, assuming that gasoline, alone, absorbs the charge. If the Argentine Government takes as long to make these adjustments as was required to effect the previous increase on June 16, the difficulties of our Argentine companies will again become acute.

It should be kept in mind that while our companies were losing over $11,000. per day on crude oil imports, the Government was collecting an equal amount in import duties. In other words, we were losing 20 pesos per ton, which is the Customs' duty rate on crude oil. Although refusing to grant the private companies any relief from import duties, Y.P.F. is exempted from paying these charges. The attached memorandum [25] shows on the first page what the companies have been allowed to retain from the 10¢ per gallon price increase on gasoline decreed on June 16. While the companies are limited to specified amounts, depending on the source of their gasoline, Y.P.F. is granted the full 10¢ regardless of source. Despite the losses incurred on crude oil imports, it will be noted from the last page of the attached memorandum that the crude imported during the first ten months of 1947 was 40% greater than during the same period of 1946.

In addition to the price problem, we are concerned about the situation created by Y.P.F.'s denouncement of the marketing agreements in effect since 1937. In order to justify the large investments required to maintain and improve our refining and marketing installations, we require some assurance that Y.P.F. will grant us import permits over which they hold complete control. Under the expiring marketing agreements, Y.P.F. was obliged to give us the permits required to import certain quantities of crude oil, as specified under the agreement, but with the termination of the agreement, this obligation will cease on March 31. What we desire is a commitment from the Government that we will have the right to import crude oil and products in sufficient quantity to maintain our operations over a reasonably long term of say, fifteen years, and that during this period, the Government's absolute control over prices will be such as to allow us a reasonable profit.

Mr. Parker and I were able to inform you personally of the Government's recent offer to purchase the producing properties of the oil companies in Argentina. The companies replied in the negative, and we believe that this matter may be forgotten for the present. Press reports of the President's speech on December 13 indicate, however, that it is the Government's intention to continue the traditional policy of excluding foreign companies from the development of indigenous crude oil. We trust that this statement is not a true interpretation of

---

[25] Not printed.

the President's intentions and that, in time, it will be possible for American oil companies to assist in the exploration and development of new sources of crude oil in Argentina.

It was indeed a pleasure and a privilege to have been able to discuss our Argentine problems with you and your associates, and I trust that the foregoing will give you a summary of our three main problems in Argentina, which are in chronological importance:

1. Prices
2. Security for our refining and marketing operations
3. Development of local crude supplies by American oil companies.

With kindest personal regards and with the Season's Best Wishes, I am,

Sincerely yours, H. A. METZGER

835.6363/1–2348

News Bulletin of the Argentine Ministry for Foreign Affairs and Worship [26]

No. 272   BUENOS AIRES, December 26, 1947.

THE PRESENT OIL POLICY OF ARGENTINA

The discovery of a new oil well—recently communicated by the Department of Fiscal Oil Fields—in the district of Barrancas, in the Province of Mendoza, is of the greatest importance for our country. It is affirmed that this oil well produces daily roughly half a million litres of oil, and is 2,720 metres in depth. The figure mentioned is exceptional for one well; it shows the importance of the oil reserves of the country and also the enormous possibilities afforded for the execution of the Five-Year Plan in this field. Oil production in 1946 amounted to 2,275,000 cubic metres, and according to the works foreseen in the Five-Year Plan, the national oil production in 1951 will total 3,575,000 cubic metres, that is, an increase of 1,500,000 cubic metres over the present yearly output.

A few days ago, on the premises of Fiscal Oil Fields, General Perón recalled the discovery of the first oil well in our country, some 40 years ago, and traced an outline of the history of the Argentine oil policy during the ceremony in which a bust of General Enrique Mosconi—first president of that department—was unveiled. The President of the Republic referred to the efforts made by the Argentine Govern-

---

[26] Copy transmitted to the Department with despatch 60, January 23, 1948, from Buenos Aires; received January 30.

ment to encourage national economy, not only furthering the development of industry, transport and the utilisation of natural sources of wealth, but also "endeavouring to nationalise our production and our means of work, recovering them from foreign ownership and international monopolies".

Further on, dealing with the problem of oil, the President stated that the only possible solution to compensate the 60% of fuel imported to cover that part of home consumption which our production cannot supply, is to increase it as far as possible, employing national elements sources of energy, especially hydraulic energy. The efforts of the Government of General Perón are directed to this end, and so is the exploitation of the coal mines of Rio Turbio, promoted in order to settle without loss of time the all-important problem of fuel.

The foresight of General Perón and of the men who have collaborated in the task of the utilisation of every source of motive power in the country and the scientific survey of 680,000 [*600,000?*] square kilometres of our territory, distribution in this area 314 oil wells—123 of which will be structural and the remaining 186 exploratory—are indispensable for our economic development and for our social welfare.

General Perón ended his speech with these words, summary of the position adopted by our government in face of the problem of fuel: "The Argentine oil policy must be based on the same principles on which all our economic policy is based: Maintenance of the Argentine sovereignty over the wealth of our subsoil; rational and scientific exploitation by the State. When the State recovers immediate and direct command over the property belonging to the Nation, it must not relinquish the privilege of administering it, nor share functions that defend interests other than those of all the Argentines".

Giving a finishing touch to the favourable prospect in what regards a greater quantity of petroleum at the disposal of the requirements of home consumption, we must mention that a commercial treaty with Venezuela will shortly be concluded whereby, in exchange for foodstuffs sent by Argentina, that sister nation will send us, for a five year period, 1,500,000 tons of petroleum per year.

The importance of this treaty is evident, since it represents the breaking up of the powerful international oil pool and is a reaffirmation of the autonomy of our country, as also an evidence of our economic greatness, which has passed from the hands of foreign monopolist interests to serve the interests of our people and our country.

The measures adopted up to now by the Government of the Revolution and the agreements to be signed with several nations are achievements leading to the independence of Argentine economy, without which nothing can be attained, as General Perón stated in the Historic

House of Tucumán, where our illustrious forefathers declared the political emancipation of our country on July 9, 1816.

EFFORTS OF THE UNITED STATES TO MAKE ARGENTINE GRAINS AVAILABLE TO COUNTRIES IN NEED [27]

835.6131/5–2247 : Airgram

The Ambassador in Argentina (Messersmith) to the Secretary of State

CONFIDENTIAL BUENOS AIRES, May 22, 1947.

A–359. Concerning the International Emergency Food Council appeal of May 8, announced by Secretary-General Fitzgerald, for an increase of Argentine exports to 1,000,000 tons monthly during May, June and July, only official public expression of Argentine Government attitude to date has been remarks by Miranda, president of Central Bank and head of the Argentine Trade Promotion Institute, during joint press conference with President Perón on May 9. In its report of the Miranda remarks pertaining to the IEFC appeal, *La Prensa* of May 10 stated:

"With reference to another question regarding the steps taken by the Secretary General of the International Emergency Food Council, Mr. Miranda said that he had answered him 'that we are shipping as much as we can and that if we are not shipping more, it is their fault. They left us without the elements to do it with and Europe will suffer hunger because of those who allowed our transportation to be destroyed without sending replacement. No more is being transported because it is impossible and as a consequence of allowing our port facilities to come to bits we must pay an increase of 55 percent on the freights. To the reproaches, I answer: If you want merchandise, send us the loading equipment. See what liberty has left us. If we had had the present system in other times, the situation would be different.'"

Present supplies in all positions in the country are unquestionably sufficient for the shipping rate urged by IEFC. In the opinion of several well-informed persons, equipment likewise is more than sufficient if grains were given top priority and maximum effort were applied. It is doubtful, however, that at best the rate could be attained in full before the end of July because of the time necessarily required for administrative reform and physical expansion of the pipe-line flow.

For one thing, only small supplies are now at ports. The Institute owns in volume only wheat and a fair proportion of the surplus, but relatively small tonnage of barley. The Institute began purchasing corn on May 5 but was offered only 2500 tons through May 9 because

---

[27] For documentation on the inter-relations of Argentine wheat and Brazilian rubber in 1946, see *Foreign Relations*, 1946, vol. XI, pp. 111 ff.

there is no premium on early delivery. On the contrary, the storage allowance to be paid farmers for unshelled corn in cribs will not become effective until July 1 and is set at a flat monthly rate. Thus, farmers seem inclined to delay deliveries to earn a larger cash return from the crop, ignoring the fact that part of the storage payment will be offset by shrink and deterioration. Also farmers having heard that the Institute has already committed itself to export something like 2,000,000 tons, may hope for the eventual addition of a bonus payment for prompt delivery, as was done with wheat.

Under the present system, the time lapse between purchases in the interior and completion of export loading is a minimum of 3 months and an average of 4 to 5 months.

Allowing for the expected seasonal progress of the corn harvest and movement and the anticipated practical adjustments to carry out the marketing program which the Argentine government is thought to have in mind in their own interest, the May–July monthly average of the five leading cereal grains may reach 700,000 to 725,000 metric tons at the May–June and July–September rates given in Embtel No. 453, April 22, 1947.[28] This compares with the February–April 1949 average of only 295,000. Equipment alone should not prevent attainment of the aforementioned May–July average, notwithstanding the present small port supplies. These figures should be reached solely for national income and political reasons irrespective of appeal from outside sources but an expected faster and more efficient matching of grain arrivals at port with the issuance of allocations and permits and the presentation of steamers will be necessary. Coordination of grain arrivals with actual readying of ships has been necessary because of clogged warehouses and docks which have caused irregular loading. Such coordination will require cereal priorities to attain volume but priorities to exceed the aforementioned May–July volume would interfere with other supply schemes included under the Five Year Plan.

While as already pointed out, it is theoretically possible that shipments could reach the requested rate of 1,000,000 tons per month towards the end of July, it is not thought that activities could possibly be concentrated toward such end in view of the current administrative over-load and preoccupation with other objectives. Because of an apparent fear of over-extension on volume commitments or unwise export price negotiations by subordinates, export supply questions continue to be channelled through only one or two key officials, thus automatically stringing out many operational matters which might be disposed of simultaneously for maximum efficiency.

---

[28] Not printed.

Under an Argentine Trade Promotion Institute resolution made known this week, but on which exporters had been forewarned April 19, efforts to increase grain exports over the next few months may be handicapped, but the present impasse in fine feed cereals should be partly resolved. All exporters with supplies of oats, barley and rye acquired before December 28, 1946, if sold to foreign accounts but not yet shipped, must now re-sell this grain to the Institute. These re-sales were supposed to have been completed by May 15. The foreign buyers involved are concerned over this decision because they fear (1) additional delay in getting export clearances, (2) a possible reduction in the volume released to them as compared with the quantity originally contracted, and (3) an increase in the price for such released volumes. The Institute has also indicated a desire to take over unshipped supplies already paid for by importing countries and this is understood to have brought a vigorous objection from at least one of the buyers, the French occupation administration of Germany.

MESSERSMITH

102.78/8-2947 : Telegram

The Acting Secretary of State to the Embassy in Argentina

SECRET   WASHINGTON, August 29, 1947—noon.

808. From Agriculture. Short U.S. corn crop and critical bread grain deficits Europe require U.S. explore possibilities acquiring large amount corn elsewhere during Sept–Dec. Agriculture interested purchase as much 16 million bushels (400 thousand L.T.) corn Argentina for delivery countries where U.S. has responsibility. Most would be used Germany and release equivalent wheat other countries.

Inform soon estimated amount corn available U.S. purchase, probable price, likely availability dates. This can be discussed with top officials, but urge secret basis this stage. Investigate possibility single purchase agreement Government covering entire amount. [Agriculture.]

LOVETT

102.78/9-447 : Telegram

The Ambassador in Argentina (Bruce) to the Secretary of State

SECRET   BUENOS AIRES, September 4, 1947—11 a. m.

1078. Deptel 808, August 29. Greenup and Thompson,[29] noon yesterday, saw Miranda and Maroglio, Presidents respectively National Eco-

---

[29] Julian C. Greenup, Counselor of Embassy for Economic Affairs, and Arthur T. Thompson, Agricultural Attaché.

nomic Council and Central Bank, who indicated delivery 30,000 metric tons monthly September–December and 60,000 January–May, all from ports up river Buenos Aires. If possible, would exceed these rates. Miranda indicated total current uncommitted surplus about 1,000,000 tons.

They ask 35 pesos per 100 kilos f.a.s. in shelled bulk, plus one-half percent commission for Argentine Trade Promotion Institute. Estimate cost to put bulk corn aboard ship at 55 centavos per 100 kilos and any necessary quantity bagged at 1.35 pesos per 100 kilos. Indicated exchange rate 335,82 pesos to $100.

In remark undoubtedly made for effect, Miranda referred to number recent corn inquiries from other countries and expressed belief price might soon reach 40 pesos.

BRUCE

102.78/9–447 : Telegram

The Secretary of State to the Embassy in Argentina

SECRET　　　　　　　　WASHINGTON, September 12 ,1947—7 p. m.

852. For the Agricultural Attaché. Reurtel 1078, Sept 4.

1. It is planned to take option of any corn fit for human consumption offered on Argentine market up to 500,000 metric tons.
2. Corn must be free of weevils, rust, and mildew.
3. As soon as your assurance is received that corn is suitable for shipment present intention is that procurement instructions will be issued.
4. Request early reply.

MARSHALL

800.5018/9–2647 : Telegram

The Acting Secretary of State to the Embassy in Argentina

SECRET　　　　　　　　WASHINGTON, September 26, 1947—5 p. m.

907. Secret for the Ambassador. Present circumstances are believed by Dept to counsel advisability of a request to Arg FonMin [30] and/or to Pres Perón personally for wholehearted Arg cooperation and participation in world-wide distribution cereals and basic foodstuffs. Unless you see serious reason why this should not be done, you are requested to make an earnest suggestion along following lines:

Estimated decline of 21,250,000 tons in US corn crop will be only partly ameliorated by an estimated increase of 6,782,000 tons in wheat crop. Even though US should find it possible by taking drastic internal

---

[30] Juan Atilio Bramuglia.

measures to export same amount cereals as during past year, i.e., approximately 14.5 million tons, crop failures in Europe will leave Western and Southern European countries with an estimated 3.5 million tons less than last year. This will bring about necessity for reducing consumption levels in those countries which are already alarming low—e.g., 2100 calories a day in France.

In present world circumstances, it has been a source of encouragement and reassurance to US Govt to feel that Arg Govt is taking a place of international leadership commensurate with the great moral and material resources Arg nation and people. This was exemplified by Pres Perón's recent message bespeaking international cooperation in reconstructing war-torn nations. That expression was warmly received by US Govt. If Arg candidacy for Security Council which is being supported by US Govt results in her election, Arg will have further opportunities for leadership in international affairs.

US Govt earnestly hopes that Arg Govt will give a further expression of its international leadership by assumption of a full share in work International Emergency Food Council. IEFC has been found by participating nations to be an invaluable instrument for allocation of basic food exports in emergency conditions in which it is particularly important to make certain that food supplies are carefully but promptly allocated in close proportion with seriousness of needs. IEFC does not control prices but only distribution. If Arg Govt wishes participate IEFC, US Govt will do its utmost to expedite this action.

In your discussion this suggestion, suggested you emphasize that this is a means by which Arg leadership in international affairs could be given currently great world-wide significance. Moreover, it would seem to be a measure that should be particularly popular among large Italian-born population Arg who must have an especially deep sympathy for current plight people of Italy who face prospect of food scarcities more drastic than last winter.

LOVETT

800.5018/9–2947 : Telegram

The Ambassador in Argentina (Bruce) to the Secretary of State

SECRET   US URGENT   BUENOS AIRES, September 29, 1947—2 p. m.
NIACT

1183. Believe Perón and Bramuglia inclined favor Argentine participation world-wide distribution cereals and basic foodstuffs. Agree wholeheartedly Deptel 907, September 26, 5 p. m. Perón will probably ask Miranda join conference when we see him. Question uppermost in Miranda's mind is in what currency payment would be made for sales. Perón stated recently Argentines worried over sterling nonconvertibility and difficulty payment to Argentina for foodstuffs sold against credits extended under trade agreements with various countries. Miranda emphasizes Argentina's desperate need for dollars and his personal position is largely dependent on ability work out supply dollar exchange. Embassy assures Argentina must look to purchasing country for payment and make arrangements for transfer exchange. Please cable immediately facts as to currency in which all purchases would be paid for.[31] Will immediately arrange appointment Perón, Bramuglia presumably tomorrow or Wednesday at latest, but urged I reply prior to interview. Army Purchasing Commission just arrived and we are having talk with them this afternoon.

BRUCE

800.5018/10–247 : Telegram

The Ambassador in Argentina (Bruce) to the Secretary of State

TOP SECRET BUENOS AIRES, October 2, 1947—3 p. m.

1202. Deptels 907 and 908, September 26.[32] Saw President and Bramuglia together this morning. President and Bramuglia were familiar with IEFC organization and would give sympathetic consideration and let us know Argentine decision soonest.

President immediately brought up question corn mission here and said difficulty was not Argentine production but possibility transportation. He said large quantities corn and wheat have rotted interior due lack transportation. He mentioned Argentina has approximately 4500 large trucks which could be used for moving corn, but Argentina handicapped current gasoline shortage; also adequate shipping facilities must be provided. He referred Argentina's commitments Chile, Bolivia, Paraguay, Brazil, other countries and said these commitments must be fulfilled. He also mentioned Argentina's commitments to Belgium, France, Italy and Spain involving large amounts which Argentina could not collect. President said would have study made immediately Argentina's possibilities under present conditions and also what they would be if adequate transportation possible. In this connection, he frequently mentioned Argentine shortage gasoline. President assured us he would issue decree immediately

---

[31] In telegram 913, September 29, 7 p. m., the Department indicated that arrangements as to price and payment were the province of buyer and seller (800.5018/9–2947).

[32] Latter not printed.

giving satisfaction American oil companies operating in Argentina. See Embdes 3033 September 25.[33]

When increased Argentine production corn arose, President said it had been useless until now urge increased production because more being produced than could be moved.

He said study would be made immediately and would call us, inform us his decision regarding IEFC [34] and possibilities increased exports.

When President brought up question of need farm machinery and additional gasoline we told him that there existed shortage of farm machinery in United States, but we would make every effort help both with regard farm machinery and gasoline, although we could, of course, make no definite commitment.

We are seeing Bramuglia this afternoon.

BRUCE

800.5018/10–947

Memorandum of Conversation, by the Assistant Secretary of State for American Republic Affairs (Armour)

[WASHINGTON,] October 9, 1947.

Participants: Dr. Oscar Ivanissevich—Argentine Ambassador
Mr. Armour—A–A
Mr. Tewksbury—RPA

The Argentine Ambassador has just returned from Buenos Aires, following a visit to his country after the Rio Conference.[35] Dr. Ivanissevich expressed the desire of his Government to cooperate with the United States in important world affairs.

During the conversation I mentioned our hope that Argentina would join the International Emergency Food Council and was pleased that President Perón had shown a favorable attitude when the matter was discussed by Ambassador Bruce. Dr. Ivanissevich expressed surprise that final action had not already been taken by Argentina and said that he thought the matter had been decided favorably before he left Buenos Aires about a week ago. He said that he would check into the matter and assured me that he would give support in attempting to obtain definite favorable action.

I extended my congratulations on the election of Argentina to a seat on the Security Council. The Ambassador appeared pleased and then pointed out that the election of a Chairman of the Governing Board

---

[33] Ante, p. 286.
[34] The Ambassador reported in telegram 1205, October 3, 1947, noon, that the Foreign Minister was confident of Argentina's entry into the IEFC in a few days (800.5018/10–347).
[35] For documentation on this Conference, see pp. 1 ff.

of the Pan American Union would come up at the Nov. 5 meeting. He stated that, for various reasons, Argentina had not been able to play the part in international affairs which its economic and political importance really warranted and expressed the hope that this action in the United Nations was an indication that favorable consideration would be given to Argentina's future role. He stated that Dr. Rocha of Colombia is at present Chairman of the Governing Board of the Union, and he stated that, in his own personal opinion, Argentina merited consideration of our support in the forthcoming election. He felt that, by holding a position of this sort, Argentina would be in a position and disposed to cooperate wholeheartedly with our plans and interests in world affairs. He expressed the hope that I would discuss this with my colleagues and said that, if I wished to discuss the matter with him further, he would be only too glad to have me call him. Brief mention was made of the Bogotá meeting [36] and other general matters relating to Latin American questions.

Prior to coming into my office Dr. Ivanissevich had a few minutes conversation with Tewksbury and he indicated that he felt that all of the problems between the United States and Argentina were being effectively handled and difficulties being ironed out. He specifically mentioned that a solution had practically been reached in the difficult problem of the *frigoríficos* and in relation to the foreign oil companies. He also mentioned a minor problem which General Motors has had with the Municipality of Buenos Aires which has also been satisfactorily settled. There was not sufficient time to discuss any one of these problems in detail.

NORMAN ARMOUR

835.61311/11–1547 : Telegram

The Ambassador in Argentina (Bruce) to the Secretary of State

RESTRICTED   BUENOS AIRES, November 15, 1947—noon.

1344. Referring accusations Argentina charging exorbitant prices wheat, Miranda stated to Corn Mission and repeated US immediately afterwards during courtesy call, Argentina would be glad sell wheat at world market price provided it could purchase equipment and material in United States at same prices any American citizen could buy similar products from manufacturer. Miranda explained Argentina frequently forced buy through two or more middlemen and sometimes paid "blackmarket" prices. Ray [37] and I have given much thought this problem and some weeks ago requested Miranda in pres-

---

[36] See bracketed note, p. 94.
[37] Guy W. Ray, Counselor of Embassy.

ence President Perón furnish us list supplies, equipment, et cetera, needed. We reminded him yesterday no such list received. He said it would be forthcoming immediately. Our conversations with Miranda made known to local press yesterday. Miranda's statement appears have substance and fact and it is hoped Dept will give serious consideration possibilities remedying situation as this most important in connection Argentina's cooperation Marshall plan and participation IEFC. Full report airmail.

BRUCE

835.6131/11-2647

Memorandum of Conversation, by the Assistant Secretary of State for American Republic Affairs (Armour)

[WASHINGTON,] November 26, 1947.

Participants: Señor Martin Luis Drago—Chargé d'Affaires, Argentine Embassy
Señor Rolando Lagomarsino—Formerly Secretary of Industry and Commerce in the Argentine Government
Mr. Armour—A-A

Mr. Drago brought Mr. Lagomarsino in to pay a courtesy call and the discussion was of a rather general character.

During the conversation Mr. Lagomarsino pointed out that Argentina was anxious to buy large amounts of equipment of various types and was particularly anxious to get equipment which would be of value even indirectly for the movement of grains. He emphasized that it was essential that purchases be made at reasonable prices and that it was only in this way that prices for cereals in Argentina could be brought down.

I pointed out that it was in the interest of us all to have conditions in Europe stabilized and specifically it would benefit Argentina if economic reconstruction could be achieved in the normal markets for Argentine products.

Mr. Lagomarsino mentioned various incidents in which Argentina has encountered difficulties in obtaining supplies, but the facts stated were only part of the problem and without long and detailed discussion it was impractical to attempt to refute his statements. In reply to his complaint that Argentina had been unable to get such equipment as oil well machinery, railroad equipment, etc., it was pointed out that our problem would be simplified if Argentina could supply moderately exact estimates of its specific requirements for various types of equipment, covering a period of six months or a year. Mr. Lagomarsino stated that any equipment which could be furnished could be utilized in Argentina and, in effect, for every ton of equipment, it would probably be possible to move an additional one hundred tons of grains to the ports. He made the statement that as much as five hundred thousand tons of cereals were lost during the current year as a result of the Government's inability to transport the cereals to ports.

NORMAN ARMOUR

835.61311/12-947

Memorandum of Conversation, by the Assistant Secretary of State for American Republic Affairs (Armour)

[WASHINGTON,] December 9, 1947.

Participants: Mr. J. C. van Essche—Belgian Food Commission
Mr. Pierre Jaspar—Belgian Economic Mission
Mr. Armour—A-A
Mr. Tewksbury—RPA

Mr. van Essche has just returned from a visit to Buenos Aires and called at the suggestion of Dr. Fitzgerald of the IEFC. Mr. van Essche had numerous interviews with Mr. Miguel Miranda and discussed with him the possibility of obtaining wheat for shipment to Belgium. He stated that, during his conversations in Buenos Aires, Mr. Miranda would not reduce the price of wheat below sixty pesos a quintal (roughly $4.88 f.a.s. Buenos Aires).

Mr. van Essche said that Miranda is definitely upset at Argentina's inability to continue to receive dollar payment for British purchases. He apparently recognizes, however, that this will not be possible unless through purchases under the European Recovery Program. He also realizes that he will probably be forced to accept a lower price for wheat—possibly approximately the Chicago price—if he is to receive dollar payments for shipments to Europe under the European Recovery Program. Mr. van Essche is of the opinion that Miranda has about reached the point where he will accept this condition.

According to Mr. van Essche, Miranda insists that he must have coal or petroleum in order to move crops to seaboard. He attempted to obtain guarantees for the shipment of these products from Belgium in return for cereals. In addition to coal and petroleum, Miranda says that he needs tinplate, agricultural equipment, railway equipment, etc. He recognizes, however, that it will not be possible to get railway equipment soon enough to assist in any early movement of crops. Miranda bitterly attacks the United States and blames it not only for Argentina's inability to get materials and equipment which it needs, but also claims that the enormous increase of cereal production in the United States has been due to the withholding of equipment for Argentina, with a resultant decline of production in Argentina. He also complains that the United States has grossly overcharged Argentina for equipment which it has purchased. In fact, Miranda lays most of the blame for any Argentine difficulties on the United States.

I asked Mr. van Essche if he thought there was any possibility of Argentina coming into the IEFC, and Mr. van Essche replied that he doubted if Argentina would do so. I pointed out that there would certainly be difficulty in using Economic Recovery Program funds for the purchase of Argentine cereals if Argentina attempted to charge the present high prices. Mr. van Essche said that he was convinced that Miranda recognized this point and that this was undoubtedly one of the factors which was bringing him to realize that there must be a sharp reduction in price for the new crop which will soon be coming on to the market. He said that Mr. Miranda is thoroughly aware of the world cereal situation both as to needs and as to availabilities.

Mr. van Essche said that Mr. Miranda brought out one interesting point in his price discussions. He recognized that Argentine wheat prices were well above those in the United States, but claimed that corn prices were approximately the same, possibly slightly lower. He then quoted United States' meat prices and explained that there was no justification for United States prices to be ten or fifteen times as high as Argentine prices. He said that the British should pay more for their meat.

Mr. van Essche was of the opinion that there should be centralized purchasing for each of those products needed in connection with the European Recovery Program. He felt that, if purchasing were undertaken by individual nations, buying might become competitive and prejudicial to the interests of all.

Mr. van Essche then took the opportunity to emphasize the seriousness of the proposal to reduce the bread ration to Belgium during the winter months. The proposal has been made, due to the difficulty in obtaining wheat shipments, that Belgium reduce the bread ration from 300 to 250 calories. He explained that the Communists were already issuing propaganda to the effect that the United States would default on grain shipments and that, as a result, bread rations would have to be decreased. He felt that any reduction in bread rations prior to the March elections would mean substantial gains by the Communists. Mr. van Essche is most anxious that the IEFC allocations covering shipments from the US and Canada be adequate to provide the ration of 250 calories and that Belgium be allocated sufficient amounts from Argentina or other sources to maintain a ration of 300 calories. If necessary, Belgium is prepared to pay the $5.00 price to Argentina for the difference between 250 and 300 calories. Mr. van Essche said that a Russian Mission is now in Belgium attempting to purchase machinery and equipment but that he is confident that his Government will not make any arrangements which do not provide for grain in return.

NORMAN ARMOUR

835.61311/12-1247

Memorandum of Telephone Conversation, by the Chief of the Division of River Plate Affairs (Tewksbury)

CONFIDENTIAL [WASHINGTON,] December 12, 1947.

Admiral Bunkley [39] has just returned from a visit to Buenos Aires and reports that, prior to leaving Buenos Aires, he had a talk with President Perón. He states that President Perón particularly requested that he bring the following message to President Truman:

President Perón stated that, approximately two years ago, the Russian Ambassador made an offer to purchase the entire wheat and grain crop of Argentina and assured the Government that Russia, in return, would supply all of the agricultural machinery, as well as other types of machinery, which the Government required. The Russians went so far as to offer not only machinery of Russian manufacture but also machinery and equipment which was being furnished to Russia and the satellite countries by the United States. President Perón said that the Russian offer was rejected and that the Russian Ambassador expressed great surprise that Argentina was not interested in his proposal. President Perón stated that he was opposed to dealing with Russia and wished to work with the United States.

President Perón further stated that Argentina desires to sell its products, including grains, meats, etc. at prices at which we sell them but that, to do so, Argentina wants to be able to obtain machinery and equipment from the United States in the quantities required and at fair market prices. President Perón complained that Argentina has had great difficulty in purchasing required products in the amounts needed and that Argentina has been charged black market prices in many instances. Argentina wants adequate supplies made available but at reasonable prices.

---

[39] Adm. J. William Bunkley, Retired.

Admiral Bunkley stated that President Perón informed him that Argentina had fourteen million tons of wheat stored away which it will be glad to give up if satisfactory arrangements can be made.

During the conversation I explained to Admiral Bunkley that one of the transactions which had been complained about by Argentine officials was the one involving the purchase of some twenty million gallons of gasoline at something over eleven cents, whereas the market price in New Orleans was in the vicinity of nine cents. (Admiral Bunkley was directly connected with this transaction which was negotiated through his representatives in Buenos Aires.) Admiral Bunkley said that this was not strictly a black market transaction and that the middleman's profit was negligible. He stated that commission of his company amounted to only $25,000 and that the Argentine agents participating in the transaction only received $50,000. All of the remaining profit went to the producers, which he claimed were the only ones able to supply the gasoline and were, therefore, in a position to demand any price. Admiral Bunkley felt that Argentine officials had only themselves to blame in this instance.

. . . .

Admiral Bunkley spoke very highly of Ambassador Bruce and said that he had succeeded in maintaining excellent relations with both the "Peronistas" and opposition factions.

HOWARD H. TEWKSBURY

800.5018/12–1647 : Telegram

The Acting Secretary of State to the Embassy in Argentina

CONFIDENTIAL   WASHINGTON, December 16, 1947—3 p. m.

1172. Dept 1058 Nov 5.[40] Nov meetings IEFC and FAO decided former should be dissolved, that commodity committees will continue under supervision new Committee (International Emergency Food Committee) of FAO Council. If Arg still unwilling join FAO and possibly regarding merger as obstacle joining IEFC, suggest pointing out that FAO Council agreed non-FAO members can be members commodity committees and of new IEFC. Latter provision adopted with Arg specifically in mind. Non-FAO members have privilege participating in FAO Council discussions on allocations questions in which they substantially interested.

LOVETT

---

[40] Not printed.

POSITION OF THE UNITED STATES WITH RESPECT TO THE OPPOSITION PRESS IN ARGENTINA

835.911/8–1447

The Chargé in Argentina (Ray) to the Secretary of State

CONFIDENTIAL BUENOS AIRES, August 19, 1947.
No. 2890

SIR: I have the honor to refer to the Embassy's despatch no. 1199 of November 13, 1946,[41] and to subsequent communications, reporting a court suit instituted by a common informer against *La Prensa* and *La Nación* for the payment of duties on newsprint imported for a number of years past.

As pointed out in that despatch, for a number of years Argentine newspapers have imported newsprint duty free on the basis of a long-standing law that "cultural organs" are exempt from the payment of such duty. In November 1946 Sr. Eugenio Alberto Marggi entered a suit in the courts charging the two newspapers mentioned with having illegally failed to pay import duties. Marggi was able to enter the suit under a law which entitled informers on tax evaders to collect a certain percentage of amounts eventually collected by the Government.

Subsequently the courts held that the matter was one for administrative action and refused to take cognizance thereof. For some months nothing more was heard of the matter and it seemed likely that the Government would let it drop.

It has been learned, however, that about July 27, 1947, the Argentine Customs sent communications to both *La Prensa* and *La Nación* demanding that they pay the retroactive import duty or else show cause why they should not do so. It is understood that at least *La Nación* has replied in the sense that the long-accepted interpretation of the law is adequate cause for granting duty-free entry of newsprint for newspapers.

The generally accepted interpretation of the abortive suit and of the new administrative action with regard to this matter is that the Government is simply using another means of putting pressure on these independent newspapers which continue to be thorns in its flesh. At this point, however, the Embassy can only speculate on the lengths to which the Government might go.

Reliable but unconfirmed sources advised the Embassy, also about July 7, that *La Prensa* had been asked by the Government to deliver the 10% of its newsprint imports which has been impounded for some time. The Department will recall a decree in 1946 which provided that

---

[41] Not printed.

all newsprint importers must deliver 10% of their newsprint to the Government at cost plus 10%, which would then distribute it "equitably" among all users. *La Prensa* obtained a court injunction and has not to date delivered any newsprint to the Government although it has earmarked and set aside the requisite quantity. In this connection reference also is made to the Embassy's despatch no. 2821 of July 24, 1947.[42]

There have been other recent evidences of Government interference with freedom of the press. In most of these cases it is American publications and journalists which are the objects of the Government's attention.

Several opposition newspapers from time to time have reported that the post office accepts their publications for distribution but that "unaccountably" (tongue-in-cheek) they fail to be delivered.

The August 11 issue of *Time* Magazine was impounded in the Argentine Customs until the night of August 13, about one week. Like *Newsweek* and several other publications, *Time* has had an arrangement whereby its shipments were exempt from customs formalities since they are not dutiable. The action against the latest issue was taken without warning, probably as a sign of displeasure against recent articles portraying Mrs. Perón [43] in a not very favorable light. The distributors expect similar trouble with a few more issues. The difficulties seem to stem from an effort to apprise *Time*'s publishers of the government's displeasure in the hope that future stories concerning Argentina will be written with a greater "sense of propriety".

The other recent event of importance in connection with press freedom was an official communiqué of August 5 excoriating the Associated Press. This was reported to the Department in the Embassy's telegram no. 968 of August 6.[42] As the Department knows, this has resulted in the recall for consultation of Associated Press Vice President Ray Ordorica. It still remains to be seen what if any solution may be found for this problem.

The Embassy recently has noted several other instances of Government displeasure with American journalists and publications. Illustrative of these are attacks in *La Epoca* and other Peronista newspapers on the *New York Times* for a recent article which in effect belittled President Perón's July 6 peace proposal; and an attack in *La Epoca* on a story filed by *Chicago Tribune* correspondent Jules DuBois, belaboring Argentine official interference with freedom of the press.

---

[42] Not printed.
[43] Wife of the Argentine President, Juan D. Perón.

Another example is a "radio editorial" on *Radio del Estado* the night of August 11, a translation of which is enclosed.[44]

In other words, it appears that the Perón Administration is growing more and more sensitive and is concomitantly determined to go to considerable lengths to obtain what it calls "fair treatment" by the "reactionary" press.

Respectfully yours, For the Chargé d'Affaires ad interim:
R. Kenneth Oakley
Second Secretary of Embassy

835.911/9-2547 : Telegram

The Acting Secretary of State to the Embassy in Argentina

RESTRICTED Washington, October 1, 1947—6 p. m.

921. UP reps here have requested Secretary send brief statement to *La Prensa*[45] Buenos Aires occasion 78th anniversary Oct 18. Apparently that newspaper plans special anniversary edition including statements and letters prominent persons many countries. Understood this customary with *La Prensa*.

Pls deliver in your discretion following message from Secretary Marshall to Dr. Gainza Paz, publisher *La Prensa:*

"Please accept my congratulations on the occasion of *La Prensa's* 78th anniversary. The prestige which your paper has achieved through its continued maintenance of the highest standards of journalism reserves for it a special place among the great newspapers of the world. I take this opportunity to wish *La Prensa* many more years of distinguished public service."

Lovett

835.911/10-247 : Telegram

The Ambassador in Argentina (Bruce) to the Secretary of State

RESTRICTED Buenos Aires, October 2, 1947—4 p. m.

1203. Deptel 921, October 1. We have given careful thought proposed message from Secretary Marshall to Gainza Paz, publisher *La Prensa* and are convinced publication by *La Prensa* would have opposite effect from that intended. Perón would interpret message as direct slap at

---

[44] Not printed.
[45] This request was made by Harry W. Frantz, Foreign Department, United Press Associations, in a letter of September 25 to the Assistant Secretary of State for Political Affairs (Armour) (835.911/9-2547).

him and net result would probably be more Government pressure and persecution *La Prensa*.

In recent conversations President has shown growing inclination favor free enterprise and removal many onerous restrictions. One reason is he is realizing artificial restrictions are detrimental Argentine commerce and trade. He discussed this morning on own initiative question freedom press and exhibited conciliatory attitude. He deplored attack in foreign press on President Truman personally and objected strongly to attacks in our press on persons of Mrs. Perón and himself. He professed have no objection constructive criticism but considered attacks on subjects of foreign states and members of their families as being uncalled for, unjust and unfair, especially since foreigners have no means defense through libel laws or otherwise.

We share Department's high esteem *La Prensa* and Gainza Paz, but believe proposed message would not only have bad repercussions for *La Prensa* but also would hamper delicate negotiations we are now carrying on with Perón.

BRUCE

835.911/10–247 : Telegram

The Acting Secretary of State to the Embassy in Argentina

RESTRICTED   WASHINGTON, October 7, 1947—6 p. m.

945. Deptel 921, Oct 1 and urtel 1203, Oct 2. Whereas Dept continues leave matter transmittal *La Prensa* message your discretion it offers following observations your consideration.

1) Embassy records doubtless show this does not constitute precedent Secretary having previously sent such messages to *La Prensa*. Conceivable public repercussions press and elsewhere resulting from omission message might be more detrimental than repercussions Perón Govt from inserting message. This might be especially true if messages received from high personages other Govts.

2) Suggest you consult your British and other colleagues view to determining what action officials their Govts, who have perhaps been similarly approached, contemplate taking.

3) Dept aware Secretaries Defense, Treasury, Agriculture, and Commerce received requests to send messages. All have been asked send statements through Dept. Altho offices other Cabinet heads report Secretaries have not received requests, other high US officials may have received them and may send direct communications to *La Prensa*.

Pls telegraph your final decision.

LOVETT

835.911/9-2547

The Secretary of State to the Embassy in Argentina

RESTRICTED
No. 43

WASHINGTON, October 8, 1947.

The Secretary of State transmits the enclosed letter from Secretary of Defense Forrestal to Dr. Gainza Paz, congratulating him on the 78th anniversary of *La Prensa*.[47] The Officer in Charge of Mission is requested to forward this letter to Dr. Gainza Paz if he transmitted Secretary Marshall's message contained in the Department's telegram No. 921 of October 1, 1947. If the Officer in Charge did not forward Secretary Marshall's message or if he deems it in any way inappropriate to transmit Mr. Forrestal's letter, he will please notify the Department to this effect.

The letter from the Secretary of Defense was sealed upon its arrival in the Department. An officer of the Department has been informed, however, that it reads as follows:

"Dear Dr. Paz:

Please accept my warm congratulations on the 78th anniversary of *La Prensa*. *La Prensa* has every reason to be proud of the high journalistic standards to which it has consistently adhered. I am confident that in the years to come these standards will be maintained and *La Prensa* will continue to champion enlightenment and international understanding.

Sincerely yours,

James Forrestal"

835.911/10-1047 : Airgram

The Ambassador in Argentina (Bruce) to the Secretary of State

RESTRICTED

BUENOS AIRES, October 10, 1947.

A-616. With reference to Department's restricted telegram No. 945 of October 7, 6 p. m. and other recent correspondence concerning the transmittal of various messages to *La Prensa*:

It seems to us that messages from Secretaries Marshall, Forrestal, Anderson and other United States Government officials might be construed by the Argentine Government as being artificial and sent for the definite purpose of warning Perón that we are in sympathy with *La Prensa* and would look with disfavor on any action he might take against that paper. In Perón's mind this would probably constitute interference in Argentine affairs.

---

[47] The Department, in telegram 952, October 8, transmitted similar congratulations from the Secretary of Agriculture (835.911/10-847).

If a message from the Department of State were signed by Assistant Secretary Armour, it would appear much more natural since Mr. Armour was Ambassador here for a long time and is a personal friend of the publisher of *La Prensa*. Such action would be considered as a very natural thing to do.

It is important in our opinion that as Secretary of Defense Mr. Forrestal should not send a statement since this could be interpreted as having political significance. We have emphasized repeatedly that relationships between armed services in Argentina and the United States are on a completely professional basis. Our Military, Naval and Air Attachés and Naval and Air Missions have done a good job and have the respect of the Argentine servicemen.

The Government here is most desirous of having a friendly press in the United States. We think it is desirable that leading United States publishers send congratulatory messages to *La Prensa*. We have consistently maintained here that the United Press is an objective news-gathering and news-distributing service and so far we have been successful in the help we have been able to render UP and AP on this basis. It would prejudice our case if we had need in the future to help them and the suspicion were aroused that they were protagonists in developing support for *La Prensa* on behalf of United States Government officials. A short time ago I gave a reception, inviting all members of the local press, except publishers, including representatives of the Argentine Government information office. The latter, although accepting, did not come and the reason was because there were going to be present members of the so-called opposition press, including representatives of *La Prensa*. A situation in which the United Press requests statements from leading U.S. Government officials to send congratulatory messages to *La Prensa* would immediately, in our opinion, be used by the Argentine Government information office, by exaggerating its importance and presenting it to the attention of the President accompanied by interpretations which were by no means intended. The objectives of the Department, of the United Press and this Embassy are the same but the means of attaining them have to be studied most carefully so that no impractical counterirritant is injected into the situation which would be upsetting to the attainment of the results we are working for.

As already stated to the Department, we know Gainza Paz personally and have the highest esteem for him and *La Prensa*. However, we do not wish to take action which might in the long run be prejudicial to him and make our delicate negotiations with Perón more difficult.

BRUCE

835.911/10–1047 : Telegram

The Ambassador in Argentina (Bruce) to the Secretary of State

RESTRICTED   BUENOS AIRES, October 10, 1947—6 p. m.

1234. Embassy records indicate no message from US officials sent *La Prensa* since 75th anniversary. British Ambassador [48] says no information regarding action contemplated his Government. Proposed messages Secretaries Defense, Agriculture so obviously solicited messages, we believe they should not be sent.

So far as Embassy can learn, only actual official sending message so far is Sforza of Italy. If Presidents, Foreign Ministers several other larger American Republics send messages, this Embassy sees no objection Secretary Marshall doing so, but suggests it be sent direct from Washington to publisher *La Prensa*. We understand this Embassy has discussed *Prensa* question with Perón informally on previous occasions expressing concern public opinion in US over freedom of press and fair treatment for *La Prensa*. We still believe Perón would interpret message from Secretary as indirect way of interfering in Argentine affairs and *La Prensa* might suffer from his resentment. Perón would realize messages have been solicited and interpret them as means bringing pressure on him.

This Embassy will take no action unless further instructions but if Department can ascertain that other Foreign Ministers or Presidents of American countries are sending messages, it sees no objection direct message from Secretary or Assistant Secretary Armour who has served here as Ambassador, knows publisher of *Prensa* and from whom message would seem natural.[49]

BRUCE

835.911/10–1547 : Telegram

The Assistant Secretary of State for American Republic Affairs (Armour) to the Publisher of "La Prensa" (Gainza Paz)

WASHINGTON, October 15, 1947.

Please accept my congratulations on the occasion of *La Prensa's* seventy-eighth anniversary.

The prestige which your paper has achieved through its continued maintenance of the highest standards of journalism reserves for it a

---

[48] Sir Reginald Leeper.
[49] In response to an inquiry from the Department, Ambassador Beaulac in telegram 695, October 14, 6 p. m., from Bogotá, stated that the Colombian Foreign Office had no knowledge about a request for a statement concerning *La Prensa* anniversary (835.911/10–1447). A similar response was received from Ambassador Thurston in telegram 1114, October 15, noon, from Mexico (835.911/10–1547).

special place among the great newspapers of the world. I take this opportunity to wish *La Prensa* and you many more years of distinguished public service.

NORMAN ARMOUR

835.911/10–2247 : Airgram

The Ambassador in Argentina (Bruce) to the Secretary of State

CONFIDENTIAL BUENOS AIRES, October 22, 1947.

A–635. With reference to the Department's telegram no. 985 of October 17, 1 p. m.,[50] quoting messages sent by Mr. Hull [51] and Mr. Armour to *La Prensa* on the occasion of its 75th anniversary, the first sentence of this Embassy's telegram no. 1234 of October 10, 6 p. m. reads as follows: "Embassy records indicate no messages from U.S. officials sent *La Prensa* since 75th anniversary." Embassy files contain record of message sent on the occasion of the 75th anniversary but there are no records of messages since that time. It seems to us that the 75th anniversary or any other anniversary the number of which would be a multiple of 25 is generally considered more significant than for instance the 78th anniversary.

We have just learned in confidence that letters from the British, Swedish, Belgian, Brazilian and Peruvian Foreign Offices addressed to the local representative of United Press stating that they were unable to comply with the United Press's request for letters of congratulations to the publisher of *La Prensa* were opened and photostatic copies made by the Argentine authorities. The local correspondent of UP was called in by the Argentine authorities and asked to explain. The letters were apparently received sealed but the authorities showed the UP correspondent photostatic copies of the letters.

This is most unfortunate development. It is known, of course, by the interested Argentine officials that UP received a large monthly fee from *La Prensa* for its services and it would be impossible to convince President Perón and other Argentine officials that UP was not interfering in the internal affairs of Argentina and probably more interested in protecting its [52] *La Prensa* than in actual freedom of the press.

. . . .

It is unfortunate that UP should become involved in this especially as it can no longer be argued that UP was not soliciting congratula-

---

[50] Not printed.
[51] Former Secretary of State Cordell Hull.
[52] Undecipherable passage.

tory messages for *La Prensa* and no one could convince Perón and his friends that UP is not primarily motivated by a desire to protect its interests and that it is interfering in the internal affairs of Argentina. This development will probably have an unfavorable effect on all American correspondents in Argentina. There seems to be little if any remedy at present other than to hope that it will eventually blow over. I sent a short message to Gainza Paz congratulating *La Prensa* on its 78th anniversary. A similar message was sent by the British Ambassador. Associated Press sent no message. This development makes more difficult our argument that news services are completely objective. According to information received by this Embassy UP gets a monthly fee from *La Prensa* of $10,000, plus certain others for unusual expenses. We have been told by a reliable newspaper man that this is the largest fee paid to any news services by any newspaper. We feel that subsequent developments have justified the position we orginally took with regard to messages from Secretary Marshall and other high officials of the United States Government. We consider that messages by Mr. Armour and me are normal and natural enough not to arouse special comment especially as British Ambassador also sent a message. However, position of UP is weakened by fact that it obviously solicited message for *La Prensa*. This information was given to Ray and me in strictest confidence with request that it be discussed with no one.

BRUCE

BOLIVIA

PROBLEMS INVOLVED IN THE PROCUREMENT OF BOLIVIAN TIN BY THE UNITED STATES [1]

824.6354/1-2347 : Telegram

The Ambassador in Bolivia (Flack) to the Secretary of State

CONFIDENTIAL   LA PAZ, January 23, 1947—6 p. m.

81. In informal conversation with Acting ForMin Saenz [2] today he told me of depression and disappointment of the Junta about slim prospects for any increase in price of tin revealed in information from Cañedo Reyes.[3]

I feel that question of price of tin is inescapably tied up with Bolivian internal economy and public order and that unless adequate increase to offset increased cost of imported foodstuffs is attained the new govt will have difficult situation dealing with mining labor in particular.

Jorje Zalles, Grace [4] Vice President, now here informed me he has been told by intimate friends that brusk statement by US that tin price resulting from negotiations would not be retroactive as heretofore, has caused very bad impressions and feeling that Bolivia is being squeezed. These people feel that they are entitled to better treatment than was the dictatorial Villarroel regime [5] and that US should contribute to stability of democratic institutions by more friendly treatment on the tin price question. This attitude was factually demonstrated by decision of producers to withhold tin shipments pending conclusion of the tin negotiations.

I hope that Dept may consider this question in the light of implications in our overall relations with Bolivia and our desire to stimulate democratic institutions which have emerged since July 21. These points might be usefully stressed in talks with RFC.

FLACK

---

[1] For documentation on obtaining Bolivian raw materials in 1946, see *Foreign Relations*, 1946, vol. XI, pp. 374 ff.

[2] Eduardo Saenz Garcia; his regular position was Minister of National Economy.

[3] Raúl Cañedo Reyes, Bolivian Director General of Mines and Petroleum.

[4] W. R. Grace and Company.

[5] For documentation on the overthrow of the Villarroel regime and the position of the United States, see *Foreign Relations*, 1946, vol. XI, pp. 340 ff.

824.6354/2–1847

Memorandum of Telephone Conversation, by Mr. James Espy of the Division of North and West Coast Affairs

SECRET [WASHINGTON,] February 18, 1947.

At 3 o'clock today Mr. Jesse Johnson, Deputy Director, Metals Reserve, RFC, telephoned me and said that at the meeting of the Board of Directors of RFC this morning, it was decided to reconsider RFC's position that RFC would not agree to enter into a new tin concentrates purchase contract with the Bolivian producers for a higher price than that of the last contract; and to offer to negotiate a new firm contract with the Bolivian producers at an "acceptable" price for the rest of the year. Mr. Johnson said that RFC would not be able to pay 76¢ which the Bolivians are asking and I gathered that RFC's top limit might be something around 72¢.

Mr. Johnson continued by informing me that he was consulting the political side of the Department for its views and also the economic side. He mentioned that the Economic Division, Mr. Kennedy's office,[6] had registered its strong opposition to any increase in price to be paid for Bolivian tin but he also wanted to know our opinion. He mentioned in this connection that he imagined that if political disturbances were occasioned in Bolivia because of the tin price they could affect the production of Bolivian tin which would be a natural concern to RFC.

I told Mr. Johnson that I believe that our views were the same as those which had been conveyed to him during the meeting in Mr. Kennedy's office on Feb. 5th. I repeated them as follows, saying that unless he received word from me to the contrary, they could be accepted as stated: (*a*) we were not requesting RFC to raise the price of Bolivian tin; (*b*) we considered that the negotiations between RFC and the Bolivian producers were a commercial transaction between that Agency and the Bolivians and that we did not enter into it as regards price or terms; (*c*) we feel however, that if RFC could not arrange a contract or other methods of purchase with the Bolivian producers for their tin concentrates at a price acceptable to the Bolivians then (*d*) tin should be placed on a free market status which would allow Bolivians to sell it wherever and at such a price and on such terms as they were able to arrange.

With respect to the last point (*d*) I said that it was my opinion that unless the Bolivians were able to sell on a free market, then—despite the fact that there was no intent to do so, despite the fact that we have and are paying a very high and fair price, despite the fact that before any hypothetical court we could without question prove that we were

---

[6] Donald D. Kennedy, Chief, International Resources Division.

fair and square with the Bolivians and that they had been remiss in not making the necessary readjustments to set their economic house in order—in the eyes of the Bolivian public, and possibly even the world at large, this country and Great Britain may well appear to be constituting what amounted to a purchasing cartel and that this again, with all the provisos that I have mentioned, laid us open to criticism on the part of Bolivia of restricting their trade in tin concentrates. Accordingly, to get this Government out of this position, we feel that our views as expressed in point (*d*) are logically justified. Mr. Johnson remarked that he fully appreciated this position and agreed with it.

824.6354/2–2447 : Telegram

The Ambassador in Bolivia (Flack) to the Secretary of State

CONFIDENTIAL   LA PAZ, February 24, 1947—noon

161. Recent press editorials and expressions of private opinions are continuing to stress Bolivia's great interest in question of tin price in current negotiations in Washington and to urge necessity of securing 76 cent prices.

Saturday evening Alberto Ostria Gutierrez, Bolivian Ambassador in Chile and former Bolivian Foreign Minister, now here on leave, came to my house at his request to express, he said, his personal views as a friend and democrat. He characterized Bolivia's situation as very grave, mentioned a previous talk he had with Ambassador Bowers in Santiago on the same matter, and speaking personally said he wished to impress upon me the seriousness of the political and economic situation of Bolivia which without our aid would place Bolivia under Perón's influence. He asserted that Argentina through recent agreement with Chile had begun to emerge as a Pacific power on the road to domination of the southern part of the hemisphere, and that Bolivia's present democratic status is an obstacle to expansion of Argentine influence since that country is seeking every opportunity to enhance its influence in this part of the world.

. . . .

Remytel 686, July 22,[7] in the early days of the regime pointing out that young Bolivian democracy would need much material help, I reiterate those statements on the basis of my subsequent experience and recommend Dept's favorable consideration of the personal viewpoint expressed by Ambassador Ostria which in main reiterates others previously transmitted.

FLACK

---

[7] *Foreign Relations,* 1946, vol. XI, p. 357.

824.6354/2–2647

The Ambassador in Bolivia (Flack) to the Secretary of State

RESTRICTED
No. 1021

La Paz, February 26, 1947.

Sir: I have the honor to refer to previous communications reporting the fact that the two presidential candidates, Drs. Enrique Hertzog and Luis Fernando Guachalla, recently requested a conference with me for the purpose of presenting their views on the above-mentioned subject.[8]

As previously stated, the two candidates then expressed their intention of submitting a memorandum setting forth more precisely the views previously expressed to me orally. This memorandum, dated February 24, was received yesterday by me and I enclose a copy with translation of the covering letter together with a copy and translation of the memorandum signed jointly by Drs. Hertzog and Guachalla.[9] A copy of the Spanish text of the original letter will be submitted at a later date since it is desirable that the present report be despatched at the earliest possible moment.

The memorandum treats chiefly with the following points:

1.) Tin is Bolivia's chief source of foreign exchange for the purchase of imported goods, mostly from the United States, and delay in the exportation and suspension of income from tin prejudices Bolivia's general economy.

2.) The point is made that the tin producing companies have either suffered considerable losses requiring the closing of certain properties, including Oploca, or they have been unable to afford the necessary equipment for modernization of their mines.

3.) Emphasis is given to the fact that the Banco Central of Bolivia has already invested all of its available assets in dollars to pay for needed imports and has been obliged to negotiate loans with the United States banks at high rates of interest, using Bolivian gold reserves in the Federal Reserve Bank as security.

4.) Emphasis is also given to the necessity of avoiding the outbreak of social conflicts and labor disturbances resulting from unemployment and the point is made that it is a high moral duty of the United States towards Bolivia to instruct its fiscal agencies to proceed to the early conclusion of a new contract for Bolivian tin at the price which the producers have solicited.

I need scarcely emphasize the importance of the views of Drs. Hertzog and Guachalla, the two leading political figures in Bolivia, one of whom will be President of the country from early March 1947 until 1951. Their views are likewise strongly supported by the members of

---

[8] i.e., higher price for tin.
[9] None printed.

the present Junta of Government and other leading figures in Bolivia's political and economic life as previous reports of this Embassy will reveal.

I therefore recommend to the Department the most favorable consideration of these viewpoints since I have the very distinct impression from all of the men of influence in Bolivia with whom I have talked that Bolivia will have a very strong feeling of having been let down, in addition to the dire economic consequences which she will confront if the United States is unable to come to her assistance at this time in this matter, and to consider the question of the tin price not alone as a commercial transaction.

Respectfuly yours, JOSEPH FLACK

824.504/3–1147

The Ambassador in Bolivia (Flack) to the Secretary of State

RESTRICTED LA PAZ, March 11, 1947.
No. 1077

SIR: I have the honor to transmit herewith two memoranda [10] from the labor reporting officer [11] concerning recent developments at the Catavi mine of Patiño Mines and Enterprises Consolidated (Incorporated). (Enclosures 1 and 2) Mr. Deringer, General Manager of Catavi, called on the Ambassador on the morning of March 8 and essentially repeated his views as quoted in the memoranda. At the request of the Ambassador, he promised that all women and children and as many of the male employees as possible would be evacuated from the Catavi area before any effort is made to bring on a showdown with the workers over the question of their pay for the eight-hour shift which took part in a sit-down strike on March 3.

The Junta of Government has issued a decree definitely characterizing the sit-down strike called by Juan Lechin [12] as illegal and relieving the mining companies of any responsibility for wages for the shift which did no work during the eight-hour strike period. (See enclosure no. 3).

Although it is expected that the workers in general, and especially those at Catavi, will make all efforts to collect the wages in question, the mining industry is determined not to pay wages for a period in which no work was done. Patiño Mines and Enterprises is especially adamant in its determination not to pay and is apparently willing to resist to the point of closing down the Catavi property. The legal position of the mining companies cannot be questioned and has been reinforced by the decree of the Junta to which reference is made above.

---

[10] Enclosures not printed.
[11] Spencer M. King.
[12] Executive Secretary, Federación Sindical de Trabajadores.

Because of the general fears of serious trouble in the mining areas, and especially at Catavi where the management was forced to sign an agreement to pay the wages in question, the Ambassador handed a note to the Sub-Secretary of Foreign Affairs at 2:30 P. M. on March 7, requesting protection for the American personnel at Catavi.[13] . . .

. . . .

Respectfully yours, JOSEPH FLACK

824.6354/3–1147

Memorandum of Conversation, by the Chief of the Division of North and West Coast Affairs (Wells)

CONFIDENTIAL [WASHINGTON,] March 11, 1947.

BOLIVIAN TIN NEGOTIATIONS

Participants: Señor Don Ricardo Martinez Vargas, Ambassador of Bolivia
Señor Don Raul Diez de Medina, Bolivian Minister Counselor
Assistant Secretary Braden
Mr. Wright, A–Br
Mr. Smith, A–Br
Mr. Wells, NWC

Repeating the history of his negotiations with RFC as stated to Mr. Briggs[14] yesterday, the Ambassador lamented the original intransigent attitude of RFC, the long drawn-out haggling over every cent increase, his successful efforts to persuade the Bolivian producers to compromise their demand for 76 cents, and the embarrassing end results. He is on a spot, having reported to his Government with much satisfaction the conclusion of an agreement at 74 cents coincidentally with the Argentine offer of 76 cents. He is not certain how to proceed, but has counseled the producers to do nothing for the moment. Before taking further steps, he wishes to ascertain the attitude of this Government, particularly as to whether RFC would contract for the 12,000 tons remaining should Argentina purchase 8,000.

He reiterated forcibly his opinion that our take-it-or-leave-it attitude and our willingness to take advantage of price controls to drive a one-sided bargain are doing immense harm to the Good Neighbor policy. He contrasted our attitude with that of the Argentine mission, which is reported to have arrived at La Paz "to do business, not to bargain over price" and had concluded an agreement in six days.

---

[13] In a note of the same date the Sub-Secretary for Foreign Affairs provided the assurances requested (824.504/3–1147).
[14] Ellis O. Briggs, Director, Office of American Republic Affairs.

Mr. Braden agreed that the Ambassador's principal points were well taken. In the Ambassador's presence, he telephoned Mr. Thorp [15] and urged that the economic divisions consider the matter urgently in order that the Bolivian Ambassador may be informed regarding our position. He suggested that the Ambassador, in the meantime, cable La Paz to inquire as to his Government's attitude toward the RFC offer in view of the draft agreement with Argentina.

824.6354/3-1747

Memorandum of Conversation, by the Assistant Chief of the Division of North and West Coast Affairs (Hall)

CONFIDENTIAL [WASHINGTON,] March 17, 1947.

Participants: Assistant Secretary Braden
Ambassador Martínez Vargas
Mr. Wright, A-Br
Mr. Briggs, ARA
Mr. Wells and Mr. Hall of NWC

The Ambassador called to ask for advice regarding the next steps to be taken in the tin negotiations. It was pointed out to him that RFC was still awaiting answer to their 74¢ offer and Señor Martínez said that he would call them to say that his Government could not accept the same.

The Ambassador expressed hopes that RFC would meet the Argentine offer of 76¢, in which case he would use his best efforts to reduce the Argentine allocation from 8,000 to say 3,000 tons, or roughly the production handled by the Banco Minero. He said that his Government would probably be willing to consider an RFC contract until September, for one year, or even for two years.

Mr. Braden replied that his officers would confer with RFC tomorrow, after which any available information would be passed on to the Ambassador.

824.6354/3-2047 : Telegram

The Ambassador in Bolivia (Flack) to the Secretary of State

SECRET   US URGENT   LA PAZ, March 20, 1947—7 p. m.

267. Information given me late this afternoon by Subsecretary Alvarado indicates that on basis of official information from Washington tin contract at 76 cents may be signed tomorrow, thus remov-

---

[15] Willard L. Thorp, Assistant Secretary of State for Economic Affairs.

ing all but Banco Minero's production of scarcely 3,000 tons from scope of proposed Argentine Agreement.

Alvarado stated further that as a result of representations made by Brazilian Ambassador the provisions in proposed agreement re Mutum iron and Beni rubber would be eliminated from draft. Also that Brazil would not only furnish funds for construction of Cochabamba-Santa Cruz railway but for La Paz–Boni railway as well thus forestalling Argentina attempts at controlling these routes and hinterland. Brazilian participation in connecting link in railway from Arica to Santos (Cochabamba-Santa Cruz sector) was stated to have been established in exchange of notes in 1943.

Alvarado stated that Bolivian counterproposal would be finished this evening taking note of points above detailed. He hopes that this will be published in line with previous decision to keep public informed and he feels that when this is made known to the Argentines they will reduce their offers of financial assistance to Bolivia by at least half if not more or make proposition unacceptable.

Foreign Office has concluded that only use Argentina could make of large amount of tin contemplated is for sale to Russia since economic negotiations with Russian delegation now taking place in Buenos Aires.

In reply to Alvarado's question about our views on draft agreement with Argentina I replied that as yet I had no official indication from Washington; this was evidently primary purpose of calling me to Foreign Office.

FLACK

824.504/3–2147

The Ambassador in Bolivia (Flack) to the Secretary of State

RESTRICTED
No. 1134

LA PAZ, March 21, 1947.

SIR: With reference to numerous previous despatches informing the Department of the steps taken by the Embassy with the Bolivian Government with a view to providing adequate protection for the lives of American citizens residing at the various mines in Bolivia, I have the honor to enclose a copy of Memorandum No. 236 of March 19, 1947 [16] which I handed to the Minister for Foreign Affairs, Dr. Urriolagoitia, on that day.

In handing him this memorandum I referred to the threats of death which had been made by the miners who in this connection had named Messrs. Deringer and Peters, two American engineers working at

---

[16] Not printed.

Catavi, and asked that the Bolivian Government take such additional steps as it might feel were necessary to safeguard the lives of these two men, their families, and other Americans at Catavi. In discussing this question Dr. Urriolagoitia said the problem was an extremely difficult one and that he realized that in addition to the personal safety of the foreigners at the mines, it was also a threat to the mine production and was a very serious matter for Bolivia from both of these standpoints. He said that the Bolivian Government is giving most careful consideration to the steps which it should take to attain the desired result and that it was considering the question of sending in some troops but that he was not sure if this would be the right thing as it might be taken by the miners as an additional cause for dissatisfaction.

Yesterday some members of the Embassy visited Catavi in the course of visits to other places in the plane of the Air Attaché of the Embassy and spent the night there. They learned that the Government is contemplating sending in a cavalry regiment composed of experienced men scheduled to arrive at Catavi on the afternoon of Saturday, March 22, as a major design to forestall any further trouble or menaces against the foreign officials working there. Likewise I am informed by our officials who just returned from Catavi that this measure is very gratifying to Mr. Deringer, the Manager, and he feels that it will be accepted by the miners without any demonstration of hostility.

Respectfully yours, JOSEPH FLACK

824.6354/3–2047 : Telegram

The Acting Secretary of State to the Embassy in Bolivia

CONFIDENTIAL   US URGENT   WASHINGTON, March 25, 1947—4 p. m.

1320. For Bugbee [17] from Karl Anderson.[18] Embtel 1748, 20th.[19] RFC made offer March 21, purchase 15,000 tons Bol tin to end this year at 76 cents.

Three weeks ago RFC offered price 74 cents. Since then Bol–Arg trade agreement signed whereby latter agrees purchase for 5 years minimum, 8,000 tons Bol tin annually and additional 12,000 tons annually if free from other contracts at price 76 cents for 1947.

After receipt latest RFC offer 76 cents Bol states impossible sell US more than 11 or 12,000 tons since cannot reduce Arg commitment below 8,000 tons. [Anderson.]

ACHESON

---

[17] Howard C. Bugbee, Attaché at the Embassy in Bolivia.
[18] Karl L. Anderson, Assistant Chief, International Resources Division.
[19] **Not printed.**

824.504/5–1947 : Telegram

The Ambassador in Bolivia (Flack) to the Secretary of State

CONFIDENTIAL   LA PAZ, May 19, 1947—2 p. m.

481. ReEmbtel 478, May 17.[20] Catavi Pulperías opened Saturday but operations not resumed as company felt insufficient guarantees to warrant return many top personnel fled to Oruro.

Effort made Sunday 6 a. m. evacuate remaining 30 top employees and families. Special train stopped by armed mob. Occupants arrested and held 2 hours by strikers before women and children permitted continue Oruro. Nine men including five Americans held virtual house arrest in homes and unable leave. Late last night managed to seek safety in army barracks. Company continuing efforts evacuate all but three who [chose] to remain.

Orders issued yesterday three additional regiments move into area cancelled last night. Hochanwe in disposition troops. Ministers Labor and Government [21] travelling to Catavi today. Deringer to join party Oruro. No announcement yet made but Embassy believes company to go through with plan close property, pay off all workers and rehire approximately 85 percent workers on new basis. Possible one month delay resumption operations. Government attempting pressure to force immediate resumption. Directors adamant before special session Cabinet last evening and appeared determined.

FLACK

824.63/5–2247 : Telegram

The Ambassador in Bolivia (Flack) to the Secretary of State

CONFIDENTIAL   US URGENT   LA PAZ, May 22, 1947—2 p. m.

493. ReEmbgram 407, December 12, 1946.[21] Request instructions position Embassy in event Bolivian Government seizes Patiños Catavi, El Allagua and Siglo Veinte properties tomorrow. Such action quite likely in view Government decree ordering resumption operations 7 a. m., tomorrow. Company may refuse since feels move would virtually present workers with property. In addition technical and administrative personnel including nationals as well as Americans, British, Argentines and Dutch almost unanimously refuse return Catavi without guarantees protection.

Government promises protection and guarantees but no steps yet taken against perpetrators incident Sunday morning (ReEmbtel 481,

---

[20] Not printed.
[21] Alfredo Mendizabal and Luis Ponce Lozada, respectively.

May 19). Public statements Ministers Government and Labor indicate strong possibility intervention unless reopened as ordered.

Embassy anticipates request by company for assistance.

FLACK

824.63/5–2247 : Telegram

The Secretary of State to the Embassy in Bolivia

CONFIDENTIAL   US URGENT   WASHINGTON, May 24, 1947—noon.

304. Urtel 481, May 19 and 493, May 22. Present issue appears to be solely internal matter for determination between Patiño Mines and Bol Govt which if eventuates into seizure [23] would not per se give grounds Emb intervention. Dept however, should be informed for its further consideration should subsequent developments result discriminatory treatment any Am interests involved or should it appear such interests would be denied just compensation.

Dept concerned safety Am citizens and assumes Bol Govt is taking effective measures protect their lives and property for which of course it has primary responsibility.

MARSHALL

824.6354/11–347

The Ambassador in Bolivia (Flack) to the Secretary of State

RESTRICTED   LA PAZ, November 3, 1947.
No. 1841

SIR: I have the honor to transmit a translation of a letter [24] received from Mr. Raúl Canedo Reyes, Director General of Mines, outlining his views on the forthcoming tin negotiations.

Mr. Canedo Reyes, on handing the reporting officer the letter, said that he wished to explain once again his apparently overly antagonistic attitude towards the RFC in Washington. He said that he has recently fought against members of the Ministry of Economy who wished to orient Bolivia completely towards Argentina. With this background, he feels he can do no less than be absolutely frank in his criticisms of the United States. However, he assured the reporting officer once again that his expressions concerning the RFC and the United States negotiators, who have in the past been unfair to Bolivia, should not be taken as any indication of an anti-American feeling. He

---

[23] The domestic turmoil subsided and seizure was not effected.
[24] Not printed.

still believes that Bolivia's economic future and independence must be based on cooperation with the United States.

This letter does not go into the question of the price which Bolivia will demand except where a vague reference is made to an appreciably increased price. Nevertheless, the general views contained therein furnish an indication of the mental attitude with which the Bolivian negotiators will be equipped when they go to Washington to draw up the contract for 1948. For this reason the letter is believed to be important.

It should be noted that Mr. Canedo Reyes states that Bolivia would like a long-term contract at prices guaranteeing Bolivian producers a steady even though small profit which would enable the country to increase production.

Another important point is the reference to economic imperialism, based on the general feeling that the United States, exercising a consumers' monopoly, refuses to allow free play of the law of supply and demand which would mean a high price. However, when Far Eastern production again creates an over-abundant supply, the United States will allow this law to operate, driving prices down, and bringing about the ruin of Bolivia. There does seem to be some justification for this argument.

There is little doubt that Bolivia is unable to compete with other producers of tin in normal times. The question for the United States to consider is, therefore, that of the importance of preserving Bolivia's capacity to produce. The Patiño and Aramayo groups can probably produce at almost any price. These two companies, even in their best years, produce approximately only 20,000 metric tons. Production by other companies depends largely on price—if the United States wants much more than 20,000 tons in the long run, it will have to pay higher prices. The Bolivian demand for $1.00 per pound is based on the assumption that such a price will revitalize the industry which has continued to deteriorate even though the demanded price of 76 cents was obtained during 1947. (The price was obtained only because of Argentina's interference.) The steady deterioration during 1947 is taken as proof that the Bolivians not only were not demanding excessive prices for 1947, but underestimated their needs. Mr. Canedo Reyes points out that he fears the implications of the Argentine treaty, since the latter country is not interested in maintaining Bolivian production of a product for which it has no use, although it is committed to purchase it. The United States, on the other hand, should have great interest in maintaining a high level of production. He therefore asks that the over-all implications of tin supply be considered by the United States and that consideration be given to strategic and political factors during the forthcoming negotiations in place of the previous cold businesslike effort to purchase tin at the lowest possible price.

Respectfully yours, For the Ambassador:
JOHN A. E. ORLOSKI
Commercial Attaché

824.6354/12-447

Memorandum by the Ambassador to Bolivia (Flack)[25] *to the Assistant Secretary of State for Political Affairs (Armour)*

CONFIDENTIAL [WASHINGTON,] December 4, 1947.

On November 3, the day before my departure from Bolivia, President Hertzog asked me to come to see him at the palace and, among other things, stated that he would like me to convey a message from him to President Truman about the price of tin in the new contract for 1948. While President Hertzog did not mention any price per pound which he may have had in mind, he said that he felt that Bolivia should have an adequate price for tin for the following reasons:

1. Bolivia is obliged to pay the high prices for the manufactured goods and foodstuffs which it must buy almost exclusively in the United States, and these prices are constantly increasing while the price of tin has been fixed by the contract with RFC.

2. An increase in the price would augment tin production in Bolivia and thus provide Bolivia with additional foreign exchange.

3. Increased production would likewise augment the national revenues which depend largely on tin which would enable the Government to pay salaries and maintain adequate administrative functions.

4. President Hertzog stated that due to the illiteracy of the Bolivian Indians and the ignorance of the laborers, Bolivia is a fertile field for Communism unless the economy of the country can be maintained on which a functioning democratic Government can rest. He said that, for a relatively small amount more each year for tin, Bolivia could accomplish all of these things and provide a stable nucleus in the southern part of South America. He considered this very important from the standpoint of Hemisphere defense and said that he felt that Bolivia was particularly open to possible infiltration of Communists and the agitation they bring with them.

5. He mentioned that, since the United States is spending such vast sums to check Communism in Europe and other places, he felt that the assistance which could be rendered to Bolivia's tin industry through an adequate price increase is fully justified and would act as insurance against possible rise of Communism in Bolivia, while stabilizing Bolivia's economy and democratic institutions.

---

[25] The Ambassador returned to Washington on November 4 and appears to have remained there for several months.

I told President Hertzog that after my arrival in Washington I would endeavor to seek an interview with the President for the purpose of conveying to him the personal message above mentioned.

JOSEPH FLACK

824.6354/11–1847

The Department of State to the Bolivian Embassy

MEMORANDUM

Reference is made to the Memorandum dated November 18, 1947 from the Bolivian Embassy [26] presented by His Excellency Señor don Ricardo Martinez-Vargas to Assistant Secretary of State, Mr. Norman Armour, on November 19, 1947.

The Memorandum referred to informal negotiations initiated with the Reconstruction Finance Corporation to determine the price and conditions of a new tin purchase contract to cover the year 1948. It states that the Government of Bolivia and the Bolivian tin producers consider the price that is to be fixed for 1948 should be substantially higher than that in the current contract. It further requests that the negotiations for the new contract be conducted in the City of La Paz. It explains that the reason for this latter request is that by holding negotiations in Bolivia representatives of the Government of the United States would have the opportunity to acquaint themselves by direct observation with the economic condition and the state of progress of the Bolivian tin mining industry as a basis for future agreements that may permit, for reciprocal benefit, a greater and closer collaboration between the United States and Bolivia.

It will be recalled that on the presentation of this Memorandum, Mr. Armour informed His Excellency Ambassador Martinez-Vargas that the questions raised in the Memorandum would be studied fully by this Government and in this respect that the Memorandum would be referred for consideration to the Reconstruction Finance Corporation, the Agency of this Government directly concerned in negotiations for the purchase of Bolivian tin concentrates.

The Department of State has just received from the Reconstruction Finance Corporation a communication submitting its views on the Memorandum under reference.

It is the opinion of the Reconstruction Finance Corporation that it would be inadvisable to conduct the negotiations in the City of La Paz. It is explained by that Agency that an acceptance of the Bolivian invitation would imply a willingness on the part of the Reconstruc-

---

[26] Not printed.

tion Finance Corporation to establish a price based on production costs. This, in its view, would be contrary to its policy of seeking to purchase commodities for the industrial needs of the United States at the equivalent of a fair market price. It states that it has been concerned in the past with production costs only in purchases that had involved subsidies and that subsidy purchases have been discontinued. It explains, furthermore, that production costs are affected by labor regulations, social laws, taxation, and other conditions of a social or political nature and that it does not consider it is proper for representatives of the Reconstruction Finance Corporation to discuss such matters with a foreign government in connection with negotiations for a commercial contract. Finally it mentions that reliable cost data could be obtained only after extensive investigation which could not be completed before the present Bolivian tin contract expires.

With respect to the price to be decided upon for the contract for the year 1948, the Reconstruction Finance Corporation advises that it does not believe that the world price for tin should again be determined solely by its negotiations with the Bolivian tin producers as has been the case in the past few years; and that in this connection, the tin apparently available to the United States from Bolivia now represents a relatively small proportion of the estimated total tin procurement by the United States for the year 1948. The Reconstruction Finance Corporation states that it is informed that as a result of diversion to Argentina, Bolivia is in a position to give the Reconstruction Finance Corporation a firm commitment only for a portion of Bolivia's 1948 tin concentrate production, estimated at nine to ten thousand long tons of fine tin. This amount is equivalent to only one-seventh of the total quantity of tin which the Reconstruction Finance Corporation expects to purchase in 1948 and only one-sixteenth of the estimated world production during the year 1948.

The Reconstruction Finance Corporation further states that by letter of October 8, 1947,[27] it advised His Excellency, the Bolivian Ambassador, that it was prepared to discuss a tin purchase contract to cover the year 1948 and suggested that negotiations with the Bolivian tin producers be held at an early date so that the new contract could be concluded before the contract now in effect expired.

The Reconstruction Finance Corporation is prepared to continue negotiations for a new contract for the purchase of Bolivian tin concentrates for the year 1948.

WASHINGTON, December 5, 1947.

---

[27] Not printed.

824.6354/12-1647

Memorandum by the Ambassador to Bolivia (Flack) [28]

CONFIDENTIAL [WASHINGTON,] December 16, 1947.

I lunched with the Bolivian Ambassador today, and he told me informally that Mr. Jewett (RFC) informed him this morning of RFC's offer of $0.88 per pound for Bolivian tin. Mr. Jewett informed him at the same time that RFC, being a purchasing agency, could only conduct this transaction on a commercial basis and it could not admit political considerations into the question of price.

The Bolivian Ambassador mentioned that he understood $1.00 a pound was being talked about in London and said that he assumed I knew that the Bolivians had asked $1.07 per pound. In the light of what he understood to be the possible London price, he felt that $0.88 was very low and that the producers would not accept it. He said he felt "very depressed" about the prospect of negotiations, and he went on to say that he had hoped that they would be concluded by December 31, 1947 in order not to further complicate Bolivia's tin relationship with Argentina.

824.6354/12-3147

Memorandum by the Assistant Chief of the Division of North and West Coast Affairs (Mills) [29]

RESTRICTED [WASHINGTON,] December 31, 1947.

Mr. Jewett of Metals Reserve, RFC, telephoned this morning to inform me that late yesterday RFC reached an agreement with Bolivian producers for the purchase of Bolivian tin by the Corporation during the years 1948 and 1949.

The contract covers all non-Patiño tin except 8,000 tons which Bolivia may be required to sell to Argentina under the recently concluded trade agreement with that country. In 1949 RFC can exercise an option and cancel the contract on six months' notice.

The base price is 90 cents a pound compared with 76 cents in the 1947 contract. There is a tie in with the RFC selling price for Grade A tin—the price paid the Bolivians will go up or down if the RFC selling price fluctuates. There is also included in the contract a deferred pricing arrangement under which the Bolivian producers can select

---

[28] Addressed to Mr. Sheldon T. Mills, Chief of the Division of North and West Coast Affairs, and Mr. James Espy, Assistant Chief, and to Mr. Paul C. Daniels, Director of the Office of American Republic Affairs.

[29] Addressed to Messrs. Daniels and Anderson and to Mr. Lyons of A-A.

the effective pricing date which cannot be before and must be within three months after the delivery date. Another provision reduces the "unit deduction" by one tenth or by 2.2 lbs. per ton. The effect of this as I understand it is that RFC pays for 2.2 lbs. more in each ton than under the 1947 contract.

There was almost a last minute hitch in the negotiations. The Bolivian producers and the RFC negotiators were congratulating each other on having concluded the agreement late yesterday afternoon. Jewett of RFC mentioned to the Bolivian Ambassador that as soon as he sent to the latter a signed copy of a draft letter regarding a guarantee of deliveries by the Bolivian Government, and the Ambassador replied, the agreement would be complete. The Ambassador replied that he was not happy about the terms and the Bolivian Government could not agree to them. Jewett was greatly surprised since the Bolivian Ambassador had had his draft letter for a week and had not raised any points with respect to it. Its provisions are the same as those which have been observed during the past seven years. He said if the Bolivian Ambassador meant that the Bolivian Government would not guarantee deliveries then the whole agreement fell to the ground. The Bolivian Ambassador talked vaguely about a free market and if higher prices were paid in such a market Bolivia should receive them.

This morning the Bolivian Ambassador told Jewett by telephone he would answer the letter guaranteeing deliveries and deliver his answer by 10:30.

At 11:15 Jewett called to say that the Bolivian Ambassador had informed him by telephone he had been delayed but he would deliver his letter of guarantee this afternoon. He authorized RFC to issue, at 11:30 as planned, the agreed press release and Jewett planned to do this.

Jewett said that agreement with the producers is complete while that with the Bolivian Government may be a little fuzzy, but probably it will do.

FINANCIAL AND TECHNICAL AID BY THE UNITED STATES FOR THE ECONOMIC DEVELOPMENT OF BOLIVIA

824.50/1–1747

The Ambassador in Bolivia (Flack) to the Secretary of State

No. 863　　　　　　　　　　　　　　　La Paz, January 17, 1947.

Sir: The General Manager of the Bolivian Development Corporation, Joseph C. McCaskill, has attempted to answer in a press statement published January 10, 1947, the various criticisms regarding its activities which have recently been leveled against that Corporation, and I have the honor to transmit herewith a copy of the article as it appeared in the press and a translation thereof [30] and to refer to Embassy's despatch no. 664 of November 29, 1946,[30] entitled "Transmitting *Boletín Comercial* for November Containing Article Criticizing Bolivian Development Corporation" calling attention to various phases of earlier criticism.

Mr. McCaskill called specific attention to the fact that the Corporation is operating with an exceedingly small capital. In the first place, he said, credits extended to the Corporation by the Export-Import Bank in Washington are restricted to the Cochabamba–Santa Cruz highway and to the petroleum program. In the latter instance, the Corporation serves merely to channel these credits from the bank to YPFB. The entire agricultural program and any other program the Corporation might undertake must be financed from funds provided by the Government of Bolivia. For this purpose the government in 1943–1944 made available to the Corporation $9,000,000. Mr. McCaskill stated that of these nine millions the government directed the Corporation to lend two millions to the Banco Agricola, one million to the Dirección General de Riegos for the construction of the Angostura and Challapata projects, and one million to the Dirección General de Ferrocarriles for the purchase of locomotives and freight cars for the Villazon–Atocha railroad. In addition, the Export-Import Bank required that before it would make advances under the road credit, the Corporation must put three millions of its own funds into the highway. This was later reduced to two and one-half millions. Thus, six and one-half million dollars of the nine million were immediately obligated before the Corporation could get a program underway. Further, the Corporation always has a million dollars tied up in the highway awaiting reimbursement from the Export-Import Bank inasmuch as the bank does not advance money except for refunds for expenditures already incurred. This accounts for seven and one-half million of the nine million dollars while loans to municipal and private industry aimed at the development of the country have required another half million.

Nevertheless, the General Manager stated, the Corporation is attempting from its limited funds 1) to develop the Beni program designed to supply meat to La Paz and much needed merchandise to the population in the vicinity of Reyes; 2) to set up a tractor unit for the clearance of land of private owners; 3) to build a large sawmill at Espejo; 4) to develop a plantation for production of rice and other products at Chané; and 5) to carry out the preliminary work necessary

---

[30] Not printed.

for the installation of the sugar mill at Saavedra. In addition, a small sum has also been set aside to aid in the development of the agricultural experimental stations under an agreement with the Department of Agriculture of the United States and the Ministry of Agriculture of Bolivia.

Mr. McCaskill stated that most of BDC's undertakings have proceeded at a much slower pace than contemplated. A major reason for this, he stated, has been the difficulty of obtaining machinery from the United States. As a result, progress on the Cochabamba–Santa Cruz highway has been slow but progress has been satisfactory in the last several months but even yet a considerable quantity of the machinery and equipment on order has not yet arrived.

In connection with the cost of the Cochabamba–Santa Cruz highway, Mr. McCaskill stated, that officials of the Export-Import Bank were not shocked when the Bolivian Ambassador in Washington [31] together with the President and General Manager of the BDC [32] laid before the bank an application for an additional credit to insure the completion of the road. As a result of increased materials and labor costs, the original estimate has been necessarily moved upward but in this connection the Public Roads Administration in Washington indicated that the unit costs to date on the highway were not out of line with similar costs in road construction in the United States and in other Latin American countries. The original estimate of twelve million dollars has now been moved up to between eighteen and twenty million dollars, although the Corporation expects that unit costs will be lowered as additional equipment arrives and that perhaps the ultimate cost may be kept below the new estimates.

Respectfully yours,

For the Ambassador:
JOHN A. E. ORLOSKI
Assistant Commercial Attaché

824.51/2–1947 : Telegram

The Secretary of State to the Embassy in Bolivia

RESTRICTED WASHINGTON, February 19, 1947—7 p. m.

96. Stambaugh [33] from Martin.[34] Board of Bank formally approved additional credit to BDC for YPFB program on Feb. 19. Following statement for simultaneous release Washington and La Paz has been

---

[31] Ricardo Martinez Vargas.
[32] Guillermo Gutierrez.
[33] Lynn V. Stambaugh, Representative of the Export-Import Bank.
[34] William McChesney Martin, President and Chairman of the Board, Export-Import Bank.

agreed upon with Mariaca and will be released here on Feb 25 upon word from you.

"Wm. McC. Martin Jr. Chairman Board Directors Export-Import Bank today announced approval by Bank of increase $3 million in an existing credit to Bolivian Development Corporation for financing petroleum development program to be conducted by Yacimientos Petroliferos Fiscales Bolivianos (the Bolivian government petroleum entity generally known as YPFB). New credit resulted from negotiations with Eximbank by Guillermo Gutierrez President Bolivian Development Corporation and Guillermo Mariaca General Manager YPFB.

Mr. Martin recalled that Eximbank authorized a credit $15,500,000 to BDC in Mar 1942. Of this amount $5,500,000 was allocated to petroleum development program and remainder to highway construction. Under terms this allocation Bank has to date advanced to Development Corporation $1 million for drilling operations in the Camiri oil fields and Corporation has in turn advanced this amount to YPFB to finance those operations. There have been no actual advances for construction costs and purchases in connection with pipeline and refinery since advances for these purposes were conditioned on reasonable assurance of a minimum stabilized production in Camiri oil fields, satisfactory plans and specifications and cost estimates, and satisfactory construction contracts with approved US engineering firms.

Bolivian and private funds equivalent to $5,650,000 have also been allocated to petroleum development program thus making together with increase $3 million in Eximbank credit a total of $14,150,000 for program as a whole. Funds to be supplied by Bank amounting now to $8,500,000 will be used to finance drilling program in Camiri fields, a part of cost of constructing pipeline from Camiri to Cochabamba, and construction of refinery at Cochabamba. Any additional funds required for completion of approved program are to be supplied from sources other than Bank and arrangements for provision of such funds have been made.

Petroleum development program in Bolivia which Bank is assisting in financing will result in production petroleum products required by Bolivian economy and is expected to produce substantial surplus revenues beginning in 1949. In order carry forward Cochabamba-Santa Cruz roadbuilding program to which Bank has already allocated $10,000,000 under the 1942 credit in favor of BDC it has been agreed that Bank funds advanced to YPFB through Bolivian Development Program will be repaid to Corporation from anticipated surplus revenues at rate to be determined by Bank but in any event not less than $3 million in each of years 1949 and 1950 and that these repayments will be dedicated by Corporation pursuant to its understanding with Bank to completion of highway program.

In announcing new credit to Bolivia for oil development Mr. Martin noted that YPFB has announced a policy subject to ratification by Bolivian Congress of opening oil resources in Chaco region to development by private capital."

[Martin]
MARSHALL

811.516 Export-Import Bank/5-2047 : Telegram

The Ambassador in Bolivia (*Flack*) to the Secretary of State

RESTRICTED   La Paz, May 20, 1947—6 p. m.

486. Export-Import Bank from Kinnear.[35] In conference today between President, Vice President, Minister Economy, Ambassador Flack [36] and myself, Bolivian Government officially requested a change in the petroleum program by reducing Cochabamba refinery to 3,000 barrel capacity and increasing Sucre refinery to 2,000 or 3,000 barrel capacity with reforming plant. Government will send an official application to Export-Import Bank along this line. I explained to President that present program had been approved by all concerned and present contracts between entities involved were drawn on this basis and that proposed change must be considered through regular channels by Board Directors Export-Import Bank and that inauguration petroleum program would thereby be delayed considerably. If revised petroleum program should be approved by Export-Import Bank, Bolivian Government offers to provide through Banco Central funds necessary to meet possible deficiencies in Cochabamba–Santa Cruz highway construction. I explained to the President I had no authority to discuss this matter and formal application therefore will be sent to Export-Import Bank. The proposed change is not favored by some officials YPFB. Have informed YPFB and Corporación that all consideration drafts of contract will naturally be suspended pending consideration by Export-Import Bank of new Bolivian Government proposal.

President reiterated that he wanted increase in Sucre capacity to balance distribution and avoid one-sided economic development in Bolivia adding that this also presented important political aspect for stability of government.

Leaving La Paz May 21 for Guayaquil, Ecuador. Letter follows reporting on Bolivian matters. Reference your telegram May 19,[37] believe Guamote–Tambo highway contract obligates Jones [38] to complete highway between the two towns. May be able offer comments after conference with Ecuadoran Government. [Kinnear.]

                                                                                                                                Flack

---

[35] Edwin R. Kinnear, Representative of the Export-Import Bank.
[36] Enrique Hertzog, Mamerto Urriolagoitia, German Costas, and Joseph Flack, respectively.
[37] Not printed.
[38] J. A. Jones Construction Company.

824.51/5–2847

The Ambassador in Bolivia (Flack) to the Secretary of State

No. 1396   LA PAZ, May 28, 1947.

SIR: As a result of the extended criticisms leveled against the Bolivian Development Corporation's various projects and the resulting Senate Investigation concerning BDC's activities in general, the need for restudying and revising the McGraw–Warren contract for construction of the Cochabamba–Santa Cruz highway was particularly pointed up and I have the honor to report that the representatives of the Export-Import Bank, of the Public Roads Administration, of Warren Brothers, of F. H. McGraw Company and of McGraw–Warren, who were requested to come to Bolivia to aid in the attempt to resolve the problems in which they were concerned, have arrived in La Paz, participated in a series of meetings with the Corporation, and have left the country convinced that the basis for general agreement regarding the various differences has been established.

. . . .

It was recommended that a new contract be drawn up containing the following points:

1. Fixed overall fee of $33,000 per kilometer.
2. Total cost under the contract to be 13.9 million dollars including engineering, construction, purchasing costs and contractor's fees.
3. A penalty is provided if the contractor's actual costs exceed by five percent the fixed fee. The penalty is to be 25% of the cost above the tolerance but not greater than one-third of the contractor's fee.
4. All engineering work and all purchases are to be made by the contractor.
5. The purchase fee will be a flat $1,500 per month instead of the former 3% commission.
6. The engineering fee will be $700,000.
7. A bonus will be paid the contractor if total costs are held 5% below the fixed amount.
8. BDC will assign an auditor to keep it informed of actual monthly costs.
9. If from audits it is apparent that the contractor cannot comply with the above terms, the contract can be cancelled.
10. The contract will be submitted for Export-Import Bank approval.
11. Through incorporation in the new contract of Public Roads Administration (PRA) specifications for the highway and periodic Board inspections the Corporation can be assured that there will be no sacrifice in quality.

The Corporation had decided to go ahead with its discussions of the contract with the contractors in the face of the Senate investigation of

BDC and the Chamber of Deputies investigation specifically of the highway contract. It was generally felt that in view of the fact that the President had appointed a new Board and had placed his confidence in that Board, that, therefore, the recommendations of the Commission, when made known, would be submitted for the Corporation's consideration, but that a specific directive would not be issued binding the Corporation to do certain things which would necessitate the rehashing of its agreement with the contractor. On Sunday, May 25th, the Committee's preliminary report appeared in the press and summarized the details of the investigation that it had made. A copy of this report as it appeared in the press is attached herewith.[40] In its conclusion the report states that work up to the present time on the Cochabamba–Santa Cruz highway had been performed on a basis of a "project" rather than a contract which could be abandoned, if necessary, or modified on the basis of experience; that in drawing up a new contract the Corporation bear in mind its experience with the other contracting work on the highway, at much lower prices, which had already been done; and that the Corporation ought to calculate the excess costs so far under the contract, considering the other construction on the road, for the purpose of accurately gauging remaining costs and their financing.

The Corporation, however, had no intention of waiting for Congressional action to come to it. It therefore requested a meeting with the Chamber of Deputies Commission investigating the McGraw-Warren contract, and in the session with that Commission, yesterday, announced what had been its conviction in the whole problem and that it had recommended the signing of a new contract. The Chamber of Deputies Commission, which had announced the results of its investigation yesterday, a press clipping of which is attached, said that since the Senate Investigating Commission as well as its own had practically denounced the highway contract, such action, in its estimation, had practically the significance of law, and that the contract ought to be rescinded. The President of BDC then informed the Commission that the opinion of the Corporation was contrary to its views in the matter, stating that "we cannot go against our convictions," and adding "I await the arrival of the President of the Republic to resolve this problem."

The President of BDC then went on to point out the reasons which guided the Corporation to take the decision it has taken. A copy of a press clipping from *Ultima Hora* of May 27, concerning the meeting of the Corporation and the Chamber of Deputies Committee is attached.[40]

---

[40] Not reprinted.

It would appear that the disadvantages of rescinding the highway contract outweigh the advantages, particularly in view of the proposed changes. It is therefore believed that General Bilbao, President of BDC, will be able to point this up to the President of the Republic and obtain his approval for continuing the work with McGraw-Warren under a new contract embodying the above modifications.

Respectfully yours,

For the Ambassador:
JOHN A. E. ORLOSKI
Commercial Attaché

811.516 Export-ImportBank/5-2047 : Telegram

The Secretary of State to the Embassy in Bolivia

CONFIDENTIAL WASHINGTON, May 29, 1947—3 p. m.

313. Eximbank on May 21 gave Bolivian Emb and BDC representative for transmission Corp and Bolivian Govt for review drafts of (1) amendment to Eximbank Corp credit agreement increasing credit $3 million and (2) letter allocating $8.5 million to petroleum program and establishing terms and conditions thereof. Additional $3 million credit and allocation to petroleum program is as indicated in allocation letter based entirely on petroleum program as presented to Eximbank Dec 1946. Bank disturbed by situation reported urtel 486 May 20 and agrees that Kinnear's statement that proposed changes in petroleum program would require complete reexamination program by Bank. This would involve considerable delay and uncertainty re outcome.

Kinnear letter May 13 from La Paz [41] informs Eximbank that YPFB Board proposes change YPFB by-laws shifting authority from manager to Board and to employ large number political appointees. If YPFB Board still plans these actions Bank would like you in whatever manner you judge best indicate emphatically to Bolivian Govt that Bank seriously objects to these steps and that they would impair Eximbank confidence in YPFB ability to conduct petroleum program. Please point out that at instance of Eximbank loan agreement between Corp and YPFB provided that manager YPFB must have full authority.

For your information and communication to Bolivian Govt at your discretion after consultation with Mariaca Eximbank fully supports position taken by Mariaca and Bank confidence in YPFB based on ability and authority Mariaca as manager. Bank desires be informed developments this matter earliest.

MARSHALL

---

[41] Not printed.

811.516 Export-Import Bank/6–1847 : Telegram

The Ambassador in Bolivia (Flack) to the Secretary of State

CONFIDENTIAL   US URGENT   LA PAZ, June 18, 1947—noon.

580. During past week pressure from Sucre politicians for change in petroleum program was intensified. Consequently I reiterated to Foreign Minister [42] Exim Bank's views as furnished in Dept's 313 of May 29. (Refer mytel 553 of June 10).[43] In this connection I also had friendly discussion yesterday morning with President Hertzog, who promised that matter would be immediately resolved. Mariaca informed me this morning that at subsequent meeting with Fomento,[44] YPFB officials and Minister of Economy, President stated that original programs approved would be adhered to and ordered that documents in this connection be prepared promptest possible. This appears to settle whole question.

However, to satisfy Sucre's aspirations, Bolivian Government may later seek separately to add to its facilities.

Dept's 313 has been most useful since it enabled me to continue discussions without requesting additional instructions.

Repeated to Lima for Sundt.[45]

FLACK

811.516 Export-Import Bank/7–1947 : Telegram

The Ambassador in Bolivia (Flack) to the Secretary of State

CONFIDENTIAL   US URGENT   LA PAZ, July 18, 1947—7 p. m.

678. Situation with regard to highway and McGraw–Warren contract has changed little since my 642, July 7.[43]

On July 15, I handed Foreign Minister two copies Exim Bank's memorandum to Bolivian Ambassador, Washington, of June 30, which he had translated and presented to Cabinet yesterday. In conversation today with Guachalla, he said government had abandoned insistence on unit price but would seek to retain services PRA in connection with plans. He is optimistic that agreement will be reached with McGraw–Warren.

However, financial difficulties corporation caused by nonpayment by Bolivian Government of its obligations to corporation amounting to $3,125,000 have complicated situation and produced published letter from president BDC to Minister Economy reiterating his previous

---

[42] Luis Fernando Guachalla.
[43] Not printed.
[44] Corporación Boliviana de Fomento.
[45] Olaf F. Sundt, Petroleum Attaché assigned to Santiago, Lima, and La Paz.

statement to Hertzog and setting forth whole situation while calling upon the government to pay amount due lacking which corporation's activities will have to terminate August 1. Although Minister Finance [46] is openly opposed payment this amount and is publicly recommending termination of Cochabamba–Santa Cruz highway work, Minister Economy told me today he strongly favors continuation of work as does Foreign Minister Guachalla.

Guachalla at Foreign Office this afternoon referred to oral statements here by Kinnear and others that Exim Bank would favorably consider financing highway work from exhaustion BDC funds to time when petroleum program may produce funds for highway termination. Guachalla asked me to ascertain for him from Exim Bank whether more concrete assurance in principle than the Kinnear statement might be secured now from Exim Bank that upon previous inauguration payment government's present obligations to BDC and satisfactory amended contract with McGraw–Warren, Exim Bank would take care of financing in the gap expected to arise in May, 1948, even with payment to BDC of government's debt.

I consider this most critical situation for corporation and related highway construction and I recommend most strongly that Exim Bank send me most specific statement possible about financing highway completion which I may convey to Foreign Minister for Bolivian Government on question above set forth. Guachalla and Costas share my view of helpfulness such step now.

Embassy informed by BDC that Holloway and Durso [47] may arrive shortly to complete negotiations re McGraw–Warren contract. Consequently I request urgent reply re Exim Bank's position.

FLACK

811.516 Export-Import Bank/7–1847 : Telegram

The Secretary of State to the Embassy in Bolivia

CONFIDENTIAL WASHINGTON, July 25, 1947—8 p. m.

433. For Flack from Eximbank. Reurtel 678, July 18 Bolivian Government payment $3,125,000 to Corporation is commitment contingent to credit agreement which was confirmed during negotiations for new petroleum program. Eximbank cannot understand why this commitment has not been fulfilled particularly because when Gutierrez was in Washington negotiating for new petroleum program and discussion of highway credit assurances were repeated that Bolivian Government

---

[46] José Alcides Molina.
[47] Francis K. Holloway, Assistant to the President of Warren Brothers, and Albert Durso, Vice President of F. H. McGraw Company.

would comply with this obligation. Refer your despatch No. 570, Nov 12, 1946,[49] Page 2.

Please reiterate to Minister Guachalla following: (1) Eximbank has informed Bolivian Amb here and Kinnear informed Corporation Board and Bolivian Govt officials there that Bank is interested in completion highway in shortest possible time and at reasonable cost and that Bank will consider application for funds to bridge gap between possible exhaustion Eximbank and Bolivian funds and beginning repayments by YPFB under Petroleum program; (2) Eximbank would not entertain such application until such time as funds now available including Bolivian Government's agreed contribution $3,125,000 near exhaustion and additional requirements if any are known; (3) it will of course also be necessary for Corporation to arrange satisfactory contract for effective and earliest possible completion engineering and construction highway; (4) Amendatory credit agreement must also be signed, but as yet Bank has not received pertinent documents, the delay of which is postponing start petroleum program and availability YPFB repayments to corporation for use on highway; (5) a flat commitment by Bank for additional funds does not appear to be necessary at this time. [Eximbank.]

MARSHALL

811.516 Export-Import Bank/8-547

Memorandum by Mr. James Espy of the Division of North and West Coast Affairs to the Assistant Secretary of State for Political Affairs (Armour)

RESTRICTED [WASHINGTON], August 5, 1947.

The purpose of the call on you this morning by the Bolivian Ambassador, Señor Don Ricardo Martinez Vargas, is to bring up the subject of a request by the Bolivian Government, through a note received by our Ambassador at La Paz dated April 28, 1947, for a loan of $30,000,000 and the services of an American engineer for the construction of a railway that would run from La Paz over the Andean cordillera down into the eastern lowlands of Bolivia. It is estimated that the construction would take about ten years, and the Bolivian Government is prepared to pay 3-1/2% interest on the loan, with amortization at 5% per annum.

The reasons presented why the Bolivian Government is so anxious to obtain the loan from the United States Government are (1) the need of the railway to connect the consuming centers of the *altiplano* with the cattle and agricultural areas of eastern Bolivia; (2) the

---

[49] Not printed.

Bolivian Government does not consider it prudent that neighboring countries collaborate in executing the project, since its construction under such conditions would mean the participation of these countries in the exploitation of Bolivia's agricultural and cattle wealth and Bolivia desires to exploit solely for its own account; (3) the railway is considered by Bolivia as a national aspiration.

With the knowledge and approval of the Export-Import Bank, the note in question has not, up till now, been referred officially to the Bank for its views. In June past Ambassador Martinez Vargas was informed orally that it was still under study and that we were seeking more information. The reason for this action was that difficulties have been experienced with the Bolivian Government in arranging for satisfactory execution of the construction work on the Cochabamba–Santa Cruz highway, which is being financed by the Bank. It was felt that this problem should be resolved first of all; but at the same time, there were also considerations of the international relations of Bolivia, involving its neighboring countries, such as Argentina and Brazil. You may recall that a comprehensive economic treaty was signed between Argentina and Bolivia last March, but it has not thus far been ratified by either country.

Observations on the economic angles to the present application for a loan may be set forth as follows:

(*a*) There is a good deal of justification for the railway's eventually being constructed.

(*b*) However, there is much doubt whether it is an economically sound project because of its high cost and of the difficult terrain through which it will have to be constructed.

(*c*) The highway, which is already well under way, should be much more economical to complete; and after the highway has opened up the area, a railway could follow.

(*d*) Most important of all, Bolivia has not carried out satisfactory arrangements for the completion of the Cochabamba–Santa Cruz highway to be financed by the Export-Import Bank. This artery of communication is much more important to the whole country of Bolivia for the integration of the nation's economy than the La Paz–Beni railway, which latter is primarily of interest to La Paz.

824.154/8–1147 : Telegram

The Ambassador in Bolivia (Flack) to the Secretary of State

CONFIDENTIAL   US URGENT   LA PAZ, August 11, 1947—11 a. m.

729. For Exim Bank. Deptel 441, August 1.[50] In brief informal conversation at airport this morning Minister of Economy Costas, who

---

[50] Not printed.

will also act as Minister for Foreign Affairs during Guachalla's absence, latter inquired whether Exim Bank would insist upon McGraw-Warren completing work Cochabamba-Santa Cruz highway.

I told Minister my opinion was Exim Bank had at no time insisted upon McGraw-Warren but at same time bank felt that this firm had gained experience and with appropriate guarantees should be able to complete the highway. He said there is very strong congressional opposition to McGraw-Warren. However, I told the Minister I would make specific inquiry and inform him bank's views as soon as possible. He intimated that the govt intended to make its payment to the corporation, details of which I shall obtain from him in forthcoming formal conversation.

FLACK

824.154/8–1347 : Telegram

The Ambassador in Bolivia (Flack) to the Secretary of State

RESTRICTED   US URGENT   LA PAZ, August 13, 1947—4 p. m.

737. Cabinet yesterday resolved basically problems of BDC highway contract, Minister Costas informed me last night. Govt to fulfill obligation 3.1 million commitment and authorize renegotiation contract cost plus basis. Minister said further discussion in Cabinet required establish working detail which will be accomplished tomorrow. Indications are that McGraw-Warren contract will be continued.

FLACK

824.154/8–1147 : Telegram

The Acting Secretary of State to the Embassy in Bolivia

CONFIDENTIAL   WASHINGTON, August 19, 1947—3 p. m.

475. For Flack from Eximbank. Urtels 726 [51] and 729. Bank believes it timely to reaffirm its position regarding highway. Bank at no time has insisted upon McGray-Warren in preference to other United States contractors, but feels changing contractors at present stage of highway job and without full justification may well cause confusion, delay and additional cost. Bank felt decision of Corporation Board on revised contract would give McGraw-Warren necessary controls and at same time hold contractor to rigid progress schedule and cost estimate, and would provide for inspection by P.R.A. If under revised contract McGraw-Warren proves incapable a change might then be

---

[51] Not printed.

justified. Eximbank feels immediate action should be taken by Government and Corporation Board to avoid further costly delay in carrying highway to completion. Request you consult President Hertzog to determine Government's immediate course of action. Following confidential. Bank feels possibly any further financing under credit should be suspended until these matters are settled. Advise if in your opinion such action would tend to hasten a solution. [Eximbank.]

LOVETT

811.516 Export-Import Bank/8-2147 : Telegram

The Ambassador in Bolivia (Flack) to the Secretary of State

CONFIDENTIAL   US URGENT   LA PAZ, August 21, 1947—6 p. m.

755. For Export-Import Bank. Deptels' 474 [52] and 475, August 18 and 19. Mourning yesterday for deceased Deputy with closure offices prevented seeing President until today. Statements made to me by President today confirmed Bolivian Ambassador's statements your 474 with addition of consideration noted my 745, August 15 [52] represent inability Bolivia to cover dollars 2 million Central Bank guaranteed.

I today reiterated to President Hertzog Bank's position as stated your 475 and left with him memorandum in Spanish. He agreed with all of the Bank's views and said that in spite of all that had been said in Congress the Govt had agreed in principle to continue with McGraw-Warren and make the payment of $1,125,000 and that the Central Bank would guarantee the additional $2,000,000 previously mentioned. He added that to confirm this he would call a Cabinet meeting tomorrow which would resolve officially the government's viewpoint after which I will again cable.

President stressed Bolivia's very difficult foreign exchange situation and the necessity of the government to obtain dollars 2 million loan or other sources guaranteed by Central Bank to cover this amount, and asked our and Export-Import Bank's assistance. In view of my knowledge very difficult Bolivian foreign exchange position, I recommend most strongly Dept and Export-Import Bank most favorable consideration this appeal by President Hertzog.

In view of President's full agreement with Export-Import Bank viewpoints, and his cordiality, I feel that it would be most unwise and paralyzing to use suspension of other credits to attempt to hasten solution already decided in principle and will be officially resolved tomorrow.

In delivering to Foreign Minister Export-Import Bank's previous

---

[52] Not printed.

expression hopes [for?] solution [of?] matter prior to signature of petroleum program credit, I stressed to Foreign Minister that this was in no sense a threat but merely the frank view of the Export-Import Bank on an important urgent business matter.

FLACK

811.516 Export-Import Bank/8–2247 : Telegram

The Acting Secretary of State to the Embassy in Bolivia

CONFIDENTIAL WASHINGTON, August 22, 1947—5 p. m.

480. For Flack from Eximbank. Amendatory credit agreement covering petroleum program signed today following assurances from Bolivian Amb that Bol Govt had advised it will promptly meet its obligations to Corporación and satisfactorily resolve highway contract with McGraw–Warren. Advance for starting petroleum program will be made soon. Eximbank confirmed to Bol Amb that Bank now ready to consider application from Corporación for interim credit to meet deficiency highway funds under terms as follows. 1, the application for interim credit not to be in excess of four and one-half million dollars. 2, term of interim credit not to exceed five years. 3, that Bol Govt make available two million dollars now obligated or its equivalent in local currency in monthly installments satisfactory to the Bank and during life of interim credit. 4, repayment of interim credit by Corporación to be made out of repayments by Y.P.F.B. for petroleum loan. 5, that highway engineering and construction be prosecuted vigorously under revised contract satisfactory to Bank. Airmail letter follows. Bank appreciates your cooperation and timely cables. Please advise when Government makes payment one million one hundred twenty-five thousand to Corporación for highway and final agreement highway contract. [Eximbank.]

LOVETT

824.51/8–2147 : Airgram

The Secretary of State to the Embassy in Bolivia

CONFIDENTIAL WASHINGTON, September 12, 1947.

A–217. Your despatch no. 1320, May 7, 1947.[53] Referring to Foreign Office note of April 28, 1947 [53] requesting opinion this government on extending $30 million credit and technical assistance in the La Paz–Beni Railway construction project the following is for your information and use at your discretion in replying to the note.

In the absence of a formal application accompanied by complete

---

[53] Not printed.

technical details, the Eximbank has no comment, since it is the Bank's policy not to give preliminary or informal indications or opinions that it will give favorable consideration to loan applications.

The Department does not desire to encourage the filing of an application with the Eximbank, and does not now look with favor upon US public financing of this project because: (1) since organization of World Bank which has the function of long-range development financing, Eximbank applications are generally confined to exporter's credits or to the financing of purchases in U.S. incident to projects which may be considered of short- or medium-term nature; (2) there does not appear to be real economic justification commensurate with the expense involved; and (3) the U.S. Railway Mission (headed by James A. Dehlsen, 1942–46) recommended against its construction.

However, should Bolivia find ways and means to go ahead with this project and then realize a need of technical assistance, this government will give consideration to such requests as Bolivia may make respecting such needs.

MARSHALL

811.516 Export-Import Bank/11–2047 : Airgram

The Chargé in Bolivia (Galbraith) to the Secretary of State

LA PAZ, November 20, 1947.

A–357. Reference Embassy's recent telegrams and despatches concerning the Bolivian Development Corporation and progress of renegotiation of contract with McGraw–Warren Corporation.

As previously reported, no real progress has been made as a result of conversations held so far, and the Bolivian Development Corporation in the first part of last week stated that it was not overly sanguine that a satisfactory arrangement could be reached. Developments came to a head on Friday, November 14, when the Corporate Directorate informed the Embassy that it had practically reached its limits and saw no possibilities other than complete cancellation of the present arrangements with McGraw–Warren Corporation. The same afternoon, however, the atmosphere improved slightly as the representatives took the stand that rather than terminate conversations, they would carry the BDC counter-views direct to their home office and would return shortly with specific instructions which would then demonstrate either definite acceptance or rejection of the Corporation's desired objectives.

The President of the Corporation, General Bilbao, told the press on November 15, that one of the new demands of the contractors was an increase of their fee from $280,000 to double that amount. He stated that under no conditions could the Corporation accede to such a request and further indicated that unless 99 percent of the Corporation's counter-proposal to the contractors was accepted by the contractors, there could be no contract.

It is now apparent that the Corporation will not concede anything beyond its last proposal to the contractors, and its views in this respect appear to have the backing of the entire country. In his regular weekly interview, the President stated to the Press on November 18 that conversations with the contractors and the Corporation had reached an impasse, but it was not possible to state categorically that the contract would not be renegotiated, in view of the return of the contractors' representatives to the United States to discuss the possibility of accepting the conditions laid down by the Corporation. That the government no longer feared the spectre of a no-contract was evidenced by the President's further statements in which he said that in the event the contractors refuse to accede to the terms of the Corporation, which already have been conciliated, the government must find another American enterprise or even a national company suitable to the Export-Import Bank to conclude the project. He added that it would be interesting should Bolivian engineers and technicians have the opportunity of demonstrating their capacity and training in this field by bringing the program to a successful conclusion.

Today's press announced the resignation of the Corporation's Vice-President, Roger D. Barneville. This resignation has been confirmed by the Corporation and the Corporation indicates that it was submitted because of the personal desire of Barneville to return to his previous undertaking involving construction programs under the Argentine-Bolivian Mixed Commission. Corporation spokesmen added that the resignation was not in any way connected with, or in any way intended to influence, present negotiations with McGraw-Warren Corporation.

Meanwhile, work on the highway continues and the next step in conversations will be developed upon the return of Messrs. Holloway and Williamson,[54] who are expected again from the United States within the next few days.

GALBRAITH

811.516 Export-Import Bank/12-1647 : Telegram

The Chargé in Bolivia (Galbraith) to the Secretary of State

CONFIDENTIAL LA PAZ, December 16, 1947—7 p. m.

982. For Export-Import Bank from Kinnear and Holbrook.[55] At interview with President this afternoon he expressed opinion that

---

[54] James S. Williamson, an engineer of the McGraw-Warren Corporation.
[55] Robert G. Holbrook, Representative of the Export-Import Bank.

cancellation McGraw-Warren contract by BDC despite agreement described ourtel 977, December 13 [56] was result misunderstanding which he regretted. To replace McGraw-Warren president proposed formation a Bolivian corporation to be composed both Bolivian and American technicians at same time accepting any controls bank might wish exercise. We did not comment on this but do not agree.

YPFB decree although signed in form which caused concern expressed ourtel 978 [56] is, on President's categorical promise over objection Minister Economy, to be replaced by decree which avoids political interference confirming present by-laws and management. President reaffirmed promise to Stambaugh to keep political interference out of both BDC and YPFB.

President requested we remain until something worked out. We agreed this saying we would ask another interview as soon as information received viewpoints bank and we had opportunity effect necessary consultations. Consequently reply ourtel 976 [56] urgently needed.

Minister Economy asked whether bank objects to removing two BDC members from board YPFB. President thought this would be desirable since it would represent a saving but said it is a point on which he will not insist. We replied this should be discussed next interview.

Since these are two of four members YPFB board supporting manager Mariaca our opinion is bank must disapprove this proposal.

Considering dangers illustrated by proposal in paragraph immediately preceeding we strongly recommend Bank and State Department despite existing contrary policy consider advisability in case Bolivia reverting to participation American members board directors BDC and YPFB. We request authority discuss this proposal with President. [Kinnear and Holbrook.]

GALBRAITH

824.154/12–1947

The Chargé in Bolivia (Galbraith) to the Secretary of State

[Extracts]

RESTRICTED LA PAZ, December 19, 1947.
No. 1959

SIR: With further reference to this Embassy's various despatches concerning the construction of the Cochabamba–Santa Cruz highway, I have the honor to now report that on December 12 President of the

---

[56] Not printed.

Bolivian Development Corporation, Bernardino Bilbao Rioja, notified the McGraw–Warren Company that the BDC was exercising its right to cancel the contract between the two parties upon 90 days notice, and was hereby issuing that notice. A copy of the resolution issued by the Corporation in this connection is attached herewith.

In the preamble to the resolution it is stated that the Bolivian Development Corporation has satisfied all of the obligations agreed upon with McGraw–Warren Company, but that the contractor has not lived up to the stipulations of the contract signed July 16, 1945. The resolution further states that the contract is being rescinded for the following reasons: (1) because of reported violations by the contractor of the stipulations agreed on; (2) because the average cost per kilometer has exceeded the calculated cost in a very appreciable proportion; (3) because the time which the contractor has taken so far for the performance of work completed is excessive and progress is slow and absolutely unsatisfactory; and (4) the rate of progress of the company would not permit the termination of the highway within the 3-½ years period stipulated in the contract.

. . . .

The action of President Bilbao, therefore, on December 12, was surprising only because of the Government's previous promise to withhold definitive action as above outlined. Construed by the Ex-Im Bank representatives here as a breach of the understanding between them and the Corporation, these representatives promptly protested the failure of the Corporation to consult with them.

When President Hertzog was queried on this point, he stated that he regretted the hasty action on the part of the Government and attributed it to a misunderstanding. The views on this development of Corporation Director, René Ballivian, however, are to the effect that the Government learned from supposedly trustworthy sources that the contractor had decided to issue, within the following 24 hours, a notice on the part of McGraw–Warren Company requesting a cancellation of the contract, supposedly because of ineffectual cooperation which the contractor was receiving in Bolivia. Ballivian indicated that such a measure on the part of the contractor, in view of the general opinion and criticism of the McGraw–Warren Company, would be most embarrassing to the Bolivian Government and lead uninformed people to believe that the major lack of performance was in reality attributable to the Government rather than to the contractor.

. . . .

Respectfully yours, For the Chargé d'Affaires ad interim:
JOHN A. E. ORLOSKI
Commercial Attaché

811.516 Export-Import Bank/12–2247 : Telegram

The Chargé in Bolivia (Galbraith) to the Secretary of State

CONFIDENTIAL LA PAZ, December 22, 1947—6 p. m.

991. For Martin from Kinnear and Holbrook. Urtel 627, December 19.[58]

1. In our opinion present disintegration BDC organization including weak and incomplete directorate and impossible Bolivian manager Knaudt, BDC Cochabamba office, makes complete reorganization BDC *sine qua non* solution highway problem. Problem law of 1947 making it possible government to interfere with Mariaca management YPFB and to turn both BDC and YPFB into political footballs must be settled at same time. Also BDC informs us changes in by-laws are contemplated and that BDC in dire financial straits since $2,000,000 Banco Central fund now authorized is only sufficient meet present BDC obligations including $248,000 interest to Exim Bank on December 31. Galbraith and Orloski agree with us that determination all Bank's views and conditions it desires to impose in order to resolve foregoing and other basic problems must precede discussion highway problem. Also we told President Hertzog that we would cover problem as a whole and feel Bank should proceed that basis.

2. In view foregoing and difficulties inherent attempts explain adequately by cable to Exim Bank our position here, our opinions and our reasons, we request authorization to advise President Bolivia, Exim Bank has ordered us return Washington for consultation and that Bank thereafter will advise Bolivian Government of decisions reached. The only apparent alternative would be for the Bank to reach decision on and instruct us regarding following points which we believe must be resolved before discussing any of Bank's views with the President:

(*a*) Modification law September 20, 1947 as condition any substantial increase loan CBF in order remove grave doubts as to future subjugation CBF and YPFB politicial pressure and interference.

(*b*) Appointment Exim Bank nominees to directorates CBF and YPFB (see recommendation our cable 982).

(*c*) Requirement Bolivian Government undertake that no laws or decrees or changes articles incorporation thereof directly or indirectly affecting CBF-YPFB will be promulgated and no changes or retentions key Bolivian or US CBF-YPFB personnel will be effected or continued without consultation with and acquiescence of Exim Bank.

(*d*) Appointment Exim Bank resident special representative; and

(*e*) Cancellation SAODC well-drilling contract with YPFB. This procedure presumably would require consultation with State and would entail considerable delay. Since such delay would not only be

---

[58] Not printed.

embarrassing for us but would weaken Bank's position we strongly urge our recall.[59]

3. We reiterate our conviction any expression Exim Bank views to Bolivia now or in foreseeable future must cover whole problem. [Kinnear and Holbrook]

GALBRAITH

824.154/12–3147 : Airgram

The Chargé in Bolivia (Galbraith) to the Secretary of State

RESTRICTED   LA PAZ, December 31, 1947.

A–407. Vice Consul Dorr, Cochabamba, telephoned Embassy yesterday stating that Bolivian Development Corporation there had obtained a legal order prohibiting Mr. Durso to leave Cochabamba and, secondly, ordering him within a two weeks' period beginning December 22nd to render complete accounts. According Dorr, Durso stated he has actually seen this order, but that he has been informed orally by Knaudt (Cochabamba superintendent for Corporation) that the order has been amended to read Republic of Bolivia rather than City of Cochabamba.

Durso informed Dorr that 2 weeks would be sufficient time solely for the preparation of an inventory, and that the rendition of complete accounts would take approximately 5 months. Dorr added that, if the order as presently standing is carried to its logical conclusion, Durso will be jailed upon the expiration of the 2 weeks. Durso said that the legal order places him in an impossible situation and that if it is not changed, he will resign as legal representative of McGraw–Warren Company, thereby leaving no legal representative against whom the order could be made operative. Durso further informed Dorr that it is not and never has been his intention to abandon Bolivia until he has arranged McGraw–Warren affairs, but that he cannot do this with the above-mentioned 2 weeks' period.

Embassy, also yesterday, discussed matter informally with General Bilbao in La Paz, who stated that the above information was not in accordance with the facts. The General stated (1) that it was the Minister of Government who issued an order that the McGraw–Warren representative be prevented from leaving Bolivia until full accounts are rendered to the Corporation, inasmuch as a definite winding up with McGraw–Warren is desired as soon as possible and the Corporation is of the opinion that the legal provisions of the contract have

---

[59] In telegram 628, December 24, 2 p. m., to the Embassy in Bolivia, the acquiescence of the Export-Import Bank in the position here taken by its representatives was indicated (811.516 Export-Import Bank/12–2247).

not been lived up to by McGraw-Warren and that therefore such action is necessary; (2) that the 2 weeks' period mentioned above refers solely to the submission of inventory data and that this period was fixed because Durso stated that inventory could be completed in 2 weeks if five Americans and one Bolivian were put back on the Corporation's payroll to do this job. The General stated that authorization to hire the additional workers had been granted but for only a 2 weeks' period. The General added that, if the inventory is not completed in 2 weeks, an extension for the individuals hired should be requested; and (3) the General categorically stated that the jailing of Durso is not contemplated in any event and that it is recognized that the completion of the accounting records could not be made in such a short time. The General further stated that no time limit has been made to Durso either for the preparation of the inventory or for the completion of the accounting records, and that such a move was never intended.

The action on the part of the Bolivian Government in taking Ministry-level steps in preventing the departure of the McGraw-Warren representative appears to be extreme, in that it could be accomplished merely through refusal of an exit visa, and points up the strained relations between the BDC and the McGraw-Warren Company brought to a head by the rescission of the highway contract. General Bilbao declared that the McGraw-Warren Company is under obligation to present an inventory of machinery and equipment and to submit proper accounting records of its activities as soon as possible so that the future of the program could be planned without delay. He added that if the McGraw-Warren Company chooses to send to Bolivia any other representative, fully empowered to act for it, to complete the windup of its activities, the Government would not insist on Durso remaining after the arrival of such official but that it would insist on some representative remaining here until the windup is completed.

Please inform Eximbank.

GALBRAITH

NEGOTIATIONS FOR AN AIR TRANSPORT AGREEMENT BETWEEN THE UNITED STATES AND BOLIVIA

711.2427/1-3047 : Telegram

The Ambassador in Bolivia (Flack) to the Secretary of State

CONFIDENTIAL   LA PAZ, January 30, 1947—3 p. m.

99. Concerning proposed bilateral air transport agreement Captain Pol, Director of Civil Aeronautics in Ministry of Defense, states that Ministry determined to amend operations contract between Panagra

and Bolivian Government signed in May 1943 and not scheduled to terminate before 1967, before signing bilateral agreement with Article 8 [60] included as proposed in United States draft. As operations contract contains no clause providing for its termination or amendment before date of expiration Captain Pol stated that Government's plan for amendment is to be as follows:

1. The Government will issue a decree directing Ministry of Defense to effect desired modifications in Panagra contract;
2. Ministry of Defense armed with the decree will approach Panagra and attempt to work out new text for contract incorporating desired modifications;
3. If agreement is reached new contract will be concluded; but if Panagra cannot find basis for agreement with government the latter will issue another decree stating that present contract is terminated due to impossibility of carrying out previous decree calling for its modification. Then Bolivia will agree to sign agreement with Article 8 intact. Pol stated desirability of issuing the first decree before Panagra informed so that latter's officials will not have time to use their influence with government Ministers to prevent its issuance. Embassy desires views of Department in matter and instructions in light of this new situation, especially if informal views of Pol are embodied in government's views soon expected through Foreign Office.

FLACK

711.2427/2–147 : Telegram

The Ambassador in Bolivia (Flack) to the Secretary of State

CONFIDENTIAL   LA PAZ, February 1, 1947—10 a. m.

106. ReEmbtel 101, January 31.[61] Jess B. Bennett, special representative Braniff Airways in La Paz to conclude operations contract with Bolivian Govt, attempting to put pressure on Embassy regarding revision Panagra's 1943 operations contract. He points out Panagra not obligated by present contract to share airport facilities in La Paz and other points with other airlines so until this is revised Braniff contract to be concluded with govt is virtually worthless, as Panagra can deny use of its facilities. He points to fact that Panagra guaranteed cabotage privileges until contract expiration in 1967 and that contract provides for controlled frequencies—both facts he asserts are in direct violation international principles subscribed to by US. He states our Government should be ashamed to sign bilateral agreement permitting con-

---

[60] This article stipulated that existing rights and concessions granted to airlines would continue in force.
[61] Not printed.

tinuance of a contract embodying those violations. He is convinced Bolivian Government will not sign bilateral agreement with Article 8 intact before revision Panagra contract. He told Embassy it is its responsibility to help Braniff, an airline certificated by US Government, to obtain satisfactory contract for operation thru Bolivia which can be effected only by proper revision of Panagra contract. He states his complete agreement with Captain Pol and other Ministry Defense authorities on necessity of this revision and thinks Embassy should share his point of view and should agitate strongly with Dept for instructions to support contract revision before government expected to sign agreement with Article 8 intact. Suggest urgent consultation with Braniff in US as Bennett clearly attempting to force issue to head and putting Embassy into position which may become difficult unless it can receive further clarifying instructions on these issues. Therefore request such views and instructions as may help to clarify this situation.

FLACK

711.2427/2–147 : Telegram

The Secretary of State to the Embassy in Bolivia

CONFIDENTIAL   WASHINGTON, February 10, 1947—noon.

77. Dept concerned lest activities Pol and Bennett reported urtels 99 Jan 30, 101 Jan 31 [62] and 106 Feb 1 result in Bolivian Govt taking action to deprive Panagra its legal rights under 1943 contract. Campbell, Vice Pres Panagra, has informed Dept his Co prepared make agreements with any certificated US carrier operating over its certificated routes for use of Panagra facilities on reasonable basis subject availability such facilities and services after Panagra needs met. He states Braniff has not sought any arrangement with Panagra for use facilities in Bolivia. No approach to Panagra has been made by Bolivian Govt re modification 1943 contract. However, Panagra has already obtained approval Bolivian Govt elimination service to Uyuni and contemplates approaching Bolivian Govt next few days looking to elimination services over Santa Cruz–Concepción–San Ignacio–San José sector and over Cochabamba–Sucre–Valle Grande–Santa Cruz sector, thus eliminating service to Sucre, Valle Grande, Concepción, San Ignacio and San José. Panagra expects obtain compensation from Bolivia or LAB for its investments at these points. Dept has advised Campbell such action should be taken soon and believes if taken prior to bilateral would improve situation from both Panagra and Dept

---

[62] Telegram 101 not printed.

point of view. You should make clear to Bolivian Govt Dept desires Article 8 left in agreement and US could not be a party to action such as Pol suggested. You should also make clear to Bennett while Dept recognizes his right to his opinion US position, it cannot tolerate any action by him, particularly representations to Bolivian officials, which impedes carrying out Govt's objectives. Dept's approval given to Braniff for Bennett proceeding to Bolivia based on understanding Bennett's activities would be subject advice and direction of Embassy. Fact that contract grants Panagra cabotage rights not inconsistent US Govt position which recognizes right each state to deal with cabotage as it sees fit. Restrictions on frequencies mentioned by Bennett do not appear real to Dept in view full reading of contract which permits modifications by Panagra upon notice to Bolivian Govt. Braniff [63] has departed US on survey tour but Dept will not hesitate requesting him recall Bennett if latter unwilling conform Embassy's directions. Advise Dept urgently any developments.

MARSHALL

724.3527/2–1247 : Telegram

The Ambassador in Bolivia (Flack) to the Secretary of State

RESTRICTED LA PAZ, February 12, 1947—5 p. m.

137. Argentine Embassy has submitted for consideration of Bolivian Government proposed Argentine–Bolivian bilateral air transport agreement. Captain Pol, Director Civil Aeronautics Ministry Defense, informed Embassy that text of agreement generally similar to that of proposed US–Bolivia agreement except that there is a provision for control of frequencies. Embassy will attempt to secure copy of agreement's text from Foreign Office for forwarding to Department.

Repeated Buenos Aires.

FLACK

724.3527/2–1247 : Telegram

The Secretary of State to the Embassy in Bolivia

CONFIDENTIAL WASHINGTON, February 18, 1947—7 p. m.

92. Embtel 137 Feb 10. Presentation Argentine draft makes desirable expeditious conclusion Air Transport Agreement. Dept anxious lest Argentine restrictive principles be accepted in view effect not only on Bolivia negotiations but on US–Argentine, US–Chilean and others where conflicting views being examined. Dept's position re Art 8 un-

---

[63] Thomas E. Braniff, head of Braniff International Airways.

changed, and that Art essential. Request Emb use all efforts expedite conclusion of agreement.

Art 6 should be revised to read as follows: "Each contracting party reserves the right to withhold or revoke a certificate or permit of an airline designated by the other party in the event it is not satisfied that substantial ownership and effective control of such airline are vested in nationals of the other contracting party or in case of failure, etc." Amendment is reversion to original draft submitted and follows Chicago standard form [64] and is definitely preferred by Dept. Negotiations should not be sacrificed to obtain new Art 6, but Dept should be informed if it appears impossible obtain this wording. Dept feels since Bolivia does not plan operate air services now objection unlikely. Keep Dept currently advised status Bolivian–Argentine negotiations.

MARSHALL

711.2427/12–346 : Telegram

The Secretary of State to the Embassy in Bolivia

CONFIDENTIAL   WASHINGTON, February 28, 1947—7 p. m.
US URGENT

113. Following rewording US route bilateral air transport agreement desired in view new Braniff operating contract Bolivia. Emb will note this combination two prior routes generally supplies greater flexibility than old description. Change follows:

"The United States of America and/or the Canal Zone to La Paz, Oruro, Cochabamba, Sucre, Valle Grande, Santa Cruz, Concepción, San Ignacio, San José, Robore, Puerto Suarez, Uyuni and beyond Bolivia."

Greater latitude in points beyond Bolivia desired because possible delay obtaining rights Arg and Chile and Uruguay may be actually terminal of line. Dept believes Pol's statement (Embdes 675 Dec 3, 1946 [65]) that only three traffic points would be granted not conclusive, Panagra representatives presently negotiating sale various airports and facilities in Bolivia. CAB's action Uyuni route is only one year's suspension and points indicated are still generally desired. Dept will advise further developments and concessions on points which might be made but would appreciate Embs views as to what traffic points,

---

[64] Type of air transport agreement formulated from the agreements reached in the Chicago Conference on International Civil Aviation of November–December, 1944. It provided for the exchange of air rights between two countries to be exercised by designated airlines, for equality of treatment with respect to airport charges, customs and inspection fees, for mutual recognition of rules and laws relating to entry, immigration, passports, licenses of personnel, etc.

[65] Not printed.

if any, should be given up. Activity Arg negotiators elsewhere South America has been generally unfavorable to pending negotiations. Therefore urge continued pressure as Emb sees proper to obtain agreement at earliest possible date.

MARSHALL

711.2427/4–2847 : Telegram

The Ambassador in Bolivia (Flack) to the Secretary of State

RESTRICTED   LA PAZ, April 28, 1947—5 p. m.

406. Late today Foreign Minister Urriolagoitia told me at Foreign Office that as result of meeting with officials of Ministry Defense, including Minister and officials handling civil aviation, with President [66] on Saturday it was decided that Article 8 proposed bilateral air agreement is after all unacceptable because in their opinion it violates Bolivia's sovereignty by freezing existing contract with Panagra. They feel that if Article 8 is retained they would be committing themselves to us as a govt not to modify Panagra's contract for its duration. There is no article in Panagra's contract providing for procedure of modification.

Furthermore, Foreign Minister said, with reference to section 1 of annex that Bolivia could only grant three stopping points for international traffic, that is La Paz, Cochabamba, Santa Cruz since they consider they could not grant such rights at airports not at present equipped for this traffic. For bargaining purposes we think we could renounce Concepción, San Ignacio, San José and Valle Grande not of value for international service.

Minister said Bolivian counterdraft incorporating above-mentioned changes would be in my hands tomorrow when I will telegraph any other minor changes suggested and transmit text by air.

I told Minister that in event my Govt was adamant in regard to retention of Article 8 I hoped that Bolivia might later present a modified version of that article acceptable to it and that with regard to the three international points of call I would inform my govt and obtain its early views. He intimated that with present Bolivian modifications agreement might be signed at once.

On basis of oral info obtained by Embassy it appears that Captain Pol, Chief Civil Aeronautics Ministry Defense is endeavoring bring about modification of Panagra contract because he feels that we are so interested in signing bilateral agreement that we would exert pressure on Panagra to agree to revising conflict [contract] with Bolivia.

---

[66] Enrique Hertzog.

This has been constantly contradicted by all of us in conversation with Bolivian officials and his conclusions are accordingly erroneous. Embassy also understands that Bolivian pressure to modify Panagra contract might lead to President bringing this question to Bolivian Supreme Court.

Repeated Buenos Aires for Bell.

FLACK

810.79611 PAA/6–1047

The Ambassador in Bolivia (Flack) to the Secretary of State

CONFIDENTIAL LA PAZ, June 10, 1947.

No. 1429

SIR: I have the honor to refer to the Embassy's despatch no. 1195 of April 9, 1947,[67] concerning difficulties between Panagra and the Ministry of Defense in the Bolivian Government over the 1943 operations contract between those two parties, and to report further on this subject. As reported in the above-mentioned despatch, the Minister of Defense at the time, Mr. Nestor Guillén, decided to allow Panagra to suspend its Uyuni diagonal route to Buenos Aires for one month (April 4–May 4) and to continue its service of increased frequencies to Arequipa and Puerto Suárez for the same period, with the understanding that in the meanwhile Panagra and the Bolivian Government would commence discussions with a view to the modification of Panagra's contract.

On April 18, Mr. Ernesto Araníbar, Manager of Grace & Company in Bolivia, which acts as Panagra's agent in this country, directed a letter to the Ministry of Defense stating that in Panagra's opinion no violation of the contract had been committed by that company when it increased its frequencies to Arequipa and to Puerto Suarez in eastern Bolivia, Panagra being at liberty under the contract to modify its frequencies as it feels traffic requirements so merit upon prior notification to the Bolivian Government. The letter also pointed out that as Panagra had decided not to suspend the diagonal route—this removed the Bolivian Government's objection on that point, and therefore, in Panagra's opinion, everything was in correct order as far as the contract was concerned and there would be no need for further discussions. No answer to this letter has as yet been received from the Ministry of Defense, nor have any further efforts been made on the part of the latter to institute negotiations with Panagra for the modification of its contract, as had been indicated by former Minister Guil-

---

[67] Not printed.

lén on April 2. This is no doubt due in part to the absence of Captain Germán Pol at the ICAO Convention in Montreal and to the assumption of office by a new Minister of Defense, Eduardo Montes y Montes.

It is Panagra's present policy in connection with its contract to continue the *status quo* and to do nothing towards the contract's modification, at least for as long a time as negotiations for the United States–Bolivia Air Transport Agreement continue. This has been made clear to the Embassy in discussions with Mr. Douglas Campbell and Mr. Thomas Kirkland, Vice Presidents of Panagra, and with Mr. Araníbar. Panagra does not wish consideration of its contract tied in with negotiations over the bilateral agreement through deliberate efforts on the part of the Bolivian Government, and it feels that its position will be considerably strengthened and that the air will be cleared when the bilateral agreement is signed first with the inclusion of an article providing for the continuance of existing contracts. Mr. Araníbar has on a number of occasions shown his keen interest in a prompt conclusion in the signing of the bilateral agreement, with the inclusion of such an article as mentioned above. The Embassy has furthermore received the impression from discussions with these officials that Panagra does not desire to modify its contract anyway, with the possible exception of clarifying certain terms to the mutual understanding of both parties.

It might be mentioned, finally, that there are indications that the anti-Panagra attitude of Captain Pol is losing influence in the Bolivian Government, and that such influential elements as the Foreign Office and General Felipe Rivera, Commander in Chief of the Bolivian Armed Forces, are dissatisfied with Pol and will aid in the establishment of a situation more favorable to Panagra's interests and to the obtaining of a prompt and favorable conclusion of the bilateral agreement. Minister Montes' opinions in this matter are not yet known.

Respectfully yours,

For the Ambassador:
JOHN A. E. ORLOSKI
Commercial Attaché

810.79611 PAA/7–2547 : Telegram

The Secretary of State to the Embassy in Bolivia

CONFIDENTIAL   WASHINGTON, July 25, 1947—8 p. m.

434. Campbell of Panagra departed for South America July 24. Will arrive Bolivia about Aug 1 and will keep self in contact with Emb reEmbtel 607 June 25.[69] Panagra position is present contract is

---
[69] Not printed.

satisfactory and no occasion to make new one. However, horse-trading between Panagra and Bolivian Govt may result in exchanging elimination Uyuni for disposal certain cabotage points, Dept believes. Pol sent Dept unofficially copy proposed new contract Panagra–Bolivia. Proposal would eliminate cabotage entirely after 3 years and has other objectionable features. Dept position is that present contract is binding and only mutually satisfactory accord between parties thereto can amend same. Campbell claims to have evidence conclusively proving no breach of contract by Panagra. Pol's communication did not contain evidence Panagra acts of bad faith reDept's memo of conversation June 10 [70] as promised, and Dept is replying personally unofficially to Pol stating its regret at failure of Pol to keep commitment and denying existence of basis for US Govt intervening in regard to new contract. Dept believes Emb should continue attitude re bilateral that same is not necessary at this time as contract rights are satisfactory and US not interested in any bilateral except on US terms including standard Art 8.

Dept requests you delicately determine whether Montes and Hertzog support Pol's position, without creating impression in their minds that Pol is not looked on with favor by US. Please keep Dept advised.

MARSHALL

810.79611 PAA/7–2847 : Telegram

The Ambassador in Bolivia (Flack) to the Secretary of State

CONFIDENTIAL   LA PAZ, July 28, 1947—6 p. m.

698. ReDeptel 434, July 25. Have been in constant close touch with Aranibar, Panagra's representative. We both feel sentiment of government is changing concerning contract and conclusion bilateral air agreement.

General Riviera, commander-in-chief armed forces wrote Jorge Zalles, New York, July 15, 1947, stating that Captain Pol, who attended aeronautical congress in Canada, had no other orders than for that congress and at no time should have offered comment on Panagra's services in Bolivia. As previously reported to Department, Foreign Office deeply resented Pol's activities in Washington. Discussed bilateral with Foreign Minister today. He informed me he wished to study matter further and would call me perhaps by the end of the week for further discussion. I stressed our view incorporation of Article 8 in eventual agreement and our opinion that proposed bilateral and Panagra contract entirely separate and that any change in the Panagra

---

[70] Not printed.

contract should be solely by mutual agreement without any intervention by US Government.

Aranibar feels it undesirable for Campbell to arrive until question of bilateral has been decided pro or con, and will accordingly regulate Campbell's plans. FLACK

810.79611 PAA/9-947

The Ambassador in Bolivia (Flack) to the Secretary of State

CONFIDENTIAL LA PAZ, September 9, 1947.
No. 1704

SIR: I have the honor to refer to the Embassy's despatch No. 1666 of August 28, 1947,[71] and to other communications between the Embassy and the Department concerning difficulties over the Panagra contract with the Bolivian Government, and in this connection to forward the Embassy's translation of a letter to Panagra from the Minister of Defense,[71] Eduardo Montes, authorizing Panagra to suspend for a period of 90 days its flight along the "diagonal" route La Paz–Oruro–Uyuni–Salta. Mr. Ernesto Aranibar, manager of Grace and Company which represents Panagra in Bolivia, confidentially gave me a copy of the original letter in Spanish.

It is the Embassy's understanding that despite previous indications to the contrary, Capt. Germán Pol, Director of Civil Aeronautics in the Ministry of Defense, has maintained strong influence with, as well as the support of Minister Montes and of President Hertzog himself in connection with matters of Bolivian civil aviation and aviation policy. Captain Pol's policy in connection with Panagra's operation contract has evidently received approval from his superiors in the Bolivian Government. That policy is to force an issue in the dispute over Panagra's contract in order to cause the cancellation or modification thereof. Apparently the Ministry of Defense will insist after the termination of the 90-day period referred to in Minister Montes's letter that Panagra reduce the frequency of several of its routes and reinstate the Uyuni diagonal route, in accordance with that Ministry's interpretation of the wording of the Panagra contract.* If Panagra should be willing to amend the contract to clarify the wording of the clauses whose interpretation is in dispute, the Ministry would use that opportunity to demand revision of other important clauses such as those affecting Panagra's cabotage rights and governmental subsidy. If Panagra should decline to agree to modification of the contract and should continue to follow its own interpretation of the contract by not

---

[71] Not printed.
*See Embassy despatch No. 1195 of April 9, 1947 and No. 1429 of June 10, 1947, concerning this subject. [Footnote in the original; despatch 1195, not printed.]

reducing its frequencies and by not reinstating the Uyuni route, the Ministry of Defense would carry the matter to the Bolivian Supreme Court claiming violation of the contract by Panagra and perhaps demanding cancellation of the same. Mr. Douglas Campbell, Vice-president of Panagra, who has recently been visiting La Paz, informed me prior to his departure on September 6 for New York that he would not be opposed to such a course, but would study it further.

There is also indication that the Government desires to take over Panagra's airport installations and facilities in the near future to be operated by a government controlled airport administration company for the use of all airlines. In this connection, another desirable amendment in the Panagra contract from the Ministry of Defense point of view would be the inclusion of a stipulation to the effect that the Government may take over these facilities from Panagra at any time it so desires, rather than at the contract's termination in 1967, as is presently provided for. Bolivian officials are careful to point out that the matter of Panagra's facilities will be dealt with within the frame of the law, and Panagra would be rendered due compensation should the transfer occur. However, it appears doubtful that the Bolivian Government has the financial resources or the technicians with which to be able to take over Panagra's facilities in the near future.

Mr. Aranibar and Mr. Douglas Campbell have kept the Embassy closely informed on the status of the situation and on their viewpoint. They have indicated that it will be Panagra's policy to resist any moves for the modification of the contract, to accept the change authorized for the 90-day period by Minister Montes, thus suspending the Uyuni flight and continuing with present frequencies, but at the end of that time to continue without further change, hoping that the natural inertia of events and that hesitation on the part of the Bolivian Government to take opposing action will serve to allow Panagra to continue more or less permanently its service as during the 90-day period. If the Ministry of Defense continues to press the issue, however, Mr. Aranibar informed the Embassy that he would prefer to have the whole matter brought before the Supreme Court, feeling that there was a good possibility that the Court would support Panagra's point of view and the Panagra interpretation of the contract. Concerning modification of the contract itself, Mr. Aranibar stated that it was undesirable to encourage or cooperate with such a step, as among other reasons, it would establish a bad precedent by which each new political regime in Bolivia would feel justified in seeking further changes in the contract according to its own point of view, which would destroy the sense of the contract's legality and permanency, and would cause the present difficulties to be endured all over again in the future.

Panagra officials have informed the Embassy that the Uyuni diagonal flight will be discontinued in the near future and that in its place direct service along the route La Paz–Arica–Antofagasta will be instituted, with passengers for Buenos Aires continuing there via Santiago, although later on an Antofagasta–Salta–Buenos Aires flight may be commenced. The new route represents a slight departure from the route authorized in the Minister's letter for the 90–day period, inasmuch as Oruro is omitted, although Panagra will continue to serve the latter point on its flight to Santa Cruz and eastern Bolivia.

Respectfully yours, JOSEPH FLACK

711.2427/11–647

The Chargé in Bolivia (Galbraith) to the Secretary of State

CONFIDENTIAL   LA PAZ, November 6, 1947.
No. 1847

SIR: I have the honor to refer to recent communications between the Embassy and the Department concerning the proposed United States-Bolivian Bilateral Air Transport Agreement . . .

The Embassy would like to review for the information of the Department the confused course of the negotiations connected with the Bilateral which has taken place during the past month. On Monday, September 29th, Mr. Alvarado, Bolivian Subsecretary for Foreign Affairs, informed the Ambassador that his Government was prepared to sign our version of the Bilateral intact with the exception of the change of one word in Article 8. The Embassy received prompt telegraphic approval from the Department for this change, and it seemed on October 2nd that the Agreement could be and would be signed in La Paz early the following week. On October 2, the Ambassador forwarded to the Foreign Ministry his full powers to conclude the Agreement. However, on Friday, October 3, Mr. Alvarado informed two officers of the Embassy that the Bolivian Government desired to introduce a further change in the text of the Annex of the Agreement reducing the number of airports in Bolivia for international traffic from 12 to 6, which information was communicated to the Department by the Embassy's telegram No. 858, of October 3.[72] Mr. Alvarado reiterated at that point his desire that the Agreement be signed before the Ambassador's departure from La Paz, then scheduled for October 14, and expressed his confidence that if the Embassy received prompt approval from Washington for the desired reduction in traffic points, the Agreement could be signed by October 8 or 9th.

---

[72] Not printed.

The reason why the Embassy had not been notified previously of this important change in the Agreement as desired by the Bolivian Government was apparently that the cabinet ministers in determining the Bolivian viewpoint during a meeting on September 27, had considered only the main part of the Agreement, but not the so-called technical points of the Annex (including the airports specified) as it was felt that the position on these latter points was the proper responsibility of Captain Germán Pol, Chief of Civil Aeronautics in the Ministry of Defense, who happened to be unavoidably absent from that meeting. It was apparently after Mr. Alvarado had informed the Ambassador on September 29 about his Government's acceptance of our version of the Bilateral, that Captain Pol entered the scene to remind Mr. Alvarado that the "technical" viewpoint of the Bolivian Government as had been previously brought out, was that a reduction was necessary in the 12 airports specified in the United States proposal. Mr. Alvarado then agreed to this viewpoint, and informed the Embassy accordingly on October 3, as related above.

Then, on October 6th, an official of the Foreign Office notified an officer of the Embassy that he, Mr. Alvarado, and others were at the moment going over our Spanish text of the Bilateral, and that the presence of the Embassy officer was desired so that the Bolivian officials might ascertain our point of view on some changes that they were introducing into the above-mentioned Spanish text. What happened in that meeting is described in the enclosed memorandum [73] prepared by the officer concerned. It seemed apparent that this meeting represented the first occasion on which the necessary responsible officials in the Bolivian Government were going over our proposed text for the Bilateral in a careful and coordinative fashion. As a result of the meeting, the Embassy was presented on the following day with a revised text in Spanish representing the Bolivian proposed version of the Bilateral. Although the Foreign Office maintained that (except for the matter of the traffic points) this text was in general different from ours only in the matter of grammar and ways of expression, the Embassy detected a number of points where, in its opinion, there was a clear difference in meaning and in substance. Subsequent meetings were held between an officer of the Embassy and officials of the Foreign Office in an attempt to reconcile these differences between ours and their versions of the Spanish text, or, more important, between the meaning of our English text and of their Spanish text, as a result of which the Foreign Office agreed to make several changes in their Spanish text so as to bring it into closer harmony with ours.

On October 9, the Embassy received the Department's **telegram**

---

[73] Not printed.

No. 540 of the same date,[74] stating the Department's unwillingness to conclude the Agreement unless all twelve traffic points were included. The Ambassador informed Mr. Alvarado of this development on the next day, stating that although an impasse had apparently been reached at this late date, he would be glad to take up personally this matter of the traffic points with the Department while he was in Washington, with a view to effecting, if possible, a conciliation of the Bolivian and United States viewpoints. Mr. Alvarado agreed with this procedure, and stated that he was confident that such a conciliation could be attained and that the Agreement could be concluded upon the Ambassador's return to Bolivia early in 1948.

The Embassy has the impression that as the Bolivian Government has already given in in our favor on most of the points of difference in the text of the Bilateral, that Government now more or less feels it a point of national honor and pride to stand up for its desired reduction in traffic points, so that on one point at least it may effect a concession in its behalf on the part of the United States Government.

. . . .

The Embassy would therefore appreciate receiving from the Department its final position on the texts of the Bilateral Agreement as submitted herewith, including what specific changes, if any, must be introduced before the United States Government is willing to sign the Agreement. It is believed that after the Ambassador, who is now en route to the United States, has had a chance to discuss personally with the Department the remaining differences between the Bolivian and United States texts, the Department will be able to state a final position which will lead promptly either to the signing of the Agreement or to the definite termination of negotiations. If the present Bolivian counterdraft meets with the Department's approval, it was the Ambassador's recommendation that full powers be telegraphed to the Chief of the Mission enabling him to sign the Agreement.

Respectfully yours, WILLARD GALBRAITH

711.2427/12–447

The Chargé in Bolivia (Galbraith) to the Secretary of State

CONFIDENTIAL LA PAZ, December 4, 1947.
No. 1916

SIR: I have the honor to refer to the Embassy's despatch no. 1847 of November 6, 1947, which forwarded to the Department the text of the United States-Bolivian Bilateral Air Transport Agreement as pro-

---

[74] Not printed.

posed by the Bolivian Government, and to enclose a copy in Spanish, along with the Embassy's translation thereof, of a confidential Memorandum dated November 28, 1947,[75] which the Bolivian Ministry for Foreign Affairs sent to the Embassy explaining the position of the Bolivian Government with regard to the points for international air traffic in Bolivia designated in the Annex of the Bilateral Agreement.

This Memorandum comes as the result of conversations between Ambassador Flack and Bolivian Sub-secretary Alvarado, and of a letter that the former sent to Mr. Alvarado on October 30, 1947, before his departure from Bolivia, expressing the opinion that a memorandum prepared by the Foreign Office concerning the airport traffic points referred to above would be of considerable benefit to him when he took the matter up with the appropriate authorities of the United States Government in Washington with a view to arriving at a fuller understanding of the viewpoints of the respective Governments. The matter of the number of traffic points designated in the Annex of the Bilateral Air Agreement remains the one outstanding point of difference between the texts for the Agreement as proposed by the United States and Bolivian Governments respectively.

It will be noted that the reason stated in the enclosed Foreign Office Memorandum for Bolivia's desire to reduce the twelve Bolivian traffic points as proposed by the United States to six, lies first of all in the need for protecting the national airline, Lloyd Aereo Boliviano, from the competition of foreign airlines. Furthermore, the memorandum points out, the reduction is necessary because Bolivia has only a very limited number of airports possessing the facilities and organization capable of handling regular international air traffic. It is stated that it would have been best to limit the airports designated in the Bilateral Agreement to three, i.e. La Paz, Cochabamba, and Santa Cruz, which alone have adequate facilities for handling international traffic, but that the Bolivian Government, desiring to offer further proof of its deference and cordiality towards the United States Government, has agreed to concede the six airports specified in its draft of the Bilateral Agreement, which the Embassy forwarded by the despatch of November 6 previously referred to, these airports being La Paz, Oruro, Cochabamba, Sucre, Santa Cruz and Roboré.

With regard to the position assumed up to the present by the Department in this matter, namely that the 12 airports must be included in the Bilateral Agreement so as to protect the monetary value of the installations that Panagra presently possesses at those airports, the Embassy may point out that Panagra's interests at those airports are protected by its operations contract with the Bolivian

---

[75] Not printed.

Government, and that Panagra officials in La Paz themselves do not see the necessity for including all 12 points in the Bilateral. International airlines of the United States would probably be interested only in handling traffic at La Paz, Cochabamba, Santa Cruz and possibly Oruro. The concern expressed by the Department that Captain Pol, with his anti-Panagra attitude, would force the price down on Panagra's installations at airports not mentioned in the Bilateral Agreement would appear to be dispelled, at least in part, by the fact that Captain Pol is no longer connected with Civil Aeronautics in Bolivia and that he appears to have lost out in his obstructionist policy connected with Panagra and the Bilateral Agreement.

It is, therefore, respectfully requested that the enclosed Memorandum of the Bolivian Foreign Ministry be referred to Ambassador Flack and to the appropriate officials of the Department for the use it may have in the final deliberations in Washington over the possibility of concluding the Bilateral Air Agreement.

Respectfully yours, WILLARD GALBRAITH

[Negotiations continued intermittently in 1948. Bolivia withdrew its opposition to Article 8, and the United States reduced its requirement of 12 traffic points to 6. The agreement was signed September 29, 1948, and is considered to have gone into effect on November 4, 1948.]

CONTINUING EFFORTS TO ELIMINATE AXIS ECONOMIC INTERESTS IN BOLIVIA [76]

740.24112A/10–947

The Ambassador in Bolivia (Flack) to the Bolivian Minister for Foreign Affairs and Worship (Elío) [77]

RESTRICTED LA PAZ, October 8, 1947.
No. 444

EXCELLENCY: I have the honor, under instructions of my Government, to invite Your Excellency's kind attention to the reported plan of the Bolivian Government which would lift altogether the restrictions imposed on the nine spearhead firms which were included in the Proclaimed List of Certain Blocked Nationals.

I have informed my Government of this proposed action and in

---

[76] For documentation on the persistence of Axis interests in 1946, see *Foreign Relations*, 1946, vol. XI, pp. 404 ff.
[77] Copy transmitted to the Department in despatch 1787, October 9, from La Paz, not printed.

reply I have been instructed to convey to Your Excellency's Government my Government's open disappointment in this proposed measure which it feels ignores the activities of these firms during the recent war.

Furthermore, it is the view of my Government that the present Bolivian Government is bound by the obligations undertaken by Bolivia's acceptance of the Chapultepec Resolutions on enemy property.[78] Bolivia has in the past itself invoked the Resolutions adopted there in notes addressed to other American Governments in the protection of its own interests.

As Your Excellency will recall, members of this Embassy have been collaborating with officials of the Bolivian Government for a number of years in an attempt to resolve the Replacement Program. Following the Bolivian revolution of July 21, 1946, the new Bolivian Government was again approached under instructions of the Department of State with the hope that it would be possible to institute an effective Replacement Program to be applied against firms and persons whose actions during the recent World War were prejudicial to the United Nations' cause. At that time the Embassy was again assured that the Bolivian Government would implement its various international obligations on this matter. After a further series of discussions between representatives of this Embassy, the Foreign Office, and the Minister of National Economy, a satisfactory program was agreed upon; namely that the Bolivian Government for economic reasons should lift her restrictions imposed on all Axis firms with the exception of the following nine:

>Juan Elsner y Cia. (Velasco y Cia.)
>Ferretería Findel
>Kyllman, Bauer y Cia. (Gumucio y Cia.)
>Quidde y Cia.
>Gustavo Schomann y Cia.
>Sickinger y Cia.
>Schweitzer y Cia.
>Zeller, Mozer y Cia.
>Fábrica de Conservas de Jorge Stege

It was further agreed that definite action would be taken regarding these remaining nine firms in order to eliminate the influences whose activities had been detrimental to the interests of the United Nations.

Upon the publication of the regulatory resolution of the Economic Defense Board to be applied to the decree of February 12, 1947, which lifted the restrictions on Axis firms in general, it was noted that the

---

[78] For texts of resolutions, see Pan American Union, *Final Act of the Inter-American Conference on Problems of War and Peace* (Washington, 1945); for documentation on the Conference, see *Foreign Relations*, 1945, vol. IX, pp. 1 ff.

resolution had been modified in a way which emasculated it by providing no time limit within which the above listed nine firms should present their cases to the Bolivian Economic Defense Board. This omission was pointed out to Dr. Luís Fernando Guachalla, then Minister for Foreign Affairs, and Mr. Germán Costas, then Minister of Economy. These officials of the Bolivian Government agreed in principle that the Minister of Economy would advise the Embassy of the action recommended by the Economic Defense Board in each case concerning the nine spearhead firms and that, if the action to be taken by the Economic Defense Board was satisfactory to this Embassy, a supplementary decree concerning them would be published. According to the Embassy's present information, the Economic Defense Board apparently has never formally met to consider the claims of these firms, nor has this Embassy received from the Bolivian Government any recommendations of the Economic Defense Board concerning their petitions. The proposal to publish a decree categorically stating that the nine firms be cleared of all charges against them thus comes as a complete surprise and a marked disappointment to the United States Government.

The position of the United States Government, in brief, is that the Bolivian Government undertook certain obligations regarding Axis dominated firms and persons within its borders. The requirements envisaged by the United States Government concerning the elimination of these Axis influences are known in a general way. The specific details of the elimination of such influences is, of course, a matter for the Bolivian Government to determine, bearing in mind its international obligations. However, in the eyes of the United States Government, the nine firms above named are dominated and controlled by influences which opposed the Allied cause during the recent war.

The United States is particularly interested in Juan Elsner y Cia., Kyllman, Bauer y Cia., and Zeller, Mozer y Cia., since these three firms are partially owned from Germany. The United States regards Enrique Elsner, Guillermo Bauer, and Germán Mozer, German nationals resident in Germany, as beneficial part-owners of the three firms. It is presumed that no matter what action the Bolivian Government may take concerning the other firms, these enemy interests will be eliminated even though they may now be held nominally by Bolivian nationals in trust for these German owners.

In conclusion I should like to point out to Your Excellency that the policy of the United States and the other members of the United Nations, despite the termination of the war and the legal abolishment of the Proclaimed List of Certain Blocked Nationals, is to continue to view firms and individuals such as the above named nine with apprehension, unless Axis influences have been removed.

My Government has asked me to request that Your Excellency be so kind as to furnish me with copies of the documents presented by these nine firms to the Economic Defense Board in order that they may be available for the records of the Department of State and of the Embassy.

Please accept [etc.]
JOSEPH FLACK

740.24112A/11–1447

The Chargé in Bolivia (Galbraith) to the Secretary of State

RESTRICTED
No. 1854
LA PAZ, November 14, 1947.

SIR: I have the honor to refer to this Embassy's despatch no. 1787, of October 9, 1947, entitled "Transmitting Copy of Embassy's no. 444 of October 8, 1947, Seeking Bolivian Compliance with Replacement Program", and to report on developments since that date in so far as the Replacement Program is concerned.

An acknowledgement of this Embassy's note no. 444 was received on October 14, under date of October 11. However, this merely stated that the Minister of Economy was being informed of the views of the United States government.

On Thursday, November 6, the Chargé d'Affaires and the reporting officer were asked to call on Dr. Julio Alvarado, Sub-Secretary for Foreign Affairs. He wished to ask specifically if the Blue Book [79] had any bearing on Bolivia's international obligations concerning a Replacement Program. He was informed that it did not, but that Bolivia had undertaken definite obligations, not only at Chapultepec, but also at the Washington Conference in 1942 [80] and the Rio de Janeiro Conference in 1943 [*1942*].[81] He then stated that the Cabinet was to consider the matter that afternoon and that he was attempting to gather together all possible information on the subject. An interesting sidelight was his request that the Embassy let him know the date upon which the Resolution of the Economic Defense Board, dated March 3, 1947, was published in the local press, since his office was unable to find

---

[79] Department of State, *Consultation Among the American Republics With Respect to the Argentine Situation* (Washington, 1946). For documentation on its issuance, see *Foreign Relations*, 1946, vol. XI, pp. 182 ff.

[80] See Pan American Union, *Final Act of the Inter-American Conference on Systems of Economic and Financial Control* (Washington, 1942). For documentation on the Conference, see *Foreign Relations*, 1942, vol. V, pp. 58 ff.

[81] The Third Meeting of the Foreign Ministers of the American Republics held in Rio de Janeiro in January 1942. See Pan American Union, *Report on the Third Meeting of the Ministers of Foreign Affairs of the American Republics, Rio de Janeiro, January 15–28, 1942* (Washington, 1942); and for documentation, see *Foreign Relations*, 1942, vol. V, pp. 6 ff.

it. He was later notified that publication occurred on March 28, in *La Razon*.

Unofficial information obtained from a member of the Foreign Office indicated that, although the Cabinet session that day did discuss the problem of a Replacement Program, no definite action was taken. The entire matter was referred to the Economic Defense Board for study. This, of course, has been done repeatedly in the past. It is doubted that any concrete action will be taken by the Economic Defense Board since representatives and friends of the spearhead firms to be considered reportedly have much influence with the Board's members. In this connection, it might be noted that many local businessmen believe that President Hertzog depends almost entirely upon his brother, Carlos Hertzog, for economic and commercial information upon which to base decisions in these fields. Carlos Hertzog is the manager of the firm Terminal, successor of C. F. Gundlach & Cia., and was included on the Proclaimed List of Certain Blocked Nationals. Although he and his firm were removed from the list early this year, largely for political considerations, it is safe to assume that he would hesitate to furnish the President with advice contrary to the interests of his long-time friends, the influences in the spearhead firms to which this Embassy objects.

As was noted in despatch no. 1787, the Embassy has discussed the Replacement Program with the British Embassy and has worked together with it, although the United States has obviously born the major burden in the matter. A copy of note no. 444 was supplied the British Ambassador.[82] The British Commercial Secretary[83] informed the reporting officer, on November 6, that instructions had been received from London to submit a note supporting this Embassy's note no. 444. He was advised that the Cabinet was to discuss the entire problem that very afternoon and he therefore agreed to telephone the Sub-Secretary for Foreign Affairs to notify him of the intention of the British Embassy to transmit a strong note on the subject. A copy of the British note, dated November 7, was supplied to this Embassy and is transmitted herewith[84] (see enclosure). This note closely follows the tenor of this Embassy's note no. 444 and, in several instances, seems to have been copied verbatim.

On November 12, the Commercial Attaché and the reporting officer called on the Minister of National Economy[85] in order to orient him regarding the views of the United States. He was supplied with a brief history of the negotiations which have been undertaken from

---

[82] Thomas Ifor Rees.
[83] F. B. Hutchinson.
[84] Not printed.
[85] Raul Laguna Lozada.

time to time and was informed that it is our sincere desire that Bolivia carry out some type of program which would not whitewash those who acted contrary to the interests of the United Nations during the recent war. He stated that he had been absent from the meeting of the Cabinet which considered the question, but that he intended to call a session of the Economic Defense Board in the near future to settle the matter. He promised to keep the Embassy informed of developments.

The Embassy is not overly optimistic that the Bolivian government will take effective steps against the spearhead firms in question, but feels that it must continue to press the matter in order to prevent a blanket clearance of Axis elements within the country.

Respectfully yours, For the Chargé d'Affaires, ad interim:
JOHN A. E. ORLOSKI
Commercial Attaché

740.24112A/12–347

The Chargé in Bolivia (Galbraith) to the Secretary of State

RESTRICTED LA PAZ, December 3, 1947.
No. 1909

SIR: I have the honor to refer to this Embassy's despatch No. 1787 of October 9, 1947 with which was transmitted a copy of Embassy's note No. 444 of October 8, 1947 [85a] to the Bolivian Foreign Office concerning the United States position regarding the Replacement Program and referring to a project of the Bolivian Government under which all present restrictions applicable to Axis firms and individuals would be completely eliminated. The Bolivian Government has finally replied to the Embassy's note and a copy and translation of its reply dated November 9, but not received until November 28, are attached herewith.[86]

The Bolivian Foreign Office, while apparently resenting the project basis of the Embassy's action, has nevertheless replied in a vein which would indicate that far from the situation developing into one of complete pessimism, there is now a definite hope that some tangible program satisfactory to the Government of the United States may be brought about. It is believed that the situation has been aided by the submission of the British Embassy's note in the matter of November 14, 1947, a copy of which was transmitted with despatch No. 1854 of November 14, 1947, because according to unofficial comment prior to the receipt of the Bolivian Government's reply, the official attitude

---

[85a] See footnote 77, p. 378.
[86] Not printed.

of the Government, influenced by pressure tactics of the spearhead firms, was that the war was over and the cases against the Axis interests were generally unpopular. On the other hand the Embassy has taken advantage of every opportunity to point out clearly to the Foreign Office and the Minister of National Economy our Government's position with regard to this program.

In view of the Bolivian Government's new official statements contained in the present note under reference, the Embassy intends to follow up these new developments by a formal meeting with the Minister of Economy, who is Chairman of the Board of Economic Defense, as soon as the atmosphere has cooled, in order to obtain the issuance of a corrected Resolution and a definitive windup of this problem.

Respectfully yours, For the Chargé d'Affaires ad interim:
JOHN A. E. ORLOSKI
Commercial Attaché

EFFORTS TO LIQUIDATE THE LEND-LEASE ACCOUNT WITH BOLIVIA

824.24/2-2647 : Telegram

The Secretary of State to the Embassy in Bolivia

CONFIDENTIAL WASHINGTON, February 26, 1947—7 p. m.

103. Dept handed Bol Amb [87] note requesting payment Bol Lend-Lease account totaling $925,000, copy of which follows air mail.[88] Recalling unfulfilled assurances of former administration that installment payments would begin March 1946 (Embdesp 2006, Dec 20, 1945 [88]), Amb was informed that while Dept earnestly desired obtain settlement of Lend-Lease accounts, matter had not been pressed recently in desire not to create difficulties Junta Govt following July revolution. For this reason we have delayed inviting his personal attention to matter until now.

Amb stated he would cable his Govt urging that, if possible, some payment be effected before March 10; and that in any case matter be given priority consideration after inauguration new administration. He expressed grave doubts, however, that Bol financial and foreign exchange position would permit early favorable action.

Unless you perceive objections, please follow up informally with FonMin stating your Govt would appreciate being informed what Bol Govt may have in mind respect settlement this account.

MARSHALL

---

[87] Ricardo Martinez Vargas.
[88] Not printed.

824.24/6-1247

Memorandum of Conversation, by the Assistant Chief of the Division of North and West Coast Affairs (Espy)

[WASHINGTON,] June 12, 1947.

Participants: Ambassador Don Ricardo Martinez Vargas
Mr. Ellis O. Briggs, Director Office of ARA
Mr. James Espy, NWC
Mr. Raul Diez de Medina, Minister Counselor, Bolivian Emb.

During their meeting this afternoon, Mr. Briggs, Director of ARA, handed to the Bolivian Ambassador a copy of Mr. Espy's memorandum dated June 5, 1947.[89] Subject—Embassy residence, La Paz.

Mr. Briggs stated that in offering to accept a part of the payment of the Lend-Lease account in bolivianos, we had in mind using some of the funds for the purchase of the Embassy residence at La Paz and possibly of other government properties in Bolivia. Mr. Briggs stressed that we were immediately concerned in keeping a "roof over our Ambassador's head."

Ambassador Vargas commented that this had been the first time that he had learned that we might be willing to receive part of the Bolivian Lend-Lease indebtedness in bolivianos. He said he thought this was a very interesting proposal. The Ambassador then informed Mr. Briggs that he would immediately telegraph his Government informing it of the substance of the memorandum and requesting that most prompt action be taken.

124.241/6-1347 : Telegram

The Secretary of State to the Embassy in Bolivia

CONFIDENTIAL WASHINGTON, June 23, 1947—7 p. m.

356. Urtel 565, June 13.[89] Dept has no knowledge basis belief lend-lease obligation would be reduced or cancelled. Possibly some confusion arose because of fact payment requested of Bolivia is only 18% of full value. Please make clear that Dept. expects payment in dollars or Bolivianos of full equivalent of dollar indebtedness of approximately $900,000.

MARSHALL

---

[89] Not printed.

824.24/6–3047 : Telegram

The Ambassador in Bolivia (Flack) to the Secretary of State

CONFIDENTIAL   US URGENT   LA PAZ, June 30, 1947—7 p. m.

623. Just received Foreign Office note 530 today's date [92] stating regarding Bolivian lend-lease amounting to $925,000, Bolivian Government accepts renegotiation on general understanding that equivalent of approximately $600,000 US currency will be used in Bolivian equivalent. In my memo No. 256 of March 31 [92] headed [handed?] to Foreign Minister,[93] no mention was made of amount to be used in bolivianos but I said orally at the time that it would probably eventually be equivalent to about $600,000.

In renegotiation conversations which will take place in Washington, we need the following immediately: $40,000 requested by owner Ernst [94] in US currency, the equivalent of $45,000 at the approximate rate of 60 or 2,700,000 bolivianos to complete payment on residence, option for which expires July 31.

Other eventual dollar needs if Cusicanqui [95] and adjacent lots on Avenida Arce not pressing at present are purchased are:

(a) Cusicanqui property $60,000;
(b) Adjoining lots (Banks Urioste, etc.) $40,000;
(c) Lot and house owned by Keenan $20,000.

Total dollar needs this heading $120,000.

Other estimated eventual Boliviano needs: Construction on Cusicanqui and adjacent property (figures in million bolivianos):

(a) Residence 6
(b) Chancery 6
(c) Additional secretary's residence 1
(d) Staff house for women 2.5
(e) Acquisition of land and construction Consulate Cochabamba 2

Total these needs 17,500,000 bolivianos

Total equivalent this amount at official rate is approximately $415,000.

This with amounts above rescinded would roughly total slightly over $600,000.

If lend-lease renegotiations are not promptly concluded enabling taking up option on residence, I recommend most strongly that Embassy be authorized to pay purchase price of $85,000 in full by draft

---

[92] Not printed.
[93] Luis Fernando Guachalla.
[94] Hugo Ernst Rivera, owner of the property housing the American Embassy.
[95] Property of Hector Cusicanqui, possible site for American Embassy.

at once, leaving question of reimbursement to lend-lease fund to emerge from forthcoming negotiations, which I think will extend several weeks before final conclusions are approved by both Governments.

FLACK

124.24/7–247 : Telegram

The Secretary of State to the Embassy in Bolivia

CONFIDENTIAL WASHINGTON, July 2, 1947—6 p. m.

389. Urtel 623 June 30. No dollars available for acquisition properties in Bolivia. Necessary all payments be made in bolivianos under renegotiated Lend-Lease agreement for property and improvements. Further instructions follow authorizing Emb submit Depts recommendation for amendment to Lend-Lease agreement.[96]

Because of present conditions necessary obtain from Ernst lowest terms payment he will accept in bolivianos for sale present residence. If Ernst prefers not receive payment from Bolivian Govt suggest he agree payment be made in bolivianos in La Paz by a bank. Emb to authorize payment out of account in which Bolivian Govt has deposited bolivianos. Report.

MARSHALL

824.51/7–1747 : Telegram

The Secretary of State to the Embassy in Bolivia

CONFIDENTIAL   US URGENT   WASHINGTON, July 18, 1947—8 p. m.

420. Re urtel 675 July 17 and Deptel 408 July 11.[97] Total [98] payment schedule is as follows:

(*a*) US Govt will require payment in July 1947 of bolivianos equivalent to $150,000.

(*b*) For subsequent payments or deliveries US presents following schedule:

(I) Property or bolivianos at option United States Govt equivalent to $150,000 on or before each of following dates: Jan. 1, 1948, July 1, 1948 and Jan. 1, 1949.

(II) Dollars, property, or bolivianos, at option United States Govt equivalent to $100,000 on or before each of following dates: July 1, 1949, Jan. 1, 1950 and July 1, 1950.

---

[96] For text of the agreement, signed December 6, 1941, see *Foreign Relations,* 1941, vol. VI, p. 428.
[97] Neither printed.
[98] Lend-Lease.

(III) Dollars, property, or bolivianos, at option United States Govt., equivalent to $25,000 on or before Jan. 1, 1951.

MARSHALL

124.24/7–2547 : Telegram

The Secretary of State to the Embassy in Bolivia

CONFIDENTIAL   US URGENT   WASHINGTON, July 25, 1947—noon.

431. Urtel 686 July 23.[99] Emb authorized acquire Ernst residence property free and clear all encumbrance at cost up to 5,500,000 bolivianos. Payment Ernst be made by Bolivian Govt through bank against delivery good and sufficient deed in fee simple. See Depcirinstr Sept 20, 1945 [99] for procedure. Bolivian Govt to receive credit for dollar equivalent of payment against its obligations to US under lend-lease.

MARSHALL

824.24/9–3047 : Telegram

The Ambassador in Bolivia (Flack) to the Secretary of State

CONFIDENTIAL   LA PAZ, September 30, 1947—5 p. m.

853. Sub-Secretary [1] informed me today Supreme Decree now in preparation which he read will authorize conclusion renegotiation Lend-Lease Agreement and enable payment first installment next week without Congressional action. However, he stated that under Bolivian law decree must recite values involved and therefore will mention publicly amount Bolivia received and amount of $916,000 now due thereunder.

Since mention these amounts inevitable I told him no objection perceived.

FLACK

824.24/10–347 : Telegram

The Acting Secretary of State to the Embassy in Bolivia

CONFIDENTIAL   US URGENT   WASHINGTON, October 3, 1947—4 p. m.

532. Publication amount Bolivia received and amount payment due may give rise to ill feeling and seriously jeopardize collection of sums due from other American republics since percentages differ with var-

---

[99] Not printed.
[1] Julio Alvarado.

ious agreements and especially since renegotiation of agreement also would be fully known. No other agreement has been renegotiated and few renegotiations are contemplated.

Dept does not understand why publicly announced decree necessary to make payment originally specified in Strictly Confidential agreement. Please explain fully as possible. Suggest communicate Dept objection to publication to Bolivians and explore possibility keeping terms confidential. Would it not be legally feasible for Bol Govt to publicly announce, if necessary, only that an installment payment was being made on lend-lease account, permitting terms of lend-lease negotiation to remain confidential?

LOVETT

824.24/10–647 : Telegram

The Ambassador in Bolivia (Flack) to the Secretary of State

CONFIDENTAL LA PAZ, October 6, 1947—2 p. m.

863. Renegotiation Lend-Lease has been rather delicate, but Subsecretary told me today enabling decree was signed by President and Cabinet October 3. He will make early appointment for meeting with Finance Minister, Guachalla,[2] to determine essential details of initial payment into bank here.

Subsecretary assured me on Saturday and today (Deptel 532, October 3) Bolivian Government will meet our wishes avoidance publicity specific figures re amount received by Bolivia and amount due, limiting itself in official announcement to statement like "a payment was made to United States on Lend-Lease obligations". He said Cabinet and some senators had necessarily been informed, but they would regard matter as officially confidential.

FLACK

124.24/10–1347 : Telegram

The Ambassador in Bolivia (Flack) to the Secretary of State

CONFIDENTIAL   US URGENT   LA PAZ, October 13, 1947—noon.

877. In conversation with Minister Finance Guachalla October 10 in presence of Subsecretary and Galbraith he promised proceed with initial payments under supreme resolution authorizing Lend-Lease payment. He promised initial payment this week of 2,500,000 bolivianos and balance of equivalent of 150,000 [3] during October or early

---

[2] Carlos Guachalla.
[3] Presumably dollars.

November. In view stringent Bolivian financial situation I accepted this as practical matter leaving question payment dates subsequent installments for future determination.

In view impending Bolivian payment I again discussed contract with Ernst. He is willing accept total price 5,738,500. This includes increase of bolivianos 238,500 based on today's free market rate 70 as against 64.70 calculated when matter first discussed (reDeptel 506 September 17 [5]).

In order to conclude this matter as Department urged, I told Ernst I felt we could accept this and request Department's promptest cable confirmation, also authorization to use my discretion in minor matters.

Ernst will deliver to us property deed on payment first installment under agreement of sale we are drafting.

FLACK

824.51/10–3147 : Telegram

The Ambassador in Bolivia (Flack) to the Secretary of State

CONFIDENTIAL   US URGENT   LA PAZ, October 31, 1947—8 p. m.

922. For Espy Assistant Chief NWC. See my US Urgent telegram No. 921 today.[5] On basis previous authorizations I proceeded point where Bolivian Government made initial payment 2,500,000 bolivianos with promise additional equivalent $150,000 during month November. On basis my negotiations Ernst had agreed deliver deed on payment initial 2,500,000 bolivianos. We now in receipt Department's telegram 566 and Department's airgram 242 [6] requesting application this late date of complicated procedure entirely unsuited conditions and situation Bolivia which will have adverse effect on residence purchase unless it can be waived as requested in my telegram cited. Please do everything possible enable Embassy treat with this matter as contemplated section 3 Department's telegram 408, July 11 [5] and as envisaged my negotiations to date. Am departing November 4 but Galbraith fully informed.[7]

FLACK

---

[5] Not printed.
[6] Neither printed.
[7] Telegram 957, November 26, 7 p. m., from the Chargé (Galbraith), indicated that Bolivia made another payment of 3,800,000 bolivianos, making a total of 6,300,000 at the Bretton Woods exchange rate of 42. The terms of the purchase of the Ernst property were also indicated. In telegram 609, December 9, 2 p. m. to La Paz, the Department indicated its approval (124.241/11–2647).

BRAZIL

THE POSITION OF THE UNITED STATES WITH RESPECT TO THE BREACH IN RELATIONS BETWEEN BRAZIL AND THE SOVIET UNION

701.3261/1–2147 : Telegram

The Ambassador in Brazil (Pawley) to the Secretary of State

RESTRICTED RIO DE JANEIRO, January 21, 1947—2 p. m.

81. Embtel 2032 of December 23.[1] Today's press carries text of Brazilian note to Moscow relating to incident involving Brazilian Embassy secretary. Note admits right of Soviet Government demand removal of secretary, but states justification not obligatory; denies that secretary's actions attributable to alcohol but to anger and reaction against unnecessary humiliation and physical violence; blames manager of hotel and State official for knowingly humiliating secretary and thus making himself responsible for damages done, which Brazilian Govt categorically refuses to pay; takes occasion to allege "lamentable happenings indirectly associated with precarious conditions of the Brazilian Embassy installations in Moscow and that there is lack of reciprocity in facilities granted Brazilian representatives in Moscow compared to treatment accorded Soviet representatives in Brazil", "a state of affairs which must not continue"; states that if conditions of installation not improved Brazilian Govt "will be forced not to maintain, at least with the present category and composition, its representation in USSR".

Foreign Minister [2] at same time announced that Brazilian Ambassador to USSR [3] has been granted permission to go to Stockholm sanitorium for medical treatment. Any connection between this and note denied.

Please repeat to Moscow.

PAWLEY

---

[1] Not printed. According to this telegram, the Brazilian Secretary of the Embassy in Moscow was said to have "committed imprudences" in a restaurant on December 8–9. The Soviet Foreign Minister protested, requested the expulsion of the offending diplomat, and payment of damages (701.3261/12–2346).

[2] Vyacheslav Mikhailovich Molotov.

[3] Pimental Brandão.

701.3261/2-447 : Airgram

The Ambassador in Brazil (Pawley) to the Secretary of State

RIO DE JANEIRO, February 4, 1947.

A-126. Reference Embassy's despatch No.1511 of January 22, 1947 entitled "Brazilian Note to U.S.S.R. on incident in Moscow involving Brazilian Diplomatic Secretary" which transmitted to the Department text of the Brazilian Note.[4] *O Jornal* of February 1 published the following communication from the Brazilian Foreign Office relating to the Brazilian Note:

"The Chargé d'Affaires of Brazil in Moscow has just informed the Itamaratí (Foreign Office) that he has received a note from the Ministry of Foreign Affairs of the U.S.S.R. in which the Soviet Government, disagreeing from our understanding as to the facts, considers it useless further to discuss the incident involving Secretary Pina.

"With reference to the installation of the Brazilian Embassy, the same Government considers it provisory, determined as a consequence of the war, but the Government explains that steps are being taken for an installation worthy of all the diplomatic missions, including that of Brazil."

PAWLEY

832.00/5-1047 : Telegram

The Ambassador in Brazil (Pawley) to the Secretary of State

CONFIDENTIAL   RIO DE JANEIRO, May 10, 1947—1 p. m.

558. Embtel 552, May 8, 1947.[5] Following official communication to Minister Justice[6] by President Superior Tribunal of Tribunal's decision cancel registration Communist Party, Minister Justice ordered stoppage all functions as political party throughout nation. Yesterday police closed all cells and committees in federal district. Police reported to have orders proceed in strict accordance law. No disturbances any kind reported from any part Brazil.

PAWLEY

832.00/5-1647 : Telegram

The Ambassador in Brazil (Pawley) to the Secretary of State

CONFIDENTIAL   RIO DE JANEIRO, May 16, 1947—10 p. m.

596. *Tribuna Popular* published on May 15 facsimile of memorandum dated May 7 issued by General Saville's[7] executive officer to personnel, US Army section air, JBUSMC, stating that it was contem-

---

[4] Neither printed.
[5] Not printed.
[6] Benedito Costa Neto.
[7] Brig. Gen. Gordon P. Saville, United States Army member, Joint Brazil-United States Military Commission.

plated that an important political decision would be rendered by Brazilian Govt on following day, May 8, and that it was possible that there might be public demonstrations during next few days.

Memo cautioned personnel to avoid public gatherings, stay off streets as much as possible and wear civilian clothes after working hours.

In reproducing Saville's memo, *Tribuna Popular* alleged that Truman was responsible for closing Communist Party and that American "imperialists" knew what vote of the electoral tribunal would be day before it took place. *Tribuna Popular* today points out that Saville's memo referred to important "political" decision of "government" not merely "tribunal". Although Saville has made no mention to anyone of fact, it is known to Embassy that he was not in town on day on which this memo was issued.

Saville yesterday gave statement to *O Globo* stating in substance that on his honor as a soldier he had no knowledge that Supreme Electoral Tribunal would cancel Communist Party registration when he issued his instruction preceding day; that this instruction was issued as matter of routine to reiterate our traditional position that Brazilian domestic affairs are reserved exclusively to Brazilians; that like other newspaper readers he learned from published accounts that the tribunal was about to render judgment; consequently cautioned personnel to be alert in avoiding any act which might even inadvertently be interpreted as indication of participation in domestic affairs of Brazil. Other papers have not featured story although several have carried Saville's statement.

I called Saville's attention to fact that it was unwise to have issued statement in effort to justify his instruction and that had I been consulted such statement would not have been made. I also cautioned Saville and other members of JBUSMC to make no written instructions of this nature in future.

PAWLEY

701.6132/7-147

The Chargé in Brazil (Key) to the Secretary of State

SECRET   RIO DE JANEIRO, July 1, 1947.
No. 2482

Subject: Departure of Soviet Ambassador from Brazil

The Chargé d'Affaires a. i. has the honor to quote below the text of a memorandum dated June 25, 1947, prepared by the Special Assistant [8] on the above subject:

1. "A usually reliable source has informed me that, according to an informant in the Brazilian Foreign Office, Soviet Ambassador Suritz,

---

[8] Randolph A. Kidder.

before his departure from Rio in May, wrote a letter to the Foreign Minister of Brazil [9] stating that he greatly regretted the occurrences which culminated in the closing of the Communist Party and which would probably cause the expulsion of Communist members from the National Congress.

2. "Suritz is alleged further to have stated that he could not continue to represent in Brazil a country whose chief of government is subjected to daily insults and injuries in the press. He reiterated his sympathy for the Brazilian people, but stated that under the circumstances he had no choice but to follow the course which he had taken.

3. "The same source states that there is considerable speculation in the Itamaratí over the question of whether or not Russia will suspend diplomatic relations with Brazil, unless for political expediency, they decide to send a new Ambassador to Brazil. The Foreign Office does not expect Suritz to return."

732.61/10–947 : Telegram

The Chargé in Brazil (Key) to the Secretary of State

SECRET   RIO DE JANEIRO, October 9, 1947—noon.

1399. During call on Foreign Minister yesterday evening I took occasion to inquire whether there was any truth to rumors which have appeared in local press that Brazil may soon break relations with Russia.

Fernandes replied that deep indignation and resentment had been caused in Brazil by scurrilous and slanderous article about President Dutra which had appeared in *Literary Gazette* (Moscow's 2985 to SecState, October 4 [10]) in view of its provocative nature as well as its perversions and fabrications and since article represented a deliberate affront by strictly controlled Soviet press, Brazilian Ambassador in Moscow was being instructed to demand an apology and retraction.

If, as Foreign Minister fears, Soviets refuse comply with Brazilian demands than Brazilian Government will sever diplomatic relations with Russia.

He added that events had already demonstrated that Brazilian collaboration with Russia was impossible. Furthermore, whereas Brazilian Mission in Moscow was isolated and its personnel ill-housed and all manner of obstacles were placed in its way, Soviet Mission in Rio had been accorded every facility and complete freedom of action. This they had abused by bringing in numerous agents and stirring up all kinds of trouble. In view foregoing, Brazil had everything to gain and nothing to lose by rupture in relations.

---

[9] Raul Fernandes.
[10] Not printed.

He realized, of course, that our position was different: US could not afford lose contact with Russia in view situation in Europe, the fact that several peace treaties awaited negotiation or ratification and for other weighty reasons. This explained why we did not take any drastic action following Molotov's rebuff to our protest against similarly venomous Soviet press articles about President Truman recently.[11]

Although none of these considerations seem to apply in case of Brazil Foreign Minister stated that he would welcome any views which Dept might care to express on course which Brazilian Government proposes pursue if satisfaction from Soviets not forthcoming.

Department repeat to Moscow.

KEY

501.BB/10–947 : Telegram

The Acting Secretary of State to the Embassy in Brazil

SECRET   WASHINGTON, October 11, 1947—2 p. m.

1167. . . .

Re urtel 1399 Oct 9, Dept naturally reproves scurrilous attack on Pres Dutra. As matter of fact first criticism of him in *Literary Gazette* was embodied in attack on Pres Truman published in its no. 39 over 2 weeks ago. In note of protest Amb Smith commented that article went so far as to imply criticism of Pres Truman for associating with Pres Dutra to whom was imputed unwarrantably prior association with Axis powers. Smith's note referred to Pres Dutra as our devoted and faithful ally in recent war and remarked that any such criticism came with extraordinarily bad taste from a Soviet writer in view of course of history since 1939. Soviet Govt rejected US protest in brusque note and we are contemplating no further action.

With regard to request of FonMin for our views on Braz intention to sever diplomatic relations with USSR in case demand for apology and retraction of attack on Pres Dutra is not met inform FonMin that Dept is appreciative of his consideration in welcoming our comments. We feel that this is matter which only Brazil can decide. He will recall that before establishing relations with USSR Brazil several times asked for our opinion and that we then maintained same attitude.[12]

LOVETT

---

[11] For documentation on this incident, see vol. IV, pp. 514 ff.

[12] In his telegram 1422, October 14, 4 p. m., the Chargé in Brazil indicated that this policy of the United States had been conveyed to the Brazilian Foreign Minister, who had informed him that the Brazilian Ambassador in Moscow knew that the United States was aware of the contemplated action of Brazil (732.61/10–1447).

821.001 Dutra, Gaspar/10–1447 : Telegram

The Chargé in the Soviet Union (Durbrow) to the Secretary of State

SECRET   Moscow, October 14, 1947—9 p. m.

3033. Brazilian Ambassador sent word in strictest confidence this afternoon about latest developments following strong protest note he addressed Foreign Office October 10th about libelous article against President Dutra (Embtel 2985, October 4 [13]). Brazilian note so worded as to make it impossible to deny that press controlled by government in USSR. Note also indicated that Brazilian Government demanded satisfactions and that "in interest of continuing reciprocal good relations" efforts be made to prevent such a matter from happening again.

This afternoon note was returned under cover of third person note from Foreign Office, curtly refusing to accept accusation against Soviet Government contained in note, and ending with statement to effect that transmission of such a note did not indicate desire of Brazilians "to continue reciprocal good relations."

Ambassador plans leave shortly and thinks it probable his government will break relations.

Ambassador asked particularly that this information be held in strictest confidence.

Department pass Rio de Janeiro.

DURBROW

732.61/10–1647 : Telegram

The Chargé in Brazil (Key) to the Secretary of State

SECRET   US URGENT   RIO DE JANEIRO, October 16, 1947—4 p. m.

1434. Mytel 1422, October 14.[14] Foreign Minister informed me this morning that in view of unsatisfactory Soviet reply to protest lodged Brazilian Ambassador Moscow Brazil decided to break relations with Soviet. He then handed me following communication which in translation reads as follows:

"In strict secrecy, I have the honor to communicate to Your Excellency, that, since the Soviet Government has refused any satisfaction for the insults printed in Moscow against the Brazilian Armed Forces and against the President of the Republic, the Brazilian Government is taking the necessary steps to break diplomatic relations with that Government, which will probably be consummated within 2 days.

"In the imminence of this event I beg Your Excellency to transmit to the Department of State a request to assist us in assuming protection for Brazilian interests in the Soviet Union, especially lending aid

---

[13] Not printed.
[14] See footnote 12, p. 395.

and assistance to the personnel of the Brazilian Mission so they may leave the territory of that country without difficulty or vexation as well as in transmitting to us the communications from our Mission which latter will be unable to transmit through its own facilities.

"With my sincere thanks in anticipation, (signed) Raul Fernandez."

Would appreciate earliest possible instructions since Foreign Minister has asked that if possible our reply be communicated to him tomorrow.

Department pass Moscow.

KEY

704.3261/10–1747 : Telegram

The Acting Secretary of State to the Embassy in the Soviet Union

SECRET   US URGENT   WASHINGTON, October 17, 1947—5 p. m.

1849. Rio's Tel 1434 Oct 16 passed to you. In addition to taking custody Braz archives you are authorized to assist personnel Braz Emb facilitating departure and transmitting through Dept (by non-confidential code or in paraphrase) messages it may wish to forward to Braz FonOff. Once you have been informed by Braz Emb that diplomatic relations have been broken you should address note to FonOff stating that Braz Govt has requested US to assume representation of Braz interests in Soviet Union and that this Govt has acceded to request.[15] Presumably Braz Amb will also inform FonOff. Advise Dept promptly of nature of any Soviet reply and date of assumption.

Sent to Moscow as 1849 repeated to Rio de Janeiro as 1186.

LOVETT

832.911/10–2247 : Telegram

The Chargé in Brazil (Key) to the Secretary of State

SECRET   RIO DE JANEIRO, October 22, 1947—6 p. m.

1458. Group invading Communist *Tribuna Popular* print shop about 4 p. m. yesterday did thorough job destroying presses, files, equipment, etc. Subsequently ransacked 13th floor *Tribuna* editorial offices different part city (first paragraph Embtel 1453, October 21 [16]). Several *Tribuna* employees reported hospitalized.

Although police headquarters only few hundred yards from print shop police arrived only after damage done. Confidential reports indi-

---

[15] In telegram 3072, October 20, 8 : 30 p. m., the Chargé in Moscow advised that this had been done (704.3261/10–2047).
[16] Not printed.

cate clearly police had foreknowledge plans and *Correio da Manha*[17] in article resenting attack on freedom press accuse police of connivance.

Being unable publish regular edition *Tribuna* distributed few hundred copies small mimeographed sheet attacking Brazilian Government, police and US.

In addition breaking several windows Soviet Embassy demonstrators tore down, destroyed (second paragraph Embtel 1453) name plate on Chancery entrance but on this occasion prompt intervention police reinforcements dispersed demonstrators before any serious damage done.

Department pass Moscow.

KEY

701.3261/10–2247 : Telegram

The Chargé in Brazil (Key) to the Secretary of State

SECRET   RIO DE JANEIRO, October 22, 1947—7 p. m.

1459. At his request called on Secretary-General Foreign Office[18] this afternoon, who asked if any word received re plans departure from Moscow Brazilian Embassy personnel beyond tentative scheme outlined Moscow's 3056, October 18.[19] I replied only additional information available this subject was Moscow's 3075, October 21[20] substance which I gave him.

Accioly said while no definite plans yet formulated for departure Soviet personnel from Rio (in fact Foreign Office as yet uninformed what country will assume charge representation Soviet interests), Foreign Office was thinking along following lines, provided reciprocal treatment is accorded by Soviets to Brazilian Embassy personnel:

1. All Soviet Embassy personnel will be permitted take with them their personal baggage without limit and without examination; all excess baggage, furniture, etc., would be handed over also without examination to representing power for subsequent forwarding.

2. Soviet personnel will be permitted select their own destination and means of transportation. All expenses, of course, will be borne by Soviet personnel.

3. Meantime Soviet personnel being permitted move freely within limits Rio and continue living in their homes but cannot send telegrams in code.

---

[17] Rio de Janeiro newspaper.
[18] Hildebrando Accioly.
[19] Not printed.
[20] According to telegram 3075, October 21, 6 p. m., the Chargé in the Soviet Union had received a noncommittal reply to his inquiry concerning arrangements for the departure of the Brazilians (701.3261/10–2147).

It is quite evident that Foreign Office will not permit Soviet personnel to depart from Brazil until it feels assured that plans for departure of Brazilian Embassy personnel are definite and that treatment accorded them is not inconsistent with above.

Foreign Office feels plans would greatly be facilitated if some power is promptly designated by Soviets to assume representation of the latter's interests here.

Department relay Moscow.

KEY

701.3261/10-2347 : Telegram

The Chargé in the Soviet Union (Durbrow) to the Secretary of State

SECRET   URGENT   Moscow, October 23, 1947—7 p. m.

3089. Upon receipt Deptel 1459, October 22, I called on Chief Protocol and gave substance proposed treatment Soviet Embassy staff Rio stressing reciprocity and asked if protecting power chosen. I also stated Brazilian Ambassador had commented on courteous treatment he and members his staff receiving here which had been reported Rio. (Mytel 3084, October 23).[21]

Chief Protocol after stating pleased to hear Brazilians here satisfied his treatment, added he had some very disquieting news to impart. FonOff had just received press report of several incidents of "hooliganism" which had taken place against both personnel and premises Soviet Embassy Rio. He stated that this was completely contrary to all international usage, could not be tolerated and that Soviet Government expected Brazilian Government take all necessary security measures to assure the protection of the Soviet staff until their departure. He added that since the press reports were fragmentary, it might be necessary for him to revert to this matter later. In informing him was sorry to hear of this unfortunate matter, I stated I would report his remarks to Washington for transmission to Rio.

When asked if he had any word re protecting power, he replied decision not yet taken.

In regard to date of departure Brazilian staff here he stated that would depend on date and arrangements made for departure Soviet staff Rio. He did not know if they planned depart by sea or air. I informed Brazilian Ambassador of above who asked me to inform his government most emphatically that he and all members his staff are being treated in exactly same manner as they were before break, they

---

[21] Not printed.

under no restraint, Ambassador and other members of staff have been permitted make private telephone calls to their wives abroad and that they are being treated with full courtesy. Ambassador expressed strong regrets that incidents had taken place and felt sure Brazilian Government would take all measures prevent any further incidents.

Department repeat Rio.

DURBROW

701.6132/10–2447 : Telegram

The Chargé in Brazil (Key) to the Secretary of State

SECRET   RIO DE JANEIRO, October 24, 1947—6 p. m.

1470. Rezov, Second Secretary Soviet Embassy, phoned today to inquire how soon transit visas could be issued 24 members Soviet Embassy staff. He was informed if passports delivered Monday transit visas would probably be ready within 2 or 3 days. Rezov expressed satisfaction this arrangement and said 9 diplomatic and 15 official passports would be delivered Monday morning.

At same time Rezov requested assistance obtaining steamer reservations. Embassy gave noncommital reply view assurances given by Brazilian Government facilitate arrangements for departure Soviet staff and in absence appointment Soviet protective power I feel Embassy should not become involved with Soviets' departure arrangements other than issuance transit visas. Department's comment would be appreciated.[22]

Department relay Moscow.

KEY

701.6132/10–2447 : Telegram

The Chargé in Brazil (Key) to the Secretary of State

SECRET   RIO DE JANEIRO, October 24, 1947—6 p. m.

1471. Moscow's 3084, October 23 to Department.[23] Called on Secretary General Foreign Office at noon today and drew his attention to complications created by inadequate police protection of Soviet Embassy premises Rio. I expressed hope that no further similar incidents would occur and enquired whether precautions were being taken in view of the large demonstration of solidarity scheduled for this afternoon in front of Catete Palace and danger that some of participants might afterwards demonstrate before Soviet Embassy.

---

[22] In telegram 1221, October 27, 6 p. m., the Department indicated approval of the Embassy's policy of avoiding involvement with the Soviet departure arrangements (701.6132/10–2447).
[23] Not printed.

Accioly stated that he would immediately telephone police to post adequate guard around Soviet Embassy premises.

Department relay Moscow.

KEY

732.61/10–2547 : Telegram

The Chargé in the Soviet Union (Durbrow) to the Secretary of State

SECRET   US URGENT   Moscow, October 25, 1947—6 p. m.
NIACT

3101. Embtel 3098.[24] I called this afternoon on Chief of Protocol and asked clarification of yesterday's announcement regarding retention Brazilian staff hotel, plans for departure and whether Soviets have named protecting power. He replied that for the moment he could not discuss Brazilian matters with me because it had not yet been decided whether Soviet Government would accept US as protecting power. When asked if this meant we could not represent Brazilian interests, he replied matter was still under study and he would advise me as soon as decision taken. I asked if Soviet Government had named protecting power and he replied decision not yet taken. I told him I would report this to Department and added that I was ready at any time to assist in working out departure arrangements in most amicable manner possible.

I added that Brazilian Ambassador had again told me this morning he receiving most correct treatment except fact he could not leave hotel. Stated that basis our reports (Rio's 1458 [25] to Department relayed) Soviet Embassy Rio had been stoned but we had no reports any Soviet personnel hit as Tass reporter implied (Embtel 3100, October 25 [24]).

While this changed attitude not clear, it possible Soviets stalling for time to make sure all agents safely included with Embassy staff before making departure proposals.

Since Brazilian staff here feeling somewhat depressed with last night's developments, I am not telling them we are not definitely accepted as protecting power. When I saw them this afternoon they expressed hope Brazilian Government would take all necessary precautions to protect Soviet staff Rio in order that no further restrictions be placed on them here.

Because of uncertainty situation, am not repeating this message Rio.

While FonOff may refuse further discuss Brazilian matter with me,

---

[24] Not printed.
[25] Dated October 22, p. 397.

would be most helpful to have full details of protection measures taken Rio and plans for departure so I could attempt resolve impasse.

DURBROW

732.61/10–2647 : Telegram

The Chargé in Brazil (Key) to the Secretary of State

SECRET   NIACT   RIO DE JANEIRO, October 26, 1947—2 a. m.

1473. Communicated substance of Deptel 1219, October 25,[27] to Foreign Minister this evening at 11:00. Fernandes then wrote in longhand a note in French which he handed me at midnight and which in translation reads as follows:

"The Brazilian Foreign Office makes known the following:
When the news of the rupture of diplomatic relations became public the chancery of the Soviet Embassy telephoned the Foreign Office advising the latter that a hostile crowd of young people had gathered in front of the building. Immediately urgent protective measures were requested of the police and the Ministry of Interior and 15 minutes later, notwithstanding the fact that the chancery is situated in an outlying area, a contingent of police arrived and dispersed the crowd, reestablishing order. There was no throwing of stones which moreover would not have been possible since the building is situated at the back of a large garden.

The same precautions were taken in order to assure the safety of the Embassy residence located in a district far removed from the Chancery.

This afternoon, having learned of the reports published in Moscow about which there was no previous knowledge the Foreign Office sent a representative to the Embassy accompanied by the Polish Minister [28] in order to ascertain from Mr. Sokolov, the Soviet Chargé, the nature of his charges against the police forces and, in the presence of the aforementioned minister, Mr. Sokolov said nothing about any attack on the chancery confining himself to a complaint that his automobile was hit by stones and eggs when, at some distance from the chancery, it was carrying himself, his young child and his secretary. The result was that the secretary's ear was struck by an egg and the child was hit on the nose. No injuries occurred from these hits.

Mr. Sokolov added that he was astonished Brazilian Ministry should have been uninformed about these occurrences since he had sent two telegrams on the subject, one in French and the other in Spanish, to the Soviet Foreign Office. Having obtained the foregoing infor-

---

[27] Not printed; it advised the Embassy in Brazil that the Soviet Foreign Office had not yet decided to permit the United States to represent Brazilian interests in the USSR, and that the Brazilian Ambassador in Moscow had expressed the hope that the Brazilian Government would take all necessary measures to protect the Soviet staff in Rio de Janeiro (701.3261/10–2547).

[28] Wojciech Wrzosek.

mation the Foreign Minister advises me (1) that the Soviet personnel can correspond freely and without censorship which explains why the Foreign Office was uninformed about the telegrams above-mentioned (2) that according to information obtained from the police the facts reported by Mr. Sokolov as outlined above are true but that the regrettable incident occurred in the street at a spot where momentarily no police were present and at such a considerable distance from the chancery building that it was impossible for the police force which was guarding the latter to intervene (3) that freedom of movement and of communication *en clair* are being permitted to the Soviet Embassy personnel (4) that Mr. Sokolov and his staff are making preparations for their departure and will be free to leave for the destination of their choice (5) that the protection of the buildings has been and will continue to be rigorously maintained (6) that a similar degree of protection against undesirable acts by irresponsible persons is difficult to achieve when the Soviet personnel is moving about unless the latter are willing to be accompanied by detectives: an offer of this kind will immediately be made to Mr. Sokolov and if he accepts it such supplementary protection will be accorded to him and to his personnel."

French text of note being forwarded airmail.

Foreign Minister orally added that Soviet Chargé has indicated his staff had nearly completed packing of their belongings and records and that all would probably be ready to depart within next three or four days. However he has no information regarding projected date of departure, means of transportation or destination of Soviet Embassy group.

KEY

701.6132/10–2847 : Telegram

The Chargé in Brazil (Key) to the Secretary of State

CONFIDENTIAL   RIO DE JANEIRO, October 28, 1947—1 p. m.
US URGENT

1488. Chief of Protocol, Foreign Office, called on me this afternoon and left with me a memorandum reading in translation as follows:

"The Ministry of Foreign Affairs has reached an agreement with the Soviet Embassy that the departure of the Soviet mission shall take place by Pan American Airways plane, via the US between November 1 and November 3, 1947.

On November 1, five members of the Soviet Embassy will depart, for New York, with most of the baggage, by the cargo vessel *Bowplate*.

The mission is composed of 35 persons which the Pan American will be able to transport between above dates (that is, the remaining 30 persons).

In order to effect this departure, it is essential that the Brazilian mission in Moscow be permitted to depart at the same time, for which purpose the Ministry would appreciate if the Embassy of the US (in Moscow) were good enough to reach an agreement with the Soviet Government to negotiate the simultaneous departure of the two missions, informing this Ministry, as urgently as possible of whatever arrangements are made through the Embassy of the US in Moscow."

He expressed hope that Soviet Government would act promptly in this matter.

Department relay Moscow.

KEY

701.3261/10–2947 : Telegram

The Chargé in Brazil (Key) to the Secretary of State

SECRET   PRIORITY   RIO DE JANEIRO, October 29, 1947—2 p. m.

1494. Re Moscow's October 28, 8 p. m., to Department,[29] Brazilian Ambassador's inquiry referred to Chief Protocol Foreign Office who requested that reply be made as follows:

(1) Soviet Chargé d'Affaires and family planning depart by plane November 3 in accordance his own wishes. Remainder of staff departing by vessel November 1 or by plane November 1 or November 2.

(2) Soviet Embassy personnel will be permitted to take as much baggage and effects as they desire. Most of baggage will go by *Bowplate*. There will be no search of persons or examination of baggage. Furthermore their departure will be facilitated every way possible.

(3) All arrangements for departure Soviet personnel are dependent on assurances from Soviet Foreign Office that at least equally favorable treatment will be accorded Brazilian Embassy staff and that latter will be permitted depart Moscow between November 1 and November 3.

In view of foregoing and since departure of Soviet Embassy personnel on November 1, 2 and 3, all necessary reservations having been made, awaits only necessary assurances from Soviet Foreign Office, I see no necessity that these measures should be carried out under responsibility of this Embassy as suggested in latter part of heading 3 of Brazilian Ambassador's message.

Brazilian Foreign Office as of noon today had not been approached re representation of Soviet interests in Brazil by Yugoslavia as reported in this morning's press under Belgrade dateline October 28.

Department relay Moscow.

KEY

---

[29] Not printed.

701.6132/10–2947 : Telegram

The Ambassador in the Soviet Union (Smith) to the Secretary of State

SECRET   URGENT   Moscow, October 29, 1947—5 p. m.
NIACT

3124. Durbrow called on Chief Protocol at 1600 today to present informal letter giving departure data contained Deptel 1488, October 28. Before letting him proceed he reminded Durbrow that he could only discuss matters with him informally. Durbrow stated that if he did not wish to discuss the question with him perhaps he might discuss it with Brazilian Embassy direct. Chief Protocol stated that he would discuss the matter informally with Durbrow at this time but stated that he would prefer not receive his informal letter. Durbrow then outlined information contained in letter pointing out plans made first group Soviet officials depart Rio by boat November 1st other leave by plane by November 3 and because of short time before projected departure believed it worthwhile pass this information on to Foreign Office in event it wished us advise Brazilian Foreign Office plans for departure Brazilian staff here.

Chief Protocol replied he could give Durbrow no concrete information on departure plans which depended upon receipt definite information re arrangements for departure Soviet staff Rio. He assured Durbrow as soon as this received immediate arrangements would be made for departure Brazilian staff by such means as they chose.

Durbrow indicated Brazilian Ambassador suggested he and staff might depart by train from Leningrad November 2 for Helsinki crossing Finnish frontier November 3. Chief Protocol made no comment on this suggestion. He then stated he had received *en clair* telegram from Rio indicating Soviet staff now being well protected and that departure arrangements proceeding rapidly but had not received definite word re departure plans. He added one of complications was that Brazilian authorities had forbidden international telephone communications to Soviet Embassy which prevented them communicating Soviet missions Buenos Aires or Montevideo to give last minute assurances final plans departure. Durbrow asked whether Brazilians here have permission to telephone and Chief Protocol assured him that they could and added that if they did not realize this there was some misunderstanding. Durbrow replied he would report that open telephone communications Soviet Embassy Rio would facilitate matters. Suggested this be done.

When Durbrow again endeavored obtain some indication departure arrangements, Chief Protocol stated Soviet Government prepared facilitate in every way Brazilian staff departure by chosen route and that soon as word was received Soviet staff departure plans were firm, matters would proceed and he advised he might get in touch with Brazilian counselor here to discuss departure arrangements direct rather than through us.

Department pass Rio.

SMITH

701.3261/10–3147 : Telegram

The Ambassador in the Soviet Union (Smith) to the Secretary of State

SECRET   US URGENT   Moscow, October 31, 1947—6 p. m.
NIACT

3144. Counselor Brazilian Embassy called 1745 to give following information:

Assistant Chief Protocol called him at 1730 to advise that Brazilian Ambassador staff no longer confined to hotel could circulate freely and that they should get in touch with Intourist (Soviet Travel Agency) to make such arrangements as they wished for their departure. Embassy staff could depart in groups between November 1 and November 3 by such means as they chose. They can take with them all personal belongings and archives which will not be opened or examined by Soviet authorities. Protocol asked passports be sent immediately Foreign Office obtain necessary exit visas (this being done).

Brazilian Ambassador has not decided definite arrangements for departure. Soon as details formulated will be cabled urgently.[30]

Department pass Rio de Janeiro urgently.

SMITH

QUESTIONS CONCERNING THE DISPOSAL OF UNITED STATES MILITARY EQUIPMENT TO BRAZIL UNDER THE LEND-LEASE AND SURPLUS PROPERTY ARRANGEMENTS [31]

811.24532/1–2147 : Telegram

The Ambassador in Brazil (Pawley) to the Secretary of State

SECRET   RIO DE JANEIRO, January 21, 1947—7 p. m.

84. Joint Brazilian United States Military Commission has effected actual transfer strategic airport installations to Brazilian Air Force.

---

[30] The Brazilian Ambassador and his party departed for Helsinki on November 3, and the Soviet staff left Rio de Janeiro in four groups on November 1, 2, and 3. (701.3261/11–347; 701.6132/11–247, 11–347, and 11–447.)

[31] For documentation on the general policy of the United States in providing military assistance and armaments to the other American Republics, see pp. 101 ff.

They now request that official acceptance these installations be obtained by Embassy from Brazilian Govt. Dept may wish to instruct Embassy regarding wording of exchange of notes officially recording transfer of title these properties in view other related considerations, such as nature of rights of Pan-American Airways to use airports, concerning which Embassy does not have detailed information.[32]

PAWLEY

832.24/1-2247

Memorandum by the Chief of the Division of Brazilian Affairs (Braddock)[33]

[WASHINGTON,] January 22, 1947.

The Brazilians having indicated their desire to hold informal exploratory conversations at a working level on this subject, Mr. Kempter[34] and I met Dr. de Mello[35] and Mr. Garcia[36] for luncheon yesterday. They indicated that their Government was considering applying for a revision of the Lend-Lease Agreement with Brazil[37] in order to scale down the rate of reimbursement provided therein. They stated that this Agreement had been entered into before Brazil was an active partner in the war, and that they believed that its terms were less favorable than the terms in our agreements with our other major Allies. Mr. Kempter and I informed them that in our opinion the United States would not consider reopening this Agreement, not only because we believed it to be a fair agreement but also because if the Agreement with Brazil were revised many other countries would most certainly also request revisions and the whole Lend-Lease system of repayments might break down. Mr. Kempter also endeavored to show Dr. de Mello and Mr. Garcia how Brazil's own credit in this country would be impaired by any request for a release or diminution of her obligations. We talked over in some detail various items and the Lend-Lease account, including the ship charters and material furnished the Brazilian Expeditionary Force. Mr. Garcia made the point that on some of the Lend-Lease equipment Brazil had been overcharged. He

---

[32] In instruction 505, February 10, the Department enclosed a draft note indicating withdrawal of the United States Forces from 13 airports and the transfer to Brazil of installations, facilities, and inventories (811.24532/1-2947). The withdrawal was formally recognized in an exchange of notes March 13 and 31 (811.24532/4-1647).
[33] Addressed to the Director of the Office of American Republic Affairs (Briggs), and the Assistant Secretary of State for American Republic Affairs (Braden).
[34] Charles W. Kempter, Chief, Lend-Lease Staff, Office of the Foreign Liquidation Commissioner.
[35] Edgard de Mello, Brazilian Commercial Counselor.
[36] Celso Raul Garcia, Second Secretary, Brazilian Embassy.
[37] Signed March 3, 1942, *Foreign Relations*, 1942, vol. v, p. 815.

was assured that full consideration would be given to any such claims which the Brazilians were able to substantiate and it was stated by Mr. Kempter that the United States for its part might also have some claims to be considered in the final settlement.

DANIEL M. BRADDOCK

832.24 FLC/3-1147

Memorandum by the Chief of the Division of Brazilian Affairs (Dawson) [43]

[WASHINGTON,] March 11, 1947.

At a meeting this afternoon in the office of Mr. Chester T. Lane, Lend-Lease Administrator in OFLC, attended by various of his subordinates, Messrs. Matlock and Miller of LP and Mr. Dawson of BA, the question of the Brazilian desire for an over-all settlement of Brazil's Lend-Lease account was gone into in detail. While, as is usual in such meetings, some of the results were not clearly defined, the consensus as to what our position should be was as follows, in broad summary:

1. Material furnished to the Brazilian Expeditionary Forces in the Mediterranean theater of operations (estimated at $54,000,000) not to be charged for, provided the Brazilians were prepared to state in writing that all such material either had been consumed or, if returned to Brazil, was in military use and had not been diverted to other purposes; this would be in line with the procedure followed with other combat allies on similar equipment.

2. No charge to be made for the use of naval vessels turned over to Brazil under charter agreement (this also in accordance with the practice in similar cases of other combat allies). The eight destroyer escorts representing some $55,000,000 of the $71,000,000 value of naval vessels Lend-Leased to Brazil cannot be disposed of by our Navy under existing legal authority which provides that destroyers (including DE's) may not be declared surplus. Title to the remaining vessels might be turned over to Brazil, if it desired, either by being declared surplus, with Brazil bidding for them, or possibly by billing for them under Lend-Lease.

3. With the equipment turned over to the Brazilian Expeditionary Forces and the chartered naval vessels eliminated from total Lend-Lease figures, the best estimate now available is that Brazil will have been advanced approximately $204,000,000 under Lend-Lease but no

---

[43] Addressed to Mr. Briggs of ARA and to Messrs. Smith, Wright, and Braden of A-Br.

precise figures are on hand. OFLC will make an effort to get more accurate data from Treasury.

4. If, as expected, the best estimate of pared-down Lend-Lease on which repayment will be expected comes to within 10% + or − of the $200,000,000 ceiling provided for in the 1942 Lend-Lease Agreement, the Brazilians might be asked to agree on $200,000,000 as the definite final figure so as to avoid further bookkeeping, et cetera. On this the repayment would be at 35% in accordance with the terms of the 1942 Agreement. Since the Brazilians have paid $35,000,000 to date, they would have an identical amount still to pay.

5. An effort should be made to get the Brazilians to assume obligation for claims against U.S. military personnel in Brazil (available figures show them to be only some $45,000 but these are purely tentative) in reaching an over-all settlement. The Brazilians have indicated a desire to assume such claims in return for our assuming obligation to pay off Italian claims against Brazilian military personnel in Italy; we cannot legally do the latter.

6. If the Brazilians ask for an extension of time in paying their remaining instalments for Lend-Lease (as they have indicated they would) no objection should be raised to having the three payments of $11,666,666 made in 1947, 1949 and 1951 provided agreement can be reached on other issues.

7. There would be no amendment to the 1942 Lend-Lease Agreement but merely an exchange of notes interpreting the loose language of that agreement.

Mr. Lane proposes to have a meeting with the Brazilians to discuss the question of an over-all Lend-Lease settlement later this week, after the latest information from the Treasury can be obtained, to see whether an agreement in principle on a settlement along the foregoing lines cannot be reached.

ALLAN DAWSON

832.34/7-2947 : Airgram

The Secretary of State to the Embassy in Brazil

CONFIDENTIAL   WASHINGTON, July 29, 1947.

A-454. There are now in the possession of the Brazilian government a number of US naval vessels leased to Brazil during the war under a charter party agreement between the two governments. By the terms of this agreement, the US retains title to the vessels and Brazil is required to return each vessel, unless lost, to this Government at a place and time to be specified by the US. This procedure was used because under the Lend Lease Act [48] it was not permitted to transfer title to these vessels.

As the Navy Department now considers the ships leased to Brazil to be surplus to its needs, it is planned to offer all of them, with the exception of 8 destroyer escorts, for sale to Brazil as surplus property at a low price. There is no legislative authority whereby destroyer escorts may be sold to foreign governments. If Brazil should agree to purchase, it is planned not to require Brazil to return the ships to a US port for actual repossession by the US, but to ask that they be returned to an appropriate US official in Brazil until a contract of sale is finalized. Failure to purchase the ships will necessitate that they be returned by Brazil to a US port for actual repossession by the US and subsequent disposal. Although the agreement states that "hire" (charge for use) of the vessels during the war shall be determined by subsequent agreement between the two governments, it is not planned to charge for use of the ships, since they were employed in the common defense effort.

Without approaching Brazilians, please report your comments regarding plan by cable and any objections you may perceive. US ships covered by agreement with Brazil are: 8 subchasers (PC); 8 subchasers (SC); 1 transport (AP); 1 repair barge (YR); 5 launches (ML); 1 gate vessel (YNg); 1 barge (YS); 1 floating drydock (YFD); 11 plane personnel craft; 19 plane rearming craft; 1 landing boat. In addition, Brazil has 8 destroyer escorts (DE) covered by the agreement, but, as indicated above, there is no legislative authority whereby these may be sold to Brazil.

MARSHALL

832.20 Defense/8–1147

The Secretary of State to the Embassy in Brazil

SECRET   WASHINGTON, August 11, 1947.
No. 824

SIR: The General Assembly of the United Nations on December 14, 1946 passed by acclamation a resolution on the Principles Governing the General Regulation and Reduction of Armaments (A/267)[49] which contained in paragraph 7 the following recommendation:

"It (the General Assembly) recommends the Members to undertake . . . the withdrawal without delay of armed forces stationed in

---

[48] Act of March 11, 1941; 55 Stat. 31.
[49] For the positions of the various powers in the United Nations Assembly on this disarmament resolution, see the United Nations, *Official Records of the General Assembly, First Session, Second Part, Plenary Meetings*, pp. 1289–1308, 1310–1316. For the text of this resolution, see United Nations, *Official Records of the General Assembly, First Session, Second Part, Resolutions Adopted by the General Assembly during the Second Part of the First Session*, pp. 65–67.

the territories of Members without their consent freely and publicly expressed in treaties or agreements consistent with the Charter and not contradicting international agreements."

In the course of the debate in the General Assembly preceding the adoption of the above-mentioned resolution, the interpretation of the term "armed forces" most generally used was one covering all uniformed members of armed services. However, members of the offices of Military and Naval Attachés can be excluded from the definition since their presence is justified by international custom and is covered by the issuance of visas and agreements.

The presence of members of the armed forces of the United States in Brazil attached to the Joint Brazil-United States Military Commission and of members of the armed forces of Brazil in the United States attached to the Joint Brazil–United States Defense Commission is based on Article 1 of the Secret Politico-Military Agreement between the United States and Brazil entered into by an exchange of notes between Ambassador Caffery and Minister for Foreign Affairs Aranha dated May 23 and May 27, 1942.[50] It would obviously be inconsistent with national policy for this document to be made public. Consequently, the Department desires to place on record in some other manner the fact that the United States members of the Joint Brazil–United States Military Commission and the Brazilian members of the Joint Brazil-United States Defense Commission are stationed within the territory of Brazil and of the United States with the full consent of the host Government in each case.

You are accordingly instructed to discuss the matter with the Minister for Foreign Affairs [51] and endeavor to effect, at the earliest possible opportunity, an exchange of notes covering the presence in Brazil and the United States of the United States and Brazilian members of the Joint Brazil–United States Military Commission and the Joint Brazil–United States Defense Commission, respectively. The text of the note which the Department desires that you address to the Minister for Foreign Affairs, if the Brazilian Government is agreeable to this suggestion, is enclosed.[52] It is expected that the Brazilian reply would, of course, be similar in phraseology, *mutatis mutandis*. You should inform the Minister for Foreign Affairs that it would be the intention of the Department to register the exchange of notes with the United Nations Secretariat.

Should the Foreign Minister suggest any changes in the wording of the proposed exchange of notes, you are requested to advise the De-

---

[50] For an explanatory note on this exchange, see *Foreign Relations*, 1942, vol. v, p. 662.
[51] Raul Fernandes.
[52] Not printed.

partment promptly by telegraph and await its instructions before proceeding further.

Very truly yours, For the Secretary of State:
NORMAN ARMOUR

832.20 Defense/9–2247

The Chargé in Brazil (Key) to the Secretary of State

SECRET   RIO DE JANEIRO, September 22, 1947.
No. 2806

SIR: I have the honor to refer to the Department's instruction no. 824 of August 11, 1947 and to subsequent telegrams referring to an exchange of notes regularizing the presence in Brazil of United States members of the Joint Brazil–United States Military Commission and in the United States of Brazilian members of the Joint Brazil–United States Defense Commission vis-à-vis the resolution passed by the General Assembly of the United Nations on December 14, 1946.

As authorized by the Department's telegram no. 1053 of September 11, 1947,[53] it has been suggested that the Brazilian Government initiate this exchange of notes and the Foreign Office has agreed to this proposal. There is enclosed a copy of the draft note agreed upon in conversations between the Ambassador and the Minister of Foreign Affairs and which will probably be addressed to the Embassy by the Foreign Ministry within the next few days.

Respectfully yours,   DAVID McK. KEY

[Enclosure]

Draft Note From the Brazilian Minister for Foreign Affairs to the American Ambassador

SECRET

EXCELLENCY: I have the honor to refer to the conversations which have taken place between representatives of the Government of the United States of Brazil and representatives of the Government of the United States of America regarding paragraph 7 of the Resolution on the Principles Governing the General Regulation and Reduction of Armaments, adopted by the General Assembly of the United Nations on December 14, 1946.

It is the suggestion of the Government of the United States of Brazil that, in order to eliminate any possible question regarding

---

[53] Not printed.

conformity with paragraph 7 of the above-mentioned Resolution, the two Governments agree as follows:

(1) Military personnel of the United States of Brazil now stationed in the territory of the United States of America, have been and are so stationed with the full and freely given consent of the Government of the United States of America.

(2) Military personnel of the United States of America now stationed in the territory of the United States of Brazil, have been and are so stationed with the full and freely given consent of the Government of the United States of Brazil.

(3) The Governments of the United States of Brazil and the United States of America mutually agree that the aforementioned military personnel shall continue to be so stationed until such time as the Government of the country in which they are stationed withdraws its consent thereto.

(4) None of the Military personnel of either government, stationed within the territory of the other government, comprises any combat forces.

I have the honor to inform Your Excellency that this note, together with your note in reply, will be considered by the Government of the United States of Brazil as placing on record the understanding of the two Governments in regard to this matter.[54]

Accept [etc.]

832.24/9–2247

The Chargé in Brazil (Key) to the Ambassador to Brazil (Pawley)

CONFIDENTIAL RIO DE JANEIRO, September 22, 1947.

Subject: Comments on Proposal to sell surplus United States Naval Vessels, except Eight Destroyer Escorts, to Brazilian Government.

In accordance with your instructions, a meeting was held on September 17, 1947, at which various points arising out of the Department's airgram A–454 dated July 29, 1947 regarding the proposal to sell to the Brazilian Government all surplus United States naval vessels, except eight destroyer escorts, were considered. The meeting was attended by Admiral Lovette, General Morris, General Beverley, Captain Cooke, as well as several of their assistants and myself.

The first subject which came under review was whether or not our records show if any definite commitment had been made to the Bra-

---

[54] In telegram 1159, October 9, 6 p. m., the Department indicated the desirability of including mention of JBUSMC and JBUSDC (832.20 Defense/9–2247). For texts of the later exchange of notes, see Agreement Relating to the Presence of Military Personnel of the United States in Brazil and the Presence of Military Personnel of Brazil in the United States, signed at Rio de Janeiro on December 15, 1947. February 2, 1948, Department of State, Treaties and Other International Acts Series No. 1759, or 62 Stat. (pt. 2) 1957.

zilian Government to convey to it the eight destroyer escorts. While it was the consensus that Brazilian officials, especially officials in the Brazilian Navy and the Brazilian Ministry of Marine, are under the impression that all United States naval vessels including the destroyer escorts, would be made available to Brazil, none of those present was able to find in the various files any evidence of a definite commitment on the part of the United States. With respect to the possibility that Admiral Ingram [55] may have made some commitment on the subject, the Embassy files contain copy of a letter dated August 2, 1945 from the Navy Department (which forms an enclosure to the Department's secret instruction 7442 of August 20, 1945 [56]) an extract of which reads as follows:

"Sir:
Reference is made to the letter from the Secretary of the Navy to the Secretary of State of July 25, 1945,[56] concerning Admiral Ingram's recent visit to Rio de Janeiro . . . Admiral Ingram has stated that in his conversations with President Vargas there was no discussion except as to the approved plans for withdrawal of United States Naval activities from Brazil and that he made no commitments as to post-war transfer of ships to the Brazilian Navy or in any other matters."

Consequently so far as the record is concerned, Admiral Ingram entered into no commitment.

Nevertheless it was agreed that the fact remains that the Brazilian Government is strongly under the impression that it will be able to retain all United States naval vessels which it is now using. Consequently it was our unanimous view that any move on our part to take away the eight destroyer escorts would cause deep resentment and dismay especially since these vessels constitute the backbone of the present Brazilian naval forces. Additionally, it was the belief of those participating in the meeting that, apart from the foregoing, any proposal to obtain payment from the Brazilian Government for the United States Naval vessels now in their possession, would be most unpopular and would be ill received, not only because of aforementioned reasons, but because almost all Brazilians feel that their cooperation in the war effort and the outstanding services performed by the Brazilian Navy entitled them to retain the vessels given to them under lend-lease.

In view of these considerations it was the earnest hope of all who took part in the meeting that the proposal outlined in the Department's airgram A–454 be left dormant. If that is not possible, it is the hope that the vessels will be sold to Brazil at a purely nominal price

---

[55] Adm. Jonas H. Ingram, Commander of the South Atlantic Force, and of the 4th Fleet, successively.
[56] Not printed.

and that some way can be found to permit Brazil to retain the destroyer escorts. In this connection it occurred to us that a possible way out would be either to declare, in Brazil's case, that the destroyer escorts are not considered "combattant" vessels or, at a later date, when the question of the implementation of the recently concluded Inter-American Treaty for the Maintenance of Peace and Security arises,[57] to convey to the Brazilian Government all presently held United States naval vessels including destroyer escorts, at that time.

There is attached a list [58] of all United States naval vessels which our Government furnished to Brazil under lend-lease. This list was compiled by Admiral Lovette who pointed out that, as of the present, no information is obtainable concerning the whereabouts and general condition of several of the categories of the list. His office is attempting to get information in this regard but he anticipates some difficulty as it is believed that most of this equipment was turned over by the Brazilian Navy to the Brazilian Air Force. This whole question is so delicate that all inquiries about these items will have to be very carefully handled: if the Brazilian Navy or Air Force suspected the purpose of the inquiries, they would unquestionably be greatly upset.

There is also attached for your information, a copy of a letter dated August 19, 1947 from the Chief of Naval Operations to Admiral Lovette bearing on this subject.[59]

832.24/9–2547

The Commissioner of Accounts of the Treasury Department (Maxwell) to the Acting Chief of the Division of Lend-Lease and Surplus Property Affairs, Department of State (Shenefield)

CONFIDENTIAL   WASHINGTON, September 25, 1947.

DEAR MR. SHENEFIELD: There is enclosed a Statement reflecting the status of our account with the United States of Brazil as of December 31, 1946 together with detailed statements supporting charges reported during the current period by the Navy Department, the Treasury Department and the various Services of the War Department.[60]

Your attention is invited to Article III of the Agreement dated March 3, 1942 [61] wherein "the Government of the United States of Brazil promises to pay in dollars into the Treasury of the United

---

[57] For documentation on this subject, see pp. 1 ff.
[58] Not printed.
[59] Letter not printed.
[60] None printed.
[61] The Lend-Lease Agreement.

States of America 35 percent of the scheduled cost of the materials delivered." This account indicates a payment of $11,666,666.64 was due on January 1, 1946 and an additional payment of $11,666,666.64 became due on January 1, 1947.

Inasmuch as an amount of $23,333,333.28 is past due and unpaid we shall appreciate any information you may have as to the possibility of early payment by the Government of the United States of Brazil or the status of any discussions between that government and the State Department relative to the above matter.

Very truly yours, R. W. MAXWELL

740.00119 EW/11–1447

The Chargé in Brazil (Key) to the Secretary of State

SECRET RIO DE JANEIRO, November 14, 1947.
No. 3053

SIR: I have the honor to refer to Department's telegram no. 1239 of November 4, 1947, and to my reply as contained in Embassy telegram no. 1549 of November 6, 1947,[62] wherein I pointed out that the Minister of Foreign Affairs had indicated that the Government of Brazil definitely desired to acquire the vessels referred to in Embassy Note No. 486 of June 27, 1947, which followed the tenor of the draft transmitted to the Department in Embassy secret despatch no. 2186 of April 30, 1947, as amended in accordance with Department's recommendation (see Department telegram no. 598 of June 9, 1947).[63]

A note confirming the foregoing has now been received from the Minister of Foreign Affairs and a copy thereof accompanied by an English translation is appended to the instant despatch as an enclosure.[64] It will be noted there from that, after consultation with the competent naval authorities, the Minister of Foreign Affairs states that the Brazilian Government accepts the offer of the two vessels on the terms and under the conditions proposed in the note under reference. The exact text of the pertinent part of Note No. 486 to which the Minister refers reads as follows:

"Mindful of Brazil's interest in reparations, the United States Government is investigating the possibility of making available to Brazil two ships from the United States share of the German navy—a measure which may be feasible as the United States share of the German

---

[62] Neither printed.
[63] None printed.
[64] Not printed.

navy was not considered as part of the reparations agreement. One ship is a torpedo boat with displacement of 1100 tons, built in 1939, operable and reported to be in good condition. The other vessel is a sailing training ship with auxiliary diesel engines, similar to that used by United States Coast Guard. It has a displacement of 1755 tons, an over-all length of 296 feet, and is reported to be in good condition. Because of certain technical and legal difficulties, the method of transfer, direct conveyance or sale at a nominal price, cannot at present be determined. Meanwhile, however, I would appreciate being informed if Your Excellency's Government would accept either or both the aforementioned ships under such method of transfer as may be determined."

The question of the manner of effecting transfer was not touched upon during my conversation with the Minister of Foreign Affairs and it is not my intention to broach this phase of the matter pending further instructions from the Department. I presume in view of Department's Airgram A–482 of August 13, 1947,[65] that the technical aspects of the problem will be handled by the Naval Mission directly with the Brazilian Ministry of Marine.

Respectfully yours, DAVID McKENDREE KEY

124.325/11–1847

The Chief of the Division of Brazilian Affairs (Dawson) to the Chargé in Brazil (Key)

CONFIDENTIAL WASHINGTON, November 18, 1947.

DEAR DAVID: I have delayed answering your letter of October 15[65] concerning the question of title to the various war vessels Lend Leased to Brazil during the late War until I could discuss it with the Ambassador and get a few reactions around here. In this connection, the Ambassador turned over to me your letter to him of September 22 on the same subject and I have that before me, too.

First, it seems well to clarify one point. Nobody here, so far as I have been able to discover, has ever had the idea of trying to repossess the 8 destroyer-escorts or any of the other vessels which were turned over to Brazil. It has been both the Navy's and the Department's idea to try to turn these ships definitely over to the Brazilians as soon as possible and on as generous terms as could legally be worked out. The difficulty has been that disposal of title to the DE's cannot be accomplished under present legislation, since they are clearly classified as

---

[65] Not printed.

combat vessels, and will have to wait passage of the legislation which has been pending before Congress for some time to arm the Good Neighborhood or some other legislative authorization.

Both the Navy and FLC have wanted to get rid of the other vessels, since they can be disposed of under the Surplus Property Act of 1944,[67] and leave the DE's under exactly the same status as they now have until the arms bill is acted upon. The FLC has placed a value of $414,128 on the vessels other than the DE's as what Brazil would be expected to pay as compared with the total original invoice price of $15,305,709 which they had when Lend Leased (incidentally, there are slight discrepancies between the FLC list and that given in the letter of August 19 from the Chief of Naval Operations to the Chief of the Naval Mission,[68] a copy of which was enclosed with your letter to the Ambassador; the FLC list carries 5 LCVP's instead of the same number of launches, 1 ML instead of 1 landing boat and does not include the YNG; these differences are, however, minor). Whether the Brazilians would consider the less than 3% of the original price a nominal charge, I do not know but there is no way, under the present set-up, in which they could be charged $1 a vessel or whatnot.

The Ambassador feels that telling the Brazilians we are ready to turn over title to the other vessels, whatever the price, would bring up in their minds the question of what would be done about the DE's and we agree with him here on the political side of the Department. We are consequently urging the Navy and FLC to hold everything until after the Bogotá Conference [69] and action on the arms legislation when we hope that it will be possible to deal with all the ships at one fell swoop. The technical boys naturally have wanted to get their books cleared as far as feasible but I think we will manage to make them see the light. In any event, there is nothing further for the Embassy to do on the matter until additional instructions come from the Department. Should the Naval Mission get anything more on the matter from the Navy Department, please let us know so that we can do the necessary at this end.

With cordial personal regards,

Sincerely,

ALLAN DAWSON

P. S. (Dec. 2) This was written a week before the Ambassador went off to Boston but reposed in my basket through inadvertence. . . .

---

[67] 58 Stat. 765.
[68] Not printed.
[69] For documentation on the preliminary discussions regarding this Conference, see bracketed note p. 94.

832.24/12-1747

Memorandum by the Assistant Chief of the Division of Brazilian Affairs (Clark) to Mr. William K. Miller of the Division of Economic-Property Policy

[WASHINGTON,] December 17, 1947.

In connection with your memorandum to Mr. Dawson dated December 7 [70] I wish to advise you that I have discussed this matter with Mr. Garcia of the Brazilian Embassy. Garcia informs me that instead of preparing a proposal to be submitted to the Department of State which would then be submitted to Rio with a recommendation for approval, the Brazilian Embassy communicated with Rio de Janeiro, provided full details and asked for instructions. Garcia has also informed me that the Brazilian Government advised the Brazilian Embassy that the matter would have consideration and study but that no immediate action was anticipated.

It appears to me that this settlement is probably stymied in Rio and I should not be surprised if the reason for the delay is at least partially due to the severe shortage of dollar currency available to the Brazilian Government. From what I know of the situation at the moment the Brazilians would find it a practical impossibility to liquidate the lend-lease settlement even in the reduced payments mentioned under one of your memoranda of December 7.

I gather that Garcia does not anticipate the possibility of any instructions on this matter from Brazil for some months to come. We are consequently faced with the necessity of either letting the matter ride or sending a note to the Brazilian Embassy reminding the Embassy of the desire of the American Government to settle these lend-lease accounts as soon as possible and requesting that the Embassy be so good as to inquire of Rio de Janeiro when some definite steps towards this settlement can be taken.

DuWAYNE G. CLARK

832.24/12-3047

The Chargé in Brazil (Key) to the Chief of the Division of Brazilian Affairs (Dawson)

[Extract]

CONFIDENTIAL

RIO DE JANEIRO, December 30, 1947.

DEAR ALLAN: I have just received your letter of December 19, 1947 [70] and we are all greatly relieved to learn that the question of

[70] Not printed.

offering the lend-leased war vessels to Brazil has been shelved for the present.

I was also interested to learn that the "nominal" price of $10,000 has been placed on each of the German vessels which were turned over to the Brazilians. This is probably $9,999 more than the Brazilians expect to pay but maybe I am wrong about this and in any event the value of these ships probably considerably exceeds the price you mention. I shall, of course, keep the figure under my hat for the present.

. . . .

Sincerely, DAVID

740.00119 EW/11–1447 : Airgram

The Acting Secretary of State to the Embassy in Brazil

SECRET   WASHINGTON, December 31, 1947.

A-668. Department pleased to advise concluding developments regarding sale to Brazil of two vessels previously of the German Navy. This refers to Embassy's secret despatch no. 3053, November 14, and Embassy's telegram no. 1549 of November 6 as well as Department's telegram no. 1239 of November 4 [72] and sundry other previous communications on subject topic.

On the basis of recommendation made by Department, it is understood that the two vessels, a T–4 type torpedo boat and a training vessel known as the *A. L. Schlageter*, will very shortly be declared surplus by the U.S. Navy to the Paris office of the Foreign Liquidation Commission. OFLC is cabling its Paris office to accept any offer made by Brazilian Government representing nominal payment for these two vessels.

Procedure now for Brazilian Government to submit offer to Paris office OFLC, care American Embassy, for these two vessels. A nominal value is understood to represent neither scrap nor commercial value. It is suggested that an offer of $10,000 U.S. currency for each of these vessels will probably receive favorable consideration from OFLC Paris.

LOVETT

---

[72] Telegrams 1549 and 1239 not printed.

DISCUSSIONS WITH BRAZIL CONCERNING TRADE AND SHIPPING QUESTIONS

611.3231/3-1247

The Acting Secretary of State to the Embassy in Brazil

CONFIDENTIAL   WASHINGTON, March 12, 1947.
No. 576

The Acting Secretary of State refers to past correspondence regarding the Brazilian consumption tax law and, in particular, to the Department's instruction no. 7571 of October 5, 1945 [73] and no. 7941 of April 5, 1946.[74] In these two instructions, there was set forth the proposal by this Government to conclude an exchange of notes with the Government of Brazil which would, in effect, grant that Government the right to impose new or increased internal taxes on any imported articles, whether or not such articles are included in Schedule I of the existing trade agreement,[75] provided that the Brazilian Government would give assurances that the rates of taxation on imported articles would be made no higher than those imposed on like domestic articles. Reference is also made to the discussion concerning the consumption tax held between an officer of the Embassy and Mr. Eduardo Pereira of the Internal Revenue Office (as recorded in the Embassy's report no. 38 of January 24, 1947 [74]). It is gratifying to note that the views expressed to Mr. Pereira have, in a concise manner, so cogently presented the Department's position in this matter. The Embassy's attention is also directed to an instruction which has not yet cleared the Department (with which were enclosed twelve copies of a preliminary list of specific tariff concessions which this Government contemplates requesting from Brazil in the multilateral negotiations at Geneva [76]) wherein it was stated that the consumption tax matter would be made the subject of a separate instruction.

As the Embassy is fully aware, in spite of numerous representations with respect to the conflict of the consumption tax with the Brazilian trade agreement, and although the offer by this Government referred to above was submitted to the Brazilian Foreign Office by the Embassy almost a year ago, the Brazilian Government has thus far given no indication that it is disposed to take any positive steps to remove the discriminatory features of the tax law. The clear and continuing violation of the existing trade agreement is regarded as

---
[73] *Foreign Relations*, 1945, vol. IX, p. 723.
[74] Not printed.
[75] Signed February 2, 1935, Department of State Executive Agreement Series No. 82.
[76] For documentation on the Geneva negotiations, see volume I.

a serious matter by this Government and, with all due allowance for necessary delay occasioned by the changing of governments in Brazil, it is felt that steps to resolve this issue might well have been taken some time ago.

At this time, however, of more immediate importance is the matter of the conflict between the Brazilian consumption tax law and the relevant provisions regarding internal taxation which have been approved by all the members of the Preparatory Committee, including Brazil, for incorporation in the Charter of the International Trade Organization.[79]

In a very short time the Preparatory Committee will hold a second meeting at Geneva to undertake multilateral tariff negotiations and to complete the drafting of the proposed ITO Charter. Article 15, Section 2, as numbered and approved by the recent New York meeting of the Drafting Committee of the Preparatory Committee, the substance of which was previously agreed to at London, reads as follows:

"The products of any Member country imported into any other Member country shall be exempt from internal taxes and other internal charges of any kind higher than those imposed, directly or indirectly, on like products of national origin."

There was complete agreement that such taxes should not be allowed to circumvent or impair tariff concessions accorded in trade agreements; if this were permitted, such concessions would prove to be valueless. Nor were such taxes considered a proper vehicle for according protection to local industry. Article 15, Section 1, states in substance that internal taxes should not be used to afford protection directly or indirectly for any national product.

This Government finds difficulty in reconciling the position taken on this question by the Brazilian delegation at London, and by the Brazilian representatives on the Drafting Committee at New York, with the actual practice at present by the Brazilian Government in the matter of the application of the consumption tax. It is not anticipated that any member of the Preparatory Committee will request at Geneva that the Charter provisions bearing on this subject be so substantially revised as to nullify the approved principle of national treatment. It is certain that this Government, as well as other Governments, would strongly oppose any attempt to nullify these provisions.

In the light of the foregoing, the Department is of the opinion that the Brazilian Government ought not to postpone further the taking of remedial measures to bring about equality of treatment in the application of the consumption tax. It is deemed of great importance

---

[79] Department of State, Treaties and Other International Acts Series No. 1700.

that the Government of Brazil proceed at once to give serious consideration to this problem in order that the Brazilian delegation at Geneva may be prepared to give assurances that measures are being taken by the Government of Brazil to remove all present conflict between the consumption tax law and the Charter provisions relating to this subject.

Unless serious objection is perceived, the Embassy is requested to convey as soon as possible the sense of the foregoing views of the Department to the appropriate Brazilian officials. Since the multilateral trade agreement which, it is hoped, will be successfully negotiated at Geneva will supersede and replace all existing reciprocal trade agreements between the United States and the parties to the multilateral accord, nothing would be gained at this stage by taking this matter up along the lines set forth in instruction no. 7941 of April 5, 1946. Therefore, while reference might be made to the past proposal of this Government to modify the existing trade agreement, the Embassy, in taking the matter up with the Brazilian authorities, should concentrate upon the need for the Brazilian Government to give urgent attention to the problem with a view to taking steps to revise the consumption tax law so that it will be in consonance with the relevant provisions of the ITO Charter, and so that the Brazilian delegation at Geneva may be in a position to give definite assurances in this regard.

611.3231/4-847

The Chargé in Brazil (Brooks) to the Secretary of State

RESTRICTED RIO DE JANEIRO, April 8, 1947.
No. 2019

The Embassy has the honor to refer to the Department's instruction no. 576 of March 12, 1947, file no. 611.3231/3-1247, instructing it to bring to the attention of the Brazilian Government the conflict of the existing Brazilian consumption tax law with the trade agreement and the provisions of the ITO Charter, and to its despatch no. 1872 of March 21, 1947,[80] enclosing a copy of a note on the subject sent to the Brazilian Foreign Office.

No reply has as yet been received to the Embassy's note, but the following data is submitted for the Department's information.

A member of the Embassy visited Mr. Arthur Simas Magalhães, Director of Internal Revenue, and, as press notices had indicated studies were to be undertaken for the revision of the consumption

---

[80] Not printed.

tax, the Director was asked whether there was anything new on that subject. Mr. Magalhães said that within a few days the Minister of Finance [81] was expected to appoint members to the committee which would undertake such studies and he would welcome any suggestions the Embassy cared to make. In reply it was said that we had one suggestion to make, which had already been made on various occasions in the past, namely, that the rates on imported and domestic goods be equalized. In reply to that statement Mr. Magalhães said that some preference should always be given to domestic commodities. In view of that reply the essence of the Embassy's note to the Foreign Office was mentioned to him and he was asked whether that note had not yet been brought to his attention. To this he replied in the negative, but expressed considerable interest therein because it might affect the studies to be undertaken.

The contemplated revision of the consumption tax is namely to bring it in line with the provisions of the new Constitution, which provides under article 15, item 6, that goods classified by law as the minimum indispensable to living quarters, wearing apparel, food and medical treatment of persons of restricted economic capacity should be exempt from the consumption tax.

Mr. Magalhães' first reaction to the information contained in the Embassy's note to the Foreign Office appeared to be that much more extensive work would have to be done in connection with the revision if taxes had to be equalized. He mentioned that consumption tax revenue from imported goods amounted to a very large sum and considerable revenue would be lost if the rates were reduced to those applicable to domestic goods. While recognizing that the Internal Revenue office was in a position to find a solution for that problem, it was mentioned that if the revenue feature was the main one to be considered a simple solution appeared to be to average the present rates, i.e., increase the taxes on domestic goods and lower them on imported ones. This solution seemed feasible to him within certain limits. He specifically mentioned the tax on alcoholic beverages, stating that in some cases the rate on those imported was 400% greater than on similar domestic beverages. He said that despite this heavy taxation imports of alcoholic beverages have not decreased, so that it was apparent the imported articles of this class could stand the taxes established, which provided considerable revenue. He added that he was sure the domestic industry could not operate on such heavy taxes and he did not see how the rates could be equalized on beverages without considerable loss of revenue.

---

[81] Pedro Luiz Corrêa e Castro.

BRAZIL 425

832.1561/3-647

The Acting Secretary of State to the Embassy in Brazil

No. 628 WASHINGTON, April 10, 1947.

SIR: There is enclosed a copy of a letter from Moore–McCormack Lines, Inc., together with its enclosures [82] requesting our assistance in bringing about the elimination of preferences being accorded Brazilian vessels in obtaining berths at Rio de Janeiro.

The Department is fully aware of the present congested situation at the port of Rio de Janeiro and realizes that under these circumstances it may be necessary at times to give preference to ships carrying certain cargoes. It is the view of the Department, however, that such priority should be given strictly on the basis of the cargoes carried without preference to the nationality of the ships, and that any regulation which gives Brazilian ships absolute priority over ships of other nationality is a discrimination and objectionable to this Government.

With reference to Section 17 of the act of June 19, 1886 [83] referred to in the attached correspondence, it is the view of the Department that its use to retaliate against foreign shipping would be most undesirable and would only lead to further discriminations and retaliations. The Department is not prepared at present to state what action might properly be taken under the provisions of the law referred to. It is hoped, however, that satisfactory arrangements can be made which would render unnecessary any possible retaliatory action.

It is requested that the Embassy investigate this matter and, unless it perceives objection, take steps with the appropriate Brazilian authorities with a view to having preference for Brazilian vessels removed. In discussing this matter with the Brazilian Government it can be stated that the Department knows no ports in the United States which grant similar preferences for American vessels.

Very truly yours, For the Acting Secretary of State:
W. A. RADIUS

832.5151/5-247

Memorandum by the Chief of the Division of Brazilian Affairs (Dawson)

RESTRICTED [WASHINGTON,] May 2, 1947.

A stabilization fund arrangement between the Brazilian and U.S. Treasuries has been in effect for some time but no use had been made

---

[82] None printed.
[83] 24 Stat. 79; this section authorized the President to exclude ships of a foreign country from those privileges in American ports which were denied American vessels in the ports of that country. Masters of ships who failed to be guided by the law were liable to arrest and trial and their ships to seizure.

of it by Brazil. Mr. Corliss of FN informs me, however, that within the past week Brazil has called on the Treasury twice for exchange under the agreement, the sums involved being $20,000,000 and $40,000,000. As I understand the procedure, Brazil merely earmarks gold which it has on deposit in New York and our Treasury turns over the equivalent in dollars.

This sudden Brazilian use of the stabilization agreement has two interesting implications. It would seem that the Brazilian exchange situation is getting tight, partly as a result of heavy imports from the United States recently. On March 27 Brazil put a long list of commodities of a "luxury or non-essential" nature under import license procedure; interestingly enough these included such items as soap and shoes so there is probably a little protection mixed up in the measure. The Brazilian efforts to get their blocked currency holdings in Great Britain unfrozen are an added indication along this line.

The other important aspect is that Brazil has not yet taken any action to participate in the Monetary Fund.[84] It has neither indicated the exchange rate it desires nor has it paid in its contribution to the Monetary Fund. We are thus in the somewhat anomalous position of supporting Brazilian exchange by a private agreement between the two Treasuries when the Monetary Fund has been set up for the very purpose and the Brazilians are delaying action to take advantage of it.

The Treasury stabilization agreement expires June 30 but presumably our Treasury would be amenable to extension, since there is no risk involved, unless somebody desires to use non-extension as a lever to get Brazil active in the Monetary Fund.

ALLAN DAWSON

832.5151/7-1147 : Airgram

The Chargé in Brazil (Brooks) to the Secretary of State

CONFIDENTIAL   RIO DE JANEIRO, July 11, 1947.

A-567. Note to FonOff reproduced in Embassy Airgram No. A-561 of July 9, 1947 was sent following receipt of Deptel 718, July 3, which was presumed to have been sent in reply to Embtel 810 of July 1.[85] This form of presentation was considered preferable to further in-

---

[84] The International Monetary Fund was established as a result of the decisions of the United Nations Monetary and Financial Conference held at Bretton Woods, New Hampshire, in July 1944. In airgram A-496, June 13, 1947, the Ambassador in Brazil reported that he had reminded the Brazilian Foreign Office that Brazil, while one of the seven countries to ratify the agreements of that Conference, had not deposited her financial commitments with the Fund (832.5151/6-1347).

[85] None printed.

formal discussions, in view completely unreceptive attitude Exchange Director reported in Embtel 805, June 30.[86]

It will be noted that Embassy's note to FonOff did not include reference to Commerce suggestion that Brazilian authorities consider requiring importers to obtain exchange permits prior to placing orders with foreign firms, providing this could be done without conflicting with Trade Agreement provisions. This subject was omitted from note in the thought that the Department and Commerce might care to consider matter further in light considerations mentioned below.

As new controls do not in themselves prohibit importation of, or payment for, any merchandise, their restrictive effect is indirect and fundamentally dependent upon the very uncertainty as regards payment which the American exporter is understandably most anxious to eliminate.

The introduction of prior exchange licensing system would inject further complications into an already confused situation at this end and might easily and logically result in the necessity of setting up an undesirable quota system not involved in current controls. To some extent the "anuência previa", or prior approval, system now in effect and which automatically confers one-time first category status on approved goods, might be regarded by the authorities as a substitute for exchange license.

From Brazil's point of view the regulations as now constituted are beautifully simple. The fact that any balance of payments' disequilibrium is absorbed by delays in payment rather than by quantitative limitations on imports, and that exchange authorizations are on a day-to-day or week-to-week basis, renders quotas and exchange budgeting unnecessary. An exchange permit system would represent little advantage to foreign firms unless necessary funds were earmarked and set aside by authorities here when permit is approved. Most of the burden resulting from the imposition of the new regulations is, in effect, now placed on foreign exporters. Prior assurance to Brazilian importers and foreign exporters regarding availability of exchange for any particular transaction, no matter how advantageous to foreign firms, would be in direct contravention of the concepts underlying the current system, and a mere suggestion to that effect would almost certainly be rejected.

Embassy accordingly feels that such a suggestion would constitute, or at least might be interpreted as constituting, a request for a basic recasting of current control system, and that if it is made it should be carefully planned in advance, particularly as regards actual and potential conflicts with international agreements in general and

---

[86] Not printed.

Trade Agreements in particular. Further and detailed instructions on this point will be awaited.

BROOKS

560.AL/7–2447 : Telegram

The Consul at Geneva (Troutman) to the Secretary of State

SECRET   US URGENT   GENEVA, July 24, 1947—6 p. m.

765. Fr[om] ITO 150. For Armour.[87] Following serious situation has arisen with Brazilians here:

Trade agreement negotiations with Brazil have for some time been practically completed except for pending problem of possible Brazilian action to increase all concession rates agreed to at Geneva by 40% as measure to offset long standing depreciation of cruzeiro. Matter has now come to a head. Brazilians argue their proposed action is no different than that by many other countries in past years. Timing however is most unfortunate and we cannot see possibility of accepting new agreement with Brazil in which all rates of duty against US products covered would be raised while were were offering bindings or reductions. Brazilians feeling they are obtaining little in tariff negotiations here except from US and claiming little to gain from charter say they will be forced to withdraw delegation unless we will approve and support their proposed action. Presumably they would be forced later also to denounce present trade agreement with US to obtain sufficient freedom of action and this has been hinted.

Discounting how much Brazilians may be bluffing, situation still serious. Support by US of their position would doubtless open door to similar requests from various other countries which could come close to wrecking tariff negotiations here, already very difficult.

We have discussed proposed action exhaustively but unsuccessfully with Brazilians in endeavor to find acceptable compromise. We recognize most Brazilian duties are now low and would probably still be moderate even after proposed increase. We also recognize their request is reasonable compared with action by other countries in past years to offset depreciation but after full discussion in delegation and weighing effect on conference here we feel our position subject to decision by Clayton [88] when he returns tomorrow must be to refuse to agree to Brazilian proposal.

---

[87] Norman Armour, Assistant Secretary of State for Political Affairs.
[88] William L. Clayton, Chairman of the United States Delegation to the meeting of the International Trade Organization Preparatory Committee at Geneva, Switzerland, April 1947.

Brazilians have discussed matter only with US but will bring question before Conference Committee July 29. Please wire urgently Department's views on possible political consequences with Brazil. [ITO.]

TROUTMAN

560.AL/7–2547 : Telegram

The Secretary of State to the Consulate at Geneva

SECRET   US URGENT   WASHINGTON, July 25, 1947—8 p. m.

891. To ITO 152. Embassy Rio has been asked to approach FonOff informally with view to latter's instructing Brazilian delegation Geneva to postpone any action along lines indicated urtel 765 July 24 FrITO 150 (which has been repeated to Rio) for at least week to enable further discussions to take place in Geneva and perhaps here and in Rio. It has been pointed out that Clayton only due return Geneva today and that Dept would like him to have full opportunity to consider matter.

Dept inclined to concur that our position must be to refuse to agree with Brazilian proposal if presented but it feels every effort should be made to convince Brazilians to withhold action. Embassy Rio of opinion that Brazilian proposed action is for protective reasons rather than to produce revenue which complicates possibility of finding acceptable compromise. Dept feels Brazilian position is probably influenced most by unbalanced trade position and resulting dollar exchange problem.

MARSHALL

560.AL/7–2847 : Telegram

The Consul at Geneva (Troutman) to the Secretary of State

SECRET   US URGENT   GENEVA, July 28, 1947—11 p. m.

781. FrITO 153. Deptel 891, to ITO 152.[88a] Clayton discussed problem exhaustively with Brazilians today. They were adamant and although agreeing to delay for a week formal presentation of case to full conference until Washington and Rio could be consulted, will submit matter to small subcommission tomorrow. This may allow Embassy Rio approach to Foreign Office to have some effect but we are not hopeful. Brazilians say their instruction specific and positive and [no?] possibility of change and they are already late in complying. We will attempt here to work out some technical device to solve problem and would appreciate suggestions but Brazilians appear unwilling

---

[88a] *Supra.*

to consider any method by which for example increases might be stated in ad valorem terms.

Until agreement was finally reached for week delay firm Brazilian position as that they could not make any trade agreements here and might withdraw delegate if not allowed to take action desired and Clayton said if pressed for answer today it would have to be no. Comments on political aspects would be helpful.

Sent Department 781, repeated Rio. [ITO.]

TROUTMAN

560.AL/8–347 : Telegram

The Consul at Geneva (Troutman) to the Secretary of State

SECRET GENEVA, August 3, 1947—9 a. m.

808. Fr ITO 165. Fr ITO 150 [89] and following. For CP and personal attention Blaisdell,[90] Commerce and Wheeler,[91] Agriculture. Brazilians have presented their case for tariff rate increases to small Conference Subcommission which agreed matter should come before entire Conference August 8. We have studied matter further in attempt to find some solution which would permit increases in low specific rates which would not affect our trade adversely and permit conclusion of agreement in the absence of which and following hinted denunciation of present US-Brazilian trade agreement Brazil would be free to increase rates much beyond proposed 40 per cent.

Trade Agreements Commission today approved informing Brazilians that we would recommend to our Government acceptance of following proposal, it to be understood that we were not committed until such acceptance obtained.

1. We would agree proposed specific duty increases in cases where resulting ad valorem equivalent would on basis of latest available unit values, still be moderate and less than prewar (big bulk of imports from US would, after increase and on basis latest available unit values, have ad valorem equivalent 20 per cent or less with most under 10 per cent).

2. There should be excepted from increases those products whose resulting ad valorem equivalent would be higher (even though less than prewar) and we would attempt negotiate further duty reductions in these.

3. Depending how successful we were in point 2, we would or would

---

[89] Department telegram 765, July 24, p. 428.
[90] Thomas C. Blaisdell, Director, Office of International Trade, Department of Commerce.
[91] Leslie A. Wheeler, Director, Office of Foreign Agricultural Relations, Department of Agriculture.

not withdraw certain Schedule II concessions on items on which it had been difficult for us to offer duty reduction on bindings.

4. A formula would be provided whereby Brazilian specific duties affected by increases would be reduced as postwar prices declined so as to maintain as maximum the ad valorem equivalents ultimately negotiated here.

. . . .

If our proposal not accepted by Brazilians, then our position would be to oppose acceptance by conference of their plan.

Comment on foregoing desired soonest.

Sent Dept 808, repeated to Rio. [ITO.]

TROUTMAN

560.AL/8-647 : Telegram

The Ambassador in Brazil (Pawley) to the Secretary of State

SECRET   RIO DE JANEIRO, August 6, 1947—4 p. m.

1053. Following telegram intended as Embassy comment on Geneva's 808,[92] repeated Rio on August 3 in connection with Brazilian proposal to increase tariff rates.

Embassy believes some difficulty to be encountered in making comparison between present and pre-war values mentioned under heading number 1. Brazilian import statistics show weights and values not number of units. It would appear unlikely that Brazilians would accept values based on US export data. Under implementation explanation it is assumed that varying unit values and specific rates would be determined by Brazilians but this difficult if not impossible due reason given above. Furthermore Brazilian import statistics usually 5 to 6 months late in preparation and serious lag in making adjustment could be anticipated.

If Dept and USDel Geneva recognize fact that current Brazilian import duties are low and can with justification be increased the Embassy is at a loss to [apparent omission] suggestion contained under item number 3. Many concessions now offered Brazil according Embassy's understanding based on desire US to reduce trade barriers and assist economic development this country. Elimination of any concessions now offered might run counter these purposes.

Embassy offers foregoing purely as comment telegram under reference and not as critique of proposal outlined by Geneva Delegation.

Sent Dept 1053, repeated Geneva.

PAWLEY

---

[92] *Supra.*

560.AL/8-647 : Telegram

The Secretary of State to the Consulate at Geneva

SECRET   URGENT   WASHINGTON, August 6, 1947—7 p. m.

962. To ITO 173. From Commerce, Agriculture and State. Com, Agric and State are in general agreement with your proposal Fr ITO 165, Aug 3.[93] In view sharp price rise and general low level existing Brazilian duties, moderate increases in duty on basis indicated urtel could be agreed to, provided firm provision made, as urtel indicates it will be, for downward revision of rates in event price decline. Depts agree, for reasons (especially possibility similar requests from other countries) indicated Fr ITO 150, July 24,[94] it is regrettable to conclude agreement which would permit later increased duties on scheduled products but feel such agreement is better than none at all, in which latter case Brazil might raise duties in any event and without limitation resulting from negotiation.

Depts offer following specific comments your proposal Fr ITO 165:

(1) Depts agree your para 1. Think "less than prewar" particularly important.

(2) Depts agree your para 2, and interpret reference to "higher" to mean higher than ad valorem equivalent specified in para 1, namely 20 per cent. As for products falling in your para 2 classification, Depts assume you will endeavor to prevent any increase in duty concessions which Brazilians have already tentatively offered. (In addition, we also assume Brazilian proposal to mean that no item now free of duty will be made dutiable and are concerned particularly on Brazil's retaining all offers for binding duty-free status.)

(3) Depts agree your para 3 and leave possible concession withdrawals to your discretion.

(4) Re your para 4, Depts agree that agreement should provide for principle of downward revision of rates in event price decline but feel your proposed formula presents great administrative difficulties and may prove unworkable. If time allows, alternative formulas might be developed here for use in connection Brazilian and similar situations that might develop. However, if Brazilians accept your formula, suggest you proceed on that basis, and difficulties which may develop subsequently can be worked out then. As final alternative, suggest you might proceed on basis commitment in principle to reduce specific rates in event postwar price decline without attempting to work out at this time specific formula for implementing this commitment.

MARSHALL

---

[93] Department telegram 808, p. 430.
[94] Department telegram 765, p. 428.

711.322/8-1847 : Telegram

The Ambassador in Brazil (Pawley) to the Secretary of State

CONFIDENTIAL   PRIORITY   RIO DE JANEIRO, August 18, 1947—8 p. m.

1124. Within past few days I have discussed with President Dutra desirability completing negotiations proposed treaty of commerce, navigation and friendship between Brazil and the United States with idea having treaty ready for signature at time of President Truman's visit to Brazil.[95] President Dutra has indicated his full agreement with this plan and is issuing a directive to the Brazilian Foreign Office for immediate initiative negotiations.

The Brazilian Government has requested that treaty be enlarged by the addition of a short chapter on economic development and investment. The Embassy has consequently drafted such a chapter which is being submitted to the Brazilians as a basis for discussion and negotiation. The text of this proposed chapter follows:

"The two high contracting parties recognize that the development and maintenance of a broad industrial and economic foundation is dependent upon, among other things, the availability, under fair and equitable terms and conditions, of capital funds, raw or processed materials, machinery and equipment, technology, trained personnel, and managerial skill. Both parties agree that no unreasonable impediments will be imposed by one against the other which might prejudice or prevent the development and maintenance of a wide and varied foundation of industrial and economic activity, and both parties undertake to extend to each other full cooperation and assistance towards this end. It is further recognized that the attainment of such industrial and economic development can be greatly facilitated by the free flow of capital funds for investment, that such capital should be available upon reasonable terms and conditions, and that it should be invested for productive purposes economically suited to the area for which it is intended and in a manner consistent with the best interests of both the supplying and recipient countries.

"The contracting powers agree not to take any unreasonable actions which might prove to be directly or indirectly injurious to the interests of the other or to its nationals and legal entities. Not by way of limitation the following special circumstances are provided for:

"(1). In all cases when one party may find it necessary to default on the service of a debt obligation to the other party, or the latter's nationals, prompt negotiations shall be undertaken with a view to arriving at an adjustment which will be fair and nondiscriminatory.

"(2). Each contracting party, its nationals and its legal entities, shall enjoy full and complete most-favored-nation treatment

---

[95] See White House press release of August 6, 1947, Department of State *Bulletin*, August 17, 1947, p. 341.

as regards the investment of capital. It is understood that this treatment is to apply to investments which have been made in the past, as well as to those which may be made in the future.

"(3). Neither contracting party shall establish any restrictions on the transfer of funds for the payment of interest, dividends, and a moderate amount for the amortization of loans or for depreciation of direct investments, except as may be mutually agreed upon after consultation and which are permitted, under the articles of agreement of the International Monetary Fund.

"It is recognized that there are numerous mutual advantages to be derived from joint undertakings involving capital and management from the territories of both contracting parties. Accordingly it is agreed that the opportunities for the voluntary participation in joint undertakings of such capital and management shall be free and unrestricted. It is further recognized that laws or regulations which compel the participation of domestic capital and management in an enterprise may reduce the amount of foreign capital available, and may impede economic development, and it is agreed that neither of the contracting parties shall adopt laws or regulations compelling such participation except in those special fields where fundamental national security may be concerned."

Department will note in foregoing draft that an effort has been made to follow proposed revision of chapter 4 of the ITO charter as approved on May 27, 1947 by Executive Commission on Economic Foreign Policy. Expropriation clause has been deleted as draft treaty appears to adequately cover this point article V, paragraph 2. The inclusion of this new chapter also presumes changes in the draft treaty article XVII paragraph 3. Conversations with Brazilian Govt are expected to begin immediately and Dept's recommendations and suggestions, regarding the draft incorporated in this telegram, are urgently requested.

PAWLEY

832.1561/8–1947

The Ambassador in Brazil (Pawley) to the Secretary of State

CONFIDENTIAL
No. 2697

RIO DE JANEIRO, August 19, 1947.

SIR: I have the honor to refer to the Department's A–462 of August 4, 1947, and to the Embassy's telegram no. 1089 of August 12, 6 p. m.,[96] regarding discriminatory treatment by the Brazilian Government in favor of Lloyd Brasileiro vessels in the ports of Rio de Janeiro and Santos.

The Embassy has been in close touch with American steamship

---

[96] Neither printed.

agencies in Rio de Janeiro, and, as the Department is aware, representations have been made to various officials including the Minister of Transportation and Public Works.[97] No improvement in the treatment accorded American vessels was noted as a result of these conversations, and during my call on President Dutra on August 12, I took occasion to discuss the entire question with him, using as an example the enclosed schedule [98] which lists comparative dates of arrival in port and docking of two Moore-McCormack vessels and four vessels of Lloyd Brasileiro. The preferential treatment accorded the vessels of the latter line is obvious, and the President expressed himself as being astonished that the discrimination was so flagrant. He promised that he would take immediate steps to see that each vessel arriving in Brazilian ports would be accorded equal treatment, the priority arrangement presumably to be based upon the type of cargo carried and in no way to relate to the flag under which the vessel operated. I mentioned to the President the fact that the only other country practicing such discrimination was Argentina,[99] and he stated that he certainly did not want Brazil placed in such a category.

I do not know that President Dutra has sufficient authority to correct this situation, even though the regulations under which the priorities have been established are executive rather than legislative. There will no doubt be strong opposition to removal of the priority in favor of Lloyd Brasileiro vessels, but I am certain that the President intends to put forth his best efforts to assure equitable treatment to United States flag vessels.

Any further developments that may take place affecting the situation in the ports of Rio de Janeiro and Santos will be communicated to the Department immediately.

Respectfully yours, WILLIAM D. PAWLEY

711.322/8–1847 : Telegram

The Acting Secretary of State to the Embassy in Brazil

CONFIDENTIAL WASHINGTON, August 25, 1947—4 p. m.

963. Embtel 1124, Aug 18, 1947. Dept does not object in principle provisions on economic development and investment if Brazil desires them. Substance most Emb's proposals generally in accord Dept's views and with its proposals at Geneva. Some important changes required in substance, however, and proposals need correlation with

[97] Clovis Pestana.
[98] Not printed.
[99] See pp. 251 ff.

commercial treaty articles and provisions ITO Charter. Improbable this work could be accomplished in time meet negotiation schedule related President Truman's visit. Charter provisions on economic development approved Geneva not yet available Dept.

In view foregoing, Dept suggests emphasis upon reaching agreement on provisions previously submitted draft commercial treaty. In meantime Dept will undertake preparation provisions on economic development and investment suitable incorporation in treaty, and, if agreement is reached on remainder of treaty, will do utmost meet timing requirements negotiation. Emb requested communicate soonest Brazilian views on content proposed new chapter.

Dept assigns great importance early negotiation treaty friendship, commerce and navigation, and desires be informed soonest acceptability draft treaty to Brazilians.[1]

LOVETT

832.1561/9–247 : Airgram

The Ambassador in Brazil (Pawley) to the Secretary of State

RIO DE JANEIRO, September 2, 1947.

A–698. At the close of business on August 29, 1947, the Association of Steamship Owners which has for some time published a list of vessels awaiting berth in the port of Rio de Janeiro advertised that no ships were awaiting berthing facilities. A letter dated August 30, 1947, was addressed to F. V. De Miranda Carvalho, Superintendent of the Rio de Janeiro Port Administration, which read as follows:

"The Association, on the occasion of announcing for the first time after trying months of prolonged delay suffered by vessels which had come to unload in this port, that there was not a single ship awaiting docking space, feels the necessity of addressing to Your Excellency its sincere congratulations in the conviction that your resolution and high degree of efficiency will result in the completion of the necessary measures for the full normalization of the port. . . ."

. . . .

The representatives of the various American shipping companies are quite pleased by the recent publication of the revised docking priorities which gave cargo ships awaiting space for more than 15 days a priority over Lloyd Brasileiro vessels (reference Embassy airgram A–694 dated August 29, 1947 [2]). Notwithstanding the general feeling

---

[1] The treaty in this form was not concluded. An exchange of notes supplementing the General Agreement on Tariffs and Trade of October 30, 1947, was effected on June 30, 1948. See Department of State Treaties and Other International Acts Series No. 1811.

[2] Not printed.

of satisfaction at the improvement of the port situation and the alteration of existing regulations it is nevertheless agreed that it would be desirable for all parties to continue to make every effort to secure the complete elimination of the priority granted to Lloyd Brasileiro vessels.

PAWLEY

832.1561/9–2547

The Chief of the Division of Brazilian Affairs (Dawson) to the Counselor of Embassy for Economic Affairs in Brazil (Brooks)

CONFIDENTIAL WASHINGTON, September 25, 1947.

DEAR CLARENCE: This is just to let you know that resentment against the continued Brazilian discrimination in favor of Lloyd Brasileiro ships is increasing here and that we may be faced by some unfortunate developments unless there are shortly some obvious results from the Ambassador's last conversation with President Dutra.

One thing which has particularly annoyed the American competition here (specifically, Moore-McCormack) is the fact that the Lloyd Brasileiro representatives in New York and New Orleans have been sounding off about their privileges in an attempt to get business away from Moore-McCormack, Delta, etc. The latter consider this dirty ball and are incensed. An example is the following excerpt from the Shipping Notes section of the September 23 issue of the *New York Journal of Commerce:*

"Lloyd Brasileiro Priorities—Lloyd Brasileiro still retains priority in the docking of both passenger and cargo vessels at Rio de Janeiro, a spokesman for the line stated yesterday. He said that cabled advices from the Brazilian capital provide that the only freighters that can be docked before those of the line are those which have been waiting in port for berthing facilities fifteen days or longer. Passenger vessels of the line get first call on berthing space. Then come those of other lines providing they do not carry more than 500 tons of cargo and then come cargo vessels which have been waiting two weeks. After these have been accommodated, Lloyd Brasileiro vessels are berthed ahead of those of all other claimants for berth space."

The Moore-McCormack people are making noises about bringing the question of discrimination up before the appropriate House and Senate Committees if remedial action is not forthcoming in the near future. I imagine that this, with stress on the angle of the loans with which Lloyd Brasileiro is getting the additions to its fleet, might well lead to a Congressional investigation. There are plenty of people anxious to discredit the Administration and to draw a conclusion that it is not sufficiently vigilant on behalf of American interests when it loans money for a rival to compete with American shipping and yet cannot prevent discrimination in favor of the rival at U.S. lines' expense.

In this general connection, I think I have already written you that the Maritime Commission suggested to the White House that retaliatory action under the enabling legislation in one of the Maritime Acts might be considered and that the White House passed this on to the Department for its comment. This would indicate that the Maritime Commission might well go along with the trade in wanting to bring the whole thing out in a public hearing.

There is another angle which may make retaliatory action more likely. I understand that the Ingalls [3] people are not satisfied with their contract with the Lloyd Brasileiro and would not be averse to getting out of it. It is consequently conceivable that they would put no obstacles in the way of suggestions that the loan on which the contract is based might be held up in the hope that this would enable them to break the contract.

All of this is pretty speculative, I know, but I have wanted to let you know that there is a good deal of smoke at this end. Frankly, I think the Brazilians have been dogs in the manger on the whole matter. They may furthermore turn out to have been stupid in pursuing a minor untenable advantage at the serious risk of losing a great deal in (*a*) good will and (*b*) actual economic benefits. It would certainly be to neither the Brazilian Government's interest nor ours to have the shipping discrimination question degenerate into a name-calling contest.

Best luck to you,
  Always sincerely,   ALLAN DAWSON

832.1561/9–3047

The Chief of the Division of Brazilian Affairs (Dawson) to the Counselor of Embassy for Economic Affairs in Brazil (Brooks)

CONFIDENTIAL   WASHINGTON, September 30, 1947.

DEAR CLARENCE: I have just talked over the telephone with the Ambassador in Miami. Although most of the conversation was about other matters, which I have more or less covered in the postscript of a letter to David Key,[4] we touched on the shipping discrimination question.

I told the Ambassador of some of the developments mentioned in my letter of September 25 to you on the subject. He reacted by telling

---

[3] Presumably the Ingalls Shipbuilding Corporation of Birmingham, Alabama.
[4] Chargé in Brazil.

me that, in his last conversation with Dutra, the latter had definitely stated, as reported by the Embassy telegraphically, that the discrimination would be brought to an end. Mr. Pawley went on to say that he thought you should push the matter vigorously, by a note to the Foreign Office if there was no progress, and commented that there was plenty of material in the Embassy's files from Moore-McCormack on which to base a strong case.

Lalley of Moore-McCormack has been in to see me twice more since I last wrote you on the subject. He says that he has been doing more talking not only with the Maritime Commission but with the Export-Import Bank people on the anomaly of our financing Lloyd Brasileiro expansion when Brazil is discriminating against American shipping. According to Lalley, his bosses are ready to "bust the situation wide open" by newspaper publicity or passing word along to an appropriate Congressional committee. I counseled him to insist with his principals that they hold off until we could see what the results were of the Ambassador's talk with Dutra. As you will gather, the pressure is getting stronger here all the time to do something.

Let us know promptly of developments, will you, so that we can try to calm down angered spirits.

Wayne Clark[5] rolled in on Saturday and is already ensconced at his desk next door. With his able assistance, perhaps I can shortly become more of a man of leisure (if not distinction) than has heretofore been practicable.

With cordial personal regards,

Yours, as ever, ALLAN DAWSON

832.1561/11–1047 : Telegram

The Secretary of State to the Embassy in Brazil

CONFIDENTIAL   WASHINGTON, November 12, 1947—6 p. m.

1269. Urtel 1566 Nov 10.[6] Braz Emb has informed Dept receipt FonOff cable making following points:

a) priority dock space granted only Lloyd Brasileiro not other Braz cos

b) purpose priority to assure supply foodstuffs from other Braz ports

c) preferences now ineffective since port Rio now uncongested

d) at present not single vessel awaiting berth.

Your comments desired. Points *a* and *b* appear specious. Are points *c* and *d* accurate? Even if so discrimination could be restored at any

---

[5] DuWayne G. Clark, Assistant Chief, Division of Brazilian Affairs.
[6] Not printed.

time. You will recall that Pres Dutra informed Amb Pawley he would immediately issue instructions cease discrimination between vessels flying Braz and Am flags (pgh 1 urtel 1324 Sept 20 [7]). FonOff explanation in no way appears to implement this assurance.

MARSHALL

832.1561/11–1447

The Chargé in Brazil (Key) to the Secretary of State

CONFIDENTIAL   RIO DE JANEIRO, November 14, 1947—1 p. m.

1582. Discussed with Foreign Minister [8] last night four points cited Deptel 1269, November 12, pointing out to him that validity of point (*a*) impaired by fact that to all practical purposes Lloyd Brasileiro sole Brazilian entity operating vessels engaged in international trade and that docking facilities coastwise trade have heretofore been ample; that since Lloyd Brasileiro vessels engaged in overseas trade do not generally carry foodstuffs from other Brazilian ports this being task almost exclusively of coastwise trade vessels which not affected by priorities. Present priority system does not therefore assure supply foodstuffs from Brazilian ports as claimed point (*b*); that point (*c*) not accurate since beginning November eight vessels have been accumulating in stream Rio and at close business November 12, five vessels were awaiting berthing facilities. Of these *Mormacsea* in number 1 position liable under present priority system to be superseded by Lloyd Brasileiro vessels in positions 2 and 3; that consequently statement point (*d*) erroneous.

I urged Foreign Minister to review question in light of foregoing and of assurances given to Ambassador Pawley by President Dutra with a view to rescinding without delay if possible pertinent sections of administrative orders extending preferences to Lloyd Brasileiro vessels.

I mentioned also that US shipping circles resented discriminations resulting from preferential treatment accorded Lloyd Brasileiro vessels, that they were becoming impatient because of failure of Brazilian authorities to correct the situation and that unless remedial action were soon forthcoming there was danger situation would get out of hand and pressure develop to point where American shipping interests would demand US Government take counter measures under existing legislation. I added that the easing in the berthing situation Rio would appear to make removal of present discriminatory measures correspondingly easier.

---

[7] Not printed.
[8] Raul Fernandes.

Fernandes agreed to review Brazilian position at once and to investigate possibility of rescinding administrative orders above mentioned which he felt would have immediate practical effect of abolishing discriminations and which could be done without requiring Congressional action which would be necessary were the decree law on basis of which the administrative orders were promulgated to be modified or repealed.[9]

KEY

EFFORTS OF THE UNITED STATES TO PROVIDE FINANCIAL ASSISTANCE FOR BRAZILIAN ECONOMIC DEVELOPMENT [10]

832.51/1–2147 : Telegram

The Ambassador in Brazil (Pawley) to the Secretary of State

CONFIDENTIAL   RIO DE JANEIRO, January 21, 1947—7 p. m.

85. I have just received memo from José Pimenta, President, Cia Vale Rio Doce,[11] reference loan $7,500,000 which Brazil is endeavoring to negotiate with Export-Import Bank for completion Rio Doce project, setting forth following items for which this money is needed:

(1) railroad equipment, cement, explosives, structural steel, trucks, and automobiles to be imported from US;
(2) payment salaries American technical personnel engaged in project;
(3) payment American engineering firms who hold contracts for completion of railway.

PAWLEY

832.51/2–1347

Memorandum by Mr. Richard F. O'Toole of the Division of Brazilian Affairs to the Chief of That Division (Dawson)

RESTRICTED   [WASHINGTON,] February 13, 1947.

Subject: Application of Cia. Vale do Rio Doce for Additional Loan of $7,500,000 from Export-Import Bank.

The attached copy of a memorandum [12] prepared in Export-Import Bank, addressed to the Board of Directors, recommends approval of

---

[9] In telegram 1681, December 6, the Chargé reported that the berthing priority accorded to Lloyd Brasileiro had been cancelled (832.1561/12–647).
[10] For documentation on the concern of the United States with Brazilian financial problems in 1946, see *Foreign Relations*, 1946, vol XI, pp. 485 ff.
[11] Brazilian governmental corporation which mined and exported iron ore. See *ibid.*, 1942, vol. v, pp. 678–679, 690, and 690n.
[12] Not printed.

the above credit. Action on this matter is now scheduled for the Board meeting on Wednesday, February 19 and ED would like BA's policy decision by Monday afternoon, February 17.

Up to now $46,000,000 has been expended on this project, of which $19,000,000 was loaned to the Company by Export Import Bank,—$5,000,000 of which is guaranteed by the Brazilian Treasury. Of the remaining $14,000,000 one-half represents participation of Lend-Lease funds.

It is now proposed to invest a further $20,000,000 in the project of which about $7,500,000 would represent new money from Export-Import Bank, the Brazilian Government agreeing to advance Cr$240,-000,000 from the Brazilian Treasury. Included in the terms governing the proposed $7,500,000, to be furnished by Export Import Bank, are the following:—

1) Repayment of principal over 15 years to commence three years after date of the contract.
2) Interest 3–1/2 percent per annum.
3) Obligation of the Company for the $7,500,000 to be unconditionally guaranteed by the Brazilian Treasury.
4) Period of application of proceeds of ore sales towards retirement of existing $14,000,000 loan of Export Import Bank, to be extended five years.

Present construction program of the project is based upon an annual production and export sale of 1,500,000 tons of ore. American steel interests apparently believe that the project could not be made to pay out either on the basis of the present production target or on the amount of the proposed increased capital investment. These same interests, according to Ambassador Pawley's airgram 1358 of December 27, 1946 and his letter of January 6, 1947 [13] to Mr. Clayton,[14] believe that it would require a further investment of $100,000,000 and an annual production and sale of 5,000,000 tons of ore to put the project on a paying basis. I understand that these same interests believe that it would be necessary to construct an entirely new standard-gauge, double-track railway and the abandonment of the present railroad to commercial uses.

In addition, Bethlehem Steel Company is putting $40,000,000 into an iron ore project on the Orinoco River, near seaboard, in Venezuela. The quality of the Venezuelan ore is reputed to be as good as that of Itabira while the hauling distance to Bethlehem Steel's Sparrows Point plant at Baltimore is only about half the distance from Victoria, Brazil.

---

[13] Neither printed.
[14] William L. Clayton, Under Secretary of State for Economic Affairs.

Unless and until it can be satisfactorily established that Itabira ore can be marketed, on a competitive basis, during the life of existing Export-Import Bank loans it is my judgment that a further investment is not justified.

832.51/2–2047

Memorandum by the Chief of the Division of Brazilian Affairs (Dawson)[15]

[WASHINGTON,] February 20, 1947.

The Eximbank Board yesterday approved the $7,500,000 loan application of the Cia. Vale do Rio Doce. The loan would be fully guaranteed by the Brazilian Government and would be contingent upon Brazilian Congressional approval including appropriation of the $12,000,000 which the Brazilian Government is to put up, $400,000 a month.

BA's memorandum of February 14 [16] routed to ED and OFD, concurred in by Messrs. Braden and Briggs, makes it clear that the appropriate political officers of the Department do not favor the granting of the loan. Whether this was brought to Mr. Clayton's attention before the meeting of the Eximbank Board I do not know.[17]

ALLAN DAWSON

832.51/3–2147

Memorandum by the Chief of the Division of Brazilian Affairs (Dawson)[18]

[WASHINGTON,] March 21, 1947.

You will recall ARA's strenuous objections to the Eximbank approval of the new $7,500,000 credit for the Cia. Vale do Rio Doce about a month ago. Figures on the interest payments on the original $14,000,000 loan not guaranteed by the Brazilian Government have just come to light. These show that $1,429,000 interest had accrued through May 7, 1946 and that payments received to that date were $267,000, leaving a balance of lapsed and unpaid interest totaling $1,162,000.

---

[15] Addressed to Messrs. Smith, Wright, and Braden, of A–Br, and to Mr. Briggs of ARA.

[16] Not printed.

[17] A notation in the margin reads: "I don't know definitely, but I am informed that he felt sure enough of the feasibility of the project to warrant giving his OK. H. G. S[mith]."

[18] Addressed to Messrs. Smith, Wright, Woodward, and Braden, of A–Br, and to Mr. Briggs of ARA.

During the rest of 1946 only $26,000 was accumulated to be applied to the current notes, a figure considerably less than in any recent preceding similar period. In other words, the unpaid interest will probably accumulate approximately another $500,000 by May 1947.

The Eximbank has given us no figures as to interest on the subsequent $5,000,000 loan guaranteed by the Brazilian Government. However, since the original loan has first lien on ore sales, transportation costs, et cetera, if anything has been paid on the $5,000,000 loan it will have been by the Brazilian Government, not by the Cia. Vale do Rio Doce.

These figures would seem to indicate that ARA's objections to the new loan were more than sound.

ALLAN DAWSON

811.516 Export-Import Bank/4–2247

Memorandum by the Special Assistant of the Division of Investment and Economic Development (Stenger) to the Director of the Office of Financial and Development Policy (Ness)

[WASHINGTON,] April 22, 1947.

Subject: Agenda for meeting of Board of Directors Eximbank April 23, 1947.

1. Minutes of meeting of April 16, 1947—to be received. They are ok.
2. Minutes of meeting of April 9, 1947—to be approved. They are ok.

For Action:

3. *Brazil—Sorocabana Railway.* The request is for a credit of $6,649,021. The Electrical Export Corporation (The International General Electric Company and the Westinghouse International Electric Company) requested the Eximbank to participate in financing the sale of 26 electric locomotives, 8 substations, transmission towers and other equipment to the Sorocabana Railway for the electrification of the line running from San Antonio to Bernadina de Campos, a distance of 185 miles. The total amount of the contract is $9,498,602. The Bank was requested to purchase, without recourse, 70% of the notes of the Sorocabana Railway, amounting to $6,649,021. The notes, to be guaranteed by the State of São Paulo, are to mature over a period of 7 years from December 1, 1947 to June 1, 1954, with interest at 4–1/2%.

The request for financing was first submitted to the Bank in June 1945, but action was deferred pending a satisfactory solution of the exchange assurances problem.

The project was again considered by the Board of Directors of the

Bank on December 13 and December 18, 1946. Action was deferred in order that additional information might be obtained regarding the financial status of the State of São Paulo. Reports have now been received which apparently indicate, to the satisfaction of the staff of the Bank, that the finances of the State of São Paulo are such that its guarantee of the obligations would be acceptable.

Recommendation: This project has been cleared with the interested divisions in the Department, and there are no objections to the approval of financing.

4. *Brazil—Sorocabana Railway.* The request is for a credit of $1,500,000. This application is from the Whitcomb Locomotive Company, a subsidiary of the Baldwin Locomotive Works, for a credit of $1,500,000 to finance, without recourse, 75% of $2 million, the cost of 15 diesel-electric locomotives purchased by the Sorocabana Railway. As in the preceding case, the Bank has been asked to accept the notes of the Railway, guaranteed by the State of São Paulo, which are to mature over a period of 5 years with interest at 4–1/2% per annum. The history in this case is similar to the aforementioned case. An application was originally submitted on July 5, 1945 for a credit to finance the sale of 30 diesel-electric locomotives, but no action was taken because it was understood that Sorocabana would arrange for other financing. Other financing had been obtained for the first 15 locomotives, but the Railway requested the builders to finance the remaining 15 in this country. It is this application which was considered at the meeting of the Board of Directors on December 18, 1946, and on which action was deferred pending further investigation of the finances of the State of São Paulo.

It might be well to remark that on February 20, 1946 a credit of $1,925,500 was authorized by the Bank to the Whitcomb Locomotive Company for similar locomotives, and that this credit was cancelled on November 26, 1946 when Whitcomb informed the Bank that the purchasers had made other arrangements for financing.

As stated in connection with the preceding application, a report has recently been received from the American Consulate, São Paulo, which indicates, to the satisfaction of the staff of the Bank, that the finances of the State of São Paulo are such that the present financing can be undertaken without any undue risk.

Recommendation: The Department has no objections to the recommendation of the staff that financing should be approved. This has been cleared with the interested divisions in the Department.[19] The political division (BA) does not feel too happy about the maturity of

---

[19] In the margin appears the notation of approval: "OK, N. N[ess]."

the notes of the Sorocabana Railway. The Bank indicates that the notes will mature over a period of 5 years, the first due 3 months after the average date of completion. The words "average date of completion" appear to disturb BA, and it is of the opinion that, in the absence of a fixed date for the first maturity, some difficulties may arise later regarding the definition of the average date of completion. ED is of the opinion that this is a matter which should be left to the discretion of the Bank.[20]

5. *Brazil—National Alkali Corporation.* This is for a proposed credit of $7,500,000. An application from the National Alkali Corporation of Brazil for a credit of $10 million was considered by the Board of Directors on January 22, 1947, but action was deferred principally because the necessary action had not yet been taken by the NAC. While the NAC on February 18, 1947 approved consideration by the Eximbank, it was felt in the Bank that additional information was necessary before a final conclusion could be reached. This information was received recently.

The National Alkali Corporation is a Brazilian Government corporation with an original capital of $50 million cruzeiros, which is to be increased to $100 million cruzeiros (from approximately $2,500,000 to about $5 million). The Corporation intends to construct a plant to manufacture soda ash and caustic soda. The total cost for construction and installation, it is estimated by the Corporation, will be in the neighborhood of $12,500,000. It will be recalled that, when the application was previously discussed, there was some question about the equity capital. As the capital is now to be about $5 million, it is the opinion of the staff of the Bank that the maximum loan required should be reduced accordingly. In other words, if the total amount required to start operation is approximately $12,500,000 and the equity capital is to be $5 million, a credit of only about $7,500,000 will be required.

The staff of the Bank is convinced that this project is economically sound, and that if the plant is constructed, it would help to solve the problem of Brazil's need for caustic soda and soda ash which is now in very short supply. The Department is in accord with this reasoning.

Recommendation: The staff of the Bank recommends approval of a credit up to $7,500,000 to finance the purchase of U.S. materials, equipment and services, the credit to be repaid in 10 years beginning December 31, 1949 and ending June 30, 1959 with interest at 3-1/2% per annum; [21] the obligations of the corporation to be guaranteed by

---

[20] In the same handwriting in the margin appears the word "yes."
[21] Approval appears in the margin: "OK, N N[ess]."

the Banco do Brasil. The Department does not object to the approval of the proposed recommendation.

* * * * * * *

832.51/6–1247 : Telegram

The Ambassador in Brazil (Pawley) to the Secretary of State

SECRET   RIO DE JANEIRO, June 12, 1947—8 p. m.

719. In effort to bring to successful conclusion number pending questions with Brazilian Government, I requested conference June 10 with President Dutra, Foreign Minister Raul Fernandes, Finance Minister Correa e Castro, and Agricultural Minister Daniel de Carvalho. Entire agenda was not covered but following items were discussed:

1. Monetary fund.[22] Brazil has been granted extension time pending final establishment rate of exchange. President and Ministers indicated definite interest and that Brazil would arrange to participate but would make no commitment regarding date. My opinion is Brazil will join fund but will require further pressure our part if to join near future.

2. Minister Agriculture has submitted memo as basis for possible request Exim Bank loan $450,000,000 to improve transportation system Brazil. I pointed out that recently Finance Minister previously refused a loan of $50,000,000 which had Exim Bank approval for same purpose. I told President Dutra that if Brazil had well-defined program of productive investments then such program could be submitted to World Bank for consideration but offered no encouragement.

* * * * * * *

PAWLEY

832.77/6–1747

The Chief of the Division of Brazilian Affairs (Dawson) to the Ambassador in Brazil (Pawley)

RESTRICTED   WASHINGTON, June 17, 1947.

DEAR MR. AMBASSADOR: With reference to my letter to you of June 3 [23] concerning the visit of various representatives of the concerns interested in the Brazil Railway Company and Port of Pará cases, I

---

[22] International Monetary Fund, an instrumentality resulting from the United Nations Monetary and Financial Conference of July 1944. It was established to promote monetary cooperation, international trade, exchange stability, and to assist in creating a multilateral system of payments in respect of current transactions.

[23] Not printed.

am enclosing a copy of a memorandum dated June 12,[23a] prepared and sent to us by Sullivan and Cromwell, who are counsel for the Chase National Bank, trustees for bonds of the Brazil Railway Company, outlining the whole case as presented to us by the representatives of the various interests involved.

The memorandum asks for our intervention with the Brazilian Government through the Embassy on three main grounds, (a) that the companies concerned are incorporated in the United States (with several subsidiary considerations which come to much the same argument), (b) that it is to our Government's general interest to support the stability of investment abroad whether we are directly concerned or not and (c) that the specific interests of two American banks were involved in the seizure of securities which they were holding as trustees regardless of the ownership of the paper in question. You will find these arguments on pages 10 to 12.

The whole matter is still under study in the Department and there is no telling just when, if ever, instructions to you will be going out. However, I thought you and Clarence Brooks [24] would be interested in the case made by Sullivan and Cromwell, particularly as Eddie Miller, the firm's representative will be in Rio before long and calling on you.

My guess is that the Department will maintain its refusal to intervene directly in the question of the seizure of the Brazil Railway and Port of Pará properties, as it has in the past, on the traditional ground that substantial American interest in the companies in the form of ownership has not been shown. So much for argument (a). Argument (b) can be discounted, of course, as too general. However, I think it very likely that the Department will feel that it is in a position to take a stand under argument (c) for the return to the Chase National Bank and Empire Trust Company of the securities held by them as trustees and seized in 1941 as part of the assets of the two companies, a very different matter than the general problem and one in which there is a direct American interest.

Incidentally, the French and Belgian Embassies have asked the Department for its support in *démarches* being made by their missions in Rio de Janeiro on behalf of the bondholders who are, of course, mainly French, Belgian and British. We have not yet been approached by the British Embassy although the French and Belgians assert that the British are also making representations in Rio. The answers which have been drafted to the French and Belgian communications but have not yet gone out take the traditional stand outlined above. Since the French and Belgians did not raise the question of the position of

---

[23a] Not printed.
[24] Counselor of Embassy for Economic Affairs in Brazil.

the Chase Bank and Empire Trust Company as trustees and this is a matter which concerns only this Government, this point has not been touched on in the draft replies.

With cordial personal regards,
Very sincerely yours,
ALLAN DAWSON

811.516 Export-Import Bank/7–2347

Memorandum by Mr. Richard F. O'Toole of the Division of Brazilian Affairs to the Chief of That Division (Dawson)

CONFIDENTIAL [WASHINGTON,] July 23, 1947.

Subject: Visit of Brazilian Ambassador to Export-Import Bank on Thursday July 17.

Mr. Stenger told me that on the occasion of this visit Ambassador Martins, accompanied by Celso Garcia (Second Secretary) visited Mr. Martin, President of Export-Import Bank.

The Ambassador, apparently in a sour mood, intimated that Brazilian financial projects were not getting the attention they deserved and said that he was leaving for Rio in four days and wished to know whether there was anything about the Bank's interest in Brazil's affairs that he ought to take back with him. Mr. Martin outlined the difficulties encountered with the Rio Doce project and read excerpts from a recent telegram about that situation, remarking that the cessation of work and the fact that a lot of valuable equipment was left lying around as a result, was not very satisfactory to the Bank's interest. Mr. Martin then said that the Bank wished to get along as harmoniously as possible with Brazil but that the situation of the Rio Doce project, and the necessity for its completion, created difficulties for the Bank.

Apparently, the Ambassador then went into a tantrum alleging, in effect, that this Government was pulling away from the good neighbor policy and he demanded to know whether Mr. Martin was implying that Brazil would get no more financial assistance until the Rio Doce project was straightened out. Mr. Martin is said to have replied that he considered that to be a fair statement of the situation.

Both the Ambassador and Garcia then brought up the question of the loan application for the petroleum refinery at Rio de Janeiro and the failure to get any action on it up to then. Mr. Martin told him that the reason that no decision had been made was that there were certain questions to be settled relating to the new Constitution, and that the Bank had not yet obtained other adequate information on which to base a decision. The Ambassador then retorted that he was willing to telegraph Rio for any information that the Bank might need and he was joined by Garcia in sarcastic comments to the effect that the real reason for the lack of a decision was because the Bank had not yet gotten Standard Oil Company's approval.

832.77/8-2147

The Embassy in Brazil to the Department of State

RESTRICTED RIO DE JANEIRO, August 21, 1947.
No. 2710

The Embassy has the honor to enclose for the Department's information and records copy of a note, dated July 24, 1947,[25] that has been submitted to the Brazilian Ministry of Foreign Affairs concerning the return of certain funds and securities removed in 1941 by government order from the Brazilian branches of the National City Bank where they had been held on deposit in the names of the Chase National Bank and the Empire Trust Company as trustees for the Brazil Railway Company and the Port of Pará Company respectively.

During the first part of July Mr. Edward Miller of Sullivan & Cromwell visited the Embassy several times to discuss on behalf of the aforementioned trustees, the Brazil Railway Company and the Port of Pará Company, the restitution of the seized funds and securities. As the result of these discussions it was agreed that the Embassy would address a communication to the Ministry of Foreign Affairs reiterating the reservation of all the rights, under Brazilian and international law, of the trustee institutions and urging compliance, at an early date, with the provisions of Minister of Finance certificate of September 28, 1946 directing that the seized cash and securities, as well as dividends on the securities, be returned to the National City Bank.

A copy of the reply [26] of the Ministry of Foreign Affairs to the Embassy's note will be forwarded to the Department when received.

832.77/9-2447

Mr. Walter G. Wiechmann of Sullivan & Cromwell to the Chief of the Division of Brazilian Affairs (Dawson)

NEW YORK, September 24, 1947.

DEAR MR. DAWSON: Please accept my thanks for your letter of September 16 [25] advising as to the action which was taken by our Embassy at Rio de Janeiro on July 24, 1947. We greatly appreciate your co-

---

[25] Not printed.
[26] Not printed, but see *infra*.

operation and that of the Embassy and feel sure that this will prove helpful in bringing about the return of the cash and securities which were formerly held by the Brazilian offices of The National City Bank of New York for account of our client, The Chase National Bank.

As you may have heard, the Brazilian Government recently made a formal offer to Brazil Railway Company to pay the sum of £2,000,000, out of the frozen Brazilian credits in London, as compensation for the seizure of the assets of the three principal operating subsidiaries of Brazil Railway Company. This offer has been accepted by the Board of Directors of that Company but the settlement is still subject to ratification by the Brazilian Congress.

Even if this settlement is consumated, we must still press our claim for return of the seized funds and other securities which belonged to The Chase National Bank in its capacity as Trustee and which have not been returned or paid for. Our local attorneys in Rio de Janeiro, Messrs. Momsen and Freeman, are conducting further negotiations with respect to these remaining claims and the continued active cooperation of our Embassy in Rio de Janeiro would be greatly appreciated.

Yours very truly, WALTER G. WIECHMANN

832.51/11–1847

Memorandum of Conversation, by the Chief of the Division of Brazilian Affairs (Dawson)

CONFIDENTIAL [WASHINGTON,] November 18, 1947.

Subject: Financial Aid for Brazil from the United States.

Participants: Mr. Carlos Martins, Ambassador of Brazil
    Mr. Arthur de Souza Costa, Brazilian Delegate to UNGA and Chairman, Finance Committee, Chamber of Deputies
    A–A—Mr. Armour [27]
    BA—Mr. Dawson

Mr. Souza Costa explained that President Dutra of Brazil had asked him to explore, while in the United States, the possibility of doing something about Brazil's difficult exchange position. Now that the General Assembly was drawing to a close, he could turn his attention to his economic mission.

Mr. Souza Costa commented that the European Recovery Program [28] had high political as well as economic importance and said that he expected Brazil could help in it. However, the situation was

---

[27] Norman Armour, Assistant Secretary of State for Political Affairs.
[28] For documentation on this program, see volume III.

complicated by the fact that half of Brazil's exports are paid for in soft currencies and only half in dollars whereas practically all of its imports require dollar disbursements. A continuation of Brazilian exports to Europe was impossible, he said, unless some dollars could be received for them as otherwise the inflationary effect would be tremendous. Any such curtailment of exports would lower production of the very goods which would be needed from Brazil in connection with the ERP.

It was Mr. Souza Costa's thought that the critical period would be between now and the putting into effect of the ERP. He wondered whether it would not be possible for the United States to do something about helping Brazil finance its trade with Europe pending the passage of the ERP legislation.

Mr. Armour stated that our Government was, of course, most sympathetic to the difficulties of Brazil and other countries faced by much the same situation but that at the present stage it was not clear what, if anything, could be done. Mr. Souza Costa was seeing Mr. Thorp later in the afternoon. Since Mr. Thorp was the Assistant Secretary in charge of economic affairs and was working on the ERP, Mr. Armour was sure that he would be glad to go over the problem in more detail.

In the later conversation with Mr. Thorp, Mr. Souza Costa suggested a credit of $100,000,000 to Brazil. That conversation is being covered in another memorandum.[31]

ALLAN DAWSON

811.516 Export-Import Bank/12–1047

The Chief of the Division of Brazilian Affairs (Dawson) to the Counselor of Embassy for Economic Affairs in Brazil (Brooks)

CONFIDENTIAL WASHINGTON, December 10, 1947.

DEAR CLARENCE: There finally reached me late yesterday afternoon the memorandum [31] which FN was supposed to prepare on Souza Costa's first visit to Thorp on November 18. Only one copy was apparently available after distribution in the economic shop although I had been promised that one would go to you immediately. Con-

---

[31] Not printed.

sequently, the girls in this office have had to go through the bad task of copying the whole kit and caboodle. I hope you are duly grateful.

You will notice that the memorandum also covers three talks which Corliss [32] had with Bulhões [33] as follow-ups to Souza Costa's approach and that the third annex is a written explanation by Bulhões of what Souza Costa was after. From a perusal of all of the papers I think it is quite clear that Souza Costa was purely on a fishing expedition and that the ground shifted.

FN will probably be equally long in getting out any memo on Souza Costa's final conversation with Thorp yesterday and having it O.K.'d by the latter so I will try to give you informally the gist of what was said.

First, I should mention that Souza Costa, accompanied by Martins and Bulhões, did go over to see Martin of the Eximbank several days ago. While we have no memorandum of the conversation and were not present, we understand that Martin made no commitments of any nature and that the talk was in very general terms.

With Thorp, Souza Costa explained that he had been to the Bank and that it was his understanding that everything would depend upon the Department's recommendations. Thorp patiently set Souza Costa straight on the present structure of the Bank's Board and where responsibilities for loan policy lay. When Souza Costa asked what the Department's reaction to his request for a loan was, Thorp said that it did not have sufficient data on which to judge, pointing out that detailed information on Brazil's exchange position, trade and balance of payments for recent months on such a basis as to see trends with projections for the future were not on hand. He courteously said that when Souza Costa got these from Brazil, we would be glad to look them over. He also enquired whether Brazil had done everything possible to restrict its non-essential imports from the United States to improve its dollar position.

Thorp brought up the fact that a $50,000,000 credit for the Brazilian Government had been granted by the Eximbank last year subject to approval of individual projects but that the Brazilian Government had withdrawn the request. Souza Costa explained that he understood that the loan in question had been for purchase of equipment in the United States in connection with a transportation program but that he supposed it had been abandoned "for budgetary reasons". The loan he was requesting was of an entirely different nature, to help solve

---

[32] James C. Corliss, Assistant Chief, Division of Financial Affairs.
[33] Octavio Bulhões, official of the Brazilian Finance Ministry.

Brazil's exchange difficulties and would be to the Bank of Brazil (this was the first time, so far as I have been able to discover, that the important point that the Bank of Brazil, not the Government, wanted the loan had been mentioned!; with this the case, it is all the more inconceivable that Vieira Machado [34] should know nothing of the "Souza Costa angle", as indicated in your telegram no. 1665,[35] if Souza Costa really had any authority).

Thorp then asked what Brazil was going to do about entering into the International Monetary Fund and indicated that failure to do so might be an obstacle to granting a loan even if the need therefor were shown. Souza Costa said that, having been at Bretton Woods, he was naturally strongly in favor of Brazil's taking full part in the Fund but that there was much opposition to it in Brazil on the grounds that the Government could not afford it and would be too restricted by the Fund limitations in view of its unsettled exchange state. He then said that he would be very much helped in his efforts to get action on the Fund if he could tell his colleagues back in Brazil that a loan would be forthcoming if Brazil fixed itself up with the Fund. Thorp corrected this interpretation rapidly and reiterated what he had said to start the discussion on this point.

An interesting thing in connection with all of this was that Martins never opened his yap once during the entire hour-long meeting. I am afraid that Souza Costa left in a rather disgruntled frame of mind, although he was pleasant enough in his urbane way, but that cannot be helped. One cannot give a man $100,000,000 to toy with just to keep him happy. Souza Costa never was able to see Lovett, who has been busy as a bird dog not only with his regular duties as Acting Secretary but in endless hearings on the Hill. I explained all of this carefully to Souza Costa and Martins and pointed out that Thorp was the top economic man to whom Lovett would refer matters such as those in which Souza Costa was interested. After all, he did see practically everyone else in the Government who would have anything conceivably to do with his quest. He said goodbye to Armour today and is off for New York tomorrow preparatory to enplaning for Brazil on Sunday.

I suppose David and Norrie [36] will be interested in this thumbnail sketch.

Best to you,
  Sincerely, if hurriedly,
                                  ALLAN DAWSON

---

[34] Acting Minister of Finance in Brazil.
[35] Not printed.
[36] Presumably David McK. Key, Counselor of Embassy, and Norris S. Haselton, First Secretary of Embassy.

811.516 Export-Import Bank/12–1147

The Chief of the Division of Brazilian Affairs (Dawson) to the Counselor of Embassy for Economic Affairs in Brazil (Brooks)

CONFIDENTIAL   WASHINGTON, December 11, 1947.

DEAR CLARENCE: With reference to my letter to you of yesterday concerning the Souza Costa negotiations, I now have a little more dope concerning the Eximbank's attitude. At a meeting of the Eximbank Board yesterday, Martin talked about Souza Costa's visit to him without saying anything very concrete and indicated that Souza Costa's approach was itself very vague, as was undoubtedly the case, judging by what he had to say to Thorp. Martin said that a memorandum of his conversation with Souza Costa would be sent to the Department in due course.

Apparently, however, Martin has no sympathy toward any loan to Brazil since he said in the Board meeting that the Eximbank was disposed not to consider any Brazilian loan applications, governmental or private, until the Vale do Rio Doce matter had been cleared up. Thorp took exception to the scope of this practical embargo and the matter was left to be discussed at the next Board meeting.

Best to you,
Sincerely,   ALLAN DAWSON

832.50 J.T.C./12–1947 : Telegram

The Acting Secretary of State to the Embassy in Brazil

CONFIDENTIAL   WASHINGTON, December 19, 1947—6 p. m.

1378. Urtels 1443 Oct 13 and 1632 Nov 25.[37] President Truman has approved formation Joint Braz-US Technical Commission each section to consist of adequate technical staff and three members with co-chairmen under these terms reference:

"The Joint Braz-US Technical Commission should endeavor to analyze the factors in Braz which are tending to promote or to retard the economic development of Braz. This might involve a broad appraisal of the manner, directions, and rates of development of the Braz economy, looking toward the most effective and balanced utilization of Braz. resources. The Comm should give particular attention to the capacity of Braz for economic expansion through the maximum use of its internal resources. The Comm shall not undertake to appraise the merits of specific projects or to evaluate the desirability of obtaining foreign financing. The Comm, however, should consider measures designed to encourage the flow of private capital to Braz and, where

---

[37] Neither printed.

appropriate, may make broad recommendations relative to measures which might facilitate economic development in Braz.

The Comm should direct its attention toward an analysis of (1) Braz natural and capital resources, (2) the supply of labor, particularly skilled labor, (3) problems in fiscal and banking fields, (4) problems of domestic and international trade, and (5) the position of Braz in the world economy."

Note proposing foregoing and requesting concurrence will go to Braz Amb shortly. Publicity should be deferred until later notice. Will keep you informed.

LOVETT

811.516 Export-Import Bank/12–2347

Memorandum by the Special Assistant of the Division of Investment and Economic Development (Stenger) to the Director of the Office of Financial and Development Policy (Ness)

[WASHINGTON,] December 23, 1947.

Subject: Agenda for Meeting of Board of Directors Eximbank December 24, 1947.

. . . .

4. *Brazil—Laminacao Nacional de Metais.* Reynolds & Company of New York, acting on behalf of Laminacao Nacional de Metais of São Paulo, has requested a credit of $4,869,923 to finance the purchase of U.S. equipment and materials required by Laminacao Nacional de Metais for the expansion of its existing facility for the manufacture of non-ferrous metal products. The application covers two credits; (1) $3,569,923 for the purchase of equipment and materials required for plant construction and equipment and (2) $1,300,000 for the purchase of U.S. raw materials to be processed in the plant. The latter to be in the form of a revolving credit.

The total cost of the expansion program is estimated at about $5.5 million, of which $4,358,000 represents the cost of U.S. equipment and materials. Virtually all contracts for the equipment and materials have been placed and an advance payment of $788,000 has already been made to U.S. supplies. The credit requested for the purchase of capital goods is, therefore, equal only to the residual payments to be made or $3,570,000.

The Company had expected to finance the entire cost of the expansion program out of earnings and borrowings in Brazil, but credit limitations imposed by the Brazilian Government in an effort to restrain inflation and a shortage of dollars in Brazil had made it impossible for the company to complete the program without foreign credits. Reynolds state they have found it impossible at this time to obtain credits from private U.S. sources.

Laminacao Nacional de Metais is one of a group of Brazilian companies reported to be the largest and most important distributors and producers of non-ferrous metals and their products in South America. The stock of the entire group, which consists of about eight affiliated companies, is owned by Francisco Pignatari. From a small beginning in 1933 Laminacao has grown rapidly, and its indicated net worth at the end of 1946 was $9,435,000 as compared with $300,000 in 1936.

The conclusions reached by the staff of the Bank are: (1) expansion of non-ferrous metal manufacturing in Brazil appears to be a sound line of development for Brazilian economy and should result in substantial foreign exchange savings equivalent to at least $2.5 million per year; (2) the prospective earnings of the company after completion of the proposed expansion program should be adequate to permit repayment of the credit within a period of 7 years; (3) the guarantee of the Banco do Estado of São Paulo, which was offered by the applicant, does not appear to be entirely satisfactory, but it should considerably reinforce the obligations of the company; (4) extension of the credit would be a material assistance to a number of U.S. manufacturers; and (5) the request for a revolving credit of $1.3 million for the purchase of raw materials should not be approved because it appears that the company should be able to finance such imports without recourse to the Eximbank.

There are really two questions to be decided, and the one of paramount importance is whether or not the Bank should delay action on this application until the Bank has received adequate assurances that the Victoria-Minas Railway (Rio Doce) will be completed. The staff of the Bank recommends that the Board not delay action on the Laminacao Nacional de Metais credit application because of the Rio Doce matter. The staff of the Bank further recommends that the Board approve a credit of up to $3,570,000 for the purchase of U.S. materials and equipment required for the expansion program, the credit to be unconditionally guaranteed by the Banco do Estado with adequate assurances of availability of exchange, the credit to be repaid in 7 years from June 30, 1949 with interest at 4 percent.

Recommendation: The interested divisions in the Department have agreed unanimously that the Bank should not withhold action on this application or any other application for Brazil, with the possible exception of a government credit, because of the delay in the execution of the Rio Doce contract. It is the firm conviction of the people in the Department that applications for exporter credits and other applications for credits which may benefit Brazilian economy should be considered on their merits. The Rio Doce project was a war-time emergency project, and the Eximbank should consider it fortunate that it has not received a request for a moratorium or for the cancellation of the credit.

Insofar as this particular application is concerned, the Department is not prepared to go along with the recommendation of the staff. In spite of much discussion and a number of meetings, the people in the Department have been unable to agree with the staff of the Bank. *ED, FN, IR and CP object to its approval until certain objections have been clarified.* (1) Laminacao has stated that it will force the competing Brazilian producers out of the market. Do we wish to assist one individual in establishing a monopoly? (2) The inability to obtain private capital financing has not been conclusively demonstrated. (3) A possible tie up with Aluminum of Canada with restrictive trade agreements. (5) Expansion of Laminacao's facilities might result in competition with the U.S. for raw materials of which there are serious shortages; such as, copper and lead. (6) Interference with the Marshall Plan.

I am not entirely in agreement with the above. I am merely reciting some of the objections, especially on the part of CP and IR. In view of this, I suggest that the Department propose that the Bank defer action until the differences of opinion have been reconciled. It may be a good idea also to clear this project with the Embassy in Rio, which I believe has not been done.

. . . .

THE UNITED STATES INTEREST IN PROPOSED BRAZILIAN LEGISLATION ON PETROLEUM AND IN CURRENT REQUIREMENTS [38]

832.6363/2–1447

The Chief of the Petroleum Division (Loftus) to the Petroleum Attaché in Brazil (Harmon)

CONFIDENTIAL WASHINGTON, January 29, 1947.

MY DEAR MR. HARMON: Your letter of January 17, 1947 [39] indicates that you have some misgivings in the interpretation of the Department's telegram no. 1566 of December 27, 1946,[40] it being your feeling that postponement of any action by the Embassy concerning petroleum legislation until that legislation may be ready for con-

---

[38] For documentation on this interest in 1946, see *Foreign Relations*, 1946, vol. XI, pp. 523 ff.
[39] Not printed.
[40] *Foreign Relations*, 1946, vol. XI, p. 557.

sideration by the Assembly would be prejudicial to our overall interest in the law.

In suggesting, in the above-mentioned telegram, that official sponsorship should not be given to any draft legislation and that official comment should not be made upon it until the draft is ready for legislative action, it was intended to imply a differentiation between a formal endorsement and informal action.

There was no intent to suggest that the Embassy should not continue to interest itself actively in the passage of this legislation nor that it should discontinue or abate in any way such informal guidance or opinions as it might be able to offer those framing the law. This latter activity is highly desirable and should be continued with all means at the disposal of the Embassy short of formal representation or comment.

The Department feels that were it to give official endorsement to the legislation or, in the name of this Government, make official comment on its provisions, such overt action could readily be misinterpreted by nationalistically inclined elements and as easily interpreted by them as being distinct interference on our part in matters of national competence. This may be, perhaps, a too cautious view of the possible results of such action, but there exists certainly the possibility which, should it become a reality, could be most embarrassing.

I believe that you should, with the Ambassador's concurrence, continue to make use of all of your valuable associations with those in any way responsible for the drafting of this legislation and, where appropriate, accord them the advantage of your professional judgment as well as your knowledge of this Government's attitude. In so doing, however, it is still felt here that the approach should continue to be on an informal basis.

If situations should arise where you and the Ambassador feel that it is necessary to make formal representation, the Department would like to be apprised of the circumstances in order that a common understanding of the approach may be arrived at.

Sincerely yours, JOHN A. LOFTUS

832.6363/2-1447

The Chief of the Division of Brazilian Affairs (Dawson) to the Ambassador in Brazil (Pawley)

CONFIDENTIAL WASHINGTON, February 25, 1947.

DEAR MR. AMBASSADOR: On receipt of your letter of February 14, 1947 [41] concerning the position of the Embassy vis-à-vis the formula-

---

[41] Not printed.

tion of Brazilian petroleum legislation, I got out the Department's telegram no. 1566 of December 27, 1946, to which you refer, and discussed the matter with officers of the Petroleum Division and others. Incidentally, the telegram and the letter from Mr. Loftus to Mr. Harmon which you enclosed with your letter to me had the same origin and were consequently intended to be complementary, not contradictory, in method of approach.

I understand that a letter has been received from you by Mr. Clayton [43] on the same general subject and that a reply is being drafted at present. This should clarify the whole question but, pending its receipt by you, a few comments from me might possibly be useful.

As I understand it, the Department's telegram no. 1566 had two objectives: (*a*) To suggest that the best means of drafting sound petroleum legislation in Brazil would be by the employment of an experienced individual or firm to act as an adviser to the Brazilian drafting committee; and (*b*) to stress the Department's feeling that, at this stage, the Embassy should limit its channels of approach on petroleum legislation to informal rather than formal ones.

So far as point (*a*) is concerned, I know from my own experience in Venezuela that the services there of Duke Curtice and Herb Hoover, Jr., were invaluable in pulling out legislation which was satisfactory to both the Venezuelan Government and the bulk of the oil companies operating in Venezuela. With the Venezuelans' lack of technical experience, there would unquestionably have been many bugs in the legislation had experienced, impartial persons knowing the oil business from all angles and in whom the Venezuelan Government had confidence not been available for consultation. The situation seems even clearer in Brazil, where nobody in the Government has much practical knowledge in petroleum matters. However, it is obviously up to the Brazilians to decide whether they want outside advice.

As regards point (*b*) the letter of January 29 from Mr. Loftus to Mr. Harmon was intended as an amplification and interpretation of the pertinent portion of telegram no. 1566. In other words, the thought is that the Embassy should continue for the present to interest itself in the proposed legislation entirely through informal channels. In this way, the Embassy can exercise some influence discreetly and still leave the way open for the Department and itself to take a formal position should the drafting turn out badly. In essence, I gather that the responsible officers on the economic side approve entirely of the

---

[43] William L. Clayton, Under Secretary of State for Economic Affairs.

manner in which you and the Petroleum Attaché have been handling the matter so far.

I hope in my fumbling efforts at explanation above I have not made the matter still more confusing.

With kind personal regards,

Very sincerely yours,
ALLAN DAWSON

832.6363/3-747 : Airgram

The Ambassador in Brazil (Pawley) to the Secretary of State

CONFIDENTIAL RIO DE JANEIRO, March 7, 1947.

A-222. At luncheon Embassy Residence on Tuesday, March 4, Dr. Daniel de Carvalho, Minister of Agriculture told me confidentially that a petroleum *projeto* had been completed and was now being studied by Brazilian Government authorities. This *projeto* contained the following general provisions:

The Brazilian Government would furnish land rights, and the companies would supply capital and technical knowledge. The first six percent return would apply as interest on the companies' investments and the second six percent would go to the Government. The balance would be divided equally between the Government and the companies.

I did not place importance on this report thinking it to be an idea presented by some outsider. However yesterday the Foreign Minister [44] while discussing many other problems informed me of this petroleum project and outlined a similar plan. I told the Foreign Minister that this project would very likely not be acceptable to foreign capital and that it would appear more logical for Brazil to study petroleum projects in existence in other countries, such as Colombia and Venezuela, and to offer something slightly better than is offered elsewhere in an effort to induce foreign companies to invest in exploration and development of the petroleum industry in this country. There still appears to be an effort on the part of influential officials to suggest schemes which will not be acceptable to foreign capital. Brazil seems to continue to follow a dog-in-the-manger attitude with reference to their petroleum law.

I am informed, however, that a new petroleum committee consisting of the following: Dr. Avelino de Oliveira, Vice President of the National Petroleum Council; Glycon de Paiva, mining engineer with the Department of Agriculture; Odilon Braga, an attorney and for-

---

[44] Raul Fernandes.

merly Minister of Agriculture; Ruy de Lima e Silva, Professor of Geology at the Polytechnical Institute; Colonel Artur Levy, member of the National Petroleum Council representing the Army; has in the last few days asked MacNaughton of DeGollyer and MacNaughton to be adviser to the petroleum committee whom the President [45] has instructed to write a petroleum law to be submitted to him at an early date.

PAWLEY

832.6363/6-2647

The Chargé in Brazil (Brooks) to the Secretary of State

CONFIDENTIAL RIO DE JANEIRO, June 26, 1947.
No. 2463

SIR: I have the honor to report that on June 23, Dr. Odilon Braga, Chairman of the Committee to Write a Petroleum Law, sent two copies of a completed draft of a law to Dr. Daniel de Carvalho, Chairman of President Dutra's Industrial Planning Committee, for the committee's consideration and recommendations.

On the same day Dr. Carvalho gave Messrs. Hoover and Curtice one of the two copies for their use as advisors to his committee. The contents of the draft law have not been made public and no copy has been given to any of the oil companies or to the American Embassy.

Mr. Hoover has confidentially informed the Embassy that the law in its present form is unworkable and that in his opinion no American oil company would be willing to attempt to operate under it. He said that it is "naive" in that many of its provisions indicate that its authors are uninformed on the policies, economics and methods of operation of the oil industry.

Mr. Hoover said that the law does not follow the pattern of other Latin American petroleum laws and that it is distinctly Brazilian in character. He further said that since many of the bad provisions of the law are due to ignorance of the industry, he believes that reasonable suggestions for changes will be accepted. He has said that he is hopeful that the law can be so revised as to make it workable.

Mr. Hoover thinks that he and Mr. Curtice will require about two weeks to complete their study of the law and to prepare their report to Dr. Carvalho.

Respectfully yours, CLARENCE C. BROOKS

---

[45] Gen. Enrico Gaspar Dutra.

832.6363/8-2147

Memorandum of Conversation, by the Chief of the Division of Brazilian Affairs (Dawson)

CONFIDENTIAL [WASHINGTON,] August 21, 1947.

Subject: Proposed Petroleum Law in Brazil; Hoover-Curtice Mission.

Participants: Mr. Arthur A. Curtice of Hoover and Curtice
 Mr. Rex Townsend of Hoover and Curtice
 BA—Mr. Dawson

Mr. Arthur (Duke) Curtice of Hoover and Curtice called with his associate, Mr. Rex Townsend, until recently an officer of the Petroleum Division of the Department, to "report" after the completion of his mission to Brazil with his partner, Mr. Herbert Hoover Jr. . . .

. . . .

Actually, six weeks elapsed before the Barreto [46] draft was turned over to Hoover and Curtice. They spent the intervening time renewing old contacts. The Barreto draft was found to be completely hopeless. Hoover and Curtice spent a month analyzing it and finally submitted a 100-page memorandum suggesting changes. These were favorably received by Dr. Carvalho who explained, however, that the memorandum would have to be turned over to the Barreto Committee which would be asked to write a "completely new law" based on it. In discussing the matter, Dr. Carvalho said he was not a completely free agent in making decisions on petroleum since General Barreto was autonomous, had practically Cabinet rank and represented the Army.

. . . .

Mr. Curtice gave it as his best judgment that in order for satisfactory oil legislation in Brazil to be feasible it would be necessary to convince the Army leaders (General, Senator, ex-War Minister and Rio Conference Delegate Goes Monteiro, General Obino, Chief of Staff, and five or six others) who were nationalistic. These men thought that keeping a close hold on Brazilian oil for strategic reasons was vital and would have to be shown that opening up production possibilities would be to Brazil's advantage and that this could only be done with foreign companies' know-how. He thought that only someone such as Secretary Marshall or Secretary Forrestal,[47] in whom

---

[46] Gen. João Carlos Barreto, President of the Brazilian National Petroleum Council.

[47] James V. Forrestal was appointed Secretary of Defense in July 1947 and took the oath of office in September.

the Brazilian Generals had complete confidence and for whose military prestige they had respect, could convince them. When I asked him whether Ambassador Pawley could not do the job, he replied "No". Mr. Curtice said that when he left Ambassador Pawley indicated to him that he hoped to get the Secretary away from Rio and Petropolis [48] for a week-end at a ranch shooting and there to indoctrinate him on the Brazilian petroleum situation with a view to having him take the matter up with General Goes Monteiro.

The memorandum has been made a detailed one because the Embassy in Rio has reported little so far as to the progress and results of the Hoover–Curtice Mission and Mr. Curtice's remarks constitute the first full picture from any point of view which is available. Mr. Curtice said that the Embassy was copying the Hoover–Curtice memorandum and that this would shortly be sent to the Department.

832.6363/10–247 : Telegram

The Chargé in Brazil (Key) to the Secretary of State

CONFIDENTIAL   RIO DE JANEIRO, October 2, 1947—6 p. m.

1374. Brazilian National Defense Council, composed Cabinet members, but army-dominated, reported have drafted project law regulating refinery concessions without reference to committee drafting petroleum law. Text project not yet obtainable, but General Barreto has indicated confidentially provides for eventual 51 percent Brazilian stock ownership with Brazilian interests contributing at outset 10 percent, with remaining 90 of 51 percent to be paid from earnings, 49 percent foreign interest to provide remainder of immediately required financing.

President Dutra signed decree September 30, published *Diario Oficial* October 1, appointing committee of Chief Staff General Obino, McNarans, Pestana and Minister Labor Figueirrio to review project and present him their opinion. Evidence points to Sampaio group with 20,000 barrel refinery concessions at Paulo as instigator project. Thought is advanced some quarters that action National Defense Council may be attempt force US hand on questions loan to Brazil. Text project will be communicated if and when available.

Emerico Kahn Sampaio's financial man now en route US to obtain financing for São Paulo refinery.

KEY

---

[48] Secretary Marshall was in Rio de Janeiro at this time as head of the American delegation to the Inter-American Conference for the Maintenance of Continental Peace and Security. For documentation on this Conference, see pp. 1 ff.

FW 832.6363/11-347

Memorandum by Mr. Richard F. O'Toole of the Division of Brazilian Affairs to the Chief of That Division (Dawson)

[WASHINGTON,] November 12, 1947.

Mr. Hoffman (PED) [49] has discussed with representatives of Standard Oil, Gulf Oil and the Texas Company the intimation contained in the Brazilian Embassy's memorandum of November 3 [50] that the inadequate supply of petroleum products for Brazil results from the retention of tankers by the United States Government. Mr. Hoffman gave me the following information with regard to the matter.

Gulf obtains its supply for Brazil from the United States and is therefore subject to export licensing control over such quantities as are allocated to Brazil. As these quantities from our supply are relatively small Gulf has no tanker problem therein. Both Standard and the Texas Company, however, obtain their supply for Brazil from Caribbean sources, and since large quantities are involved both companies do have a tanker problem under existing conditions.

The current supply problem stems from a greatly increased worldwide demand for petroleum products, the transportation of which is hampered by an inadequate supply of tankers. In the case of Brazil, 1947 petroleum requirements are 40% higher than they were in 1946, while those for 1948 are estimated to be from 48 to 60% higher. Neither Standard nor the Texas Company has taken off tankers from the Brazilian run nor have they supplied less than Brazil's normal supply of petroleum products. Their difficulty is to obtain enough tankers to meet the increased requirements.

Such tankers as are available for purchase (and they are very few) have jumped from 50 to 100% in price. Standard says that it is doing everything possible to increase its tanker fleet and in so doing is completely disregarding the extra premium costs. Tankers used to transport petroleum products to Brazil are either privately owned or chartered and at no time in the past has the Maritime Commission allocated any of its tankers to Brazil, contrary to a current belief in that country. Up until recently the Commission has allocated tankers to such countries as England, France and Italy but as of November 1 the Commission has ceased tanker allocations to all foreign countries in order that tankers, under its control, may be used exclusively in meeting United States domestic requirements.

Representatives of American oil companies point out that both

---

[49] Malvin G. Hoffman of the Petroleum Division.
[50] Not printed.

Lloyd-Brasileiro and the Brazilian Navy have a number of tankers which are not being used on a full-time basis and they suggest that if these could be chartered by private oil companies, during the periods when not in use, it would help out the Brazilian petroleum supply situation. The tanker shortage is critical and is expected to continue so for some months.

RICHARD F. O'TOOLE

832.6363/12–2447 : Telegram

The Chargé in Brazil (Key) to the Secretary of State

CONFIDENTIAL   RIO DE JANEIRO, December 24, 1947—8 a. m.

1740. Under pressure from President Dutra urgent solution Brazil's petroleum problem General Barreto, President National Petroleum Council, has approached Embassy requesting following information:

1. Can U. S. Government charter or sell to Brazil up to four fuel oil tankers; if so how many, carrying capacity, what price.

2. Can U. S. guarantee or assure Brazil's minimum requirements petroleum products first 6 months 1948, amounts as submitted by Brazilian Embassy Washington to Office International Trade July 1947 in reply to latter's request for such information.

Would appreciate Department's comment soonest.

KEY

832.6363/12–2447 : Telegram

The Secretary of State to the Embassy in Brazil

CONFIDENTIAL   WASHINGTON, January 6, 1948—4 p. m.

6. Dept concerned over statements attributed to Barreto that revised draft petroleum law now in Dutra's hands provides for control refineries and inland transportation facilities by Brazilian nationals. Such restrictions would probably be so unacceptable to Amer oil cos that they would be unwilling enter Brazil and would thus go counter to Dutra's repeated assurances to Amb Pawley that law will be acceptable to foreign capital.

Braz requests covered urtels 1740 and 1744 Dec 24 [51] would appear to give opening for requesting informally from Dutra copy proposed law now before it is sent to Congress. If obtainable and it contains unacceptable clauses you are authorized to request Dutra delay presentation until you can consult Dept for comments. You will appreci-

---

[51] Latter not printed.

ate difficulty of obtaining favorable amendments after draft reaches Congress.

Tels 1740 and 1744 point up world shortage oil and transportation therefor. So far as can be foreseen situation will become progressively worse. Only way for Brazil to be sure eventually of sufficient oil for its needs is by adequate production therein. We believe firmly that this can be obtained only through utilizing experience of established oil industry. It is for this reason that satisfactory oil law seems so essential for Brazil's own interests. While Dutra is aware of these arguments it might be well to stress them in your conversations with him.

For your own info it may be difficult to justify special measures to aid Brazil in present emergency unless it modifies present development criteria which will effectively prevent any real utilization its own resources in future.

Supply Govt-owned surplus warbuilt tankers earmarked for foreign sale exhausted. Marit Comm will only charter govt-owned tankers for discharge in US ports.

All petroleum products including gasoline, diesel and fuel oil are short in US. Gas oil and diesel 15 percent short Middle Atlantic and New England States, 10 percent short in area east of Rockies. Residual fuel about 10 percent short same area. US endeavoring reduce own consumption to available supplies. Under these conditions not possible for US guarantee Brazil's minimum petroleum requirements first 6 months 1948 or any other period especially since US has not been normal supplier for Brazilian petroleum products.

MARSHALL

THE RESPONSE OF THE UNITED STATES TO THE BRAZILIAN REQUESTS FOR WHEAT

832.61311/1-2247 : Airgram

The Ambassador in Brazil (Pawley) to the Secretary of State

CONFIDENTIAL   RIO DE JANEIRO, January 22, 1947.

A-98. I have just received a letter from Foreign Minister Raul Fernandes from which I quote a translation concerning the supply of wheat to Brazil:

"I wish to take advantage of this opportunity to inform Your Excellency confidentially that I have serious reasons to believe that Argentina will place us during the month of February in the dilemma of not receiving wheat or of paying the exorbitant price of 45 pesos per hundred kilos. Because of this disagreeable prospect, I have instructed our Embassy in Washington to endeavor to obtain relief in the United States and I will greatly appreciate the assistance of the good offices of Your Excellency toward this request and thus put us above the extortion with which we are threatened."

Under the Brazilian-Argentine agreement, Argentina is obligated to ship 120,000 tons of wheat monthly to Brazil, beginning January 1, 1947. As far as the Embassy has been able to ascertain, there has been no wheat whatever shipped under this agreement. In view of this situation and the above-quoted request of the Foreign Minister, the Embassy recommends that a temporary allocation of wheat for shipment to Brazil be established in the United States until such time as the present difficulties regarding the shipment of wheat from Argentina have been resolved.

PAWLEY

832.6584/3-347

Memorandum by Mr. Richard F. O'Toole of the Division of Brazilian Affairs to the Chief of That Division (Dawson)

[WASHINGTON,] March 3, 1947.

Subject: February 27 Memorandum of Brazilian Embassy Proposing Agreement for Supplying American Wheat to Brazil.

Pursuant to the request contained in the above memorandum for a discussion of this matter Mr. Highby (IR) and I joined Mr. Carneiro,[52] of the Brazilian Embassy, at Mr. Glen Craig's [53] office in the Department of Agriculture this afternoon.

Mr. Craig remarked to Mr. Carneiro that he felt sure that since Brazil is represented in IEFC Mr. Carneiro was probably acquainted with the overall difficulties of the wheat supply situation. However, he went into some detail to demonstrate that UK, Belgium, Holland, France and Italy are in a particularly difficult supply situation. He then said that in this country we had no surplus wheat available, and therefore to meet Brazil's request it would be necessary to take it away from those countries mentioned above, which he was sure Mr. Carneiro would not expect. Mr. Craig then assured Mr. Carneiro that there were no supply agreements with any country other than current allocations on a monthly or quarterly basis as the case may be. He added that both he and his associates deeply regretted that Brazil or any other country had to look to Argentina for wheat in light of all circumstances but that he could hold out no hope that Brazil could obtain wheat other than from Argentine sources, even if the price went to $4.00 a bushel. Mr. Carneiro was told that even if it came to the worst we could do nothing for Brazil or any country until the

---

[52] Octavio Augusto Dias Carneiro, Second Secretary in the Brazilian Embassy.
[53] Director, Office of Requirements and Allocations, Department of Agriculture.

middle of June when the new crop came in. He expressed the opinion that even then the situation would be almost as bad as it is today. However, he conceded, that if Brazil should by any chance find herself completely bare of supplies, as she was last summer, undoubtedly an effort would be made to dig up a small spot supply to help out but that this could not be viewed as a definite commitment.

Mr. Carneiro referred to the fact that so far this year Argentina has not met the monthly target of 100,000 tons of wheat for Brazil. Mr. Craig then sent out for figures of actual export liftings of flour to Brazil, from this country, which in January were equivalent to 111,000 tons of wheat. Mr. Craig then pointed out that this flour, plus the amount of wheat received from Argentina, heavily exceeded the IEF allocation for Brazil for January. He went on to say that these flour shipments were a heavy drain on our flour supply and that if it continued to go to Brazil in the same proportion he would not be surprised to see the amount allowed to be exported limited to the 15,000 or 20,000 tons per month normally supplied to northern Brazil.

Mr. Carneiro was undoubtedly disappointed at the result of the meeting but he appeared to accept the decision gracefully, although he did say, in semi-jocular vein, that he thought perhaps Brazil ought to raise the price of her rice.

832.6584/4–2347

Memorandum by Mr. Leo I. Highby of the International Resources Division to the Chief of the Division of Brazilian Affairs (Dawson)

[WASHINGTON,] April 23, 1947.

Subject: Flour Allocation to Brazil

I note your revision of the last sentence in your memorandum of conversation of April 15 [54] on "Controversy over Export Licensing of 200,000 Bags of Flour for the Government of the State of São Paulo", as well as the revision of the second page as of April 16. The last sentence suggests that the State Department might intervene to attempt to assure the State of São Paulo of receipt of the necessary flour for the special uses contemplated, <u>in view of the nature of the transaction and of the fact that it had been initiated before the removal of wheat flour from general license.</u>

A stand in the Department reflecting the underlined words would involve the Department in difficulties, since the embargo announced on March 20 and made effective on April 1 was intended to cut off such contracts, permitting only those to be completed where the flour had

---

[54] Not printed.

already been started on its way on April 1. In fact, if it had been permitted to fulfill outstanding contracts, it is estimated that perhaps 200,000 tons more would have moved to general license areas and the embargo would have had little meaning. As laid down by the Department of Agriculture, the procedure henceforth will be to send flour to the general license areas only on an emergency basis and with need well established. The Department of Commerce, which administers licenses covering any allocations made by the Department of Agriculture, awards licenses to applicants for the same on the basis of historical experience of United States exporters in shipping to the market in question and without reference to contracts made before the cut-off day of the embargo. This principle is also acceded to by the flour trade.

Consequently, granting of a license on the basis of initiation of a transaction before removal from general license would open the door to a demand for like consideration by all other exporters who had negotiated deals before the embargo and would make it impossible to administer the flour control. Only if altogether convinced of a need which cannot be met by equalization of supplies within the importing country in question would it appear that the State Department should support requests for allocations. The need does not appear to have been established in this case. The allocation was apparently established only because of the activities of a well-known lobbyist. I should perhaps also mention that it was especially the excessive shipments of flour to Brazil while grave shortages were developing elsewhere, that caused Mr. Clayton [55] to urge Secretary Harriman [56] and Secretary Anderson [57] to agree to flour being put back on specific license some time ago.

832.61311/6–547

Memorandum by Mr. Harold M. Midkiff of the Division of Brazilian Affairs, to the Acting Chief of the Division of River Plate Affairs (Tewksbury)

[WASHINGTON,] June 5, 1947.

Subject: Brazilian Wheat Requirements.

	Tons per Month	Tons per Year
Normal imports	100,000	1,200,000
Minimum import quota set by IEFC	70,000	840,000
Domestic production	17,500	200,000
Total normal consumption	117,500	1,400,000
Total minimum consumption (IEFC)	87,500	1,050,000

---

[55] William L. Clayton, Under Secretary of State for Economic Affairs.
[56] W. Averell Harriman, Secretary of Commerce.
[57] Clinton P. Anderson, Secretary of Agriculture.

Imports (Wheat & Flour)	Tons per Month	Total Tons
July–December 1946	40,000	240,000
December 1946–March 1947	102,500	410,000
April and May 1947	48,000	96,000

U.S. allocation now authorized permits exportation of 25,000 tons of flour or wheat equivalent in July, to arrive in Brazil in July or August.

In view of Argentine shipments described below it is obvious that imports from that country are unsatisfactory to Brazil.

IMPORTS FROM ARGENTINA

1946	Tons	1947	Tons
July	43,955	January	14,322
August	17,135	February	61,790
September	566	March	13,233
October	2,564	April	64,487
November	—	May	16,530
December	—		

Total July 1946–May 1947—234,582 tons, an average of 21,326 tons per month.

In January the price charged by Argentina was $2.33 per bushel, in February $3.00 and at present Argentina is demanding $3.75.

800.5018/8–1547

Memorandum by Mr. Richard F. O'Toole of the Division of Brazilian Affairs

RESTRICTED [WASHINGTON,] August 15, 1947.

Yesterday morning I attended a meeting in Mr. Highby's office (IR) during which he supplied tentative wheat allocation figures for October, on the basis of an exportable surplus of 14 million tons from the US production.

Brazil has been omitted from the October allocations and I asked Mr. Highby the reason for this. He prefaced his reply with a statement that "it is not for punitive reasons" and went on to say that Brazil's stock position, plus the fact that Canada had recently supplied her with some wheat, made it appear that no provision was necessary under the circumstances. I told him that we had heard that Brazilian stocks were expected to be exhausted by the end of September and that we anticipated that political pressure would be brought for assistance in October. The following wheat statistics regarding Brazil were given to me at the meeting:

IEFC tentative allocation, July–December	90,000 tons
Shipped, July–September	50,000 "
Balance, October–December	40,000 "
Recommended October program	0
1946–1947 shipments	609,000 "

The evident purpose of the meeting was to try to impress upon those present that the tentative figures, based upon the assumed surplus of 14 million tons, would very likely be reduced through re-calculation upon the basis of 13 million tons.

I received the impression that final allocations will depend upon several contingencies, including the unsettled question of increasing per capita food calories for Germany and Italy, the size of our exportable surplus of corn, etc., and that if Brazil really has to have wheat she will be supplied through a readjustment of allocations.

800.5018/8–1847

The Secretary of State to the Embassy in Brazil

RESTRICTED WASHINGTON, August 18, 1947.
No. 832

The Secretary of State transmits for the Embassy's information, a copy of the note [58] which the Department recently addressed to the Brazilian Ambassador in Washington expressing this Government's regret at Brazil's decision to withdraw from the International Emergency Food Council, and requesting that the Brazilian Government continue to cooperate, insofar as possible, with the Council's recommendations.

As previously reported to the Embassy, Mr. Valentim Bouças,[59] in conversation with officers of the Department encouraged the belief that Brazil might reconsider its decision and seek reinstatement. The Department would, of course, welcome such a development but will make no further approach to the Brazilian authorities on this subject, in view of the Embassy's report that Mr. Bouças' comments were made without authorization. Under existing circumstances, it is to be ex-

---

[58] Not printed.
[59] Head of President Dutra's special mission to the United States to buy wheat.

pected that any wheat requirements submitted by Brazil to the IEFC will be closely scrutinized.

832.61311/8–3047 : Telegram

The Ambassador in Brazil (Pawley) to the Secretary of State

CONFIDENTIAL   RIO DE JANEIRO, August 30, 1947—5 p. m.

1202. During past week the subject of Brazil's wheat supply has been broached by Rubens de Mello, Chief Economic Division Foreign Office, Aranha,[60] Goes Monteiro,[61] Foreign Minister Fernandes and finally President Dutra. All are alarmed because present supply of wheat will be exhausted by October.

We are informed Argentine reluctance to fill quotas established under agreement probably due to fact they are selling wheat to Britain and Spain at 60 pesos the quintal whereas Brazilian agreement is at rate of 40 pesos the quintal.

All persons mentioned requested urgent assistance from US, either directly or through IEFC, to meet minimum requirements of 40,000 tons per month during September, October, November and December. All expressed deep concern over political repercussions should Brazil run out of bread, which would be case if new supply wheat is not obtained. Brazil would accept flour as readily as bulk wheat in this emergency.

I offered no encouragement but took occasion to inquire whether, if able obtain allotments with US help either from IEFC or US direct, Brazil would be willing rejoin IEFC. Both Foreign Minister and President stated categorically that they would rejoin immediately and would welcome opportunity correct original error of withdrawing without loss of face.

Foreign Minister and Rubens de Mello added if US desired Brazil would make available to Britain its surplus rice to extent latter requires for sterling area, not however for resale in dollar area.

If wheat problem develops unfavorably and Brazil is confronted with no bread in November or December, the political difficulties of the Dutra Government would be indeed serious. Such a situation would play directly into hands Communist Party in their efforts to embarrass and hamper administration.

PAWLEY

---

[60] Oswaldo Aranha, former Minister for Foreign Affairs.
[61] Gen. Pedro Goes Monteiro, former Minister of War and Chief of Staff.

832.61311/8–3047 : Telegram

The Secretary of State to the Embassy in Brazil

CONFIDENTIAL   WASHINGTON, September 12, 1947—6 p. m.

1062. For the Ambassador from Armour.[62] World grain situation is becoming so much more critical daily that it is complicating our efforts to meet Braz needs expressed in your 1202 Aug 30 and telephone call to me.

After canvassing situation thoroughly, best procedure appears to be for Braz to request IEFC for new wheat and flour quotas, justifying its request with figures as to Braz minimum needs, recent production and imports and stocks on hand. It would of course help Braz position immeasurably if it were at same time to rejoin IEFC. We as a govt have undertaken to follow IEFC recommendations and exception would place us in a most difficult position. However if Braz can make case we will support it strongly with IEFC.

Our efforts have been severely handicapped by failure of Braz to give us data on which to work and by indications from Braz sources here that situation is not as critical as represented to you. For example officer of Braz Emb has given Braz minimum requirements as 65,000 tons monthly. If this correct Braz has in last 9 months obtained enough wheat and flour for consumption of over year. Furthermore when suggestion in second pgh made to Braz Emb officer did not want to act pending return of Amb Martins saying that immediate action unnecessary. Also Rio port regulations issued Aug 26 place ships carrying wheat in only fifth of nine priority classes.

Another complication has been dissatisfaction our authorities with Braz Army efforts to circumvent quota system by purchasing 25,000 tons from Overseas Trading Corp (32,000 tons in wheat equivalent) and then asking for special permission to ship. To grant this would disrupt entire quota system. Not a single supplier has been an exporter and normal shippers up in arms over transaction. Commerce adamantly opposed. Attempt has only prejudiced chances of getting needed wheat for overall Braz consumption by arousing natural resentment of tactics.

We are doing all possible but our hands will be strengthened if Braz will coordinate its activities and give us urgently necessary basic info in concrete form. We can get no action without figures justifying it. [Armour.]

MARSHALL

---

[62] Norman Armour, Assistant Secretary of State for Political Affairs.

800.5018/9-2247

Memorandum by the Chief of the Division of Brazilian Affairs (Dawson) to the Assistant Secretary of State for Political Affairs (Armour)

CONFIDENTIAL [WASHINGTON,] September 22, 1947.

Subject: Brazilian Desire for Wheat.

GENERAL

The Brazilian Embassy today delivered a note to the IEFC applying for readmission to that organization and asking for a quota of 40,000 tons of wheat monthly until the end of the year from non-Argentine sources, i.e., from the United States to all intents.

President Dutra discussed the general problem of Brazil's wheat shortage with President Truman in Rio de Janeiro.[63] Ambassador Pawley reports that our President promised to take action and designated Admiral Leahy [64] to follow up the matter in Washington. It might be well to check with Admiral Leahy as to what he has done.

Brazil was granted no grain quota in the USDA's export allocations for October and 15,000 tons for November. 25,000 tons remain for possible December distribution from IEFC recommendations for the second half of 1947 but there is no assurance this figure will be followed.

ARMY WHEAT

The Brazilian Government has also been most concerned with getting export licenses for 25,000 tons of wheat bought by the Brazilian Army (and already paid for; irrevocable letter of credit) from sources which have not been engaged in the export trade and for which no quotas are available. This wheat is largely in New Orleans piling up storage charges.

The Brazilian Army wheat case has important political connotations since the man who handled the deal at this end was Vieira Machado of the Bank of Brazil who has just become Acting Brazilian Minister of Finance in replacement of the titular Minister who is taking leave of absence (the Minister's illness is believed to be diplomatic). Also the leading generals in the Brazilian Army were responsible for the transaction and the Army is a potent internal political

---

[63] President Truman attended and addressed the closing session of the Inter-American Conference for the Maintenance of Continental Peace and Security on September 2. For summary of President Truman's address, see p. 78.

[64] Adm. William D. Leahy, Chief of Staff to the Commander in Chief of the U.S. Army and Navy.

force. For all or part of the $3,500,000 spent for the Army wheat to be dissipated would cause a serious loss of face for Vieira Machado and the generals.

Suggested Solution

My suggestion would be to endeavor to have Brazil granted a monthly quota of 25,000 tons for each of the last three months of 1947, counting the Army purchases as the October quota and procuring export licenses for these. This would entail raising the November quota from 15,000 to 25,000 tons and fixing the December quota at 25,000 tons also.

This suggestion would not meet the Brazilian Government's desires since it hopes for a total of 120,000 tons for the quarter. However, an allotment for October would normally be impossible at this late date. The suggestion would give Brazil 75,000 tons over three months instead of 80,000 over two months.

In order to accomplish what is suggested, it would be necessary to enlist the assistance of Messrs. Anderson and Harriman or their Under Secretaries as well as the IEFC. The latter has indicated a sympathetic attitude. Ambassador Martins informed me that he would personally take the matter up with Mr. Anderson and Under Secretary of Commerce Foster.

Future

The best estimates we have as to Brazil's wheat and flour position is that 95,000 tons are on hand or in transit. Taking Brazil's minimum requirements as 65,000 tons a month (it has ordinarily consumed about 100,000 in recent years), the quotas from United States sources suggested above should enable it to get through the year with slight imports from Argentina. The situation could be reviewed again in October or November when it becomes more evident whether Brazil can get much wheat from Argentina.

ALLAN DAWSON

632.119/10–447

Memorandum by the Assistant Secretary of State for Political Affairs (Armour) to the Under Secretary of State (Lovett)

CONFIDENTIAL [WASHINGTON,] October 4, 1947.

The Brazilian Ambassador, Mr. Carlos Martins, has asked for appointments with the Secretary and the President concerning the two matters of which I spoke to you on September 25, that of getting a wheat quota of 40,000 tons a month for Brazil and obtaining export licenses to cover a purchase of flour for the Brazilian Army. When told that the Secretary was in New York, Mr. Martins asked for an appointment with you for October 6, if possible.

Brazilian Army Flour

In August the Brazilian Army bought and paid for 500,000 bags of flour from the Overseas Trading Corporation which has had no historic basis as a flour exporter. Export licensing is based largely on this factor. The price paid was $7.15 a bag (cwt) as compared with a market price of around $5.00 a bag at the time. 300,000 bags reached New Orleans where they have been building up storage charges, deteriorating and using needed warehouse space.

The Brazilian Embassy and Dr. Vieira Machado, then exchange director of the Bank of Brazil, through which the purchase was made, approached the Department and the Departments of Agriculture and Commerce in an attempt to get export licenses (there was no available export quota against which the shipment could be charged). OIT absolutely refused to countenance this procedure, pointing out that it would be completely irregular and bring the whole export licensing program into disrepute. The Brazilians were told repeatedly that the only solution was a sale of the flour in the open market, with the Brazilian Army pocketing its losses.

There is no question but that the Brazilians were fully aware that the transaction was not in accord with regular procedure, of which they had thorough knowledge. They managed to cancel the purchase of the 200,000 bags which had not been delivered but continued to try to flout established procedure by attempting to purchase an additional 200,000 bags from at least two other sources. Apparently they were counting on the Department's being able to get Commerce and Agriculture to back down from their opposition as a result of the Brazilian representations on political grounds.

Ambassador Martins has received several scorching telegrams from President Dutra demanding that he get favorable action, taking the matter to the "highest level". According to Mr. Martins, President Dutra has stressed Brazilian cooperation with the United States during the Rio Conference, the lavish entertainment of President Truman and Brazilian support on a series of problems, including atomic energy, and has complained bitterly at the lack of United States cooperation in return in the flour question. Obviously, Ambassador Martins is worried that failure on his part will force his resignation.

The tremendous Brazilian interest and pressure in the matter is due to a number of factors. President Dutra's political position has been deteriorating and he needs the continued support of the Brazilian Army, top officers of which were responsible for the deal (there is reason to suspect, from the price paid, that somebody got a sizable cut). The old Minister of Finance, Mr. Correa e Castro, who approved the flour purchase without reference to the Foreign Office, is being dropped, partly as a result of his part in the matter. However, Dr. Vieira Machado is the new Acting Minister of Finance and his personal prestige is manifestly tied up in the case.

Commerce and Agriculture's opposition, which is shared by the economic divisions of the Department, is based not only on the factors outlined above but on the fact that a previous Brazilian attempt to get export licenses for flour from non-traditional exporters was refused. A reversal of policy now would not only be inconsistent but give ammunition to Thurman Arnold, attorney for the sellers in the previous transaction, who has threatened to sue Commerce. The Millers Association, which knows of the 300,000 bag affair, can be expected to protest vigorously if approval is given to it.

The only possible way to meet the Brazilian desires in this matter would be by a decision by you that this should be done for political reasons and pressure on Agriculture and Commerce. Agriculture would have to grant a special export allocation to cover the 300,000 bags of flour (roughly 19,000 tons in wheat equivalent) since the only allocation now available to Brazil is one of 15,000 tons for November which is needed for flour for civilian consumption. Commerce would in turn have to grant equivalent export licenses. Perhaps a path toward the latter might be found in having the Brazilian Government or one of its agencies figure as the shipper but this would, of course, be a subterfuge.

The Brazilian request leaves a distinctly bad taste but, in view of President Dutra's marked interest in the matter and the possibility of increased instability in Brazil in case of a turn-down, I am inclined to feel that the Department should try to get affirmative action from Agriculture and Commerce. Failing this, I believe that arrangements should be made for Ambassador Martins himself to carry the case to Secretaries Harriman and Anderson, properly briefed by their subordinates, so that the onus of the unfavorable decision will be distributed among the three Departments and not borne solely by State.

Wheat Quotas for Brazil

The concentration on the flour situation has taken attention from the civilian wheat quota problem which is a most serious one with future consequences. Ambassador Martins will also take this up with you.

Brazil, of course, withdrew from the IEFC some months ago in the belief that it would profit by withdrawing its rice from IEFC control and counting on Argentina for its wheat. These hopes have been blasted and Brazil has now rejoined the IEFC. It is asking for quotas of 40,000 tons of wheat a month from United States sources for the remainder of the current calendar year and will presumably want such allocations to be continued thereafter. The IEFC Cereal Committee is about to consider the Brazilian request.

At present, IEFC grain recommendations for Brazil are only on a basis of 15,000 tons a month (in flour) and our information is that a similar figure is now projected for December, January and February.

Mr. Highby of IR has calculated that Brazil has not yet reached the bottom of the wheat barrel and that, if consumption is held down to 65,000 tons a month and if Argentina ships an average of 10,000 tons a week to Brazil for the remainder of the year stocks of some 85,000 tons will remain on January 1, 1948. However, the Embassy at Rio de Janeiro calculates Brazilian minimum needs as considerably in excess of 65,000 tons a month and Ambassador Pawley has been informed by Ambassador Bruce [65] that there will be no further Argentine shipments to Brazil this year. Ambassador Pawley estimates that Brazil will be out of wheat in November if relief is not forthcoming.

I recommend that our representatives on the IEFC Cereals Committee be asked to consider the Brazilian request most carefully and to support it if the Brazilians can present a prima facie case of need. One difficulty in this respect has been the dilatory nature of Brazilian representations and the lack of adequate statistical evidence.

632.119/10-1747 : Telegram

The Acting Secretary of State to the Embassy in Brazil

RESTRICTED   US URGENT   WASHINGTON, October 17, 1947—5 p. m.

1189. At request Amb. Pawley Commerce officials again considered license problem on Braz Ministry War flour. They have now notified Dept impossible to license this flour because not bought from regular exporter. Mexican Govt willing buy about one-third this flour at $6.05 a bag, tentatively quoted to it. Braz Emb now trying to confirm this offer.[66] After this settled, Dept will be glad cooperate, if requested by authorized Braz authorities here, in seeing if remainder cannot be

---

[65] James Bruce, Ambassador in Argentina.
[66] The Acting Secretary of State notified the Embassy at Rio de Janeiro in telegram 1200, October 20, 6 p. m., that the Brazilian Government had notified its Ambassador in Washington to sell the Army flour at New Orleans (832.6584/10-2047).

disposed of to CCC to avoid possible spoilage with resultant complete loss.

LOVETT

800.5018/11–347

The Chief of the Division of Brazilian Affairs (Dawson) to the Counselor of Embassy for Economic Affairs in Brazil (Brooks)

RESTRICTED [WASHINGTON,] November 3, 1947.

DEAR CLARENCE: We thought we were getting 25,000 tons of wheat or wheat equivalent in flour for Brazil for December as compared with 15,000 tons for November and zero for October but a little fly came into the ointment. The figure of 25,000 was approved in the lower strata of Agriculture and would have brought the wheat allocations for Brazil for the whole of the second semester of 1947 right up to the IEFC's original recommendation of 90,000. However, when the December allocations got up to Secretary Anderson, he slashed those for almost all countries and the Brazilian one was reduced to 20,000 tons. The December allocations were officially announced on October 30.

In my conversations with the people in the Brazilian Embassy, I am taking the optimistic line that, while we did not meet their desire for 40,000 tons a month, at least the trend has been up. We hope to keep the monthly figures at 20,000 in early 1948 but, of course, what success we will have is in the laps of the Gods. One good aspect is that the White House has taken an interest in the general problem and that Jim Stillwell, who is acting as an assistant to Steelman,[67] on detail from the Department, is sympathetic.

. . . .

Yours, as ever, ALLAN DAWSON

PROBLEMS IN THE LIQUIDATION OF THE RUBBER DEVELOPMENT CORPORATION

103.9151/2–1947

Memorandum by Mr. Richard F. O'Toole of the Division of Brazilian Affairs to the Chief of That Division (Dawson)

RESTRICTED [WASHINGTON,] February 19, 1947.

Subject: Liquidation of RDC's Investment in the Banco de Credito da Borracha

In 1942 the predecessor of RDC invested $3 million in 40 percent of the capital stock of Banco de Credito da Borracha—the remainder

---

[67] John R. Steelman, Assistant to the President.

having been furnished by the Brazilian Government through the Bank of Brazil. The Rubber Bank was established for the purpose of financing rubber production and development in connection with the war emergency.

In addition to paying 6 percent dividends on its stock, part of the Bank's profits, amounting to several million dollars, was diverted to a fund for development of the Amazon country. The administration and disposal of this fund was exclusively vested in the President of Brazil. Rubber Development Corporation was represented on the Board of the Bank by two American directors.

In August 1946, when RDC began to liquidate its affairs and, following resignation of RDC's directors on the Board of the Rubber Bank, our Rio Embassy addressed a formal note to the Brazilian Foreign Office regarding the desire of RDC to recapture its investment in the Bank. The note stated, substantially, that the US Government would appreciate prompt arrangements permitting withdrawal of RDC's investment, on the basis of full reimbursement of its holdings in the Bank. Mention was also made that since the war emergency had ended further participation by this Government in the affairs of the Bank was considered both unnecessary and unwise.

A short time later RDC sent a representative (Holt) to Rio de Janeiro to assist in the negotiations while Valentim Bouças (Executive Director, Committee for the Control of the Washington Agreements) was authorized to act for the Brazilian Government. Mr. Bouças took the position that there was no obligation requiring the Brazilian Government to take over RDC's investment in the Bank, a fact that was conceded. However, he claimed that during the preliminary discussions which led to the formation of the Bank it was understood that RDC's investment would remain for the duration of the Bank's charter,—20 years. Mr. Holt immediately challenged this statement and Bouças said that he would produce the minutes of a certain meeting to prove his statement. He was not able to do so, however, and announced that he would go to Washington to see Mr. Clayton [68] who would confirm his statement. In the meantime officials of RDC, as well as Mr. Clayton, who had been informed of the matter, discussed it with former officials of Rubber Development Corporation who in every case denied that any such agreement had been made.

On several recent occasions Mr. Bouças has discussed the Banco de Credito da Borracha case with Mr. Clayton and a few days ago, during a telephone conversation from New York with RDC officials, referred to a letter he had written to Mr. Clayton on February 10 [69] and said

---

[68] William L. Clayton, Under Secretary of State for Economic Affairs.
[69] Not printed.

that Mr. Clayton had told him that the matter was being studied. A copy of his letter has been obtained and it is important to note that it implies the possibility of the shares being purchased from the Bank at their nominal value, although on a trading basis whereby the consideration would be extension of our rubber purchase agreement from the present expiry date (June 30, 1947) to March 1948. RDC officials have told him that this is out of the question.

In my judgment the Minister of Finance [70] is not so much opposed to taking over the investment as he is concerned with the practical consideration of the terms of payment. In recent discussions with officers of our Rio Embassy, regarding re-imbursement of a loan for surplus property purchases, he said that it would be easier for Brazil to liquidate this transaction with dollar exchange rather than to make available to the US Government cruzeiro currency. It is well-known that the Minister is adamant against any further currency issues for any purpose. In my judgment, our strategy should be that of trying to obtain an agreement of the Minister of Finance to take over RDC's investment at its nominal value. The terms of repayment as to currency and time of repayment are really secondary matters and could be adapted to any reasonable proposal of the Brazilians.

. . . .

It is my belief that during recent negotiations in the Department Bouças has sensed a tendency in certain places to agree to a compromise in settling this case, probably along the lines of reduction in the amount of repayment and he therefore hopes to capitalize on this situation. I am convinced that if we stand pat and decline to take any reduction or to permit a tie in with any other proposal, that we shall get the agreement we desire.

103.9151/3–1947

The Acting Secretary of State to the Embassy in Brazil

[Extract]

CONFIDENTIAL WASHINGTON, March 19, 1947.
No. 590

The Acting Secretary of State refers to the Department's telegram No. 287 of March 13 [71] and to previous communications regarding the Banco de Credito da Borracha.

Representatives of the Department and of the Rubber Development Corporation met with Mr. Bouças on February 18 to discuss the

---

[70] Pedro Corrêa e Castro.
[71] Not printed.

disposal of the Rubber Development Corporation stock in the Bank. No agreement was reached. Mr. Bouças pointed out that there is no contract or obligation for the Brazilian Government to repurchase Rubber Development Corporation stock and contended that the United States should hold the stock for 20 years, representing the life of the Bank, rather than basing the date of withdrawal on the life of the Rubber Development Corporation or on the termination of the rubber agreement.

If the reasons for the organization of the Bank and the discussions concerning repurchase of the Rubber Development Corporation stock which were held prior to the Bank's organization both are disregarded, and if the written documents concerning the Bank are taken as the sole evidence in the case, there is some support (although as indicated below, such support is considered weak) to Mr. Bouças' contention that continued participation by the United States for 20 years is implied. For example, in the Decree Law which was forwarded as an attachment to the Embassy's despatch No. 7936 of July 14, 1942,[72] Article 4 gives the duration of the Bank as 20 years from the date of installation, and Articles 1, 5, and 6 mention Rubber Reserve and the American Directors of the Bank. Similarly, in the statutes of the Bank, which were forwarded as an attachment to the Embassy's despatch No. 8139 of August 10, 1942,[72] Article 3 gives the duration of the Bank as 20 years from the date of organization, and Articles 5, 8, 9, and 20 mention the Rubber Development Corporation or its representatives on the directorate of the Bank. Nowhere in either document is there any mention of the withdrawal of the American interest from the Bank, and it is difficult to argue that the paragraphs dealing with American participation are separable from the equally important paragraphs concerning the duration of the Bank.

It has never been contended that there was a written obligation of the Brazilian Government to repurchase the Rubber Development Corporation stock. However, it is considered from the viewpoint of the United States that the Brazilian Government should repurchase the stock in view of the fact that the subscription by the Rubber Development Corporation was for the sole purpose of implementing the rubber program, as contemplated in the agreement of March 3, 1942 [73] (as extended to June 30, 1947). This agreement was entered into by both parties only for the purposes of the United Nations and hemispheric defense; consequently both the United States and Brazil benefited from this cooperative undertaking.

A recent interview with the representatives of the United States

---

[72] Not printed.
[73] Department of State Executive Agreement Series No. 371 or 57 Stat. (pt. 2) 1318.

Government who arranged for participation by the Rubber Development Corporation in the Bank revealed that the question as to whether or not the Brazilian Government would purchase the Rubber Development Corporation stock was discussed at length at that time. The representatives stated that no agreement could be reached on this point, and it was recognized that the question would have to be left for subsequent determination. However, it is significant that provision was made at that time in the statutes governing the Bank for withdrawal of the Rubber Development Corporation from the Bank by the sale of its stock.

The Department and the Rubber Development Corporation consider that neither Mr. Bouças nor the Commission for the Control of the Washington Agreements is the proper party to negotiate for disposal of the stock, since, for the reasons given above, the problem becomes purely a policy and political question for settlement between the Embassy and the Foreign Office. Apparently previous messages from the Embassy to the Foreign Office and the Minister of Finance have not been answered except indirectly by the suggestion of the Commission for the Control of the Washington Agreements that the matter be discussed with Mr. Bouças. This is not considered satisfactory, and the Embassy is instructed again to call the matter to the attention of the Foreign Office and to insist upon immediate discussion of arrangements for disposal of the stock.

103.9151/4–1047

Memorandum by Mr. Richard F. O'Toole of the Division of Brazilian Affairs to the Chief of That Division (Dawson)

RESTRICTED [WASHINGTON,] April 10, 1947.

Subject: RDC Investment of $3 Million in Banco de Credito da Borracha.

A few days ago I told Mr. Consley, General Counsel of RDC, that Ambassador Pawley was not disposed to negotiate for a settlement of this matter, on a political basis, unless and until RDC had exhausted its remedies,—and then only with the understanding that the Embassy would be given a free hand in negotiating any settlement.

In another conversation with Mr. Consley, this morning, he told me that RDC considers that it has exhausted all its remedies in this matter and would like the Ambassador to take it up with the Brazilian authorities. He added that RDC would not want to settle on too low a basis say, for example, $10,000. I answered that while I had no knowledge of Ambassador Pawley's ideas along these lines I felt that his thinking would undoubtedly run along substantial lines. I also said that I would arrange to have his (Mr. Consley's) wishes brought to the Ambassador's attention and that no doubt the latter would see that there was a prior exchange of viewpoints in the event that he should decide to take up the case. He asked me to keep him informed of developments.

103.9151/7-1647 : Circular airgram

The Secretary of State to Certain Diplomatic Representatives and Consular Officers in the American Republics [74]

WASHINGTON, July 16, 1947—9 a. m.

From Hadlock RFC.[75] . . .

. . . .

You are requested to inform appropriate officials of local Government that coincident with termination of all remaining rubber agreements, RDC has dissolved as of June 30, 1947, and all of its assets and liabilities, functions and duties, transferred to Reconstruction Finance Corporation. Since RDC's obligation to purchase rubber will have been satisfied by June 30, 1947, even though rubber has not actually been shipped or paid for in certain instances, there remains only matter of liquidating RDC's activities.

Dissolution of RDC will not involve for the present any change in personnel nor in the methods of operation heretofore followed by RDC. Existing personnel will act for Reconstruction Finance Corporation in winding up affairs of RDC.

You are further requested to inform local banks with which RDC funds are deposited to change designation of such accounts to "Reconstruction Finance Corporation–Working Fund". Previously authorized RDC field representatives and Treasurer of RFC authorized to make withdrawals and deposits. [Hadlock.]

MARSHALL

103.9151 : Telegram

The Acting Secretary of State to the Embassy in Brazil

RESTRICTED   US URGENT   WASHINGTON, October 3, 1947—6 p. m.
NIACT

1134. BCB notified RDC–RFC of stockholders meetings Oct. 6 Belem. Emb requested inform BCB that Dept. and RDC–RFC con-

---

[74] Sent to the Embassies in Brazil, Bolivia, Colombia, Costa Rica, Ecuador, Mexico, Peru, and Nicaragua; and to the Consulates at Belem, Georgetown, and Port of Spain.
[75] Gerald B. Hadlock, Executive Director, Office of Rubber Reserve, Reconstruction Finance Corporation.

sider inappropriate further U.S. representation in affairs of Bank, since rubber program ended and corporate life RDC terminated June 30, 1947. (Complete authority liquidation RDC delegated RFC, Dept. Cir. tel. July 1 [76])

Emb also requested inform Dept. present status attempts obtain reimbursement RDC $3,000,000 stock in BCB and prospects settlement. (Dept. Instruction 590, March 19).

Sent to Rio as 1134, repeated to Belem as 133.

LOVETT

[The Ambassador reported in telegram 276, March 17, 1948, 7:10 p. m., that the Brazilians had agreed to acquire the bank shares at the proposed price and conditions. However, at the end of 1948 the Brazilian legislature had failed to approve, according to the Embassy's telegram 1312, December 31, 1948, 4 p. m. (103.9151)]

INTEREST OF THE UNITED STATES IN BRAZILIAN PROBLEMS INVOLVING FORMER ENEMY PROPERTY AND PERSONS [77]

800.515/12–1846 : Airgram

The Secretary of State to the Embassy in Brazil

CONFIDENTIAL WASHINGTON, January 28, 1947.

A–75. Reference is made to your despatch no. 1295 of December 18, 1946 [76] concerning a proposed Brazilian law affecting property of enemy nationals.

The Department has not raised objections to the lifting of restrictions in other countries if the main objectives of the Replacement Program or other security measures are not prejudiced thereby, but it prefers lifting of restrictions on an *ad hoc* basis after review of individual cases and has so indicated to several American Republics. The Department realizes, however, that such individual review would be extremely difficult to administer in Brazil in view of the broad scope and application of Decree Law no. 4166. The Department further realizes that it is the apparent intention of the AGEDE to prevent certain highly undesirable elements from being benefitted by the proposed law, but the question arises whether Article 7 is sufficiently broad or whether it would be desirable to extend this Article 7 in any respect, e.g. so as to include other persons who have actively engaged in inimical activities or who may be qualified candidates for repatria-

---

[76] Not printed.
[77] For previous documentation, see *Foreign Relations*, 1946, vol. XI, p. 462 ff.

tion to Germany. The Department would appreciate receiving your comments on this point and suggests that you may wish to discuss this point with officers of the AGEDE, if you consider such action feasible.

MARSHALL

740.00119 EW/2–1147

The Brazilian Ministry for Foreign Affairs to the American Embassy in Brazil [78]

[Translation]

DPC/DPO/48/949.4 (00)

The Ministry of Foreign Affairs presents its compliments to the Embassy of the United States of America and has the honor to communicate that, by note presented on January 22, 1947 to the Council of Foreign Ministers presently meeting in London, the Brazilian Government had occasion to formulate some opinions on the question of the independence of Austria and on the future statute for Germany.

2. In the case of Germany, in addition to considering in its note certain questions relative to reorganization of that country to exercise its role as a member of the international community, the Brazilian Government brought up the matter of reparations [79] which it thought it could rightfully demand from its ex-enemy; it recalled that notwithstanding its active belligerency, Brazil was not invited to participate in the Paris Conference of Reparations and it ended by strongly urging the Council under reference to review Brazil's claim and to examine the possibility of recognizing its right to a part of the enemy assets located in German territory and intended for the payment of reparations.

3. Addressing itself today to the Embassy of the United States of America on the subject, the Ministry of Foreign Affairs wishes to call its attention to the fact that the Paris Conference did not make up the chart of reparations to be claimed from Germany solely with data relative to losses and damages of the war. It is known that the countries, participants in the Conference, were invited also to compute in their account of reparations various other factors among which stands out that relative to the war effort expressed in costly expenditures of war, loss of human life and days of labor lost.

4. It is necessary to make clear that, at first, the Brazilian Government proceeded only with the calculation of losses and damages caused by the enemy to Brazil and to the Brazilians. Notwithstanding the

---

[78] Copy transmitted to the Department by the Ambassador in Brazil in his despatch 1669, February 11, 1947; received February 18.
[79] For documentation on this subject, see vol. II, pp. 391 ff.

modest amount of its claims, it soon became evident that, deprived of the means of reparation conceded to the other Allies and having to indemnify itself only with liquidated German property under its jurisdiction, Brazil would be able to indemnify itself for the losses suffered only in greatly reduced proportions.

5. Taking into consideration today the criterion adopted by the Paris Conference on the matter of reparations and reserving the right to claim in equity the application of the same treatment in its case—the Brazilian Government must review the amount of its losses. This act by itself is justifiable. It is well known that, from the early days, hostilities in Europe began badly and as a result of its various agreements with the Government of the United States of America Brazil mobilized itself to cooperate in the war effort of its sister of the North. The rubber campaign, the minerals campaign, the contribution of its merchant marine and the furnishing without limitation of primary materials of all types in favor of the Allied cause—all this caused a considerable dislocation of manual labor in the country with the consequent disequilibrium of its means of production and distribution, of daily aggravation caused by the constant drain on its transportation system and its industrial equipment, a situation that still continues.

6. But now, being compelled to compute in its calculations, as the Allies are doing, the costly expenditures of war, Brazil sees its reparations account growing in terms out of proportion to the recourses for indemnification that it has.

7. It is necessary to add—and the Brazilian Government made the observation in its note to the Council of Foreign Ministers—that with the dissolution and liquidation of the industrial and commercial enterprises of the Axis which operated in Brazilian territory and contributed thus to national prosperity, Brazil certainly fulfilled its duty as an ally, but was not indemnified for what it lost. In effect, if the State uses such liquidations as a means of covering the losses of its nationals, the Nation will bear a double loss because having received nothing from the outside, it is still depriving itself of future collaboration with such enterprises in the development of its economic life.

8. It is hoped that the question of reparations will be revised when reviewed in London in terms of conciliation with certain territorial readjustments claimed by neighboring countries of Germany. The ex-Secretary of State, Mr. James Byrnes, foresaw this in his speech of last September 6 delivered in Stuttgart.[80]

9. If such should be the case, as everything indicates it will be, the

---

[80] Department of State *Bulletin*, September 15, 1946, p. 496.

proportional division made at Paris will have to suffer the necessary changes (*deducçãos*). The Inter-Allied Agency of Brussels will remain, then, with an expendable balance corresponding to territorial compensations that the Council of Foreign Ministers was asked to approve.

10. The Ministry of Foreign Affairs has the honor to submit the present considerations to the Embassy of the United States of America, requesting its courtesy in transmitting them to the Department of State, with anticipated assurance that the Brazilian Government will appreciate the support that the case merits at the hands of the Government of the United States of America, at the time when the question will be discussed at the meetings of the Council of the Four Great Powers.

11. The Ministry of Foreign Affairs extends its thanks to the Embassy of the United States of America for its courtesy in transmitting this note to its destination.

Rio de Janeiro, January 31, 1947.

710.62115/2–1247 : Airgram

The Ambassador in Brazil (Pawley) to the Secretary of State

CONFIDENTIAL　　　　　　　Rio de Janeiro, February 12, 1947.

A–167. Reference is made to the Department's instruction no. 366, November 23, 1946,[81] which reads in part as follows:

"It is suggested that the Foreign Office be informed of the United States Government's continued interest in removing dangerous Germans from this hemisphere and preventing a resurgence of German influence in the American Republics. It is further suggested that, if practicable, some expression be obtained from the Brazilian Government as to what steps, if any, it is planning to initiate pointing towards the removal of those dangerous Germans still remaining in Brazil."

The Department's telegram no. 62, January 17, 1947,[81] instructs the Embassy "to make no further effort to obtain repatriation or punishment of comparatively minor offenders which still remain unpunished in Brazil".

The Embassy will appreciate receiving clarification of these conflicting instructions.

Pawley

---

[81] Not printed.

740.00119 Council/2–2047 : Telegram

The Chargé in the United Kingdom (Gallman) to the Secretary of State

SECRET LONDON, February 20, 1947—11 a. m.

1154. Delsec 1255 from Murphy.[81a] Brazil, in presenting its views on Germany and Austria, complains because it was not invited to participate in the Paris Conference on Reparations and that the German assets over which it has jurisdiction and which, according to a note from the Govts of France, the US and UK in September 1946, is authorized to liquidate and use for purposes of reparations, will not be sufficient to compensate Brazil in the same proportion as countries participating in Paris will receive. For this reason, Brazil asks to participate in the sharing of assets situated in Germany which will be used for reparations purposes.

It is my understanding that the US undertook to make satisfactory arrangements with Brazil in the matter of reparations outside the scope of the Paris Act.[82] Hence, this complaint of Brazil which is addressed to the four countries participating here is in fact a complaint that Brazil is not receiving proper treatment from the US. Dept's comment would be appreciated.

Repeated Rio de Janeiro 4. [Murphy.]

GALLMAN

710.62115/2–1247 : Airgram

The Acting Secretary of State to the Embassy in Brazil

CONFIDENTIAL WASHINGTON, March 10, 1947.

A–176. There is no inclination by Department to deviate in any degree from joint commitments agreed to by all the American republics at Chapultepec and set forth in Resolutions VII and XLII [83] which were specifically created to eliminate the continuance and prevent the resurgence of Nazi influence in this hemisphere. Therefore the Embassy may well carry out the suggestion contained in the Department's instruction no. 366 of November 23, 1946 as quoted in Embassy's A–167 of February 12, 1947.[84] Department perceives no con-

---

[81a] Robert D. Murphy, U.S. Political Adviser for Germany.

[82] See the multilateral agreement of January 14, 1946, Department of State Treaties and Other International Acts Series (TIAS) No. 1655, or 61 Stat. (pt. 3) 3157; for documentation on the subject, see *Foreign Relations*, 1945, vol. IX, pp. 650 ff.

[83] Pan American Union, *Final Act of the Inter-American Conference on Problems of War and Peace*, pp. 38–40 and 80–81.

[84] Not printed.

flict between this instruction which is aimed at the removal of those Germans considered dangerous who still remain in Brazil and instructions quoted from Deptel 62 of January 17 [85] which referred to minor offenders only.

As requested in reference instruction, an up-to-date list of Germans now in Brazil who could be considered dangerous according to standards adopted at Montevideo in Resolution XXVI [86] would be useful to the Department.

ACHESON

740.00119 Council/3-1147 : Telegram

The Ambassador in Brazil (Pawley) to the Secretary of State

SECRET   RIO DE JANEIRO, March 11, 1947—7 p. m.

288. London's telegram 1154, February 20. Embassy is not aware of any undertaking "to make satisfactory arrangements with Brazil in the matter of reparations outside the scope of the Paris Act".

This Embassy will be interested in learning if any conversations this regard were carried on either Washington or London.

PAWLEY

740.00119 EW/2-1147

Memorandum by the Chief of the Division of Brazilian Affairs (Dawson) to the Acting Assistant Chief of the Division of German and Austrian Economic Affairs (Todd)

[WASHINGTON,] March 12, 1947.

The attached despatch from the Embassy at Rio de Janeiro encloses a note from the Brazilian Foreign Office [87] again bringing up the question of Brazilian reparations aspirations. The note asks that the considerations in it be passed on to the Department. There is no indication that our Embassy in Rio has made any reply, so instructions from the Department to the Embassy embodying what we wish it to say are in order.

This is particularly advisable since the Brazilian Chargé at London [88] complained to Murphy there on January 20 (see telegram 412, January 20, 8 p. m. from London [85]) that his Government was put out

---

[85] Not printed.
[86] Of the Emergency Advisory Committee for Political Defense. See the *Third Annual Report of the Emergency Advisory Committee for Political Defense*, Montevideo, 1945.
[87] Despatch 1669, February 11, 1947, not printed; for its enclosure, see p. 487.
[88] Hugo Gouthier de Oliveira Gondim.

at never having received an acknowledgment of its note no. 104 of April 26, 1946 [90] to our Chargé at Rio on the subject of German reparations. This accusation may be technically correct as Ambassador Pawley appears to have presented no formal note, but he did take up the whole matter informally with the Brazilian Foreign Office in detail on the basis of airgrams A–442, A–443 and A–444 of June 24, 1946,[91] drafted by Mr. Surrey of ES.

I should think it would be preferable for ES or GA to draft a reply to the attached despatch. There seems to me to be nothing much to do except to reiterate the position consistently taken by the Department and definitely instruct the Embassy in Rio to present a note embodying it so the Brazilians can have no grounds for further complaint that we have not studied their position and made our own clear in a formal fashion.

ALLAN DAWSON

740.32112A/1–3147

The Acting Secretary of State to the Embassy in Brazil

RESTRICTED
No. 596

WASHINGTON, March 21, 1947.

The Acting Secretary of State refers to the Embassy's despatch no. 1589 of January 31, 1947,[90] concerning the desire of the Companhia Cervejaria Brahma to be released from its undertaking.[92]

The Department appreciates the reluctance expressed by the Embassy to grant such release, since it appears that the firm has not complied with all of the provisions of the undertaking, and the firm's failure to comply may be said to constitute an act of bad faith. The Department wishes, however, to make the following comments with regard to the termination of undertakings in general:

It is felt that, with the withdrawal of the Proclaimed List and in the absence of other sanctions to be applied against violators, the effective enforcement of undertakings has by and large become difficult, if not impossible. For this reason the Embassy was instructed in the Department's airgram no. 841 of November 29, 1946 [93] to release firms or persons from undertakings when such release is requested by the signatory, unless circumstances were found to be present which would make it desirable to retain the undertaking in force. The purpose of granting such release only upon request was to avoid creating

---

[90] Not printed.
[91] None printed.
[92] A pledge taken by a person or firm to have no business dealings with Axis companies appearing on the Proclaimed List.
[93] *Foreign Relations*, 1946, vol. XI, p. 463.

the impression that this government had effected a wholesale whitewash of firms or persons previously considered objectionable or that it is no longer interested in economic security measures in general, and in the affairs of such firms or persons in particular. The clause "unless a review of the case reveals any circumstances which would make it desirable to retain the undertaking in effect for the period specified therein" is interpreted as referring to consideration of such factors as (*a*) the accomplishments which can be achieved through observance of the undertaking, (*b*) any adverse effects of release (e.g. release may compromise an effected elimination of undesirable elements by removing the obstacle to readmission), (*c*) the possibility of obtaining full compliance, and (*d*) the desirability of insisting on compliance for the sake of principle.

In the case at hand, and with reference to point (*c*) above, the Department wonders whether refusal to grant the requested release could be expected to result in complete fulfillment of the firm's obligations at this time, since full compliance was not obtained at the time when reinclusion of the firm in the Proclaimed List remained a possibility. In this connection, it is noted that in the Embassy's despatch no. 3640 of December 4, 1945,[94] in which a proposal was submitted for the termination of the fiscalization of the firm, the Embassy stated that there had been substantial compliance with the principal conditions of the undertaking, including elimination of the most objectionable employees.

On the other hand, and with reference to point (*a*) above, if the firm should decide to comply with the terms of the undertaking, it would presumably be obliged under Brazilian law to pay indemnification to the employees dismissed; in addition to receiving such a windfall, these persons would not be hindered in any way in seeking employment with other firms in which they might be more dangerous than in a brewery.

With regard to those persons named by the Embassy who are shareholders in the company, the Department perceives certain practical difficulties surrounding any attempt to remove them from the affairs of the firm. It would appear that none of these persons are subject to Brazilian expropriation measures either on the basis of nationality or inimical activities, since such action has not been taken and the Department's files do not indicate that such action has been contemplated or has been requested of the Brazilian authorities. Elimination of these shareholders would, therefore, have to be accomplished by persuasion which, if successful, would result in placing into their hands funds available for investment elsewhere.

---

[94] Not printed.

The Department believes, therefore, that the Companhia Cervejaria Brahma should be released from its undertaking, unless the Embassy feels that retention of the undertaking may still accomplish a useful purpose, or that continued fiscalization of the firm is desirable in view of the presence of objectionable employees and shareholders, or that withdrawal of the undertaking at this time would be embarrassing to the Embassy.

740.00119 EW/2-1147 : Telegram

The Acting Secretary of State to the Embassy in Brazil

SECRET WASHINGTON, April 9, 1947—6 p. m.

376. Dept requests you make written reply Braz FonOff notes April 26, 1946 [95] and Feb 11, 1947 [96] re German reparations. General line this reply shld be similar position stated A442, A443 and A444 of June 24, 1946 [97] with exception that portion indicating US govt wld consider attempting arrange Brazil's participation IARA which is no longer considered feasible. In addition you are authorized mention current negotiations with reference possible sharing proceeds liquidation Ger assets in Amer Republics with further indication that Dept believes any such sharing would increase Brazil's receipts. May also state consideration being given possibility delivery Brazil large torpedo boat from US share Ger Navy. Ur statement shld emphasize tentative nature this possibility. Vessel being considered is approximately 1100 tons and reported excellent condition.

Suggest ur note be brief in anticipation more detailed reply to be made after receipt Braz response which undoubtedly will be forthcoming without delay. Dept chiefly interested this stage avoiding further Braz complaint re US failure give formal answer their representations.

Telegraph summary ur note & forward text earliest airmail.

ACHESON

740.00119 EW/4-3047

The Chargé in Brazil (Brooks) to the Secretary of State

SECRET RIO DE JANEIRO, April 30, 1947.

No. 2186

The Chargé d'Affaires ad interim refers to the Department's secret telegram No. 376 of April 9, 1947, and has the honor to enclose here-

---

[95] Not printed.
[96] Reference is to note of January 31, 1947, transmitted in despatch 1669, February 11, 1947 : for text of note, see p. 487.
[97] None printed.

with the draft of a note prepared for submittal to the Ministry of Foreign Affairs. It has been considered desirable to prepare the note in draft form as some clarification may be required in connection with the statement to the effect that the United States cannot cede any part of its reparations and the indication that the Government of the United States is contemplating the cession of one large torpedo boat. The Embassy presumes that vessels received as the United States share of the German Navy are not to be considered as reparations and has so stated in the appended note.

. . . .

[Enclosure]

Draft Note From the American Embassy to the Brazilian Ministry for Foreign Affairs

The Embassy of the United States of America presents its compliments to the Ministry of Foreign Affairs and has the honor to refer to the Ministry's note (DPC/DPO/48/949.4(00)) dated January 31, 1947), the Embassy's reply, Note No. 336 of February 11, 1947,[98] and previous communications concerning the reparations which the Brazilian Government feels it can rightfully demand from Germany.

The Embassy has been instructed by the Department of State to point out that at the time that plans were being made for holding the Paris Reparations Conference, it was recognized that nations which declared war against Germany would have an interest in obtaining reparations from Germany. It was also recognized that certain of these countries, particularly those which were overrun by Germany and those which had devoted a totality of their resources, human and material, to the waging of war, would have claims against Germany for reparations which would be so extensive as to prohibit anything approximating a reasonable satisfaction of such claims. It was also clear that certain countries could satisfy a comparatively large share of their claims against Germany out of German assets located within their borders. Countries in this latter situation, if invited to participate in the Paris Reparations Conference, would have been in a position of having to yield up certain of the German assets within their borders in order that the percentage of total satisfaction that they would realize would equal the percentage realized by other countries with considerably larger claims. This would have seriously interfered with the establishment of uniform procedures and mechanisms of reparations by the countries participating in the Conference, since it would have divided participants into those who would have to yield a certain proportion of assets within their borders and a second cate-

---

[98] Latter not printed.

gory of those who would have to obtain assets from other sources in addition to the German assets within their borders. It was therefore believed equitable and, from the point of view of formulating procedure, desirable not to ask Brazil to participate in a conference wherein she would lose rather than gain by such participation.

The Brazilian Government in an earlier note suggested that the Government of the United States might be able to devote part of its reparations share to the satisfaction of Brazil's claims. Under the reparations agreement this is, unfortunately, not possible as the United States when it relinquished, prior to the formulation of shares, a portion of the shares of Category B assets to which it would have been entitled on a statistical basis, left itself no recourses to that part which it had sacrificed. Nor is the United States authorized to devote any part of the reparations which it obtains through the removal procedure to any nationals other than its own.

The attention of the Brazilian Government is invited to the current negotiations with reference to the possible sharing of the proceeds of German assets in the American Republics. The Department of State believes that such sharing will increase Brazil's total receipts.

The Embassy has been instructed to stress to the Brazilian Government that the United States of America, for its part, has not forgotten the contributions which Brazil made during the war to the common cause. On the contrary as stated above the Government of Brazil was not invited to the Paris Reparations Conference in order, within the terms of the Mexico City Conference, to protect her interests and to assure her a greater satisfaction of her claims than she could otherwise secure.

Furthermore consideration is currently being given to the possibility of delivery to Brazil of one large torpedo boat from the United States share of the German Navy—a measure which may be feasible as the United States share of the German Navy was not considered as part of the reparations agreement. The vessel under consideration is approximately 1100 tons and is reported to be in excellent condition. The Department of State, however, has requested that the tentative nature of this possibility be emphasized.[99]

The Embassy takes this opportunity [etc.].

---

[99] In telegram 598, June 9, 4 p. m., the Department indicated certain modifications of language in the draft and added to this offer of a torpedo boat, a sailing training ship with auxiliary diesel engines (740.00119 EW/4–3047).

CHILE

ATTITUDE OF THE UNITED STATES TOWARD LABOR VIOLENCE IN CHILE AND THE ENSUING BREACH OF RELATIONS BETWEEN CHILE AND THE SOVIET UNION, CZECHOSLOVAKIA, AND YUGOSLAVIA

825.6362/6–1147 : Telegram

The Ambassador in Chile (Bowers) to the Secretary of State

SECRET　　　　　　　　　　SANTIAGO, June 11, 1947—4 p. m.

472. Mytel 438, June 4 [1] and previous correspondence. Foreign Minister [2] asked me again today about possibility.[3] There is a grave crisis and while the miners have agreed increase output to make up for loss during short strike, the coal in reserve is very short and strike would be disastrous in extreme. With this coal asked in reserve, position of government in dealing with subversive element involved would be greatly strengthened. Government is now compelled resort to rationing coal, and, because coal shortage, to rationing electricity and gas.

BOWERS

825.5045/6–1347 : Telegram

The Ambassador in Chile (Bowers) to the Secretary of State

RESTRICTED　　URGENT　　　SANTIAGO, June 13, 1947—1 p. m.

477. Late last night government declared Santiago province an "emergency zone" for initial period 30 days following armed attacks yesterday evening against busses carrying armed guards by striking Communist-controlled bus drivers in four sections of city. Army now in charge with General Rafael Fernandez commanding second division named "Jefe de Plaza". Armed forces called to barracks. Interior Minister Cuevas stated government had proof attack planned at meeting of Communist strikers June 11.

Fire from strikers returned by Army and *carabineros* after dispersal attempts failed. Four bystanders killed, several wounded.

---

[1] Not printed.
[2] Raul Juliet Gomez.
[3] i.e., the possibility of U.S. compliance with a Chilean request for coal shipment.

All papers except Communist *El Siglo* fix responsibility on Communists. Socialist *La Opinion* report headlined "Communist rebellion" states Communists attempted revolt using bus strike as pretext.

City calm this morning with busses operating under armed guard and authorities in full control.

BOWERS

825.5045/6–1547 : Telegram

The Ambassador in Chile (Bowers) to the Secretary of State

RESTRICTED   US URGENT   SANTIAGO, June 15, 1947—1 p. m.

484. Political committee Communist Party published statement yesterday placing responsibility of bus strike disturbances of June 12, in which four persons killed, on armed forces, govt and President of Republic. Last night President Gonzalez Videla gave to press forceful declaration asserting that disturbances were perpetrated by persons armed by Communist Party and constituted part of a preconceived plan to alter public order. In condemning Communist attempt to place responsibility on govt, he states that "they are mistaken if they believe that President of the Republic can be used as an instrument of their designs". He promises that he will "fulfill national program and will give laborers and employees betterment they ask for; will never use public force to restrict constitutional and social rights of people; and will not permit that Communist Party with its treacherous demagogy pretend exclusive representation of the working classes of Chile".

President's declaration enthusiastically received by all sectors except Communists who today publish statement that it will be studied by political committee and reply issued at later date. Communist organ on other hand publishes front page direct attack on govt, listing raises in foodstuffs and utilities as well as failure to create copper monopoly, delivery of exchange to Yankee bankers to pay foreign debt, North American control of Magallanes petroleum, Yankee control of Chilean steel industry, repression of public liberties, and definitive abandonment of national program.

Bus strike continues but almost normal service maintained by govt with police and armed guards. Situation calm. Communists are trying to organize general strike for June 23.

I suggest situation set forth above be taken into consideration in connection with Chile's request for coal stockpile for use in its struggle to combat Communism.

BOWERS

CHILE 499

701.2561/7–947 : Telegram

The Ambassador in Chile (Bowers) to the Secretary of State

RESTRICTED   SANTIAGO, July 9, 1947—noon.

556. Vice President Cuevas [4] yesterday urgently called to his office Soviet Ambassador Zhukov and presented formal Chilean Government protest against treatment being accorded Chilean diplomatic representation in Moscow.

Son of former Chilean Ambassador David Cruz Ocampo married to Russian has not been allowed leave Soviet Union with wife. Furthermore, Chilean Chargé d'Affaires Carlos Valenzuela and Military Attaché Colonel Armando Martin have systematically been refused assistance in obtaining living quarters or given any other facilities since arrival in Moscow. Chargé has been forced use room in house of young Cruz Ocampo and Colonel Martin has to sleep in quarters unbefitting his rank.

Since all Chilean Government protests to Soviet Government have remained unanswered, Vice President informed Ambassador Zhukov that Soviet procedure was inexplicable in view cordial treatment being accorded Soviet representation in Santiago. *El Mercurio* reports Vice President gave Ambassador Zhukov period 48 hours obtain from his government full explanation. If at termination this period satisfactory explanation not received Chilean representation would be recalled and Ambassador would be declared *persona non grata* and given his passports.

Government organ *La Nacion* only newspaper not carrying account interview; even Communist *El Siglo* gives mild version of incident. Foreign Office official, however, states press announcement substantially correct.

BOWERS

825.00B/9–1747 : Telegram

The Ambassador in Chile (Bowers) to the Secretary of State

CONFIDENTIAL   SANTIAGO, September 17, 1947—7 p. m.

745. In speech before Rotary Club today President Gonzalez Videla according to reliable American businessman made his strongest condemnation of communism to date. Speech not for publication but no other restrictions placed upon it.

Outstanding points made by President:

1. He said world divided into two sections: That part dominated by Asiatic Russia in which all human and personal liberties have been

---

[4] Also Minister of the Interior.

denied individuals and which subscribed to vile and vicious practices; and the occidental or Anglo-Saxon section which is sole remaining haven for such rights and liberties. He added that Chile had to align herself with one or the other and that his strongest efforts in past and future would be assure that Chile takes her place with the occidental group—only one in which she would be able preserve her democratic way of life.

2. He stressed that inasmuch as Communists had assisted him in his election he had felt duty bound recognize such assistance by including three Communist officials in his Cabinet but that his effort to fit Communist representation into a democratic government completely hopeless and unavailing. He added that every Communist placed in public office had double-crossed him either upon instructions from foreign power or for own personal benefit.

3. President stated emphatically that as long as any of "leftist" parties had anything to do with Communists or Communist Party he would have nothing further to do with them.

Embassy attempting obtain stenographic transcript speech.

BOWERS

825.00B/9–2347

The Ambassador in Chile (Bowers) to the Secretary of State

CONFIDENTIAL
No. 15,633

SANTIAGO, September 23, 1947.

SIR: With reference to Embassy's despatch 15,586 of August 27, 1947,[5] I have the honor to report that the President has since then been gradually eliminating Communist functionaries from their various Government posts.

After getting rid of the Communist *Intendentes* and Governors, steps were then taken to remove Party members from the various pension funds, some twelve of these functionaries having already been officially separated from their positions. On September 14 the President signed a decree issued by the Ministry of Economy and Commerce removing Messrs. Bernardo Araya (head of the Communist C.T.Ch.), José Campusano, José Diaz Iturrieta, Raúl Gatica, Reinaldo Nuñez from the National Economic Council.

As and when the corresponding decrees are actually prepared, signed and placed into effect, the few remaining Communist functionaries will also most probably be forced out.

With respect to Communist functionaries in the Government, the Department is respectfully referred to a report submitted to his principals by Attaché William B. Caldwell, dated August 28, 1947 and entitled "Communists in the Chilean Government."[5]

---

[5] Not printed.

The Government can for the moment take no steps against those Communist officials holding elective positions but the President seems to be gradually ensuring that no administrative posts of any importance are left in the Communists' hands.

Respectfully yours, CLAUDE G. BOWERS

825.5045/10-647 : Telegram

The Acting Secretary of State to the Embassy in Chile

CONFIDENTIAL WASHINGTON, October 7, 1947—6 p. m.

491. Following is situation coal allocations for export. November allocations made Oct 3.

Due very tight coal situation US and critical winter requirements Europe total set aside for all LA countries drastically reduced. Allocation Chile 9,000 tons November compared 18,000 tons October.

You should tell Pres (urtel 776 Oct 6 4 p. m.[6]) possibility obtaining anywhere near 100,000 tons next month extremely remote. Dept however will have Chilean allocation reexamined at highest level but several days may be required for final decision.

To strengthen Dept's discussion with allocation authorities telegraph miner's current employment conditions, their demands, and differences between latter and wages and working conditions assured by govt but rejected by miners.

LOVETT

825.00B/10-847

Memorandum by the Deputy Director of the Office of American Republic Affairs (Woodward) to the Assistant Secretary of State for Political Affairs (Armour)

CONFIDENTIAL [WASHINGTON,] October 8, 1947.

On October 6, 1947, the President of Chile, Gonzalez Videla, declared war on communism as a result of what he claims is a communist plot to overthrow the Government and obtain control of the production (in order in an emergency to deprive the US of the use) of strategic raw materials, namely copper and nitrates.

This action followed the elimination of communists from appointive public office in Chile several weeks ago, and was precipitated by a strike on October 4 of 18,000 Chilean coal miners. On October 6 the miners refused to return to work despite the Government's assurance

---

[6] Not printed.

of a 40 percent wage increase, a house allowance, and a guarantee of their right to work.

The Government of Chile publicly announced that the Legation of a country which is a satellite of Russia has been intervening in the strike. The President privately identified the satellite country as Yugoslavia and told Ambassador Bowers Chilean communists were receiving orders from Belgrade and a Yugoslav General [7] recently had come to Chile with specific instructions to precipitate a test of strength. He added that Chile was chosen for this test because of the heavy US investment there. Furthermore the President stated that the Communists had despatched agents to the American owned copper and nitrate mines to foment solidarity strikes, but 30 of these agents had been apprehended and were being held on warships. Later 30 armed communist pickets who were terrorizing workers at the coal mineheads were arrested and sent to the far South.

Other steps taken by the Chilean Government to date include:

1) Mobilization of the 1946 conscripts and of all coal technicians and specialists.
2) Application of emergency powers, voted by the Chilean Congress about a month ago, in the coal zone emergency area. This means all those inciting to disorder or urging miners not to return to work will be arrested. The first to be arrested were the Communist ex-Mayor and ex-Secretary of Colonel.
3) Rationing of gas, electricity, and out train schedules and the closing of power plants at Santiago and Valparaiso.

The President informed Ambassador Bowers that he intends to conscript 16,000 coal miners into the army but the army is convinced that even then they will not work since 60 percent of them have been keyed up to a pitch of fanaticism by communist agents. He expects they will have to be replaced by new elements, an operation which will take three months. Whether this attempt is made depends upon whether Chile can count on the moral and material help of the US.

It is possible that the drastic action already taken by the Government of Chile will induce the miners to return to work in a day or two. If this does not occur, however, Chile requests that the US provide 100,000 tons of coal per month during November, December and January while fanatically communist labor at the coal mines is being replaced.

The allocation of coal for export to Chile from the US is 18,000 tons for October and only 9,000 tons for November. The latter figure compares with total export allocations of 3,500,000 tons for November, a reduction of 500,000 tons from the October figure. Of this 3,500,000

---

[7] Gen. Ljubonier Ilic.

tons, 3,000,000 tons are destined for Europe. This means only 500,000 tons are destined for all other sources.

Of the 500,000 ton allocation to destinations other than Europe, Argentina and Brazil have separate allocations. All other countries of Latin America are given a lump allocation of 6 cargoes or about 54,000 tons.

In other words the set aside for November for Latin American countries other than Argentina and Brazil is only slightly over half the request of Chile for that month and also for December and for January.

I consider we should instruct Ambassador Bowers to assure the President of Chile that the United States is prepared to provide 100,000 tons of coal during November as a one time operation*, the allocations to Chile for December and January to be considered later in the light of subsequent developments.

It is at least possible that Chile will not have to avail itself of such an allocation since knowledge that the US is prepared to keep essential services in Chile in operation during November may well undermine the communist test of strength and induce the miners to return to work.

Robert F. Woodward

825.00B/10–847 : Telegram

The Ambassador in Chile (Bowers) to the Secretary of State

CONFIDENTIAL   Santiago, October 8, 1947—11 p. m.

786. For Lovett and Armour. Tonight President informed me of the action of the govt this evening in sending across the frontier the Yugoslav Chargé and the Secretary of the Yugo Legation in Buenos Aires who was here.[8] Later he sent me a full statement which will be sent later by air mail. The purport of this statement follows:

The Govt has precise information that instructions to the Communists in Chile directing their activities are being sent by the Agrupacion Regional Latin Americana which has its center in Buenos Aires and Rosario which has intimate contact with the Communist international center in Belgrade. The work of this organization intensified immediately after the visit to Chile of the Yugo General Ilic who came for the President's inauguration. During his visit he held conferences with the Communist leaders in Santiago and the provinces, he took the initiative in organizing groups for Communist

---

*Chile's normal consumption averages about 160,000 tons per month. [Footnote in the original.]

[8] Andres Cunja and Dalibor Jakasa, respectively.

propaganda. Since he left numerous agents have appeared in Chile mostly Yugoslavs bearing Chilean passports forged by the Agrupacion Regional Latin Americana, bearing instructions from the Communist International in Europe.

Before leaving Chile General Ilic had accredited as Yugoslav Chargé Andres Cunja who had lived in Chile since 1937. He established contacts with the Communist Party here and organized groups of Yugoslavs and descendants and made possible the entrance to Chile of Communist agents. Plans had been announced that Yugoslav Minister in Buenos Aires [9] would visit Chile but because of the attitude of Chilean Govt this was abandoned. But a few days ago a Secretary of the Legation in Buenos Aires, Dalibor Jakasa, arrived with instructions for the Chargé. These called on the Communists to (a) intensify the campaign against the US and the western democracies, (b) to attack the policy of continental defense, (c) to carry out sabotage of production through slowing down production or through strikes.

These instructions are now being carried out by the Communist Party here and the purpose was to create strikes in the mines of coal, nitrate and copper.

With full information as to these activities the Chargé was summoned to the Foreign Office this afternoon, informed that his functions were terminated, and since he had gravely infringed the hospitality of the country and attacked it through subversive activities, "the govt had decided in conformity with the practice of international law to put him and the Argentine secretary on the frontier." This measure carried out this afternoon.

BOWERS

825.5045/10–947 : Telegram

The Ambassador in Chile (Bowers) to the Secretary of State

CONFIDENTIAL SANTIAGO, October 9, 1947—8 p. m.

783. Issue raised in Chile by Communist coal strike is now on purely political ground and should be so considered. Our war with Communists is on two fronts, Europe and South America. Issue on latter front concentrated on revolutionary lines in Chile is now acute and while serious in its possibilities is being met forcefully by President with staunch support all political parties but Communists. Coal strike if continued will stop ships, trains, close factories, create unemployment and distress which is Communist strategy. Our cooperation in

---

[9] Gen. Franjo Pirc.

fight would be in standing by to supply as much coal as possible which would carry with Italians [*Chileans?*] proof of our moral support so much desired by Chilean Govt and people. To meet this crisis with actual reduction in coal allocations (Deptel 491, October 7) will inevitably create impression here we are indifferent to struggle now in decisive state.

While we probably cannot supply all coal asked, we feel situation demands material increase in allocations especially for November. Any other course will have serious repercussions, discourage our friends and have bad effect on armed forces (which today called up 5,500 reserves). It is common belief here that result of test international Communism now concentrating on here will have decisive effect throughout South America. It would, therefore, in my opinion be grave mistake overlook predominant political significance Chilean situation which overshadows lesser issues and that it is our duty stand by. I believe that with reasonable cooperation from US battle will be won and will not last through December–January for which President prefers make provision. With the knowledge that through our help in supplying coal the Communist purpose is defeated, I think it probable miners will resume work especially in view unprecedented concessions (mytel 782, October 8, 6 p. m.[10]) government gave in drastic (40 percent) wage increase, housing, family allowance, weekly wage et cetera.

BOWERS

825.5045/10–1347 : Telegram

The Ambassador in Chile (Bowers) to the Secretary of State

CONFIDENTIAL　　　　　　　　SANTIAGO, October 13, 1947—8 p. m.

796. Vergara Foreign Minister [11] summoned me at 7:00 to Moneda. He was sitting with Council of Ministers on the crisis when I arrived. He was very serious and emphatic. He reports conditions not improving, with but few miners returning to work who can produce but 6% of necessary output. Sees a thoroughly organized Communist push intended as incentive to Communism through SA. If coal cannot be had from outside and unemployment on large scale results with hunger and suffering, confesses does not know where it will end. Government knows today that Communists are preparing similar strike in nitrate and copper mines. Chile has but 42,000 tons on hand and using Navy stock. Normal coal consumption 240,000 tons; by closing some factories, drastic rationing on light and heat, reduc-

---

[10] Not printed.
[11] Germán Vergara Donoso took office as Foreign Minister on August 2, 1947.

tion rail operations can manage with sacrifices on 105,000 tons per month. Reports our Coal Control Board offers 18,000 tons from Pacific at $10 ton; that private companies are asking payment before shipment but Chile unable to get dollars. Asks if some credit arrangement cannot be made in consequence.

He made it clear that he came from President and Council Ministers to say Chile must know positively what if any moral support can expect from the US. Says unless shipment begins within 3 days supply here be exhausted before arrival. He understands large coal stock in Balboa.

Vergara's statement no exaggeration. The strike is Communistic and revolutionary and result will have inevitable effect throughout SA. No possible doubt that strike is ordered from outside as a major effort of Communism to take over in Chile as first step toward the Continent. The issue is clear as crystal—Communism or democracy. With such an issue earnestly urge that we stand by for this fight is ours. It seems to me our clear duty in our own interests. Dribs of coal will not suffice. All parties but Communists, all sectors of society and opinion warmly supporting the President who thinks it may mean a struggle of two to three months. In view of the world contest between Communism and democracy it seems incredible that we should be indifferent to the major battle Communism is waging in Chile, and that we cannot be better than heretofore indicated. Unless we can and do we may prepare ourselves for a grave Communist triumph in our backyard and which will spread to other American nations.

BOWERS

701.6125/10–1347

The Ambassador in Chile (Bowers) to the Secretary of State

RESTRICTED SANTIAGO, October 13, 1947.
No. 15, 666

SIR: With reference to my telegram No. 792, October 10, 1947[12] regarding the shots which were fired at the Soviet Embassy building on the morning of October 10, I have the honor to report certain additional information.

The police court declaration states that the shooting took place at 3:15 in the morning from an automobile speeding by the Embassy. The shots entered the second floor apartment occupied by Civil Attaché Sergei P. Eguiazarov and family. The Soviet coat of arms over the

---

[12] Not printed.

main entrance was also hit. An examination of the bullets revealed that they were 12 millimeter machine gun bullets.

In the declaration made by the policeman detailed to guard the Soviet Embassy he stated that upon hearing the shots he had tried to enter the Embassy to ascertain whether there had been personal injuries, but that he was told by direction of the Ambassador that he would not be allowed to enter the building until after 10 o'clock in the morning.

At a reception on October 10 Ambassador Zhukov told an officer of my staff that when the shots were heard two of his secretaries went out to look for the policeman on guard and that not only was he not at his place of duty, but that no policeman could be found within an area of several blocks from the Embassy. (Referring to the shooting, the President's anti-Communist measures and the expulsion of the Yugoslav diplomats, Ambassador Zhukov jokingly remarked "these must be interesting days for the American Embassy.")

Up to the present no progress has been made in identifying the perpetrators of this act or even the automobile from which the shots were fired.[13]

While the Chilean Government has presented its official apologies for the incident, it is evident the Soviet Embassy feels the protection afforded by the Chilean Government was insufficient. (In this connection, however, it should be borne in mind that owing to the serious coal strike situation numerous policemen have had to be withdrawn from the capital and only one was assigned to protect two Embassies, the other being about two blocks away from the Soviet Embassy. At the time of the shooting the policeman happened to be at the other end of the beat.)

The Acting Under Secretary for Foreign Affairs [14] stated privately today that the Chilean Government was embarrassed over this and other disagreeable incidents of which the Soviet Ambassador has been the victim. On several recent occasions he has been hooted by the public and yesterday at the annual banquet given by the powerful National Agricultural Society, to which all chiefs of missions were invited, insults were shouted at the Ambassador as he was leaving the function. The Under Secretary said that while this was not a matter in which the Government could intervene, the Foreign Minister had insinuated to the president of the organization that apologies be made to the Ambassador.

Respectfully yours, CLAUDE G. BOWERS

---

[13] According to the Ambassador's despatch 15, January 8, 1948, the tribunal before which the case was presented suspended proceedings because of lack of evidence to identify the perpetrators and because the Russians failed to participate in the proceedings (701.6125/1–848).

[14] Enrique Bernstein.

725.61/10–1347 : Telegram

The Chargé in the Soviet Union (Durbrow) to the Secretary of State

Moscow, October 13, 1947.

3019. Soviet press October 12, carried following Tass communiqué: Ministry Foreign Affairs USSR received communication from Santiago [apparent omission] was fired on by machine gun from auto passing Embassy building. Regarding this, October 11 Deputy ForMin USSR R. A. Malik summoned Chilean Ambassador USSR Cruz Ocampo and according instructions USSR Government registered protest to Chilean Government against scandalous infringement diplomatic immunity USSR's representatives in Chile, pointing out this could only occur as result unbridled campaign hostility to Soviet Union which being carried on in Chile without opposition from Chilean authorities. Malik pointed out Soviet Union insists on immediate investigation and firm punishment those responsible. Ocampo, after expressing regrets with regard what had occurred in Santiago, assurred Malik Soviet Government's communication would be immediately brought notice Chilean Government.

DURBROW

825.5045/10–1347 : Telegram

The Acting Secretary of State to the Embassy in Chile

CONFIDENTIAL   WASHINGTON, October 14, 1947—6 p. m.

506. Chil Amb [15] following tel conversation Pres Gonzalez last night described current situation substantially as presented urtel 796 Oct 13. Told Amb reasonable certainty eight cargoes (about 72,000 tons) can be made available Chile remainder Oct and Nov not counting second cargo Oct allocation scheduled shipment Mobile next week in nitrate bottom. With one cargo already en route from Oct allocation this makes total 90,000 tons before end Nov. No guarantee can be given now but Dept will make every effort allocate stated minimum needs Dec and Jan if required. Investigating possibility release Balboa coal. Panama Ry has no coal for sale.

Amb told payment may present greater obstacle than finding coal. Urged Amb vigorously explore every possibility short term commercial credit since doubtful Eximbank authorized grant credit for coal and decision possibly adverse may take 10 days. Nevertheless Dept immediately presented situation Board Eximbank which promised careful consideration any request Chil Amb. Amb should be author-

---

[15] Felix Nieto del Rio.

ized give security appropriate to short term credit including possibly gold.

LOVETT

825.5045/10–1747

Memorandum by the Assistant Secretary of State for Political Affairs (Armour) to the Secretary of State

CONFIDENTIAL [WASHINGTON,] October 17, 1947.

With great effort the Department has obtained for Chile assurances of export licenses for October and November totalling 12 cargoes or about 108,000 tons. The Chilean Ambassador has been advised to exhaust every possibility of obtaining privately short term credits to finance these extraordinary coal imports since the Eximbank may be unable or unwilling to extend such a credit. At the same time the Department requested the Board of the Eximbank to do what it could to assist Chile in financing emergency coal imports.

On October 16 the Board agreed to authorize immediate advances up to $4,000,000 against the credit established for a Chilean steel mill to reimburse the Chilean Development Corporation for dollar expenditures it has made to date on this project from its own funds. The Development Corporation can turn over the dollars it thus will receive from Eximbank to the Chilean Government and the latter can thus pay for coal purchases immediately necessary. The Bank considers it important that its action be understood as exclusively related to the steel mill and not connected with Chile's emergency needs of coal.

NORMAN ARMOUR

825.5045/10–1747 : Telegram

The Ambassador in Chile (Bowers) to the Secretary of State

CONFIDENTIAL US URGENT SANTIAGO, October 17, 1947—5 p. m.

813. Although press this morning reports coal strike broken and miners returning work, situation still doubtful.

Press states Defense Minister General Barrios reported President last night that coal miners resistance ended shortly afternoon yesterday. This was confirmed to Embassy by Secretary General of Government this morning. Barrios attributed end resistance (1) arrangement secure coal US, (2) importation coal zone 1500 workers from other areas, (3) strict enforcement conscription in coal area, (4) tranquility imposed coal zone by calm attitude troops. Rationing to continue until amount production known and begin build stock. Further evacuation Communist leaders and those refusing work from zone began yesterday afternoon. 2300 reported Lota first two shifts yesterday.

Barrios' statement reflects confidence determination military authorities handle situation possibly due prestige considerations. Also reflects probable government propaganda policy paint optimistic picture benefit public and undermine Communist influence. Optimism not shared Foreign Office and government coal officials, former possibly to maintain pressure US provide more coal and latter due anticipation production delays.

Embassy believes strike finishing as claimed but probability early resumption substantial production doubtful. Even though miners return work and coal is produced may be delay of month or more before supply situation materially eased due transportation disruption and possible technical difficulties. Shipments US coal essential maintain strength government position and as a safeguard since no assurance emergency is over. Communist *El Siglo* plays down settlement and points out government decree provides further discussion dispute.

BOWERS

825.5045/10–2147

Memorandum on the Situation in the Coal Mining Area[16]

CONFIDENTIAL SANTIAGO, 20 October, 1947.

The control which the Communists had in the mining area is astonishing. A miner was compelled to join the Communist Party. If a miner was sick and did not belong to the Party, he was given one peso a day; but if he did belong to the Party, he was given thirty-one pesos per day. The Communist Party controlled the majority of public officials and such agencies as the post office, telegraph system, and treasury. There were some Communists who lived in the zone, officials and organizers, who were on the pay roll of the Communist Party. One such individual indicated that the Party paid him two thousand five hundred pesos monthly plus expenses for his work of agitation and propaganda. All these officials and organizers will be sent to Quiriquina. One of the principal women agitators was Blanca Sanchez, a school teacher in Lota, who has now been removed from

---

[16] Transmitted to the Department by the Ambassador in Chile in his despatch 15,681, October 21, 1947, not printed.

the mining area. It appears that the company on many occasions had requested through the Ministry of Education that this Communist agitator be removed, but nothing was ever done about it.

825.5045/10–2147 : Telegram

The Ambassador in Chile (Bowers) to the Secretary of State

CONFIDENTIAL   URGENT   SANTIAGO, October 21, 1947—7 p. m.

825. For Lovett and Armour. With understanding coal strike finished last night, 2,000 miners of night shift entered the mines; this morning when day shift reported was met at entrance with some inside with dynamite and refused entrance and those inside would not come out. Small detachment soldiers under a lieutenant entered mine to investigate and met by explosion of dynamite, no one hurt. The soldiers took out a deputation to parley with military authorities and their proposition was would return to work on three conditions: (1) that state of emergency be called off; and (2) that the armed forces be withdrawn; and (3) that all the Communist agents and agitators arrested and sent away be released and brought back. This arrogant demand naturally not considered and deputation told that if miners did not emerge by 2 p. m. would be declared in state of rebellion. At 2, tear gas put in the mine and miners emerged and were taken into custody by army who will institute proceedings to determine guilt. Government understands that of the 2,000 in mines about 200 were armed Communists who kept others in by terrorism.

Council of Ministers in continuous session today. President furious and proposed breaking relations with Russia, with Vergara and others urging nothing be done without specific proof of Embassy's implication. But at 5:30 this evening Vergara sent for me to say that Chile is breaking relations with both Russia and Czechoslovakia.

Russian Ambassador summoned for 6:30. This done on President's conviction revolutionary strike ordered and engineered from without on instructions he is sure come from Communist diplomatic missions. Czechoslovak Chargé [17] who clings to Zhukov like a burr on public occasions and looks like a sneak will be no loss. Vergara stressed break with Russia due to recent developments and nothing to do with Brazil's action.[18]

Government heard yesterday of threat which materialized and intercepted message instructions to miners from Communist headquarters

---

[17] Frantisek Cejka.
[18] For documentation on the Brazilian break with the Soviet Union, see pp. 391 ff.

in Santiago. Government ordering all Communist leaders in Chile aside from parliamentarians be detained. Clearly concerned lest the conspiracy involve nitrate.

Since miners' demands, and more, granted at beginning strike this clearly revolutionary. Clear I think that the Comintern determined to make desperate effort in Chile as first step toward the Continent. Situation may become very serious. President who thought that 100,000 tons coal from United States sufficient now begs that we will not yet abandon the original plan of standing by beyond November. Says since this involves the very life of nation and democratic institutions all the resources of the nation will be put behind the credit.

Will keep advised any important development.

BOWERS

725.61/10–2247 : Telegram

The Chargé in the Soviet Union (Durbrow) to the Secretary of State

CONFIDENTIAL   Moscow, October 22, 1947—7 p. m.

3080. Learned following from Chilean Ambassador re rupture:

Matter of firing on Soviet Embassy Santiago having been regulated satisfactorily Ambassador believed Chile would now follow Brazil's example and Ambassador planning advise Chilean Government against any precipitous move.

First news of break came this morning when American correspondent called Chilean Secretary to ask confirmation BBC radio report. Ambassador did not receive telegram announcing break till about noon. He does not know who will represent interests. I informed him I also have no information.

Ambassador very perturbed because of family situation involving his son's Soviet wife who for some time has been refused exit visa. He most anxious take her but fears he will be forced leave her behind.

Department pass Santiago.

DURBROW

725.60H/10–1147 : Telegram

The Ambassador in Yugoslavia (Cannon) to the Secretary of State

SECRET   BELGRADE, October 11, 1947—3 p. m.
[Received October 23—5 : 29 a. m.]

2095. Today's *Borba* published FonOff statement connection breaking relations with Chile. Statement accuses Chilean Government "gross violations elementary principles international relations". Statement alleges Chilean Government's charges without foundation and adds that "series most fantastic abuses directed by Chilean Government against Yugo".

Statement adds that inasmuch Yugo innocent of accusations clear action by Chilean Government part of planned campaign which is being conducted not in interests of Chile but rather in interests of expansionistic policy certain powers who are assuming ever increasing role in direction Chilean domestic and foreign policy.

Statement concludes Chilean Government's behavior demonstrates antagonistic attitude involved and therefore Yugo considers it no longer necessary to continue diplomatic relations with government which is no longer free to conduct its relations with other countries.

Activity Yugo representatives in Chile supplements growing list of complaints reaching Embassy made by representatives other governments in Belgrade concerning work of Yugo representatives abroad (Embtel 1098, September 25 [19]) and is further evidence that Yugo Government is using its diplomatic missions to carry out work of subversive nature principally under cloak of commercial activities and that Yugo has far-flung network of Communist agents abroad. Embassy feels that choice Belgrade as center new Communist info bureau had additional advantage Yugos highly developed network of trained agents operating abroad.

Please relay interested missions.

CANNON

725.60F/10-2447 : Airgram

The Ambassador in Chile (Bowers) to the Secretary of State

SANTIAGO, October 24, 1947.

A-455. In exclusive interview granted UP correspondent re motives for breaking relations with Czechoslovakia, FonMin Vergara declared, "Czechoslovakia is no longer a silver bridge between occidental democracies and Soviet Russia. We have decided to break with those nations which are the center of Communist international influence." He said Chile based action on serious internal developments related to recent Communist revolutionary strikes. Vergara added that while Chile appreciated efforts to maintain political independence being made by certain statesmen of countries which, like Czechoslovakia, on account of geographic position are submitted to direct Soviet influence, it could not disregard fact that those efforts are annulled by predominant power exercised by respective Communist Parties in service of USSR.

[19] Not printed.

Diplomatic relations with Poland, he explained, not severed because no diplomatic representatives accredited. Had there been relations Rumania and Bulgaria, these would also have been broken. Chilean action not aimed at Czechoslovakia itself, but merely directed against Soviet influence on Chilean affairs through indirect action of its satellites. Vergara said he had told Secretary Chilean Czechoslovakian Chamber of Commerce Kocian, as unofficial representative local Czechoslovakian community, they could count on full protection Chilean laws in all legitimate activities. He terminated interview with statement, "Commercial relations with Czechoslovakia will continue as before. Chile recently purchased beet sugar refinery from Skoda in exchange agricultural products and copper."

BOWERS

701.6125/10–3047 : Telegram

The Ambassador in Chile (Bowers) to the Secretary of State

RESTRICTED   SANTIAGO, October 30, 1947—5 p. m.

852. Members Soviet diplomatic representation here, consisting 51 persons, have made arrangements leave in four groups. First group left yesterday, but departure of rest (which includes Ambassador Zhukov) postponed because safe conduct not yet issued Chilean representatives in Moscow.

BOWERS

725.60F/10–3147 : Telegram

The Ambassador in Czechoslovakia (Steinhardt) to the Secretary of State

TOP SECRET   PRAHA, October 31, 1947—10 a. m.

1445. Impact on Czech Government of unexpected rupture of diplomatic relations by Chile cannot be overemphasized. It is no exaggeration to say that Gottwald and Clementis [20] were stunned. They have made no effort to conceal their extreme anxiety lest Brazil and Argentina follow suit.

As a result of Chilean rupture and fear that Brazil and Argentina will pursue same course Communists in Cabinet are for first time in many months on defensive. At Cabinet meeting last night anti-Communist leaders made a severe attack on Communist leaders. They accused them of having sent only Communist diplomatic representa-

---

[20] Klement Gottwald and Vlado Clementis, Prime Minister and Minister of Foreign Affairs, respectively, of Czechoslovakia.

tives to South America and insisted that rupture by Chile and what they described as "probable" rupture by Brazil and Argentina should be ascribed primarily to these appointments. I am told that defense made by Clementis was unusually weak and that he was frank in expressing grave concern at economic consequences of a rupture by Brazil and Argentina.

Should Brazil or Argentina break off diplomatic relations with Czechoslovakia such action at this time would probably do more to strengthen hands of anti-Communist leaders in Czechoslovakia and to cause Communist press to tone down its attacks on US than any other single measure.

STEINHARDT

701.2561/12-347

The Ambassador in Chile (Bowers) to the Secretary of State

CONFIDENTIAL SANTIAGO, December 3, 1947.
No. 15,783

SIR: With reference to my despatch No. 15,672 of October 16, 1947 [21] I have the honor to report that after prolonged negotiations the Chilean Government has announced it will hold the 42 remaining members of the former Soviet Embassy in Chile until the entire Chilean group in Moscow, including Ambassador Cruz Ocampo's Russian daughter-in-law, is issued exit permits.

Last week Sr. Enrique Bernstein, Under-Secretary for Foreign Affairs, informed the Embassy privately that Argentina, which had agreed to represent Chilean interests in Moscow, had been unable to persuade the Soviet authorities to allow the departure of the Russian daughter-in-law, and that negotiations had therefore reached an impasse. Sr. Bernstein, at this time, said he believed Chile would have to give in on this point. On November 28, however, the Foreign Office issued a communiqué declaring categorically that, in view of the intransigent and inhumane position taken by the Soviet Union in this case, the Chilean Government had decided to prevent the Soviet diplomats from leaving the country until the entire Chilean group was allowed to depart in accordance with accepted diplomatic practice and international law. A copy and translation of this communiqué [21] are attached.

The Under-Secretary informed an officer of my staff that the Chilean Government had changed its position after receiving indirect reports from Sr. Cruz Ocampo on the treatment he was receiving from the

---

[21] Not printed.

Soviet authorities. The Ambassador said he and the members of his household were being held under the most disagreeable and undignified conditions, that he was denied the use of the cable, that he was kept under strict surveillance, and that he was not allowed to speak or communicate with any ranking Soviet officials. Furthermore, the Soviet Government had refused to allow Argentina to represent Chilean interests in Moscow.

In view of these circumstances, the Chilean Government has retaliated by submitting the Soviet group to similar treatment. The use of cable communication has been prohibited, and surveillance increased. Visitors are carefully questioned and inspected on entering or leaving the Soviet residence. Telephone communications are controlled, and several other minor measures have been taken. It is the hope of the Chilean Government that these annoyances might become disagreeable enough for the Moscow Government to request that a foreign power represent its interests in Santiago, in which case it would have to accept Argentine representation of Chilean interests in Moscow.

Sr. Bernstein said the Foreign Office was studying the technical aspects of this case further, but that it believed it would soon be in a position to bring up the matter at the United Nations Human Rights Commission and other international organizations, in order to embarrass Soviet Russia with the denunciation of its totalitarian system.

The Chilean position has elicited considerable favorable comment in the country. Brief summaries of this editorial comment are enclosed.[23]

Respectfully yours,   CLAUDE G. BOWERS

725.61/12–1147

Memorandum of Conversation, by Mr. James H. Webb of the Division of North and West Coast Affairs

CONFIDENTIAL [WASHINGTON,] December 30, 1947.

Participants: Señor Mario Rodríguez, Minister Counselor of Chilean Embassy
  Mr. Bechhoefer—IS
  Mr. H. B. Wells—OA
  Mr. Mills—NWC
  Mr. Webb—NWC

Mr. Mills explained to Mr. Rodríguez that, although it was not a formal request, the Chilean Embassy in its note No. 2586/294 of

---

[23] Not printed.

December 11, 1947,[24] had asked for the Department's comments on press statements made by the Chilean Foreign Office in connection with the refusal of the Soviet Government to permit the departure of the Russian wife of the son of the former Chilean Ambassador to the USSR. The object in inviting him to call at the Department was to discuss informally means the Chilean Government might employ to bring the question before some form of international arbitration.

Mr. Bechhoefer pointed out that the case might, in his opinion, very well fall within the consideration of the General Assembly under Article 14 as a "situation, regardless of origin, which it deems likely to impair the general welfare or friendly relations among nations." On the other hand, Mr. Bechhoefer did not consider it appropriate for presentation to the Interim Committee because it does not require preliminary study, one of the conditions requisite to consideration by that body. Refusal by the Interim Committee to consider the case on whatever grounds, however technical, might react unfavorably to the Chilean cause. Non-representation of the USSR on the Interim Committee, precluding a chance to state its side of the question, would in Mr. Bechhoefer's opinion further weaken the Chilean position.

Mr. Rodríguez said that while he had not heard that presentation to the Interim Committee was under consideration, he was glad to have Mr. Bechhoefer's opinion. It was explained to Mr. Rodríguez that the Interim Committee had been mentioned informally in conversations between the Foreign Office and Ambassador Bowers.

In the opinion of all present the question might appropriately be taken to the Court of International Justice. Although the Russians no doubt would refuse to recognize the validity of the case and would also refuse to accept the Court's decision if unfavorable to them, this refusal itself would strengthen the Chilean position if the case later is taken before the United Nations General Assembly.

The Human Rights Committee was mentioned as a third means of bringing the case to arbitration. While this was considered a possibility and worth further investigation, Mr. Wells felt that the case was more important, involving political (i.e. diplomatic) in addition to human rights.

Mr. Rodríguez showed Mr. Mills a telegram the Chilean Embassy had received from the Foreign Office proposing the following steps:

(1) Another effort by the Argentine Embassy in Moscow, acting in behalf of the Chilean Government, to obtain the release of the daughter-in-law and her son;
(2) If this fails, a demand by the Argentine Embassy that the case be referred to arbitration;

---

[24] Not printed.

(3) If this fails, the direct request by Chile to the Court for arbitration by the International Court;

(4) A joint approach by the representatives of those American countries having diplomatic representation at Moscow.

The telegram also stated that any suggestions the Department might have would be appreciated.

Mr. Rodríguez was told, in reply to a question as to the probable US attitude toward step No. (4), that it would be impossible to give even an informal opinion on that point until it had been given further study. Otherwise, the program as outlined by the Chilean Foreign Office appeared sound.[25]

UNITED STATES POLICY IN PROVIDING ARMS TO CHILE [26]

825.248/2–2147 : Telegram

The Ambassador in Chile (Bowers) to the Secretary of State

CONFIDENTIAL SANTIAGO, February 21, 1947—2 p. m.

130. Deptel 442, September 4.[27] Chief Air Mission [28] tells me airplanes under interim program now ready be turned over to Chile. Chief Chilean Air Force [29] says Chile prepared pay approximately $400,000 as first payment above mentioned airplanes. Grateful for any details these negotiations. Can FLC turn over these planes against said first payment with balance payment installments as in other sales contracts of surplus equipment through FLC?

BOWERS

825.248/2–2147 : Telegram

The Secretary of State to the Embassy in Chile

CONFIDENTIAL WASHINGTON, February 25, 1947—6 p. m.

93. Urtel 130 Feb 21. Total sales price air force interim program Chile approximates $2,000,000. Of this almost $900,000 worth con-

---

[25] In airgram A–423, August 31, 1948, the American Chargé in Argentina indicated that only then were arrangements being made for the departure for home of the Soviet diplomatic mission to Chile (701.6125/8–3148).

[26] For documentation on the general policy of the United States in providing military assistance and arms to the other American republics, see pp. 101 ff. For documentation on the provision of arms to Chile in 1946, see *Foreign Relations, 1946*. vol. XI, pp. 559 ff.

[27] *Ibid.*, p. 573.

[28] Lt. Col. Wilson T. Jones.

[29] Gen. Manuel Tovarias.

sists aircraft and parts already flown to Chile now assigned to air mission pending sale and transfer.[30]

Chilean representatives here requested 5 year credit for purchase this equipment but informed this Govt's policy not extend credit interim arms sales. FLC has, however, offered take payment for $1,000,000 worth in Chilean pesos to be used for acquisition real estate needed by this Govt in Chile. Details on this offer now being discussed with Chilean representatives by FLC here.

Chile indicated could pay 25% of total price air equipment, or approximately $500,000, in cash dollars.

MARSHALL

825.24/3–447

The Chilean Embassy to the Department of State

[Translation]

CONFIDENTIAL WASHINGTON, March 4, 1947.
No. 535/59

The Government of Chile desires to obtain, in the United States of America, the war matériel indicated in this Memorandum. The plan for acquisitions, concerning which the Commander in Chief of the Chilean Army [31] has already spoken with Colonel Cleland, Military Attaché of the Embassy of the United States in Santiago, and, also, the Head of the Chilean Military Mission [32] with the Department of War in Washington, takes into consideration the minimum elements for the instruction of officers and troops, in accordance with the Army's needs for preparation.

The list of war matériel which the Government of Chile proposes to purchase from the Government of the United States, on the terms of payment and time-limit on delivery indicated, is as follows:

[Here follows list of war matériel.]

The matériel and arms must be of the model which the United States Army will keep in use, and not obsolete, for that would completely destroy the idea of standardization.

Munitions. Weapons must be provided or furnished with a 30-day supply of ammunition, and in accordance with the estimates and provisions made by the United States Army.

---

[30] Department's telegram 430, August 29, 1947, to Santiago, indicated that Chile had agreed to pay Chilean pesos equivalent to $616,293.66 for aviation equipment in the hands of the United States Military Air Mission in Chile (825.24 FLC/8–2947).

[31] Maj. Gen. Guillermo Barrios.

[32] Col. Milciades Contreras.

Spare Parts. Spare parts must be added for those parts which the United States Army has determined, through experience, to be the most indispensable.

Financing. Conditions of long-term payment, in order to determine whether the economic possibilities of Law 7144 could meet the commitments being made through the acquisition of the aforesaid matériel.

Time for Delivery. It is of the utmost importance that the Army have the munitions at its disposal as soon as possible.

The Government of Chile has informed this Embassy that it would like to obtain the agreement of the Government of the United States to these acquisitions, in order that the respective contracts may be signed by Major General Guillermo Barrios T., Commander in Chief of the Chilean Army, during the official visit he will make to the United States at the end of the present month of March.

WASHINGTON, March 4, 1947.

825.248/3–1347 : Telegram

The Ambassador in Chile (Bowers) to the Secretary of State

CONFIDENTIAL   SANTIAGO, March 13, 1947—7 p. m.

188. Retiring Chief US Air Mission now submitting report to CDC with copy for Embassy on types airplanes he recommends for Chilean Air Force. I am forwarding copy this report to Department. One point which I feel calls for early action is following: Chief, Air Mission believes B–25 bombers of which 12 now in Chile under interim program and have not yet been transferred to Chile are not suitable for Chilean Air Force program. Furthermore he has gained impression from conversation with Chilean Air Force officers that Chile would prefer not to purchase these planes owing very great expense operation and other important limitations. Should Chilean Air Force actually express wish not to purchase these B–25's would appropriate American officials be agreeable? What disposition would be made these aircraft?

In view imbalance Chilean budget I of course feel any steps which forces might wish to make toward economy operation Expelles are highly desirable. Please telegraph urgently.

Repeated Panama for CDC.

BOWERS

825.248/3–1847

The Ambassador in Chile (Bowers) to the Secretary of State

SECRET
No. 15,033

SANTIAGO, March 18, 1947.

SIR: With reference to my telegram no. 188 of March 13, 1947, I have the honor to transmit herewith a report [33] submitted at my request by the retiring chief of our Air Mission in Chile.

The report in question is, I believe, self-explanatory, and contains recommendations for Chilean aircraft strength which are practical and take into consideration the many limitations under which the Chilean Air Force operates.

Hampered by severe budgetary difficulties, with limited personnel, inadequate servicing facilities and a paucity of air fields suitable for tactical aircraft, it is the Air Mission Chief's opinion that Chile should be supplied not with many types of planes, but rather with adequate supplies of a reduced number of types which could best serve the Chilean Air Force's present needs. Due to Chile's long coast line, the necessity for transport planes is evident. It will be noted that, while the Interim Allocation Plan calls for the supplying of six C–47's, the Air Mission Chief's report recommends twelve of these planes and eighteen C–45's (AT–11) instead of ten. Furthermore, it is suggested that Chile be supplied with six OA–10 or PBY flying boats instead of the proposed two.[34]

Although purchase of the planes recommended in the attached report would cost some $320,000 more than the Interim Allocation Plan's budget, it should be borne in mind that annual operating expenditures would be cut some $307,000, an important consideration considering local budgetary difficulties.

A copy of this report has been submitted to the Chilean Air Force, but no official comments have yet been received. Nevertheless it is believed that the return of the Mitchell A–25 bombers referred to in my above-mentioned telegram would be appreciated by the Chileans, as they realize that a plane more economical to run and which can be used for transport purposes is of greater use in the long run.

Respectfully yours, CLAUDE G. BOWERS

---

[33] Not printed.
[34] The C–47's, C–45's, and AT–11's were transport planes; the OA–10's and PBY's were navy patrol planes.

825.248/3–1347 : Telegram

The Acting Secretary of State to the Embassy in Chile

CONFIDENTIAL WASHINGTON, March 21, 1947—7 p. m.

130. Embtel 188, March 13. Contract for aircraft now in Chile scheduled for sale to Chile under interim program not yet signed. Neither State nor War Dept. wishes encourage Chile purchase aircraft which it cannot afford to maintain, and decision of course rests with Chilean Govt. B–25's were, however, sent to Chile at specific and urgent request Chilean Air Attaché here, and only recently Chilean Amb wrote letter confirming desire Chilean Govt purchase all interim aircraft now in Chile plus 8 AT–11's and 4 C–47's. Decision by Chile not to buy B–25's would probably require their return to US by Army.

ACHESON

825.24/3–2747

Memorandum by the Chief of the Division of Special Inter-American Affairs (Dreier) to the Director of the Office of American Republic Affairs (Briggs)

RESTRICTED [WASHINGTON,] March 27, 1947.

The Chilean Military Attaché [35] is pressing very hard for permission to buy military equipment for one more regiment of infantry (the interim ground program for Chile included one regiment of infantry and some artillery).

Colonel Ordway is very anxious to have this approved because it has been indicated to him that, if we make this equipment available, the Chileans will ask for a ground mission from the United States Army.

I recommend that we do not approve this sale because it will amount to getting us considerably more involved than we already are in providing arms to the Chilean Army when we still do not know what the top policy decision will be in regard to future arms transfers. We have a military air mission in Chile, so a ground mission is not quite so urgent as if we had none. Furthermore, I do not like the idea of a deal whereby we would make equipment available just to get an invitation to a mission.[36]

JOHN C. DREIER

---

[35] Col. Ernesto Medina.
[36] In the margin beside the final paragraph appears the following: "Agree B[riggs], Ditto S B[raden]".

825.34/5–747 : Airgram

The Secretary of State to the Embassy in Chile

CONFIDENTIAL WASHINGTON, May 7, 1947.

A–177. There are now in the possession of the Chilean government a number of US naval vessels leased to Chile during the war under a charter party agreement between the two governments. By the terms of this agreement, the US retains title to the vessels and Chile is required to return each vessel, unless lost, to this government at a place and time to be specified by the US. This procedure was used because under the Lend Lease Act [37] it was not permitted to transfer title to these vessels.

As the Navy Department now considers the ships leased to Chile to be surplus to its needs, it is planned to offer them for sale to Chile as surplus property at a low price. If Chile should agree to purchase, it is planned not to require Chile to return the ships to a US port for actual repossession by the US, but to ask that they be returned to an appropriate US official in Chile until a contract of sale is finalized. Failure to purchase the ships will necessitate that they be returned by Chile to a US port for actual repossession by the US and subsequent disposal. Although agreement states that "hire" (charge for use) of the vessels during the war shall be determined by subsequent agreement between the two governments, it is not planned to charge for use of the ships, since they were employed in the common defense effort.

Please report your comments by cable and any objections you may perceive. US ships covered by agreement with Chile are: 3 aircraft rescue vessels, 6 aircraft rearming vessels.[38]

MARSHALL

825.24 FLC/5–1947 : Telegram

The Ambassador in Chile (Bowers) to the Secretary of State

CONFIDENTIAL SANTIAGO, May 19, 1947—8 p. m.

388. My telegram 387, May 19.[39] Chilean Air Force also informs me that they desire utilize balance between one million dollars authorized and expenditures covering delivery air equipment already in

---

[37] 55 Stat. 31.
[38] Memoranda of February 26 and March 11, 1947, from the Deputy Field Commissioner for Military Programs, Foreign Liquidation Commissioner's Office, to the Chief of the Division of Special Inter-American Affairs, indicated that 6 LCI(L)'s and 4 LSM's were transferred to Chile (825.34/3–1747).
[39] Not printed.

Chile to purchase eight Beechcraft AT–11's and 556,000 rounds 50 caliber ammunition which they state would cover one year's training. Shipping expenses will be for account of Chilean Government.

Air Attaché [40] urgently recommending to his superiors that Beechcrafts and ammunition be supplied to Chile. I strongly concur.[41]

BOWERS

825.24 FLC/5–2747 : Telegram

The Secretary of State to the Embassy in Chile

CONFIDENTIAL   WASHINGTON, May 27, 1947—8 p. m.

254. Embtel 387, May 18.[42] Presidential decree authorizing payment for Air Force equipment is subject. Understanding here was that Chilean representatives would acquire broad authority to negotiate contract for purchase aircraft and equipment offered and that details of contract would be negotiated here under this authority. Urtel indicates Chilean Air Force is apparently drafting Presidential decree in such form as to leave no area for negotiation but to conform exactly with the tentative draft which was furnished by General Wooten.[43] General Wooten's draft was not intended as offer to sell on exact terms set forth therein but simply an indication of general nature of an agreement which might be negotiated as to specific terms.

It is Department's view that certain provisions of draft contract, primarily monetary clause, should be modified. Dept regards it as highly desirable that Presidential decree grant broad authority to Chilean Emb Washington to negotiate contract with only general limitations as to amount and terms of payment. If this impossible request Chilean Air Force delay temporarily final submission Presidential decree pending submission through you revised form agreement.

MARSHALL

825.24 FLC/5–1947 : Telegram

The Secretary of State to the Embassy in Chile

CONFIDENTIAL   WASHINGTON, May 28, 1947—3 p. m.

256. Urtel 388 May 19. Million dollars in pesos may be used for purchase aircraft and supporting equipment now in Chile and 10

---

[40] Lt. Col. Robert Lewis Coffey, Jr.
[41] In telegram 483, September 29, 1947, to Santiago, the Department indicated the consummation of a contract for the AT–11 planes (825.24 FLC/9–2947).
[42] Not printed.
[43] Maj. Gen. Ralph H. Wooten, Field Commissioner for Military Programs, Office of the Foreign Liquidation Commissioner.

AT-11's not yet flown Chile. Chile has made firm commitment for these aircraft. In addition, there were originally approved for program 13 P-47's, 4 C-47's, and 8 AT-11's. These withdrawn by War Dept from program and therefore no longer available because Chileans did not make firm commitment by March 15, necessary deadline imposed by War Dept on acceptance offers of aircraft to all countries participating program. Price of aircraft and spare parts which Chile committed to purchase is about $860,000. Remainder of million dollars in pesos may be used to purchase other air equipment in program such as training ammunition and base maintenance equipment. Field Commissioner for Military Programs is best qualified to discuss details of program and Chileans should be advised to conduct further negotiations with Fld. Comm. through Chilean Emb Wash.

MARSHALL

825.34/6-1047 : Telegram

The Ambassador in Chile (Bowers) to the Secretary of State

CONFIDENTIAL   SANTIAGO, June 10, 1947—2 p. m.

461. 1. Military Air Attaché approached Chilean authorities re possible acquisition vessels mentioned Depgam 177 May 7. Chileans interested but unable discuss details at moment (Deptel 266 June 4 [44]).

2. Chief Naval Mission [45] states vessels are scattered along Chilean coast and strongly recommends their remaining Chilean custody pending negotiations; mission lacks funds or personnel properly safeguard vessels if possession taken.

3. Embassy reluctant press negotiations re vessels pending completion arrangements sale aircraft mentioned Embtel 403 May 26.[46] Please advise status aircraft deal and expedite instructions.

BOWERS

825.24/6-2047

The Secretary of State to the Chilean Ambassador (Nieto del Rio)

CONFIDENTIAL   WASHINGTON, June 20, 1947.

EXCELLENCY: I have the honor to refer to this Department's note of May 26, 1947,[44] concerning charges to the Government of Chile under the Lend-Lease Agreement.[47]

---

[44] Not printed.
[45] Capt. Oberlin C. Laird.
[46] Not printed, but see *supra*.
[47] For a note on the agreement, see *Foreign Relations*, 1943, vol. v, p. 816.

There are transmitted herewith two copies each of Statements LL–11 and LL–12 and supporting schedules reporting charges through December 31, 1946.[50] It will be noted that charges reported under Statement LL–11 total $12,674.32 and that charges reported under Statement LL–12 are counterbalanced by credits to a total of $202,892.83 credit. Charges through December 31, 1946 aggregate the grand total of $20,171,705.30.

Of this grand total the appropriate percentage due to the Government of the United States under the terms of the Agreement is $6,051,000. Since the Government of Chile has already paid $5,000,000, the sum now due is $1,051,000.[51]

It is requested that these statements and schedules be treated by your Government on a most confidential basis.

Accept [etc.]   For the Secretary of State:
[File copy not signed]

811.34525/6–1347

The Under Secretary of State to the Secretary of War (Patterson)

SECRET   WASHINGTON, July 14, 1947.

MY DEAR MR. SECRETARY: The Embassy of the United States in Santiago, Chile, has informed me that the Chilean Air Force Chief of Staff recently had a conversation with our Military Air Attaché, in which the former displayed interest in the establishment of a joint United States-Chilean air base in the Magallanes area of Southern Chile. The files of the Department of State show previous correspondence with the Departments of War and Navy on the general subject of a base in this area.

It will be recalled that when previously consulted, the War and Navy Departments were of the opinion that while it might be desirable to obtain rights to establish a base in the Magallanes area when and if needed, there was then no immediate need for such a base. Unless the views set forth in the War Department's letter of April 19, 1945 [50] have changed to the extent that a definite need for such a base has now developed, it is the intention of the Department to inform the Embassy at Santiago that it is not advisable to entertain discussions with the Chilean Government concerning the acquisition of a base.

An identical letter has been sent to the Secretary of the Navy.

Sincerely yours,   ROBERT LOVETT

---

[50] Not printed.
[51] A memorandum of conversation of July 14, 1947, indicated that the Chilean Minister Counselor delivered a check for this amount (825.24/7–1447).

POSITION OF THE UNITED STATES ON THE PROVISION OF ECONOMIC ASSISTANCE TO CHILE [52]

825.51/2-2147 : Airgram

The Ambassador in Chile (Bowers) to the Secretary of State

RESTRICTED   SANTIAGO, February 21, 1947.

A-78. *El Diario Ilustrado* of February 21 published interview with Minister of Economy and Commerce Bossay who was reported as saying that recent decision of the Eximbank to grant new loan of 5,300,000 to Fomento Corporation [53] was of great significance as regards future economic support for Chile's production. He stated this loan was proof of the favorable attitude existing in the United States relative to strengthening of economic relations between the two countries and willingness of the United States to collaborate in Chilean plans for increased production.

Bossay said loan would be used to acquire machinery for agriculture and for electric power plants. He referred to the "magnificent conditions" of the loan which bears 3.5 per cent interest and is payable in ten years as compared to previous loan at 4 per cent interest payable in five years. Bossay said this was proof of the excellent and favorable atmosphere in which Chile's relations with the United States are developing. Embassy assumes Bossay referring to Eximbank loan approved Oct., 1946.[54]

BOWERS

825.51/3-647 : Telegram

The Ambassador in Chile (Bowers) to the Secretary of State

CONFIDENTIAL   SANTIAGO, March 6, 1947—7 p. m.

162. Vice President Joseph Cussen of Cía Chilena de Electricidad, Electric Bond and Share Subsidiary, has discussed with me at length problems affecting future this important US investment. He is convinced Chilean authorities have decided upon squeeze policy by refusing company increased rates to meet higher costs occasioned by inflation or any other form of relief on basis similar to procedure which forced company to sell Santiago street car system to govt after several years futile efforts to avoid such step.

---

[52] For previous documentation on financial problems, see *Foreign Relations*, 1946, vol. XI, pp. 591 ff.

[53] Corporación de Fomento de la Producción, a Chilean governmental instrumentality.

[54] See telegram 1364, October 18, 1946, 7 p. m. to Rio de Janeiro, *Foreign Relations*, 1946, vol. XI, p. 602.

Cussen says his fears strengthened by conversation Finance Minister Pico Canas inadvertently held with company director last week revealing squeeze policy which would discourage company and permit eventual acquisition properties by Fomento Corporation subsidiary "Endesa". Company has publicly stated its willingness to sell out but Cussen believes any reasonable deal looking toward nationalization impossible because lack of funds and foreign exchange.

Cussen has furnished Embassy copies of five memoranda setting forth problems of company here and says New York office will supply copies to Department. He has given me these data for background purposes and has requested no immediate assistance from Embassy.

Department is of course aware of potential danger facing important American investment, especially at this time when Fomento Corp. seeks substantial loans for increased power production. Cussen points out that because Fomento Corp's hydroelectric program is financed by Exim Bank loans his company could hardly undertake expansion its facilities. Hence possible electricity rationing this winter with ensuing public resentment for inadequate planning and service (see Embtel 897, October 8 [56]).

Embassy as yet unaware present status Exim Bank credits to Chile (Embtel 129, February 20 and Airgram A-51, February 4 [57]). Although I strongly favor proper and reasonable economic support to Chile I consider it paradoxical to finance competing or parallel activities here without due consideration of existing American investments in same field (Deptel 143, June 2, 1941 [56]). Clarification of Department's policy toward such problems would be appreciated, particularly in connection Exim Bank and International Bank financing.

BOWERS

825.51/2–2047 : Airgram

The Acting Secretary of State to the Embassy in Chile

CONFIDENTIAL WASHINGTON, March 19, 1947.

A–106. Urtel 129 Feb. 20, 2 p. m.[56] Chile's application for a $40 million credit is still being considered by the International Bank but no part of it is about to be approved. U.S. Executive Director of Bank still awaiting instructions from National Advisory Council which

---

[56] Not printed.
[57] Neither printed.

desires to learn more about possible repercussions of the recent Argentine-Chilean Agreement.[58] (Above for your information only.)

Instead of the $15 million credit (Deptel 473, Oct. 1, 1946, 7 p. m.[59]) the Eximbank on Oct. 16, 1946, authorized credits of $5 million to Chilean State Railways and $5.350 million to Fomento Corporation (Deptel 515, Oct. 21, 1946, 6 p. m.,[59] your A–78, Feb. 21, 1947). Chile has no applications pending with the Bank at present.

Total credits of $76,351,260 to Chile have been authorized by Eximbank (as of January 31, 1947) of which $49,524,468 has not yet been disbursed. Repayments on principal already made by Chile amount to $9,286,351. The following table summarizes status of Eximbank credits to Chile:

EXIMBANK CREDITS TO CHILE

(Millions of U.S. Dollars)

	Purpose	Amount	Not Yet Disbursed	Expiry Date
Fomento Corporation				
	Machinery	15.751	0.	0
	Machinery	13.0	6.0	6/30/48
	Steel Mill Equipment	28.0	28.0	12/31/48
	Materials & Equipment	5.350	5.350	6/20/48
	Total	62.101	39.350	
State Railways				
	Railway Equip.	5.0	.924	*3/31/47
	Locomotives	1.2	1.2	6/30/47
	Electrical Equipment	2.8	2.8	6/30/48
	Materials & Equipment	5.0	5.0	6/20/48
	Total	14.0	9.924	
Ingeneiria Electrica, S.A.C.				
	Dollar Exchange	.250	.250	6/30/47
	Grand Total	76.351	49.524	

*Extended to June 30, 1947. [Footnote in the original.]

ACHESON

---

[58] An economic and financial agreement signed December 13, 1946, envisaged immediate credits from Argentina to Chile of some $12.5 million and a long-term arrangement of $175 million. The agreement provided for reciprocal free entry of most goods and a stipulation against extension of the provisions to a third party. (825.50/1–1347 and 625.3531/1–247)

[59] Not printed.

825.51/3-2047

Memorandum of Conversation, by Mr. Phil R. Atterberry of the Division of Investment and Economic Development

RESTRICTED [WASHINGTON,] March 20, 1947.

Participants: Robert Vergara—Fomento Corporation, Attorney
Burr Brundage—NWC
Mr. Cady—ED
Mr. Atterberry—ED

A general discussion covered the Fomento Corporation's projects in Chile, including economic and financial aspects, i.e., Eximbank credit already authorized and Chile's credit application pending with International Bank.

Mr. Vergara stated the International Bank had the application under active consideration, but that the US Executive Director was awaiting advice from the NAC. He indicated his intention to call at the International Bank within the next week or so with a view to urging final action on the application.

Mr. Vergara related that the application included the following projects:

Power (3 hydro-electric plants)	$9,000,000
Timber Development	6,000,000
Trolley coaches	5,000,000
Port Equipment	2,000,000
Electrification of Railways	18,000,000
	$40,000,000

Replying to Mr. Cady's question, Mr. Vergara observed that any indication that Chile might nationalize American-owned power plants is political talk; that such move, which would involve purchase or indemnification by Chile, would, it is believed, not be economically justified. No mention was made about other methods of nationalization, such as legislating American interests out of existence or unfair competitive infiltration in the power field by ENDESA (a Fomento Corporation subsidiary).

825.51/4–347

Memorandum of Conversation, by Mr. Burr C. Brundage of the Division of North and West Coast Affairs [61]

RESTRICTED [WASHINGTON,] April 3, 1947.

Participants: Señor Guillermo del Pedregal
Señor Victor Santa Cruz
Señor Flavian Levine

Señor del Pedregal stated that the Mission of which he is the Chief is in the United States to explain Chile's position. The Mission is bringing no specific projects nor requests. It hopes that a better understanding, however, will result from the discussions which it will entertain and that it can make certain clarifications in respect to the Chilean Government's program which is intended to further Chile's progress.

He explained that it was President Gonzalez' desire that he speak frankly; in fact, he stated that the Mission is here not only to talk but also to listen. Mr. Braden replied that he also desired to speak frankly and that if some of his remarks should seem harsh, it was only because he had the future interests of Chile at heart.

Pedregal stated that his Mission wished to hold a more detailed discussion after it has approached the various financial and governmental entities in this country. Mr. Braden assured him that he personally and others in the Government are at the service of the Mission in this respect.

825.51/4–447

Memorandum of Conversation, by the Deputy Director of the Office of American Republic Affairs (Woodward) [62]

SECRET [WASHINGTON,] April 4, 1947.

At lunch today, Señor Enrique López-Herrarte (former Counselor of the Guatemalan Embassy who is now employed by the World

---

[61] On the occasion of the introductory visit of the Pedregal Economic Mission.
[62] Addressed to Milton K. Wells, Chief, and Burr C. Brundage, of the Division of North and West Coast Affairs; Ellis O. Briggs, Director, Office of American Republic Affairs; Spruille Braden, Assistant Secretary of State for American Republic Affairs, and James H. Wright, Special Assistant to Mr. Braden.

Bank) informed me that it is his primary responsibility to make recommendations concerning such loans as the $40,000,000 loan for which the Chileans have applied. He said that the Chilean negotiations may prove to be a very important test case for the Bank, to decide whether security and probability of repayment of the loans, in accordance with conventional banking traditions, will be a principal criterion in issuing the loans, or whether the emergency needs of weak or unbalanced economies will take definite priority over the question of risk.

López-Herrarte said that the present inclination of Mr. John McCloy and other principal officers whose background is identified with commercial banking, is to place primary emphasis upon the question of financial risk.[63] López-Herrarte favors the other point of view, and he believes that failure to make some response to the Chilean application might be a denial of one of the most fundamental reasons for the existence of the Bank. Moreover, he is afraid that the Chileans, if completely rebuffed, would probably withdraw from the Bank and that this would be a serious reflection upon the Bank in the present state of its development.

López-Herrarte confided that the result of the deliberations within the Bank would probably be a counterproposal to the Chileans that they be given a preliminary loan of $10,000,000, and he thought this might be raised, by compromise, to as much as $15,000,000. He has recommended that, if this is done, the credits be released piecemeal in amounts of not more than $250,000 and that the Chileans be required to present satisfactory information to show that they have not paid exhorbitant prices for materials and services. (As is probably well known, none of the credits of the World Bank may be converted into the currency of the country receiving a loan for expenditure within that country; the entire loan must be spent outside of the country receiving the loan). Likewise, López-Herrarte said that he is insisting on a provision that the Bank may inspect freely and at any time the results being produced by the loan within the country receiving the loan.

López-Herrarte believes that Chile will probably have a fairly permanent market for as much as 800,000 tons of nitrate per annum, as compared with present production of about 1,300,000 tons. He bases his hopes for Chilean copper upon the desire of the United States Government not to deplete copper reserves within the United States. With these bases for Chilean exports, López-Herrarte thinks Chile can maintain a fairly stable economy, upon a somewhat lower level than at present, provided the Chileans can develop a substantial additional

---

[63] In the margin appears the following: "Checks with first impression gained by Chilean mission."

local manufacture of staple products (with the loan money) that will enable Chile to reduce its imports to the level of its exports.

In order to stimulate a greater interest in the American Republics and their problems on the part of Mr. McCloy, the President of the Bank, López-Herrarte is urging him to make a trip through the American Republics. Of more immediate importance with respect to the views of Bank officers concerning loans to the American Republics, Emilio Collado [64] has now been re-employed by the Bank as a consultant (being paid on a day-to-day basis for the memoranda of recommendations and other advice he provides). López-Herrarte said that Collado was a very active exponent of the thesis that the Bank should make loans to assist sagging economies in the American Republics as well as in war-torn areas.

From time to time during the conversation with López-Herrarte, I lamented the situation in Chile which made it a poor "bankable risk" and implied that the Bank might express its concern to the Chileans about the political factors that reduce confidence in the Chilean economy.

ROBERT F. WOODWARD

825.00/4–1847

Memorandum of Conversation, by the Assistant Secretary of State for American Republic Affairs (Braden) [65]

SECRET [WASHINGTON,] April 18, 1947.

Pedregal, pursuant to his previous request that he wished to have a long conversation with me alone, called yesterday afternoon at 4:00 P. M. He began by saying that he wished to have an entirely frank and confidential talk with me because (1) the President had particularly charged him to take up two matters with me; and (2) I was such a close friend of Chile.

The two special messages of Gonzalez Videla:

1. The President, having been elected by a combination of parties in which the Communists had played the decisive role, had to remain loyal to them, both by naming them to the Cabinet and otherwise, but this by no means meant that he was in favor of Communism. On the contrary, he would restrict their activities rigidly to the official functions with which they were concerned.[66]

Pedregal was glad to call to my attention that this whole Com-

---

[64] Formerly Deputy to the Assistant Secretary of State for Economic Affairs, and one-time member of the Board of Trustees of the Export-Import Bank.
[65] Addressed to Mr. Briggs, ARA, and to Messrs. Wright and Mann of A–Br.
[66] For documentation on the Communist situation, see pp. 497 ff.

munist situation had now been resolved by the new Cabinet reorganization in which both the Communists and Liberals had gone out, being replaced by radicals. However, since the Communists had such great influence among the masses in Chile, the President had to handle the matter with utmost caution, since otherwise he might provoke serious trouble, strikes, et cetera, by the working classes of Chile.

2. The President had charged Pedregal to assure me that he, Gonzales Videla, had not changed one iota his complete dislike for Perón and the Argentine Government—opinions he had expressed to me when he visited me in the Department in October 1945. However, his views as a senator and as a private citizen could not interfere with his obligations as Chief of State and because of Chile's situation, he had to seize any opportunity wherever it might lie. Therefore, when the chance had been presented to reach an agreement with Argentina, he had sent a mission to Buenos Aires; upon its arrival it had been presented with a finished draft of the treaty which might give valuable assistance to Chile and since Chile would protect herself at all times, could not possibly do any harm.

Gonzalez Videla had instructed Pedregal to assure me that a fundamental of Chilean policy would be friendship with the United States and the greatest possible desire to cooperate with this country, and he hoped that we would continue our cooperation. Gonzalez Videla had further instructed Pedregal to say that there was no question but that Argentina was endeavoring to form the *bloque austral*, but Chile being alert to this danger would not permit herself to become a cat's paw of Perón.

As a matter of fact, Pedregal observed he doubted that the treaty would ever become really effective because Argentina, as in the case of the oleaginous seeds, had insisted on selling the manufactured product, the oil, to Chile instead of allowing Chile to manufacture herself. When it came to the actual working out of the treaty, if Argentina tried to do this with Chile, Chile, in turn, would insist on selling Argentina the finished iron, copper, or other products. Thus they would probably come to an impasse and nothing would result.

. . . .

Pedregal then went on to say that he had had a series of very agreeable conversations with the people here in Washington but he was disturbed when, for instance, Mr. Black of the International Bank had made it a condition precedent to the issuance of a credit by that Bank that Chile satisfactorily adjust its debt situation in this country.*
Pedregal felt that this was unfair pressure and that self-evidently it

---

*Note: Mr. Black tells me he merely expressed hope to Pedregal that the Bondholders Protective Council could be induced to write to the Bank approving such credit as might be extended to Chile. [Footnote in the original.]

would do Chile no good to get a 40-million dollar credit if, on the other hand, she had to increase her debt service charges by 10 or 15 million dollars per year. He was extremely downcast by this development—he called it imposition—and felt that it was unbearable pressure.

I replied by reciting the story of the conversation at the White House between Presidents Truman and Rios, Secretary Byrnes, and those accompanying Rios,[67] repeating what I had said at that time. I said that unquestionably if Chile wished to reestablish her credit, she would have to do something about the debt and particularly in reference to the 22 million which had been taken out of what was practically a trusteed fund. I then said, however, that while perhaps admitting I was influenced by my knowledge of the subject, nevertheless my thoughts were mostly induced by genuine friendship for Chile and my desire to see that country prosper. I continued the only way Chile could prosper would be by getting private capital, which certainly she could not unless she so reestablished her credit. And this could only be accomplished if the copper companies situation, with the exorbitant and discriminatory taxes and exchange regulations, were satisfactorily adjusted. I added that every word that I had said in my speech before the American Institute of Mining Engineers was true and that, as a matter of fact, in writing that speech, because of my personal knowledge, I had had Chile very much in mind. I went into some details in this connection.

Pedregal responded that the difficulty was that Chile had to have the 40 million dollar credit before she could take care of the tax situation because she must live from the taxes. I replied, "In other words, you claim it is a vicious circle". He said, "Exactly". I then said that I agreed it was a vicious circle which had to be broken at some point but that since the taxes and other impositions on the copper companies were so self-evidently unjust, discriminatory, and counterproductive to Chile and to our relations, that in my opinion Chile should break the vicious circle by demonstrating her willingness and ability satisfactorily to adjust these matters and that once she had done so, thus reestablishing her credit, then she might expect to get the private capital and the consideration otherwise which she desired.

I also said the rumors about Chile setting up a copper sales company were very disturbing since it would be tantamount to an expropriation. Pedregal deprecated the idea of any such plan being attempted.

The interview ended by Pedregal inviting me to luncheon on April 25. I accepted.

Spruille Braden

---

[67] In October 1945.

825.50/5-2247

Memorandum of Conversation, by Messrs. Edgar L. McGinnis and Burr C. Brundage of the Division of North and West Coast Affairs

CONFIDENTIAL [WASHINGTON,] May 22, 1947.

Subject: Report of Pedregal Economic Mission

Participants: Señor Guillermo del Pedregal, head of the Chilean Economic Mission
Señor Victor Santa Cruz and Señor Flavian Levine, members of the Mission
Señor Roberto Vergara, Chilean Fomento Corporation
Assistant Secretary Thorp
Mr. Brundage—NWC
Mr. McGinnis—NWC
Mr. Cady—ED

. . . . . .

Mr. Santa Cruz, spokesman for the Chilean group, explained that prior to departing for Chile on May 24 he desired to review the activities of the Chilean Mission in this country and to pay a farewell call on Mr. Thorp. He itemized the results of the Mission as follows:

(1) *Copper*—The Mission conferred at length with representatives of the copper companies in New York and arrived at a statement of principles which was satisfactory to the copper companies.* Chile would abolish the copper dollar and permit the companies to purchase exchange at the regular rate of 31 pesos to the dollar. The various taxes and charges on copper production would be consolidated into one income tax so that the firms would know exactly where they stood. The profits of the copper companies after payment of taxes would be divided with one portion employed by the companies for dividends, etc., and the other would be required to be invested in Chile. While substantial agreement had been arrived at, further and conclusive discussions would be held in Chile on these matters, and, in fact, company representatives are already in Chile. The Mission appeared to be very satisfied with the copper conversations.

(2) *Debt*—The Mission had met with no success. Conversations were held with Mr. Rogers, President of the Foreign Bondholders Protective Council, wherein the two parties were unable to reach a satisfactory agreement. The Chileans said that they were able to pay

---

*While the Chilean Economic Mission gave the impression that substantial agreement had been reached in negotiations with the copper companies, it appears that neither Anaconda nor Kennecott are by any means satisfied with the Chilean proposals. [Footnote in the original.]

on their external debt (sterling and dollars) between $7,000,000 and $8,000,000 per annum. They did not wish to make an agreement now which Chile could not live up to in the long run, thereby precipitating another default. They preferred to arrive at a modest settlement which would be within Chile's economic means to fulfill. Mr. Rogers was firm in insisting that the FBPC would not accept less than 3% interest and 1% amortization. The Mission stated that this would be impossible within the sum which Chile could afford to set aside for debt purposes. Chile would either have to offer less than 3% interest or scale down the face value of the outstanding bonds in order to stay within this figure.

(3) *International Bank Loan ($40,000,000)*—The Mission was told by Bank officials that they could not consider Chile's application until Chile had arrived at a settlement of its foreign obligations with the FBPC. The Chilean Mission was taken aback by this categorical statement. They insisted that since the Bank was established for the purpose of making rehabilitation loans the Bank should not insist that applicants come to them with their financial houses completely in order. In fact, they said, loans should be made for the very purpose of assisting foreign countries to reestablish their credit rather than insisting that their credit be first established before a loan would be made. They referred, heatedly, to the recent loan made to the French Government and to the financial position of that country, which they compared unfavorably with Chile's present situation. They further said that they did not see how Chile could look forward to lifting exchange restrictions and to following the principles of the ITO unless through foreign loans its economy could be balanced and stabilized. The Mission felt strongly that by insisting on a prior debt settlement the Bank had put a strong and unfair bargaining weapon in the hands of the FBPC.

The Mission added that it was considering a recommendation that an American expert be employed to study Chile's financial and monetary situation. The Mission felt that, while complete information and statistics were available regarding Chile's financial and economic position, a report from an impartial expert would carry more weight with authorities in this country.

Mr. Thorp expressed his appreciation for the Mission's visit and stated that he was glad the Chileans had at least made progress toward the arrangement of the copper matter. With respect to the sending of an expert to study financial conditions, Mr. Thorp agreed that while complete statistics might be available on this subject, the findings of an impartial expert on these matters would doubtless be given more attention in this country.[68]

825.51/5–2347 : Airgram

The Ambassador in Chile (Bowers) to the Secretary of State

SANTIAGO, May 23, 1947.

A–219. The President's annual speech at the opening of Congress on May 21, 1947, laid special emphasis on the precarious state of government finances at the end of 1946 and at the present. Most of the ten points in the legislative program which he requested concerned revenue and tax measures. Some of these had already been drafted and sent to Congress. The source of new revenues was not stated.

While the 1946 budgetary deficit was 528.6 million pesos, as shown by the Comptroller General's report, he pointed out that the effective deficit was 979.1 millions, arrived at as follows:

	(Pesos, millions)
Budgetary Deficit 1946 (as carried by Treasury)	528.6
Sugar Subsidy funded by Central Bank purchase of internal debt bonds	225.0
Salary advances made to Armed Forces	221.1
Loss on collections from various debtors	4.4
Total	979.1

He stated that this sum, added to the cumulative deficit of previous years in the amount of 575.2 million pesos, less 96.2 million pesos which represented unspent funds from special law bonds financing, resulted in an effective, cumulative Treasury overdraft of 1,458.1 million pesos. Because of this situation, he stated that normal expenditures of the administration since January 1, 1947 had required cash overdrafts of 549.9 million pesos; that the government could only meet its current bills promptly if the total Treasury overdraft were reduced to a maximum of 700 millions. Point (1) of his legislative program was the partial financing of this cumulative deficit that apparently would require approximately 750 million pesos to reduce it to the workable sum mentioned. He pointed out that, despite savings which had been effected in public expenditures, it was impossible to cover the deficit plus 1947 cash overdrafts without providing special revenues to normalize the situation.

---

[68] Two handwritten notes appended read as follows:

"The net of this is that the Pedregal Mission is returning with a large goose egg. I am apprehensive that this may force the Chilean Govt. to recement its relations with the Communists. B. C. B[rundage]."

"All in tone with Pedregal's last talk with Mr. Braden; Dept should give careful consideration to attitude of Bank vis-à-vis Chile's external debt. M. K. W[ells]."

In addition to the Treasury, similar financial problems faced most of the semi-fiscal institutions, according to the President. He specifically mentioned the Fomento Corporation's budget of 1,000 million pesos for investments already approved, with no funds available in its treasury as of December 31, 1946; the Low-Cost Housing Bank whose overdraft as of the same date financed by the commercial banks was 191 million pesos, with its needs for this year estimated at 204 million pesos; the Reconstruction and Aid Corporation to which the government owed 57 million pesos, which it had been unable to pay; the Workers' Social Security Fund (Caja de Seguro Obligatorio) which carried an old actuarial deficit of 4,800 million pesos.

He called attention to the fact that most appropriation measures which had been enacted by the Congress in the past has specified financing by the sale of government internal debt bonds, authorization for the sale of which had been far in excess of the market potential.

The ten points of his legislative program were as follows:

1. Financing of the cumulative legislatory deficit.
2. The enlargement and improvement of the Department of Internal Revenue.
3. A capital gains tax.
4. Re-appraisal of the capital assets for tax purposes.
5. A change in the basic law of the government-sponsored National Savings Bank to permit greater credit facilities.
6. Modification of the basic Banking Law.
7. A tax on obsolete buildings in the business center of Santiago.
8. Increase financial resources for the Agricultural Credit Bank and the Low-Cost Housing Bank (both semi-fiscal agencies).
9. Further financing for the Fomento Corporation, the State Railroads, and the government's Transit Company.
10. A law to strengthen the enforcement of the government's economic laws and regulations.

BOWERS

825.50/5–2747

Memorandum by the Assistant Secretary of State for American Republic Affairs (Braden) to the Director of the Office of American Republic Affairs (Briggs)

CONFIDENTIAL [WASHINGTON,] May 27, 1947.

With further reference to Mr. Wells' Memorandum of Conversation of May 21, subject, "Pedregal Economic Mission",[69] and Mr. McGinnis' Memorandum of Conversation of May 22, "Report of Pedregal Eco-

---

[69] Not printed.

nomic Mission", I think the following additional observations are important for the record:

Messrs. Pedregal and Santa Cruz endeavored to convey the impression that an agreement had been reached with the American copper companies, Kennecott and Anaconda. This agreement could be further amplified by discussions which would be carried on in Chile, in point of fact as Sr. Pedregal admitted, when I twice emphasized the fact no agreement has been reached but merely a starting point from which further discussions can be carried on in Chile.

The copper companies received no "guarantee" of "a reasonable return on their present investment." In essence what was discussed in New York was:

(1) That a system of labor courts should be established and other measures taken to reduce strikes to a minimum and to eliminate illegal strikes, it being understood that wages would be raised or lowered in proportion to the cost of living in each mining camp. Sr. Pedregal, while observing that all labor difficulties could not be eliminated, was hopeful that this procedure would in large measure obviate future difficulties.

(2) The copper companies will no longer have to purchase pesos in exchange at the 19.37 rate but will be allowed to purchase pesos at the official rate, presently 31.00 or such future rate as may be established.

(3) By means of new legislation all present taxation will be put into one basket, whereby normal profit of each of the companies for the average of the last ten years will be established. Thereafter any profits made in excess of this normal, the companies may retain 50 percent in the United States but will have to return the other 50 percent to Chile, purchase pesos with it and then will be allowed to invest these pesos either in their own plants in extirpation [*exploration?*] and development of other properties, copper fabrication or such other enterprise and/or Chilean bonds as may be decided upon.

In short, the Chileans while offering some hope of alleviating existing bad labor conditions and promising relief from the present discriminatory exchange situation, actually force the companies to return a still larger proportion of their net income to Chile than presently is the case, so that in effect it is the Chileans who are endeavoring to set a floor below which the Chilean Government returns may not decrease, while at the same time grabbing off rather more than they presently receive from the copper companies. This is apparently done exclusively with the American owned companies and therefore if anything continues the present discrimination.

The attempt by Messrs. Pedregal and Santa Cruz to put words into other peoples' mouths as they did in my case at the luncheon tendered me by them on April 25 and by stating that an agreement had been reached with the copper companies is a discouraging beginning to such negotiations.

Similarly, in their communication to Mr. Rogers, President of the Foreign Bondholders Protective Council, Inc., it will be observed from my marginal notations that they have not made an honest approach to this problem.

Spruille Braden

825.51/6-447 : Telegram

The Ambassador in Chile (Bowers) to the Secretary of State

CONFIDENTIAL   US URGENT   Santiago, June 4, 1947—2 p. m.

436. My conversations with President Gonzalez reveal deep concern over attitude toward Chile encountered by Pedregal mission and fear lest door has been closed to further economic cooperation between our two countries. President even states they may be forced to withdraw from all Bretton Woods [70] commitments unless better understanding can be reached.

Chile is key country in struggle against Communism, and I feel that we should make every effort to overcome present impasse. Following my instructions Dunn [71] has sounded out Minister of Finance Pico Canas, as to possibility of implementing program here which would tend to inspire confidence in US financial circles and rehabilitate Chile's admittedly vulnerable debt record. Pico Canas stated that he was ready to take concrete steps to this end and expressed confidence that a mutually satisfactory agreement could be reached with bondholders. He hinted that he would be disposed to undertake negotiations personally if given encouragement by Department directly or indirectly. He undoubtedly desires invitation to visit US some weeks hence for this purpose.

If Department approves, Embassy will continue exploratory conversations with Pico, but before doing so, I should appreciate information as to feasibility of further negotiations with bondholders and what Chile must do to reopen loan negotiations with International Bank. I believe Pedegral mission was constructive in opening eyes of Chilean authorities to real situation in US and that they will be more readily disposed now to put their financial house in order. Please instruct.

Bowers

---

[70] Department of State, Treaties and Other International Acts Series No. 1502.
[71] William E. Dunn, Counselor of Embassy for Economic Affairs.

825.51/6–1147

Memorandum by Mr. Frederick Livesey of the Office of Financial Development Policy to the Assistant Chief of That Office (Cady)

[WASHINGTON,] June 11, 1947.

At your suggestion, I telephoned Mr. Rogers, President of the Bondholders Council, and asked him for details to enable us to interpret such phrases from Santiago as "the terms on which the bondholders insisted". Mr. Rogers said that he told Messrs. Pedregal and Santa Cruz that Chile ought to work out an agreement from an agreed arrangement for a fixed interest rate and a fixed amortization rate. He suggested 3% interest rate on the outstanding bonds. They were prepared for this, and had apparently assumed that that would be the suggested rate, and the whole discussion proceeded on that basis. The possibility of issuing new bonds with extended periods of payment, et cetera, was raised and discussed. The subject of amortization was left very vague. Various possible rates, such as ½% or 1% were mentioned but the matter was never pushed.

The Chileans raised the problem that a settlement which increased the market value of the bonds would greatly slow down the rate of decreasing the debt by amortization. They asked if it would be possible to reduce the principal of the bonds, perhaps 20%, to offset this feature. When Mr. Rogers said that this had never been done, they asked him to submit the question to the Council. The Council declined the proposal. Mr. Rogers told the Chileans that the Council might possibly consider alternative proposals such as it had accepted in the Brazilian settlement, one of them providing for a reduction in prinicpal compensated by a cash payment and the other providing for interest payments on bonds in the original face value. In the end the Chileans said that they could not consider a settlement which would increase the value of their bonds, as they expressed it.

I said that I had somewhere heard 3% and 1% amortization as the terms which the Council had offered. Mr. Rogers said that both the Chileans and he had gone over the figures of their current situation and both had agreed that they were enough at the present time to permit payments on that basis. However, the talks had never crystallized in respect of amortization beyond the point of proposing a "reasonable" rate of amortization.

I said Communist papers in Santiago were apparently suggesting that the Mission had fallen into the hands of New York financial imperialists. Mr. Rogers said that the Mission had visited and talked with many banks in New York and was quite critical of the attitude it found in some of them. However, they had given a big party, which he did not attend, at the end of their New York visit and all their discussions with the Council had been on a very courteous basis.

I did not mention the International Bank and Mr. Rogers gave no indication of having anything about it in mind.

825.51/8–2547

Memorandum by the Assistant Chief of the Division of River Plate Affairs (Lyon)

[Washington,] September 10, 1947.

Summary of Mr. McCloy's Memorandum Regarding "The Application of Chile for a Loan" [72]

Ambassador Bowers' letter of July 21 to the President [73] is full of misconceptions. The Bank is far from unsympathetic to Chile and has given more time and thought to Chile's application than to any other one in the Bank. It is true that a loan has not yet resulted but for good reasons. The Bank insists upon receiving satisfactory assurances that a country to which it makes a loan is actually taking steps to remedy unsound budgetary practices which in most cases have necessitated the country's applying for a loan.

It is felt that Chile should take the following steps before a loan would be justified:

(1) Reduce non-essential imports. Build up foreign exchange and gold reserves. Chile receives large dollar returns from copper and nitrate exports but is dissipating these.

(2) Attempt to check inflation. There has been much talk but no action in this line. Chile proposes a large scale plan of development, the economic soundness of some of which is doubtful.

(3) Balance the budget.

(4) Revise the tax system.

(5) Make reasonable efforts to come to an agreement with foreign bondholders.

Prior to 1931, Chile never failed to meet its obligations. However, service on its foreign debt was suspended that year. The serious earthquake in 1939 necessitated diverting debt service funds to relief. This continued until 1945 and amounted to $23,000,000.

The Bank has never insisted that Chile reach an agreement with its bondholders. Its position has been that it must consider, before granting the loan, the reason for default on previous loans. The Bank has offered to send representatives to Chile to be employed as con-

---

[72] John J. McCloy, President of the International Bank; memorandum not printed.

[73] Not printed.

sultants. The Bank desires to assist Chile and other countries similarly situated to restore their credit positions.

No Latin American country has yet received any loan from the Bank. The same test will be made for all Latin American countries applying for loans, as well as all European countries.

Cecil B. Lyon

825.51/10-247

The Ambassador in Chile (Bowers) to the Assistant Secretary of State for Political Affairs (Armour)

Santiago, October 2, 1947.

Dear Norman: The other day the finance expert of the Nitrate Company, a Chilean greatly respected by the Americans, was brought to me by the head of the Company, to convey an unofficial, very confidential message, from Jorge Alessandri, Minister of Finance. It is to the effect that the Central Bank of Chile had notified the International Monetary Fund [74] on September 13, 1947, that, in accordance with the privileges granted in Article V, Section 3, Letter a) of the Final Act of the Fund, it wishes to purchase $8,900,000 with the equivalent in gold which Chile has deposited with the Fund. Chile then proposes to use these dollars to get goods, practically all American, now backed up in the Chilean customhouses for lack of dollars to take them out. As you know, most of the goods are seriously needed since they include machinery for farms and factories and railroads, and are productive.

It is the stated purpose of the Finance Minister to sell these dollars to Chilean importers in order that the supply of articles, which the country urgently needs and which are in the customhouses because of the lack of dollars, can be secured. It will require 275.5 million paper pesos to purchase these dollars, at the official rate of exchange, and it is the purpose and pledge to retire these pesos from circulation, and credit them to the account of the International Monetary Fund. The retirement of these pesos would have a deflationary effect on the economy of Chile and would serve to offset partially the inflationary effect of the revaluation of the old gold reserve, which is also proposed.

I understand that Mr. Maschke, Manager of the Central Bank of Chile and Chile's representative as a Governor of the International Monetary Fund, now in London, has reported by cable that the administrative authorities of the Fund may be doubtful as to the Fund's acceding to the request unless serious efforts are made to restrain any

---

[74] Established on the basis of a provision in the Final Act of the United Nations Monetary and Financial Conference, July 22, 1944.

inflationary processes. Alessandri believes this is taken care of in his plan. The necessary data and information have been sent by air mail to Maschke to enable him to explain in London that this measure is part of the Government program to strengthen and stabilize finances, and that the Government believes that the proposed dollar purchase will be deflationary rather than inflationary. I am enclosing a memorandum [75] on the plan and purpose submitted at my request by the Nitrate man.

In view of the energetic steps which are being taken by the present Cabinet and the apparent sincerity of the Minister of Finance, in whom the country clearly has confidence, I hope that our representative on the International Monetary Fund may be able to support Chile's request.

Another matter: Very earnest efforts are being made by the Government to reduce the cost of living by ending speculation and the criminal arbitrary raising of prices in the stores to fantastic heights. Many merchants, an average of 25 a week, are being convicted and sent into exile to small villages in the north of Chile. The President's wife has gone on the radio, urging housewives to report immediately to a designated person and place any exorbitant price asked in the stores, and the women are responding.

I was shocked by the death of Wright.

Warmest regards.

Sincerely,

CLAUDE G. BOWERS

825.51/10–247

Memorandum of Conversation, by the Assistant Chief of the Division of North and West Coast Affairs (Mills)

CONFIDENTIAL [WASHINGTON,] October 13, 1947.

Participants: Señor Nieto del Rio, Chilean Ambassador
Norman Armour, Assistant Secretary
Roberto Vergara, Chilean Representative of the Fomento Corporation
Norman Ness, OFD
Sheldon T. Mills, NWC

Accompanied by the Chilean Ambassador, Señor Nieto del Rio, Roberto Vergara, head of the New York Office of the Fomento Corporation, called on Assistant Secretary Armour today. He explained to Mr. Armour that during a recent visit to Chile he had prepared for the Finance Minister, Jorge Alessandri Rodriguez, a memorandum

---

[75] Not printed.

recommending a settlement with the foreign bondholders. Señor Alessandri had instructed him to try to reach such a settlement. Before approaching Rogers of the Bondholders Council, however, Señor Vergara wished to obtain the reaction of the Department of State and a promise of its cooperation. He outlined the plan which he would present to Rogers, namely amortization payments of 1% per year and interest payments to a rising scale starting at 1% in 1947, 1–½ in 1948, 2% in 1949 and 1950, 2–½% in 1951 and 1952, and a final figure of 3% in 1953 and thereafter. The plan contains other "stipulations," including cancellation of back interest, the return to the amortization fund of $27 millions diverted to other uses, and the retention of the present fiscal agents.

Señor Vergara was in Washington on October 1 and 2 when he discussed the plan with Mr. Mills and other officers of NWC. Also prior to today's meeting he had discussed it with Mr. Ness and Messrs. Corliss and Livesey of OFD. These departmental officers were in agreement that the Vergara plan was a most encouraging development and that, if Mr. Armour agreed, this should be conveyed to Mr. Vergara.

Mr. Armour expressed to Mr. Vergara his satisfaction in hearing that a serious attempt would be made to settle the debt problem. Mr. Ness suggested that an officer in OFD this afternoon telephone to Rogers of the Bondholders Council and advise him that the Department knew Vergara well and had confidence in his integrity, and that the Department had studied the proposals which Vergara would lay before him and felt that they offered a solution to the long standing disagreement between Chile and the Bondholders Council. Mr. Ness suggested that after a discussion with Vergara, Rogers probably would come to Washington at which time the Department could consider with him the terms of the Vergara plan.

Mr. Armour approved this proposed procedure.

825.51/10–3047

Memorandum of Conversation, by Mr. James H. Webb of the Division of North and West Coast Affairs

RESTRICTED [WASHINGTON,] October 30, 1947.

Participants: Mr. Ness—OFD
Mr. Mills—NWC
Mr. Webb—NWC

Mr. Ness stated that negotiations between Roberto Vergara and representatives of the Bondholders' Protective Council had been going extremely well. Vergara was so encouraged that he cabled Minister of Finance Alessandri on Friday, October 24, requesting permission to sign the agreement on terms essentially the same as those outlined in Vergara's proposal.

Unfortunately, Minister Alessandri was having his own troubles in Santiago as the result of passage by the legislature of a bill proposed to extinguish the Chilean 1947 budget deficit of some 2,000,000,000 pesos. The bill included, among several sources of revenue, a 20 percent increase in the extraordinary tax on copper exports. Alessandri, who had opposed this provision of the bill, felt that whatever difficulties had been anticipated in the attraction of American capital to investment in Chile would be greatly increased by the passage of this bill.

Mr. Ness, who said he was expecting a telephone call from Vergara at any moment, was doubtful that we could afford to offer too much encouragement in pushing the debt settlement, since a successful solution of that problem would not necessarily produce the ultimate objective, which was a loan from the International Bank. Mr. Ness pointed out that settlement of the debt was only one of several conditions, named by the International Bank as prerequisite to a loan, ranking in fact only fifth in a list of such conditions enumerated in a memorandum from John J. McCloy, President of the International Bank, to Secretary of the Treasury Snyder.

Mr. Mills pointed out that notwithstanding such low placement, he himself knew from conversations with International Bank officials that debt settlement was actually the first consideration in their minds. Mr. Mills recommended that Vergara be encouraged to proceed with the settlement if possible, taking up the problem of possible antagonism of the copper interests when that problem arose. Mr. Ness agreed to proceed on that basis.

In reply to a question from Mr. Ness, Mr. Mills stated he would be glad to give him full backing if there were any repercussions as a result of his urging Vergara to proceed with the debt settlement. If the copper companies should approach the Department regarding the increase in taxation in Chile, the problem could be considered separately, in the opinion of Mr. Mills.

(NOTE: Embassy Santiago's telegram No. 851 of October 30, 1947,[76] indicates that since the proposed export tax on copper is temporary, to operate only until December, little opposition is anticipated from the copper companies.)

---

[76] Not printed.

825.51/10–247

The Assistant Secretary of State for Political Affairs (Armour) to the Ambassador in Chile (Bowers)

CONFIDENTIAL   WASHINGTON, November 3, 1947.

DEAR CLAUDE: I have your letter of October 2, 1947, regarding Chile's desire to buy dollars from the International Monetary Fund to the extent of her contribution to the Fund which amounted to about $8,900,000. I have noted that Chile desires to employ the dollars thus obtained for the purpose of moving essential merchandise from Customs, which have accumulated there owing to the dearth of dollar exchange.

It is my understanding that Mr. Maschke presented Chile's request to the International Monetary Fund during its recent meeting in London, and that officials of the Fund were reluctant to authorize Chile to purchase dollars equivalent to Chile's full contribution to the Fund unless she took radical steps to control inflation. I am told that the Fund was desirous of authorizing Chile to purchase a lesser amount of dollars and that Chile was finally authorized to buy $2,500,000 for pesos for the purpose above mentioned. Later the Chileans again brought up this matter and the Fund authorized the purchase of an additional $2,500,000 for pesos to be effective October 24. In making this latter authorization the Fund indicated that they would give full consideration to later applications from the Chileans for additional amounts of dollars, but that they hoped that the $5,000,000 already authorized would be sufficient to meet Chilean needs. Inasmuch as the Fund is, as you well know, an international organization, and is apparently fully cognizant of Chile's difficult financial situation, I do not feel that it is desirable at this point for the Department to request the United States member to support Chile's request for dollars. However, I should be glad to go into this matter at a later date if the Chileans encounter difficulties with the Fund.

In view of the Fund's position in this matter, I trust that the Chileans will utilize the dollars already obtained for the release from Customs of essential imports which will help increase the output of Chilean industries, and that none of these funds will be employed for the importation of unessential merchandise. Although it may be somewhat trite, it is apparent that the principal solution to Chile's financial difficulties lies in the direction of greater production.

I am thankful for your comments on general economic conditions in Chile and am completely sympathetic with the efforts of the Chilean Government to stabilize its economy. However, I agree with you that the Government's efforts to reduce the cost of living through prosecution of speculators will not alone solve the problem of high prices unless its plan to increase production, reduce unessential Government expenditures, and to curtail the money supply through increased taxation is carried out.

Sincerely yours,

NORMAN ARMOUR

825.51/11–2547 : Telegram

The Acting Secretary of State to the Embassy in Chile

CONFIDENTIAL   WASHINGTON, November 25, 1947—11 a. m.

563. For Emb info only. Robert Vergara informed Dept that on Nov 18 he had reached agreement with Rogers, Pres, For Bondholders Protective Council, on terms settlement of Chil debt which provide initial interest 1–½ percent rising to 3 percent after 1953 and 1 percent amortization. Announcement agreement probably be delayed few weeks since related negotiations with British and Swiss bondholders groups not concluded.

LOVETT

CHILE'S RELUCTANCE TO ENTER INTO AN AGREEMENT WITH THE UNITED STATES REGARDING TRADE [77]

711.252/2–747 : Airgram

The Ambassador in Chile (Bowers) to the Secretary of State

RESTRICTED   SANTIAGO, February 7, 1947.

A–57. On two occasions during 1947 Chilean officials have indicated some misunderstandng concerning pending United States–Chile Treaty of Friendship, Commerce and Navigation. Economic Counselor Dunn mentioned this on Feb 5 to FornOff Acting Under-Secretary, Sr. Bernstein, who stated that perhaps some Chilean officials considered this Treaty unimportant in view of current multilateral negotiations. He also said FornOff Commercial Policy Section very much disorganized lately and that very few in Section knew very much about Treaty. He said he would see that erroneous impression is cleared up and that study of proposed Treaty is resumed.

BOWERS

---

[77] For previous discussions, see *Foreign Relations*, 1941, vol. VI, pp. 596 ff.

711.252/5–1947

Memorandum by the Counselor of Embassy for Economic Affairs in Chile (Dunn) to the Ambassador in Chile (Bowers) [78]

SANTIAGO, May 16, 1947.

This afternoon I called at the Chilean Foreign Office to talk to Messrs. Bernstein or Vergara [79] about the proposed Treaty of Friendship, Commerce and Navigation, and found them in conference together, so that I was able to get their joint views at the same time.

. . . .

I then asked them frankly what their attitude toward the treaty was at this time. Mr. Bernstein said that until the results of the multilateral treaty negotiations at Geneva [80] were apparent, Chile would prefer not to discuss the broader treaty. Mr. Vergara then said that as a matter of fact Chile had always been afraid of such broad treaties. He said that former Ambassador Culbertson had proposed something of the same nature in 1927, and that they had turned it down. He went on to say that some apparently very innocuous and innocent looking article in such a treaty would often turn up later to haunt them, and that they preferred to make separate treaties covering the various matters involved and not combine them into such an all-inclusive document.

I argued that our proposed treaty was quite elastic and would provide a set of principles on which our relations could be based; that we were trying to negotiate a number of such treaties, and had hoped that Chile would be one of the first countries with which we could sign up; also that it would be to Chile's interest to conclude such a treaty. I said that now that we were in such excellent practice as a result of our recently concluded bilateral aviation agreement,[81] we should not lose the momentum we had acquired, but should continue our discussions on this new basis.

Mr. Vergara smiled and said that if it had taken us a week to negotiate the comparatively simple aviation agreement, it would take at least seven weeks of continuous work to do the broader treaty, and even then he doubted that we could reach an agreement on certain of its articles. He again said that they would prefer to await the

---

[78] Copy transmitted to the Department by the Ambassador in his despatch 15,297, May 19, 1947, not printed.
[79] Germán Vergara Domoso, Legal and Economic Adviser of the Chilean Ministry for Foreign Affairs.
[80] Negotiations that ended in the General Agreement on Tariffs and Trade, signed October 1947. For documentation, see volume I. For text of the agreement, see Department of State, Treaties and Other International Acts Series (TIAS) No. 1700.
[81] TIAS No. 1905.

results of the Geneva conference, as a number of the articles in the proposed treaty of Friendship, Commerce and Navigation seemed to be embodied in the multilateral negotiations. He concluded by saying that if we were really interested in getting started with such a treaty, it would be necessary for Ambassador Bowers to speak about it to Foreign Minister Juliet, since the present views of the Foreign Office were as they had outlined them to me.

In view of this conversation, I deem it futile to press the matter further at this time, unless the Department gives instructions to the contrary. After the Geneva conference is over, however, further inquiries might then well be made.

W. E. DUNN

711.252/5–1947 : Telegram

The Secretary of State to the Embassy in Chile

CONFIDENTIAL WASHINGTON, June 11, 1947—7 p. m.

283. Dept surprised coolness Bernstein, Vergara and statement treaty ultimately dependent results Geneva conference ref Embdes 15297 May 19, 1947.[82] Under circumstances considered desirable now above all secure reaffirmation Chilean interest in treaty.

Unless strongly felt attitude Vergara, Bernstein accurately and fully reflects views FonMin or other serious objection perceived, Emb instructed approach FonMin with view securing reaffirmation even in general terms pointing out not immediately seeking opening formal negotiations.

Urinfo only Dept feels present inopportune press further for Chilean views specific articles US draft or attempt conduct concrete discussion.

MARSHALL

711.252/6–1747 : Telegram

The Ambassador in Chile (Bowers) to the Secretary of State

CONFIDENTIAL SANTIAGO, June 17, 1947—6 p. m.

494. Deptel 283, June 1[*11*]. Vergara (on way trip to Rio de Janeiro) informed Dunn today he saw no objection to reaffirmation Chilean interest in treaty of friendship, commerce and navigation. Since Bernstein already in Rio, Vergara said he would discuss matter with Abelardo Silva, chief FonOff commercial policy section, re in-

---

[82] Not printed.

serting reaffirming clause in text of forthcoming note renewing Chile–US *modus vivendi*. Vergara suggested preparing and exchanging notes extending *modus vivendi* now without waiting for actual expiration date and said would suggest this procedure to Silva. Embassy requests authorization follow matter up with Silva with view to effecting exchange of notes within next week or two.

BOWERS

711.252/6–1747 : Telegram

The Secretary of State to the Embassy in Chile

CONFIDENTIAL WASHINGTON, June 30, 1947—7 p. m.

322. Ref Embtel 494 June 17. Preparatory steps renewal 1945 provisional commercial agreement authorized. Urinfo only Dept continues feel attitude Vergara negative and surprised apparent indifference FonOff officials to concrete progress on matter such importance to US and Chile, in view assurances Bernstein Ref Embgram A–57 Feb 7 ChilGov study proposals would be resumed.

Dept desires if possible obtain statement specific period within which propose concrete negotiations be initiated, preferably six months to one year. Emb requested inquire FonMin whether agreeable include such statement reaffirmation clause forthcoming exchange notes to implement general interest expressed notes last renewal July 30, 1946. Point out US not immediately seeking Chil views specific articles US proposals but on contrary recognize complex questions involved require full deliberation. Emb should delay actual renewal if possible until this matter explored FonMin. Urinfo only Dept feels general reaffirmation little continuing value unless sincere and accompanied assurances resumption ChilGov actual study treaty draft. Emb authorized none the less proceed, submitting draft proposed note for Dept approval prior exchange.

MARSHALL

611.2531/7–2247 : Telegram

The Ambassador in Chile (Bowers) to the Secretary of State

CONFIDENTIAL SANTIAGO, July 22, 1947—10 a.m.

595. Dunn saw Vergara yesterday on renewal provisional commercial agreement. Vergara said Chile willing insert reaffirmation clause along lines desired by Department (Deptel 322, July 1 [83]) provided

---

[83] Not printed.

clearly understood that negotiations on treaty friendship would be on basis other than our proposed draft which he said unacceptable on political and psychological grounds and which Foreign Office considers too all-embracing with many points therein already covered in constitution and laws. Chilean Treaty Commission scheduled inform Embassy today of decision on draft of provisional agreement proposed by Embassy. Will cable draft soon as possible.[84]

BOWERS

---

[84] The exchange of notes renewing the 1945 Provisional Commercial Agreement between Chile and the United States took place on July 30 and 31, 1947. For text, see TIAS No. 1642.

COLOMBIA

DISCRIMINATORY TREATMENT OF AMERICAN SHIPPING INTERESTS BY COLOMBIA

821.85/8–1347

The Acting Secretary of State to the Embassy in Colombia

RESTRICTED
No. 1273

WASHINGTON, August 20, 1947.

SIR: With reference to the Department's circular instruction of April 7, 1947 entitled "Shipping Discriminations" and to despatches Nos. 2492 of May 30, 1947 and 2578 of July 17, 1947,[1] you are requested, unless objection is perceived thereto, to deliver a note along the following lines to the Colombian Minister for Foreign Affairs, and at that time to express concern about the present practices of discriminating against American shipping:

"Excellency:
"I have received instructions from my government to protest to your government in connection with a number of shipping discriminations recently adopted by it. Information has been received that preferential treatment is being accorded Flota Mercante Grancolombiana S. A., in the following respects:

"1. by Law 10 of 1946 exempting Grancolombiana from income and inheritance taxes and from payment of port dues, and

"2. by a policy of the Federación Nacional de Cafeteros de Colombia, a government organization of the Republic of Colombia, under which it will sell coffee to merchants, dealers and exporters only upon condition that such coffee be exported in steamships of Grancolombiana.

[Here follows a historical explanation of United States policy including quotations from the treaty of 1846 between the United States and the Republic of New Granada (Colombia), and from certain United States Statutes.]

"The Governments of the United States and other trading nations of the world have recognized the necessity of adopting sound principles of non-discriminatory multilateral trade in effectively promoting and encouraging international trade and international peace. A program of shipping discriminations if permitted to flourish would inevitably act as a restraint on international trade in that it would provide a monopoly to national interests with subsequent large increases in freight rates.

---

[1] None printed.

"Looking toward future relations it is sincerely hoped that the Government of Colombia will abandon its present discriminations against the shipping of the United States. In the past 150 years the possibilities of a discriminatory program have been fully explored, and the disadvantages have been found to far outweigh any possible advantages."

Very truly yours,   For the Acting Secretary of State:
WILLARD L. THORP

821.85/9–1047 : Telegram

The Chargé in Colombia (Warner) to the Secretary of State

RESTRICTED   Bogotá, September 10, 1947—11 a. m.

585. Bogotá liberal newspapers of September 9 sensationally headlined news agency account originating New York of interview with shipping spokesman who announced delivery by this Embassy of protest note to Colombian Government over discriminations against US shipping by National Coffee Federation and Flota Gran Colombiana. Spokesman indicated possible US retaliation to ships of Colombian flag if discrimination or suspension of commercial privileges in US not discontinued.

This publicity and threat of retaliation has extraordinarily inflamed public opinion and brought a rousing public pre-trial with decision adverse to US of his case. *El Liberal* editorialized that Secretary Marshall at Rio Conference [2] counselled Latin American nations to help themselves economically, but that no one would have expected that US obstruct rather than help in this process. *El Espectador* characterizes US action as an "audacious attempt at economic aggression". Elsewhere frequent references were inevitably made to the contradiction of US action with the good neighbor policy, the return to dollar diplomacy, et cetera. Communist Party and CTC chimed in with calls for support of citizens in freeing country from chains of imperialistic monopolies.

Colombian House of Representatives indulged in heated debate of question September 9 where US action was labeled as "imperialistic", "— one of compulsion", "insult" and "menace", but it finally approved a motion to obtain the facts about the note from the government before doing anything further.

Embassy despatched note set forth in Department's instructions 1273 on August 27. It deliberately avoided use of word "protest" but expressed "deep concern" in connection with shipping discriminations recently adopted. Rest of note exactly like that suggested by Depart-

---

[2] For documentation on the Conference, see pp. 1 ff.

ment with specific additional request for Foreign Office views in premise. In view of change in wording Foreign Office yesterday was able to inform press that note simply states problem of violation of 1846 treaty in connection with the measures taken by Coffee Federation. If no additional fuel is added to the flames from US press, it is hoped that local excitement will subside.

WARNER

821.85/9–1047 : Telegram

The Chargé in Colombia (Warner) to the Secretary of State

RESTRICTED   BOGOTÁ, September 10, 1947—1 p. m.

586. ReEmbtel 585 September 10. Crowd of approximately 500 university students later augmented by others assembled in front of Embassy 11:30 a. m. this morning. They threw stones breaking windows, overturned one Embassy car, deflated tires of others, sang national anthem, yelled "down with Truman and with imperialism" and other epitaphs [epithets]. The few regular police present were apparently afraid take action. Although a students' manifestation was announced in the morning press in support of the Gran Colombiana, no special police were in evidence. It took over 23 minutes to communicate with Foreign Office by telephone and when it was finally reached reinforcements and riot squad arrived within 5 minutes and streets were immediately cleared. Grace[3] office sacked, employees escaped injury; United Fruit Office not attacked.

WARNER

821.85/9–1047 : Telegram

The Secretary of State to the Embassy in Colombia

RESTRICTED   US URGENT   WASHINGTON, September 11, 1947—6 p. m.

453. Unjustified and rowdy attacks student and hoodlum mobs against Emb and office Grace and Co have been source much concern to Dept. Fact that Chief of Protocol spontaneously called at Emb to express his regrets for disorders deters Dept from making protest which it otherwise surely would be called upon to lodge. You may say to FonOff that we accept apology of Col Govt without prejudice, however, to any claims for damage which may have been done to American property. It is noted from urtels that certain windows in front Emb were damaged, an Emb car was overturned, and Grace and

---

[3] W. R. Grace and Company.

Co office was sacked. You should point out these facts to FonOff and immediate assessment damage should be made for sake record.

Dept has noted several newspapers, in particular *El Tiempo*, *El Liberal* and *El Espectador*, wrote precipitately in a condemnatory vein before possession facts. Dept confident . . . that upon explanation they will be glad to publish true facts. Such statements as "audacious attempt at economic aggression" are offensive and misleading. . . .

In your conversation with FonOff you should make clear that Emb expects adequate police protection in event imminence any further disorder.

MARSHALL

821.85/9–1147 : Airgram

The Chargé in Colombia (Warner) to the Secretary of State

BOGOTÁ, September 11, 1947.

A–451. Reference Embassy's telegram No. 596 of September 11.[4] Following speech by Dr. Diego Montawa Cuéllar[5] to anti-U.S. gathering in front Communications Building, National Federation Petroleum Workers (Fedepetrol) issued declaration urging all classes and political groups of Colombia "to organize great national movement to defend Flota Grancolombiana threatened by the illicit intervention of the North American Government, with grave ignominy to our sovereign nation". Declaration said petroleum workers are prepared cease working for imperialist companies if U.S. Government "maintains the position taken in its note, which is a dangerous manifestation of the rapacious, anti-democratic tendencies of Yankee imperialism and deeply wounds the national dignity".

National Association of Bank Employees of Colombia called note "total disregard for the liberty and sovereignty of our nation", published protest, and voted full support for "every manifestation effected by Governments and peoples of Gran Colombia tending to prevent any abusive interference of Yankee imperialism in the legitimate interests and rights of our nations".

Executive Committee of National Federation of Railway Workers, in declaration asserted note shows clearly United States wants to continue 40-year-old monopoly of shipping trust and resolved: Support all measures that may be adopted by Flota Mercante Grancolombiana and National Coffee Federation, to preserve right "dispose freely of

---

[4] Not printed.
[5] Communist legal adviser to Fedepetrol.

the shipment of our products": Support the "virile protest" of the Colombian Congress against the "Dollar Dictators" and to "protest to the world" against the U. S. stand which is a "frank violation of the already much betrayed 'Good Neighbor' policy".

Numerous other labor organizations issued similar protest declarations, the general tone of which was keyed to official statement issued Tuesday by Confederation Colombian Workers (CTC) simultaneously calling on laborers throughout Colombia to organize in defense of Flota Grancolombiana. CTC's statement said it had welcomed organization of merchant fleet as "step toward liberation of our peoples from the monopoly of imperialism in the transportation of their imports and exports". When the Grancolombiana was organized, the CTC said, it had warned that "shipping monopolies of imperialism would spare no effort to torpedo this initiative which is an encouraging step on road to the economic and political liberation of our nation, and reduce it to impotency".

The statement added, "The imports and exports of our country must be moved, preferentially, in our own merchant marine units, with an eye to strengthening the Grancolombiana, until it is in such condition that our country can free itself definitively from the tutelage of the imperialist monopoly. This is not discrimination. It is simply an essentially patriotic policy that corresponds to the desire of our people in open struggle for the independence and sovereignty of our peoples of Latin America.

"We trust the Government will adopt a patriotic stand toward the barefaced protest of Yankee imperialism, in keeping with the deep patriotic feeling of our people, in whom it will find the fullest support, and the determination to defend our country's patrimony."

WARNER

821.85/9–1147 : Telegram

The Consul at Medellín, Colombia (Ragland), to the Secretary of State

MEDELLÍN, September 11, 1947.

32. Angry anti-United States demonstration front Consulate between 6 and 6:45 last night. Crowd apparently led by students estimated 150 screamed such things as "*abajo* Truman and *viva* La Flota Gran Colombiana". Speeches referred to United States imperialists and allegedly contained coarse language regarding United States and

President Truman. Of interest crowds also shouted *"abajo los Liberales"*.

Police on hand and no damage done. Consulate building and residences Consular officers under police guard which continues. Apparently no arrests and no information yet available regarding mob leaders.

While further trouble unlikely, am keeping official car under cover as precaution. Incident unreported in local press. Embassy informed.

RAGLAND

821.85/9-1247 : Telegram

The Chargé in Colombia (Warner) to the Secretary of State

RESTRICTED   BOGOTÁ, September 12, 1947—noon.

599. ReDeptel 453, September 11. Department has apparently misinterpreted my telegram reporting Chief of Protocol "expressed regrets" as apology. No apology has yet been made. When news despatches from Washington reached Bogotá September 11 reporting that spokesman for Department had stated that "the Colombian chancellery, as well as Chief of Police had presented excuses to the Embassy of the United States in Bogotá" the Secretary to the Presidency "emphatically" informed press that "the Government of Colombia has not presented excuses". As to press report of Department's statement that chief of police had also "made excuses" to Embassy, the Secretary to the Presidency informed press that "General Torres Duran had limited himself, as was his duty, to offering all protection to the US Embassy building and to all other dependencies". At same time Presidency informed press that Chief of Protocol "went himself yesterday to the Embassy to deplore what had happened". In view of foregoing, Embassy unable to inform FonOff of acceptance of Colombian Government's apology.

Chief of Protocol has indicated informally that FonOff is taking up question of payment of damages to Embassy property. President issued statement last night that note would not be made public until decision in premises has been reached. In view thereof, the Embassy refraining from giving facts to press which now attributes confusion and manifestations which took place to lack of facts at that time.

Embassy awaiting further instructions from Department. However, contents of Deptel 453 brought informally to attention of Secretary General FonOff this morning as friendly gesture.

WARNER

821.85/9–1247 : Telegram

The Chargé in Colombia (Warner) to the Secretary of State

RESTRICTED   Botogá, September 12, 1947—6 p. m.

603. Re mitel 599, September 12. Acting Foreign Minister Urdaneta [6] called me to Foreign Office this afternoon. He stated that government deplored and emphatically condemned incident of September 10. He explained that government has refrained from "making excuses" because in Spanish "making excuses" implies active participation and he again emphasized that government emphatically condemned incident and was in no way a party thereto. He admitted police were taken by surprise. Subsequently chief of protocol stated that Foreign Office would send workers to repair broken glass and asked that repair bills for damage to cars be sent to him for payment.

Embassy considers statement of Foreign Minister, coupled with action of Foreign Office with respect to damages, as adequate amends and as satisfactory as a literal apology. Embassy requests Department's authorization to inform Foreign Minister that Department finds his statement satisfactory, — without prejudice however to any claims for damages which may have been done to American property other than Embassy.[7]

WARNER

821.85/9–2347 : Telegram

The Chargé in Colombia (Warner) to the Secretary of State

CONFIDENTIAL   Bogatá, September 23, 1947—6 p. m.

644. From the Ambassador. Foreign Minister [8] called me this morning to discuss note 598, August 27,[9] Department's instruction 1273, August 20, concerning shipping discriminations in favor of Flota Mercante Gran Colombiana.

He referred to delicate position of Government as result of premature and inaccurate publicity concerning note. . . . inquired informally and in very friendly way if our Government would be willing to eliminate from note reference to provisions of United States code which to Colombian people would sound like a threat.

I told Minister I was under impression note already known to certain people in United States and that any effort to modify it now might lead to undesirable complications. He did not press point.

---

[6] Roberts Urdaneta Arbelaez, Prime Minister and Minister of Interior.
[7] In telegram 460, September 13, 2 p. m., the Department advised the Embassy that the Foreign Office statement was adequate (821.85/9–1247).
[8] Domingo Esquerra.
[9] Not printed; the Chargé's note was transmitted to the Department in despatch 2714, September 24, 1947.

With reference to remainder of note he said he believed our objections to exemption of Flota from income and inheritance taxes not well taken but our objection to exemption from ports dues, etc., was well taken.

He thought whole matter of Law 10 might be handled in one of two ways, either by decision of Council of State declaring law invalid or by decreeing regulations which would remove discrimination.

I agreed solution one of these methods desirable. In reply to my inquiry he said he thought President might press Council of State for early decision on law.

Minister then said he considered Coffee Federation a private entity and our objection on that score therefore unfounded. I told him that after studying statutes of Federation and its contract with Government I could assure him our Government would not recede from its view that Federation is official entity.

I told him my Government wished Colombia to have healthy merchant marine as it wished Colombia to have healthy economy and that I would do everything appropriate and desirable to assist Colombia to these ends but it must be on basis of no discrimination. Discrimination would only hurt Colombia in long-run and make it impossible for our government to be of help. I added that in United States as in Colombia there were interests seeking quick victories and easy solutions and that when Colombia discriminated against United States it was giving support to forces in our country which would be willing to discriminate against Colombia and other countries. I said Colombia would be in bad way indeed if United States began to discriminate against it. Minister agreed and said it was in Colombia's interest to settle this right away. He said I could inform my Government that matter would be settled in manner satisfactory to it. [Beaulac.]

WARNER

821.85/9–2447 : Telegram

The Acting Secretary of State to the Embassy in Colombia

CONFIDENTIAL WASHINGTON, September 25, 1947—7 p. m.

488. For Ambassador. Dept approves deletions from note recommended urtel 646 Sept 24 [10] in view your belief this will be effective in reaching settlement satisfactory to US and benefit future relations.

You should be aware shipping interests here will press for action under statutes in question unless satisfactory adjustment coffee matter reached.

---

[10] Not printed.

If FonOff contemplates publishing your note and its reply you may wish indicate your desire see reply before publication.

Dept appreciates (urtel 644 Sept 23) and commends capable manner you conducted discussion with ForMin.

LOVETT

821.85/10-1747 : Telegram

The Ambassador in Colombia (Beaulac) to the Secretary of State

RESTRICTED   BOGOTÁ, October 17, 1947—6 p. m.

711. Embassy today received Foreign Office reply dated October 15 [11] to Embassy note 596 [*598*] of August 27 Embassy despatch No. 31 October 10 [12] concerning discriminations against American shipping. With reference to Law 10 of 1946, Foreign Office points out foreign companies have access to Colombian courts and Council of State. With reference to discrimination by Coffee Federation, Foreign Office maintains latter is private entity. It also reminds Embassy that by virtue of Public Resolution 17 passed by 73rd Congress [13] exportation of American products obtained through loans made by official entities must be exported exclusively in ships of American registry.

BEAULAC

821.006/11-1147

The Secretary of State to the Embassy in Colombia

RESTRICTED   WASHINGTON, November 11, 1947.
No. 38

The Secretary of State refers to the Embassy's report No. 163 dated May 6, 1947, to the Embassy's airgram A-275 dated May 29, 1947, to the Embassy's report No. 254 dated July 10, 1947, and to subsequent reports [14] which have indicated an early intention of the Colombian Office of Exchange Control to establish quotas in licensing the importation of certain articles, including cigarettes, automobiles, trucks, tires, liquors, radios and refrigerators.

The Department is concerned over these developments, since establishment of the quotas contemplated and their application to articles of United States origin listed in Schedule I of the 1936 [*1935*] trade agreement with Colombia [15] would clearly be in contravention of that

---

[11] Not printed; it was transmitted to the Department by the Ambassador in his despatch 49, October 21, 1947.
[12] Not printed.
[13] 48 Stat. 500.
[14] None printed.
[15] Signed September 13, 1935; for text, see Department of State Executive Agreement Series No. 89, or 49 Stat. 3875.

agreement. Article V of the trade agreement with Colombia provides that no prohibition or restriction shall be imposed by the United States or by the Republic of Colombia upon importation of products included in Schedules II and I respectively, with certain exceptions enumerated in paragraph 2 of Article V, none of which would appear to be applicable in the present case. The establishment of the system of quotas contemplated by the Colombian Office of Exchange Control for importation of these Schedule I products from the United States would therefore in the Department's opinion be precluded by the terms of the trade agreement.

For the Embassy's information, however, the Department recognizes the serious difficulties in Colombia which have resulted from an increasingly unfavorable balance of payments and the continuing decline in the exchange reserves of that country. The Department is additionally inclined to agree not to invoke provisions of the existing trade agreements with respect to measures adopted by other Governments which conflict with provisions of the agreements in question but which are nevertheless in harmony with the relevant provisions of the Geneva draft Charter for the International Trade Organization. This inclination is of course qualified in the sense that this Government reserves all of its established rights in such matters in the interim period pending installation of the International Trade Organization, and the adherence of other Governments to the Organization, and by the expectation that the terms of existing agreements will be respected as fully and completely as possible until formally superseded.

The Embassy will note in referring to the copy of the Geneva draft of the Charter for an International Trade Organization in its hands that Article 21 [*12*] allows for restriction of the quantity or value of merchandise permitted to be imported into any country to the extent necessary to halt a serious decline in its monetary reserves, or, if they are very low, to increase them reasonably. A country so restricting imports may also classify products so as to give priority to the importation of those products more essential to its economy. However, these provisions are qualified in several important respects, permitting their maintenance only to the extent that unchanged exchange conditions continue to justify their application, requiring that they do not unnecessarily damage the commercial interests of other countries, providing for their progressive relaxation as far as possible, and requiring their administration in a non-discriminatory manner. The Embassy will note these and other requirements outlined in Articles 20, 21 and 22 of the Charter.

The Embassy is requested to approach the appropriate Colombian authority at an opportune moment to inquire what the intention of the Colombian Government may be with regard to the application of the quotas to imports of United States origin listed in Schedule I of the trade agreement.

The Embassy should attempt to dissuade the Colombian Government from the institution or extension of such a system of quotas insofar as possible. The Department is fully aware of the current balance of payments problem in Colombia and recognizes that the Government of that country may find full compliance with all provisions of the trade agreement difficult at this time. The Embassy therefore is authorized to indicate that this Government would be willing to agree to refrain for the time being from invoking Article V of the trade agreement, in return for an agreement by the Government of Colombia to establish and administer such temporary quota arrangements in accordance with the principles outlined in Articles 20, 21 and 22 of the Geneva draft of the International Trade Organization Charter. This waiver would apply only pending the decision of the Government of Colombia at an early date following the Habana conference to adhere to or reject the Charter. In the event of a negative Colombian decision with respect to membership in the International Trade Organization the United States would be free to claim its rights under the agreement. Of course this Government continues to expect that the Government of Colombia will afford the opportunity for consultation prior to imposition of such restriction, as implicitly provided in Article V of the agreement, even though no disposition may exist to invoke its provisions.

The Department would appreciate prompt and full report of the progress of any discussion which the Embassy may undertake, as well as being informed of the details of any concrete system of import quotas which may be elaborated by the Colombian Government. Any indication of the attitude of the Colombian Government towards the International Trade Organization which may appear in the course of these discussions would be of great interest to the Department in view of the forthcoming Habana conference.

821.85/10–2147

Memorandum of Conversation, by Mr. Albert H. Gerberich of the Division of North and West Coast Affairs

RESTRICTED [WASHINGTON,] November 12, 1947.

Participants: SD—Mr. Falck   NWC—Mr. Mills
               Mr. Wallace   Mr. McGinnis
               Mr. Havemeyer   Mr. Post
               RPA—Mr. Tewkesbury   Mr. Owen
               Le—Mr. Gray   Mr. Gerberich

Mr. Mills began the discussion by calling attention to the last paragraphs of the Colombian note enclosed with the Embassy's despatch no. 49 of October 21,[16] which contain inferentially a counter-accusation that we ourselves have violated the 1846 treaty by imposing discriminations in favor of our shipping interests. The Colombian Government refers specifically to P.R. No. 17, which expresses the sense of Congress that articles purchased through Eximbank loans must be exported in United States ships.

The representatives of SD said they feel that our discriminations are of quite a different nature from those of the Colombians, and that we would have no objection if they imposed the same kind that we have. Mr. Mills said this viewpoint might be considered hypocritical on our part; that the Colombians might equally well say that they would not object if we discriminated in their way.

Mr. Falck and Mr. Wallace said that there is another thing to consider—that P.R. No. 17 operates solely in connection with purchases made with United States money advanced to other countries, and that it is not administered 100% against a foreign country; if the foreign country does not like the terms, there is no obligation for it to negotiate the loans. Mr. Mills said that he thought that this was splitting hairs, and that the first thing we should do if we want to be sure our skirts are clean is to repeal P.R. No. 17, Mr. Tewkesbury said he agreed with this.

Mr. Wallace said that he very much doubted that even if P.R. No. 17 were repealed it would make any difference in the Colombian attitude.

It semed to be the consensus of those present that the courts of Colombia are not the proper medium to appeal to in the case of a treaty violation, but that recourse must be had to normal diplomatic channels. Mr. Gray said that he felt that we have a pretty good case in contesting the exemption of port dues, but not a very good one on the inheritance and income tax issue. It was pointed out that the port dues and other taxes do not divert any freight to the Colombian line; exemption from them may increase its profits, but the freight rates are set by the Conference, to which the Gran Colombiana adheres.

Mr. Mills recommended that Mr. Gray prepare a statement regarding the port dues, outlining the arguments we could use with the Colombian Government, especially citing precedents.

It was agreed that in the dispute with Colombia the most important problem is discrimination in the shipment of coffee. Mr. Havemeyer said that 70% of Colombia's export trade is in coffee, and to lose all this trade is therefore a serious matter for United States lines. He asked how many vessels the three sections of the Gran Colombiana now have in service, and the information on hand indicated that there

---

[16] Not printed.

are now three vessels being operated by the Venezuelan section and three by the Colombian section, all bought in the United States, averaging 5000 tons each, while the Ecuadoran section has one boat apparently dating back to pre-war years. The Colombians have bought six more boats which are being outfitted at Pascagoula, Mississippi, and are believed to be of the same tonnage as the three now in service; and there have been repeated rumors that they are trying to buy seven more freighters and a tanker. The Venezuelans apparently have no plans to increase their fleet, and we have no information on the Ecuadoran plans.

Mr. Mills suggested that a last resort but effective way for United States shipping to bring to the attention of the Colombians the seriousness with which it regards the policy of the Coffee Federation would be to refuse to call at Colombian ports. Mr. Falck agreed that the Gran Colombiana and other than United States lines would not be able to take care of all the cargo to Colombia in such an event. He said he believes that in a matter of two or three years the Gran Colombiana will have plenty of difficulties when its vessels stand in need of major repairs, as they doubtless will by then.

Mr. Tewkesbury outlined the type of discrimination practised by Argentina and Brazil against foreign steamship companies, and it was plain that it is different from the type confronting us in Colombia.

Mr. Wallace stated that he knows of no important discriminations by the United States except in P.R. No. 17, other than possibly subsidies. Mr. Falck added that SD would have no objection if Colombia should choose to subsidize its merchant marine in some such form as that adopted by us, or almost any other way.

It seemed to those present that to reply to the Colombian note by sending another note would be unsatisfactory: the Colombians will probably be in the same mind after they read our new arguments in any case. Moreover, it is impossible to get into an instruction to the Embassy all the information and suggestions that would be helpful in pursuing the case. Finally, since the coffee problem is the most important one, it would seem to be better to have it handled personally by a man sent to Bogotá to discuss it with the Ambassador and Colombian officials.

For these reasons it was recommended that SD discuss this further and consider sending a special representative to Bogotá to advise Ambassador Beaulac regarding future negotiations and inform him of certain facts that would be difficult to develop in an instruction. After this we could call another conference, if it is felt desirable.

It was further recommended, at Mr. Owen's request, that we take up with the Ecuadoran Embassy here discriminations with regard to invoice fees, but not on the basis of a treaty, as we do not have a commercial treaty with Ecuador.

It was further recommended that, in meeting pressure from United States shippers, SD might be well advised to urge the Federation to come out strongly against any type of discrimination favoring United States vessels.

621.006/11-2547

The Ambassador in Colombia (Beaulac) to the Secretary of State

RESTRICTED BOGOTÁ, November 25, 1947.
No. 143

SIR: I have the honor to refer to the Department's Restricted Instruction No. 38 of November 11, 1947, in which concern is expressed over the establishment of quotas by the Colombian Office of Exchange Control in licensing the importation of certain articles which fall within Schedule I of the 1936 [*1935*] Trade Agreement with Colombia.

. . . .

With respect to the Department's statement that it "recognizes the serious difficulties in Colombia which have resulted from an increasingly unfavorable balance of payments," the Embassy believes that the existing restrictions on imports are directly related to Colombian exchange difficulties and can be defended on that ground. As of the end of October 1947 Colombia's unfavorable balance of exchange totaled over $71,000,000.00 for the calendar year, and represented an unfavorable balance in each of the ten months. It should be noted that the restrictions have served to put an effective brake on the earlier alarming outflow. In October, the unfavorable dollar movement was less than $7,000,000.00, and there are indications that for the month of November, a small favorable balance will be reported.

There are reasons to believe that as Colombia's exchange situation improves, the Office of Exchange Control will lessen some of the restrictions and permit an increased volume of imports. For instance, it has already been announced that for the first quarter of 1948, holders of import quotas covering the second, third and fourth priority groups will be permitted to use 7 percent of their quotas, as compared with 5 percent during the current quarter, and 3 percent in the previous quarter. Also, this month the Office of Exchange Control called for applications for, and approved, quota increases governing agricultural, industrial and mining equipment and machinery, and other essential items. The Embassy had been informed that approximately $20,000,000.00 in additional quotas were thus approved. As far as the Embassy has been able to determine, the various restrictions on imports have resulted from a sincere attempt on the part of the Colombian Government to accommodate the volume of imports into Colombia to the realities of a dwindling supply of dollars.

The Embassy, therefore, believes the moment is not opportune to invoke Article V of the Trade Agreement. Consequently, it will not approach the Colombian Government on the matter in the absence of further instructions.

Respectfully yours, For the Ambassador:
J. A. SILBERSTEIN
Third Secretary of Embassy

621.006/11–2547

The Acting Secretary of State to the Embassy in Colombia

RESTRICTED WASHINGTON, December 30, 1947.
No. 60

The Acting Secretary of State refers to the Embassy's despatch No. 143, dated November 25, 1947, concerning the establishment of quotas by the Colombian Office of Exchange Control in licensing the importation of certain articles included in Schedule I of the 1936 [*1935*] trade agreement with Colombia.

It was not the intention of the Department, as the Embassy will note in referring again to the Department's instruction No. 38 of November 11, 1947, that Article V of the trade agreement be invoked at this time. On the contrary it was the Department's intent that the Colombian Government be informed of this Government's willingness temporarily to waive the provisions of Article V with respect to the contemplated quotas, in view of Colombia's precarious foreign exchange position, and in recognition of the fact that the Government of that country might find full compliance with all the provisions of the trade agreement difficult or impossible under present circumstances. In return, the Department wished it to be clearly understood by the Colombian authorities that this Government's willingness to refrain from protesting such a contravention of the agreement was based upon the assumption that Colombia would continue to respect the agreement as fully and completely as possible, and that in those instances where deviation from its provisions was necessitated, the remedial measures adopted would be instituted and administered in accordance with the broader principles and provisions of Articles 20, 21, and 22 of the draft Charter for an International Trade Organization. The principles and provisions in question were outlined in the Department's instruction under reference.

The Department is gratified to note that additional exchange control measures which have been adopted in Colombia to correct the current balance of payments problem are in general in harmony with Articles 20, 21, and 22 of the Charter. The provisions of Colombian Resolution No. 169 of April 30, 1947, envisaging quotas for the importation only of tires of sizes "not manufactured in the country" would appear to constitute an exception, by which protection of the local industry rather than simple control remedial of the balance of payments would seem to be the object. The Department is somewhat relieved to note that in actual practice tires of all sizes, including those manufactured in the country, continue to be licensed at least for the present, and is hopeful that the protective aspect of the exchange allocation for tires may be eliminated.

In summary, the Department concurs with the Embassy that the various restrictions adopted by Colombia, which are discussed in the Embassy's despatch No. 143, represent a sincere attempt on the part of the Colombian Government to meet its current exchange problems, and that the remedial measures undertaken satisfy the requirements of the ITO Charter in general, with exception as noted. Under these circumstances the Department continues to feel that a discussion of these questions with the Colombian authorities in the sense of the foregoing would be helpful, lest otherwise these authorities be led to believe that this Government is unaware of or indifferent to both the present exchange difficulties confronting the Government of Colombia and the contravention of the trade agreement in the remedial measures which the Colombian Government has felt itself required to take, and to make clear the sympathetic understanding and cooperative spirit with which these problems are viewed in the Department.

The Embassy is therefore again requested, unless substantial objection is perceived, to approach the appropriate Colombian authorities at an early opportunity to broach a discussion of these questions along the lines indicated above, reporting any developments to the Department promptly.

AGREEMENT BETWEEN THE UNITED STATES AND COLOMBIA RESPECTING A CIVIL AVIATION MISSION

[For text of the agreement, effected by exchange of notes signed at Bogotá, October 23, December 3 and 22, 1947, see Department of State, Treaties and Other International Acts Series No. 1738.]

DISCUSSIONS CONCERNING COLOMBIA'S DEBT AND NEED FOR CAPITAL

821.51/3-2247 : Telegram

The Ambassador in Colombia (Wiley) to the Secretary of State

SECRET   US URGENT   BOGOTÁ, March 22, 1947—3 p. m.

161. Confidential for Braden. Rogers [17] here on unpublicized exploratory mission on behalf of Council to study possibilities of debt settlement. President Ospina [18] professes great interest in seeing matter cleared up but considerable difficulty may be foreseen. While Rogers' mission here is his responsibility I propose to facilitate his task in every discreet way, particularly in establishing his contacts and giving strong moral support.

WILEY

821.51/4-1147 : Telegram

The Ambassador in Colombia (Wiley) to the Secretary of State

CONFIDENTIAL   BOGOTÁ, April 11, 1947—3 p. m.

207. With great tact and skill Dr. Rogers has concluded his conversations with Dr. Esteban Jaramillo and Dr. Carlos Lleras Restrepo [19] for settlement of bonds of six departments and two municipalities which have been in default for approximately 16 years. Agreement in principle has been reached which includes reduction of interest rate to 3 percent per annum and refunding of interest arrears on basis of 20 percent of capital value to be added to face value of bonds outstanding. A new bond issue will be made with each department and municipality separately responsible for its part but with national government guarantee of whole. Aforesaid agreement is subject to approval by Departmental assemblies and municipal councils concerned, by Colombian Congress and of course, by Bondholders Council in US. Both Jaramillo and Lleras seem confident that terms of proposed settlement are such that no serious obstacle is to be foreseen in obtaining Colombian approval. President Ospina has expressed himself as delighted. President Ospina has ordered that everything be done to prevent any further Colombian transactions in defaulted bonds.

WILEY

---

[17] James Grafton Rogers, President of the Foreign Bondholders Protective Council.
[18] Mariano Ospina Pérez.
[19] Messrs. Jaramillo and Lleras Restrepo represented the interests of the two towns and the departments of Colombia.

821.51/5-147 : Airgram

The Ambassador in Colombia (Wiley) to the Secretary of State

RESTRICTED   BOGOTÁ, May 1, 1947.

A-191. Reference is made to my confidential telegram #289 of April 30, 1947,[20] requesting the Department to inform Dr. Rogers that Drs. Esteban Jaramillo and Carlos Lleras Restrepo, representatives of the six governors and two alcaldes in the matter of foreign debt settlement, had issued a statement to the press last night for publication today, May 1, and that Dr. Rogers would be at liberty to publish all details concerning the agreement. The Bogotá press of May 1 carried the statement in full, which is as follows: (in translation)

"As has been appropriately reported, the Departments of Antioquia, Caldas, Cundinamarca, Santander, Valle del Cauca and Tolima, and also the municipalities of Medellín and Cali, commissioned Drs. Esteban Jaramillo and Carlos Lleras Restrepo to start negotiations with the Foreign Bondholders' Protective Council with offices in the United States, regarding foreign loans obtained by the aforesaid entities in the years prior to 1930. These loans are in default and the interest and amortization payments have been stopped since 1932.

"Drs. Jaramillo and Lleras Restrepo had several interviews with Dr. James Rogers, President of the Council, in the course of which a conversion formula was reached, which the Council accepts in principle and which requires for presentation to the bondholders, the approval of the Departmental Assemblies and Municipalities.

"The proposed solution covers the following loans, for each of which are given the rate of interest, the due date, the initial amount of issue, the sums normally paid before the moratorium, and the outstanding balance, that is, the difference between the initial amounts and the normal amortization payments for each debtor entity:

	Issue	Amortization	Balance
Antioquia 7% 1945	20,000,000	2,828,000	17,172,000
Antioquia 7% 1957	12,350,000	843,000	11,507,000
Caldas 7½% 1946	10,000,000	1,409,000	8,591,000
Cundinamarca 6½% 1959	12,000,000	463,000	11,537,000
Santander 7% 1948	2,000,000	209,000	1,791,000
Valle del Cauca 7% 1948	4,500,000	635,000	3,865,000
Valle del Cauca 7½% 1946	4,000,000	591,500	3,408,500
Tolima 7% 1947	2,500,000	388,000	2,112,000
Municipality of Medellín 6½% 1954	9,000,000	622,000	8,378,000
Municipality of Medellín 7% 1951	3,000,000	356,000	2,644,000
Municipality of Cali 7% 1947	2,885,000	477,000	2,408,000
Totals	82,235,000	8,821,500	73,413,500

[20] Not printed.

"The following are the conditions reached during the course of the negotiations between Drs. Jaramillo and Lleras Restrepo and Mr. Rogers:

"*a*) The future rate of interest for all the above mentioned loans will be 3% per year. This represents reductions which range from 3½ to 4½% per year.

"*b*) The coupons of interest due as of the date when the new conditions become effective will be redeemed in exchange for departamental or municipal foreign bonds at 3% per year, in an amount equal to 20 per cent of the principal of the bond to which such coupons belong. The bonds to be issued in the above mentioned manner will be in every way equal to those issued for the exchange of the original bonds actually in circulation.

"*c*) Not only the bonds allotted for the conversion of the principle of those now in circulation, but also those to be issued for the capitalization of the interest, as mentioned above, will be amortized through an amortization fund equivalent to 0.6 per cent of the nominal value of the bonds during the first five years and 1.0 per cent of such nominal value from the sixth year on, and such funds will be increased by the amount of interest due on the bonds as amortized. The amortization fund will be invested in buying bonds in the open market.

"*d*) The time for the total amortization of the bonds will be thirty years.

"*e*) The security given as specific guarantee for the loans now in force will not be offered as specific guarantee for the new bonds. But the Departmental Governments will try to get the nation's guarantee for the latter. Regarding the unpaid interest, it should be noted that the amount thereof is today more than 100 per cent of the principal of the bonds in circulation. Consequently, the reduction obtained is equivalent to more than 80 per cent of the total amount of interest due.

"Dr. Jaramillo and Dr. Lleras Restrepo have already presented to the Governors and Mayors of the interested entities a copy of the proposal contained in the present communication, which will be submitted for consideration to the respective Assemblies and Municipal Councils.[21]

Bogotá, April 30, 1947."

WILEY

---

[21] In a letter of July 15, 1947, to Rogers, not printed, Lleras Restrepo advised that five of the six departments (Santander being the exception) and the two municipalities had approved the settlement (821.51/7–1547). Ambassador Wiley's successor, Willard L. Beaulac in telegram 801, December 15, 1947, not printed, advised that the Colombian Congress had agreed to guarantee service on the debt (821.51/12–1547).

COLOMBIA 573

821.51 Bondholders/8–1447 : Telegram

The Chargé in Colombia (Warner) to the Secretary of State

RESTRICTED BOGOTÁ, August 14, 1947—4 p. m.

536. ReEmbtel 364, May 24.[22] Welsh [23] and Barranca[24] latter representing Citibank Farmers Trust Company,[25] returned US last week after several days in Colombia on debt negotiation. While here Welsh attempted influence Rogers to telegraph Colombian representatives Carlos Lleras Restrepo and Esteban Jaramillo advising them reopen negotiations in view new bondholder opposition. This Rogers apparently refused to do but Welsh prevailed upon two or three trustees to wire Minister of Finance their nonconformity with Rogers agreement terms. Welsh and Citibank then appointed Dario Echandia as representative and stated preliminary steps toward bringing suit against the municipality of Cali. Later Echandia advised Welsh against suit to which he agreed temporarily.

During two conferences Welsh subsequently had with Lleras Restrepo latter first refused reopen negotiations whereupon Welsh reports he threatened publicity in United States regarding:

(1) Colombian purchase of approximately 50% outstanding bonds during same period Office Exchange Control blocked transfer of accumulated services to American bondholders.

(2) Regarding Welsh's belief that capacity of Colombian debtor entities to pay is three or four times better now than when loans were originally made and considering 50% bond repurchase is actually six or eight times better and

(3) That Colombian banks had made loans to departments and municipalities using pledges revenues of US loans. During second conference Lleras is reported to have informed Welsh he would write Rogers for his recommendations concerning renewal negotiations and that Lleras had seen the President who agreed call Governors and Mayors within 10 days.

Yesterday Lleras on President's instructions called at Embassy leaving copy his and Jaramillo's letter to Rogers dated August 12. Letter explains that project is now before Congress providing government guarantees on refunded bonds accordance with Rogers agree-

---

[22] Not printed.
[23] Chicago investment banker.
[24] Trustee for Cali, Caldas, and Antioquia bonds.
[25] Affiliate of the National City Bank of New York.

ment: That Welsh and trustees have been asking Colombians to reopen negotiations as follows:

(1) After agreeing with Rogers on fair and practical basis cannot commence new negotiations with every group bondholders wishing obtain more favorable conditions, which practice would prolong situation indefinitely.

(2) Although willing to discuss agreement terms with trustees, Colombia does not believe even now that Welsh opinions representing small group of bondholders could be sufficient cause deny Rogers proposal.

(3) Department assemblies recessed until next year; reopening negotiations would require special session to request authority for entire new basis of agreement.

(4) It is Colombian considered opinion that such authority should not be granted.

(5) In view of new municipal elections special sessions of assemblies at this time would risk undesirable political complications.

(6) If necessary present new project for federal guarantees to Congress there would be risk of bill not passing this session.

(7) Would be difficult obtain authority open negotiations *ad referendum* and such steps would be necessarily prolonged.

(8) Manner of reopening negotiations under threats legal action and publicity campaigns would change cordial atmosphere of previous negotiations.

(9) Colombia believes Rogers plan fair and is sure large proportion bondholders willing accept it.

Letter adds that Colombian representatives not disposed recommend terms Welsh settlement particularly under pressure of Welsh alternatives. Letter nevertheless requests Rogers opinion on reopening negotiations and states discussions with trustees will be postponed until answer received.

Lleras was told that matter was one between bondholders and debtor entities and that consequently Embassy position was only on sidelines. Lleras explained that he hoped Embassy could reinforce through knowledge local conditions Colombian contention of risk of prolonged complications and delays by not proceeding under Rogers agreement.

Although Welsh's stiffer terms may be fully justified by present financial situation in Colombia, Embassy does believe that reopening negotiations would cause indefinite delay and create atmosphere of general resentment here which might adversely affect other important American activities. Reopening negotiations would most likely have political repercussions adverse to President Ospina and his National Union Government, which has just completed first and difficult year in office. While growing Colombian desire to reestablish nations public credit is so strong that terms better than those provided for in Rogers agreement might eventually be obtained, Embassy believes that because of the delay, risk, hard feeling and other factors involved it would be advisable to settle this long, drawn out matter promptly even though on basis of Rogers agreement.

WARNER

821.51 Bondholders/8-1547 : Telegram

The Chargé in Colombia (Warner) to the Secretary of State

CONFIDENTIAL   BOGOTÁ, August 15, 1947—11 a. m.

537. ReEmbtel 536, August 14. President Ospina called me to Palace last evening to stress how serious he considered reopening of the proposed foreign debt settlement would be. He reviewed history of negotiations starting with his discussion as to debt settlement with Assistant Secretary Braden, US bankers, and others when he visited US last year. He noted that he was able to obtain agreement to Rogers proposals from the departmental governors, and municipality representatives. He repeated arguments set forth in Lleras letter to Rogers. The President believes that a reopening of negotiations or failure to carry through Rogers plan would cause him considerable political embarrassment, would be basis for new attacks by Communists and other extremists against so-called US imperialism, and would in general be contrary to US interests.

The President regrets such possibility especially at this time when he is highly satisfied with relations with US. He attributes good relations to oil companies' present policy of publicity and to rise in coffee prices which not only benefits economy of country, but especially permits the buying of machinery et cetera to improve lot of workers. He called Welsh's attitude unfortunate and expressed fervent hope that it would not delay final settlement on basis of Rogers agreement especially since proposal was sponsored by Department and Ambassador Wiley. I told him that his views would be conveyed to the Department.

WARNER

821.5151/12-547

The Ambassador in Colombia (Beaulac) to the Secretary of State

CONFIDENTIAL   BOGOTÁ, December 5, 1947.
No. 165

SIR: With reference to the Department's confidential telegram No. 587 of December 3, 1947,[26] I have the honor to enclose a memorandum

---
[26] Not printed.

of a conversation I had with Mr. Victor Rose, Manager of the local branch of the National City Bank on November 21, 1947. Since the date of my conversation, the Embassy has been endeavoring to obtain additional background on the controversy between the National City Bank and the Colombian Government. It will be noted that during my conversation with Mr. Rose, I invited him to submit a memorandum concerning his difficulties, but he has not taken advantage of the invitation. However, he has orally volunteered much of the information given below.

It will be noted also from the memorandum that I declined to support the National City Bank's position vis-à-vis the Colombian Government. So far, I see no reason for the Embassy to intervene in this matter nor am I impressed with the National City Bank's statement that unless its position is accepted by the Colombian Government, it will close its branches in Colombia.

The following is the background of the case so far as Embassy has been able to obtain it.

The Colombian branch of the National City Bank, according to information received by the Embassy from the Manager of the bank, is considering liquidation because the Colombian Banking Superintendent has recently called upon it to import three million dollars of capital, and because of the onerous effect of Law 95 of December 30, 1946. It is understood that the importation of the capital was requested in order to relieve the foreign exchange shortage in Colombia. According to the Government, the National City Bank is legally obliged to import the capital and to substitute it for Colombian Government notes of more than two millions which the bank has been holding since 1929 and which it has tried to induce the Colombian Government to regard as its capital in Colombia.

Although the National City Bank agreed in writing, according to its Manager's statement to the Embassy, to import the 3 millions into Colombia whenever the Banking Superintendent might request it, the Bank now contends that economic conditions in Colombia have changed so from what they were at the time the agreement was made, that the Bank can ill afford to import the capital now. The Bank is prepared, however, to live up to its agreement, but it has informed the Embassy in confidence that if it does accede to the Government's present demands for the capital importation, it will serve immediate notice of its intention to liquidate its interests in Colombia.

. . . .

The Embassy considers that the Colombian Government's request for the capital importation is justified. At the same time, it sympathizes with commercial banks in Colombia because of the burdens of recent social legislation. But the Embassy cannot agree with the position that the National City Bank is not legally bound to import the capital being requested by the Colombian Government. Article 21 of Law 45 of 1942 states that the Banking Superintendent is authorized to regulate the manner of importing money to increase the capital of foreign banks, and on the basis of National City's written promise to the Superintendent to import the capital when called upon, it would seem that the Bank has no legal out. Although the National City Bank defends its position by referring to Section 9 of Article 85 of Law 45 of 1923, this section goes no further than to state that investment in Colombian Government bonds is the only exception to the rule that commercial banks cannot invest more than 10 percent of their capital and reserves in bonds.

The Embassy does consider that Law 95 is a definite discouragement to private capital in Colombia, and Mr. Rose has been informed that the Embassy intends to make known its opinion on this subject to the Colombian Government.

Meanwhile, the National City Bank has contested the legality of the Banking Superintendent's demand for the capital. As a result, the Government has requested the legal section of the Bank of the Republic to study the legislation in question and to render an opinion.

There is before the Congress now in session a petition signed by the majority of commercial banks in Colombia raising strong objection to the financial burdens imposed on the banks by the social benefits of Law 95 of 1946. The Embassy will report on this petition as soon as the Congressional committee assigned to its study makes a report.

Respectfully yours,

For the Ambassador:
CARLOS J. WARNER
First Secretary of Embassy

COSTA RICA

UNITED STATES POLICY OF NONINTERVENTION IN THE INTERNAL AFFAIRS OF COSTA RICA

818.00/1–947

The Ambassador in Costa Rica (Johnson) to the Assistant Secretary of State (Braden)

SECRET   SAN JOSÉ, January 9, 1947.

DEAR MR. BRADEN: My despatches No. 2764 of January 3rd and 2774 of January 9, 1947,[1] show a highly disturbed political condition in Costa Rica.[2] A bomb was recently exploded in the San José water works, and 60 or 70 other bombs have been found by the inadequate police.

February 2nd, the day of the Nicaraguan elections, has been mentioned to me by both members of the Government and of the Opposition as the day on which things may well come to a head and further bombings and even attempts at assassination take place.

There are other rumors, as you know, of a Guatemalan effort on that date to further a revolution in Costa Rica in order to use this weak country as a base for operations against Honduras and Nicaragua. I put little faith in these rumors, but fear serious local troubles . . .

Since I naturally regard Costa Rica as the Central American country by far the most advanced in democracy, I am anxious to do everything possible to prevent possible chaos, with the conceivable result of another dictator. As a purely preventive measure I therefore suggest that a good will trip be made by an American destroyer so that it will be at a Costa Rican port during the last days of January and the first days of February. No ship of ours has been here since a visit of sub-chasers in November of 1945. A small Colombian warship visited Costa Rica a month ago and a British ship in September, 1946. If the destroyer came from the North it might well touch at El

---

[1] Neither printed.
[2] The campaign was under way for Presidential and Congressional elections to be held in February 1948. Presidential candidates for the office of the incumbent, Teodoro Picado, included Rafael Angel Calderon Guardia, candidate of the National Republican Party (PRN), and Otilio Ulate, candidate of the National Union Party (PUN), popularly known as the Opposition party. For additional information on the situation, see despatch 269, October 9, p. 589.

Salvador, and if it came from Panama it would probably be best to come straight here. Its presence could be advertised as a good will visit and this idea be followed up by a baseball game in the local port, or other means. I believe that the mere presence of such a ship in Costa Rican waters would give pause to those who are possibly planning to bomb the San José water works and electric plants, to set fires in the city, and in the confusion to take over the Government, perhaps by means of assassination of the President and his friends. Should such an event have partial success, the so-called shock battalions of the Leftist Vanguardia Popular Party would undoubtedly make a counterattack and chaos would result, from which chaos a dictator might emerge, and the best experiment in and advertisement for democracy in Central America would go down in complete failure.

I can foresee no complications to the presence of a destroyer here at that time, and recommend it strongly, since it might have a moral effect deterrent to subversive acts.

I may add that Mr. John Carrigan [3] and our Military Attaché, Colonel Hughes, concur in my recommendation.

Very sincerely yours, HALLETT JOHNSON

818.00/1-947

The Assistant Secretary of State (Braden) to the Ambassador in Costa Rica (Johnson)

SECRET WASHINGTON, February 3, 1947.

DEAR HALLETT: Thank you for your letter of January 9 advising me of the possibility of trouble in Costa Rica at the time of the Nicaraguan elections on February 2. I have been following with interest your continuing despatches on the disturbed political situation there and the tactics being followed by the Opposition.

We have given careful consideration to your suggestion that an American destroyer pay a good will visit to a Costa Rican port during the first days of February. While such a call might possibly serve the purpose you have in mind, the consensus here is that it would be risky under present conditions and might result in allegations of intervention by groups unfriendly to us who are only too ready to take advantage of any opportunity to criticise. I believe, therefore, that it would be advisable to defer a visit by an American naval vessel until a later date when conditions in Costa Rica are more settled.

Very sincerely yours, SPRUILLE BRADEN

---

[3] First Secretary of Embassy and Vice Consul.

818.00/7-2547 : Telegram

The Ambassador in Costa Rica (Donnelly[4]*) to the Secretary of State*

SECRET SAN JOSÉ, July 25, 1947—2 p. m.

345. Dr. Alberto Oreamuno, Dr. Antonio Peña Chavarría and Dr. Francisco Jiménez Rodriguez, prominent pro-Ulatistas, called on me last night at their own request. They said they wished explain the facts of the present crisis as they saw it. I observed that while I would be pleased to receive their views, I wanted to make it perfectly clear to them that this Embassy was wholly neutral and that I was confident they would understand our position. I asked them if they were representing Ulate and they replied they came of their own accord; they were not to be considered as officially representing Ulatista Party.

They said they considered our Government partially responsible for events of yesterday which according to them resulted in 10 persons killed and 20 wounded (Embstel 341, July 24 [5]) by reason of fact our Government had sent arms and ammunition to Picado administration and that our military mission here had trained the men who had "murdered these unarmed innocent by-standers". They said they understood the justification for the military mission during war but that they could not understand reason for keeping the mission in Costa Rica since termination of war.[6] I interjected with statement to the best of my knowledge my Government had not authorized shipments arms to Costa Rica since end of war with the exception of some ammunition and with respect to their statement that military mission has trained 300 or more men that this figure was considerably exaggerated.

DONNELLY

818.00/7-2947

Memorandum of Telephone Conversation, by the Assistant Chief of the Division of Central America and Panama Affairs (Wise)

RESTRICTED [WASHINGTON,] July 29, 1947.

Mr. Carrigan [7] called attention to his telegram 366 of July 28 [8] concerning the looting of shops in San José. He said that no effort was

---

[4] The nomination of Walter J. Donnelly as Ambassador in Costa Rica was confirmed by the United States Senate on April 9, 1947.

[5] Not printed.

[6] For the United States-Costa Rican agreement relating to a military mission, signed at Washington December 10, 1945, see Department of State Executive Agreement Series No. 486, or 59 Stat. (pt. 2) 1682.

[7] In the absence of Ambassador Donnelly, Mr. Carrigan was acting as Chargé in Costa Rica.

[8] Not printed.

being made to curb the looters and that there had been two or three cases of damage to stores owned by U.S. citizens. He said the attitude of police and Government was that the store owners were getting what they deserved because of noncompliance with the Presidential Proclamation directing that business houses re-open under penalty of loss of license. In this connection, Mr. Carrigan referred to his telegram 337 of July 24.[9] He said he could confirm the fact that the police had been instructed not to interfere with looters. He said there would be a repetition of looting in San José today and that there had been rioting in Cartago last night which had likewise been uncontrolled by the police.

Mr. Carrigan said the situation was serious enough to warrant an official protest to the Government. His position is that during a situation of open public disorder our American business interests are entitled to protection. It is obvious that the firms failing to open business in compliance with the Government order would be subject to the penalty, but that the Government should not permit the extraction of penalties beyond the scope of law. Mr. Carrigan said that the Government was being very casual about the whole situation. I asked if there were any evidences of Communistic activities in the picture. He said there definitely were, because the Vanguardia partisans were particpating in the looting. I asked Mr. Carrigan whether he expected this situation to continue, and he replied that in his opinion it would for some time.

Mr. Carrigan said that unless he heard from the Department by return call, he would present an official note of protest immediately.

Mr. Carrigan asked that Ambassador Donnelly be advised that his family was well and that all was quiet in the vicinity of the Embassy residence.

Comment:

Upon consultation with Ambassador Donnelly and Mr. Wright, Director of ARA, it was decided that Mr. Carrigan should be called immediately and informed that the official protest should be made informally and verbally. . . . It was decided also that Mr. Carrigan be instructed to approach Costa Rican authorities in a conciliatory attitude and with the statement that unless American interests were protected from further damage by disorderly elements, this Government would have to present a formal written protest.

M[URRAY] M. W[ISE]

---

[9] Not printed.

818.00/7–2947

Memorandum of Telephone Conversation, by the Assistant Chief of the Division of Central America and Panama Affairs (*Wise*)

[WASHINGTON,] July 29, 1947.

Participants: Mr. John Carrigan, Chargé d'Affaires at San José
Walter J. Donnelly, Ambassador to Costa Rica (in Washington)
M. M. Wise—CPA

After discussing with Ambassador Donnelly and Mr. Wright the subject of Mr. Carrigan's inquiry of this morning (see memorandum of telephone conversation) I telephoned Mr. Carrigan and said that the Department desired that he protest informally and verbally rather than in writing about inadequate protection of American property. I stated that we believed his attitude should be conciliatory, although firm, and that he should say that unless American interests were adequately protected a formal written note of protest would have to be submitted. I stated further that he might frankly inform the appropriate Costa Rican authority that the protest was being made at present informally inasmuch as we did not wish to give any appearance of interfering in the internal affairs of Costa Rica.

Mr. Carriagan said that he would like to go on record as very deeply regretting the decision not to protest in writing. He said that two American stores had been damaged, one American gassed, and that the trolley company operated by American interests had been ordered to resume service and that it did not have insurance to cover damages which might occur under the present circumstances. He felt that it should be definitely on record in writing with the Costa Ricans that we were protesting against inadequate protection. He said another reason for his request was that Vanguardia partisans were now apparently openly participating in the disorders.

Mr. Carrigan did say that in support of our position was the fact that the President had just sent him word that protection would be extended to all American interests and that the demonstration scheduled for this afternoon had been cancelled. Mr. Carrigan was not sure that the President could guarantee this. . . .

Mr. Donnelly asked Mr. Carrigan whether he had received protests from American business and received the reply that Americans had visited the Embassy expressing concern. In describing the situation further, Mr. Carrigan stated that the banks had not opened, many business houses were still closed, railways were still operating, Pan-American Airways was operating in San José with three employees, and that TACA was operating internationally but not within the country. Mr. Carrigan reported that there were stray shots yesterday but no killings and that there was no shooting today.

Mr. Donnelly then stated that the Department and he would prefer Mr. Carrigan's approach to the Costa Rican authorities be informal and that if this did not bring the required results he should advise the Department immediately for he felt certain that instructions would then be given to make a written protest.

Mr. Carrigan was informed of the visit to Mr. Armour [10] by the Costa Rican Ambassador today, as covered by separate memorandum.[11]

M. M. WISE

818.00/7-2947 : Telegram

The Chargé in Costa Rica (Carrigan) to the Secretary of State

SECRET   US URGENT   SAN JOSÉ, July 29, 1947—4 p. m.

372. Pursuant to Department's instructions as contained in telephone call this morning, I called on Under Secretary Foreign Affairs [11a] just before noon. I told him my Government had instructed me to call and talk to him in the most conciliatory, friendly and informal way. I said I wished to invite his attention to possible effect of situation which prevailed yesterday and which might again prevail today upon United States private interests. I referred to proclamation of July 23 to effect that shops or other business institutions which remained closed would incur as a penalty for not having opened the loss of their operating licenses. I said that of course such a sanction would be predicated I assumed upon the maintenance by the appropriate authorities of a degree of order which would permit business institutions to open without fear of damage. I said that as he knew yesterday stores and other business institutions were broken into without there being any effort on part of police to stop the looting. I said that if a store or business institution through not opening were in fact violating the law of the land I assumed the only penalty applicable would be revocation of institution's license to operate. I said I felt the mere fact of a store not opening would not prevent the police and other government authorities from affording protection.

At the same time I expressed once again our deep appreciation for the excellent and continued cooperation which has been given by authorities of Casa Presidencial and I expressed the confidence of our

---

[10] Norman Armour, Assistant Secretary of State for Political Affairs.
[11] Memorandum not printed.
[11a] The Under Secretary of State, Ricardo Fournier, was in charge during the absence of the Minister for Foreign Affairs, Julio Acosta.

Government that adequate and effective protection would be afforded to United States interests in Republic of Costa Rica.

I found this an exceedingly difficult conversation. Under Secretary inquired why it was we had not complained in connection with an attack which had been started by Ulatistas against Perry Girton's radio store (Perry Girton has been broadcasting for the government) and why it was that we had not complained in the case of breaking of windshield on Embassy's pickup truck. He seemed to feel that we were being unfair.

He went on to the extent of remarking that once in New York he had been bitten by a dog on the leash of an intoxicated person and that while he had made every attempt to find a policeman in order obtain redress he had not been able to do so.

He seemed bent on having me make the statement that I considered the undisciplined mob of yesterday a group organization and under the control of the Government of Costa Rica. He seemed also bent on having me say the government was directing attacks on stores which remained closed. These instances are cited simply to show that there has been and is rather a startling attitude about this matter.

He went on to say that stores which refused to open were really outside the law and that no protection need be afforded them. Upon my demurring very forcefully insofar as American interests were concerned, he agreed that adequate protection should be afforded them. He said he would talk with the President and would let us have his views later this afternoon. He told me I could assure the Department that in event of any American store being threatened in any way, shape or form, we could ask for police protection and he would see that it was given. He inquired if we had a list of American business interests in Costa Rica and particularly in San José. Unfortunately, we do not have such a list and it is almost impossible prepare one, reason being there are many instances of Costa Rican business houses in which there are substantial American interests which would be naturally affected should the institution in question be damaged.

As matters now stand, we have his word every effort will be made to protect any American institution for which we may request protection.

With reference to events of yesterday, he told me that in the specific case that I personally had seen where the police did not interfere, they had failed to do so because of an error on their part. He said that in every other case the police had immediately intervened. I made no comment.

CARRIGAN

818.00/7-3147

The Chargé in Costa Rica (Carrigan) to the Secretary of State

CONFIDENTIAL
No. 79

SAN JOSÉ, July 31, 1947.

SIR: I have the honor to refer to despatch No. 78 of July 29, 1947, transmitting a copy of a letter [12] which had been sent to the Dean of the Diplomatic Corps, the Papal Nuncio, on July 28th by a group of pro-Ulate medical men.

The previous day Dr. Alberto Oreamuno, Ulatista, informed Mr. Carter of the Embassy staff [13] that 200 United States-educated doctors, lawyers, and other professional men, all Ulatistas, proposed to come to the Embassy in a body to protest against the Government and to explain their views concerning the proposed demonstration which was to take place against closed stores and businesses.

The Embassy was naturally disturbed by this report. At that time Government troops and police were breaking up groups of more than three or four persons, and for a group of 200 persons suddenly to appear in front of the Embassy might have created serious trouble in which the Embassy might very easily have been involved, particularly since the police would have attempted to disperse these men by force. Undoubtedly, whatever attitude we would have taken would have been susceptible to misinterpretation, probably by both sides.

With this in mind, I arranged for Dr. Oreamuno to call at the Embassy. I explained the neutrality of our position, and went on to say that if such an attempt were made and the Embassy found itself involved in any difficulties, we could not feel that Ulate was without blame. At the same time I referred to a story which appeared in the *Diario de Costa Rica*, Ulate's own paper, concerning the departure of Ambassador Donnelly (Embassy's telegram No. 356 of July 27th [14]), in which the *Diario* had indicated its assurance that the Ambassador's journey was connected with the present political situation in Costa Rica. I also referred to other comments in the *Diario* involving the military mission. I said that we were really doing our best to be neutral, and that I found it particularly unfortunate to read stories such as this in a local newspaper. I said that we had made it very clear, not only to the Government but also to Dr. Oreamuno himself, that we did not intend to have the slightest partiality for either side, and that this was still our position, and that it was somewhat annoying to find people trying to drag us in against our will.

---

[12] Neither printed.
[13] Albert E. Carter, Cultural Attaché.
[14] Not printed.

With respect to the proposal that a large group of professional men come in to the Embassy to talk politics with us, I said that I did not feel that this would be a particularly friendly act. I said that I was not prepared to talk politics. I said I would always be very happy to see Dr. Oreamuno or any other distinguished professional Costa Rican, but that in doing so I wished to avoid any action which might indicate that I were taking sides. For this reason, I told him that if this group should call at the Embassy I would refuse to discuss politics with them, and might even refuse to see them.

Dr. Oreamuno told me that he was very sorry that this had come up and that he had not realized the possible consequences. . . . He said that instead of these men calling on me, a letter would be addressed to the Dean of the Diplomatic Corps. In this connection, the letter transmitted with my despatch No. 78 is the one referred to. It is interesting to note that this letter was considerably toned down.

With respect to articles which might appear in Ulate's newspapers involving the Embassy, Dr. Oreamuno assured me that during this present critical period any article which might appear in the Ulate newspapers would be personally cleared by Otilio Ulate if it mentioned the Embassy. He pointed out that this would mean that Ulate himself would take the responsibility for anything that was said. I said that I felt that this was a very wise approach to this matter and that, in the premises, he might dismiss from his mind any thought that there might be annoyance on our part for what had been done. Since that time the Embassy has not been bothered.

Parenthetically, I asked the Nuncio what he had done with the note. He said that he had filed it away. I told him that I felt this was a simple and effective solution of a matter which really did not concern the Corps.

Respectfully yours, JOHN WILLARD CARRIGAN

818.00B/9–1747 : Telegram

The Ambassador in Costa Rica (Donnelly) to the Secretary of State

CONFIDENTIAL SAN JOSÉ, September 17, 1947—3 p. m.

452. *La Tribuna* today published text President Picado's press release referring to statements by opposition that Sept 15 parade was "Communist demonstration for Communist chief of state". The President labeled it as malicious statement and added "the govt over which I preside is not and never has been Communist" and said "the ideology and spirit of this country is identified with the United States foreign

policy and with the democratic doctrines of the bloc of the western nations as generally referred to".

... Late yesterday afternoon President Picado asked me to call on him. He reiterated his strong opposition to Communism and his loyalty to the foreign policy of the U.S. Calderon Guardia sent word thru Dr. Anderson [15] that he would welcome a meeting with me to inform me of his views on Communism and his loyalty to U.S. ...

DONNELLY

---

123 Donnelly, Walter J.

Memorandum of Conversation, by Mr. W. Tapley Bennett, Jr., Area Specialist, Division of Central America and Panama Affairs

CONFIDENTIAL [WASHINGTON,] September 30, 1947.

Participants: Sr. Don Francisco de P. Gutiérrez, Ambassador of Costa Rica
A–A—Mr. Armour
CPA—Mr. Bennett

Ambassador Gutiérrez said that he was calling on Mr. Armour to express his Government's feeling of profound loss at the departure of Ambassador Donnelly from Costa Rica.[16] ...

Ambassador Guitiérrez then launched the conversation into a discussion of the Nicaraguan political situation. ...

The Picado administration was determined to cooperate with the other American republics in a common policy. He said, however, that the present non-recognition policy represents great sacrifice and very real danger for Costa Rica. He remarked that there is already disorder in Nicaragua and that internal cleavages are widening, and he predicted that the eventual result is likely to be civil war.

Ambassador Gutiérrez called attention to the common border of the two countries and asserted that civil strife in Nicaragua would inevitably have serious consequences in Costa Rica. He declared that in any armed struggle within Nicaragua the losers would attempt to flee to Costa Rica and that the forces of the stronger side would attempt to cross the border in pursuit. He also stated that there are between 50,000 and 100,000 Nicaraguans in Costa Rica. (Note: The Ambassador's estimate is substantially larger than the number believed

---

[15] Dr. Luis Anderson, Costa Rican statesman, lawyer, and professor.
[16] Mr. Donnelly was to serve as Ambassador in Venezuela; the United States Senate confirmed his nomination on December 8, 1947.

to be correct). . . . He asserted that all these facts make the question of recognition of the Román Government [18] a very serious one for Costa Rica.

Ambassador Gutiérrez remarked that in his opinion the non-recognition policy affects Costa Rica most seriously of any American republic and, after Costa Rica, the United States. He said that he realizes that instability in Nicaragua represents a constant preoccupation for the United States. In that connection, he made reference to previous instances of armed intervention by the United States in Nicaragua and said that he was confident that the United States would not wish to send troops into Nicaragua again. Mr. Armour in his reply to this statement made it clear that such a course would be completely out of the question and that it had not the slightest possibility of being entertained by this Government.

Mr. Armour said that he understood that Mariano Arguello had made certain statements to President Picado concerning a purported discussion with him, Mr. Armour, at Petropolis.[19] He said that he was glad to be able to clear up the matter since, in point of fact, he had not talked with Arguello at all during the recent inter-American conference. He remarked that he had received Sevilla Sacasa [20] at the latter's request and had replied to a query of Sevilla regarding a visit by Somoza [21] to the United States for medical treatment. . . .

Mr. Armour inquired as to whether the Costa Rican Government had any suggestions as to steps which might be taken to bring about a solution of the Nicaraguan problem. Ambassador Gutiérrez replied that his Government had no definite plans to suggest but that it merely desired to emphasize the need for an early formula. The Ambassador said that in his opinion most of the other republics are awaiting proposals by the United States. There followed then a discussion of possible means of resolving the situation.

Mr. Armour said that in essence what is needed in Nicaragua is a broadening of the base of the Government to make it truly representative of the nation as a whole and to restore the country's confidence. . . . Mr. Armour proposed that one way of restoring confidence would be for all political parties to agree on one man to serve as an impartial successor to Somoza in the Guard. He said that he did not know whether there was such a person but that action of that nature

---

[18] Victor Manuel Román y Reyes, had been selected by the Constitutional Assembly as President of Nicaragua, August 15, 1947 (817.00/8–1547).
[19] For documentation on the Inter-American Conference for the Maintenance of Continental Peace and Security, Quitandinha, Brazil, August 15–September 2, 1947, see, pp. 1 ff.
[20] Guillermo Sevilla Sacasa, Nicaraguan Ambassador in the United States.
[21] Gen. Anastasio Somoza García, former President of Nicaragua; at this time head of the National Guard.

would make possible a broadening of the governmental structure and would, in his opinion, be worthy of the consideration of the other American republics as a positive move on the part of Nicaragua to put its house in order. He emphasized to Ambassador Gutiérrez that no Government is more anxious than the United States to see the matter settled and that we maintain a constant hope that action will be taken in Nicaragua to make a settlement possible.

. . . . .

W. T[APLEY] B[ENNETT]

818.00/10-947

The Ambassador in Costa Rica (Donnelly) to the Secretary of State

CONFIDENTIAL SAN JOSÉ, October 9, 1947.
No. 269

SIR: I have the honor to report below my appraisal of the current political situation in Costa Rica.

POLITICAL PARTIES

The political parties in Costa Rica are presently engaged in a bitter and sometimes violent campaign in preparation for the Presidential and Congressional elections to be held in February, 1948. The successful candidate will take office in May, 1948.

The principal political parties involved in the campaign are the Partido Republicano Nacional which is supported by the present Government and whose candidate is Dr. Rafael Angel Calderon Guardia, President of Costa Rica from 1940–1944. The second party, the Partido Union Nacional, is commonly referred to as the opposition party with Otilio Ulate as the Presidential candidate. Ulate is the editor-owner of the *Diario de Costa Rica*, a daily newspaper in San José. The Vanguardia Popular, the third political party, has not designated a Presidential candidate and for the time being appears to be interested only in the elections for the Assembly. Vanguardia follows the Communist line and its leaders are confirmed Communists. The present policy of the party is to support the candidacy of Calderon Guardia for President.

. . . .

. . . It is logical to assume that in supporting Calderon Guardia for President they will expect him to reward them with key positions in the Government, the Social Security Department, and to endorse their legislative agenda.

The Vanguardia party has as its Secretary-General Dr. Manuel

Mora who is regarded as the most intelligent of the upper echelon of the Costa Rican Communist Party. He is a member of Congress and is very popular among the laboring classes. He is a protégé of Carmen Lyra, Costa Rica's ace Communist instructor and an ardent believer in the Lenin brand of Communism. While the party is not conducting an open campaign against the United States, it is not friendly to the United States. . . .

. . . . . .

As regards the United States, it would be a mistake to proceed on any other premise than that Mora is anti-United States, anti-United States foreign policy and anti-United States business interests. He is against private enterprise and sincerely believes that labor can progress only under State owned and managed enterprises. Mora, not a militant Communist, is intelligent, honest, with a carefully balanced program. The question is frequently asked "With whom would Mora side in case of armed hostilities between the United States and Russia?" The consensus of opinion here is that Mora would accept the judgment of the Government and the people, but that he would not actively support the Government in case it should ally itself with the United States. As to the other question "What would be the policy of the Government and the people in case of an armed conflict between the United States and Russia", there can be no doubt that they would side with the United States the same as they did in World War I and World War II. Costa Rica is proud of the fact that she was the first nation in this hemisphere to declare war on the Axis.

. . . . . .

Summary

Present indications are that Rafael Calderon Guardia, with the support of the Vanguardia party and the Communist leaders, will be elected President in February, 1948. While he has openly solicited their backing, he tries to allay the fears of anti-Communists by saying that he is doing so for political expediency and that he "never has been, is not, and never will be a Communist". The fact is, however, that he is aligned with them and in doing so has contributed to their standing and influence in Costa Rica.

Ulate is making a strong and determined fight, marked by occasional acts of violence, but barring unforeseen developments, the importance and seriousness of which should not be discounted, he will lose the election, but the party will probably win several seats in the Assembly. Reports are current that the opposition will not permit elections to be held; that they will attempt to overthrow the Government and take possession by forceful means, etc. The situation is undeniably tense and anything can happen. The opposition is presently encouraged by the new Russian policy which they feel will bring about a wave of anti-Communism in Costa Rica to the detriment of Calderon Guardia.

Relations With United States

Regardless of who is elected President of Costa Rica for the term 1948–1952, the position of the United States here will in all probability continue favorable. This is a truly democratic country. The people are free and want to continue free. All of the freedoms exist here and though the country is passing through what is said to be the most bitterly contested election in its history, there are no political prisoners, no political exiles, and Costa Ricans may return to their country, regardless of their political convictions. Few countries in the world enjoy the same degree of economic, social, religious, press and political freedoms as does Costa Rica. The people are proud of their heritage and are determined to preserve it.

President Teodoro Picado, whose term of office expires in May, 1948, has been a reasonably successful President. He too is a confirmed believer in democracy. He has tried to serve the people in strict accordance with their democratic ideals and practices. He has always been friendly to the United States and is a staunch supporter of the inter-American way of life.

Respectfully yours, Walter J. Donnelly

FINANCIAL AND MILITARY ASSISTANCE BY THE UNITED STATES TO COSTA RICA [22]

818.24/1–247

Memorandum of Conversation, by the Second Secretary of Embassy in Costa Rica (Snow) [23]

CONFIDENTIAL [San José,] December 31, 1946.

This morning at 10 o'clock, I called by appointment to see the Finance Minister [24] on the subject of surplus property and the possibility that his Government might be willing to negotiate a contract with us similiar to the Colombian, Salvadoran and Guatemalan surplus contracts.[25]

---

[22] Continued from *Foreign Relations*, 1946 vol. xi, pp. 682–690.
[23] Copy transmitted to the Department in despatch 2751, January 2, 1947, from San José; received January 7.
[24] Alvaro Bonilla Lara.
[25] Contracts not printed.

I first explained that we had a three-fold purpose in bringing the matter up. In the first place, we were desirous of disposing of our war surplus as soon as possible. Secondly, we desired a suitable piece of land in the vicinity of San José on which to build a new Embassy residence. Thirdly, we wished to offer the Costa Rican Government the same opportunity as that given to Colombia, El Salvador and Guatemala, as well as various other Latin American countries, in so far as acquiring material was concerned.

I gave him copies of the three agreements cited above, and briefly went over their terms with him. As for the discounts offered therein for purchases in excess of $300,000, I told him we realized that Costa Rica might not wish to go up that high. Therefore, we might not be able to grant discounts, but could possibly negotiate advantageous financing and credit terms for a sum below $300,000.

He asked if we had any specific plot of land in mind, or if we knew how much money we wished to spend for it. I replied that we did not,[26] but that we would also be incurring expenditures in colones for the building of our new chancery. Any surplus property credit could also be used in that direction. He asked when we proposed to begin construction of the chancery. I replied that I understood July 1, 1947, to be the new date set.

We then discussed the nature of the surplus property available in the Canal Zone and Trinidad, with an explanation about the catalog system and a statement on my part to correct his impression that we were also selling arms and ammunition. I told him that we were merely disposing of tools, machinery, automotive equipment, surplus aircraft, food, clothing, etc. The Minister felt that although the Costa Rican Government could not at present attempt such a contract, the National Bank of Costa Rica conceivably might. For example, the Bank had credit while the Government did not, as he frankly put it. The Bank could obtain the land and the National Production Council affiliated with it might be able to use tools, automobiles, and the like, in its program of fostering the agricultural development of the country. He would present the matter at the next meeting of the Production Council, which would take place on Thursday, January 2, and let me know the results on the following day.

[Here follows a discussion of other financial matters.]

W. P. Snow

---

[26] Real property belonging to Victor Manuel Yglesias was transferred to the United States Government on June 13, 1947, to be used as a site for the construction of the Embassy residence.

818.248/11-1446

The Secretary of State to the Embassy in Costa Rica

SECRET WASHINGTON, January 20, 1947.
No. 732

The Secretary of State refers to the Embassy's despatch no. 2552 of November 14, 1946,[27] which quoted a statement published locally to the effect that Costa Rica was included on a list of American republics to which the United States was preparing to make available airplanes and military equipment and which stated that the Embassy would be glad to be informed as to the accuracy of this information.

Reference is made to the Department's instruction no. 646 of October 30, 1946 [27] relative to rejection by the Department of a request from the Costa Rican Government for assistance in purchasing military aircraft and to the Department's telegram no. 357 of December 12, 1946 [28] concurring with the position of the Ambassador in disapproving a proposed requisition for military equipment by the United States Military Mission in Costa Rica.

The Embassy's further attention is called to a Departmental memorandum of March 14, 1946 [27] a copy of which was furnished the Embassy. That memorandum referred to a conversation held by officers of the Department with the Costa Rican Ambassador,[29] during which it was explained to him that this Government was not disposed to make military equipment available as long as Costa Rica was in complete default on its Lend Lease account.

There has been no change in the Department's policy with respect to the furnishing of military equipment to Costa Rica since the transmission to the Embassy of the material under reference.

818.24/2-1347

The Secretary of State to the Costa Rican Ambassador (Gutiérrez)

CONFIDENTIAL WASHINGTON, February 13, 1947.

EXCELLENCY: I have the honor to transmit herewith two copies each of Statements LL-10 and LL-11 and supporting schedules [27] reporting charges made against Your Excellency's Government during the period from June 1, 1946 through September 30, 1946, covering defense material transferred in accordance with the terms of the

[27] Not printed.
[28] *Foreign Relations*, 1946, vol. XI, p. 689.
[29] Francisco de P. Gutiérrez.

Lend-Lease Agreement signed on January 16, 1942 [32] by representatives of the Republic of Costa Rica and the United States of America.

It will be noted that charges during the period under reference were $1,534.55, and that charges through September 30, 1946 aggregate the grand total of $153,502.07. Of this grand total the sum of $83,000 represents the appropriate percentage due on account from the Government of Costa Rica under the terms specified in the Agreement. . . . No payments have been received to date.

I bring this matter most earnestly to the attention of the Government of Costa Rica in the hope that there may be received as soon as possible from the Government of Costa Rica a check in the amount of $83,000, which would cover sums due including arrears. . . .

. . . .

Accept [etc.]

For the Secretary of State:
SPRUILLE BRADEN

818.51/4–2447

The Ambassador in Costa Rica (Johnson) to the Secretary of State

CONFIDENTIAL

SAN JOSÉ, April 24, 1947.

No. 3130

SIR: I have the honor to report that in my opinion a recent editorial in the *New York Times* regarding the death of the Bolivian tin king Patiño made certain observations which are relevant to the situation in Costa Rica.

The editorial said, in part:

"In most Latin American countries today the majority of wealth is still held in a few hands. This is the basic reason for Communist penetration there. It is soil in which the weed of totalitarianism grows most verdantly."

I believe that the majority of Costa Rican wealth, apart from foreign interests, is held in a few hands. . . .

This group pays what amounts in many cases to near starvation wages and in general are opposed to social change or to reasonable social legislation. Their forebears controlled the country and they wish to maintain such control. They resent the fact that the Government has gotten out of the hands of the wealthy group and, alleging distrust of the Government, evade as far as possible the payment of taxes. This year there were less than one thousand people who were paying any income tax at all.

Moreover, the taxes on the statute books, both as regards income and real estate, are infinitesimal compared to comparable taxes in the United States. Whenever the Government makes an effort to raise

---

[32] *Foreign Relations,* 1942, vol. VI, p. 235.

taxes in order to secure money to pay its employees—which payment is continually in arrears—the wealthy landowners, business and professional men sabotage the effort through one means or another.

It is obvious to me that this situation is a basic reason for possible Communist penetration. On the other hand, it may give rise to an effort toward totalitarianism government of another sort. Moreover, although the banks are in sound financial condition and merchants' accounts paid up, business cannot continue to prosper under a semibankrupt government.

The above situation makes the formation of our own policy vis-à-vis Costa Rica more difficult. We do not wish to see chaos in a country which after all is comparatively more democratic than other countries in Central America. We must, therefore, I think be sufficiently lenient in the readjustment of loans and even in the granting of small loans in the future, if such action is necessary, to avoid complete bankruptcy of the Government.

On the other hand, Costa Ricans must be taught that the United States is not a Santa Claus and that they must take steps to put their house in order before we are willing to help them financially in a measure which we otherwise might favorably consider.[33]

Respectfully yours, HALLETT JOHNSON

818.00/8-747

The Chargé in Costa Rica (Carrigan) to the Secretary of State

CONFIDENTIAL SAN JOSÉ, August 7, 1947.
No. 102

SIR: I have the honor to report that on August 6, 1947, General René Picado, Secretary of Public Security, came to call upon me in connection with a visa matter involving certain Polish relatives of his.

During the course of the conversation he made certain rather interesting remarks:

[Here follow remarks on the Rio Conference, re-inauguration of President Trujillo, General Picado's visit to the United States, and the Presidential designates.]

Costa Rican Arms Situation

General Picado said that during the last two weeks [34] the Costa Rican Army had fired only its old ammunition, that is, certain am-

---

[33] In airgram A-80, March 19, 1947, the Department informed the Embassy in Costa Rica that the Export-Import Bank had not been approached either formally or informally regarding any credits since 1946, and the Department would not at that time recommend approval by Eximbank of any application for credit for domestic expenditures or for projects which were not self-liquidating and exchange-saving (818.51/2-1147).

[34] See documentation on the disturbed political situation, pp. 578 ff.

munition which had been bought through Raúl Gurdián from Mexico. He said that they still had some three million rounds left of this old ammunition. He said that none of the new ammunition had been used, and that there were about three million rounds of this new ammunition.

I asked him how much Lend-Lease armament had been used in the last two weeks. He said no Lend-Lease arms at all had been used. He said that the only sub-machine guns used had been Swiss Neuhausen, and that the only Thompson sub-machine guns used were pre-war stock.

He told me that he had purchased commercially from the United States some 25 Colt .45-calibre automatics, and that these automatics had arrived in Port Limon yesterday or the day before. He said that they had just completed negotiations and signature on a deal with the Madsen Arms factory of Denmark. He reminded me that a representative of this firm had been in Costa Rica within the last five weeks. He said that they bought 50 light machine guns from this firm. He said that delivery of these machine guns would be completed by October 15, 1947, and that they would be brought over by the Dutch KLM Airlines as air freight.

He said that he had originally planned to buy these machine guns in the United States, but that after a rebuff from Washington he had decided that it would be better to try to buy his arms elsewhere. He said that he had been interested in Mexican arms but that he had found the Mexicans unwilling to help him. He said that he had then turned to Argentina, but found that Argentine prices were too high. Accordingly, he said, he had only one alternative, and that was to buy from Europe.

Parenthetically, he remarked that he was able to buy all the arms he needed from Europe, and would be forced to do so if we continued in our present refusal of authorization for the Government of Costa Rica to buy arms in the United States.

It is perhaps pertinent to remark that, irrespective of where he buys his arms, the general public will assume that they came from the United States.[35]

Respectfully yours,   JOHN WILLARD CARRIGAN

---

[35] In despatch 103, August 8, 1947, Mr. Carrigan referred to the often-made charge that the lend-lease arms which the United States furnished for continental defense were being used in the suppression of civic liberties in Latin America, and added: "As far as the Embassy is aware, with the exception of two weapon carriers, no arms furnished Costa Rica under the Lend-Lease Act were used by the government during the recent civic disobedience campaign. As a matter of fact, in the case of Costa Rica, it is felt that a grossly exaggerated idea exists in the public mind as to the quantity of arms and equipment actually supplied as lend-lease equipment." (818.24/8–847)

800.48 FAA/12-1147

Memorandum of Conversation, by Mr. W. Tapley Bennett, Area Specialist of the Division of Central America and Panama Affairs

CONFIDENTIAL [WASHINGTON,] December 11, 1947.

During a conversation on other matters, Ambassador Gutiérrez took occasion to express the fear that the United States will "over-extend" itself in the carrying out of the projected aid programs for Europe.[36] He said that in his opinion we, as the nation with the highest living standard in the world, often fail to realize that citizens of other countries exist on a great deal less than we would consider necessary. He said that he did not want in any way to imply criticism of our effort, which he considers magnificent, and that he considers such mistakes as we make to be mistakes of the heart.

I pointed out to the Ambassador that our programs have the aim of helping European countries to help themselves. He said he realizes that this is the aim of the program but that he personally does not feel that the European nations are doing their full part in the program. He mentioned the 16-nation aid conference in Paris last summer,[37] asserting that the Europeans asked for a great deal but made very few concrete suggestions as to economic cooperation among themselves and contributions to the overall program. He offered the opinion that, while the United States has been and is outstanding in its generosity for other nations, it cannot go on being Lady Bountiful forever without undesirable dislocations at home and a dangerous depletion of national resources.

Ambassador Gutiérrez eventually reached the point which perhaps was the real reason for his reference to the subject of aid. He said that he was concerned lest United States aid to Europe should result in our forgetting the needs of the other American republics. He said that this feeling was quite prevalent in the Latin American diplomatic group here at the present time. He said that he had heard numerous heated discussions among his colleagues on the subject, and he mentioned the Mexican Ambassador[38] as one individual with whom he himself had talked.[39] The Ambassador concluded that, while it is realized that the

---

[36] For documentation on the European Recovery Program, see volume III.
[37] See a summary of the report of the Committee of European Economic Cooperation, which was signed on September 22, 1947, by representatives of the sixteen European countries meeting in Paris between July 12 and September 22, 1947, Department of State *Bulletin*, October 5, 1947, pp. 681–687.
[38] Antonio Espinosa de los Monteros.
[39] In a letter of December 1, 1947, to President Truman, the Ambassador in Mexico (Thurston) stated: "Remarks recently made to me by the Minister for Foreign Affairs indicate that official feeling here is that we are placing undue emphasis on shoring up and rebuilding European states (some of which were our opponents in the last war) and neglecting near neighbors and friends (some of whom were our active allies in the war) whose need for immediate development—both for economic reasons and as fortification against ideologies—is quite as great and urgent as that of a remote and probably ungrateful Europe." (711.20/12-1247)

problems of Latin America are simpler of solution than those of Europe, he maintains the hope, which he is sure is shared by his colleagues, that the needs of Latin America will not be overlooked. I, of course, assured the Ambassador that we desire to be helpful economically in every way possible within our natural economic limitations and that discussions to that end are under way at the present time.

UNITED STATES INTEREST IN COSTA RICAN FISHERIES LEGISLATION

818.628A/5–2947 : Telegram

The Secretary of State to the Embassy in Costa Rica

CONFIDENTIAL WASHINGTON, June 6, 1947—8 p. m.

189. Costa Rican Emb requested Dept make available fisheries expert purpose advising on pending fisheries legislation. Foregoing and Embtels 219 May 28 and 223 May 29 [40] indicate no immediate Costa Rican legislation.

2. Issuance Mex declaration Oct 1945 asserting jurisdiction over subsoil continental shelf and control high seas conservation zones prompted US note Jan 1946 [41] stating US–Mex fisheries agreement considered prerequisite US recognition establishment high seas conservation zones. Privately proposed amendments Costa Rican legislation similar problem. Dept approves Emb action (Embtel 223 May 29). In Embs discretion additional *aide-mémoire* may be presented along following lines:

3. "US Emb understands certain Costa Rican organizations advocate extension Costa Rican jurisdiction for fisheries conservation purposes beyond usual limits of territorial waters. Since somewhat similar proclamation re fisheries was issued by US Govt Sept 28, 1945,[42] it may be helpful to Costa Rican Govt to have summary of principles recognized by US Govt in issuance of this proclamation.

4. Since due regard must be given conditions peculiar to each region and situation and to special rights and equities of coastal State and any other State which may have established legitimate interest therein, it is felt that prior to establishment of jurisdiction over high seas areas, coastal State must reach agreement with states having legitimate fishing interests in area concerned. Further, fisheries control and regulation must be based on valid scientific evidence, and jurisdiction established must be for purposes of fisheries conservation only.

5. The US, as a state whose nationals have legitimate interest based in substantial fishing activities in waters contiguous to Costa Rica, is willing to cooperate with Costa Rica in agreement re fisheries con-

---

[40] Neither printed.
[41] For note of January 24, 1946, to the Mexican Ambassador (Espinosa de los Monteros), see *Foreign Relations*, 1946, vol. XI, p. 1054.
[42] Department of State *Bulletin*, September 30, 1945, p. 4884.

servation and necessary scientific investigation connected with establishment of conservation measures."

6. Info Emb only, Dept likely reserve all fisheries rights pertaining high seas areas in proposed extension territorial jurisdiction unless agreement assuring no taxation applicable such areas no restrictions there on purse seiners, freezer ships or vessels without shore bases in Costa Rica. If Costa Rican legislation imminent despite indications paragraph 1 this tel or if Emb action now appears useful Emb requested take interim action suggested paragraph 3 sentence 2 Deptel 166 May 22 [43] and report soonest.

7. Re fishing within presently defined Costa Rican territorial limits Dept favors views sentences 3 and 4 paragraph 3 tel under reference also paragraphs 2, 3 and 4 Instruction 366 Feb 21, 1946.[43] Dept suggests possibility charge US intervention less if US fisheries expert, in employ Costa Rican Govt, proposed para 1 above, would urge action along these lines with Emb prepared to give added support position if expert fails convince Costa Rican authorities advisability this course. However, if Emb should see indication immediate legislation barring directly or indirectly through prohibitive taxes purse seining in territorial waters, floating canneries or freezers, or vessels not based Costa Rica, or if Emb action now appears useful, Emb should take whatever action deemed appropriate to urge Costa Rican acceptance US views, avoiding action which could reasonably charge intervention. None fees proposed by any group thus far appear prohibitive.

MARSHALL

818.628A/6-347

The Secretary of State to the Embassy in Costa Rica

[Extracts]

CONFIDENTIAL WASHINGTON, July 17, 1947.
No. 1

The Secretary of State refers to previous correspondence concerning the assignment to the Costa Rican Government of fisheries expert Dr. John L. Kask for the purpose of giving technical advice on fisheries legislation and on other fishery matters.

On June 3, 1947 the Ambassador of the Costa Rican Government presented a note to the Department (a copy of this note is attached [43] as Appendix I) requesting the services of a technical expert to advise

---

[43] Not printed.

and assist in developing fishery legislation to protect the natural rights of the parties concerned with it.

Officials of the Department in discussion of this request with officials of the Fish and Wildlife Service of the Department of the Interior decided that it would be preferable to make available to the Government of Costa Rica the services of a technician who was not at present employed by the Federal Government or the State of California. It was believed that in the circumstances the assignment of such a government official might more readily be interpreted in Costa Rica by interested groups as a device for securing more favorable treatment for special United States interests to the detriment of certain other groups or as a means for furthering American economic advantage to the detriment of Costa Rican interests. For this reason, it was believed appropriate to make available the services of an outstanding scientist who had a reputation for objectivity and who was familiar with the west coast fisheries problems.

. . . .

Upon Dr. Kask's departure it is expected that a press release [45] will be issued, after consultation with the Costa Rican Embassy, in the following sense:

. . . .

Officials of the Department and of the Fish and Wildlife Service of the Department of the Interior have discussed with Dr. Kask the objectives of this mission. So far as the Government of the United States is concerned, these objectives, which are to be confidential, are:

(a) To advise the Government of Costa Rica on the proposed fishery legislation with a view to influencing the Government of Costa Rica to adopt measures which will contribute to: (1) Conserving and developing the fishery resources of common concern to Costa Rica and to the United States, and (2) Both short and long range economic benefits to both nations.

(b) To stimulate an active interest in Costa Rica for an improved fishery program, with a view to collaboration by the Costa Rican Government with the United States Government in the near future, on a joint program for the fisheries of common concern.

(c) To advise the United States Government on matters relating to fisheries which are or may be of joint concern.

Dr. Kask was informed that the United States officials considered that these objectives could be served with respect to proposed Costa Rican legislation by:

(1) Opposing prohibition upon or discriminations against any type of fishing gear which scientific evidence does not show to be necessary to conservation of the fishery,

---

[45] Department of State *Bulletin*, July 27, 1947, p. 201.

(2) Supporting taxes and regulations which are easily understood and complied with by American fishermen and involve minimum administrative burden on the Government and minimum opportunity for administrative abuse,

(3) Opposing taxes which are prohibitive and which discourage the development of the fishing industries.

. . . .

[In despatch 69, August 14, the Chargé in Costa Rica reported that an *aide-mémoire* following outline in the Department's telegram 189 of June 6 was left at the Foreign Office on June 18; it included reservation of full rights in the event of any attempt by Costa Rica unilaterally to assert jurisdiction outside territorial waters. Dr. Kask, he reported, had arrived on July 14, and left for Washington on August 8. (818.628a/8–1447)]

818.628/10–2347

The Chargé in Costa Rica (Carrigan) to the Secretary of State

[Extracts]

CONFIDENTIAL SAN JOSÉ, October 23, 1947.
No. 312

Subject: Suspension of Costa Rican Fisheries Decree of September 24, 1947.

SIR: I have the honor to refer to the series of correspondence regarding the Costa Rican fisheries decree which recently was issued and subsequently suspended. . . .

It will be recalled from prior reports that the fisheries regulation, based on the work of the American scientist, Dr. John L. Kask, was promulgated in the *Official Gazette* of September 27. (The full text was submitted with despatch 246 of October 1.) [46]

Immediately following the promulgation of this decree, a press campaign was instituted against it. . . .

. . . .

Meanwhile it had been intimated in the press on October 17 that the fisheries decree would be revoked. On that same morning the Acting Foreign Minister, who is also the Finance Minister, requested that a member of the Embassy staff call upon him. It appears that at a meeting on the preceding evening it had been decided to suspend the decree and it developed that he wished to propose that the Embassy seek an interview with the Minister of Agriculture and Indus-

---

[46] Not printed.

tries. Since it appeared that the Acting Foreign Minister, who was known to favor the decree, might have had the idea in mind of using the Embassy to bring pressure upon the Minister of Agriculture and Industries, great care was taken not to become entangled in the domestic aspects since in the existing state of mind of those opposed to the decree a cry of interventionism could easily have arisen. . . .

The Minister's decision to do that may have resulted from the fact that President Picado signed on October 18 Decree No. 5, promulgated on the following day, which suspends the fisheries decree until such time as a General Fisheries Department may be established. . . .

. . . . . .

The fisheries question in Costa Rica now returns to the *status quo ante*. Precise definition of that status is difficult since the Government itself has left it rather ambiguous. . . .

It is evident that the recently concluded campaign against the fisheries decree has found its origin in commercial and financial motives and was not primairly a gear fight.

It is quite possible that entry of American purse seine boats into Costa Rican ports or their activity in proximity to Costa Rica might again cause the controversy to be renewed in the future. The Embassy, upon instruction from the Department, previously set forth certain basic views in the *aide-mémoire* left at the Foreign Office in June 18, 1947 [47] (embodied in Enclosure No. 1 to despatch 69 of August 14 [47a]). The Embassy is quite prepared in event that American vessels should again encounter difficulties to address any communication to the Foreign Office which the Department may instruct.

Respectfully yours, For the Chargé d'Affaires a.i.:
JULE L. GOETZMANN
Second Secretary of Embassy

818.628/10–2347 : Airgram

The Acting Secretary of State to the Embassy in Costa Rica

RESTRICTED   WASHINGTON, December 8, 1947.

A-276. Reference is made to Embassy's despatch No. 312, October 23, 1947 regarding suspension of the Costa Rican Fishery Decree promulgated in the *Official Gazette* on September 27, 1947, with particular reference to the last three paragraphs.

[Here follow data concerning planned purse seine tuna operations by American companies off the coast of Costa Rica.]

---

[47] Not printed.
[47a] Not printed, but see bracketed note printed *supra*.

At the moment the Department does not anticipate entering into fishery treaty discussions with Costa Rica. It would appear unlikely that Dr. Kask can take an active part on any treaty discussions since he is now serving as part-time consultant to the Department on the Northwest Atlantic Treaty Program and therefore would not be available to serve the Costa Rican Government until his service with the Department is terminated. Dr. Kask has agreed to serve with the Department until early spring, at which time he will accept the position as full-time permanent Chief Biologist to the Fisheries Division of the Food and Agriculture Organization.

The thinking of the Department on the general question of fisheries relations between this Government and the Government of Costa Rica is along the following lines. While it is recognized that the appearance of American purse seiners off the coast or in the ports of Costa Rica may cause the controversy to be renewed, there appears a possibility that the Costa Rican Government will, under existing law and without further representations from the Embassy, permit the purse seiners to enter Costa Rican ports for supplies and for the transfer of fish and to make it possible for them to fish for tuna outside the territorial waters of Costa Rica. If the Govt of Costa Rica should grant such permission, it is probable that there would be no impediment to effective purse seine operation, and further discussion at this time between the Embassy and the officials of Costa Rica on these matters would be obviated. It seems appropriate that since the Embassy has made clear the views of this Govt on fisheries problems in Costa Rica, this Govt should avoid any further involvement in these policy questions so long as there is not actual undue interference with American commercial operations. However, should the American vessels find it difficult or impossible to carry on their operations, or should a change in circumstances warrant, it may be necessary for the Dept to request the Embassy to bring the matter again to the attention of the Government of Costa Rica. In the meantime the Embassy should, of course, extend the usual and normal courtesies to the American operators.

LOVETT

CUBA

EFFORTS TO SETTLE OUTSTANDING PROBLEMS BETWEEN THE UNITED STATES AND CUBA [1]

837.61351/2–1247

Memorandum of Telephone Conversation, by the Chief of the Foods Section of the Division of International Resources (Mulliken)

[WASHINGTON,] February 12, 1947.

I telephoned Mr. Marshall [2] to ask whether my understanding that the Department of Agriculture was recommending an additional one-year extension of the Sugar Act of 1937 [3] was correct. Mr. Marshall stated that his report on Senate 246, a bill recently introduced by Senator O'Mahoney to amend the Sugar Act of 1937 [and incidentally to improve the position of domestic beet growers] [4] had not yet gone forward, but that he did expect to recommend a further extension for one year.

I pointed out that the 1947 Cuban Sugar Purchase Contract [5] contains the following provision [6]:

"In the event that the United States of America should enact legislation extending, modifying, or supplanting the Sugar Act of 1937, as amended, in a manner detrimental to the position of Cuba as a future supplier of sugar to the United States market, then and in that event all provisions of this Contract shall, at the option of the Institute, become null and void as to the portion of the products sold hereunder and undelivered at the time of such cancellation. For the purposes of this clause, a simple one-year extension of the Sugar Act of 1937, as amended, is determined not to be detrimental legislation."

This contract was signed prior to the 1946 renewal of the Sugar Act, and it was clearly understood that the reference to a "one year re-

---

[1] For previous documentation on this subject, see *Foreign Relations*, 1946, vol. XI, pp. 702 ff.

[2] James H. Marshall, Director, Sugar Branch, Production and Marketing Administration, Department of Agriculture.

[3] For text, see Department of State, Treaties and Other International Acts Series (TIAS) No. 990, or 59 Stat. (pt. 2) 922.

[4] Brackets appear in the original.

[5] The 1946 and 1947 Cuban Sugar Crops Purchase and Sale Contract, July 16, 1946, not printed; for documentation on this subject, see *Foreign Relations*, 1946, vol. XI, pp. 799–804.

[6] Part IV, article 8, of the Contract.

newal" applied to a renewal extending to December 31, 1947, and not beyond that date. Mr. Marshall acknowledged that that was the understanding, but stated that he intended to claim, in the Cubans' own interest, that the phrasing of the Contract implies that any number of one-year extensions may be made without detriment to Cuba's interest. It is his belief that this is not the time for a general revision of sugar quotas, since quotas will probably remain in suspense for several years anyway in view of the sugar shortage, and that the Cubans would gain nothing by campaigning for an increase in a suspended quota. He asked that State support Agriculture's position that another one-year extension of the Sugar Act is not contrary to the terms of the Sugar Purchase Agreement.

I pointed out that this is the time, if ever, when Cuba could apply a little leverage in obtaining an increase in its quota by threatening to cut off our sugar supply. Mr. Marshall said that if Cuba actually took such a step its quota would probably be reduced to zero, that he was sure the Cubans were aware of that fact, and that he thought they would not run the risk of antagonizing the American public by any such action.

I called Mr. Marshall's attention to the fact that the Secretary of State, in a recent confidential letter to Senator Vandenberg,[7] a part of which had been released by the Senator, had listed legislation which the Department hopes to see enacted by this Congress and that point 17 on the list was "an increase in the Cuban sugar quota". I said I thought this was probably a tactical error, since we are not actively sponsoring legislation, but merely suggesting, in our report on S. 246, that in any revision of quotas recognition be given to performance during a recent representative period. The inclusion of late years in the base period for sugar quotas would, of course, result in an increase in the Cuban quota. I said I would have preferred that the emphasis be laid on the more general problem of securing a "representative" base for import quotas rather than on the Cuban aspect of the question, but that since the statement had been made, and had received wide press notice, I thought the Department would not be prepared to reverse itself and state that all it really had in mind was a one-year renewal of the present act. I also expressed doubt that we would wish to support Agriculture's interpretation of the contract, even if no statement regarding our intentions had appeared in the press, because of the unfortunate effect which such obvious distortion of the meaning of the contract might have upon our relations with Cuba. I agreed, however, to raise the question with the other interested divisions and inform Mr. Marshall promptly of the Department's views.

---

[7] Letter of February 5, 1947, not printed.

800.8836/3-547

Memorandum of Conversation, by the Assistant Chief of the Division of Caribbean Affairs (Walker)

CONFIDENTIAL [WASHINGTON,] March 5, 1947.

Participants: Señor Guillermo Belt, Ambassador of Cuba
Assistant Secretary of State Braden (A-Br)
Mr. Ellis O. Briggs, Department of State (ARA)[8]
Mr. William W. Walker, Department of State (CRB)

Ambassador Belt, at Mr. Braden's request called at the Department this afternoon. Mr. Braden said that he wanted to discuss with the Ambassador in an unofficial but friendly and frank manner certain issues which have created a great deal of ill will against Cuba. By way of example, he referred to several remarks made by a group of Republican Congressmen who attended a meeting of the Wednesday Night Club last month. They had heard about the Seatrain issue,[9] Mr. Braden stated, and asked him what the State Department was doing about it. They stated quite frankly that unless this problem were resolved, Cuba would certainly not receive favorable consideration with regard to sugar quotas, tariffs, etc. In this connection, Mr. Braden called the Ambassador's attention to the fact that despite any efforts made by the State Department, the Department of Agriculture or any other agency of this Government to assist Cuba in getting a more equitable share of the sugar quota, it is most unlikely that Cuba would receive favorable consideration in view of its record regarding the Seatrain matter and claims of U.S. citizens.

Mr. Braden informed the Ambassador of the assurances which he received from the Minister of Finance (Supervielle) and President Grau when he was Ambassador to Cuba in 1944, that in accordance with an agreement which they worked out, the claims of the Isle of Pines Steamship Company [10] would be paid. He also informed the Ambas-

---

[8] Ellis O. Briggs, Director of the Office of American Republic Affairs.
[9] The Seatrain Lines Inc. (a special steamship service, transporting goods in railroad cars, between the United States and Cuba, in operation since 1929) had suspended operations at the end of 1946 as a result of Cuban customs regulations which made it impracticable to continue operations. The Department of State, in a note delivered to the Cuban Ambassador on January 7, 1947, protested against these regulations as restrictions upon international trade. (800.8836/4-2646)
[10] This company's claims against the Cuban Government were for freight services between the Isle of Pines and Cuba.

sador of repeated assurances on the Stowers claim.[11] The failure of the Cuban Government, he said, to carry out these commitments cannot be satisfactorily explained. Mr. Braden then referred to other claims, most of which have been either adjudicated by the Cuban Supreme Court or acknowledged by administrative agencies of the Cuban Government. The Cuban Government, he said, has been urged on a number of occasions to settle the adjudicated and recognized claims and to establish a mixed claims commission for those claims concerning which there may be some doubt. These matters, Mr. Braden stated, are causing much unfavorable comment which will inevitably prejudice Cuba's position so far as sugar legislation is concerned.

The Ambassador stated that he understood that these conditions were harmful to Cuba's best interests and that he had on a number of occasions urged President Grau to settle some of the outstanding claims. He explained that arrangements for the payment of the Lend-Lease debt [12] were difficult and required considerable effort on his part. With regard to the Seatrain matter, he said that he had discussed it with Representative Bradley [13] and Admiral Smith, Chairman of the Maritime Commission, at luncheon today. When Congressman Bradley asked him about labor conditions in Cuba, he stated that he replied that they were better than in the United States. He mentioned that in discussing the Seatrain matter with Mr. Falck (Assistant Chief, Shipping Division) last January, he had suggested that if the Seatrain would continue operations for a period of two months, he would go to Habana and arrange with President Grau for the conclusion of an agreement which would be satisfactory to both the Seatrain and the

---

[11] An American citizen, John L. Stowers, sought compensation for his property which was overrun by squatters whom the Cuban authorities regarded it as impolitic to dislodge. According to despatch 4331, September 8, 1947, from Habana, Mr. Stowers had on that date informed the Embassy that he understood the Ministry of Public Works had prepared a check to his order for the amount of $34,900, the sum which the Council of Ministers appropriated in order to bring about the purchase of his property by the Cuban Government (837.52/9–847).

Ambassador Norweb reported in airgram A–347, March 19, 1948, as follows: "Stowers has just informed this Embassy that he today received 34,690.88 Cuban pesos, the proceeds of the Government check in payment of his claim. While he indicated that the bulk of this amount would be needed to pay expenses and his outstanding debts, he expressed his deep appreciation of the assistance he had received from the Embassy." (837.52/3–1948)

[12] On February 26, 1947, the Cuban Government had made a payment of $2,400,000 on its Lend-Lease account.

[13] Representative Fred Bradley, Chairman, Committee on Merchant Marine and Fisheries, House of Representatives.

government. He added, however, that since Mr. Falck appeared disinterested in this suggestion, nothing was done.

The Ambassador stated that he was planning another trip to Habana within the next few weeks and that he would endeavor to resolve some of the problems.[14]

. . . .

837.61351/3–2947

Memorandum by the Director of the Office of American Republic Affairs (Briggs)[15]

CONFIDENTIAL [WASHINGTON,] March 29, 1947.

CUBA: RECOMMENDATION REGARDING PROPOSED TREATY OF FRIENDSHIP AND ESTABLISHMENT, AND REGARDING ANNUAL ALLOCATION OF SUGAR QUOTA

Recommendation: That the following two provisions be included in the next basic United States sugar legislation:

1) That any increase over the prevailing 28% which our Congress may grant as the Cuban share of the United States domestic sugar market be made contingent upon the acceptance by Cuba of a satisfactory treaty of friendship and establishment.

2) That in connection with the annual allocation of the Cuban quota, a provision be included specifying that such allocation shall not take effect until the Secretary of Agriculture is satisfied that the distribution of the Cuban share of the U.S. quota has been made in a fair and equitable manner.

Discussion:

1) The number one problem in Cuba is government corruption, and the secondary problem is the subservience of the Cuban Government to the local Communist Party, whose objective is the liquidation of American interests. Both problems bear heavily on American enterprises in Cuba, which total approximately $750,000,000.

It is clear from the record that relations with Cuba to be even relatively satisfactory must be based on "strength and justice" on our part, and that in the absence of some effective continuing leverage American interests cannot count on protection by the Cuban Govern-

---

[14] In airgram A–593, August 18, the Department informed the Embassy in Cuba that a check for $103,488.94 in payment of the 1943 peanut seed debt had been received from the Cuban Embassy on August 12 (837.613/8–1847). For documentation regarding the Cuban peanut seed purchase, see *Foreign Relations, 1943*, vol. VI, pp. 223 ff.

[15] Addressed to Messrs. Braden, Wright, and Smith, A–Br; Messrs. Woodward and Nufer, ARA; Mr. Turkel, CP; Mr. Thorp, A–T; and Mr. Walker, CRB.

ment. Our Government has tried at various times all forms of presentation in defense of American interests and our arguments (in the absence of leverage) have generally been met with indifference, or even derision.

Continuing protection for American interests in general would be afforded by the proposed treaty of friendship and establishment,[16] but there is scant prospect that Cuba will accept such a treaty unless we make some benefit ardently desired by Cuba and within our power to bestow or withhold, contingent upon Cuba's agreeing to the treaty. An increase in the Cuban share in the U.S. sugar market constitutes such a benefit.*

2) The second provision is designed specifically to protect American sugar interests from discrimination. Although those interests have not fared badly during the period since Pearl Harbor merely because *all* sugar producers have prospered and because there has been no important conflict of interest between Cuban and American producers, this situation will shortly change. American mills are generally large low-cost producers and they are greatly outnumbered by Cuban mills many of which are small high-cost producers. When the time comes for contraction of Cuban sugar production, the temptation—politically and historically—will be for this reduction to be disproportionately at the expense of the foreign (i.e. American) producers. Experience gives no basis for anticipating that the Cuban Government, if left to its own devices, would adopt a quota allocation system even remotely fair to American producers. Our experience with Decree Law 522 adopted in 1935 and maintained thereafter in circumstances of mounting insecurity illustrates this point.

To protect U.S. sugar producers there should be inserted in American sugar legislation a provision in general terms that the Secretary of Agriculture before making each year the global allocation of quota to Cuba shall have satisfied himself that the distribution of quota in Cuba has been fair and equitable. The inclusion of such a provision would give our Government the necessary leverage in dealing with the Cuban Government, and our Habana Embassy could see to it each year that a "fair and equitable" allocation had in fact been made. (An alternative suggestion that distribution of the Cuban quota

---

[16] The Ambassador in Cuba reported in despatch 2790, February 13, 1947, that a draft of the proposed Treaty of Friendship, Commerce and Navigation had been presented to the Cuban Minister of State under cover of the Embassy's memorandum of January 27, 1947 (711.372/2–1347). As of December 31, 1947, no reply to the memorandum of January 27 had been received (711.372/12–3147).

*The possibility is not overlooked of using a reduction in the sugar duty, contemplated in the ITO negotiations, as the *quid pro quo;* should the treaty be obtained in those negotiations it would of course not be necessary to handle the matter as suggested herein. [Footnote in the original.]

destined for the U.S. be made by the U.S.—or that the same end be obtained through the establishment of an import permit system—is not practical. It would expose us to criticism for intervening in Cuban domestic affairs, and it would place a complicated additional administrative burden on the U.S.)

Should these two provisions be included in permanent U.S. legislation the way would be paved for the establishment of genuinely good relations with Cuba based on respect by Cuba for American rights, as well as on the respect which the United States has traditionally shown for Cuban rights.

ELLIS O. BRIGGS

611.3731/4–347

Memorandum of Conversation, by the Assistant Chief of the Division of Caribbean Affairs (Walker)

RESTRICTED [WASHINGTON,] April 3, 1947.

Participants: Under Secretary Clayton
             Ambassador Belt of Cuba
             Sr. Sergio Clark, Cuban Minister of Communication and Chairman of Cuban delegation to Geneva Conference on Trade and Employment

During the course of the luncheon which Mr. Clayton gave for Señor Clark yesterday at the Blair House, Ambassador Belt indicated that he would like to discuss some of the problems between the United States and Cuba. Mr. Clayton remarked that such discussion would be very helpful. He then stated that he wanted Ambassador Belt to know that the difficulties being experienced by American business men have reached the ears of members of Congress and that unless they are resolved satisfactorily, it is unlikely that Cuba will get a larger sugar quota when new sugar legislation is enacted. Mr. Clayton referred to the inability of American corporations to send technical and executive personnel to Cuba to operate their business enterprises, to the restrictive measures which forced the Seatrain to discontinue operations, and to the pending claims of American nationals against the Cuban Government. If, Mr. Clayton added, the Department were in a position to inform Congress that it had concluded with Cuba a treaty of commerce, friendship and navigation which would eliminate these problems, its efforts to obtain for Cuba a more equitable sugar quota would be immeasurably more effective.

The Ambassador expressed the hope that before the end of his mission in Washington, he would be able to resolve all of the problems between Cuba and the United States. He pointed out, however, that it would not be possible for his President to give favorable consideration to a treaty of commerce until Cuba is given a larger sugar quota. The treaty, he stated, was, in his opinion, a reasonable one but contained some provisions which would be contrary to the Cuban constitution. He went on to say that the treaty, while reciprocal in theory, would actually be far more advantageous to the U.S. than to Cuba since there are many American firms in Cuba, but no Cuban firms to speak of in the United States.

Mr. Clayton stated that as a matter of right and amity, these difficulties affecting American business firms should be resolved and a solution should not hinge upon a larger sugar quota for Cuba. He further stated that, in his opinion, members of Congress would not react favorably to a suggestion that they would have to give Cuba a larger sugar quota in order to have these matters settled. The Ambassador referred to Cuba's contribution of sugar during the war, stating that his country was fully entitled to fair and equitable consideration for this contribution. Mr. Clayton admitted that Cuba should be given a larger sugar quota and stated that an effort would be made to obtain a larger quota, but added that this is a matter that rests with Congress. The Ambassador reiterated that it would be absolutely impossible for Cuba to conclude a treaty of commerce until it is given what it considers a fair sugar quota.

The Ambassador stated that when the Seatrain matter was brought to his attention last January, he had suggested through Mr. Falck (SD) that he would be very glad to go to Habana with Mr. Brush [17] in order to discuss the over-all problem with President Grau. Mr. Brush, he added, rejected this suggestion. Mr. Clark said that Brush had adopted an unreasonable attitude and seemed to feel that he could force the Cuban Government to accept his terms. He went on to say that a few weeks ago the Cuban Cabinet agreed to pass a resolution suspending temporarily the Decree Law affecting the Seatrain in order to permit the Company to make three trips to Habana to transport some steel freight cars badly needed by the Northern Railroad Company. The matter, he stated, was discussed with the Seatrain representative in Habana who communicated with Mr. Brush and who received instructions to inform the Cuban Government that any proposition of that sort would have to be handled through the State Department. Sr. Clark stated that this attitude on the part of Brush was entirely unjustified.[18]

---

[17] Graham H. Brush, president of the Seatrain Lines.
[18] Telegram 199, April 24, 1947, 8 p. m., to the Embassy in Cuba stated the following: "Dept informed by Maritime Commission that Seatrain New Orleans will depart for Habana within next two or three days with shipment of railway box cars under contract arrangement with Consolidated Railways. It is Dept's understanding this trip and others to follow for sole purpose of shipping railway cars should not be interpreted to mean regular service will be resumed." (800.8836/4–2447)

Sr. Clark said that the Decree requiring the use of additional labor would have added very little cost to the operation of the Seatrain, and that the Decree governing the inspection of certain cargo at the port of arrival was designed to prevent the entry of contraband material and would not actually require the inspection of much cargo generally handled by the Seatrain. He explained that the Car Ferry Company, which is subject to the same regulations which the Seatrain Company objects to, is operating so profitably that it intends to purchase two additional vessels.

800.8836/5–147

Memorandum by the Director of the Office of American Republic Affairs (Briggs) [19]

[WASHINGTON,] May 1, 1947.

I telephoned Ambassador Belt this morning in regard to the Seatrain matter, pointing out that according to information from our Embassy in Habana the vessel has been approximately ten miles off Habana for the past two days but hasn't entered the port because of apprehension on the part of the company lest difficulties (which Ambassador Belt and I discussed last week) should occur. In the meantime the port workers who a few days ago were demanding $20,000 which they alleged was due them from the company, had successively reduced the figure to $10,000 (and yesterday) to $3,000. The position of the company is that it will of course entertain any properly presented request, provided it is formulated in the prescribed legal manner and handled through the established legal procedure. The company is not however prepared to enter the harbor unless and until it has received an assurance in writing from the Director General of Customs to the effect that clearance will be given for departure if unloading operations should be delayed or suspended due to circumstances beyond the vessel's control.

I observed that although the Department has no information concerning the basis for the alleged claim against the vessel, the fact that the workers have not proceeded through established channels, and that the demand has been reduced from $20,000 to $3,000 supports the view that the Communist-dominated union is trying to blackmail the company.

Finally, I stated that the company's position has been taken on the advice of competent Cuban counsel, and furthermore that the vessel

---

[19] Addressed to Assistant Secretary of State Braden and to the Assistant Chief of the Division of Caribbean Affairs (Walker).

had embarked on the voyage to Habana following our conversation last week—see previous memorandum reporting Ambassador Belt's assurances from the President.

Ambassador Belt said that he expected to speak to President Grau by telephone during the morning and that he would again take up the matter with him. He said that he would then inform me of the President's comments.[20]

ELLIS O. BRIGGS

837.61351/5-2947

Memorandum of Conversation, by the Assistant Chief of the Division of Caribbean Affairs (Walker)

RESTRICTED [WASHINGTON,] May 29, 1947.

Participants: Señor Guillermo Belt, Ambassador of Cuba
A-Br—Mr. Braden
ARA—Mr. Briggs
CRB—Mr. Walker

Ambassador Belt stated that during his recent visit to Cuba he had discussed with President Grau and with several members of the American Chamber of Commerce of Cuba the question of a larger and more equitable share of the U.S. market for Cuban sugar. The Chamber of Commerce members, he added, were concerned over some of the difficulties confronting American businessmen in Cuba and felt that a treaty of commerce was absolutely essential.

The Ambassador said that he had spoken with President Grau regarding the desirability of satisfactorily resolving the problems (including a larger sugar quota for Cuba) between the United States and Cuba. The President, he stated, agreed that it would be advisable to settle these problems and instructed him to open discussions with this Government in an effort to reach a basis for satisfactory settlement.

---

[20] Mr. Briggs informed Assistant Secretary Braden and Mr. Walker in a memorandum of May 2 that Ambassador Belt had telephoned him the night before to say that he had just finished speaking with President Grau who, after learning of the further apprehensions of the Seatrain, had asked Ambassador Belt to convey a message to Mr. Brush assuring him on behalf of the Cuban Government that the departure of the vessel from Habana would not be delayed in any way, and should there be any claim on the part of workers against the company, that would be handled through established channels (800.8836/5-147).

Mr. Nufer reported in telegram 234, May 1, noon, that Seatrain had entered Habana the evening of May 1 and normal unloading operations were commenced May 2 after Customs officials had given oral assurances the vessel would not be held up (800.8836/5-147).

In airgram A-559, May 13, Mr. Nufer reported that Seatrain had announced resumption of its regular New Orleans-Habana Service on May 16 (800.8836/5-1347).

The Ambassador then presented a note to Mr. Braden [21] setting forth his Government's suggestion that this was the opportune moment to settle outstanding problems between the two countries and that discussions be undertaken as early as possible.

Mr. Braden stated that the matter raised in the Ambassador's note would be studied by the Department and other interested government agencies. He added that upon the completion of these studies the Department would of course communicate with the Ambassador.

Mr. Braden handed Ambassador Belt the Department's preliminary reply to the Ambassador's note of May 20,[21] expressing the Cuban Government's preoccupation over efforts being made in Congress to have the Sugar Act of 1937 extended for a period of one year.

837.61351/6-1747

Memorandum by the Director of the Office of American Republic Affairs (Briggs) to the Under Secretary of State for Economic Affairs (Clayton)

[WASHINGTON,] June 17, 1947.

In regard to sugar legislation, in addition to the overriding question of good faith (our note of January, 1946, sent to the Cubans at Secretary Anderson's request [22]), and the tremendously important economic factors involved, our relations with Cuba are of prime political importance.

1) Unless we fulfill our commitment to recommend an improved position for Cuba, the Cubans, who have a low boiling point in addition to much articulateness, are likely to denounce us to the hemisphere, to the detriment of our general Latin American relations.

2) Unless Cuba gets an equitable share of our market the present "flash flood prosperity" can rapidly be converted into economic distress which can in turn plunge the island into political chaos.

3) Whenever Cuba ignites, the United States invariably has to step in and put out the fire. This in the past has been an expensive business and could easily be more costly in the future.

4) A proposal unfair to Cuba (or even one generally regarded by Cubans as unfair) would be a bonanza for the Communists, not only in Cuba where they are already very strong but elsewhere in the hemisphere. The prospect of a Communist Cuba 90 miles from our doorstep is one which I want no part in promoting.

---

[21] Not printed.
[22] For note of January 4, 1946, to the Cuban Ambassador, see *Foreign Relations*, 1946, vol. XI, p. 772. Clinton P. Anderson was Secretary of Agriculture.

All of which seems to me to make it advisable that Secretary Anderson be informed in the most vigorous terms that this Department cannot approve, much less endorse, any sugar legislation which does not stand four square (1) with our commitments, and (2) with our national interests.

ELLIS O. BRIGGS

837.61351/6-2047 : Telegram

The Secretary of State to the Embassy in Cuba

CONFIDENTIAL WASHINGTON, June 20, 1947—9 p. m.

290. Hearings start tomorrow morning draft sugar bill having full support all segments domestic sugar industry, strong approval Agriculture, and concurrence State. Sec Agri Anderson will testify in behalf Administration. Pertinent provisions:

1. Cuba assured, at any level of consumption, no less than would receive under Section 202(b) Sugar Act of 1937.
2. Cuba will receive 95 percent of Philippine deficit.
3. Cuba receives all domestic deficits when consumption is below seven million tons and shares therein with other domestic areas if consumption above that level.
4. Domestic areas guaranteed 1,800,000 tons; mainland cane, 500,000; Hawaiian 1,052,000; Puerto Rican 910,000; Virgin Islands 6,000; Philippines 952,000. These amounts, which are in short tons, constitute both floors and ceilings and Cuba gets 98.64 percent of difference between these amounts and total consumptive requirements. Accordingly, Cuban share increases as US consumption rises and is never less than amt under 1937 Act.
5. Cuban refined quota 375,000 tons, unchanged.
6. Section 202(e) reads as follows: If the Secretary of State finds that any foreign country denies fair and equitable treatment to the nationals of the United States, its commerce, navigation or industry, and so notifies the Secretary (Agri), the Secretary (Agri) shall have authority to withhold or withdraw any increase in the share of the domestic consumption requirements provided for such country by this Act as compared with the share allowed under Section 202(b) of the Sugar Act of 1937.

Dept believes this bill if enacted will give Cuba most favorable treatment possible. Alternative was one-year extension which would have given Philippine deficit to full-duty countries.

Cuban Emb advised informally of pertinent points except 202(e).

Strategy of tariff reduction will be discussed in subsequent telegram to USDel Geneva.

Repeated to Geneva.

MARSHALL

837.61351/6-2647

Memorandum by the Secretary of State to President Truman

SECRET WASHINGTON, June 26, 1947.

The Cuban Ambassador, Dr. Guillermo Belt, is seeking an appointment with you to express his government's opposition to Section 202(e) of a proposed sugar act which authorizes the Secretary of Agriculture to withhold from any foreign country which denies fair treatment to U.S. citizens, any increase in the sugar quota granted that country. In a conversation with Mr. Acheson [23] on June 24, the Ambassador alleged that such a provision was in violation of the Act of Chapultepec,[24] of Pan-Americanism, and of the UN Charter.[25] He stated that if the provision were not removed, he would appeal to the Pan American Union and the UN Assembly. He also stated that if the proposed legislation is enacted, it should be vetoed.

Mr. Acheson informed the Ambassador that there was nothing unusual or unfair about the provision and that for years there had been provisions in our General Tariff Act for steps to be taken in the event any country discriminated against the United States. He added that he saw no violation of the UN Charter or conflict with the inter-American system in Section 202(e).

It is reported that the Ambassador subsequently informed an American sugar producer that his government will take economic reprisals against all American nationals in Cuba unless Section 202(e) is removed. While it seems doubtful whether these somewhat hysterical threats and allegations will be acted upon by the Cuban Government, they are at least indicative of the Ambassador's desire to have us deprive ourselves of our bargaining power in future relations.

I regard Section 202(e) as essential to the protection of American investments in Cuba, valued at approximately $750,000,000, and to the settlement of the many long-pending problems affecting United States-Cuban relations. This conviction derives from the refusal of the Cuban Government over many years to grant reasonable and moderate requests for fairer treatment of U.S. nationals. It is strengthened by statements recently made to officers of this Department by the Cuban Ambassador that Cuba would place import restrictions on American products and take other measures which would be objectionable to American commerce if sugar legislation considered unfair to Cuba is enacted. Repeated assurances and promises from the President

---

[23] Dean Acheson, Under Secretary of State.
[24] TIAS No. 1543, or 60 Stat. (pt. 2) 1831.
[25] Department of State Treaty Series No. 993, or 59 Stat. (pt. 2) 1031.

of Cuba and other high officials that remedial action would be taken have proved meaningless.

The bargaining power provided in Section 202(e) will be of indispensable help in achieving the following important objectives:

1. Protection of U.S.-owned Cuban sugar mills against inequitable treatment. Indications have already been received that when the Cuban Government attempts to reduce sugar production to a normal level, it may be unable to resist pressure that reduction be accomplished at the expense of U.S. sugar mills.

2. Conclusion of a commercial treaty which our Government for years has been endeavoring to negotiate with Cuba. Such a treaty is of paramount importance to American business interests because of discriminatory practices against U.S. firms and of a rising tide of nationalism.

3. Settlement of claims of United States nationals amounting to approximately $9,000,000, some of which have been pending for over thirty years.

A copy of Section 202(e) is attached.[26]

G. C. MARSHALL

837.61351/7-1147

Memorandum of Conversation, by Mr. Duncan A. Mackay of the Division of Caribbean Affairs

RESTRICTED [WASHINGTON,] July 11, 1947.

Participants: Señor Guillermo Belt, Ambassador of Cuba
Mr. Norman Armour, Assistant Secretary of State
Mr. James Wright, Department of State (ARA)
Mr. William W. Walker, Department of State (CRB)
Mr. Duncan Mackay, Department of State (CRB)

Ambassador Belt called this afternoon at his own request to discuss his government's protest of June 24, 1947 over the inclusion in the proposed sugar legislation of Section 202(e) (which gives to the Secretary of Agriculture the authority to withhold from any foreign country that denies fair and equitable treatment to United States interests any increase in the sugar quota) and to inquire whether the State Department could exercise its influence to have it deleted. The Ambassador observed that the House Conference Report indicated that it was at the instigation of the Department that this clause was included. He referred to the provision as a violation of the Drago doctrine, and said that his government would consider the inclusion of this clause as an unfriendly act. He foresaw the possibility that Cuba

---

[26] Not printed.

might (1) not be present at the Rio or Bogotá conferences [27] and (2) refer the matter to the governing board of the Pan-American Union, should this clause be included in the legislation.

The Ambassador was informed that a reply to his note was awaiting the Secretary's signature. Mr. Armour brought to the Ambassador's attention the fact that the bill had already cleared the House earlier in the day and that it was presumably even now on the Senate calendar, since it had already passed the Senate Finance Committee. He indicated, therefore, that it was highly improbable at this juncture that such an amendment would be made. Mr. Armour expressed surprise that this clause should be regarded as discriminatory to Cuba since it has often been included in previous tariff acts, and since it was not expected that Cuba would willfully render itself subject to the conditions of this clause. Information from the Embassy at Habana had indicated, furthermore, that only the Communist newspaper *Hoy* has so far objected to the proposed bill. Mr. Armour stressed the fact that the Executive Committee which considered the bill had actually felt that the wording was not strong enough and that Mr. Walker had testified at the final hearing against stronger wording of the clause. Mr. Armour told the Ambassador that it would be regrettable if Cuba should not be present at the Río and Bogotá conferences. The Ambassador was further informed that since this particular legislation was a domestic matter, referring it to the Pan-American Union or other international body would be an infringement of the sovereign rights of this country. Mr. Wright remarked that on numerous occasions the Ambassador had been acquainted with the dissatisfaction of the Congress over the failure of the Cuban Government to settle the pecuniary claims of American interests in Cuba. Lack of positive action on the part of the Cuban Government was probably responsible, in part, for the inclusion of this clause in the legislation. The Ambassador would not admit that the Tribunal de Cuentas still lacked the authority to settle all American claims. Mr. Wright then made reference to the unsatisfactory practice of including American claims in the "floating debt". The Ambassador felt that pressure was being brought to bear on Cuba which might mar the historically good relations between the two nations. He was reminded of the efforts of this Government to negotiate a mutually satisfactory treaty of friendship, commerce and navigation.

[27] Inter-American Conference for the Maintenance of Continental Peace and Security, Quitandinha, Brazil, August 15–September 2, 1947; for documentation on this Conference, see pp. 1 ff; and Ninth International Conference of American States, scheduled to be held at Bogotá, March 30–May 2, 1948; for documentation on preparations in 1947 for this Conference, see bracketed note p. 94.

The Ambassador then brought up the desire of the Cuban Government to purchase four coastal cargo ships from the Maritime Commission. He was informed that our reply of May 28, 1947 to the Cuban note of April 16, 1947 [28] in this regard still stood, since no satisfactory written agreement has been effected which would guarantee protection to U.S. shipping against some of the discriminatory regulations recently promulgated by the Cuban Government.

837.61351/6–2447

The Secretary of State to the Ambassador in Cuba (Norweb)

CONFIDENTIAL WASHINGTON, July 16, 1947.
No. 1477

SIR: There is enclosed a copy of a note recently presented to Ambassador Belt in reply to the Ambassador's note of June 24, 1947 [28] expressing his government's opposition to section 202(e) of the proposed Sugar Act of 1948. A copy of the latter note is also enclosed.

You should seek an early interview with President Grau and hand him a copy of the Department's note. In discussing the matter with the President, you should explain that this Government is naturally anxious to maintain mutually advantageous relationships between the United States and friendly neighboring nations. It should also be explained that the bill makes a sincere endeavor to distribute fairly and equitably the United States market for an important food supply. You should point out that, naturally, this Government feels that United States interests abroad should be given assurances of fair and equitable treatment.

You should inform President Grau of the constant desire of this Government to find a mutually satisfactory basis for resolving the problems which confront United States nationals in Cuba. In this connection, you may wish to refer to some of your previous conversations with him and the Foreign Minister, and also to the numerous discussions held in Washington between Ambassador Belt and officers of the Department.

It would be well to mention to the President that on January 30, 1947 you presented a complete draft of a proposed commercial treaty [29] to the Cuban Minister of State in accordance with the desire of this Government to make every possible effort to negotiate mutually satisfactory assurances of fair and equitable treatment for the nationals, commerce, and industry of each of the two countries in the territory

---

[28] Neither printed.
[29] Not printed.

of the other. Copies of this draft were also presented to Ambassador Belt on June 8, 1947.

You should call the President's attention to the fact that no response has been received to a copy of a note which you presented to him on December 30, 1946 [31] concerning this Government's position with respect to the settlement of pecuniary claims of United States nationals against the Cuban Government. In reviewing this matter with the President, you should allude to Cuba's exceptionally favorable financial position and express the hope that these long-pending obligations will be promptly discharged. It should again be made clear to the President that this Government cannot regard seriously the inclusion of any American claims in the "floating debt" as an acceptable excuse for nonpayment of such claims pending the establishment of a Tribunal of accounts, since no state can justify its failure to fulfill its international obligations on the ground that its municipal legislation is defective.

In your conversation with the President, you should emphasize that comparatively little action on the part of the Cuban Government would be required to resolve almost all of these problems. You should also emphasize that since the requests that have been made from time to time by this Government are all moderate and reasonable, it should not be difficult for the Cuban Government, if it wishes to do so, practically to eliminate any possibility that section 202(e) of the proposed Sugar Act could be applicable to Cuba.

Very truly yours, For the Secretary of State:
NORMAN ARMOUR

837.00B/7–1847

The Ambassador in Cuba (Norweb) to the Secretary of State

RESTRICTED HABANA, July 18, 1947.
No. 4177

SIR: I have the honor to enclose a report [32] which brings up to date my impressions of the Communist movement in Cuba and the position of the Communist Party.

This report may seem to the Department to be repetitious, presenting an old picture in no particularly new light. If this is so, it is because the Cuban political scene is per se repetitious; and in again summarizing the play of forces and the vacillation of personalities, it is my intention to stress the almost unvarying monotony of the theme current to such reports, almost any month of any recent year.

---

[31] *Foreign Relations*, 1946, vol. XI, p. 770.
[32] Not printed.

One reason for this is, I believe, that in the plethora of political parties and intra-party groups one can only with difficulty find any real principles to which men have committed their public careers, any concrete or far-sighted program which would warrant their control of public affairs and the public purse. The slogan "Cubanidad" was at best a formless rallying-cry, and the great expectations which seemed justified in the beginning of the present administration have faded into a weary general acceptance of "Plus ça change . . ." We have now the familiar spectacle of the same people jockeying for place and power, first in one alignment and then another. The combinations and re-combinations change, but the main participants seldom, and I am unable to recall a significant or plausible public statement of any principles involved in these shifts. To invoke principles might indeed have been too cynical.

There is one group which can, however, conjure up a more solid symbolism and some form of apologia for its actions: the Communist Party, which, perhaps because it is not called upon to implement it, can produce the clearest blue-print of them all. Perhaps it is this factor which gives the Party its value as a makeweight in the political scales, for while its active membership may not be as large nor as influential as claimed, its voice is loud and insistent and there is in Cuba no countervailing party voice that can match its public pronouncements in evoking the good will and the good hopes of the politically immature masses. (The President, and also Senator Chibás, speak with authority to a wide audience: but I am referring to the influence of parties, not the impact of personalities—and in any case the voice of the President no longer seems to reach his people from Sinai.)

The attached report will show that the situation which obtained when President Grau was a candidate in 1944 is again crystallizing. The leaders, in "choosing sides" for the game, may not wish to give the nod to the Communists, but cannot ignore them. While the old associations, between the President and the Party are on the wane, they have used each other in the past and, having ridden each other's tiger, each now wonders how best to dismount. I have on several occasions in informal conversation made an appeal to Grau's broader statesmanship (as in the talk reported on page 2 of the enclosure), pointing out that the Communist movement is a world-wide phenomenon with no real nationalist allegiance, in which we may all be engulfed unless action so concerted on its part is met with equally concerted action among ourselves. Others, I know, made similar representations as to the danger of his course, and the cumulative effect of this pressure—plus the impact of the East-West cleavage—is becoming manifest in his attitude. I believe, however, that it is his personal disenchantment with the Party on local political issues that has made him receptive to any idea of a break.

As the enclosed report indicates, there is no way of judging at this time to what extent the split in the ranks of Labor will reduce the effectiveness of the Communist Party; but though this may be lessened, it will not be negligible, and the status of the Party will be better revealed when we can see into what part of the Cuban political jigsaw it next fits itself. There will be many factors: whether the opposition can unite, whether an honest election will and can be staged, what the political climate is elsewhere in the world. One of the more controlling factors, however, will be the price of sugar. Some continued measure of prosperity will have as much effect as the slogans of any party—if not more; and this again is one of the great repetitions in the Cuban scene.

Respectfully yours, R. HENRY NORWEB

837.61351/8-847 : Telegram

The Secretary of State to the Embassy in Cuba

RESTRICTED WASHINGTON, August 8, 1947—7 p. m.

394. President signed Sugar Act 10:30 a. m. today. White House released 1:00 p. m. letter to President from me dated yesterday body of which reads:

"It is my understanding that you have before you for consideration the General Sugar Act of 1948.[33] During recent days I have been impressed by the fears expressed in certain quarters that section 202(e) of the Act constitutes an economic threat to sugar supplying nations of this hemisphere. This section reads as follows: (Text)
Section 101(a) of the Act reads: (Text)
These fears should be allayed.
I wish to emphasize that the permissive provisions of section 202(e) of the Act do not refer to basic quotas, but rather give discretion to withhold an increase in the quotas under certain conditions. It is not intended to substitute for or replace the orderly processes of settling differences, including international arbitration."

MARSHALL

837.61351/7-847

Memorandum of Conversation, by the Assistant Secretary of State (Armour)

RESTRICTED [WASHINGTON,] August 8, 1947.

The Ambassador [34] called this morning by appointment made at his request by telephone from New York where he had been staying.

---

[33] Public Law No. 388, August 8, 1947, "Sugar Act of 1948", 61 Stat. 922.
[34] The Cuban Ambassador, Guillermo Belt.

I opened the conversation by asking him when he planned to leave for Rio. He said this would depend somewhat on how far we could go in reaching a satisfactory arrangement over the controversial clause in the Sugar Bill, which was the particular object of his visit. He said he wondered whether this could perhaps be accomplished by an exchange of notes. He understood the Bill would be signed by the President today.

I confirmed this and then showed him the letter from the Secretary to the President which it was planned to have released at the White House at the time the Bill was signed, probably about one o'clock. The Ambassador read the note and expressed himself as pleased with it, particularly the reference to arbitration in the last sentence. He said that this was exactly what he, himself, had at one time proposed and he felt sure the publication of the letter would go far to help things. In any event, he proposed to telephone to the President (Grau San Martin) at once and read the letter to him, a copy of which I furnished him.

The Ambassador then told me that he hoped after his return from Rio we could get together with a view to exploring the possibilities of concluding the long deferred treaty of friendship, commerce and navigation. He believed that these conversations would lead to a settlement of many of the outstanding questions and was convinced that the signing of such a treaty would go a long way to put our relations on the firm and friendly basis where they belonged.

I told the Ambassador that I felt the negotiation of such a treaty would be a constructive step forward. I then told him that I had frankly been disappointed by the attitude he had shown regarding Article 202e of the Sugar Bill. Admitting that he had objected to this clause, his action in taking his case to the American press, Members of Congress, and particularly his extensive remarks before the Pan American Union had, I felt, not only confused the issue, but had created an erroneous impression as to the meaning of the article itself. The issue had even reached Rio where the Brazilian Foreign Minister had consulted our Ambassador as to its significance.

I told the Ambassador I thought he would agree that the general situation in the Caribbean area, notably the Dominican Republic, and certain sections of Central and South America, was not a particularly happy one as the curtain-raiser to the Conference and I regretted that he had found it necessary to make such an open issue of this particular clause in the Sugar Bill, which had had the effect of adding one more confusing element to the general picture. For this reason, I hoped, if he felt the publication of the Secretary's letter had clarified the situation, that he or his Government would make this clear. After Rio, as he had suggested, we could then proceed to consider the more fundamental problems.

The Ambassador after further attempt to explain his position, said that he would see to it that his Government's approval of the action taken to clarify the issue was made officially known both in Cuba and the other American republics.

Ambassador Belt later telephoned to say that he had read the letter to President Grau San Martín and that the latter had expressed himself as entirely satisfied with it. The Ambassador said that they would have liked to have had the language a little more specific but assured me they were not disposed to question it and repeated that they were entirely satisfied.

NORMAN ARMOUR

837.852/8-2847 : Telegram

The Acting Secretary of State to the Embassy in Cuba

CONFIDENTIAL WASHINGTON, August 29, 1947—5 p. m.

431. Prior to telling Barón [35] that we would recommend Maritime Commission release ships if Order 20 were revoked, we gave most complete study to possibility of making some agreement which would provide necessary safeguards for US vessels. (Urtel 511, Aug 28).[36] It was concluded this would be impracticable owing to fact that even in US, agreement, which would have to be reciprocal could not by-pass our Congress without its consent. We could not ask Cuba to freeze *status quo* if we were not prepared to do so in this country which we definitely are not. We will simply have to await treaty and Dept does not feel that holding up these ships will hasten treaty in proportion to amount of other differences it will create.

LOVETT

---

[35] The Acting Secretary of State informed the Embassy in Cuba, in telegram 425, August 26, 1947, 4 p. m., that the Cuban Chargé (Barón) had been informed that the Department would recommend the sale of four merchant vessels provided Resolution 20 was abolished (837.852/8-2547). General Order No. 20 of the Cuban Maritime Commission, concerning the utilization of small vessels, was one of the more objectionable shipping decrees considered by the Department to be detrimental to United States shipping.

[36] Not printed: in this telegram Ambassador Norweb emphasized that cancellation of Resolution 20 would not prevent issuance of new and more drastic resolution once the ships were delivered. It was accordingly recommended by the Embassy that special agreement affording necessary safeguards for US vessels be obtained as contingent requirement in proposed transaction, and that such agreement could be superseded by suitable provisions in the commercial treaty if and when negotiated. (837.852/8-2847)

[By telegram 537, September 15, 4 p. m., the Embassy informed the Department that General Order No. 20 of the Cuban Maritime Commission was cancelled on September 12, 1947 (837.852/9–1547).

The Department recommended in a memorandum of September 24, 1947, that the Maritime Commission favorably consider the sale to the Cuban Government of the four vessels of the C1MAV1 type (837.852/9–1547).

The Commissioner, United States Maritime Commission (Parkhurst), in letter of October 29, informed Assistant Secretary of State Armour that the Commission had authorized the sale of four C1MAV1's to the Republic of Cuba (837.852/10–2947).]

437.11/11–1247

The Secretary of State to the Cuban Ambassador (Belt)

WASHINGTON, November 12, 1947.

EXCELLENCY: I have the honor to refer to the Department's note of December 30, 1946 [37] concerning the possible satisfaction of various claims of United States nationals against the Government of Cuba, and to Your Excellency's acknowledgment of January 20, 1947.[38]

As the nature of the recognized claims appeared to be well understood by both Governments, it was hoped that Your Excellency's Government would find it possible to effect an early settlement. It was also hoped that Your Excellency's Government would furnish this Government with its views on the draft claims convention which was suggested in the Department's note of December 30, 1946.

Numerous inquiries have been received in regard to the status of these claims, both from members of Congress and from claimants whose efforts to arrange a satisfactory settlement with the Cuban Government have been unavailing. I am sure that Your Excellency will appreciate that this problem, which has been the subject of numerous conversations between representatives of our Governments, will doubtless evoke additional inquiries. It would be greatly appreciated, therefore, if Your Excellency's Government would be so kind as to give my Government the benefit of its views concerning the proposals in the Department's note of December 30, 1946, and in particular the

---

[37] *Foreign Relations*, 1946, vol. XI, p. 770.
[38] Not printed.

proposal for an arbitral Mixed Claims Commission to determine the extent of the validity of claims that have not as yet been adjudicated.[39]

Accept [etc.] For the Secretary of State:
NORMAN ARMOUR

837.61351/11–2847

Statement Released to the Press by the White House, November 28, 1947

The President today issued a proclamation, under authority of the Sugar Act of 1937, as amended, which will make possible the establishment of sugar marketing quotas by the Department of Agriculture in 1948. Because of wartime shortages, sugar quotas have been in suspension, also by Presidential proclamation, since April 13, 1942.

However, because sugar supplies in the areas which normally supply the U.S. market are expected to be more than ample to meet United States requirements in 1948, it now appears that sugar quotas again will be required to insure orderly marketing of sugar. This proclamation is issued now in order to permit the holding of several public hearings and the completion of other preparatory work necessary for the establishment of quotas in 1948. In the event of any significant change in either supply or demand conditions, the quota provisions of the Sugar Act could again be suspended, under authority of the Sugar Act of 1948, the Act which succeeds the Sugar Act of 1937.

Title II of the Sugar Act of 1948, which succeeds the Sugar Act of 1937, contains the quota provisions of the Act. Section 201 provides

---

[39] Acknowledging receipt of the Secretary's note of November 12, Ambassador Belt informed Secretary Marshall in a note of November 21 that while the Executive branch of the Cuban Government was "most anxious" to make some arrangement for the settlement of the claims, the matter was, under the Constitution, not for the Executive branch but for the Legislative branch and also the Tribunal of Accounts (437.11/11–2147).

In a memorandum of December 9, 1947, to the Assistant Chief of the Division of Caribbean Affairs (Walker) the Assistant Legal Adviser for International Claims (English) stated: "It is not believed that the provisions of the Constitution support that position", taken by Ambassador Belt, adding: "Even it be assumed that the allegations made in the note are true, that is, that under Cuban law the responsibility for making settlement is in the Legislative branch and a non-existent agency of the Cuban Government, that situation cannot operate to relieve the Cuban Government of its international obligation under international law . . . the principle of international law that the failure of a state to give effect to the decisions of its own courts in favor of aliens, particularly judgments against the state, constitutes a denial of justice, is so well settled as to require no citation of authority. It is also well settled that a state cannot be permitted to evade its responsibilities in that regard under international law by setting up its own municipal law." (437.11/12–947)

that the Secretary of Agriculture shall determine the amount of sugar needed to fulfill U.S. requirements, each year—and in the case of 1948, this amount is to be named during the first ten days of January 1948. Section 202 sets total domestic quotas at 4,268,000 short tons, raw value, divided as follows: Domestic Beet Sugar, 1,800,000 tons; Mainland Cane Sugar, 500,000 tons; Hawaii, 1,052,000 tons; Puerto Rico 910,000 tons; Virgin Islands, 6,000 tons.

The quota for the Republic of the Philippines is 952,000 short tons of sugar. The balance of the required sugar is prorated to other foreign countries, with Cuba receiving 98.64 percent of such amount and all other foreign countries receiving 1.36 percent of such amount. Cuba also benefits substantially from any Philippine production deficit. Provision is also made for distributing production deficits in other areas.

611.3731/12-3147

The Acting Secretary of State to President Truman

WASHINGTON, December 31, 1947.

MY DEAR MR. PRESIDENT: On December 17, 1947 the Protocol for the Provisional Application of the General Agreement on Tariffs and Trade, concluded at Geneva on October 30, 1947,[40] was signed on behalf of the Cuban Government, and a few days later an agreement was reached between this Government and the Government of Cuba that the exclusive supplementary agreement concluded by the two governments at Geneva shall be applied on January 1, 1948.[41] Because of the particular language of the Trade Agreements Act relating to the modification of the preferential treatment of Cuban products imported into the United States, it has been considered desirable to proclaim this exclusive supplementary agreement with Cuba as a separate trade agreement. This agreement continues preferential treatment for some of the most important imports from Cuba, and eliminates the preference on numerous other products which are in most cases of little or no importance to Cuba.

There is enclosed for your signature, if you approve, a draft proc-

---

[40] For the General Agreement on Tariffs and Trade, with annexes and schedules and protocol of provisional application, concluded at Geneva, October 30, 1947, see TIAS No. 1700, or 61 Stat. (pts. 5 and 6). For documentation on this subject, see volume I.

[41] For exclusive agreement supplementary to the General Agreement on Tariffs and Trade, exchanges of notes and memoranda, signed at Geneva October 30, 1947, and supplementary exchange of notes signed at Washington December 19 and 22, 1947, see TIAS No. 1703, or 61 Stat. (pt. 4) 3699.

lamation carrying out this exclusive trade agreement as from January 1, 1948.[42]

Faithfully yours,

ROBERT A. LOVETT

AGREEMENT BETWEEN THE UNITED STATES AND CUBA AMENDING AND EXTENDING THE AGREEMENT OF JULY 17 AND AUGUST 2, 1944, RESPECTING A COOPERATIVE PROGRAM FOR WEATHER STATIONS IN CUBA

[Effected by exchange of notes signed at Habana August 21, 1947, and January 27, 1948. For texts of notes, see Department of State Treaties and Other International Acts Series (TIAS) No. 1847, or 62 Stat. (pt. 3) 3134. For texts of notes of July 17 and August 2, 1944, see TIAS No. 1842, or 61 Stat. (pt. 4) 3699.]

---

[42] For the President's Proclamation of December 16, 1947, putting into effect the General Agreement on Tariffs and Trade as of January 1, 1948, see Department of State *Bulletin*, December 28, 1947, pp. 12–58.

The President issued on January 1, 1948, a proclamation putting into effect as of January 1, 1948, the provisions of the exclusive agreement, signed by the United States and Cuba on October 30, 1947, supplementary to the general agreement on tariffs and trade signed at Geneva on the same date (see statement in Department of State *Bulletin*, January 11, 1948, p. 60).

DOMINICAN REPUBLIC

UNITED STATES POLICY OF NONINTERVENTION IN DOMINICAN POLITICAL AFFAIRS [1]

839.00/12-2446

The Secretary of State to the Ambassador in the Dominican Republic (Butler)

SECRET   WASHINGTON, February 19, 1947.

No. 131

SIR: Reference is made to your recent recommendations with respect to possible multilateral action by the American republics to deal with the political situation in the Dominican Republic, which constitutes a flagrant departure in practice from basic principles to which all the American republics have pledged themselves with respect to the protection of human rights. These recommendations were contained, specifically, in the Embassy's secret despatches nos. 223 of November 22, 1946, and 306 of December 24, 1946, and in the Embassy's secret telegram no. 380 of December 2, 1946.[2]

As you know, these recommendations raise the question of the nature of "intervention" within the meaning of the nonintervention commitments assumed by this Government in common with the other governments of the American republics. These commitments are contained in Article 8 of the Convention on Rights and Duties of States (Montevideo, 1933)[3] and the Additional Protocol Relative to Non-Intervention (Buenos Aires, 1936).[4] It is this Government's belief that action by the organized community of nations with respect to transgressions by one of their number, in accordance with established principles of

---

[1] For previous documentation on delineation of policies for guidance in the conduct of general relations of the United States with the Dominican Republic, United States rejection of Dominican requests for military aid, and attitude of the United States with respect to Communist activities in the Dominican Republic, see *Foreign Relations*, 1946, vol. XI, pp. 805 ff.

[2] For despatch 306 of December 24, 1946, see *ibid.*, p. 811; despatch 223 and telegram 380 not printed.

[3] For text, see Department of State Treaty Series No. 881, or 49 Stat. (pt. 2) 3097; for documentation concerning the Seventh International Conference of American States, held at Montevideo, December 3-26, 1933, see *Foreign Relations*, 1933, vol. IV, pp. 1 ff.

[4] For text, see Department of State Treaty Series No. 923, or 51 Stat. 41; for documentation concerning the Inter-American Conference for the Maintenance of Peace held at Buenos Aires, December 1-23, 1936, see *Foreign Relations*, 1936, vol. V, pp. 3 ff.

the community, does not constitute intervention. On the contrary, the Department believes that such multilateral action is the alternative to, and, in a sense, the antithesis of intervention. Such action by the community would be in substitution for arbitrary intervention by individual nations that have the power to practice it.

The agitation of this problem among the American republics in the past two years has, however, led the Department to believe that, for the most part, the majority of them are not yet prepared to accept this view. You will recall that the response of the majority to the proposal made by the Uruguayan Foreign Minister in November, 1945 [5] (that the protection of human rights within any particular American republic be considered in certain circumstances a proper subject for action by the community of American republics) was not favorable. In fact, that proposal and the support of it by the United States appeared to have the effect of arousing the suspicions of many of them and of putting them on guard against any proposal that would appear to limit their respective sovereignties, whether that limitation was imposed by individual powers or by the organized inter-American community.

The fact that the United States has such preponderant power in the Hemisphere argues the necessity of particular caution on its part in dealing with this problem. The experience of the Department indicates that any move by this Government at this time in support of the principle of action by the community is more likely to arouse resistance among the majority of the other American republics than to win their favor. This may be accounted for by the suspicion that the United States might practice what was, in effect, unilateral intervention under the guise of community action. This kind of suspicion is, perhaps, the penalty of power.

Under the circumstances, the Department believes that the community of American republics is not yet prepared to accept the principle of multilateral action for the protection of human rights. It is also persuaded that any proposal for such action would have less chance of acceptance if it should come from the United States than if it should come from other American republics. Consequently, while the Department looks forward to the time when the authority of the organized community in these matters is generally acknowledged and supported, it believes that for the present that objective is most likely of early attainment if this Government refrains from pressing the other American governments with respect to it.

In this connection, it should be noted that there is at present no

---

[5] For documentation on this subject, see *Foreign Relations*, 1945, vol. IX, pp. 185 ff.

provision in the agreements on which the inter-American system is based for action by the community of nations to deal with such a situation as exists in the Dominican Republic.

The Department appreciates, of course, that the situation in the Dominican Republic might become aggravated to such a critical point as to arouse a greater willingness than would now be found among the American republics to take joint action with respect to it. In such case, the United States would undoubtedly support the taking of such action, within the limits imposed by the Charter of the United Nations.

The Department is in full agreement with the following statement in your secret despatch no. 306 of December 24, 1946:

"Again, hope seems to lie in multilateral action based on democratic principles which have been proclaimed, if not observed, by all of the American Republics. If the American Republics wish to handle their affairs under a mutually satisfactory arrangement with the United Nations, then they must make the inter-American system a live force devoted to the attainment of the general welfare, peace and security of the peoples of the Americas. Problems of armament and hemisphere defense, of the duties as well as the rights of states, of the protection of individual rights and civil liberties, and of real freedom of information in all countries must be faced and workable solutions found which will be genuinely supported by a substantial majority of the American nations."

The difficulty at present would be to obtain the requisite support of "a substantial majority of the American nations".

The Department is in accord with the further suggestion in your despatch no. 306 of December 24 regarding the desirability of this Government's issuing a press release concerning the policy of the United States in inter-American affairs, and it is the Department's present intention to take steps in this direction as soon as the moment is opportune. Meanwhile, the Department wishes you to know of the appreciation with which it has received your views on this and the other matters discussed in your despatches under reference.

Very truly yours, For the Secretary of State:
SPRUILLE BRADEN [6]

837.00/3–1347

The Secretary of State to the Embassy in Cuba

SECRET WASHINGTON, March 13, 1947.
No. 1322

The Secretary of State refers to reports originating in Havana, Caracas and Ciudad Trujillo, regarding reported revolutionary plot-

---
[6] Assistant Secretary of State for American Republic Affairs.

ting in the United States by political exiles of Cuba, Venezuela and the Dominican Republic.

As many of the informants have been of unknown reliability, it has been difficult to evaluate the reports. However, the Department, in conjunction with other agencies of the Government, is making every effort to discover whether or not American laws are being violated by these exile groups.

Should the Government to which you are accredited make inquiry concerning this matter, you are authorized, at your discretion, to inform the Foreign Office of the action being taken by this Government. You may also inform the Foreign Office that, in the event it has any concrete evidences of revolutionary expeditions being planned in the United States, the Department would be glad to receive such information for appropriate action.

A similar instruction has been sent to Caracas and Ciudad Trujillo.

839.00/3–2447

The Acting Secretary of State to the Embassy in the Dominican Republic

SECRET WASHINGTON, April 15, 1947.
No. 178

The Acting Secretary of State refers to the Department's airgram No. A–41 of February 26, Embassy's airgram No. A–76 of March 4, and the Embassy's telegrams No. 51 of March 13 and No. 56 of March 24.[7] These communications deal with the appearance of suspicious aircraft, apparently originating in the United States and appearing in the Dominican Republic.

This situation has received consideration in the Department. The following information is provided for the Embassy's use in dealing with this situation. The only aircraft among those mentioned for which export licenses were issued are the PBY–5A and the OA–10. It is believed that these are the same amphibious planes observed at Santiago and Ciudad Trujillo. These planes were to be sold to the Compañía Aviación Dominicana and were to be converted to cargo carriers. If these planes were resold to the Dominican Army or if they are being used to train Dominican Air Force personnel, such action is contrary to the understanding held at the time the export licenses were issued and was not contemplated in the issuance of the licenses. Any information which can be obtained locally as the actual manner in which the transfer of the planes from the Compañía Aviación Dominicana to the

---

[7] None printed.

Dominican Army was accomplished should be reported to the Department, so that further transactions of this type may be forestalled.

No licenses have been issued for the export of any B–14 or P–38 type planes to the Dominican Republic or any of the adjacent areas. If planes of this type seen in the Dominican Republic were flown out of the United States, this was done illegally and no records are available concerning them.

It is desired that any further information obtainable in the Dominican Republic concerning the source of these suspicious aircraft be reported to the Department so that it may be forwarded to the agencies investigating this situation.

The information concerning these aircraft has been made available to Military Intelligence for use in an Army investigation of this problem, particularly the desire of the Dominican Government to obtain planes from Borinquen field. Similarly, a report has been made to the Federal Bureau of Investigation, with a request that these aircraft be investigated, as well as the attempts to export other contraband implements of war to the Caribbean and Central American areas.

. . . .

711.39/5–647 : Telegram

The Ambassador in the Dominican Republic (Butler) to the Secretary of State

CONFIDENTIAL CIUDAD TRUJILLO, May 6, 1947—10 a. m.

97. Recent Embassy despatches have reported on the critical attitude of several chiefs of mission of resident diplomatic corps to the Trujillo Government.[8] During a conversation with Foreign Minister [9] last evening he spoke informally about political situation and attitude of diplomatic corps. He made a direct plea for my assistance in bringing about a more friendly and cooperative attitude so as to help him in his task. He claimed that for his part he always has been able to get along very well with the diplomatic corps and always is ready to extend every cooperation.

I pointed out to the Foreign Minister that the Embassy has cooperated in cases where such action is to the mutual advantage of the two peoples and governments. I reiterated the policy of absolute nonintervention—neither opposition to nor support of the Trujillo administration—in Dominican political affairs. I told him that I was making a very conscientious effort to be objective and fair but that, speaking very frankly, I was forced to the conclusion that democratic institu-

---

[8] Gen. Rafael Leonidas Trujillo Molina, President of the Dominican Republic.
[9] Arturo Despradel.

tions and practices, as we conceive of them in the US, did not exist in the Dominican Republic. I told him that that was the job of the Dominican people and that the US did not intend to interfere. I reminded him that President Truman had instructed me to cooperate fully on the basis of the inter-American system, as outlined by President Truman in his Pan-American Day address last year.[10]

The Foreign Minister then made the usual argument that cooperation is essential to combat Communism. I assured him that the last desire or intention of this Embassy was to give any encouragement or support to Communists, but I expressed the opinion that all political opposition is not necessarily Communist. The Foreign Minister could see no problem except the world wide and extremely dangerous Communist threat. I repeated that my own government intended to continue the fight for real democracy and all that it implied, and that in my opinion any anti-democratic forces, whether of the right or the left, were contrary to the democratic principles of the inter-American system.

It is possible that the Foreign Minister will seek permission from President Trujillo to talk to me again in order "to convince me that real democracy exists in the Dominican Republic and that Trujillo has the overwhelming support of the Dominican people". This development of course is directly related to the coming elections and to an obviously critical attitude on the part of some chiefs of mission here. Unless instructed to the contrary, I shall continue to express to the Foreign Minister views similar to those outlined above. I should like to add that the Government of the US necessarily must base its policies on conclusions drawn from all of the information available to the Department over a period of 20 years and more, and to emphasize again that our present relations with the Dominican Government indicate neither support of nor opposition to President Trujillo.

BUTLER

839.00/5–2847

The Ambassador in the Dominican Republic (Butler) to the Secretary of State

SECRET   CIUDAD TRUJILLO, May 28, 1947.
No. 790

SIR: Referring to the Department's secret telegram no. 75 of May 5, 7 p. m.,[11] I have the honor to report upon the results and some of the probable effects of the Dominican elections held on May 16, 1947.

---

[10] April 14, 1962, Department of State *Bulletin*, April 28, 1946, p. 720.
[11] Not printed.

President Trujillo was re-elected for another five-year term by an overwhelming majority. That was a foregone conclusion. Congress will be composed almost entirely of members of the Dominican (Trujillo) Party. There never was any doubt about that. The elections were technically free according to Dominican constitutional and legal requirements. In view of our non-intervention policy, we cannot challenge the "freedom" of these elections, although the "campaign", the electoral procedure, and the whole business of the elections certainly did not conform in any way to our standards of free and democratic elections.

As a result of the elections, President Trujillo now can: (*a*) continue almost unchallenged in the exercise of his dictatorial powers, (*b*) continue to claim credit for the material progress of the country under his administration, (*c*) bring pressure to bear for active cooperation with the United States and other countries against the great danger of communism—a danger which probably is comparatively insignificant in the Dominican Republic, (*d*) give renewed drive to his constant effort to obtain credit and publicity as a leader in inter-American and international affairs, and (*e*) claim a direct and overwhelming mandate from the Dominican people as approval of and support for his program and actions. His position is a strong one.

The Department and the Embassy, as matters stand at present, are severely restricted in any effort to counteract the anti-democratic influences of the Trujillo regime. We still can insist upon our policy that American firms and citizens should not be involved in any way in Dominican politics. We can refuse to be drawn into any program of cooperation against alleged communists, when the latter—as so often happens—are merely anti-Trujillo rather than communist. The force of public opinion is a factor; but Trujillo has proved time and again that he has the cash and the will to obtain favorable publicity abroad. Unfortunately, he has been able, by one means or another, to persuade prominent Americans and other foreigners, in public, business or private life, to plead his cause and to support him. There is little evidence of any strong anti-Trujillo feeling among the Dominican masses. Further, since we are not in a position to challenge the "freedom" of the May 16 elections, it is useless to reiterate that we have a warmer feeling of friendship for and greater desire to cooperate with governments that rest upon the periodically expressed consent of the governed. Finally, multilateral action to protect human rights appears not to be feasible at present (see Department's secret airmail instruction 131, dated February 19, 1947).

Before making suggestions about future courses of action, comment will be made on several phases of the Dominican elections and political situation.

[Here follow data under headings "Background", "Election Results", and "Factors in New Phase of United States-Dominican Relations".]

Conclusions and Recommendations:

The foregoing review of the Dominican political situation and of relations between the United States and the Dominican Republic forces me to the conclusion that a more direct and positive approach to our policy will be necessary during the coming five years of the Trujillo administration. Either we will have to make clear to the Trujillo Government why we do not intend to cooperate with it as we would cooperate with a genuinely democratic government, or we will have to overlook the fundamental matter of principle involved and accept at face value many of Trujillo's trappings of democracy. The Embassy recommends the former course of action, but such a course would have to be approved of and supported by the President and the Secretary of State, as well as by the Department officers directly concerned with Dominican affairs.

In my despatch no. 199 of November 18, 1946, I raised the question of whether or not it would be desirable and useful to have an Ambassador here as Chief of Mission rather than to have a competent officer as Chargé d'Affaires for a period of time. The Department's secret airmail Instruction no. 96 of December 26, 1946, in reply to my despatch,[12] states in part as follows:

"Should the relationship between the Embassy and President Trujillo develop in such a way that you feel the conduct of Embassy business is being severely hindered, you might consider the formulation of a specific recommendation in the above sense."

I wish now to suggest two alternative courses of action for the Department's consideration:

1) The first alternative involves a full and frank exchange of views, the substance and form to be worked out by the Department and the Embassy, between the Governments of the United States and the Dominican Republic. It should be made clear that on the basis of its records and information over a period of twenty years, the Department is forced to the conclusion that many of the basic principles and institutions of democracy, which the United States believes in and which are written into inter-American and United Nations documents, have not been observed in the Dominican Republic over a long period of years. Consequently, the Government of the United States cannot in good faith maintain as friendly and cooperative a relationship with the Dominican Government as it does with governments and peoples which are so much closer in principle and practice to the Government

---

[12] For despatch 199, November 18, 1946, and instruction 96, December 26, 1946, see *Foreign Relations*, 1946, vol. XI, pp. 809 and 815, respectively.

and people of the United States. I realize fully the complications and difficulties which would result from such a course of action, but I believe it to be the honest and the best solution from the point of view of our long range policies and interests.

2) So far as I know, a new American Ambassador has not been designated to succeed Ambassador Warren in Nicaragua. If this is a matter of policy, the second alternative would be to apply the same policy to the Dominican Republic. While President Trujillo would keenly resent not having an American Ambassador accredited to his country, it also would substantially weaken the prestige of his Government, both at home and abroad, if our Mission here were headed by a Chargé d'Affaires for an appreciable period of time. Experience during the time that Mr. George Scherer was in charge for several months shows that the essential interests of our country need not suffer through such an arrangement. If the Department, for any reason, would not wish to recall me openly, I would be perfectly willing and able to give personal reasons to justify my absence from my post for as long a time as the Department might consider desirable.

Respectfully yours, GEORGE H. BUTLER

839.00B/6–1247

The Ambassador in the Dominican Republic (Butler) to the Secretary of State

CONFIDENTIAL CIUDAD TRUJILLO, June 12, 1947.
No. 858

SIR: I have the honor to refer to the Embassy's despatch no. 854 of June 10, 1947 [13] entitled "President Trujillo appoints new Commission to deal with Communism", and to enclose a clipping and translation from *La Nación* of June 11, 1947,[13] consisting of a presidential message to the Congress requesting passage of a law to outlaw Communist and Communist-type parties or groups, thus forbidding their legal activity in Dominican politics. The bill itself has not been published, but it was rushed through two readings in the Senate on June 10 and now, presumably, passes to the House for consideration and action.

In his message, the President differentiates between Communists in the Dominican Republic and those in other countries. He claims that most Communists limit themselves to propagandizing certain ideals within the legal framework of the particular country, but that here, far from maintaining any constructive belief, the Communists are striving to break down the institutions and governmental machinery by violence and to do this in a brief period of time. The President, furthermore, does not fail to point out the Communists' blind obedi-

---

[13] Not printed.

ence to groups outside of the Dominican Republic who are striving to accomplish a world imperialism by old-fashioned methods.

It is possible that President Trujillo does feel some genuine fear of the local Popular Socialist (Communist) Party and the Democratic Youth, both of which are at present practically helpless opposition groups. It is more likely that President Trujillo is putting on a clever show of opposition to Communism (without, however, mentioning the USSR except by implication) in order to ride certain currents now becoming clearly noticeable in the United States. If this latter supposition is correct, the objective of the President is to use his anti-Communist program as a basis for a fairly close *rapprochement* with the United States Government; without, however, his having to yield one inch in his arbitary manner of ruling the Dominican Republic.

The Embassy's basic analysis of the Dominican political situation is contained in secret despatch no. 790 of May 28, 1947.

Respectfully yours, GEORGE H. BUTLER

839.00/6–1947

The Ambassador in the Dominican Republic (Butler) to the Secretary of State

SECRET CIUDAD TRUJILLO, June 19, 1947.
No. 886

SIR: Referring to my secret despatch No. 790 of May 28, 1947, I have the honor to supplement my report regarding the Dominican political situation, foreign policy, and relations between the United States and the Dominican Republic. The Embassy's secret telegrams 119, June 1, 3 p. m. and 125, June 11, 4 p. m.[14] contain similar additional information.

1. Developments during the past several months furnish justification for questioning the good faith of the Dominican Government in its relations with the United States and in its foreign policy:

The Venezuelan Case

In secret despatch No. 812 of June 3, 1947,[15] reference is made to a Navy Department report regarding statements of General Eleazar Lopez Contreras . . . This report clearly implicates President Trujillo and the Dominican Government in plans for an armed attack against the Betancourt Government.[16] Yet my secret telegram 10 of

---

[14] Neither printed.
[15] Not printed.
[16] Romulo Betancourt, President of the Venezuelan Revolutionary Junta.

January 10, 1947, 11 a. m.[17] reports the categorical assurance given me by the Dominican Secretary of State for Foreign Affairs that the Dominican Government was not intervening in any way in Venezuelan affairs. It seems to be established beyond reasonable doubt that General Lopez Contreras actually was in the Dominican Republic a few weeks prior to this assurance, and that he came in connection with a force being assembled here to attack Venezuela.

Meanwhile, the Dominican Government was throwing up a great smoke screen of charges that there were plots, encouraged abroad, to overthrow the Trujillo Government. Preparations were supposed to include activities in the United States, Puerto Rico, Canada, Cuba, Haiti, Mexico, Dutch West Indies, and Venezuela. This Embassy and the Department made a conscientious effort—at no small cost—to investigate these rumors and to prevent any illegal operations in the United States. . . .

Arms from the U.S.:

The Dominican Government is trying by all sorts of devious means to obtain arms and munitions from the United States. Some of these may be for use against the Betancourt Government. The considered opinion of this Embassy is that there is no justification for additional armament for the Dominican Republic. Its armed forces are larger and better equipped than those of Haiti. Inter-American commitments provide assurance of aid in case of foreign aggression against the country. The unarmed Dominican people are completely at the mercy of the well armed and well treated police and army. The Embassy's attitude has been reasonable and in accord with the Department's policy. . . .

Cooperation between U.S. and Dominican Republic:

This Embassy believes that President Trujillo's idea of cooperation with the United States involves: (*a*) acceptance of his government as democratic, in spite of substantial evidence that it is a ruthless dictatorship; (*b*) the same treatment in all respects by the United States as that accorded to other American Republics including, of course, such democratic countries as Uruguay and Colombia; (*c*) a joint anti-communism campaign on the basis of accepting the mere statement of the Dominican police that individuals are communists, when it is fairly certain that the label "communist" is indiscriminately applied to any political opponents of Trujillo; and (*d*) participation in the sickening campaign of adulation of Trujillo as a great "democrat", "statesman", savior of his country, and admired friend of the United States.

---

[17] Not printed.

With President Truman's approval, I made clear in an interview with President Trujillo, shortly after my arrival last September, the basis for cooperation, namely, along the lines of President Truman's Pan American Day address in 1946. Nothing resembling that basis exists (see, for example, confidential despatch no. 885 of June 19, 1947 [19]), as I intimated rather clearly to the Dominican Foreign Minister recently when he made the astounding request that I try to bring about a more sympathetic attitude toward the Trujillo Government on the part of the resident diplomatic corps (confidential telegram 97, May 6, 10 a. m.). The latest despatches referring to the attitude of the diplomatic corps are No. 878 of June 18, 1947,[19] regarding my conversation with the Colombian Minister, and No. 885 of June 19, 1947, referred to above.

The subject of communism has been thoroughly covered in the Embassy's despatches. It is extremely unlikely that any serious communist threat exists in the Dominican Republic. Articles in La Nación of Ciudad Trujillo make suspect the motives and measures of the Trujillo regime. Nothing of importance would be published in this newspaper—the principal one in the country—without government approval. Recent articles have accused Mr. Braden, Assistant Secretary of State, of encouraging communism in Latin America, and have made similar charges against reputable American newspaper correspondents who wrote critically of the Trujillo regime.

. . . .

2. The position of U.S. business is an important factor in the Dominican situation (see specific reference in despatch 790, May 28, 1947).

There has been a consistent effort by the Trujillo regime to use U.S. firms and citizens for political ends. Now there is the case of a Dominican police warning to a reputable U.S. businessman for alleged derogatory remarks about Trujillo (see despatch 877 of June 18, 1947 [19]).

. . . .

Since the May 16 elections I have been trying to assess the importance of factors having a bearing on our relations with the Trujillo Government. On the evening of June 18, I talked with one of the most reliable and best informed American businessmen in the Dominican Republic. Mr. McArdle of the Embassy staff [20] was present during the interview. I outlined the situation described in the preceding paragraph. I said that I knew that business has to go along to

---

[19] Not printed.
[20] Robert J. McArdle, Attaché.

a substantial extent with the established government here if it is to avoid trouble. I then asked for a frank opinion regarding the extent to which American business thought it necessary to cooperate with Trujillo.

The American businessman replied that he would be entirely frank. He agreed about the necessity of getting along with the local government. He said that, in general, American business experiences little difficulty during the initial period of a substantial investment in a foreign country. Once established, however, and faced with the necessity of protecting the investment and earning a profit, relations with the local government become much more important and difficult. He expressed the opinion that, in spite of what businessmen had told me about their attitude toward the Department's policy, an honest answer from the majority would be that American business prefers to deal with foreign governments itself. The implication, of course, is that business and economic conditions should not be interfered with for political or ideological reasons. That confirms the opinion expressed in despatch No. 555.[21] While the opinion expressed by this one man does not necessarily reflect the majority view, I suspect that it does. At any rate, I respect the man's honesty and good judgment.

. . . .

Concluding the conversation, I made the following observations: (*a*) that I did not think Trujillo could afford to make things difficult for American business if his regime were to come under scrutiny on the basis of international protection of individual rights and civil liberties, or if the Government of the United States made it officially and publicly clear that its cooperation would be limited to that in accord with such a democratic inter-American system as President Truman outlined in his April 14, 1946 speech at the Pan American Union; (*b*) that I thought either of these two courses of action might mean some temporary inconvenience to U.S. business but would be to its long range advantage; and (*c*) that I thought dictatorships and economic and political oppression made for the spread of communism, and that our own national interests would best be served by measures which might gain for us the support and confidence of Latin American labor rather than the opportunistic cooperation of "strong men" and of an indifferent array of armed forces. I added that the development of Latin American national economies probably would have to be the job of private enterprise rather than government; that this would require assurance to U.S. business of fair treatment and the opportunity to make a reasonable profit, and that this in turn would almost certainly involve intergovernmental relations and assistance by our govern-

---

[21] Not printed.

ment to U.S. business abroad. While the American businessman listened attentively, he made no comment.

Conclusion:

The factors discussed in this despatch may make it more difficult for the Department to reach a decision regarding the alternative courses of action suggested in my despatch No. 790 of May 28, 1947. I regret that I have no other more constructive recommendations to make.

Respectfully yours, GEORGE H. BUTLER

839.24/7-847

Memorandum of Conversation, by the Secretary of State

SECRET [WASHINGTON,] July 8, 1947.

Participants: The Secretary of State, Mr. Marshall
Sr. Don Julio Ortega Frier, Dominican Ambassador
Mr. Ellis O. Briggs [22]

The Dominican Ambassador called this morning to discuss the following matters:

1) An invitation for the United States to have a special representative at the reinauguration of President Trujillo on August 16. He handed me a note conveying this invitation. [23]

2) In accordance with President Trujillo's instruction the Ambassador expressed the hope that the U.S. Government would see fit to reverse its policy of not furnishing arms to the Dominican Republic, as set forth in a communication to his predecessor by the Department of State in December, 1945.[24] The Ambassador summarized the contents of this communication, indicating that the Dominican Government took particular exception to the stated reasons for the Department's position. He went on to say that the Dominican Government endorsed the standardization plan contained in legislation pending before Congress [25] and that although it had obtained certain arms during the past eighteen months from other sources, and had in particular an offer to supply munitions from the British Government before it now, President Trujillo preferred to meet his requirements in the United States. He reiterated therefore the hope that the Dominican

---

[22] Director, Office of American Republic Affairs.
[23] Neither the Dominican note nor the United States note of July 24 in reply, printed.
[24] For the *aide-mémoire* of December 28, 1945, see *Foreign Relations*, 1945, vol. IX, p. 994; for the Dominican reply, January 8, 1946, see *ibid.*, 1946, vol XI, p. 816.
[25] For documentation on United States policy with respect to provision of military assistance and armaments to other American Republics, see pp. 101 ff.

Government could shortly anticipate being permitted to make purchases in the U.S. market.

3) Likewise under direction of President Trujillo, the Ambassador stated that his government looked forward to collaborating with our Government toward the success of the forthcoming Rio de Janeiro Conference,[26] to which the Dominican Government attributed great importance. In particular the Ambassador said he wished to assure me that "other rumors to the contrary" the Dominican Government did not propose at the Conference to make any statements critical of any other American country. He went on to explain that the country in reference was Venezuela.

I told the Ambassador that I had not had an opportunity to consider prior to his call the first two points which he had made, but that I would do so at an early date and would then indicate the Department's position. With respect to representation at the inauguration I mentioned that our recent practice has been to have our resident Ambassador represent this Government.[27]

GEORGE C. MARSHALL

839.00/7-2547 : Telegram

The Secretary of State to the Embassy in Cuba [28]

SECRET   US URGENT   WASHINGTON, July 26, 1947—1 p. m.
NIACT

363. Dept heartily approves careful manner in which you are following incipient Dominican revolutionary situation which seems to be developing in Cuba, possibly with aid from Venezuelan and Guatemalan nationals. Dept approves your having taken matter up with FonOff. You will receive at about same time you receive this telegram longer message describing visit to Dept of Dominican Ambassador on July 25.[29] Ambassador at that time indicated that points covered in his discussion at Dept had been taken up with Cuban authorities by Dominican representative in Habana.

Info received this morning from Ciudad Trujillo and yesterday from Port-au-Prince gives rise to further fears that there may be

---

[26] For documentation on the Inter-American Conference for the Maintenance of Continental Peace and Security, Quitandinha, Brazil, August 15–September 2, 1947, see pp. 1 ff.
[27] The Department informed Ambassador Butler in telegram 165, August 12, 1947, 10 a. m., that President Truman had approved his appointment as his Personal Representative with the rank of Special Ambassador, to attend the inaugural ceremonies of General Trujillo (839.001 Trujillo, Rafael/8-947).
[28] Repeated as telegram Nos. 296, 210, 138 and 180 to Caracas, Guatemala City, Ciudad Trujillo, and Port-au-Prince, respectively.
[29] See telegram 139, July 26, to Ciudad Trujillo, *infra*.

something more than rumor and amateurish activity to alleged revolutionary reports. It would be a severe blow to concept of pacific settlement and to Inter-American system if, particularly on eve of important Rio Conference, there were to occur in our midst outburst of kind which Dominican Republic feels is under way and which reports from several of our Caribbean diplomatic missions indicate is at least under some degree of preparation.

It is desired that you seek an immediate interview with Pres Grau [30] to express to him concern which this Govt has and which it is sure he will share that there occur no action which is likely to cause any upheaval or even substantial fear of upheaval within Hemisphere. Of course Dept knows that you will make it clear that we do not feel in any way that President Grau's Govt has anything to do with these plans any more than U.S. Govt had to do with alleged revolutionary plans against Cuba some months ago and during recent weeks and months alleged revolutionary plans against Venezuela from Dominican sources. In these cases U.S. Govt has since Jan of this year, through Federal Bureau of Investigation, Dept of Justice proper and through Customs Bureau taken every precaution including stringent measures to prevent fulmination of violence in this area. Nature of your remarks to President should, I believe you will agree, be along line that we are sure his views in this respect parallel ours and that he will leave no stone unturned to investigate the alleged revolutionary plotting and, if he perceives any concrete evidence thereof, to promptly and effectively squelch it.

Dept will await with interest receipt of your reply.

MARSHALL

839.00/7–2447 : Telegram

The Secretary of State to the Embassy in the Dominican Republic

SECRET WASHINGTON, July 26, 1947—1 p. m.

139. Dominican Amb called on Assistant Secretary Armour yesterday and stated his Govt had reliable report of impending substantial well-armed invasion Dominican Republic from Cuba. Participants stated to consist of Cubans, Venezuelans, Spaniards and Guatemalans. He said Cuban Government informed but unable take effective preventive measures. He mentioned large influx suspicious persons into Puerto Rico and stated Puerto Rico frequently used in past as jump-

---

[30] Ramón Grau San Martín, President of Cuba.

ing off point for attacks on Dominican Republic though he had no other evidence expedition being launched from Puerto Rico. Dept alerting appropriate US officials re this possibility. Amb referred to possible armed attack by same elements from Haiti.

Amb said his Govt's principal reason bringing this matter our attention aside from general info was assertion by these and other anti-Trujillo elements of sympathy if not support from US. Amb stated he knew no justification for these assertions but referred to statements by US officials being used for this purpose by Trujillo enemies. He cited particularly Pres Truman's remarks on presentation his credentials [31] as being publicly distorted throughout other American republics to indicate anti-Trujillo slant by US. He said something should be done to stop circulation these false interpretations US attitude and intimated US officials should take care not to make public statements capable being used this purpose.

Amb was advised this Govt has taken no action justify alleged remarks anti-Trujillo groups cited by Amb and that we cannot undertake control form and tenor press reports. Amb then informed we have received over past six months constant stream reports revolutionary activities and plots against various countries bordering on Caribbean and requested full investigation appropriate agencies this Govt to prevent and punish violations US laws. He was frankly told one such rumored plot investigated had revealed evidence of attack planned on Venezuela from Dominican Republic, that we intend to prosecute certain individuals and that unpleasant publicity may ensue.

Amb stated he fully realized our obligation to enforce laws and prosecute violations thereof. He added Minister Counselor Nouel of his staff here was recalled when he became aware of Nouel's involvement with Lopez Contreras' activities.

Amb told we welcome any info from him on matters this nature and he was given substance Habana's tel 379 July 24 and Port-au-Prince's tel 256 July 24.[32] It was emphasized our reports from Cuba did not indicate rumored attack from Cuba is of magnitude described by Amb.

Repeated to AmEmbassies Habana, Caracas, Port-au-Prince and Guatemala City.[33]

MARSHALL

---

[31] The newly-appointed Ambassador (Ortega Frier) presented his credentials to President Truman on February 27, 1947.
[32] Neither printed.
[33] As telegram Nos. 362, 297, 181, and 211, respectively.

839.00/7-2847

Memorandum of Telephone Conversation, by the Director of the Office of American Republic Affairs (Wright)

CONFIDENTIAL [WASHINGTON,] July 28, 1947.

I called Ambassador Norweb [34] Sunday evening, July 27, to say that two of the telegrams we had received from him (Nos. 402 and 405 [35]) spoke of informing us of the "time of departure of aircraft and vessels". This had thrown a bit of a scare into me, for I had thought that we had made it clear that we wanted all possible done with the Cuban Government to prevent the departure of the aircraft and vessels. We greatly appreciated his reporting which was excellent and approved the action he had taken up to date. However, we wanted him, if necessary, to go back to the authorities to make it clear to them, if it were not already clear, how dimly we would view the departure of the aircraft and vessels. We wanted to avoid a pitched battle. Ambassador Norweb said that he would take it up further and, if necessary, try to get in touch with President Grau.[36]

839.00/7-2847 : Telegram

The Ambassador in Cuba (Norweb) to the Secretary of State

SECRET US URGENT HABANA, July 28, 1947—6 p. m.
NIACT

410. Thoroughly reliable source in Cuban Government working with Dominican revolutionaries states:

1. Due to outside pressure President Grau has given them until Wednesday, July 30, to leave Cuban shores. Failing this he will utilize Cuban Army for eviction.

2. Although many prominent members Cuban Government are included in the movement they failed to approach General Genovevo Perez Damera chief staff Cuban Army. General Perez highly incensed and has made several trips to assembly areas. He also has approximately 50 trained soldiers at Las Chivas with others alerted.

3. Sunday afternoon one small boat containing approximately 50 Dominican exiles departed for isolated port of Dominican Republic. This group to infiltrate and warn natives of impending revolution and enlist internal aid.

4. (Cancelled).

---

[34] R. Henry Norweb, Ambassador in Cuba.
[35] Neither printed.
[36] Ambassador Norweb saw the Cuban Foreign Minister on July 27 and stated that it was hoped that no action would occur which would disturb the peace of the Western Hemisphere. The Minister admitted that the Government was aware of what was occurring, and that the Government was following activities in order to prevent any abuse of hospitality.

5. Five transport type aircraft from Venezuela are available for use on a moment's notice. Some of these aircraft are expected at Rancho Boyeros this afternoon.

6. The air operations are to be in charge of a former Dominican colonel who answers to name of "Freddie".

7. The air operations section has procured "belly tanks" which will be used as incendiary bombs (possibly "nazalm") also demolition bombs.

8. Planes are to be manned by a group of 30 Americans.

9. Groups need $100,000 at once to permit of its prompt departure. Mario Salabarria, Chief secret police, and Manolo Castro [37] soliciting funds. Castro in Miami now. Believe aircraft crews demanding cash deposit prior to take off. Estimate venture has now cost between five and seven million dollars.

10. Headquarters Habana announced this a. m. that no change in plans following newspaper revelations and Grau orders.

11. Troops are being assembled in Holguín and transported to Antilla. Estimate 4,500 to 5,000 now. Group is exceedingly well equipped with rifles, machine guns and ammunition.

12. Landings will be made on shore of Dominican Republic. Air attacks will be made on Ciudad Trujillo. Internal assistance heavily counted upon for success of the revolution. Approximately 20 days training has been given troops. Training has been for revolution, not military attack.

13. Comment. This information substantially as received piecemeal other sources and given high rating as to accuracy. We are checking further on reports re aircraft. At 5 p. m. I am still awaiting a reply from Foreign Minister, who I am sure has seen President. He evidences increasing resistance and is critical of press stories headlined as "US probe".

Inform War, Navy.

Sent Department 410; repeated Ciudad Trujillo and Port-au-Prince.

NORWEB

839.00/7–2847 : Telegram

The Ambassador in Cuba (Norweb) to the Secretary of State

SECRET   US URGENT   HABANA, July 28, 1947—7 p. m.
NIACT

411. President Grau late this afternoon informed me that energetic measures are being taken to suffocate revolutionary activity based on

---

[37] Manolo Castro del Campo, Cuban Director General of National Sports in the Ministry of Education.

Cuban soil and directed against Dominican Republic which has been subject recent telegrams. He further declared public statement this effect will be issued and subsequent ones as situation warrants.

Inform War and Navy.

Sent Department 411, repeated Ciudad Trujillo and Port-au-Prince.

NORWEB

839.24/7–1747 : Telegram

The Secretary of State to the Embassy in the Dominican Republic

SECRET   US URGENT   WASHINGTON, August 1, 1947—7 p. m.

147. Dominican Amb called on me July 8 to request that our policy of not supplying his Govt with arms be reversed. He made it clear that it was not question whether Dominican Republic would buy arms but rather where it would buy them. If they were not purchased from us they would be purchased elsewhere and he simply wanted to know whether U.S. would authorize their sale or whether his Govt should purchase them from another source of supply. Since Ambassador's call matter has been carefully studied within Dept and it has now been concluded that we should consider D. R. and all other Amreps on same basis insofar as permission for export or transfer of arms is concerned. This means, in accordance with Dept's general policy on arms exports, that proposed exports arms to D. R. will be permitted when Dept concludes such transfers are reasonable and necessary for maintenance internal order or to provide for the exercise of right of self-defense or to fulfill international obligations to provide contingent forces to Security Council.[38]

Consideration will also be given to approval small interim program for D. R. if War Dept so recommends.

Our restrictive arms policy toward D. R. and certain other Govts worked well so long as this Govt had a virtual arms monopoly, which is far from case at present time. Political factors which argue for embargo are as cogent today as ever and present reversal is on pragmatic grounds. If D. R. is to arm (as apparently arm itself it will) then our position is stronger to have some voice therein.

MARSHALL

---

[38] The Secretary of State indicated in telegram 151, August 4, to Ciudad Trujillo (839.24/8–447), that the Dominican Ambassador had called at the Department on that date and was given the substance of this paragraph.

839.00/8–147

Memorandum of Conversation, by the Under Secretary of State (Lovett)

TOP SECRET [WASHINGTON,] August 1, 1947.

Following luncheon with Admiral Ramsey [39] and in accordance with the instructions of the Secretary of State in connection with the threatened Dominican revolutionary invasion launched from Cuba, I showed Admiral Ramsey the full file of telegrams and went over them with him. Following the Secretary's conversation with Mr. Forrestal [40] the Navy Department had already prepared a message to the Commander in Chief, Atlantic Fleet, requesting reconnaissance in an effort to locate the vessels which had sailed from Cuban ports, and ordering prompt reports, whether affirmative or negative in character. This message was dispatched immediately after it was shown to me at 1:15 P. M.

In discussing the situation with Admiral Ramsey it was emphasized that there should be no interference of any type with the operation at this stage and no show of force. The only thing that we wished at present was intelligence reports and such information as could be obtained through reconnaissance supplemented by some sort of continuous supervision of these boats if located by small craft such as PT's. The Navy expressed full agreement with the program, offered complete cooperation, and agreed with the approach suggested as well as with the sense of urgency which we felt.

The Navy Department showed me the full disposition of its vessels in the Guantánamo area which, by pure coincidence, represent some of the most powerful Fleet units because the Midshipmen's cruise arrived at Guantánamo yesterday and expects to be there until August 6. The vessels include, among others, two aircraft carriers, a couple of battleships, two divisions of destroyers, etc., etc. Admiral Ramsey indicated that the air reconnaissance was a simple matter and that they fully understood the necessity for exercising caution. He stated further that the training maneuvers being undertaken thereabouts would provide in his opinion a cover plan if needed.

We further discussed the next logical steps in the event the boats were discovered in Haitian waters or in landing operations.

I told Admiral Ramsey that it was our present feeling that we must avoid anything approaching interference and that it was our

---

[39] Adm. DeWitt C. Ramsey, Vice Chief of Naval Operations.
[40] James Forrestal, Secretary of the Navy.

present intent to move through the United Nations machinery, using either Article 39, Chapter VII, or Article 51,[41] or both, and that we might simultaneously or alternatively move through the Havana Conventions [42] or under the Act of Chapultepec.[43] I explained to him that it was my personal feeling, with the Rio Conference coming up, that the Havana and Chapultepec routes might be an embarrassment and that other United Nations procedures might be more immediately effective or less embarrassing.

Admiral Ramsey agreed to keep me posted by telephone of any intelligence reports, either affirmative or negative.

It was also agreed that Admiral Ramsey would telephone Admiral Leahy [44] on behalf of both Departments and inform him of the situation and steps we had taken, in view of the fact that Admiral Leahy on hearing that the matter had been brought to the attention of the White House by the State Department had requested the Navy Department to keep him posted.

ROBERT A. LOVETT

839.00/8-1347 : Telegram

The Ambassador in Cuba (Norweb) to the Secretary of State

SECRET   US URGENT   HABANA, August 13, 1947—2 p. m.

469. Considerable confirmatory information obtained since yesterday ranging from depositions four British seamen sworn at British Legation to rumor and gossip. Now clear that vessel LCT *Libertad* departed New York July 9 has connection with Cruz Alonso [45] (see Embassy's 450, August 7 [46]) and engaged end July in transport ordnance munitions and men from Nipe Bay to Cayo Confites where military camp established which by last week reported contain about 1,000 men. *Libertad* probably renamed *Aurora*. Additional vessel probably LST *Victoria* renamed *Berta* also engaged.

---

[41] United Nations Charter, June 26, 1945; for text, see Department of State Treaty Series No. 993, or 59 Stat. (pt. 2) 1031.

[42] Signed at the Sixth International Conference of American States, Habana, January 16–February 20, 1928 (Department of State Treaty Series No. 814, or 46 Stat. (pt. 2) 2749), and at the Second Meeting of the Ministers of Foreign Affairs of the American Republics, Habana, July 21–30, 1940 (Resolution VI, *Report of the Secretary of State* . . . Department of State publication No. 1575, p. 64).

[43] Department of State Treaties and Other International Acts Series (TIAS) No. 1543, or 60 Stat. (pt. 2) 1831.

[44] Fleet Adm. William D. Leahy, Chief of Staff to the Commander in Chief of the Army and Navy.

[45] Rodriguez Cruz Alonso, a Cuban who took a leading part in procuring vessels and arms for the expedition; the *Libertad* was seized by the Cuban Navy and brought to Antilla about September 30, 1947.

[46] Not printed.

Regarding telephone call from Dept yesterday and Cuban pressure obtain release LCI at Balto,[47] Cruz Alonso called at Commercial Section, Embassy, today, requesting information on detention. Various reports indicate lack of transport as a serious handicap to effort especially for troop movement. Several rumors maintenance discipline difficult at training centers with Venezuelan Communists in group now thrown out and some executions of which one reliably reported.

Dominican revolutionaries tightening on loose talk and have reprimanded Juan Bosch.[48] Dr. Rosell of Cuinair [49] said to have double-crossed revolutionaries on purchase price B-24 aircraft and fears violence.

Revolutionary attempt cannot be discounted yet but problems continue to multiply.

Unless movement to other areas has been made recently, which I doubt, it is still on Cuban territory or in Cuban waters. Does Department desire inquire of Cuban Government under what conditions revolutionaries are on Cuban territory? [50]

Pass War Navy.

Sent Department 469, repeated Ciudad Trujillo, Port-au-Prince.

NORWEB

839.00/9-147 : Telegram

The Ambassador in the Dominican Republic (Butler) to the Secretary of State

CONFIDENTIAL   CIUDAD TRUJILLO, September 1, 1947—3 p. m.

241. ReEmbtel 238 and 240.[51] Following comment is made with reference to Dominican note regarding revolutionary force reported to

---

[47] LCI (landing craft infantry) No. 534 renamed *Patria* was detained early in August 1947 at Baltimore by United States customs authorities at the Department's request.

[48] Member of the Dominican Central Revolutionary Committee, duty of which was declared to "bring about in the Dominican Republic an armed revolution, the immediate purpose of which shall be the overthrow of the tyranny of Rafael L. Trujillo and the establishment of a revolutionary government . . .".

[49] Reinaldo Ramirez Rosell, head of Aerovias Cubanas Internacionales, was one of the purchasing agents for the expedition.

[50] Replying in telegram 406, August 15, 6 p. m., the Department stated: "Dept is under impression our position is clear to Cuban Govt (urtel 469, August 13) but if you feel it is not fully clear you have discretion to make it so. We would be inclined at this time not to make the inquiry mentioned in last sentence of your message." (839.00/8-1347)

[51] Neither printed. Reference is made to notes presented by the Acting Dominican Minister for Foreign Affairs on August 30 (not printed), to the Chiefs of Mission of the other American Republics requesting any information that they might have concerning Dominican revolutionary activities in their respective territories.

be preparing attack against Dominican Republic from Cuban territory.

1. Dominican note, with one exception mentioned in subsequent paragraph, appears to be technically in accord with provisions of 1928 Habana Convention on rights and duties of states in the event of civil strife, and Resolution 6 of second consultative meeting American Foreign Ministers at Habana in 1940.

2. Since US is party to Habana Convention and Resolution 6 and since Dominican note twice refers to possible involvement of US citizens or officials, we have a special interest in the case.

3. Dominican intention to request inter-American investigation of activities in Cuba does not appear to be contemplated under provisions of Resolution 6. Article 1 provides that state directly interested may request inter-American consultation. This seems to be quite distinct from a specific investigation of activities in only one country.

4. Dominican request for strictly confidential exchange of information probably is legally in accord with Article 3 of Resolution 6, although the exchange of information referred to in Article 2 is a part of consultation which has not yet been requested or initiated.

5. When a similar state of tension existed between Venezuela and the Dominican Republic a few months ago, with the latter country apparently in the position it now charges that Cuba occupies, I recommended inter-American consultation. I repeated that recommendation recently in connection with the present Cuba case. I still am of the opinion that inter-American consultation on friction in the Caribbean area is necessary and desirable. The present revolutionary activity in Cuba is a symptom of a basic trouble. A limited investigation of one symptom does not seem fair or constructive. A full and impartial consultation regarding basic causes for friction among Caribbean countries would be difficult and unpleasant but it might lead to at least a partial remedy. As long as internal political situations in many countries are such that political exiles must plot from abroad, there probably will be a continuation of these difficulties. I believe that the US should assume leadership in an effort to assure wider and more genuine observance of the democratic processes which in theory are the basis of the inter-American system.

6. Finally, this Embassy is convinced on the basis of information available, and I believe Embassy Habana concurs, that revolutionary movement is primarily one of Dominicans opposed to Trujillo's dictatorship and is not one directed by Communists either foreign or Dominican.

BUTLER

839.00/9-347

Memorandum of Conversation, by the Assistant Chief of the Division of Caribbean Affairs (Walker)

CONFIDENTIAL [WASHINGTON,] September 3, 1947.

Participants: Dr. Joaquin E. Salazar, Dominican Chargé d'Affaires
Mr. James H. Wright, Department of State (ARA)
Mr. William W. Walker, Department of State (CRB)

Dr. Salazar, at the Department's request, called at Mr. Wright's office this morning. Mr. Wright opened the conversation by stating that the Department had received from Ambassador Butler a telegram furnishing the substance of a note delivered to him and to other Chiefs of Mission by the Acting Dominican Minister of Foreign Affairs, requesting information on the activities of Dominican revolutionaries in their respective territories. He went on to say that for some months this Government has been exercising the closest vigilance over the activities of Latin-American exile groups in this country and that every precaution has been taken in an effort to prevent any illegal activity on the part of such groups. The Department, he explained, has maintained the closest cooperation with Ambassador Ortega Frier, Dr. Salazar and other members of the Dominican Embassy, and has exchanged information on the activities of the Dominican revolutionaries. He referred particularly to the frequent conversations that officers of the Department have had with Señor Herrera, of the Dominican Embassy, and to the almost daily conferences for the exchange of information.

Mr. Wright cited the detention of the LCI vessel at Baltimore as an example of the vigilance exercised by this Government and assured Dr. Salazar that no stone would be left unturned in continuing the closest possible surveillance. Dr. Salazar expressed complete satisfaction over the action being taken by this Government.

Mr. Wright referred to that section of the Dominican note concerning a statement attributable to the Dominican revolutionaries that their movement was supported by public officials of this Government and pointed out that the movement did not have the support of any officials of this Government. Dr. Salazar agreed with Mr. Wright that such information was undoubtedly false. Mr. Wright then referred to the Dominican allegation that some of the leaders of the movement were American citizens and stated that the Department would appreciate it very much if the Dominican Government would furnish it with any available information regarding this matter.

Dr. Salazar stated that his government was concerned over the failure of the Cuban Government to take steps against the Dominican revolutionaries and particularly disturbed over evidence that elements of the Cuban Government were openly assisting and abetting the conspirators. He mentioned that latest reports indicate that the revolutionaries have several small boats, twelve airplanes, and about 1700 men on Cuban territory. He also mentioned that of late there had been some movement of the ships belonging to the revolutionary group, particularly in the vicinity of Nuevitas and Holguín. Mr. Wright remarked that such movements were subject to almost daily air reconnaissance.

Dr. Salazar said that his government was fearful that the Cuban Government was making available to the revolutionaries arms and ammunition obtained from the United States. In this connection, he mentioned that Sr. Ramirez, whom he referred to as a Cuban citizen, had made frequent trips to the United States, presumably in an effort to purchase arms and weapons of war for the revolutionaries. He admitted, however, that because of the considerable travel between United States and Cuba, and the fact that Cubans entering this country for 29 days or less do not require visas, it would be utterly impossible to check the movements of all incoming passengers from Cuba. Mr. Walker pointed out that it was his understanding that Sr. Ramirez is now in Habana.

Mr. Wright stated that the Department had received a telegraphic report from Caracas saying that Sr. Rodriguez had recently left Venezuela, presumably for Cuba. The report, he added, went on to say that while Rodriguez was in Caracas he allegedly visited a number of Dominican exiles and that the feeling among them seemed to be that of disillusionment. Their plans, Mr. Wright added, apparently had been altered somewhat by their inability to get the LCI vessel from Baltimore. Mr. Wright took occasion at this point to reiterate that this vessel would be detained at Baltimore indefinitely.

839.00/9-1547

Memorandum of Conversation, by Mr. Charles C. Hauch of the Division of Caribbean Affairs

CONFIDENTIAL [WASHINGTON,] September 15, 1947.

Participants: Assistant Secretary Armour
Mr. Wright—ARA
Ambassador Ortega Frier—Dominican Republic
Mr. Hauch—CRB

The Dominican Ambassador called at his request and discussed in a very grave and at times agitated manner the revolutionary activities against the Dominican Government centered in Cuba. He reviewed some of the alleged facts regarding concentration of forces and other details. He said that the plot was backed by a fund of $3,000,000. Part of this money had come, he said, from President Betancourt of Venezuela. He emphasized the communist influence in the plot, although admitting that a number of the principals were not communists.

The Ambassador then passed to the main purpose of his call, which was to solicit certain assistance from this Government. He prefaced his remarks by adverting to the alleged plan of the revolutionaries to destroy the Dominican sugar industry by bombing sugar centrals from the air. (See Department's memorandum of conversation of Friday, September 12 entitled "Reported forthcoming attack on United States sugar properties in Dominican Republic".[52]) He pointed out that the Dominican sugar industry was for the most part American-owned and that American interests would consequently suffer. He said the obvious objective of this plan was to destroy the principal source of the Dominican Government's revenues and thus precipitate a financial and economic crisis in the Dominican Republic. He said that while this was the plan of the revolutionaries, it had the support of certain Cuban Government officials and Cuban sugar men who hoped the Dominican sugar industry and economy would be ruined in this way. He said the revolutionaries had adequate planes at their disposal to carry out this operation.

The Ambassador then requested that the delivery of the arms, ships, and aircraft his Government has solicited our assistance in obtaining be expedited. He pleaded in the strongest manner that the United States must assist the Dominican Republic in obtaining the means to defend itself. He said that the Dominican Government has only thirty aircraft and that most of these are training planes. (*Note:* Mr. George C. Stamets, technical advisor to the Dominican air force, had informed Messrs. Hauch and Spencer earlier in the day that the Dominican Government had only nine aircraft. Presumably, he meant aircraft capable of being used in combat.)

Mr. Wright explained that the State, War and Navy Departments were doing everything possible to expedite deliveries of an appropriate quantity of armament . . .

. . . .

Mr. Armour observed that assistance in obtaining arms and military advice would appear not to be the immediate problem from the Dominican point of view. He said that an effort to resolve the problem of the Cuban Government's toleration of and assistance to the revolu-

---

[52] Not printed.

tionary movement based on its territory would seem to be the most important step. Mr. Wright added that since the Dominican Republic is the offended party, it has the primary responsibility to initiate action in this direction, and that the Dominican Government could not and should not expect other Governments to take the initiative in this case. To this the Ambassador replied that this was precisely what the Dominican Government intended to do. He said his Government had obtained no satisfaction from dealing directly with the Cuban Government and now intended to have the matter considered in accordance with Resolution XIV adopted at the Second Meeting of the Ministers of Foreign Affairs of the American Republics at Habana in 1940. Under this Resolution the Governing Board of the Pan American Union has designated a committee of five countries "which shall have the duty of keeping constant vigilance to insure that states between which any dispute exists or may arise, of any nature whatsoever, may solve it as quickly as possible, and of suggesting, without detriment to the methods adopted by the parties or to the procedures which they may agree upon, the measures and steps which may be conducive to a settlement." Pursuant to this resolution, the Governing Board had appointed Cuba, the United States, Argentina, Mexico and Brazil to serve as members of this committee, but only the Cubans had actually appointed a representative. This was former Ambassador Concheso.[53] (*Note:* The Dominican Ambassador incorrectly stated that Ambassador Belt [54] was the Cuban representative.)

The Dominican Ambassador requested that this Government appoint its representative on the committee as quickly as possible in order that the committee might be ready to handle the case. He intimated, and subsequent investigation confirmed, that he was endeavoring to have the other countries on the committee likewise appoint their representatives. Mr. Wright stated that if the United States had not appointed anyone to serve in this capacity, we would probably designate our representative on the Governing Board, Ambassador William Dawson, to serve on the committee. (*Note:* It was subsequently decided to address a letter to the Pan American Union so designating Ambassador Dawson).

In the course of the discussion the Ambassador referred to the possibility of land attacks from Haiti. He said that the Haitian Government was doing what it could to prevent its territory from being used as a base, but intimated that it was not able to act effectively to avoid all such possibilities. He said that it was of grave concern to

---

[53] Aurelio Fernandez Concheso, formerly Cuban Ambassador in the United States.

[54] Guillermo Belt, Cuban Ambassador in the United States.

his Government that in the event of Haiti's being used as a base it might be necessary for the Dominican land forces to cross the frontier. He asserted his concern at the effect this would have on Dominican-Haitian relations. He said that President Trujillo had discussed this with Haitian Ambassador Price-Mars and Ambassador Ortega Frier understood that Price-Mars had left for Haiti to report to President Estimé. The Ambassador also stated that President Trujillo had advised him that Estimé's position was becoming weaker and that in the event it deteriorated completely a "military circle" headed by Col. Paul Magloire might take over the Haitian Government in a *coup d'état*.

The whole tone of the Ambassador's conversation was very serious and he implied that he expected drastic developments shortly.

837.00/9-2147 : Telegram

The Ambassador in Cuba (Norweb) to the Secretary of State

SECRET   US URGENT   HABANA, September 21, 1947—2 p. m.

549. Further Embtel 546, September 19.[55] Friday night [56] President Grau appointed Army's Colonel Enrique Hernández Nardo supervisor of National police who assumed charge yesterday and appointed army supervisors each police district and made many transfers high police officials. Police Chief Ruiz Rojas has gone on leave.

Today's press featured army seizure yesterday afternoon 13 truck loads munitions including aerial bombs and depth charges on farm belonging Alemán Minister Education (Embtel 490, August 20 [57]). Chief Staff facilitated extensive reporting and photos.

As consequence these developments army control police promises more peaceful domestic situation. Cabinet shifts likely view implication Alemán. President's prestige will suffer further but there are no indications rift with army.

Above developments and other information indicate rapid crumbling Dominican invasion attempt.[58]

Pass War, Navy.

Sent Department 549, repeated Port-au-Prince.[59]

NORWEB

---

[55] Not printed.
[56] September 19.
[57] Not printed. José Manuel Alemán had been entrusted with the organization of the revolutionary movement.
[58] On September 29 an Army investigator informed the press that the Dominican expeditionary force had been liquidated.
[59] Text of telegram 549 repeated also to Ciudad Trujillo in telegram 200, September 22, 1947, 6 p. m.

839.00/9-2647

The Secretary of State to the Dominican Ambassador (Ortega Frier)

The Secretary of State presents his compliments to His Excellency the Ambassador of the Dominican Republic and has the honor to acknowledge receipt of the Embassy's notes 3069 of September 13, 3105 of September 16, 3103 and 3104 of September 17, 3223 of September 25 and 3224 of September 26,[61] all with reference to the activities of an armed expedition stated to have been intending to proceed against the Dominican Republic. The Department appreciates the courtesy of the Embassy in keeping it informed of developments in this connection and has communicated the information contained in the Embassy's notes to the other interested agencies of this Government.

The Department of State has noted with particular interest statements in the Embassy's several notes under reference regarding the alleged acquisition of equipment in the United States for the expedition, as well as the alleged participation in the undertaking of United States citizens and other persons residing in this country. As has been orally explained to officers of the Embassy on several previous occasions, this Government has taken all possible precautions to assure compliance with its international obligations in this connection and the enforcement of its pertinent legislation. Consequently, any further information the Embassy may be able to supply the Department with respect to the points mentioned in the first sentence of this paragraph would be greatly appreciated.

WASHINGTON, October 23, 1947.

839.24/10-647

The Secretary of State to the Dominican Ambassador (Ortega Frier)

WASHINGTON, October 24, 1947.

EXCELLENCY: I have the honor to refer to your notes Nos. 2974, 3011, and 3361, dated September 9, September 11, and October 6, 1947, respectively,[61] concerning your Government's interest in acquiring certain arms, ammunition, and implements of war for the Navy of the Dominican Republic.

The Department is pleased to inform you that it is prepared to approve licenses to export to your country the quantities of naval arms,

---

[61] None printed.

ammunition, and implements of war set forth in the attached list.[62] . . .

The Department regrets that it is not in a position to approve at this time licenses to export to the Dominican Republic arms and ammunition for the five corvettes and for the Las Calderas naval base.

. . . .

Accept [etc.] For the Secretary of State:
NORMAN ARMOUR

839.00/11–1947

Memorandum by Mr. Charles C. Hauch of the Division of Caribbean Affairs [63]

SECRET [WASHINGTON,] November 19, 1947.

Subject: Increasing Terrorism in Dominican Republic

The attached despatch from Ciudad Trujillo [64] makes clear that since Trujillo's reelection and the revolutionary activities against him, he has embarked on a new campaign of terrorism against both Dominicans and foreigners. He has apparently given a blank check to the head of the local Gestapo, Major General Federico Fiallo, to suppress all enemies and alleged enemies of the regime. General Fiallo seems to be running amuck in this task despite a lack of sympathy in the Foreign Office.

The Embassy is currently following several cases of alleged arbitrary action and mistreatment of American citizens. The remaining 100 Spanish Loyalists in the Dominican Republic are being forced to leave the country under one pretext or another, and General Fiallo has stated that any enemy of General Franco, even if not a Communist, must be considered an enemy of Trujillo. Refugees of other nationalities have likewise been advised to leave in the near future. The campaign of terrorism, of course, is unrelenting against Dominicans, and a number of executions have been reported.

A markedly increased number of applications for American immigration visas have been received from close relatives of high ranking Government officials, although very few of them have been able to obtain passports and exit permits. An unconfirmed report is that the

---

[62] Not printed.
[63] Addressed to the Assistant Secretary of State for Political Affairs (Armour), the Director (Daniels), and the Deputy Director (Woodward), of the Office of American Republic Affairs, and to the Assistant Chief of the Division of Caribbean Affairs (Walker).
[64] Despatch 1260, November 4, 1947, not printed.

President's mother has been attempting to convince him he should leave the country for residence in a safer spot abroad.

839.248/11–2647

Memorandum of Conversation, by Mr. Charles C. Hauch of the Division of Caribbean Affairs

CONFIDENTIAL WASHINGTON, November 26, 1947.

Participants: Ambassador Luis F. Thomen—Dominican Republic
Mr. Daniels—ARA
Mr. Hauch—CRB

The Dominican Ambassador called at his initiative and requested that the Department's decision with respect to the licensing of military aircraft for the Dominican Republic be reconsidered again. He referred to his previous call on Mr. Armour on this subject and the information he had received from me that it would not be possible to make this type of aircraft available to the Dominican Republic. The Ambassador said that if the decision of the Department should remain unchanged, then he would like to have transit and refueling privileges given to some thirty mosquito planes which the Dominican Government could obtain in Canada.[65] He stated his Government would much prefer to obtain its equipment in the United States, in view of its desire to cooperate with us in the arms standardization program, but that if planes of the desired type could not be secured here at the present time they would have to endeavor to obtain them elsewhere.

The Ambassador then went on to reiterate that his Government urgently needed these planes for defensive purposes against the revolution based in Venezuela against his country. Mr. Daniels made clear that he did not believe any such threat to the Dominican Republic exists. He also stated his view that the atmosphere of charges and counter-charges of revolutionary activity and involvement of one government against another should be played down. The Ambassador said he was in accord with this approach, but that his Government could not ignore the fact that the Government of Venezuela is actively aiding a revolutionary attempt against the Dominican Republic in

---

[65] On November 26, the Third Secretary of the Canadian Embassy (Rogers), was informed that the Department had disapproved the acquisition by the Dominican Republic of aircraft of this type and was asked whether the Canadian Government would have any objection to the State Department's refusing a transit license. On December 2, Mr. Rogers telephoned to say that it was the policy of the Canadian Department of External Affairs not to approve the sale of weapons of any kind to the Dominican Republic and that any Dominican request for the purchase of combat aircraft would be referred to the Canadian Cabinet with the recommendation that the aircraft not be sold.

Venezuelan territory. Mr. Daniels reiterated several times his view that this danger is grossly exaggerated.

During the discussion Mr. Daniels inquired whether the Ambassador would be willing to discuss this situation on a personal and unofficial basis with the Venezuelan Ambassador in Mr. Daniels' presence. Mr. Daniels made clear he was not proposing this, but was merely inquiring as to the Ambassador's views on the subject. The Ambassador stated his belief that this would be impossible. He said that his Government plans to communicate its position on this subject to the Government of Venezuela through the Pan American Union.

The Ambassador referred to the armament and aircraft obtained by other American republics, including Venezuela, during the period when the Dominican Republic was unable to obtain equipment in the United States.[66] He said this had brought about a disequilibrium which the Dominican Government was now attempting to overcome. He obviously felt that Venezuela had been disproportionately armed by the United States and that we should, therefore, enable the Dominican Republic to restore the balance.

Mr. Daniels said he would look into the Dominican aircraft requests again and would get in touch with the Ambassador later.

810.248/12–147

Memorandum by Mr. George O. Spencer of the Division of Special Inter-American Affairs to Mr. Charles C. Hauch of the Division of Caribbean Affairs

[WASHINGTON,] December 1, 1947.

The underlying tabulation [67] indicates, for 7 Caribbean countries, (1) the number of planes in the Air Forces long range program, (2) the number of planes in the interim program, and (3) the number of planes actually purchased in the interim program. The following conclusions may be drawn:

1. For 4 of the countries, the Dominican Republic, Haiti, Honduras and El Salvador, no aircraft larger than advanced trainers are planned for the over-all or interim programs. Two of the countries, Cuba and Venezuela were offered a few bombers and fighters in the interim program and have purchased some of those offered. A few more bombers and fighters are planned for Cuba and Venezuela in the over-all program. Guatemala has nothing in the interim program beyond the advanced trainers, but a few fighters are planned for the over-all program.

---

[66] See memorandum of December 1 on this subject, *infra*.
[67] Not printed.

2. Although the Dominican Republic was not offered an interim program, she has been able to purchase commercially and to export, more planes than the Army Department has planned for the Dominican Republic in the over-all program.

3. Venezuela, which was offered a few bombers and fighters in the interim program, has purchased all of those which were offered and has purchased 30 AT–6's in addition, from commercial sources.

On the basis of the underlying tabulation, I do not believe it would be in order, nor do I believe that the PCA would approve, fighters or bombers for the Dominican Republic, whether procured from US surplus stocks, US firms, or Canada. This would mean rejecting all Dominican requests, including the request for a transit license for Canadian mosquito aircraft, with the exception of the request for 30 AT–6's which the Dominicans say they can obtain from the Babb Co. I think we might approve some of these AT–6's, although 30 of them would seem to be a rather large order.

839.24/12–547 : Telegram

The Chargé in the Dominican Republic (Burrows) to the Secretary of State

CONFIDENTIAL   CIUDAD TRUJILLO, December 5, 1947—3 p. m.

336. Re Rio's 1671 December 4.[68] Secretary Foreign Affairs [69] this morning admitted readily Dominican Republic had been attempting secure arms wherever possible for defense purposes since US not willing supply needs. Emphasized Cayo Confites invasion would have been complete success if properly organized since government did not have planes and defensive armaments in anything like necessary quantities. Said ridiculous for Venezuela fear attack; his country's only interest defense.

Secretary evinced sincere concern over developing events re Venezuela attributing situation in large part personal feelings between President Betancourt and Trujillo kept at fever pitch by statements and activities Dominican exiles there and Venezuelan exiles here. Voiced somewhat ingenious [*ingenuous?*] hope for understanding and friendship; thinks if there somehow were simultaneous change in Venezuelan and Dominican Governments there would be no further trouble since no basic cause exists for enmity between two peoples. Regrets deeply his government's present expenditures for armaments and

---

[68] Not printed.
[69] Virgilio Días Ordóñez, Acting Secretary for Foreign Affairs in the absence of Foreign Minister Arturo Despradel, was designated Secretary for Foreign Affairs on December 9, 1947.

fears economic complications for country may develop. He personally also fears other complications of pre-marine days such as periodic revolutions if large supplies armaments brought into country. Somewhat innocently explained he has presented this point of view to President but said pessimistically that despite best intentions he feels his efforts will bear little fruit, particularly since he is only interim Secretary. Expressed personal hope that US could intervene in interest friendly relations.

. . . .

Sent Department 336, repeated Caracas, Rio and Habana 41.

BURROWS

TERMINATION OF UNITED STATES-DOMINICAN CUSTOMS CONVENTION OF 1940

[On July 18, 1947, President Trujillo proclaimed, unilaterally, the termination of the convention between the United States and the Dominican Republic providing for the assistance of the United States in the collection and application of the customs revenues of the Dominican Republic, signed at Washington, September 24, 1940 (Department of State Treaty Series No. 965, or 55 Stat. (pt. 2) 1104), and declared that conditions set forth in the exchange of notes of September 24, 1940, had been met as regards bona fide claims. On July 21, 1947, a check was delivered to Oliver Newman, Representative of the Holders of Bonds of the Dominican Republic, toward redemption in full of the Dominican bond issues of 1922 and 1926 together with accrued interest (839.51 Bondholders/7–2147). For statement released by the Department of State to the press on August 6, 1947, see Department of State *Bulletin*, August 17, 1947, page 341.

On August 9, 1951, the Secretary of State and the Dominican Ambassador (Thomen) signed an exchange of notes on behalf of their Governments recognizing the automatic termination of the convention of September 24, 1940, on October 1, 1947 (Department of State, Treaties and Other International Acts Series (TIAS) No. 2365). The 1951 exchange of notes gave recognition to the fact that the Dominican Republic had redeemed in full its external debts of 1922 and 1926 in accordance with the bond contracts and had fully discharged the last financial obligation to the United States assumed under the terms of the 1940 financial convention (411.392/8–951). For statement released to the press on August 9, 1951, see Department of State *Bulletin*, August 20, 1951, page 299.]

ECUADOR

THE QUESTION OF RECOGNIZING THE MANCHENO, THE SUAREZ, AND THE AROSEMENA REGIMES IN ECUADOR

822.00/8–2347 : Telegram

The Ambassador in Ecuador (Simmons) to the Secretary of State

SECRET   NIACT   QUITO, August 23, 1947—11 p. m.

344. Political situation flared into action tonight about 9 : 30. Troops and armored cars appeared throughout city. Many shots were fired. Group of army officers appeared at President's residence and demanded he resign. Last information is that President had not agreed so to do but that he accompanied officers to armored car headquarters to confer with Mancheno [1] who seems to be taking control of the government. My Military Attaché [2] quotes Mrs. Mancheno as saying that Velasco [3] has resigned.

Apparently crisis came as result of Mancheno reopening Ernesto Villacis incident [4] by reinstating him temporarily on August 11 as Acting Under Secretary Defense. This action was apparently taken without President's previous knowledge or consent. Velasco demanded his transfer to post outside of Quito. Mancheno refused. Velasco then demanded Mancheno's resignation, but latter stated he had once before resigned under pressure (last January) but that he refused to resign a second time. Mancheno then apparently took action to oust Velasco. The matter consequently resolved itself into a show of strength between the two, the chief determining factor being army support. Plans seem to have been well laid in advance and confidential source reports that Mancheno has also recently consolidated to considerable extent opposition to Velasco among various civilian groups including Conservatives, Liberals, Socialist and more particularly Communists. In this connection one source states that only condition of Communist

---

[1] Col. Carlos Mancheno, Minister of National Defense.
[2] Col. Paul K. Porch.
[3] The Ecuadoran President, José Maria Velasco Ibarra.
[4] An officer of the Ecuadoran Tank Corps whose conduct caused differences between the Mayor of Quito and the National Government. The latter rescinded the action of the former, releasing Villacis from prison and restoring him to his rank.

support was a promise that if coup successful Trujillo [5] would be recalled from Rio Conference.

Mancheno apparently has gained full support of army and *guardia civil*. Troops generally in control; no opposition evident. No casualties, looting or disorder so far ascertained.

Armed forces this evening seized telegraph, telephone and cable facilities. No information as to situation Guayaquil or other sections of country.

Nothing has been heard concerning situation Vice President Suarez Veintimilla in relation to possible formation new government.

Message not sent to Petropolis because lack facilities.

SIMMONS

822.00/8–2547 : Telegram

The Ambassador in Ecuador (Simmons) to the Secretary of State

SECRET   US URGENT   QUITO, August 25, 1947—1 p. m.

349. Question of recognition of new Ecuadoran regime undoubtedly will arise immediate future in connection actions either deliberate or implying our policy. Rumors from two sources quote Colon Eloy Alfaro [6] as stating that US recognition will be extended within 24 hours. Mancheno is reliably reported to have stated his political and economic policy must closely parallel that of US.

. . . .

Present *de facto* regime appears thoroughly to control the machinery of government. With exception of the Cabinet most government employees are continuing at their posts.

There is no apparent active opposition to present regime. Evidence of degree of popular support not yet accurately ascertainable although public indicates attitude of general acceptance without enthusiasm. Conservatives have been given a minor role and probably are disgruntled. Mancheno is reported as saying that the Communists shall have no part in his government. In fact he is reported to have refused to talk to the Communist delegate who went to the meeting for the formation of the Cabinet in the hope that a Communist member of the government could be appointed.

Two highly reliable sources report Mancheno as stating that all in-

---

[5] José Vicente Trujillo, Ecuadoran Minister of Foreign Affairs and Delegate to the Inter-American Conference for the Maintenance of Continental Peace and Security which met at Petropolis, August 15–September 2, 1947.

[6] Former Ecuadoran Ambassador to the United States.

ternational treaties, agreements and obligations entered into by previous regime will be observed and complied with. Mancheno reportedly friendly to US and, as it appears he is in strong position and may well remain in power for some time, position of Ambassador to retain this goodwill without performing an act of recognition will become increasingly difficult.

It must be remembered however that Mancheno seized power through the illegal strong-arm method of a military *coup d'état* and that he did not even permit a normal constitutional succession to the presidency. As to the latter point he caused the arrest and detention of the Vice President for a few hours yesterday morning although later ordering his release. If the method of coming into power were to be a norm for recognition, his position would obviously be weak as regards that particular point. However, he is believed to be very well disposed toward the US, considerably more so than was Velasco Ibarra.

As to the point, which he is now stressing, that after all Velasco did resign and did hand the presidential power over to him, my observation is (1) that he only resigned under strong compulsion and (2) that the decision as to who should succeed him was not his to make but rather should be a constitutional question. He unquestionably has by his action disavowed the Congress recently elected by free expression of opinion of the people.

Summing up, I believe that recognition of Mancheno regime, if based upon the three criteria now usually observed under international law and under the policy of the US would have considerable justification but that, if the manner of his coming into power should be an important consideration, his case would obviously be greatly weakened.

I am adopting a course of personal conduct which could not possibly be construed as recognition of new regime. It is my intention not to call on Mancheno although my Argentine colleague is reported to have done so. I have instructed the chiefs of the various other US Government agencies and missions here to be very circumspect, maintaining their usual contacts on an informal and cooperative basis and avoiding all possible indications of unfriendliness, at the same time refraining from actions, particularly at higher governmental levels, which could possibly be interpreted as an indication of our recognition.

Embassy would appreciate knowing as soon as possible any developments on this question particularly whether consultative procedure with other American Republics is contemplated.[7]

SIMMONS

---

[7] For the most part the other American Republics indicated a disposition to await events. Peru, Chile, and Bolivia revealed a strong disinclination to recognize the Mancheno regime (822.01/8-2647, 8-2847, 8-2947, and 9-147).

822.01/8–2747

Memorandum of Conversation, by Mr. George H. Owen of the Division of North and West Coast Affairs

CONFIDENTIAL [WASHINGTON,] August 27, 1947.

Participants: Señor Dr. Neftali Ponce, Ecuadoran Ambassador in Washington
Mr. Sheldon Mills, Chief,[8] NWC
Mr. George H. Owen, NWC

Ambassador Ponce of Ecuador called at the Department of State this morning.

He inquired whether the Department had taken any decision with regard to the new government of Ecuador. He was told by Mr. Owen and again by Mr. Mills that a reasonable period of time was required before any decision with respect to recognition of the new government could be made.

The Ambassador later inquired of Mr. Mills whether, specifically, the Department takes the position that a problem of recognition exists or not. It was made clear to the Ambassador that in all similar changes of government the question of recognition does exist and that formal relations with Ambassador Ponce remain suspended until the new government is recognized.

The Ambassador then also inquired whether the Department had received any word regarding the attitude of the Rio Conference [9] toward the new Government of Ecuador. He was told in reply that the Department had received no news from Rio on this point.

In the course of conversation it was pointed out to the Ambassador that formal business with the Embassy has had to be suspended and that there would be some delay in the carrying out of day to day business; that this includes transactions with the Export-Import Bank and contracts for the delivery of military supplies under the Interim Program. Señor Ponce said that he had received word from the Export-Import Bank today that the decision on the Quevedo Manta loan [10] which was to be made today had been postponed. He said he has reported this to the Ecuadoran Foreign Office expressing his regrets.

When asked about his views on the overthrow of Velasco, Señor Ponce stated that the fundamental cause of the coup lay undoubtedly in a personal dispute between Velasco and Colonel Mancheno and that the change in Government could not be said to have been caused by

---

[8] Mr. Mills became Assistant Chief on August 1 and Chief on October 19.
[9] For documentation on this Conference, see pp. 1 ff.
[10] For documentation on the financing of Ecuadoran economic proposals, see pp. 690 ff.

any fundamental conflict of political parties. He stated his belief that a Presidential election would be held. He certainly left no impression that he was personally enthusiastic in support of the new government.

822.01/8–2847 : Circular telegram

The Acting Secretary of State to the Diplomatic Representatives in the American Republics

CONFIDENTIAL   WASHINGTON, August 28, 1947—7 a. m.

For your confidential info Dept has suggested to USDel, Petropolis, policy respecting recognition or nonrecognition Mancheno regime Ecuador (1) should involve appropriate waiting period to make certain New Govt can maintain order, will comply its obligations, etc., and (2) Dept considers US should not take lead in proposing recognition, but if neighboring countries start move that direction we could fall in line.

LOVETT

822.01/8–2947

Memorandum by the Assistant Chief of the Division of North and West Coast Affairs (Mills) to the Desk Officers of That Division

RESTRICTED   [WASHINGTON,] August 29, 1947.

United States policy with respect to recognition of new Ecuadoran regime of Col. Mancheno, based on views expressed to Chilean Ambassador by Mr. Wright: [11]

1. It is wise to wait an appropriate period to see whether *de facto* regime has all required elements of stability.

2. The change in government does not appear to us to have the attributes of constitutionality, although we have not completed our studies in this respect.

3. The revolution does not seem to have any special significance, being similar to 40 or 50 others in Ecuador's history.

4. We have to be sure that our action in the case of Ecuador is not over hasty, in order to avoid charges, however unfounded, of discrimination in respect of Nicaragua.[12]

5. We have heard that Rio Conference has decided not to allow Foreign Minister Trujillo of Ecuador to sign treaty. This certainly was an important international action which involves us all.

---

[11] James H. Wright, Special Assistant to the Assistant Secretary of State for American Republic Affairs.

[12] For documentation on the Nicaraguan situation, see pp. 841 ff.

ECUADOR 669

6. The United States prefers not to take the lead, but is rather awaiting with interest the views and actions of the other American governments.

SHELDON T. MILLS

822.00/9–147 : Telegram

The Ambassador in Ecuador (Simmons) to the Secretary of State

SECRET   QUITO, September 1, 1947—11 a. m.

372. Immediate struggle for control situation between Mancheno and "Constitutionalist" troops confined Ambato-Riobamba area. Mancheno troops reported to have passed through Latachunga. Radio message received through Shell Company facilities this a. m. said guardedly "Situation not good. No one allowed to leave Ambato." A later rumor that insurgents in Riobamba had surrendered seems unlikely.

Leaflet dropped from airplane this a. m. says a battalion of infantry, a squadron pursuit planes and a company civil guard have joined the Oppositionist movement dated August 31, Tulcan, and signed by officers known to oppose Mancheno.

Message from Guayaquil dated last night says troops and Junior Officers Ninth Infantry Battalion apparently have revolted. Mancheno forces resisting them with tanks. Attitude of civil guard there still uncertain. There were possibilities of imminent serious conflict that city although an unclear report this a. m. indicates tank group may have joined insurgents. City reported momentarily tranquil.

Disaffection seems to be spreading throughout country thus making it extremely difficult for Mancheno to maintain control.

.   .   .   .

SIMMONS

822.00/9–247 : Telegram

The Ambassador in Ecuador (Simmons) to the Secretary of State

CONFIDENTIAL   URGENT   QUITO, September 2, 1947—11 a. m.

375. Mancheno at 11 a. m., today sent message asking asylum this Embassy. I declined citing our general position in such matters. His message delivered to me by Mrs. Salinas wife of Major Salinas of our military ground mission at whose house he now is. I suggested possibility other Embassies here. Mancheno troops at Ambato reported demoralized. Guayaquil confirmed in opposition hands. In other words Mancheno is through although situation highly confused as to who

will now take power. Possibility exists civil disturbance Quito which now has no adequate police or military protection. Crowds now milling in center city. Atmosphere tense.

SIMMONS

822.00/9-447

Memorandum of Conversation, By Mr. George H. Owen of the Division of North and West Coast Affairs

RESTRICTED [WASHINGTON,] September 4, 1947.

Participants: Ambassador L. Neftali Ponce of Ecuador
Mr. Sheldon T. Mills
Mr. James Espy
Mr. George H. Owen

Ambassador Ponce of Ecuador called at the Department this afternoon at his request. He stated that, according to the latest information from Ecuador available to him, the government of Mariano Suarez Veintimilla, constitutionally designated Vice President under Velasco's administration, was, unquestionably, in effective control of the country with a cabinet of distinguished Ecuadorans.

He added that there probably remained some differences originating in conflicting views of certain Army officers, but that these were undoubtedly of minor importance and that public opinion overwhelmingly is in support of the Suarez government. He stated that he had heard of the reported movement in Guayaquil or Ambato under Colonel Girón but that it was not clear whether Girón was acting in opposition to Suarez or not, since Girón is reported to have announced that he had taken charge of the government of the Guayaquil area by order of Colonel Angel Baquero, who is the minister of Defense of the Suarez Government.

Señor Ponce then read the attached memorandum No. 201, dated September 4, 1947,[13] which states that Constitutional order, momentarily deranged, has been restored in Ecuador. The memorandum describes the coup of Colonel Mancheno as a "censurable act of force" which has been rejected by public opinion, and that Vice President Suarez, from the very beginning of Mancheno's regime had requested that the Government be transferred to him in accordance with the Constitution, which Colonel Mancheno refused to do; that this movement to re-establish constitutional order has now triumphed completely. The memorandum then states that the Council of State, on

---

[13] Not printed.

September 3, 1947, has called on Suarez to assume the Presidency in accordance with the Constitution and has convened the National Congress for September 15. The Memorandum concludes with an assurance that the restoration of the constitutional regime has been welcomed with general approval.

Mr. Mills inquired whether a statement such as this memorandum had been made to other governments. Ambassador Ponce replied that he was leaving the memorandum with the Department in accordance with a circular instruction which the Ecuadoran Foreign Office had sent to all the Ecuadoran Missions in the American Republics. He added that he was also instructed to say that the Government of Suarez maintains that, since constitutional government has been restored, the matter of recognition is now solved and relations between Ecuador and other countries should be considered normal.

It was made clear to Señor Ponce by Mr. Mills that the memorandum was accepted informally, without implication of any decision on behalf of the Department on the matter of recognition, since the Department would have to study this matter in the light of current developments. Señor Ponce agreed that the Department was, of course, within its rights in wishing to study the matter of recognition further in the light of these events.

Mr. Mills inquired whether it was suggested that matters be held in abeyance until September 15 when the Congress convenes and takes appropriate action under the provisions of the constitution. Señor Ponce replied that, while it is true that Congress actually has the last word in deciding the issues involved, the decision of the Council of State of September 3, calling on Suarez to assume the Presidency may be considered decisive since the Council of State is established by the Constitution to determine constitutional questions.

Mr. Espy inquired as to what Señor Ponce considered to be his personal status as Ambassador. Señor Ponce replied that he had sent his resignation on the day following Mancheno's assumption of power, but that no action had been taken on his resignation, and that since the lawful government has been re-established, he considers himself to be the regularly appointed Ambassador of Ecuador.

Señor Ponce also pointed out that one further difficulty may arise in the event that former President Velasco should enter Ecuador and wish to be reinstated as President. Ponce believes that there would be considerable opposition to this and that further difficulties would then have to be expected. He stated that it was unlikely that Velasco would succeed in entering Ecuador since the group in power in Guayaquil had specifically denied him permission to land there.

822.01/9-747 : Telegram

The Secretary of State to the Embassy in Ecuador

CONFIDENTIAL   WASHINGTON, September 8, 1947—1 p. m.

266. Urtel 388, Sept 7.[14] Dept does not wish to take any action in respect of Ecuadoran recognition at this time. Situation is not yet considered clear and it is considered preferable to await developments particularly from Sept 15 meeting of Congress and in general to have clear picture of whether regime manifests all qualities of stable *de facto* govt. Also we will probably wish to await views of a rather substantial body of other American republics.

MARSHALL

822.01/9-847

Memorandum of Conversation, by the Assistant Chief of the Division of North and West Coast Affairs (Espy)

RESTRICTED   [WASHINGTON,] September 9, 1947.

Participants: Ambassador L. Neftali Ponce of Ecuador
                Mr. Sheldon T. Mills
                Mr. James Espy

Ambassador Ponce of Ecuador called on his request at the Department this afternoon. Referring to his previous call on September 4, Ambassador Ponce stated that he had brought with him two Memoranda giving additional information on the situation in Ecuador which he wished the Department to consider with respect to the possible reestablishment of relations with Ecuador. Copies of these Memoranda are attached.[14] The one quotes a resolution of the Ecuadoran Council of State declaring that President José Maria Velasco Ibarra abandoned his office as President and that, therefore, the Presidency of Ecuador was constitutionally assumed by Vice President Mariano Suarez Veintimilla, and summoning a special session of the Ecuadoran Congress for Monday, September 15 for the purposes as stated in article 87 of the Ecuadoran Constitution of 1946. (The article provides that Congress shall be called into extraordinary session in order to issue "la resolucion corespondiente" after the Council of State has found that the President has abandoned his office.) This resolution is dated September 3, 1947. The other Memorandum states that order has been reestablished in Ecuador and conveys information reported to the Ecuadoran Ambassador by the Ecuadoran Foreign

---

[14] Not printed.

Ministry to the effect that the constitutional government of Dr. Suarez Veintimilla is exercising effective jurisdiction in all territory of Ecuador; that there is peace and tranquillity throughout the Republic; that all the army units have returned to their barracks and recognize the authority of the constitutional government; that the people of Ecuador have manifested their support of the government; and that it is unanimously agreed that the present actual government of Ecuador is the constitutional continuation of the previous government that was temporarily overthrown by the attempted dictatorship of Colonel Mancheno.

Following his reading of these Memoranda Ambassador Ponce said that he was convinced that all was quiet in Ecuador and that the Suarez Veintimilla government had been accepted as the constitutional administration of the country and was supported by all elements in Ecuador. In reply to various questions asked him by Mr. Mills he said that on September 4 Colonel Vellacis, the leader of the dissident military at Ambato which had been supporting Colonel Mancheno, capitulated to Colonel Baquero, Minister of Defense of the Suarez Veintimilla Government; that the military at Guayaquil were also disposed to accept the Suarez Veintimilla government; and that apparently Major Giron had also acceded to this (he explained that all along Major Giron has been in opposition to Colonel Mancheno and supporting the constitutional government, but it was not clear whether Major Giron would accept Suarez Veintimilla as the constitutional President); that former President Velasco Ibarra was not returning to Ecuador and that if he tried to do so, it would be very improbable that he could obtain any support for his restitution as President; and that the Foreign Minister, Dr. Trujillo, had returned to Quito and reassumed charge of the Foreign Ministry on September 6.

Ambassador Ponce also stated that as he understood it, Dr. Suarez Veintimilla would on September 15 appear before the Congress as the constitutional President and report on the events that had occurred and thereafter submit his resignation to the Congress. The Ambassador explained that Suarez Veintimilla is a member of the conservative party of Ecuador which has the largest single membership in the Congress, but does not have a majority over the combined liberal and socialist party members and therefore could not hope to obtain the continued support of Congress. The Ambassador said that he did not know who would be the candidate for the provisional Vice President. According to the constitution, however, the President of the House of Deputies would normally succeed the Vice President. In any event, the provisional Vice President would only hold office until national elections were held next year.

At the end of the conversation Ambassador Ponce said he had received word today that the government of Bolivia had announced that it would continue to maintain relations with the constitutional Ecuadoran Government and he hoped that the United States Government would soon see its way clear also to do so.

822.00/9-1647 : Telegram

The Ambassador in Ecuador (Simmons) to the Secretary of State

QUITO, September 16, 1947.

402. Congress elected Carlos Julio Arosemena Vice President by vote 103 to 3; next session scheduled 4:30 p. m. Arosemena arrives Quito this afternoon. Resignation Suarez expected to be acted upon immediately and Arosemena may be installed as President today.

SIMMONS

822.01/9-1847 : Telegram

The Ambassador in Ecuador (Simmons) to the Secretary of State

URGENT   NIACT   QUITO, September 18, 1947—10 a. m.

410. In regard to political situation here is [I] submit following points:

1. Constitutionality now completely restored (see mytel No. 388 September 7 [16]).

2. Interim President Arosemena elected by overwhelming majority and has unopposed support of country including army. Situation stable and new administration has full control of machinery of government. Existence discontent in army (mytel 401, September 16 [16]) considered at present a minor factor.

3. Our withholding recognition now is very different from our doing so before president coming into office last evening. Other countries apparently contemplating acts of recognition. Four have already taken action tantamount to this. Our withholding favorable action further might easily be interpreted as a positive act of unfriendliness.

4. Ecuadoran delegation already admitted as full member forthcoming sessions GA UN.

5. I consequently recommend that I be authorized immediately to take some positive step such as delivering a routine note or calling on FonMin which would indicate our position as recognizing continuity between new government after a short hiatus and previous constitu-

---

[16] Not printed.

tional regime thus implying that no question of recognition has arisen in usual sense of word. I also recommend simultaneous announcement by Department that normal cordial diplomatic relations have been resumed.

SIMMONS

822.01/9–1947

Memorandum of Conversation, by Mr. George H. Owen of the Division of North and West Coast Affairs

RESTRICTED [WASHINGTON,] September 19, 1947.

Participants: Señor Dr. L. Neftali Ponce, Ambassador of Ecuador in Washington
Mr. Sheldon T. Mills, NWC
Mr. George H. Owen, NWC

Ambassador Ponce of Ecuador called at the Department this afternoon at his request and left the attached informal note [17] which gives account of the election by Congress and the inauguration of President Carlos Julio Arosemena and Vice President José Rafael Bustamante and the composition of the new Cabinet.

Mr. Mills invited Señor Ponce to call on Mr. Wright on Monday, September 22 and informed him that we would consider this visit as constituting establishment of normal diplomatic relations with the Government of Ecuador. Mr. Mills also stated that we were instructing our Ambassador in Quito to call on the Ecuadoran Foreign Minister on September 22 and resume normal relations thereby.

Mr. Mills stated to the Ambassador that the reason for delaying official announcement of the resumption of normal relations until Monday was our desire to consult thereon with other American Governments.

822.01/9–1947 : Circular telegram

The Acting Secretary of State to the Diplomatic Representatives in the American Republics

RESTRICTED WASHINGTON, September 19, 1947—2 a. m.

Please inform Govt to which you are accredited that US Govt is instructing US Amb at Quito to enter into normal relations with new Govt of Ecuador on Monday, Sept 22.

LOVETT

---

[17] Not printed.

UNITED STATES MILITARY ASSISTANCE TO ECUADOR; THE GALÁPAGOS BASES [18]

811.24522/1–3047

The Ambassador in Ecuador (Scotten) to the Assistant Secretary of State for American Republic Affairs (Braden)

RESTRICTED   QUITO, January 30, 1947.

DEAR SPRUILLE: Since Illescas' [19] return I have given a luncheon for him attended by Trujillo [20] and others. He came in to see me previous to that luncheon, and he discussed in general terms the Galapagos matter. When I say in general terms, I mean exactly that. He did not have one concrete plan or suggestion of a plan. I told him I understood that he would receive detailed instructions from his government to take back to Washington. He replied that it was true that Trujillo had told you that he would receive these instructions but that on thinking it over, he had decided and had told both the President [21] and Trujillo that he did not desire such instructions, but that he be allowed a free hand to see what he could do. He was completely vague, and I am wondering whether in fact he will actually try to arrive at a definite agreement for the future of the Base. He did mention, however, the desire of Ecuador to obtain military equipment for its armed forces, and he seemed to think we would be delighted to furnish Ecuador everything it needed in return for the right to maintain the Base. When I asked him just what equipment he had in mind, he shied off this subject, and I received the impression that he had not even talked the matter over with the Ecuadoran military authorities. He said he would discuss the matter further with me, but so far has not done so. This may not be very helpful, Spruille, but it is really the best I can do.

With kindest regards, please believe me,

Sincerely yours,   ROB

---

[18] For documentation on the general policy of the United States in providing military assistance to the other American Republics, see pp. 101 ff.; and for documentation concerning the negotiations on United States bases in Ecuador and other defense problems in 1946, see *Foreign Relations*, 1946, vol. XI, pp. 836 ff.
[19] Francisco Yllescas, Ecuadoran Ambassador to the United States.
[20] José Vicente Trujillo, Ecuadoran Minister for Foreign Affairs.
[21] José Maria Velasco Ibarra.

822.248/2–1347

The Ambassador in Ecuador (Scotten) to the Secretary of State

CONFIDENTIAL
No. 4962

QUITO, February 13, 1947.

SIR: I have the honor to report that the United States Military Attaché in Quito [22] has today furnished me with a copy of his report also dated today entitled "Threatened Resignation of Officers of Ecuadoran Air Force." It is pointed out in the report that the resignation of these officers and possibly of others later is based upon the non-availability of suitable aircraft for military training. The Chief of the Ecuadoran Air Force [23] and the Minister of Defense [24] have been criticized directly for failing to obtain the aircraft which has been purchased from the United States or, in fact, to obtain even an approximate date as to when it may be expected. Reference is made to aircraft which had been purchased and paid for. This is understood to mean the one C–47, three C–45, and six P–47 airplanes [25] which were reported to have been ready for delivery in Texas last fall. (Note: Number of airplanes involved is quoted from an oral statement by the Chief of the Ecuadoran Air Force.)

No direct mention was made of any other aircraft which Ecuador desires but which has not become available, due to difficulties in the way of delivery by the United States and in the way of financing by Ecuador. It is doubtful if the junior officers concerned will recognize all of these difficulties. The fact remains that resentment against the United States is being built up and much of the good work of the military missions in Ecuador is being lost.

It is earnestly recommended that at least some definite indication as to when the aircraft already purchased will be available for delivery to Ecuador be furnished to this Embassy or to the United States Military Air Mission in Quito.

A copy of the report referred to above is attached hereto.[26]

Respectfully yours,

For the Ambassador:
GEO. P. SHAW
Counselor of Embassy

[22] Col. Paul K. Porch.
[23] Col. Victor Tobar Albuja.
[24] Cesar Jaramillo.
[25] C–47's and C–45's were transport planes; P–47's were dive bombers.
[26] Not printed.

811.24522/3-1047

The Secretary of War (Patterson) to the Secretary of State

CONFIDENTIAL WASHINGTON, March 10, 1947.

MEMORANDUM FOR THE DEPARTMENT OF STATE

Attention: Mr. Carlos Hall, Division of North and West Coast Affairs

1. Reference is made to State Department correspondence of 5 March 1947,[27] requesting the following information regarding the Galápagos Base:

   a. Total cost to the War Department of installations and equipment;
   b. Book value of remaining installations and equipment;
   c. Estimated surplus value of installations and equipment now at Galápagos.

2. The total cost to the War Department of the installations and equipment on the Galápagos Base, as of this date, is $10,021,006.01. Additionally, there is an AWS station in the Galápagos, but not on the base itself, which cost $834,641.79. Both installations are still active and their book value is carried as the cost value. Estimated surplus value can only be determined by on the spot sale evaluation, which the Foreign Liquidation Commission advises probably could be provided by their Panama representative upon request, such evaluation being properly a function of that agency.

For the Secretary of War:
J. E. BASTION, JR.
Colonel, GSC

822.248/2-1347

The Chief of the Division of Special Inter-American Affairs (Dreier) to the Ambassador in Ecuador (Scotten)

CONFIDENTIAL WASHINGTON, March 19, 1947.

DEAR MR. AMBASSADOR: I believe a personal letter may be the best way of giving you some background on the rather confused situation, repercussions of which, in Ecuador, were discussed in the Embassy's despatch No. 4962, February 13. This despatch reported the resentment of officers of the Ecuadoran airforce over the failure to acquire aircraft promised them by the United States in the so-called interim program.

The aircraft in the interim program for Ecuador totaled 22 planes

---

[27] Not printed.

as outlined in the Department's telegram No. 90 of March 12, 1946.[28] Their availability was first mentioned to the Ecuadorans by the Department in March, 1946. Due to protracted delays in connection with the administration of the program under the Surplus Property Act,[29] involving determinations of availability, establishment of prices, etc. a formal offer of these aircraft to Ecuador at a specified price was not made until August 27, 1946. Two days later a representative of the Ecuadoran Government sent to the Foreign Liquidation Commission a check for $131,500 to cover the cost of ten of these aircraft, namely, 1 C–47, 3 C–45's, 6 P–47's. Deposit of this check was not called for since no contract had been signed but it was indicated by the Ecuadoran representative that he wished to deposit the money anyway to insure against its being diverted to other purposes.

At that time, it was not clear at all how long it would take the War Department to put these aircraft in operable condition since they were sealed up, stripped of some equipment, etc. However, it is quite probable that the persons in the Foreign Liquidation Commission who discussed the matter with the Ecuadorans expressed the hope that these ten aircraft would be ready in 60 days, namely, early in November. I am quite confident, however, that no promise or formal statement of availability was ever made to the Ecuadorans since the War Department itself did not know at that time when the aircraft could be delivered.

In fact the War Department has, insofar as I have been able to find out, not yet been able to start work on these aircraft paid for by Ecuador, let alone do anything about the other 12 aircraft in the interim program for which the Ecuadorans recently placed a firm order. It is the practice of the FLC on this interim program not to sign a contract with the purchasing country until they know when the material will be available. So far no contract has been signed by the FLC, I am told, covering the interim aircraft because of uncertainty as to their readiness.

The principal reason for the delay of the War Department in getting around to the Ecuadoran aircraft is that the Ecuadoran Government did not wish to have the aircraft ferried to Ecuador by United States Army personnel as did most of the countries to which such an offer was made. The War Department, anxious to complete the ferrying project, naturally reconditioned first the planes which they had agreed to fly to the purchasing country. Planes ordered by Ecuador, Brazil and Uruguay (the three countries which wanted to fly their planes south with their own pilots) were left at the end of the list and are only now being worked on.

---
[28] Not printed.
[29] Of October 8, 1944; 58 Stat. 765.

I have several times talked with the War Department and pointed out the good will which they were losing by failing to make good on delivery of at least some of the aircraft for which Ecuador has already paid. In my last conversation I referred to the report of the Military Attaché [30] attached to your despatch under reference, which the War Department had not seen. I am hopeful that when they see it they will make some energetic move to get at least a few of the Ecuadoran planes into flying condition within the next few weeks. However, we have not yet obtained any firm date from them. I do know, moreover, that the Ecuadoran Military Attaché [31] has himself been going after the War Department on the matter.

The foregoing will not be of much help to you but will at least give you an indication why all this delay is taking place. We shall, of course, let you know as soon as we hear anything definite from the War Department on the delivery of any of the aircraft which Ecuador is purchasing.

With best regards,

Sincerely yours, JOHN C. DREIER

P.S. Since writing the above, the Army has informed me that they are putting the Ecuadoran aircraft at the top of the list of those to be reconditioned from now on. They are not, however, able to give a definite date of delivery as yet.

811.24522/4–1047

Memorandum by Commodore J. E. Maher of the Office of the Chief of Naval Operations, Navy Department

CONFIDENTIAL WASHINGTON, April 10, 1947.

Memorandum for: Chief, Division of North and West Coast Affairs, Department of State

Ref: (a) Dept of State ltr NWC dated 5 March 1947 to Navy Dept.[30]

1. The following information concerning the former Naval Air Facility, Galápagos, is submitted in accordance with the request contained in ref (a):

(a) Total cost to the Navy Department of installations and equipment.

The original cost of construction and equipment for the Naval Air Facility Galápagos, was $1,700,705. The total cost of the Naval installations now remaining on the site at Galápagos was $1,474,935 of

---

[30] Not printed.
[31] Gen. Luis Larrea-Alba

which $500,000 represents the cost of existing water lines, fuel lines, electrical distribution system, sewer system, roads, etc.

(*b*) Book value of remaining installations and equipment.

All remaining Navy buildings and installations were stripped of salvageable material when the Naval Air Facility was disestablished on 16 May 1946. However, it is estimated that to replace the numerous frame buildings remaining, would cost approximately $800,000. In addition, a small amount of Navy equipment, valued at $2,000 has been loaned to the United States Army and is now in use at Galápagos.

(*c*) Estimated surplus value of installations and equipment now at Galápagos.

It is not possible for the Navy Department to determine the surplus sale value of installations and equipment now at Galápagos inasmuch as sales possibilities are not known to this Department. However, the salvage value to the Navy of buildings and equipment remaining at Galápagos is nil, because of the excessive cost of dismantling and shipping the buildings to a location where they could be utilized by the Navy.

2. All figures given above are approximations.

J. E. MAHER

822.24 FLC/7–1147

The Chargé in Ecuador (Shaw) to the Secretary of State

RESTRICTED QUITO, July 11, 1947.
No. 5357

SIR: I have the honor to inform the Department that Mr. Robert F. Edgar, Central Field Commissioner for Latin America, Office of the Foreign Liquidation Commissioner with headquarters in Balboa, Canal Zone, came to Quito on about May 15, 1947 to discuss with the Minister of National Defense of Ecuador the matter of signing an agreement and contract of sale between Ecuador and the United States whereby Ecuador would have the privilege of purchasing on credit up to $350,000 in United States currency surplus movable property, including maritime and aviation equipment. The agreement in effect is an open credit payable in five annual installments and bearing interest at 2⅜% per annum.

The Minister of Defense was very much interested and indicated that he was willing to sign the contract within a few days. Mr. Edgar was traveling in a United States Government plane and took a commission to the Galápagos Islands to survey certain property whose sale was contemplated. A list of said property was drawn up and agreed upon.

Mr. Edgar was informed, upon returning to Quito, that the Minister of Defense would have to clear the contract with the Minister of Treasury and, therefore, he could not sign it prior to Mr. Edgar's departure. Mr. Edgar delegated me to sign the contract for him at such time as it should be approved by the Ecuadoran Government.

On taking off on Saturday morning, May 17, Mr. Edgar's airplane was wrecked and was declared a total loss. Incidentally, it is understood that the remains of the plane, which contained a lot of undamaged instruments and other equipment, were turned over to the Ecuadoran Government for the insignificant sum of $300.

Mr. Edgar and a commission of Ecuadoran officers proceeded to Panama by other means and the commission went on to Trinidad where it drew up an additional list of property that Ecuador desired to acquire.

In the meantime, and despite frequent urgings by the Embassy, the Minister of Defense ran into difficulties not only with the Minister of Treasury but with the Council of State as well. It was decided that, in view of the terms of the contract, the Council of State would have to approve it. The Council of State at that time was in conflict with the Minister of Defense and it is understood that the matter was held up for political reasons. It was only when the contents of Mr. Edgar's telegram of June 25,[33] stating that unless the agreement were executed before June 30 the privilege of purchasing the property would be cut off, was brought to the attention of the Ecuadoran Government through the Ministries of Foreign Affairs and of National Defense that the Council of State acted. It approved the contract except for the provision whereby the Government of Ecuador might transfer Government property to the Government of the United States. This situation confronted me on the evening of June 27 and I realized that if the contract and the opinion of the Council of State were both interpreted strictly and literally it would be impossible to sign any agreement. Therefore, I acquired the verbal assurance of the Foreign Office and the Ministry of Defense that the contract and the opinion of the Council of State both would be given the most liberal interpretation and I was assured that the Government was disposed to assist the United States in acquiring property to liquidate this account, as the use of sucres for this purpose was very advantageous to Ecuador. Also, I was assured that property could be transferred to the United States through a third person or with the special permission of Congress. In order not to declare that Ecuador had lost its opportunity to purchase this property, and confident that a practical solution for the

---

[33] Not printed.

technical difficulties would be found, I signed the document and it was forwarded by airmail to Mr. Edgar in Balboa. I have since received a communication from him stating that the contract was found to be acceptable. It was pointed out, however, that the principal object of the contract was to carry out the property acquisition program, and that if the Ecuadoran Government failed to cooperate as it had promised, the obligation to pay in United States dollars would remain.

In view of the various conversations which I had had with the Minister of Defense and officials of the Foreign Office concerning this matter, I deemed it advisable to reduce my statements to the form of a memorandum and deliver it to the Foreign Office for the information of the Minister of Defense so there would be no misunderstanding as to the objectives that the United States had in mind when the offer was made and the property was transferred.

One signed copy of the contract in English together with a copy of the opinion of the Council of State and a copy of my memorandum today to the Foreign Office are transmitted herewith to the Department as a matter of record and for possible use should any question arise as to the circumstances under which this agreement was signed and the understanding of the signers as to interpretation at that time.

General Alfonso Jaramillo Zumarraga, who signed the contract as Minister of National Defense, resigned immediately after signing the contract and was succeeded by Colonel Carlos Mancheno, former Minister of Defense. Colonel Mancheno has evinced great interest in this matter since assuming the duties of Minister and has assured me personally and even more emphatically than did General Jaramillo that the contract will be given the most liberal interpretation and that there will be no practical difficulties encountered in acquiring property or material desired by the United States in liquidation of the account. As a matter of fact, Colonel Mancheno already has brought to me tentative propositions for certain pieces of property in which he thinks the United States Government might be interested. He has suggested that the site of the present military hospital might be used to much more advantage as a site for an Embassy chancery and if a transfer of some kind could be worked out he could move the hospital to the suburbs which would be much more advantageous to him. This incident is cited merely to show the good will which exists on the part of the present Minister of Defense at this time.

The matter of suitable property which may be acquired is being investigated actively as it is believed advisable to take advantage of the aid and assistance proffered by the Minister of Defense before further changes may occur in the administration.

Respectfully yours, GEO. P. SHAW

822.24/8-1647 : Telegram

The Ambassador in Ecuador (Simmons) to the Secretary of State

SECRET   US URGENT   QUITO, August 16, 1947—1 p. m.
NIACT

328. Colonel Macherey [34] has just informed me that two official representatives Prague office of Empresa Nacional Zbrojovka Brnpn [sic] an organ of Czechoslovak Govt who are now in Quito have offered Ecuadoran Govt a contract for supplying Ecuador with 30 million cartridges ball steel point calibre 7.92 millimeters for Mauser short rifles and ZB automatic rifles for first delivery 5 million rounds promised within 30 days subsequent deliveries on similar monthly basis until completed, six equal semi-annual payments beginning August 31 continuing on last days of June and December until completed for total amount of $2,189,400.

Colonel Macherey convinced that only method of forestalling signature this contract would be for us to offer immediate facilities purchase comparable US material at substantially cheaper prices. Minister of Defense expresses definite wish to purchase from US and has given Macherey verbal commitment to withhold signature Czechoslovak contract pending prompt information on US prices, the terms of credit and payment to be worked out at later date.

Would appreciate reply as soon as possible giving indication Dept's attitude and if latter favorable a statement on price per thousand rounds which we would be able to offer for large purchase of type contemplated in order to forestall signature of contract for which Czechoslovaks are now exerting strong pressure. Macherey convinced that Czechoslovak offer bona fide and that Ecuadoran representations are not to be considered as high pressure method of securing US ammunition at cheaper price.

Repeated Petropolis.[35]

SIMMONS

822.24/8-1647 : Telegram

The Acting Secretary of State to the Embassy in Ecuador

SECRET   WASHINGTON, August 19, 1947—7 p. m.

250. Urtel 328, Aug 16. War Dept does not use or stock 7.92 caliber ammo and thus none is or will be available. Maximum amt comparable

---

[34] Lt. Col. Earl J. Macherey, Chief of the United States Military Ground Mission in Ecuador.
[35] Petropolis was the site of the Inter-American Conference for the Maintenance of Continental Peace and Security which opened on August 15 and which the Secretary of State attended as head of the U.S. delegation.

ammo possible War Dept supply Ecuador is (1) three yrs training supply each weapon purchased interim program, and (2) three yrs supply each weapon transferred lend-lease. This formula being applied all countries participating program and in opinion War Dept provides sufficient ammo to meet normal requirements.

Ecuador has ordered all ammo eligible receive under (1) above. This amounts to approx 1,500,000 rounds small caliber ammo at bargain price of 5 per cent cost to US or about $9,000. Ecuador eligible receive under (2) above, approx 812,000 rounds small caliber ammo priced at about $4,500. Ecuador has ordered some but not all ammo this category. No commitment should be made supply ammo excess these amounts.

Although not possible at present undertake commitments additional those indicated above par, future program envisaged Ecuador includes additional 30 caliber and other weapons to replace non-standard weapons. It therefore would not appear in best interest Ecuador purchase large quantities non-standard ammo, particularly since prices quoted by Czechs are many times higher than prices it has so far been possible quote for interim program ammo, i.e., approx $4.65 per thousand rounds rifle ball ammo. Acquisition at this time of such large quantities ammo commit Ecuador to Mauser rifle. Over extended period cost of ammo used by one rifle will greatly exceed cost of new rifle.

Implementation envisaged program is of course dependent upon passage by Congress of arms bill.[36] Hence no commitment beyond paragraph 2 shld be made. For Emb's conf info War Dept is exploring possibility second interim program under which Ecuador may be offered small amt additional military equipment later this yr.

Amdel Rio has referred urtel Dept for action. Problems this nature should not be referred Rio in future. Also your message was overclassified for security purposes.

LOVETT

811.24522/10–2347

The Ambassador in Ecuador (Simmons) to the Secretary of State

CONFIDENTIAL QUITO, October 28, 1947.
No. 6188

SIR: I have the honor to refer to my despatch no. 6157 of October 17, 1947 [37] and to previous recent correspondence concerning conditions

---

[36] Known also as the Military and Naval Collaboration Bill. For documentation, see pp. 101 ff.
[37] Not printed.

in the Galápagos Islands, particularly with reference to local criticism of the American armed forces now stationed in those islands.

For the Department's information, I enclose copies of a telegram addressed to me under date of October 23, 1947 by Lieutenant General Willis D. Crittenberger, the Commanding General of the Caribbean Defense Command, Canal Zone, and of my letter of yesterday in reply to this telegram,[38] both referring to certain specific measures which General Crittenberger has now taken in order to correct the Galápagos situation as revealed by a recent investigation which he ordered to be conducted in the Galápagos.

I feel that these measures, which include the imminent replacement, without prejudice, of the present commanding officer, the assignment of a Spanish-speaking officer to assist him in his relations with the Ecuadoran garrison and other improvements mentioned in his telegram, will go far towards correcting the present situation and towards silencing a considerable amount of criticism recently published in the local press concerning the activities of our armed forces now stationed in the Galápagos Islands.

A copy of this despatch is being forwarded to General Crittenberger for his information.

Respectfully yours, JOHN F. SIMMONS

811.24522/11-847

The Ambassador in Ecuador (Simmons) to the Secretary of State

RESTRICTED QUITO, November 8, 1947.
No. 6219

SIR: I have the honor to refer to previous correspondence concerning training maneuvers which the United States Navy Department was contemplating carrying out in the vicinity of the Galápagos Archipelago, using Seymour Island as a base.

The Ecuadoran Foreign Office was notified by this Embassy on October 27, 1947, of the contemplated plans. The Minister for Foreign Affairs, Dr. José Vicente Trujillo, returned the original note and suggested that it be made a request for permission to carry out the operations, rather than that it be a mere notification. The Embassy on October 30, and before any further communications had been passed concerning this matter, advised the Foreign Office that the Navy Department had cancelled its plans for these training operations.

---

[38] Neither printed.

Yesterday evening, November 7, the Foreign Office delivered to the Embassy two antedated memoranda, No. 252–DDP dated October 28, 1947, and No. 253–DDP dated October 31, 1947, the first setting out clearly that the Government of Ecuador denies that there is any understanding in existence for the unlimited use of the waters in the vicinity of the Galápagos Islands by United States Forces, and stating further that mere notification of the intention to carry out operations in this area is not sufficient but that, in case the Government of the United States desires to do this, formal request through diplomatic channels should be made. The second memorandum is merely an acknowledgment of our two notes and refers to what had been stated on the subject.

Copies and translations of the memoranda No. 252–DDP and No. 253–DDP are transmitted herewith for the information of the Department.[39]

No further communication is being sent to the Foreign Office on this subject for the present. Further comment on this matter will be forwarded to the Department in a subsequent despatch as soon as it can be prepared.

Respectfully yours, JOHN F. SIMMONS

811.24522/11–747

Memorandum by Mr. George H. Owen of the Division of North and West Coast Affairs [39a]

CONFIDENTIAL [WASHINGTON,] November 13, 1947.

Ambassador Simmons proposes to accompany the Chief of United States Air Mission[40] in Ecuador on flight to Galápagos and would invite editor Mantilla of newspaper *El Comercio* to go along, and possibly other prominent Ecuadoran.

Ambassador Simmons believes this to be an opportunity to give good impression of United States participation at Seymour Island base and has so informed General Crittenberger. Propaganda value is enhanced by purpose of flight, viz. to return a doctor who has attended wife of Ecuadoran Commanding Officer.

Ambassador Simmons wishes to know if Department has any objections.

---

[39] Neither printed.
[39a] Addressed to Sheldon T. Mills, Assistant Chief of the Division of North and West Coast Affairs, Robert F. Woodward, Deputy Director of the Office of American Republic Affairs, and Stephen V. C. Morris of the Division of Foreign Activity Correlation.
[40] Col. Joshua T. Winstead.

I believe it is good opportunity, as Ambassador says, and strongly recommend advising him to go ahead with trip and using it to create favorable impression desired.[41]

822.24/12–247

Memorandum by Mr. George H. Owen of the Division of North and West Coast Affairs [42]

RESTRICTED [WASHINGTON,] December 2, 1947.

While General Larrea Alba was Ecuadoran Military Attaché in Washington he bought $571,000 worth of maintenance parts under so-called "post V–J lend lease" contracts, payable in full and in cash. We were informed by the Chief of the U.S. Military Mission in Ecuador [43] that, in doing this, Larrea exceeded instructions from his government not to spend more than $150,000.

All the matériel involved has been delivered to Ecuador. The Treasury has sent bills for the total amount to the Ecuadoran Military Attaché. No reimbursement has been made and no word received concerning this matter from the Ecuadoran Government. Our last instructions to Embassy Quito were that we will not give consideration to reduction of the bill until Ecuador makes a formal request in this regard. (Department's instruction no. 1958, August 19, 1947).[44]

Mr. Kempter of Lend-Lease has now suggested that, since FBO state they can use $500,000 in sucres (in addition to $500,000 OFLC surplus property credit extended to Ecuador reimbursable in sucres and available to FBO) for the Embassy building program in Ecuador, we direct the attention of the Ecuadoran Embassy in Washington to the existence of this account and mention the possibility of our accepting payment in sucres. No commitment would be made, but we would give the Embassy opportunity to request instructions.

General Larrea is no longer Military Attaché and is now Chief of Staff of the Ecuadoran Army.

I agreed with Mr. Kempter that the next time I see Señor Arosemena, Ecuadoran Chargé d'Affaires in Washington, I would mention the matter in accordance with the foregoing.

Please indicate approval.

---

[41] A handwritten note at this point reads: "Tel. this sense attached."
[42] Addressed to Sheldon T. Mills of the Division of North and West Coast Affairs, Messrs. George O. Spencer and John C. Dreier of the Division of Special Inter-American Affairs, and Robert F. Woodward of the Office of American Republic Affairs.
[43] Col. John F. Stodter.
[44] Not printed.

811.24522/12–447

The Ambassador in Ecuador (Simmons) to the Secretary of State

CONFIDENTIAL

QUITO, December 4, 1947.

No. 6286

SIR: I have the honor to refer to my despatch no. 6265 of November 24, 1947,[45] entitled "Conversation Concerning Galápagos Islands Situation, with Ecuadoran Minister of Defense Colonel Angel Vaquero Davila and Brigadier General Glen C. Jamison", and to inform the Department that Captain Michael P. Russillo, shortly before his final departure from Ecuador on December 1 as Chief of the United States Naval Mission here, was given by Captain J. Alberto Sanchez L., Chief of the Ecuadoran Naval Forces, informally and confidentially, a statement embodying Captain Sanchez's views and presumably those of the Minister of National Defense in regard to the terms of an agreement concerning the Galápagos Islands base which presumably would be acceptable to the Ecuadoran Government.

Captain Russillo, in telling me of this statement of Ecuadoran views, emphasized that it could not be considered as official in character at the present time. He said, however, that he considered it as a kind of tentative offer made informally to him in the hope that it might be transmitted to the American Government for its informal consideration. It naturally would not require a definite answer from our Government, but he felt that, should we wish later to give any unofficial or informal comments on it, such comments would be welcomed.

I would emphasize that this action was taken entirely without any suggestion on our part, either definite or implied, and it would indicate a revived interest of the Ecuadoran Government in coming to a definite basis of settlement for the Galápagos Islands base question. I believe that this revived interest may be traced directly to the recent trip made to the Galápagos by a group of Ecuadorans, including the Minister of National Defense, as described in my despatch no. 6264 of November 24,[45] entitled "Trip to the Galápagos Islands".

Captain Russillo will arrive shortly in Washington and will be available for any discussions which the Department may wish to make in regard to the present matter.

It is his opinion that, although certain terms of the present proposals would probably be unacceptable, the proposal is basically a fairly reasonable one and, with proper modification, might form the basis for definite action on this controversial issue in the near future.

---

[45] Not printed.

I would emphasize once more that the Embassy has taken no initiative in this matter whatever, although the question was discussed in general terms during my visit to the Gálapagos Islands as reported in my despatch first referred to above.

A translation of the informal proposals in question [46a] is transmitted herewith as an enclosure to the present despatch.

Respectfully yours, JOHN F. SIMMONS

FINANCING ECUADORAN HIGHWAY DEVELOPMENT AND OTHER ECONOMIC PROPOSALS [47]

811.516 Export-Import Bank/3–1147

The Ambassador in Ecuador (Scotten) to the Secretary of State

[Extracts]

CONFIDENTIAL QUITO, March 11, 1947.
No. 5045

SIR: I have the honor to refer to the Department's telegram No. 29 of February 5, 7 p. m., 1947,[48] concerning the scheduled visit to Ecuador of the Export-Import Bank Mission headed by Director Lynn Stambaugh, and to transmit herewith information concerning the activities of the Mission while in Ecuador.

The members of the Mission arrived in Guayaquil on March 3 from La Paz, remaining in Guayaquil until March 5, when they departed for and arrived in Quito. The Mission consisted of the following: Mr. Lynn Stambaugh, Mr. Elmer Chase, Mr. Edwin R. Kinnear, and Mr. Bernard Bell. Their activities in Guayaquil were confined to discussions with officials of the Municipality and the Frederick Snare Corporation concerning the credit agreement whereby $4,000,000 will be made available to the Municipality for improvement and construction of water facilities . . .

. . . The Municipality of Guayaquil will authorize the Ecuadoran Ambassador in Washington, Sr. Francisco Illescas Barreiro, to sign the agreement in Washington in behalf of the Municipality. The Ambassador will also have authority to sign in behalf of the Government of Ecuador. With all questions now resolved, the agreement is ready for signature, and, according to the Mission, should be signed soon.

[46a] This statement, not printed, proposed that the United States Department of Defense send a delegation to Quito to participate in the formulation of a ten to twenty year contract for the joint use of Seymour Base by Ecuador and the United States.

[47] For documentation on the participation of the United States in the economic development of Ecuador in 1946, see *Foreign Relations*, 1946, vol. XI, pp. 873 ff.

[48] Not printed.

On March 5 at 5 p. m. the members of the Mission, accompanied by the Ambassador and the Acting Commercial Attaché, held a conference with the Ecuadoran Minister of the Treasury, Sr. Enrique Arízaga Toral. The first part of the conference was concerned with matters pertaining to the Consolidation Agreement signed in Washington on February 28. The Consolidation Agreement consolidated Ecuador's outstanding obligations under Loan Agreement No. 262, authorized on May 7, 1940 for a total amount of $1,480,000, and Agreement No. 316, authorized on March 6, 1942 for $5,000,000. The latter was a joint obligation of the Republic of Ecuador and the Corporación Ecuatoriana de Fomento. By the terms of the Consolidation Agreement the Republic of Ecuador became the sole debtor. The aggregate principal amount outstanding on the notes held as of the date of signing of the Consolidation Agreement on February 28 was $5,650,248.67. Information concerning the Consolidation Agreement was transmitted to the Embassy in the Department's telegram No. 53 of February 28, 7 p. m., 1947,[49] for Stambaugh and Chase from Eximbank.

. . . .

After the conclusion of the discussion concerning the Consolidation Agreement, the Minister asked the members of the Mission for the attitude of the Bank concerning an additional credit for completion of the Quevedo–Manta Highway. The Mission pointed out that the Tucker McClure estimate could not be utilized since it was not a recent report. They added that the report of the Resident Engineer of the Public Roads Administration in Ecuador, Mr. Vincent Johnkoski, who is supervising the construction of the Quamote–Tambo Highway, was likewise insufficient to enable the Bank to arrive at a decision. Mr. Johnkoski's report, which estimated that it would require $3,100,000 to complete the Quevedo–Manta Highway as planned, or $3,600,000 if a bridge over the Rio Quevedo were included, did not make it clear whether or not additional machinery and equipment would be required. According to the Mission, if additional machinery and equipment are required or if presently available equipment is unsatisfactory, Mr. Johnkoski's estimate of the cost of completion would have to be increased. They stated that they would discuss that matter with Mr. Johnkoski on the following day and would then talk further with the Minister concerning an additional line of credit for completion of the highway.

Since the $1,000,000 credit previously approved for engineering studies has been transferred by the Bank to construction of the Quevedo–Manta Highway and since the Government of Ecuador has

---
[49] Not printed.

deposited $780,000 for the same purpose, the Government of Ecuador desires an additional credit in an amount equal to the estimated cost of completion less $1,780,000.

In conclusion the Minister stated that he was interested in the following matters:

1) Additional credit for the Quevedo–Manta Highway
2) Completion of negotiations on the $4,000,000 loan for Quito water project
3) Completion of negotiations for the Guayaquil water project
4) Continuation of construction of the Guamote–Tambo Highway

. . . .

At 11:00 a. m. on March 6 the members of the Mission, accompanied by the Acting Commercial Attaché, held a conference with the Mayor of Quito concerning the credit for the Quito water project. In addition to the foregoing, the Municipal Engineer, Sr. Enrique Rivadeneira, and the Vice President of the Council, Sr. Ricardo Espinosa, were present.

The members of the Mission first referred to the exchange of correspondence they had had with the Municipality since their visit to Quito last August. The Mayor said that the Municipality had transmitted to six American firms interested in the engineering and construction work specifications prepared by the Municipality. A copy of the specifications had been sent to the Export-Import Bank during the absence from Washington of the members of the Mission. The text of the specifications is attached as enclosure No. 1 to this despatch.

At the present time an American engineer, Mr. Harold T. Smith, is engaged in the construction of water facilities in the North Zone of the city. The Municipality estimates that it will require approximately $500,000 to complete the North Zone project. The Municipality therefore intends to use $500,000 of the $4,000,000 for such construction. Consequently, the specifications transmitted to the six American firms called for construction of water facilities in the South Zone of the city in an amount not to exceed $3,500,000. The six American firms which received the specifications are the following:

Walsh Construction Company
Harold T. Smith
Jones Construction Company
Parsons, Brinkerhoff, Hogan & MacDonald
Morrison-Knudson Company
The Pertuitut Company

The Export-Import Bank has tentatively approved all of the foregoing, with the exception of the Morrison–Knudson Company. Members of the Mission informed the Embassy that although the Bank had not yet approved the Morrison–Knudson Company, there was no doubt that it would do so. It should be noted, however, that actual plans and specifications of the successful American firm must be approved by the Bank before the $4,000,000 credit is made available.[50]

The specifications call for individual estimates on each of the following phases of the project:

1) Determination of source of water supply
2) Design
3) Construction
4) Maintenance or Administration

. . . .

The Export-Import Bank Mission left Quito on March 7, to return directly to Washington.

Respectfully yours, For the Ambassador:
ALVORD L. BOECK
Acting Commercial Attaché

822.51/5–2947

The Chargé in Ecuador (Shaw) to the Secretary of State

No. 5274 QUITO, May 29, 1947.

SIR: I have the honor to report that in a conference in Guayaquil on May 26 in which I participated, together with the Minister of Treasury, Enrique Arízaga Tora; the Minister of Public Works, Pedro Concha Enríquez; Mr. Vincent Johnkoski, U.S. Public Roads Administration; and Mr. Edwin R. Kinnear of the Export-Import Bank, the matter of financing the Quevedo–Manta Highway was discussed and the following points were brought out. (Figures approximate—see note in last paragraph of this despatch).

1) A sum of $780,000 is presently available in the Banco Central del Ecuador to be used for this work. (See memorandum of conversation between Acting Commercial Attaché Alvord L. Boeck and Mr. V. Johnkoski of the Public Roads Administration—dated April 28, 1947, attached hereto.[51] Regardless of the seeming authenticity of Mr. Johnkoski's statement, the Minister of Treasury stated in the conference of May 26 that the $780,000 was intact.)

2) The sum of $1,000,000 previously approved by the Export-Import Bank for engineering studies has been set aside and earmarked for the construction of the Quevedo–Manta Highway.

---

[50] In instruction 1888, of May 29, 1947, the Department advised the officer in charge in Quito that representatives of Ecuador and of the Export-Import Bank had signed an agreement on May 22 providing a credit of $4,000,000 for the waterworks of Quito and an equal amount for a similar purpose for Guayaquil (822.51/5–2247).

[51] Not printed.

3) Preliminary estimate by Mr. Johnkoski of the cost of completing this highway was about $3,100,000.

4) In view of the above, it has been accepted that additional financing of at least $1,320,000 would have to be arranged.

5) It now appears, in light of the experience of the Jones Construction Company on the Guamote–Tambo Highway, (Despatch No. 5273 of May 28, 1947 [52]), the rising cost of material and labor, and the fact that the calculations were made from incomplete data on actual terrain, the estimate of the total cost of completing the road, according to Johnkoski, probably should be nearer $3,500,000 than the original figure of $3,100,000.

6) Mr. Johnkoski was asked to review his original estimates in light of the additional information available, and it was anticipated that his revision would result in an estimate of cost of approximately $4,000,000. However, he has just submitted his letter dated today (May 29) a copy of which, with enclosure, is attached,[52] showing his revised estimate to be only $3,500,000.

7) The Minister of Treasury made the statement, concurred in by the Minister of Public Works, that while all available funds for road construction for the fiscal year 1948 were already obligated, it would be possible for the Ecuadoran Government to provide an additional $400,000 contemplated by the increased estimates in its regular budget for 1949. It would appear, therefore, that the Ecuadoran Government is prepared to assume the responsibility of providing funds for the completion of the highway over and above the $3,100,000 originally estimated, and it is willing to accept the fact that the cost of terminating the road probably will be in the neighborhood of three and a half million dollars.

8) Regardless of the statement made in paragraph 7 above, both the Ministers were in agreement that the matter of setting aside $400,000 in the regular budget of 1949 would be a somewhat difficult task and, while they would not admit the possibility that the Ecuadoran Government might fail to provide these funds, they both stated it would be much more desirable if the Export-Import Bank would agree to finance the additional $400,000, which would make a total of $1,720,000 to be considered instead of the amount mentioned in paragraph 4. The Ministers desire a statement, if possible, as to whether the Bank would look with favor upon an application for this additional financing. (It is the opinion of this Embassy that, with the prospect of lower world prices for its exports and a general return to a normal level of economic activity, it would be more difficult for the

---

[52] Not printed.

Ecuadoran Government to set aside $400,000 in 1949 than it would be at the present time.)

It probably should be pointed out at this time that some difficulty may be expected in getting an experienced American construction company to accept a contract for the completion of this road with one of the terms being the payment of the last $400,000 under the ordinary budget of the Ecuadoran Government two years hence. It may be assumed that an experienced company would suggest some such arrangement as setting up a $400,000 revolving fund which would remain intact or be securely blocked for the completion of the work after the original $3,100,000 portion of the work had been completed.

It is respectfully recommended that this phase of the situation be considered carefully in any final arrangement that is made in order to avoid future embarrassment to the United States Government and possible loss of prestige for American engineering and construction companies, not to mention any political repercussions which might result.

Note: As a matter of fact the conversations of May 26 were held without having documentary references at hand. The first assumptions were based on the following figures:

Sum presently available	$780,000
Sum earmarked by Eximbank	1,000,000
Additional sum needed	1,720,000
Present estimated cost to complete Quevedo–Manta Highway	3,500,000
Guess that revised estimate would be	4,000,000
Guarantee or additional financing needed for	500,000

Although the conversations were conducted on the above assumption that the present estimate was $3,500,000, Mr. Johnkoski did not mention the fact that his figure was about $3,100,000 until he submitted his letter of May 29. Therefore, while his estimate has been raised some $400,000, the total as revised is $3,500,000. Mr. Johnkoski says that this works out about $23,000 a kilometer and is his best estimate. Also, the figures have been checked and concurred in by the Director of Public Works of Ecuador.

Regardless of the above it is desired to point out that the so-called estimates are not based on accurate engineering studies and are really only considered guesses. Therefore, in light of the experiences of American engineering companies on works of this kind in Ecuador and in consideration of the costly operating difficulties that probably will have to be overcome, the final cost of the work to be done may well be nearer $4,000,000 than $3,500,000.

Respectfully yours,

GEO. P. SHAW

811.516 Export-Import Bank/8–1247

Memorandum by the Special Assistant in the Division of Investment and Economic Development (Stenger) to the Director of the Office of Financial and Development Policy (Ness)

CONFIDENTIAL WASHINGTON, August 12, 1947.

Subject: Agenda for Meeting of Board of Directors Eximbank August 13, 1947.

. . . .

For Consideration:

6. *Ecuador–Quecedo–Manta Highway.* In August 1946 Ecuador indicated that it would need $3.5 million to complete the Quevedo–Manta Highway. Ecuador earmarked $780,000 of its dollar funds for this purpose, and requested the Bank to finance the balance by making available the $1,000,000 credit, which was authorized in July 1945 to finance engineering services, and by a new credit of $1,720,000. On September 18, 1946 the Board approved the diversion of the $1,000,000 credit provided the engineering and construction services were performed by approved U.S. contractors. At that time, the Board also indicated its willingness to consider the additional $1,720,000 provided that Ecuador could support its estimate of completion costs with detailed engineering estimates satisfactory to the Bank.

This project was originally undertaken by the Ecuadoran Development Corporation under a credit of $2.5 million from the Eximbank.

This project has a long history of frustration and mismanagement for which American contractors, as well as the Ecuadorans, are partly to blame. The Department (politically) can also accept some of the responsibility for the unsatisfactory manner in which this project has been handled.

The Department and the Bank feel that there is at least a moral if not an actual commitment on the part of the U.S. Government to assist in the completion of the Quevedo–Manta Highway.

The staff recommends the approval of a credit of $1,720,000; that this credit be merged with the $1,000,000 credit previously authorized; and that Ecuador be required to finance any amount above the $3.5 million estimated cost of completion of the highway. The suggested term of repayment is 15 years with interest at 3–½%.

Recommendation: The political division strongly recommends approval of the proposal. It is suggested that the Department concur in the approval.

822.51/8-2547

Memorandum by Mr. George H. Owen of the Division of North and West Coast Affairs [54]

CONFIDENTIAL [WASHINGTON,] August 25, 1947.

An application presented by the Government of Ecuador for a loan of $2,720,000 for the completion of the Quevedo–Manta Highway is now under consideration by the Board of the Export-Import Bank.

Mr. Chase of the Export-Import Bank indicated in a telephone conversation that the recent overthrow of the government of President Velasco will adversely affect the question of the approval of this application by the Bank.

The Board of the Export-Import Bank is to consider this matter on Wednesday, August 27. Mr. Stenger of ED is of the opinion that it is extremely unlikely that the Bank will approve the loan, in view of the recent showing of political instability in Ecuador. Mr. Stenger believes that if the Department is interested in the approval of the loan it is better to seek postponement of its consideration rather than risk rejection by the Bank at this time. Mr. Stenger will accordingly attempt to postpone final decision of the matter by the Export-Import Bank.[55]

822.51/9-2947 : Telegram

The Ambassador in Ecuador (Simmons) to the Secretary of State

RESTRICTED QUITO, September 29, 1947—5 p.m.

419. Embassy records show US has moral commitment to finance completion Quevedo-Manta Highway as this seems to be a generally accepted point of policy. Financing should be for completion and not merely for assisting (reDeptel 289, September 26.)[56]

Johnkoski of PRA states project status same as last report. He recommends contract on per kilometer or unit basis but not cost plus. This point of view endorsed by Embassy. However, it is believed US

---

[54] Addressed to Sheldon T. Mills of the Division of North and West Coast Affairs, and to Messrs. James H. Wright and Robert F. Woodward of the Office of American Republic Affairs.

[55] The following handwritten note appears in the margin: "Isn't this a new doctrine? i.e. to condition action on a loan on whether or not a country refrains from revolutions. After all Mancheno has already announced he will abide by all Ecuadoran international commitments. Delay might be a good idea—in fact inevitable. But if the new regime is eventually recognized the highway's merits should still be the basic criterion. S. T. M[ills]."

[56] Not printed.

objective namely goodwill and establishment of record for compliance with commitments will be lost if road not completely financed. Recommend sufficient funds be made available for that purpose. Ecuador probably would fail to put up funds to complete any lacking last section, appeal to US for extension of loan and be resentful if it was not obtained thus defeating objectives mentioned above.

Johnkoski stated today he felt that last hundred kilometer road should cost about $25,000 a kilometer to construct.

Embassy's remarks above are made because of fact that estimates of amount needed are not based on thorough engineering studies (re Embassy's despatch 5274, May 29, 1947).

SIMMONS

822.51/9–1847 : Telegram

The Acting Secretary of State to the Embassy in Ecuador

RESTRICTED   WASHINGTON, October 24, 1947—6 p. m.

316. Eximbank Oct 8 approved $1,720,000 credit to complete Quevedo–Manta highway but withheld notification and publicity for purpose recommended your A–202 Sept 18 [57] and will do so for another 10 days.

Quito waterworks credit was approved some time ago but disbursement thereunder not imminent. Other possible Eximbank credits you mentioned not now under active consideration.

Dept prefers generally not using for purposes this kind bargaining potential Eximbank or other credits.

LOVETT

---

[57] Not printed.

EL SALVADOR

AGREEMENT BETWEEN THE UNITED STATES AND EL SALVADOR RESPECTING A MILITARY AVIATION MISSION

[For text of the agreement effected by exchange of notes, signed at Washington August 19, 1947, see Department of State, Treaties and Other International Acts Series No. 1633, or 61 Stat. (pt. 3) 3002.]

AGREEMENT BETWEEN THE UNITED STATES AND EL SALVADOR FOR THE ONE-YEAR RENEWAL OF THE AGREEMENT OF MAY 21, 1943, PROVIDING FOR THE DETAIL OF AN OFFICER OF THE UNITED STATES ARMY TO SERVE AS DIRECTOR OF THE MILITARY SCHOOL AND OF THE MILITARY ACADEMY OF EL SALVADOR

[Effected by exchange of notes signed at Washington March 4 and April 7, 1947; notes not printed (816.223/3-447). For text of agreement of May 21, 1943, see Department of State Executive Agreement Series No. 328, or 57 Stat. (pt. 2) 1000.]

GUATEMALA

AGREEMENT BETWEEN THE UNITED STATES AND GUATEMALA RESPECTING UNITED STATES ARMED FORCES IN GUATEMALA

[Effected by exchange of notes signed at Guatemala City August 29, 1947; for texts of notes, see Department of State, Treaties and Other International Acts Series No. 1663, or 61 Stat. (pt. 3) 3289.]

SETTLEMENT OF THE REMAINING OBLIGATION OF THE UNITED STATES UNDER ITS MUTUAL AID AGREEMENT WITH GUATEMALA [1]

814.24/3-2147

Memorandum by the Director of the Office of American Republic Affairs (Briggs) to the Under Secretary of State for Economic Affairs (Clayton)

CONFIDENTIAL [WASHINGTON,] March 21, 1947.

Shipments of supplies to Guatemala in settlement of our lend-lease obligation have been suspended, by order of the General Accounting Office.[2] The failure to make these deliveries leaves us owing Guatemala about $1,000,000 in materials under our Lend-Lease Agreement of 1942.[3] It is important that shipments be resumed and the obligation liquidated.

It will be recalled that this secret Lend-Lease Agreement provided that Guatemala should receive without charge $3,000,000 worth of Lend-Lease supplies in return for letting us occupy two air bases in that country. When hostilities ended, we had shipped only about $1,500,000 of lend-lease supplies to Guatemala. It was then proposed that our remaining obligation be liquidated by transferring to Guatemala all the materials included in her interim arms allocation. After President Truman approved this proposal [4] (see attachment), it was presented to the Guatemalan Government and accepted.[5]

---

[1] Continued from *Foreign Relations*, 1946, vol. XI, pp. 885–889.
[2] A ruling was issued by the Comptroller General (Warren) on January 10, 1947, that not only could the funds appropriated in Public Law No. 521, Seventy-Ninth Congress, July 23, 1946, not be used for any of the expenses incident to the shipment abroad of lend-lease articles after December 31, 1946, but in addition, funds deposited by the foreign governments could not be used for that purpose (800.24/4-2447).
[3] Signed November 16, 1942, *Foreign Relations*, 1942, vol. VI, p. 444.
[4] See memorandum of May 14, 1946, by Acting Secretary of State Acheson to President Truman, *ibid.*, 1946, vol. XI, p. 885.
[5] See notes of May 23 and October 18, 1946, to the Guatemalan Embassy, *ibid.*, pp. 886 and 888, respectively.

Some of the shipments to Guatemala were completed before the G. A. O. ordered the suspension. The bulk of the material, however, is yet to be transferred.

In emphasizing the importance of expediting deliveries, it should be noted that Guatemala has already paid a large part of the accessorial charges for suspended shipments.[6] These Guatemalan payments apparently satisfy the G. A. O. requirement that accessorial funds be paid by the foreign government.

Inasmuch as your office has been at work on the general question of the suspended lend-lease shipments, the particular problem of Guatemala is brought to your attention with the hope that some action can be taken with a view to removing G. A. O.'s objections. Anything that can be done to enable us to meet our obligation to Guatemala will be very much appreciated.

814.24/3–2847

Memorandum of Telephone Conversation, by the Chief of the Division of Central America and Panama Affairs (Newbegin)

[WASHINGTON,] March 28, 1947.

Colonel Morales López[7] called this morning to inquire regarding the status of deliveries to Guatemala under the arrangement terminating our lend-lease obligations. He said he was very much concerned over the delay; that he had discussed the matter on various occasions with Mr. Kempter[8] but that he also wanted to bring the matter to my attention. I told him that I understood his concern; that the matter was at the moment a technical one; we were giving it our full attention and hoped that we would be able to find a satisfactory solution. In this connection, I reminded him that ever since the exchange of notes on this subject, I had been urging speedy action by the Guatemalans so that the whole arrangement could be terminated without any further complications. It had been a matter of constant concern that Guatemala had not submitted her requisitions more promptly. Colonel Morales López concurred. He stated that as things now stood, his Government was under the impression that he was doing nothing effective about the matter and said "you know these Latin American Governments don't always understand what is happening". I replied that for just that reason I hoped he would point out to his Government that it was largely to blame for the situation in which we now found ourselves; that if requisitions had been submitted promptly we would not be hav-

---

[6] A payment of $65,000 had been made in December 1946.
[7] Col. Oscar Morales López, Military and Air Attaché, Guatemalan Embassy.
[8] Charles W. Kempter, Chief of Lend-Lease Staff, Office of Foreign Liquidation.

ing our present difficulty. I said in pointing this out that I did not wish to excuse the present delay on our part but I was extremely sorry that the situation had developed as it had and that he might be certain we would do everything we could to clear the matter up. At the same time a further delay was probably inevitable. Colonel Morales López expressed his appreciation.

814.24/5-2747

The Secretary of State to the Guatemalan Ambassador (Garcia Godoy)

CONFIDENTIAL WASHINGTON, May 27, 1947.

EXCELLENCY: I have the honor to transmit herewith two copies each of Statements LL-10, LL-11, and LL-12 and supporting schedules [9] reporting charges made against the Government of Guatemala during the period from June 1, 1946 through December 31, 1946 for material transferred in accordance with the Lend-Lease Agreement signed on November 16, 1942. It will be noted that charges through December 31, 1946 for all defense material transferred to the Government of Guatemala aggregate the grand total of $2,108,839.20.

It is requested that the enclosed statements and supporting schedules be treated by Your Excellency's Government on a most confidential basis.

Accept [etc.] For the Secretary of State:
SPRUILLE BRADEN

811.24514/7-147

The Secretary of State to the Secretary of War (Patterson)

SECRET WASHINGTON, July 1, 1947.

DEAR PATTERSON: I refer to a secret memorandum of October 14, 1946 [10] prepared by Colonel Mark A. Devine, Jr., Military Attaché at the Embassy at Guatemala City, concerning the disposition of United States Army property in Guatemala. A copy of the aforementioned memorandum was transmitted to the Department by the Embassy at Guatemala City under cover of a secret despatch No. 2000 of December 6, 1946,[10] a copy of which has been referred to the War Department.

According to information supplied by Colonel Devine and by the Embassy, it would appear that during the evacuation of United States

---

[9] None printed.
[10] Not printed.

Army personnel from the Guatemala City air base in 1944, General George H. Brett, who was then Commander of the Caribbean Defense Command, directed that certain United States Army property, having an approximate value of $30,000, be transferred to the Guatemalan Government on memorandum receipt. The action of General Brett was doubtlessly the result of informal representations made by the Guatemalan Government that the property should be transferred to Guatemala without reimbursement under the terms of the Base and Lend-Lease Agreement with Guatemala. Approximately two years after the transfer of the property in question, the Caribbean Defense Command, on November 22, 1946, notified Colonel Devine that the records of the Caribbean Defense Command did not indicate that a transfer of the property under the provisions of lend-lease had taken place. Subsequently, the Office of the Foreign Liquidation Commissioner catalogued the property and is presently prepared to offer it for sale to Guatemala or to other prospective purchasers. However, the Embassy, the United States Military Attaché and a representative of the Foreign Liquidation Commissioner in Guatemala have investigated the circumstances of the transfer and have recommended that the property be withheld from sale. In discussing these recommendations with the Office of the Foreign Liquidation Commissioner, the Department has been informed that the property must be sold, unless the War Department withdraws the declaration of surplus by which jurisdiction over the property was transferred by the War Department to FLC.

In view of the fact that the property was, in fact, transferred to the Guatemalan Government, the latter is of the opinion that the transfer was made under the terms of the lend-lease agreement, no reimbursement being required. The grounds for Guatemala's permanent possession of this property would appear to be Article 4 of Note 337 attached to the Lend-Lease Agreement of November 16, 1942, which provides that the bases, with all fixed installations "except the organic equipment of the troops", shall become the property of the Guatemalan Government when the "emergency" is ended and the peace treaty is signed. Moreover, it is believed that the opinion held by the Guatemalan Government is justified, in part, by the circumstances of the transfer.

The Department would appreciate being informed if the War Department is able to furnish the Foreign Liquidation Commissioner a statement that this material is to become the permanent property of the Guatemalan Government under the terms of the Lend-Lease Agreement of November 16, 1942. This would make it unnecessary for the Commissioner to proceed with the sale of the material as surplus property.[11]

Faithfully yours, G. C. MARSHALL

814.24/12–1747

Memorandum of Conversation, by Mr. Robert E. Wilson of the Division of Central America and Panama Affairs

RESTRICTED [WASHINGTON,] December 17, 1947.

Participants: Sr. Don Francisco Linares Aranda, Guatemalan Embassy [12]
Lt. Col. Offer [13]
Col. Oscar Morales López
Mr. Charles Kempter
Mr. George Spencer, IA [14]
Mr. Robert Newbegin, CPA
Mr. Robert E. Wilson, CPA

The meeting was called by Mr. Newbegin, who opened it with the statement that he hoped that at long last it would be possible to make final arrangements on the question of the Guatemalan lend-lease settlement program which had been pending for so many months. Mr. Newbegin said he understood the agreement had finally been reached as to what equipment Guatemala wants under the interim program but that unfortunately, because of the unavoidable delays, some items not desired had already been shipped to Alabama and it is now too late to eliminate them. It will still be possible, however, to eliminate the items not ordered from what remained to be shipped. He said that he understood that the amount of the accessorial charges which Guatemala would now be obliged to pay, taking into consideration the elimination of items not desired, had been reduced to $35,000 and that he hoped that Guatemala would be able to pay this sum promptly so that the whole matter could be brought to an early conclusion.

Turning to Señor Linares, he asked whether he anticipated any difficulty in making a prompt settlement of $35,000. Señor Linares said he could not say, but would consult his Government and hoped to be able to reply at an early date.

Colonel Morales López then asked if this $35,000 was in addition

---

[11] On March 29, 1948, the Secretary of the Army, Kenneth C. Royall, replied as follows: "After examination of all available data relative to the claim by the Government of Guatemala, the Department of the Army is able to inform you that the material in question will be withdrawn from the Foreign Liquidation Commissioner and will become the permanent property of Guatemala under the terms of the Lend-Lease Agreement of 16 November 1942." (811.24514/3–2948)
[12] First Secretary of the Embassy.
[13] Lieutenant Colonel Offer of the War Department.
[14] George O. Spencer of the Division of Special Inter-American Affairs.

to what had already been paid. Colonel Offer said that it was in lieu of the $110,000 which were to have been the accessorial charges before the undesired items were deleted, and that it brought the total accessorial charges to only $100,000 instead of $175,000 ($65,000 have already been paid). Colonel Morales López then said "O.K., I will pay you tomorrow." [15] . . .

Mr. Newbegin said, "Then we all agree that that closes the deal?" All present agreed that it did. Colonel Offer said that of course it might take some time to get the equipment together. Colonel Morales López said they were badly in need of certain of the instruments, parts, tires, etc. and that arrangements would probably be made to have part of the order flown from Mobile to Guatemala City.

The meeting broke up with all participants in good spirits and there was a general feeling of satisfaction that final agreement has been made.

UNITED STATES CONCERN OVER PROVISIONS OF NEW GUATEMALAN LABOR CODE APPEARING TO DISCRIMINATE AGAINST AMERICAN COMPANIES

814.504/5–2847

The Department of State to the Guatemalan Embassy

MEMORANDUM

With reference to the Guatemalan Ambassador's conversation with Mr. Braden on May 24, 1947,[16] on the subject of the new Guatemalan Labor Code,[17] the Department of State calls the Embassy's attention to several provisions of this code which appear to discriminate in practice against American companies.

These provisions are in articles 105, 116, 121, 238 and 243, which make special regulations for companies employing 500 or more agricultural laborers and for companies employing 1,000 or more workers of any sort and operating in more than one department or economic area. Such distinctions would serve to apply to certain American employers restrictions and obligations different from those under which other concerns operate. So far as is known the only concerns with more than 1,000 employees are the United Fruit Company, Compañía Agrícola de Guatemala, and International Railways of

---

[15] Col. Morales López enclosed a draft for $35,000 in his letter of December 30, 1947 (not printed), to the Acting Chief, Division of Lend-Lease and Surplus War Property (Shenefield) (814.24/12–3047).

[16] Memorandum of conversation between Ambassador Garcia Granados and Assistant Secretary of State Braden, not printed.

[17] The Guatemalan Government promulgated a Labor Code by legislative decree No. 330, published in the *Diaria de Centro America* on February 24 and 26, 1947, which became effective May 1, 1947.

Central America, all American enterprises. With one possible exception, the only employers of more than 500 agricultural laborers are the American-owned Compañía Agrícola de Guatemala and United Fruit Company.

The Department of State does not presume to express an opinion upon the merits of the Guatemalan labor code beyond pointing to this apparent discrimination, which is a matter of serious concern to the Department of State. Therefore, the Department would appreciate any action which the Embassy may be able to take with a view to exploring the situation with the Guatemalan Government and eliminating any discriminations against American-owned enterprises.

WASHINGTON, May 28, 1947.

814.504/7–1547 : Telegram

The Secretary of State to the Embassy in Guatemala

RESTRICTED   WASHINGTON, July 24, 1947—8 p. m.

205. Urtel 244, July 15.[18] Emb Guatemala has now replied[19] to Depts memo of May 28 saying Govt has carefully studied articles 105, 116, 121, 238, and 243 and has reached conclusion they do not contain juridical or practical discrimination against American companies.

Reply states that besides American companies referred to in Dept's memo the following *fincas* in Guatemala employ more than 500 agricultural laborers: Hacienda Nacional Chocolá, Finca Nacional "El Porvenir"; *Fincas:* La Unión, Alabama, El Rosario, Nahuatancillo, La Soledad, San Francisco Cotzal y Anexos.

Finally reply states Govt in capacity of manager of Fincas Nacionales Rústicas e Intervenidas counts larger number of laborers than total employed by all foreign companies and "this does not mean that it is not affected by the dispositions contained in the Labor Code, because if it approved said body of laws, it was with the intention of protecting the laboring class".

Dept would appreciate your immediate comment on statement concerning *fincas* which are apparently nongovernment organizations employing more than 500 agricultural laborers. Comment is also desired regarding statement on Govt-managed *fincas* as well as any other observations which Emb may now care to make on entire Guatemalan reply.[20]

MARSHALL

---

[18] Not printed.
[19] Guatemalan note dated July 23, 1947, not printed.
[20] No record found in Department files of an immediate reply from the Embassy on these specific points.

814.504/8-447

Memorandum by the Chief of the Division of Central America and Panama Affairs (Newbegin)[21]

CONFIDENTIAL [WASHINGTON,] August 4, 1947.

In accordance with instructions from the Department, I proceeded to Guatemala on July 29 and met with the Foreign Minister [22] on July 30 to discuss the Guatemalan Labor Code and its effect on the United Fruit Company. A copy of the memorandum of that conversation is attached. It will be noted that it follows closely the Department's stand, as agreed upon before my departure. It was unfortunate that the visit coincided with the resignation of the Foreign Minister who announced his action during the conversation itself. He did however bring the substance of the conversation to the attention of the President,[23] and was himself in complete accord with the views of the Department.

In a conversation with President Arévalo on July 31 Ambassador Kyle was informed that the President would be pleased to receive the views of the company, in as much as certain changes in the code would have to be made at the September session of Congress. The company presented its views in a communication to the President dated August 1. It emphasized not only the two articles, 13, 243, which the Department viewed as discriminatory but mentioned a number of other articles which the company itself regarded as discriminatory. Unfortunately, the communication to the President was not presented in person by representatives of the company, although the latter expected to see him within a few days following the presentation.

Before my departure Mr. Corcoran of the United Fruit Company suggested that a formal protest be made. He was informed that in view of my comment to the Foreign Minister, and in as much as the company officials had not yet seen the President, this did not appear to be the appropriate time to make such a protest. Furthermore, clearance had not been obtained from the Department on this point.

In a conversation with Senator La Follette [24] this morning, I informed him of my views in this regard. He said that while he had come to the Department prepared to urge that a protest be sent immediately, he felt it well to postpone this action until he had communicated again with his representatives in Guatemala.

It was most regrettable that my visit to Guatemala coincided with

---

[21] Addressed to the Director (Wright) and the Deputy Director (Woodward), Office of American Republic Affairs.
[22] Eugenio Silva Peña.
[23] Juan José Arévalo.
[24] Ex-Senator Robert M. La Follette.

a cabinet crisis, the outcome of which is not yet clear. It appears, however, that President Arévalo has definitely decided to throw in his lot with PAR and the more radical Guatemalan groups. It is still too early to tell what the effect of this will be, or even whether any very useful purpose was served by my trip.

[Annex]

Memorandum of Conversation, by the Chief of the Division of Central America and Panama Affairs (Newbegin)

CONFIDENTIAL   GUATEMALA, July 30, 1947.

Present: Minister for Foreign Affairs
          Ambassador Kyle
          Mr. Donovan [25]
          Mr. Newbegin

Accompanied by Ambassador Kyle and Mr. Donovan, I called on the Foreign Minister, Silva Peña, on July 30. I began the conversation by informing the Foreign Minister that the purpose of my trip was solely to discuss with him the Guatemalan Labor Code and its effect upon the United Fruit Company.

I explained that the United States Government was most seriously concerned, both with regard to certain discriminatory Articles of the Code and the over-all result as it related to the operations of the Company. I told him that I had not come prepared to present any formal protest, although we felt there were at least two provisions of the Code which would justify it. It was our hope that no formal protest would become necessary.

Reference was then made specifically to Articles 13 and 243 of the Code, relating to employment of aliens and the right to strike against agricultural enterprises respectively. The Foreign Minister stated that no reference had been made to Article 13 in the Department's Memorandum of May 28, and that he himself, because of his many duties, had been unable to give the attention to the Code which it deserved. Upon reading Article 13 he expressed complete surprise and said that he had been unaware of the fact that employment of aliens could be limited to the extent set forth therein.

With regard to Article 243, he at first claimed that, since the products of the United Fruit Company were subject to deterioration during the harvest period in case of a strike, he felt that there was no danger involved. However, he subsequently admitted that the wording was ambiguous and that our cause for concern might well be justified.

---

[25] Andrew E. Donovan, 2d, First Secretary of Embassy in Guatemala.

The Foreign Minister was then informed that there were various other articles in the Code which appeared discriminatory, but upon which we were not prepared at this time to determine whether they might serve as the basis for any formal protest. I then told the Foreign Minister that, aside from the question of discrimination, we were very much preoccupied lest the effect of the law be such as to seriously interfere with and possibly make impracticable the further operations of the company. I told him that I knew that the company officials were studying the matter with great care, taking into account the possibility that they might find it necessary to withdraw from Guatemala. I said that, whereas I could give no definite information as to whether they would do so or not, I believed the possibility should be taken into consideration. I said that I was mentioning this not by way of any threat of any sort, but merely because it was desirable to face the situation as it was. It was pointed out that any such development might well have a serious effect upon relations between the two countries; that, whereas the United Fruit Company might take a serious loss in any such move, the importance to Guatemala likewise would be paramount.

Reference was made to the many contributions which the United Fruit Company had made and was making to the economy of Guatemala, specifically with reference to the large amounts of money paid in salaries, the purchase of bananas from independent growers, the payment of taxes, and other contributions of a social nature. Reference was likewise made to the effect which the United Fruit Company withdrawal would have upon possible investors from the United States who would, of course, be ultra-cautious if it were felt that the United Fruit Company had been treated unfairly here. The point was made again that the United Fruit Company was entirely willing to meet any requirements of law which applied to all other enterprises but that the company felt that in adopting the Code, the Guatemalan Government had definitely had the Fruit Company in mind and had drafted its provisions accordingly. I expressed the hope that in its own interest as well as that of the Company and of the relations between our two countries the Guatemalan Government would find it possible to review the Code in an effort to amend it so that the Company could operate with sufficient guarantees and assurance. It was suggested that it would, of course, be preferable to make such an arrangement directly with the Company itself. The Ambassador pointed out that foreign investments at this stage of its development were particularly desirable for Guatemala. He said that in the early days of American history there were large-scale investments on the part of the British, particularly in railroads and in Texas ranches. He asserted that these investments had been particularly beneficial to us and had played a very important part in our development. He continued that the British no longer had holdings of such importance and that they had passed to American owners naturally and not as a result of pressure or legislation.

The Foreign Minister replied that he was in entire accord with our views set forth during the conversation, but that he thought that in all frankness he should inform us that he would probably no longer be a member of the Government after a day or so, and that he had already submitted his resignation to the President. He stated that his views on a number of subjects were not in accord with those of the administration and he did not feel that he could retain his present position when he foresaw certain obligations which other members of the Government were unwilling to meet. He said that he would in any case inform the President of our conversation. He was requested to do so, emphasizing:

1. The existence of the two discriminatory Articles under reference;
2. The existence of a number of other Articles which appeared discriminatory and would seriously affect the operations of the Company; and
3. Notwithstanding 1 and 2, the desirability, in the interest of Guatemalan economy and of relations betwen the two countries, of reaching an arrangement which would not prejudice the Company's operations.

814.504/8-847

Memorandum of Conversation, by the Ambassador in Guatemala (Kyle) [26]

CONFIDENTIAL [GUATEMALA, August 8, 1947.]

On Thursday, July 31, at 5:00 P. M. I called on President Arévalo to discuss with him two important matters: First, the forthcoming trip of Governor Beauford Jester of Texas to Guatemala, around August 14, and, second, the troubles which the United Fruit Company is having because of the provisions of the Labor Code of Guatemala approved by Congress some months ago, and which we believe detrimental to the interests of the United Fruit Company and discriminatory against American interests in this country.

Since the pleasantries had already been exchanged at the beginning of the conversation about Governor Jester's trip, I said I had this unpleasant matter to bring up regarding the trip of Mr. Robert Newbegin to Guatemala and the conferences he had had with the Foreign

---

[26] Copy transmitted to the Department by the Ambassador in Guatemala in his despatch 2594, August 8; received August 14.

Minister about the alarm of the United Fruit Company officials in the United States regarding the effect the Labor Code was having on its interests here. The President had apparently been talking earlier in the day with the Foreign Minister regarding Mr. Newbegin's visit, so he immediately cited Article 243 of the Labor Code as the source of trouble. President Arévalo attempted to explain the said article in terms of the whole Code by indicating that although the Code appeared to be radical, in fact it was not, that under the provisions of the Code, there could be no strikes. The Code, he went on, provided for the economic and moral improvement of the workers of Guatemala and definitely had not been aimed against the foreign interests in the country; that if anyone said something else, it was possibly due to a misunderstanding or mis-translation of Article 243. I then said that the provision authorizing the workers of corporations employing more than 500 persons to strike at any time would only be aimed against the United Fruit Company and perhaps the International Railways of Central America, which was also an American company; that the United Fruit Company could not possibly feel the security it needed for its interests when the workers could refuse to collect the crop when the bananas were about to ripen. Such conduct could undoubtedly cause tremendous losses to the company.

I also made reference to the provisions of the Code which limit the number of foreigners which may be employed by any one organization and which hinders the development of new American enterprises especially in their early stages when normally no nationals of this country have been trained to do essential jobs. To this he replied that the Code applied only to workers (*trabajadores*), not to executives or technical personnel (*directores o personal técnico*). I stated that I had a different understanding of the said provisions of the Code based on their actual application and that the matter should receive careful consideration.

The President then read the article and after reading it twice, he himself agreed that it was rather obscure, but he could assure us that there was no intention whatsoever to hurt the interests of the United Fruit Company. He added that last year when the Company had a strike, the workers, to a certain extent, had been encouraged in the movement, which was more or less aimed against the Government. When the Government wanted a settlement, it was the Company that hindered such settlement. Furthermore, he said that the lawyer of the Company, whose name he did not mention, was one of the people who were definitely against his Government and who had been prominent in every activity against "my Government". After some other comments on the Labor Code, he said that if United Fruit Company would present to him or to the Minister of Economy and Labor a series of suggestions for amendments, he would give them very serious consideration and together with other amendments suggested by local labor organizations and that the Government itself was thinking of putting before Congress, they would be submitted as soon as Congress met in September.

He added that he would be most willing to have the Company do so because he knew what the interests and the activities of the United Fruit meant for this country and they certainly would want to offer every possible cooperation so that they could help develop the country further. I then asked if I could understand I was authorized to indicate to the Company that they could present this memorandum and the possible amendments to him, and he said by all means to do so at the earliest possible date because he was most willing to have this matter cleared as soon as possible.

814.504/9-2247

The Ambassador in Guatemala (Kyle) to the Secretary of State

RESTRICTED GUATEMALA, September 22, 1947.
No. 2641

SIR: I have the honor to report that on Saturday, September 20, I called on President Arévalo to ascertain his views in connection with the conversations which he has been holding with officials of the United Fruit Company concerning the application of the Guatemalan Labor Code to that Company.[27] Mr. Donovan accompanied me and acted as interpreter during the conversation.

I told the President that Mr. Taillon had kept me informed regarding his conversations and that I had followed them with great interest. I explained that the Department was most anxious that a satisfactory solution of the problems which had arisen be arrived at and I inquired regarding the present status of the matter. President Arévalo stated that, as I knew, he had requested the United Fruit Company to present to him suggestions for amendments to the law which would overcome the difficulties which they foresaw. He said that this had been done and that he had turned over the Fruit Company's suggestions to trust-

---

[27] A memorandum of conversation, between President Arévalo, W. E. Turnbull, General Manager for Central America, and W. L. Taillon, General Manager for Guatemala, on August 6, was transmitted to the Department in despatch 2597, August 11, from Guatemala, not printed (814.504/8-1147); on August 13 Mr. Taillon again met with the President and presented to him another memorandum setting forth provisions which the Company considered discriminatory and proposing certain changes (despatch 2605, August 19 from Guatemala, not printed, 814.504/8-1947).

worthy attorneys (*de mi confianza*) for study. He said that the report had not yet been rendered by the attorneys in question but that I need not be worried, since the Government did not propose to bring the matter before Congress until a later date. The President remarked that, in addition to the suggested amendments presented by the Company, other amendments had been or would be presented by the Agricultural Association, the labor organizations, and the Chamber of Commerce. All of these would be studied and presented to Congress in such form as to endeavor to obtain at least a certain measure of satisfaction for the several interests concerned. President Arévalo then said that he understood that one of the chief objections on the part of the United Fruit Company was to a provision of the law which provided that agricultural enterprises employing more than 500 workers were not exempt from strikes.

I asked the President whether in his view of the matter he felt that there was discrimination against the Company. He immediately said that he would be the first to admit that there were several articles directly discriminatory against the United Fruit Company and that they were a virtual "machine gun" held against the head of the Company. He went on to say that these provisions had not been included in the original draft of the law presented to Congress and that they had been inserted in the heat of the debates in Congress, apparently without much attention having been paid to them at the time. He added that the laborers on the other hand felt that there were certain provisions of the Code which did not sufficiently protect their rights and that they also had certain justification for their requests for revisions of the Code.

In answer to my query concerning the approximate date of action on this matter, the President said that for political reasons and in view of the present situation, no action would be taken during the present month nor would any action be taken prior to the October holidays in connection with the Anniversary of the 1944 Revolution. He said that the matter might be presented to Congress during the latter part of October or possibly during November. He remarked on the similarity of the situation where so many different interests were endeavoring to obtain modifications of the Code and the situation which has arisen owing to the debate in the National Congress on the suspension of constitutional guarantees. He said that the three parties which support the Government, presumably the PAR, the FPL and PRN, were quarrelling among themselves but that this was only a step in their democratic education and that the differences between the various interests desirous of modifying the Labor Code were not dissimilar.

Respectfully yours,

EDWIN J. KYLE

814.504/5-2847

Memorandum by Mr. Robert E. Wilson of the Division of Central America and Panama Affairs [28]

[WASHINGTON,] September 29, 1947.

The attached is the long-awaited reply of the Guatemalan Government [29] to the memorandum presented to the Guatemalan Embassy on May 28, 1947, following Assistant Secretary Braden's conversation with the Ambassador held on May 24, 1947. A copy and a translation of the Memorandum are being forwarded to the Embassy in Guatemala for its information and comment. Meanwhile, the following observations may be made:

It has been noted that with respect to Article 105, which provides for the creation of special Parity Commissions for Minimum Wages for individual companies having not less than 1000 workers and activities in various departments or economic areas, that according to the Report these commissions could not be set up unless the companies themselves specifically request it.

With respect to Articles 116 and 121 concerning the normal work day, work week for pay purposes, and overtime pay, establishing differences for the large agricultural companies, the Report seeks to justify these discriminations, referred to as "a greater economic burden", on the grounds that because of their size they must have a more efficient organization and are therefore in a better situation to share with the workers their economic benefits, and it is asserted that greater economic capacity rightly carries with it greater social obligations, such obligations being adjusted more to the economic capacity of the giver than the needs of the recipient.

Referring to the provision of Article 238 which places the rural syndicates of the large companies on the same level as urban syndicates, in contradistinction to rural syndicates composed of workers of the smaller companies, the Report states that the limitation on the activities of the smaller companies' rural syndicates is due to the fact that most of the workers, because of lack of education, have not yet reached a cultural level justifying their assumption of these activities, whereas, on the other hand, the large companies, because of their better organization, require a greater number of educated employees,

---

[28] Addressed to the Chief, Division of Central America and Panama Affairs (Newbegin), the Deputy Director, Office of American Republic Affairs (Woodward), and the Chief of Area Problems Branch, Division of International Labor, Social and Health Affairs (Fishburn).

[29] Memorandum from the Guatemalan Embassy dated September 16, 1947, with an attached Report rendered on September 5 by the Juridical Division of the Guatemalan Ministry for Foreign Affairs; neither printed.

resulting in a higher cultural level in their syndicates, justifying their assumption of the same activities as urban workers' syndicates.

The exclusion of large agricultural companies from the classification of public services, for strike purposes, in Article 243, is admitted by the Report to be contradictory, but is held to be justified in the light of the fundamental principle of the Law, which is tutelary and devised to give labor a greater bargaining position in its deals with powerful companies which have economic advantages on their side.

In its summary, the Report asserts that the seemingly discriminatory features of the Law are consistent with the tutelary function of the state, but insists that the Law is not discriminatory against American firms in particular, or even foreign firms, since it applies equally to Guatemalan firms, whether private or public, and it provides the names of seven Guatemalan firms which are affected by it. Finally, it closes with the reassuring statement that "These measures cannot be cause for reasonable concern for foreign capital invested or about to be invested in Guatemala, or for national capital which is also affected, because the obligations they establish are reasonable and do not destroy the legitimate margin of profit to Capital."

814.6156/11–2247 : Telegram

The Acting Secretary of State to the Embassy in Guatemala

CONFIDENTIAL WASHINGTON, November 22, 1947—1 p. m.

337. Since Dept has received no info indicating that question of proposed modifications of Labor Code has been presented Congress, you requested seek interview with President and remind him of his conversation with Ambassador Kyle Sept 20, in course of which he agreed certain provisions of code are discriminatory against United Fruit Company, and agreed present proposed modifications to Congress probably in late October or early November.

You may, if you see fit, point out that enforcement of discriminatory conditions such as Article 13(*b*) paragraph 3 and Article 243(*b*) only serve to increase difficulties of reaching satisfactory solution and cause serious concern in US business circles interested in economic development in Guatemala and elsewhere in Latin America.

You may also wish emphasize fact that proposed development plan of United Fruit Company in Guatemala and its relation to pest control is of fundamental importance in continuation of banana industry and that it would be most unfortunate for national economy if Company, because of uncertainty of future labor relations, would be forced curtail this activity.

LOVETT

814.6156/11-2647

The Chargé in Guatemala (Wells) to the Secretary of State

RESTRICTED GUATEMALA, November 26, 1947.
No. 2733

SIR: I have the honor to enclose for the Department's information a memorandum [30] covering a conversation between Messrs. Turnbull and Taillon and President Arévalo on November 21 concerning the application of the Labor Code to the United Fruit Company.

The salient points brought out during the conversation were: (1) the President confirmed his intention to propose modification by Congress of the discriminatory clauses of the Labor Code, holding in abeyance the application of these clauses in the meantime; and (2) that the proposed amendments will not be presented to Congress before the opening of the next ordinary session in March of next year.

This memorandum covers some of the points raised in the Department's telegram No. 337 of November 22, which will be the subject of a separate despatch.

Respectfully yours, MILTON K. WELLS

814.6156/12-1847 : Telegram

The Chargé in Guatemala (Wells) to the Secretary of State

CONFIDENTIAL GUATEMALA, December 18, 1947—4 p. m.

434. Deptel 337, November 27 [*22*]. During interview with President Arévalo today to discuss discriminatory features Labor Code, President reaffirmed favorable attitude indicated his conversation with Ambassador Kyle on September 20; likewise referred recent assurances given Turnbull and Taillon of United Fruit to effect these clauses are being studied for purpose submitting proposed amendments to Congress in March. (Embassy's despatch 2733, November 26.)

I felt it opportune to cover all points mentioned Deptel 337, particularly comments re Article 13 of Labor Code since only two days ago Minister of Economy and Labor [31] reminded President International Railways [32] of existence government's discretionary authority under this article to reduce percentage foreign employees, as thinly veiled threat, during discussion re labor demands on railway. (Embassy's A-434, December 17.[30])

---

[30] Not printed.
[31] Augusto Charnaud MacDonald.
[32] Thomas A. Bradshaw, President, International Railways of Central America.

The President readily admitted matter should have been taken care of sooner, but said that time did not permit consideration by Congress of proposed amendments during session which ended November 30. Twice during interview he suggested we again remind him of matter some two weeks before Congress reconvenes.

WELLS

814.504/12–1947

The Chargé in Guatemala (Wells) to the Secretary of State

CONFIDENTIAL GUATEMALA, December 19, 1947.
No. 2770

SIR: I have the honor to refer to the Embassy's telegram No. 434 of December 18 concerning my interview with President Arévalo with regard to the proposed modification of certain discriminatory clauses of the Guatemalan Labor Code; and to the Department's instruction No. 898 of November 28, 1947,[33] inviting comments in regard to the contradictions between the Guatemalan position as stated in the Foreign Office memorandum delivered to the Department by the Guatemalan Embassy on September 16, and the statements made by President Arévalo in his conversation with Ambassador Kyle on September 20, 1947.

During our conversation on December 18, the President reaffirmed the position taken in his previous talk with Ambassador Kyle, stating that the discriminatory clauses are being studied by the Executive with a view to presenting proposed modifications to Congress in March. While, admittedly, he did not give categoric assurances that such modifications would be satisfactory in every respect, he definitely conveyed the impression of being determined to eliminate from the Labor Code those features which are the cause of legitimate concern to foreign enterprise. He did reserve his position somewhat, however, by calling attention to the conflicting demands from employers and labor for revision of the Code, implying that neither may be satisfied with the compromise which the Government may have to effect. During our talk, I mentioned the report prepared by the Juridical Division of the Guatemalan Foreign Office, remarking that since this document rejected our contention that certain clauses of the Code are discriminatory in character, my Government would be glad to have his renewed assurances that consideration was now being given to their modification. Although I had hoped he would do so, he offered no direct comment (which could mean he was uninformed regarding this Guate-

---

[33] Not printed.

malan memorandum, or at least unfamiliar with its substance), but permitted me to continue the conversation at that point.

It is not unlikely the position stated by the Ministry for Foreign Affairs represents the thinking of many key officials in the Arévalo administration, particularly in the Ministry of Economy and Labor which is under the direction of Sr. Augusto Charnaud MacDonald, whose record identifies him as extremely pro-labor and hostile to foreign enterprises. Many observers believe Charnaud MacDonald's extremism will be his undoing; that his days as a Cabinet minister are numbered. The more optimistic think that his resignation will be demanded as a result of the FPL victory in the municipal elections. (Charnaud MacDonald is a leader of PAR). Nevertheless, as long as he remains Minister of Economy and Labor, the United Fruit Company and other American enterprises cannot count upon sympathetic consideration in that Ministry.

It must also be borne in mind that the Labor Code (and the question of labor-employer relations in general) is decidedly a hot political issue in Guatemala today. The extremism of labor leadership and the complacency of the Arévalo Administration were considered by competent observers as an important underlying issue in the recent municipal elections. While the results were regarded as a rebuff to labor radicalism and a mandate for moderation, the triumphant political party, Frente Popular Libertador, naturally received much abuse, however unjustified, for having turned its back on labor. It is not unreasonable to expect that this political party, now in the saddle, will be inclined to appease labor to some degree during the forthcoming months when revision of the Labor Code will be debated as a means of demonstrating that it has not gone "reactionary". Likewise, it must be borne in mind that President Arévalo's express policy is one of "protecting labor". He considers himself the maximum champion of the underprivileged; and takes great pride in boasting that he enjoys the full confidence of the masses, and can manage labor. Therefore, while he appears to have a realistic approach to the problem, an inherent sympathy for the laboring classes may sway him at the crucial moments.

In considering the Labor Code as a whole, as well as the discriminatory features thereof, it is important to note that many provisions are subject to Executive interpretation or discretion; and the actual administration thereof is more significant than purely legal concepts.

Having in mind the political pressures that will be brought to bear pro and con when time comes for Congress to consider proposals for modification of the Labor Code, it is likely that a satisfactory solution will be largely contingent upon the President's personal intervention.

In this connection, Mr. Taillon, Manager of United Fruit, is confident that if the matter were left in the President's hands there would be no difficulty in obtaining congressional modifications to remove the offensive features, but that certain members of the Cabinet and other sub-officials are working at cross purposes.

Therefore, I feel we will have to rely heavily upon the President and that it would be highly advisable for the Ambassador again to discuss the situation with him in mid-February, especially since the President himself has extended the invitation [34] (last paragraph my telegram No. 434).

Respectfully yours, MILTON K. WELLS

---

[34] In airgram A-10, January 20, 1948, the Department requested the Ambassador to bring this matter to the personal attention of Arévalo sometime in mid-February (814.504/12-1947).

HAITI

UNITED STATES EFFORTS TO ASSIST HAITI IN SOLVING FINANCIAL AND OTHER PROBLEMS [1]

838.51/2–2147

The Acting Secretary of State to the Members of the Haitian Special Mission [2]

WASHINGTON, March 17, 1947.

EXCELLENCIES: I have the honor to refer to Your Excellencies' notes of February 11 and February 21, 1947 [3] amplifying the earlier proposals of your Mission with respect to certain financial adjustments as first set forth in the Mission's note of December 23, 1946,[4] to which the Department of State made reply in its note of February 13, 1947.[4] This Government has followed with great care economic and political developments in Haiti and, mindful of the good relations prevailing between our two countries, has endeavored to view in the most sympathetic light possible the Mission's several requests.

With regard to the request for funds with which to redeem the bonds issued under the private loan contracts of 1922 and 1925, you will recall that in its note of February 13, the Department of State expressed its full concurrence in the position of the Export-Import Bank as stated in the latter's memorandum of January 27, 1947 presented to the Haitian Mission,[4] concerning the Bank's inability to accede to this request. In this connection it may be pointed out that there is no agency of the Government of the United States empowered to effect a refunding loan at a lower rate of interest or to extend the term of amortization and reduce the interest rate of the present bonds.

In its note of February 21 the Mission requested the immediate termination of the Executive Agreement of September 13, 1941.[5] It alleged intervention of the United States in the internal affairs of

---

[1] For previous documentation on several aspects of United States relations with Haiti, see *Foreign Relations*, 1946, vol. XI, pp. 931 ff.
[2] The Mission consisted of the Haitian Minister of Foreign Relations (Price-Mars), the Ambassador in the United States (Charles), the Minister of Finance (Margron), and the former Minister of Agriculture and Commerce (Rigaud).
[3] Neither printed.
[4] Not printed.
[5] Department of State Executive Agreement Series No. 220, or 55 Stat. (pt. 2) 1348; for documentation on this subject, see *Foreign Relations*, 1941, vol. VII, pp. 322 ff.

Haiti in connection with the terms of payment of 1922–23 bonds envisaged in that Agreement and stated in support of this opinion that the Agreement of September 13, 1941 does not permit the Haitian Government to prepare its budget or to amend its present budgetary laws except to put them in harmony with the Agreement. The Government of the United States has carefully reexamined the provisions of the Agreement and is unable to discover the basis for the statements of the Mission respecting the Haitian budget.

With respect to the allegations of the Mission concerning intervention, it should also be pointed out that the present situation is the result of negotiations freely entered into by both Governments in 1941, and in the opinion of this Government the Executive Agreement of September 13, 1941 is, therefore, not to be considered as an act of intervention.

My Government wishes to emphasize that the Executive Agreement of September 13, 1941 involves the interests not only of the Government of Haiti and the United States but also of Haiti's private creditors. Consequently, in considering the Mission's request, this Government must take into account the views of the bondholders, who have not indicated their willingness to approve an abrogation of the Executive Agreement.

Accordingly this Government feels it must advise the Haitian Mission that it is unable to agree to a termination of the Executive Agreement except in conformity with the express terms thereof. Article XI of the Agreement provides in part as follows:

"The present agreement shall continue in full force and effect during the existence of the outstanding external bonds of 1922 and 1923. After the redemption of the said bonds, the provisions of this agreement shall automatically cease to have effect."

In connection with the foregoing, the Department of State is mindful of the statements made by the Mission's counsel respecting the possibility of retiring the present bonds through a private refunding loan, and will continue to follow developments in this direction with sympathetic interest.

With regard to the Mission's request for a readjustment in the interest rate and terms of amortization of the Export-Import Bank public works credit of 1938,[6] no reason is perceived for modifying the reply to this question previously communicated to the Mission by

---

[6] A loan of $5,500,000 to the Haitian Government by the Bank for public works purposes; the J. G. White Engineering Company was engaged by the Haitian Government to carry out projects which that Government desired and approved, such as roads and water supply for Port-au-Prince.

the Bank and concurred in by the Department of State, to the effect that present circumstances do not justify a second refunding of this credit. It may be pointed out that the interest rate for this loan is exactly the same as has been provided in all similar loans to other governments.

The comments of the Mission regarding the SHADA obligation were considered carefully by the Export-Import Bank in its memorandum of January 27 [8] and the Department of State fully concurs in the views expressed therein.

With respect to the Mission's remarks regarding the Cryptostegia program, this Government, for reasons set forth in a separate note [9] being addressed to the Mission, regrets that it is unable to accede to the Mission's request to reopen the settlement on this subject reached with the Haitian Government in 1944.

The remaining request set forth in the Mission's notes under reference concerned the desire of the Haitian Government to obtain a new loan from the Export-Import Bank. The Department of State is fully appreciative of the reasons which have been advanced by the Mission in support of its request for this loan and accordingly expresses its concurrence with the position taken by the Bank during conversations on this subject with the Mission on March 7 and confirmed in the Bank's memorandum of that date,[10] to the effect (1) that the Bank is not in a position to consider the program as a whole, both because of its size and because of the lack of up-to-date or detailed information on individual projects; and (2) that if the Haitian Government wishes to select the most urgent and most desirable project from the Haitian point of view and secure competent engineering and other technical assistance in developing all of the relative information regarding this selected project, the Bank would be prepared to consider it on its merits and in the light of prevailing conditions in Haiti at that time and the status of Haiti's external indebtedness.

Accept [etc.] For the Acting Secretary of State:
SPRUILLE BRADEN

---

[8] The $5 million loan from the Export-Import Bank, authorized in May 1941 and thereafter extended to Haiti through the medium of the Société Haitiano-Américaine de Développement Agricole (SHADA), had been utilized for the purpose of diversifying and developing profitable Haitian enterprises; in its January 27 memorandum, not printed, the Bank expressed its inability to find any valid basis on which Haiti could request cancellation of the SHADA credit; the Bank was therefore not disposed to make any readjustment at that time (838.51/1–2747).

[9] Infra.

[10] Memorandum not printed.

838.51/2–2147

The Acting Secretary of State to the Members of the Haitian Special Mission

WASHINGTON, March 17, 1947.

EXCELLENCIES: I have the honor to refer to Your Excellencies' notes dated December 23, 1946 and February 11 and 21, 1947,[11] as well as to your conversations with representatives of the Department of State in which statements have been made concerning damages alleged to have been sustained by the economy of Haiti as a result of the Cryptostegia project. It will be recalled that this was a wartime project undertaken in Haiti from 1942 to 1944 through agreement between our two governments.[12] Your Excellencies' note of February 21 estimates this damage at twenty million dollars.

Although representatives of this Government have, of course, been willing during the visit of the Mission to discuss this matter in the spirit of frankness and friendship which has traditionally animated our two governments, I wish to point out that an exhaustive examination of the project and its effects was made with the Government of Haiti at the time of the conclusion of the Cryptostegia program in 1944, as a result of which examination definitive termination arrangements were made and plans for restoration of the affected lands to productive food crops were agreed upon. It was for this reason that in its note of February 13 this Government expressed its full accord with the statement on this subject contained in the Memorandum of January 27 presented to Your Excellencies by the Export-Import Bank, to the effect that settlement with respect to the Cryptostegia program was reached in 1944. In this connection, I wish also to call Your Excellencies' particular attention to a Memorandum delivered by the Government of Haiti to the American Embassy at Port-au-Prince on May 29, 1944, a copy of which is enclosed in translation.[13] This Memorandum recorded the intention of the Haitian Government to make no further claim with respect to alleged damages to landholders arising out of the Cryptostegia program.

Despite the fact that this Government is unable to consider reopening the settlement arrangements made in 1944, it wishes to take this opportunity to point out certain facts in connection with the Mission's allegations regarding damage to the Haitian economy from the

---

[11] None printed.
[12] For data on the program's initiation in 1942 and termination in 1944, see *Foreign Relations*, 1942, vol. VI, p. 460, and *ibid.*, 1944, vol. VII, 1169 ff., respectively.
[13] Not printed, but see telegram 162, May 30, 1944, 3 p. m., from Port-au-Prince, *ibid.*, 1944, vol. VII, p. 1172.

Cryptostegia program. All information available to this Government indicates that in the years since 1944, when the Cryptostegia program was abandoned, the Haitian economy has reached an almost unprecedented high level, with increased production, export, and government revenue figures demonstrating that Haiti's economic condition is, in fact, considerably better than in pre-war years. Included among those exports enjoying a favorable or improved position are several agricultural commodities the production of which the Mission has asserted suffered as a result of the Cryptostegia program.

As for the years during which the Cryptostegia program was in operation in Haiti, it is this Government's view that funds expended by it in Haiti in connection with the program played a significant role in maintaining the Haitian economy at a time when that economy was suffering because of adverse world shipping and market conditions caused by the war. Moreover, at the time of termination of the program, a large amount of valuable United States Government-owned property which had been used in the program was made available to SHADA, a Haitian Government Corporation, at drastic reduction in price, for use in continuing SHADA's activities in developing long run aspects of the Haitian economy.

With respect to the Mission's oral statements that losses to individual landholders in Haiti from the Cryptostegia program amounted to twenty million dollars beyond the cash remuneration received for rental of their lands, and damages to their crops and other property, this Government regrets it is forced to express its complete disagreement. The particular attention of the Mission is called in this connection to the informal memorandum of December 6, 1946 [15] delivered to His Excellency the Foreign Minister of Haiti by this Government's Embassy at Port-au-Prince, following the Embassy's receipt of the former's note of October 9, 1946,[15] the fourth paragraph of which was concerned with the Cryptostegia program. A copy of the Embassy's memorandum is attached for ready reference.

In addition to the foregoing memorandum, the Government of the United States wishes to make certain other observations with respect to the Cryptostegia program. One of the principal assertions of the Mission alleges the indiscriminate and widespread destruction of fruit trees. This Government feels that this statement is refuted by the evidence. It is known that more than half the approximately 70,000 acres of land actually prepared for Cryptostegia plantings had originally been almost devoid of trees. In the case of large trees, it was found more economical to top them back than to remove them.

It is understandable that in the prompt execution of a program

---

[15] Not printed.

which, by Haitian Government decree, requisitioned some 111,000 acres of land involving somewhat less than 40,000 families, a few of the property holders may have felt inadequately compensated for the payments received for rental of lands and crop damages.

However, when it is considered that the $328,242 paid as rents and damages to landowners were those considered as just and equitable by the Haitian Government; when it is considered that the $3,162,759 paid to peasants as wages during the twenty-two months of program operation were the wages specified by the Haitian Government, and were fifty per cent higher than the labor scale previously in effect; when it is considered that for twenty-two months the average number of peasants employed on the program per month was 31,000; when it is considered that the peasant families themselves were urged to work at the high local wage rate for the program and were given preference in such employment; when it is considered that at the conclusion of the program there was full provision for clearing lands of Cryptostegia at the expense of the Government of the United States; and when it is further considered that following the termination of the Cryptostegia project, the major part of the first year's work of the Institute of Inter-American Affairs' agricultural assistance program was directed not only to restoring former Cryptostegia lands to production of food crops by distributing seeds and tools to the returning landowners and by growing and distributing some one million fruit trees and plants, but also to planting in food crops a not inconsiderable amount of previously uncultivated land cleared at the expense of the United States Government as part of the Cryptostegia program, when all of the above facts are considered, it appears that this Government has not only fulfilled its legal obligations, but has also made a substantial contribution to the improvement of the Haitian economy.

It is believed that the foregoing shows the fairness and generosity of the United States Government (1) in paying for the loss to individual landholders resulting from the temporary use of not more than five per cent of the tillable land of Haiti in an emergency war project on behalf of the United Nations, including Haiti, and (2) in assuming the major share of the cost of restoring this land to peacetime use when the Cryptostegia project was terminated. The Government of the United States further feels that these facts are of particular cogency when it is recalled that the attempt to produce Cryptostegia rubber in Haiti was declared at that time to be the major contribution of the Haitian Government and people to the joint war effort which was rendered in a true spirit of cooperation in a cause for which the United Nations expended so much in blood and treasure.

Accept [etc.]　　　　　　　　For the Acting Secretary of State:
　　　　　　　　　　　　　　　　　　　　　Spruille Braden

838.51/3–2747

Mr. Charles C. Hauch of the Division of Caribbean Affairs, to the Haitian Ambassador (Charles)

WASHINGTON, March 27, 1947.

DEAR MR. AMBASSADOR: I am enclosing two copies of the Department's press release of last night setting forth the exchange of correspondence with the Haitian Good Will Mission.[18] As you are aware, release of this correspondence was suggested by the Haitian Government to the American Embassy at Port-au-Prince and this Government was pleased to give publicity to these documents simultaneously with their release in Haiti.

Sincerely yours, CHARLES C. HAUCH

838.24/5–1347

The Ambassador in Haiti (Tittmann) to the Secretary of State

CONFIDENTIAL PORT-AU-PRINCE, May 13, 1947.
No. 464

SIR: With reference to the Department's telegram No. 110 of May 1, 1947,[19] stating that the Department would consider sympathetically a Haitian request to purchase from surplus small amounts of arms and equipment to meet an urgent and immediate need, I have the honor to report that the content of this telegram was conveyed by me personally to President Estimé on May 3, 1947. The President expressed satisfaction, and it is understood that shortly thereafter he forwarded to the Haitian Embassy in Washington for presentation to the Department a list of arms and ammunition desired by the Army of Haiti (since the Law of March 29, 1947, no longer known as the Garde d'Haiti) which was furnished by General Lavaud, Chief of Staff of the Haitian Army.

There is enclosed a copy of a report dated May 9, 1947,[19] from the Military Attaché of this Embassy to the War Department which I believe is of sufficient importance to be called especially to the Department's attention. Therein is found what amounts to a declaration of Haitian Military policy by the Chief of Staff of the Haitian Army.

---

[18] The press release consisted of a statement by the Department, printed in Department of State *Bulletin*, April 6, 1947, p. 634, together with the exchange of correspondence comprising 26 pages of notes and memoranda. The correspondence was issued in mimeographed form but was not printed. Two of the Department's notes, dated March 17, are printed *ante*, pp. 720 and 723.

[19] Not printed.

In broad outline this policy is to (1) provide first of all for internal security; (2) have a small army to act as a covering force if Haiti is attacked and to train civilian officer and NCO reserve; (3) have only sufficient equipment for training purposes; (4) not be the aggressor; (5) request assistance from the United States, if attacked; (6) have reserve personnel trained to use United States arms and equipment; (7) obtain now United States arms and equipment for internal security and training purposes.

With regard to paragraph 3 of the Department's telegram No. 110 of May 1, 1947, which is for my information only, perhaps I should say that the Haitians have been aware for some time of the possibility of some sort of an interim program for Haiti,[20] although it may be assumed that the present status of the matter as set forth in the telegram is not known to them.

Respectfully yours, HAROLD H. TITTMANN

Press Release Issued by the Department of State, July 10, 1947

The Government of Haiti, acting under the provisions of the Executive Agreement of September 13, 1941, entered into between the Governments of Haiti and the United States, has requested the acquiescence of this Government to the flotation of an internal loan in Haiti of $10,000,000. The acquiescence of this Government was given in an exchange of notes signed at Port-au-Prince on July 4, 1947.

Article VII of the Executive Agreement of 1941 provides that until the amortization of the whole amount of the bonds of the external debt of 1922 and 1923 of the Government of Haiti shall have been completed, the public debt of the Republic of Haiti shall not be increased except by previous agreement between the two governments. The Government of Haiti, in requesting such an acquiescence at this time, stated that the proceeds of the internal loan would be used in part for amortization of the 1922 and 1923 bond issues.

The translation of the note from the Haitian Government and the text of the reply of the American Ambassador at Port-au-Prince are as follows:

[Here follow the two notes, constituting agreement between the United States and Haiti respecting Haitian finances, printed in Department of State, Treaties and Other International Acts Series (TIAS) No. 1643, and in 61 Stat. (pt. 3) 3097.]

---

[20] The first installment of arms and equipment under the Interim Program did not arrive in Haiti during 1947.

838.51/9–1747

Memorandum of Conversation, by Mr. Charles C. Hauch of the Division of Caribbean Affairs

RESTRICTED [WASHINGTON,] September 17, 1947.

Participants: Mr. Maffry, Export-Import Bank
Mr. Lucien Hibbert—Director of the University of Haiti and former Finance Minister
Mr. Hauch—CRB

Following Mr. Hibbert's call on Assistant Secretary Armour on September 9 (see Department's Memorandum of Conversation of that date entitled "Proposal for Export-Import Bank Loan to Haiti" [23]), Mr. Hibbert's memorandum presented at that time was considered by the interested officers of the Department and the Export Import Bank. Although it was felt that there was little the Bank could do other than to refer Mr. Hibbert to its memorandum of March 7, 1947 [23] in replying to the request of the Haitian Financial Mission for a $20,000,000 loan, it was decided after discussion with Mr. Armour to have Mr. Hibbert received by Mr. Maffry of the Bank.

Accordingly, I accompanied Mr. Hibbert to the Bank on September 17. Mr. Maffry confirmed the Bank's previous position that in order for it to consider any loan proposal from Haiti, the Haitian Government must present it with a well-justified and thought out project. Mr. Hibbert said that this approach was impossible for the Haitian Government because (1) it did not have the funds to have a private or technical organization undertake a survey and justification of this type and (2) the publicity attendant on any such survey being made would have unfortunate results if a request for a loan were turned down by the Bank after time and money had been spent on the survey. Consequently, he wished the Department and/or the Bank to arrange to have an economic mission go to Haiti and help the Haitian Government decide which projects should be undertaken. Mr. Maffry said it would be impossible for the Bank to participate in a survey of this kind and that having such a survey made was the Haitian Government's responsibility. He said he could give to Mr. Hibbert the names of several persons or firms whose ability to make a survey of this kind was known to the Bank. Mr. Hibbert evinced no interest in pursuing the matter further, and consequently no names were given to him.

Mr. Hibbert emphasized the "guaranties", which he had outlined in his memorandum. These included certain provisions whereby the management of SHADA would be turned over to the Bank and

---

[23] Not printed.

SHADA's income would be used to repay the loan, as well as a pledging of returns from the sisal export tax to this end and the organization of the National Bank of Haiti in such a way as to protect the Export-Import Bank's investment. Mr. Maffry said that these "guaranties" were not required by the Bank and that the Bank would not consider making a loan on these terms. He said the Bank's requirements were that the project be sound from the Bank's point of view and that the Bank have confidence in the ability and promise of Haiti to repay the loan. He added that these "guaranties" would not get Haiti any more favorable treatment than she would receive without them. He emphasized further that the Bank in no circumstances would undertake the administration of SHADA. To this Mr. Hibbert replied that the Bank is in effect already managing SHADA.

Mr. Hibbert stated he considered the Bank's attitude to be a complete shutting of the door in Haiti's face as regards the possibility of a loan. Mr. Maffry said it did not seem so to him in view of the Bank's memorandum of March 7, but Mr. Hibbert said it was quite impossible for Haiti to proceed on the terms of that memorandum.

838.51/9-1947

Memorandum of Conversation, by Mr. Charles C. Hauch of the Division of Caribbean Affairs

RESTRICTED [WASHINGTON,] September 19, 1947.

Participants: Mr. Lucien Hibbert—Director of the University of Haiti and Former Finance Minister
Mr. Robert F. Woodward, ARA [24]
Mr. Hauch—CRB

Following Mr. Hibbert's call at the Export Import Bank on September 17, further discussion on his proposal was held by Assistant Secretary Armour and other officers of the Department. It was decided that Mr. Hibbert should be received again by Departmental officers in an effort to explain to him why the door is not closed on consideration of an Export-Import Bank credit for Haiti and to assure him of this Government's sympathy with Haiti's problems.

Accordingly, Mr. Hibbert was received by Mr. Woodward and myself, and a two and one-half hour discussion ensued touching on many aspects of Haiti's past and her present problems. Mr. Woodward assured Mr. Hibbert of our sympathy and desire to cooperate with Haiti, and said the problem was to find the means of doing this. He said that the Export-Import Bank was the only agency which could make

---

[24] Deputy Director of the Office of American Republic Affairs.

a loan to Haiti and that the only basis on which the Bank was prepared to consider such a loan was set forth in its memorandum of March 7, 1947.[25]

Mr. Hibbert reiterated that this memorandum did not offer a satisfactory approach to the Haitian Government, for reasons set forth during his conversation with Mr. Maffry of the Bank (see Department's Memorandum of Conversation of September 17 entitled "Proposed Export-Import Bank Loan to Haiti"). He then discussed Haiti's criticisms of previous Export-Import Bank loans to Haiti. This afforded an opportunity for Mr. Woodward to state that this was precisely what we wished to avoid in our future relations with Haiti, and that consequently, we wished to be careful about the terms and conditions on which any future loan might be made. Mr. Woodward specifically referred to certain statements made in the notes of the Haitian Financial Mission visiting Washington last winter charging the United States with intervention and responsibility for injuries to Haiti's economy. He also referred to Ambassador Charles' recent statement to a press conference as reported in article by James L. Tuck entitled "Haiti—America's Test". Ambassador Charles was quoted as stating: "One cannot question the good intentions of the United States, but every time the United States has tried to help us, they have increased our confusion and poverty instead of lessening it." Mr. Hibbert made no reply to Mr. Woodward's statements other than to say that certain United States Government projects in Haiti had been beneficial to that country.

The discussion then passed to consideration of an informal list of projects Mr. Hibbert had prepared for further study and possible submission to the Export-Import Bank in connection with a loan request. A list of these projects is appended.[25] Mr. Hibbert stated he considered projects 1, 2 and 5 of the most importance for Haiti.

In reference to the first numbered project, i.e. the development of the Artibonite Valley and the Hinche Plateau, Mr. Hibbert again inquired whether any assistance in developing this project as a loan possibility could be obtained from this Government. Mr. Woodward inquired as to whether the Haitian Government itself did not have technical experts capable of presenting the plan, to which Mr. Hibbert replied in the negative. Mr. Woodward then suggested that it might be possible for the IIAA's food mission in Haiti to work with the Government in surveying and developing this project. He added that our Embassy would be glad to give informal advice and assistance and mentions specifically Ambassador Tittmann's sympathy for and

---

[25] Not printed.

his interest in the problems of Haiti and Agricultural Attaché Tanner's technical abilities in the agricultural field.

Mr. Hibbert felt this was a worthwhile suggestion and said he would discuss it with President Estimé. He wondered whether it might not be possible to secure the services of some other expert recommended by the United States to assist in any such survey. Mr. Woodward said he felt that the beginning should be by personnel presently in Haiti and added that any sending of additional experts to Haiti might cause undue hopes to be aroused in that country. I cautioned Mr. Hibbert that even after any such survey and plan were completed, there would be no guaranty that the Export Import Bank would consider it favorably as the basis for a loan. It was emphasized throughout the discussion that any advice given the Haitian Government by the IIAA or the Embassy on this matter would be informal and that responsibility for the plan would rest with the Haitian Government.

Mr. Hibbert then discussed his second proposed project, i.e., the development of the Tourist business in Haiti. He wished to have some tourist expert sent to Haiti to survey possibilities in this field. Mr. Woodward stated this would appear to be a project on which the advice of the transportation companies might profitably be sought, since they are interested in increasing travel. It was obvious this did not satisfy Mr. Hibbert who persisted in his idea of a United States Government-sponsored expert to give advice to Haiti on this problem. Mr. Hibbert inquired regarding the attitude of the Bank on a loan for this purpose and was told that of course the Department could not speak for the Bank. It was pointed out, however, that the Bank had advanced funds for the construction of the Jaragua Hotel in the Dominican Republic. Mr. Hibbert stated that Mr. Armour had expressed considerable interest in tourist possibilities in Haiti.

Mr. Hibbert passed over points 3 and 4 and stated that he personally considered point 5 to be of the most importance. This called for financial assistance in taking what would be the first complete census in Haiti in 1950. He felt the information obtainable in such a census was absolutely essential before any basic economy projects could be planned. He estimated the cost of the census at a million dollars, and stated Haiti expected to have the assistance of a United States census expert. It was pointed out to him that obtaining a credit from the Export Import Bank for this purpose seemed highly doubtful, although the Department of course could not speak for the Bank. In this connection it was noted that taking a census in itself was not an income-producing undertaking and the Bank in general requires that projects on which it loans money have a more direct effect in improving the economy of the country and in providing the means for repaying the loan. It was pointed out that financing a census is usually a regular charge on the government's revenues. Mr. Woodward wondered whether it was worth $1,000,000 to Haiti to take a census.

In the course of the conversation Mr. Hibbert made reference to the loans the United States has made to European countries and stated that the Haitian public was sometimes unable to understand why we were willing to advance money to other countries but not to Haiti. In reply, he was again informed that the Export Import Bank stands ready to make loans to the American Republics under certain circumstances. As for other economic assistance, reference was made to Secretary Marshall's comments at the Rio Conference [27] and the fact that plans for economic cooperation among the American Republics will be one of the subjects on the agenda of the Bogotá Conference. Mr. Hibbert did not appear impressed, and stated Haiti's need was of an immediate character in view of the rising cost of living and the concentration of underpaid wage earners in the cities.

Mr. Hibbert seemed somewhat uncertain at the close of the conversation as to the recommendations he should make to President Estimé. He thought he might discuss the Artibonite project with him as an Export-Import Bank loan possibility, but on the other hand felt the Bank's conditions for making a loan were distasteful to Haiti. He said that his recommendation might well be that Haiti should "tighten its belt" and proceed on its own initiative and resources.

838.51/10–347

The Chargé in Haiti (McBride) to the Secretary of State

RESTRICTED
No. 715

PORT-AU-PRINCE, October 3, 1947.

SIR: With reference to Embassy's telegram number 368 of September 30 and previous correspondence [28] regarding the termination of the Financial Agreement between the Governments of the United States and Haiti, signed on September 13, 1941,[29] I have the honor to transmit herewith a copy of the Note which was left with the Minister of Foreign Affairs on October 1, formally stating that the Government

---

[27] For documentation on the Inter-American Conference for the Maintenance of Continental Peace and Security, Quitandinha, Brazil, August 15–September 2, 1947, see pp. 1 ff.
[28] None printed.
[29] Department of State Executive Agreement Series No. 220, or 55 Stat. (pt. 2) 1348; for documentation on this subject, see *Foreign Relations*, 1941, vol. VII, pp. 322 ff.

of the United States considered the agreement automatically to have ceased to have effect.[30]

Respectfully yours, ROBERT H. MCBRIDE

838.51/10–1047

Memorandum of Conversation, by Mr. Charles C. Hauch of the Division of Caribbean Affairs

CONFIDENTIAL [WASHINGTON,] October 10, 1947.

Participants: Assistant Secretary Armour
Ambassador Tittman—Haiti
Mr. Hauch—CRB

During a discussion on current United States-Haitian relations, the following points were mentioned:

1. Mr. Armour felt that in view of this Government's past close association with Haiti, it has a particular moral responsibility to guide and assist Haiti in meeting its problems and in improving conditions in Haiti. He said he was quite disturbed by the present state of opinion towards the United States in Haiti, as evidenced by the recent Tuck article. Ambassador Tittmann agreed that it would be extremely desirable for political reasons to make a substantial gesture of cooperation with Haiti in solving that country's problems. The Ambassador observed that the Department has recently pursued a hand-off withdrawal policy towards Haiti, and his estimate of our present policy is to do just enough for Haiti to keep the country's head above water. Mr. Armour stated that this should not be and that we should be doing considerably more.

2. Mr. Armour agreed that informal advice in working with the Haitian Government in drawing up and executing a plan for the development of the Artibonite Valley might be helpful as a gesture of this Government's desire to cooperate with Haiti. He wondered, however, whether this would be sufficient and thought perhaps that additional technical personnel should be sent from the United States to assist the Government of Haiti. Ambassador Tittmann said it was his view that since the Food Mission had achieved such marked success in Haiti and had the good will of the Haitian Government, it would be best to continue to work through that channel, perhaps enlarging the personnel and funds of the Mission. Mr. Armour observed that this might be a problem in view of the limited funds at the disposal of the

---

[30] For Understanding Between the United States and Haiti Respecting Haitian Finances, effected by exchange of notes signed at Port-au-Prince October 1, 1947, see TIAS No. 1862, or 61 Stat. (pt. 4) 4111.

Institute. It was agreed that the matter would be discussed with officers of the Institute. As for a Haitian application for a loan from the Export-Import Bank in connection with this project, it was felt that this would have to await development of a detailed plan by the Haitian Government assisted by the IIAA Food Mission.

3. Mr. Armour thought that the development of tourism, and particularly hotel construction, in Haiti might offer a real opportunity for this Government to assist in Haitian development. He referred to the visit of Georges Leger and the French citizen, Georges Maurin, regarding their hope of obtaining funds from the Export-Import Bank for hotel construction in Haiti, and thought this might be worked out within the framework of the Bank's policy.

4. Ambassador Tittmann mentioned that Finance Minister Margron had inquired of him regarding the possibility of the Export-Import Bank's granting a five or ten year extension of the J. G. White loan. The Ambassador thought this might be a tangible gesture of good will towards Haiti which would assist our relations with that country. It would mean that the Haitian Government would have additional funds to carry on developmental projects during the next decade. Mr. Armour agreed that this would be a worthwhile gesture and that Ambassador Tittmann should suggest it to the Export-Import Bank during a meeting scheduled for the same afternoon.

5. In general, Mr. Armour felt that Ambassador Tittmann might express to the Board of directors of the Export-Import Bank our concern with Haitian-United States relations and inquire of them whether they would be sympathetic to some tangible evidence of the Bank's willingness to cooperate in improving these relations. Ambassador Tittmann noted particularly the unanimous opinion of Haitians that they had been given a bad deal by the United States on the SHADA and Cryptostegia programs, and stated his opinion that perhaps a neutral commission might proceed to Haiti in order to ascertain the truth of the Haitian belief. I said that the Cryptostegia settlement in 1944 had been agreed to, perhaps reluctantly, by the Haitian Government which itself had declared the question closed at that time. As for present SHADA operations, they are currently showing a profit and consequently it was my understanding that the Bank felt this is no time to go into the question of a SHADA debt readjustment. Mr. Armour said that regardless of this the anti-United States feeling engendered by the SHADA and Cryptostegia programs was the important thing to placate, particularly in view of the use to which it might be put by communist influences.

6. Mr. Armour said he had seen Mr. Blackmon of Standard Fruit briefly the previous day and that Mr. Blackmon had expressed great

HAITI   735

concern for the future of United States business in Haiti. Ambassador Tittmann outlined briefly the situation with respect to Standard's present difficulties, and Mr. Armour expressed concern at the Haitian Government's present policy. He agreed that a telegram should be sent to Port-au-Prince authorizing the Embassy again to express our concern and inquire specifically of President Estimé why he had refused to conclude a new agreement with Standard on the terms of his recent written statement to the Embassy. (Note: This telegram went out as no. 291 of October 10 [33]).

838.12/11-2147

The Ambassador in Haiti (Tittmann) to the Secretary of State

RESTRICTED   PORT-AU-PRINCE, November 21, 1947.
No. 792

SIR: I have the honor to inform the Department that I was disturbed when I was in Washington recently to learn that there was a plan on foot to terminate the Sanitary Mission,[34] leaving the Food Supply Mission [35] as the only activity of the Institute of Inter-American Affairs in Haiti. I am convinced that such a step would have unfortunate political repercussions here and desire to recommend strongly that the Sanitary Mission be continued along with the Food Supply Mission.

The Sanitary Mission has done an outstanding job. There is no doubt but that its achievements have a widespread popular appeal. The results of the yaws and malaria control programs are immediately apparent and often dramatic, building up good will toward us generally and especially among the Haitian masses who are the principal beneficiaries. The results of the construction program, such as sewer and water projects in the Haitian General Hospital, toilets, health centers, laundries, et cetera, are also readily visible to the man-in-the-street. These construction projects have in addition brought about a

---

[33] Not printed.
[34] For agreement initiating a cooperative program of health and sanitation in Haiti, effected by exchange of notes signed at Washington April 7, 1942, see Department of State Executive Agreement Series No. 425, or 58 Stat. (pt. 2) 1439.
[35] For memorandum of agreement between the Haitian Government and the Institute of Inter-American Affairs, signed at Port-au-Prince, August 28, 1944, initiating a cooperative food production program in Haiti, see TIAS No. 2061, or 62 Stat. (pt. 3) 3953.

For agreement between the United States and Haiti respecting a cooperative food production program in Haiti, confirming and extending the agreement of August 28, 1944, as modified and extended, effected by exchange of notes signed at Port-au-Prince December 19, 1947, and January 5, 1948, see TIAS No. 2061, or 62 Stat. (pt. 3) 3950.

strong feeling of cooperation between the Haitians and the Americans who have worked together on them.

. . . .

It can be said without hesitation that the Sanitary Mission enhances our prestige and is therefore a definite political asset. Its termination would mean not only the loss of the foregoing advantages, but also could cause positively unfavorable reactions among the Haitians, who would be keenly disappointed. Finally, its termination would eliminate a well-established unit of cooperative action, and activity which for reasons stated above should not be curtailed, but instead increasingly developed in Haiti.[36]

Respectfully yours, HAROLD H. TITTMANN

838.24/12–2947 : Airgram

The Acting Secretary of State to the Embassy in Haiti

CONFIDENTIAL WASHINGTON, December 29, 1947.

A-287. In the absence of relevant advices from you since your talks in the Department last October when it was understood that you would initiate informal action to secure the payment of the $20,000. obligation outstanding under the Haitian lend-lease agreement [37] the status of the account is unchanged.

Fiscal offices continue to report total aid furnished as $1,342,308.22 whereas agreement authorized "about $1,100,000". Full repayment responsibility under agreement is $60,000. of which $40,000. has been paid; however, no proposal for settlement for the value of over-deliveries has been made to date.

The Department is very desirous of concluding settlements for all outstanding unresolved lend-lease matters soonest possible. Therefore, with sympathetic understanding of Haiti's financial position and after consultation between interested offices, the Department is now willing to offer to the Government of Haiti those materials which were furnished at its request although in excess of the agreement limitation at approximately the same repayment rate as applied under the agreement. In actual figures, for such over-deliveries, valued at $242,308.22 under procurement prices, the Department is willing to accept in full

---

[36] An agreement between the United States and Haiti respecting a cooperative health and sanitation program in Haiti, extending the agreement of April 7, 1942, as amended, until June 30, 1948, was signed September 30, 1947, and effected by change of notes signed at Port-au-Prince September 25 and 27, 1947; for text of agreement and exchange of notes, see TIAS No. 1693, or 61 Stat. (pt. 4) 3651.

[37] For the Lend-lease agreement between the United States and Haiti, signed at Washington, September 16, 1941, see *Foreign Relations*, 1941, vol. VII, p. 319.

payment the sum of $13,000. and will consider the payment now of the aggregate sum of $33,000. as a full and final settlement of all lend-lease responsibility of the Government of Haiti with the sole exception of that concerning the Coast Guard Cutter which was leased under Charter Party and will be offered for sale as a separate transaction.

You are requested to bring this proposal to the attention of the appropriate officials of the Government of Haiti. As it is believed that a prompt settlement of the lend-lease account would benefit Haiti's credit position in the United States it is suggested that you stress the fact that this consideration proved an important factor in reaching final determination to extend these favorable terms. It is further suggested that, if you perceive no objection, preliminary conversations with Mr. Daniel Théard, Secretary of Haitian Embassy here and due in Port-au-Prince for the holidays, might prove helpful in developing eventual action.

LOVETT

HONDURAS

THE QUESTION OF MILITARY COOPERATION WITH THE HONDURAN REGIME [1]

815.24/1–447 : Telegram

The Secretary of State to the Embassy in Honduras

CONFIDENTIAL WASHINGTON, January 4, 1947—6 p. m.

1. As indicated Deptel No. 153 Dec 31 [2] Dept does not object Honduras obtaining non-military engineering equipment provided equipment is purchased outside interim program in which Honduras currently not included. However, War Assets Administration, which disposes of equipment of this type located in U.S., states informally that most of equipment desired by Honduras is unavailable for sale to foreign governments because of regulations requiring that it be offered to veterans and domestic purchasers. FLC, which disposes of surplus equipment located outside U.S., states that practically all surplus equipment in Pacific area has been turned over to Philippine and Chinese governments.[3] It is very unlikely that engineering equipment would be available from these sources and negotiations for the sale of any equipment would have to be conducted by Honduras directly with those governments.

If notwithstanding above Col Adams [4] still wishes to come to Washington Dept would have no objection provided such a visit does not coincide with that Col Bertrand.[5]

BYRNES

---

[1] Continued from *Foreign Relations*, 1946, vol. XI, pp. 955–968.
[2] Not printed.
[3] In an unnumbered telegram of September 18, 1947, the Ambassador in Honduras reported to the Department that he had sent a telegram to the American Embassy, Panama, for FLC, expressing concern that there was some hesitation on the part of FLC to sell to Honduras badly needed heavy engineering equipment and requesting their full cooperation in releasing this equipment for sale to Honduras immediately, adding, "as you know Honduras has benefitted very little either by FLC program or previously by Lend-Lease activities". (815.24 FLC/9–1847) In telegram 101, October 20, 1947, 6 p. m., the Department informed the Embassy in Honduras that FLC had approved the transfer of heavy engineering equipment (815.24 FLC/10–2047).
[4] Lt. Col. James Y. Adams, Chief, United States Military Mission in Honduras.
[5] Col. Francisco Bertrand, Honduran Army. The Honduran Ambassador had requested in December 1946 that Colonel Adams be authorized to come to the United States with Colonel Bertrand on what was believed to be a purchasing mission for military supplies for Honduras (815.24/12–2446).

815.24/8-1147

The Secretary of State to the Honduran Ambassador (Cáceres)

CONFIDENTIAL WASHINGTON, August 11, 1947.

EXCELLENCY: I have the honor to transmit herewith two copies each of Statements LL-11 and LL-12 and supporting schedules [6] reporting charges made against the Government of Honduras during the period from September 1, 1946 through December 31, 1946 for defense material transferred under the terms of the Lend-Lease Agreement of February 28, 1942.[7]

It will be noted that charges during the period under reference were counterbalanced by credits to a net sum of $8,779.62 (credit), and that charges through December 31, 1946 aggregate the grand total of $367,118.17. Of this amount a total reimbursement of $34,000 is due from Your Excellency's Government under the terms of the Agreement. Since payments in the amount of $33,000 have been received, however, the balance outstanding is $1,000.

It is requested that the enclosed statement and supporting schedules be treated by Your Excellency's Government on a most confidential basis.

Accept [etc.]   For the Secretary of State:
NORMAN ARMOUR

815.24 FLC/8-2547

The Ambassador in Honduras (Daniels) to the Secretary of State

RESTRICTED TEGUCIGALPA, August 25, 1947.
No. 2899

SIR: With reference to the Embassy's despatch No. 2844 of June 30, 1947 and the Department's telegram No. 67 of July 23, 1947, 6: 00 P. M.,[8] I have the honor to report that this morning a contract was concluded between the Government of Honduras and the Foreign Liquidation Commission whereby the latter opened a credit of $450,000 available to the Government of Honduras for purchases of surplus war material now being liquidated by the FLC.[9] The contract, a copy of which is enclosed, was signed by the Ministers of Foreign Affairs and War for the Honduran Government,[10] and by Mr. Robert F. Edgar,

---

[6] Not printed.
[7] For text of agreement, see *Foreign Relations*, 1942, vol. VI, p. 479.
[8] Neither printed.
[9] An amendment to the contract was signed on December 3, 1947, extending it to January 31, 1948.
[10] Silverio Laínez, Minister of Foreign Relations; Juan Manuel Galvez, Minister of War, Navy, and Aviation.

Central Field Commissioner for Latin America, on behalf of the FLC. The signatures were witnessed by Dr. Marcos Carías Reyes, Private Secretary of President Carías, and by Colonel James Y. Adams, Chief of the United States Military Mission.

The Government of Honduras plans to make immediate purchases of material now in the Canal Zone, particularly heavy engineering equipment. Colonel Adams plans to proceed to the Canal Zone to assist in the selection and purchasing of this material, though all responsibility for purchasing and shipping equipment to Honduras will rest with the Honduran Government.

Article First, Section 4(b) provides that the Government of Honduras may make payment for the material purchased in the form of real property and improvements to real property in Honduras. It is anticipated and recommended that this procedure be followed, so that all payments by Honduras for surplus material may be applied to the acquisition of Embassy sites and the construction of suitable buildings, both for the Chancery and for the residence. Mr. Edgar has told me that his office will keep the Department and the Embassy currently informed regarding actual purchases made by Honduras under this contract and the corresponding amount of dollar obligations incurred by Honduras which may be applied to the building program under this clause.

Respectfully yours, PAUL C. DANIELS

815.248/9–247

The Ambassador in Honduras (Daniels) to the Secretary of State

RESTRICTED TEGUCIGALPA, September 2, 1947.
No. 2907

SIR: I have the honor to enclose a memorandum dated September 2, 1947 [11] addressed to the Embassy by Colonel Royal S. Thompson, Acting Chief of the United States Military Mission here, giving information regarding the forthcoming trip to the United States of Major B. F. Matthews, Chief of the Maintenance Section of the Honduran Air Force. The aircraft which Major Matthews has in mind purchasing for the Honduran Air Force are as follows:

Six (6) AT–6 type aircraft
One (1) AT–11 type aircraft
One (1) C–47 type aircraft

Major Matthews plans to be in Washington in the latter part of September. It is suggested that this information be brought to the

---

[11] Not printed.

attention of the interested agencies of the Government in order that appropriate assistance may be extended to him in connection with his mission.

Although Major Matthews is an American citizen, his only employment here in Honduras is as Chief of Maintenance of the Honduran Air Force. As such he has been doing, from all accounts, an outstanding job in keeping the equipment, repair shops and mechanical facilities of the Honduran Air Force and School at a high level of efficiency.

I assume that Major Matthews will encounter no unusual difficulty in carrying out his mission, inasmuch as it appears that the Department already authorized some three months ago the exportation of six converted AT-6 airplanes to Honduras. I recommend that official contact be established with Major Matthews when he is in Washington, through the medium of the Honduran Embassy there, and that within the limits of the Department's policy in such matters he be given the assistance to which a high official of a friendly foreign Government is entitled. It is likewise recommended that the Embassy be kept currently informed of the progress of Major Matthew's mission insofar as the Department is able to do so.[12]

Respectfully yours, PAUL C. DANIELS

---

123 Daniels, Paul C.

Memorandum of Conversation, by the Chief of the Division of Central America and Panama Affairs (Newbegin)

CONFIDENTIAL [WASHINGTON,] October 24, 1947.

I called on Ambassador Cáceres this morning to inform him for his personal and confidential information that Ambassador Daniels, after his return to Washington from Honduras, would not go back to Honduras again as Ambassador, in as much as he was being appointed Director of the Office of American Republic Affairs.[13] . . . I told him that no selection had been made as yet and that several months may

---

[12] In a memorandum of December 6, 1947, Mr. Daniels, then Director of the Office of American Republic Affairs, stated that on December 5, Maj. Ben Matthews had telephoned him from Miami and referred to the airplanes he had been procuring for the Honduran Government and said that everything had moved smoothly with regard to the AT-6's and a C-47, but that there might be some delay in getting an export license for the AT-11 he was buying as an advanced trainer (demilitarized). Mr. Daniels told Major Matthews he would look into the AT-11 matter immediately. (815.248/12-647) Secretary Marshall informed the Embassy in Honduras in telegram 1, January 13, 1948, 6 p. m., that one AT-11 was licensed January 12 for export to the Honduran Air Force (815.248/1-1348).

[13] Ambassador Daniels returned to the Department on November 13 and was appointed Director of the Office of American Republic Affairs on that date.

well elapse before a new ambassador reached Tegucigalpa. Ambassador Cáceres expressed his satisfaction that a new ambassador would be sent and emphasized that any failure to do so would inevitably be misunderstood. He likewise emphasized that it was particularly desirable to have an American Ambassador in Tegucigalpa during the pre-election period [14] in order that he might give stability and see for himself the efforts being made to have an entirely free election. He then digressed on the local political situation stating that Carías and the National party had the support of a minimum of 80 percent of the people. He asserted that the so-called white-collar group was opposed to him but actually that had no particular importance and received no support whatsoever from the great illiterate masses.

The Ambassador then referred to previous conversations with Mr. Braden and Mr. Briggs,[15] particularly one with the latter [16] when he had been told quite frankly that this Government was indisposed to cooperate in a military way with Honduras since it had a regime which did not permit periodic free elections. He said that he had found this conversation very disturbing and that there were various remarks which he might have made at that time but which he refrained from making in order to continue friendly relations. He added further that he had not been able to inform his government in writing of this conversation with Mr. Briggs because of its delicate nature. He had however discussed it during his recent visit to Tegucigalpa when President Carías had asked whether the policy enunciated by Briggs was still in effect now that Briggs had proceeded to Montevideo.[17] The Ambassador said he had informed his Government that he felt that that policy was largely in the discard and that he thought it was primarily the policy of Mr. Braden and Mr. Briggs rather than the continuing policy of the Department of State. I told the Ambassador that was not quite correct, that we still had a warmer feeling for those governments which were periodically and freely elected than for those that adopted a policy of *continuismo* without adequate opportunity for popular

---

[14] The Presidential election was scheduled for October 1, 1948.
[15] Spruille Braden, Assistant Secretary of State, and Ellis O. Briggs, Director of the Office of American Republic Affairs.
[16] For memorandum of conversation of December 26, 1946, see *Foreign Relations*, 1946, vol. xi, p. 966.
[17] Mr. Briggs was appointed Ambassador to Uruguay on July 3, 1947.

expression, that there was perhaps a difference in approach but that our outlook remained very much the same.[18]

R[OBERT] N[EWBEGIN]

810.20 Missions/11–1047

Memorandum of Conversation, by the Chief of the Division of Special Inter-American Affairs (Dreier)

SECRET   [WASHINGTON,] November 10, 1947.

Participants: ARA—Mr. Daniels
CPA—Mr. Newbegin
Colonel Ordway and Lt. Colonel Smith—Army
IA—Mr. Dreier

Colonel Ordway called Mr. Daniels by arrangement to discuss the specific question of the plans advanced by Colonel Adams, Chief of US Military Mission to Honduras for the training of a group of Honduran Army personnel in parachute jumping, in regard to which the issue had been raised as to whether the Chief of Diplomatic Mission and the Department could intervene in regard to the nature of the Military Mission's activities.

Colonel Ordway expressed the desire to reach full agreement with the State Department on this matter and said he was prepared to recognize that the Department could intervene in regard to any aspect of the Mission's work which it considered involved political considerations, and furthermore that the Department had to be the judge of what was political. He did, however, wish to argue in favor of Colonel Adams' plan of training Hondurans in parachute jumping.

Mr. Daniels expressed his satisfaction with Colonel Ordway's views in regard to the role of the State Department in such matters. He

---

[18] For statement of the Department's policy, placing all American Republics on the same basis with respect to the procurement in the United States of arms, ammunition, and implements of war, subject to certain criteria, see enclosure to letter of August 22, 1947, from the Acting Secretary of State to the Secretary of the Army (Royall), p. 120.

Mr. J. Harold Darby, of the Munitions Division (Licensing Section), indicated in a memorandum of telephone conversation of November 24, 1947, that Mr. Gordon S. Reid, of the Division of Central America and Panama Affairs, had informed him on that day that in view of the elections to be held in Honduras on October 1, 1948, a strict policy would be followed with regard to all requests for any shipments of munitions materials to that country for the six-month period preceding the election date; therefore, after April 1, 1948, it was likely that applications for export licenses would not be considered favorably during that time. (815.24/11–2447)

pointed out that the Chiefs of Military Mission, according to their instructions, were to be guided by the Chiefs of Diplomatic Mission in their dealings with the officials of the foreign government, and in all matters of political character. He pointed out furthermore that the Mission agreement with Honduras called for the agreement of both the State and War Departments to any changes in the Mission program. Mr. Daniels explained that the extension of the proposed type of training to the Honduran Army would be interpreted in Honduras as an action of the United States to equip the Honduran Army better to control internal situations, since no one would conceive of Honduran parachutists being used in hemisphere defense. He pointed out that under any conditions such an interpretation of a Mission's activity was undesirable politically, and that it was particularly so this year when political maneuvers are already being undertaken looking toward the election of a successor to President Carías next October.

Colonel Ordway said that he appreciated those views and would be glad to be guided by them. He wishes, however, to point out that in his opinion this type of training had definite military advantages to the United States. He said that in time of war or international emergency it would handicap the United States from a military viewpoint to have revolutions take place in Latin America, and that it was therefore desirable that the armies of Latin American countries be equipped and trained with a view to maintaining civil order and avoiding outbreaks of violence which might hamper the cooperation of the governments in hemisphere defense.

Mr. Daniels challenged this view on the grounds that it could not be assumed that the maintenance of the political *status quo* in Latin American countries was automatically in the interests of the United States, or that any overturn of an existing government would necessarily lessen the cooperation of established authorities with the United States. However, he pointed out, if it were widely believed that the United States was aiding a military dictatorship to retain its power such a feeling might definitely increase any [anti?] U.S. sentiment and encourage political forces antagonistic to the United States. He recognized, at the same time, that in time of war these problems had to be considered realistically and carefully.[19]

---

[19] In a memorandum of telephone conversation of December 8, 1947, the Chief of the Division of Central America and Panama Affairs (Newbegin) stated that Colonel Ordway had called him that afternoon concerning a letter which he had sent to Colonel Adams. According to the memorandum, "Colonel Ordway informed him that the parachute training matter could be considered as closed for some time to come. He referred to his conversation here with Colonel Adams in which he had expressed his own personal views as being favorable to the proposal, but said that that was before he had had an opportunity to discuss the matter with State Department officials. He mentioned that political considerations took precedence over all others, and that, since the view of the State Department was that the program should not be put into effect for political reasons, there was nothing further to be said on it." (815.223/12-847)

[Here follows a summary of suggestions regarding the necessity of writing a more definite policy statement on activities of Military Missions in Latin American countries.]

Mr. Newbegin brought up the question of the request delivered to him this afternoon by Ambassador Cáceres for some military equipment for Honduras.

It was agreed that the note left by the Ambassador [20] would be considered by the Department and transmitted to the Department of the Army for consideration.

AGREEMENT BETWEEN THE UNITED STATES AND HONDURAS RESPECTING A COOPERATIVE HEALTH AND SANITATION PROGRAM IN HONDURAS, FURTHER AMENDING AND EXTENDING THE AGREEMENT OF MAY 8, 1942

[Effected by exchange of notes signed at Tegucigalpa May 13, 1947. For text of notes, see Department of State, Treaties and Other International Acts Series (TIAS) No. 1646, or 61 Stat. (pt. 3) 3114. For texts of notes of May 5 and 8, 1942, and April 18 and 19, 1944, see TIAS No. 1557, or 61 Stat. (pt. 3) 2319.]

---

[20] On November 7 Ambassador Cáceres had presented to Mr. Newbegin a note addressed to Secretary Marshall by the Honduran Secretaries of Foreign Affairs and War, Navy, and Aviation requesting assistance in obtaining certain military supplies, primarily equipment for an infantry battalion and a battery of field artillery. No action was taken on this request during 1947.

MEXICO

DISCUSSIONS OF THE PROBLEM OF LEND-LEASE OBLIGATIONS OF MEXICO TO THE UNITED STATES [1]

812.24/1–2047

The Ambassador in Mexico (Thurston) to the Secretary of State

CONFIDENTIAL MEXICO, January 20, 1947.
No. 2551

Subject: Lend Lease Indebtedness of Mexican Government

SIR: Supplementing despatch no. 2542 dated January 17, 1947,[2] on the subject noted, and for purposes of official record, there is transcribed below the text of a personal letter addressed by me on January 10 to Guy W. Ray, Esquire, Chief, Division of Mexican Affairs:

"Confidential MEXICO, D. F., January 10, 1947.

My dear Guy:
This will answer your letter of December 23, 1946 [2] and Ellis Briggs' letter of December 18, 1946,[3] and will supplement my telephone call on the morning of January 8, 1947—all of which concern the Department's desire that I obtain a reply from the Mexican Government to the Department's several Notes to the Mexican Embassy in Washington regarding Mexico's Lend Lease indebtedness to the United States.

I took up this topic in an interview last night with Señor Jaime Torres Bodet, the newly-appointed Mexican Minister for Foreign Affairs. Señor Torres Bodet did not let me finish my presentation of the subject before interrupting me to say that his Government felt that Mexico's war sacrifices in the Philippines, at sea, and through the emigration of its *braceros* [4] placed the inescapable obligation on the Mexican Government to obtain adequate recompense—and that it was the position of the Mexican Government, which found itself excluded from the peace arrangements for Italy [5] and threatened with similar

---

[1] Continued from *Foreign Relations*, 1946, vol. XI, pp. 978–987.
[2] Not printed.
[3] Not printed; Mr. Briggs was Director of the Office of American Republic Affairs.
[4] Day laborers.
[5] For the Mexican point of view on the draft peace treaty with Italy, see memorandum submitted by the Mexican Delegation before the Paris Peace Conference, August 30, 1946, Department of State publication No. 2868, *Paris Peace Conference, 1946: Selected Documents*, p. 335. See also *Foreign Relations*, 1946, vol IV, pp. 815–816, 827–828, 830–831.

exclusion as regards Germany,[6] to defend its position as strongly as possible and that in this effort it felt that it should make its Lend Lease settlement with the United States contingent upon adjustment of its claims against Italy and Germany. With respect to the *braceros*, he said that while it was true that some of them brought small savings back to Mexico, these in the aggregate were not important and did not offset the loss to Mexico's industry and agriculture resulting from their absence from the country in crucial years. He then said that perhaps I did not know that President Roosevelt had stated, when the Lend Lease arrangements were being made, that Mexico would not be expected to make any outlay in connection with those arrangements.[7]

When Señor Torres Bodet had concluded these remarks, I stated to him that if he would permit me to do so, I would say that I felt that the position he had outlined was not entirely defensible and that I regretted that he had felt it necessary to link Mexico's general claims against the Axis powers with her concrete contractual obligations with the United States under the Lend Lease Agreement.[8] I stated that I was certain that the sacrifices made by Mexico as a loyal and active participant in the War against the Axis were fully recognized in the United States, and that they had created a most sympathetic atmosphere in that country which would be reflected when negotiations for a settlement of Mexico's Lend Lease obligations were held. I said that with respect to President Roosevelt, we had no record of any such commitment on his part nor could we confirm it from those who were associated with him, and that furthermore it seemed to me unlikely that in the face of such a commitment Mexico would have been called upon to sign a formal agreement on Lend Lease requiring payments. I added that regardless of what I had just said, all that I requested him to do was to address a Note to me in response to the numerous Notes sent by the State Department to the Mexican Embassy in Washington on this subject, in which he would say merely that the Mexican Government is ready to negotiate a settlement of its Lend Lease indebtedness. He requested me to give him the dates of the Notes to which I had alluded, and from the two or three documents I had in my possession when speaking to him, I cited those dated March 27, 1945, June 1, 1945, August 30, 1945, and October 1, 1946.[9] I further pointed out that oral statements of intention to negotiate a settlement had already been made to the Secretary of the Treasury of the United States [10] during his recent visit to Mexico, and that a similar and equally definite statement had been incorporated in the memorandum written by the Mexican Secretary of Finance, Licenciado Ramón

---

[6] For documentation on the Moscow session of the Council of Foreign Ministers, March 10–April 24, 1947, see vol. II, pp. 139 ff.

[7] See letter from Assistant Secretary of State Braden to the Mexican Ambassador, July 2, 1946, *Foreign Relations*, 1946 vol. XI, p. 985.

[8] For United States-Mexican lend-lease agreements of March 27, 1942, and March 18, 1943, see *ibid.*, 1942, vol. VI, p. 485, and *ibid.*, 1943, vol. VI, p. 397.

[9] The Department's notes of March 27, June 1, and August 30, 1945, requesting reimbursement, not printed; for note of October 1, 1946, see *ibid.*, 1946, vol. XI, p. 985.

[10] John W. Snyder.

Beteta, which Señor Torres Bodet had handed to me on December 16.[11] The Note that I requested consequently would constitute no new decision on policy but merely a formal ratification thereof. In conclusion, I remarked that the formal affirmation of the readiness of the Mexican Government to negotiate a settlement of its Lend Lease indebtedness would not preclude the presentation and discussion of the general and particular views he had expressed at the beginning of our conversation. I recommended that these views be omitted from the Note he might send me in the sense tentatively agreed upon, and that if he desired to present them to me in writing he do so in a separate communication—which would not, however, limit or qualify the Note. I was confident, I said, that Mexico's views would be taken into full account and that I felt that we might possibly be able, in the negotiations following the receipt of the Note I had requested, to work out a plan whereunder some portion of the Lend Lease indebtedness could be discharged without drawing against Mexico's foreign exchange reserves through the transfer to us of lands on which we might build diplomatic or consular premises.

The Minister for Foreign Affairs appeared to be impressed by these arguments and while I was speaking, drafted a brief Note along the lines I had indicated. He stated that he would prepare this Note and if authorized to do so by the President and his Cabinet colleagues he would forward it to me within the near future.

Cordially and sincerely yours,
(signed) Walter Thurston"

Respectfully yours,   WALTER THURSTON

812.24/11–1947

The Secretary of State to the Embassy in Mexico

CONFIDENTIAL   WASHINGTON, November 19, 1947.
No. 1585

SIR: I refer to the Department's airgram no. A–305 dated April 10, 1947,[12] concerning modification of the terms of repayment to the United States Government by the Government of the United Mexican States of obligations incurred under the Lend-Lease Agreement of March 18, 1943, and to conversations of recent date between officers of the Department and yourself on the same subject.

It was agreed in the discussions referred to that conversations leading to the revision of the payment in terms embodied in the exchange of notes accompanying that agreement could best be held in Mexico. Accordingly, you are requested to approach the Mexican Government

---

[11] Not printed, but see *Foreign Relations*, 1946, vol. XI, p. 987, footnote 19.
[12] Not printed; the Department indicated that it was then giving further serious consideration to revision of the terms of lend-lease payment to permit part payment in real estate or local currency for the Division of Foreign Buildings Operations program (812.24/3–1147).

and proceed with revision of the payment terms through an exchange of notes on the basis outlined in the attached draft note to the Mexican Ministry of Foreign Affairs.[13]

For your information, the sum now due from the Mexican Government under the present terms of the above-mentioned exchange of notes is $8,800,000. An additional sum is scheduled to become due January 1, 1948. According to the latest reports of the lend-lease fiscal authorities (Statement LL-12), this will be $957,000, making a grand total of $9,757,000. This sum represents 33 per cent of lend-lease charges reported through December 31, 1946 of $29,566,805.27. It is not final since reporting and auditing of lend-lease accounts has not yet been completed.

The Mexican Embassy in Washington was informed of the sum now due in a note dated March 24, 1947, a copy of which was transmitted to the Embassy under cover of instruction no. 971 dated March 28, 1947.[14]

The undetermined amount of the final payments specified in paragraph B of the draft note is due to the fact that reports of lend-lease charges are not yet final. Charges and credits in connection with lend-lease transfers effected during the past several years are still being reported to the Treasury Department fiscal authorities by the United States procuring agencies. Consequently the net bill is likely to be somewhat higher than the total of $9,757,000 mentioned above, or it may possibly be somewhat lower. This point should be made clear to the Mexican Government. In the event that the indeterminate amount of the final payments should prove an obstacle to the success of your negotiations, however, the Department would consider an agreed total, if it should be proposed by the Mexicans.

The draft note attached of course is not intended to be absolutely final in respect to specific language. Any substantial revision of the proposed terms, however, except the substitution of alternate paragraph C concerning interest charges, should be referred to the Department for clearance. There is no chance that a proposal for reduction of the 33 percent payment originally specified would be accepted.

The proposed exchange of notes should be *Confidential*, as it is felt that publicity regarding this matter might seriously jeopardize prompt collections of sums due from other countries. You may inform the Mexicans accordingly at your discretion.

Very truly yours,   [For the Secretary of State]
NORMAN T. NESS
*Director, Office of Financial and
Development Policy*

---

[13] Not printed.
[14] Neither printed.

812.24/12–1847

The Ambassador in Mexico (Thurston) to the Secretary of State

CONFIDENTIAL
No. 5225

MEXICO, December 18, 1947.

SIR: I discussed yesterday with the Minister for Foreign Affairs the subject of a modification of the terms of the Lend-Lease Agreement of March 18, 1943 along the lines set forth in the Department's confidential airmail instruction Number 1585 of November 19, 1947 and the draft of a note that accompanied it.[14a] For the convenience of the Minister, I had embodied my contemplated remarks in a draft of a note, to which I attached a copy of the draft note transmitted with the instruction just cited.

Señor Torres Bodet stated to me when I had terminated my introductory remarks that he wished to reiterate at the outset Mexico's intention to negotiate a settlement of its Lend-Lease indebtedness to the United States. He then stated that an arrangement along the lines described in the draft notes I had just shown to him would probably be welcome, inasmuch as Mexico's dollar position would make it impossible for some time yet to come for it to undertake the liquidation of this indebtedness in dollars. At the same time, he said, the budget for the coming year has virtually been completed and is about to be submitted to Congress—and in consequence it is not likely that any schedule of payments, even on a peso equivalent, can be undertaken at this time. He then tentatively suggested that such payments under the contemplated modified program begin in 1949.

I then mentioned that I had observed in the morning newspapers that legislation whereunder foreign governments may obtain ownership of land in Mexico for their diplomatic establishments is now before the Mexican Congress. The Minister stated that the Senate had approved the bill to which I had referred and that it would next come before the Chamber of Deputies. He added that he was not sure that this legislation would embrace land for consular establishments and suggested that if this should prove to be the case and we could not utilize the full Mexican payment for the acquisition of diplomatic property in Mexico City, perhaps the settlement could be partly in land and partly in pesos. In this connection, he expressed the desire to know approximately how much the American mission and its affiliates here spend in pesos per annum. I said that as far as I was aware, such information could be made available and that I would endeavor to supply it, provided no objection to such action appeared on the part of my

---

[14a] Draft note not printed.

Government. It would be appreciated if the Department would inform me of its decision with respect to this request.

The Minister then stated that the proposal I had presented would of course require study by several other ministries and departments, and requested that I leave with him for translation and reference to those agencies the texts of the two drafts I had shown him. I accordingly handed to Señor Torres Bodet the two documents alluded to, with the understanding that they are informal, unofficial, and tentative. In view of the impending Christmas and New Year's holidays, it is unlikely that there will be any developments in this negotiation until mid-January or even later.

Respectfully yours, WALTER THURSTON

BREAKDOWN OF UNITED STATES-MEXICAN NEGOTIATIONS ON A PROPOSED BILATERAL AIR TRANSPORT AGREEMENT [15]

711.1227/5-1547

Memorandum by Mr. Joseph J. Wolf of the Aviation Division to the Associate Chief of that Division (Bell)

[Extracts]

CONFIDENTIAL [WASHINGTON,] May 15, 1947.

Subject: Status of Bilateral Air Transport Agreement Negotiations with Mexico

1. *U. S. Routes sought.*

By its decision in the Latin American Case, the Civil Aeronautics Board (in accordance with the desires of the President as expressed in his letter to the Civil Aeronautics Board commenting upon their proposed decision in that case, date May 16, 1946 [16]) found that the public convenience and necessity required the operation of the following routes to Mexico by U. S. airlines:

A. Braniff: San Antonio and Laredo to Monterrey and Mexico City.
B. American: Fort Worth-Dallas and San Antonio to Monterrey and Mexico City.
C. American: El Paso to Monterrey and Mexico City.
D. Western: Los Angeles and San Diego to La Paz and Mexico City.
E. Pan American Airways: Houston and New Orleans to Merida and beyond.
F. Pan American Airways: Miami via Havana to Merida and beyond.

---

[15] Continued from *Foreign Relations*, 1946, vol. XI, pp. 992-997.
[16] Not printed.

G. Pan American Airways: Houston, Corpus Christi and Brownsville to Tampico, Mexico City, Tapachula and beyond.

H. Eastern: New Orleans to Mexico City.

Operations by American and by Pan American Airways over the routes indicated have been maintained for a number of years.

2. *Mexican Airlines and Operations.*

The Mexicans originally asked for the following nine routes:

1. Mexico City or Mexicali to Los Angeles.
2. Torreon, Nogales (Ariz.) and Phoenix to Los Angeles.
3. Mexico City and Monterrey to San Antonio and Fort Worth–Dallas.
4. Torreon to Houston.
5. Monterrey to Houston.
6. Mexico City, San Antonio and Detroit to Canada.
7. Tampico to Brownsville and Houston.
8. Mexico City and Tampico to New Orleans and New York.
9. Mexico City or Vera Cruz to Miami and beyond.

. . . .

Mexico has almost no airlines of solely Mexican nature. CMA, LAMSA, and, indeed, all of their lines, have some good amount of American backing, financially. CMA is controlled by Pan American through the ownership of a large minority block of stock.

. . . .

3. *Negotiations with Mexico.*

In the summer of 1946 negotiations were held in Mexico City. According to despatch 593 of July 29, 1946,[17] these negotiations failed primarily and publicly because Mexico felt that some sort of division of traffic should be agreed upon between the two countries as a means of protection for Mexican airlines from strong competition from U.S. airlines. As the policy of the United States did not permit the entering into of agreements along such lines, negotiations were suspended after an appeal to the President of Mexico[18] resulted in his espousing the restrictive philosophy above referred to.

It appears both from the referred despatch and from personal conversations with Mr. Bohan, Economic Counselor of the Embassy, that a further point was of great importance. The route certificated to Western Airlines from Los Angeles to Mexico City would parallel the route served by CMA. The route certificated to Braniff Airways from San Antonio to Mexico City would parallel the route already served by American Airlines. Pressure was exerted and is continuously exerted at present by both Pan American Airways and American

---

[17] *Foreign Relations,* 1946, vol. XI, pp. 993 ff.
[18] Miguel Alemán Valdes.

MEXICO 753

Airlines to prevent competition to CMA and American from being initiated as the result of the conclusion of a bilateral which would incorporate those two U.S. routes.

[Here follow sections on subsequent developments and recommendations.]

711.1227/7-2447

The Secretary of State to the Ambassador in Mexico (Thurston)

CONFIDENTIAL　　　　　　　　　　　WASHINGTON, July 24, 1947.
No. 1374

SIR: You will recall the conversation you held with officers of the Department, at the time of your recent sojourn in the United States, concerning a program to be pursued in order to accomplish the proposed bilateral air transport agreement between the United States and Mexico.

In accordance with the understanding expressed at that time, the Department has obtained from the President a letter to President Alemán, expressing President Truman's personal interest in this matter. This letter, and copies thereof, are enclosed herewith. It is requested that you personally deliver this letter to President Alemán on behalf of the President at the earliest time convenient to yourself and to President Alemán.

It is suggested that at the time of your visit with President Alemán, you orally reiterate the desire of the United States to reopen negotiations at the earliest possible date if it appears probable that a satisfactory agreement will follow. It is believed that there is a great advantage to be obtained from holding these negotiations in Mexico City: the presence of President Alemán at the place of negotiations makes available the procedure of personal intercession by you to him in case the negotiations should arrive at a seemingly insurmountable impasse, and he could then personally instruct his representatives to proceed with the matter. On the other hand, it is true that if negotiations were held in Washington, the Mexican representatives would be free, at least to a certain extent, from the pressure which would otherwise be exerted by certain special interests. It is true that it is the turn of the United States to act as host in this matter; but it is also true that if negotiations are held in Mexico, travel expenses will be borne by the United States. The Department believes that greater advantage will be obtained if the discussions can be held in Mexico City, but in view of all the circumstances, considers it desirable that you do not eliminate the possibility of the negotiations being held in Washington, if the Mexicans insist.

Assuming that conversations will be held in Mexico, it is suggested that negotiations be conducted, on the part of the United States, by the Embassy's staff. It is felt that you may not wish to take part in all of these conversations, so that you may be more free to intercede with President Alemán should circumstances so require. It is assumed that Messrs. Bohan and Sharp [19] would actively conduct the conversations, and, as was discussed in Washington, the Department will make available to you the services of a departmental official familiar with these problems as a technical adviser.

In view of this suggested organization of the American delegation, it is proposed that you might orally suggest to President Alemán that the United States believes that success can best be obtained by conversations strictly between governmental officials whose positions would let them represent the technical thinking of the governments concerned, rather than by delegations composed of people outside of government who, consciously or not, might not approach this proposal from the governmental point of view which is the spirit of Mr. Truman's letter.

[Here follow details on arrangements for negotiations.]

Very truly yours,   For the Secretary of State:
GARRISON NORTON

[Enclosure]

President Truman to the President of Mexico (Alemán)

WASHINGTON, July 15, 1947.

MY DEAR MR. PRESIDENT AND FRIEND: While I was your guest,[20] and a guest of the great Mexican nation whose leader you are, and when my fellow countrymen and I had the pleasure of your visit to the United States,[21] we had full opportunity to appreciate the importance of an informal and direct relationship between heads of state in the satisfactory accommodation of important problems of mutual interest. In the spirit of our recent conversations, I therefore take this occasion to discuss one of these problems.

I am sure you share my belief that the fullest possible development of international air routes between the two countries would be of the greatest benefit to the economies of Mexico and the United States.

---

[19] Frederick D. Sharp, 3d, Third Secretary of Embassy and Vice Consul.

[20] For an address by President Truman at Mexico City, March 3, 1947, on United States relations with Mexico and the other American Republics, see Department of State *Bulletin*, March 17, 1947, p. 498.

[21] For an address by President Alemán before a Joint Session of Congress, May 1, 1947, see *Congressional Record*, vol. 93, pt. 4, p. 4508.

For this reason I should like to invite your attention to the matter of an air transport agreement between the Governments of Mexico and the United States which I believe will, when completed, make possible the achievement of such mutual benefits. When I visited Mexico, I proceeded by air in a few hours on a journey that once took months, and later took weeks and days. It was possible for you to use this same modern means of transport on your visit to the United States. We are truly living in an air age.

As you know, several meetings have been held during the past two years between representatives of Mexico and the United States for the purpose of negotiating a mutually satisfactory air transport agreement.[22] To date these negotiations have resulted in only partial accord, the principal matters on which disagreement existed being predetermined division of airline capacity and the precise routes to be flown by carriers of both countries.

In connection with the first point, it is my firm belief that air transportation can achieve the ends we both desire only if it is allowed to develop unhampered by artificial restrictions. As in the case of several agreements to which the United States is a party, the representatives of the United States are prepared to incorporate in the proposed agreement with your government provisions which guarantee fair and reasonable competitive practices over the routes to be agreed upon. I also feel confident that our negotiators can reach agreement concerning the routes to be flown by airlines designated by Mexico and the United States.

I hope in the near future to see a steadily increasing amount of safe and efficient air transportation available between Mexico and the United States offered alike by airlines which are truly Mexican in character, by those representing United States interests, and by others in whose operations citizens of both nations participate. With these facts in mind may I suggest that you personally review this matter of mutual concern to the two countries to the end that negotiations may be resumed in the near future with every hope of reaching an early accord.

I shall always treasure the recollections of my Mexico trip and the pleasant associations with you and your country. I hope that I shall have the pleasure of welcoming you again to the United States and that I may in the not too distant future again visit your great country.

With assurances of my warm friendship and highest esteem, I am, my dear Mr. President,

Very sincerely yours,

HARRY S. TRUMAN

---

[22] For documentation on the last meeting, in the summer of 1946, see *Foreign Relations*, 1946, vol. XI, pp. 993 ff.

711.1227/S-447 : Telegram

The Ambassador in Mexico (Thurston) to the Secretary of State

CONFIDENTIAL   MEXICO CITY, August 4, 1947—3 p. m.

854. Reference Department's instruction 1374 July 24. President Alemán, after reading President Truman's letter handed him by Ambassador August 1, stated he also wished reach early agreement on aviation. He remarked he had not followed carefully negotiations held June 1946, but surmised these failed because of too many technical representatives on both sides. He felt settlement could be reached if matter handled informally and suggested that in place of delegation Embassy appoint representative discuss bilateral agreement with person to be designated by him. Ambassador expressed agreement and stated we were ready initiate conversations immediately. Named Bohan as Embassy's representative. President then said he would talk with Minister[s] Foreign Affairs and Communications [23] and designate representative. If these representatives could not reach agreement, it would be easy bring matter to his personal attention for decision.

THURSTON

711.1227/S-447 : Telegram

The Secretary of State to the Embassy in Mexico

CONFIDENTIAL   URGENT   WASHINGTON, August 7, 1947— 6 p. m.

746. Instructions re bilateral air transport agreement negotiations Embtel 854, Aug. 4,[24] are:

(1) Text of agreement and annex to conform to Chicago and Bermuda principles,[25] with form enclosed in instruction preferred by Dept.

(2) Dept's aims in resuming negotiations are to make all out effort implement President's Latin American decision [26] *in toto*. Conversations should pursue that aim without concession. Failure to obtain all US routes will probably require review of Latin American decision in all details, affecting all carriers and routes involved.

---

[23] Jaime Torres Bodet, Minister for Foreign Affairs; Augustin García López, Minister for Communications and Public Works.
[24] Not printed.
[25] For convention on International Civil Aviation, opened for signature at Chicago, December 7, 1944, see Department of State, Treaties and Other International Acts Series (TIAS) No. 1591, or 61 Stat. (pt. 2) 1180; for documentation on the conference at Chicago, November 1–December 7, 1944, see *Foreign Relations*, 1944, vol. II, pp. 355 ff. For agreement between the United States and the United Kingdom relating to air services between their respective territories, signed at Bermuda February 11, 1946, see *ibid.*, 1946, vol. v, p. 50.
[26] See memorandum by Mr. Wolf, May 15, p. 751.

(3) Therefore, as agreed in conversation with Amb, Dept assumes that if talks between Mexican representative and Bohan fail, Amb to appeal personally to Alemán.

(4) Failure on Presidential level may result in suspension of talks or interim agreement pending review Latin American case. Latter possibility of course should not be disclosed.

(5) Emb requested to keep Dept informed all stages of negotiation, and to make no commitments without Dept's specific approval.

(6) Dept will send J. J. Wolf to assist Amb and Bohan as technical adviser, when requested.

(7) No publicity to negotiations being given by Dept, even to airlines. Emb requested to pursue like policy and endeavor convince Mexicans to do likewise.

(8) Full powers for Thurston have been requested.

MARSHALL

711.1227/8–1447 : Telegram

The Ambassador in Mexico (Thurston) to the Secretary of State

CONFIDENTIAL   URGENT   MEXICO CITY, August 14, 1947—7 p. m.

900. For Reveley, Mexican Division,[27] and Bell, Aviation. First stage conversations with Martín Pérez [28] terminated today. He will see President and Secretary Communications weekend hoping resume talks Monday.[29] He stated Mexico prepared include all existing US routes and either Eastern or Braniff, maintaining Mexico should have monopoly New Orleans–Los Angeles nonstop route. He suggested these views be communicated Washington. He was informed that while this would be done, Embassy could answer at once re Eastern and Braniff. These routes essential if objective increased tourist trade is valid since economic benefits to be derived by Mexico from agreement promised in competition between Eastern–American and Braniff–American and fullest traffic potential could not and would not be developed by any other means. Therefore Embassy impelled be adamant and Martín Pérez requested to so inform superiors. Embassy agreed explain Mexican views respecting Western.

Fact that foregoing conversation preceded and followed by definite statements, Alemán wants agreement and Martín Pérez strongly feels agreement in sight strengthens Embassy's opinion that both Eastern and Braniff routes can be secured and that Western only real issue.

---

[27] Paul J. Reveley, Assistant Chief, Division of Mexican Affairs.
[28] Angel Martín Pérez, Private Secretary of the Mexican Minister of Communications and Public Works.
[29] August 18.

Embassy's interpretation Mexican position re Western is that Mexico feels CAB certificated carriers entirely on basis US interests without consideration or allowance legitimate interests Mexican carriers; that while US insistence goal routes understandable up to certain point, continued stand that Latin American route decision sacrosanct tantamount imposing US will and no negotiating inter-agreement.

Embassy feels its case airtight respecting US pattern except for Western. In this case Mexican company with enviable record and responsible developing Mexico City–Los Angeles route already faces real competition from American, non-stop schedule 7 hours 45 minutes elapsed time DC–4 equipment versus American [*Mexican*] 8½ hours DC–6 equipment. American schedule including inspection time lost El Paso so that travelers' time approximately same. It is difficult refute Mexican contention competition already present and Mexican Company cannot compete two US carriers.[30]

Embassy also wishes point out poor policy of attempting reach agreement which is not mutually satisfactory or wherein grave danger exists that only successful Mexican international operator might fail.

Mexico asks same eight routes requested last June, including Mexico City–Detroit and beyond. Embassy made no comments to Mexicans re routes but wishes indicate Department favors giving Mexico as many routes as consistent with other inter-agreements. Through routes requested can never be profitably operated without cabotage rights. Mexico cognizant this fact, but wishes sufficient routes give appearance reciprocity and satisfy internal political considerations.

Time has arrived for policy as distinguished from technical decision. Mexican Division should emphasize probability US–Mexican economic relations entering period strain as foreshadowed by foot and mouth, trade agreement, protection of industry, and balance of payments difficulties.[31] Also present conversations deliberately timed coincide with keen interest tourist promotion as means increasing dollar balances, an

---

[30] In telegram 780, August 18, the Department stressed that "giving up of Western route and granting of monopoly to CMA would be extremely distasteful to US and might well be bar to agreement", and continued: "Argument advanced urtel re comparative times American and CMA schedules fails take account fact that competitive disadvantage of CMA due to equipment easily remedied and also fact that traffic statistics indicate clearly growing increase in CMA traffic over this route and corresponding decrease American traffic via El Paso. Dept in agreement your views re forcing agreement not mutually satisfactory and is making every effort propose solution mutually acceptable. Nevertheless we believe you should exert every effort convince Mexicans validity our requirement for Western route" (711.1227/8–1447).

[31] For documentation on these subjects, see pp. 811 ff., pp. 772 ff., and pp. 764 ff.

interest publicly and privately displayed by Alemán and key Cabinet officers. In short, no better opportunity foreseeable for prompt settlement mutually beneficial and therefore lasting agreement.

Instructions requested by August 16.

THURSTON

711.1227/8–1947 : Telegram

The Acting Secretary of State to the Embassy in Mexico

CONFIDENTIAL   US URGENT   WASHINGTON, August 21, 1947—7 p. m.
NIACT

792. For Ambassador and Bohan. Dept has carefully reviewed Embs views re air transport agreement: First. U.S. route proposals based upon decision by President after recommendations of Board and must be accepted as those required in US public interest. Second. Letter from President part of program designed exert every possible effort obtain agreement including these routes. Third. Dept can not recommend to President accepting less from Mexico unless Dept can honestly say and establish on record that every argument and effort has been applied with result impasse in which must choose between something less than route pattern and no agreement all. Fourth. As matter of negotiating tactics Dept believes very unwise to indicate or imply any compromise on route proposals or any other point prior to time Dept knows specifically all points of difference and can review them. In this connection Dept envisages possibility developing numerous points of difference re preferred language of text of agreement most of which might be conceded in ultimate trading out. Fifth. Unless there is clear record of points of difference on entire agreement and annex indicating exactly what we would get if we were willing to concede something impossible for Dept press issue either with Board or at higher level. For example now have no formal assurance Mexican position on division of traffic, fifth-freedom [32] restrictions, non-stop privileges, etc. Dept desires Emb to exert all efforts without reservation along lines indicated.

---

[32] Under the International Air Transport Agreement (Five Freedoms), Fifth Freedom rights are defined as follows: "The privilege to take on passengers, mail and cargo destined for the territory of any other contracting State and the privilege to put down passengers, mail and cargo coming from any such territory." (Department of State, *Proceedings of the International Civil Aviation Conference*, Chicago, November 1–December 7, 1944, vol. I, p. 179)

Dept assumes views stated Embtel 909 [33] have been expressed solely to Dept since most unwise to permit Mexicans obtain impression US negotiator doubtful as to validity or wisdom of US position. In this connection Dept disturbed fifth sentence Embtel 900 which indicates negotiator may have implied possible doubt need for Western route. Dept assumes Emb is aware political aspects involved any ultimate route sacrifice and that neither Dept nor Emb can afford to take any action which can be interpreted in any way as prejudicial to one carrier in favor another. Decision must be made by President on basis recommendation CAB. Senators George and Overton this week have approached Dept and President re status negotiations.

Apart from foregoing, views expressed Embtel 909 not acceptable to Dept. Value to US establishing these routes exactly same as value thereof to Mexico in that they provide arteries for fullest development of trade and commerce and improvement of knowledge and understanding between two countries. US desires no monopoly for itself nor for Mexico. We are fully convinced monopolies restrain development and prevent benefits of air service from being obtained. US believe its form of agreement provides adequate safeguards for preventing unfair competitive practices and that Mexicans would not be estopped either legally or practically from development their air services in competition with ours. We would strongly favor such development as guaranteeing to both countries exertion of best efforts of all operators to improve service offered. Treating areas of competition as suggested simply another and equally objectionable way of dividing traffic. Dept does not believe establishment Western route would adversely affect CMA except to deprive it of monopoly that is contrary best interests Mexico and to require it constantly develop and improve its services to meet fair competition which could only inure to benefit of Mexico. Provisions our form agreement safeguard against any abuse superior resources of US operators although comparison financial status Western and CMA (backed by PAA) leaves no doubt as to fallacy of argument Western would choke CMA out.

Dept believes best course at this point is to follow procedure suggested Deptel 784 [34] in light contents this message. Joseph Wolf who is completely familiar with US position all points is proceeding at once to advise Emb.

LOVETT

---

[33] In telegram 909, August 19, 7 p. m., Ambassador Thurston suggested a pattern from four standpoints as basis of a possible agreement (711.1227/8–1947). The English translation of the Mexican draft air transport agreement was transmitted to the Department in telegram 1067, October 3, 4 p. m., from Mexico City; not printed.

[34] Not printed.

711.1227/10-3147 : Telegram

The Ambassador in Mexico (Thurston) to the Secretary of State

CONFIDENTIAL MEXICO CITY, October 31, 1947—5 p. m.

1183. For Armour and Norton. Embassy bespeaks most careful consideration action outlined Department's telegram 1032.[35]

Department requested consider Embassy's comments spirit desire reach correct decision and no sense critical either CAB or AV.

Original Latin American decision was domestic and did not consider established or prospective interests Mexico. Needless point out agreement not taking cognizance and not giving reasonable equitable protection those interests can never be successful. Demanding six airlines into Mexico's only real traffic terminal raises grave danger US would soon completely monopolize international air traffic. Mexico has legitimate pre-existing interests west coast and expects equitable treatment eastern seaboard. While our policies must not be prejudiced by Mexican settlement we must realize route pattern wanted Mexico requires special treatment permit Mexico enjoy fair opportunity share US-Mexico traffic.

President Mexico informed both verbally and in writing that only points at issue question over-flight El Paso and equal rights New Orleans. Embassy perfectly willing seek west coast eventual nonstop formula providing it can also suggest some solution present New Orleans impasse. Embassy reported October 20 Minister Communications desirous signing agreement and only looking for some possible settlement New Orleans. Embassy, therefore, suggested at Minister's request Eastern discuss matter within provisions Bermuda agreement and Section 412 Civil Aeronautics Act. Embassy does not believe conversations would lead solution but would place Embassy in position see President and Minister Communications and assure them all possible done meet legitimate Mexican rights and ask agreement be signed based on general provisions Bermuda agreement which Minister now states so loosely drawn and defined as constitute little if any protection for a weaker foreign line.

Clearly evident private carriers both nations exercising undue influence negotiations. Fairly reliable report indicates President Alemán fully realizes this but states political influences so great he does not feel he can override them unless some concessions obtained. This confirms same information given Bohan by Minister Communications October 18. Department should not underrate described political pressures.

---

[35] This telegram, dated October 30, 6 p. m., was concerned with a proposed conference with President Truman on the air transport negotiations and his personal intervention with President Alemán. (711.1227/10-3047).

Embassy thoroughly believes in basic aviation policies our government but still persistent idea we can impose our domestically conceived route pattern on Mexico must be abandoned if negotiations successful. Air transport agreement under discussion Mexico since 1945 and sufficient experience should have been gained indicate some modification our original position essential.

Embassy feels most strongly it would be grave mistake request President Truman write President Alemán this time. Ball is not in Mexican court, as stated in Department's telegram 1008 October 24,[36] but is bouncing up and down in our own.

THURSTON

711.1227/11–647 : Telegram

The Secretary of State to the Embassy in Mexico

CONFIDENTIAL URGENT WASHINGTON, November 6, 1947—3 p. m.

1068. Armour, Landis and Barringer conferred with President Nov 4 re air transport agreement. Decision that level was that matter of primary importance is to connect two capitals and New York and New Orleans for airlines of both countries. On presentation impossibility obtaining western route, elimination of same was reluctantly authorized with President expressing desire that strong last effort be made obtain maximum rights possible at present or in future on direct route Los Angeles-Mexico City.

Pursuing desires so expressed, Armour, Landis and Barringer agreed would probably be best notify Mexicans that matter being pursued to very highest level, but that such strong opposition being met that Mexican case would best be presented if Martin Pérez were to come to Wash. Idea would be, pursuing Bohan's thought, that he would thus satisfy himself last stone had been turned. Contemplated that on arrival here he would meet adamant reaction from Barringer, Armour and Landis on New Orleans proposition, and, if necessary, at end of his visit, Armour to inform him decision of President. Re West Coast situation, best possible transaction would be evolved, in view all circumstances.   Dept hopes Bohan, as Amb's designee, will be able accompany Pérez, if other duties so permit.

Request matter not be discussed telephonically, as any leak would greatly prejudice contemplated US position. Request views Emb foregoing plan, and if Emb agrees, request communicate ideas above set forth to Pérez.

---

[36] Not printed.

No mention made at meeting with President of proposed further top-level letter.

MARSHALL

711.1227/12–1247 : Telegram

The Acting Secretary of State to the Embassy in Mexico [37]

CONFIDENTIAL   WASHINGTON, December 16, 1947—7 p. m.

1276. Dept believes firm but friendly gesture should be made at this time to Mex Govt to indicate that US not being fooled by their tactics re air transport matters. Emb requested make oral approach to appropriate Mex authority along following lines:

(1) That Palavicini indicated at Geneva [38] that he believed his report might eliminate obstacles in way of signing agreement and that it is hoped that his return about Jan 1 will herald new Mex position; that US interested in effects of his report, and would appreciate being advised.

(2) That US believes it unfortunate that Guest applications have been filed with CAB at this time as this procedure complicates picture. In addition, CMA application has been filed for right for cargo service between any and all points on CMA network and Brownsville and/or Laredo. It is impossible to continue approach to matter on long-range basis and on basis discussion routes mentioned by Mex Govt if such piecemeal procedure pursued. Dept believes it will be extremely difficult for aeronautical authorities to establish long-range workable air transport pattern between Mex and US on such a basis and believes these applications obscure ultimate goals to be obtained in the interest of the public. Therefore believe matter should be further approached

---

[37] A memorandum of December 12, 1947, by the Acting Deputy Director of the Office of Transport and Communications (Merchant) to the Assistant Secretary of State (Armour) with reference to this telegram (No. 1276 transmitted on December 16), stated as follows:
"The attached telegram is proposed in light of the following three developments:
"1. Opposition on the part of Mexico to the United States position at the Multilateral Air Transport Conference in Geneva.
"2. Apparent stalemate in bilateral air transport negotiations with Mexico.
"3. The collaboration in Washington by Colonel Gonzalez Gomez, Director of Civil Aviation of Mexico, with representatives of Aerovias Guest in attempting to push action on two applications filed by Aerovias Guest for routes to be granted outside of any bilateral agreement.
        Livingston T. Merchant"
[38] Manuel Palavicini, head of Mexican Delegation at the meeting of the Commission of the International Civil Aviation Organization on Multilateral Agreement on Commercial Rights in International Civil Air Transport, Geneva, November 4–27, 1947. For summary reports on this meeting, see Department of State, *Participation of the United States Government in International Conferences*, July 1, 1947–June 30, 1948, p. 109; and *ICAO Monthly Bulletin, January 1948*, pp. 4–7 (Montreal, Inland Press Ltd., 1948).

on basis of intergovernmental agreement rather than such piecemeal approach, result of which latter approach will undoubtedly not be satisfactory to the public or to the airlines concerned. Since Guest and CMA applications filed through diplomatic channels, believed desirable that Mex should appreciate US thoughts on this matter.

Request report of effect this conversation.

LOVETT

EXPORT-IMPORT BANK LOANS TO MEXICO FOR PURCHASE OF UNITED STATES EQUIPMENT, MATERIALS AND SERVICES FOR PUBLIC WORKS AND INDUSTRIALIZATION PROJECTS [39]

812.75/4–1847

Memorandum by the Assistant Secretary of State for American Republic Affairs (Braden) [40]

WASHINGTON, April 18, 1947.

The IT&T states that in recent years it has been losing money with its company in Mexico and that it needs financial assistance to purchase the Ericsson Company there and to combine the two systems; or it will have to negotiate a sale of its own Mexican interests to Ericsson.[41] The latter development would be highly undesirable. A–Br and ARA believe it extremely important that telephone communications in Mexico be in American hands. Arrangements should be concluded for the IT&T to purchase the Ericsson system.

During the war the Ericsson company in Mexico, like the Swedish legation there, tried to convince us it was friendly to us while at the same time it did the same with the Germans, and in fact actively furnished information to the Nazis.

---

[39] Continued from *Foreign Relations*, 1946, vol. XI, pp. 997–1005. For additional information on these credit authorizations and allocations, see Export-Import Bank of Washington: *Fifth Semiannual Report to Congress for the Period July–December 1947*, pp. 10–11.

[40] Addressed to Under Secretary of State Acheson and Under Secretary of State for Economic Affairs Clayton.

[41] Letters of March 12 and April 14, 1947 (not printed) from the International Telephone and Telegraph Corporation (IT&T) inquired whether or not the Department of State would recommend and support a plan for financial assistance by United States Government agencies (1) for the consolidation of the Mexican Telephone and Telegraph Company and the Swedish Ericsson Telephone Company in Mexico under American control subject to IT&T's purchasing the L. M. Ericsson Company (LME), or (2) advance to a Mexican Government controlled company, with both Mexican Governmental and private capital, for the acquisition of the two companies. Both letters stated that failing a favorable answer, the IT&T would have no other alternative than to negotiate the sale of IT&T's Mexican Company to the L. M. Ericsson Company. (812.75/4–2247)

The Ericsson company amongst other foreign companies makes a practice of furnishing commercial information to their own nationals competing with Americans, thus giving them an unfair advantage over American interests.

Russia since VE day has imposed an increasing political and economic influence on Sweden. The Ericsson company may already have Russian agents in Mexico but if it obtained control of the entire telephone system there, Russian agents would undoubtedly filter in. This is a most important reason why IT&T should purchase Ericsson in Mexico. In the event of war, telephone communications in Mexico would be far more important to us than they have ever been.

With Ericsson controlling all telephone communications in Mexico, an effective weapon would be placed in the hands of the Russians in promoting the communist cause in Mexico. The necessity of preventing the application against us of geopolitical actions by non-hemisphere powers makes it prudent to facilitate the acquisition of IT&T of the entire telephone system in a contiguous country.

The Secretary of State, on March 4, 1946, wrote Colonel Sosthenes Behn, president of IT&T,[42] that "no objection will be interposed by the Government of the United States to the sale or other disposition of your telephone subsidiary in Mexico". Prior to writing this letter, Mr. Acheson addressed letters to the Acting Secretary of War and to the Secretary of the Navy, dated January 17, 1946,[43] asking for the advice of these Departments as to whether considerations of national security would justify the financial support of this Government to enable IT&T to acquire the Ericsson interests in the Mex-Ericsson Telephone Company. As replies were not received early in March, 1946, and as IT&T desired a reply to its inquiry, the Department, in the March 4, 1946 letter, referred to above, stated that no objection would be interposed by the Government of the United States to the sale or other disposition of IT&T's telephone subsidiary in Mexico. ARA has always felt strongly that no foreign interest should acquire this property. However, the lack of timely information from the War and Navy Departments resulted in the March 4, 1946, letter, which apparently expressed the views of the economic divisions of the Department, but not the opinion of ARA.

The Secretary of War, in a letter dated April 25, 1946,[43] to the Secretary of State, stated that: "The War Department desires to inform the State Department of its conviction that it is of utmost importance to

---

[42] For letter of March 4, 1946, see *Foreign Relations*, 1946, vol. XI, p. 1000.
[43] Not printed.

national interest and security that all communications facilities in the Western Hemisphere be owned by hemispheric interests and, if possible, by companies controlled by citizens of the United States." The Secretary of the Navy, in a letter dated April 11, 1946,[43] informed the Secretary of State that: "The Navy Department favors the acquisition by hemisphere interests of all communications systems now owned, directly or indirectly, by non-hemisphere interests—a position previously taken by this Department." We believe that the above-quoted opinions of the two defense departments express in definite terms the importance which these Departments attach to the acquisition by an American-controlled company of Ericsson telephone interests in Mexico. ARA concurs fully, as it has done consistently in the past, with this point of view.

We believe in ARA that the political considerations in favor of the purchase of Ericsson interests in Mexico by IT&T are so overwhelming and so important to our security that we should use every means in our possession to make possible the consummation of this transaction.

SPRUILLE BRADEN

812.51/4-2047

Memorandum by the Chief of the Division of Investment and Economic Development (Havlik) to the Director of the Office of Financial and Development Policy (Ness)

CONFIDENTIAL WASHINGTON, April 29, 1947.

Subject: Mexico—Proposed Export-Import Bank loans.

With the exception of the Poza Rica–Mexico City gas line project,[44] there is no objection to the proposal contained in the Export-Import Bank document dated April 22 [45] that the Board [46] approve the extension of credits to Nacional Financiera, S.A.,[47] to finance the dollar cost of certain projects, as follows:

---

[44] This was item No. 1 in the list of tentative projects given in this document.
[45] Not printed.
[46] The Board of Directors of the Export-Import Bank of Washington.
[47] A financing agency of the Mexican Government. On behalf of that Government the Mexican Ambassador had applied to the Export-Import Bank on February 26, 1947, for a series of loans intended to promote the economic development of Mexico and requiring financing in the aggregate amount of $175,000,000. On May 13 the Export-Import Bank issued a press release stating that the Bank was prepared to approve $50,000,000 of additional credits for Mexico to finance the dollar requirements of projects which fully met the Bank's specifications.
See press release by the Treasury Department, May 13, 1947, concerning a Stabilization Agreement entered into with the Banco de Mexico and the Mexican Government, printed in Department of State *Bulletin*, May 25, 1947, p. 1043.

	Current Estimates of Dollar Requirements
2. Fertilizer plant near Mexico City utilizing Poza Rica natural gas	$5,500,000
3. Coke oven and by-products plant in Monclova (To supply coke for steel plants at Monclova and Monterrey)	3,600,000
4. Colomilla hydroelectric power plant and associated transmission lines and pumping stations (To enlarge power output of Chapala Co. which serves power-short area of Guadalajara and vicinity)	3,700,000
5. Meat, fish, fruit, and vegetable packing	13,000,000
6. Highway construction	10,000,000
7. Hotel construction	5,000,000
Total	$40,800,000

Poza Rica Pipeline

With respect to the financing of the construction of a natural gas pipeline from Poza Rica to Mexico City which is estimated to require $4,200,000 it has been the position of the Department that this project should not be financed by a US Government loan. (See letter from Mr. Clayton to Mr. Martin, dated September 11, 1946, and Mr. Martin's reply, dated September 17, 1946.)[48]

The interpretation that a natural gas pipeline falls within the category of "commercial development of Mexican petroleum resources" is a narrow one, and may be subject to challenge. However, PED has specifically objected to the pipeline as being contrary to the President's policy (see copy of memo attached)[49] and MA informs us that Mr. Braden concurs in PED's view.

812.75/4-1447

The Under Secretary of State (Acheson) to the President of the International Telephone and Telegraph Corporation (Behn)

WASHINGTON, April 30, 1947.

MY DEAR COLONEL BEHN: I refer to your letter of March 12, 1947[50] and the letter from Mr. Francis White of April 14, 1947[51] setting

---

[48] For letter of September 11 from the Under Secretary of State for Economic Affairs (Clayton) to the President of the Export-Import Bank of Washington (Martin), see *Foreign Relations*, 1946, vol. XI, p. 1001; Mr. Martin's reply of September 17 not printed.

[49] PED's office memorandum of April 28, 1947, not printed; for documentation on policy as set down by Presidents Roosevelt and Truman in the extension of credits to Mexico for development of the oil industry, see *ibid.*, 1944, vol. VII, pp. 1336 ff., *ibid.*, 1945, vol. IX, pp. 1159 ff., and *ibid.*, 1946, vol. XI, pp. 1005 ff.

[50] Not printed.

[51] Letter of April 14 from the Vice President of IT&T (White) not printed.

forth the proposals of the International Telephone and Telegraph Corporation concerning the consolidation of the two telephone companies in Mexico. I also refer to Mr. White's letter of April 22, 1947 [51a] relating to his conversation with Mr. C. Tyler Wood [52] on April 18, at which time Mr. Wood presented the views of the State Department on the above-mentioned proposals of the International Telephone and Telegraph Corporation.

The Department is unable to support your request for government financial assistance to the International Telephone and Telegraph Corporation for the acquisition of the Ericsson Telephone properties in Mexico. While the Department is still of the opinion that it cannot formally object to the sale of your telephone subsidiary in Mexico, it would nevertheless at this time take a serious view of such action.

The Department does not support the proposal that a loan be made to the Mexican Government for the purpose of financing a Mexican Government controlled mixed company.

The Department has carefully explored the possibilities of the United States Government financing of the acquisition of the Ericsson company by the International Telephone and Telegraph Corporation and, while it is unable to support that proposal, it would however support a request for financial assistance to help finance the export of equipment which might be needed for the modernization and development of the Mexican telephone system, should the International Telephone and Telegraph Corporation acquire the Ericsson company there. The Department would also be disposed to be of assistance through such good offices as it might deem appropriate.

Sincerely yours,

DEAN ACHESON

811.516 Export-Import Bank/10-647 : Airgram

The Acting Secretary of State to the Embassy in Mexico

RESTRICTED   WASHINGTON, October 6, 1947.

A-770. Credit application for $3.5 million behalf Nueva Compañía Electrica Chapala, S.A., to finance purchases in U.S. of equipment and materials for Colomilla Hydro-electric Power Plant,

---

[51a] Not printed.
[52] Deputy to Assistant Secretary of State Clayton. The Department's views, as set forth by Mr. Wood in a memorandum of April 21 to Under Secretary Acheson, not printed, were that the Export-Import Bank, under its charter, could not help IT&T in financing the purchase of the competing company, but it might be possible to have the Eximbank assist IT&T in financing the provision of the equipment to the Mexican Telephone Company if IT&T could itself arrange to finance the acquisition of the competing company; by no other means, apparently, could this Government give assistance to IT&T (812.75/4-2147).

two associated transmission lines, and the pumping station was approved by Eximbank Board of Directors October 1. This is the first specific credit approved under the $50 million commitment made to Mexico in April 1947.

. . . .

LOVETT

812.51/11–1447 : Airgram

The Secretary of State to the Embassy in Mexico

RESTRICTED WASHINGTON, November 14, 1947.

A–837. The Board of Directors of the Export-Import Bank on November 12 approved a credit of $5 million, under the $50 million commitment in favor of Nacional Financiera, to assist that agency in financing the purchase in Mexico, through normal channels, of U.S. agricultural equipment under the following arrangements:

(*a*) that all sales financed under the credit shall be made through established distributors in Mexico to purchasers certified by the Joint Commission for Eradication of Foot and Mouth Disease,[53] or by another appropriate agency in Mexico as agricultural operators in the infected zone;

. . . .

In conversations with the Export-Import Bank the Washington representatives of the Mexican Government informed the Bank that the Government was unwilling to use the credit entirely for the benefit of the infected zone, and that only one-half of the credit should be made available to finance purchases in that zone, because the Mexican Department of Agriculture considers the infected zone to be smaller in area and production than the non-infected zone, and also because equipment is needed in the non-infected zone to open up new lands. The Board of the Bank, however, with the concurrence of the Department, approved the use of the credit to finance purchases only in the infected zone, because of the most urgent need for tractors and associated implements in that zone. If this machinery is not made available land already in cultivation could not be worked because oxen, the prime source of farm power in the infected zone, are being removed. This action does not prevent the Mexican Government from extending credits in other zones without refinancing by the Bank.

MARSHALL

---

[53] For documentation on this subject, see pp. 811 ff.

812.51/12–1547 : Airgram

The Acting Secretary of State to the Embassy in Mexico

RESTRICTED   WASHINGTON, December 15, 1947.

A-918. On December 3 the Board of Directors of the Eximbank approved the following credits to Nacional Financiera under the $50 million commitment all to be guaranteed by the Mexican Government:

(1) $7 million to assist in financing purchases in U.S. of railway equipment including principally rails and accessories, and also three diesel electric locomotives for National Railways; credit available until June 30, 1948, at 3–½ percent repayable in ten years beginning December 31, 1948;

(2) $5 million to assist in financing purchases in U.S. of materials, equipment and services required to complete construction of the Guayalejo and Sanalona sugar mills; credit available until June 30, 1948 at 3–½ percent repayable in 20 equal semiannual installments beginning six months after date of obligation; credit to be equally divided between the two mills, the interest rate charged by Financiera not to exceed 4–¼ percent for a term not less than ten years.

For Embassy information only. Although the Department believes that economic justification for the project is doubtful and while it concurs with Embassy's views and recommendations, Department did not press these objections since it is believed a moral commitment to finance project existed and other members of the Board favored approval of credit.

(3) $1 million to assist in financing purchases in U.S. of equipment, materials and supplies required to establish in Mexico those meat canneries with which U.S. Department of Agriculture is concluding a contract for the purchase of canned beef; credit at 2–½ percent is available until April 30, 1948, is repayable in two semiannual installments, the first due six months after date of advances; interest charged by Financiera on Eximbank funds readvanced to canneries not to exceed the above rate by more than 1–½ percent.

The foregoing credits bring the aggregate total to date to $21.5 million under the $50 million commitment.

Also December 3, Bank Board denied Nordberg Manufacturing Company's application for an advance commitment of $900,000 to assist the company in financing sale of diesel electric generating units to the Federal Electricity Commission. This negative action is based upon apparent fact that installation of these units would not serve industrial or agricultural demand and, therefore, would make little contribution to Mexican economy; also that a balance of approximately $3 million of the $20 million credit to the Federal Electricity Commission authorized on March 21, 1945 remains uncommitted.

LOVETT

812.51/12–1547 : Airgram

The Acting Secretary of State to the Embassy in Mexico

RESTRICTED WASHINGTON, December 15, 1947.

A–917. On December 10, 1947 Board of Directors of the Eximbank approved a credit of $12 million in favor of Nacional Financiera (under the $50 million commitment) to finance 25 percent of expenditures made by Mexico on the Nogales–Guadalajara highway subsequent to January 1, 1948, under contracts let as a result of competitive bidding open to U.S. as well as Mexican contractors. . . .

LOVETT

812.75/12–2247

The Acting Secretary of State to the Secretary of Defense (Forrestal)

WASHINGTON, December 22, 1947.

MY DEAR MR. SECRETARY: On November 4, 1947, representatives of the International Telephone and Telegraph Corporation met with Department officials to discuss the problem now confronting the I.T.&T. in connection with its majority-owned Mexican subsidiary, the Mexican Telephone and Telegraph Company. As a result of that meeting, and at the Department's request, the I.T.&T. prepared a memorandum on the Mexican telephone situation and delivered it to the Department on November 24, 1947. A copy of that memorandum is enclosed.[54]

As indicated in the enclosure, the Department is now being requested to sponsor a government loan to effect the purchase for American or Mexican interests of the two telephone companies now operating in Mexico, or to declare that it would have no objection to a sale by the International Telephone and Telegraph Corporation of its holdings in the American Mexican Company to the L. M. Ericsson Company, a Swedish corporation, in the manner and under the circumstances as outlined in the enclosed memorandum.

Before taking a position in this matter, the Department would appreciate having the views of your Department on the security features

---

[54] Not printed.

which might be involved were the sale to be consummated along the lines as stated in the enclosed memorandum.[55]

Sincerely yours,   For the Acting Secretary of State:
GARRISON NORTON
Assistant Secretary

DISCUSSIONS BETWEEN THE UNITED STATES AND MEXICO REGARDING MEXICAN IMPORT RESTRICTIONS AND TRADE AGREEMENT REVISION [56]

611.1231/1–1047

The Secretary of State to the Ambassador in Mexico (Thurston)

RESTRICTED   WASHINGTON, March 4, 1947.
No. 879

SIR: I refer to your despatch No. 2517 of January 10, 1947,[57] reporting your conversation with the Minister of Foreign Relations [58] during which he expressed the hope that this Government might find it possible to open negotiations for the revision of the present trade agreement between the United States and Mexico [59] not later than April or May, 1947, and that in the meantime experts from the United States might go to Mexico to study conditions there and to initiate preliminary conversations.

Your remark to the Foreign Minister that this Government would probably be unable to enter into trade-agreement discussions or negotiations during the next few months reflects the views of the Department. You may inform the Foreign Minister of this Government's regret that, for the reasons set forth in this instruction, it will not be in a position, during the next several months, to comply with the request of the Mexican Government. The documents referred to in the

---

[55] In his reply, of January 2, 1948, Secretary Forrestal stated as follows: "I can see no security problems involved in the consummation of the sale of the telephone companies in Mexico, as outlined in the enclosure to your letter." (812.75/1–248) Under Secretary of State Lovett reported to Colonel Behn in a letter of January 20, 1948, that the Department would interpose no objection to the sale by IT&T of its holdings in the Mexican Telephone and Telegraph Company to foreign interests (812.75/11–1947).

The Assistant Secretary of State for American Republic Affairs (Miller) informed the Director of the Office of Middle American Affairs (Reveley), in a memorandum of December 13, 1949, that Colonel Behn had called him from New York to say that an agreement had been reached in principle with reference to the consolidation of the two telephone companies in Mexico providing for operation of the properties on a joint basis, subject to approval of the Mexican Government (812.75/12–1349).

[56] Continued from *Foreign Relations*, 1946, vol. XI, pp. 1030–1048.
[57] Not printed.
[58] Jaime Torres Bodet.
[59] For text of the reciprocal trade agreement of December 23, 1942, see Department of State Executive Agreement Series No. 311, or 57 Stat. 833.

following discussion are identified in detail at the end of this instruction.

By a resolution of February 18, 1946 (See Annexure 1 of Report,[60] page 60) the Economic and Social Council of the United Nations set forth its decision to call an International Conference on Trade and Employment, and, for the purpose of preparing for the Conference, including an agenda and a draft charter for a proposed international trade organization, created a Preparatory Committee consisting of 18 members, including the United States. The Preparatory Committee held its first meeting in London during October and November, 1946, and made progress in the preparation of a draft charter for an international trade organization, basing its deliberations largely upon the *Suggested Charter for an International Trade Organization*[61] which had been submitted by the delegation of the United States. The *Suggested Charter* was an elaboration of the *Proposals for Expansion of World Trade and Employment*[62] which the Government of the United States, in December 1945, transmitted to the Government of Mexico and to other governments for consideration.

The second meeting of the Preparatory Committee will convene in Geneva, Switzerland on April 10, 1947 (See Annexure 5 of Report, page 74), at which time it will complete its work on the proposed Charter[63] and will prepare definite recommendations for submission to an International Conference on Trade and Employment. It is now anticipated that the International Conference will be held shortly after the conclusion of the Preparatory Committee's second meeting, perhaps before the end of the present year.[64] The Government of Mexico has stated its intention to participate in the Conference.

Since specific action to reduce, modify or eliminate barriers to trade is essential to the establishment and success of an international trade organization, the Preparatory Committee at its first meeting in London recommended (See Annexure 7 of Report, page 75) to the Governments concerned that the Committee sponsor trade-agreement

---

[60] See *Report of the First Session of the Preparatory Committee of the United Nations Conference on Trade and Employment, London, October–November, 1946;* the Annexures of the Report are not printed.

[61] Department of State publication No. 2598.

[62] Department of State publication No. 2411.

[63] For draft Charter for the International Trade Organization of the United Nations, (ITO) embodied in the report of the second session of the Preparatory Committee of the United Nations Conference on Trade and Employment at Geneva, April 10–Oct. 30, 1947, see Department of State publication No. 2947. For the General Agreement on Tariffs and Trade (GATT), completed at this meeting on October 30, see Department of State Treaties and Other International Acts Series (TIAS) No. 1700, or 61 Stat. (pt. 5) and (pt. 6), A 3–A 2054.

[64] For documentation on the United Nations Conference on Trade and Employment, Havana, November 21, 1947–March 24, 1948, see Department of State publication No. 3117, *Havana Charter for an International Trade Organization, and Final Act and Related Documents.*

negotiations among its members, and approved a Memorandum on Procedures for the conduct of those negotiations (See Annexure 10 of the Report, pp. 77–86). The negotiations accordingly are scheduled to be held at Geneva during the second meeting of the Preparatory Committee, and it is expected that they will continue for several months.

This Government, on November 9, 1946, announced its intention to conduct trade-agreement negotiations with the 18 countries which are members of the Preparatory Committee. The major attention of the interdepartmental trade-agreements organization of this Government must at present be focused upon preparations for those negotiations and later upon the negotiations themselves. The burden of this work on the entire organization now and until the conclusion of the Geneva meeting is such as to preclude consideration of trade-agreement discussions or negotiations with other countries for the next several months.

Moreover, in consonance with this Government's policy of participating in the work of the Preparatory Committee looking to the establishment of an international trade organization, its current program of trade-agreement negotiations provides exclusively for the announced negotiations with members of the Preparatory Committee.

Following the conclusion of the Geneva meeting, this Government's program for trade-agreement negotiations will be integrated within the framework provided by the Charter of the proposed international trade organization, as developed at the second meeting of the Preparatory Committee for presentation to the International Conference on Trade and Employment. Such a course of action is implicit in the adherence by this Government to the principles of the Charter.

The Memorandum on Procedures, to which reference has been made, suggests alternative procedures for tariff negotiations involving members of the United Nations which are not parties to the General Agreement (See Section J. Annexure 10, second part, page 85). The Preparatory Committee will, at its second meeting, consider the suggestions and determine procedures for future negotiations.

Following the establishment of such procedures, the Government of the United States will be pleased to consider the possibility of entering into trade-agreement negotiations with the Government of Mexico, although it is not possible to state at the moment whether such negotiations may be considered prior to the International Trade Conference, concurrently with it, or following its conclusion.

The following documents mentioned in this instruction are enclosed, in duplicate, for the information and use of the Embassy:

1. *Suggested Charter for an International Trade Organization.*

(The *Suggested Charter* was submitted to the Preparatory Committee of the United Nations Conference on Trade and Employment for use as a basis for discussion at its first meeting, which was held in London during October and November, 1946).

2. *Preliminary Copy of Redraft of a Charter for an International Trade Organization.*[65]

(This was prepared in the Department as an interim working paper to show the provisions of the proposed Charter on which agreement was reached by the Preparatory Committee at its London meeting).

3. *Report of the First Session of the Preparatory Committee of the United Nations Conference on Trade and Employment, London, October–November, 1946.*

(As reproduced in part [Charter and Annexure to the Charter omitted] [66] by United States Delegation to the United Nations).

The foregoing statement of this Government's policy with respect to future trade-agreement negotiations, together with copies of any or all of the documents enclosed, may, in your discretion, be conveyed to officials of the Mexican Government and discussed with them in whatever manner you may consider appropriate.

Very truly yours,   For the Secretary of State:
C[LAIR] WILCOX [67]

611.1231/4–2347

The Secretary of State to the Mexican Ambassador (Espinosa de los Monteros)

WASHINGTON, June 12, 1947.

EXCELLENCY: I have the honor to acknowledge the receipt of your Excellency' note of April 23, 1947,[65] transmitting a memorandum proposing an agreement for the modification of the reciprocal trade agreement between the United States of America and the United Mexican States signed December 23, 1942, under the provisions of Article X thereof, which would terminate in part the concessions accorded under Schedule I of the trade agreement with respect to automobiles, radios, wearing apparel, refrigerators and iron and steel furniture, and wool carpets. The memorandum suggests that Article X, paragraph 2 of the trade agreement be interpreted as authorizing increases in import duties above the rates stipulated in Schedule I annexed to the agreement.

---

[65] Not printed.
[66] Brackets appear in the original.
[67] Vice Chairman, United States Delegation, Second meeting of the United Nations Preparatory Commission, and Vice Chairman, United States Delegation, United Nations Conference on Trade and Employment, Havana.

My Government would be particularly unhappy to see any increase in barriers to trade at this time since, as your Excellency is aware, my Government has taken the initiative in a broad program for the expansion of world trade through the lowering of tariffs and other barriers. Even now, at Geneva, Switzerland, the delegations of 18 countries are conducting definitive negotiations for the lowering of such barriers.

In particular, my Government cannot agree that Article X of the trade agreement, even when read in the light of Article XI, can serve as a basis for modification of the provisions of Article VII, which provides that no other or higher duties or charges shall be levied on the importation of United States products listed in Schedule I than these stipulated therein.

My Government recognizes that there is an adverse trend in Mexican balance of payments of the character described in the memorandum under reference. If the Mexican Government is of the opinion that the point has been reached at which curtailment of some imports of secondary essentiality is now desirable as a temporary measure to alleviate the drain on foreign exchange reserves, and if it considers that the curtailment must be extended to certain items listed in Schedule I of the trade agreement, it will no doubt wish to give due notice thereof in writing as provided in the agreement, in order that there may be an opportunity for consultation on any action proposed. On the part of this Government I may say that it appreciates the difficulties confronting the Mexican Government, and is prepared to designate promptly representatives to discuss any measures of relief consistent with the existing trade agreement which may be proposed. I wish to repeat that this Government stands ready to enter into negotiations for a general revision of the trade agreement at the earliest possible moment.

Accept [etc.] For the Secretary of State:
WILLARD L. THORP

612.003/6-1647

The Ambassador in Mexico (Thurston) to the Secretary of State

CONFIDENTIAL   FIRST PRIORITY   MÉXICO, D. F., June 16, 1947.
No. 3905

SIR: I have the honor to refer to the Department's confidential airgram A-474 of June 2, 1947,[69] regarding the present exchange situation in Mexico.

An answer to the Mexican note of April 23 [70] must be expedited or

---

[69] Not printed.
[70] See instruction 1283, June 19, *infra*.

this country will undoubtedly be forced to take unilateral action to reduce the drain on its exchange reserves, as indicated by the following figures:

GOLD AND FOREIGN EXCHANGE RESERVES
(millions of U. S. dollars)

Date	Total	Legal Reserve	Int'l Mon. Fund	Balance
1/31/47	259. 6	143. 4	----	116. 2
2/28/47	245. 1	142. 5	----	102. 6
3/31/47	233. 4	142. 0	22. 5	68. 9
4/30/47	222. 6	140. 3	22. 5	59. 8
5/31/47	214. 6	140. 3*	22. 5	51. 8

*Provisional. [Footnote in the original.]

A study of the foregoing table shows that Mexico only had 51.8 million dollars on May 31, 1947 immediately available for international commercial transactions. This small amount will be quickly exhausted if measures are not taken to conserve it. The possibility of reducing the legal reserve should be discounted since it is believed that such action would create so much lack of confidence in the stability of the peso as to cause a flight of capital from this country. Likewise, the use of either the International Monetary Fund or the stabilization credit extended by the United States Treasury could only be viewed with approval if the present situation were patently temporary in character. Unfortunately, there is no such evidence and the Embassy is strongly of the opinion that, for the present at least, our actions should be predicated on the assumption that Mexico is facing a rather long period of exchange disequilibrium. It would be foolish to encourage Mexico to have recourse to either the Fund or the Stabilization Agreement and to create an obligation repayable at a later time when the United States will be in the position of desiring to stimulate its exports to this country. Hence, any sound appraisal of the situation, in the opinion of the Embassy, conclusively establishes the fact that the soundest long-range policy is for Mexico to restrict imports of non-essential items and to institute measures to this end with the least possible delay.

The Embassy agrees with the Department that quantitative restrictions are the measures to be favored in the present emergency because tariffs, unless prohibitory, would not stem the present drain on exchange reserves and because quantitative restrictions are contemplated not only in the trade agreement, but also in the draft charter of the International Trade Organization. In agreeing, the Embassy wishes to go on record in stating its belief that quantitative restrictions, whether in the form of quotas or import licenses, are far greater obstacles to international trade than reasonable tariffs and that such restrictions should be condoned only when temporary and the objective sought is exchange equilibrium. They should never be agreed to for any other purposes, especially when used for the protection of domestic industry.

The insincerity of the Mexican memorandum should not blind the Department to the need for decision with regard to the two immediate problems which are facing Mexico, i.e., the conservation of exchange and the protection of domestic industry. The Department has apparently reached a satisfactory decision with respect to the former, but it is equally important to lay down policy with respect to the latter. Our Government can let events take their course which will probably result in many unwise and prohibitory duties being imposed in Mexico or it can realistically face the problem and stand more than an even chance of influencing Mexican tariff policy along conservative lines. If it is the policy of the United States Government to promote the sound industrialization of Latin America, the necessary corollary to that policy must also be accepted, i.e., reasonable tariff protection. Mexico must not only revise its tariffs on products manufactured in Mexico because of the lower ad valorem equivalent of its present specific duties, but also because of the greater diversity of local production. The Embassy is confident that if it were authorized to informally discuss the problem with the Mexican authorities that it could greatly influence both the timing and extent of such increases and effectively combat the unreasonable and prohibitive tariffs which the powerful Chamber of Manufacturing Industries are promoting. Furthermore, the Embassy might also be successful in destroying the present import license system and the bureaucratic organization which is administering it and obtain acceptance of the principle that quantitative restrictions be limited to protection of the exchange value of the peso and have such measures administered by the Bank of Mexico, an institution far less subject to undue influence than any direct bureaucratic organization of the Mexican Government.

There is a third problem which will become increasingly important in coming months and that is the revenue aspect of tariffs. Revenues from export taxes are decreasing and revenues from import duties will become relatively more important in the fiscal situation. There is much logic in the position of the Mexican Minister of Finance that imports should shoulder their just burden of taxation which, with rising price levels and specific duties, is not the case today. However, if a satisfactory solution were found for the first two major problems, consideration of the third might be postponed until a more appropriate time.

The Embassy fully concurs with the Department that duties on items in Schedule I of the Trade Agreement cannot be changed until formal negotiations have been concluded.

Respectfully yours, For the Ambassador:
MERWIN L. BOHAN
Counselor for Economic Affairs

611.1231/4-2347

The Secretary of State to the Embassy in Mexico

CONFIDENTIAL WASHINGTON, June 19, 1947.
No. 1283

The Secretary of State encloses, for the information of the Embassy, a copy of the Department's note of June 12, 1947 to the Mexican Ambassador,[71] in response to his note of April 23 [72] relating to the Mexican Government's proposal that the existing trade agreement be modified to permit the imposition of increased duties on certain products included in Schedule I of the trade agreement.

A proposed draft reply was summarized for the Embassy's information in the Department's airgram A-474 of June 2,[72] as were the considerations which led to its preparation in that form. The definitive reply, which represents the general agreement of representatives of various interested agencies in Washington and which has received the approval of the Committee on Trade Agreements meeting at Geneva, does not differ essentially from the proposed draft reply.

It will be noted that the reply has been related directly and exclusively to the application of the trade agreement to the problem presented by the Mexican Government. It states that this Government cannot agree with the Mexican suggestion that, broadly interpreted, Article X could serve as a basis for permitting duty increases on certain scheduled products, and suggests indirectly that the agreement provides methods other than increased rates of duty for restricting imports in certain circumstances.

A consideration which prompted the preparation of the reply note in its present form was the thought that the Mexican Government was, in effect, seeking to shift to this Government the responsibility, properly belonging to itself, for a decision made necessary largely as a result of internal political pressure for tariff protection.

No specific reference was made in the reply to the provisions of the trade agreement pursuant to which the Mexican Government may take action to relieve the situation. That course was followed in view of the strong preference expressed by one of the interested agencies

---

[71] *Ante*, p. 775.
[72] Not printed.

for recommending the use of internal taxes to meet the Mexican problem, and its vigorous objection to a recommendation that quantitative restrictions be used. However, the action which this Government regards as least undesirable under the described circumstances is, in fact, the imposition of temporary quantitative restrictions pursuant to Article X.

As stated in airgram A–474,[73] the imposition of temporary quantitative restrictions "to protect the exchange value of the currency" is provided for by the trade agreement, and their use by Mexico in the present instance would maintain the agreement unimpaired during the Geneva meeting and possibly until such time thereafter as general negotiations with Mexico may be undertaken. Such action would be defensible in the event of discussion in connection with congressional opposition to the trade-agreements program.

The Department desires to reiterate that the general position of this Government with regard to quantitative restrictions remains unchanged, namely, that their use as regular long-term methods of import control is most undesirable. Without prejudice to that general position, it is considered, however, that their temporary use is admissible as a flexible means of meeting emergency situations of a financial character, such as a short-run disequilibrium in a country's balance of payments.

The foregoing has been set forth as background information for officers of the Embassy in connection with possible discussion of the Department's note with Mexican officials.

The Embassy will be interested to learn that, in a discussion of the reply note with an official of the Mexican Embassy, it was brought out that the trade-agreement items in the list of projected tariff increases mentioned in the Mexican note amounted to a very small proportion of Mexico's total imports and that it was therefore doubtful whether action taken by Mexico to control imports of the specified trade-agreement items would have much, if any, effect on the general situation described in the note. The Embassy may find it desirable to emphasize this point in any discussions of the reply note which it may have.

611.1231/7–947

The Secretary of State to the Mexican Ambassador (Espinosa de los Monteros)

WASHINGTON, July 28, 1947.

EXCELLENCY: I have the honor to acknowledge the receipt of your note No. 4538 of July 9, 1947, enclosing a copy of a memorandum

---
[73] Not printed.

dated July 3, 1947,[74] which was delivered to an officer of the United States Embassy at Mexico City and to representatives of this Government who were in Mexico City for the purpose of consulting with authorities of the Government of Mexico pursuant to Article X of the trade agreement now in force between our two countries.[75] The note and memorandum refer to the intention of the Government of Mexico to impose quantitative restrictions upon the importation into Mexico of certain products regarded as non-essential, including a number enumerated in Schedule I of the trade agreement, for the purpose of checking the present drain upon its foreign exchange reserve resulting from continued heavy imports.

You request that the note and memorandum be considered by my Government as formal notice by the Government of Mexico, in accordance with Article X, of its intention to restrict imports of certain products enumerated in Schedule I of the agreement.

In accepting the note and memorandum as due notice of the action, I have noted that the commercial policy objective of the Government of Mexico continues to be the elimination of barriers to international trade and that it regards its action to restrict imports as a temporary emergency measure which will be withdrawn as its balance of international payments improves.

I also have the honor to acknowledge the receipt of your note No. 4539 of July 9, 1947,[76] courteously informing my Government of the intention of the Government of Mexico to increase import duties on certain products with a view to discouraging excessive imports which have been adversely affecting its balance of international payments.

Accept, Excellency, the renewed assurances of my highest consideration.

For the Secretary of State:
NORMAN ARMOUR

611.1231/10–847

The Secretary of State to the Embassy in Mexico

CONFIDENTIAL
No. 1530

WASHINGTON, October 22, 1947.

The Secretary of State refers to the Embassy's telegram No. 1089 of October 8, 1947,[76] reporting the receipt of a note from the Foreign Minister adverting to the conversation of October 1 between Mr.

---

[74] Neither printed.
[75] See statement released to the press on July 11, entitled "Mexico Limits Importation of Nonessential Goods", Department of State *Bulletin*, July 20, 1947, p. 151.
[76] Not printed.

Armour and the Chargé d'Affaires of the Mexican Embassy,[77] and proposing that the exploratory trade-agreement conversations, discussed at that time, be undertaken on October 20. Reference is also made to despatch No. 4767 of October 9 [78] transmitting a translation of the note and its annexes, together with the Embassy's analysis of the Mexican proposals.

The following statement with respect to the projected conversation is made in order that this Government's position may be clear to the Embassy, and explained by the Embassy to the Mexican Government.

The Officer in Charge is of course aware of the reluctance with which the exploratory conversations were agreed to, in view of the full preoccupation of this Government's interdepartmental trade-agreements organization since the closing months of 1946 with matters relating to the establishment of an International Trade Organization and the negotiation of a General Trade Agreement. In that connection reference is made to instruction No. 879 of March 4, 1947, in which this Government's program for the ITO Charter and General Trade Agreement work at Geneva was outlined, its policy with respect to trade-agreement negotiations thereafter suggested, and authorization given officers at the Embassy to convey the information to Mexican officials and discuss it with them in any manner considered appropriate. The statement was made in that instruction that United States trade-agreement negotiations in the post-Geneva period would be integrated within the framework provided by the Charter and would follow procedures established for that purpose, such a course of action being implicit in this Government's adherence to the principles of the Charter. It was also stated that no commitment could then be made as to whether negotiations with Mexico pursuant to the principles and procedures adopted at Geneva could be undertaken prior to the United Nations International Conference on Trade and Employment (subsequently scheduled to convene on November 21 at Habana, Cuba), concurrently with it, or following its conclusion.

There has been no lessening in the intervening months of this Government's intention to negotiate future trade agreements within the framework of the ITO Charter. It is of course the strong hope of the United States that the Government of Mexico will participate in the International Trade Conference at Habana and become a member of the International Trade Organization to be established there. Membership in the ITO entails "negotiations directed to the substantial reduction of tariffs and other charges on imports" (Article 17, Geneva Draft of the Charter).

Pending the conclusion of the Habana Conference and the determi-

---
[77] Vicente Sánchez Gavito.
[78] Not printed.

nation of procedures for negotiating with countries which have not yet entered into the General Trade Agreement concluded at Geneva, the United States is not ready to enter into new trade-agreement negotiations with Mexico or any other country. In that connection, attention is directed to Article XXXIII of the General Trade Agreement a copy of which was forwarded to the Embassy by airmail on October 17. The Article provides in effect that future trade-agreement negotiations between governments which are not parties to the Agreement will not be conducted bilaterally, but on terms agreed upon between each non-contracting party and all contracting parties. It is believed probable that this Article will be approved in substantially its present form.

In view of the repeated and urgent requests of the Mexican Government for trade-agreement discussions, the United States agreed to the holding of exploratory conversations with a view to discussing informally, in the light of the draft Charter of the projected International Trade Organization, changes which the Mexican Government may wish to have made in the existing trade agreement, and to ascertain whether there appear to be promising bases for holding in due course the negotiations envisaged in Article 17 of the Charter. However, it must be reiterated, as it was stated to the Mexican Chargé d'Affaires, that the agreement to enter into exploratory discussions is not a commitment to negotiate. Should promising bases for an agreement be found to exist, this Government will undertake formal negotiations as soon after the conclusion of the Habana Conference as it is able to do so. However, the timing of the negotiations must necessarily depend upon the views of the other governments which are parties to the General Agreement as well as upon the situation in the United States. In so far as the United States is concerned, negotiations will of course be undertaken pursuant to established trade-agreement procedure, involving public announcement and hearings.

Reference is made to paragraphs (2) and (3) of the Foreign Minister's note of October 6 expressing the hope that the period between the completion of the exploratory conversations and the negotiation, under established United States procedure, of a revision of the existing agreement may be as brief as possible. There appears to be an implication in those paragraphs that the Mexican Government expects the exploratory conversations to lead to an agreement which subsequent formal negotiations will have the effect of formalizing. The Department desires to emphasize that the exploratory conversations must be general and informal, and must in no sense take on the character of negotiations such as may be undertaken by this Government only after the customary trade-agreement procedures of public announcement and hearings have been followed. Any other course would be contrary to the law and regulations governing the operation of the trade-agreements program.

The Mexican officials should be informed of the limited character of the exploratory conversations, and that this Government considers an understanding of the following basic formulae to be essential to the successful outcome of any negotiations which may be undertaken eventually by the two Governments. Such an understanding should precede any study of the Mexican proposals set forth in the October 6 note.[78a]

1. In its future trade-agreement negotiations, the United States Government will adhere to the principles and procedures of the ITO Charter relating to the reduction of tariffs and other trade barriers and the elimination of discriminatory treatment in international trade. It will therefore not consider the negotiation of a trade agreement which is inconsistent with any of the provisions or objectives of the Charter as approved at Habana. Pending conclusion of the Habana Conference this Government will be guided by the Charter in the form in which it was approved at Geneva.

2. The United States is willing to consider requests for increases in Schedule I products to the extent needed for the reasonable protection of sound economic industries as contemplated in Articles 8 and 13 of the Geneva Draft Charter. It is likewise prepared to entertain Mexican requests for further concessions in Schedules II and III. However, the final agreement must be equally advantageous to both parties.

The Department appreciates the valiant efforts which have been made by officers of the Embassy to maintain the integrity of the trade agreement and to minimize the effects on United States trade of Mexican import restrictions,[79] and recognizes that the foregoing statement of this Government's position as to timing of formal negotiations may cause some difficulty from the Embassy's point of view in carrying on the exploratory conversations. The fact remains that this is the only position which can be taken at the present time.

611.1231/1–1648

The American Ambassador in Mexico (Thurston) to the Mexican Secretary for Foreign Relations (Torres Bodet) [80]

No. 1556   MÉXICO, D. F., December 12, 1947.

EXCELLENCY: I have the honor to refer to Your Excellency's note of October 6, 1947 [78a] and ensuing exploratory conversations with

---

[78a] Not printed.
[79] On November 13, 1947, the Mexican Government decreed a general increase in all import duties not covered by the trade agreement.
[80] Copy transmitted to the Department in despatch 101, January 16, 1948, from Mexico City (not printed).

reference to the revision of the trade agreement between the United States of America and the United Mexican States, signed December 23, 1942.

The Government of the United States has recognized that the Government of Mexico must take appropriate action to achieve equilibrium in its balance of international payments, and is prepared to collaborate in meeting the problem by concurring in any further action to suspend imports of products listed in Schedule I of the trade agreement which the Government of Mexico may consider it advisable to take pursuant to Article X of that agreement. With respect to Your Excellency's proposals to effect a change in Articles X and XI of the trade agreement, my Government is also prepared in any further revision of that Agreement, to include provisions with respect to restrictions to safeguard balance of payments similar to Article XII of the General Agreement on Tariffs and Trade signed at Geneva, October 30, 1947.

The Government of the United States has also recognized the desire of the Government of Mexico to accord increased protection to domestic industry, and I am authorized to state it is prepared to negotiate a revision of Schedule I of the existing trade agreement between our two countries immediately upon the conclusion of the United Nations Conference on Trade and Employment, now in session at Habana, on the following basis:

1. The Government of the United States will consent to the conversion of specific rates on items enumerated in Schedule I to ad valorem or compound rates at 1942 levels, subject to points 3 and 4 below. It is understood that in such compound rates the specific element will be given approximately one-third weight and the ad valorem element approximately two-thirds weight.

2. The Government of the United States will consider proposals of the Government of Mexico for increases in rates of duty on Schedule I items above the restored 1942 levels, wherever necessary to provide reasonable and adequate protection for sound Mexican industries.

3. The Government of Mexico will consider a selected list of items within Schedule I to be submitted by the Government of the United States proposing the binding of present rates of duty or reductions from the restored 1942 rates or present rates of duty.

4. The Government of Mexico will consider a list of items not now included in Schedule I to be submitted by the Government of the United States for inclusion in the renegotiated Schedule I at the rates stipulated in the recently revised Mexican Customs Tariff, or decreases therefrom.

5. All adjustments in Schedule I will be negotiated in terms of the merits of each specific item, so that the resulting agreement, taken as

a whole, will be equally advantageous and mutually satisfactory to both countries.

6. The revised rates of renegotiated Schedule I would be accepted by the Government of the United States as a proper basis for any more extensive future renegotiation of the trade agreement, either bilaterally or within the framework of a multilateral agreement. The Government of the United States would be prepared to support the propriety of this basis with other Parties to the General Agreement on Tariffs and Trade, signed at Geneva, October 30, 1947.

With reference to Annexes IV and V of Your Excellency's note of October 6, 1947, for reasons which have already been made known to Your Excellency my Government is not in a position to consider reductions in duty or additions to Schedules II and III of the trade agreement immediately after the conclusion of the United Nations Conference on Trade and Employment. It is understood, however, that in any more extensive future renegotiations, referred to in point 6, the Government of the United States will consider proposals for reductions in duty on items enumerated in Schedules II and III, and additions to those Schedules.

In view of the circumstances which have led Your Excellency's Government to conclude that the conversion of present Schedule I rates to 1942 ad valorem equivalents is immediately necessary, my Government consents to the immediate provisional conversion of the specific rates enumerated in Schedule I in accordance with point 1 above and with the understanding that the Government of Mexico is in agreement with the objectives of and procedures for the more definitive revision of Schedule I in accordance with points 1 through 6. In agreeing to the provisional increase of rates of duties on items now within Schedule I, pending a more definitive revision, my Government would expect that such increases in duty would not be effective until five days after publication of the decree imposing such increases. It is understood that the Government of Mexico will, moreover, permit entry at the present rates of duty for all shipments actually en route from points within the United States to Mexico on the date of the publication.

I should be happy to have Your Excellency's confirmation of my understanding of this agreement.[82]

I avail myself [etc.]　　　　　　　　　　　　　　　Walter Thurston

---

[82] Note No. 2243, December 12, 1947, from the Mexican Secretary for Foreign Relations (Torres Bodet), not printed. For a press release issued by the Department December 13, 1947, concerning the provisional agreement embodied in the December 12 exchange of notes with Mexico modifying trade agreement, see Department of State *Bulletin*, December 21, 1947, p. 1219. For a press release of December 31, 1947, concerning the formal notice of intention to conduct negotiations for the revision of Schedule I of the trade agreement between the United States and Mexico, see *ibid.*, January 11, 1948, p. 59.

UNITED STATES POLICY REGARDING THE PARTICIPATION OF FOREIGN OIL COMPANIES IN THE MEXICAN OIL INDUSTRY [83]

812.6363/1–1047

The Ambassador in Mexico (Thurston) to the Secretary of State

SECRET   MÉXICO, D. F., January 10, 1947.
No. 2384

SIR: The Department's instructions numbered 100 and 209, of July 24 and August 27, 1946,[84] indicated "the Department's interest concerning the reopening of informal negotiations with the Mexican Government in the matter of petroleum". The latter instruction was accompanied by a memorandum on the United States Government's policy regarding Mexican petroleum, prepared for my information and guidance in any conversations that I might initiate with the Mexican Government under the authority of the two instructions cited. It was recognized that no negotiations on this subject would be undertaken until after the inauguration of the new Government on December 1, 1946.

Immediately following Licenciado Miguel Alemán's assumption of the Presidency on the date cited, it became apparent that the economic and other problems confronting Mexico would be attacked promptly and with energy. With respect to the petroleum industry, his appointment of Senator Antonio J. Bermúdez as Director General of "Petróleos Mexicanos", commonly known as Pemex, was universally regarded as being most wise and as promising intelligent management of that vitally important organization and possibly its complete reorganization. Events since then seem to have justified such opinions, for Señor Bermúdez, with the strong support of President Alemán, has successfully met a challenge on the part of the petroleum workers and is known to have undertaken measures for essential exploration and drilling work. I have described these developments in informal communications addressed to Assistant Secretary of State Braden, and to Mr. Guy Ray of the Mexican Division, and to Mr. Charles Rayner, Petroleum Adviser.

In the light of these circumstances and developments, it seemed to me that it would be unwise to delay the initiation of the informal conversations to which allusion has been made. It seemed to me that further delay under these conditions might be construed as indifference, or might result in the initiation of programs or measures about which we might fail to obtain timely information and which might ultimately constitute an obstacle to negotiations or even to the return to

---

[83] Continued from *Foreign Relations*, 1946, vol. XI, pp. 1005–1016.
[84] Instruction 100 not printed; for instruction 209 and enclosure, see *ibid*, 1946, vol. XI, pp. 1008.

Mexico of American and other foreign petroleum interests. Accordingly, some days ago I requested an audience with the Mexican Minister for Foreign Affairs, Señor Jaime Torres Bodet, which took place last evening.

At this interview I informed Señor Torres Bodet of the general purport of pages one and two of the memorandum transmitted with instruction no. 209 and stated that in view of recent developments affecting Pemex, and in particular in view of reports that had reached me of contractual arrangements being concluded with American firms for certain works in Mexico under the auspices of that organization, I felt that perhaps it would be opportune for me to resume the informal conversations regarding Mexico's petroleum industry that had been carried on by Mr. Messersmith.[85] I said that if President Miguel Alemán were agreeable, I would be happy to be received by him so that we might resume such conversations on an informal basis. The Minister for Foreign Affairs said that he would convey my message to the President within the next few days and would let me know the President's response as soon as might be possible.

Respectfully yours, WALTER THURSTON

812.6363/1-2147

The Ambassador in Mexico (Thurston) to the Secretary of State

SECRET MEXICO, January 21, 1947.
No. 2553

SIR: Supplementing secret despatches nos. 2384 and 2534, dated January 10 and January 15, 1947,[86] respectively, on the subject cited, I have the honor to inform the Department that I was received by President Miguel Alemán in his private residence last evening. As in the case of my preliminary discussion of petroleum matters with the Minister for Foreign Affairs, I informed the President of the substance of the first few pages of the "Memorandum on United States Government's Policy regarding Mexican Petroleum" that accompanied the Department's secret instruction no. 209 of August 27, 1946.[87] I added that in view of the energetic manner in which the new Government had undertaken to deal with the problems confronting it, and in particular of developments affecting Pemex itself, I felt that perhaps the time had come for me to ascertain the views of the Government with respect to the Mexican petroleum industry and the part that

---

[85] George S. Messersmith, former Ambassador in Mexico.
[86] Despatch 2534 not printed.
[87] *Foreign Relations*, 1946, vol. XI, p. 1008.

might be played in the development thereof by American and foreign enterprises and capital.

President Alemán replied that he had for some time past been a close student of the Mexican petroleum problem and the world petroleum problem, and that he was well aware that the United States has seriously depleted its petroleum stocks and is in urgent need of readily accessible supplies abroad. He said that it was the firm policy of his Government to cooperate with the United States and that in any emergency that might arise Mexico's petroleum would be at the disposal of the United States. He remarked that perhaps some government-to-government arrangement might be brought about, and suggested that possibly a loan might be extended to Mexico for the development of new oil reserves.

I stated to the President with respect to the foregoing observations that while it is true that the United States had drawn very heavily upon its petroleum reserves in prosecuting World War I and World War II, there were two schools of thought with respect to our present oil position—one of which maintains that we have depleted our reserves and must hereafter rely upon foreign stocks, and the other of which maintains that our known and potential reserves, together with improvements in exploration, extraction, and refining processes, assure us of adequate supplies for a very extended period of time. I said that I had not intended, in bringing up the topic of Mexico's petroleum policy, to suggest any government-to-government arrangement, and that as far as any loan for the commercial development of Mexican petroleum resources is concerned, I thought it had been made clear in the past that there was no likelihood of any loan of that nature being granted. I then stated that what I desired to ascertain was the attitude of the Mexican Government with respect to the participation in the development of the Mexican oil industry by American and other foreign enterprises and capital. I remarked that it was felt by some observers that Pemex could not alone carry the burden of the development of the Mexican petroleum industry which in the past had been distributed among a group of oil companies of unusual individual and collective economic strength, and who possessed all the skills and facilities requisite for that task, and that moreover while Mexico should be deriving abundant foreign exchange from the export of its petroleum products it actually was expending heavy amounts in order to purchase such products to supply the northern and western areas of the Republic. I remarked that added to these conditions was the fact that while operating at a constant annual budgetary deficit, Mexico's balance of trade presumably would be adverse for some time as a result of the postwar trend of diminishing exports and increasing imports. Under all these circumstances I suggested there might be some advantage in the collaboration of American and foreign enterprises and capital in the development of Mexico's petroleum industry.

The President made no comment whatever with respect to the observations regarding Mexico's economic position described in the preceding paragraph but confined his next remarks to a statement of the plans which Pemex will undertake to carry into execution during 1947. He stated that it is intended to drill one hundred wells during the present year which will be distributed throughout Lower California, Chihuahua, northern Tamaulipas, lower Veracruz, Tabasco, and Oaxaca. He spoke with confidence when describing these plans and seemed to believe that the prospects for bringing in large new pools are very good. He stated that suitable American oil drilling contractors and independent oil companies will be selected by the Pemex agency in Houston to undertake drilling and exploitation work under contractual arrangements.

I inquired whether these plans precluded general participation in the development of the Mexican petroleum industry by American and foreign companies. The President replied that this was the fact and that the Mexican petroleum law (which could not be changed because of the political consequences that would follow any tampering with it) made it impossible for any other than strictly Mexican companies to operate in Mexico excepting under such contractual terms as were contemplated with respect to the companies that are to be approached by the Houston agency of Pemex.

This morning Señor Valentín Garfias, the local representative of the Cities Service Company, called to inform me that he had seen Señor Antonio J. Bermúdez, the Director General of Pemex, last night and that Señor Bermúdez had stated to him categorically that it is not the intention of the Mexican Government to permit foreign capital to participate in the Mexican petroleum industry. I asked Señor Garfias if he could suggest any explanation that would account for such a complete reversal of the views of Señor Bermúdez—who as recently as January 9 had submitted to Señor Garfias a draft of a press release in which it was stated that foreign capital was essential to the development of the Mexican petroleum industry. Señor Garfias stated that he was unable to account for the abrupt change but that he suspected that it might be related to the presence in this city during the past few days of Mr. DeGolyer, the well-known American geologist and oil industrialist. Señor Garfias is of the opinion that Mr. DeGolyer, who has frequently served as adviser to Pemex, may have convinced the Mexican Government that the reorganization of Pemex now under way will enable it to operate and expand the Mexican petroleum industry through contractual arrangements with independent oil companies.

During our conversation President Alemán was alert and friendly—but I sensed that he was somewhat on the defensive and that he was not interested in exploring the possibility of participation in the development of the Mexican oil industry by American and other foreign companies and capital as a general arrangement. His chief concern appeared to be to make it clear to me that in any emergency affecting the United States or this hemisphere, Mexico's oil resources would be instantly at our disposal. As to the current and peace-time development of the Mexican oil industry, it appeared to be his opinion that this is a domestic matter, and that the appropriate agencies of the Mexican Government will seek out such American capital or instrumentalities as they may deem necessary to the prosecution of their plans, and that such capital and such instrumentalities will work for the Mexican Government under mutually acceptable terms.

In the light of this general attitude, I did not consider it to be advisable to press for a further discussion or to bring up such points as that mentioned in the memorandum already cited to the effect that the Mexican Government "by its present nationalization of its oil industry . . . is not carrying out the spirit . . . of the Economic Charter of the Americas signed at Chapultepec on March 7, 1945".[88]

I have not informed the local representatives of American oil companies of my conversation with President Alemán, and would appreciate an indication of the Department's views as to the advisability of doing so at this time. I am of the opinion that it might be better to await further developments, and not to interpret the attitude assumed yesterday by President Alemán as constituting a definitive rebuff.

Respectfully yours, WALTER THURSTON

812.6363/10-647

The Under Secretary of State (Lovett) to the Under Secretary of the Navy (Kenney)

CONFIDENTIAL WASHINGTON, October 8, 1947.

DEAR MR. KENNEY: Prior to his departure for Mexico City, Ambassador Thurston [89] discussed with me certain aspects of the Mexican oil

---

[88] For the "Economic Charter of the Americas", Resolution LI of the Final Act of the Chapultepec Conference, see Department of State, *Report of the Delegation of the United States of America to the Inter-American Conference on Problems of War and Peace, Mexico City, Mexico, February 21–March 8, 1945*, p. 120.

[89] Ambassador Thurston had visited the United States for consultation on the Mexican oil situation.

matters which Secretary Forrestal [90] had previously talked to me about on a personal basis. In the course of conversation, Mr. Thurston told me that he did not feel it was proper to disclose in a large meeting which he attended in the Navy Department certain matters which have a direct bearing on the Government-to-Government transactions with Mexico. Accordingly, I asked him for a memorandum, a copy of which I enclose for your confidential information in the hope that it may be of some value to you.

With kind regards, I am

Very sincerely yours, ROBERT A. LOVETT

[Enclosure]

Memorandum by the Ambassador to Mexico (Thurston) to the Under Secretary of State (Lovett)

[WASHINGTON,] September 30, 1947.

I have some misgivings about our current activities with respect to the development of Mexican petroleum resources.

Background: In 1938 the Mexican Government expropriated the majority of the foreign owned oil companies operating in Mexico.[91] An Agreement was subsequently reached between the Mexican and American Governments [92] whereunder the American companies affected by the expropriation would receive compensation, and the last payment under this Agreement will be made today.[93] A similar Agreement with respect to the British and other foreign interests affected by the expropriation was concluded in Mexico City one month ago.

It has been the policy of this Government not to condone the expropriation proceedings of the Mexican Government by advancing United States funds, through any agency of this Government, for the development of the Mexican oil industry in its commercial phases. This policy has been set down in a Presidential Directive initialled by President Roosevelt in 1944 [94] and in a Presidential Directive approved by President Truman in 1945.[95]

---

[90] James V. Forrestal, Secretary of the Navy until September 17, 1947 when he became Secretary of Defense.

[91] For documentation on this subject, see *Foreign Relations*, 1938, vol. v, pp. 720 ff.

[92] For United States-Mexican exchange of notes on expropriated petroleum properties, September 25 and 29, 1943, see Department of State Executive Agreement Series No. 419, or 58 Stat. (pt. 2) 1408.

[93] See press release entitled "Final Compensation for Petroleum Properties Expropriated in Mexico", Department of State *Bulletin*, October 12, 1947, p. 747.

[94] For memorandum by President Roosevelt to the Secretary of State, July 19, 1944, see *Foreign Relations*, 1944, vol. VII, p. 1346.

[95] See instruction 8098 to Mexico City, November 8, 1945, in *ibid.*, 1945, vol. IX, p. 1161.

The organization (Petróleos Mexicanos or Pemex) created by the Mexican Government to administer the expropriated petroleum industry soon demonstrated its inability to operate the industry in such a fashion that adequate quantities of petroleum might become available to world use. Official conversations have been held by my predecessor and myself with the Presidents of Mexico in an effort to ascertain whether foreign oil companies might again be permitted to collaborate in the development of Mexico's oil resources. These conversations have thus far produced no results—in part because the American oil companies are reluctant to engage in operations in Mexico until certain provisions of the Mexican petroleum law shall have been modified, and in part to the feeling of hostility of some of the Mexican people to the foreign oil companies and to the idea of their return to Mexico.

Recent Developments: Since the inauguration of President Alemán, the affairs of Pemex have been administered more efficiently and an attempt has been made to discover and to bring into production new oil reserves. This effort has taken the form of the granting of drilling contracts to American companies and tentative negotiations with American oil companies—one of which, the Cities Service Company, may soon conclude an agreement—for participation contracts. The pattern of the drilling contracts is roughly that of a cost plus agreement with payment in 6% Government bonds convertible into oil, if any of the wells are productive, at the election of the bondholders. The participating contracts call for financing by the companies of development operations by Pemex, reimbursement to be in the form of Government bonds and of marketing rights on 50% of any oil produced. It is generally believed that the effort of Pemex to develop the national petroleum resources through drilling contracts will fail because of insufficient funds and the dubious character of some of the contractors involved. The Cities Service contract, on the other hand, if it is consummated, may produce satisfactory results.

In the meanwhile, the general economy of Mexico has been seriously disturbed by the curtailment of its wartime exports, by the great increase of imports following the reconversion of American industry, by the closing of the American frontier to exports of cattle following the out-break of the foot and mouth disease in Mexico, and by a more or less general economic recession not entirely related to these factors. At the same time, President Alemán not only has initiated a large scale and very costly program of national improvement involving the construction of highways, irrigation projects, power plants, air fields, and the development of agriculture and industry, but has repeatedly promised his people that he would lower the cost of living. Under all these conditions, the development of the Mexican petroleum industry with the resultant inflow of dollar exchange assumes special importance in Mexican eyes.

Last July, the Technical Petroleum Committee, which I understand is a body representative of all United States Government departments interested in petroleum, addressed an inquiry to the American Embassy in Mexico with respect to the general situation regarding petroleum and with specific reference to the advisability of initiating formal discussions with the Government of Mexico looking to the development of that country's petroleum resources. The Embassy's reply to this instruction stated that such negotiations could prudently be initiated in the near future and recommended that they be begun with the Mexican Foreign Minister and President Alemán, possibly, in the case of the latter, on the basis of a personal letter from President Truman.

Without apparent reference to the development just described, Mr. Paul Shields, an American business man residing in New York City, who has promoted arrangements of considerable importance in Mexico in the past, has held discussions on behalf of the Navy Department with the Head of the Bank of Mexico and the Mexican Minister of Finance, and others. These negotiations also have been participated in to some extent by the Mexican Ambassador to Washington and seem to have led the Mexicans to believe that in return for certain arrangements resulting in the delivery of adequate quantities of Mexican oil to the United States Navy a cash advance of perhaps as much as one hundred million dollars may be made to the Mexican Government by the United States Government or some dependency thereof. They seem furthermore to have touched upon the formation of a company which would in some fashion involve itself in the situation. There is reason to question the motives of the Mexican officials and others who presumably would constitute this organization. It appears to be contemplated by Mr. Shields that these negotiations, which at least for a certain period should be conducted by himself or by representatives of the Navy Department with the Mexican Minister of Finance, could be so guided that they would result in the return to Mexico of private foreign oil companies. At the present moment, the Mexican Embassy is awaiting a reply to a letter addressed to Mr. Forrestal proposing that representatives be sent to Mexico to discuss the suggested arrangements.

Comment: The willingness of Mr. Shields to place at the disposal of our Government his knowledge of Mexico and its present authorities and his desire to contribute to the solution of our own need for petroleum and of Mexico's economic and petroleum difficulties is appreciated. I feel, however, that it is unwise and dangerous as a general policy to by-pass the recognized and established channels of intercourse between states, and that it is particularly hazardous to do so in the present instance. There has been no greater source of misunderstanding between the United States and Mexico than petroleum and any mishandling of this question might easily and speedily impair relations between the two countries—which are on a better basis now than ever. Mr. Shields of course can have no knowledge of the secret Presidential Directives precluding United States Government aid in the commercial development of Mexico's oil industry (which was seized in part from American ownership), nor is it to be expected that he should be aware of the danger of encouraging expropriation of American and other foreign owned petroleum interests in other countries of this hemisphere, such as Colombia.

Moreover, . . . the Mexicans could easily be aroused to active hostility against us should injudicious action create the impression that the United States Government itself is seeking domination of Mexico's petroleum resources. In the event that we should acquire direct Government to Government interest in Mexico's petroleum, we would thereby set up a target for those hostile to us, with the result that any minor labor conflict in the petroleum industry could be exploited to the disadvantage of harmonious relations between the two countries.

I recommend therefore that high policy within our own Government regarding Mexican petroleum be immediately and definitely coordinated and operated through one official channel only. I further recommend that when this has been done, normal negotiations be instituted with the Mexican Government designed to ascertain whether there is any likelihood that American and other foreign petroleum companies may be permitted to operate in Mexico legally, normally, and on a competitive basis.

If it should be ascertained that there is no possibility of the establishment of conditions under which bona fide American and other foreign companies may return to Mexico, then our policy should be re-examined with a view to decision whether our need for petroleum for defense or other purposes is sufficiently great to warrant the risks involved in United States Government support of the Mexican Government's administration of the expropriated Mexican petroleum industry.

WALTER THURSTON

812.6363/10–3147

The Secretary of State to the Ambassador in Mexico (Thurston)

CONFIDENTIAL WASHINGTON, October 31, 1947.

SIR: Reference is made to the growing interest and evident need of the Mexican Government substantially to increase petroleum production in order to meet domestic requirements for petroleum products and to provide additional urgently needed dollar exchange. Reference also is made to your recent conversations in Washington with officials of this Government interested in the same problem because of the desirability and urgency of developing additional hemisphere oil resources necessary for increasing peacetime requirements and for hemisphere defense. The Department believes that the urgency and coincidence of these needs make the time appropriate for immediate discussions with the Mexican Government with a view to formulation of an oil program under which foreign oil companies would be permitted to operate in Mexico on a competitive and non-discriminatory basis, the only basis upon which it is believed the needed development of Mexican oil resources can be efficiently and promptly achieved. At the earliest opportunity you are instructed to enter into discussions with the President of Mexico along the lines suggested below and to pursue the matter as may seem appropriate and advisable. To the extent feasible such discussions at the outset should be of an informal and preliminary nature and, should the President so indicate, may be continued with Señor Ramón Beteta [96] or any other official of the Mexican Government designated by the President. For your background information there is enclosed a copy of recent correspondence between the Mexican Ambassador in Washington and Secretary Forrestal relative to this problem.[97]

In your discussions the following views of the United States Government should be made known to the Mexican Government:

1. The United States Government recognizes and respects the position of the Mexican Government regarding the national ownership of its sub-soil resources, as stated in Article 27 of the Mexican Constitution of 1917, and does not seek the accomplishment of any arrangement which would in any way violate that position or conflict with the freely expressed wishes of the Mexican people.

2. The United States Government does not seek any preferential rights or privileges for its nationals in the development of the Mexican petroleum industry. It is interested only in arrangements under which its nationals would participate in the development of the Mexican petroleum industry on a basis of equality with the nationals of other foreign countries.

Your Government believes that the only method by which Mexico can obtain any substantial increase in oil production, such as would make a substantial contribution to helping solve Mexico's foreign exchange problem, is through reentry of foreign oil companies into Mexico. You should make it clear that your Government is completely

---

[96] Ramón Beteta, Mexican Minister of Finance and Public Credit.
[97] Not printed.

open-minded with respect to the basis of reentry of foreign oil companies, and that it recognizes and appreciates that any basis of reentry must be determined by and be fully acceptable to the Mexican Government. On the other hand, any proposal of the Mexican Government which would not offer the foreign oil companies reasonable compensation for the risks involved and which as a result would not induce the foreign oil companies to return to Mexico, would fail of its purpose. You might also find it desirable in connection with the above points to make it clear that the views of your Government are not based upon any preconceived notions or prejudices with respect to Pemex. In its opinion what is required of Mexico is access to the best petroleum technology, great diversity of effort, and access to virtually an unlimited volume of risk capital, all of which can be met only by drawing fully and freely upon the world petroleum industry.

It is believed that the following reasons, which at your discretion may be used in your discussions, provide the Mexican Government with ample justification for the most serious consideration of some plan for the reentry of foreign oil companies into Mexico:

1. The expansion of production which could be expected to ensue would provide Mexico with substantial additional quantities of urgently needed dollar exchange. It is believed that development at a relatively early date of Mexico's petroleum resources offers a practical means for Mexico to earn additional foreign exchange essential for its economy.

2. The development of Mexico's petroleum resources would yield to Mexico additional internal revenues from taxes and from the sales of its share of the expanded output of petroleum and petroleum products, thus contributing to the budget of the Mexican Government. There should result also substantial general improvement in the Mexican economy from the large expenditures of the oil companies for capital investment, payment of wages to workers, and related operations such as the construction of housing, camp facilities, roads, telegraph lines, and other forms of transportation and communication facilities.

3. From an expansion of its petroleum industry Mexico would derive special benefits in the form of increased employment for its nationals, the development of skills, and the construction of schools and hospitals for its workers.

4. The expansion of the Mexican petroleum industry would make possible a more rapid industrial development by furnishing low cost power for its industries and for the various means of transportation and communication. It also would provide a basis for and stimulate the growth of related industries requiring similar engineering skills and petroleum by-products.

5. Increased oil production in Mexico is necessary to meet Mexico's anticipated requirements, which in the near future are expected to exceed production under present operating conditions in the Mexican petroleum industry.

6. The surplus petroleum which Mexico would be able to export

would find a ready market not only in the United States but also in other American markets whose requirements are already in excess of their supply; United States petroleum requirements already exceed domestic supplies, and demand is expected to continue to increase at a rapid rate.

7. Increased petroleum production and reserves in Mexico would be available for Mexican defense in time of emergency and would enable Mexico to make a material contribution to the defense of the Western Hemisphere. Such a development would enable Mexico better to discharge its responsibilities in the Mutual defense commitments made by the American Republics at Chapultepec and Rio de Janeiro.

Should the Mexican Government raise the question of the creation of a United States and/or Mexican Military or Naval petroleum reserve in Mexico, it should be made clear that your Government is not prepared to give any consideration to this approach to the Mexican and hemisphere petroleum problems. Experience has shown that the petroleum resources most readily available in time of emergency are those already developed and being actively operated on a non-discriminatory and commercially competitive basis. Moreover, the political and other complexities involved would render such an approach wholly undesirable.

In the event the Government of Mexico takes up with you the general subject of a petroleum loan, you should state that it is your understanding that under present United States Government lending practices public funds are not made available for economic development projects when private funds are available for such projects on reasonable terms.

Should you feel the need of assistance, advice or consultation in the course of your discussions, Departmental personnel and personnel of the defense agencies will be available at your request in the capacity you deem advisable.

Very truly yours, For the Secretary of State:
NORMAN ARMOUR
Assistant Secretary

812.6363/12–1247

The Ambassador in Mexico (Thurston) to the Secretary of State

SECRET MEXICO, December 12, 1947.
No. 5217

SIR: The Department's confidential unnumbered instruction dated October 31, 1947, directing me to enter into discussions at the earliest opportunity with the President of Mexico with respect to the desirability and urgency of developing Mexico's petroleum resources reached me on November 6—on the eve of the departure of President Alemán on an extended visit to the northern districts of this Republic. President Alemán returned from this tour on the afternoon of December 3 and on December 4 I called on the Minister for Foreign Affairs, informed him of the general nature of my instructions, and requested an appointment with the President.

President Alemán received me yesterday afternoon. At this interview I reminded the President of my inquiry shortly after he had assumed office with respect to Mexico's petroleum policy and the likelihood that American and other foreign oil companies might be permitted to participate in the development of Mexico's petroleum resources, and of my brief conversation with him on this subject shortly before my last visit to Washington in mid-September. I stated that upon my arrival in Washington I had found that considerable interest existed in connection with the need for petroleum for peacetime requirements and hemisphere defense, and that I was of course aware of Mexico's own increasing need for petroleum for the development of its economy and as a source of urgently required dollar exchange. I mentioned that I had been informed of the conversations held here by Mr. Paul Shields with Licenciado Ramón Beteta and others, and that I had discussed all these matters with our officials and that as a result it had been decided that upon my return to Mexico I would discuss with the President the general subject of the development and expansion of oil production in Mexico. I added that there had been some exchange of views on these matters between the Mexican Ambassador in Washington and Secretary Forrestal, and that the Secretary had informed Señor Espinosa de los Monteros [99] that I would undertake these discussions.

The President in reply recalled his earlier statements to me to the effect that while yet a Presidential candidate, he had recognized that should he be elected one of the most important problems with which his Government would have to deal would be that of petroleum. For this reason he had conducted extensive studies of the subject, and since his election he had followed developments in the field of petroleum and was aware of the present situation in the United States and of the growing demands for this product in Mexico itself. He repeated the statement made to me at our first interview on this subject that Mexico's petroleum would always and instantly be at the disposal of the Government of the United States in the event of an emergency. I thanked the President for this renewed assurance but stated that in the event of an emergency, undeveloped petroleum resources would be of little avail. I then read to him the first six points of the memo-

---

[99] Antonio Espinosa de los Monteros, Mexican Ambassador in the United States.

randum I had prepared for this interview, into which were incorporated the essential points of the Department's instruction No. 209 dated August 27, 1946,[1] and the Department's instruction above cited of October 31, 1947. A copy of this memorandum is attached hereto.[2]

The President indicated during my reading his understanding and appreciation of the several points developed, and with specific reference to point number six stated that the initiative regarding the creation of a military or naval petroleum reserve had been taken by us in the conversations held by Mr. Paul Shields on behalf of our Navy Department. He added that the initiative had been well-received and that it would again receive friendly consideration should it be revived. Nonetheless he made it quite clear that he understood that this subject has been dropped.

The President then stated that Pemex is currently in negotiation not only with American drilling contractors on a fee basis but also with several small independent American oil companies, and that he believes that some of these negotiations may be carried to a successful conclusion. In consequence, he said, American companies would be permitted to undertake "wild cat" operations—which operations, he said, have constituted the basis of the development of the oil industry in the United States. At this point I remarked that some American oil companies have indicated an unwillingness to participate in the development of Mexico's oil industry until the present Petroleum Law should be modified by the removal of the restriction against foreign participation in exploration and exploitation. The President stated that he does not agree that operations of the kind contemplated under the negotiations now pending with Pemex are precluded by the Petroleum Law, adding that it would be very difficult for political reasons to change the law. He said that the arrangements now under discussion with Pemex contemplate that the company concerned would be allocated a tract of land on which it might explore for petroleum. If these explorations should be fruitless, the cost of the exploration would be borne by the company; if they were successful, the company would receive a share of the oil produced. I repeated that in the opinion of some companies, this arrangement, which seems to provide for exploration and exploitation, would be in conflict with the Petroleum Law. To this observation, the President again assured me that he did not agree, inasmuch as the company concerned would be operating on the basis of a contract extended by Pemex. I infer that in the President's mind (and a similar view was advanced by Foreign Minister Torres Bodet when I spoke with him on December 4) the paramount

---

[1] *Foreign Relations*, 1946, vol. XI, p. 1008.
[2] Not printed.

fact is that Pemex is the Government agency possessing monopoly faculties for the development of Mexico's petroleum resources. Hence, no violation of the Petroleum Law would result from operations of Pemex even though these take the form of the delegation to a foreign oil company of certain operations and the payment therefor should be made in Mexican oil. I stated to the President that his opinions in this regard led me to hope that a formula might be found whereunder American and other foreign companies could operate in the development of Mexico's petroleum industry, and that in this hope, and if it were agreeable to him, I would be glad to explore this possibility further with Licenciado Beteta or any others whom he might designate for the purpose. The President stated that he felt that upon the return of Foreign Minister Torres Bodet and Finance Minister Ramón Beteta, it would be well if they and I and Senator Antonio Bermúdez should enter into such discussions, and that he would communicate with them following their return and arrange for a meeting.

Toward the close of our conversation I mentioned the position of the Government of the United States in regard to the employment of United States public funds for the development of Mexico's oil industry, and in this connection read to him paragraph number seven of the memorandum already mentioned. President Alemán said that he had understood this to be our position but made no further comment.

As is stated in the telegram I despatched to the Department last evening following my meeting with President Alemán, I received the impression that President Alemán's attitude toward a frank and thorough discussion of the matter of American and foreign participation in the development of the Mexican petroleum industry is favorable. When I mentioned, for example, the existence of a hostile public attitude toward such participation, the President remarked that this could be overcome by a suitable public presentation of the Government's views, and that, moreover, the frequent references in the public press to negotiations between Pemex and American oil companies had provoked no adverse reaction. He displayed, furthermore, an understanding of the time factor, although he did not agree with the view that were strong oil companies to be admitted into Mexico immediately, full beneficial results would not accrue for several years. He was of the opinion that in certain areas, strong companies could bring in important production within as short a time as one year. In brief, the President's attitude was one of optimism and readiness to hold serious discussions. It is expected that Licenciado Beteta will return from Havana over the weekend, and it is understood that the Foreign Minister has returned today from his brief vacation. Senator Bermúdez is already here. It is possible, therefore, unless Beteta must return to Havana, that our conversations may take place in the near future.

In so far as I am aware, only the Standard Oil Company of New Jersey has asserted that it could not and would not operate in Mexico until the Petroleum Laws have been changed. I believe that the Trumbull Asphalt Company, the Phillips Petroleum Company, the Signal Oil Company, the Cities Service Company, and perhaps others have sought contracts from Pemex without raising this issue. I shall, of course, in my conversations with Messrs. Beteta, Torres Bodet, and Bermúdez go very thoroughly into this subject. Should the Department, however, have any information as to the attitudes of other companies or any opinions of its own, it would be helpful if they might be imparted to me.

Respectfully yours, WALTER THURSTON

CONFLICTS IN UNITED STATES-MEXICAN FISHERIES RELATIONS AND EXCHANGE OF VIEWS ON A PROPOSED FISHERIES TREATY [3]

812.628/1–3147

The Acting Secretary of State to the Embassy in Mexico

RESTRICTED WASHINGTON, April 16, 1947.

No. 1030

The Acting Secretary of State refers to the Embassy's despatch no. 2719 of January 31, 1947 [4] transmitting a memorandum of observations of the Mexican Government [5] on the United States proposals for a fisheries treaty between the United States and Mexico.[6] Reference is also made to subsequent communications on this matter.

The Department is now studying the suggestions contained in the Mexican memorandum. As one phase of this study, and in view of the Mexican suggestion that the proposed treaty include fisheries of both the Pacific and Gulf of Mexico coasts, it was considered advisable to consult informally with fishery conservation officials and representatives of the fishing industry of the several Gulf Coast states. Accordingly, officers of the Department and of the Fish and Wildlife service of the Department of the Interior met in New Orleans, Louisiana, on March 3 to 5, 1947 with such officials and representatives.

---

[3] For documentation on the continental shelf policy of Mexico and its effect on United States-Mexican fisheries relations, see *Foreign Relations*, 1946, vol. XI, pp. 1054 ff.
[4] Not printed.
[5] Mexican memorandum dated January 27, 1947, not printed.
[6] The United States draft fisheries treaty of August 20, 1945, which was to apply to waters of the Pacific Coast, was submitted to the Mexican Government for its consideration on August 31, 1945 (not printed).

While several questions, such as the possibility of imposing a tariff or quota on the importation of Mexican shrimp into the United States, appeared to overshadow interest in a fisheries treaty with Mexico, representatives of the industry made helpful statements and suggestions and contributed information which will be useful in relation to the proposed fisheries treaty with Mexico. There appeared to be general agreement that it would be desirable to conclude a treaty establishing a well-defined line between Mexican territorial waters and the high seas areas in which United States industry could operate freely.

[Here follow data on the possibility of Cuban participation in negotiations.]

In considering the suggestion that a single fisheries treaty with Mexico should include the fisheries of both the Pacific and Gulf of Mexico coasts, the Department recognizes that such a treaty might require a somewhat longer period of time for negotiation than would a treaty covering only the Pacific coast area. However, in view of recent developments, careful consideration is being given to the Mexican suggestion with respect to the area which might be included in the treaty. It is hoped that, prior to consulting the Cuban Government on aspects of the proposed treaty which may be of interest to that country, the United States and Mexico may reach substantial agreement on all other phases of the matter.

The Department is assembling pertinent information and views on the Mexican memorandum under reference and will communicate further with the Embassy on this matter at as early a date as practicable.

It appears appropriate for the Embassy to acknowledge by note, if it has not done so, the Mexican memorandum of January 27, 1947, indicating at the same time that the matter is under study by this Government and that, at a later date, a further communication will be forwarded to the Mexican Government. At the time of presenting such note to the Mexican Ministry of Foreign Relations, or at some other appropriate time, the Embassy should, in its discretion, indicate informally that this Government has received information relative to rumors among the fishing industry of this country to the effect that the Mexican authorities might increase the fees applicable to foreign fishing vessels. The Embassy might indicate in this connection that this Government understands that the informal agreement with the Ministry of Foreign Relations that no changes would be made in fees during the negotiation of the pending fisheries treaty is applicable until the United States has had a reasonable period of time in which to reply to the suggestions contained in the Mexican memorandum of January 27, 1947.

812.628/2–447

The Secretary of State to the Ambassador in Mexico (Thurston)

CONFIDENTIAL WASHINGTON, September 11, 1947.
No. 1463

SIR: Reference is made to the Embassy's despatch no. 2730 of February 4, 1947, transmitting a translation of note no. 51347 from the Mexican Government [7] containing observations on the draft fishery treaty dated August 20, 1945 between Mexico and the United States, and to other communications on the same subject.

Careful consideration has been given by the Department to the views of the Government of Mexico as contained in the observations, and to the Embassy's comments thereon transmitted with despatch no. 2950 dated February 21, 1947.[8] While there appear, at the present time, to be certain substantial differences between the views of the two Governments with respect to the provisions of the proposed treaty, it is believed that it may be possible to resolve these differences in direct and informal negotiation. Accordingly, if you perceive no objection, you are requested to inform the Government of Mexico that this Government is prepared to enter into informal negotiations on the subject, at as early a date as may be convenient. It is suggested that a note along the following lines be transmitted to the Mexican Minister for Foreign Affairs:

"Reference is made to the note of the Ministry of Foreign Relations no. 51347 dated January 27, 1947 transmitting a memorandum of comments on a draft of a proposed Treaty between Mexico and the United States with respect to the Pacific Fisheries of Common Concern and Protocol, and to previous communications on the same subject.

"Careful consideration has been given by the Government of the United States to the comments on the draft treaty, as transmitted with note no. 51347. While there appear, at the present time, to be certain substantial differences between the views of the two Governments with respect to the provisions of the proposed treaty, it is believed that it may be possible to resolve these differences in direct and informal negotiation. Accordingly, the Government of the United States is now prepared to enter into informal negotiations with a view to formulating a draft in terms satisfactory to both our Governments. The Government of the United States of America would appreciate being informed of the earliest date that would be convenient to the Government of Mexico for such negotiations."

Officers of the Department would prefer that the negotiations take place in Mexico City in order that the representatives of the Mexican Government may have full opportunity for technical advice and con-

---

[7] Neither printed.
[8] Not printed.

sultation with other officials of their Government. The present plan of the Department is that the negotiators on behalf of the United States would not carry full powers to sign an agreement but that the draft which will result from the conference will be in substantially final form, subject only to minor modifications which may be effected by telegraph, so that no further conferences will be required. If, however, the Government of Mexico should indicate a preference for the negotiations to be conducted by representatives with full power to sign, the Department would not interpose objections to such an arrangement.

Officers of the Department are holding consultations with representatives of industry on the West Coast and it is probable that similar consultations wil be held with the Gulf Coast industry prior to the commencement of negotiations. These plans for consultation should not, however, be taken into consideration in such manner as to delay the setting of as early a date as possible for the negotiations.

Very truly yours, For the Secretary of State:
WILLARD L. THORP
Assistant Secretary

812.628/12-1047

The Acting Secretary of State to the Ambassador in Mexico (Thurston)

CONFIDENTIAL WASHINGTON, December 10, 1947.
No. 1616

SIR: Reference is made to your despatch No. 2961 of February 26, 1947,[9] concerning the interception and detention by Mexican authorities in September, 1946, of United States fishing vessels which had been operating off the coasts of the State of Campeche.[10]

In view of the proposed negotiation of a fisheries treaty between this Government and Mexico, the Department does not at this time deem it advisable to take definitive action in this matter. However, it feels that the attention of the Government of Mexico should be directed to three points brought out by the Mexican note enclosed with the despatch under consideration. These are (1) the statement that the limit of territorial waters, as between the United States and Mexico, is established by treaty to be nine nautical miles; (2) the assertion of jurisdiction, in the particular case under reference, at a point four

---

[9] Not printed.
[10] For documentation on the four Louisiana shrimp vessels apprehended in the Bay of Campeche and released through the Embassy's representations after payment of a fine of 1,000 pesos each, see *Foreign Relations*, 1946, vol. XI, pp. 1058–1067.

miles from the coast by virtue of the General Law of National Wealth published August 26, 1944; and (3) the claim that the vessels were four miles from land at the time of apprehension, a claim which is not substantiated by depositions and other evidence in the files of the Department, which indicate rather that the seizure occurred seventeen miles from land.

With reference to the purported establishment of the nine mile limit by the Treaties of 1848 and 1853,[11] the United States, by the note of March 7, 1936,[12] to the Government of Mexico reserved all rights of whatever nature so far as effects on American commerce are concerned from enforcement of the Decree of August 29, 1935, which essayed to extend Mexican territorial waters from three miles to nine miles in breadth, and in subsequent correspondence pointed out that the Treaty of 1848 mentioned furnished no authority for Mexico to claim generally that its territorial waters extend nine miles from the coast. The claim of extension of territorial waters to nine miles was repeated in Article 17, Section II, of the General Law of National Wealth (published August 26, 1944), under which article the present seizures were made. It is felt necessary, therefore, that this Government should reiterate its position that it does not recognize general Mexican sovereignty in waters beyond the three mile limit, and that it reaffirms the reservations of rights of American commerce, made in 1936, against the enforcement of the law of August 26, 1944, and of all other laws purporting to extend general jurisdiction beyond three miles.

You are requested, therefore, unless you perceive objection, to transmit to the Mexican Ministry of Foreign Affairs a note along the following lines:

"I have the honor to refer to Your Excellency's note No. 52602 of February 18, 1947, concerning the interception and detention, in September, 1946, of four United States fishing vessels which had been operating off the coasts of the State of Campeche.

"In the note under reference the statement is made that the territorial waters of Mexico, in the relations between the United States and Mexico, have an extension of nine miles, which extension, it is stated, is derived from interpretations of Article V of the Treaty of 1848 and of Article I of the Treaty of 1853 between the United States and Mexico. The Government of the United States maintains, and has consistently maintained, that the general territorial jurisdiction of

---

[11] For the treaty of Guadalupe Hidalgo, February 2, 1848, and the Gadsden treaty, December 30, 1853, see Department of State Treaty Series Nos. 207 and 208, respectively, or 9 Stat. 922 and 10 Stat. 1031, respectively.
[12] *Foreign Relations*, 1936, vol. v, p. 759.

Mexico, so far as United States nationals are concerned, extends three miles seaward from the coast measured from the low-water mark. In this regard Your Excellency's attention is invited to this Embassy's note of June 3, 1936,[13] addressed to Your Excellency's Government, which, after discussing at length the Treaty of 1848, pointed out that it furnished no authority for the Government of Mexico to claim generally that the territorial waters of Mexico extend nine miles from the coast. The same conclusion necessarily applies to the Treaty of 1853 which, in regard to the question of territorial waters, introduced no change in the terms or meaning of the Treaty of 1848.

"With reference to Article 17, Section II, of the General Law of National Wealth referred to in Your Excellency's note and stated to be the justification of the seizures, the United States cannot, so far as that law purports to define the territorial waters of Mexico as coastal waters to the distance of nine nautical miles from land, accept its application to United States fishing vessels operating between three and nine miles off the coast. Further, the Government of the United States continues, as in 1936, to reserve all rights of whatever nature so far as concerns any effects upon American commerce from enforcement of this legislation, or of similar legislation which purports to extend the limit of general jurisdiction beyond three nautical miles.

"Your Excellency's note states also that the vessels at the time of apprehension were four miles from the coast. Although on the basis of evidence available at this time it would appear that the actual distance was seventeen miles, it is not the intention of this Government to discuss this question which is one of fact. The violation of American rights is equally serious whether the seizure took place at the lesser or the greater distance, both being outside the territorial waters in which general jurisdiction could properly be exercised under the circumstances.

"In the sincere hope that the proposed negotiations between the Government of the United States and Your Excellency's Government with respect to fisheries matters will remove all future difficulties in what Your Excellency rightly terms a routine matter of coast patrol, this Government does not at this time desire to press the issue of the unwarranted seizures of the vessels mentioned above or of other seizures which occurred recently.[14] It does, however, desire to indicate to the Government of Mexico that it has not changed the position set forth in the note of June 3, 1936, and that it cannot recognize as justified any interference of this character with fishing vessels flying the flag of the United States when such vessels are situated at a distance of more than three miles from the coasts of Mexico."

Very truly yours,   For the Acting Secretary of State:
WILLARD L. THORP

---

[13] Not printed.
[14] Four American fishing vessels were taken into custody and detained at the port of Obregon in January 1947, and another vessel was detained at Tampico in April and released by Mexican authorities on July 2.

812.628/12-947 : Airgram

The Acting Secretary of State to the Embassy in Mexico

CONFIDENTIAL WASHINGTON, December 16, 1947.

A-923. Reference Embassy's telegram 1406 December 9, 1947.[15] Department concurs Embassy's recommendation.

Department would appreciate receiving promptly Embassy's evaluation past publicity regarding proposed United States-Mexican fisheries treaty in Mexican publications and probable effect these newspaper accounts on opinions of government officials or public; also recommendations with reference desirability of later release in Mexico of U.S. 1945 draft. In view Lindner's [16] statement that additional publicity at this time will stimulate opposition to treaty, Embassy is instructed not approach Mexican Government to request permission release in this country or give permission release U.S. 1945 draft in Mexico until further instructed by Department.

Department being criticized for failure inform and consult with fishing industry and Congress on international problems of concern to fishing industry. Believe essential, if proposed treaty is to receive support in this country, that all important segments industry affected must be consulted on all phases before commencement Mexican treaty negotiations. For this reason public release in this country of substance U.S. 1945 draft and Mexican memorandum thereon is considered highly desirable. If, however, a simultaneous release substance these documents in Mexico would have repercussions inimical to welfare treaty negotiations, some other course of action must be considered. Industry consultation in this country might be achieved by informing interested persons on confidential basis of all pertinent points for their consideration and advice, without releasing contents U.S. or Mexican documents to newspapers or periodicals. Department would like Embassy's views in order to help determine desirable course of action.

LOVETT

812.628/12-2247 : Airgram

The Ambassador in Mexico (Thurston) to the Secretary of State

RESTRICTED MEXICO CITY, December 22, 1947.

A-1146. Referring to the Department's telegram No. 1255 of December 11, 1947 and to the Embassy's reply, telegram 1437 of De-

---

[15] Not printed; it concerned the undesirability of any additional publicity at that time regarding the fisheries treaty (812.628/12-947).

[16] Milton J. Lindner, Chief of the United States Fisheries Mission to Mexico.

cember 16, 1947 [17] regarding the raising of tuna fish taxes by the Mexican authorities, the Department is further informed that on December 18 at the request of the Under-secretary of the Ministry for Foreign Affairs [18] the Counselor of the Embassy [19] called at the Foreign Office with regard to the above-mentioned matter. His memorandum in the premises reads as follows:

Señor Tello, Undersecretary of the Ministry for Foreign Affairs, requested me to call at the Foreign Office where he received me in the presence of Mr. Sánchez Gavito.[20] Señor Tello said that after my visit of last Saturday, December 13, he had investigated in the files at the Foreign Office the matter which I raised, namely, the commitment not to raise taxes on tuna fishing boats pending the negotiation of a fishery treaty between the two Governments. Señor Tello had in his hand the official file and pointed out that the commitment which was made originally when the time of the first reduction of tuna fish taxes expired was given, as he finds, temporarily, namely, until the submission of the draft of the treaty. When the draft treaty was submitted, he explained the commitment no longer existed. To this he added that he felt obliged to tell me officially that he did not know whether or not the Mexican Government was intending to raise the taxes on American tuna fishing boats.

"I said to Dr. Tello that the commitment was mentioned in the Department's telegram [21] which he will recall I read to him during last Saturday's interview. I said that I remembered distinctly before Mr. Reveley [22] left a year ago he had repeatedly mentioned the fact that the Mexican Government had agreed not to raise taxes on American tuna fishing boats or alter the *status quo* of our mutual fishing relations until both governments had an opportunity to negotiate a treaty. I said to Dr. Tello that I would inform the State Department of his observations with regard to the status of the commitment as it exists in the Foreign Office files but I pointed out that the American Government, as expressed in the Department's telegram, is desirous of negotiating a fishery treaty as soon as possible; so all questions of

---

[17] Neither printed. In telegram 1255, the Department requested the Embassy's views on new Mexican fishery laws and informed the Embassy that an instruction was en route "to reiterate to Mex (if Emb perceives no objection) this Govt's refusal recognize justification interference by Mex with US fishing vessels outside three mile territorial waters", and that in view of the hopes for an early reconciliation of any fisheries conflicts between the two nations by treaty, previous unwarranted vessel seizures would not be further protested at that time (812.628/12–1147). In telegram 1437, Ambassador Thurston reported: (1) No decision had been made to submit new fishery law to the Mexican Congress; (2) Question of raising tuna taxes was still pending and had been pending since last year; (3) As to renewal of conversations on the fishery treaty, the matter would be taken up with the Foreign Minister the next day on his return; and (4) presentation of note respecting US territorial-waters position might preferably wait until the Embassy had received commitment date treaty discussions from Mexico as the note might create delay in Mexico's designating date for conference. The Department indicated approval of these suggestions in telegram 1289, December 19, 1947, 5 p. m., not printed. (812.628/12–1647)
[18] Manuel Tello.
[19] Raymond H. Geist.
[20] Vicente Sánchez Gavito, Mexican Counselor of Embassy in the United States.
[21] Reference is apparently to telegram 1255, December 11, 1947, 3 p. m., to Mexico City.
[22] Paul J. Reveley, formerly Second Secretary of Embassy and Consul in Mexico.

interest to the two Governments can be settled and I said I was sure that the Mexican Government shared the views of the United States Government to the effect that under such circumstances it would be helpful in getting on with the negotiations not to alter conditions under which present fishing relations are carried on and that I was sure that the Foreign Office was disposed to share this view.

"Señor Tello assented in general to this but reiterated that he was obliged to tell me officially that the commitment not to raise tuna fish taxes was a temporary one.

"I reminded Señor Tello that he expected during the course of this week to advise the Embassy as to the possible date of beginning negotiations for a fishery treaty. He replied that he was leaving presently for a short vacation to be gone until the second of January and that in the meantime Señor Córdova,[23] who had returned from Habana, would get in touch with me in a few days with regard to this matter which was depending upon the decision of the Foreign Minister.[24] He said Señor Córdova would be able to advise the Embassy whether the Mexican Government would be able to proceed with negotiations for a fishery treaty or whether it would be delayed for some time longer.

"I gathered from the tenor of Señor Tello's conversation that some conflict may be going on between the Foreign Office and the Ministry of Marine with regard (1) to the question of raising tuna fish taxes and (2) the date for commencement of negotiations, it having been indicated by the cautious reservations made by Señor Tello that probable some action is in the offing before the Mexicans are willing to lay their cards on the table for the negotiation of a fishery treaty."

THURSTON

812.628/12–2347 : Airgram

The Ambassador in Mexico (Thurston) to the Secretary of State

RESTRICTED MEXICO CITY, December 23, 1947.

A–1150. Referring to the Department's airgram A–923 of December 16, 1947 in which it is stated that the Department would appreciate receiving the Embassy's evaluation of past publicity regarding proposed United States-Mexican fishery treaty in Mexican publications and probable effect of these newspaper accounts on opinions of Government officials or of the public, the questions raised in the Department's airgram under reference have received the careful attention of both the Embassy and Mr. Milton J. Lindner, Chief, Fishery Mission to Mexico and the following suggestions are made with the approval of both:

In view of Mr. Lindner's statement that additional publicity at this time will stimulate opposition to the treaty, the Embassy, as directed by the Department, will not approach the Mexican Government to request permission to release in Mexico or in the United States the

---

[23] Roberto Córdova, Mexican lawyer and diplomat.
[24] Jaime Torres Bodet.

text of the 1945 draft until this matter is the subject of further instruction from the Department. In this connection Mr. Lindner has observed that, in his opinion, if the 1945 draft is released in Mexico, it will probably be impossible to negotiate successfully a fishery treaty with Mexico on account of the opposition which certain provisions of that draft will raise among Mexican fishing interests and other interested parties.

The Embassy understands the Department's observation with regard to importance of consulting the American fishing industry and the Congress on international problems of concern to the fishing industry; it is considered essential, however, in this connection that these consultations be conducted on a confidential basis, particularly avoiding publicity which would have the effect, as stated above, of raising probable insuperable barriers through arousing pressure upon the authorities here by Mexican fishing interests. The Embassy is of the opinion that no public release of substance of treaty should be made until conclusion of the negotiations with Mexico; and then release should be simultaneous by both Governments. However, the Embassy considers a confidential disclosure to United States fishing industry is highly advisable.

Further with reference to past publicity, it is thought that past publicity has not adversely influenced the attitude of Government officials. Nevertheless, the reaction of the public and particularly of Mexican fishing interests on the west coast has been the cause of inordinately stirring up opposition with the probable results that responsible officials have hesitated and delayed making definite decisions toward getting on with negotiations for a United States-Mexican fishery treaty, not only vis-à-vis the Mexican commercial interest involved but certain powerful political personalities who have a definite interest in exploiting Mexico's fishing resources.

THURSTON

JOINT UNITED STATES-MEXICAN CAMPAIGN AGAINST FOOT-AND-MOUTH DISEASE [25]

611.1256/1–2347 : Telegram

The Ambassador in Mexico (Thurston) to the Secretary of State

CONFIDENTIAL   U.S. URGENT   MEXICO CITY, January 23—11 p. m.
NIACT

87. For Guy Ray, Mexican Division, for immediate delivery to Under Secretary Acheson.

---

[25] Continued from *Foreign Relations*, 1946, vol. XI, pp. 1048–1051. See also an article by John A. Hopkins, Acting Head of the Latin American Division, Office of Foreign Agricultural Relations, Department of Agriculture, entitled "The Joint Campaign Against Foot-and-Mouth Disease in Mexico", Department of State *Bulletin*, April 20, 1947, p. 710.

1. Acting upon instructions conveyed by telephone by Mr. Guy Ray, I suggested this evening to the Minister for Foreign Affairs [26] that a written request for our assistance in controlling and eradicating the outbreak of foot-and-mouth disease in Mexico be addressed to the Government of the United States by the Mexican Government. Señor Torres Bodet informed me with emphasis that the Mexican Government would not and could not present such a written request.

2. I said to the Minister that I perceived although I did not agree with the element of "amour propre" that presumably governed the feelings of the Mexican Government in this respect and that I felt that the situation called for equal perception on the part of the Mexican Government of the situation in the United States. I pointed out that an intransigent attitude by Mexico at this time might well provoke active resentment in the United States and charges that the danger threatening our cattle industry had been brought on by Mexico in disregard of the Sanitary Convention [27] and specific warnings based on the earlier violation of that Convention. I suggested accordingly that we endeavor to devise an arrangement that might achieve the results desired in Washington while meeting the views of his Government.

3. Señor Torres Bodet then drafted with me, in the understanding that the proposal is tentative and may well be rejected by his Government when it is laid before it tonight or tomorrow, the following suggested course of action.

4. The Sub-commission on Animal Industry of the United States-Mexico Agricultural Commission the first meeting of which will take place tomorrow afternoon and on which our representatives are Dr. Fladness [28] and Mr. Don Stoops,[29] should draft a joint report setting forth the facts of the situation resulting from the presence of foot-and-mouth disease in Mexico and recommending to the Government of the United States and to the Mexican Government that an arrangement be concluded for scientific, economic, and technical cooperation. Upon receipt of this report an exchange of notes should be effected by

---

[26] Jaime Torres Bodet.
[27] For convention safeguarding livestock interests through the prevention of infectious and contagious diseases, signed at Washington, March 16, 1928, see Department of State Treaty Series No. 808, or 46 Stat. (pt. 2) 2451.
[28] Severin O. Fladness, Assistant Chief of the Bureau of Animal Industry, Department of Agriculture.
[29] Assistant Agricultural Attaché in Mexico.

the two governments citing the report and indicating the readiness of each Government to engage in a campaign for the control and eradication of the disease through technical, economic, and scientific cooperation to be conducted under the auspices of the Mixed Commission.

5. It is the Minister's thought that by this procedure the question of a direct appeal for our assistance can be obviated and that any reluctance on our part to proffer assistance or any impediment to such action would be overcome.

6. The Minister told me quite frankly that widely divergent views are entertained by the several highest members of the Mexican Government with respect to the methods by which the outbreak of foot-and-mouth disease should be dealt with. I believe that those who are opposed to the slaughter method, which they assume we advocate, base their attitude upon the belief that that method would be resented and opposed by the owners of stock to be slaughtered with possible political repercussions and I suspect that these feelings are being fomented probably by the advocacy which we must assume is being engaged in by the Argentine and Brazilian veterinary experts in favor of milder alternative methods.

7. Dr. Fladness arrived this afternoon but has not yet been in consultation with the Mexicans. I have discussed the foregoing text with him and he authorizes me to say that he feels that the proposed course of action worked out with the Minister for Foreign Affairs and described in paragraphs above would be feasible although he fears that a joint report by the Mixed Commission could not be agreed upon and signed before Monday next.[30]

THURSTON

---

[30] United States-Mexican agreement was reached by exchange of notes of January 28 and 29, 1947, providing for a general plan of action; notes not printed. An exchange of notes of February 7 and 8 (not printed) was concluded with further reference to United States-Mexican cooperation toward control and eradication of foot and mouth disease.

Public Law 8, an Act to authorize the Secretary of Agriculture to cooperate with the Government of Mexico in the control and eradication of foot-and-mouth disease and rinderpest was approved on February 28, 1947 (61 Stat. 7). Public Law 22, making an appropriation for expenses incident to the control and eradication of foot-and-mouth disease and rinderpest ($9,000,000.00) was approved on March 27, 1947 (61 Stat. 24).

By a United States-Mexican exchange of notes, March 17 and 18, 1947, a resolution was approved as constituting the basis of an agreement for cooperation between the two countries for the control and eradication of the foot and mouth disease; for texts of notes, see Department of State, Treaties and Other International Acts Series (TIAS) No. 2404.

612.325/4-147

Memorandum of Conversation, by Mr. William G. MacLean of the Division of Mexican Affairs

[WASHINGTON,] April 1, 1947.

Subject: Withdrawal of note no. 1030 of February 26, 1947, regarding Zebu cattle, by the Mexican Ambassador.

Participants: His Excellency Señor Dr. Don Antonio Espinosa de los Monteros, Ambassador of Mexico;
Señor Don Vicente Sánchez Gavito, Counselor of the Mexican Embassy;
Mr. Ellis O. Briggs, Director, Office of American Republic Affairs;
Mr. William G. MacLean, Division of Mexican Affairs.

The Mexican Ambassador came in as prearranged to request the return of his note no. 1030 of February 26, 1947, a copy of which is attached,[31] regarding testimony on the importation into Mexico of Zebu bulls from Brazil by Mr. Guy W. Ray, Chief of the Division of Mexican Affairs, before a Congressional committee.[32] The Ambassador had stated in his note that his Government was firmly convinced that the importation was in no way a violation of the Sanitary Convention of March 16, 1928, between the Government of the United States and the Government of Mexico.

The Ambassador stated that it was now his conviction that the important thing was for the two Governments to cooperate in every possible way for the eradication of the foot and mouth disease in Mexico and that the question of antecedents should not be allowed to threaten that cooperation. He enlarged on this thesis and included a statement that his Government considered that the importation of bulls was not a violation of the Convention. Mr. Briggs replied that this Government had demonstrated by its action that its viewpoint was that every other consideration should be subordinated to the fullest cooperation in stopping the progress of this destructive disease and to bring about its complete eradication as soon as possible. He said that this Government, as the Mexican Government knew, was of the opinion that the importation of these cattle into Mexico from infected areas was a violation of the Convention. He said that the situation was one on which it was desirable to agree to disagree in the interests of insuring complete cooperation in the wiping out of the disease at the earliest possible date. The note was then returned to the Ambassador.

---

[31] Not printed.
[32] See Hearings Before the Committee on Agriculture, House of Representatives, 80th Cong., 1st sess., on H.R. 1819 (S. 568), February 10, 11, and 12, 1947.

The Mexican Ambassador referred to the appropriations made to carry on the campaign to June 30 and expressed the hope that this Government would take the necessary steps to participate in the work until the disease was completely stamped out.[33] He was assured of the continuing interest of this Government in assisting Mexico, as well as preventing the spread of the disease toward or into the United States.

(Attached hereto for the records of the Department is a copy of the note which had been prepared in the Department as a reply to the Mexican note under reference.[34] The Mexican Embassy had been informally advised of the nature of this proposed reply, and apparently the strong evidence therein supporting the Department's stand led to the Mexican Ambassador's request that his note of February 26 be returned to him.)

611.1256/8–447 : Telegram

The Ambassador in Mexico (Thurston) to the Secretary of State

CONFIDENTIAL   US URGENT   MEXICO CITY, August 4, 1947—1 p. m.

853. For Reveley, Mexican Division.[35] See my confidential airmail letter July 29.[34] President Alemán[36] spoke to me at length and with great earnestness with respect to what he described as the political dangers of the campaign for the eradication of the foot and mouth disease as it is now being conducted. He stated that the position of prominence occupied by the American appraisers and paymasters directs resentment toward them which may produce anti-American sentiment and exposes them to danger. Moreover the procedure of the American appraisers and paymasters retards the campaign because they operate on an individual appraisal and payment basis whereas the President feels that a more rapid mass appraisal and payment system with the Americans in the background would be more efficacious and would make for greater speed.

The President then stated that he has reports from scientists familiar with the foot and mouth disease in France, Denmark and England which lead him to believe that a simultaneous program of vaccination should be carried out together with the present American slaughter

---

[33] Public Law 122, approved June 27, 1947, Public Law 161, approved July 30, 1947, and Public Law 271, approved July 30, 1947, made appropriations for expenses incident to the control and eradication of foot-and-mouth disease, amounting to $1,500,000, $5,000,000, and $100,000 respectively; for texts, see 61 Stat. 185, 245, and 617, respectively.
[34] Not printed.
[35] Paul J. Reveley, Assistant Chief of the Division of Mexican Affairs.
[36] Miguel Alemán Valdes, President of Mexico.

campaign. He proposes accordingly that a commission of experts from the countries named, together with American experts, be created to work out such a combined vaccination and slaughter campaign. He made it clear that he is not opposed to slaughter but feels that is not the solution of Mexico's problem and that the vaccination method should be given a full trial.

Licenciado Alemán then stated that he has found it impossible to cause his views to be acceded to by the Joint Commission with respect to methods of operation and plan of campaign, and that he had been led to believe that if he were to insist upon the installation of the vaccination system American cooperation might be jeopardized.

All these considerations, the President stated, have caused him to feel that it is necessary to give the campaign political as well as technical guidance, and he accordingly urgently proposed that a person of high political standing be designated by President Truman to reside in or frequently visit Mexico for the purpose of supervising and exercising broad control based on other than technical considerations over the American section of the Joint Commission. At the same time he would designate a Mexican citizen of comparable high political experience and understanding to collaborate with the agent appointed by President Truman in concurrent control over the Mexican-US Commission. Each agent would have direct access and would report to his President.

I undertook to convey the foregoing message directly to the President and I accordingly request that it be forwarded to him at once. A second message follows.

THURSTON

611.1256/8-447 : Telegram

The Ambassador in Mexico (Thurston) to the Secretary of State

CONFIDENTIAL   US URGENT   MEXICO CITY, August 4, 1947—6 p. m.

858. For Reveley, Mexican Division. Dr. Shahan,[38] Messrs. Bohan,[39] Gibbs, Stoops, and Geist [40] have reviewed with me the opinions and suggestions of President Alemán as reported in confidential tel 853, August 4, and have drafted the following comment thereon:

1. With respect to American personnel, this problem has been recognized by both sections of Joint Commission and general agreement

---

[38] Maurice S. Shahan, Bureau of Animal Industry, Department of Agriculture; American Co-Director of the Joint Mexican-United States Foot-and-Mouth Disease Commission.
[39] Merwin L. Bohan, Counselor of Embassy for Economic Affairs.
[40] Raymond H. Geist, Counselor of Embassy.

has been reached whereby Americans will remain in background on all possible occasions. It is felt, however, that it is essential to have Mexican [*American?*] personnel operating close enough to the front to make sure that appraisals are just and reasonable and that American funds are handled properly. In this connection it is agreed in the Commission that the greatest need is for a more ample corps of qualified Mexican appraisers and paymasters with which American counterparts can collaborate. At present the ratio of Mexicans to Americans is one to three. Where qualified Mexicans have been provided there have been few difficulties in appraisals and little untoward public reaction. Under overall plan for prosecution of campaign it is felt that the classes of susceptible animals to be appraised and slaughtered are too variable to set general blanket appraisal values. Furthermore, it is contemplated that number appraisers and paymasters requested from US, if matched by similar qualified Mexicans, will be sufficient slaughter all possible susceptible animals during coming year on basis present appraisal and reimbursement procedures and will present no impediment to campaign. It should be pointed out that basic delay in program during past several days has been lack Mexican Govt funds with which to pay indemnities for small animals *designed* for slaughter. There have been cases where hogs, sheep and goats were slaughtered and have not yet been paid for by Mexican paymasters. In some such cases owners have refused to submit cattle for slaughter even though they have been shown cash for payment by American paymasters.

During the recent Commission meeting it was proposed that Mexico make monthly contribution to the Joint Commission indemnity fund of $1,500,000, US currency per month, and that indemnities for all classes susceptible livestock be paid from that common fund, US to bear all expenses above $1,500,000 monthly, excepting expenses of Mexican Army and Mexican Government personnel. Such plan believed essential basis experiences to date. It is felt that all slaughter operations must be simultaneous and coordinated if campaign is to succeed. Although Joint Commission felt that such plan would be advantageous to Mexican Govt, its approval has not yet been forthcoming.

Another important element causing delaying slaughter and inciting resentment among owners has been lack authority under Mexican law to outright condemnation affected and exposed animals. A proposed decree along these lines has been drawn up by Joint Commission and has been in hands of Mexican Govt for approximately 10 days without definite action.

2. Proposed vaccination-slaughter program regarded by American

Section Commission as contrary US policy and interest inasmuch as they feel chances eradication will be lessened if not eliminated thereby. They have expressed doubt of continued American support if program is so compromised. Proposed International Commission, supposedly to be resident in Mexico, might lead to controversy prejudicial to US. American Section Commission feel that in view US is bearing bulk financial burden campaign its views should not be subjected to compromising actions other countries not actively participating financially and otherwise in campaign. It does, however, recommend consultation between research scientists of US and Mexico with those of selected countries, and definitely favors cooperation of US and Mexican research scientists with countries having established research facilities. It also strongly favors establishment soon as possible foot and mouth disease research institute outside Mexico.

3. As regards designation of person of high political standing by President Truman to collaborate with person of similar qualifications appointed by President Alemán in concurrent control of Mexican-US Commission, we feel that President of US should be protected from engaging so directly in a campaign which, although basically technical in nature, has many political ramifications. It is our understanding that US Secretary of Agriculture [41] has direct responsibility to President and people of US for success this campaign and we believe by-passing Secretary on matters such importance, particularly where so many technical aspects are involved, would only lead to confusion and overall weakening of campaign. Members of Commission are well aware of political and economic significance of this eradication program.

It the course of our examination of this problem, we came to the conclusion that President Alemán either has not been convinced by the views of the American section of the Joint Commission with regard to the manner in which the campaign should be conducted (which views are shared by the technical members of the Mexican section of the Commission) or has been influenced by foreign and Mexican advisers hostile to the slaughter method. We believe that the situation created by President Alemán's present attitude toward the campaign is sufficiently critical to warrant the recommendation that the American viewpoint be authoritatively explained to him by the US Secretary of Agriculture in person and we accordingly recommend that Mr. Anderson be directed by the President to visit Mexico at an early date for this purpose. Such a course of action would remove the necessity for designating the special representative requested by Alemán, a

---

[41] Clinton P. Anderson.

measure which we are convinced would only result in confusion and delay.

THURSTON

611.1256/8-647 : Telegram

The Acting Secretary of State to the Embassy in Mexico

CONFIDENTIAL WASHINGTON, August 15, 1947—6 p. m.

772. Meeting August 12 Agriculture of representatives Agriculture including Under Secretary,[42] Bureau Animal Industry, representative Dr. Steelman's office [43] and Dept for purpose determining policy current aphthous problems reurtels 853, 858, 859, August 4 and 869, August 6.[44]

Agreed with MexGovt US appraisers and paymasters should not occupy prominent position beyond necessary assure just appraisals and disbursements US funds consistent responsibility American Section. Correction present situation requires employment additional Mex personnel. Agriculture agrees to appraisals group basis whenever practical. US Govt cannot agree to simultaneous vaccination program because inadequate but will consider holding conference Mexican, American and European scientists preferably in Washington lay groundwork further research England where large staff trained and experienced personnel available. Proposes adequate publicity showing that both Mex and US actively pursuing research all phases disease.

Concerning broad control this Govt cannot agree designation special Presidential representative. Secretary Agriculture responsible to President and Congress operations American Section and disbursement American funds, and Ambassador is personal representative President Truman in Mex. Designation of another person to make political decisions would create confusion and hamper campaign.

US Govt holds agreement immediate future re financial participation essential future effectiveness joint campaign. Would accept plan whereby MexGovt maintains army units and Mex personnel in field and pays 6 million pesos monthly into Joint Commission toward *all* other expenses, US to supply all additional funds needed estimated at $5,000,000 US. Arrangement would permit coordinated field operation including immediate indemnities *all* domestic animals slaughtered, purchase and delivery costs of mules, harnesses and plows, and salaries

---

[42] N. E. Dodd.
[43] John R. Steelman, Assistant to the President; Merle E. Colby, representative of Mr. Steelman's office.
[44] Telegrams 859, August 4, and 869, August 6, not printed.

of American personnel. Whereas Mex contribution would remain fixed our contribution would increase with tempo of campaign. Mex financial participation therefore on basis of not more than one peso for each US Govt dollar. Proportionately greater American participation could not be justified before Congress.

Airmail instruction follows with request that Embassy prepare detailed analysis those aspects of campaign having political and economic significance in Mex and probable effects of continuance of present program.[45]

LOVETT

611.1256/10–2747 : Telegram

The Ambassador in Mexico (Thurston) to the Secretary of State

SECRET   US URGENT   MEXICO CITY, October 27, 1947—10 a. m.

1158. Dr. Shahan and Dr. Clarkson informed me last night that they have reluctantly but definitely reached the conclusion that the campaign for the eradication of the foot-and-mouth disease from Mexico cannot succeed. Clarkson left by air last night for Washington where he will present to the Department of Agriculture his views and a tentative plan for containment and vaccination. I requested that the State Department be informed promptly of any decisions reached. In view of our adamant insistence upon the slaughter campaign and opposition to the employment of the vaccination method of treatment; in

---

[45] In instruction 1422, August 16, the Acting Secretary of State transmitted a copy of the memorandum prepared by the Division of Mexican Affairs at the conclusion of the August 12 meeting; also, a copy of a memorandum by Dr. M. R. Clarkson of the Bureau of Animal Industry, Department of Agriculture, to Dr. B. T. Simms, Chief of that Bureau. He also informed Ambassador Thurston that President Truman had approved the general policy decisions agreed to by the representatives of the Departments of State and of Agriculture at the meeting of August 12, and continued as follows:

"The Department desires that you convey the substance of the policy decisions contained in Dr. Clarkson's memorandum of August 12 orally to President Alemán and that you endeavor to convince him of the desire of this Government to continue its participation in the joint campaign to the fullest possible extent consistent with the obligations of this Government to Congress for the most efficacious expenditure of United States public funds in the conduct of the campaign. You may inform him that the President has and is according full and sympathetic consideration to the serious political and economic problems confronting President Alemán and his administration because of the eradication program, and that the United States Government desires to assist in every practical way in reaching solutions to these problems concurrently with the energetic and efficient conduct of the campaign."

In despatch 4477, August 25, from Mexico, Ambassador Thurston reported on an interview with President Alemán on August 22 at which time he had conveyed to the President the substance of the Department's telegram 772 of August 15.

For text of an exchange of notes of September 26 and October 3, 1947, making effective an agreement between the United States and Mexico, namely, a joint agreement of the Mexican-United States Commission, see TIAS No. 2404.

view of the economic consequences of the slaughter thus far accomplished of some 300,000 cattle, 20,000 oxen and large numbers of sheep, goats and swine; and in view of the resultant resentment of that part of the population affected by these measures, it is essential to our good relations with President Alemán and general Mexican-American relations that no abrupt or tactless unilateral action be taken by US. Alemán must be informed in due time of the new course to be taken and, if feasible, should be permitted to take the initiative.

THURSTON

611.1256/11-2447 : Telegram

The Ambassador in Mexico (Thurston) to the Secretary of State

RESTRICTED   MEXICO CITY, November 24, 1947—10 p. m.

1324. Mexican-American Aftosa Commission today agreed upon following recommendations: Mexican Section has presented text to Foreign Office which tomorrow will communicate to Embassy by note. Embassy requires immediate instructions to enable it complete exchange of notes endorsing recommendations.

"The session of November 24, 1947.

On this date in the offices of the Mexican–US Commission For the Eradication of Foot and Mouth Disease, 5 de Febrero, 73 Mexico D.F., the following representatives of Mexico and the US met at 5 p. m.: for Mexico, Lic. Oscar Flores, Dr. Ignacio de la Torre, Drs. José Figuero, Federico Rubio Lozano and Lauro Ortega; for the US, Dr. M. S. Shahan, Mr. Don Stoops, Drs. L. R. Noyes, F. M. Shigley and Mr. R. M. Gottfried.

The Mexican Section proposed that in view of the fact that inspections that have been carried out indicate that apparently clean zones which had not been reported with outbreaks of foot and mouth disease are actually infected, and even though the only proven method of rapid and infallible eradication is that of destruction, but considering that the destruction of the great number of susceptible animals in the infected zone would mean a tremendous economical and social impact to the country, it is necessary so as to better control and to continue on progressive eradication to adopt a combined plan of quarantines, vaccination, and destruction when necessary.

As a result of this proposition, and after an ample exchange of impressions, the following recommendations were approved:

1st: Although it is recognized that the only proved effective method by which foot and mouth disease can be eradicated is by slaughter, and although the Mexican-US Commission for the eradication of the foot and mouth disease has for the past 7 months exerted all the means at its disposal to overcome the existence of this disease in Mexico by the slaughter method, inherent conditions beyond the Commission's control have prevented accomplishment of this purpose to that degree which would justify the continuation of the slaughter method alone.

Therefore, in view of these conditions and the economic and social consequences of the continuation of the present method, it is agreed that a plan of combined quarantine, vaccination and, when necessary, slaughter should be adopted.

2nd: It is proposed that the details of this plan of operations be immediately developed and applied by the Mex-US Commission for the Eradication of Foot and Mouth Disease.

3rd: That the aforementioned resolution be brought to the attention of the two governments.

For Mexico: Lic. Oscar Flores, Ignacio de la Torre, Federico Rubio Lozano, José Figuero, Lauro Ortega.

For the United States: N. E. Dodd, B. T. Simms, M. S. Shahan, Don Stoops."

Repeat to Agriculture.[46]

THURSTON

61.1256/12–1047 : Telegram

The Acting Secretary of State to the Embassy in Mexico

RESTRICTED WASHINGTON, December 10, 1947—6 p. m.

1251. Mex-U.S. members Foot and Mouth Commission today signed eight-point agreement changing procedure in campaign.[47] Agri has requested Dept authorize exchange of notes with MexGovt. Instruction with copies of agreement will be forwarded tomorrow.

Principal changes campaign effected are (1) establishment of northern and southeastern quarantine lines with buffer zones with slaughter method exclusive north of northern quarantine line; (2) regrouping of commission forces along quarantine lines; (3) provisions research and study effect of disease; (4) setting up facilities for vaccine research and testing; (5) stoppage of salvage operations. It is doubtful Congress will appropriate funds for participation vaccination program in central infected zone, other than for research and testing. Shahan and Stoops returning this weekend.

LOVETT

[In despatch 69, January 13, 1948, from Mexico, Ambassador Thurston summarized statements he had made to Under Secretary of

---

[46] By an exchange of notes of November 24 and November 26, 1947, the United States and Mexico agreed to these recommendations; for texts of notes, see TIAS No. 2404.

[47] In instruction 1621, December 12, 1947, there was enclosed a copy of the December 10 agreement, and the Ambassador in Mexico was instructed to take the necessary steps to effect the agreement by means of an exchange of notes with the Mexican Government. For the United States-Mexican exchange of notes of December 15, 1947, and January 3, 1948, see TIAS No. 2404.

Foreign Affairs Manuel Tello on December 15, 1947, in delivering the Embassy's note which was based on the Department's instruction no. 1621 of December 12, as follows:

". . . considerable concern now prevails in the United States with respect to the existence of foot-and-mouth disease in this country and the threat it constitutes to our own animal industry. I said that this concern was reflected in the attitude of our Congress and that it would be most unfortunate indeed if the disease should be allowed, under the new procedure, to get out of control. I said that the consequences of such a tragic development could be very disagreeable in the international field. I urged that the Mexican authorities be informed of my remarks and that in particular the Mexican Army be urged to give its fullest cooperation to the campaign so that this time, and under the new procedure, it might be successful. I made these statements in such a meaningful manner that there can be no doubt whatsoever that Señor Tello fully grasped their import." (611.1256/1–1348)]

ARRANGEMENTS BY THE UNITED STATES AND MEXICO REGARDING TEMPORARY MIGRATION OF AGRICULTURAL AND OTHER WORKERS INTO THE UNITED STATES [48]

811.504 Mexico/2–747

The Ambassador in Mexico (Thurston) to the Secretary of State

RESTRICTED   FIRST PRIORITY   MÉXICO, D. F., February 7, 1947.
No. 2498

SIR: I have the honor to refer to the Embassy's telegram No. 1147 of December 30, 1946, the Department's telegram No. 73 of January 17, 1947, subsequent exchanges of messages [49] concerning the threat of the Mexican authorities to impede the return to this country of Mexican laborers found to be illegally in the United States and to the conversations between the representatives of the two governments conducted in Mexico City during the ten days ending February 4, 1947.[50]

Participants in the conversations were as follows:

For the United States:

    Mr. William G. MacLean, Mexican Division, Department of State.
    Mr. Ugo Carusi, Commissioner of Immigration and Naturalization, Department of Justice.
    Mr. Albert Del Guercio, Director of the Los Angeles District, Immigration and Naturalization Service.

---

[48] Continued from *Foreign Relations*, 1946, vol. XI, pp. 1017–1036.
[49] None printed.
[50] For a statement released to the press on February 6 on the United States-Mexican discussions, see Department of State *Bulletin*, February 16, 1947, p. 303.

Mr. Maurice L. Stafford, First Secretary and Consul General, American Embassy, Mexico.
Mr. Harry F. Brown, as observer for the Office of Labor, Department of Agriculture.

For Mexico:

Señor Alfonso Guerra, Oficial Mayor of the Secretaría de Relaciones Exteriores.
Licenciado Benito Coquet, Oficial Mayor of the Secretaría de Gobernación.
Licenciado Jesús Castorena, Oficial Mayor of the Secretaría de Trabajo.
Señor Arcadio Ojeda García, Jefe del Departamento de Migración, Secretaría de Gobernación.
Arquitecto Jorge Medellín, Secretaría de Trabajo.
Señor Manuel Aguilar, Jefe del Departamento de Asuntos Comerciales y del Servicio Consular, Secretaría de Relaciones Exteriores.

The interested officials in the Department were kept currently informed of the progress of the conference by Mr. MacLean and this despatch is prepared as a matter of record and to present certain phases which were brought out during the various sessions.

At the outset, the political implications of the Mexican proposals were evident and towards the close of the session, during the discussions of certain disputed points, this was disclosed by Mr. Guerra, the *Oficial Mayor* of the Foreign Office, and later confirmed by Dr. Manuel Tello, the Under-Secretary, in a conversation between him and Messrs. MacLean and Stafford.

Before the sessions commenced the Mexican delegation presented the following agenda for discussion:

1. Illegal status of Mexican workers in the United States, because of their entry without a previous contract.
2. Illegal status of workers employed in the United States, after expiration of their contracts.
3. Comparison between status of the workers employed in the United States, with that of those workers who initially entered without a contract.
4. Use of the Mexican workers in the United States in new employment.
5. Reports from the Mexican Consulates on the number of workers employed along the border areas, as well as on deportees.

It was evident also the Mexicans wished that any agreement which might result would involve commitments on the part of the Government of the United States in connection both with the work contracts between American employers or employers' associations and the Mexican workmen, as well as with the enforcement of such contracts. They insisted virtually on a government-to-government agreement. This was successfully opposed by the American delegation in view of the instructions given to Mr. MacLean prior to his departure from the United States.

. . . .

Villanueva Garza, while stationed at Mexicali, a post to which his acquaintances state he wishes to return, objected to the admission of the illegal entrants through the ports of the territory and for a time refused to receive any who were unable to prove at least six months' previous residence in the territory. This for a time compelled the transportation of many at United States government expense to Nogales and El Paso.

The presence of Messrs. Carusi and Del Guercio and of Mr. Harry F. Brown, the latter as observer for the Office of Labor of the Department of Agriculture, was of great benefit and their knowledge of the laws and procedure governing the temporary admission of aliens was availed of.

The draft protocol in English and Spanish was finally signed after the departure of Messrs. Carusi and Del Guercio of the American delegation and of Mr. Coquet of the Mexican delegation. Their signatures will be obtained at a later date and when completed will be transmitted to Mr. MacLean who will attach the proper copies to the original of this despatch.

The protocol finally accepted and signed, and which is subject to approval by an exchange of notes,[51] provides for the following:

(*a*) That a proposal be submitted to the Government of the United States for the return to Mexico of all Mexican laborers illegally in the United States, preferably via Mexicali, Ciudad Juárez, and Reynosa, with the view of making selections which may permit their legal return to employment in the United States under protection of contracts.

(*b*) Work contracts to be entered into by the laborers and the American employers or associations of employers after permission has been granted to the latter by the United States Immigration and Naturalization Service; the contracts to be signed at stations to be established by the Mexican authorities at certain as yet not designated ports, and the signing to be witnessed by representatives of the Immigration Service and of the Mexican government.

---

[51] In instruction 873, March 3, 1947, Ambassador Thurston was authorized to exchange notes with the Mexican Foreign Office to make effective the recommendations contained in the memoranda of conversations under consideration (811.504 Mexico/2–747). For the United States-Mexican exchange of notes signed at Mexico City on March 10, 1947, on the subject "Mexican Agricultural Workers: Legal Employment of Certain Workers Who Entered the United States Illegally", see Department of State, Treaties and Other International Acts Series (TIAS) No. 1857. For a supplementary but separate agreement of the same date providing that the March 10 agreement was applicable to the State of Texas, see TIAS No. 1858.

(c) Both governments will continue their efforts to impede the illegal crossing of farm workers. The Mexicans agree to take steps to prevent the sale of railway and bus tickets to contingents of workers at strategic points, especially at Punta Peñasco, and to discourage the congregation of workers along the border.

(d) That the possibility of punishing the employers of illegal crossers will be made the subject of study, and that employers who hire illegal entrants be denied the right of contracting.

(e) That the employers pay the cost of transportation of contracted workers from the American border towns opposite the places of recruitment to the localities of their employment, and return.

(f) That as a special consideration to prospective employers in Texas and in recognition of the friendly attitude of the present governor and the efforts of the Texas Good Neighbor Commission, the right to contract Mexicans for ranch work in that state will be extended, with the understanding that such action is to be considered as temporary and as not to constitute a precedent.

(g) That the present practice of granting immigration visas to male members of the working class only to those bearing passports specifically approving their emigration, except those with close family ties in the United States, be continued.

Respectfully yours,

For the Ambassador:
M. L. STAFFORD
Consul General

811.504 Mexico/4-247

The Ambassador in Mexico (Thurston) to the Secretary of State

FIRST PRIORITY
No. 3237

MÉXICO, D. F., April 2, 1947.

SIR: I have the honor to refer to the Embassy's Note No. 697 of March 25, 1947,[52] a copy of which is in the Department's records, regarding certain supplementary provisions in relation to the employment of Mexican agricultural workers in the United States. As stated in that note, it was understood that the note, together with the Foreign Minister's reply in the same terms, would constitute an agreement between the Government of the United States and the Mexican Government on the provisions cited.

The Embassy is now in receipt of a note from the Foreign Minister

---

[52] For U.S.-Mexican exchange of notes signed at Mexico City March 25 and April 2, 1947, effecting agreement on the temporary migration of Mexican agricultural workers, supplementing the agreement of August 4, 1942 (Department of State Executive Agreement Series No. 278) as revised April 26, 1943 (Department of State Executive Agreement Series No. 351), see TIAS No. 1710. For documentation on the 1942 and 1943 agreements, see *Foreign Relations*, 1942, vol. VI, pp. 537 ff., and *ibid.*, 1943, vol. VI, pp. 531 ff.

which quotes in translation the Embassy's note referred to above. It then concludes, in translation, as follows:

"In reply I am pleased to inform Your Excellency that, recognizing the willingness of the representatives of the United States Department of Agriculture to coordinate their point of view with that of the Mexican Intersecretarial Committee, my Government manifests its conformity with the terms of the above quoted note, considering them as supplementary to the agreement of April 26, 1943, on the understanding that if, in practice, differences of interpretation should arise regarding the application of the above-mentioned agreement of 1943, or the additional clauses above cited, my Government hopes that the text most favorable to the worker will apply".

Respectfully yours, For the Ambassador:
DOUGLAS FLOOD
Second Secretary of Embassy

811.504 Mexico/8-647 : Airgram

The Secretary of State to the Embassy in Mexico

RESTRICTED WASHINGTON, August 6, 1947.

A-653. Reference is made to your exchange of notes of March 10, 1947,[53] with the Mexican Foreign Office, making effective an arrangement for the recruiting of Mexican workers, illegally in the United States, by American growers through recruiting centers established at three border points in Mexico. The Commissioner of Immigration and Naturalization, Department of Justice, has requested the Department under date of July 29, 1947, to approach the Mexican Government with a view to arranging, if possible, for the recruitment of 10,000 additional Mexican agricultural workers for employment in the border states as cotton pickers during the coming season. Mr. Carusi states that the conditions of admission would be those applicable to aliens now admitted under contract pursuant to the agreement contained in the exchange of notes under reference. He further states that the original period of admission would not extend beyond December 31, 1947.

You are requested to make representations to the Mexican Government with a view to securing its agreement to the recruiting of these additional 10,000 workers through the presently operating recruiting stations and under the pertinent conditions set forth in your notes no. 673 and 675 of March 10. Please inform the Department by telegram or telephone of the reply since the workers specified will need to be recruited beginning shortly after September 1. The workers requested

[53] TIAS No. 1857.

are in addition to the so-called "wetbacks", the recruiting of which will continue; the additional workers requested are not the so-called "wetbacks". Recruiting of "wetbacks" will continue as long as they are available, but their numbers are not considered sufficient.

MARSHALL

811.504 Mexico/8–2547

The Ambassador in Mexico (Thurston) to the Secretary of State

RESTRICTED   FIRST PRIORITY   MEXICO, August 25, 1947.
No. 4458

SIR: I have the honor to refer to the Department's telegram No. 774 of August 15, 1947,[54] instructing that the contents of its airgram No. 653 of August 6, 1947, relating to the recruitment of 10,000 additional Mexican agricultural workers under the agreement of March 10, 1947, be submitted formally to the Mexican Foreign Office.

There are enclosed a copy of the Embassy's Note No. 1307 dated August 19, 1947, and a translated copy of Note No. 3949 dated August 22, 1947,[55] received today from the Foreign Office in reply, from which it will be observed that the request for additional workers under the agreement of last March has been refused. The Mexican Government is willing, however, to furnish workers if they are contracted in accordance with the agreement entered into on August 4, 1942, amended in 1943.

In informal conversations at the Foreign Office it was pointed out by the *Oficial Mayor* that the agreement of last March contained no provision for the recruitment of workers who are not wetbacks. That official stressed the fact that the March agreement dealt solely with Mexican workers who were found illegally in the United States and who were returned to Mexico for documentation, which would permit their legal reentry into the United States. He mentioned that the Ministry had to consider the pressure of public opinion, which would censure recruitment on a wetback basis, depriving workers of the advantages accruing under the 1942 agreement, such as, higher pay, medical attention, and provision for transportation. He also stated that to his knowledge approximately 130,000 wetbacks are in the United States and that only 3,000 have been processed through the recruiting stations established in April following the agreement of last March. He complained that farmers in Texas were not disposed to cooperate in returning wetbacks in accordance with the agreement and that the Mexican Government could not expose itself to justifiable

---

[54] Not printed.
[55] Neither printed.

public criticism by acceding to this request, which would only aggravate the border problem and result in further exploitation of Mexican labor, particularly in the State of Texas, where the greatest problem of racial discrimination exists.

Respectfully yours,

For the Ambassador:
FORREST K. GEERKEN
Second Secretary of Embassy

811.504 Mexico/10-1647 : Telegram

The Ambassador in Mexico (Thurston) to the Secretary of State

RESTRICTED   US URGENT   MEXICO CITY, October 16, 1947—7 p. m.

1124. Embassy today received Foreign Office note 34231 October 15 [56] referring supplementary agreement for contracting workers in Texas signed January 31 confirmed in exchange of notes of March 10, 1947 (Embsdes 3090 March 14 [56]) and stating that in view fact that as regards Mexican workers in Texas stimulation [*stipulations?*] of general agreement have not been fulfilled at least to desired extent and taking account hopes not realized favorably for solving discrimination against Mexicans in Texas. Mexican Government resolved terminate supplementary agreement and consequently will no longer authorize contracts Mexican laborers found illegally in Texas. Copy and translation note being forwarded by pouch.

THURSTON

811.504 Mexico/10-1647 : Airgram

The Acting Secretary of State to the Embassy in Mexico

RESTRICTED   WASHINGTON, October 27, 1947.

A-803. Reference is made to the Embassy's telegram 1124 of October 16, 1947, in reference to the contracting of workers for the State of Texas under the agreement of March 10, 1947, and to the agreement of April 26, 1943, providing for the recruiting of Mexican agricultural workers. The termination of the supplementary agreement of March 10, 1947 by the Mexican Government, which prevents workers being contracted for the State of Texas, has caused considerable concern to agricultural employers in that State, and the Immigration and Naturalization Service and the Department have been receiving urgent requests for assistance as is indicated by the various memoranda of conversations with American growers, copies of which have been forwarded to the Embassy through usual channels.

---

[56] Not printed.

The termination of the administration of workers under the agreement of April 26, 1943, as of December 31, 1947, in accordance with an Act of Congress,[57] has also resulted in numerous approaches to the Immigration Service and the Department by agricultural employers in various states who wish to retain the majority of the workers now in the United States under a system of private contracts.

In reply to petitions for assistance in the two cases cited above, the Immigration Service and the Department have indicated that the availability of workers ultimately depends upon the willingness of the Mexican Government to make its nationals available and that that willingness in large part will no doubt depend upon the terms offered and the guarantees which would insure compliance with those terms. The Immigration Service has received applications from certain groups of growers in regard to these matters and has written the Department requesting that the Department arrange with the Mexican Government for a conference on these labor matters at the earliest possible date with a view to clarifying the present situation and to continuing the supply of workers which may be needed in the coming months or for an even longer period. You are therefore requested to approach the Mexican Government with a request for such conversations between representatives of the two Governments. The Immigration Service and the Department would prefer to have these conversations in Washington, especially so in view of the fact that the large majority of previous conversations on this matter have been in Mexico City. It is considered desirable to include among the representatives of each country at least one official who has had direct experience with these programs at the border and the American representatives will include one or more officials of this kind at least on an advisory basis. The Immigration Service will probably be represented by either Assistant Commissioner Joseph Savoretti or Assistant Commissioner Willard F. Kelly, or both, and the Department by William G. MacLean, Division of Mexican Affairs.

LOVETT

811.504 Mexico/11–1347 : Telegram

The Ambassador in Mexico (Thurston) to the Secretary of State

RESTRICTED   US URGENT   MEXICO CITY, November 13, 1947—7 p. m.
NIACT

1264. ReDepgam A-803, October 27. Formal note dated November 13 received today Mexican Minister Foreign Relations[58] agreeing to

---

[57] Public Law No. 40, approved April 28, 1947, provided that the farm labor supply program should be extended to December 31, 1947, and thereafter liquidated in 30 days (61 Stat. 55).

[58] Jaime Torres Bodet; his note was in reply to Ambassador Thurston's note of November 10, 1947, neither printed.

conduct intergovernment conversations and expressing hope American authorities willing agree to accept following points as basis for conversations:

a. Contracting Mexican laborers not to be authorized in states of United States where discriminatory acts against Mexicans have been committed.

b. US Government to adopt necessary administrative or legal measures to prevent movement Mexican workers from one state to another without consent of worker and previous authorization of Mexican Government.

c. Basis for contracting to be agreement of April 26, 1943, with necessary amendments offsetting increases cost of living since that date.

Mexican delegates will have instructions to examine practical result of recommendation following discussions last January, February whereby US authorities would study possibility adopting legal measures adequately punishing American employers who either contract or utilize Mexican workers who are illegal immigrants.

Foreign Office requests approval US Government of foregoing points as initial basis discussions whereupon names Mexican representatives will be communicated this Embassy. *Oficial Mayor* Guerra proposes depart for El Paso November 17 arriving there 18th for initial discussions with Consul Aguirre, Ciudad Juarez, Mexican Consul General El Paso, prior arrival remainder Mexican delegation November 20. He expressed hope that Mr. William MacLean would be present El Paso November 18.

Embassy informed informally Mexican desire incorporate April, 1943 agreement and March, 1947 wetback agreement into one new agreement suggesting its possible enforcement by utilizing existing farm organizations in US.

Department requested inform Embassy urgently whether points by Mexican Government given above acceptable for discussion.

THURSTON

811.504 Mexico/11-1447

The Acting Director of the Labor Branch, Production and Marketing Administration, Department of Agriculture (Holley) to the Acting Chief of the Division of Mexican Affairs (Reveley)

WASHINGTON, November 14, 1947.

DEAR MR. REVELEY: This is in reference to your letter of November 13, 1947,[59] and will confirm your understanding that this Department has no objection to the proposed transfer of Mexican agricultural workers transported by this Department under the agreement of

---

[59] Not printed.

April 26, 1943, to direct employment under contracts between growers and the workers, subject to the approval of the Mexican Government to such transfer.

Since legislative instruction (Public Law 40) calls for the termination of the Farm Labor Supply Program by December 31, 1947, and thereafter shall be liquidated within 30 days, plans have been set in motion to repatriate all Mexican national agricultural workers within the allotted period. Should the Mexican Government contemplate approving the transfer of at least a part of the workers now in this country under contract to this Department, to growers or associations of growers, it is recommended that they act immediately in order to retain the greatest number of workers possible.

In transferring these workers from our program, we will, of course, want to be released of all further obligations under our work agreements with the transferred workers. A form of release is enclosed. It is respectfully requested that your Department obtain the approval of the Mexican Government on the use of such form.

Sincerely yours, W. C. HOLLEY

811.504 Mexico/11–1347 : Airgram

The Acting Secretary of State to the Embassy in Mexico

RESTRICTED WASHINGTON, November 19, 1947.

A–846. Reference is made to the Embassy's telegram no. 1264 of November 13, 1947, regarding conversations to be held in El Paso, Texas, between representatives of this Government and the Government of Mexico in regard to future contracting of Mexican agricultural laborers. This will confirm the Department's position on the lettered points in the telegram as it was given to Mr. Forrest K. Geerken of the Embassy by telephone by Mr. William G. MacLean of the Division of Mexican Affairs on November 14 :

A. This Government wishes to reserve the right to discuss the contracting of Mexican laborers without the limitations suggested in order to be fully informed as to the Mexican attitude regarding Texas, and in order that representatives of both Governments may be free to reach a mutually satisfactory agreement on as comprehensive a basis as possible.

B. The Mexican proposal for measures to prevent the movement of Mexican workers from one state to another without the consent of the workers and previous authorization of the Mexican Government is acceptable to this Government.

C. The adaptation of the work contract under the April 26, 1943, agreement is presently under study as a possible practical basis for future contracting. These studies are not completed, and therefore this

Government does not wish to commit itself on this point prior to the discussions.

The representatives of this Government will be prepared to discuss the other items mentioned in the Embassy's telegram. In regard to the desire of the *Oficial Mayor* of the Ministry for Foreign Affairs to have an initial discussion on November 17, this will confirm that Mr. MacLean expects to arrive in El Paso on the evening of November 18 and will get in touch with the *Oficial Mayor* early on November 19.

LOVETT

811.504 Mexico/12–1647

The Acting Secretary of State to the Ambassador in Mexico (Thurston)

RESTRICTED   WASHINGTON, December 16, 1947.
No. 1631

SIR: Reference is made to the conversations between representatives of this Government and of the Government of Mexico at El Paso, Texas, from November 20 to December 3, 1947, with a view to the continued employment in the United States of Mexican agricultural workers, and to the draft over-all agreement and contract form which was prepared during that conference,[60] copies of which were forwarded directly to Consul General Maurice L. Stafford of the Embassy on December 9, 1947. Reference is also made to Ambassador Thurston's memorandum of conversation, dated December 5, 1947,[60] covering comments made to him by the Mexican Minister for Foreign Affairs in regard to the agreement and contract.

As Consul General Stafford was informed by telephone on December 9 by an officer of the Department, most of the points raised by the Foreign Minister were definitely covered in the documents under reference. Article 10 of the over-all agreement and Article 4 of the individual work agreement, for example, assure workers of free lodging and travel expenses. Article 8 of the over-all agreement does not establish Torreon and Saltillo as recruiting centers but establishes a line from coast to coast through Torreon and Saltillo as the limit to which transportation for workers is to be paid by employers. The Mexican Government, as stated in the agreement, is free to establish recruiting centers wherever it wishes. For your own strictly confidential information, considerable pressure is being brought to bear on certain committees of the Congress to provide funds for the United States Employment Service which it could use to cover transportation costs

---

[60] Not printed.

of workers from recruiting centers in Mexico to the international border, from which point the travel cost would be obligatory on the employer. As this is merely in the proposal stage, it of course should not be communicated to the Mexican Government, but you will recognize that it would simplify the travel problem for both Governments if action were taken along this line.

In regard to the desire for guaranteed wages for 75 per cent of contract period and the Minister's emphasis that Mexico did not expect better than the 1943 terms in this regard, it was pointed out to the Mexican Delegation at El Paso that the 1943 agreement was a wartime measure of so much importance that the Mexican workers were given guarantees far beyond those available to domestic agricultural workers. With the cessation of hostilities, there is no longer justification for this discrimination, nor is there any fund or appropriation which would permit continuance thereof. Notwithstanding the above, the El Paso documents still represent considerable preferential treatment for the Mexican workers. Domestic agricultural workers do not receive free lodging, have no subsistence guarantee, and usually must cover their own transportation both to and from the place of employment. Workers presently being brought in from other countries in the Caribbean region, incidentally, are not receiving transportation. All of these things illustrate the earnest and sincere efforts of the United States Delegation to provide for these workers from Mexico in the best possible manner within the existing framework of laws and customs in the United States.

The United States Delegation offered a 50 per cent guarantee of wages and pointed out that the amount of money that employers would have invested in these workers would insure the great majority of them fulltime and probably overtime work. However, the Mexican Delegation turned this proposal down as not "looking like enough." It accepted as preferable the present wording of Article 24. If the Mexican Foreign Office presses for a guarantee, this Government will accept a revision of Article 24 in the over-all agreement to read somewhat as follows:

"The employer guarantees the worker employment for one-half of the work days of the period during which the contract is, in fact, in effect. If the employer offers the worker less employment, the worker shall be entitled to the amount which he would have earned had he, in fact, worked for the required guaranteed period. In determining whether the guarantee provided for in this paragraph has been met, days on which the worker refuses employment without justification shall be added to the number of days of actual employment.

"Furthermore, the United States Department of Labor will use its good offices in order that Mexican workers under this agreement may obtain maximum employment and wage rates. Information in regard to salary and working conditions is to be circulated among the workers in the contracting centers in the manner specified in the final paragraph of Article 3 of this agreement with a view that the workers themselves may be in a position to decline employment offered if the contracting conditions and wage rates do not appear to be to their interest."

The above is independent of and additional to, of course, the provisions guaranteeing subsistence to the worker on any day in which he is not given at least four hours of employment (see Article 19 of the individual work contract).

The Department, the Immigration and Naturalization Service, and the United States Employment Service of the Department of Labor are under heavy pressure from employers and from members of Congress for the earliest possible approval and functioning of the El Paso agreement. They are particularly interested in the continuance of employment through the present crop cycles of workers now in the United States both under the agreement of April 26, 1943, and under the agreement of March 10, 1947. Especially in the southwest, including California, these workers are engaged in the harvesting of important crops, and there will be heavy losses if their services do not continue to be available. There is also great interest in completion of the agreement in order that workers may be assured from Mexico for the new crop year beginning in March 1948, and the uncertainties caused by the lack of decision on the part of the Mexican Government in regard to the proposed agreement and contract has resulted in the very interested examination of possibilities for bringing in workers from Puerto Rico and the Philippines. The Mexican worker, however, is preferred because of his experience and because of the general understanding that it is mutually advantageous to have a sound economy in Mexico, to which the earnings of these workers can make a very substantial contribution.

You are therefore instructed to take every appropriate action with a view to early adoption of this agreement and contract by the Mexican Government, and you are authorized to exchange notes making them effective on the part of this Government upon the earliest date which can be arranged with that Government.[61] The Department has received communications from both the Immigration and Naturalization Service of the Department of Justice and from the Department of Labor expressing approval of the terms of the proposed agreement and asking that it be made effective between the two Governments as soon as

---

[61] An agreement between the United States and Mexico respecting temporary migration of Mexican agricultural workers, superseding the agreements of April 26, 1943, and March 10, 1947, was effected by exchange of notes signed at Mexico City February 20 and 21. 1948. For texts, see TIAS No. 1968.

possible. It will be appreciated if you will keep the Department informed of developments and progress by telephone or telegraph in order that immediate steps can be taken, when approval is received, to extend any contracts of Mexican workers now in the United States who wish to remain.

Very truly yours, For the Acting Secretary of State:
PAUL C. DANIELS
Director for American
Republic Affairs

UNITED STATES EFFORTS TO ELIMINATE ILLICIT TRAFFIC IN NARCOTIC DRUGS BETWEEN MEXICO AND THE UNITED STATES

812.114 Narcotics/8-947

The Secretary of State to the Embassy in Mexico

No. 1407 WASHINGTON, August 9, 1947.

The Secretary of State encloses herewith, in duplicate, for the information of the Embassy a copy of a statement made by Mr. Harry J. Anslinger, United States Representative on the Commission on Narcotic Drugs of the Economic and Social Council of the United Nations, at Lake Success, New York, on July 30, 1947, in regard to the narcotics situation in Mexico.

There is also enclosed herewith, in duplicate, a copy of a report, dated July 28, 1947,[62] concerning a shooting affray that occurred near Calexico, California, between Mexican smugglers and United States narcotics and customs enforcement officers, which Mr. Anslinger made available to the Commission on Narcotic Drugs for its information.

[Enclosure]

STATEMENT OF THE UNITED STATES REPRESENTATIVE ON THE COMMISSION ON NARCOTIC DRUGS OF THE UNITED NATIONS, MR. HARRY J. ANSLINGER, REGARDING THE NARCOTICS SITUATION IN MEXICO

JULY 30, 1947.

I have received information from the representative of the United States [63] who accompanied the Mexican officials engaged in making an aerial survey in Mexico last spring that the cultivation of the opium poppy in Mexico covers a large area and is increasing year after year. It is estimated on the basis of observation and photographs of

---
[62] Not printed.
[63] Treasury Representative D. J. Delagrave.

an area of about 1,000 square miles that the poppy fields now number close to 10,000, averaging one-half hectare (1–1¼ acre) or more per field. The total area is between 4,000 and 5,000 hectares (10,000 and 12,500 acres), producing from 32 to 40 metric tons of opium. The principal opium producing area is roughly 6,000 square miles in extent. It forms a rectangle east of Bodiriguato, Sinaloa. It extends in a northwesterly direction with the eastern boundary on the western slopes of the Sierra Madre mountains.

The aerial survey I have mentioned was made northeast of Bodiriguato. In this limited area of approximately 1,000 square miles, 1500 to 1700 fields were observed. Outside of the 1000 square miles main area an additional 3000 fields were observed.

For various reasons, notably the change in the administration, a misconception of the extent of the task, the lack of manpower and finances, the 1947 opium poppy destruction campaign conducted by the Attorney General achieved poor results. Approximately 200 poppy fields, having a total area of only 36 hectares (90 acres) were destroyed by a ground expedition.

The cultivation of the opium poppy in Mexico, although prohibited by Mexican law, appears to be tolerated by the state and local authorities in the producing areas, with the possible exception of the State of Sonora.

It is reported that between 20 and 30 secret landing strips for airplanes have been constructed in Mexico to handle the transportation of narcotics from Mexico to the United States. There is confirmation of this on both sides of the border. The Mexican Government recently seized a plane loaded with narcotics in Mexico and a crashed plane containing the bodies of two known narcotic smugglers was found in the United States. We also have information that underworld groups in the United States have their representatives in Mexico to promote the cultivation of the opium poppy, to purchase the crop and to arrange for its transformation into more valuable and less bulky derivatives, thereby facilitating transportation.

Information received from reliable sources indicates that there are twelve or more clandestine laboratories in Mexico, a few of which are large and well equipped. Two of the laboratories have been seized during the last few months. It is estimated that at least one-half of the raw opium produced in Mexico is being processed into either morphine or heroin.

The United States is concerned over the narcotics situation in Mexico because most of the narcotics produced are intended for smuggling across the border into our country and are a serious menace to the health of our people. In order to present a picture of the present situation along the border, I have in a separate paper described in detail a shooting affray that occurred a few weeks ago at Woodbine near Calexico between desperate Mexican smugglers and narcotics and customs enforcement officers of the United States. I am authorized to state that my Government hopes that the Mexican Government will increase its activity without delay, in consonance with its international obligations, with a view to suppressing the illicit cultivation of opium poppies within its borders.

812.114 Narcotics/9-2647

The Secretary of State to the Ambassador in Mexico (Thurston)

CONFIDENTIAL   WASHINGTON, October 14, 1947.
No. 1518

SIR: Reference is made to the Department's instructions nos. 1193 of May 19, 1947, 1407 of August 9, 1947 and 1495 of September 26, 1947,[64] in regard to the traffic in narcotic drugs between Mexico and the United States.

The information transmitted by the Embassy during the past year clearly indicates that narcotic conditions have worsened and that the Mexican Government has relaxed its vigilance.

The Department concurs with the Embassy's view that the situation is a difficult one for the Mexican Government to handle and that the cost of strictly enforcing prohibition of the cultivation of opium poppies would be great. The Government of Mexico does, however, have the inescapable duty of trying to prevent illicit traffic in narcotic drugs. It cannot pass this responsibility on to any other government. All the United States Government can do is to cooperate with the Mexican authorities in every appropriate way with a view to keeping the traffic at a minimum.

This Department and the Treasury Department believe that it would be advisable for you to have a frank discussion with the Mexican Minister for Foreign Affairs[65] about prevailing conditions. This discussion might be based, in your discretion, on parts of the report dated August 19, 1947 of Treasury Representative Delagrave addressed to the Commissioner of Customs, Washington, D.C., and other information in the possession of the Embassy, which is believed to be reliable.

You are authorized to impress upon the Mexican Foreign Office the concern felt by our Government over existing conditions, which are a serious menace to the health of our people, and again to urge the Mex-

---

[64] Instructions 1193 and 1495 not printed.
[65] Jaime Torres Bodet.

ican Government to exert every effort to prevent the cultivation of opium poppies this fall and to combat actively other forms of the illicit traffic.

Very truly yours, For the Secretary of State:
GARRISON NORTON [66]

812.114 Narcotics/12–1847

The Ambassador in Mexico (Thurston) to the Secretary of State

CONFIDENTIAL MÉXICO, D.F., December 18, 1947.
No. 5226

SIR: I took up yesterday with the Minister for Foreign Affairs the general subject of the Department's confidential airmail instruction Number 1610 dated December 5, 1947 [67] with respect to the illicit traffic in narcotic drugs in Mexico. I stated that my Government had learned with pleasure from Mr. DeLagrave of the program outlined to him by the Mexican Attorney General for an energetic campaign in 1948 to prevent the cultivation of opium poppies in this country, and I inquired whether the Foreign Minister was in a position to assure me that such a program would actually be undertaken and prosecuted.

Señor Torres Bodet stated in reply that he knew of the Attorney General's program and that it was his understanding that it was already in operation and that it would be continued throughout the coming year. He then called the Attorney General by telephone and informed him of my statements and of my request for assurances of the nature just described. At the termination of this conversation, Señor Torres Bodet stated that the Attorney General had authorized him to assure me most formally that the campaign described by him to Mr. DeLagrave was in progress, and that it would be vigorously continued through the next year. I expressed appreciation of these assurances.

The Foreign Minister then stated that the Mexican Government had been offended and embarrassed by the statements made by Mr. Anslinger during the Second Session of the Commission on Narcotic Drugs at Lake Success some months ago. He implied that the Mexican Government was considering the advisability of attempting at the forthcoming session of the Economic and Social Council (which he said begins February 2, 1948—not in January) to bring about the retraction of some of Mr. Anslinger's accusations and remarks with

---

[66] Assistant Secretary of State for Transportation and Communication.
[67] Not printed.

respect to Mexico's laxity in enforcing control over the traffic in illicit narcotics. When, however, I asked him specifically if this was the intention of the Mexican Government, he replied that no decision had been reached although since the subject of the charges made by Mr. Anslinger would of necessity be discussed at that session, Mexico would of course present its own views. There are some, he said, who are angry over Mr. Anslinger's remarks and who wish it to be pointed out that Mexico is virtually the victim of this traffic, which is financed in Mexico and in the United States by American capital, and to call upon us to put our own house in order. He gave me to understand, however, that no intemperate action along these lines would be taken.

In view of the Mexican attitude as just described and in view of the assurances given to me by the Minister and the Attorney General with respect to the 1948 campaign, I considered it to be inadvisable to say to the Mexican Foreign Minister, as directed in the last paragraph of the Department's instruction under reference, that the United States Government intends to urge the Economic and Social Council to recommend that the Government of Mexico take measures to suppress the illicit cultivation of opium poppies in Mexico. It seemed to me that by obtaining the assurances mentioned, I had gone far enough for the present. I venture to suggest to the Department that it likewise give consideration to the broader aspects of this situation: If the United States Government officially endorses Mr. Anslinger's remarks and assumes a critical attitude of the Mexican Government for permitting the production of poppies and opium, it is quite apparent that this attitude will provoke resentment and very likely hostile remarks with respect to conditions in the United States and the connivance of American capital and gangster organizations, which we seem no more able to control than do the Mexicans seem able to control the production and shipment of narcotics.

Respectfully yours, WALTER THURSTON

NICARAGUA

POLITICAL UPHEAVAL IN NICARAGUA: UNITED STATES POLICIES OF NONINTERVENTION AND NONRECOGNITION [1]

Editorial Note

As the 1947 national elections approached, political tensions grew between President Anastasio Somoza, who was supporting Leonardo Argüello, candidate of the Liberal Party, and the Conservative opposition, which supported Enoc Aguado. Each side hoped for some overt support by the United States.

817.00/1–1747 : Telegram

The Ambassador in Nicaragua (Warren) to the Secretary of State

SECRET   US URGENT   MANAGUA, January 17, 1947—5 p. m.

20. For Assistant Secretary Braden. President Somoza yesterday afternoon definitely requested me to communicate with General Chamorro [2] and to tell him that the President is desirous of talking with Chamorro in an endeavor to reach conciliation between the regular Liberals and the Nationalist Conservatives on one side and the regular Conservatives and the independent Liberals on the other. President Somoza realized that the Embassy cannot comply with his request without the expressed authorization of the Department of State. He asked specifically that the foregoing be conveyed to the Department and authorization to act requested. Since only 16 days remain before election the Department's prompt instruction would be appreciated.

[WARREN]

817.00/1–1747 : Telegram

The Secretary of State to the Embassy in Nicaragua

RESTRICTED   WASHINGTON, January 18, 1947—3 p. m.

12. Situation set forth your recent communications has received careful consideration. Dept considers your reply to Pres Somoza accu-

---

[1] For previous documentation on reaffirmation of United States policy of nonintervention in the internal affairs of Nicaragua, see *Foreign Relations*, 1946, vol. XI, pp. 1068 ff.

[2] Gen. Emiliano Chamorro Vargas, former President of Nicaragua, head of the Conservative party.

rate reflection of its own views.[4] It is inconceivable that if Somoza is sincere in his wish to reach fair agreement with opposition meeting cannot be arranged without intervention of Emb. On other hand if approach to you is merely a political maneuver it would be even more undesirable for Emb to have anything whatsoever to do with proposal. Dept of course is most anxious to see fair elections which accurately reflect will of Nicaraguan people but as repeatedly emphasized this is a problem to be worked out by Nicaraguan people and government.

You are authorized to convey orally substance this telegram to Pres Somoza.

BYRNES

817.00/1–2047 : Telegram

The Secretary of State to the Embassy in Nicaragua

CONFIDENTIAL   WASHINGTON, January 22, 1947—3 p. m.

14. Urtel 25 Jan 20.[5] Were Embassy to comply with President Somoza's request, it would be acting as intermediary between him and opposition, a procedure which Dept has considered undesirable. No objection is perceived, however, to your confirming facts if inquiry is made by opposition leaders.

MARSHALL

817.00/1–3047

Memorandum of Conversation, by Mr. Gordon S. Reid of the Division of Central America and Panama Affairs

WASHINGTON, January 30, 1947.

Participants: Sr. Dr. Don Guillermo Sevilla Sacasa, Nicaraguan Ambassador.
Spruille Braden, Assistant Secretary of State.
Mr. Reid—CPA

Ambassador Sevilla Sacasa called on Mr. Braden today to acquaint him with the latest information of the political situation in Nicaragua.

---

[4] In despatch 1321, January 13, 1947, Ambassador Warren had reported as follows: "I have consistently answered all inquiries about assistance from this mission in getting General Somoza and General Chamorro to come to some agreement with the statement that I can do nothing that can rightly be considered as intervening in the internal affairs of Nicaragua, and that should I receive a direct and explicit request for the good offices of the Embassy in the present situation I would have to refuse. I have always added, however, that in the event that the request is made by General Chamorro or General Somoza I would immediately inform the Department of State and ask for instructions. In doing so, I have discouraged any optimism regarding the possibilities of the Department's giving its approval to the request." (817.00/1–1347)

[5] Not printed; Ambassador Warren reported that he had conveyed orally to President Somoza the substance of Department's telegram 12 of January 18, and the latter had asked that Ambassador Warren let General Chamorro and others know of his request to the Department and its refusal (817.00/1–2047).

The Ambassador expressed to Mr. Braden at great length the desire of President Somoza to reach an agreement with the Opposition which would prevent any rumors of electoral malpractice and reminded Mr. Braden that Ambassador Warren had been asked to aid in this attempt at conciliation. He stated that despite the President's most sincere efforts, his conciliatory hand had been refused by the Opposition and, in turn, General Chamorro had threatened revolution, the use of incendiary bombs and terror tactics leading to civil war.

Somoza wants no revolution and is attempting to assure free elections in Nicaragua and to turn over the presidency in an orderly manner, the Ambassador went on, yet he is faced with threats everywhere and may be called upon to use force to keep order. His opponents will then unjustly charge him with dictatorial practices. The Ambassador further stated that United States newsmen have been invited to be on the scene and he seemed to feel that representatives of the *New York Times*, the *New York Herald Tribune* and *Time* Magazine would be present.[6]

Mr. Braden stated that a revolution would be looked upon by the whole hemisphere as a catastrophe and a breach of the democratic processes that have been built up on these two continents.

. . . .

The Ambassador stated to the writer later that it was Somoza's desire to keep Mr. Braden frankly and fully informed to offset the many rumors which they were certain would reach his ears from the Opposition.

817.00/2–1447

Memorandum of Conversation, by the Chief of the Division of Central America and Panama Affairs (Newbegin)

WASHINGTON, February 14, 1947.

Ambassador Sevilla Sacasa reviewed the conduct of the elections in Nicaragua held on February 2 [7] stating that there was remarkably little disturbance and no deaths. He emphasized that the elections were free and gave great praise to Somoza for the manner in which they were conducted. He pointed out also that henceforth, because of

---

[6] In telegram 41, February 1, 11 a. m., Ambassador Warren reported as follows: "Somoza has striven to please American representatives by issuing special press cards, instruction to telegraph and cable companies to facilitate transmission of their uncensored messages, and by offers of unrestricted transportation to any part of the republic." (817.00/2–147)

[7] Leonardo Argüello, declared by President Somoza the winner of the February 2 elections, was proclaimed President-elect by the National Council of Elections on February 23, to take office on May 1, 1947.

the large vote which they received, the Conservatives will enjoy major party status which they lost during the last election. He conceded that the Opposition had won in Managua and several other places. He accused the Opposition of bad faith in describing the elections as fraudulent although he thought this natural in view of the fact that Nicaragua was not so far advanced in democracy as certain other nations and the losing side did not accept its defeat with the same degree of reasonableness as more advanced countries.

The Ambassador suggested that Chamorro would probably come to Washington [12] laden with documents and accompanied by certain of his assistants in order to enlist the support of the Department. . . . He emphasized once more the fact that the Government candidate had won in a fair election. Mr. Braden said that he did not have as yet, of course, all the data relating to the election but that he had seen a number of reports some good and some bad. He did not, however, feel in a position to comment on it at this time. He said that he was an ardent exponent of democracy and that he defended it from Communists on the left and fascists on the right. He continued that he did not, of course, expect perfection and it should not be expected that countries which had been subjected through their history to a series of revolutions and dictatorships and which were not fully advanced could attain democracy over night—the important thing was to progress along democratic paths as had Mexico and certain other countries in the hemisphere. The Ambassador said that this was just what had happened in Nicaragua; that "they" did not pretend to be angels but that the recent elections had marked a great step forward.

In connection with the Nicaraguan application for a license to export airplanes, the Ambassador stated that he expected to make a new request within a few days that their export now be permitted since the election was over. Mr. Braden said that he was under the impression that this question was tied up to the Lend-Lease problem. Mr. Newbegin confirmed this fact pointing out that the Ambassador had been informed many months ago that this Government was not disposed to facilitate the acquisition of arms and ammunition by the Nicaraguan Government while the lend-lease debt remained unpaid.

Following his call on Mr. Braden, the Ambassador stated that only a few technicalities remained to be completed in order for the Bank

---

[12] Visits to Washington by the President-elect, Presidential candidates, and Opposition leaders, were discouraged by the Embassy, in accordance with Departmental instructions, inasmuch as "such visits would tend to put Dept in position of arbiter of elections, position it particularly desires to avoid". (Telegram 33, February 13, 2 p. m., to Managua, filed under 817.00/2–1247)

of America loan to Nicaragua to become effective. He said he had been in touch with the Federal Reserve Board and Secretary Snyder [13] on this score. He continued that as soon as Nicaragua received its first payment of $500,000 under the terms of the loan, he expected that a portion of it would be set aside for Lend-Lease payments. He asked if that would clear up the matter entirely as far as the planes were concerned. Mr. Newbegin informed him that in his opinion, the answer was probably negative; that an arrangement for the payment of Lend-Lease was essential but that it was also unlikely that any favorable action would be taken before the next presidential term commenced. He explained that as the Ambassador knew, the situation in Nicaragua at this time was somewhat unstable and we would prefer to wait until the new presidential term began.

817.24/3–2847

Memorandum of Conversation, by the Chief of the Division of Central America and Panama Affairs (Newbegin)

WASHINGTON, March 28, 1947.

In the course of a conversation at Blair House yesterday afternoon, the Ambassador [14] referred to the initial Nicaraguan payment on lend-lease which he said involved naturally some sacrifice on the part of the Nicaraguans but that they recognized their debt and were glad to meet their obligation.[15] I expressed my appreciation.

I then told the Ambassador that speaking informally, I was not sure whether he understood thoroughly that it was unlikely that we would be able to supply any arms or ammunition to Nicaragua until the entire lend-lease debt was paid. I told him that I hoped that he had understood this because I wished our respective positions to be entirely clear and our relations handled on the basis of complete frankness. The Ambassador indicated that he had so understood . . . He inquired as to whether it would be possible to obtain replacement parts for equipment prior to full payment on lend-lease as distinct from any new items. I told him I could not give him a categoric reply

---

[13] John W. Snyder, Secretary of the Treasury.
[14] The Nicaraguan Ambassador, Guillermo Sevilla Sacasa.
[15] In a letter of February 10, 1947, to the Nicaraguan Ambassador, transmitting copies of Statement LL–10 and supporting schedules covering charges made against the Nicaraguan Government for the period June 1–August 31, 1946, for Lend-Lease material, the Department expressed the hope that payment would be made in the near future of $608,000 on the grand total of charges amounting to $878,878.80 (817.24/2–1047). A payment on account in the amount of $100,000 was made by the Nicaraguan Government and transmitted to the Department in despatch 1508, March 26, 1947, from Managua (817.24/3–2647).

but that speaking personally, I believed that replacement parts would be considered as a category apart and would be obtainable.

R[OBERT] N[EWBEGIN]

817.00/4–847 : Telegram

The Acting Secretary of State to the Embassy in Nicaragua

[Extract]

CONFIDENTIAL   US URGENT   WASHINGTON, April 8, 1947—6 p. m.

79. Aguado received yesterday by Braden at request former. Aguado described "Nicaraguan situation" saying it has more gloomy aspect now than before elections. Aguado claimed to speak in interest democracy and of stable political regime in Nicaragua rather than of personal ambition. He expressed hope that US, for moral political effect that would result, could in some way support cause he represented.

Braden replied forthrightly that our established policy is one of non-intervention, that we have international commitments to maintain that policy, and that standing firm as regards policy and commitments will in long run have more beneficial moral political effect than would any other position we might take.

On other hand, Braden pointed out that in 1944 we had made known that Govt and people US could not help but feel a greater affinity and warmer friendship for those Govts which rest upon the periodically and freely expressed consent of the governed. . . .

ACHESON

817.00/4–2347

The Ambassador in Nicaragua (Warren) to the Secretary of State

RESTRICTED   MANAGUA, April 23, 1947.
No. 1560

SIR: I have the honor to report that the now generally conceded failure of Dr. Enoc Aguado's trip to Washington has led to increased anti-American feeling in opposition circles and to a marked sense of relief in Government quarters.

As reported in the Embassy's despatch no. 1412 of February 15, 1947,[18] the Embassy's frequent reiteration to Dr. Aguado and other opposition leaders of the United States' non-intervention policy had

---

[18] Not printed.

apparently dispelled their previous hopes of unilateral United States action on their behalf. However, whether through a willful policy of deceit on the part of opposition leaders, or whether through a genuine hope of a sudden reversal in United States policy, Aguado's trip and subsequent conversations in Washington was allowed to lead to a growing hope amongst the rank and file that the United States Government might refuse to recognize the Argüello regime after all. When these hopes were dashed by the designation of a special American emissary to the inauguration, speculation centered around the possibility that the United States might accord only conditional recognition, based on the condition that General Somoza relinquish his position as Jefe-Director of the Guardia Nacional. Most recently even this hope has faded and it is now generally acknowledged that Aguado failed completely in obtaining United States aid. With this realization has come a marked increase in the already present anti-American feeling in Opposition ranks and a tendency to accuse the United States of hypocrisy, selfishness and insincerity. Typical Opposition feeling is displayed in the enclosed translation [19] of an editorial which recently appeared on the front page of the Conservative *El Heraldo*.

While the opposition has thus come to condemn the United States for the failure of Aguado's trip, the Government has loudly applauded the United States' steadfast refusal to intervene in Nicaraguan affairs. Although at first a certain nervousness was displayed lest Dr. Aguado discredit the Government and perhaps even secure outside assistance, confidence returned with the announcement that the United States would be represented at the inauguration on May 1. Current Government attitude was summarized by President Somoza in his last press interview, copies of which are enclosed,[19] in which he comments extensively on Dr. Aguado's trip. In answer to certain statements allegedly made by Aguado in the United States and in reply to local Opposition speculation growing from the trip, President Somoza bluntly and emphatically made the following points:

1. He never had pictures of Hitler and Mussolini in his office, as Dr. Aguado has reportedly asserted in the United States.
2. His relations with the notorious Nazi, Wilhelm von Brayman, were exclusively of a commercial nature.
3. He has fulfilled his promises of not seeking reelection and of giving free elections "to the extent humanly possible".
4. "With respect to (retiring from) the Command of the Army, I have never made any promise to anybody nor to the Department of State, for I could not make such a promise as long as I was not asked, and the Department of State has been very far from asking such a

---

[19] Not printed.

question, conduct which truly brings honor to that Government, not asking of me what is a matter only for the future government of Dr. Argüello".

5. "If (the United States) refused to intervene in the most important question of electing a President, how much less would it be disposed to intervene in the appointment of an official, which, as I have said before, is a matter for the President of the Republic".

6. Dr. Aguado has gotten nowhere in the United States and "I hope that this defeat will teach Dr. Aguado a lesson and that he will return to this country with more disposition to work for the prestige and advancement of his native country".

Respectfully yours, FLETCHER WARREN

817.00/5-947 : Airgram

The Chargé in Nicaragua (Bernbaum)[20] *to the Secretary of State*

CONFIDENTIAL MANAGUA, May 9, 1947.

A-190. I saw President Argüello[21] this morning at his request. The President's call followed the publication yesterday morning of General Somoza's repeated announcement that he had been designated Jefe-Director of the Guardia Nacional; and a meeting held last night between General Somoza and President Argüello at the Casa Presidencial.

After repeating substantially what he had told Ambassador Warren on May 3 (see my A-181 of May 5, 1947[22]), the President informed me that General Somoza had visited him last night by appointment for an interview lasting well over an hour. Somoza, he stated, expressed his dissatisfaction over not having been consulted on the recent reorganization of the General Staff.[23] ... The President then informed Somoza that he had deliberately by-passed the office of the "Jefe-Director" to demonstrate to Somoza as well as to the people of Nicaragua that he is actually in command of the situation. ... He emphasized to the ex-President that he was following a carefully thought out plan and would allow nothing to divert him from its fulfillment. He reproached Somoza in that regard for having attempted to intimi-

---

[20] Ambassador Warren had departed for the United States on May 4.
[21] In telegram 184, May 2, Ambassador Warren reported that Argüello was inaugurated President of Nicaragua on May 1, without incident (817.001 Argüello, Leonardo/5-247).
[22] Not printed.
[23] Undertaking to establish a reform government free from military control, President Argüello had issued an order on May 2, without consulting General Somoza, reorganizing the General Staff with officers of his own choice. On May 6 he had appointed a Cabinet of men noted for their alleged honesty, integrity, and, for the most part, their opposition to General Somoza (despatch 1646, June 6, 1947, from Managua, filed under 817.00/6-647).

date him by a display of military force and for having stirred up public unrest by talking too much, especially of his having been appointed Jefe-Director. Upon being reproached by Somoza for the Oppositionist character of the newly-appointed Cabinet, the President replied that the Ministers had been carefully selected for their reported honesty and industry as well as for their being representative of all parts of the country, and of the opposing sectors of the Liberal Party. He then pointedly stated that since he could create Ministers, he could always get rid of them. He gave Somoza a lengthy lecture on the advantages to them both as well as to Nicaragua of bringing about quiet political conditions and economic improvements. This, he stated, would not only work to the advantage of Argüello, but also to Somoza's benefit for having given to Nicaragua a successor who really helped the country. Argüello added that Somoza agreed to this.

The President confirmed that Somoza is *de facto* head of the Guardia in the sense that he has not been deprived of the position previously held. He explained that to have completely deprived Somoza of this position would have served only to bring about a conflict. . . .

[The President then spoke of Nicaragua's fiscal problems and budget deficits.]

The President told me that he hopes to secure a loan from the United States to tide him over, and in that connection he is thinking of sending the Foreign Minister, Dr. León Debayle, to the United States to sound out the situation. I did not encourage any hopes of success, but suggested that any application made be well-documented and thought out.

The President confirmed rumors that his son-in-law, Frank M. Townsend, has returned from Colombia to become Director [National?] Railway and will be formally designated at the press conference to be held tomorrow morning. He also expects to name various other new secondary officials. . . .

He described his program as being based on the improvement of education, of road communications, and of sanitation and that United States help in that regard would be greatly appreciated.

The "old man" spoke at length of his prospects to bring about a clean and efficient Government and stated that he himself expects no remuneration other than the satisfaction of doing a good job. He is optimistic about the future in the belief that the good moral effect of his program and the growing prestige it is bringing him from both within and without Nicaragua will carry far more weight in the final solution than Somoza's control of the Guardia Nacional and all available arms. I left with the feeling that he truly believes this and will not be deterred by military considerations.

BERNBAUM

817.51/5–1547

Memorandum by Mr. Fred G. Heins of the Division of Central America and Panama Affairs [25]

CONFIDENTIAL WASHINGTON, May 15, 1947.

The following is a brief résumé of Nicaragua's confused financial situation, made in view of A–190 of May 9, 1947 from Managua indicating that President Argüello may send his Foreign Minister to Washington to try to obtain a loan from the United States to tide him over his present financial difficulty. . . .

Although the public debt is said to have increased from 14,999,000 cordobas in 1938 to 29,217,000 cordobas in 1945, government revenues are reported to have increased from 7,493,825 cordobas for the fiscal year 1937 to 63,762,659 cordobas for the fiscal year 1945 with a surplus for each except two (1943 and 1945) of these nine years. The net surplus of revenues over expenditures for this period was reported to be 24,229,142 cordobas. The budgets for 1946 and 1947 amount to 70,391,338 cordobas and 77,359,608 cordobas respectively, but information is not available as to how they will balance.

The history of Nicaragua's external debt is more favorable than that of many other countries. All outstanding loans previous to 1909 were converted into or paid from the proceeds of the Sterling 6% loan of 1909. Sinking fund payments due in 1911 and interest due January 1, 1912 were suspended. Under an agreement of 1912 interest was reduced to 5% and sinking fund fixed at 1% per annum. Service was interrupted in 1915–16 and again in 1917–20 when part cash–part scrip payments were agreed upon. Service was resumed in 1920 and maintained to November 1931, after which date sinking fund remittances through 1936 reduced. New arrangements were concluded in July 1937, reducing the rate of interest to 4% per annum and extending the maturity to 1957. Sinking fund payments on the outstanding 4% bonds of 1909 were temporarily suspended in September 1941, and resumed on January 1, 1945. On December 31, 1945 the outstanding balance of this Sterling debt was 9,437,116 cordobas.

The 1945 public debt, which was reported to be 29,217,000 cordobas, included external debts (Sterling bonds and Export–Import Bank credits) of approximately 24,242,000 cordobas. While exact figures

---

[25] Copy transmitted to the Embassy in Nicaragua in instruction 506, June 16, 1947, not printed.

are not readily available concerning the public debt at this time, it appears that the total external obligations now amount to approximately 77,373,465 cordobas as explained by the following:

Outstanding Principal on Export-Import Bank Loan	$2,396,000
Outstanding Interest on Export-Import Bank Loan	656,994
Outstanding Lend-Lease Credits	508,000
Outstanding Stabilization Fund	5,263,699
Outstanding Bank of America Loan	2,000,000
Outstanding Sterling Bonds (approximately)	1,850,000
Quota for International Fund	2,000,000
Subscribed for Shares of International Bank	800,000
Total	$15,474,693

The total Export-Import Bank loans of 1939 and 1941, outstanding on May 13, 1947, amount to $2,396,000 in principal and $656,994.78 in interest. Payments were current as of April 1, 1947, but are delinquent at the present time because $35,000 principal and $3,275.14 interest, due on April 30, 1947, have not been made as yet. In addition, $37,000 principal and $1,805.05 interest will become due on May 31, 1947, as well as similar amounts in succeeding months. Furthermore, payments due on principal will increase substantially before the end of 1947, because $2,000,000 of the above-mentioned loans are payable in 8-½ years, semiannually, beginning December 31, 1947.

As of May 1, 1947, Nicaragua owed a balance of $508,000 on its Lend-Lease account.

The Exchange Stabilization Fund on December 31, 1946 amounted to 26,318,499 cordobas, or 19.8% less than on December 31, 1945 and 29.4% less than on December 31, 1943.

Nicaragua is obligated, and may be called upon at any time, to make a considerable financial payment to the International Monetary Fund and the International Bank. According to a decree dated December 21, 1946, which became effective on February 17, 1947, the Issue Department of the National Bank of Nicaragua is fully authorized to pay in the name of and for the account of the Nicaraguan Government its quota for the Fund and also for its subscribed shares of the Bank. These two obligations total $2,800,000.

During the early months of 1947 the National Bank of Nicaragua negotiated a 3-½% loan of $4,500,000, in behalf of the Nicaraguan Government, from the Bank of America in San Francisco. The entire loan is to be made available by July 31, 1948. Quarterly repayments ranging from $100,000 to $175,000 are to begin in 1947 and are due until July 31, 1955. $2,500,000 is to be devoted to the indirect assumption of "frozen" agricultural loans held by the National Bank and $2,000,000 to the extension of new agricultural and industrial loans Two million dollars were advanced to Nicaragua in March.

The general economy of the country in recent years has been fairly good, but the Embassy reports that business in the first quarter of 1947 was stagnant. The passed due loans by the National Bank as of December 31, 1946 amounted to 9,611,829 cordobas, or 19.05% of the bank's total loans.

In 1946 Nicaragua's receipts for exports exceeded payments for imports and showed a favorable balance of $129,929, as compared with an unfavorable balance of $247,329 for 1945. The first quarter of 1947 would have shown an unfavorable balance of over $134,000 had it not been for a two million dollar advance received in March by the National Bank against the above-mentioned $4,500,000 loan from a California bank.

At the close of 1946, the frozen deposits against import orders amounted to 23,243,254 cordobas and as of March 31, 1947 they amounted to 18,997,751 cordobas, showing a reduction of 18.3%. This reduction is due to the large imports of merchandise received during the quarter against back orders some of which had been placed nearly a year before.

F[RED] G. H[EINS]

817.00/5–2447 : Telegram

The Chargé in Nicaragua (Bernbaum) to the Secretary of State

CONFIDENTIAL U.S. URGENT MANAGUA, May 24, 1947—8 p. m.

202. President Argüello today informed me intends tonight to request Somoza's resignation.[26] Decision based on two Somoza circular telegrams attempting to subvert Guardia commanders.[27] I gained impression that President had not yet decided whether to force resignation in event Somoza's refusal. President will inform me tomorrow morning of results.

BERNBAUM

---

[26] In despatch 1613, May 20, Chargé Bernbaum had reported on the apparent intention of General Somoza to force a showdown with President Argüello resulting either in his resignation as Jefe Director of the Guardia Nacional or in his confirmation as sole commander, as revealed in a conversation between General Somoza and the Embassy's Military Attaché, Lt. Col. Harry H. Towler, Jr. (817.00/5–2047)

[27] The first telegram warned that the Guardia was in danger and gave instructions that only General Somoza's orders be obeyed, and the second ordered the arrest of any officer attempting to take over commands on the President's orders (despatch 1646, June 6, 1947, filed under 817.00/6–647).

817.00/5-2647 : Telegram

The Chargé in Nicaragua (Bernbaum) to the Secretary of State

CONFIDENTIAL MANAGUA, May 26, 1947—4 a. m.

204. ReEmbtel 203, May 25, 10 p. m.[28] In surprise move taking President and loyal Guardia unaware, Somoza tonight seized control of Managua key points including Palacio Nacional, police barracks, communications system, Guardia hospital, Campo De Marte, Defensa Nacional and others. Casa Presidencial surrounded and cut off.

Embassy assistance was telephonically requested by Minister of Sanitation.[29] He was told that Embassy could not accede in absence instructions. A presidential messenger who escaped from the Casa Presidencial later conveyed President's request that I visit him there. After an unsuccessful attempt to telephone him, I telephoned General Somoza who advised against making the visit owing to the danger involved.

Somoza stated that he had been driven to the wall and forced to take drastic measures to protect his life. He alleged having already secured complete control of the country and stated he will communicate with me in the morning. He mentioned something about mediation.

Embassy will maintain neutral position and refuse any request by Somoza or the President for mediation or other assistance. The Department will be kept currently informed.

No news yet available of developments outside of Managua. City quiet with most inhabitants apparently yet unaware of what is going on. Military operations have been most discreet and effected with minimum, if any, firing.

Delay in transmittal of this and previous telegram due to strange absence from offices, stations and homes of all responsible personnel All America Cables and Tropical Radio.

Due restricted communications, Military Attaché requests this pass to War Dept without delay.

BERNBAUM

---

[28] Not printed; in this telegram, the Chargé reported that President Argüello had informed him that General Somoza had agreed to leave for the United States, that he would not permit General Somoza to delay departure, and would, if necessary, publicly force his resignation (817.00/5-2547).

[29] Jacinto Alfaro.

817.00/5-2647 : Telegram

The Secretary of State to the Embassy in Nicaragua

CONFIDENTIAL   US URGENT   WASHINGTON, May 26, 1947—6 p. m.

108. In conversation with Nicaraguan Chargé [30] this afternoon Asst Sec Braden expressed Depts very serious concern regarding developments reported urtel 204 May 26. He pointed out that Argüello had taken office after elections which had been characterized in many quarters as questionable but which Somoza himself had declared to be free and honest, and less than a month later spectacle is reported of Somoza's snatching power away from Pres whose candidacy he himself sponsored. Allegation Somoza took this action because he was "forced to take drastic measures to protect his life" hardly impressive. Mr. Braden emphasized unfortunate effects this action can have and our profound preoccupation with trend events are taking.

Use of Guardia Nacional deplored. Chargé informed we continue to recognize Argüello.

While this Govt will not intervene and wishes to avoid any steps which could be interpreted as intervention, you are authorized in your discretion to bring the above to the attention of Sevilla Sacasa.

You should endeavor to see Pres Argüello (taking into account of course necessary precautions for your own safety) in order to inform him of conversation with Chargé.

This telegram is forwarded with reference to and in amplification of your conversation with Asst. Secy Braden this afternoon.[31]

MARSHALL

817.00/5-2647 : Airgram

The Chargé in Nicaragua (Bernbaum) to the Secretary of State

[Extracts]

CONFIDENTIAL   MANAGUA, May 26, 1947.

A-206. See Embassy's telegram no. 204 of May 26, 1947. Following the telephone conversation of this afternoon with Mr. Braden, I arranged with General Somoza for the appointment agreed upon earlier this morning. The Military Attaché and I saw him at La Curva. It was quite obvious when I began to relate what Mr. Braden had said

---

[30] Col. Camilo González-Cervantes.
[31] Following the Nicaraguan Chargé's visit, Mr. Braden that afternoon called Mr. Bernbaum on the telephone and informed him of his conversation. Mr. Bernbaum said that former President Somoza was in complete control of the situation and that Argüello was being held in the presidential palace incommunicado (817.00/5-2647).

that Somoza had already been apprised of Mr. Braden's viewpoint. . . .

. . . .

He confirmed that Congress had been called to meet this afternoon for the purpose of considering Dr. Argüello's resignation. He insisted that this move had originated entirely within Congress, although admitting at one point that he might have had some influence in it. When asked what he proposed to do in the event that President Argüello should refuse to resign, Somoza smiled and remarked "there is no food in the Casa Presidencial". He insisted, however, that he had no intentions of harming Argüello. He confirmed the arrest of General Medina, General Reyes, Colonel Balladares Torres, Colonel Baca, Colonel Prado and others who had supported the President and stated that they are now eating off his table in La Curva.

Somoza proudly stated that the unprecedented success of his *coup d'état* is eloquent evidence of his popularity within the Guardia Nacional. In that connection he mentioned that the commanding officers and men of the Guardia detachments in most of the Departments had unanimously answered his call to report for duty in Managua. The large influx of troops has already been reported in Embassy's telegram no. 207 of May 26, 1947.[32]

. . . .

In closing the conversation I told him that I believed myself to be echoing the thoughts of Mr. Braden and of Ambassador Warren in earnestly advising him to think long before making any drastic move which he might later regret. I told him that his grievances against Dr. Argüello as related to Colonel Towler and me (see my despatch no. 1613 of May 20, 1947 [33]) had already been described in detail to the Department of State and presumably taken into consideration by Mr. Braden. I reminded him of the emphatic statements he had made to us regarding his complete lack of any intention to use force against Argüello under any circumstance and of his proposal to resign from the Guardia in the event that he could not get along with the President. In that connection I pointed out that he was the one who had requested the Department's authorization for this Embassy to witness his signed declaration of loyalty to the President and that he had then stated his intention of resigning should the Department refuse its authorization (see my despatch no. 1613 of May 20, 1947). Naturally, I stated, the Department of State was considerably disturbed and puzzled over Somoza's precipitate coup. I also expressed my regret that in resorting to force, however great may have been the provocation, he had undone

---

[32] Not printed.
[33] See footnote 26, p. 852.

all the good work in the achievement of democratic institutions in Nicaragua. He smiled wryly, admitted the truth of what I had said but reaffirmed that he was thinking only of Nicaragua.

Somoza stated that he had been disturbed to learn from Colonel Camilo González that Mr. Braden felt he had not permitted me last night to see President Argüello. He added that in advising me not to make the visit, he had been thinking primarily of the danger from "trigger happy" Guardia troops. I told him that I understood his motive, realized that the time might not have been propitious and had planned to see the President today. General Somoza immediately agreed and promised to telephone the Casa Presidencial guard to authorize my entrance.

My subsequent conversation with President Argüello is covered in A-207 of May 27, 1947.

BERNBAUM

817.00/5-2747 : Airgram

The Chargé in Nicaragua (Bernbaum) to the Secretary of State

CONFIDENTIAL MANAGUA, May 27, 1947.

A-207. See my A-206 of May 26, 1947. After my conversation with General Somoza in La Curva yesterday afternoon I proceeded directly to the Casa Presidencial. Much to my amazement I saw approximately 6 or 8 women and no less than 25 Guardia officers and men in the waiting room. Among them were Panchito and Horacio Aguirre, and Colonel Balladares (Somoza had apparently been in error when he told us that Balladares was under arrest at La Curva). The President appeared solemn and somewhat depressed. He did not, however, show any signs of nervousness.

With Panchito Aguirre present he told me that it was not until his inability at about 11:30 Sunday night to make connection with La Curva and the American Embassy that he and his people realized what had taken place. He had since received no word from Somoza or any information regarding what had been going on. Nobody had eaten since that morning owing to the lack of food. In this connection he expressed anxiety over the aged parents of Mrs. Argüello, but stated firmly that he would under no circumstance accede to General Somoza's wishes by resigning.

The President handed to me for transmittal to President Truman a message describing his reactions to the *coup d'état*, the text of which is given in the Embassy's telegram no. 210 of May 26, 1947.[37] Copies of

---

[37] Not printed.

this message will also be handed to the various diplomatic representatives in Managua for transmittal to the heads of their respective governments.

Prior to my departure I gave the President a summary of my telephone conversation of this afternoon with Mr. Spruille Braden. He grimaced a bit over Mr. Braden's reference to the elections, but expressed pleasure over the remainder of the message, especially with regard to the question of recognition. I made it clear, however, that the Department's apprehension and disapproval of General Somoza's actions did not in any way indicate a relaxation of the Department's nonintervention policy. He replied that this policy was well enough understood to require no lengthy comment.

I assured the President I would be glad to visit him at any time he considers convenient.

Reference my telephone conversation of this morning with Mr. Ellis Briggs.[38] Shortly before my departure he [Argüello] handed me a letter addressed to the Dean of the Diplomatic Corps (Mexican Ambassador), requesting that the Diplomatic Corps as a whole and any of its individual members visit him. The letter was personally handed the Mexican Ambassador who was then conducting a meeting in the Mexican Embassy of the Diplomatic Corps.

The final resolution at about 7:30 p. m. was to immediately visit President Argüello as a body. General Somoza was informed in advance in order to avoid trouble with the troops surrounding the Casa Presidencial. His one condition, which was accepted after considerable debate, was that the President not be removed from the Casa Presidencial for asylum. An important part of the preliminary conversation was devoted to this question and to the inhumane character of General Somoza's apparent plan to starve the President into submission. Having only a short time before returned from the Casa Presidencial and in view of the possibility that there might be raised the question of asylum, I did not participate in the visit. The Mexican Ambassador promised to inform me of the outcome.

Upon visiting the Mexican Embassy this morning en route to the Chancery, I learned that President Argüello had for himself, his family and supporters accepted the invitation for asylum which was extended. The invitation had been extended despite the promise made to General Somoza and was confirmed upon Somoza's subsequent acquiescence to the departure of the President and his retinue. . . .

At this moment, President and Mrs. Argüello and eleven officers are enjoying asylum at the Mexican Embassy. The others are scattered among the various Legations. Captain Francisco (Panchito) Aguirre

---

[38] Director of the Office of American Republic Affairs.

Baca and his brother Horacio were this morning issued immigration visas by this office and left this morning by plane. They were escorted to the airfield by the Panamanian Minister.

Rumors of President Argüello's impending departure were this evening denied to me by the Mexican Ambassador who stated that no definite plans had yet been made. The President's acceptance of asylum was taken up this afternoon by Somoza in a conversation with a news correspondent as evidence of unresponsibility and criminal desertion of his duties which would alone have justified his removal from the Presidency.

BERNBAUM

817.00/5–2847

The Chargé in Nicaragua (Bernbaum) to the Secretary of State

RESTRICTED
No. 1628

MANAGUA, May 28, 1947.

SIR: I have the honor to refer to the Embassy's telegram no. 213 of May 27, 1947,[39] and to elaborate on Congress' action in deposing President Argüello and in naming Benjamin Lacayo Sacasa as provisional President of Nicaragua.

The combined Houses of Congress met in the evening of May 26 in the National Palace. Only two Deputies were absent, one Independent Liberal and one Conservative. No spectators or reporters were allowed and the meeting place was closely guarded by Guardia troops.

Deputy Arturo Cerna presented a bill which was later passed as resolution No. 112, copies of which are enclosed.[39] This bill, which was reportedly drawn up during the day by the Nationalist Liberal Deputies in conference with General Somoza, charges President Argüello of "incapacity for the administration and governing of the State, thereby creating an abnormal situation which compromises the internal tranquility and international credit of the country"; of not obeying the Constitution, as evidenced by his "publicly applauding a reporter's proposal for dissolving Congress", and of ignoring the Designates to the Presidency recently elected by Congress; and of provoking division in the armed forces thereby endangering the peace. The bill thereupon deposes President Argüello and names Benjamin Lacayo Sacasa to fill the Presidency "until normalcy is completely restored and new elections are held".

---

[39] Not printed.

Opinion is unanimous that impeachment proceedings as carried through by Congress were unconstitutional. Witness of this is the fact that the decree mentioned no articles of the Constitution as the legal basis of its extraordinary action. By selecting one of the three Designates to be President, Congress performed the function given to the President by the Constitution. By its action of Monday night, Congress followed the military coup with a legislative coup.

Respectfully yours,
MAURICE M. BERNBAUM

817.00/5-3147 : Telegram

The Secretary of State to the Embassy in Nicaragua

CONFIDENTIAL WASHINGTON, June 3, 1947—6 p. m.

114. Urtel 222, May 31.[40] It is appreciated that General Somoza may find it desirable to communicate with you again. Should you have occasion for further conversations with him you should be certain that it is unequivocally understood by Somoza that you are communicating with him as a private citizen only and not in his official capacity as Minister of War or as Director of the Guardia Nacional. The same procedure would apply of course with respect to any other member of the Lacayo regime.

MARSHALL

817.00/6-1047 : Telegram

The Chargé in Nicaragua (Bernbaum) to the Secretary of State

RESTRICTED MANAGUA, June 10, 1947—5 p. m.

241. See Embassy's telegram 234, June 6.[40] Decree calling Constituent Assembly finally released to press this afternoon after long delay, occasioned by difficulties in negotiations between Somoza and Conservatives. Signed by President Lacayo and his cabinet and taking effect upon publication in *La Gazeta*, decree provides for: Elections to a Constituent Assembly August 3; Assembly convened August 29; Conservatives given principal party status only after presentation electoral tickets for Assembly; nominations due within 15 days from effective date of decree; each department allowed Representatives equal to number of Deputies and Senators; use of same electoral lists used in past elections; Congress dissolved immediately; Provisional President empowered legislate by decree during interim period.

---

[40] Not printed.

Assembly empowered to write new constitution, elect new President and Congress, and reorganize judiciary.

Repeat to War Department.

BERNBAUM

817.00/6–1647 : Telegram

The Secretary of State to the Embassy in Nicaragua

CONFIDENTIAL   WASHINGTON, June 24, 1947—7 p. m.

138. Reference your A–228, June 16.[43] For your info only: Formal consultations are not contemplated at this time. Informal consultations have resulted in failure of *de facto* govt to obtain recognition from any of the American Republics and difficulty in obtaining unanimity on any joint statement or joint course of action would make formal consultations inadvisable.

Further informal exchanges of views are anticipated should a change in Nicaraguan situation occur.

MARSHALL

817.20 Missions/6–2647

The Chargé in Nicaragua (Bernbaum) to the Secretary of State

[Extracts]

CONFIDENTIAL   MANAGUA, June 26, 1947.
No. 1664

SIR: I have the honor to refer to Mr. Gordon Reid's letter of June 18, to the Department's telegram no. 137 of June 24, and to the Embassy's telegram no. 251 of June 25,[44] concerning the present status of the American Military Mission in Nicaragua and of the ammunition belonging to the Mission which had until recently been stored at the Casa Presidencial.

As reported in the Embassy's despatch no. 1592 of May 9,[43] Colonel Greco sent a memorandum on May 6 to the Jefe Director of the Guardia Nacional (Somoza) requesting that the ammunition in question be returned to him for transfer to American Army Headquarters in Panama. Shortly thereafter, Major Francisco Boza, Guardia Supply Officer, informed Colonel Greco that he had been authorized by General Somoza to say that due to the recent transfer of the Government Arsenal from the Presidential Palace to La Curva, the arsenal

---

[43] Not printed.
[44] None printed.

was considerably disarranged and the ammunition belonging to the United States Army could not be readily located. At that time, however, Major Boza stated that as soon as the ammunition was located it would be returned in accordance with Colonel Greco's request. Although Colonel Greco frequently reiterated his request to Major Boza by telephone during the next few weeks, the answer was always the same and the ammunition was not returned.

On June 24, following the receipt here of Mr. Reid's letter, Colonel Greco once again called Major Boza. This time he stated that the United States War and State Departments were interested in the ammunition and insisted that it be returned to him at once for shipment by air to Panama. After some hesitation Major Boza finally agreed to return it on the following evening (June 25), when he delivered the 214 rounds of 16 mm. mortar. The remaining 60 grenades were promised for tomorrow.

As to the status of the agreement which placed Colonel Greco at the Military Academy,[45] there is nothing in the files of the Embassy or of the Military Mission which would indicate that it is valid after May 22, 1947. In accordance with my request, Colonel Greco, who has always understood that his detail here would not end until July 1948, sent a cable on June 24 to the Commanding General of the Caribbean Defense Command in the Canal Zone [46] asking for information on the subject. No answer has yet been received.

Following our discussion yesterday on the matter, Colonel Greco handed me a memorandum, copies of which are enclosed,[46] in which he states that even if the agreement in question has terminated, it is his belief that he should carry on as heretofore and that as soon as a recognized Government emerges in Nicaragua the agreement in question should be extended for another two years. . . .

. . . .

As reported in the Embassy's telegram no. 251 of June 25, 1947, there has already been some criticism of the apparent contradiction between non-recognition and continued United States participation in the Military Academy. Should the fact that the agreement has lapsed become known, such criticism would undoubtedly grow. It is the Embassy's belief that the withdrawal of the Mission pending negotiation of an agreement with a recognized Government would emphasize to both Somoza and the people that the United States Government is serious in its non-recognition, [and] would re-emphasize its displeasure with the Somoza coup. . . .

. . . .

---

[45] For documentation on extension of the 1943 Military Mission agreement to May 1947, see *Foreign Relations*, 1945, vol. IX, pp. 1193. For the 1943 agreement, see Department of State Executive Agreement Series No. 344, or 57 Stat. (pt. 2) 1109.

[46] Not printed.

Should such action be taken, it would be desirable in the interest of at least consistency, that the same be done temporarily with the Aerial Mapping Plan and staff of the Public Roads Administration. As reported in this Embassy's telegram no. 253 of June 25, 1947,[54] the PRA representative has already advised the Embassy that his participation on Rama Road activities will cease on June 28 and that he advocates a temporary return to the United States of PRA personnel due to the current political situation. Similarly, it is informally understood that the first phase of the Ground Survey work of the Mapping Mission is nearing completion. This will be checked with Mr. Gee, Chief Engineer, upon his return to Managua during the next few days.

Respectfully yours, MAURICE M. BERNBAUM

817.20 Missions/7-147 : Telegram

The Chargé in Nicaragua (Bernbaum) to the Secretary of State

CONFIDENTIAL MANAGUA, July 1, 1947—2 p. m.

270. Deptel 146 of June 28.[54] Upon receipt from Greco of copy of ComGenCarib telegram instructing immediate evacuation of military mission, following statement given to press in Spanish:

"Colonel John Greco, chief of the United States military mission and director of the Nicaraguan Military Academy, has been instructed by the United States Government to withdraw from Nicaragua together with his personnel and equipment, pending the establishment of an internationally recognized Nicaraguan Government."

I informally apprised Somoza prior to release of foregoing to press. He expressed regret but stated he intends continue in present position until new President elected by Constituent Assembly when he plans proceed States for medical attention and possible visit in Washington.

Initial reaction from reporters and Dr. Enoc Aguado was enthusiastic and congratulatory. Dr. Alejandro Argüello Montiel visited Embassy shortly after Somoza conversation in another attempt to explain Somoza's position and necessity for our assistance to help him solve political problem. He was visibly depressed and left even more so.

Two representatives ComGenCarib arrived this morning from Panama to assist in mission evacuation. We tentatively arranged to store mission equipment at Las Piedrecitas and office Military Attaché on latter's responsibility. I expressed desire to cooperate fully in minimizing evacuation burden and stated I have no objection to unhurried

---

[54] Not printed.

evacuation since *de facto* government and public have already been made aware of US Government position.

BERNBAUM

817.00/6–3047 : Telegram

The Secretary of State to the Embassy in Nicaragua

CONFIDENTIAL WASHINGTON, July 7, 1947—7 p. m.

151. During past few weeks Dept has received many Nicaraguans representing various parties. In all conversations Dept has made it extremely clear that this govt does not and has not advocated that any party either abstain from or cooperate in the Constituent elections (reurtel 267, June 30 [55]).

Furthermore, Dept has not made any statement as to possible recognition of any govt emanating from Constituent Assembly (reurtel 266, June 30). Obviously we cannot commit ourselves as to future action.

MARSHALL

817.00/7–1147

The Department of State to the Bolivian Embassy

MEMORANDUM

Reference is made to the Department's memorandum of June 28, 1947 [55] in connection with the Bolivian initiative suggesting that consultation be held among the American republics relative to Nicaragua. In the memorandum under reference it was pointed out that the Government of the United States would support the Bolivian initiative as therein set forth provided the Bolivian Government obtained approval of a substantial majority of the other American republics and provided agreement was also reached on the question of Nicaraguan participation in the Rio de Janeiro conference.[56]

In view of the fact that the question of Nicaraguan participation in the conference is now being handled through other channels [57] at the instance of the Brazilian Government as host, the United States Government is now prepared to support the initiative on the single proviso

---

[55] Not printed.
[56] Inter-American Conference for the Maintenance of Continental Peace and Security, Quitandinha (Rio de Janeiro), Brazil, August 15–September 2, 1947; for documentation on this conference, see pp. 1 ff.
[57] i.e., through the Governing Board of the Pan American Union.

that the Bolivian Government obtain approval of a substantial majority of the other American republics.

WASHINGTON, July 11, 1947.

[A copy of the memorandum printed *supra* was transmitted to the Embassy in Bolivia in telegram 409, July 12, 1947, 3 p. m., concluding as follows:

"Please see FonMin and discuss matter with him. For your background information Dept hopes consultations suggested by Bolivia be proceeded with so that consensus of American republics as to non-recognition of Lacayo Sacasa regime be put on record regardless of what steps may be taken in connection with its participation in Rio Conference which question is now being considered by Gov Bd PAU at request of Brazil. Marshall." (817.01/7–1247)]

817.00/8–747 : Airgram

The Chargé in Nicaragua (Bernbaum) to the Secretary of State

[Extracts]

CONFIDENTIAL MANAGUA, August 7, 1947.

A–287. Reference this Embassy's telegram no. 298 of August 6, 1947,[58] regarding a conversation held at my home yesterday with General Anastasio Somoza. He was exceedingly amiable throughout the conversation, and repeatedly stressed his past, present and future loyalty to and cooperation with the United States.

. . . He confirmed at this time that convening of the Constituent Assembly had been advanced to August 15 from August 29 over the strong objection of the *de facto* President, Benjamin Lacayo Sacasa. . . . Somoza recapitulated the qualifications of each candidate. . . . The final decision, announced as if it had been reached during the interview, was that the septuagenarian Dr. Victor Roman y Reyes be the President and Dr. Mariano Argüello Vargas the Vice President. The former, he indicated, would be elected by the Constituent Assembly shortly after convening and the latter would be designated Vice President after completion and approval of a suitably amended Constitution. Somoza did not conceal the belief that Argüello Vargas might be too furious to accept the Vice Presidency, and insisted that Argüello Vargas' participation in the *coup d'état* was the only factor disqualifying him for the Presidency.

Somoza's preoccupation with United States non-recognition and his policy of effecting recognition as the reward for cooperation were

---

[58] Not printed.

further illustrated in a lengthy exposition of the changes to be effected in the new Constitution. Of these the most heavily stressed were: "Concrete and effective dispositions against Communist propaganda and activities"; and "ample powers to the executive for the negotiation of agreements to permit, without violating national sovereignty, the temporary use of Nicaraguan territory for the establishment of military, naval and air bases in times of continental emergency." He reaffirmed his desire for the return of the United States Military Mission and promised unconditional support for United States policies at all times, including the Rio Conference.

Dr. Guillermo Sevilla Sacasa is to attend the Rio Conference as observer, and delegate in the event of later recognition and the extension of an invitation. Dr. Mariano Argüello Vargas will be requested to accompany him, but Somoza believed that he would probably be too angry to accept. Dr. Carlos Cuadra Pasos would be another choice if permitted by General Chamorro to accept the designation. In view of the foregoing, Somoza gave it as probable that Octavio Salinas (delegate to the United Nations Assembly) or another Nationalist Conservative will attend with Sevilla Sacasa.

Upon questioning, Somoza admitted that his departure for the United States for medical attention will be dependent upon international recognition. Should that not be forthcoming he will remain to face the "inevitable revolution". Although repeatedly emphasizing that he was motivated only by the desire to protect his friends and had no desire or intention to remain in politics, he further admitted that he plans to return after recovery from his operation and an extended vacation trip. I gathered he was thinking in terms of about six months. Somoza predicted that the Conservative Party will wait only for his departure before initiating attempts to overthrow the new Government, and affirmed that he would in such case return immediately.

· · · · · · ·

Somoza expressed considerable concern over refusal of the Bank of America to make its contractual advance of $500,000 to the account of the Nicaraguan National Bank. He understood from Bank of America telegrams that the refusal was based either on the advice or instructions of the State Department.[59] With about US$300,000 in Na-

---

[59] The Department informed the Embassy in Nicaragua in airgram A-156, August 18 (817.51/8-647), that it did not offer advice to the Bank of America as to the policy the Bank should follow, but had stated in telegram of August 8 to the Bank as follows: ". . . Lacayo Govt not recognized by US Govt which cannot therefore undertake to make confirmation of agreements made by officials of Lacayo Govt or of advances for use of Lacayo Govt, a condition precedent to recognition of any future Nicaraguan Govt. Dept is not prepared to express legal opinion on effectiveness your lien on gold in Federal Reserve bank of New York for all purposes."

tional Bank drafts outstanding and gold reserves immobilized in the Bank of America and the Federal Reserve Bank of New York, he gloomily mentioned the possibility of a run on the National Bank as soon as the situation becomes known. It was evident that he, as well as previous visitors to the Embassy, believed that this move signified the beginning of economic sanctions.[61]

Comment:

. . . . .

BERNBAUM

817.00/8–1947

The Chargé in Nicaragua (Bernbaum) to the Secretary of State

[Extracts]

RESTRICTED
No. 1729

MANAGUA, August 19, 1947.

SIR: In continuation of the Embassy's despatch no. 1726 of August 15, 1947 [62] concerning the meeting of the Constituent Assembly, I have the honor to enclose a clipping of the address of Dr. Victor Manuel Román to the Assembly subsequent to his selection by it as President.

It may be interjected here that there is some question as to whether Dr. Román is a "constitutional" or "provisional" President in the technical sense of the term. The Government press invariably describes him as a "constitutional" magistrate while the opposition press, the majority, describes his office as "provisional". As a matter of fact, it is difficult to understand how a constitutional president can be selected before there is a Constitution.

. . . . .

As the Embassy reported telegraphically (see Embassy's telegram no. 306 of August 15, 1947 [62]), the selection of Dr. Román has provoked a general reaction of respect for him as an individual but no respect whatsoever for the maneuver which put him into office and which is considered as nothing less than a continuation of the Somoza regime. . . .

. . . . .

Respectfully yours,

MAURICE M. BERNBAUM

---

[61] In telegram 187, August 14, 6 p. m., the Department informed the Chargé that "Dept does not favor economic sanctions and will take no action to that end". (817.51/8–1347)
[62] Not printed.

817.01/8-2147 : Airgram

The Acting Secretary of State to the Embassy in Nicaragua

CONFIDENTIAL WASHINGTON, August 21, 1947.

A-159. For your information the following telegram was sent to the U.S. Delegation at the Rio Conference [63] in reply to a request from the Delegation asking for the Department's views:

"It has been our consistent position, both in Pan Am Union debate prior to Rio [64] and in our informal conversations with Sevilla Sacasa and members of diplomatic corps here, that we would 'follow the majority' in so far as possible in connection with question of Nicaraguan attendance at Rio and, for that matter, eventual recognition. We have expressed hope both in circular telegram to our missions in field [65] and in Wright's statement before Pan Am Union [66] that there would exist in Nicaragua a Govt recognized by majority of American Republics in sufficient time to permit Nicaragua's attendance at Rio. We continue to feel that this is wise policy and that our present attitude should be very judicious one waiting for substantial body of Govts to act without our giving impression of taking lead in manner which might be interpreted as pressure or tutelage. Our information here is that Honduras should be added to list of countries you mention urtel 26, Aug 19,[67] as ones not likely to recognize new Govt. Honduras will of course go along with majority but we have definite information that Caceres' instructions are to follow our lead.

"Telegram went forward today giving you composition of 'Argüello' delegation which is going solely as observers. Also Dept has been informed that Argüello Vargas, who, as you know, is Vice Pres in new regime, will attempt to present credentials tomorrow in Rio as representative of newly elected Govt. We are told that if he is not accepted, he will present credentials as representative of 'Nicaragua' and credentials will state that acceptance does not imply recognition of regime but rather recognition only of right of Nicaragua to have a delegation seated.

"In all honesty we must take into account fact that, like it or not, present regime in Nicaragua has all attributes and qualities of stable *de facto* Govt. It is maintaining public order. It is so far as can be ascertained meeting its international commitments, et cetera. Given the situation in Nicaragua and admitting that the regime is certainly a puppet one and a creature of Somoza (using oppressive measures such as recent detention of leading members of opposition), one of questions for us to decide is whether it is likely that in foreseeable future there will be any other stable regime in Nicaragua composed of other than these same or similar elements. Without condoning methods

---

[63] Telegram 41, August 19, 8 p. m., to the United States Delegation, Petropolis (Brazil), p. 39.
[64] For data on decisions reached at close of debate at the Pan American Union, see circular telegram, July 29, 1947, 2 a. m., p. 27.
[65] Circular telegram of July 24, 1947, p. 24.
[66] Statement by the Director of the Office of American Republic Affairs (Wright), July 28, not printed.
[67] Not printed.

by which regime has placed itself in power, it is our view that likelihood of strictly constitutional and more representative Govt in near future is slight."

LOVETT

817.51/8–2147

The Chargé in Nicaragua (Bernbaum) to the Secretary of State

CONFIDENTIAL MANAGUA, August 21, 1947.
No. 1736

SIR: I have the honor to refer to my telegram no. 307 of August 15 [68] and previous correspondence with the Department regarding the local financial flurry aroused by refusal of the Bank of America to continue advances under its loan agreement with the Nicaraguan National Bank.

As previously reported, the unexpected action of the Bank of America left the Nicaraguan National Bank with only about $60,000 in liquid dollar balances as of August 12. With refusal of the Federal Reserve Bank of New York to make an otherwise normal 90–day advance of $500,000 against earmarked gold owing to the *de facto* character of the Government (see Embassy's A–291 of August 12, 1947 [68]), it was then considered that the National Bank's gold assets in the United States had been frozen. Such assets comprised:

Gold
Collateral with Bank of America	$2,750,000
Earmarked with Federal Reserve Bank of New York	1,594,385
International Monetary Fund	500,000

Dollars
Collateral with Bank of America	904,159
Total	$5,748,544

As against this, the National Bank has already received from the Bank of America and expended net advances of $2,155,000 on loan account.

The crisis broke on August 13 when, as a result of the foregoing situation, the National Bank discontinued dollar operations: all new and pending import applications as of that day were rejected and importers attempting to meet sight drafts covering merchandise already at Corinto were told that the National Bank was not in a position to furnish the dollars.

---

[68] Not printed.

The immediate result was a sharp rise in the black market rate for dollars and a state of panic and confusion in commercial circles. With replacement costs uncertain, some merchants discontinued sales and others raised prices markedly. Rumors of economic sanctions were prevalent, and anxiety was, if anything, accentuated by the following statement to the press on August 13 by Rafael Huezo, Manager of the National Bank:

"Commerce has been abusing the law of October 15, 1945 which authorizes applications for foreign exchange through the deposit of 60 percent of the total value of the imports involved. The National Bank has been forced to issue an order temporarily restricting the entry of imported goods, since there are in warehouses and in the customs stocks of goods which could not be consumed in a year. Commerce has violated its obligations by absorbing more than its share of foreign exchange. The Bank is now disposed to maintain an equilibrium between imports and exports."

The situation remained tense until August 15 when the admittedly* unexpected purchase by the Federal Reserve Bank of New York of 15,000 ounces of earmarked gold valued at $525,000 permitted the limited resumption of dollar operations. Although not yet restored to normal, economic conditions have as a result receded from the panic stage. Black market dollar quotations have declined from a momentarily frenzied high of C$9.00 to about C$5.50–5.75. The quotation on April 12 was C$5.35. Shops have been reopened and general business activity has returned to the limited levels consonant with the currently acute political situation.

An examination of the National Bank's foreign exchange position reveals that the action of the Bank of America has merely served to precipitate the initiation of severe import and exchange restrictions which were in any case inevitable. As itemized above, current gold and exchange assets prior to the recent sale of gold amounted to $5,748,544. Taking into consideration outstanding gold-secured loans from the Bank of America of $2,155,000 and the non-liquid character of the $500,000 deposit with the International Monetary Fund, liquid foreign exchange assets totalled only $3,093,500. (This represents a decline of $2,170,250 from the comparable balance on December 31, 1946 of $5,263,800 †). As against this, collection accounts payable aggregated $1,200,000 ‡ and pending import orders to approximately $5,000,000 §.

---

*By Rafael Huezo, Manager of the National Bank. [Footnote in the original.]
†See Report No. 15 of February 11, 1947 (Nicaraguan Foreign Exchange Position). [Footnote in the original.]
‡According to Rafael Huezo (see telegram no. 304 of August 14, 1947). [Footnote in the original.]
§ Deposits (60%) with the National Bank against imports amounted on July 31 to C$14,900,517. [Footnote in the original.]

With estimated foreign exchange receipts during August–December estimated by the National Bank at only $1,500,000 ‡, the end of the year will, even assuming the discontinuance of all import licenses and non-import dollar transactions, find the National Bank with an exchange deficit for the year well in excess of $6,000,000, and dollar-bankrupt. Resumption by the Bank of America of its loan obligations would, in view of the stringent repayment terms provided by the loan contract, only reduce the pending deficit by about $1,000,000 for the current year (see despatch no. 1346 of January 22, 1947).[70]

As stated to me yesterday by Rafael Huezo, the anticipated foreign exchange shortage has led to the decision to restrict all future import applications to only scarce and essential items. Pending the elaboration of a new schedule by the National Bank, no new import applications are being accepted. He assured me, however, that existing dollar obligations are being fulfilled, and in illustration stated that only $200,000 is left of the $525,000 sale of gold last week to the Federal Reserve Bank of New York. Further gold sales are contemplated. It is also planned to liquidate the loan account with the Bank of America in the event the latter does not see its way clear to comply with the loan contract.[71]

From the political viewpoint, the incident is generally interpreted as having been related to economic sanctions by the United States, and has reportedly reinforced the belief of opposition leaders, including General Chamorro, that "further" sanctions will soon eventuate. I shall, of course, do my utmost to discreetly disabuse them of this idea as running counter to our repeatedly-declared policy of non-intervention.

The foregoing belief is, so far as can be ascertained, based on: a widely publicized prediction from Washington by Dr. Fernando Sacasa during the first days of August that economic sanctions were in the offing; the wording of the Federal Reserve Bank's refusal to grant the requested 90-day loan; and the apparently evasive policy of the Bank of America. . . .

Although under the circumstances virtually swamped by appeals for information from the press, businessmen, and "politicos", the Embassy refrained from any comment pending news from the Department. Following an earlier statement to General Chamorro that there was no

---

‡ According to Rafael Huezo (see telegram no. 304 of August 14, 1947). [Footnote in the original.]

[70] Not printed.

[71] In airgram A–298, August 22, the Chargé reported that Rafael Huezo, Manager of the Nicaraguan National Bank, had informed him that morning that the Bank of America had on that date telephoned to advise him that advances under the loan contract would be resumed (817.51/8–2247).

reason to believe sanctions were contemplated, comment was restricted to conversations with General Somoza (see Embassy's A–287 of August 7, 1947), Rafael Huezo and the Panamanian Minister (see Embassy's A–293 of August 13 [72]) in which I expressed the opinion that the matter was of a legal rather than political nature. This was confirmed to Rafael Huezo upon receipt of the Department's telegrams no. 187 and 190 of August 14 and 16,[73] and made public following a concurrent telephone call from José Sandino in Washington to the then *de facto* President, Benjamin Lacayo Sacasa (see Department's telegram no. 191 of August 16, 1947 [72]). A reporter's request for confirmation of United States sanctions was on August 15 answered with substantially the following statement: "the Department of State has not and is not exercising sanctions in accordance with its already well known international policy." It is still, however, apparently considered in both official and opposition circles that sanctions are either in effect through coercion on the Bank of America or were discontinued in the face of an unexpectedly strong reaction. Characteristic press clippings are enclosed.[74]

It appears that the net result of the incident has been to further weaken Somoza's political position and encourage opposition hopes that international action will force him out.

Respectfully yours, MAURICE M. BERNBAUM

817.01/8–2447

Memorandum of Conversation, by Assistant Secretary of State Armour, Political Adviser, United States Delegation, Rio de Janeiro Conference

SECRET PETROPOLIS, August 24, 1947.

Dr. Sevilla Sacasa having expressed through Mr. Sanders [75] a desire to see me, I had a talk with him this morning at the Copacabana Hotel. He brought up three points:

1. The question of presentation of the credentials of his delegation as representatives of the new government in Nicaragua. He asked me whether I felt that they should present their request for decision on this point. I said that I thought that no useful purpose would be served since I did not believe there had been any radical change since

---

[72] Not printed.
[73] Telegram 190 not printed; for extract from telegram 187, see footnote 61, p. 866.
[74] Not reprinted.
[75] William Sanders, Associate Chief of the Division of International Organization Affairs; Adviser at the Rio Conference.

the decision taken after the vote at the Pan American Union in Washington.[77]

2. He reminded me that when he had seen me in Washington he had told me that General Somoza had for some time been planning to leave the country in order to have a serious operation and he wondered whether this would not be a good time for him to do so. In other words, whether the departure of Somoza would not help in clearing up the situation and making recognition easier. I told him that I entirely agreed: that so long as General Somoza remained in the country it would be difficult to convince the other governments withholding recognition that any steps taken were not under the direction of General Somoza himself. I told Dr. Sevilla Sacasa that while of course I did not wish to appear to be telling them how they should arrange their affairs, I believed that if after the departure of General Somoza they would broaden the government by bringing in representatives of certain of the other groups this might also improve the situation. The important thing was to convince us and the governments of the other American Republics that the Government in Nicaragua was representative of the will of the majority of the people and that naturally the broadening by the inclusion of other elements in the Government would appear to be a step in this direction.

. . . .

N[orman] A[rmour]

817.01/9–2047 : Telegram

The Ambassador in Costa Rica (Donnelly) to the Secretary of State

SECRET   SAN JOSÉ, September 20, 1947—8 p. m.

465. Embtel 463, September 20, 4 p. m.[78] President Picado received Mariano Argüello last night and again this morning. Argüello gave President letters from Román y Reyes and from Somoza both requesting Costa Rica's immediate recognition current Nicaraguan regime. Somoza reminded Picado of his friendship toward him and his noninterference Costa Rican affairs as evidenced by his refusal aid opposition during Picado's presidential 1943 campaign . . . Foreign Minister this morning told me Picado, while greatly disturbed and resentful of Argüello's remarks, told him last night and

---

[77] In Airgram A–308, September 2, the Chargé reported as follows: "Ministers of State of the Argüello Government detained since the Somoza *coup d'état* were released Friday evening [August 29]. This action apparently taken owing to the decision of the Rio Conference not to accept the Argüello delegation or representatives of the *de facto* Government. Those released include the Minister of Foreign Affairs, Dr. Leon DeBayle, who for the past three weeks has been confined in General Somoza's fortress residence. Bernbaum". (817.00/9–247)

[78] Not printed.

again this morning when Argüello called on Picado ostensibly to say good-by that his government would continue to be guided by principle of consultation among the American Republics and that it would accept the position of the majority of the countries. Nevertheless the Acting Foreign Minister called me to the Foreign Office late today to tell me that his government was alarmed over possibility of trouble for Costa Rica as result of failure Argüello mission to Costa Rica . . .

Minister went on to say that a protracted delay in solving Nicaraguan problem would result in increasing Costa Rican domestic tension and while Costa Rica desired to continue to adhere to consultative principle the situation here is critical and that he felt an immediate solution was imperative. With this in mind, he requested our views as to possibility of solution through Somoza leaving Nicaragua for Philadelphia and then American Republics recognizing the Román y Reyes regime. I told him that in my opinion such a solution would not provide for a restoration of democratic principles in Nicaragua. He then suggested an alternate plan which he asked that I send to Washington as my idea and not as his, namely, that Somoza leave for the United States and not return to Nicaragua; formation of a coalition Cabinet with Román y Reyes as President and the new government to determine whether general elections would be held and when.

I asked him if his government had received any assurances that such a plan would be workable and he replied that his government was confident that it could be realized. He said he knew that Honduras would endorse this or any other plan acceptable to our Government. I asked the Minister if Argüello had suggested this or any other solution and he said he had not (I question his sincerity). He requested our views as to either of these two proposals or as to any other solution we would find acceptable, stressing once again his government's grave concern over the turn of events and the need for a prompt solution in order to prevent trouble here.

I told him I would convey the substance of our conversation to my Government and said that I assumed his government would be willing to take the lead in consulting with the other American Republics as to any solution which might be found. He assured me that his government would be disposed to do so.

As Department knows, pressure from Nicaragua is of fundamental concern to Costa Rica. Last night Minister told me very definitely that President was determined to adhere to consultative procedure and to abide by majority view. This afternoon he and the President had weakened to a point where they were looking for an immediate out without antagonizing either, on one hand Somoza or on the other the US and domestic public opinion. He repeated several times that no solution was practicable unless it were on terms acceptable to the U.S.

In the balance there are on one side Somoza and on the other the US and domestic public opinion: . . . While I realize that efforts are being made to draw me in as an intermediary, efforts for which I do not plan to fall, I feel that I must warn the Department that, unless some formula is promptly found, Costa Rica may very easily recognize Román y Reyes.

I request the Department's telegraphic views of the formulae suggested by the Acting Foreign Minister or a statement of what we consider to be the minimum requirements for recognition of some Nicaraguan regime.

Repeated to Managua.

DONNELLY

817.01/9–2047 : Telegram

The Acting Secretary of State to the Embassy in Costa Rica [79]

SECRET WASHINGTON, September 23, 1947—1 p. m.

316. This Govt's position in respect of Nicaraguan recognition question has been made abundantly clear in previous telegrams and circulars. Our policy has not beeen changed. We do not wish to influence in any way what Costa Rica may do. We have consistently resisted repeated efforts to have this Govt indicate what type of a solution to Nicaraguan problem would be acceptable. It is hoped that our action in either recognizing or not recognizing a Nicaraguan govt can be in harmony with similar action by a broad cross section of the other American govts.

LOVETT

817.51/9–2347 : Airgram

The Acting Secretary of State to the Embassy in Nicaragua

RESTRICTED WASHINGTON, September 23, 1947.

A–173. The following telegram was sent today by the Federal Reserve Bank of New York to the Banco Nacional de Nicaragua.

"Owing to continued absence of official relations between US Government and the regime in power in Nicaragua, we regret that we continue to be unable to grant you a loan at this time".

This was sent in reply to a direct request to the Federal Reserve Bank from the Banco Nacional for a loan for $500,000 for three months against gold held by the Federal Reserve Bank of New York.

LOVETT

---

[79] Repeated to the Embassy in Nicaragua in telegram 216, September 23, 1947, 6 p. m.

817.00/9–2347 : Telegram

The Acting Secretary of State to the Embassy in Nicaragua

CONFIDENTIAL   WASHINGTON, September 24, 1947—6 p. m.

217. Reurtel 331, Sept 23.[80] Dept believes safe conduct is part of right of asylum not granted by this Govt except when immediate danger to life involved. Should you believe Chamorro's life immediately endangered, Dept authorizes you to request informally safe conduct to airport. Above is predicated on Dept's belief you concur in Chamorro's statement of his situation. In such case, Dept suggests you consider possibility asking entire diplomatic corps to accompany you. Thus onus of unilateral action could be avoided.[81]

LOVETT

817.00/10–647

Memorandum of Conversation, by the Chief of the Division of Central America and Panama Affairs (Newbegin)

CONFIDENTIAL   [WASHINGTON,] October 6, 1947.

Participants: Don Julián R. Cáceres, Honduran Ambassador
Mr. Armour, Assistant Secretary
Robert Newbegin, CPA

Ambassador Cáceres called this morning to discuss the Nicaraguan political situation with Mr. Armour. He said that he was calling at President Carias' suggestion in order to clarify the Honduran position vis-à-vis the Nicaraguan problem. He stated that Honduras intended to follow the lead of the United States as it had been doing in the past. He mentioned the fact that the non-recognition policy had been adopted more or less simultaneously and after consultation by the American republics and he hoped that when the time came for recognition it would likewise be done more or less simultaneously. He emphasized that non-recognition of Nicaragua carried with it perhaps greater problems for the Central American countries than for others since there was a tendency to assist opposition groups in exile which led to obvious complications. He stressed that Carias himself would much prefer to have more satisfactory relations with Nicaragua than existed at present, but that he felt this was a question of political morals and he had no intention whatsoever of deviating from the stand which he had taken originally.

---

[80] Not printed; it concerned General Chamorro's request that the Embassy secure safe conduct for his departure to Mexico (817.00/9–2347).

[81] In telegram 336, September 27, noon, the Chargé reported that General and Mrs. Chamorro had left on that date by PAA for San Salvador, and that at the Embassy's request he had been granted safe conduct by General Somoza the day before (817.00/9–2747).

Mr. Armour asked if Ambassador Cáceres had any idea as to how the problem could be solved. The Ambassador replied that speaking personally he felt that there could be no solution until Somoza left the country. He said that this view was also that of the Chilean Government and certain of the other American republics. Mr. Armour said that he felt that the departure of Somoza would undoubtedly make a solution easier but it should be perfectly clear that this Government was not making his departure a condition for recognition, that what appeared to be necessary was a broadening of the Government in which all parties could participate and a selection of a Director of the Guardia Nacional in whom all parties had confidence. Ambassador Cáceres intimated that it would be helpful if the United States could take the lead in finding a solution, although he appreciated the danger of being accused of intervening. He referred to Mariano Argüello Vargas' visit to Costa Rica and stated that maybe some solution along the lines suggested by him might eventually be reached. He further stated that he considered part of the present difficulty in Nicaragua due to the fact that Somoza was continuing to remain there . . .

R[OBERT] N[EWBEGIN]

817.00/10-647 : Telegram

The Chargé in Nicaragua (Bernbaum) to the Secretary of State

RESTRICTED   MANAGUA, October 6, 1947—noon.

342. Renato Argüello, son of Dr. Leonardo Argüello, called this morning to request this Embassy's aid in procuring safe conduct for his father to leave country. After expressing sympathy, I told him nothing could be done in view of long standing policy of US on asylum which allowed aid only in case of immediate danger to life.

Mexican Embassy Secretary told this Embassy today that state Dr. Argüello's health considered critical. Friday night he suffered heart attack which doctors diagnosed as result of his enforced sedentary life. This complication is added to his existing diabetes, amoebas, hemorrhoids and mental anxiety. This office expressed fears that Dr. Argüello might die within Embassy because of complete impasse which had developed in the case between Mexican Embassy, acting on Dr. Argüello's behalf, and Foreign Office. Latter has now refused to grant exit visa whether or not Dr. Argüello should agree to renounce presidency. On other hand Dr. Argüello absolutely refused accept Somoza's offer of safe conduct to go to his home or to any local hospital.

BERNBAUM

[In telegram 227, October 8, 10 a. m., Acting Secretary Lovett stated as follows: "You are authorized in your discretion as a humanitarian measure to extend informal good offices (urtel 342 Oct 6) with a view to obtaining safe conduct permitting Dr. Leonardo Argüello to leave Nicaragua." (817.00/10–647) On October 8, the Chargé informed the Mexican Ambassador that the American Mission would be glad to be of informal assistance in the Argüello matter; the Mexican Ambassador confirmed that authorities were not disposed to permit Argüello to leave the country (817.00/10–847). Despatches 1783 and 1791, October 7 and 14, respectively, reported (1) the issuance by the Nicaraguan Foreign Office of a communiqué declaring that the Government would not allow Dr. Argüello to leave his asylum in the Mexican Embassy for exile abroad, and (2) Constituent Assembly decree of October 13 prohibiting the departure from Nicaragua of the deposed President without the express authorization of the Constituent Assembly (817.00/10–747; /10–1447).]

817.01/11–2547 : Telegram

The Chargé in Costa Rica (Carrigan) to the Secretary of State

SECRETSAN JOSÉ, November 25, 1947—5 p. m.

549. Foreign Minister this morning informed me Costa Rica convinced several South American presidents (he referred Betancourt [82] among others) would exchange New Year's greetings with Somoza, thus effecting *de facto* recognition.

Foreign Minister then reviewed well-known previous argument Costa Rican position.

He then said he wished formally to request I inquire of Department for his government's information answer following questions: Since government cannot afford avoid consideration similar action, will its recognition Nicaragua be considered by US (*a*) action hostile to US

---

[82] Romulo Betancourt, President of Venezuela.

policy or (*b*) regrettable but understandable in view Costa Rican position.

I made no comment other than to say I would, of course, transmit inquiry to my Government. He has already been thoroughly informed our position.

CARRIGAN

817.01/11–2547 : Telegram

The Acting Secretary of State to the Embassy in Costa Rica

SECRET   WASHINGTON, November 28, 1947—7 p. m.

382. It is not clear to Dept why Costa Rican govt feels impelled to follow action mentioned urtel 549 Nov. 25.[83] It is equally difficult to believe Betancourt would participate. You may however inform Fonmin that Dept would not interpret action as "hostile" to US policy although definitely not in line with it. You may also inform Fonmin that in opinion this govt exchange of messages with Somoza would not constitute recognition since Somoza is not technically head of state. Dept does not anticipate acknowledging or sending any holiday messages to Román, Somoza or any other Nicaraguan official.

LOVETT

817.00/12–247

The Chargé in Nicaragua (Bernbaum) to the Secretary of State

[Extract]

RESTRICTED   MANAGUA, December 2, 1947.
No. 1861

SIR: With reference to this Embassy's telegrams nos. 374 and 376 of November 27 and 29, respectively,[84] I have the honor to submit the following preliminary observations on the political situation following the departure for Mexico on November 29 of the deposed president, Dr. Leonardo Argüello, after a record asylum of six months and two days in the Mexican Embassy.

In line with the information previously made available to this office by the Mexican Embassy, Dr. Argüello's departure had been authorized on November 27 by the Constituent Assembly on terms indicating

---

[83] The Chargé in Costa Rica replied in telegram 553, December 1, 1947, 4 p. m., as follows: "Foreign Office has now informed me Acting Foreign Minister meant greetings with Román and not Somoza and (2) he was mistaken concerning Betancourt (817.01/12–147).

[84] Neither printed.

that the Mexican Government had substantially yielded to General Somoza's demand for guarantees that Dr. Argüello would not be allowed to take any part in political activities against the *de facto* regime.[85] . . .

. . . .

Respectfully yours,   MAURICE M. BERNBAUM

817.00/12-1047

Memorandum of Conversation, by the Director of the Office of American Republic Affairs (Daniels)

RESTRICTED   [WASHINGTON,] December 10, 1947.

Dr. Sevilla Sacasa called on me at my home on December 9, at 6:30 p. m., by appointment made at his initiative. It was largely in the nature of a personal call, since we had known each other for several years.

During the course of his call, we—or, more accurately, he—talked at length on a variety of subjects. In the course of the conversation the Nicaraguan situation naturally came up. I found occasion to reiterate what Dr. Sevilla Sacasa had been told on earlier occasions, to the effect that the attitude of the Department of State had not changed in regard to the extension of recognition to the Román y Reyes regime. Dr. Sevilla Sacasa pointed out more time had passed during which peace and order had been maintained by the Government, economic activities were continuing, international obligations were being punctually met, and a cooperative policy had been followed with regard to the United States in world affairs. I admitted all of those points, although with some qualifications on economic conditions, but said that there was still no sentiment in the Department for extending recognition, in view of the antecedents of which he was well aware, and the broad principles and precedents involved.

. . . I . . . suggested that it might be desirable for the Nicaraguans to work out some solution which would permit a transition into more stable political conditions with consequent benefits which should be appreciated by most, if not all, Nicaraguans, Dr. Sevilla Sacasa agreed that the solution should come primarily from Nicaraguans.

With regard to the possibility of Somoza's leaving Nicaragua and going to the United States, Dr. Sevilla Sacasa said that he was sure Somoza not only would do that, but was, in fact, very desirous of

---

[85] The death of Leonardo Argüello on December 14, 1947, attributed to a heart attack, was reported by the Ambassador in Mexico (Thurston) in airgram A-1131, December 15, 1947 (817.001 Argüello, Leonardo/12-1647).

doing so, as soon as he felt that conditions in Nicaragua would permit. He said that Somoza was tired and desirous of giving up his grave responsibilities. However, he said that Somoza did want to see a recognized and stable Government in Nicaragua before leaving the country, to avoid the possibility of bloodshed.

I said that we were equally interested in avoiding internal disturbances and bloodshed, and repeated my expression of hope that some way could be worked out to the satisfaction of all concerned.

Towards the close of our conversation I inquired of Dr. Sevilla Sacasa when the United Nations General Assembly was to be convened at Paris and who the Nicaraguan Ambassador in Paris was. He gave me the name of the Nicaraguan Minister there, and after some thought, I let the subject drop.

817.01/12–3147 : Circular telegram

The Acting Secretary of State to Diplomatic Representatives in the American Republics Except Costa Rica, the Dominican Republic, and Nicaragua [86]

CONFIDENTIAL WASHINGTON, December 31, 1947— 4 a. m.

Extension of recognition by Costa Rica and the Dominican Republic to *de facto* regime of Román y Reyes in Nicaragua [87] constitutes important change in previously existing situation where all American Republics were pursuing similar course of action in withholding recognition.

In accordance with our desire to consult with other American Republics on matters of mutual interest, Dept desires to ascertain views of Govt to which you are accredited in regard to this action by Costa Rican and Dominican Govts. In discussing matter with FonMin you may state that there has been no change in Dept's policy over recent months, but that this Govt desires to be fully informed of present attitude of other Govts in light of changed situation and will be largely influenced in its policy towards Nicaragua by views of other American Republics.

LOVETT

---

[86] Repeated to San José, Ciudad Trujillo, and Managua for information only.
[87] Recognition on Christmas Day by the Costa Rican Government of the *de facto* Government of Nicaragua was closely followed on December 27 by recognition on the part of the Dominican Republic (despatch 1894, December 29, 1947 from Managua, filed under 817.01/12–2947).

PANAMA

REJECTION BY THE PANAMANIAN ASSEMBLY OF THE DEFENSE SITES AGREEMENT [1]

711F.1914/1–1747 : Telegram

The Ambassador in Panama (Hines) to the Secretary of State

CONFIDENTIAL   PANAMÁ, January 17, 1947—5 p. m.

33. At the request of the Foreign Minister [2] I went to his office this morning and found that he had arranged a conference consisting of himself, Minister of Government and Justice Sucre and Minister of Public Works Vallarino.[2a] He opened the conversation by advising me that they had been discussing the defense sites agreement and the existing situation with reference to our occupation of the bases and that they desired to take up with me a solution which they felt would be most helpful and lead to final agreement upon the occupation of the bases. The Foreign Minister talked from a memorandum hastily prepared he said and which he promised to furnish me with a copy later in the day. He again referred to the lengthy new agreement and the many matters in the proposed new agreement that were not included in the 1942 agreement [3] which he said would require considerable time to study and reach a conclusion on. The proposition which he made may be summarized as follows:

First. That a communiqué be issued jointly by the two Governments indicating their obligations under the 1936 treaty [4] and announcing that the 1942 agreement would be superseded by a new agreement, for one year, that under the new agreement the bases would be occupied under a joint trusteeship consisting of General Crittenberger [5] and Minister of Government and Justice Sucre.

Second. On a given date the bases would be—as he put it—symbolically returned by the holding of a ceremony at some suitable base which would mark the ending of the old agreement and the commencement of the new tentative arrangement for one year. The new

---

[1] For previous, documentation, on the defense sites, see *Foreign Relations*, 1946, vol XI, pp. 1095 ff. For documentation on the acquisition of the defense sites in 1941 and 1942, see *ibid.*, 1941, vol. VII, pp. 414 ff., and *ibid.*, 1942 vol. VI, pp. 577 ff.
[2] Ricardo J. Alfaro.
[2a] Octavio A. Vallarino.
[3] Department of State Executive Agreement Series No. 359.
[4] Department of State Treaty Series No. 945.
[5] Lt. Gen. Willis D. Crittenberger, Commanding General of the Caribbean Defense Command.

agreement would cover only those things necessary for the administration of the bases as they are now. The Foreign Minister said there were only five points in the new agreement which he had agreed to send me. After he had concluded his statement on the new agreement which he proposed I asked him definitely what the "symbolic return" contemplated. He indicated that the radar stations and those needed at all times would continue in their present status; that he was hopeful that a short interval would intervene marking the end of the 1942 agreement and the signing of the tentative agreement for one year. I told him that I felt sure that we could not agree to abandon the bases where we had valuable property and installations which required guarding at all times. He then asked if it would not be possible to reduce the care-taking detachments to a minimum for a short interval and then reman them to the extent necessary. At this point Minister Sucre offered the suggestion which the Foreign Minister accepted—that because of the value of installations and property on the bases—that by an exchange of notes agreed upon beforehand it would be indicated that it was agreeable to the Panamanian Government for such detachments as may be determined necessary by the Commanding General be retained on the bases: That during the interval of one year from the signing of the tentative agreement careful study and consultation under Article 10 of the 1936 agreement would be undertaken and a new long term agreement be worked out. It was quite evident that the new plan contemplates finding a way to reestablish in the minds of the people confidence that we do not desire to retain Panamanian territory under our control unless it is mutually agreed to by the Panamanian Government. It is their feeling that this arrangement will work out in such way that it will in no way jeopardize the protection of the Canal and that it will remove the present barrier to the negotiation of a satisfactory new agreement. I was with the members of the conference for one and three-quarter hours and near the [end?] thereof Minister Sucre again referred to those needs of Panama which I have previously reported to the Department. It was quite evident that he feels strongly that at the time they make an announcement on the renewal of an agreement on the occupation of the bases that some statement should be made at the same time indicating that the United States contemplates doing certain things that will be of assistance to Panama. This preliminary report is being made pending the receipt of the memorandum used by the Foreign Minister which he promised to have delivered to me either later in the day or early tomorrow.

HINES

711F.1914/1–1747 : Telegram

The Secretary of State to the Embassy in Panama

CONFIDENTIAL   WASHINGTON, January 20, 1947—7 p. m.

30. It appears urtel 33 Jan 17 Fonmin plan contains factors which this Govt consistently has found basically objectionable. Dept most anxious for progress on new defense agreement and thereafter to meet Panama's justifiable requests on other pending matters. Accordingly, Dept feels it advisable send Murray Wise [6] to Emb with Dept's instructions to assist in pressing negotiation these matters. If this proposal agreeable to you Wise would plan arrive Panama by Sun 26. Please advise immediately.

BYRNES

711F.1914/1–2147

The Secretary of State to Mr. Murray M. Wise, on Special Mission to Panama

WASHINGTON, January 24, 1947.

SIR: In accordance with arrangements made by the Department and Ambassador Frank T. Hines, United States Embassy, Panamá (see Department's telegram no. 30 of January 20, 1946 [*1947*] and the Ambassador's reply telegram no. 38 of January 21 [7]) you are to proceed to Panamá and assist the Ambassador in the negotiation of a new defense sites agreement in accordance with the following instructions:

The Department is interested in the prompt agreement with Panamá on the provisions of a new defense sites agreement. Our need for the continued use of sites still held under the 1942 accord, and for certain additional ones, to insure the security of the Panamá Canal has been made known to the Panamanian Government. The basis for the defense negotiations in which you are to participate is Draft "D" prepared jointly by the State, War and Navy Departments and transmitted to the Department with the Embassy's despatch no. 3090 of December 18.[8]

The Department is of the opinion that the agreement in its present form is too lengthy and detailed, that leases should not exceed a maximum of thirty years, (if the Panamanians will assent to such duration), that the additional acreage requested for the Rio Hato site should be reduced, and that rental for private lands should not exceed $50 per hectare per year while that for public lands should be $1 per year for all tracts.

---

[6] Assistant Chief, Division of Central America and Panama Affairs.
[7] Latter not printed.
[8] Not printed. The draft was dated December 17, 1946.

The Department is also of the opinion that the War Department's desire to establish post offices on the Panamanian sites is not in keeping with the principle of Panamanian sovereignty and that all reference to them should be eliminated from the draft. The Department recognizes as justifiable the Panamanian request that the Inter-American Highway at Rio Hato should be realigned in such a way as to by-pass the airstrip and thus avoid any cause for our Armed Forces to interrupt Panamanian traffic at any time. The Department is informed that the Army is willing to reroute the road at that point.

The Department believes that Panama should feel obligated by the provisions of the 1936 General Treaty to negotiate and sign a new defense sites agreement and that Panama should not condition its approval on extraneous economic or other unrelated matters (see Embassy's telegrams no. 317 of May 10, 1946 and nos. 770 and 776 of December 24[23] and 28, 1946,[9] and Enclosure 5 to despatch 3013 of December 8, 1946 [10]).

This Government recognizes and supports the full sovereign and independent status of the Republic of Panama. Recognition is made of the position in which the Panamanian Government now finds itself with respect to its publicly declared interpretation of the expiration date of the 1942 Agreement, an interpretation which this Government cannot accept (see Department's telegram no. 499 of September 24, 1946 [11]). The Department understands that the Panamanian Foreign Minister insists that his Government requires a "face-saving device" or "symbolic return" of the presently held defense sites before it can announce the signing of a new agreement. Accordingly, if insisted upon by Panama, the Department is prepared to enter into an interim agreement, provided that in so doing there is no compromise of this Government's interpretation of the termination clause of the old agreement; provided that the interim agreement remains in operation until the new definitive agreement becomes effective (in the Department's opinion, the duration of the interim agreement should not exceed a few hours or at the most a few days) and provided the interim agreement contemplates a "trusteeship" rather than a so-called "joint" control over the old bases until such time as the new agreement shall have entered into effect. The War Department has advised that short of the extinguishment of the 1942 Agreement before the signing of a new one, it will be agreeable to any provisions for an interim agreement which meet the minimum requirements of the Commanding General, Caribbean Defense Command. The Department agrees with the War De-

---

[9] For texts of these telegrams see *Foreign Relations*, 1946, vol. XI, pp. 1098, 1138, and 1140, respectively.
[10] Not printed.
[11] For text, see *Foreign Relations*, 1946, vol, XI, p. 1115.

partment that it would be inadvisable from every consideration to withdraw, even temporarily, from the bases now occupied under the 1942 Agreement.

The Panamanian authorities may be informed that it is to the best interests of both governments, in compliance with their joint treaty obligations to provide continuous security for the Panama Canal, a security which likewise insures the defense of Panama and figures greatly in the defense of the hemisphere. It may be added that this Government is most anxious to negotiate, (seriatim and daily during your presence in Panama until agreement is reached) the provisions of the defense sites agreement before announcing publicly and before discussing in any detail the Panamanian requests on which the United States is now prepared to make commitments. In the negotiation of the defense sites agreement, it is believed that the only commitment which can be proposed, other than possible modifications to the provisions of Draft "D", is an agreement to realign the Inter-American Highway in such a way as to bypass the Rio Hato airstrip.

Should Panama so desire, once an agreement has been reached on the defense sites, announcement thereof may be deferred until agreement is reached on other matters.

In connection with matters other than the defense sites, this Government is prepared:

(1) To reiterate its assurances of fulfillment of the following previous commitments:[12]

(a) to transfer the Panama Railroad station to a new site provided by Panama,
(b) to maintain our public policy of granting to Panamanians the same opportunity and treatment of employment accorded citizens of the United States,
(c) to consult and cooperate with Panama in the prevention of the smuggling of commissary items from the Canal Zone into Panama,
(d) to give assurances of a permanent market in the Canal Zone for Panamanian produce,
(e) to negotiate a convention for the realignment of the Colon Corridor,
(f) to improve transportation facilities over the Canal at Balboa

(2) To offer the following new commitments:

(a) to realign the Inter-American Highway in such a way as to bypass the airstrip at Rio Hato,
(b) to enter into an aeronautical agreement for the coordination of air traffic over Panama,

---

[12] Department of State Executive Agreement Series No. 452.

(c) to furnish through the Civil Aeronautics Administration both general and private service radio communications for all commercial aviation over Panama and to furnish to the extent deemed necessary for defense purposes a system of air traffic control in Panama in conjunction with air traffic control in the Canal Zone,

(d) to construct a dock at cost for Panama at the Coiba Penal Colony,

(e) to provide Panama insofar as military requirements permit with circuits in existing telegraph and telephone lines and cables,

(f) to transfer Paitilla Point to Panama subject to the approval of the Congress,

(g) to transfer to Panama the Aspinwall, Vialette, and Huerta San Doval tracts subject to the approval of the Congress,

(h) to consult with Panama on the advisability of revising the existing monetary agreement,

(i) to eliminate immediately the 25% cargo differential charged by the Panama Railroad Company.

(3) While no commitment can be entered into with respect to Panama's expressed interest in receiving financial assistance, the appropriate officials of this Government are prepared at any time to enter upon an examination of the problem. The relevancy of the Encanto Claim to any financial assistance to Panama is already known to the Panamanian Government.

Sincerely yours, For the Secretary of State:
SPRUILLE BRADEN

711F.1914/1–2947 : Telegram

The Ambassador in Panama (Hines) to the Secretary of State

CONFIDENTIAL   US URGENT   PANAMÁ, January 29, 1947—8 a.m.

46. On Sunday I discussed with Wise Department's instructions relative his assistance on defense sites negotiations and went over with him current situation in Panama. Monday morning General Crittenberger was acquainted with Department's current plan to press for agreement.

At noon Monday I accompanied Wise on informal courtesy visit to Foreign Minister who said President Jimenez wished to see Wise informally at earliest convenience and that arrangements should be made directly with Presidencia. No mention was made of defense sites to Foreign Minister. During afternoon Vallarino, Minister of Public Works and Cabinet member closest to President, called informally at Embassy. He referred to Foreign Minister as main obstacle to progress on negotiations and expressed President's interest in seeing Wise first thing Tuesday morning. Vallarino said President was anxious to reach agreement and would listen to proposals.

Tuesday Wise conferred with President for 1-½ hours. President at outset offered assurances his cooperation on defense negotiations. He brought up matter proposed claims convention and of own accord said he knew Department was justifiably concerned over Panama's delay in replying. He admitted difficulties with Foreign Minister on both defense and claims, gave indication he would take stronger hand with Cabinet, and stated now was psychological time to press forward for defense agreement. He agreed to appoint representative to serve on joint committee to re-draft at once and continuously provisions proposed new defense agreement in manner acceptable to Embassy, Army and Panama. It is believed this is important wedge.

President said that while he was willing now to negotiate new agreement, some plan for symbolic return of bases would be necessary before it could become effective. He mentioned Panama's desire for joint communiqué which would state that on some date to be decided upon 1942 accord would have served its purpose, that US would return remaining bases and that pending consideration by two govts of need for new agreement, bases could be re-occupied for fixed period under an arrangement providing (joint control) arrangement. President said return of bases would be merely "symbolic". President was immediately informed that this procedure previously proposed by Foreign Office was entirely unacceptable to this Govt, that we could not withdraw from bases for one moment thus weakening defense of canal, nor could we remain on them without some written agreement in force. It was also stated that to assume before the public that bases were being returned when actually they were not was likewise considered unwise.

Department's suggestion was presented that new agreement be negotiated and followed by public announcement along with simultaneous release of list of Panama's requests which Department is willing to undertake and to recommend to Congress in those cases requiring Congressional action. President appeared very interested but insisted that some interim arrangement would be necessary. He was told that occupation under "joint control" was not acceptable and that while this govt definitely desired to avoid an interim arrangement particularly one with fixed time limit, consideration might be given to some trusteeship plan. It was emphasized that trusteeship would necessarily have to be well-defined and that it should be understood that it merely meant assignment of a Panamanian official as trustee to represent interests of Panama as regards bases but in no way could imply that Panama would participate in any phase of military control or jurisdiction which must be sole responsibility of Commanding General.

President said he would consider matter further and asked Wise to call again on Wednesday at 1 o'clock for informal luncheon during which he wished to continue discussion.

HINES

711F.1914/2–447 : Telegram

The Ambassador in Panama (Hines) to the Secretary of State

CONFIDENTIAL   PANAMÁ, February 4, 1947—1 p. m.

58. Emtel 57, February 3.[13] Following Cabinet session yesterday, First Secretary Foreign Office met with Wise. This time De Diego [13a] appeared to speak with confidence and authority, and to represent a much more united Panamanian front than formerly.

It would seem that President and Cabinet, including Dr. Alfaro, have decided: (1) to make no further issue of interpretation termination clause 1942 agreement; (2) to abandon position of refusing to discuss or negotiate new agreement until remaining defense sites are returned; and (3) to abandon request for a symbolic return of presently held defense sites or for an interim agreement. Using each article draft "D" as a basis for discussion, De Diego offered suggestions for a new draft agreement. His proposition may be summarized as follows:

The negotiation of an executive agreement which would become effective upon signature and which, according to De Diego, would not require the approval of the National Assembly, although it would later be presented to that body. It would consist of an opening paragraph or preamble referring to the obligations of the two countries under the 1936 treaty to provide for the adequate defense of the Canal. This would be followed by approximately six articles which in rather general terms would give the impression that the occupation and use of defense areas in Panama would be a joint or partnership undertaking of the two governments. Rights, duties, special relationships between the two governments, and legal specifications would be defined in an exchange of notes to accompany the executive agreement. Apparently the principal document of the executive agreement would be made public while the accompanying notes would not.

De Diego said that in the proposed "partnership" or "joint" agreement, the Commanding General, Caribbean Defense Command, would retain the military authority which his position and responsibility required. De Diego explained that the object of the Panamanian proposal is to avoid the use of such expressions as "leased", "lands

---

[13] Not printed.
[13a] Mario de Diego.

granted", "sites returned", etc., so that neighboring countries and the world in general would have the feeling that whatever is decided with respect to defense sites in Panama is based on the 1936 treaty and on consultation and mutual agreement rather than on a basis of the United States "requesting" and Panama "giving". Wise told De Diego that his proposal would be considered to determine whether there was sufficient common ground for beginning a revision of draft "D". De Diego said he would present informally a very rough draft of what he thought Panama would want in the proposed executive agreement.

It is believed his draft will be basically different in form and approach from our draft "D". Nevertheless, Embassy will maintain stand that all legal rights established for military in draft "D", approved by Department and War Department, are required even though form and phraseology may be changed.

HINES

711F.1914/2–747 : Telegram

The Ambassador in Panama (Hines) to the Secretary of State

CONFIDENTIAL   US URGENT   PANAMÁ, February 7, 1947—11 a. m.

65. Embtel 58, February 4. Foreign Office this morning presented its rough draft of proposed executive agreement on defense sites. As was expected, draft is basically different from draft "D". Embassy and commanding general are now drafting counterproposal. In considering Panamanian proposal and draft "D" following questions have arisen upon which I would like to have the Dept's advice:

(1) Can defense sites needs satisfactorily be covered and can we sufficiently be legally protected by an executive agreement? Panamanians might wish to negotiate same without approval of National Assembly to which agreement might be submitted for information only.

(2) Would the necessary accompanying exchange of notes signed at the same time be as binding as executive agreement itself (*a*) if notes are referred to in executive agreement; and (*b*) if not mentioned in executive agreement. The Panamanian proposal for a short basic document, the provision of which would be general in tone, would necessarily oblige us to insist on an exchange of notes to define in some detail our legal rights and jurisdiction. It is believed that Panama might desire not to publish accompanying notes. Please advise.

HINES

711F.1914/2-747 : Telegram

The Secretary of State to the Embassy in Panama

CONFIDENTIAL   WASHINGTON, February 11, 1947—10 a. m.
US URGENT

51. Dept considers this Govt's interests would be sufficiently protected by executive agreement as outlined Emb's first question Embtel 65 Feb 7. As regards second question Dept's opinion is that accompanying exchange of notes would be equally binding provided sentence is inserted in notes specifically referring to agreement and stating that notes form integral part thereof. Dept would agree to non-publication of accompanying notes if Panamanian officials consider that point vitally important but would feel it necessary to include notes with agreement in submission to UN Secretariat under Article 102 of UN Charter.[14] Publication by UN would follow as a routine matter. Routine publication would be given by Dept several months after signature, but no press release would be made.

While Dept considers US would be legally protected on defense sites by executive agreement, question arises as to whether agreement entered into by Pres of Panama would be similarly binding legally on his Govt. Study of Panamanian constitution appears to indicate agreement would have to be submitted to National Assembly for consideration. Dept requests clarification this point by Emb and notification to Dept before Emb proceeds further with plans for possible executive agreement. Dept also desires Emb's opinion on whether agreement negotiated while Panama is still in state of war would be equally binding under peacetime conditions.

If executive agreement should be decided on as preferable to treaty, Emb is directed to advise Dept as soon as that decision taken in order that prior to signature Congressional leaders may be advised informally of reasons for choice.

                                                                                       MARSHALL

711F.1914/2-1347

Memorandum by Mr. W. Tapley Bennett of the Division of Central America and Panama Affairs to the Director of the Office of American Republic Affairs (Briggs)

[WASHINGTON,] February 21, 1947.

I believe you will be interested in the following paragraphs from a memo of conversation with Acting Foreign Minister Sucre (also Minis-

---

[14] Department of State Treaty Series No. 993.

ter of Government and Justice and one of the two men in the Cabinet closest personally to President Jimenez). . . .

"Sucre also pointed out very firmly that it was Panamá's intention to negotiate an agreement whereby the United States would be responsible for all costs of expropriation, damages, etc., etc., arising out of the occupation of defense sites. Sucre said that he understood that the actual suit by the individual would be against the Government of Panamá but that the United States must be ultimately responsible. . . ."

"The next point discussed by the Ambassador was the question of rentals. He pointed out to Minister Sucre that Rio Hato had at the present time a special rental rate of $10,000 for the entire 7,000 hectares and that if Rio Hato were rented at $50.00 per hectare per year the annual rental would be $350,000 rather than $10,000. He pointed out that any scheme whereby all lands to be occupied and paid for at $50.00 per hectare would, because of the fact that we desired to take over the entire Island of San José, raise the annual compensation a great deal and make it probably unacceptable to the War Department and Congress. Sucre said he could not understand why we were not willing to pay the regular rate for all of Rio Hato as Rio Hato was our most important base and that he still hoped to make some arrangement whereby all lands used as defense sites would be expropriated by the Government of Panamá and then we would pay $50.00 per hectare for public and private lands. There was considerable discussion on this point. An effort was made to convince Sucre that any raising of the rentals to this extent each year would meet with Congressional disapproval and cause a great deal of trouble. This point of the actual rental rate will have to be adjusted."

711F.1914/3-1747

Memorandum by Mr. W. Tapley Bennett of the Division of Central America and Panama Affairs [15]

[Washington,] March 17, 1947.

The following paragraph is quoted from a personal letter from Second Secretary Lansing Collins [16] at Panamá under date of March 11:

"We have not been able to get the Army to agree to certain features of this draft and we have not come to any final conclusions with the Army as to the most important question which is how much to pay. I feel that the atmosphere is fairly favorable, and I have gotten word from a number of sources in Panama that it is now becoming politically expedient for the President to settle the defense sites question. For example, I was informed several days ago that every effort will be made to postpone the national convention of the Liberal party until this fall because of two factors: (1) the fact that selection of a nominee will result in four or five disappointees who will be fed up with the

---

[15] Addressed to Messrs. Wise and Newbegin of CPA; Mr. Briggs of ARA; and to Mr. Braden, A–Br.
[16] Not printed.

present regime; and (2) the fact that politicos do not dare to hold any kind of a convention with the defense sites question unsolved. General Crittenberger is meeting with us today and promises to have an answer to all the unanswered points in the draft agreement. A miracle might take place and we may make some rapid progress."

Aside from the amount of compensation to be paid for site acreage, the principal question at issue now is the inclusion of the term "joint authority" in the agreement. General Crittenberger continues adamant that language of the agreement must not interfere with exclusive U.S. military responsibility on the defense sites; to meet his objections, Ambassador Hines has been attempting to get Panamanian acceptance to removal of the reference to joint authority from the body of the agreement to the preamble, where it would serve to emphasize the mutual obligation aspect of the agreement. Meanwhile, War Department General Staff sources have indicated to Mr. Wise that Crittenberger undoubtedly will eventually accept the inclusion of "joint authority".

Ambassador Hines and General Crittenberger met with Foreign Minister on Saturday morning, March 15, at which time the Ambassador stressed the urgency of arriving at an agreement, per the Department's telegram no. 79 of March 12.[17] In that connection, the Embassy concurs in the Department's view that Ambassador Vallarino's [18] recent statements have been motivated by his personal political aspirations.

The pressures of internal politics in Panama, along with the Embassy's urgent representations, combine to present a fairly optimistic picture now as regards agreement on the defense sites problem.

711F.1914/4–1047 : Telegram

The Ambassador in Panama (Hines) to the Secretary of State

SECRET   PANAMÁ, April 10, 1947—2 p. m.

186. Embtel 185, April 10.[17] Following is office translation of Alfaro's proposed defense sites agreement:

"Preamble. Governments of Republic of Panama and of US of America have consulted together to consider all of phases of situation existing since termination of wartime emergency as well as to discuss experiences of last war in relation to defense of Panama Canal; and after complete interchange of information with relation to present needs, have reaffirmed their joint interest in providing for continued security of Canal, of Republic, and of entire hemisphere,

---

[17] Not printed.
[18] J. J. Vallarino, Ambassador of Panama in the United States.

have reiterated their mutual determination to assure continued and effective protection of Panama Canal as is stipulated in general treaty of March 2, 1936, and exchange of notes relating thereto; and have come to conclusion that in present circumstances functioning of certain defense sites existing in territory under jurisdiction of Panama should not be interrupted, but on contrary that it is imperative to continue for prudent time maintenance and functioning of certain of them; in virtue of which undersigned Dr. Ricardo J. Alfaro, Minister of Foreign Relations of Republic of Panama and His Excellency, Frank T. Hines, Ambassador of US of America representing their respective Governments by whom they have been duly and legally authorized have agreed as follows:

Article I. High contracting parties declare terminated agreement of May 18, 1942, it having accomplished its purposes.

High contracting parties at same time declare ended occupation of all defense sites under terms of that agreement and agree that hereafter maintenance of defense sites in territory under jurisdiction of Panama will be regulated by conditions set forth in preamble and stipulations set forth in following articles.

Article 2. Republic of Panama designates temporarily areas specified in Annex A [19] attached to this agreement and of which it forms an integral part, to serve as sites intended for defense of Panama Canal for limited period specified for each one. These defense sites will be maintained under joint authority of Governments of Panama and of US.

Article 3. For exercise of joint authority of Republic of Panama and US over defense sites which this agreement covers, Government of Republic of Panama designates Minister of Government and Justice and Government of US of America, Commanding General of Caribbean Defense. Two Governments will determine through agreement means by which this joint authority will be exercised.

Article 4. Republic of Panama retains its sovereignty over areas used as defense sites and over air space corresponding to same, as well as jurisdiction in civil matters, it being understood, nonetheless, that Government of US will have exclusive jurisdiction over civilian and military personnel of US to be stationed on defense sites and over their families.

Article 5. Government of US will pay to Government of Panama on first day of February of each year, or before, an annual compensation of blank Balboas per hectare for preceding year for all lands used as defense sites in accordance with terms of this agreement. Pay-

---

[19] Not printed.

ment will be reduced proportionately in case of periods of less than a year.

Government of Republic of Panama will assume, with respect to lands used as defense sites, all expenses of expropriation, as well as indemnifications and reimbursements for installations, cultivated lands, or other improvements that may exist.

There will be expressly excepted from provisions of paragraphs 2 and 3 (*sic*) of this article:

(*a*) Piece of land in township of Rio Hato designated as number blank in Annex A for which Government of US will pay to Government of Republic of Panama an annual compensation of blank Balboas.

(*b*) Entire area of Island of San Jose, in Archipelago of Las Perlas in Bay of Panama, designated as number blank in Annex A, for which Government of US will pay to Government of Republic of Panama an annual compensation of blank Balboas.

Compensation established in this article will be paid in Balboas as they were defined in exchange of notes effected March 2, 1936, to which Article 7 of treaty of that date between US of America and Republic of Panama refers, or equivalent in dollars, and shall be paid from date on which use of each defense site shall have been commenced, in accordance with terms of this agreement.

Representatives of Republic of Panama and of US will inform their respective govts of date on which each use has commenced within 30 days following that date.

Article 6. When defense site or part of same is not needed for defense of Canal its use will be discontinued on date which representatives of 2 Govts will agree upon. Representatives of Panama and US will notify 2 Govts not less than ninety days prior to date they have set unless 2 Govts are in agreement to accept lesser period of time.

All buildings construction, installations or accessories which may have been erected or placed by US on defense sites will be property of US and may be taken away by it before cessation of use of defense site. Buildings, constructions, accessories, crops, cultivated areas or whatever other improvements exist at time defense site commences to be used, may be used for same purposes. US will not be obligated to pay for damages caused in whatever manner on same, and Republic of Panama will not be obligated to pay compensations to US for improvements made on defense site or for buildings, constructions or properties left on them, all of which will become property of Republic of Panama on discontinuance of use of defense site.

Article 7. Republic of Panama and US reiterate their understanding with respect to temporary nature of occupation of defense sites to which this agreement refers. Consequently US recognizing importance of cooperation rendered by Panama in making available these temporary defense sites, and recognizing also burden that maintenance of these sites signifies for Republic of Panama will obligate itself expressly to conform with necessary measures so that disoccupation of said sites will be effected no later than date of expiration of period stipulated with respect to each site in Annex A, if in opinion of 2 Govts causes and circumstances which have determined maintenance of defense sites should have ceased.

Article 8. Civilian and military personnel of US which by agreement between 2 Govts function at defense sites or are employed in relation to operation of those sites and families of such personnel as well as property and effects destined to sites will be free of all duties, contributions or taxes of any sort on part of Republic of Panama or its political subdivisions during period of this agreement.

It is established however that with respect to customs duties there will only be exempt merchandise and articles for consumption of civilian and military personnel and for families of such personnel when such merchandise and articles are produced in US.

Article 9. This agreement may be terminated by contracting parties through an agreement between each other even prior to expiration of terms stipulated in Annex A for maintenance of defense sites, but its operation will terminate in any case on expiration of greatest of said periods.

Article 10. This agreement will be submitted to National Assembly of Panama, in accordance with constitutional precepts governing public treaties, but in view of circumstances set forth in preamble, 2 Govts agree that this agreement, maintaining its character of referendum, will enter into effect on date of its signature by representatives of Panama and U.S.

In faith of which plenipotentiaries of high contracting parties have signed this agreement in duplicate in English and Spanish, both texts of equal authenticity, and have affixed their respective seals.["] [20]

HINES

711F.1914/4–1947 : Telegram

The Ambassador in Panama (Hines) to the Secretary of State

CONFIDENTIAL PANAMÁ, April 19, 1947—2 p. m.

202. Have just completed one-hour conference with General Crittenberger on defense sites draft submitted in despatch 3741, April 10.[21]

---

[20] The annex to this draft is not printed, but see p. 939 for the annex accompanying the final text of the agreement dated December 10, 1947.

[21] Not printed. This despatch transmitted the full text of the draft of which telegram 186, *supra*, gave an abbreviated form.

The draft is unacceptable to General Crittenberger because it violated three important principles:

First, the use of language indicating the agreement is temporary in nature and therefore not in accordance with the principles of the general treaty of March 2, 1936.

Second, it does not cover clearly and differentiate on the manner of military command and maintenance of defense bases.

Third, that it lacks flexibility and makes no provision for additional defense sites needed.

General Crittenberger talked from a draft of notes which he promises to put in definite form so that I may transmit to Department. Taking up the preamble and articles of the agreement in order, the objections raised by General Crittenberger are the following:

The preamble—the use of the language "the wartime emergency" he feels is misleading and emphasizes the trend of the temporary nature of the agreement: also the use of the language "complete interchange of information" is incorrect, General Crittenberger's feelings being that this is actually a misstatement of facts. Also feels the language "for a prudent time the maintenance and functioning of certain of them" would still emphasize the temporary nature of the agreement. In other words, the preamble does not consider the long range defense policy of the Panama Canal, in its present form.

Article 1—the language declaring the termination of that agreement on [of?] March 18, 1942 when read in connection with Article 10 is considered dangerous in that failure on the part of the National Assembly to ratify the agreement might find the US having terminated the 1942 agreement without having a new agreement in its place.

Article 2—the words "temporarily" in first line and "limited" in the fourth line are objectionable; also the last sentence will require modification to indicate that maintenance of the bases is a military function of the US and not of both governments.

Article 3—is objectionable and ambiguous in that it sets up the joint authority by naming the Minister of Justice of Government of Panama and the Commanding General of the CDC on part of US and then in the last sentence indicates "the two governments will determine by agreement".

Article 4 is incomplete and General Crittenberger feels should be modified more in keeping of Article 4 of the 1942 agreement, particularly in relation to jurisdiction of civilian and military personnel not only on defense sites but those who have access thereto.

Article 5 is acceptable provided the rate per hectare is less than $50 per year. Also 3rd paragraph requires modification in regard to the exceptions from provisions of 1st and 2nd paragraphs of the article rather than paragraphs 2 and 3 as indicated.

Article 6—General Crittenberger feels that function of determining when a defense site is no longer needed is that of the military authorities and should not require decision on the part of the representatives of Panamanian Government.

Article 7—the use of word "temporary" in second line further emphasizes temporary nature of the agreement and requires clarification.

Article 8—this article should be clarified in order to indicate that all personnel will be free of all duties, taxes, etc., whether supplies come from Canal Zone or outside it. It is no more restrictive than the provisions of the 1942 agreement.

Article 9 still carries forward the temporary nature of the agreement and General Crittenberger feels that provisions should be such as to emphasize that the 1936 obligation of defending the Canal is not of a temporary nature.

Article 10—no objections.

General Crittenberger indicates that he will furnish me on Monday data requested by Foreign Minister relative to cost operation bases now in use. His estimate is approximately one million dollars per month. President and Foreign Minister are exceedingly anxious that I give them some reaction on their last draft. In lieu of draft submitted by Panama General Crittenberger recommends we submit to Panama Government in regular form our draft of March 13, 1947 (reEmbdesp 3614, Secret).[22] I recommend using Panama draft making necessary changes to meet important objections.

HINES

711F.1914/4–747 : Telegram

The Acting Secretary of State to the Embassy in Panama

SECRET   U.S. URGENT   WASHINGTON, April 25, 1947—8 p. m.

139. Urtel 186 Apr 10 [22] and des 3741 same date; [23] see also Embstels 181 Apr 7, 189 Apr 14 and 199 Apr 16.[24] Dept views respect Panamanian proposal defense sites agreement are as follows: Theory of "joint authority" running through Panamanian proposal is basically different from our proposal and appears to provide for more Panamanian participation than Dept originally contemplated, as our draft

---

[22] Not printed.
[23] See footnote 21, p. 895.
[24] None printed.

of Mar 13 transmitted your des 3614 Mar 17 [25] discloses and as Amb and Gen Crittenberger are fully aware (Embstel 202, Apr 19). Panamanian suggestions are based on theory that agreement is of temporary nature and that it and all annexes, including A, may be cancelled even sooner than would presently be contemplated. No specific provision is made for extension agreement although final thought in Article VII implies there may be cause for continued use of defense sites.

In view Panamanian political situation and effect which continued delay in negotiations has on overall relations with Panama, Dept desires to go as far as is practicable in accepting Panamanian suggestions on a relative short term basis rather than continue press for what we consider ideal from our point of view. Accordingly, instead striving in this agreement obtain document long range character Dept will for practical purposes consider time limits stipulated in Annex A (preferably 10 years for all sites except Rio Hato which would be requested on 15-year basis) as "temporary" periods. It is hoped that Panama will agree on 10-year rather than 5-year maximum for sites other than Rio Hato in view our willingness to go along on theory of joint authority. Dept does not consider that 10-year period would obviate temporary nature of agreement as desired by Panama. This in no way precludes possibility negotiating new agreement of more permanent nature upon expiration agreement now being considered.

Dept has come to conclusion that type agreement suggested by Panama, because it is more general in terminology than our proposal, will provide us with a better basis for operating militarily in Panama than would agreement terms of which were too specific.

Dept considers most important sentence in Panamanian proposal to be that in Article III which reads "The two Governments will determine through agreement the means by which this joint authority will be exercised". Dept interprets this sentence as providing for not one exchange of notes but for continuing exchanges when necessary during the life of the agreement if such are needed to establish definitely that matters of military nature or involving exercise of command remain exclusive responsibility of military authorities of US. Dept believes that this sentence also provides means for establishing that actual authority for determining when a site is no longer needed (see Article VI below) will be prerogative our military authorities. Also it provides that authority for criminal jurisdiction which had been established in last two sentences of our Article II

---

[25] Not printed.

(draft of Mar 13 referred to above) but which Panamanian proposal omits could be established under the provision of Article III. However, Dept suggests that there be added to sentence under reference the following words: "such accords being an integral part of this agreement."

Our views with respect to the specific articles of the Panamanian proposal are as follows:

Preamble. Acceptable, if the expression "of the Republic and of the entire hemisphere" is omitted on grounds that subsequent paragraphs of agreement refer exclusively to defense of Canal. Since agreement will be registered with UN, inclusion of this expression might open way for multilateral rather than strictly bilateral interest which is intent of document.

Article I. Acceptable.

Article II. Acceptable.

Article III. Acceptable if the expression "such accords being an integral part of this agreement" is added to the last sentence and provided (as explained above) exchanges of notes establish our exclusive authority in all military matters pertaining to defense of Canal, the practical necessity for determination by us when a site is no longer needed, possibility of extending periods of use of sites or of negotiating new agreement on expiration arrangement under negotiation, and our authority for criminal jurisdiction as expressed in Article II our draft (Mar 13). These notes would of course be exchanged simultaneously with signature master agreement and would bear same date.

Article IV. Acceptable, if authority for criminal jurisdiction is agreed to by Panama in form indicated in previous paragraph.

Article V. Acceptable, provided first paragraph begins "Subject to its constitutional procedures with respect to appropriations the Government of the United States will pay to the Government of Panama on the first day of February of each year" and provided there is added to second paragraph after word "exist" the following: "thereon, saving the United States harmless from all claims arising therefrom or incident thereto".

Article VI. Acceptable, if specific notes are exchanged under Article III to insure that authority for determining discontinuance of site use remains with US officials and that their notification will be binding on the joint representatives.

Article VII. Acceptable, if provision is made for possibility of extending periods for use of sites or negotiating new agreement as discussed under Article III above.

Article VIII. Acceptable, if there is added to end of second paragraph after words "United States", the phrase "or in the Republic of Panama". It is inconceivable that Panama would expect defense sites personnel to pay customs duties or local taxes not imposed on local citizens with respect to merchandise or articles produced in Panama. Such expectation on the part of Panama would be entirely inconsistent with spirit of 1936 Treaty or this agreement. In addition, to cover possible future needs for importation of foodstuffs and other necessities from other countries, the following should be added to end of second sentence: "except for designated countries and specified articles which may be agreed on from time to time by the joint representatives".

Article IX. Acceptable, provided clause reading "but its operation will terminate in any case on the expiration of the greatest of said periods" is eliminated. Without this elimination Article IX would be inconsistent with revision suggested for Article VII.

Article X. First paragraph not acceptable since US Senate criticized Dept for terminology in 1942 agreement which recognized need for submission to National Assembly of Panama but which made no provision for consideration by our Senate. Accordingly, phraseology suggested in Article IX of enclosures to despatch 3702 of Apr 2 [26] is preferable. It reads as follows: "This agreement will enter into effect upon the signature of the representatives of the Republic of Panama and of the United States of America duly and legally authorized". This language leaves question of submission to National Assembly or to Congress to discretion of respective negotiating powers.

The foregoing is submitted for your consideration and discussion with Gen Crittenberger. Dept agrees with Amb's recommendation that Panamanian draft be used and that appropriate changes be made to meet important objections (last sentence Embstel 202, Apr 19).

Revised proposal should be presented formally soonest possible to FornMin with statement that War and State Depts are becoming increasingly concerned over fact that uncertainty surrounding defense sites matter has reached US Congress which may become less sympathetic to Panama if this issue is not settled.

In summary Dept reiterates its position that Panamanian draft is acceptable as master document only provided accompanying exchanges of notes under Art III obtain for military authorities all essential protection of exercise of command and other necessary rights and authority.

Our formal proposal to Panama which would be master agreement accompanied by all essential exchanges of notes should be presented by official note.

---

[26] Not printed.

We of course assume that you and Gen Crittenberger will collaborate in drafting notes.[27] Until these are ready no approach should be made to FonMin in response its latest draft.

ACHESON

711F.1914/5-547

The American Ambassador in Panama (Hines) to the Panamanian Minister for Foreign Affairs (Alfaro)

No. 410   PANAMÁ, May 5, 1947.

EXCELLENCY: I have the honor to refer to the proposed new defense sites agreement which Your Excellency handed me on April 9, 1947.[28] This proposal incorporated certain principles which Your Excellency has stated are basic in the consideration of your Government, as regards the continued use of defense areas in the Republic of Panama.

In compliance with instructions which I have now received from the Department of State,[29] I am pleased to inform Your Excellency that my Government has accepted, with certain modifications, the proposal submitted by Your Excellency. Accordingly, I transmit herewith an English translation of Your Excellency's proposed defense sites agreement, embodying the above referred to modifications and including notes accessory to the agreement, which are to be considered an integral part thereof.[30]

Once Your Excellency's Government shall have approved these modifications, I am confident that any details which may be pending solution can be negotiated expeditiously by the respective representatives of Panama and the United States, as provided for in Article III.

The accessory notes submitted herewith cover matters which my Government considers essential in order that the orderly and efficient administration of the defense sites is assured, from the time of the transition from the 1942 Defense Sites Agreement to the new one providing for the principle of "joint authority".

I am confident that the Government of Panama shares the views of the Government of the United States of the importance of reaching an immediate agreement on this matter, and I therefore anticipate receiving Your Excellency's acceptance.

Accept [etc.]   [File copy not signed.]

---

[27] In telegram 230, May 2, 1947, 11 a. m., from Panamá, the Ambassador indicated that General Crittenberger agreed to this procedure (711F.1914/5–247).
[28] See telegram 186, April 10, 2 p. m., from Panamá, p. 892.
[29] *Supra.*
[30] Enclosures not printed.

711F.1914/5–1247 : Telegram

The Ambassador in Panama (Hines) to the Secretary of State

CONFIDENTIAL PANAMÁ, May 12, 1947—3 p. m.

257. Embtel 255, May 12, 9 a. m.[31] After presentation Embassy's note May 5 to Foreign Minister local press, reacting on indications from Foreign Office, reported agreement on principles had apparently been reached, negotiations would begin and likely would lead to prompt agreement. Few articles originating radical sources criticized Alfaro's change in position about necessity our returning bases before further negotiations.

Tuesday p. m. May 8 Minister Vallarino, at President's request, requested two members my staff see him urgently. In his possession was approximately 10-page analysis prepared by Alfaro of our May 5 draft proposal. He found most our modifications his previous document unsatisfactory and in strong language criticized and found unacceptable accessory notes as integral part of agreement. Analysis called for return to Alfaro's language of April 9 for most part and stipulated that proposed exchange of notes be left to joint authority. Vallarino said Alfaro would call session for preliminary discussion following day.

Discussion was held at Foreign Office late Friday, May 9. Present were Minister Alfaro, Vallarino and [Obarrio?], Comptroller General and Panamanian Ambassador to Washington. Wise and Collins accompanied me. Foreign Minister began saying our May 5 note had opened way for negotiations and that he was desirous taking up in preliminary way enclosures to note. Conference lasted 3 hours. Main point of difference centered around definition joint authority and method it would be exercised. Department's insertion in Article 5 that availability of funds for rentals would be subject to Congressional appropriations was objectionable.

Alfaro pointed out that with few exceptions our modifications his April 9 draft were unsatisfactory and that Panama could not go along with accessory notes in present form for they completely nullified any plan for joint authority set up in main document. He said many matters covered were unnecessary and irritating to Panama. He believed all specific details must be given to joint representatives who could issue regulations through "joint orders". Alfaro believed agreement must be based on Article 10 of 1936 treaty and therefore temporary. We insisted the second paragraph Article 2 was equally applicable, if not more so than Article 10. Memo of conversation forwarded today's pouch.

News soon got around city that first conference had not gone well. Duque of *Star and Herald* to member of staff has severely criticized

---

[31] Not printed.

Alfaro for giving false impression to press after conference that all was going well. . . .

Saturday p. m. President called for Wise and stated his concern over Friday meeting and said he would give matter full consideration over weekend, would call meeting certain Cabinet members for 8 o'clock this morning, and that perhaps discussions could be continued with Alfaro this afternoon.

HINES

711F.1914/5–1547

Memorandum by the Assistant Chief of the Division of Central America and Panama Affairs (Wise) [32]

[WASHINGTON,] May 23, 1947.

It is suggested that the Department's position with respect Panama's latest proposal on defense sites agreement should be as follows:

Alfaro's most recent suggestion (Embstel 265, May 15 [33]) handed to Ambassador Hines informally on May 15 and carried to Washington personally by Wise comprises:

(*a*) draft basic agreement of nine articles. This is Alfaro proposal April 10 (Embs desp 3741 same date [34]) further modified apparently as result Embassy's representations. However, falls short of including all Embassy's suggestions May 5 and in certain aspects is basically difficult in principle and less definite than language military has wanted.

(*b*) draft proposals for seven joint recommendations to be signed by Panamanian Minister of Government and Justice and the Commanding General. These represent entirely new procedure for making "joint authority" more realistic. Idea is they be signed simultaneously with bases agreement but not as integral part thereof, although reference is made in them to main agreement. They represent modifications of Embassy's May 5 proposed simultaneous exchanges of notes planned to be accessory to defense agreement. Alfaro proposal of joint recommendation omits three of Embassy's proposed notes and definitely shortens and simplifies several others beyond limit military authorities have shown willingness to go.

(*c*) draft proposed form for exchanges of notes between Foreign Minister and Ambassador to correspond to and make effective each joint recommendation. There is no positive indication that notes are to be signed simultaneously with joint recommendations and bases agreement.

Embassy should insist on formal official reply to its note of May 5. If found substantially same as proposition presented informally now

---

[32] Addressed to Messrs. Bennett and Newbegin of CPA; and Mr. Briggs of ARA.
[33] Not printed.
[34] Not printed, but see telegram 186, April 10, 2 p. m., from Panama, p. 892.

under consideration Department will accept plan (1) provided documents described in (c) above are signed simultaneously with (a) and (b); (2) provided it is understood by all parties concerned that further joint recommendation and corresponding notes may be required from time to time pursuant to developments and needs; (3) provided plan is acceptable to military and phraseology of documents and contents of joint recommendations can be worked out to assure essential rights needed by military; and (4) provided the time limits stipulated in Annex "A" are no less than ten-year periods.

M. W[ISE]

711F.1914/5-3147 : Telegram

The Ambassador in Panama (Hines) to the Secretary of State

CONFIDENTIAL   PANAMÁ, May 31, 1947—11 a. m.

299. Minister of Public Works, Octavio Vallarino, has made available to Embassy a copy of a press release to be made by President Jimenez on Sunday June 1, when the new airport is inaugurated. This release will take the form of an answer to a reporter's question and is the Panamanian definition of joint authority as promised by Vallarino May 22 (see Embtel 282, May 23 [35]).

Embassy will forward release in clear after it has been made. Briefly, it states that Panama is waiting for the US to take the next move in defense site matter. Release then pointed out that as Panama is not a military power, it has been decided that the US will assume exclusively all technical, military and economic maintenance of defense sites, but that this comes about as an emanation from the joint authority of the two nations over defense sites and not as an exercise of unilateral power by the US. Release states that it is planned that the defense sites will not be a concession to the US but an example of cooperation between the two governments.

HINES

711F.1914/6-1347

Memorandum of Telephone Conversation, by the Assistant Chief of the Division of Central America and Panama Affairs (Wise) [36]

[WASHINGTON,] June 13, 1947.

Colonel Lutes [37] called to say that a letter has now been drafted in answer to our request that a decision be reached immediately concerning requirements for defense sites in Panama. He said that the

---

[35] Not printed.
[36] Addressed to Mr. Newbegin, CPA, and Mr. Briggs, ARA.
[37] Col. R. Lutes, War Department General Staff.

letter would be addressed to the Secretary of State and signed by the Secretary of War.

The letter will say that the less formal Panamanian proposal has been found acceptable to the War Department provided that:

(a) in the basic agreement itself there be a statement that the Commanding General will have exclusive military control over the sites;

(b) in either the basic agreement or in the accompanying notes there be a provision specifying that the Army can abandon a site by giving prior notification to Panama but *without* Panamanian approval; and,

(c) we accept a new proposal for Annex "A" to the agreement.

Colonel Lutes said that the new proposed Annex "A" is rather specific in requesting certain rights which, from past experiences in these negotiations, Panama may not be willing to accept. He says that the Army is asking for Rio Hato and only 13 additional sites. The latter are for small air warning stations. Rio Hato is being requested on a 50-99-year basis or a 30-year basis with our option to renew. The smaller ones are being requested for ten years with our option to renew. The letter goes on to say that if Panama is not willing to accept this proposition, then the War Department suggests breaking off negotiations. If negotiations are broken off the War Department will withdraw from the 36 sites now in use with the exception of Rio Hato and the 13 to be listed in the new proposed Annex "A". If this procedure does not bring Panama around to agreement then the War Department probably will begin to release the remaining sites.

711F.1914/6–1647

Memorandum of Telephone Conversation, by the Assistant Chief of the Division of Central America and Panama Affairs (Wise)[38]

CONFIDENTIAL [WASHINGTON,] June 17, 1947.

I called Colonel Lutes and brought to his attention the Embassy's telegram no. 326 of June 16.[39] It reports that we have now received through the Foreign Minister Panama's agreement to state in the basic defense sites document that the United States will have exclusive military command of the areas. Colonel Lutes emphasized that this has been one of the main points for which the Army has been insisting. He added that General Crittenberger probably would be surprised that Alfaro made this move inasmuch as he (General Crittenberger) told the War Department in a recent letter that he did not believe the Foreign Minister would go so far.

---

[38] Addressed to Messrs. Bennett and Newbegin of CPA, and Mr. Briggs of ARA.
[39] Not printed.

Colonel Lutes said that the Secretary of War has now signed a letter to the Secretary of State accepting the Panamanian proposal provided it is modified to include certain basic minimum requirements of the Army. One of these is exclusive command as referred to above. The letter encloses a revised list of sites needed and a copy of General Crittenberger's recent letter to the War Department arguing against acceptance of the Panamanian proposal.

General Eisenhower has been in on the discussion of the Panamanian problem and has pointed out that the War Department appreciates that it is primarily within the province of the State Department to determine how and when an agreement embodying the above is to be arrived at with the Republic of Panama.

Colonel Lutes said that a copy of the War Department's letter and enclosures was being sent to General Crittenberger. He believes Crittenberger probably will not like it, but that there will be attached to the file sent to Crittenberger a strong indication that he should be pretty much guided by Washington's position, although he has the War Department's full powers to negotiate with Ambassador Hines.

M. W[ise]

711F.1914/8-1947

Draft "G" of the Defense Sites Agreement Between Panama and the United States [40]

CONFIDENTIAL   [WASHINGTON,] 8 July, 1947.

PREAMBLE

The Governments of the Republic of Panama and of the United States of America have consulted together to consider all the phases of the existing situation as well as to discuss the experiences of the last war in relation to the defenses of the Panama Canal and the Republic of Panama; and, after an exchange of information with relation to the present needs, have reaffirmed their joint interest in providing for, and their mutual determination to assure the continued and effective protection of the Panama Canal and of the Republic of Panama as stipulated in the General Treaty of 2 March 1936 and the exchange of notes relating thereto; and, have come to the conclusion that a limited number of defense sites in territory under the

---

[40] Transmitted by the Acting Secretary of State (Lovett) to the Secretary of War (Royall) in communication of August 19, 1947, not printed. This draft originated with Lt. Gen. Willis D. Crittenberger, Commanding General, Caribbean Defense Command. It was informally turned over to the Department of State in mid-July.

jurisdiction of Panama should be maintained; in virtue of which the undersigned, Dr. Ricardo J. Alfaro, Minister of Foreign Relations of the Republic of Panama, and His Excellency, Frank T. Hines, Ambassador of the United States of America, representing their respective Governments by which they have been duly and legally authorized, have agreed as follows:

Article I

The High Contracting Parties, coincident with the entering into effect of this agreement, declare ended the occupation of all the defense sites now in use under the terms of the Agreement of May 18, 1942 and agree that hereafter the defense sites in territory under the jurisdiction of Panama will be regulated by the conditions set forth in the Preamble and the stipulations of the following articles of this agreement.

Article II

The Republic of Panama designates the areas specified in Annex "A"[41] attached to this Agreement and of which it forms an integral part, to serve as sites to be used by the armed forces of the United States for the defense of the Panama Canal and of the Republic of Panama, for the limited period specified for each one.

Article III

The Republic of Panama retains its sovereignty over the areas used as defense sites and over the air spaces corresponding to the same, as well as jurisdiction in civil matters, it being understood, nonetheless, that the United States will have exclusive jurisdiction over its civilian and military personnel, when employed or engaged in any manner whatsoever in connection with the operation of a defense site, and their families. The United States will have the right to arrest, try, and punish all persons who, in any defense site, wrongfully commit any act against the safety or security of the site, of the military installations therein, or of the personnel situated thereon, provided, however, that any Panamanian citizen arrested or detained on any charge will be delivered to the authorities of the Republic of Panama for trial and punishment. National authorities of both governments will be accorded adequate facilities for access to the defense sites but the military authorities of the United States may exclude from the defense sites such other persons as they see fit.

---

[41] Not printed.

Article IV

The Republic of Panama accords to the United States the powers and authority necessary to assume full military, technical and economic responsibility for the defense sites. The United States will exercise, therefore, all the rights and authority within defense sites and the air space thereover, which are necessary for occupation, use, operation and defense thereof or appropriate for their maintenance and control, and rights essential for access to, security and proper functioning of the defense sites, such as the right to improve or use roads, territorial waters, air spaces, subterranean waters, and waters of rivers and streams adjacent to or in the vicinity of defense sites. The Government of the United States may employ contractors and other personnel in the exercise of such rights as exist under this agreement.

Article V

To assure the efficient and mutually satisfactory functioning of the defense sites as well as to assure the exercise of the Republic of Panama's sovereign rights, the Government of the Republic of Panama designates the Minister of Government and Justice as its representative and the Government of the United States of America designates the local Commander of the Armed Forces as its representative to form a joint commission. The above-mentioned representatives will consult on all matters arising from the use of the defense sites and which are not specifically provided for in this agreement, provided, however, that all matters of a military nature or involving in any way the exercise of military command are to remain within the exclusive responsibility and jurisdiction of the military authorities of the United States. Following such consultation, the two Governments will adopt by an exchange of notes, which shall become an integral part of this agreement, the recommendations of the mentioned representatives.

Article VI

The Government of the United States will pay to the Government of Panama on the first day of February of each year or before an annual compensation of ———— balboas per hectare for all the lands used as defense sites during the preceding calendar year in accordance with the terms of this Agreement. The payment will be reduced proportionately in the case of periods of less than a year. There will be expressly excepted from the above provisions of this article:

(*a*) The piece of land in the township of Rio Hato designated as No. ——— in Annex "A" for which the Government of the United States will pay to the Government of the Republic of Panama an annual compensation of ——— balboas.

(*b*) The entire area of the Island of San José, in the archipelago of Las Perlas, in the Bay of Panama, designated as No. ——— in Annex "A" for which the Government of the United States will pay to the Government of the Republic of Panama an annual compensation of ——— balboas.

The Government of the Republic of Panama with respect to the lands used as defense sites will assume all the expenses of expropriation as well as the indemnifications and reimbursements for installations, cultivated lands, or other improvements which may exist thereon saving the United States harmless from all claims arising therefrom or incident thereto.

The compensations established in this article will be paid in Balboas as they were defined in the exchange of notes effected on March 2, 1936, to which Article VII of the Treaty of that date between the United States and Panama refers, or the equivalent in dollars, and will be paid for each defense site listed in Annex "A" from the effective date of this agreement.

Article VII

When a defense site or part of the same is no longer required for the defense of the Panama Canal and the Republic of Panama, its use will be discontinued on a date set by the United States. The Republic of Panama will be notified of the contemplated discontinuance no less than 90 days prior to the date set, unless the two Governments agree to a shorter notice.

All the buildings, constructions, installations, or accessories which may have been erected or placed by the United States on a defense site may be removed by the United States at any time prior to the date set for discontinuing the use of the site. The buildings, constructions, accessories, crops, cultivated areas, or other improvements existing at the time a defense site is first occupied by the United States may be used by the United States without obligation to pay for damages caused in any manner to the same. The Republic of Panama will not be obligated to pay compensation to the United States for improvements made on a defense site or for the buildings, constructions, or assets left thereon by the United States, all of which will become the property of the Republic of Panama when the use of the defense site is discontinued in accordance with this agreement.

Article VIII

Government owned and/or operated aircraft of the Republic of Panama will be authorized to land at and take off from air bases established within defense sites in accordance with regulations established by the joint commission created pursuant to the provisions of Article V.

In case of flight emergency or in time of national emergency, Government-operated aircraft of the United States will be authorized to use all airports established in the Republic of Panama.

Civil aircraft and aircraft of governments other than those of the Republic of Panama and the United States will not be authorized to land at or take off from any defense site established by the terms of this agreement, except in the case of emergency, or for strictly military purposes under supervision of the Armed Forces of the United States.

The Republic of Panama will not permit the erection or existence of obstacles which may constitute hazards to the safe operation of air bases established on defense sites. If it is necessary to alter or remove and/or relocate any existing structures the United States will bear all costs involved.

Article IX

The Republic of Panama agrees that all roads under its jurisdiction used for movements by the armed forces of the United States from one defense site to another, and between defense sites and the Canal Zone, will be well and properly maintained at all times. The Republic of Panama may ask for the assistance of the United States in the performance of repair or maintenance work on the said roads whenever such assistance is necessary to fulfill the aforesaid undertaking. In the case of emergencies or other situations which require prompt remedial action, the United States may voluntarily undertake the necessary emergency repairs, immediately notifying the Republic of Panama of its action. For normal or routine maintenance requirements the United States may offer assistance for the performance of repair and maintenance work whenever it appears to be appropriate.

The United States will pay annually to the Republic of Panama on on before the first day of February of each year ———— balboas or the equivalent in dollars as its contribution to the preceding calendar year's cost of repair or maintenance work on the roads used by the armed forces of the United States for movement from one defense site to another and between defense sites and the Canal Zone. First of such payments shall be made on or before the last of February 1948 to cover the calendar year 1947. In the event that in any calendar year the United States performs repair or maintenance work in accordance with the provisions of the first paragraph of this Article, the expenses incurred by the United States in so doing will be subtracted from the next annual payment made by the United States to the Republic of Panama. If the expense incurred by the United States in any calendar year is greater than the annual payment for that year, the annual payment will be cancelled and no claim will be made by the United States as a result of the amount spent in excess thereof.

In consideration of the aforementioned contribution by the United States to the cost of maintaining roads in the Republic of Panama, the United States is granted free right of transit on all roads under the jurisdiction of the Republic of Panama. The foregoing free right of transit shall be applicable to the routine, or tactical movement of members of the armed forces of the United States and civilian employees of such armed forces, and their families, as well as animals, animal-drawn vehicles and motor vehicles, employed by the armed forces, or by contractors employed by the armed forces, or by others whose activities are related to the defense of the Panama Canal.

The United States will maintain and permit the free use of any existing public roads which cross the defense sites or may relocate such roads in accordance with the recommendation of the joint commission.

Article X

The Republic of Panama accords to the United States, free of charge, right of ways for the maintenance, operation and use of such aerial telegraph and telephone lines, submarine cables, subterranean cables, and aerial cables, as are presently established.

The United States will, under such regulations as may be recommended by the joint commission and insofar as military requirements permit, share with the Republic of Panama the use of existing military telegraph and telephone lines and cables and any similar additional facilities of the armed forces of the United States which hereafter may be constructed in the Republic of Panama.

Article XI

The Republic of Panama accords to the United States the authority to install, operate, and maintain within defense sites such radio communication facilities as may be required by the armed forces of the United States to provide for the defense of the Panama Canal and the Republic of Panama. Similarly, the United States may use radio communication facilities with any elements of its armed forces in territory and territorial waters of the Republic of Panama.

Article XII

The Government of the Republic of Panama agrees that neither it nor its political subdivisions will impose any duty, tax, or charge on civilian or military personnel of the United States, employed in connection with the operation and defense of the defense sites, and their families, nor will any duty, tax or charge be levied on property belonging to or destined for this personnel, for any agency of the Government of the United States, or for a contractor employed by the United States in connection with a defense site.

Article XIII

The Republic of Panama accords to the United States the right to operate its naval vessels into, through and away from the territorial waters of the Republic of Panama, including the Perlas Islands, and to anchor such vessels in these areas without restriction. In exercising these rights, the United States will have the following attendant rights:

(1) To refuel, take on supplies, and/or effect repairs.
(2) To contract with persons, companies, or government agencies for services and supplies locally required.
(3) To permit military and naval personnel to enter the Republic of Panama for recreational liberty.

Article XIV

This Agreement may be terminated by the Contracting Parties by mutual accord even prior to the expiration of the periods stipulated in Annex "A".

Article XV

This Agreement will enter into effect upon the signature of the representatives of the Republic of Panama and of the United States of America duly and legally authorized.

In faith of which the plenipotentiaries of the High Contracting Parties have signed this Agreement, in duplicate, in English and Spanish, both texts being of equal authenticity, and have fixed their respective seals.

711F.1914/7–1947 : Telegram

The Secretary of State to the Embassy in Panama

SECRET WASHINGTON, July 19, 1947—2 p. m.

292. Gen Crittenberger and Asst Secy of War Petersen yesterday conferred with Asst Secy Armour on Panama defense sites issue.

Crittenberger's theses are: (1) Panama would now favorably consider a defense sites agreement proposal of the nature which the Army believes is required to meet its essential requirements; (2) our official silence since May has been effective in softening Panamanian resistance to our numerous proposals; (3) the immediate return of a number of sites now held under the 1942 agreement but no longer needed will bring added pressure to bear on Panama; (4) the Alfaro idea of "joint recommendation" and of treating essential Army requirements in notes ancillary to a basically short meaningless defense sites agreement is wholly unsatisfactory; and (5) while a commendable effort has been made to revise the Alfaro proposition our present draft [42] is still not acceptable.

Accordingly, Crittenberger urges (1) that we continue temporarily our present strategy of silence and of returning unneeded bases; (2) that we stand firm with Panama in requesting by way of an agreement language and requirements essential to the military; (3) that we give serious consideration to a new draft agreement [43] which the War Dept will take up with us; (4) that any new draft be presented to Panama formally on a "take it or leave it" basis; and (5) that if the proposal is unacceptable to Panama we withdraw from all bases now held under the 1942 Defense Sites Agreement.

Dept believes that circumstances may currently be more favorable than before to obtaining from Panama an agreement incorporating reasonable US requests but would not wish to press Panama into action on a new draft if it ignores most of the points insistently urged by Panama or many of its justifiable requests concerning form or phraseology of the agreement. Dept has no objection to temporary further silence and delay in negotiations nor to continued return of defense sites not to be requested under new accord. Furthermore, Dept favors submission our counter proposal simultaneously to both President and Foreign Minister on a "take it or leave it" basis. The advisability of complete withdrawal from Panama and its long run consequence in case of unacceptability our proposition to Panama would seem to be matter for further serious contemplation. While defense sites issue is most important matter pending there are other problems of far-reaching consequences in relations between two countries which must be negotiated soon. Consequently, atmosphere must be left conducive to the friendly settlement of other problems. The general sense of the Depts views as recorded above was expressed at the meeting. You will be advised of further developments.

MARSHALL

---

[42] The Alfaro draft as modified by the Department of State.
[43] Draft "G", *supra*.

711F.1914/8–1247 : Telegram

The Acting Secretary of State to the Embassy in Panama

CONFIDENTIAL   US URGENT   WASHINGTON, August 16, 1947—1 p. m.

337. Dept interprets urtel 445 Aug 12 [44] as meaning Emb wd find Crittenberger's draft G satisfactory for presentation to Panama provided it is revised to cover your detailed criticisms with which Dept concurs in general. It is further understood Emb wd favor presenting draft G modified rather than Dept's revision of Alfaro proposals containing ancillary notes.

In case draft G can be modified in line your suggestions to mutual satisfaction War and State Depts is it believed chances acceptance by Panama great enough to risk presentation on firm "take it or leave it" basis? Wd it be advisable try draft G on customary basis and if strongly opposed by Panama then fall back to presentation our revision of Alfaro plan on basis negotiations wd definitely be broken off if not accepted?

Dept wants this issue concluded before Sept 1 if possible and does not desire further protracted negotiations. Pls reply urgently.

LOVETT

711F.1914/8–1747 : Telegram

The Ambassador in Panama (Hines) to the Secretary of State

CONFIDENTIAL   PANAMÁ, August 17, 1947—10 a. m.

457. Deptel 337, August 16. Embassy favors presenting to Panama draft G with recommended modifications. This would avoid number of auxiliary notes.

Should Panama strongly oppose, we should then present Department's revision of Alfaro proposal on "take it or leave it" basis.

Embassy believes issue if handled as indicated can be concluded by September.

HINES

711F.1914/8–2947 : Telegram

The Acting Secretary of State to the United States Delegation to the Inter-American Conference for the Maintenance of Continental Peace and Security

SECRET   WASHINGTON, August 29, 1947—5 p. m.

130. To Armour from Wright. Dept strongly recommends Secretary brief Senator Vandenberg [45] on status defense sites negotiations with

---

[44] Not printed.
[45] Senator Arthur H. Vandenberg, Chairman, Senate Foreign Relations Committee, and a member of the Delegation to the Conference meeting in Rio de Janeiro.

Panama. In view controversy over expiration date 1942 agreement, desirability making new agreement effective urgently, and fact that only Congress action needed to fulfill US obligations under agreement is appropriation funds for War Department, either earmarked or general, for rental payment, Dept hopes contemplated agreement can become effective as executive agreement without treaty procedure. However, most important that questions on that point not hinder signing agreement.

Advisable obtain Vandenberg reaction because during 1943 hearings Senate Foreign Relations Committee on matters affecting relations with Panama Dept criticized for not sending 1942 defense agreement to Senate as treaty. Committee was concerned particularly over language 1942 agreement expressly requiring approval by Panamanian National Assembly without any reference to Senate approval. Language 1942 agreement was justifiable because Panamanian Constitution specifically requires National Assembly approval of every agreement made by executive authority.

Contemplated agreement provides for bringing into force by notification of approval from each government to the other, leaving each free to take action deemed necessary before giving notification. This permits approval agreement by Panamanian National Assembly pursuant constitutional requirement and likewise makes it possible, if subsequently found necessary, to submit agreement for Senate approval before notification. Accordingly agreement can be signed without express commitment on national procedure to be taken before notification.

Proposed agreement will commit US Govt to certain financial obligations to Panama in annual rentals for sites obtained. Although no reference in agreement to need for appropriations, contemplated that 1942 procedure of payment through War Department appropriations will be followed. Agreement intended give effect US rights and obligations regarding defense Panama Canal under treaties 1903 and 1936 with Panama. US obligations can be fulfilled under appropriate legislation. Dept believes agreement can properly be entered into without treaty procedure. However, discussion this matter need not be obstacle to signing agreement since national procedure prior to notification left open by agreement. [Wright.]

LOVETT

711F.1914/9-1847 : Telegram

The Ambassador in Panama (Hines) to the Secretary of State

SECRET   URGENT   PANAMA CITY, September 18, 1947—9 a. m.

518. Embtel 517, September 17.[46] Immediately after interview with Hall[47] yesterday, De Diego[48] and Filós consulted with President regarding some points in Panama counter-proposal[50] found objectionable by Embassy and they now agree to avoid mention of 1942 convention in Article 1, thus removing one of two principal difficulties in reaching agreement on sites. . . .

Panama also agrees to use our version of phrases "or involving" in Article 3 and "accords" in Article 4 (Embtel 517).

. . . I am now hopeful that we may reach agreement on periods of occupancy without resorting to ultimatum. However, I consider figures set in Annex "A" draft G are impossible of achievement and would appreciate urgent instruction giving shortest periods acceptable to War Department.

HINES

711F.1914/9-1847 : Telegram

The Acting Secretary of State to the Embassy in Panama

SECRET   US URGENT   WASHINGTON, September 26, 1947—6 p. m.

412. Urtel 518, Sept 18, 1947. Emb is authorized to inform Acting Fonmin that the changes proposed by Panama to Draft G of Defense Sites Agreement and as modified in conversations between Panamanian authorities and Emb are acceptable to this govt.

This leaves two important points unresolved: (a) amount of rent to be paid for sites and (b) duration of leases. Emb has already been requested to discuss point (a) with Panamanian authorities. (Deptel 403 Sept 23 [46]).

As re point (b) you should inform Filós that absolute minimum period acceptable this Govt is lease of 15 years for Rio Hato with option to renew additional 15 years. Five year period for other sites is acceptable.

In discussing Rio Hato you should inform Acting Fonmin that this Govt fully appreciates that period specified by it is considerably

---

[46] Not printed.
[47] Carlos Hall, First Secretary of Embassy in Panama.
[48] Mario de Diego, First Secretary of the Panamanian Foreign Office.
[49] Francisco A. Filós, Panamanian Minister of Government and Justice; in the absence of the Minister, he acted as Minister of Foreign Relations.
[50] Forwarded by the Ambassador in Panama in despatch 4299, September 18, 1947, not printed.

longer than that contemplated by Panama. While we would like to meet Panama's wishes in this regard we are unable to do so because of enormous sums which we must invest in area and which cannot possibly be justified for lease of shorter duration. You should point out further that if Panamanian Govt is not disposed to grant lease for period indicated no useful purpose would appear to be served by further negotiations. You should be careful not to convey impression that we are "threatening" Panama but rather to convey idea that this point is so basic that no agreement which omitted it would be of any use to this Govt.

You may also inform that in event they do not feel able to grant this request Dept of Army is disposed to withdraw in near future from all sites in Panamanian territory now occupied by our forces.

LOVETT

711F.1914/10-247 : Telegram

The Ambassador in Panama (Hines) to the Secretary of State

SECRET   US URGENT   PANAMA CITY, October 2, 1947—11 a. m.

565. Embtel 563 October 1.[51] Following note number 476 delivered personally last night to De Diego:

"I have the honor to refer to your note number DP 2103 of September 13, 1947 enclosing a draft counter proposal [52] of a new defense sites agreement which document has received the most careful study and consideration on the part of my Government.

I am pleased to state that, with the exception of articles I, III, IV, the US Government accepts textually the proposal made by the Foreign Office. However, in order to permit effective compliance with its obligations relative to the defense of the Panama Canal, my Government deems essential that some modifications for the Panamanian draft of the above-mentioned articles be made. The Embassy has discussed these modifications on various occasions with His Excellency the President, with Your Excellency, and with the First Secretary of the Ministry of Foreign Relations and, as a result of such conversations, I submit herewith the form which I consider such changes should take and which I understand is acceptable to the Government of Panama.

    Article I. The two Governments agree that the defense sites referred to in the present agreement will be regulated by the conditions set forth in the following articles.

    Article III. To assure the efficient and mutually satisfactory functioning of the defense sites as well as to assure the exercise of the sovereign rights of the Republic of Panama, the Government of the Republic of Panama designates the Ministry of Gov-

---

[51] Not printed.
[52] Neither printed.

ernment and Justice as its representative and the Government of the US of America designates the local Commander of its armed forces, or his designated representative, as its representative to form a joint commission whose members, the above-mentioned representatives, shall consult on all matters relating to the use of the defense sites, provided, however, that all matters of a military nature or involving in any way the exercise of military command are to remain within the exclusive responsibility and jurisdiction of the military authorities of the US. Following such consultation, the two Governments, carrying out the stipulations of this agreement, shall adopt by an exchange of notes the recommendations of the above mentioned representatives.

Article IV. The Republic of Panama accords to the US the powers and authority necessary to assume full military, technical, and economic responsibility for the defense sites. The US shall exercise, therefore, all the rights and authority within defense sites, and the air space thereover, which are necessary to make effective such responsibilities. The Government of the US of America may employ contractors and other personnel in the exercise of such rights.

Two important questions still require solution. The first relates to the compensation to be paid by the US for the use of the defense sites and the amount to be contributed by my Government as its share of the cost of maintenance of roads in the Republic. This is now under active consideration by officials of the Foreign Office and of the Embassy and, while no difficulty in reaching an understanding on this matter is anticipated, it is hoped that this may be effected at an early date.

The second point involves the period of occupancy of the defense sites, prescribed in the enclosure to my note number 456 of August 25, 1947 [54] as 30 years for Rio Hato and 10 years for each of the other defense sites described therein. Since these periods seemed unduly long to Your Excellency, your oral objections thereto were communicated to my Government which, after careful consideration, has instructed me to inform you that the minimum periods of occupancy acceptable to it are of 20 years for Rio Hato and of 5 years for the other defense sites under discussion.

My Government fully appreciates that the period specified for Rio Hato is considerably longer than that contemplated by Panama. While the United States would wish to meet the Republic's desire in this regard, it is impossible to do so in view of the enormous expenditures which my government contemplates making in that area in order that such defense site may adequately serve the purposes for which it is intended, and which outlay cannot in any manner be justified for a lesser period. Indeed, this minimum period is considered to be of such vital importance, that no agreement embodying a shorter period of occupancy would be of any practical value to my Government.

The return to Your Excellency of the Panamanian proposal, with the incorporation of the modifications found necessary by my Government, is made in a spirit of full and frank cooperation, with the great-

---

[54] Not printed.

est regard for the needs and requirements of Panama, and is indicative of the desire of the United States to meet as fully as possible the views of the Panamanian Government. It is based on the joint responsibility of the United States of America and the Republic of Panama to provide adequate protection for one of the invaluable assets of the hemisphere. I believe that steps should now be taken promptly to draw up the final agreement for signature.

As will be appreciated, our proposal as amended represents the minimum requirements of the United States. It is hoped that it also meets the requirements of Panama. During the 13 months that this matter has been under discussion, both Governments have evidenced every wish to reach a mutually satisfactory solution. It is believed that each thoroughly understands the considerations which have motivated the other. In view of the above, should the Government of Panama not find the present proposal acceptable, it is the opinion of my Government that no useful purpose would be served in attempting further negotiations for a new defense sites agreement at this time."

HINES

711F.1914/9-2347

Memorandum of Conversation, by the Secretary of State [55]

SECRET [NEW YORK,] October 8, 1947.

Participants: Secretary Marshall
Panamanian Foreign Minister Dr. Ricardo J. Alfaro
Mario de Diego
Murray M. Wise

At his request Dr. Alfaro called on me again this morning to discuss matters relating to the negotiation of a new defense sites agreement. The conversation lasted about thirty minutes.

Dr. Alfaro began by saying that during the interview of September 24 I had mentioned the possibility of talking to him again on this subject once I had seen the defense sites documents. At that point I interrupted the Minister and said that I had now been advised fully of the status and details of the negotiation and understood that he was not pleased with the phraseology, nor the proposed term of occupancy for Rio Hato.

Dr. Alfaro said that there were certain matters of phraseology that had not yet been satisfactorily ironed out, but he gave no indication of wanting to discuss details of phraseology with me. He said that he was primarily concerned with the term of occupancy for Rio Hato, and stated that he thought we were asking for Rio Hato for too long a period and that we must appreciate the opposition in Panama to

---

[55] The Secretary was in New York in connection with the General Assembly of the United Nations.

long-term grants to the U.S. Dr. Alfaro said that Articles II and X of the 1936 treaty were ample protection for the defense needs of the U.S. in Panama and that the Panamanian Government would, therefore, find it difficult to justify ceding Rio Hato on a long-term basis. I told Dr. Alfaro that I thought that I had a good understanding now of the Panamanian problem with respect to long-term leases and that I had hoped that I could persuade the people intimately connected with these negotiations that Rio Hato should be requested on a 15-year basis. I added, however, that political leaders in Washington and those in a position to advise on appropriations felt that a longer term was needed for Rio Hato. I said that it was the consensus among our people that we should either obtain Rio Hato for 20 years or proceed with a decision which was fast forming, to withdraw entirely from Panama. I said that in my opinion this would be very regrettable, and that such a decision would be tragic. I said that I had been most hopeful that these negotiations would be worked out in a manner satisfactory to both Governments. I said, however, that if we could not negotiate an agreement which would give us Rio Hato on a basis by which we could prepare and equip it for the use of new planes now under construction, we would (if we obtained Rio Hato on a shorter term) be forced to use smaller planes considered today as inadequate for the proper defense of the Canal. Accordingly, the decision which apparently is being reached with respect to withdrawing from Panama is based on the theory that it would be better to run the risk of being able to defend the Canal from within the Canal Zone itself than to have an unsatisfactory agreement. I repeated that I realized well the embarrassment which might be caused Panama by the negotiation of a long-term agreement for Rio Hato. I stated that I had been encouraged by recent reports from Panama with respect to the negotiations on phraseology, and I told Dr. Alfaro in this connection that I was sure he could understand that any agreement must necessarily provide a very clear basis for our use of sites in Panama during the interim period which would come between the conclusion of the negotiation of the new agreement and the date it actually would come into effect (here I was obviously referring to the Minister's objection to our language for Article I).

Dr. Alfaro said that he could not understand, if listening posts, radar stations, etc. were so essential to protection as had been explained by General Crittenberger, why we would ask for Rio Hato for a period longer (20 years) than we sought for the listening posts (5 years). He thought this was an inconsistency and that if Rio Hato were to be of any value to us, it would have to be always supported by the listening posts. Therefore, he thought we should ask for Rio Hato on the same basis as we asked for the other sites.

I told Dr. Alfaro that I could not see his point. I said that a radar station could be set up on short notice, while the extension and equipping of Rio Hato was a much different proposition. I said that upon very short notice we could at the slightest indication of need for listening posts go out and set them up. I referred to my explanation to Dr. Alfaro on September 24 that we could not be too certain at any moment, in view of the situation in the world today, as to just what threats we might have to face, and that since time is such a necessary factor in providing adequate defense, we wanted to take every precaution now and not allow ourselves to get into a position of unpreparedness such as existed prior to the last war. I added that it would be unfortunate to come out with a statement to the effect that we were on the verge of military action, but that I could not consider any procedure of disarmament such as had been followed in 1921. I said with great firmness and conviction that the casualties we had suffered during the past war were tremendous and that we had paid a terrific price for victory, and while I was determined to avoid another international conflict, I had no intention of disarming as we had after the last war. I told Dr. Alfaro that this was a practical element in our considerations and that with respect to the defense of the Panama Canal there was a need for adequate preparation. I said that it would be deplorable to have to withdraw from Panama and that I was really surprised that the military authorities were even considering it, but that apparently the decision was fast being reached that there would be less risk in withdrawing from [*to?*] the Canal Zone than there would be in agreeing to the use of Rio Hato on a basis which would force us into a defense setup inadequate for our needs.

At this point Dr. Alfaro said that if Rio Hato were not obtained on a long-term basis we could always fall back on the 1936 treaty, which provided for consultation on defense needs in cases of "an international conflagration" or "a threat of aggression". I questioned Dr. Alfaro's reference to "aggression" and endeavored to have him see what a broad interpretation might be given to that word and how it would be difficult today to determine when there was or was not a threat of "aggression".

Dr. Alfaro had no answer except to say that President Truman had just publicly stated that "peace is near" and that he wondered how I could reconcile my desire for such defense measures in Panama as I was discussing, with the President's statement. I told Dr. Alfaro that I had not been aware of the President's statement and that I was sure that whatever the President said could in no way be interpreted as a willingness to let down our guard. I told Dr. Alfaro that I thought his point was not well taken and that he could certainly find a better argument than President Truman's statement as support for the Panamanian position as regards Rio Hato.

Dr. Alfaro said that there was another point he would like to mention. He said that while he had always felt that the defense sites negotiations were pursuant to treaty commitments, there was a strong feeling that Panama was not receiving economic benefits from the U.S. equal to Panama's moral sacrifice in making sites available to the U.S. He said that it would be a very easy matter for the U.S. to build roads in Panama and to pay for certain other public works which for the Republic of Panama would be most costly, and asked if in connection with the negotiation of the defense sites agreement the U.S. would not be willing to announce a policy of economic cooperation with Panama with respect to certain needed public works. Dr. Alfaro referred to the economic assistance we were extending to Greece. I said I didn't think the Panamanian situation was in any way comparable to the case of Greece. I added that I had not given the question of economic benefits to Panama any consideration in connection with the present negotiations.

Mr. Wise stated that, of course, the fact should not be overlooked that Panama's so-called "moral sacrifices" made by the granting of defense bases was certainly in great part compensated for by rental payments. Wise added that it had consistently been the position of the U.S. Government that its request for defense sites was pursuant to treaty commitments and, accordingly, the defense sites matter should not be related to negotiations on pending economic matters. Wise said that it was felt most important that neither Panama nor the U.S. in these negotiations give any cause for criticism to the effect that defense sites were being obtained through processes of economic bargaining. Wise remarked, however, that at one time the Department had shown a disposition, once negotiations on the defense sites agreement had been concluded, to enter into the discussion of economic matters. He said that in fact the Department had previously been willing even to withhold the announcement of the conclusion of a defense sites agreement if Panama so desired, until pending economic problems had been discussed or at least until such time as a public announcement could be made that the U.S. would agree to negotiate immediately various pending economic problems. Wise said he could not state that this was still the position of the Department without further consultation. This matter was not pursued further.

I told Dr. Alfaro that I was sorry that I would have to leave for other business but that if he wished, I would be pleased to receive him again.

Following the conversation with the Secretary, Dr. Alfaro continued the discussion with Wise on the question of Rio Hato. He said that he could not see how Panama could agree to accept from the U.S. a special arrangement for rentals to cover Rio Hato and San José Island, when other private land owners in Panama would receive $50.00. He said this was a most important item and that while no protest had ever been received over the 1942 arrangement for the U.S. to pay a lump sum of $10,000 yearly for the use of Rio Hato, he was sure that if Panama accepted less for Rio Hato than was allowed private owners in other parts of the Republic of Panama there would definitely be a protest this time. He recalled that a claim had already been received from the Hurtematte family because the Army had used all of San José Island rather than the site originally agreed to. Dr. Alfaro said that the Army had occupied the whole island continuously, on the basis that the use of the major part of the island was for maneuvers. He said he had never seen the Army contract for the use of Rio Hato, since it was made behind the Government's back, and that he would like to know its terms. He said that until he knew them he could find no basis for accepting less than $50.00 per hectare for Rio Hato. Wise told him that his considerations with respect to the above would be made known to the State Department.

Mario de Diego referred to the some 750 hectares which would comprise the land needed for all bases other than Rio Hato. He said that he thought since the total area was so small the U.S. should pay $50.00 per hectare per year for all 13 bases, even though some of them might be on public land. He said he had been discussing this matter with Mr. Hall in Panama.

In conclusion Dr. Alfaro told Wise that personally he believed that Panama should not and could not enter into an agreement which would cede Rio Hato to the U.S. for 20 years. He said he could not and would not recommend this at all. He said he would communicate a summary of his interview with the Secretary immediately to President Jimenez, whom he said would have to make the final decision with respect to our request.

711F.1914/10–1347 : Telegram

The Ambassador in Panama (Hines) to the Secretary of State

SECRET   US URGENT   PANAMA CITY, October 13, 1947—4 p. m.

596. Embtel 594, October 12.[56] Assurances desired by President are textually as follows with Embassy's comments in parentheses:

1. Construction within a definite period, at the expense of US, of

---

[56] Not printed.

a concrete highway following a route to be indicated by Panama from a point on the highway to Rio Hato, to the Costa Rican frontier. (If accepted by US agreement should include cancellation of our commitment to build tunnel under Canal. See Embdesp 3550, March 7.[57] Route selected would naturally take into account our strategic needs as well as Panamanian political considerations.)

2. Return without cost to Panama of Pantilla Point and other areas in Taboga which will be determined later. (Covered by Department's instruction to Wise Jun 24).[57]

3. Reiteration of assurances of effective fulfillment of commitments regarding equality of treatment and opportunities for Panamanians in Canal Zone. (Foreign Office believes statement of what has been and is being done in this sense would be sufficient.)

4. Our conclusion of a bilateral agreement covering the following points: (*a*) regulations prohibiting the sale, manufacture or importation of alcoholic beverages into Canal Zone, in accordance with stipulations of ex-President Roosevelt's executive order (Foreign [apparent omission] states EO is no longer in effect, enforcement of its provisions being discretionary with CDC); (*b*) assurance of a Canal Zone market for products of Panama, under analogous conditions with regard to costs and reasonable comparison in quality. (Although drafting is murky, upon questioning Foreign Office admitted that what is sought amounts to a subsidy, i.e. prices obtaining in domestic US market); (*c*) prohibition of the sales of civilian goods in Canal Zone post exchanges, to include groups garrisoned in the Isthmus as established in prohibitions contained in Secretary of War's order of August 15, 1947; (*d*) limitation of sales in commissaries and post exchanges to merchandise produced or manufactured in US and Panama, (Foreign Office admits point 4 inspired solely by Panama Chamber of Commerce).

Embassy realizes difficulty in giving Panama written assurances regarding points 1 and 2 since both would require Congressional action. No objection, if Department sees fit, to write note covering point 3.

De Diego was informed that consideration of matters so completely extraneous as those included in point 4 would not only cloud and prolong the issue but possibly preclude its favorable conclusion. Hall reminded him that even Alfaro had stated that defense sites negotia-

---

[57] Not printed.

tions should not be conducted with a view to a *quid pro quo* but on a much higher ethical level.

I repeat recommendation last paragraph Embtel 594, believing there is still chance of securing Assembly's approval if President has courage to present our final proposal unchanged.

HINES

711F.1914/10–1247

Memorandum of Telephone Conversation, by Mr. W. Tapley Bennett of the Division of Central America and Panama Affairs

SECRET [WASHINGTON,] October 13, 1947.

Participants: Colonel O. H. Moore, Deputy Chief of Western Hemisphere Branch, War Department General Staff
W. T. Bennett— CPA

Colonel Moore telephoned in response to my earlier conversation with Colonel Gerety, during which I had inquired as to the Army Department's reaction to the Panamanian proposal of a 10–10 period at Rio Hato (Embassy's telegram no. 594 of October 12 [58]).

Colonel Moore stated that he had discussed the matter with appropriate authorities in the Army and Air Force Departments and that their position is as follows:

As regards the Rio Hato site, a period of 10 years with unconditional option for an additional 10 is, in the opinion of the Army and the Air Force, no different from the outright 20-year term requested. Since even this possible revision represents an improvement in their view over the 15-year period discussed at one stage of the negotiations, they are willing to go along with it and do not anticipate any particular difficulties with the Congress or the Budget Bureau as a result of the change from a straight 20-year term. Colonel Moore said, therefore, that the Department has the "blessing" of the Army and Air Force in negotiating on the 10–10 basis. He remarked, however, that if the Department should consider further revision of the United States proposal to a 15-year term or to a period less than that, then the Army and Air Force would have to consider the matter with some care.

I made it clear to Colonel Moore that we were ascertaining their reaction in order to be able to transmit it along with ours to New York for the attention of the Secretary. I said that we would, of course, clear any proposed action with his Department before going ahead.

---

[58] Not printed.

711F.1914/10–2947 : Telegram

The Ambassador in Panama (Hines) to the Secretary of State

SECRET   URGENT   PANAMÁ, October 29, 1947—noon.
NIACT

631. Through Minister Vallarino, President has informed Embassy that, while he is ready to sign draft G on straight 10–10 basis for Rio Hato, he feels approval of Assembly impossible in view of Alfaro's continued insistence on 5 years with no renewal. Latter has told Jimenez he is sure United States will accept his terms if only Panama stands firm (Embtel 616, October 23 [59]).

President offers to sign tomorrow if we will accept renewal subject to existence at end of 10 years of same or similar international conditions. This would provoke a Cabinet crisis and he is ready to accept Alfaro's resignation, offering him post in Washington and bringing J. J. Vallarino into Cabinet as well as Florencio Arosemena and Carlos Sucre. Latter would be offered Foreign Ministry. Jimenez feels sure he could then obtain Assembly's ratification, and requests immediate reply.

Vallarino asked Hall what would be next step if Panama replies that it can only grant 10 years without renewal and latter answered that Army would proceed to evacuate all bases.

I believe this is President's last desperate effort to secure better terms in order to facilitate approval by Assembly and recommend that we maintain present position.[60] If possible, please telephone reply I may give him.

HINES

711F.1914/10–3147 : Telegram

The Ambassador in Panama (Hines) to the Secretary of State

SECRET   URGENT   PANAMA CITY, October 31, 1947—7 p. m.
NIACT

637. In note delivered to me this afternoon Foreign Minister accepts unchanged our counterdraft of Articles 1, 3 and 4 of draft G and expressed confidence there would be no difficulty in reaching agreement on rentals and road maintenance, going on to state "My Government cannot accept the request of Your Excellency's Government that a period of 20 years be fixed for the operation of the Rio Hato sites;

---

[59] Not printed.
[60] A memorandum of conversation of October 30, 1947, by the Chief of the Division of Central America and Panama Affairs (Newbegin) indicated that the Department was standing firm (711F.1914/10–2947).

but conscious of its responsibility for the defense of the security and neutrality of Panama Canal and on behalf of continental solidarity, it is willing that a fixed period of 10 years be indicated for Rio Hato, this period being renewable up to 10 more years, if the periodic consultations to be made by the joint commission, created in conformity with Article 3 of the proposed agreement, determine that circumstances justify a renewal".

He adds that this proposal does not imply the intention of initiating new negotiations and is offered in spirit of conciliation and good will.

Above note was approved by Cabinet this morning to be supplemented by new consideration embodied in *aide-mémoire* also presented this afternoon and planned to cover our objection that short period would not justify heavy investment we intend to make at Rio Hato. They propose that Panama expropriate or buy the Rio Hato lands and, through an agreement which Foreign Minister assures me would meet with approval of Assembly and of Panamanian people, at the end of shorter period proposed air base would become property of the Republic, to be maintained in good condition so that in case of international conflagration it could be used by US Armed Forces in accordance with provisions of 1936 treaty. "The above-mentioned air base would thus remain converted in a defense installation of the Republic under its exclusive jurisdiction, and the maintenance of its efficiency and utility could be assured through the technical and economic cooperation of the US. This measure would assure that, for the mere reason that a shorter period for Rio Hato is suggested, there would not be lost to the defense of the Republic, the Canal and the whole continent, the costly improvements which the Government of the US proposes to make thereat. An arrangement such as suggested would permit Panama to own an additional air field for its aerial services and at the same time assure Panama and the US, interested in and committed to the defense of Panama and the Canal, an adequate air base which could be rapidly utilized in case of an international conflagration."

Questioned whether the President still proposes to present the agreement to the Assembly, Foreign Minister replied affirmatively, but only if signed in the form last proposed. This would indicate possibility that, if we do not accede, President may dismiss Assembly and then sign as proposed by US. Filós said his Government is certain Assembly would not approve straight 10–10 for Rio Hato and feels rejection would leave President in worse position than if no agreement whatsoever is signed.

Department's telephonic reply to Embtel 631, October 29,[63] was communicated to President yesterday afternoon.

Copies of note and *aide-mémoire* will be forwarded by first available courier. Newbegin should see letter from Hall arriving tomorrow night's air pouch.

HINES

711F.1914/11-147 : Telegram

The Ambassador in Panama (Hines) to the Secretary of State

SECRET PANAMÁ, November 1, 1947—9 a. m.

638. Deptel 478, October 31.[63] Virtual agreement has been reached on rentals [as] follows: No change in previous rental for Rio Hato and San Jose; 25 dollars per hectare for all other lands both public and private. Road maintenance payment still under discussion at my having suggested 100,000 and Panama asking 150,000. Believe we can settle for 125,000 or a little less. With exception of roads, arrangements so far conform to army expectations.

HINES

711F.1914/11-147 : Telegram

The Secretary of State to the Embassy in Panama

SECRET US URGENT WASHINGTON, November 8, 1947—1 p. m.
NIACT

493. Dept received Embdesp 4387 on Nov 1, 1947 [63] this afternoon. Panama should be aware now we are unable make further alterations our position regarding terms proposed defense sites agreement. Further concession on Rio Hato base along lines suggested by Panama as reported Embtel 637 Oct 31, 1947 is unacceptable both to State and Army Depts.

Inasmuch as note and *aide-mémoire* delivered to Emb Oct 31, 1947 by Panamanian Fonmin suggest further modifications of proposal submitted Panama by Emb on Aug 25, 1947,[64] Emb is instructed transmit note in reply to Panamanian communication. Emb note should point out in friendly tone the following: Within framework of mutual obligation US and Panama under Article II 1936 Treaty to provide effective protection of Canal, US has endeavored consistently

---

[63] Not printed.
[64] None printed.

to coordinate its estimates defense necessities with Panama's statements her national requirements. In effort reach agreement this Govt had prior to transmission its proposal of Aug 25 abandoned original estimate of need for 50–99 year term at Rio Hato in response Panama's exposition her position in matter, and our formal request was for 30-year rights. Following presentation that note this Govt has, in effort to meet Panamanian desires and requirements, successively reduced its request for Rio Hato rights to 15–15 term, to straight 20-year period and finally now to 10–10 term. Occupancy rights requested for all other sites have been reduced from 10 to 5 years. Reasons for need of longer period at Rio Hato have been explained on numerous occasions by Emb and have been discussed by Secy Marshall personally with Fonmin Alfaro both at Petropolis and New York.

It is of course entirely within discretion of Panamanian Govt to accept our current proposal, which represents absolute minimum US requirements, or to reject if it does not consider it possible accept terms. While we would very much regret rejection our proposal, the Republic of Panama may nevertheless be assured this Govt's continued desire maintain most friendly and cooperative relations.

MARSHALL

711F.1914/12–247

Memorandum of Conversation, by Mr. W. Tapley Bennett of the Division of Central America and Panama Affairs

CONFIDENTIAL [WASHINGTON,] December 2, 1947.

Participants: Norman Armour, Assistant Secretary of State
J. J. Vallarino, Ambassador of Panama
W. T. Bennett, CPA

Ambassador Vallarino opened the conversation by saying that, while he had talked with Ambassador Hines last week on defense sites matters, he was glad for the opportunity to come in to discuss the problem once again with Mr. Armour. He reiterated to Mr. Armour, as he has on numerous occasions to other officers of the Department, that he had returned to Washington from Panama solely with the hope of bringing about a solution to the impasse on the defense sites negotiations. He repeated that he is desirous of rendering any possible assistance.

The Ambassador again broached the question of a change in phraseology in the agreement with respect to continued occupation of the Rio Hato site following the initial 10-year period. He said that Foreign Minister Alfaro is still unwilling to agree to more than five years for Rio Hato but that he himself is convinced of the necessity for a longer period and is willing to work for the acceptance of the 10–10 period by the National Assembly of Panama. He said, however, that the Assembly would not be disposed to ratify the signed accord in the absence of some written expression of this Government's willingness to grant "compensations" following signature of the agreement. He said that the Panamanian people, with the example of the twelve-points accord [65] signed at the same time as the 1942 Defense Sites Agreement, would expect certain concessions (he mentioned roads as the principal field of interest of his Government and also suggested an Executive Order restricting the Canal Zone commissaries to the handling of goods produced in the United States or Panama) and that he is doubtful of ratification by the Assembly without such assurances. The Ambassador said that President Jimenez under present circumstances would not be prepared to present the agreement to the Assembly.

Mr. Armour replied that, while this Government would view with regret such a decision by the Government of Panama, we are unable to make further changes in our position relative to the defense sites agreement. He reiterated the view of this Government that the matter of economic concessions must be kept separate from the defense of the Canal, which is a mutual obligation of the two Governments under the 1936 Treaty. He said that he was glad to repeat again our previously given assurances of willingness to discuss economic matters following conclusion of the defense sites agreement.

Mr. Armour pointed out that we have made repeated concessions in an effort to meet the viewpoints of Panama and that we have reached a point beyond which we can go no farther. He mentioned that Secretary Marshall has followed the course of the negotiations personally and with a great deal of interest and that our position is the result of detailed consideration of the problem in the Department and with officials of the Army, Navy and Air Force Departments. Mr. Armour offered the opinion that the members of the Panamanian Assembly should be able to understand that our requests are based on defense needs of the Canal, defense of which is of vital interest to the entire Hemisphere, and to recognize the numerous concessions we have made from our original proposals.

Ambassador Vallarino showed considerable disappointment at Mr. Armour's remarks. At one point he declared that he had been a failure here as his country's representative and that, therefore, he did not want to retire and return home at the present time. He said that he regretted not having been given a larger part by his Government in

---

[65] Department of State Executive Agreement Series No. 452.

the conduct of the negotiations and pointed out that he had not been brought in to the problem until the very end of the discussions. He expressed confidence that a more satisfactory solution would have been found had he been in charge of the negotiations on the Panamanian side. He then said that he had been advised by his doctor of the necessity for a thorough physical check-up and that under the circumstances he was not desirous of entering the presidential race for next year's elections in Panama. He asked what would be the result of failure to reach agreement and inquired whether it would mean evacuation from all bases in Panamanian territory of United States troops. Mr. Armour replied that it would.

Mr. Armour took occasion once again at the end of the conversation to assure the Ambassador that our present position must be considered firm and that it remains as presented by Ambassador Hines last week and by him today. He said that if Ambassador Vallarino wished he would be glad to review the matter once again with the Acting Secretary but that he desired to express in all frankness his opinion that there will be no change in our position.

Ambassador Vallarino said that he appreciated Mr. Armour's courtesy in offering to take up the matter with the Acting Secretary and that he would await word as to the results of that conversation. He seemed aware of the small likelihood of any change in our position.

NOTE: Mr. Armour talked with Ambassador Vallarino at the President's reception to the Diplomatic Corps on the evening of December 2 and informed him that Mr. Lovett had confirmed this Government's position on the defense sites agreement as expressed by Mr. Armour earlier in the afternoon and by Ambassador Hines on November 25. Mr. Armour explained to Ambassador Vallarino that our position had been determined through study and consultation among all the Departments concerned. He said that if the latter were sending a message on the matter he should inform his Government that this was our final position.

711F.1914/12–547

Memorandum of Telephone Conversation, by the Chief of the Division of Central America and Panama Affairs (Newbegin)

CONFIDENTIAL [WASHINGTON,] December 5, 1947.

Mr. Hall [66] telephoned to state that the Panamanian authorities called him in at one o'clock today to say that the Cabinet had taken a definite decision to accept the final draft of the defense sites agreement.

---

[66] Carlos C. Hall, First Secretary of Embassy in Panama.

He said that the President wished to sign it on Tuesday or Wednesday, and that he planned to call the Assembly into session on Friday. Mr. Hall stated that he hoped the Ambassador could return by Tuesday if possible, so that the signing could be completed. He said that he would receive a note from the Foreign Office probably in the course of the day, accepting the agreement. The draft of the note had been shown to him, as had another note which would accompany it. The other note refers to the question of economic assistance from the U.S. Mr. Hall was informed orally that this note should not give us much concern, that it was written essentially for its political effect in the Assembly. However, if we were in a position to answer before the Assembly met, it would undoubtedly help in obtaining approval from the Assembly. It was pointed out by Mr. Hall that the note regarding economic assistance was not intended to have any connection with the defense sites agreement as such. If I understood him properly, I gathered that we should not be too concerned about the debate and probable charges which would be made in the Assembly.

Mr. Hall added that Alfaro was returning on Monday and would undoubtedly resign.

I, of course, congratulated Mr. Hall sincerely for his very good work in connection with the agreement.

R. N[EWBEGIN]

711F.1914/12–1047

Defense Sites Agreement, Signed on December 10, 1947, But Not Subsequently Ratified Between Panama and the United States [67]

The Government of the United States of America and the Government of the Republic of Panamá have consulted together to consider all the phases of the existing international situation as well as to discuss the experiences of World War II in relation to the defense of the Panamá Canal; and, after an exchange of information with relation to the present needs, have reaffirmed their joint interest in providing for that which is necessary for the continued and effective protection of the Panamá Canal and the security of the Republic as stipulated in the General Treaty signed at Washington March 2, 1936 and in the exchange of notes relating thereto; they have reached the conclusion that under present circumstances a limited number of defense sites in territory under the jurisdiction of Panamá should be maintained temporarily; in virtue of which they have decided to conclude an

---

[67] Transmitted by the Ambassador in Panama in his despatch 4489, December 10, 1947, not printed.

agreement in order to effectuate the foregoing objectives, and for that purpose have appointed as their respective representatives:

His Excellency Frank T. Hines, Ambassador Extraordinary and Plenipotentiary of the United States of America to the Republic of Panamá, and

His Excellency Doctor Francisco A. Filós, Acting Minister of Foreign Relations of the Republic of Panamá, who, having been duly authorized by their respective Governments, have agreed as follows:

Article I

The two Governments agree that the defense sites referred to in the present Agreement will be regulated by the conditions set forth in the following articles.

Article II

The Republic of Panamá designates the areas specified in the Annex attached [67a] to this Agreement, and of which it forms an integral part, to serve as sites to be used for the defense of the Panamá Canal and of the Republic of Panamá, for the limited period specified for each site.

Article III

To assure the efficient and mutually satisfactory functioning of the defense sites as well as to assure the exercise of the sovereign rights of the Republic of Panamá, the Government of the United States of America designates the local Commander of its Armed Forces, or his designated deputy, and the Government of the Republic of Panamá designates the Minister of Government and Justice as its representative, to form a joint commission whose members, the above-mentioned representatives, shall consult on all matters relating to the use of the defense sites, provided, however, that all matters of a military nature or involving in any way the exercise of military command are to remain within the exclusive responsibility and jurisdiction of the military authorities of the United States. Following such consultation, the two Governments carrying out the stipulations of this Agreement, shall adopt by an exchange of notes, the recommendations of the above-mentioned representatives.

Article IV

The Republic of Panamá accords to the United States the powers and authority necessary to assume full military, technical, and eco-

---

[67a] Not printed.

nomic responsibility for the defense sites. The United States shall exercise, therefore, all the rights and authority within defense sites and the air spaces thereover, which are necessary to make effective such responsibilities.

The Government of the United States of America may employ contractors and other personnel in the exercise of such rights.

Article V

The Republic of Panamá maintains its sovereignity over the areas used as defense sites and over the air spaces corresponding thereto, as well as jurisdiction with respect to civil and criminal matters in these areas, it is being understood, nonetheless, that the United States shall have exclusive jurisdiction over any offenses which may be committed within the defense sites by its civilian or military personnel employed or engaged in any manner whatsoever in connection with the operation of the defense sites and by members of their families. The United States, by virtue of the military responsibility which it assumes in conformity with Article IV, shall have the right to arrest, try, and punish, if necessary, all persons who, in any defense site, commit any act against the security of the site, of the military installations therein, or of the personnel situated thereon, provided, however, that any Panamanian citizen arrested or detained on any charge shall be delivered to the authorities of the Republic of Panamá. National authorities of both Governments shall be accorded adequate facilities for access to the defense sites, but the military authorities of the United States may exclude other persons from the defense sites.

Article VI

The Government of the United States of America shall pay to the Government of the Republic of Panamá on or before the first day of February of each year an annual compensation of seventeen thousand two hundred fifty Balboas (B/17,250.00) for all the lands used as defense sites during the preceding calendar year in accordance with the terms of this Agreement. The payment shall be reduced proportionately in the case of periods of less than a year. There shall be expressly excepted from the above provisions of this Article:

(A) The piece of land in the township of Río Hato designated as No. 1 in the Annex, for which the Government of the United States of America shall pay to the Government of the Republic of Panamá an annual compensation of ten thousand seven hundred and fifty Balboas (B/10,750.00).

(B) The entire area of the island of San José, in the Archipelago of Las Perlas, in the Bay of Panamá, designated as No. 2 in the

Annex, for which the Government of the United States shall pay to the Government of the Republic of Panamá an annual compensation of fifteen thousand Balboas (B/15,000.00).

The Government of the Republic of Panamá shall assume, with respect to the lands used as defense sites, all expenses of expropriation as well as the indemnifications and reimbursements for installations, cultivated lands, or other improvements which may exist on those lands.

The compensations established in this Article shall be paid in Balboas as they were defined in the exchange of notes effected on March 2, 1936, to which Article VII of the treaty of that date between the United States of America and the Republic of Panamá refers, or the equivalent in dollars, and shall be paid proportionately for each defense site listed in the Annex, from the effective date of this Agreement.

Article VII

When a defense site or part thereof is no longer required for the defense of the Panamá Canal and the Republic of Panamá, its use shall be discontinued on a date set by the United States. The Republic of Panamá shall be notified of the contemplated discontinuance no less than 90 days prior to the date set, unless the two Governments agree to a shorter notice.

All the buildings, constructions, installations, or accessories which may have been erected or placed by the United States on a defense site may be removed by the United States at any time prior to the date set for discontinuing the use of the site. The buildings, constructions, accessories, crops, cultivated areas, or other improvements existing at the time a defense site is first occupied may be used by the United States without obligation to pay for damages caused in any manner thereto. The Republic of Panamá shall not be obligated to pay compensation to the United States for improvements made on a defense site or for the buildings, constructions, or assets left thereon by the United States, all of which will become the property of the Republic of Panamá when the use of the defense site is discontinued in accordance with this Agreement.

Article VIII

The United States and the Republic of Panamá reiterate their understanding regarding the temporary character of the occupation of the defense sites to which this Agreement refers. Consequently, the United States, recognizing the importance of the cooperation rendered by Panamá in making these temporary defense sites available, and also recognizing the burden which the maintenance of these sites signifies for the Republic of Panamá, expressly undertake to reach agreement with the latter upon the measures necessary in order that the evacuation of said sites will be effected no later than the date of expiration of the period stipulated with respect to each site in the Annex, or before, if in the opinion of the two Governments the causes and circumstances which have determined the maintenance of the defense sites should have ceased.

Article IX

Government owned or operated aircraft of the Republic of Panamá shall be authorized to land at and take off from air bases established within defense sites, in accordance with regulations to be established by the Joint Commission created pursuant to the provisions of Article III.

Civil aircraft and aircraft of Governments other than those of the Republic of Panamá and of the United States shall not be authorized to land at or take off from any defense site established by the terms of this Agreement, except in the case of emergency, or for strictly military purposes.

The Republic of Panamá shall not permit the erection or existence of obstacles which may constitute hazards to the safe operation of air bases established on defense sites. If it is necessary to alter, remove or relocate any existing structures, the United States shall bear the costs involved.

Article X

The Republic of Panamá agrees that all roads under its jurisdiction used for movements by the Armed Forces of the United States from one defense site to another, and between defense sites and the Canal Zone, shall be well and properly maintained at all times. In the case of emergencies the United States may undertake the necessary repairs, immediately notifying the Republic of Panamá of its action. For normal or routine maintenance requirements the United States may offer assistance for the performance of repair and maintenance work whenever it appears to be appropriate.

The United States shall pay annually to the Republic of Panamá on or before the first day of February of each year one hundred thirty-seven thousand five hundred Balboas (B/137,500.00) or the equivalent in dollars as its contribution to the preceding year's cost of repair or maintenance work on the roads used by the Armed Forces of the United States. The first of such payments shall be made on or before the last day of February 1948 to cover the calendar year 1947. In the event that in any year the United States performs repair or maintenance work in accordance with the provisions of the first paragraph of this Article, the expenses incurred by the United States in so doing shall be subtracted from the next annual payment made by the United States to the Republic of Panamá. If the expense incurred by the United States in any year is greater than the annual payment for that year, the annual payment shall be canceled and no claim shall be made by the United States as a result of the amount spent in excess thereof.

In consideration of the aforementioned contribution by the United States to the cost of maintaining roads in the Republic of Panamá, the United States is granted free right of transit on all roads under the jurisdiction of the Republic of Panamá. The foregoing free right of transit shall be applicable to the routine or tactical movement of members of the Armed Forces of the United States and civilian employees of such Armed Forces, and their families, as well as animals, animal-drawn vehicles, and motor vehicles, employed by the Armed Forces, or by contractors employed by the Armed Forces, or by others whose activities are related to the defense of the Panamá Canal. The United States shall not obstruct the free use of any of the roads under the jurisdiction of the Republic of Panamá by virtue of the routine or tactical movement of United States Armed Forces, except in cases of emergency.

The United States shall maintain and permit the free use of any existing public roads which cross the defense sites or may relocate such roads in accordance with the recommendation of the Joint Commission.

Article XI

The Republic of Panamá accords to the United States the right to maintain and use such aerial telegraph and telephone lines, submarine cables, subterranean cables, and aerial cables, as are presently established.

The United States shall, under such regulations as may be agreed upon by virtue of recommendation by the Joint Commission and insofar as military requirements permit, share with the Republic of Panamá the use of existing military telegraph and telephone lines and cables, and any similar additional facilities of the Armed Forces of the United States which hereafter may be constructed in the Republic of Panamá.

Article XII

The Republic of Panamá accords to the United States the authority to install, operate, and maintain within defense sites such radio-communication facilities as may be required by the Armed Forces of the

United States for the defense of the Panamá Canal and the Republic of Panamá. Similarly, the use of radio-communication facilities by the Armed Forces of the United States in territory and waters under the jurisdiction of the Republic of Panamá shall be permitted, in accordance with the regulations to be established by recommendation of the Joint Commission.

Article XIII

The civilian and military personnel of the United States functioning on the defense sites or employed in connection with the operation of said sites, including contractors working exclusively on the defense sites, and the families of such personnel, as well as the property and effects destined for the bases, shall be exempt from all taxes, contributions or imposts of any kind imposed by the Republic of Panamá or its political subdivisions, during the terms of this Agreement.

The authorities of the Government of the United States of America shall impede the sale or transfer of merchandise and articles imported into or sold in the defense sites for the use or consumption of civilian and military personnel employed thereon to persons having no right to buy such merchandise or articles. Said authorities shall, in addition to preventing the abuse of the exemptions conceded by this Agreement, cooperate with the authorities of the Republic of Panamá for the purpose of precluding the contraband of said merchandise and articles.

Article XIV

This Agreement may be terminated by the two Governments by mutual accord prior to the expiration of the periods stipulated in the Annex.

Article XV

This Agreement shall enter into force on the day on which each of the Governments notifies the other Government in writing of its approval of the same, if such notifications are given on the same day; and if the notifications are given on different days, the Agreement shall enter into force on the date of the notification later in time.

In faith of which the plenipotentiaries of the High Contracting Parties have signed this Agreement in duplicate in English and Spanish, both texts of equal authenticity, and have affixed their respective seals.

Done at the city of Panamá, the tenth day of December, 1947.

Frank T. Hines

Francisco A. Filós

[Annex]

MEMORANDUM DESCRIBING THE DEFENSE SITES AND STIPULATING THE PERIOD OF OCCUPANCY OF THE SAME, ANNEXED TO THE DEFENSE SITES AGREEMENT BETWEEN THE UNITED STATES OF AMERICA AND THE REPUBLIC OF PANAMA, AND FORMING AN INTEGRAL PART OF THAT AGREEMENT

The exact boundaries of the defense sites are shown in detail on the United States Army maps and drawings listed below, copies of which are in the possession of the Ministry of Foreign Relations of Panamá. For further identification, where possible, there are given the numbers under which said bases appeared in the Annex to the Agreement for the Lease of Defense Sites in the Republic of Panamá, of May 18, 1942.[68]

DEFENSE SITE NO. 1, RIO HATO, formerly known as No. 12, is located in the township of that name and Province of Coclé approximately 57 miles westward, along the National Highway from the Canal Zone and extends from the shore of the Gulf of Panamá northward across the National Highway for a distance of approximately 16 miles. The site consists of two parcels, one with an area of 7,675.96 hectares and the other of 12.32 hectares, or a total area of 7,688.28 hectares. The boundaries are shown on Department Engineer Drawings Nos. 5889 and 5889–1. *Period of occupancy:* Ten years, renewable for an additional period of ten years, at the option of the United States of America.

DEFENSE SITE NO. 2, SAN JOSÉ ISLAND, comprises the entire island of that name and is located in the Bay of Panamá, in the Perlas Archipelago, approximately 55 miles S 40° E of Balboa, Canal Zone. Its area is approximately 4,460 hectares. *Period of occupancy:* Five years.

DEFENSE SITE NO. 3, TABOGA ISLAND, located on the island of that name which lies in the Bay of Panamá approximately 11 miles due S of Fort Amador, Canal Zone. It comprises three parcels of land formerly known as No. 17 with an aggregate area of 26.79 hectares, the boundaries of which are described in Department Engineer Drawings 6020, 6026, 6073, 6075, 6077 and 6078; and of another parcel of 14.5 hectares, formerly known as No. 56 and described in Department Engineer Drawings 6020 and 6022; the total area of this site being 41.29 hectares. *Period of occupancy:* Five years.

DEFENSE SITE NO. 4, TABOGUILLA ISLAND, formerly known as No. 18, is located on the island of the same name, in the Bay of Panamá less

---

[68] For text, see Department of State Executive Agreement Series No. 359; 57 Stat. (pt. 2) 1232. For documentation on negotiations of this Agreement, see *Foreign Relations,* 1942, vol. VI, pp. 577 ff.

than one mile E of Taboga Island which has been previously identified. The site comprises 132.06 hectares, the boundaries of which are described in Department Engineer Drawings 5311, 5820, 5821 and 5885. *Period of occupancy:* Five years.

DEFENSE SITE NO. 5, SALUD, is located in the Province of Colón on the Caribbean Sea, approximately 19 miles SW along the coast from Fort Sherman, Canal Zone, between the villages of Salud and Lagarto. It comprises 49.996 hectares and is delimited in Sheet 122, Terrain Map, Military Survey of Panamá, Scale 1: 20,000. *Period of occupancy:* Five years.

DEFENSE SITE NO. 6, REY ISLAND, is located on the southernmost part of the island of that name, the largest of the Perlas Archipelago, lying in the Gulf of Panamá approximately 69 miles S 40° E of Albrook Field, Canal Zone. The site, formerly known as No. 32, consists of two parcels with a total area 100.05 hectares and is shown on Department Engineer Drawing 5672. *Period of occupancy:* Five years.

DEFENSE SITE NO. 7, JAQUE, with a total area of 149.01 hectares, consists of one parcel of 9.02 hectares, formerly known as No. 20, located at Piñas Bay in the Province of Panamá, approximately 30 miles NW along the Pacific Coast from the Colombian border, and described in Department Engineer Drawing 5865; and of another parcel of 139.99 hectares, previously known as No. 21, located inland approximately 1 mile from the former and shown on Department Engineer Drawing 6039. *Period of occupancy:* Five years.

DEFENSE SITE NO. 8, POCRI, formerly known as No. 7, is located in the Province of Los Santos peninsula, approximately 92 air-miles S 26° W of Albrook Field, Canal Zone and 10 miles E from the town of Las Tablas. It consists of two parcels with an aggregate area of 157.2 hectares and is shown on Department Engineer Drawings 2002-1 Revised, 6002-1-2 and 6002-3. *Period of occupancy:* Five years.

DEFENSE SITE NO. 9, CAPE MALA, is located in the Province of Los Santos at the SE extremity of Los Santos peninsula, approximately 108 air-miles S 16° W from Albrook Field, Canal Zone and comprises two parcels with a total area of 20.07 hectares. The first, of 15.03 hectares, formerly known as No. 8, is shown on Department Engineer Drawing 6061; while the other, previously known as No. 126, has an area of 5.04 hectares and is shown on Department Engineer Drawing 6356. *Period of occupancy:* Five years.

DEFENSE SITE NO. 10, SAN BLAS POINT, formerly known as No. 24, is located in the Comarca of San Blas on the Caribbean Coast on a peninsula at the western end of the Gulf of San Blas and approximately 61 air-miles N 82° E from France Field, Canal Zone. It has an area of 23.87 hectares and is shown on Department Engineering Drawing 4781. *Period of occupancy:* Five years.

DEFENSE SITE NO. 11, ISLA GRANDE, formerly known as No. 96, is located in the Province of Colón, on a small island of that name on the Caribbean Coast, approximately 30 air-miles N 51° E of France Field, Canal Zone. It consists of two parcels having a total area of 8.66 hectares, the boundaries of which are shown on Department Engineer Drawing 6167-Revised. *Period of occupancy:* Five years.

DEFENSE SITE NO. 12, VICTORIA, formerly known as No. 36, has an area of 5.4 hectares, lies approximately 5 miles NE of the town of Pacora in the Province of Panamá, and is shown on Department Engineer Drawing 6019. *Period of occupancy:* Five years.

DEFENSE SITE NO. 13, LAS MARGARITAS, formerly known as No. 127, is located near the village of the same name, in the Province of Coclé. The site has an area of 2.13 hectares and is shown on Department Engineer Drawing 6438-A-Revised. *Period of occupancy:* Five years.

In witness whereof, this memorandum is signed in duplicate in English and Spanish, in Panamá, this tenth day of December, A.D. 1947.

FRANK T. HINES

FRANCISCO A. FILÓS

711F.1914/12–1047 : Telegram

The Acting Secretary of State to the Embassy in Panama

RESTRICTED   U.S. URGENT   WASHINGTON, December 10, 1947—11 a. m.
NIACT

549. Dept plans issue following press release at 4 p. m. today:

The US Amb to Panama, General Frank T. Hines, and the Acting Fonmin of the Republic of Panama, Sr. Don Francisco A. Filós today signed an agreement on behalf of their Govts which provides for the continued use of certain sites in the territory of the Republic for the defense of the Panama Canal.

This new agreement exemplifies and continues the spirit of cooperation evidenced by Panama in the accord of May 18, 1942. Under the former agreement the Republic of Panama made available 134 areas in its national territory for use during World War II. The new accord provides for use by the US of 13 sites, principally technical installations essential to safe aerial navigation, for a period of five years. A 14th site at Rio Hato, an important military air base some 70 miles west of Panama City, will be leased by the US under terms of the agreement for a period of 10 years, with option for an additional 10 years.

The agreement signed in Panama today at noon is the result of a lengthy study by the two Govts of lessons learned during the recent conflict relative to Canal defenses and takes into account its current and future security requirements. It is designed to insure continuous operation and effective protection of the Canal as provided in the Treaty of Friendship and Cooperation signed by the two countries in 1936. It gives recognition to the fact that requirements of modern defense make essential the use of certain areas outside the 10-mile wide Canal Zone for the protection of the international waterway which is so vital to the interests of the US and Panama.

The agreement provides for the appointment by the two Govts of representatives who will jointly administer the agreement. Under terms of the accord the US assumes authority and responsibility for all technical, military and economic matters connected with the operation of the 14 defense sites.

The text of the agreement will be released in the near future.[68a]

LOVETT

711F.1914/12–1147 : Telegram

The Ambassador in Panama (Hines) to the Secretary of State

CONFIDENTIAL   URGENT   PANAMÁ, December 11, 1947—10 a. m.
NIACT

723. Accompanied by General Hale,[69] I called on President this morning to thank him for cooperation shown in signing agreement. He is extremely anxious that reply to note transmitted in Embtel 710, December 6 [70] be received by time Assembly convenes tomorrow since he feels certain that, if couched in favorable terms, it would make certain ratification by that body.

Confirming today's conversation with Newbegin I most strongly urge I be authorized immediately to reaffirm in writing the verbal assurances previously given Panama. Even if we only state that Department will make appropriate recommendations to Congress, such assurance if made at this time would have powerful effect on Assembly and on critical political situation now brewing.

The opposition is presently organizing behind Alfaro who recently told Jimenez that, if he did not get promise from US of economic assistance before signing agreement, he could whistle for it after. This is the impression we must combat at once.

Furthermore, I believe that our promise to return Paitilla and other parcels to Panama, which involves no drawn-out negotiations, should be presented as a "must" to the present Congress if we are not to be exposed to accusations of bad faith.

HINES

[68a] Department of State press release 967, December 12, 1947.
[69] Gen. Willis F. Hale, Commanding General, Caribbean Air Defense.
[70] Not printed; for reply, see *infra*.

711F.1914/12-647 : Telegram

The Acting Secretary of State to the Embassy in Panama

CONFIDENTIAL   WASHINGTON, December 11, 1947—8 p. m.
US URGENT
NIACT

555. Urtel 710 Dec 6.[71] Desire of Panamanian Govt to initiate conversations on economic assistance fully appreciated and Dept disposed to cooperate. There is some concern however lest our assurances this regard be greatly exaggerated by Jimenez administration in effort secure ratification defense sites agreement by Assembly. Any such exaggeration would of course in long run be detrimental to over-all relations were actual possible assistance to fall materially short Panamanian expectations. You should convey this concern to FonMin and President at time of replying to Panamanian note of Dec. 6, making it clear that our concern should not be interpreted as modifying in any way our desire cooperate to fullest possible extent.

In reply to Dec 6 note you are requested present following note FonOff:

"I have the honor to acknowledge the receipt of Your Excellency's note of Dec 6 in which you refer to the aspirations of the Govt of Panama with reference to the economic cooperation which your Govt hopes to receive in accordance with the joint obligations of our two governments as provided for in Article I of the general Treaty of 1936.

In this note Your Excellency expresses the hope that there will be initiated as soon as possible conversations and negotiations on this subject.

In reply I am glad to inform Your Excellency that my Govt is in entire accord with the procedure suggested, and is prepared to initiate conversations on economic matters with the Govt of Panama on any date after Jan 1, 1948 which the Govt of Panama may care to designate. It is understood that such conversations will take fully into account the legitimate aspirations and interests of both countries under the broad principles of the Treaty of 1936.

Please accept etc."

LOVETT

711F.1914/12-1347 : Telegram

The Ambassador in Panama (Hines) to the Secretary of State

RESTRICTED   PANAMA CITY, December 13, 1947—11 a. m.

730. Yesterday afternoon in defiance Mayor's refusal to permit demonstration against agreement, at time National Assembly convened, students clashed with police. Tear gas and even side arms had to be used by latter to defend themselves from infuriated students

---

[71] Not printed.

who threw rocks, used clubs, etc. One student critically shot and a dozen others hurt while 17 policemen were reportedly hospitalized. A number of demonstrators arrested.

National Police Chief [72] has issued statement complimenting police on restraint in face extreme provocation, pointing [out] that more police than students were hurt and blaming trouble on Moscow paid agitators behind demonstration. He named Deputy Josca Brouwer (Socialist), his alternate Gilberto Bazan Villalaz and Communist Celso Selano, Secretary General of Partido del Pueblo, as having actively participated and directed students' attack tactics.

HINES

711F.1914/12–1747 : Telegram

The Chargé in Panama (Hall) to the Secretary of State

CONFIDENTIAL   PANAMA CITY, December 17, 1947—noon.

743. Embtel 738 December 16.[73] Estimated 10,000 women and children gathered in front of Assembly after march from De Lesseps Park last night in demonstration against agreement. All speeches were anti-American and probably made considerable impression on Assembly whose president replied weakly. Further demonstration was made in front of President's palace, all without violence since police were kept out of sight.

Minister of Education [74] unable to bring about end of students' and professors' strike presented resignation which was not accepted by Jimenez.

Air of pessimism regarding ratification prevails. Of many leaders interviewed in past 3 days only Florencio, Arosemena and Villarango still hopeful.

All of Panama is off limits to our troops, since further demonstrations are expected and agitators might provoke incident with US in order to embarrass government.

·   ·   ·   ·   ·   ·   ·

HALL

711F.1914/12–1847 : Telegram

The Chargé in Panama (Hall) to the Secretary of State

CONFIDENTIAL   PANAMÁ, December 18, 1947—1 p. m.

745. Principal feature of yesterday's Assembly session was motion by Renovador Party to suspend discussion of agreement by Assembly

---

[72] José Remón.
[73] Not printed.
[74] José Daniel Crespo.

and return same to executive for renegotiation "along lines more in accord with Rooseveltian spirit which inspired 1936 treaty". Motion was defeated 24 to 9 but Renovadores, on whom President counted to swing to agreement, are now aligned against it. An informal poll yesterday by *Panama-American* believed by Embassy to be too optimistic showed 26 votes against ratification which would constitute one vote majority. (Embtel 743, December 17).[75]

1. Amazing development is actual physical fear which has seized most deputies. President of Assembly spoke of "10,000 boys with knives" which might await them, and several Colón deputies have stated privately that, while they promised Jimenez their votes, they did not promise to allow themselves to be shot at. This sentiment may be favorably affected by speech radioed by President last night, the first word yet spoken in defense of the agreement, and by admission to committee of Alfaro and Harmodio Arias [76] that threat of agression definitely exists. Most political parties in their proclamations admit obligation of Panama to participate in defense of the Canal but all object to terms of agreement. Jimenez, president Supreme Court and members of Cabinet are bringing pressure on Harmodio Arias to elicit favorable comment his papers on President's speech. For the second time in two days I have been asked . . . to exert Embassy's influence on Harmodio, which I have refused to do for obvious reasons.

More demonstrations of students are in prospect. They have been urged by Roberto Arias not to relent in their endeavors. Efforts are reportedly being made to organize a general labor strike, beginning with chauffeurs' union in Colón.

Octavio Vallarino informs me in strict confidence that, since Renovadores have failed him, President intends to ask for Florencio Arosemenas' resignation, to be accepted at an opportune moment. He would be replaced as Foreign Minister by De Diego.

HALL

711F.1914/12–2247 : Telegram

The Chargé in Panama (Hall) to the Secretary of State

SECRET   PANAMA CITY, December 22, 1947—noon.

756. Embtel 752, December 20.[75] While normally all Deputies would wish to be heard on subject, it is anticipated that mob of students in Assembly galleries as well as on street will demand immediate vote today to reject agreement.

After gaining this objective the students, having tasted power, will

---

[75] Not printed.
[76] Former President of Panama.

not be satisfied but will most likely continue agitation for our withdrawal from bases.

I believe we should anticipate this move after rejection by Assembly, by public statement by Department that such is our intention, as previously made clear to Alfaro by Secretary and to Filos by Ambassador Hines, further strengthening our position by an offer to submit interpretation of 1942 agreement to arbitration.

Soldier was stabbed by four students last night in Colón causing extension of off-limits to entire provinces of Colón and Panama. Two Canal Zone employees here also involved in altercation with Panamanians in this city last night. Army is considering withdrawal of six soldiers now on duty at David airport. Topographic crews operating in Darien have all returned to their posts for holidays.

HALL

711F.1914/12–2347 : Telegram

The Chargé in Panama (Hall) to the Secretary of State

CONFIDENTIAL   PANAMA CITY, December 23, 1947—11 a. m.

760. Embtel 758 December 23.[78] Assembly was in session almost 6 hours yesterday reaching final decision at 9:50 p. m. Most of time was taken up by questioning of Harmodio Arias, Ricardo Alfaro, Octavio Fabrega, Raul De Roux, and Narciso Garay,[79] by Deputies Fabrega and De la Rosa, and by a violent peroration by the other Socialist Deputy Brower. There were constant interruptions from the galleries, demanding an immediate vote for rejection. Foreign Minister Arosemena was questioned briefly regarding his attitude toward the agreement. He weaseled saying that it was too clear that the Panamanian people were against it. Alfaro impugned our good faith saying that the continuous reduction of our original demand of "999 years" for Rio Hato only proved that we intended to occupy that base permanently. Brower and De la Rosa brought up all of Panama's old woes and complaints, the latter saying that bringing about the rejection of the agreement did not complete the students' work which had only just begun.

According to proper procedure Assembly would have first voted on minority report of agreement committee, which embodied complete rejection without prejudice to initiation of new negotiations and, if this were not adopted, majority report (Embtel 775, December 20 [78]) would have been considered. This course was forestalled by the intro-

[78] Not printed.
[79] Former Ministers of Foreign Relations.

duction of an independent motion presented by Deputy Felipe Perez and 10 other deputies objecting to the constitutionality of the majority report and reading as follows:

"The agreement signed in this city on the 10th instant by the representatives of the Governments of the Republic of Panama and the United States of America is hereby rejected, because the said agreement is not inspired in the principle of the juridical equality of the contracting states nor does it adhere to the norms of international law and the spirit of the inter-American system of defense."

Due to the galleries' insistence this was voted upon at once by roll call resulting in 51 "yes". In voting, presidential candidate Fabrega was successful in making a statement that for two years he had consistently and fervently opposed the agreement, but another deputy, Mrs. Paez, was shouted down when she endeavored to say that, unfortunately but inevitably, the destinies of the two countries are inseparable.

In addition to the galleries, a large crowd outside the Assembly, armed with sticks and stones, kept up a continuous uproar. Merchants along the line of march to the Assembly were threatened and forced to close their shops. The session ended with the singing of the national anthem. Mild street demonstrations followed.

President Jimenez had had resignation of Foreign Minister Arosemena since December 17 (Embtel 745 December 18) but will probably not act on it until after Christmas when general reorganization of Cabinet is expected.

The approaching presidential campaign plus continued agitation by students and others will make atmosphere decidedly unfavorable to further negotiations of any kind for several months.

HALL

711F.1914/12–2347 : Telegram

The Acting Secretary of State to the Embassy in Panama

US URGENT   NIACT   WASHINGTON, December 23, 1947.

573. Following statement has been released to press:

"According to official reports the National Assembly of Panama has rejected the ratification of the defense sites agreement signed on December 10, 1947 by the Governments of the Republic of Panama and the United States of America. This agreement was reached in accordance with the 1936 Treaty of Friendship and Cooperation providing for joint responsibility of the two countries for the effective protection of the Canal.

Throughout the period of more than 15 months during which negotiations for a defense sites agreement have taken place the United States Government has endeavored at all times to share with the Government of Panama its estimates of the minimum defense needs of the Canal. It has been the constant aim of the United States negotiators to consult with the appropriate Panamanian authorities in all frankness with respect to the considerations underlying these estimates which have provided the basis for the recent defense proposals of this Government.

Substantial and repeated concessions were made during the lengthy negotiations on the agreement in an attempt to reconcile Panamanian desires with the defense requirements of the Canal. The negotiations were concluded on December 10 by the signature of the agreement in terms which were intended to take into account the legitimate interests of both countries.

In accordance with oral statements made to the Panamanian Government in the course of the negotiations, the necessary steps will be taken immediately with a view to evacuation of all sites in the Republic of Panama outside the Canal Zone where United States armed forces are now stationed. This withdrawal will be completed as quickly as possible consistent with the number of personnel and the amount of materiel involved.

Failure to conclude an agreement will not, of course, affect the normal friendly relations between the two countries."

LOVETT

DISCUSSIONS OF ALLEGED DISCRIMINATORY TREATMENT OF CERTAIN LABOR CLASSES IN THE CANAL ZONE [61]

811F.504/1–2747

Memorandum by the Secretary of State to President Truman

CONFIDENTIAL [WASHINGTON,] January 27, 1947.

Subject: Racial-Labor Problem in the Canal Zone

In view of the interest which you have shown in this problem, I should like to inform you that by agreement among the State, War and Labor Departments Brigadier General Frank J. McSherry, retired, has been appointed as special adviser on labor relations to the Governor of the Canal Zone.

This step has been taken in order to determine what measures may be adopted to reduce to a minimum such racial-labor friction as now

---

[61] For documentation on the Panamanian accusations of discriminatory labor practices in 1946, see *Foreign Relations*, 1946, vol. XI, pp. 1149 ff.

exists in the Canal Zone. General McSherry's mission will have three purposes:

(1) he will make recommendations to the Governor on current policies relating to the opportunities and treatment accorded labor groups in the Canal Zone and will recommend a long-range program;
(2) since General McSherry possibly will be a United States representative to the ILO meetings at Geneva next summer, he will seek background information on labor conditions in the Zone;
(3) to the extent that his other duties permit, he will endeavor on behalf of the Governor to submit a proposal for coordination of the labor policies of all Government agencies operating in the area.

As a result of discussions at the ILO meeting at Montreal [82] and with the Foreign Minister and other Panamanian officials, the Government of Panama is fully aware of our desire to remove all reasons for charges of discrimination in the Canal Zone. It has welcomed enthusiastically the assignment of General McSherry.

GEORGE C. MARSHALL

811F.504/3–1947 : Telegram

The Ambassador in Panama (Hines) to the Secretary of State

PANAMÁ, March 19, 1947.

144. In weekly press conference March 18 President Jimenez released text of a cable sent March 17 by Foreign Minister Alfaro to Ambassador Vallarino as follows:

"The Government has been informed that certain North American labor groups and affiliated individuals are carrying out a campaign to obtain the revocation of President Truman's fair executive order [83] whereby Panamanian citizens are admitted to positions in the Panama Canal and the Panama railroad classified within the civil service. The National Government has fought for the full and effective enforcement of the principle of equality of opportunity and treatment for Panamanian citizens working or seeking work in the Canal Zone which principle is incorporated in treaties, agreements and pacts over and over again throughout the nation's history. The Government maintains unaltered this stand which meets the legitimate interests, rights and aspirations of our working classes. Therefore I request you to be on the alert for the aforementioned adverse negotiations, to inform this Ministry of any developments and to take quickly whatever measures should be required for the protection of the national interests in this regard."

HINES

---

[82] For documentation on this meeting, see *Foreign Relations*, 1946, vol. XI, pp. 40 ff.
[83] No. 9830; for text, see 12 *Federal Register* 1259.

811F.504/3–2847

Memorandum of Conversation, by Mr. W. Tapley Bennett of the Division of Central America and Panama Affairs

CONFIDENTIAL [WASHINGTON,] March 28, 1947.

Participants: Mr. Briggs, ARA
Mr. David Morse, Assistant Secretary of Labor
Mr. John W. Martyn, Office of the Secretary of War
Admiral Nibecker, Navy Department
Mr. Arthur Flemming, Civil Service Commissioner
Mr. Stanley Burdick, Office of the Panama Canal
Captain Bird, Navy Department
Mr. Ewing, Labor Department
Mr. King, Office of Panama Canal
Mr. Wise, CPA
Mr. Bennett, CPA

Mr. Briggs [84] explained that the meeting had been called to enable representatives of the interested Departments and Agencies to hear General McSherry on his recent study of labor problems and policies in the Canal Zone.

General McSherry opened his remarks by stating flatly his opinion that there has been both official and unofficial labor discrimination in the Canal Zone. He believes that the U. S. Government has not lived up to the commitments made in the notes accompanying the 1936 treaty [85] promising equality of opportunity and treatment for citizens of Panama in the Canal Zone. He mentioned the Third Locks Act [86] which restricts employment under that Act to U.S. citizens as one official violation. He called attention to the Philadelphia Agreement of the ILO [87] calling for no discrimination, and charged that U.S. agencies have not lived up to the meaning and spirit of that Agreement despite adherence to it by the U.S. Government.

In General McSherry's opinion, the heart of the problem is the Gold and Silver rolls. He described the rolls as the vehicle through which discrimination is practiced administratively. Wage rates for the Silver roll range from 44 to 66 cents per hour; only 20 persons in a total of 19,000 Silver employees receive a higher wage. The minimum gold wage is $1.07 per hour. He produced a tabulation showing that the charge of equal work without equal pay has much foundation. For instance, Gold and Silver carpenters do the same work but are paid at

---

[84] Director of the Office of American Republic Affairs.
[85] Department of State Treaty Series No. 945.
[86] 53 Stat. (pt. 2) 1409.
[87] The 26th session of the International Labor Conference, Philadelphia, April 20–May 12, 1944; see *Foreign Relations*, 1944, vol. II. pp. 1007 ff.

an hourly rate of $1.81 and 66 cents respectively. As another example, Gold teachers receive monthly salaries on an average of three times the amounts earned by their Silver counter-parts; General McSherry considers that in the primary grades the Silver teachers are doing a better job under much more trying conditions and with larger numbers of students per teacher. General McSherry made it clear that he did not mean to imply that all Silver employees are equal to all Gold employees and should be paid at the same rate. There are sufficient instances, however, of Silver employees doing the same type of work as Gold as to call for reform in the wage system.

Mr. Morse asked why reforms were not made by local administrators to remedy the more glaring of these inequities. General McSherry replied that for one thing legal difficulties stand in the way and went on to mention the lack of job analyses for Silver positions in the Panama Canal and Panama Railroad. He emphasized that in his opinion the Governor [88] has done a great deal for the Silver employees in the Zone. He cited the institution of the 40-hour week with the same take-home pay for Silver employees. The Governor's interest in and improvement of Silver schools and his desire to raise the wages of some 200 Silver employees under authority given by the Secretary of War (to raise 10% of non-Panamanian aliens) were also reviewed. The construction of new theaters in Silver districts, in numerous instances better than corresponding Gold facilities, was mentioned. It was brought out, however, that there is considerable resistance to reform in the Canal Zone hierarchy beneath the top command (which comes and goes), that U.S. citizens in the Zone are jealous of their rights and privileges, as well as their jobs, and that the tradition of Gold and Silver and what General McSherry termed the Gold roll psychology influences the whole situation. He called attention to differing leave regulations as evidence of further inequities and pointed out that, while the Army and Navy establishments in the Zone apply Civil Service retirement rules for their Panamanian and alien employees, the Canal does not. Mr. Wise asked whether raising Silver rates too much would upset the economy of Panama. General McSherry said he was not worried about Panama. He added that it eventually might change the whole Caribbean wage scale, which he says is very low.

Admiral Nibecker asked whether General McSherry would recommend bringing the Silver employees up to the United States pay level. General McSherry answered that he did not have that in mind, that he would never recommend paying the 25% differential (paid to U.S. employees on the thesis that they have left their homes in the United States to go to the Canal Zone) to native labor. The General

---

[88] Maj. Gen. Joseph C. Mehaffey.

stated that he does favor strongly the abolition of Gold and Silver rolls and the preparation of job analyses for all positions with an adequate number of grades within each classification.

Mr. Morse asked what would happen in the Zone if we abolished Gold and Silver, explaining that his question had to do with the psychological effects. General McSherry replied that in his opinion nothing would happen. He spoke of the mixture of nationalities and varying degrees of color in the Panama Air Depot, an Army installation, where there is no Gold and Silver and where normal classification procedures are followed, and described the excellent morale and relations among the personnel there.

Mr. Morse expressed the view that the Gold and Silver question should definitely be put on the committee agenda for future discussion. He warned of the trouble to be expected at the ILO conference at Geneva in June, where we may anticipate the raising of the old question of discrimination. Mr. Wise agreed that the question was bound to come up there and asserted that we should either take positive steps looking toward settlement of the Gold and Silver problem or be prepared to defend the existing situation. Mr. Briggs believed that the latter would be impossible.

Mr. Martyn asked how wages in the Zone compared with those in the Republic of Panama. General McSherry reviewed the practices of a number of U.S. corporations in Panama showing that for comparable jobs, wages and accompanying benefits are perhaps somewhat higher. General McSherry expressed the opinion that the Canal Zone *is* the economy of Panama and that practices there set the pattern for the Republic. He is opposed to across-the-board increases, such as the 24 cents per hour raise asked by the CIO, but considers that there are many individual injustices. He feels that a man's fate is at present too much in the hands of his foreman and reiterated his strong belief that there should be job descriptions for all positions.

Mr. Briggs asked whether General McSherry planned to make definite recommendations. The General replied that he was going back soon to spend an additional month in the Canal Zone and was planning to make recommendations at the end of his study. Mr. Briggs offered the view that it seemed to be the feeling of the meeting that the Gold and Silver rolls should be eliminated and job descriptions instituted to shrink the area of inequality.

General McSherry next emphasized the difficulties caused in the Zone by non-uniform legislation and regulations established for the various agencies operating there. In his opinion it would not be too difficult to make a detailed study of all legislation now in effect and to amalgamate it into one general pattern applying to all U.S. agencies on the Isthmus. He favors the establishment on the Isthmus of a general board representing all agencies which would consider labor problems to draw up uniform regulations, especially for alien employees. Problems incapable of solution there should come before the Washington Committee, which would determine major policy.

The McCarran Amendment [90] was mentioned and it was brought out that it does raise exceedingly difficult administrative problems in the Zone. The General asked whether U.S. policy is really to uphold the 1936 treaty providing for the equality of employment opportunities or whether we are merely paying lip service to the idea. Whatever our policy, he argued that all U.S. Agencies should follow the same one. He agreed with Admiral Nibecker that Civil Service rules should be followed throughout the Zone in so far as practicable.

Mr. Flemming warned of the possibility of imminent legislative difficulties. He stated his conviction that a majority of the House Civil Service Committee will attempt to nullify the recent Civil Service regulation admitting Panamanians to examinations for Civil Service positions in the Canal and Railroad organizations. He said the matter had been presented to the Attorney General for an opinion.

It was decided that interim meetings to explore further the problems raised at this conference would be desirable. Members present agreed to name representatives to attend a working committee with General McSherry during his current stay in Washington in order to have the benefit of his suggestions.

811F.504/4-947

Memorandum by the Governor of the Panama Canal (Mehaffey)[91]

[PANAMÁ,] April 9, 1947.

THE MCCARRAN AMENDMENT QUESTION

Below is quoted the McCarran Amendment which since 1940 has been regularly incorporated in appropriation acts for The Panama Canal, Army and Navy covering expenditures on the Isthmus of Panama:

No part of any appropriation contained in this Act shall be used directly or indirectly, except for temporary employment in case of emergency, for the payment of any civilian for services rendered by him on the Canal Zone while occupying a skilled, technical, clerical,

---

[90] See *infra*.
[91] Transmitted by Governor Mehaffey to the Assistant Chief of the Division of Central America and Panama Affairs (Wise), in his memorandum of April 9, 1947, not printed.

administrative, executive, or supervisory position unless such person is a citizen of the United States of America or of the Republic of Panama: *Provided, however*, (1) That, notwithstanding the provision in the Act approved August 11, 1939 (53 Stat. 1409), limiting employment in the above-mentioned positions to citizens of the United States from and after the date of the approval of said Act, citizens of Panama may be employed in such positions; (2) that at no time shall the number of Panamanian citizens employed in the above-mentioned positions exceed the number of citizens of the United States so employed, if United States citizens are available in continental United States or on the Canal Zone; (3) that nothing in this Act shall prohibit the continued employment of any person who shall have rendered fifteen or more years of faithful and honorable service on the Canal Zone; (4) that in the selection of personnel for skilled, technical, administrative, clerical, supervisory, or executive positions, the controlling factors in filling these positions shall be efficiency, experience, training, and education; (5) that all citizens of Panama and the United States rendering skilled, technical, clerical, administrative, executive, or supervisory service on the Canal Zone under the terms of this Act (*a*) shall normally be employed not more than forty hours per week, (*b*) may receive as compensation equal rates of pay based upon rates paid for similar employment in continental United States plus 25 per centum; (6) this entire section shall apply only to persons employed in skilled, technical, clerical, administrative, executive, or supervisory positions on the Canal Zone directly or indirectly by any branch of the United States Government or by any corporation or company whose stock is owned wholly or in part by the United States Government: *Provided further*, That the President may suspend from time to time in whole or in part compliance with this section in time of war or national emergency if he should deem such course to be in the public interest: *Provided further*, That the President may, if he finds it necessary because of a shortage of housing, suspend, for the fiscal year 1947, the application of those portions of this section which require the employment of citizens of the Republic of Panama or of the United States in skilled, technical, clerical, administrative, executive, or supervisory positions.

Each year since fiscal year 1941 Congress has seen fit to add the McCarran Amendment in substantially the form quoted above to the War Department Civil Functions Appropriations Bill which includes The Panama Canal funds. It appears probable that the McCarran Amendment will again be put in the appropriation bill for The Panama Canal unless Congress can be persuaded it should be dropped.

Thus far each year the President has deemed it advisable to suspend the McCarran Amendment as provided by the penultimate proviso contained therein.

3900 EMPLOYEES WOULD BE DISCHARGED

While there is some disagreement as to the interpretation of "skilled, technical, administrative, clerical, executive or supervisory positions" as it might be applied to alien workers, a survey based on interpretations of the Legislative Representative of the American Federation of Labor in his remarks in hearings on this amendment indicates that application of the McCarran Amendment would necessitate the discharge of approximately 3900 employees distributed as follows:

The Panama Canal	2,450
Panama Canal Department	650*
15th Naval District	400*
Caribbean Air Command	400*
Total	3,900

This means the loss of the services of approximately 3900 experienced aliens with varying degree of skill from all agencies. On the basis of estimates submitted to the Governor by supervisory officials of long experience on the Isthmus, it would be necessary to replace these aliens almost man for man by either Panamanians or Americans. In some cases, such as chauffeurs, an average of almost six Americans would be required to replace five natives because of differences in vacations. It is not difficult to picture the chaos that would prevail if these people were dropped from the rolls on July 1, 1947. Based on previous recruiting experience, it would require approximately a year and one-half to get 3000 new employees (the estimated number required for replacement) in the United States for work in the Canal Zone. During the war emergency it was necessary to recruit skilled workers away from Panama as early as February 1940, readily illustrating that the Republic of Panama has no surplus of skilled workers on which we can draw. Aside from the costs in transportation, wages, housing and facilities expansion of bringing great numbers of American workers to the Isthmus of Panama, it is questionable that a large number of skilled American workers could be recruited in the United States at this time.

. . . .

PANAMANIAN ECONOMY WOULD BE UPSET

The dumping of 3900 unemployed aliens and their families in a country the size of Panama would also create a series of economic problems not easily solved. Hundreds of former contract workers are married to Panamanian women and have received permission to reside indefinitely in the Republic of Panama. Some have repatriation deposits with the Panamanian Government and could be sent home as transportation becomes available but many others have entered illegally and would probably become public charges.

---

*Estimate made by using same percentage as shown affected by Panama Canal survey. [Footnote in the original.]

Although on the surface it appears that the McCarran Amendment is favorable to the Republic of Panama, it is questionable whether the number of positions gained by Panamanian citizens would compensate for the problems created by homeless aliens.

The McCarran Amendment provides that the selection of personnel for positions affected by it is to be based on efficiency, experience, *training* and *education*. Panama has only one minor trade school and very limited facilities for training office personnel. Most of the present native Canal Zone workers received their training, as such, by working in the Zone. The Panamanian is unable to compete with Americans when training and education are major factors in selection. At present they are able to compete with personnel nearer their own level of training and education.

POTENTIAL THREAT TO SECURITY

Those persons repatriated would be but a temporary problem. However, more serious problems to all would be:

(1) Those displaced aliens unable to find employment and
(2) Those displaced aliens compelled through economic necessity to take jobs in the Canal Zone as common laborers despite their qualifications as semi-skilled workers or office employees.

Unquestionably, these people who had been displaced from their jobs by an Act of the U. S. Government would provide a most fertile field for Communism. Under present conditions there is no reason to question the loyalty of these people. However, a dissatisfied and destitute group such as this could easily form the nucleus of extensive subversive activities which would threaten the security of the Canal.

TRADE UNION POSITION

The American trade unions in the Canal Zone are the only strong advocates of the McCarran Amendment on the Isthmus of Panama. They have consistently opposed the placement of any aliens, Panamanian or otherwise, on the so-called Gold Roll. This is one of the primary reasons the Treaty of 1936 has not been duly observed.

Fear of job security for themselves and for their children, as well as fear of losing their 25% pay differential if too many Panamanians go on the Gold Roll, are admittedly the reasons for the union support of the McCarran Amendment. Even though the McCarran Amendment has been in suspension since its enactment only 60 of 5900 Gold Roll employees are aliens. If after 43 years operation only 1% of the Gold Roll is made up of aliens it seems highly questionable that the American worker need now worry about the encroachment of foreigners.

THE PANAMA CANAL POSITION

Because of the various factors stated above The Panama Canal is seeking the elimination of the McCarran Amendment except the proviso contained therein relative to the Third Locks Act which should be continued in the form quoted below:

"Notwithstanding the provision in the Act approved August 11, 1939 (53 Stat. 1409), limiting employment in certain positions to citizens of the United States, citizens of Panama may be employed in such positions."

811F.504/5-847

Memorandum by the Director of the Office of American Republic Affairs (Briggs) to the Under Secretary of State (Acheson)

[WASHINGTON,] May 8, 1947.

Executive Order 9830 [92] published in the *Federal Register* on February 25, 1947 provided that citizens of the Republic of Panama might be admitted to examinations for employment by the Panama Canal and the Panama Railroad Company. This regulation went into effect on May 1.

As a result of hearings by the Senate and House Civil Service Committees the Attorney General has been requested to render an opinion whether this action was mandatory under provisions of our 1936 General Treaty of Friendship and Cooperation with Panama. The Justice Department has informally requested the Department's views on that question.

One of the notes exchanged by the two Governments simultaneously with the signature of the Treaty, and regarded as an integral part thereof, commits this Government to maintain as our public policy the principle of equality of opportunity and treatment of Panamanian citizens in employment in the Panama Canal and Railroad. This Government is further committed to take such measures as may be necessary to put this into effect.

The Department therefore believes that this Government is specifically committed to admit Panamanian citizens to Civil Service examinations for Canal and Railroad positions. It was the intent of the parties negotiating the 1936 Treaty that the words "equality of opportunity and treatment" should mean exactly that.

The attached letter to the Attorney General [93] emphasizes that the Department considers the recent action of the Civil Service Com-

---

[92] 12 *Federal Register* 1259.
[93] *Infra.*

mission to have been necessary to fulfill this Government's obligation and to be in accord with our established national policy.

811F.504/5-747

The Under Secretary of State (Acheson) to the Attorney General (Clark)

[Extracts]

WASHINGTON, May 9, 1947.

MY DEAR MR. ATTORNEY GENERAL:

. . . .

The Department has for many years maintained a special interest in labor legislation concerning the Canal because of the inevitable effect of that legislation on citizens of the Republic of Panama and on existing commitments of the United States Government to the Panamanian Government. While the basic treaty between the United States and Panama, dated November 18, 1903, contained no stipulations with regard to labor in the Canal Zone, the United States Government has steadily moved toward the establishment of equality of opportunity and treatment between United States and Panamanian citizens in matters pertaining to employment.

. . . .

Finally, in 1936, after lengthy negotiations, a General Treaty of Friendship and Cooperation was concluded at Washington between the United States and Panama. This agreement sought to meet many of the complaints of Panama during the preceding third of a century and at the same time to take cognizance of changing conditions, including the need for increased defenses for the Canal, which is of vital importance in the defense of the United States and of the entire Hemisphere.

. . . .

Examination of the minutes of the treaty negotiators indicates that their purpose was to provide for equality of employment opportunity and treatment with respect to the Panama Canal and the Panama Railroad, and that no distinction was drawn between positions which are filled by examination and those which are not. In other words, the negotiators intended to expand the principles inaugurated in the earlier orders and practice.

The 1936 Treaty, together with its accompanying notes, having the force and effect of law, is the basic document governing our current relations with Panama. This Government stands committed to Panama under the document to maintain as our public policy the principle that Panamanian citizens shall have equal rights with our own citizens in employment opportunities in the Panama Canal and the Panama Railroad. This Government is committed to take such measures as may be necessary to put this principle into effect.

In pursuance of this policy, the Department believes that this Government is specifically bound to admit Panamanian citizens to civil service examinations for Canal and Railroad positions. It was the clear intent of the parties negotiating the 1936 Treaty that the words "equality of opportunity and treatment" should mean exactly that.

There was no desire on the part of the United States representatives merely to codify and give treaty sanction to administrative practices existing in the Canal Zone in 1936, but rather there was an intent to establish a pattern for the future in which heed would be given to the legitimate aspirations of Panamanians for employment in the operations of the international waterway which bisects their national territory and which they have pledged themselves to defend jointly with us. I should like to stress, therefore, that the Department supports fully the recent action of the Civil Service Commission in providing for the admission of Panamanian citizens to civil service examinations for positions in the Panama Canal and the Panama Railroad.

The Department considers, therefore, that the Commission's action is necessary to fulfill this Government's obligations and is in accord with established national policy.[94]

Sincerely yours, DEAN ACHESON

811F.504/6-2047

Memorandum of Telephone Conversation, by Mr. W. Tapley Bennett of the Division of Central America and Panama Affairs

[WASHINGTON,] June 20, 1947.

I called Commissioner Flemming [95] to ascertain his opinion on despatch no. 4032 of June 10, 1947 from the Embassy at Panama,[96] describing the raising by the *Panama American* of the issue of Panamanian citizens taking an oath of allegiance to the United States in order to accept civil service positions in the Canal Zone. The Embassy in the same despatch mentioned reports that Foreign Minister Alfaro is planning to protest the necessity for Panamanians to take this oath.

---

[94] In instruction 746, August 4, 1947, to Panamá, the Department indicated that the Attorney General held that the action of the Civil Service Commission in opening certain examinations to citizens of Panama was mandatory under the General Treaty of 1936 (811.504/8-447).
[95] Arthur S. Flemming, Civil Service Commission.
[96] Not printed.

Mr. Flemming stated that this question had been raised at an executive session of Senator Thye's subcommittee of the Senate Civil Service Committee attended by him and by Governor Mehaffey of the Canal Zone. He also said that so far as he knew there would be no statutory authority to permit an exception to the rule that all persons entering on civil service positions must take an oath of allegiance in support of the United States. Mr. Flemming asserted that he personally did not feel that we should make an exception to the rule. He further stated that the U.S. Government has many aliens in its employment, such as British subjects working on various matters and the German scientist projects. All these individuals have taken the oath of allegiance, and Mr. Flemming knows of no instance where the procedure has been questioned.

NOTE: Following my conversation with Commissioner Flemming, I took occasion to inquire of Mr. Burdick, Office of the Panama Canal,[97] as to the policy in effect with respect to employees in the Canal Zone. Mr. Burdick informed me that while the no-strike pledge is mandatory for all employees, the oath of allegiance is not required of aliens employed on the silver rolls. He was not able to say whether a similar exception is made in the case of Panamanian citizens on the gold roll but indicated that he would investigate the matter and inform me as to the policy presently in effect relative to that category.

I agree with Mr. Flemming that it would be inadvisable to seek an exception to the rule requiring an oath of allegiance for persons taking civil service positions, particularly in view of the fact that exceptions have not been made for the many other aliens already on civil service rolls. If there is a dilemma here, it is one for the Panamanians, not for us. They are the ones who want the jobs.

W. T[APLEY] B[ENNETT]

811F.504/7-1047 : Airgram

The Ambassador in Panama (Hines) to the Secretary of State

CONFIDENTIAL   PANAMÁ, July 10, 1947.

A-734. Reference Department's airgram 449 of July 8, 1947 [98] regarding the taking of oath of allegiance by Panamanian citizens appointed to positions in Panamá Canal and Panamá Railroad.

Citizens of Panamá now occupying "gold-roll" positions have all been required to take standard oath of allegiance. "Silver-roll" employees no longer subscribe to any oath upon employment.

---

[97] B. F. Burdick, Chief of Office and General Purchasing Officer.
[98] Not printed.

The taking of our standard oath of allegiance would not affect Panamanian citizenship, this point being covered by Section 2, Article 15 of the new Constitution of Panamá which states that Panamanian citizenship is tacitly renounced "When the employ of another Government is accepted without the permission of the Executive, *except* in the case of employment on a project in which the Republic is interested in conjunction with another nation."

Despite the above exception, the Embassy is reliably informed that the Government of Panamá will require all prospective Panamanian appointees to our Civil Service to seek its permission before accepting employment with the Canal or the Railroad. This would result in giving the Government a political veto over such appointments.

HINES

811F.504/7–2547

The Secretary of State to Senator Chan Gurney [99]

CONFIDENTIAL   WASHINGTON, July 25, 1947.

DEAR SENATOR GURNEY: It has been pointed out to me that the Senate has added the following proviso, pertaining to the Panama Canal, of the War Department Civil Functions Appropriation Bill:

"that no alien employed on the Canal Zone, who may secure United States Civil Service status, shall be paid a salary or wages, wholly or in part, from monies appropriated by this Act."

This proviso, if it becomes a law, will violate our 1936 Treaty with Panama which was ratified by our Senate in 1939. As you know, steps have been taken to implement this Treaty whereby Panamanian citizens may participate in a few classified positions in the Canal Zone. This action on the part of the United States has been favorably received in the Republic of Panama. To nullify this action by law would create the impression that the United States does not live up to its international agreements and would definitely jeopardize our present negotiations with Panama in regard to defense sites for the protection of the Canal. We have already been accused of bad faith by Panamanians and by various anti-American elements throughout Latin America with respect to the defense sites. A definite case of bad faith, such as this would be, would be of invaluable aid to these elements in their anti-American campaign. Further, if this proviso becomes law, it may well have serious effects on the United States carrying out its

---

[99] Member of the Senate Appropriations Committee.

program at the Rio de Janeiro Conference[1] scheduled for the near future.

I urge you most sincerely to eliminate this proviso in the final bill.

Faithfully yours,

G. C. MARSHALL

811F.504/7-2547

Memorandum by Mr. M. M. Wise of the Division of Central America and Panama Affairs

[WASHINGTON,] July 28, 1947.

It will be recalled that on July 16 the Department in response to a request from the Senate Appropriations Committee sent to Senator Gurney a letter[2] setting forth our position which was one of objection to an amendment to H.R. 4002 reading as follows:

"that no alien employed on the Canal Zone, who may secure United States Civil Service status, shall be paid a salary or wages, wholly or in part, from monies appropriated by this Act."

On Thursday afternoon, July 24, from a source outside this Department, CPA was informed that the Senate Appropriations Committee had reported on H.R. 4002, leaving in the bill the amendment to which we had expressed objection. Our informant advised that the bill was at that moment on the floor of the Senate being considered.

Within the next few minutes a contact was established with Senator Green, who on the floor of the Senate objected to this amendment on a point of order. The Chair overruled Senator Green and a decision vote sustained the Chair. The bill was enacted with the amendment and sent to conference.

On Friday morning the seriousness of the above development was brought to Mr. Armour's[3] attention with the recommendation that the Secretary of State lose no time in getting in touch with Senator Gurney and Representative Engel,[4] pointing out our objection to the amendment and urging that the conference eliminate it. In the meantime CPA had a telephone call from the Embassy of Panama requesting that the Department do everything possible to have eliminated the amendment under reference inasmuch as its inclusion in our legislation would be highly embarrassing to the diplomatic relations between the two countries.

---

[1] For documentation on this Conference, see pp. 1 ff.
[2] Not printed.
[3] Norman Armour, Assistant Secretary of State for Political Affairs.
[4] Albert J. Engel, member of the Committee on Appropriations, House of Representatives.

At 3:45 p. m. Friday Mr. Armour and Mr. Wise delivered a letter signed by Mr. Marshall to Senator Gurney who was at that moment in conference on H.R. 4002. The letter was left with him.

On Saturday morning CPA received another telephone call from the Embassy of Panama officially protesting in the name of the Foreign Minister of Panama the enactment of legislation including the above-mentioned amendment. At about the same time a representative of the Associated Press telephoned to say that the matter had broken wide open in the Panamanian press, which was being very critical of the Senate action. Upon checking with the Senate Appropriations Committee it was learned that the conferees' report was being written but that there was no chance of finding out what action the conferees had taken with respect to the elimination of the amendment. However, a short while later the Department was advised by Senator Gurney's office that the amendment had been eliminated and that during the course of the day the House and the Senate would pass H.R. 4002 without it.

CPA then advised the Embassy of Panama which expressed extraordinary appreciation for the Department's efforts in the cooperation of the Senate. CPA then telephoned Ambassador Hines at Panama to report the action of the conferees and authorized Ambassador Hines to pass the information along to the Panamanian Foreign Minister. The Ambassador said this news would be most pleasing to Panama and added that it was most fortunate that the amendment had been eliminated. In my conversations with the Embassy of Panama and Ambassador Hines I endeavored to stress the fact that appreciation should be felt for the cooperation of the Senate rather than for anything which this Department had done.

M. M. WISE

811F.504/9–2447

Letter Drafted in the Department of State for the Signature of the President [5]

CONFIDENTIAL

During the past several years the Government of Panamá has charged that United States employment practices in the Canal Zone are discriminatory. Panamá also maintains that these practices are at

---

[5] To be addressed to the Secretaries of State, Defense, and Labor, the President of the Civil Service Commission, and the Chief of Office, The Panama Canal. The letter was not approved and signed by the President. The draft was attached to a communication from the Secretary of State to the Secretary of Labor (Schwellenbach), September 24, 1947.

variance with the General Treaty of 1936 between the United States and Panamá, wherein this Government agreed to maintain in the Zone opportunity and treatment for Panamanians equal to that accorded American citizens. These complaints are detrimental to our general relations with Panamá and have come to be a source of embarrassment at various international conferences, where our employment practices on the Isthmus have been openly criticized. Of late, criticism has been more frequent and has been utilized by elements in the other American republics hostile to the United States in campaigns against our national interest.

A detailed investigation of United States labor practices in the Canal Zone was completed recently by Brigadier General Frank J. McSherry (ret.) on special assignment as advisor on labor relations to the Governor of The Panama Canal. General McSherry reported that there is substantial truth in allegations of discrimination in Canal Zone labor practices. His study revealed that there is considerable variation in the laws, executive orders and departmental regulations applicable to Panamanian employees of the several departments and agencies operating in the Zone. General McSherry found further that there is confusion and difference of opinion as to our national policy with respect to the employment of Panamanians in the Canal Zone by Federal agencies.

It is essential that the United States abide by the obligations of the General Treaty of 1936 with Panamá and the notes attached thereto regarding equality of opportunity and treatment for Panamanians in the Canal Zone. The extension of such employment opportunities must, of course, as provided in the Treaty notes, be consistent with the efficient operation and effective protection of the Canal.

In order to ensure a proper understanding of United States policy and to encourage uniformity of legislation and regulations concerning personnel practices in the Canal Zone, it is my desire that an interdepartmental committee be established. This committe shall consist of representatives of the State, Defense and Labor Departments, the Civil Service Commission and The Panama Canal. In order that the committee may function properly, your representative thereon should have the rank of an Assistant Secretary or a Commisioner, or, in the case of The Panama Canal, should be the ranking official present in Washington.

The committee shall concern itself solely with matters of broad policy with a view to the coordination of legislation governing the operations of the several Federal departments and agencies active in the Canal Zone. The committee shall not be concerned with the administration of the Canal Zone, which is the responsibility of the Governor of The Panama Canal.

It shall be the responsibility of the Department of State to proceed at once with the organization of the committee. The committee should meet at the earliest practicable date and from time to time submit to me a report of its progress.

811F.504/12–3047

The Secretary of Defense (*Forrestal*) to the Assistant Secretary of State (*Armour*)

CONFIDENTIAL [WASHINGTON,] 18 December 1947.

DEAR MR. SECRETARY: The Departments of the Army, Navy, and Air Force have given very careful consideration to your letter which suggested the establishment by the President of an inter-departmental committee to (1) clarify United States policy with respect to non-United States citizens employed in the Canal Zone and (2) insure uniformity of legislation and regulations with respect to personnel practices on the Isthmus. This proposal follows the recommendations of General McSherry's report, a report which has been studied by officials of the three Departments both here and in the Canal Zone.

We agree that there are certain important problems relating to American policies with respect to employment in the Canal Zone and that some of these are of mutual interest to several of the federal departments. However, we do not think that these problems are generally of such a character as to justify the formation of another inter-departmental committee, particularly a high level committee of the kind suggested. On the contrary, we believe that each such problem, as it arises, should be handled through informal consultation among the particular departments which are directly concerned with it. There is not identical mutuality of interest among all the departments in all cases. Many policy issues which affect personnel in the Canal Zone have no foreign relations implications whatsoever, and they should be decided by the three Services and the Panama Canal, either in joint consultation with one another, or through such mechanisms for the coordination of personnel matters which may be established by them. In such cases we do not believe that representatives of the State Department, Civil Service Commission and Department of Labor would wish to participate. Other problems will clearly depend for their intelligent solution upon the most thorough examination by the State Department, or by other agencies, of those aspects thereof for which they have an important responsibility. In such cases, we agree, there should be full joint consideration which is participated in by all of the agencies concerned. However, it would appear that this type of consultation, whenever the occasion for it arises, should be worked out on an *ad hoc* basis and that those agencies and individuals most familiar with the particular subject involved should be invited to participate.

In a given case, the specific problem might well be one that did not require decisions at the Assistant Secretary level. We also feel that to the extent that coordination of legislation affecting the operations of the several federal departments and agencies active in the Canal Zone is necessary, this can be satisfactorily accomplished through existing government procedures established for such purpose.

In the event that the President should conclude that the establishment of an inter-departmental committee along the lines recommended by you is desirable, the National Military Establishment would wish the Departments of the Army, the Navy, and the Air Force each to be directly represented on such committee in lieu of a single representative for the entire Establishment who might be designated by me. Each of these Departments has important responsibilities within the Canal Zone and it would be important that its point of view and problems be directly before the Committee. The conclusions of any such committee might well be unsound if they did not fully take into account the kind of considerations which these three Departments would alone be in a position to present.

You will be interested to know that I have requested the Department of the Army, through the Commanding General, Caribbean Area, to obtain the views of the various federal officials who have active responsibilities within the Canal Zone on the report of General McSherry. In this way, I hope to secure a clearer picture from people at the operating level of those recommendations in the report which require action at this level, either in the form of policy decisions or implementing legislation. When these views have been collected, I am certain that representatives of the Army, Navy and Air Force will be in a much better position to judge which problems can be handled by them jointly without burdening outside agencies, and which of them are matters which other agencies must also consider. Those three Departments will, of course, be glad to discuss any Canal Zone problems with the State Department whenever you believe such discussions are in order.

Sincerely yours, JAMES FORRESTAL

811F.504/12–3047

Memorandum by the Chief of the Division of Central America and Panama Affairs (Newbegin) to the Director of the Office of American Republic Affairs (Daniels)

CONFIDENTIAL [WASHINGTON,] December 30, 1947.

There is attached for your attention a letter received from Secretary Forrestal [6] relative to the proposed establishment by the President of

---

[6] *Supra.*

an inter-departmental committee on the Assistant Secretary level to clarify U.S. policy with respect to non-U.S. citizens employed on the Isthmus and to ensure uniformity of legislation and regulations concerning personnel practices in the Canal Zone. There is also attached a copy of Mr. Armour's letter of September 24, 1947,[7] to which Secretary Forrestal's communication is a reply.

The recommendation for an inter-departmental committee to consider Canal Zone employment policies was made by Brig. Gen. Frank McSherry (ret) in his report of June 1, 1947. General McSherry's report resulted from a four-months' study made by him on the Isthmus under arrangements made jointly by the State, War, and Navy Departments. Consideration of such a committee was also given continuing study—and seeming approval—by a working group composed of representatives of the three departments mentioned above, along with officials of the Labor Department, the Civil Service Commission and The Panama Canal.

The Labor Department and the Civil Service Commission responded promptly and favorably to the proposals contained in Mr. Armour's letter of September 24. During the period of almost two months before the Secretary of Defense replied, Panama Canal Governor Mehaffey made known in a conversation with Mr. Armour his strong opposition to the creation of the committee under the terms suggested. Secretary Forrestal's letter is in effect a statement of Governor Mehaffey's views.

In as much as employment practices in the Canal Zone are of fundamental importance in our relations with the Republic of Panama and have an effect on relations with other countries of the area, I believe that careful attention should be paid the letter from the Secretary of Defense, and consideration given as to our further course with respect to the Canal Zone labor problem.

It is my understanding that Mr. Armour did not see Mr. Forrestal's letter before his departure on leave.

THE REGULATION OF RADIO COMMUNICATIONS IN PANAMA AND THE CANAL ZONE

819.74/9-347

Memorandum by Mr. William E. O'Connor of the Telecommunications Division to the Assistant Chief of That Division (Otterman)

CONFIDENTIAL [WASHINGTON,] September 3, 1947.

The question of the regulation of radio communications in the Republic of Panama, a subject of recurrent controversy since the Canal was built, was revived last November in the form of a request from the

---

[7] Not printed.

Chief Signal Officer [8] and the Canal Zone authorities that the regulation of Panamanian radio should be made the subject of a treaty. This proposal, which is concurred in by Ambassador Hines at Panama City, involves the revising and renegotiating of the unratified Radio Communications Convention of 1936. A summary of the historical background of this problem follows:

The Treaty of 1903 [9] between the United States and the newly organized Republic of Panama, which provided for the perpetual use and control by the United States of the Canal Zone, granted to the United States certain rights and privileges over the Republic of Panama, especially as related to the operation and security of the Canal. No mention of radio was made in the Treaty, since at that time radio was largely in an experimental stage. In 1914, under pressure from the United States, the Panamanian President issued a decree [10] giving the United States full control over radio communications throughout the Republic of Panama; this decree stated that the general provisions of the Treaty of 1903 gave the United States the right to demand such a prerogative. From 1914 on, regulation was in the hands of the United States Navy. In 1926 an executive agreement was drawn up which would have put radio regulation back in the hands of Panama, at least in appearance, but the United States would have retained the rights:

1. To veto any license application for radio operation;
2. To insist upon enforcement of license provisions;
3. To resume full control over radio in Panama in the event of actual or impending hostilities.

This agreement, however, was never put into effect.

In December, 1930 the Panamanians suddenly abrogated the decree of 1914. Panama contended that its adherence to the International Radio Convention of 1927 [11] made it responsible for the regulation of its own radio matters. For over a year discussions were held by the State, War, and Navy Departments as to what attitude the United States should take towards this abrogation. Finally the Panamanians were formally advised that the United States claimed the right to regulate Panamanian radio activities as a right deriving from the Treaty of 1903, but that we would not insist on the exercise of this right if some adequate measure of control could be set up agreeable to Panama and at the same time providing for the efficient protection of the Canal. Along with this statement there was submitted to the Panamanians a proposed agreement similar to the agreement drawn up in

---

[8] Letter from Brig. Gen. W. O. Reeder to Francis Colt de Wolf of the Telecommunications Division, November 8, 1946, not printed.
[9] Department of State Treaty Series No. 431.
[10] *Foreign Relations*, 1914, p. 1051.
[11] Department of State Treaty Series No. 767.

1926. This agreement went so far as to specify that the Panamanian Government should, upon request by the United States, close without delay any radio transmitter which in the opinion of the United States was detrimental to the safety and operation of the Canal.

In 1936, along with a series of treaties on other subjects negotiated with Panama, there was drawn up a Radio Communications Convention [12] which was ratified by Panama but which did not receive the consent of the United States Senate apparently due largely to the opposition of Senator White [13] (to whom many Senators look for advice on radio matters). Senator White was particularly opposed to the provision turning regulation of the mobile services over to Panama with only partial supervision being retained by the United States. It seems that opposition to the Convention was also voiced by United States Naval authorities who were apparently concerned at possible ambiguities which could conceivably result in leaving the military authorities powerless to cope with interference or illegal operation in Panama in an emergency. The problem consequently seemed to resolve itself to keeping the United States in a position to prevent any undesirable radio operation anywhere in the Republic of Panama, but to do this with the minimum possible infringement on Panamanian sovereignty and with careful regard for Panamanian sensibilities.

Ever since the Panamanian abrogation, in 1930, of the Decree of 1914, no formal arrangement has existed between the United States and Panama regarding the regulation of radio communications. In practice an informal cooperation has been maintained by a Mr. Richard D. Prescott, a United States citizen, who has worked for many years for the Panamanian Government as telecommunications adviser. Besides being an employee of the Panamanian Government, Mr. Prescott is also a Reserve Officer in the United States Army, and from 1940 until shortly after the end of the War he served as a Colonel on active duty with the United States Army, at the same time keeping his status as an employee of Panama. This extremely informal arrangement appears to have worked satisfactorily through the War but it is, of course, undesirable since a Panamanian Government could terminate Mr. Prescott's services at any time. It should also be remembered that Mr. Prescott is an old man and in the event of his death or resignation there is no assurance whatever that the Panamanians would appoint an American to handle radio matters. Consequently, there is an urgent need for a formal arrangement.

A summary of the principal points in the proposed revised convention follows:

---

[12] See bracketed note, *Foreign Relations*, 1936, vol. v, p. 855.
[13] Senator Wallace H. White, Jr., Chairman of the Senate Interstate and Foreign Commerce Committee.

This Convention would require the Panamanian Government to license all transmitters in its territory and to license all radio operators. Licenses would be granted only to Panamanian citizens and companies (and, if Panama wishes, to United States citizens and companies). Two Boards would be established—one an agency of the United States Government, the other an agency of the Panamanian Government. All actions by one government affecting the licensing and operation of any privately owned radio station would have to be submitted for study to its Board, and "in matters concerning the common interests of the two Parties", both Boards would have to be consulted. If either government "submits substantial reasons in writing" to the other that the present or proposed operation of a specified private station is endangering or would endanger the security of the Canal or the security of the Republic of Panama, the government responsible *must* require suspension of operations. . . . It is, of course, uncertain who would be the judge of what constituted a "substantial" reason, but this is about as strong phraseology as we are likely to get the Panamanians to accept. The Division of Central American and Panamanian Affairs (CPA) agrees that while this wording is vague, it would not be advisable to try to make it stronger and we shall have to depend upon a reasonable amount of good faith on the Panamanian side.

It is also provided that whenever *either* of the two Boards so recommends, either government must inspect any private radio station under its jurisdiction to ascertain whether the approved licensing regulations are being complied with. Members of both Boards may accompany the inspecting authorities. (In effect, this provision would permit the United States to require an inspection of any Panamanian private station and to send United States technical personnel along on the inspection.)

In case of war or threat of aggression, the 1936 Convention stated that the two governments would act jointly and the two Boards unite into a joint Board. The wording of this section was rather vague and its effective operation would appear to have depended entirely on the voluntary cooperation of the Panamanian authorities. The Convention now proposed would allow the United States in case of war or threat of aggression to "exercise the degree of control deemed by it to be necessary regarding everything relating to radio communications" throughout the Republic of Panama. The United States, however, in such a case would "consult" Panama before acting, except in an emergency, in which event it would "consult" as soon as possible after taking the required action. The significant difference in this regard between the presently proposed Convention and the 1936 Convention should be noted. Whether Panama will accept this change remains to be seen.

Other minor provisions of the Convention provide for the reciprocal free emergency use of radio facilities for official business of the two governments and for the reciprocal training by each country of ten men as radio operators.[14]

. . . . . .

---

[14] The proposed agreement was not acceptable to Panama, and the bilateral approach to the Communications problem was dropped. Panama subscribed to the multilateral telecommunications agreement of October 2, 1947, for which see Department of State, Treaties and Other International Acts Series No. 1901.

PARAGUAY

THE POSITION OF THE UNITED STATES TOWARD THE INSURRECTION IN PARAGUAY

834.00/3-1747 : Telegram

The Acting Secretary of State to the Embassy in Paraguay

SECRET   U.S. URGENT   WASHINGTON, March 18, 1947—7 p. m.

68. Urtel 116, Mar 17, 2 p. m.[1] While we view present difficulties Paraguayan Govt with concern, we are confident that on reflection Pres[2] will appreciate that it would be wholly inconsistent with our hemisphere commitments for this Govt to accede to his request for planes and tanks.

In conveying substance foregoing orally you should of course reiterate our earnest hope that a solution may be reached without further bloodshed and that Paraguay will herself be able to settle her internal problems.

ACHESON

834.00/3-1947 : Telegram

The Chargé in Paraguay (Trueblood) to the Secretary of State

SECRET   ASUNCIÓN, March 19, 1947—5 p. m.

128. I conveyed substance Deptel 68, March 18, 7 p. m., to Foreign Minister this morning. He seemed stunned by our refusal but I cannot believe either he or President sincerely thought we could take request seriously. Chaves then suggested we extend aid indirectly by agreeing to let Brazil transfer a few lend-lease planes to Paraguay. I gave him no encouragement on this. See Military Attaché's secret telegram No. 105, March 16.[1]

Especially after Liberal Party statement telegram 122,[3] it is becoming clearer that only insuperable obstacle to pacific settlement of Paraguay's political situation is continuance of President Morínigo in office. Although Colorados profess confidence and some talk of fight to finish, I believe they would jump at compromise which would stop

---

[1] Not printed.
[2] Higinio Morínigo.
[3] March 18, 1947, 5 p. m., not printed.

present insane course events here, ruinous to a poor country and with infinite possibilities chaos and confusion. Unfortunately Colorados feel honor bound stand by Morínigo. Brazilian Chargé [4] also of opinion that there is no reason why this situation should be allowed to degenerate into unnecessary civil war and is so informing his Government.

TRUEBLOOD

834.00/3-1847 : Telegram

The Acting Secretary of State to the Embassy in Paraguay

CONFIDENTIAL   US URGENT   WASHINGTON, March 19, 1947—6 p. m.

71. Urtel 121 Mar 18 noon [5] Spanish text telegram from FonMin [6] for Secretary reporting rebellion and characterizing it as Communist and possible threat to continent, received yesterday.

In absence specific info on question of international Communist domination Concepción movement or other significant factors threatening continental peace and security, Dept has no basis for concluding at this moment that situation calls for multilateral action. Inter-American agreements (Declaration of Lima 1938 [7]) provide that American republics coordinate their respective sovereign wills by means of consultation when peace or security any one of them threatened. Dept hopeful Paraguay by own efforts will be able to reestablish and maintain order within its boundaries. However, should it develop that situation calls for action by other American republics, proper procedure in accordance with Inter-American agreements would be for immediate consultation of all American republics with a view to determining facts, to deciding whether multilateral action advisable and, if so, agreeing what action.

Communicate above to FonMin, expressing appreciation his courtesy in telegraphing Secretary Marshall and Dept's earnest hope for prompt settlement conflict.

Please report urgently all info bearing on question Communist domination.

This telegram being repeated to Buenos Aires and Rio de Janeiro for info respective foreign offices, in view fact they have received similar communications from Paraguayan FonMin.

ACHESON

---

[4] José Fabrino de Oliveira Baião.
[5] Not printed.
[6] Federico Chaves.
[7] For text, see *Report of the Delegation of the United States of America to the Eighth International Conference of American States, Lima, Peru, December 9–27, 1938* (Washington, Government Printing Office, 1941), p. 189.

834.00/3-2147 : Telegram

The Chargé in Paraguay (Trueblood) to the Secretary of State

SECRET   Asunción, March 21, 1947—10 a. m.

133. Conveyed yesterday orally substance Deptel 71, March 19, 6 p. m. to Under Secretary Foreign Affairs: [10] Told him we must have more precise information, pointing out we were still uninformed regarding identity and connections men involved in March 7 police station affair and as to connection between that and Concepción revolt, Moreno blamed police for failure get data together sooner but stated he would press. He has just phoned me to meet 5 p. m. with Brazil Chargé and Argentine Ambassador [11] reference further evidence Communist complicity.

. . . [Embassy] assembling data on officers known to be in Concepción revolt. As Department aware, not believed to be any officers in Paraguayan armed forces members Communist Party; only possible link with Communist Party would come thru Febrerismo, one sector of which during last July–January period drifted close to Communist Party line. Colonel Galeano, leader at Concepción, is Febrerista involved in several past revolutionary attempts but . . . [source] states from his information regarding Galeano that latter is not Communist.

                                                                            Trueblood

---

834.20 Missions/3-1947 : Telegram

The Acting Secretary of State to the Embassy in Paraguay

CONFIDENTIAL   US URGENT   Washington, March 21, 1947— 7 p. m.

77. Urtel 125 Mar 19 11 a. m.[12] Dept and War concur undesirable cancel military missions contracts. While such unilateral action provided for in present circumstances by art. 5 [13] which could be invoked if Paraguayan Government not amenable to temporary suspension of activities, it is believed that immediate agreement between mission chiefs and Commander-in-Chief should be reached under art. 7 (air mission agreement) [14] whereby missions withdraw from active duty during hostilities. War advises that Crittenberger [15] has already cabled

---

[10] José Antonio Moreno González.
[11] Isaac Arriola.
[12] Not printed.
[13] Of Military Mission Agreement between the United States and Paraguay, Department of State Executive Agreement Series No. 354.
[14] Department of State Executive Agreement Series No. 343.
[15] Lt. Gen. Willis D. Crittenberger, Commanding General, Caribbean Defense Command.

orders both missions to cease activities. Please advise status Brazilian and Argentine missions under State of War.

ACHESON

834.00/3-2147

The Chargé in Paraguay (Trueblood) to the Secretary of State

RESTRICTED   ASUNCIÓN, March 21, 1947.
No. 2549

SIR: I have the honor to transmit herewith copies and translations of a declaration [16] addressed to the people of Concepción and of the Republic of Paraguay by the Command of the insurrectionist forces in Concepción. This statement was broadcast by the Concepción short-wave radio on March 9 and mimeographed copies have clandestinely been circulated in Asunción.

It will be noted that the declaration states that the movement does not answer any political end but has as its purpose the formation of a transitional military government which will (1) grant full liberty to all political parties, including Communist; (2) form a Central Electoral Board with the participation of all parties; (3) effect a cleanup of the Police and Army to eliminate elements supporting the Morínigo régime; (4) guarantee free elections in the near future; and (5) undertake measures to combat the high cost of living.

Respectfully yours,   EDWARD G. TRUEBLOOD

834.00/3-2547 : Telegram

The Acting Secretary of State to the Embassy in Paraguay

SECRET   WASHINGTON, March 25, 1947—7 p. m.

83. Braz Amb [17] called at Dept today on instructions his Govt to report receipt request by latter from emissary Par Govt that airplanes be furnished by Brazil for use in overcoming present rebellion in Paraguay. Amb stated that his Govt's oral reply was that request could not be complied with because (*a*) inter-American commitments and (*b*) fact that available planes were Lend-Lease from US; only assistance which Brazil could offer would be mediation if both parties in Par desired it on basis of calling election and this only as joint action with other neighboring countries, i.e. Argentina and Bolivia. He added

---

[16] Not printed.
[17] Carlos Martins.

that his Govt was appropriately advising Arg Govt through its Amb in BA but made no mention of any advice to Bol Govt.

Keep Dept and interested Embs informed any developments concerning possible mediation which come to your attention.

Repeated to Rio de Janeiro as 323, to Buenos Aires as 216 and to La Paz as 156.

ACHESON

834.00/3-2847 : Telegram

The Acting Secretary of State to the Embassy in Paraguay

SECRET   US URGENT   WASHINGTON, April 1, 1947—7 p. m.

89. Dept considering sending following message to BA if you believe opportune in light latest local developments. Please comment urgently on probable reaction to mediation offer suggested. BA has been requested repeat Embtel 339 [18] to you if not already done.

"Inform FonMin Dept's views as follows re Embtel 339, March 28:

1. Present situation Para, especially Morínigo's public rejection idea of mediation March 27, 28, makes prospects of success of mediation offer doubtful now. However, Dept entirely sympathetic to suggestion of Arg and Braz Govts that some steps be taken on behalf Inter-American system to prevent further bloodshed destruction.

2. Any offer mediation should be undertaken in accordance inter-American procedures and on behalf inter-American system as Arg FonMin [19] suggests.

3. Should situation in Para further deteriorate as seems possible from Liberal party manifesto Mar 28, or should events make acceptance of mediation by both parties more likely, Dept would favor general plan Braz initiative as modified Arg suggestions. Dept would recommend Arg and Braz ForOffs initiate consultation Amreps through diplomatic channels suggesting Arg, Braz, and third govt offer Para Govt mediation services. Dept considers Res 107, 8th Conf Lima [20] best basis for consultation in view absence any international dispute.

4. For third govt mentioned above, Dept suggests Colombia as preferable either Bolivia or Chile because of Colombia's traditional friendly relations with Para and desirability giving more continental character to mediation procedure. Dept has not broached suggestion to Col Govt."

ACHESON

---

[18] From the Ambassador in Argentina, March 28, 1947, not printed.
[19] Juan Atilio Bramuglia.
[20] *Report of the Delegation of the United States*, p. 188.

834.00/4-247 : Telegram

The Chargé in Paraguay (*Trueblood*) to the Secretary of State

SECRET   US URGENT   Asunción, April 2, 1947—5 p. m.

171. Have not received Buenos Aires 339 [21] but Lyon [22] and I heartily approve purpose of Deptel 89, April 1, 7 p. m. in belief that any step offering any hope of pacific settlement this situation here is worth exploring. As Department suggests however prospects of Paraguayan Government inviting mediation are dim at this moment. Immediately prior receipt Deptel Brazilian Chargé informed us government here had advised him they consider Brazil's offer of mediation "inopportune" at this time, but would be glad to keep under advisement. Last night in call on Argentine Ambassador he reiterated intention his government to act in harmony with Brazil and US in event mediation appears feasible, which he did not think was the case now.

Trueblood

834.00/4-847 : Telegram

The Chargé in Paraguay (*Trueblood*) to the Secretary of State

SECRET   Asunción, April 8, 1947— 9 a. m.

185. Brazilian Chargé informed me last night in strict confidence that Paraguayan Government had delivered to him the memorandum replying to Brazil's offer of mediation, which was referred to in paragraph 3, Embtel 177, April 4, 4 p. m. [21] Fabrino did not give me full details but said reply insists on unconditional surrender of rebels before conditions can be discussed, then outlines conditions and states Government's intention proceed with elections, etc. Memorandum is being sent to Brazilian FonOff, which will presumably, in due course, inform the Department.

Trueblood

834.00/4-547 : Telegram

The Acting Secretary of State to the Embassy in Paraguay

SECRET   US URGENT   Washington, April 9, 1947—2 p. m.

97. Dept repeated urtels 177 Apr 4 and 180 Apr 5 [23] to Rio BA for inf. In view time lag reception here from Asunción and delays retrans-

---

[21] Not printed.
[22] Presumably Cecil B. Lyon, Assistant Chief, Division of River Plate Affairs.
[23] Neither printed.

mission please repeat your future messages re mediation direct to those Embassies.

Since Para Govt as such still seems adverse mediation by neighboring states and has given no definite indication it would view multilateral action Amreps as more acceptable at this time, Dept does not wish to sponsor consultation Amreps outlined Deptel 89 Apr. 1. However, if Brazil continues press direct mediation you may point out to Fonmin Chaves that while, in principle, the US believes in desirability following procedures inter-American system on multilateral consultation and sees possible advantages in Pan-American designation mediatory states, we do not object to Brazilian initiative if acceptable to Paraguay and hope for its prompt success if accepted.

Rebel formation *de facto* govt which may seek recognition makes multilateral consultation towards mediation at this time more complex since, if Morínigo administration can overcome the rebels promptly (which apparently it still believes it now can), as the acceptedly legitimate Govt of Para it might charge overt action by the other Amreps tended to give hope if not legal status to insurrectionists at very time Govt was about to quell rebellion. If the facts change, matter can be reexamined.

You may discuss our position informally with Fonmin if circumstances warrant. Sent to Asunción as 97. Repeated BA as 282 and Rio as 375.

ACHESON

834.00/4-847 : Telegram

The Chargé in Paraguay (Trueblood) to the Secretary of State

SECRET   ASUNCIÓN, April 11, 1947—5 p. m.

197.[25] I have reported Chaves' outspokenly unfavorable reaction when he learned of Argentina's interest in mediation on a multilateral basis. The Paraguayan Government also took us to task re our reply to their circular of March 18 for intimating that multilateral consultation might be in order. On March 26, the government here hastily revoked the decree of March 18, declaring a state of war. All of these circumstances combined with Brazil's course of action lead me to believe Brazil's insistence from the outset on mediation by adjoining countries was a position worked out with the government here and designed to exclude from any consideration of Paraguayan situation, countries with strong leftist groups such as Uruguay and Chile which might exert their influence against the Morínigo Government here.

---

[25] First section of this telegram not printed.

The Brazilian Chargé has consistently defended Morínigo in our conversations because in his opinion (1) latter is aggressively anti-Communist hence his ouster at this stage would be inconsistent with present anti-Communist trends in US and elsewhere; (2) Morínigo was helpful to US and Brazil during war; (3) Morínigo is more sinned against by scheming and treacherous politicians here than a sinner in his own right; (4) Morínigo was prevented from democratizing Paraguay earlier than June, 1946 by cavalry clique but since then he has been sincere in his efforts to do so; (5) if Morínigo steps out, he has no legal successor, which would force country back to another military junta at a time when armed forces are disrupted.

If the foregoing hypothesis is correct, Brazil, motivated by a strong desire for peace here, and due to a belief that this would be best served by saving the Morínigo-Colorado Government, has successfully preempted the situation here by shutting off any chance of multilateral consultations in favor of regional mediation, for which the memorandum of April 6 [26] can pave the way. It now remains to be seen whether Argentina, in the event mediation can get underway, will consent to cooperate on basis of a formula developed entirely by Brazil. Buenos Aires telegram April 10, 3 p. m.,[27] implies this will be the case.

Fabrino tells me in strict confidence that he thinks the forthcoming conference between Dutra and Perón [28] will offer a splendid opportunity to thresh out the Paraguayan situation and for the two nations to agree on a political hands-off policy here implemented by a coordinated economic approach so that any rivalries and friction between Argentina and Brazil here can be effectively eliminated.

Sent to Department; repeated to Rio as 23 and Buenos Aires as 39 and brings them up to date.

TRUEBLOOD

834.00/4-1447 : Telegram

The Chargé in Paraguay (Trueblood) to the Secretary of State

SECRET   ASUNCIÓN, April 14, 1947—11 a. m.

201. Since present Paraguayan situation developed the observation has been frequently heard that it is fortunate US has not supplied this country with a greater supply of modern instruments of warfare under proposed hemisphere arms program. The destructive consequences of a

---

[26] Not printed.
[27] Telegram 394, not printed.
[28] The Presidents of Brazil and Argentina, respectively.

supply here at present time of modern bombing planes, tanks, etc., are obvious and underline the dangers involved in arming even on a modest scale countries such as Paraguay which have no institutional stability.

As it is, all except one of the few airplanes in flying condition and the bulk of the small amount of modern equipment in use by both sides such as machine guns, mortars and 105–mm guns were supplied under Lend-Lease. Most of equipment on both sides was captured from Bolivians during Chaco War.

TRUEBLOOD

834.00/4–1547

Memorandum of Conversation, by the Chief of the Division of Brazilian Affairs (Dawson)

CONFIDENTIAL [WASHINGTON,] April 15, 1947.

Participants: Carlos Martins, Ambassador of Brazil
Octavio Carneiro, Second Secretary, Brazilian Embassy
A-Br—Mr. Braden
BA—Mr. Dawson

Ambassador Martins referred to Brazil's qualified offer of mediation in the present internal difficulties in Paraguay and outlined in general terms the Paraguayan memorandum in reply thereto, the substance of which had already been reported to the Department by our Embassy at Asunción.[29] The Ambassador said that he had been asked by his Government to review this matter with the Department.

Mr. Martins then stated that his Government had informed him that the Argentine Government had approached the various Chiefs of Mission of the American Republics at Buenos Aires with regard to inter-American consultation on the Paraguayan question, referring to Resolution No. 107 of the Eighth International Conference of American States at Lima in 1938 as giving a basis for such action. Mr. Martins went on to say that his Government felt that this Resolution was inapplicable since the Paraguayan affair was an internal one. Inter-American consultation on the question would be subject to delays and the Brazilian Government felt that the Brazilian *démarche* looking toward the offer of good offices of neighboring countries would be more fitting.

Mr. Braden agreed that the general terms of Resolution No. 107 did not appear to apply to the Paraguayan case except by the broadest of interpretations.

---

[29] Despatch 2596, April 16, 1947, not printed.

834.00/4-2147

Memorandum by the Assistant Secretary of State for American Republic Affairs (*Braden*) *to the Under Secretary of State* (*Acheson*)

SECRET [WASHINGTON,] April 23, 1947.

During March the Paraguayan Government requested the United States, Brazilian and Argentine Governments to supply it with certain arms (we were asked for tanks and advanced trainers) to help suppress what it termed a Communist revolt. All three Governments declined. More recently the Paraguayan Government has made efforts to purchase from private sources in the United States advanced trainers and machine gun ammunition; and it has formally requested the Department to license the export of these arms.

Ambassador Beaulac believes that we should, as a matter of general policy, license the export of arms during times of domestic revolt to recognized, friendly and cooperative American Governments; and that the Paraguayan Government should receive arms under this general rule. I attach a copy of his memorandum dated April 21[30] which sets forth these views.

I have reached the conclusion that we should not license the export of arms to the Paraguayan Government at this time because:

a) Our motives would be interpreted by various unfriendly groups as intervention in Paraguay's internal affairs aimed at propping up a "reactionary dictatorship" by the suppression with United States arms of a "popular revolt." There is a danger that this charge might gain considerable acceptance throughout the Hemisphere and that faith and confidence in United States principles and motives would be impaired.

b) Our arms would probably be used to kill Paraguayans, perhaps including non-combatants. This would tend to stigmatize the United States in the minds of many people.

c) Our action might in the future be used by other American Governments (such as Argentina) as a precedent for supporting with arms to their selfish political advantage governments opposed by the popular will.

I recognize that the Paraguayan political picture shows a potential Communist danger, but I do not believe that the danger can now be said to be sufficiently certain or immediate to justify us in incurring these hazards. We may soon have to take the initiative in working out a program to combat Communist tactics in this Hemisphere, but the program should, in my opinion, be an inter-American one which has been carefully considered by all concerned and which will have the support of not only the American Governments but of the people as well.

---
[30] Not printed.

I have indicated informally to the Paraguayan Chargé [31] the possibility of inter-American consultation on the arms question. I said that we were not presently disposed to take the initiative in arranging for consultation if the Paraguayan Government was opposed to the idea. That Government has now replied that it is opposed to consultation; it has not renewed its request for export licenses.

Recommendation:

I recommend that we continue to decline to approve export license applications for arms to be shipped to Paraguay. If the situation changes, the problem can be reexamined. This memorandum is submitted to you since it may conflict with broad policy at some point.

834.00/4–2147

Memorandum by the Under Secretary of State (Acheson) to the Assistant Secretary of State for American Republic Affairs (Braden)

[WASHINGTON,] April 30, 1947.

I concur for the present in the recommendation on page 2 of your attached memorandum of April 23.[32] This morning in discussing the matter with Ambassador Beaulac I [he?] referred to a suggestion which I [he?] wished to make on his return to Paraguay and which he said had your approval to the effect that the President of Paraguay might make an offer to the other parties to invite representatives of some of the other American Republics to observe elections which he was offering to hold. If the other parties refused an offer of this sort the Ambassador thought that we might well reconsider the decision not to permit the export of arms to Paraguay.

I said to the Ambassador that this seemed to me an excellent suggestion and that I thought if the offer was made and refused we should reconsider this question.

DEAN ACHESON

834.00/5–2247 : Telegram

The Ambasador in Paraguay (Beaulac) to the Secretary of State

SECRET   ASUNCIÓN, May 27, 1947— 5 p. m.

285. President told me this morning he told *Newsweek* correspondent yesterday that he was placing his hopes for political peace following the suppression of the rebellion on free elections and that he hoped

---

[31] César R. Acosta.
[32] *Supra.*

persons might come to Paraguay from other American republics to assure themselves that elections are really free.

President said he was sounding out Colorado Party leaders concerning a formal suggestion in the above sense and had encountered no opposition so far. He said he was hopeful government might extend some formal invitation to other American republics to send observers, although he gave no promise in this regard.

BEAULAC

834.00/6-447 : Telegram

The Chargé in Paraguay (Trueblood) to the Secretary of State

SECRET   ASUNCIÓN, June 4, 1947—10 a. m.

300. Negrão [33] informed me last night results of his first talk with President Morínigo were disappointing. Latter emphasized impossibility of accepting mediation at moment when government forces, after hard struggle involving great sacrifices, were approaching final victory. President reaffirmed his intentions of inviting outside observers to witness elections. Negrão will see President again today.

Sent Department 300; repeated Rio de Janeiro 54; Buenos Aires 84.

TRUEBLOOD

834.00/6-547

Memorandum by the Ambassador to Paraguay (Beaulac) Temporarily in the United States [34]

CONFIDENTIAL   [WASHINGTON,] June 5, 1947.

The *New York Herald Tribune*, in its edition of June 5, 1947, publishes a dispatch from its representative in Asunción, Mac R. Johnson, in which he quotes President Morínigo as saying "I invite all nations in the inter-American system to send observers to Paraguay for the elections so they may observe and testify to the honesty and fairness of the balloting."

President Morínigo told me on Tuesday, May 27, that he had extended such an invitation to the other American republics through the correspondent of *News Week*. The latter confirmed the President's statement.

By issuing this public invitation, which any or all of the Governments of the other American republics may follow up, President

---

[33] Francisco Negrão de Lima, formerly Brazilian Ambassador to Paraguay.
[34] Addressed to the Secretary of State, the Under Secretary, and Mr. Briggs, ARA.

Morínigo has cut the ground out from under the military rebellion, and exposed it for what it is, a selfish attempt by a heterogeneous group of military and politicians, including international communists, to seize power in Paraguay.

The suggestion that the other American republics be invited to send persons to observe elections in Paraguay was made to President Morínigo by me with the prior authorization of Under Secretary Acheson and Assistant Secretary Braden. I made the suggestion after President Morínigo had told me he was placing all his faith for permanent peace in Paraguay on free elections participated in by all the political parties, or at least by the two major political parties which together comprise nearly the total electorate of Paraguay.

President Morínigo's invitation, made on what appears to be the eve of military victory over the rebels, is a courageous, imaginative step, which if intelligently and imaginatively followed up and if repeated by the Presidents or Governments of certain other American republics may help to break the vicious circle of bad government; rigged elections, bad economic and social conditions, and revolution, which has retarded progress in those countries and which constitutes a potential threat to our security.

Since President Morínigo has extended this invitation following a suggestion from us, and since it is in our interest that the invitation lead to tangible results in the form of improved democracy in Paraguay and perhaps in other American republics, I earnestly recommend that the Department show by words and by acts that it recognizes the contribution which President Morínigo is trying to make to peace and solidarity in this Hemisphere and that it is prepared to cooperate with him.

WILLARD L. BEAULAC

834.00/6–347 : Telegram

The Secretary of State to the Embassy in Paraguay

SECRET   WASHINGTON, June 6, 1947—3 p. m.

152. Urtel 299 June 3, 6 PM and 300, 301 June 4, 10 AM and noon.[35] Fol for your own info: No approach made to date by Brazilian Govt but shd matter be raised Dept wd not at this juncture favor any action that might be construed as pressure by this Govt on Morínigo Admin to accept mediation.

Repeated to Rio as 591 Montevideo as 192 BAires as 485.

MARSHALL

---

[35] Telegrams 299 and 301 not printed.

834.00/6-847 : Telegram

The Chargé in Paraguay (*Trueblood*) to the Secretary of State

CONFIDENTIAL   US URGENT   ASUNCIÓN, June 8, 1947—2 p. m.

313. Negrão De Lima leaves here this afternoon for Porto Murtinho on Brazil–Paraguay frontier where he will confer again with rebels. He states govt will not consent to restore to active duty officers participating in rebellion but will pension them, offering full amnesty to all others connected with revolt. Will not agree to give freedom to Communists but will leave decision to Constituent Assembly.

Negrão doubtful rebels will accept these terms but points out that since he saw them 2 weeks ago tide of battle has gone against them, hence they may be more receptive now.

Negrão stated Paraguayan Govt wishes United States included among mediatory group in event mediation proceeds which was agreeable to Brazil. (FonMin confirmed this to me yesterday. Chaves again expressed view that govt needed military victory, but thought mediation to assist in pacification would be of great utility.) Negrão does not however see any place for mediation if struggle is fought to finish. He said President had reiterated intention of inviting foreign observers to witness elections here.

Negrão will proceed to Rio following contact with rebels.

Sent Dept 313, repeated Rio 57, Buenos Aires 88.

TRUEBLOOD

834.00/6-1647 : Telegram

The Secretary of State to the Embassy in Paraguay

CONFIDENTIAL   WASHINGTON, June 16, 1947—8 p. m.

158. *Herald Tribune* June 5 carried delayed copyright desp by Mac R. Johnson datelined Asunción June 3 quoting Pres Morínigo as saying:

"I invite all nations in the Inter-American System to send observers to Paraguay for the elections so they may observe and testify to the honesty and fairness of the balloting."

Amb Beaulac confirms that Pres Morínigo told him that he had extended such an invitation to the other American republics thru correspondent of *Newsweek*.

While this Govt is naturally gratified at any move in direction establishment democratic institutions in Paraguay, we believe subject delicate one to be approached with caution. In authorizing you to discuss matter with Pres it is suggested you seek to obtain some indication his conception how this project wd operate. For example, having in mind practical problems in presence foreign govt representatives in period of probable political tensions, consideration might be given to inviting instead representatives of foreign press. In any case, terms of ref shd be specifically clear and it shd be understood that at least several other American republics wd also participate.

For your conf info we wd prefer to see press rather than govt reps invited.

MARSHALL

834.00/6-2447 : Telegram

The Chargé in Paraguay (Trueblood) to the Secretary of State

CONFIDENTIAL   US URGENT   ASUNCIÓN, June 24, 1947—5 p. m.

341. Negrão de Lima returned here yesterday. He tells me rebels will not accept government's terms of unconditional surrender, feeling that they can prolong struggle indefinitely and eventually win. Rebels will accept, however, following terms:

Free elections guaranteed by either non-partisan or coalition government, Morínigo to finish out his term, and armed forces to be reorganized on basis of professional officers, which will in turn guarantee government.

Negrão feels situation has changed radically since he was last here with government now faced by 4–6-month struggle to defeat rebels, whereas earlier they spoke of an end by June 15, etc.

He is conferring now with Foreign Minister.

Sent Department 341; repeated Rio 66, Buenos Aires 100.

TRUEBLOOD

834.00/7-1747 : Telegram

The Chargé in Paraguay (Trueblood) to the Secretary of State

SECRET   ASUNCIÓN, July 17, 1947—3 p. m.

389. Brazilian Ambassador presenting credentials this morning. Last night he told me that Foreign Minister yesterday declared offensive in the north (Embassy's telegram 387, July 16 [36]) did not represent any change in government's decision to proceed with mediation as proposed. Chaves explained to Barboza that the offensive had been planned for some weeks past and got under way on July 14 before the

---

[36] Not printed.

government here was notified of the Itamarati's [37] approval of proposed plan. Offensive obviously represents final attempt on part of government to administer decisive military defeat to rebels which has been leitmotif of government thinking all along (Embassy's telegrams 313, June 8 and 346, June 27 [38]). Barboza and I feel this 11th hour offensive which is sure to result in considerable bloodshed is unfortunate and scarcely in keeping with spirit of current negotiations. He is undeterred, however, from pressing forward.

Negrão is at frontier waiting to consult rebels. Once their assent is obtained Barboza states Itamarati will invite the mediating powers to name their representatives and constitute the board of mediation. Chaves informed Barboza yesterday that Paraguayan Government will probably instruct Enciso [39] today or tomorrow to issue formal invitation to United States to participate in mediation which if accepted will enable Itamarati to request our government to appoint representative. The Brazilian Government is understandably anxious to get the mediation machinery set up at the earliest possible moment in order to call an armistice and stop further fighting. Barboza inquired if I had any instructions regarding United States participation in mediation; I hope Department will be able to advise me shortly its views on this. Barboza was also interested in Argentine Government's attitude at this stage and that of Paraguayan exiles in Buenos Aires; I stated I had no reports from our Embassy there. Barboza and Fabrino envisage that the work of the mediators may well be of considerable duration, possibly extending until holding of elections, which as suggested in Embassy's telegram 383, July 14 [40] will require many months to prepare properly. They also foresee that Argentina, Brazil and the United States may be called on to cooperate in the development of a program of economic rehabilitation and development for Paraguay. In weighing the pros and cons of our participating in the mediation the foregoing factors are of pertinence. If we desire to continue our policy of actively cooperating in Paraguay's development I believe it will be essential for us to act affirmatively in view of the likelihood that plans of far-reaching scope will emerge from the mediation.

Sent Department 389, repeated Buenos Aires 123, Rio 82.

TRUEBLOOD

---

[37] The Brazilian Foreign Office.
[38] Latter not printed.
[39] Guillermo Enciso Belloso.
[40] Not printed.

834.00/7–1747 : Telegram

The Chargé in Paraguay (Trueblood) to the Secretary of State

CONFIDENTIAL   ASUNCIÓN, July 17, 1947—4 p. m.

391. Embtels 376, July 11 and 387, July 16.[41] The following is a literal translation of the mediation proposals as presented by the Brazilian Embassy in Asunción on July 11 to US Government for approval:

"Established the conditions decided upon at Concepción to the effect that the revolutionists do not challenge the authority, which they recognize, of the presidential mandate of General Higinio Morínigo, a council of mediators will be immediately constituted.

Within this meaning the soldiers in arms against the Government will cease hostilities, in order to fulfill the stipulations of the memorandum 6 April (1947)[42] and they will deliver their arms to the mediators, who will be the guarantors, of them (the rebels) before the Government and of the Government before them, of the fulfillment of the present commitments.

The revolutionists will be respected in their military dignity; therefore, they will keep their rank and will remain in the army lists, awaiting orders of the Paraguayan Government.

The Government and the revolutionists in confidence entrust the task of pacification to the high sense of justice of the mediators, preserving always the principle of the presidential authority of General Higinio Morínigo until the completion of his term."

Sent Department 391; repeated Rio de Janeiro 83, Buenos Aires 124.

TRUEBLOOD

834.00/7–1747 : Telegram

The Secretary of State to the Embassy in Paraguay

SECRET   WASHINGTON, July 18, 1947—8 p. m.

191. Urtel 389 July 17, 3 p. m. For your guidance in conversations FonMin and colleagues US is prepared to give favorable consideration if formal invitation is extended by Paraguay to participate in mediation.

For your info Enciso has not approached Dept on mediation question but in light your cables we are exploring availability mediator of adequate grade and regional experience should invitation be forthcoming and Brazil request we appoint representative. Pls inform Dept all info re probable points reference in proposed mediation,

---

[41] Neither printed.
[42] Not printed.

estimates time required for successful conclusion, locale proposed and local travel involved.

Repeated Rio and BA for like action.

MARSHALL

834.00/7-2147 : Telegram

The Chargé in Paraguay (Trueblood) to the Secretary of State

SECRET   ASUNCIÓN, July 21, 1947—9 a. m.

395. Brazilian Ambassador yesterday morning flew to Campo Grande to confer with Negrão who is due Rio this morning. On return here yesterday, Barboza informed me Negrão stated rebels had accepted formula quoted in Embtel 391, July 17. Barboza, Argentine Ambassador and I in agreement that this clears way for immediate setting-up of mediation machinery. FonMin expressed his agreement thereon to us yesterday without mentioning point reported in paragraph 1 Embtel 394, July 19.[43]

Regarding US participation Chaves and Barboza have agreed on plan now before Itamarati whereby Paraguayan and Brazilian Ambassadors in Washington jointly issue invitation. Deptel 191, July 18.

Fighting near Concepción continues with govt moderating its initial optimism. Barboza informs me in confidence Brazilian officers who made Concepción trip with Negrão feel rebels position still strong and that issue of present battle by no means decided.

Repeated Rio 86; Buenos Aires 128.

TRUEBLOOD

834.00/7-2347 : Telegram

The Chargé in Paraguay (Trueblood) to the Secretary of State

SECRET   ASUNCIÓN, July 23, 1947—6 p. m.

401. Brazilian Ambassador informs me of receipt of instructions from Itamarati altering on request Argentine Government mediation formula quoted in Embtel 391, July 17, in respect that rebels will not be required deliver their arms to mediators. Each group will merely cease fighting and maintain *status quo*. Change is due to Argentine belief that actual turning over of arms to mediators would humiliate rebels and would also place mediators in undesirable position of having to return arms to rebels if mediation broke down. Itamarati stated Argentine Government impatient to reach accord here.

---

[43] Not printed.

Barboza regrets need to re-present formula to Government here, but feels it is improvement. He will consult Arriola and see President or Chaves on this, but not until he has received reply from Rio to question raised by Government yesterday as to whether acceptance of armistice given to Negrão only represents decision of Military Junta or whether it also binds the political parties backing the Concepción movement. Judging by telegram 895, July 22,[44] from Buenos Aires, the Liberals do not consider themselves so bound since they propose ouster of President as *sine qua non* which present formula does not of course contemplate.

Barboza saw Chaves this morning and he said latter spoke in terms reminiscent of our talk on 19th (Embtel 394 [44]), emphasizing difficulties faced by Government to sell mediation plan to Colorado Party, fact that army in north is not National but Party army which has fought hard and is now on threshold of victory, etc. Chaves again suggested need for some kind of post-victory mediation to assist in "spiritual pacification", pointing out problem of bringing the Colorados and Liberals together again, with numbers of Paraguayans now in exile. Barboza told him that he could not visualize the role for mediation under such circumstances.

As for US participation, Itamarati thinks Paraguayan Government should issue invitation with Chaves still favoring action by three-power group which would be accompanied by his approaching our Embassy here.

The way matters are shaping up question US participation is becoming distinctly secondary—with the Government stalling for time to give its army a chance to win a military victory and opposition apparently divided in its view toward mediation, the immediate outlook is dim. If Argentina is genuinely anxious to get this situation settled it may be able to apply some pressure on the Liberals residing within its borders in order to get all of the opposition behind the present formula. Taking into account however disparity of objectives among the opponents of the Paraguayan Government, bringing them together may be an impossible task.

In any event the prospect of getting all groups together and arranging an armistice before the Government wins in the north appears increasingly remote. When and if the Government's victory takes place and events reported in Embtel 399, July 22,[44] tying it closer the situation will then have to be reexamined to see whether mediation in some form will still be feasible.

Sent Department 401, repeated Rio 90, Buenos Aires 131.

TRUEBLOOD

---

[44] Not printed.

834.00/8-647 : Telegram

The Chargé in Paraguay (*Trueblood*) to the Secretary of State

SECRET ASUNCIÓN, August 6, 1947—11 a. m.

427. Government forces now reported to have lost further ground to rebels who are approaching Salado line which is 35 kilometers from city. Government still holds Altos and Arroyos to east. Cannon fire now [audible?] in Asunción. Issue depends on arrival of government troops from north who General Staff claims are now close to rear of rebels. Gunboats attempted force passage of Paraná at Perritos yesterday but government report they were put out of commission by artillery.

Argentine Ambassador has ordered two minesweepers to stand by at Puerto Pilcomayo and Brazilian Ambassador has two planes in readiness at Brazilian frontier if conditions should require evacuation. We consulted all Americans within reach yesterday and offered fly women and children to Foz Iguassu today. Air Attaché proceeded Rio this morning with several women and children but most preferred remain. We are recommending citizens living in especially exposed locations move to Grand Hotel if fighting reaches city.

Understand government here in event of loss of Asunción will join its army in north.

Ordinary business in city practically at standstill, refugees are crowding Argentine and Brazilian Embassies and foodstuffs getting scarce.

Sent Dept 427, repeated Rio 104, Buenos Aires 145.

TRUEBLOOD

834.00/947 : Telegram

The Chargé in Paraguay (*Trueblood*) to the Secretary of State

CONFIDENTIAL   US URGENT   ASUNCIÓN, August 9, 1947—11 a. m.

441. At 10:00 this morning Brazilian Ambassador was still without reply from President on mediation. In meantime military situation of government has apparently deteriorated considerably, with treachery, and dissension undoubtedly partly responsible. Rebels reported to be drawing closer to city from northeast and from east although no cannonading audible. Last government reserves except those in city have entered into action. If rebels succeed in getting up to city it is doubtful whether government can hold Asunción, but in any event, civilian population can expect bad going. In event rebels capture city there is real danger of chaotic conditions, opening of jails (releasing Communists), looting, reprisals, etc. Some Colorado families already fearful and asking asylum.

If government loses Asunción they will presumably try to concentrate their troops at some point nearby and try to retake. Advance units government First Army Corps (from north) now at Mercedes by Manduvari River. If government continues lose ground at present rate they will not arrive in time to save city.

We are worried about safety of our military planes here but reluctant to send them out of country since they may be of great value in days to come, although airfield unfortunately is in exposed position northeast of city.

Cable service may possibly be suspended if fighting reaches city. Will use Almon's facilities in emergency.

Sent Dept 441, repeated Rio de Janeiro 110, Buenos Aires 149.

TRUEBLOOD

834.00/8–1247 : Telegram

The Chargé in Paraguay (Trueblood) to the Secretary of State

RESTRICTED   ASUNCIÓN, August 12, 1947—6 p. m.

449. . . .

Thirty Americans, principally women and children, now living Grand Hotel, two blocks from chancery. Embassy officer Harmon residing there designated in charge. This Embassy maintaining close contact with heads our various missions and other Americans. A few Americans in outlying district now cut off from communication with city and Embassy will attempt contact them soon as possible.

No commercial airplanes have arrived Asunción since August 6 and little likelihood service will be resumed for present. Dodero boats coming only as far as Pilcomayo. Embassy will have no mail service until shipping and air line traffic resumed.

Business in Asunción at standstill and many government offices are closed although public utilities still functioning. Six p. m. curfew in effect since Sunday. Food supply becoming increasingly difficult with no milk, butter or bread now available. Limited amount meat and vegetables still found but unless roads opened to surrounding producing areas within the next few days even these products likely disappear.

Repeated to Buenos Aires, repeated to Rio de Janerio.

TRUEBLOOD

834.00/8–1647 : Telegram

The Chargé in Paraguay (Trueblood) to the Secretary of State

CONFIDENTIAL   ASUNCIÓN, August 16, 1947—6 p. m.

462. At regular weekly meeting Chiefs of Mission at noon there was extended discussion of problem created by haphazard bombing of

city by rebel planes which seems to serve no military purpose. Bomb fell and exploded this morning close to Mexican Embassy only 50 yards from Secretary Hoyt's house. Mexican Ambassador proposed a collective exhortation that such attacks cease. Brazilian and Argentine Ambassadors recommended instead that each envoy report sense of meeting to his govt and request instructions. This was agreed to. The French Minister and Uruguayan Chargé favored advising rebels "informally" of view of Corps; Argentina led general objection to this course on grounds Corps has no contact with rebels and should have none.

Peruvian Ambassador also urged statement by Corps to effect that it would welcome immediate solution of Paraguayan problem. Venezuelan Chargé agreed vehemently on ground Corps is being accused of indifference to this situation and that this misconception ought to be corrected. Argentina violently disagreed, insisting everything humanly possible to do has been done.

Repeated Rio 127, Buenos Aires 167, sent Dept 462.

TRUEBLOOD

834.00/8–1847 : Telegram

The Chargé in Paraguay (Trueblood) to the Secretary of State

CONFIDENTIAL ASUNCIÓN, August 18, 1947—4 p. m.

465. Government's position much improved and safety Asunción apparently assured as result govt offensive beginning yesterday which has broken up rebels into three main groups. Three govt combat teams totalling some 2,400 men mainly from First Corps now operating to clear up countryside. Civil airport, Lugue and San Lorenzo all retaken. Foregoing confirmed personally by Military and Air Attachés. Our military planes intact and gasoline supplies, tools, etc., not taken, although undetermined amount damage done to Air Mission HQ.

Air mission OGT Allen, whose home near airport, taken prisoner by rebels but later released after being robbed of some personal belongings and subjected to questioning by rebel major. Latter specifically asked how many US aviators had come down to help Morínigo and seemed convinced that this had happened. Rebel officers stated that they were out to get US pilots. Fact that Communist leader Barthe reliably reported to be with rebel troops obviously pertinent with respect to foregoing statements.

Govt has started to use airport again. No rebel plane over city since Saturday when it was reported one plane shot down by govt gunfire.

Food shortage in Asunción acute, but can be expected improve rapidly now that rebels pushed back out of nearby producing areas. Fresh milk should be received city tomorrow from Sfica dairy which came through heavy fighting intact and is now within govt lines.

Fighting during past few days reported bloodiest of war, and many wounded now in Asunción hospitals. Reports of atrocities both sides prevalent with some unconfirmed rumors to effect that both sides shooting volunteer soldiers rather than take them prisoners. However, govt has set up prison camp near city and has undetermined amount prisoners there now.

Air Attaché flying Rio tomorrow with mail pouch and will bring back women previously evacuated and supplies (Embtel 449, August 12). No information yet as to when regular airmail service will be resumed.

Sent Dept 465, repeated Rio 131, Buenos Aires 170.

TRUEBLOOD

834.00/8-1647 : Telegram

The Acting Secretary of State to the Embassy in Paraguay

CONFIDENTIAL   WASHINGTON, August 19, 1947—4 p. m.

209. Urtel 462 Aug 16, Buenos Aires 167, Rio 127. Authorized in your discretion join other powers in concerted informal protest to revolutionaries. Protest, however, should be based on danger to lives and, if agreed to, property of foreign nationals, rather than on humanitarian grounds in view general practices such as saturated bombing followed in last war, and should state action taken has no implication support for either side.

Filing of informal advice with revolutionaries would not in any manner constitute recognition of belligerency in absence of clear intention to so treat them. If you consider advisable, protest might be drafted to include disavowal of intention recognize belligerent status revolutionaries.

Since responsibility still remains in Paraguayan Government, as recognized government, to protect foreign lives and property, copy of protest should be furnished Parag Govt.

Sent Asunción 209, repeated Rio 935, US Del, Petropolis (Brazil) 34, Buenos Aires 776.

LOVETT

834.20 Missions/8-2147 : Telegram

The Chargé in Paraguay (Trueblood) to the Secretary of State

CONFIDENTIAL   ASUNCIÓN, August 21, 1947—5 p. m.

481. Department's telegram 77, March 21. With situation here rapidly returning normalcy can be expected Embassy will shortly be

in position recommend resumption activities our military missions. Would therefore appreciate information as to what consideration and action being taken re renewal of contracts which expire October and December. Embassy concurs with Military Attaché and heads of missions that it highly desirable contracts be renewed and that arrangements be made at earliest date.[46] Government officials informally state they desirous missions continue. Military Attaché today similarly cabling War Department.

TRUEBLOOD

834.00/9-947

The Second Secretary of Embassy in Paraguay (Hoyt) to the Secretary of State

CONFIDENTIAL   ASUNCIÓN, September 9, 1947.
No. 2853

SIR: With reference to previous despatches concerning communist participation in the revolution, I have the honor to enclose a memorandum from Special Assistant Almon containing further information on the part played by communists and their leaders in the rebel campaign. An international communist brigade composed of Paraguayans, Bolivians, Brazilians and Argentines was formed, under the direct leadership of the number two communist in Paraguay, Obdulio Barthe, and took an active part in troop movements. In addition other important communists operated the rebel radio station "La Voz de la Victoria" when the rebel forces came down from Concepción in their attack on the capital.

The Paraguayan Government reported the existence of this international brigade as the war ended, and stated that Barthe and his followers had fled to the interior of the country to escape capture. The attached memorandum [47] substantiated this government claim and states that the group may have numbered as high as 350 men. The brigade was with the rebel troops in the fighting around Asunción, and the Embassy has received numerous reports regarding the active participation of Barthe in the events of the last few weeks of the war. It appears evident that he exerted considerable influence in the rebel ranks. The Embassy received an unconfirmed report that the members of this international brigade wore special arm bands to distinguish them from the regular troops.

The importance of communist operation of the rebel radio station cannot be overlooked. The station had a large radio audience, and was

[46] See bracketed notes on the renewal of these missions, p. 997.
[47] Not printed.

continually cited by those persons in opposition to the Government as the only source of authentic news of the progress of the war. News, rumors, and propaganda broadcast over "La Voz de la Victoria" were given out the next day on the streets of Asunción as confirmed facts. That communists should be handling this news, propaganda, etc., indicates that they had at least substantial influence in rebel activities.

Although, as the Embassy has consistently reported, this was far from a communist-dominated rebellion, it is obvious that the communists did play a certain part in it and were taking advantage of the situation to advance their own ends at every opportunity. Reviewing this participation, and considering just how close the rebels came to winning, one cannot help but surmise that the communists would have necessarily participated to some extent in any government which might have been set up by the rebels; this despite Liberal assurances that the communists would have been dropped once the victory was won.

Respectfully yours, HENRY A. HOYT

834.00/12–1247 : Airgram

The Ambassador in Paraguay (Warren) to the Secretary of State

CONFIDENTIAL ASUNCIÓN, December 12, 1947.

A–249. Reference Embassy's despatch No. 2953 dated November 3, 1947, Embassy's airgram No. 230, of December 1, 1947, and Embassy's telegrams Nos. 630 and 628 both dated December 6, 1947.[48]

In the last two weeks the Embassy has noticed what may be a change of attitude on the part of President Morínigo and members of his official family toward the United States and its activities in Paraguay in contrast to what the Embassy considered to be an unfriendly atmosphere prevailing prior to, during, and immediately after the holding of the Colorado convention. This possible change is indicated by the following:

[Here follows an eight-point explanation of instances of greater personal friendliness of Paraguayans of high station toward the United States.]

Embassy realizes that perhaps it is possible to explain the foregoing in such a way that it would not indicate a change in the attitude of the Paraguayan Government. However, in view of the absence in Argentina of Natalicio González [49] whom the Embassy does not consider to be pro-USA and his rumored failure to obtain an Argentine loan or Argentine support of his plans, it believes that these eight points do

---

[48] None printed.
[49] Paraguayan Minister of Finance.

indicate a turning toward the United States of the President in an effort to balance somewhat Argentine pressure on this country. This view is strengthened when it is recalled that both Prieto [50] and Vasconsellos [51] were placed in the Cabinet as announced González men and that previously neither had shown any particular friendliness toward the United States.

Please send a copy of this message to the Department of the Army.

WARREN

AIR TRANSPORT AGREEMENT BETWEEN THE UNITED STATES AND PARAGUAY

[For text of the Agreement, signed at Asunción, February 28, 1947, see Department of State, Treaties and Other International Acts Series, No. 1753.]

AGREEMENT BETWEEN THE UNITED STATES AND PARAGUAY ON RECIPROCAL TRADE

[For texts of the Agreement and Exchange of Notes, signed at Asunción, September 12, 1946, effective, April 9, 1947, see Department of State, Treaties and Other International Acts Series, No. 1601.]

AGREEMENT BETWEEN THE UNITED STATES AND PARAGUAY RENEWING THE AGREEMENT OF DECMBER 10, 1943, PROVIDING FOR A MILITARY MISSION FROM THE UNITED STATES TO PARAGUAY

[Effected by an exchange of notes signed at Washington October 25 and November 20, 1947, not printed. Fort text see Department of State, Treaties and other International Acts Series, No. 2578.]

AGREEMENT BETWEEN THE UNITED STATES AND PARAGUAY RENEWING THE AGREEMENT OF OCTOBER 27, 1943, WHICH CONSTITUTED THE UNITED STATES MILITARY AVIATION MISSION TO PARAGUAY

[Effected by an exchange of notes signed at Washington on October 25 and November 20, 1947, not printed. For text, see TIAS No. 3339.]

---

[50] Leandro Prieto, Paraguayan Minister of Economy.
[51] César Vasconsellos, Paraguayan Minister of Foreign Affairs.

PERU

CONVERSATIONS CONCERNING A PERUVIAN DEBT SETTLEMENT AND PERU'S NEED FOR LOANS [1]

823.51/1–347

Memorandum of Conversation, by the Director of the Office of Financial and Development Policy (Ness)

[WASHINGTON,] January 3, 1947.

Participants: Mr. Juan Chavez, Minister and Commercial Counselor of the Peruvian Embassy
Mr. Livesey, OFD
Mr. Ness, OFD

On December 27 Mr. Chavez called at my office to tell me that he was instructed to approach the Eximbank with a loan application covering construction of a zinc and lead refinery in the Santa River Basin of Peru. He said he was calling to determine whether the Department would object to such an application. I told him that he could of course approach the Eximbank but that I anticipated he would be there informed that the Bank could consider no additional credit so long as the present default on Peru's bonded indebtedness continues unchanged. I reminded him that such a condition attached to the $25 million credit due to expire on December 31, 1946 and pointed out that it would be inconsistent for the Bank to extend other credits under the circumstances.

Today, having talked in the meantime to Mr. Maffry [6] of the Eximbank and having had the reply I had anticipated, Mr. Chavez called again to clarify the nature of the condition which had been imposed on loans to Peru. In response to direct questions, I informed Mr. Chavez that (1) the policy in question was not confined to the Eximbank but represented the viewpoint of the State Department as well, (2) that the condition had been attached to the $25 million credit from its beginning and not, as he professed to understand, from the date of the breakdown of the Montero Bernales proposal of November, 1945. [7]

---

[1] Continued from *Foreign Relations*, 1946, vol. XI, pp. 1251–1265.
[6] August Maffry, Vice President and Economic Adviser, Export-Import Bank.
[7] For documentation on the Montero Bernales mission, see *Foreign Relations*, 1945, vol. IX, pp. 1358 ff.

Mr. Chavez referred to the Section of the first Semi-Annual Report of the Eximbank to Congress dealing with "loans to governments in default" and inquired whether Peru was not in an exceptional position. He was told that such might be taken to be the case. He then inquired for the reason of this exceptional treatment, and was informed that by the early 1940's the feeling had grown up in the Department that Peru was (a) well able to undertake debt-service resumption and (b) had persistently failed to do so. When Mr. Chavez objected that when the present (Bustamente) administration had assumed power it had early undertaken to correct the default situation and had accordingly sent the Finance Minister, Mr. Montero Bernales, to this country to negotiate with the Bond Holders Council it was then observed that the subsequent failure of the Peruvian Congress to ratify the agreement had only added weight to the earlier impatience with Peru.

Mr. Chavez left saying that he felt he had a clear understanding of the conditions attaching to Eximbank credits to Peru. (Incidentally, Mr. August Maffry, during the course of an NAC Staff Committee meeting yesterday afternoon, observed that the National Advisory Council might have occasion to reconsider shortly this government's bond-default policy in light of a possible Peruvian application for credit.)

N. T. N[ESS]

823.51/2–447 : Telegram

The Ambassador in Peru (Cooper) to the Secretary of State

SECRET LIMA, February 4, 1947—6 p. m.

110. Foreign Minister [8] noon today, after advising that Peru had failed through Chavez of Peruvian Embassy at Washington to secure Export-Import Bank loan, again appealed to me to help Peru get a loan before Peru did anything about settling old debt. Foreign Minister stated Bustamante Govt might fall unless loan was immediately forthcoming from the US. He likened Peru to a drowning man asking for immediate help. I pointed out to the Foreign Minister that United States had high regard for Bustamante Govt and that on Dec 11, 1946, I had informed President Bustamante that no loan would be forthcoming until satisfactory settlement of debt (Embtel 1251 Dec 12 [9]) and that apparently no effort had been made to arrange satisfactory settlement from that time to date and that if Peru was in earnest

---

[8] Enrique García Sayán.
[9] *Foreign Relations*, 1946, vol. XI, p. 1258.

about settling the debt a measure might be passed through the Peruvian Senate with great expedition provided the President took the leadership in sponsoring satisfactory debt settlement. Foreign Minister did not deny this and stated that he hoped I would see the Minister of Finance Echecopar. When Minister of Finance was contacted this afternoon, he stated that he was at this time not ready to take up discussion of debt settlement on account of having to advise with various sources but that in possibly a few days time he would have a proposition formulated.

COOPER

823.51/2-2147

Memorandum of Telephone Conversation, by Mr. James H. Wright, Special Assistant to the Assistant Secretary of State for American Republic Affairs

[WASHINGTON,] February 21, 1947.

Participants: Ambassador Prentice Cooper, American Embassy, Lima
Assistant Secretary Spruille Braden
Mr. James H. Wright

Ambassador Cooper telephoned Mr. Braden this morning to refer to his telegram no. 143 [10] in respect of the Peruvian unilateral offer looking to the resumption of partial service on its defaulted dollar bonds. The Ambassador stated that he wanted to get our reaction as quickly as possible, owing to the fact that Congress would go out of session on February 28. Mr. Braden said that the offer was such a poor one that there was nothing we could do about it and that we did not want to give the Peruvians any encouragement that the offer might be acceptable to the Foreign Bondholders Protective Council, Inc., who would have to be the judge. The low rate of payment was striking and particularly with interest of only ½ per cent, the remainder being dedicated to amortization to buy the bonds on the open market at distressed values. Ambassador Cooper said that was the best the Peruvians could do. Mr. Braden replied that they could do better and everyone knew they could do better, what with a military budget of 45 per cent of the total early outlay. Ambassador Cooper said that he too realized they could do better. Mr. Braden said that we wanted to do everything we possibly could to help Peru and particularly to help the incoming administration, but this was something we could not do anything on. The best thing the Ambassador could do was simply to

---

[10] Dated February 19, 1947, not printed.

state our view that the present offer was too low and then rest our case without further to-do.

823.51/2–2447

Memorandum of Telephone Conversation, by Mr. Alexander Schnee of the Division of North and West Coast Affairs

CONFIDENTIAL [WASHINGTON,] February 24, 1947.

Participants: Ambassador Cooper, American Embassy, Lima, Peru
Mr. Livesey—OFD
Mr. Schnee—NWC

Early this afternoon Ambassador Cooper called Under Secretary Clayton [11] to report terms of a debt settlement which the present Peruvian Administration has under consideration. As Mr. Clayton was not clear as to whether the terms of settlement referred to interest only or interest and amortization, he requested that a call be put through to Ambassador Cooper to clarify this question.

The Ambassador informed me that the terms of settlement were as follows:

	Interest	*Amortization*
1947	1%	1%
1948	1–1/4%	1%
1949	1–1/2%	1%
1950	1–3/4%	1%
1951 and thereafter	2%	1%

The Government would buy in the bonds at the market value or at par if they reached that figure.

The Ambassador stated that the Peruvian Government understands that it will not receive a loan from this Government as a *quid pro quo* for the debt settlement, but that the Government is endeavoring to bring about a settlement of the debt because it recognizes the necessity of restoring its credit position. The Ambassador expressed the opinion that the Council should accept this offer which is superior to the offer reported in the Embassy's Telegram 143 of February 19,[12] and, according to the Ambassador, is in some respects better than the Montero Bernales' offer. The Ambassador thought the Council should bear in mind the fact that the bondholders had received no service at all for seventeen years. The Ambassador believes the present Finance Minister is very competent and considers it important that this matter be settled before the adjournment of the Peruvian Congress on February 28.

---

[11] William L. Clayton, Under Secretary of State for Economic Affairs.
[12] Not printed.

Several times during the conversation I pointed out to the Ambassador the fact that the Department could only transmit the terms suggested by the Peruvian Government to the Council which alone could accept or refuse an offer by the Peruvian Government.

823.51/2–2447 : Telegram

The Secretary of State to the Embassy in Peru

SECRET   WASHINGTON, February 24, 1947—7 p. m.

90. Reur telephone conversation Under Secretary this date [13] Dept endeavoring communicate to Council substance Peruvian Govt's proposed settlement together with your comments. Dept will communicate with Emb by phone when Council's reaction ascertained.

Dept hopes President Peru understands that even favorable action by Bondholders Council on any proposal for debt settlement would not carry assurance that any loan or credit will necessarily follow. With expiration of credit on books of Eximbank on Dec 31, 1946 (subject of conversations between Commercial Counselor of Peruvian Emb and Dept and Eximbank in December and also referred to in Art VII of draft credit agreement [14] forwarded with letter of Dec 11, 1945 to Montero Bernales from Taylor, then Pres Eximbank) there no longer exists commitment on part present statutory lending authorities this Govt. They would have to consider afresh any credit request from Peruvian Govt.

Dept finds no evidence Pres fully understands this and it is anxious avoid any possibility embarrassment to either US Govt or Pres that might originate in misunderstanding these facts. Dept would therefore request that at earliest possible opportunity you approach Pres and restate situation. Please telegraph when this done.

MARSHALL

823.51/2–2547

Memorandum of Telephone Conversation, by the Chief of the Division of North and West Coast Affairs (Wells)

[WASHINGTON,] February 25, 1947.

I telephoned the Ambassador [15] a summary of the Bondholders' Council's comments and counter offer to the Peruvian proposal which

---

[13] See *supra*.
[14] Not printed.
[15] The Ambassador in Peru.

the Ambassador telephoned to the Under Secretary yesterday. The terms compare as follows:

PERUVIAN OFFER			COUNCIL'S COUNTER OFFER	
Interest	*Amortization*		*Interest*	*Amortization*
1%	1%	1947	1%	½%
1-¼%	1%	1948		½%
1-½%	1%	1949	increasing	½%
1-¾%	1%	1950		½%
2% and			to	
thereafter	1%	1951		½%
		1952	3% and	
			thereafter	½%

I added that a telegram is already on the wires and suggested that he await its receipt before communicating the Council's counterproposal to the Peruvian Government.

The Ambassador at considerable length reviewed his arguments for acceptance of the Peruvian proposal. He appeared to feel strongly that the Peruvian offer represents the maximum, especially since there is only a hope for future credits even should the offer be accepted by the Bondholders' Council, and that it is extremely doubtful whether another proposal would have any chance of approval by Congress this session. Therefore, for these reasons (and while realizing the Embassy is only an intermediary) he asked whether he should, in transmitting the Bondholders' counterproposal, encourage the Peruvian Government to push its own offer through Congress and take chances on its being ultimately accepted by the Council. I replied, "No, I wouldn't do that", and suggested that he merely transmit the Council's counterproposal and ascertain the reaction. He agreed.

823.51/2–2547

Memorandum of Telephone Conversation, by Mr. Alexander Schnee of the Division of North and West Coast Affairs

[WASHINGTON,] February 25, 1947.

Participants: Ambassador Cooper, Lima, Peru
Mr. Wells—NWC
Mr. Schnee—NWC

Ambassador Cooper called at 5:45 to report that he had been informed by the Finance Minister that the maximum terms which Peru could offer in an effort to reach a debt settlement would provide for annuities totalling 3%. Peru would be willing to maintain amortization at ½%, thereby leaving 2-½% for interest. The Finance Minister said that, although he personally might be willing to increase the annuities to 3–½% in order to meet the Council's offer of 3% interest and ½% amortization, he was convinced that the Senate would not approve a debt settlement providing for annuities in excess of 3%. On the basis of personal conversations with some of the leading Senators, the Ambassador agrees with the Finance Minister that the extra half per cent could not be forced through the Senate.

The Ambassador commented to the effect that he thought the Council would make a mistake if it rejected this latest offer. Although he has not supported any proposal other than that advocated by the Council, after a long period of negotiations he is now convinced that the current Peruvian proposal should be accepted.

With reference to the Department's Telegram 90 of February 24, the Ambassador has been assured by the Finance Minister that the President fully understands that any settlement of the external dollar debt does not carry any assurance whatsoever that a loan or credit will necessarily follow. While he does not consider that it will help the negotiations, the Ambassador will, as instructed, see the President tomorrow (February 26) and inform him of the substance of the telegram.

Mr. Wells said he thought the Ambassador had handled this matter very well and that it now appears that there is nothing more we could do at this time.

823.51/2–2547 : Telegram

The Secretary of State to the Embassy in Peru

SECRET   US URGENT   WASHINGTON, February 26, 1947—noon.

95. Council rejects 2–½% top interest rate proposal ur 158 Feb 25.[16] Question thoroughly canvassed recently. Rogers [17] sure Council members if polled would vote unanimously against it.

MARSHALL

823.51 Bondholders/2–2547 : Telegram

The Secretary of State to the Embassy in Peru

RESTRICTED   WASHINGTON, February 26, 1947—noon.

96. Supplementing suggestion paragraph 3 Deptel 93 Feb 25 [16] Rogers has telegraphed:

"Council will expect Peruvian legislation establishing these terms will contain provision that original contract rights will be restored

---

[16] Not printed.
[17] James Grafton Rogers, President of the Foreign Bondholders Protective Council.

if any failure occurs in prompt payment of interest and amortization as scheduled in new plan; also that if any more favorable terms are granted by Peru hereafter to any other holders of foreign national or guaranteed debt now existing, Peru will extend proportionately equal treatment to dollar bonds of nation and Callao. These provisions become important as extended step-up period increases risk and sterling bonds are not now included in settlement. We assume new legislation will repeat reference to Lima dollar bonds as contained in project of law of Dec 31, 1945 second paragraph of first article. Rogers"

Proposal assumes retention all Montero bill terms it does not necessarily alter.

MARSHALL

823.51/2–2747

Memorandum by the Director of the Office of American Republic Affairs (Briggs) to the Assistant Secretary of State for Economic Affairs (Thorp)

CONFIDENTIAL [WASHINGTON,] February 27, 1947.

The Administration of President Bustamante is engaged in a desperate effort to maintain civil liberties and to avoid seizure of the Government by radical elements of the Left or the Right. Should President Bustamante fail in this effort, there would be a distinct possibility of a bloody and costly civil war with marked repercussions throughout the hemisphere.

A critical lack of dollar exchange has given rise to a basic economic problem which, if unsolved, will sharply reduce the President's chances of creating stable political conditions.

Peru requires a long-term federal credit of at least $20,000,000 to create greater economic stability. There is presently under consideration in the Treasury a Peruvian request for a $20,000,000 stabilization loan. There is doubt in many quarters of the Department that short-term loans such as Treasury is authorized to extend will be sufficient to permit a solution of the problem. Development loans through the Eximbank or the International Bank would also be insufficient to meet the immediate problem in that results would not accrue for several years. The most hopeful possibility that occurs to me is that the World Bank is authorized to grant long-term stabilization credits.

As it is a matter of major interest to this Government to provide President Bustamante with such economic assistance as will strengthen his hand in the present crisis, it would be appreciated if you would endeavor to find some way in which assistance might be extended. Specifically, I would like to suggest three steps:

(1) To request the NAC to make a determination as to whether the American representative on the World Bank would be authorized to approve a long-term stabilization credit to Peru of between $20,000,000 and $30,000,000.

(2) To request a prompt determination from the Treasury with respect to the pending Peruvian request.

(3) The Department should use its good offices with a view to persuading the Foreign Bondholders Council to issue a moderate rather than harsh statement to the bondholders if the Peruvian Congress approves a unilateral settlement which is close to the most recent suggestion by the Finance Minister, i.e., annuities after six years of 2–1/2% interest and 1/2% amortization.

ELLIS O. BRIGGS

823.51/3–1347

The Secretary of State to the Embassy in Peru

No. 918　　　　　　　　　　　　　WASHINGTON, March 14, 1947.

The Acting Secretary of State transmits the text of the statement on the Peruvian debt legislation of February 28, 1947 released by the Foreign Bondholders Protective Council for publication in morning papers March 12, 1947. The Department understands that it was unanimously approved by the Council members and that there is some disposition among them to issue a stronger statement if Peru comes out with the plan authorized by the legislation.

"Foreign Bondholders Protective Council, Inc. sends herewith for your information the text (in translation) of legislation, passed February 28, 1947 by both houses of the Peruvian Congress, empowering the Executive authority of Peru to resume service on the Dollar bonds of the 7% and 6% issues of Peru, and on the 7–1/2% issue of Callao, under a plan which would call for (1) cancelling all interest arrears earned until December 31, 1946 (or for more than 16 years), and (2) depositing funds in the Central Reserve Bank of Peru for its opportune conversion into dollars for annual interest at 1% for 1947 and 1948, 1–½% for 1949 and 1950, 2% for 1951 and 1952, and 2–1/2% for 1953 and thereafter, and for annual accumulative amortization at 1/2%. The legislation empowers also the Provincial Council of the City of Lima to resume service on its foreign debt in the manner that it may deem convenient.

"The Council calls attention to the fact that no formal offer has been made to the bondholders under this legislation.

"If the Government of Peru undertakes to resume service of its dollar bonds on the basis of the legislation of February 28, 1947, the

Council will not recommend to the holders of the dollar bonds acceptance of the plan proposed. Peru, in our judgment, can and should resume service on terms considerably nearer a recognition of its contract obligations.

"The Council's principal objections to the legislation may be summarized briefly as follows:

"(a) The ultimate interest rate (2–1/2%) reached in the seventh year) is below standard. The Council has not considered so low a rate adequate in the case of any other country attempting to rehabilitate its credit after a default.

"(b) The cancellation of all interest arrears, covering service earned and due for approximately sixteen years is a departure from the principles required for a reasonable debt adjustment.

"(c) The legislation is not clearly an obligation to pay service promptly in dollars but contains (in Section III) an ambiguity or implication that Peruvian soles deposited for service may be converted into dollars only when considered opportune.

"(d) The legislation does not purport to authorize an offer, subject to acceptance by bondholders (as is customary and necessary in bond adjustments) but to be a unilateral change made by Peru in its contracts with all bondholders, with or without their consent.

"(e) The service obligation assumed is disproportionately low. Peru faces just now an acute shortage of foreign exchange, but according to the best figures available to the Council, the money called for in the year 1947 is less than 1% of the current Peruvian national budget and only about 1% of the value of Peruvian world exports last year.

"The Council refused to acquiesce in the service rates set forth in this legislation when informed of them before the law was enacted and the Peruvian Government was so advised. The Council now reiterates its position for the public information. It thanks the American Government for its good offices through many years given to the Council in its effort to arrive at a debt settlement with Peru which the Council could recommend, and hopes that Peru may later come to face its debt problem more nearly in the light of its contractual obligations and its own best interests.

[Here follows the text, in translation, of the Peruvian law of February 28, 1947.]

823.51/5–2247

The Chargé in Peru (Ackerman) to the Secretary of State

CONFIDENTIAL   LIMA, May 22, 1947.
No. 1624

SIR: I have the honor to report that during the course of a rather lengthy conversation with the Minister of Foreign Affairs when making my first official call on Monday, May 19, he expressed keen disappointment that the American Foreign Bondholders Council had reacted unfavorably to the legislation enacted by the Peruvian Government for the resumption of interest payments on the dollar level. He is still hopeful that the Peruvian representative in the United States will be able to convince Mr. Rogers and his associates that the payments set forth under the Peruvian legislation represent the maximum sacrifice which Peru can make and that this evidence of intention to resume services on the debt will be interpreted as a sincere desire of the present administration to solve a problem which it inherited. Should the Council continue its objections, the Minister stated, the Peruvian Government is determined to approach Bondholders direct. This decision has been reached after consultation with the New York law firm of Sullivan & Cromwell. It is the understanding of the Minister that the Central Hanover National Bank has signified its willingness to act as the agent of the Peruvian Government for making payments against the bonds.

The Minister also referred to the discussions being held in Washington concerning a $20,000,000 stabilization loan. All of the data requested by the Treasury Department have been supplied except as pertains to Government budgets for the next several years.

As the Congress has the final word concerning appropriations and as, obviously, future developments cannot be foreseen with accuracy, the only data which could be supplied in answer to questions on future budgets had to be of a general instead of a specific nature. The Minister expressed the hope that the information supplied and that which Ambassador Cooper can give concerning the existing situation and the basic soundness of Peruvian economy will induce the Treasury Department to take early favorable action on the pending application. Unless Peru can obtain support for the sol it will be extremely difficult to arrest present inflation, to maintain the present economy or to provide for an expansion to meet growing needs. If this is not done the Minister fears the present social unrest will reach dangerous proportions. Although aware that stabilization loans are usually short term credit operations, he side-stepped an answer to my question as to whether Peru would be able to repay such loan at the end of 12 or 24 months.

The Minister expressed his sincere appreciation for the favorable comments made by Ambassador Cooper to the press concerning the Peruvian situation and stated that he had telegraphed to the Ambassador personally thanking him for his kind words.

Respectfully yours,

RALPH H. ACKERMAN

823.51/6-1847

Memorandum by the Chief of the Division of North and West Coast Affairs (Wells)[19]

RESTRICTED [WASHINGTON,] June 18, 1947.

Rogers telephoned Livesey this morning to report that Ambassador Cooper's presentation of the Peruvian case did not favorably impress the Council; and that the Council instructed Rogers to issue a firm statement denouncing the offer should the Peruvians proceed on a unilateral basis.

The Peruvian representative, Barreda,[20] will receive the same news when he calls at Mr. Rogers' office this morning.

MILTON K. WELLS

823.51/6-1347 : Telegram

The Secretary of State to the Embassy in Peru

CONFIDENTIAL WASHINGTON, July 1, 1947—11 a. m.

340. From Treasury. Re your A-391 June 13.[21] In view limited resources and specialized objectives of United States Stabilization Fund Treasury has decided it would not be appropriate under present circumstances to conclude Stabilization Agreement with Peru. Ambassador Prado[22] so advised June 27. [Treasury.]

MARSHALL

711.23/7-847

Memorandum of Conversation, by Mr. James Espy of the Division of North and West Coast Affairs

CONFIDENTIAL [WASHINGTON,] July 8, 1947.

Participants: Peruvian Foreign Minister, Dr. Enrique Garcia Sayán
Peruvian Ambassador, Don Jorge Prado
Assistant Secretary of State, Mr. Norman Armour
Mr. Wright, ARA
Mr. Cecil Lyon, RPA
Mr. Wells, NWC
Mr. Espy, NWC

The Foreign Minister opened the conversation with an expression of pleasure at being in this country and he stressed the long friendly and cooperative relations between Peru and the United States.

---

[19] Addressed to Messrs. Woodward and Briggs.
[20] Presumably José Barreda Moller, an official of the Peruvian Ministry of the Treasury.
[21] Not printed.
[22] Jorge Prado, Peruvian Ambassador to the United States.

The Minister then spoke of the internal affairs of Peru saying that they had reached politically and economically a stage of confusion and strain. He described the situation in the following effect: Politically, the Graña murder in January of this year brought into the open the conflict between the Aprista party and the conservative elements in the country. Antonio Graña was a leading conservative newspaper editor and the conservatives immediately assigned a political character to his murder endeavoring to implicate the Aprista party in the crime. The danger in the conflict is that one side or the other might endeavor to overthrow the democratic and liberal regime of President Bustamante and take over the government. Contrary to rumors that have been circulated the President has no intention on his part to assume arbitrary powers to meet this threat such as suspending the Peruvian Congress and is determined to follow democratic practices and to steer a middle of the road course. But the most important factor with which the President is faced in this problem is the economic stability of the country.

Dr. Garcia said that Peru is now confronted with serious economic difficulties which arise primarily from insufficient foreign exchange for the purchase of necessary commodities from abroad and that are needed for the welfare of the country. He cited as examples the fact that there had to be cancelled the construction of a paper mill, using sugar cane pulp, because the $300,000 foreign exchange could not be made available for the purpose. Another example he said was the cancellation of $100,000 worth of fertilizers required for Peruvian agriculture.

The Minister stated that to meet the situation Peru needs financial assistance from the United States. Dr. Garcia declared that he feared that if Peru was unable to obtain such assistance there might well be an economic and political upset in the country which would not only have serious effects in Peru but as well to the hemisphere. He explained this remark by saying that Peru is on the Pacific the counterpart of Brazil on the Atlantic and that they form, so to speak, a transverse axis through South America. Therefore due to this geographical and political position should Peru be shaken by internal disturbances this might well affect all the other American nations. He concluded by reiterating the hope that the United States could render assistance to his country.

The remarks of the Foreign Minister were followed by an emphatic statement by the Peruvian Ambassador. The Ambassador averred that his country had shown a warmer friendship toward and a longer record of close cooperation with the U.S. than any other nation of this hemisphere. He made particular reference to Peru's successful efforts to thwart an attempted plan, at the time of the Rio de Janeiro

Conference,[23] to create a division of American hemispheric solidarity. Despite this attitude of Peru toward the U.S. the door had been closed to it to obtain any financial assistance, the most recent example of which was the announcement of the Treasury Department [24] declining to grant a stabilization loan to Peru. He pointed out that in contrast to this position taken toward Peru, we had been granting financial assistance in large amounts to other countries, even to former enemy states. He said he felt that Peru was entitled to more consideration than this and should be accorded preferential treatment.

Mr. Wright [25] suggested to the Minister and the Ambassador that the question of these economic matters should be presented and discussed frankly at the meeting with Assistant Secretary Thorp on Wednesday at 3 p. m. July 9th.

. . . .

711.23/7–947

Memorandum of Conversation, by Mr. James Espy of the Division of North and West Coast Affairs

CONFIDENTIAL [WASHINGTON,] July 9, 1947.

Participants: Dr. Enrique García Sayán, Minister of Foreign Affairs, Peru
Señor Jorge Prado, Peruvian Ambassador to the U.S.
Señor Juan Chavez, former Peruvian Commercial Counselor
Señor Carlos Alzamora, Peruvian Commercial Counselor
Mr. Willard L. Thorp, Assistant Secretary
Mr. Norman T. Ness, Director OFD
Mr. James H. Wright, Acting Director, ARA
The Honorable Prentice Cooper, U.S. Ambassador to Peru
Mr. James Espy, NWC

A meeting was held this afternoon at 3:30 p. m. in Assistant Secretary Thorp's office for the purpose of discussing the economic and financial problems of Peru which the Foreign Minister had indicated he desired to take up with the Department.

The Minister presented briefly the present financial and economic

---

[23] The Third Meeting of the Foreign Ministers of the American Republics held at Rio de Janeiro, January 1942. For documentation, see *Foreign Relations*, 1942, vol. v, pp. 6 ff.
[24] *Supra*.
[25] James H. Wright, Acting Director, Office of American Republic Affairs.

situation in Peru stressing the current difficult foreign exchange position. In remedy he said Peru was in need of loans from the U.S. He explained that what would be particularly helpful would be dollar credits to help finance a number of industries in the country.

Mr. Thorp asked the Minister what projects the Peruvian Government had in mind. In reply the Minister said that he had not brought with him to the meeting all the material that had been prepared on the subject but that offhand he could mention such enterprises as irrigation, railroads, petroleum and coal. He then went on to say that the Banco Industrial of Peru had applications for loans aggregating an amount of some $30 million dollars which had been received from small enterprises in the country. He inquired whether an open credit could be granted by the Export-Import Bank to the Banco Industrial in approximately this amount for re-loaning, by the latter Institution, to the enterprises.

Mr. Ness informed the Minister there would be no possibility of such a credit from the Export-Import Bank for the reason that it was against the Bank's policy to make available such open credits. He explained that the Bank only made loans for specific projects.

The discussion then turned to the $30 million dollar line of credit which had been previously established for Peru by the Export-Import Bank but which the Peruvian Government had been informed could not be drawn upon until a satisfactory settlement had been made of the Peruvian Foreign Debt in this country. The Minister asked whether this credit which had lapsed as of December 31, 1946 could be reestablished and used by Peru. In reply he was informed that such was not feasible.

Mr. Thorp then said that the Department had consulted the Export-Import Bank during the past few days and that it had been decided that the Bank would now be prepared to give appropriate consideration, on their economic merits, to applications for loans made by the Peruvian Government. Mr. Thorp added that this was, of course, no assurance of the granting of loans by the Export-Import Bank to Peru but that, in effect, it lifted the previous ban and that Peru was to be considered as one of the countries whose loan applications could now be presented to the Bank. The Minister expressed his gratification on hearing this announcement.

The question then arose whether some sort of formal communication should be addressed to the Peruvian Government to this effect. It was suggested that possibly the Export-Import Bank could send a letter to the Peruvian Ambassador. Mr. Thorp and Mr. Ness expressed doubt as to the appropriateness of such action but it was agreed that the matter would be broached, later in the day, to Mr. Martin [26] of the Bank.

Ambassador Cooper then said that speaking on behalf of Peru he believed the question of timing was of great importance. He pointed out that the Peruvian Congress would meet on July 28th and that, naturally, the Peruvian Government would want to go before it with something concrete in the way of evidences of a financial character. This point was left with the understanding that the door had now opened for the application for credits by the Peruvian Government to the Export-Import Bank and that the next step would be for the Peruvian Government, if it so wished, to submit sound project applications.

Following the discussions on this subject, Mr. Thorp referred to the recent import restrictions imposed by the Peruvian Government and inquired whether the Peruvian Government proposed to initiate further restrictions. Mr. Thorp explained that this question did not imply criticism or representations in the matter but that we hoped, as provided by the United States-Peruvian Trade Agreement, consultations would first be held between the two Governments before any further restrictions would be placed on imports from the U.S. The Minister said that he could give no assurances that there would be no further restrictions but upon his return to Peru, he would immediately get in touch with the Ministers of Finance and National Economy and bring this to their attention.

. . . .

811.516 Export-Import Bank/10–1047 : Telegram

The Ambassador in Peru (Cooper) to the Secretary of State

CONFIDENTIAL LIMA, October 10, 1947—4 p. m.

733. Mr. August Maffry, Vice President Export-Import Bank, exploded bombshell in field Peruvian economic relations with US by stating in letter Peruvian Commercial Counselor Washington, September 23 that barrier that had existed since 1942 against Peru using Export-Import Bank credits still stood. Foreign Minister stated President and Cabinet greatly disturbed and discouraged in view all President Bustamante and Peruvian Congress had done to try to reconstruct Peru's credit standing this year, notably by passage Peruvian law last February 28 to resume service on Peru's external dollar debt despite Peru's extreme dollar shortage.

Foreign Minister said statement of Maffry directly contrary his

---

[26] William McChesney Martin, President of the Export-Import Bank.

understanding, obtained in Washington when Foreign Minister visited US, and mentioned specifically the conference he had with Assistant Secretary Thorp on July 8 in which Mr. Thorp stated that "the Department had consulted the Export-Import Bank during past few days and that it had been decided that the Bank would now be pleased to give appropriate consideration on their economic merits to applications for loans made by Peruvian Government". Mr. Thorp also stated that "in effect this lifted the previous ban and that Peru was to be considered one of the countries whose loan applications could now be presented to the bank".

Foreign Minister stated that talks with both President Truman and the Secretary of the Treasury [27] tended to confirm this understanding. He further said that President Bustamante's talk with Secretary Snyder in Lima last July 29 confirmed Peru's understanding that credit door was now open to Peru provided Peru could submit sound economic projects.

Foreign Minister and Finance Minister in recent talks with me have evidenced little short of alarm at Maffry's apparent reversal previously stated policy.

I was present with Foreign Minister in Washington at conference with President Truman and Assistant Secretary Thorp and Secretary Snyder and was present with President Bustamante when Peru's credit standing with US was under discussion with Secretary Snyder. My impression from these talks is contrary to the policy stated by Mr. Maffry in his letter of September 23, copy of which given me by Foreign Minister.

This Embassy would appreciate being informed as to whether Mr. Maffry's letter correctly states present US financial policy with Peru.

COOPER

823.51/10–1747

The Assistant Secretary of State for Economic Affairs (Thorp) to the Acting Chairman of the Export-Import Bank (Gaston)

WASHINGTON, October 17, 1947.

MY DEAR MR. GASTON: For the records of the Export-Import Bank I wish to confirm that on July 8, 1947, during his visit to Washington, I informed the Peruvian Foreign Minister that after consultation with the Export-Import Bank I was able to advise him that the Bank

---

[27] John W. Snyder.

would be prepared to give appropriate consideration on their economic merits to applications for loans which might be made by the Peruvian Government.

Sincerely yours,

WILLARD L. THORP

811.516 Export Import Bank/10–1347 : Telegram

The Acting Secretary of State to the Embassy in Peru

CONFIDENTIAL   WASHINGTON, October 30, 1947—5 p. m.

549. Urtels 733 Oct 10, 738 Oct 13.[28] Maffry Eximbank Oct 29 informed Peru Commercial Counselor by letter that "Board Directors has given new consideration to matter (reference Bank's letter Sep 23 [29]) and has reviewed with Dept conversations held with Formin in July regarding offer settlement made by Peru Govt to holders its defaulted obligations. Dept has informed Bank that these conversations removed obstacle which had heretofore stood in way consideration by Bank of Peru loan applications. Accordingly Bank is prepared consider proposals for financing projects in Peru on their individual merits".

You may inform Peru Govt.

LOVETT

CONFLICT BETWEEN PERUVIAN TRADE REGULATIONS AND THE UNITED STATES–PERU TRADE AGREEMENT

611.2331/1–3147

The Ambassador in Peru (Cooper) to the Secretary of State

RESTRICTED   LIMA, January 31, 1947.
No. 1098

SIR: I have the honor to refer to the Department's Instruction No. 797 of December 26, 1946, concerning the Embassy's despatch No. 416 of September 26, 1946,[30] and to previous correspondence on the subject of Peruvian contraventions of the Trade Agreement between the United States and Peru.[31]

. . . .

---

[28] Latter not printed.
[29] Letter from the Export-Import Bank to the Peruvian Commercial Counselor, referred to in the Ambassador's telegram 733, October 10, p. 1013.
[30] Neither printed.
[31] Of May 7, 1942, Department of State Executive Agreement Series No. 256.

Application of Most-Favored-Nation Duty Rates to Products of United States Origin

The Department will recall that, as last reported, Peruvian officials promised to instruct the Superintendent of Customhouses henceforth to apply automatically and unconditionally and without invocation by the importer or his agents all most-favored-nation duty rates to imported products of United States origin. Although this explicit undertaking was given in September of last year, it was not until after a further interview on this subject was had with the Director General of Hacienda [33] on November 14 that the Embassy received, per copy enclosed, letter No. 1962, dated November 15, 1946,[34] instructing the Superintendent of Customs to extend automatically and without invocation by the importer to goods of United States origin the duty rates specified in Schedule 1 of the Trade Treaty with the United States. This action, however, remedied the situation only in part, and on December 2 there was forwarded to the Director General of Finance and Commerce a communication from the Embassy calling his attention to this fact and requesting that amended instructions be issued to the end that United States products upon importation into Peru likewise be given the benefit of all preferential duty rates to which such products are entitled under the provisions of the most-favored-nation article (Article I) of the trade agreement. Accordingly, there was subsequently received under cover of letter dated December 26, 1946, a copy of letter No. 2160 from the Director General of Finance to the Superintendent of Customhouses amplifying previous instructions to include also the duty rates specified in Schedule I of the commercial treaty between Peru and the United Kingdom, dated October 6, 1936. A copy of this communication is likewise enclosed.[34]

In so far as the Embassy has been able to ascertain, the aforementioned trade treaty between Peru and Great Britain is the only extant treaty under which products of United States origin upon importation into Peru are entitled to preferential import duty rates other than those specified in the Trade Agreement between Peru and the United States. Preferential customs duties specified in existing commercial treaties between Peru and countries other than Great Britain are not applicable to similar products of United States origin by virtue of paragraph one of Article XIII of the Trade Agreement with the United States excepting from the application to United States products the advantages accorded to adjacent countries or by virtue of

---

[33] Ernesto Alayza G.
[34] Not printed.

customs union agreements. Therefore unless and until Peru promulgates additional trade treaties involving preferential duty rates to products from nonadjacent countries or other than in connection with customs union agreements, this important point in our bill of complaints appears to have been successfully negotiated.

Violations Arising From Taxes and Charges Authorized by Laws Antedating the Trade Agreement

. . . .

In view of the definite negative position previously assumed by the Peruvians as reported in the Embassy's despatch under reference,[35] no further discussions have taken place with reference to this group of taxes and charges as a whole pending receipt from the Department of appropriate legal references or other evidence as to the retroactive effect of the general provisions of the Trade Agreement. However, in several recent interviews with the Director General of Finance the question has been repeatedly but informally raised by an officer of the Embassy as to the propriety under Peruvian law of Supreme Decree of August 24, 1936, which administratively applies taxes on tobacco products of as much as 18 percent based upon Law 8433 which authorizes a tax of only two percent on those products. An officer of the Embassy was orally informed by the Director General on February 1, 1947 that the entire schedule of tobacco taxes is now under study with a view to a suitable revision thereof.

Following receipt of the Department's instruction under acknowledgement providing additional information concerning the retroactive aspects of the general provisions of the Trade Agreement, the Embassy's Note No. 360 dated February 6 on this subject has been forwarded to the Minister for Foreign Affairs,[36] per copy enclosed.[37] The Department will be opportunely informed with regard to developments in this connection.

In the meantime it may be mentioned that just prior to forwarding the Embassy's aforementioned note of February 6 an unofficial translation thereof was shown to the Director General of the Commercial office of the Ministry of Foreign Affairs, Sr. Vicente Cerro Cebrian, with a view to obtaining his unofficial observations on the subject in the light of the contents of that note. According to Sr. Cerro, his office and the Ministry of Finance and Commerce remain in complete agreement as to the nonretroactive effect of the general provisions of our trade agreement with Peru. Sr. Cerro undertook to explain his attitude by

---

[35] Despatch 344, September 11, 1946, not printed.
[36] Enrique García Sayán.
[37] *Infra.*

saying that any interpretations that might be given to substantially similar provisions in trade agreements between the United States and other countries in no way affected the meaning of the provisions of the particular agreement between the United States and Peru in so far as the latter country is concerned. Had retroactive application been intended, Sr. Cerro stated, explicit language to that effect would have been required.

Moreover, it has been Peru's understanding, Sr. Cerro continued, that a revised trade agreement between Peru and the United States is to be negotiated in the not distant future at which time all outstanding differences in views, such as that at hand, might be settled. Sr. Cerro was then informed that the Embassy is unaware of any current plans on the part of the Department to renegotiate our trade agreement with Peru. Sr. Cerro concluded with the opinion, which he carefully labelled as his own, that our Government would be completely unsuccessful in obtaining acceptance by Peru of the views expressed in the note under reference. Otherwise, he stated, there would be required a downward revision in Peru's revenue budget which would be most inconvenient at this time. The latter statement is believed significant in that it probably explains in large part the determined resistance by the Peruvians to any arguments that can be adduced in support of our Government's views on the point in question.

VIOLATIONS ARISING FROM TAXES AND CHARGES AUTHORIZED BY LAWS DATED SUBSEQUENT TO TREATY (EXCEPT PORT TAXES AND CHARGES)

Other than the instances of port taxes and charges (mentioned below) apparently only two laws are involved in discriminations arising from taxation undertaken subsequent to the signing of the Trade Agreement; namely, Law 10090 of December 22, 1944, and Law 10576 of May 16, 1946. The former provides a tax of ten centavos per package of imported tobacco (cigars, cigarettes, pipe or other) and five centavos per package of domestic cigarettes of certain brands only. It will be recalled that, as previously reported, the Peruvians claim that a change from the present specific tax to an *ad valorem* tax would involve serious administrative difficulties on the part of the Peruvian Government without improving the competitive position of United States tobacco products. Moreover, it is argued, this tax is not discriminatory in practice if there be taken into account the *ad valorem* equivalent of the present specific taxes collected. It was promised that the Embassy would be furnished with a written communication in substantiation of that contention.

After repeated conversations and reminders the Embassy finally received, under date of December 26, letter number 2166 from the Director General of Finance enclosing a memorandum on this subject, copies of both of which are enclosed.[38] It will be noted that in claiming non-discrimination on an *ad valorem* equivalent of the specific taxes applied the Peruvians do not refer to the fact that only a few brands of national manufacture are taxed at all under Law 10090. Their point of view on this, as orally expressed, is that the non-taxed brands of domestic cigarettes are a poor quality low-priced article and therefore, practically speaking, can not be considered as competitive with the United States product. Thus to insist upon rigid and exact compliance under those circumstances, the Peruvians insist, is to distort the real purposes and objectives of the Trade Agreement. The Embassy awaits the Department's further views and observations on this point.

With reference to Law 10576, there is enclosed a copy of letter number 2164 of December 26, 1946, from the Director General of Finance to the Manager of the *Caja de Depositos y Consignaciones*, the Government's tax-collecting agency, instructing that cigars of United States origin are to be considered exempt from the tax authorized by that law.

Port Taxes and Charges

In accordance with the Department's instructions under reference the Embassy will defer until later further discussions with the Peruvian authorities with regard to the port-tax matters. In the meantime the Embassy is investigating with a view to reporting to the Department whether these taxes are levied on domestic products of a nature similar to imported products and in a similar manner.

Respectfully yours, For the Ambassador:

Thomas S. Campen
Acting Commercial Attaché

611.2331/1–3147

The American Ambassador in Peru (Cooper) to the Peruvian Minister[39] *for Foreign Affairs (García Sayán)*

No. 360 Lima, February 6, 1947.

Excellency: I have the honor to address Your Excellency once again with reference to apparent contraventions of the Trade Agreement between the United States and Peru. Your Excellency will doubtless recall that this matter has been made the subject of several

---

[38] Not printed.
[39] Copy transmitted to the Department by the Ambassador in his despatch 1098, January 31, 1947, *supra*.

communications to Your Excellency's Government, the most recent being the Embassy's note of August 23, 1946,[40] in which the various points at issue have been mentioned in detail together with my Government's views and observations with respect thereto.

. . . .

I am informed, however, that in view of the circumstance that the above-mentioned laws antedate the signing of the Trade Agreement on May 7, 1942, they are considered by Your Excellency's Government to be unaffected by the general provisions of the treaty under reference. More specifically, in discussing this matter on September 21, 1946, the Director General of the Ministry of Finance and Commerce together with Sr. José Barreda Moller of that Ministry orally informed representatives of the Embassy that although desirous of reaching an understanding regarding the retroactive effect of the Trade Agreement the Ministry of Finance and Commerce considers it can not do so in the absence of legislative clarification of the meaning of that treaty with respect to Peruvian laws of a date prior to the signing of the trade agreement.

In the absence of a written confirmation of the above-mentioned orally expressed opinion of Your Excellency's Government on this important subject, I have informed my Government accordingly and I must now advise Your Excellency that my Government does not concur with those views. In this connection, I am instructed to invite Your Excellency's attention to the fact that the national treatment article appears in substantially the same form in trade agreements negotiated between the United States and seventeen other countries and that this is the only instance in which the opinion is expressed that this article does not apply to laws in effect prior to the signature of the trade agreement.

That the article is intended to cover such laws, and that it has been so understood by many countries, may be seen from the fact that in trade agreements between the United States and ten other countries exceptions have been made in the national treatment article for certain laws already in effect. The trade agreements containing exceptions of this nature are those with the following countries:

Argentina,	Article II
Brazil,	Article VII
Canada,	Article V
Colombia,	Article VIII
Haiti,	Article IV
Netherlands,	Article V
Sweden,	Article VI
United Kingdom,	Article III
Uruguay,	Article II
Venezuela,	Article V

---

[40] Not printed.

In the absence of the mention of specific exceptions, it appears clear that the wording of Article II of the Trade Agreement between the United States and Peru is intended to indicate that products imported into either country from the other shall be exempted for all discriminatory internal taxes regardless of whether or not such taxes were in effect at the time when the agreement was signed.

. . . . . .

It is suggested that if the general provisions of the trade agreement were to be considered applicable only to laws and regulations which come into effect after date of signature of the trade agreement, the result would be to continue in effect many of the very conditions which the agreement was intended to remedy. The national treatment article in trade agreements embodies a recognized principle, just as does the unconditional most-favored-nation provision, both of which are applicable from the effective date of agreement to all the commerce between the two signatory countries regardless of what the practice to the contrary may have been in the past. Hence, it is suggested that the above-cited discriminations in the form of taxes on tobacco products, toilet articles and beverages, which are higher on imports from the United States than on like national products and which were in effect when the trade agreement was signed, should have been removed just as any discrimination in favor of a third country should have been removed because of the unconditional most-favored-nation provision.

. . . .

My Government is of the opinion that this discrimination in favor of foreign countries other than the United States not only infringes the last phrase of Article II of the trade agreement but likewise constitutes a violation of the most-favored-nation provisions set forth in Article I. The wording of Article I indicates that these provisions apply to charges of any kind and with respect to all laws or regulations in connection with the importation, and to all laws or regulations affecting the sale, taxes or use of imported articles within the country. Furthermore, Article I clearly has retroactive effect since it states that "any advantage, favor, privilege or immunity which has been or hereafter may be granted by the United States of America or the Republic of Peru to any article originating in or destined for any third country shall be accorded immediately and unconditionally to the like article orginating in or destined for the Republic of Peru or the United States of America, respectively."

My Government considers that the foregoing comments apply equally in the case of differences in taxes and charges on toilet articles, tobacco, and beverages provided under the above-mentioned Laws numbered 5049, 7612 and 9507, as well as to such differential treatment in any other instances as may not yet have come to the attention of the Embassy and the Department of State.

My Government is most interested in and attaches importance to implementation of the reciprocal provisions of the Trade Agreement and in view of the long-standing nature of the above-mentioned taxes and charges so clearly appearing to contravene the terms of that Agreement, I am confident that Your Excellency's Government will wish to examine this matter at its earliest convenience and to take remedial measures considered appropriate. In order that I may fully inform my Government in the premises I would appreciate a reply from Your Excellency's Government as soon as circumstances permit.

I avail myself [etc.] PRENTICE COOPER

611.2331/1–3147

The Secretary of State to the Embassy in Peru

RESTRICTED WASHINGTON, March 5, 1947.
No. 903

The Secretary of State refers to the Embassy's despatch no. 1098, dated January 31, 1947, relating to the status of negotiations over contraventions by Peru of its trade agreement with the United States. For the Embassy's information and in accordance with its request, page four, paragraph three, of the despatch under reference, the Department's further views as regards the memorandum enclosed with letter no. 2166 of December 26, 1946 [41] received by the Embassy from the Director General of Finance, and supplementary oral remarks made by the Peruvian officials on this same point, are summarized below.

The fact that non-taxed brands of domestic cigarettes may be of poor quality and low in price is, in the Department's opinion, irrelevant to the question whether taxation of the United States tobacco products under Law 10090 of December 22, 1944 constitutes a contravention of the trade agreement between this country and Peru. The continued assessment of a ten-centavo tax per package of imported tobacco [including cigars, cigarettes, pipe, or other] [42] while domestic cigarettes of certain brands are subject to a lower tax of five centavos, or exempt from such tax entirely, clearly imposes an additional and

---

[41] Not printed.
[42] Brackets appear in the original.

discriminatory burden upon the imported product, in violation of Article II of the trade agreement.

The Department does not consider that this point of view is purely formal and cannot agree with Peruvian officials that insistence upon it distorts the real purposes and objectives of the trade agreement. These objectives are exactly the reduction or elimination of restrictions, discriminations and barriers to trade such as the tax in question. The Peruvian argument that this tax is not discriminatory in practice if the *ad valorem* equivalents of the present specific taxes collected are taken into account is unacceptable from the Department's point of view, even were these equivalents found to be roughly identical, since this accidental correspondence is a factor of the current price of the products compared; the provisions *per se* of Law 10090 are none the less unequal and discriminatory in fact. The discriminatory nature of the legislation is not altered by coincidence nor diminished by demonstration of its present effect in application, calculated upon the basis of formulae not provided by the language of the law itself.

It might also be noted that even in terms of its own premises the memorandum submitted by the Director General of Finance with his letter no. 2166 of December 26, 1946 could not be considered satisfactory. Not only, as the Embassy has pointed out, does the table enclosed exclude consideration of the many brands of national manufacture not subjected to the tax, but figures for foreign brands of cigarettes other than of United States origin imported into Peru are not included. The *ad valorem* equivalents in the case of many of these brands, as reported on page 4 of the Embassy's despatch no. 286 of September 17, 1945,[43] range considerably lower than for United States cigarettes.

The Embassy is authorized to make use of these views as it may consider appropriate in any further discussions with Peruvian officials in connection with the Embassy's note no. 360 of February 6, 1947 or the Ministry of Finance and Commerce memorandum submitted by the Director General of Finance under cover of his letter no. 2166 of December 26, 1946. If the attitude of the Peruvian authorities with regard to the violation of the trade agreement arising from taxes and charges authorized by laws antedating the agreement itself continues unchanged and adamant, it may be that final settlement of these questions will not be reached until such time as new trade-agreement negotiations with Peru are undertaken. It is not the Department's intent, however, that efforts to secure remedial action in the matters concerned should be relaxed, pending any such new negotiations.

In this connection, and with reference to the remarks of the Director

---

[43] Not printed.

General of the Commercial Office of the Ministry of Foreign Affairs, Sr. Cerro, the Embassy was correct in its statement that there exist no specific current plans on the Department's part to undertake such new negotiations. The major attention of the interdepartmental trade-agreements organization of this Government must at present be focused upon the multilateral trade-agreement negotiations [45] scheduled to begin at Geneva on April 10, 1947.

Following the conclusion of the Geneva meeting, however, it is contemplated that negotiations with other countries not members of the Preparatory Committee of the International Conference on Trade and Employment, including Peru, may be initiated. This Government's program for trade-agreement negotiations subsequent to the Geneva meetings will of course be integrated within the framework provided by the Charter of the proposed International Trade Organization. For the Embassy's information, there is enclosed a copy of a memorandum entitled *Procedures for the April 1947 Trade-Agreement Negotiations*,[46] which outlines, pp. 12–14, both the relation which will obtain between any general agreement on tariffs emergent from the Geneva negotiations and the proposed International Trade Organization, and alternative procedures by which additional tariff negotiations with countries not parties to such general agreement, including Peru, will be undertaken.

623.003/4–2547 : Telegram

The Acting Secretary of State to the Embassy in Peru

RESTRICTED   WASHINGTON, April 25, 1947—8 p. m.

203. Dept not yet received Embs report on specific proposals tariff project Embtel 303 Apr 18.[46] Nevertheless in view short time remaining prior to promulgation new tariff schedule Peru, Emb requested express to appropriate high officials Peru Gov Depts deep concern contemplated tariff increases as at variance with negotiations now being conducted Geneva at which major trading nations endeavoring elaborate concerted program to reduce or eliminate restrictive barriers trade all types including reductions tariff rates. Geneva Conference to be followed by fuller general conference of the nations in which Peru will undoubtedly wish participate in accordance common aspiration all American Republics expressed Article 51 *Final Act Inter-American Conference on Problems of War and Peace at Mexico City*

---

[45] For documentation on these negotiations, see volume I.
[46] Not printed.

1945 [47] "to find practical international formulae to reduce all barriers detrimental to trade between nations". Emb should express strong hope this Gov that tariff increases may be held in abeyance Peru Gov pending outcome Geneva trade conference. If placing increased schedule in effect unavoidable prior to general conference referred to above assurances desired this Gov that there will be no change dutiable status of those United States products for which tariff reductions or bindings were granted in 1942 trade agreement.

In event any upward revision however limited occurs this Gov strongly hopes reasonable notice new schedule and terms its operation will be given and that Peru Gov will grant adequate exemption for United States goods en route and for other hardship cases goods under contract such as products being especially prepared for Peruvian market.

ACHESON

611.2331/5-247

The Chargé in Peru (Ackerman) to the Secretary of State

RESTRICTED LIMA, May 2, 1947.
No. 1510

SIR: I have the honor to report the promulgation of Law No. 10880 dated April 1, 1947 (see clipping enclosed) [48] paragraphs (*a*), (*b*), (*c*) and (*d*) of Article I of which contain provision for taxation of imported commodities when consumed in the Province of Jauja at rates in excess of taxes applied to similar commodities of national origin. In the event the higher charges were to be applied to goods of United States manufacture, this would appear clearly to contravene Article II of our trade agreement with Peru.

This matter was discussed by the Commercial Attaché with the Minister of Finance [49] on April 25. It was the Minister's contention that although Law No. 10880 does not in itself contain provision for any exceptions in the application of the taxes under reference, the appropriate authorities of the Peruvian Government would naturally take into account any agreements or treaties having the effect of law and providing for exemption from internal charges at rates in excess of those applicable to national products.

Nevertheless, the Minister agreed that for the purpose of avoiding possible errors in the application of the law his Ministry would perceive no objection to the issuance at the Embassy's request of a letter

---

[47] Published by the Pan American Union, Washington, 1945.
[48] Not reprinted.
[49] Luis Echecopar Garcia.

to the appropriate Peruvian Government authorities calling to their attention the existence of Article II of the United States-Peruvian trade agreement. There is accordingly enclosed a copy of the Embassy's communication of April 29 [50] on this subject to the Minister of Finance. A copy of the Minister's reply, when received, will be forwarded promptly to the Department.

Respectfully yours, For the Chargé d'Affaires, a. i.
THOMAS S. CAMPEN
Commercial Attaché

623.003/5–1947

The Chargé in Peru (Ackerman) to the Secretary of State

RESTRICTED　　　　　　　　　　　　　　　　　　LIMA, May 19, 1947.
No. 1593

SIR: I have the honor to refer to the Department's telegram No. 203 of April 25, 1947, expressing our Government's deep concern at the promulgation by Perú of a new tariff schedule involving import duty rates substantially higher than heretofore and to enclose a copy of the Embassy's note No. 510 of May 6 on that subject to the Ministry for Foreign Affairs.[51]

In order to add emphasis to our Government's formal expressions in the premises the matter was promptly discussed informally and at length by the Commercial Attaché with Sr. Domingo Parra at the Customs Advisory Board and with the Minister of Finance, subsequent to which there was forwarded the Embassy's telegram No. 340 of May 7 (per copy enclosed). Although agreeing as to the desirability of a temporary postponement of the application of the new duty schedule the Minister is of the emphatic opinion that it is highly essential for financial reasons that such delay be limited to a brief period only since national revenues needed to balance the current budget otherwise would be adversely affected.

The Minister's attention was then invited to the omission in the new tariff of any mention of the preferential rates, specified in Schedule I of the trade agreement, to which American merchandise is entitled upon importation into Perú. It was recalled to the Minister that the Peruvian customs authorities had not always and uniformly applied minimum tariff rates in the absence of specific invocation of those benefits by the importer or his customs agent (see Embassy's despatch No. 1098 of January 31, 1947, reporting settlement of this difficulty). The suggestion was accordingly offered that appropriate reference in

---

[50] Not printed.
[51] Enclosures to this despatch not printed.

the new tariff to existing preferential rates, where applicable, would probably prove helpful in avoiding recurrences of similar difficulties as well as be of assistance to customs officials, local importers and the business public in general. The Minister requested that a written reminder be addressed to him in that connection and there is enclosed a copy of the Embassy's letter of May 8 to the Minister on that subject.

In the meantime the Lima Chamber of Commerce also requested that the application of the new tariff be deferred (clipping attached) and there shortly thereafter appeared in the public press the text of an Executive Decree (clipping attached) fixing June 15 as the date when the new tariff will go into effect. This development was reported in the Embassy's telegram No. 348 of May 10 (per copy enclosed), together with the substance of another conversation between the Commercial Attaché and the Minister of Finance upon occasion of the delivery of the Embassy's above-mentioned communication dated May 8.

In an interview on May 8 with the Director of the Department of Foreign Trade of the Ministry for Foreign Affairs, Sr. Vicente Cerro Cebrian, the Commercial Attaché again raised the question of the new tariff as being at variance with the objectives of the Geneva and subsequent general conference of the United Nations for the reduction or elimination of trade barriers of all types including tariff rates. The opportunity was not lost again to express the hope that the Peruvian Government would not take action which would serve to hinder the full participation by the Peruvian delegate in the proceedings of the general conference of United Nations on trade and employment scheduled to be held following the termination of the Geneva Conference. At his request Sr. Cerro was handed a Spanish translation of the "Suggested Charter for an International Trade Organization" (he had misplaced a similar copy previously furnished him by the Embassy) at which time the provisions of Chapter IV "General Commercial Policy" were brought to his attention. Although expressing a polite interest Sr. Cerro was obviously preoccupied with matters which he considered of more immediate urgency such as the prospective early exhaustion of Perú's wheat supplies (see the Embassy's telegram No. 346 of May 9 [52] and despatch No. 1578 of May 14 [53] entitled "Emergency Wheat Shipment for Peruvian Government") to which subject he reverted frequently with the fervent hope that our Government would effectively assist Perú in her hour of need.

A second conference was held on May 16 with officials of the Customs Advisory Board for the purpose of obtaining advance unofficial information as to which of the new tariff items—some of which have

---
[52] *Post*, p. 1036.
[53] Not printed.

been reworded and otherwise altered—are held by the Peruvians to correspond with the items specified in Schedule I of our trade agreement with Perú. Apparently as a result of the Embassy's request of May 8 to the Minister of Finance (see enclosure No. 3) the Board was then engaged in compiling that information and there is enclosed an item-by-item comparison based on such data as are currently available from the Board.[54] In order that our Government's observations and objections, if any, may be made known to the Peruvian authorities prior to the issuance of official dispositions on the subject (probably to be made not later than June 15), the Department may wish to examine the comparisons and appropriately instruct the Embassy at its earliest convenience.

Respectfully yours, For the Chargé d'Affaires a.i.
THOMAS S. CAMPEN
Commercial Attaché

102.81/6–2747 : Airgram

The Chargé in Peru (Ackerman) to the Secretary of State

LIMA, June 27, 1947.

A-422. Reference Embtels 465 June 26 and 466 June 27.[55] Based upon Supreme Decree of June 19, 1947 as first published on June 26 (see Embsgam A-420 of June 27 [56]) the National Council of Foreign Commerce (Consejo Nacional de Comercio Exterior) issued on June 26 new regulations, effective as of July 1, involving important modifications of existing import, export and foreign exchange controls. Text of communiqué in translation reads as follows:

"In accordance with the Supreme Decree of June 19, 1947, the Council has agreed today that as of July 1, 1947, foreign trade will be subject to the following regulations [57] :

. . . .

ACKERMAN

---

[54] The Chargé in his despatch 1727, June 23, 1947, indicated the receipt of a note from the Peruvian Foreign Office, but it was not responsive to the concern of the Embassy at the prospective tariff increases nor to the request that Peru defer the application of the new rates (623.003/6–2347).
[55] Neither printed.
[56] Not printed.
[57] These provided that official exchange would be granted only for essential foods, commodities needed by state and government corporations, merchandise given priority by the National Council of Foreign Commerce, payment of interest, dividends, etc., in foreign countries, and amortization of capital. Imports not in category A were to be made with unofficial exchange and did not require an import license. Imports of luxury items were, for the most part, suspended.
Applicants for official exchange were required to make a deposit returnable up to 60 days if importation was made or license issued therefor. Applications to cancel licenses were to be honored only for certain specified reasons.

623.116/12–2347

The American Ambassador in Peru (Cooper) to the Peruvian Minister of Finance and Commerce (Echecopar García) [58]

LIMA, September 4, 1947.

MY DEAR MR. MINISTER: As suggested by you I had the pleasure of attending on August 21 a conference with the Director General of Finance, Dr. José Barreda Moller, and the Administrator of the Tobacco Monopoly, Ing. Raymundo Quintana, concerning various Peruvian tax laws whose application appears to be contrary to the provisions of the trade agreement between Peru and the United States.

Opportunity was taken on that occasion to discuss with Dr. Barreda another matter, involving the provisions of the trade agreement, to which Your Excellency's attention is invited. I refer to the communiqué of June 26 [59] issued by the National Council of Foreign Trade under which there was established as of July 1, a list of articles which may not be imported into Peru. On that list are several commodities, classified under Items 2886, 2961, 2962 and 2963 of the new import tariff, which are included in Schedule I of the trade agreement and accordingly are subject to the provisions of Article X specifically providing for exemption from prohibition or restriction of imports except under certain conditions and then subject to prior written notification and opportunity for consultation. My Government did not, of course, receive prior notification of the action taken by the Council nor was there extended an opportunity for previous consultation with Your Excellency's Government on that subject.

The Embassy is informed that this matter was discussed during the recent visit to the United States of His Excellency the Minister for Foreign Affairs in the course of his interview with the Assistant Secretary of State, Mr. Willard Thorp. The Assistant Secretary was informed that the subject would be brought to the attention of Your Excellency.

My Government is fully aware of the circumstances and conditions giving rise to the above-mentioned action by the Council. In view of the provisions of the trade agreement, however, my Government considers that if any restriction must continue the establishment and administration of temporary quotas in accordance with Article III of the trade agreement is highly preferable to outright prohibition. I am therefore instructed to request Your Excellency's assurances that the present prohibition, insofar as it applies to commodities of United

---

[58] Copies of this communication and the answer thereto were transmitted to the Department by the Ambassador in his despatch 2242, December 23, 1947, not printed.

[59] See *supra*.

States origin specified in Schedule I of the trade agreement, will be of the shortest duration pending replacement by the quota system and establishment of the necessary administrative machinery.[60]

With assurances [etc.]

For the Ambassador:
THOMAS S. CAMPEN
Commercial Attaché

611.2331/12–2947

The Ambassador in Peru (Cooper) to the Secretary of State

[Extracts]

RESTRICTED
No. 2245

LIMA, December 29, 1947.

SIR: I have the honor to report that with reference to the Embassy's despatch 1835 of July 21, 1947,[61] in which there was submitted an interim report on negotiations re trade agreement violations by Peru, an official reply, per copy and translation enclosed,[61] has at long last been received to the Embassy's note 360 of February 6, 1947, on this subject.

While agreeing in principal with our Government's point of view that discriminatory tax laws although enacted prior to the date of the Trade Agreement nevertheless cannot under the terms of that Agreement be applied to articles imported from the United States, the Peruvian Government's reply is deficient in that (1) the remedy offered would be extended only to products included in Schedule I of the Agreement, and (2) in the case of the measure individually most burdensome (Supreme Decree of August 24, 1936, governing application of the tax on tobacco authorized by Law 8433) the remedy is made contingent upon future legislative action, the possibility of which now appears distinctly remote. Moreover, and contrary to repeated promises in this connection, the Embassy has not received copies of official communications or indications of any other nature confirming the Peruvian Government's statement in the subject note that "measures have been taken so that in the future products included in Annex I of the Agreement of May 7, 1942, will not be taxed differently than similar national products." Reference in paragraph six of the subject note to Laws 10576 and 10806 is altogether superfluous, matters relative thereto having long ago been settled satisfactorily

---

[60] In his reply of October 20, 1947, the Minister of Finance provided the assurances requested.
[61] Not printed.

(see Embassy's despatches 1098 of January 31 and 1727 of June 23, 1947).[62]

. . . .

In summary, the present status of the Embassy's representations on discriminatory taxation is as follows:

1—Peru has officially recognized the validity of our claims re applicability of the general provisions of the Trade Agreement to discriminatory taxation based on laws antedating the Agreement.

2—The Embassy has been promised and is now awaiting receipt of a supplementary note correcting the Peruvian Government's note of November 12, 1947, to include as susceptible to the limitations imposed by Article II of the Agreement all, instead of merely a portion, of the articles imported into Peru from the United States.

3—With respect to Laws 5049, 9507 and 10880, immediate corrective action has been promised.

4—Depending upon the Government's success in promulgating by edict a new 1948 budget, remedial action of a similar character has been promised in connection with Supreme Decree of August 24, 1936.

5—For the sake of convenience to the Peruvian Government, corrective measures affecting other taxation on tobacco products—i.e. Laws 7612 and 10090 as well as Supreme Decree of June 12, 1946—is postponed temporarily to permit action simultaneous with that relating to the decree of August 1936.

The Department will be opportunely informed in respect of future developments.

Respectfully yours,

For the Ambassador:
THOMAS S. CAMPEN
Commercial Attaché

EFFORTS OF THE UNITED STATES TO MEET PERUVIAN FOOD REQUIREMENTS [63]

102.78/1–1047

Memorandum by the Director of the Office of American Republic Affairs (Briggs) to the Director of the Office of International Trade Policy (Wilcox) [64]

RESTRICTED [WASHINGTON,] February 19, 1947.

On the basis of information exchanged between the Department of Agriculture and our Embassy in Lima, as contained in the Embassy's Airgram A–17 of January 10,[65] and Department's Telegram 14 of

---

[62] Neither printed.
[63] For documentation on the wheat crisis in 1946, see *Foreign Relations*, 1946, vol. XI, pp. 1265 ff.
[64] At the end of this memorandum appears the note: "Concur, J. H. W.[ilcox]"
[65] Not printed.

January 9, I am extremely reluctant to go along with the flat refusal incorporated in the Department's reply [66] to A-17 attached.

The minimum wheat requirements for Peru total about 8,000 tons per month. The Embassy reports arrivals expected in December and January totalling 33,000 tons, which should provide Peru with supplies through the early part of April.

The present unstable political situation in Peru requires that the United States, as a matter of self-interest, make every effort to provide Peru with assurances that their wheat requirements will be met by this country if imports from Argentina do not materialize. During the last year Argentina has repeatedly demonstrated its unwillingness to accept responsibility for supplying Peru's requirements. In the light of this experience, I do not believe this Government is warranted in relying upon Argentina to resume regular shipments to Peru this year, and I can not, in confidence, recommend to the Peruvian Government that it place full reliance upon Argentina as a source of supply.

The efforts of this Government to force Peru to take flour instead of wheat impress me as being contrary to general commercial policy, in that they favor American millers as against Peruvian millers, and as a violation of our repeated promises to sustain Peru's economy on a basis equal to our own. In addition, the disruption which is bound to take place in the Peruvian milling industry will have a very harmful effect on the Peruvian economy, which is presently in a precarious position, and upon the political situation which is of considerable concern to me at this time.

The price differential of roughly 22% is a matter of vital importance to Peru. As Argentina is not contemplating importing Peruvian coal until mid-1947, when it is reported they will not want more than 3,000 tons at a time, the price of Argentine wheat delivered in Peru may be expected to increase. It appears to me that a spread of 20% or over as between Argentine and United States wheat justifies Peru's request for assurances of future supplies. I suggest that so long as this price discrepancy exists, or until such time as Peru's economic position improves, the United States should consider Peru as a legitimate claimant upon our wheat supplies.

The constant refusal of the Department of Agriculture to recognize Peru as a claimant upon our wheat supplies has placed a heavy burden on those officers of my staff concerned with this problem, which confronts us anew every month, or at the most, every three months. More importantly, our past policy has encouraged political instability by keeping Peru in a constant state of uneasiness by withholding assurances that this Government will fill Peruvian wheat requirements.

---

[66] Not printed.

For reasons set forth above it appears to me that enlightened self-interest requires the United States to make available for shipment to Peru not later than the 15th of March one boat load of wheat, and that provisions be made for the shipment of minimum requirements during the second quarter of this year. In addition, it is important that Peru be given early and unqualified assurances that the United States is prepared to take such action.

ELLIS O. BRIGGS

623.3531/3-2247 : Telegram

The Ambassador in Peru (Cooper) to the Secretary of State

SECRET   US URGENT   LIMA, March 22, 1947—4 p. m.

231. Argentina is pressing Peru for quickest possible answer to Argentine commercial treaty proposal. Answer demanded today, but probably will not be given by Peru until Monday or possibly Tuesday. Terms demanded by Argentina appear contrary to some American interests in Peru, and indications are Peru would prefer to deal with US provided US in position to furnish fats and vegetable oils and some wheat to meet her comparatively small requirements. . . . Is possible proposed agreement may work against American interests since exportable supply of oil of International Petroleum Company, whose stock is more than two-thirds owned by American citizens, would be commandeered to extent of 300,000 tons per year by Peruvian Govt to service Argentine treaty requirements, resulting in destroying the framework of International Petroleum Company's present export commitments. . . . the actual terms which Peru will probably agree to, unless Peru is informed next Monday that she may look to US for same amounts of fats and vegetable oils, are as follows:

The following commodities would be furnished annually to Argentina for next five years in amounts shown:

100,000 tons anthracite; 400,000 tons petroleum; 30,000 tons sugar; 1,200 tons cotton; 30 tons rotenone; 1,000 tons rubber.

In return for above Argentina would agree to furnish Peru annually following commodities in amounts indicated:

130,000 tons wheat; 4,000 tons meat; 1,500 tons fats; 3,500 tons pork grease; 3,000 tons vegetable oils; 500 tons butter; 100 tons linseed oil; 300 tons cheese; 100 tons milk powder; 76 tons lambs' wool; 2,500 tons quebracho; 800 tons leather.

Understand so far no prices are specified or any of above articles by terms of agreement which stipulates 50% all freight to be carried in Argentine flag vessels.

It is urgent that I receive reply by telephone or otherwise by Monday whether Peru could look to US for assistance in meeting its requirements for fats, vegetable oils and wheat . . . I recommend that such assurance be given if practicable as being in best interests of US.

COOPER

611.2331/3–2547 : Telegram

The Acting Secretary of State to the Embassy in Peru

SECRET WASHINGTON, March 25, 1947—7 p. m.

152. Confirming Ambassador's conversation with Briggs, we cannot give Peruvians long-term commitment re wheat, fats or other short supply items mentioned for inclusion proposed Argentine-Peruvian agreement. You may inform Peruvians however, this Govt would naturally endeavor do its best in light of over-all situation to meet specific Peruvian requests from time to time. You will appreciate, however, Peruvian decision as to agreement with Arg is one for Peruvians alone and we do not wish to be in any position that might be misinterpreted as interfering with making of Peruvian decision.

For your info only (and not for communication to Peruvian Govt) Arg may have committed itself under various trade agreements to supply more wheat than may actually be available for export this year. In your discretion you may express on personal basis your assumption that Peruvians will naturally have investigated ability of Argentina to fulfill commitments re wheat.

ACHESON

623.3531/4–747 : Telegram

The Ambassador in Peru (Cooper) to the Secretary of State

SECRET LIMA, April 7, 1947—5 p. m.

263. Mytel 231, March 21 [*22*]. Foreign Minister informed me this morning Argentine wheat price to Peru "nearly double", apparently to stimulate Peruvian action on Argentine trade proposals still pending. On c.i.f. Callao basis present quotation 510 pesos equivalent US $149.50 per metric ton against approximately US$105 for American wheat. Under these conditions additional purchases Argentine wheat will further weaken Peru's exchange position and contribute to existing economic dislocation. Recommend re-examination US wheat position (urtel 152, March 25) with view offering shipments covering third quarter requirements of about 40,000 tons.

[COOPER]

623.3531/4-747 : Telegram

The Acting Secretary of State to the Embassy in Peru

SECRET   WASHINGTON, April 21, 1947—7 p. m.

193. Urtel 263 Apr 7. Agri officials verify that soft wheat could be bought on West Coast at cost including transportation $105 long ton but point out cost #2 hard wheat bought Kansas City would come to about $123. Relative cost to Peru of Arg and US wheat would presumably have to take into account matter of quality.

Position on question shipment wheat US to Peru has not changed from that communicated in Deptel 152 Mar 15 [*25*]. Third quarter allocations have also not yet been considered for any country and will not be developed until after recommendations have been developed with regard world distribution pattern in IEFC.

ACHESON.

102.81/4-2447 : Airgram

The Acting Secretary of State to the Embassy in Peru

WASHINGTON, April 24, 1947.

A-172. Following from Commerce: Reference your despatch no. 1324 March 17 [68] concerning possibility of Peruvian purchase of wheat from U.S. and export of anthracite coal to the U.S.

Inasmuch as Peru and U.S. taking part in International Wheat Conference, believe action regarding any long term arrangements should await outcome of this Conference. In negotiations, Peru has tentatively agreed to import 4,400,000 bushels wheat each year for 5-year period from exporting countries—U.S., Canada and Australia. Argentina has announced her unwillingness to join in agreement at this time. London conference still in session and will require approval of participating governments.

For your information, while this Government would not be directly involved in the import of coal, it seems unlikely that Peru would find satisfactory market west coast U.S. for anthracite type coal since it would have to compete with fuel oil and western produced coal. There may be possibility coking type coal such as produced in Oyon field might compete with or supplement coking coal from Utah for use in California steel industry. In either case, much sales research would be required. [Commerce.]

ACHESON

---

[68] Not printed.

611.2331/5-947 : Telegram

The Chargé in Peru (De Lambert) to the Secretary of State

SECRET   US URGENT   LIMA, May 9, 1947—4 p. m.

346. Reurtel 152 March 25 and subsequent communications. FonOff formally requests Dept's assistance in obtaining emergency allocation 15,000 tons wheat for earliest shipment plus monthly quota 12,000 tons through December. In view our Government's previously negative response to long term wheat commitment request Peru now negotiating with Argentina (mytel 341 May 7 [69]); but Peru Embassy, Buenos Aires, warns extreme difficulties to be encountered this direction, at least until availability new crop November/December. Present Peruvian stocks 6,500 tons wheat and 40,000 quintals flour to last with rationing 51 percent normal consumption Lima 24 percent provinces, until first week June only. Embassy strongly recommends appropriate assistance and requests telegraphic reply results.

DE LAMBERT

611.2331/5-947 : Telegram

The Secretary of State to the Embassy in Peru

SECRET   WASHINGTON, May 19, 1947—3 p. m.

247. Embs 346 May 9. In view stock position Peru, Dept Agri has told Peruvians they are now permitted buy 10,000 tons flour for as early shipment as can be arranged. Peruvian Emb says flour acceptable. Most other countries taking a far larger percent of imports in form of flour than is Peru.

US July export program just announced includes 8,500 tons wheat for Peru.

It is hoped that these emergency allocations will improve Peru's bargaining position in its current negotiations with Argentina.

MARSHALL

823.61311/6-2447

Memorandum by Mr. Edgar L. McGinnis of the Division of North and West Coast Affairs [70]

CONFIDENTIAL   [WASHINGTON,] June 24, 1947.

. . . .

On Thursday, June 19, I arranged for a meeting in Mr. Stillwell's [71] office for the purpose of affording Ambassador Cooper an opportunity

---

[69] Not printed.
[70] Addressed to Messrs. Espy and Wells of NWC, and to ARA and A–Br.
[71] James A. Stillwell, Adviser in the International Resources Division.

of expressing his views regarding the urgent wheat requirements of Peru. The meeting was attended by Mr. Epsy and myself—NWC, Messrs. Highby and Linville—IR, Mr. Craig—UE, and Mr. Andrews of the Department of Agriculture. Ambassador Cooper explained that he was anxious to present the overall situation in Peru as a background for its present difficult situation with respect to wheat. He stated that he had received the utmost cooperation from the present Administration in Peru and that it was extremely friendly to the United States. He stated that he was repeatedly called upon by the Department to request favors of Peru and had not yet been refused on any major issue. He specifically cited Peru's cooperation with us respecting an air transport agreement and her withdrawal . . . of an aviation mission sent to Argentina for the specific purpose of negotiating an air transport agreement. He cited other evidences of cooperation on the part of Peru including her military cooperation during the war. Ambassador Cooper asserted that Peru was a bulwark against communist infiltration in Latin America and that Peru's stand against communism was undoubtedly as strong as that of any country in South America.

Ambassador Cooper then referred to Peru's rich resources in petroleum, non-ferrous metals, sugar, cotton and other commodities. He spoke of the strenuous efforts of Argentina to conclude with Peru . . . arrangements with respect to petroleum, banking and other economic matters. He said that Peru had thus far resisted Argentine efforts . . . but that the latter had two things which Peru required, namely wheat and money. Ambassador Cooper said that through the withholding or reduction of wheat shipments to Peru, Argentina had already brought considerable pressure to bear upon Peru, and that they would undoubtedly continue to do so until they obtained the desired concessions from Peru.

Ambassador Cooper then stated that if this Government could promise Peru to furnish her wheat requirements from the U.S., this . . . severe pressure from Argentina could be obviated. He stated that he strongly felt the best interests of the U.S. required that we furnish Peru with a long-term commitment to supply its needs for wheat and that, in his opinion, wheat could well be diverted from less cooperative foreign countries for this purpose.

. . . . Mr. Linville stated that to make such a commitment to Peru would involve a change in basic policy in that this Government had never acceded to the demands of other countries for long-term commitments on wheat. He said that the world wheat situation was so tight that allocations were made only on a monthly basis and that this policy would have to be adhered to [to] enable the most equitable distribution of wheat supply. He cited the pressing demands of Europe and other areas. Mr. Linville said that Argentina was the historical supplier of wheat to Peru and that it was the policy of the IEFC to insist that those countries which ordinarily obtained their wheat supplies from Argentina should continue to do so in order to relieve the U.S. of the enormous obligation of supplying the major portion of the world wheat deficit. Mr. Linville also stated that, if a commitment were made to Peru to furnish wheat over an extended period, that country would relax its efforts to obtain wheat from Argentina since the price of Argentine wheat was greatly in excess of that of American grain. He asserted, however, that IR as well as IEFC would be willing to examine sympathetically the emergency wheat requirements of Peru, and in the event that Peru could not obtain her requirements from Argentina after exhausting all possibilities, the IEFC would be disposed to furnish emergency supplies. Mr. Linville said that during June, July and August this Government was committed to furnish 34,000 tons of wheat, or flour in wheat equivalent, to Peru, and that this amount formed a large part of Peru's annual import requirements (fixed by IEFC at 100,000 tons). Mr. Linville concluded by saying that since Peru was represented in the IEFC, her requests for wheat allocations should be made in the first instance through that body with the necessary supporting data.

Ambassador Cooper stated that he felt other countries . . . should be required to meet their wheat requirements by imports from Argentina and that Peru should be given assurances by this country that her needs would be filled here. This, he said, would relieve Peru of the . . . pressure exerted by Argentina and would not reduce the total availability of grain to needy areas.

Since the guarantee to Peru of wheat shipments from the U. S. over an extended period would entail a modification of our basic food policy, it appears that this matter must be resolved at high levels in the Department.

823.61311/6–947 : Airgram

The Secretary of State to the Embassy in Peru

RESTRICTED WASHINGTON, July 16, 1947.

A–286. Embs A–379, June 9, 1947.[72] The report communicated to the Embassy by the International Petroleum Co. that "the United States proposed to supply Peru with approximately 8,000 tons per month for the balance of the year" is unfounded and must rest upon some misunderstanding. US commitments do not extend beyond the periods covered by publicly announced export programs. At present this means not beyond August except in cases where allocations of

---

[72] Not printed.

flour have been announced for both August and September. The supply situation in all claimant countries and imports made and in prospect from other sources than the US are taken into account in the preliminary study leading up to the announcement of the export programs.

Embassy's recent reports (No. 7 of January 8, and No. 121 of June 12 [73]) indicate that Peru's commercial demand for wheat is increasing over the 150,000 tons hitherto regarded as a normal import requirement. The figure of 150,000 was used for Peru's stated requirement to IEFC in 1946–47 and the recommendation of the Cereals Committee after study of Peru's case was for shipments during that crop year to Peru from all sources of 100,000 tons. The reduction in imports recommended by IEFC was therefore 50,000 tons and represented an overall reduction in Peruvian consumption of wheat of about one-fifth. Against this figure known shipments July 1, 1946 to June 30, 1947 have, according to information here available, been about 120,000 tons inclusive of the recent emergency allocation of 10,000 tons of flour from the US. We note that Embs report No. 7 places imports during the calendar year 1946 at 112,745 metric tons. These figures indicate that Peru has, by reducing consumption of wheat, made a contribution to the alleviation of world shortages, roughly equivalent to what was recommended by IEFC.

Questionnaire replies of claimant countries to IEFC indicate total world import requirements for the crop year ending June 30, 1948 exceeding estimated world availability by over 50 percent. Under these circumstances it clearly will not yet be possible for countries dependent upon imports, of which Peru is one, to return to normal consumption and it is not probable that the IEFC Cereals Committee will be able to recommend a figure for total import for Peru in 1947–48 greatly different from that recommended for the crop year 1946–47. The Peruvian representative in that Committee will of course be given full opportunity to present Peru's case before the Committee and its Executive Committee. Any reduction in Peru's indigenous production of wheat or change of availability of other foods would of course be taken into account.

In view of the continuing critical shortage in cereals which keeps the supply situation this year on the same basis as a year ago, the request of the Peruvians for monthly quotas of 12,000 tons (Embs telegram 346, May 9 and despatch No. 1578, May 14 [74]) suggests that the Peruvian Government may assume that the world supply situation has improved. Since this is clearly not the case, the Embassy may

---

[73] Neither printed.
[74] Latter not printed.

wish, if circumstances in Peru make it advisable, to bring this aspect of the matter to the attention of the Peruvian Government so that its planning for the crop year 1947–48 as to level of consumption may be placed on as realistic a basis as possible.

MARSHALL

823.6584/7–2447 : Airgram

The Ambassador in Peru (Cooper) to the Secretary of State

CONFIDENTIAL LIMA, July 24, 1947.

A–490. Effective July 22, Peruvian Ministry of Agriculture lifted regulations on wheat which previously required 85% flour extraction and directed distribution under Ministry quotas for each locality. Simultaneously, Government subsidy is being withdrawn for wheat entering into white flour, whose price will be drastically higher than for whole wheat flour as latter will continue to receive subsidy. One mill is being directed, however, to devote its production solely to 85% flour extraction (estimated 12.5 per cent of total domestic output) and more will be added if warranted by demand.

Total wheat and flour supplies now in sight for July–December 1947 indicated approximately 60,000 tons. This includes (1) United States emergency allocation 10,000 long tons flour, wheat equivalent, June shipment, (2) United States allocations 17,000 long tons wheat, July–August shipment, (3) Argentine shipments 13,500 metric tons, in transit, (4) tentative Argentine commitments 20,000 to 25,000 metric tons, shipment next few months.

Embassy has brought to Minister's attention the fact that world supply situation has not improved (reference last paragraph Department's A–286, July 16) and that apparent liberalization of Peruvian controls might prejudice United States assistance in wheat supply. Minister indicated urgent need for further United States allocations to mitigate Argentine exploitation of Peru's deficit position, and explained that his present action was essential and not conducive to increased consumption, for the following reasons: (1) Ministry efforts to control flour distribution by localities had caused serious maladjustments, because of inadequate personnel and flexibility; (2) compulsory 85% extraction has proved inadvisable because of mill evasion, consumer resistance, and reduced millfeeds needed for dairy feed; (3) heavy subsidy on wheat imports must be abandoned and this can be accomplished by elimination first on white flour, with subsidy maintenance at least temporarily for whole wheat flour; (4) higher price for white flour is expected to restrict total consumption more effectively than previous controls; and (5) political factors, including strategy in reducing subsidies, raising prices, and freeing internal commerce, require this immediate step which can be reconsidered when the initial purpose has been accomplished (after Congress session beginning July 28 is well under way).

COOPER

623.3531/10-247 : Airgram

The Ambassador in Argentina (Bruce) to the Secretary of State

RESTRICTED BUENOS AIRES, October 2, 1947.

A-600. ReDeptel 903, September 25, 6 p. m.[75] Competent Peruvian officials made the following comment on the current negotiations in Buenos Aires of a Peruvian-Argentine commercial treaty:

A treaty will be signed for reasons of political expediency, but the document probably will not contribute a great deal toward strengthening trade relations. Mr. Miranda[76] inflexibly insists on pesos 60 per 100 kilos of wheat but will not accede to Peru's counter-argument that prices of Peruvian products for Argentina should be increased proportionately. However, even if Mr. Miranda should accede, Peru would not wish to adopt the Argentine system of taking a part of the profit which rightfully belongs to producers.

Mr. Miranda has made various offers of financial assistance. One was a credit of 50 million pesos for buying wheat at the 60-peso level. Other large credits were suggested for developing Peruvian coal mines and oil production, on condition that large amounts of these products be supplied to Argentina at world market quotations. The exact sums were not definitely stated but from the tenor of Mr. Miranda's conversations, either one could amount to 100 to 200 million pesos, or even more.

Peruvian policy at present is opposed to incurring further large-scale indebtedness, and Mr. Miranda's proposals probably will receive consideration only if necessary to obtain wheat. Peru will evidently have to take more of Mr. Miranda's 60-peso wheat, but only so long as it remains impossible to obtain this cereal at lower quotations in other markets.[77]

. . . .

BRUCE

---

[75] Not printed.
[76] Miguel Miranda, President of the Argentine Economic Council.
[77] In telegram 786, October 31, 1947, 6 p. m., not printed. Ambassador Cooper warned that Peru might be forced into an undesirable commercial agreement with Argentina if wheat or flour shipments were not obtained from the United States or Canada (823.6584/10-3147).

823.61311/11–1747 : Airgram

The Secretary of State to the Embassy in Peru

CONFIDENTIAL WASHINGTON, November 17, 1947.

A-429. ReEmbs 786, October 31.[78] The situation with regard to world export availability is no less grave now than when pictured in Department's A-286 of July 16. In fact, a great reduction of the wheat crop in Canada and of the corn crop in the United States have greatly worsened the situation. The Secretary General of the International Emergency Food Council in a report of October 27 stated that "cereal production in Europe falls below 1946 by the equivalent of about 75 grams of bread per person per day for the entire 1947–48 cereal year" and "imports of cereals (for the world as a whole) would need to be six or seven million tons larger than they actually were last year just to maintain last year's Spartan bread rations and restricted level of livestock feeding. Actually, export availabilities now appear to be no larger than last year's shipments. It is inevitable, therefore, that either bread rations or livestock feeding, or both, will have to be reduced in many countries."

Under these circumstances, it will be understood that there is greater need than ever for the United States to support low consumption levels in Europe, particularly in view of the European Recovery Program. The United States policy still pursued in allocations is not to make commitments beyond the monthly export programs announced publicly about five or six weeks in advance. Importing countries are urged to secure, if at all possible, the supplies allocated to them by IEFC from sources other than the United States, in spite of greater cost, so that needs can be met as fully as possible. The policy with regard to Peru remains as before, namely, that, for your confidential information, the United States is prepared within IEFC recommendations to assist with shipments to that country on an emergency basis if grain is not forthcoming from Argentina or other sources and supplies in Peru run low.

Weekly reports received from our Embassy in Buenos Aires based on manifests of ships departures show movement from Argentina for Peru of 52,687 tons of wheat in the four months July to October. From the United States in the period July–September 18,000 tons of wheat and 7,000 tons of flour were shipped. This constitutes a total of about 78,000 tons within four months. Since 14,200 tons were shipped from Argentina in June, Peru must have had some stockpile in July 1. On the basis of stocks and imports as reported in Embassy's report No.

---

[78] See footnote 77, p. 1041.

121 of June 12,[79] disappearance of imports in the period January to May 1947 is calculated at about 11,000 tons per month, as compared to 8,000 during the period of lowest consumption in the spring of 1946. Embassy's A-379 of June 9 [79] also refers to 11,000 tons a month as the minimum monthly import requirement. At this rate of consumption shipments to Peru the first four months of the present crop-year would cover seven months' consumption and stocks would become quite low by February 1948, if no further shipments were made in the meantime from Argentina.

MARSHALL

823.61311/11-1747

The Acting Secretary of State to the Peruvian Chargé (Fernández-Davila)

WASHINGTON, December 12, 1947.

SIR: I have received your note No. 5-3-M/242 dated November 17, 1947,[79] in which you point out that the high price of Argentine wheat and the obligation to furnish to that country large quantities of oil in exchange for grain shipments make it desirable for the Peruvian Government to suspend all wheat purchases from Argentina. It is observed that the Peruvian Government will suspend these wheat purchases if the Government of the United States can give assurances that it is able to supply 12,000 tons of wheat per month to Peru, which quantity, it is stated, represents the estimated minimum consumption needs of Peru for imported wheat.

While this Government appreciates the reasons which impel the Government of Peru to seek to obtain its wheat import requirements from the United States, it is regretted that the many demands upon the United States for shipments to low consumption areas and the limitations of United States export availability do not permit this Government to declare itself the main source for wheat for Peru. As a member of the International Emergency Food Council, in which Peru also has membership, the United States is guided by the recommendations concerning world grain distribution which are developed in that body. It is also the policy of the United States, dictated by the emergency world grain supply situation, not to make actual commitments for export of grain beyond announced allocations.

The demand now placed upon United States grain export availabilities is greater than ever before. In his report of October 27, 1947,

---

[79] Not printed.

the Secretary-General of the International Emergency Food Council stated that, because of reduced cereal production in Europe, world imports of cereals would have to be six or seven million tons greater than last year just to maintain last year's Spartan bread rations and a restricted level of livestock feeding for 1947–48. Under the circumstances it is imperative that all sources of wheat supply be utilized to the utmost. The International Emergency Food Council has consistently urged that those nations who have traditionally obtained their wheat requirements from non-member states such as Argentina continue to fill their needs in so far as possible through imports from those sources. Many of the nations of Europe as well as countries in the Western Hempisphere have been securing grain supplies from Argentina as indicated by International Emergency Food Council recommendations.

In the spirit of inter-American collaboration this Government has in the past shipped quantities of wheat and wheat flour to Peru to meet urgent needs not supplied from other sources. You may be assured that the United States will be pleased, within International Emergency Food Council recommendations, to assist on an emergency basis with shipments of wheat or flour to Peru if such supplies are not available from Argentina or other sources.

Accept [etc.]

For the Acting Secretary of State:
NORMAN ARMOUR

URUGUAY

THE POSITION OF THE UNITED STATES WITH RESPECT TO URUGUAY'S DEFENSE NEEDS AND THE LEND-LEASE ACCOUNT [1]

833.34/1–3047

The Ambassador in Uruguay (McGurk) to the Secretary of State

CONFIDENTIAL   MONTEVIDEO, January 30, 1947.
No. 228

SIR: With reference to the Embassy's despatch no. 178 of January 22, 1947, transmitting a memorandum [2] on military matériel pending delivery from the United States which the President-elect of Uruguay [3] handed to me, I have the honor to enclose a further memorandum [4] prepared by the Uruguayan Navy and entitled "Purchases in the United States" which the President-elect delivered to me.

It will be observed that the Uruguayan Navy states that it has available the sum of approximately $3,200,000 for purchases, and that it desires to acquire at least one destroyer, indicating that it would accept a used vessel in good general state which has been modernized, and that the destroyer could be of the types constructed in the years 1935–36. The Navy Department is fully aware of the long-standing desire of the Uruguayan Navy to acquire a vessel of the destroyer class.[5]

The President-elect in handing me the memorandum made no comment other than to say that it was one of the matters that he would wish to discuss during his stay in Washington [6] and that he presumed we should like to have the memorandum before his arrival.

Respectfully yours,   For the Ambassador:
EDWARD J. SPARKS
Counselor of Embassy

---

[1] For documentation on these subjects in 1946, see *Foreign Relations*, 1946, vol. XI, pp. 1270 ff.
[2] Neither printed.
[3] Tomás Berreta.
[4] Not printed.
[5] In his despatch 349, March 13, 1948, Ambassador Briggs indicated that the request for a destroyer was dropped in favor of four frigates (833.34/5–1348).
[6] In telegram 95, undated, received March 1, 1947, Ambassador McGurk noted that President Berreta in his inaugural address stressed that during his visit to the United States in February, 1947, he had requested, not financial aid, but machines and tools to increase production (833.001 Berreta, Tomás/3–147).

711.33/2–2547 : Telegram

The Secretary of State to the Embassy in Uruguay

[Extracts]

TOP SECRET   WASHINGTON, February 25, 1947—6 p. m.

71. Berreta's visit apparently highly successful in strengthening relations between new Govt and US and he and party deeply appreciative attentions throughout sojourn.

. . . .

Berreta in secret conversations expressed grave concern Uruguay-Argentine relations and fear of pressure which his Govt might be unable to resist. Our assurances of continuing solicitude for Uruguay's political independence and economic freedom of action gratefully received although President-elect has presentiment his country might be faced with a direct threat from Argentina if at some future crisis US attention sharply distracted from Plate Area.

MARSHALL

833.34/5–1747 : Telegram

The Chargé in Uruguay (Sparks) to the Secretary of State

CONFIDENTIAL   MONTEVIDEO, May 17, 1947—3 p. m.

217. Depgam 103, May 7.[7] Informally explored Uruguayan Navy requirements with Inspector General Uruguay Navy[8] but without revealing plans of US Navy to offer four ships for sale as surplus property at low price.

Uruguay will probably wish to acquire aircraft rescue vessel, motor launch and picketboat but retain subchaser only until replaced by destroyer. Inspector General claims subchaser does not meet Uruguay's requirements. He referred to two Paraguayan gunboats now lying off Carmelo declaring Uruguay has no unit strong enough to control them. He insisted on destroyer to permit naval and not merely maritime training.

President Berreta and Uruguayan Navy are obsessed with necessity of having destroyers (see my letters Ellis Briggs April 8 and May 7[9]). Financing of its purchase is partly based on credit which will accrue to Uruguayan Navy appropriation authorizations when subchaser returned. President May 14 again raised question of destroyer and I again outlined to him and later to Inspector General legal obstacles

---

[7] Not printed.
[8] Rear Adm. Juan Angel Battione.
[9] Neither printed.

to our transferring title at this time. Both understand our position but President stressed Uruguay must have destroyer promptly to bolster Navy morale and prestige.

SPARKS

733.35/12-1847

Memorandum of Conversation, by the Ambassador in Uruguay (Briggs) [10]

[Extracts]

SECRET   MONTEVIDEO, December 15, 1947.

At luncheon today at the Naval Air Station near Punta del Este I was seated next to President Batlle Berres and talked with him for something over an hour. The subjects discussed are as follows, and unless otherwise noted were introduced by the President:

. . . .

In these circumstances,[11] the President declared, he could not view without concern the increased military potential of Argentina. In the event of trouble between Argentina and Brazil, Uruguay would inevitably be involved: Uruguay has 7,000 kilometers of highway (soon to be increased to 10,000) and a modern telephone system. With these facilities and her protected harbors, Uruguay could hardly fail to be involved. Obviously Uruguay cannot aspire to match Argentine military strength, but the President said he had concluded—with great reluctance—that some form of compulsory military training must shortly be established here. But even with compulsory military service Uruguay cannot hope to have a formidable army. The President expressed the opinion that there would be little point in Uruguay's purchasing, for example, bombers or jet planes, but that he thought it should have a small competent air force and that in particular additional training planes should be made available.

. . . .

ELLIS O. BRIGGS

---

[10] Transmitted to the Department by the Ambassador in his despatch 2083, December 18, 1947, not printed.

[11] The "circumstances" were the dominant position of Argentina among her neighbors and the ties that united Argentina and Uruguay.

833.34/5–1747 : Telegram

The Acting Secretary of State to the Embassy in Uruguay

CONFIDENTIAL　　　　　　　　　　WASHINGTON, December 18, 1947.

A–263. Reference Department's airgram No. 852 of May 7, 1947,[12] and Embassy's airgram No. 217 of May 17, 1947.

For your information, Field Commissioner for Military Programs, OFLC, expects to offer to Uruguay, at an early date, the U.S. naval vessels leased to Uruguay under the Naval Lease Agreement negotiated during the war. Offer will be made in letter addressed by OFLC to Uruguayan Naval Attaché, Washington. Uruguay will not be charged for use of vessels, as contemplated in Article VI of the agreement. Although total cost of vessels to U.S. was $1,323,883, they will be offered to Uruguay at total price of $35,361. Since sale of ships individually would be unfeasible, price quoted presupposes all will be purchased and none returned to U.S. Uruguayan request for destroyer or destroyer escort cannot be made a part of negotiations for sale of these ships, in as much as there is no legislative authority for sale of destroyers or destroyer escorts, pending enactment by Congress of Inter-American Cooperation Bill or other necessary legislation.

　　　　　　　　　　　　　　　　　　　　　　　　　　　　LOVETT

733.35/12–1847

The Director of the Office of American Republic Affairs (Daniels) to the Ambassador in Uruguay (Briggs)

SECRET　　　　　　　　　　　　WASHINGTON, December 24, 1947.

DEAR ELLIS: I have just received your secret letter of December 18 enclosing a copy of your secret Despatch No. 2083 of December 18 [13] on the subject of your recent conversation with President Batlle Berres. I have read the attached memorandum of conversation [14] with great interest, and, in response to your inquiry as to what you should tell the President, suggest for your consideration the following informal comments:

1) URUGUAYAN-ARGENTINE RELATIONS

It is quite natural that Uruguay does not wish to be subjected to undue Argentine pressure. It seems clear that the present Argentine Government is seeking energetically to extend its economic and political influence in southern South America, as many previous Argentine Governments have attempted to do. It does not necessarily follow that the United States should put itself in the position of seeking to

---

[12] Not printed.
[13] Neither printed.
[14] Dated December 15, p. 1047.

block Argentine efforts to strengthen political and economic ties with its neighboring and nearby countries. Naturally, Uruguay can "continue to count on the United States" in any normal and fair interpretation of this phrase, and in view of the mutual confidence, traditional friendship and absence of major controversies between Uruguay and the United States, it would seem reasonable to anticipate a continuation and strengthening of friendly cooperation between the two countries during the years to come. As you have pointed out, our concept of the Inter-American System is one of a friendly association of independent and sovereign republics, all enjoying political and juridical equality. The creation of blocs within the Inter-American System, and the domination of some countries by others would, of course, be inconsistent with this concept.

It is not quite clear to me what steps, if any, President Batlle Berres thinks the United States might take with a view to cooperating with Uruguay in the latter country's desire "to have close and friendly relations with her southern neighbor, but on the basis of complete Uruguayan independence". If the President should make some specific suggestions along this line, we would be most interested in having them (at his initiative).

I am seriously disturbed at the President's statement that he has concluded that some form of compulsory military training must shortly be established in Uruguay. That puts Uruguay into the same category as the Dominican Republic, which is considering similar measures. Obviously Uruguay cannot hope to compete in military strength with either Argentina or Brazil, and speaking personally, I should think the wiser policy might be to hold down their military expenditures rather than increase them. It seems that you are quite correct in pointing out the relevance of the Rio treaty.[15] It has been my hope; perhaps overoptimistic, that one result of that treaty might be to relieve individual American republics of the fear of aggression from their neighbors, and permit an orderly transition from competitive armaments and their heavy economic burden to the concept of hemispheric defense on an efficient and more economical basis. In fact, I should say there would probably be less chance of Argentina (or Brazil) attacking an unarmed Uruguay than one attempting to arm itself.

With reference to General Crittenberger's visit to Argentina, in so far as I am informed, he made no commitments to Argentina on the occasion of his visit. At the same time, it must be realized that Argentina is included in the hemispheric defense scheme; is a relatively large and wealthy country; and will undoubtedly wish to standardize and modernize its military establishment. This will undoubtedly mean

---

[15] Of September 2, 1947; see Department of State, **Treaties** and other International Acts Series No. 1838.

forthcoming requests from Argentina for military equipment from the United States. As things now stand, these probable requests will be given consideration on the same basis as requests from other American Republics. I do not see why this should necessarily give Uruguay any just cause for concern.

Sincerely yours, PAUL C. DANIELS

833.24/1–1648

The Secretary of State to the Uruguayan Ambassador (Blanco)

CONFIDENTIAL WASHINGTON, January 16, 1948.

EXCELLENCY: I have the honor to transmit herewith two copies of Statement LL–14 and supporting schedules [16] reporting charges made against the Government of Uruguay during the period from April 1, 1947 to June 30, 1947, covering defense materials transferred in accordance with the terms of the Lend-Lease Agreement signed January 13, 1942 [17] by representatives of the Republic of Uruguay and the United States of America.

It will be noted that charges reported for the period under reference have resulted in a net credit of $8,250.75 and that the total charges to June 30, 1947 aggregate $5,183,798.80.

The following statement summarizing the status of the Uruguayan lend-lease account as of December 31, 1947 is based upon records of this Department and the United States Treasury Department:

Total payments		$7,800,000.00
Net charges under Lend-Lease Agreement through June 30, 1947	$2,378,326.89	
Funds transferred to cash lend-lease account through December 31, 1947	172,561.51	
Funds transferred to the account of the Foreign Liquidation Commissioner through December 31, 1947	938,158.11	
		3,489,046.51
Current balance due to the Government of Uruguay		$4,310,953.49

[16] Not printed.
[17] See bracketed note, *Foreign Relations*, 1942, vol. VI, p. 703.

The figure representing net charges is based upon Statement LL-14 and should not be necessarily considered final due to possible unreported retroactive charges by the United States procurement agencies.

Accounts for vessels leased under the Charter Party Agreements are not included in the foregoing figures and the settlement of the account covering such vessels is being treated apart from normal lend-lease operations.

It is requested that this statement of account and also the enclosed statement and supporting schedules, be treated by your Government on a most confidential basis.

Accept [etc.]

For the Secretary of State:
NORMAN ARMOUR

THE END OF THE CAMPAIGN AGAINST AXIS INFLUENCE IN URUGUAY [18]

740.34112A/6-2747 : Airgram

The Acting Secretary of State to the Embassy in Uruguay

SECRET WASHINGTON, October 27, 1947.

A-231. Please report to the Department whether the agenda of the Uruguayan Congress lists the subject of a bill for liquidation and replacement of Axis firms? Reference is made in this connection to your despatch No. 798 of June 27, 1947 [19] referring to a statement by Dr. Pratt de María that efforts would be made to obtain the necessary legislation.

The continuing active interest of this Government in this matter should be made known to the Uruguayan Government at the earliest appropriate opportunity in whatever manner you deem most effective. The Department now considers it advisable, however, to lower its sights to a replacement program covering only firms clearly representing important German and Japanese external assets in the hope that limitation of this program may in some measure aid in strengthening the hand of the Uruguayan administration in pushing for enactment of suitable legislation. With respect to such firms as Staudt, Quincke, Brehmer, Rabe and any others previously recommended to the Uruguayan Government for expropriation (or intervention) solely or principally on grounds of inimical activities, no further representations should be made by you or information proffered unless it is specifically requested by the Uruguayan Government. For your information in this regard, the last shadow of control by the Argentine Government over the principal office and

---

[18] For documentation on German penetration in 1946, see *Foreign Relations,* 1946, vol. XI, pp. 1276 ff.
[19] Not printed.

assets of the Staudt firms in Argentina has now been removed with the return to Ricardo Staudt of the 570 shares in Staudt y Ciá. owned by his German sisters. A copy of despatch No. 3032 of September 25, 1947 [20] from the Embassy at Buenos Aires reporting this development is being forwarded to you by the Department.

If the Uruguayan Government should inquire whether this Government is still interested in Staudt, Quincke *et al*, you should reply that this Government has not changed its view respecting these firms, but regards liquidation of branches and subsidiaries of firms in Germany and Japan of greater immediate importance. For your guidance in discussing this subject with the Uruguayan authorities, the Department believes that the following firms should be regarded by the Uruguayan Government as the most important targets for action:

Complete Ownership from Germany (Direct):

    Banco Alemán Transatlántico
    La Quimica Bayer Wescott y Cia.
    La Mannheim, Cía. de Seguros
    Productos Farmaceúticos Schering (trademarks)

Partial Ownership from Germany (Direct):

    Bayer y Cia.—about 80%

Complete Ownership from Japan (Direct):

    Omura, Matsutaro
    Yamada y Cia.

Partial Ownership from Germany through Head Office in Argentina (Indirect):

    Lahusen y Cia.—21.57%. With respect to this case it should be made clear to the Uruguayan authorities that adequate action contemplates removal from the firm of the German interest only.

. . . .

Copies sent to Buenos Aires.

LOVETT

740.35112A/12–2447 : Airgram

The Ambassador in Uruguay (Briggs) to the Secretary of State

SECRET   MONTEVIDEO, December 24, 1947.

A–537. Re Department's secret A–231, October 27, 1947, requesting information concerning status of Uruguayan replacement bill. Draft of bill to provide for liquidation of Axis firms has long been before Uruguayan Congress. It has been referred to Committee on Social Legislation for study and report, but Embassy informed orally that

---

[20] Not printed.

Committee has no intention of bringing out bill in foreseeable future. (It is well to recall in this connection that in Uruguay the Congress is traditionally—and at present—fully as powerful as the Executive; that is, this program is not one for decision by the Executive alone.)

The interest of our Government in this matter has been repeatedly expressed to Uruguayan officials, including the "Commission on the Intervention of Enemy Firms", of which Dr. Pratt de María of Foreign Office is a member. While in general sympathetic with objectives of replacement program, those officials have consistently expressed orally opinion that passage of replacement program for Uruguay in form suggested by us is now impossible. Furthermore in confidential legal study by the Foreign Office the conclusion is reached that proposed replacement bill is unconstitutional.

Another factor is undoubtedly pressure brought by the intervened firms. Also, the strong opposition (Herrerista) party has from the outset attacked the bill, and the present administration is seeking a working agreement with the opposition. Hence the administration would be reluctant to press a matter tenaciously opposed and for which there is at present no discernible public demand.

A further factor is Argentina. After observing with interest the course of our negotiations with that country on the replacement program, the United States announcement last May was widely interpreted (or misinterpreted) here in the sense that since we were discontinuing our efforts in the much wider and more important Argentine field, we could not consistently continue to press for action by Uruguay, a country which had collaborated genuinely and effectively on many matters having to do with the war.

Finally the development recently reported by the press that an American firm had entered into a contractual arrangement with Staudt & Company in Buenos Aires has not escaped notice in Montevideo and has a definite bearing on this whole situation.

In short, the Uruguayan Government regards the replacement program as a dead issue. In the opinion of the Embassy further efforts to revive it would have scant prospects of success and would not now be well received.

BRIGGS

VENEZUELA

THE POSITION OF THE UNITED STATES WITH RESPECT TO REVOLUTIONARY ACTIVITY IN VENEZUELA

831.00/1–747 : Telegram

The Chargé in Venezuela (Maleady) to the Secretary of State

SECRET   US URGENT   CARACAS, January 7, 1947—6 p. m.

10. Betancourt [1] called me Presidential Palace today and exhibited document bearing apparently genuine signature Lopez Contreras [2] turned over by Army officer. Reminding recipient he is Andino, document exhorted him join movement oust Acción Democrática and Dictator Betancourt, common enemies. It said Lopez has placed all political capital, moral credit, personal services and material so far available to him at disposal Col. Julio Cesar Vargas [3] for purpose indicated.

"Betancourt aware Lopez visited St Domingo (mytel 587 Dec 20, 6 p. m. and 594 Dec 24 12 p. m.[4]) said abundant evidence exists of which we undoubtedly aware that expedition to invade Venezuela being fitted out St Domingo with aid abettance Trujillo [5] (mygam 3 Jan 3, 1947 [6]). He expressed fullest confidence ability repel invasion, adding if expedition sets out he would consider Trujillo guilty act of war and immediately send Constellation bombard Ciudad Trujillo."

He said he felt time had come for US demand Lopez, Vargas and others now in US desist conspiring, and likewise refuse permission their departure from US order prevent carrying out plans from other places. While he admitted arms, ammunition and other material obtained thru cloaks, he added most thereof must be American and that fact alone would look bad. He said he felt assured if invasion attempted Argentine would offer aid hoping thereby add to Perón's [7] anti-US bloc. He said no blocks should exist, all Republics should form single group, but one could help another as we can in this instance. Went on to say he is realist and aware we may have no particular

---

[1] Romulo Betancourt, President of the Revolutionary Junta of Government.
[2] Eleázar López Contreras, former President of Venezuela.
[3] One-time Inspector General of the Venezuelan Army.
[4] Neither printed.
[5] Rafael Leonidas Trujillo Molina, President of the Dominican Republic.
[6] Not printed.
[7] Juan D. Perón, President of Argentina.

sympathy for him personally or even as head of govt, but continued he felt sure we do not approve civil war, this for loftier reasons than that we need Venezuelan oil. He feels we can help him now.

Betancourt requested I cable foregoing. Despite some faults, Oct election conducted more less cleanly overall and Constituent Assembly now sitting represents free will of people. I feel time has come to do something. Betancourt expects be advised Dept's reaction. Please advise.

MALEADY

831.00/1-747 : Telegram

The Secretary of State to the Embassy in Venezuela

SECRET   WASHINGTON, January 10, 1947—7 p. m.

13. For the Ambassador. Dept deeply concerned info contained Embtel 10, Jan 7 and by your estimate Ven political situation as described your recent conversations with officers Dept.

Re friction between Dom Rep and Ven (Ciudad Trujillo's tel 8, Jan 9 [8]), Dept of opinion that, while Act of Chapultepec [9] would be applicable should either country believe the circumstance and evidence indicate a threat of aggression, initiative toward consultation should be taken by country concerned. Should Betancourt open discussion with you re alleged activities Ven exiles in Dom Rep, you are authorized in your discretion suggest he give consideration initiating consultation among Am Reps if in his judgment facts appear to bring case within scope Resolution 8, Mex City Conf.

Dept also disturbed by Betancourt's apparent reference his talk with Maleady to lack sympathy for him on part U.S. This Govt has demonstrated every good will and all proper sympathy toward Junta Govt and its general objectives, a fact which we trust Betancourt and his colleagues fully appreciate. Also, we have demonstrated our desire to cooperate in every appropriate manner. However, it is obvious that ultimate solution Venezuela's exile problem is essentially matter Ven internal politics.

Repeated to Ciudad Trujillo.

BYRNES

---

[8] Not printed.
[9] Pan American Union, *Final Act of the Inter-American Conference on Problems of War and Peace* (Washington, 1945). The Act of Chapultepec was Resolution VIII of the Final Act, *ibid.*, p. 40. For documentation on the Chapultepec Conference, see *Foreign Relations*, 1945, vol. IX, pp. 1 ff.

831.00/1–1447 : Telegram

The Ambassador in Venezuela (Corrigan) to the Secretary of State

SECRET   CARACAS, January 14, 1947—noon.

28. ReDeptel 13, January 10. In regard Betancourt's request that we demand López Contreras, Vargas *et al* cease conspiring in US and prevent their departure therefrom I was informed while in Curaçao, by Dutch Governor, that Betancourt had also requested him expel General León Jurado. Dutch Governor informed me he has no intention expelling or intervening with political refugees, who have been coming to Curaçao from Venezuela throughout its history. He did promise however that Jurado would be kept under strict surveillance.

I am inclined to credit Dominican Foreign Minister's [11] statement as reported by Ambassador Butler in his telegram 10, January 10 to Department.[12] Venezuelan antipathy to Trujillo so general I question that Lopez would accept direct aid from former because to do so would bring unfortunate political repercussion. I also question authenticity document shown Maleady bearing "apparently genuine" signature Lopez turned in by army officer.

In my opinion threat of aggression too nebulous to warrant initiative toward consultation under Mexico City resolution VIII, and I feel Department correct in concluding solution Venezuela's exile problem rests within Venezuela.

                                                           CORRIGAN

831.00/4–1447 : Telegram

The Ambassador in Venezuela (Corrigan) to the Secretary of State

CONFIDENTIAL   CARACAS, April 14, 1947— 1 p. m.

171. Situation continues tense. Junta yesterday released copy document termed as attempt to win military members Junta to Lopez Contreras' side. Number political arrests large. Many civilians and officers have gone into hiding. Embassy has had several requests for asylum. AD sponsored mass meetings held at Caracas and announced elsewhere have contributed to great public unrest. Workers proclaim readiness to take up arms in support government. Julio César Vargas still hiding in private home. Reliable source reports Vargas expects counter-revolution start quickly, perhaps tomorrow. Other sources confirm this possibility, but very drastic steps being taken may have disrupted opposition plans.

                                                           CORRIGAN

---

[11] Arturo Despradel.
[12] Not printed.

831.00/6-3047

Memorandum of Conversation, by Mr. Charles C. Hauch of the Division of Caribbean Affairs

SECRET [WASHINGTON,] July 10, 1947.

Participants: Mr. Lyon—A-A   Mr. Wells—NWC
Mr. Wright—ARA   Mr. Barber—CRB
Mr. Woodward—ARA   Mr. Hauch—CRB
Mr. Gray—Le   Ambassador Corrigan—
Mr. Peterson—MD   Caracas

This meeting was held to discuss the advisability of bringing charges against the persons allegedly involved in the revolutionary plot to overthrow the Government of Venezuela. The Department of Justice had requested the opinion of the Department of State on this subject in several conversations and had formalized its request by a letter of June 30.[13]

Mr. Gray [14] outlined the case, as set forth in his secret memorandum of July 8 entitled "Revolutionary plot against the present Venezuelan Government".[13] He explained that four of the principals in the case have been charged with theft of United States Government property. In investigating this theft the FBI discovered this was merely incidental to a plot to overthrow the Venezuelan regime, which involves a large number of other persons including . . . Venezuelans, as well as several Dominicans. The plot appears to have the backing of the Dominican Government, which is assisting in the obtaining of war material for use against Venezuela and is permitting its territory to be used as a base of operations.

The basic question was whether charges on counts other than the theft of Government property should be pressed against the Venezuelans and Americans concerned. It was pointed out by Mr. Wright and Mr. Wells that (*a*) it would probably be undesirable politically to prosecute the Venezuelans involved; (*b*) if the foreigners were not prosecuted, it would not appear proper to press the same charges against the Americans involved; and (*c*) if the charge of organizing a revolution against a friendly power were pushed, full publicity would ensue during the trials with undesirable results for inter-American relations.

Mention was made that confining the trial to the four individuals charged with theft of Government property would mean that persons who have been bringing planes and perhaps other war material into

---

[13] Not printed.
[14] George O. Gray, Assistant to the Legal Adviser.

the Dominican Republic, in violation of various statutes, would not be apprehended at this time, with the result that they might continue to participate in the clandestine and irregular shipment of arms and aircraft to that country. Note was taken of the fact that some of them have continued to fly aircraft into the Dominican Republic even after questioning by the FBI and the arrest of Eisenhardt [16] and his three associates on the theft charge. Ambassador Corrigan expressed concern regarding the seriousness of the action of these flyers. It was pointed out, however, that the actual bringing of the four persons to trial on the theft charge would probably cause the others involved in the plot to desist from their activities, and that if it did not, further consideration could then be given to taking action against them.

Mr. Peterson stated that if any of these individuals were involved in violation of export control laws, he thought MD would take the position they should be prosecuted on this charge. He did not feel that complete publicity on the plot need ensue were charges of export control violation to be pushed. He also doubted that trying the foreigners on this charge would necessarily reveal their complicity in the plot, since it would be in their interest not to mention this, and the prosecution need not bring it out. Mr. Wells said that if it was deemed undesirable for political reasons to prosecute the foreigners concerned, he felt it likewise undesirable to bring the Americans to trial on this charge, since in such trials they would probably make public statements implicating the foreigners as their principals. Mr. Peterson reiterated his view that any violation of the export control law should be punished.

After considerable discussion, it was decided (with Mr. Peterson of MD later reserving MD's position) to acknowledge the letter of the Department of Justice by stating (1) that the Department has no objection to the immediate prosecution of the four persons already apprehended on the charge of the theft of Government property and (2) that with regard to the institution of additional criminal prosecutions as the result of the alleged revolutionary plot, the Department is of the view that, although investigations of any activities relating to this subject should be continued, it is desirable that prosecutions be held in abeyance, if the Justice Department has discretion in the matter, owing to the international political repercussions which would probably ensue.

---

[16] Karl John Eisenhardt, said to have organized a number of commercial companies useful in smuggling weapons, planes, and boats.

831.00/7-1747

Memorandum of Conversation, by the Chief of the Division of North and West Coast Affairs (Wells)

SECRET [WASHINGTON,] July 17, 1947.

Participants: Mr. James H. Wright, Director, ARA
Mr. Robert F. Woodward, Deputy Director, ARA
Colonel Woodson F. Hocker, War Department (G-2, American Republics Section)
Commander Edgar G. Thompson, ONI
Mr. Allan Dawson, BA
Mr. Milton K. Wells, NWC

At the Under Secretary's [17] suggestion, representatives of the War and Navy Departments were called in to be informed of the very serious view the Department is taking of Venezuelan political developments, which threaten a new revolutionary attempt with possible international complications due to aid being given Venezuelan exiles by the Dominican Republic. A general discussion was had of the situation.

Mr. Wright expressed the Department's feeling that a revolution would likely result in a bloody and drawn-out civil war. While the crisis may pass, information regarding revolutionary plotting disclosed by the Eisenhardt investigation requires that we be particularly alert. The potential danger to the Venezuelan oil supply is cause for serious concern. The consensus of those present was that the period between now and the forthcoming elections (date not yet fixed but probably in November) is likely to be the most critical; that, if a revolution does not occur before then, the new administration will be in a better position to effect a conciliation with the opposition. Mr. Wright said he had no specific suggestions to make, except to urge that War and Navy follow the situation as closely as possible by maintaining adequate coverage in the field, and to be thinking about what steps, if any, would be called for in case trouble breaks out.

831.00/8-147

The Secretary of State to the Embassy in Venezuela

SECRET WASHINGTON, August 12, 1947.
No. 3815

The Secretary of State refers to previous correspondence regarding the investigation of certain individuals alleged to be involved in a

---

[17] Robert A. Lovett.

revolutionary plot against the Venezuelan Government and transmits copies of two letters [18] on this subject which were recently sent to the Attorney General. One letter, dated July 15, 1947, expresses the Department's approval of the immediate prosecution of those who have been charged with the theft of United States Government property, including Karl J. Eisenhardt. The other letter, dated July 28, expresses the desirability of preparing the remaining cases for prosecution but requests the Department of Justice to issue no process against persons who are not of American nationality without prior consultation with the Department.

The Venezuelan Embassy has been informed that the Department of Justice has turned over the cases against the four individuals mentioned in the Department's letter of July 15 to the competent District Attorneys and that hearings will commence before a Grand Jury in Augusta, Georgia, and possibly Miami, Florida, probably in late September or early October. The Embassy expressed its satisfaction.

The progress of these hearings will be communicated to the Embassy at a future date.

831.00/8-1447

Memorandum by Mr. Richard H. Post of the Division of North and West Coast Affairs [19]

SECRET   WASHINGTON, August 14, 1947.

The following excerpt is presented from *Weeka* dated August 8:

"Widespread subversion discovered existing among enlisted men in Caracas garrisons fomented 70% by local Communists . . .

"Maracay mutiny last month now believed by General Staff to be similarly Communist inspired. Delgado Chalbeaud [20] states his belief this subversion not aimed to achieve Communist coup but to embarrass weakened government generally. Entire development not published yet but being hushed. 37 sergeants arrested this connection to date. Plot discovered in San Carlos barracks Caracas. As one result Ministry National Defense has organized Disciplinary Company vicinity Eldorado far south Orinoco River in area used past penal camp. This is very positive and to knowledge this office first step toward real punishment guilty military personnel."

A further note on Communism in Venezuela: the Constitutional Assembly took a very firm attitude in quashing an attempt of the two

---

[18] Not printed.
[19] Addressed to Messrs. Mills and Wells of NWC.
[20] Carlos Delgado Chalbaud, Venezuelan Defense Minister.

Communist delegates to create trouble during its sessions July 21–July 26.

831.00/9–1247 : Telegram

The Chargé in Venezuela (Maleady) to the Secretary of State

SECRET US URGENT CARACAS, September 12, 1947—10 a. m.
NIACT

363. All Caracas barracks and those La Guaira area alerted early this a. m., as were presumably all others throughout country. Traffic being rerouted in all streets adjacent Caracas *cuartels*. Military guards are dressed full equipment. Radio stations under guard. Armored and other military cars in evidence all downtown streets. Approximately twelve well-known civilians including Director Geology in Ministry of Fomento, Victor Lopez, arrested.

Some informants state show military force made intentionally by administration in Junta to impress populace and prevent attempt break up meeting here at which Gallegos' [21] presidential candidacy to be publicly proclaimed tonight. Others feel alert occasioned by matter mentioned mytel 361, September 11, 4 p. m.[22]

Reports of uprisings at various places outside Caracas wholly unconfirmed.

Miraflores Palace source states situation under control and has promised furnish me full details this noon.

MALEADY

831.00/9–1247 : Telegram

The Chargé in Venezuela (Maleady) to the Secretary of State

SECRET US URGENT CARACAS, September 12, 1947—4 p. m.

365. Junta President Betancourt on nationwide hook-up this p. m., said attempt made before dawn today block off presidential palace and Ministry Defense with autobuses but these quickly seized and arms they carried confiscated. Uprising Puerto de la Cruz quickly put down by army troops from nearby Barcelona, and disturbances various Andean towns likewise promptly smothered.

He announced attempt overthrow government frustrated; situation under control therefore no need suspend civil guarantees.

Also said had gone on air himself at request Junta Cabinet members who felt his doing so would in itself be reassuring.

MALEADY

---

[21] Romulo Gallegos, candidate of the governing Junta.
[22] Not printed.

831.00/10–1347

Memorandum by Mr. Richard H. Post of the Division of North and West Coast Affairs [23]

[Extracts]

SECRET [WASHINGTON,] October 13, 1947.

Ambassador Corrigan is quite worried because of the failure of the opposition . . . to find a candidate for the presidential elections, scheduled for December 14. . . .

Dr. Corrigan feels that if the only rival of Gallegos should be the Communist candidate Machado, the opposition elements would have no safety valve, a situation which would seriously increase the chances of revolution.

. . . .

831.00/10–2347

The Acting Secretary of State to the Attorney General (Clark)

WASHINGTON, October 23, 1947.

MY DEAR MR. ATTORNEY GENERAL: Further reference is made to letters from the Department of State to the Department of Justice dated July 28, 1947 and August 15, 1947,[24] regarding investigations which were made of the activities of Karl John Eisenhardt and others in a reported plot to form a revoluntionary expedition against the Venezuelan Government.

The Department of State requests that the Department of Justice, if it is possible to do so, continue to hold in abeyance prosecutions against . . . Venezuelan nationals involved in the cases.

The Department of State has no objection, however, to the prosecution of any persons who have violated Section 452 of Title 22 of the United States Code, involving the illegal exportation of arms and ammunition. In view of the fact that Venezuelan presidential and congressional elections are to take place on December 14, 1947 the Department requests that no action regarding these cases be taken prior to that time which might lead to publicity.[25] . . .

Sincerely yours, ROBERT A. LOVETT

---

[23] Addressed to Messrs. Espy and Mills, NWC, and Mr. Woodward, ARA.
[24] Neither printed.
[25] The Acting Assistant to the Attorney General, in a letter of October 29, 1947, to the Secretary of State, indicated the difficulty of prosecuting some offenders and not others in the same plot (831.00/10–2947). In a letter to the Attorney General, March 23, 1948, the Secretary of State requested that charges be preferred against plotters of the overthrow of certain American republics' governments, where United States law was violated and regardless of nationality (831.00/10–2347).

831.00/11-2847

Memorandum by Mr. Richard H. Post of the Division of North and West Coast Affairs [26]

SECRET [WASHINGTON,] November 28, 1947.

The attached memo [27] from the Department of the Army indicates the possibility of the Venezuelan Army making a *coup d'état* and ousting Acción Democracia.

The Embassy, the Military and Naval Attachés have pointed out the possibility of such a coup in recent months.

Since AD is supported actively and devotedly by a vast majority of the populace (it expects 1,500,000 voters to register for the December 14 elections, in a population of between 4 and 4.5 millions.) and since the party is known to be armed, as stated in this memo, I fail to see how such a coup could be bloodless.

If the coup should be attempted and should lead to protracted civil war, it would seriously endanger oil production and installations.

---

[26] Addressed to Mr. Espy, NWC; Mr. Woodward, ARA; and Messrs. Lyon and Armour, A-A.
[27] Not printed.

INDEX

INDEX

Accioly, Hildebrando, 33, 34, 89–90, 398n, 400–401
Acevedo, Carlos Leonidas, 52, 57–58
Acheson, Dean:
 Argentina: Air transit agreement negotiations, 239–240, 242–243; British policy on supply of arms to, 171–172
 Brazil: Elimination of Nazi influence in, 490–491; German reparations to, 494
 Chile, 522, 528–529
 Cuba, U.S. sugar legislation, 616
 Emergency Advisory Committee for Political Defense, functions of, 98–99, 100
 Inter-American Arms Program, economic aspects, 104–106, 113, 114
 Mexico, IT&T consolidation with Ericsson Corporation, 764–768
 Nicaraguan politics, U.S. policy of non-intervention, 846
 Panama: Canal Zone, equality of employment opportunity, 958–959; defense sites agreement negotiations, 897–901
 Paraguay, U.S. position on insurrection in, 972, 973, 974–975, 977–978, 982
 Peruvian discriminatory trade legislation, 1024–1025; wheat requirements, 1034, 1035
Ackerman, Ralph H., 1007–1008, 1028
Act of Chapultepec, 1945, 1–93 passim, 163, 170, 223
Adams, Lt. Col. James Y., 738, 740, 743, 744n
Aguado, Enoc, 841, 846–848, 862
Alemán Valdes, Miguel, 752n, 753–761 passim, 787–794 passim, 799, 800, 815–816
Alessandri Rodriguez, Jorge, 544, 545–546, 547
Alfaro, Ricardo J., 49–51, 881–905 passim, 919–949 passim
Alvarado, Julio, 332–333, 374–389 passim
American Airways, 751, 752–753
Anderson, Clinton P., 470, 471, 478, 480, 818
Anslinger, Harry J., 836–838, 839, 840
Antarctica, Chilean claims, 17, 75, 80
Aranha, Oswaldo, 473
Aranibar, Ernesto, 369, 371, 372, 373
Arévalo, Juan José, 134, 707–717 passim

Argentina, 163–325
 Air transit problems between the United States and Argentina, 238–251, 261; Flota Aérea Mercante Argentina, 238–239, 247
 Argentine grains, U.S. efforts to make available to countries in need, 304–316
 Argentine Trade Promotion Institute, 304, 306, 307
 Belgium needs, 232, 233, 314–315
 Brazil, delays and shortages in wheat supplies to, 467–479 passim
 Corn, negotiations for purchase of, 306–310
 Currency for payment, problems regarding, 309, 313
 European Recovery Program, 15, 308, 313, 314–315
 International Emergency Food Council, 304–316 passim
 Peru, wheat for, 1032–1043
 Soviet offer to purchase grain and supply machinery, 315
 Wheat: Peruvian attempts to purchase, 1032–1043; supply to Brazil, 467–479 passim
 Armaments, U.S. policy on provision of (see also Armaments and military assistance), 117n, 117–121, 208, 215–238, 1049–1051
 Aircraft, 217–235 passim
 Belgium Overseas Trading Corporation, sales of arms, 226–238 passim
 British policy on sales of arms, 171–172, 219–235 passim
 Naval vessels, 115, 168, 215–226 passim, 244
 "Reasonable and necessary", requirement of, 227
 Soviet Union, question of reshipment to, 228–236 passim
 Aviation agreement with United Kingdom, question of, 239–240
 Bolivian trade and other relations, 328–340 passim, 353, 366, 367
 Chilean economic and financial agreement, 252, 256, 529, 534
 Commercial agreements with other American Republics, 252, 256–257
 Commercial ship sales by U.S. firms and effect of Argentine discriminatory shipping practices, 251–269 passim

1067

Argentina—Continued
  Committee on Political Defense, question of return of Argentina to, 98, 99
  Communist influence, U.S. evaluation, 31, 42–43, 44, 206–207, 208–209
  Czechoslovak sales of arms to, 230–231
  Discrimination against American and other foreign shipping and trade, 251–278, 320, 435
    Bilateral discriminatory (shipping clause) agreements of Argentina with other countries, 252–259 *passim*
    Income tax decree on foreign freight profits, 253, 258, 259–260, 267, 268
    Trade and financial controls, 270–271, 273–276
    U.S. retaliatory measures, questions of 252, 258, 260, 262–263
  Economic and financial situation, 205, 207, 273–276
  Falkland Islands, claims to, 75
  International Emergency Food Council, question of participation in, 308–316 *passim*
  Linseed oil shipments to United States, 244, 259, 260–261, 262
  Nazi influences, U.S. interest in efforts to extirpate, 163–215, 1053
    British position, 171, 175, 177, 194
    Deportation of German agents, 166–215 *passim*
    Educational institutions, 166–193 *passim*
    Enemy property rights, titles, and interests in certain enterprises, disposition of, 165–166, 167, 180–181; Argentine decree for liquidation of enemy property, 167–184 *passim*
    Staudt & Co., 167n, 1051–1052, 1053
  Opposition press, 317–325
    Government closing of certain papers, 85, 206
    Import duty on newsprint, demands for payment of retroactive charges, 317–319
    La Prensa's 78*th* anniversary, U.S. congratulatory message, questions of policy regarding, 319–325
  Peru, attempts to purchase Argentine wheat, 1032–1043
  Petroleum problems of Argentina, and problems of American oil companies in Argentina, U.S. concern regarding, 278–304, 309–310, 316
    Argentine oil policy, 302–304; President's Petroleum Day Speech, *Dec. 13*, 294–299, 301, 302–303
    Decrees regarding profits, 290–292; decree regarding YPF, 290
    Development and exploitation of resources, 284–303 *passim*

Argentina—Continued
  Petroleum problems of Argentina—Continued
    Export and import license problems, 292–293, 301
    Expropriation or forced sale of private companies, question of, 278–298 *passim*
    Mixed companies, ban on, 278, 279
    Venezuelan oil, agreement on exchange for Argentine foodstuffs, 303
    Wage and price increases, effects on profits, 279–282, 285, 286–288, 300–301, 302
    YPF intervention in operation of private companies, 293–294
  Political situation, 196–197, 222, 257
  Soviet influence, question of, 206–207, 208–209
  United Kingdom: Policy on sales of arms, 171–172, 219–235 *passim*; question of aviation agreement, 239–240
  U.N. Security Council, election to seat on, 310
  Uruguayan relations, 1047n, 1048–1049
  U.S. Technical Mission, proposed, 247
Argüello, Leonardo, 11, 12, 147n, 841–858 *passim*, 876–877, 878–879
Argüello Vargas, Mariano, 40, 588, 864, 865, 867, 872–873, 876
Arias, Harmodio, 945, 946
Arias, Roberto, 945
Arízaga Toral, Enrique, 691, 693–694
Armaments and military assistance, U.S. policy with respect to provision of (*see also under individual countries*), 101–130, 684–685
  Aircraft, 122–124, 125–126, 130, 661–662
  Airports, disposition of, 101–102, 112–113
  Arms manufacturing plants, 124
  Canada, 108, 110, 113, 114
  Commercial sales, 116, 117–118, 122–124, 125, 126
  Dominican Republic, Venezuela, and other Caribbean countries, comparative armament, 661–662
  Economic considerations, 104–110, 111–112, 126, 127
  Foreign Liquidation Commission Field Commissioner for Military Programs, 115–116
  Inter-American Military Cooperation Bill, 103–115 *passim*, 115n, 125, 129, 130, 685
  Kilgore Committee, 102
  Lend-lease pipeline agreements, 103, 112, 121–122, 127–128
  Military and naval missions, 111, 113–114, 127, 128, 129
  Naval vessels, 103–104, 109, 115
  Policy Committee on Arms and Armaments, 117–120, 124, 125

INDEX

Armaments and military assistance—Continued
"Reasonable and necessary", requirement of, 119-128 *passim*, 648
Soviet Union, delivery of lend-lease materials to, discontinued, 121-122
Transportation and related costs, 114
Armed forces, U.N. General Assembly resolution on principles governing the regulation and reduction of, *1946*, 410-413
Armour, Norman, 41-51 *passim*, 72, 451, 545, 617, 625-626, 654, 762, 962, 963, 1009; Argentina, 310-311, 312-315, 322, 323-324; Bolivia, 339; Brazil, 410-412, 474, 476-479; Chile, 546, 548-549; Cuba, 618, 622-624; Dominican Republic, 655-656, 658-659; Haiti, 733-735; Honduras, 739; Inter-American Highway, 148-149, 150-151; Mexico, 780-781, 795-798; Nicaragua, 587-589, 871-872, 875-876; Panama, 912, 929-931; Peru, 1043-1044; Rio Treaty, 37-38; Uruguay, 1050-1051
Arosemena, Carlos Julio, 674-675
Arosemena, Florencio, 926, 944, 946, 947
Atwood, Rollin S., 285-286
Austin, Warren, 60
Axis influence. See Axis *under* Bolivia, Brazil, and Uruguay.

Baquero, Col. Angel, 670, 673
Barboza da Silva, Edmundo Penna, 987, 989-990, 991
Barreda Moller, José, 1009, 1020, 1029
Barreto, Gen. João Carlos, 463, 464, 466
Barrios Tirado, Maj. Gen. Guillermo, 519n, 520
Barros, José Constantino, 294, 295, 298
Batlle, Berres, Luis, 1047-1049
Beaulac, Willard L., 323n, 560-561, 562, 572n, 981, 982-984, 985
Becker, Johannes Siegfried, 167, 189-215 *passim*
Behn, Col. Sosthenes, 767, 772n
Belgium, Overseas Trading Corporation, sale of arms to Argentina, 226-238 *passim*
Belize, Guatemalan claim to, 57, 75
Bell, John O., 242, 245-246, 250
Belt, Guillermo, 16, 30, 32, 39, 59, 69-70, 606-626n *passim*
Bennett, W. Tapley, 587, 597-598, 891-892, 925, 929-931, 950, 959-961
Bermúdez, Antonio J., 787, 790
Bernbaum, Maurice M., 848-879 *passim*
Bernstein, Enrique, 507n, 515, 516, 549, 550, 551, 552
Berreta, Tomás, 36, 1045, 1046
Betancourt, Romulo, 131, 132, 144, 655, 877, 878, 878n, 1054-1056, 1061
Beteta, Ramón, 747-748, 796, 799, 801
Bevin, Ernest K., 224-225, 233, 234-235
Bilbao Rioja, Gen. Bernardino, 348, 349, 357-358, 360, 362-363
Black, Eugene, 534-535

Bloom, Sol., 36
Bogotá Conference, 93, 94, 99, 223, 224
Bohan, Merwin L., 752-779 *passim*, 816
Bolivia, 326-390
Air transport agreement with the United States, negotiation of, 363-378
Art. 8 on continuance of existing rights and concessions of airlines, 364-378 *passim*
Panagra *1943* contract, proposed revision, 363-366, 368-374
Signing of agreement, Sept. 29, *1948*, 378
"Substantial ownership and control" provision, 367
Traffic points, 367-368, 374-378
Argentine influence, 328-340 *passim*, 353, 366, 367
Axis economic interests, U.S. efforts to eliminate, 378-384
Communist influence, 338
Economic development, U.S. financial and technical aid, 342-363
Cochabamba-Santa Cruz highway construction, revision of McGraw-Warren contract and subsequent cancellation, 343-363 *passim*
Eximbank credits, restrictions on, 343
Guamote-Tambo highway construction, 346
La Paz-Beni railway construction, 68, 352-353, 356-357
Petroleum program, 343-359 *passim*
Lend-lease account, efforts to liquidate, 384-390
Payment in dollars, property, or bolivianos, 385, 386-388, 389-390
Publication of amount received, question of, 388-389
Railway construction, Brazilian aid, 333
Tin, problems involved in U.S. procurement of, 326-342
Labor problems, 329-336 *passim*
Price increases, negotiations with RFC, 326-342 *passim*
Protection of American citizens, 333-334, 335, 336
U.S. purchase of Embassy and other government buildings, 385, 386-388, 390
Bolivian Development Corporation, 342-349 *passim*, 357-363 *passim*
Bosch, Juan, 651
Bouças, Valentim, 472, 481, 482-484, 484
Bowers, Claude G., 22, 79-80, 502, 503-507, 513-528 *passim*, 538-539, 541, 544-545, 549, 551-553
Braden, Spruille, 4, 166-168, 331, 332, 522n, 702, 1000; Argentina, elimination of Axis influence from, 176-178, 180-181, U.S. arms policy, 215-216, 218-219, 220; Chile, U.S. economic aid to, 531, 533-535, 539-541; Costa

Braden, Spruille—Continued
  Rica, 579, 593–594; Cuba, interests of U.S. nationals, 606–608, 613–614; Haitian Special Mission for financial arrangements, 720–725; human rights, multilateral approach for protection of, 629–631; Inter-American highway, 147–148; Mexico, IT&T consolidation with Ericsson Co., 764–766; Nicaraguan politics, U.S. policy of non-intervention, 842–843, 844, 846, 854, 854n, 855, 856, 857; Panama, defense sites agreement negotiations, 883–886; Paraguayan insurrection, 980–982; Rio Treaty, 1–3
Bradshaw, Thomas A., 716n
Bramuglia, Juan Atilio, 15, 21, 32–44 passim, 84, 85, 98, 163–165, 183–185, 240, 276–309 passim, 903, 906
Braniff Airways, 239, 364–365, 366, 751, 757
Brazil, 391–496
  Arms sale to Dominican Republic, 131–144
    Brazilian position, and reports regarding sale, 132–133, 134–135, 143, 144
    Cuban concern, 133–134, 135, 137–138, 142–143
    Venezuelan concern and consideration of oil embargo, 131–132, 136–137, 138, 140–142
    Request for U.S. intercession, 132, 138–140, 140–141, 142
    U.S. decision not to intercede, 140n
  Axis persons and property, U.S. interest in problems concerning, 486–496
    German reparations, question of Brazilian share, 487–492, 494–496
    Property of enemy nationals, U.S. views regarding Brazilian plans for disposition of, 486–487, 489, 490–491
    Undertakings regarding Proclaimed List firms, U.S. policy regarding, and question of release of Companhia Cervejaria Brahma from, 492–494
  Breach in relations with Soviet Union, 391–406, 511
    Attack on President Dutra in Soviet press, Brazilian protest, followed by severance of relations, 394–397
    Communist Party in Brazil, cancellation of registration of, 55, 392–393, 394
    Demonstrations in Brazil following severance of relations, 397–398, 399, 400–401, 402n, 402–403
    Discord preceding break in relations, 391, 394–395; departure of Soviet Ambassador from Brazil, 393–394; incident involving Brazilian diplomatic secretary in Moscow, 391–392
    Embassy personnel, treatment and repatriation, 398–406
    Protection of interests: Brazilian, by United States, 396–397, 401, 405–406; Soviet, question of, 398, 399, 400, 401, 402n, 404
    U.S. policy regarding expression of views, 395
    Communist Party in, 31, 39, 473; cancellation of registration, 55, 392–393; mob attack on Communist newspaper, 397–398
  Economic development and investment:
    Brazil Railway and Port of Pará properties, seizure of, 447–449, 450–451
    Private capital investment, 433–434, 435–436
    U.S. efforts to provide financial assistance, 441–458, 461–462
    Joint Brazil-U.S. Technical Commission, establishment of, 455–456
    Laminação Nacional de Metais loan request, 456–458
    National Alkali Corporation, 446–447
    Orinoco River iron ore project, 442
    Sorocabana Railway project, 444–446
    Stabilization fund arrangement with U.S. Treasury, 425–426
    Transportation system, Eximbank loan proposed, 447
    Vale Rio Doce project, 441–458 passim
  Exchange position, problems of, 451–452, 453–455
  International Emergency Food Council, withdrawal of Brazil and subsequent reinstatement, 468–479 passim
  International Monetary Fund, participation in, 426, 447, 454
  Joint Brazil-U.S. Defense Commission, 411, 412
  Joint Brazil-U.S. Military Commission, 406–407, 411–412
  Lend-lease and surplus property arrangements, disposal of U.S. military equipment under, 406–420
    Airport installations, 406–407
    Brazilian Expeditionary Forces materiel, disposition of, 408–409
    Destroyer escorts, legislative restriction regarding disposal. See Naval vessels, infra.
    German vessels, former, sale of, 416–417, 420

INDEX

1071

Brazil—Continued
  Lend-lease and surplus property arrangements—Continued
    Naval vessels under charter agreement, 408, 409, 410, 413–415, 416–418, 419–420
    Overall settlement, consideration of, 408–409, 415–416, 419
    Revision of lend-lease agreement, questions of, 407, 409
  Paraguayan insurrection, armament policy, 975–976, 981; mediation, 975–991 *passim*
  Petroleum, 458–467
    Legislation regulating development of resources, proposed:
      Preparation of draft by Brazil, 461–462, 464; advisory work of Hoover-Curtice Mission, 462–464
      U.S. policy regarding presentation of U.S. views, 458–461, 466–467
    Requests for U.S. assistance:
      Loans for construction of refineries, 449–450, 464
      Petroleum products to supply minimum requirements, 466, 467; problem of tanker shortage, 465–467
  Political situation, 477–478
  Proclaimed List. *See* Axis persons and property, *supra.*
  Reparations from Germany, and position on non-participation in Paris Conference, 487–489, 490, 491–492, 494–496
  Rubber Development Corporation, liquidation of, 480–486
  Soviet Union. *See* Breach in relations, *supra.*
  Trade and shipping questions, 421–441
    Alcoholic beverages import taxes, 424
    Brazilian consumption tax law, 421–424
    Discriminatory practices in Brazilian ports, 425, 434–435, 436–441
    Prior exchange licenses, 426, 427–428
    Tariff increases, 428, 429–432
    U.S. trade agreement negotiations, 428–431, 433–435
  Tribuna Popular, 392–393, 397–398
  Truman, visit of, 4–5, 436, 475
  U.S. armed forces, agreement on presence of, 410–413
  War efforts, 487–489
  Wheat, U.S. response to Brazilian requests for, 467–480
    Argentine wheat, problems involved in procurement of, 467–479 *passim*

Brazil—Continued
  Wheat—Continued
    Army purchase of wheat from Overseas Trading Corporation, and export license problem, 474–480 *passim*
    Flour shipments, 469–470, 480
Brett, Gen. George H., 703
Briggs, Ellis O.: As Ambassador to Honduras, 742, 1045n, 1047, 1052–1053; as Director of Office of American Republic Affairs, 4, 13–14, 19n, 166, 221–224, 332, 385, 522n, 606–608, 612–615, 642–643, 814, 857, 950, 952, 957–958, 1005–1006, 1031–1033
Brooks, Clarence G., 11–12, 423–424, 426–428, 448, 462, 494–495
Brown, Harry F., 824, 825
Bruce, James, 227, 230–231, 232–233, 272–273, 283–284, 295–297, 298–300, 306–307, 308–310, 311–312, 316, 319–320, 321–323, 324–325, 479, 1041; presentation of credentials as U.S. Ambassador to Argentina, 283–284
Burdick, B. F., 960
Burrows, Charles R., 88–89, 134–135, 662–663
Bustamente, José Rafael, 675
Butler, George H., 633–642, 643n, 651–652
Byrnes, James F., 163–166, 488, 738, 841–842, 883, 1055

Cáceres, Julián R., 20, 22–23, 70–71, 741, 742, 745n, 875–876
Calderón Guardia, Rafael Angel, 578n, 589
Cale, Edward G., 155–156, 158
Campbell, Douglas, 365, 370, 371, 372, 373
Campen, Thomas S., 1015–1019, 1025–1028, 1030–1031
Canada: Inter-American Military Cooperation Act, applicability to, 108, 110, 113, 114; observer to Rio Conference, 21, 23, 24; policy on sale of arms to Argentina, 221, 227
Canedo Reyes, Raúl, 326, 336–337
Carbajal Victorica, Juan José, 97–98
Carías Andino, Gen. Tiburcio, 742
Carnevali, Gonzalo, 136, 137
Carrigan, John W., 579, 580–581, 582–586, 595–596, 596n, 877–878, 878n
Carvalho, Daniel de, 447, 461, 462
Censorship of communications, recommendation by Committee for Political Defense for abolition of, 96–97
Cerro Cebrian, Vicente, 1017–1018, 1024, 1027
Chamorro Vargas, Gen. Emiliano, 841, 842n, 843, 844, 875, 875n
Chantrain, Alfonso (Joseph Schröel), 198, 210, 212, 213
Charles, Joseph D., 730
Chaves, Federico, 65–67, 972, 973, 978, 985–990 *passim*

Chavez, Juan, 998–999, 1011
Chile, 497–553
 Argentina, commercial relations with 252, 256, 529, 534
 Armaments, U.S. policy on supply of, 518–526
  Air base in Magallanes area, question of, 526
  Aircraft, number and financing of, 518–519, 520–522, 523–524
  Lend-lease account, status of, 525–526
  Naval vessels, sale to as surplus, 523, 525
 Breach of relations. See Czechoslovakia, Soviet Union, and Yugoslavia, infra.
 Communist-inspired labor violence and consequent breach of certain diplomatic relations, 497–518
  Bus strike, 497–498
  Coal strike, and importing of U.S. coal to counteract, 497, 498, 501–503, 504–506, 508–512
  Communist complicity, and removal of Communists from Government, 497–598, 499–501, 501, 503–506, 510–511, 511–512, 533–534, 541; Communist press attacks on Government, 498, 499, 542
  Czechoslovakia, breach of relations with, 511, 513–514, 514–515
  Repatriation and treatment of diplomatic staffs, 499, 514, 515–516, 518n; refusal of exit visa for Soviet daughter-in-law of Chilean Ambassador, 499, 512, 515, 517–518
  Shots fired at Soviet Embassy, and Soviet protest, 506–507, 508, 512
  Soviet Union, breach of relations with, 511, 512, 514, 515–516. See also Repatriation, etc., and Shots, supra.
  Yugoslavia, breach of relations with, 502, 503–504, 512–513
 Czechoslovakia, breach of relations with, 511, 513–515
 Economic assistance, U.S. position on provision of, 46, 527–549
  American copper companies, taxation and exchange problems, 532, 535, 536, 537–538, 540–541, 547
  Amortization of Chilean debt, 536–538, 542, 546–547, 549
  Eximbank credits to Chile, table of, 529
  Hydroelectric power production, 527–528, 529, 530, 539
  International Monetary Fund, Chilean requests for dollars from, 544–545, 548–549
  Nationalization of American interests, questions of, 528, 530, 535

Chile—Continued
 Economic Assistance—Continued
  Pedregal Economic Mission, 531–542 passim
  World Bank financing, conditions for, 528–547 passim
 Economic condition and prospects, 45–46, 532–549 passim
 Labor violence in Chile. See Communist-inspired labor violence, supra.
 Nazi agents, refuge in, 199
 Soviet Union. See under Communist-inspired labor violence.
 Trade agreement with United States, Chilean reluctance to conclude, 549–553; GATT negotiations, effect of, 549, 550, 551
 Yugoslavia, breach of relations with, 502, 503–504, 512–513
Clark, Duwayne G., 139, 419, 439
Clark, Sergio, 610–612
Clayton, William L., 429, 470, 481–482, 610–612
Clementis, Vlado, 514n, 514–515
Colombia, 554–577
 Anti-American propaganda and sentiment, 555–556, 557–560, 575
 Boundary treaties with Venezuela, Ecuador, and Peru, question of revision, 56
 Civil aviation mission, agreement with United States respecting, 569
 Debt situation and need for capital, 563, 567, 570–577
 Discriminatory treatment of American shipping interests, 554–569
  Flota Mercante Gran Colombiana and National Coffee Federation, preferential treatment of, 554–566 passim
  Import restrictions, 562, 564, 567–569
  U.S. Embassy and Grace Co. office, incidents involving, 556–557, 559, 560
  U.S. Public Resolution 17, effect of, 562, 565, 566
Communist Party (see also Communist entries under country headings), 67, 314
Concha Enríquez, Pedro, 693, 694
Connally, Tom, 187
Cooper, Prentice, 83–84, 999–1022 passim, 1033–1041 passim
Corominas, Enrique, 31–32
Correa e Castro, Pedro, 447, 478, 482n
Corrigan, Frank P., 1056–1058, 1062
Costa Rica, 578–603
 Civil disorders. See under Election, infra.
 Communism in, 581, 586–587, 590, 591, 594–595
 Election campaign, 578–591
  Civil disorders, 578–580, 595–596
  Good will visit by U.S. destroyer, proposed, 578–579

Costa Rica—Continued
  Election campaign—Continued
    Civil disorders—Continued
      U.S. protest regarding inadequate protection of property of American nationals, 580–584
      Nicaraguan situation, effect of, upon Costa Rica (*see also* Recognition, *infra*), 578, 587–589
      President Picado's statement of position, 586–587
      Summary report on candidates, and prediction of outcome, 589–591
      Ulatistas, 580, 585–586
      U.S. policy of nonintervention, 579, 580, 582, 585–586
  Financial and military assistance by by the United States, 591–598
    Aircraft and military equipment, U.S. policy, 593
    Surplus property sales negotiations, 591–592
  Fisheries legislation, U.S. interest in, 598–603
    Purse seine operations, 598–599, 602–603
    Suspension of Costa Rican Fisheries Decree, 601–602
    U.S. fisheries expert, Dr. Kask, mission to Costa Rica of, 598, 599–601, 603
  Lend-lease account, status of, 593–594
  Lend-lease arms, question of use for suppression of civil liberties, 596*n*
  Recognition of Nicaraguan government of Roman y Reyes, 587–589, 872–873, 877–878, 878*n*, 880
  U.S. military mission, 580, 585
  U.S. policy of nonintervention in Costa Rican internal affairs, 579, 580, 582, 585–586
Costas, German, 346*n*, 351, 353–354, 380
Crittenberger, Lt. Gen. Willis D., 686, 886, 892–913*n*, 974–975, 1049
Cruz Alonso, Rodriguez, 650, 651, 654
Cruz Ocampa, 499, 512, 515–518
Cuba, 601–628
  Brazilian sale of arms to Dominican Republic, concern over, 133–134, 135, 142–143
  Claims of U.S. nationals and protection of interests of, 608–626*n passim*; Isle of Pines Steamship Co., 606; Seatrain issue, 606–612 *passim*; Stowers claim, 607
  Communist movement in, 608, 612, 614, 620–622
  Discriminatory shipping legislation, cancellation of, 624*n*, 625
  Inter-American Conference, delegation, 16, 617–618
  Labor conditions, 607
  Lend-lease account, status of, 103, 128
  Peanut seed debt, settlement of, 608*n*
  Political situation, 620–622

Cuba—Continued
  Revolutionary expeditions against Dominican Republic based in Cuba, 643–648, 649–659, 662; Venezuelans, involvement of, 632, 644, 645, 655
  Sugar crop, 70
    Discussions and negotiations on U.S. purchase of, conditional on conclusion of treaty of friendship and establishment, 59, 604–628 *passim*
    U.S. Sugar Act of *1948*, 626–627; Cuban protests, 30–39 *passim*, 59, 615–619, 622
  Supplementary trade agreement with United States, conclusion of, 627–628
  Treaty of friendship and establishment with United States, importance, 608–624 *passim*
  U.S. merchant ships, purchase of, 619, 624–625
  U.S. policy on military assistance and armaments. *See* Armaments.
  Weather stations, agreement with United States amending and extending cooperation program agreement of *1944*, 628
Curtice, Arthur A. (Duke), 460, 462, 463–464
Czechoslovakia, severance of relations with Chile, 513–515

Daniels, Paul C., 136, 137, 139, 155–156, 660–661, 738*n*–745 *passim*, 833–836, 879–880, 1048–1050
Dawson, Allan, 4–5, 13, 22–23, 408–409, 417–418, 425–426, 437–464 *passim*, 475–476, 480, 491–492, 980, 1059
Dawson, William, 6–7, 41–51 *passim*, 656
De Diego, Mario, 888, 889, 919, 923, 945
De Golyer, E. L., 790
De Gruben, Baron, 228, 232
Despradel, Arturo, 52, 64–65, 633–644
Díaz Bialet, 238, 239, 247
Diez de Medina, Raul, 331, 385
Dodero Shipping Lines, 244, 247, 254–278 *passim*
Dominican Republic, 629–663
  Arms supply, U.S. policy (*see also* Armaments), 125, 639–662 *passim*
  Gen. Andrews Airport, disposition of, 101, 101*n*–102*n*
  U.S. transit licenses for Canadian-bought aircraft, denial of, 660–661, 667
  Communism, Dominican position on, 634–640 *passim*
  Customs convention of *1940*, termination of, and redemption of Dominican *1922* and *1926* bond issues, 663
  Economic situation, 65
  Intervention in Venezuelan affairs, 638–639, 662–663, 1054, 1055, 1056

Dominican Republic—Continued
  Invasion from Haiti, question of, 645, 656–657
  Lend-lease account, status of, 103, 127–128
  Political situation and U.S. policy of nonintervention, 629–663
    Elections, May 16, 634–635
    Trujillo government, 633–637, 645
    Revolutionary invasion based in Cuba, 643–648, 649–659, 662
      Communist influence, questions of, 652, 655
      U.N. or American Republic consultation, proposals, 650–661 passim
      U.S. citizens, alleged participation of and supplies of U.S.-bought vessels and aircraft, 631–633, 650–658 passim
      Venezuelan support of, 632, 644, 645, 655, 660–661
      Sale of arms by Brazil. See under Brazil.
    Treatment of American citizens, 659–660
    Trujillo inauguration, U.S. representation, 642, 643
    U.S. business, necessity for cooperation with Trujillo regime, 640–642
    U.S. diplomatic representative, question of levels, 636, 637
    U.S. relations, summary and recommendations, 639–640
    Venezuelan relations, 638–662 passim, 1054, 1055, 1056
Donnelly, Walter J., Ambassador to Costa Rica, 55, 58, 580–591 passim, 872–874; Ambassador to Venezuela, 131–132, 138, 587n
Dorr, Vice Consul, 362
Dreier, John C., 5–6, 13–14, 95–96, 104–105, 125–127, 221n, 233, 522, 678–680, 743
Dunn, William E., 541, 549, 550–551, 552–553
Durbrow, Elbridge, 396, 399–400, 401–402, 405, 508, 512
Dutra, Eurico Gaspar, 35, 137, 140, 142, 394–396, 433–478 passim

Echecopar Garcia, Luis, 1000, 1025, 1026
ECOSOC International Conference on Trade and Employment, Preparatory Committee, 773–774
Ecuador, 664–698
  Boundary dispute with Peru, 46–47, 84, 162
  Colombian boundary treaty, question of revision, 56
  Communist influence, questions of, 664–665
  Czechoslovak sale of arms to Ecuador, question of, 684

Ecuador—Continued
  Economic and highway development, proposals, 47, 690–698
    Consolidation Agreement (principal debts), 691
    Export-Import Bank Mission, 690–693
    Guamote-Tambo Highway project, 692, 694
    Quevedo-Manta Highway project, 667, 691–692, 693–698
    Water facilities, improvement and construction project, 690, 692–693, 698
  Galapagos bases, 676–690 passim
    Cancellation of naval training maneuvers, 686–687
    U.S. good will visit, 687–688
    Military assistance from U.S., under interim program, requests for and U.S. policy, 676–688 passim
    Participation in Inter-American Conference, effect, 69, 665, 667, 668; Suarez, 670–674
    U.S. acquisition of property, 682–683
Eisenhardt, Karl John, 1058, 1060, 1062
Eisenhower, Gen. Dwight D., 906
El Salvador:
  Military aviation mission, agreement with U.S., 699
  Military school and military academy, detail of U.S. Army officer to serve as director of, 699
  U.S. arms supply program, 661
Enciso Belloso, Guillermo, 987, 988
Engel, Albert J., 962
Emergency Advisory Committee for Political Defense, competence to include political defense against all totalitarian infiltrations, 95–100
Esguerra, Domingo, 55–56, 560n
Espinosa de los Monteros, Antonio, 799, 814
Espy, James, 139, 327–328, 352–353, 385, 670–671, 672–674, 1009, 1011, 1037
Estimé, Dumarsais, 657, 726, 735
European Recovery Program, 15, 78–79, 307–308, 314–315, 451–452, 468, 597, 1042, 1044
Export-Import Bank, see Export-Import Bank and related entries under countries.

Falck, L. James, 262, 564–567, 607, 608, 611
Falcón-Briceño, M. A., 47, 49, 136
Falkland Islands, 75
Fernandes, Raul, 56, 140, 394–403 passim, 440–441, 447, 461, 467–468, 473
Filós, Francisco A., 916, 927
Flack, Joseph, 80–81, 326–390 passim
Fleming, Maj. Gen. Philip B., 145–146, 148n
Flemming, Arthur, 950, 953, 959–960

INDEX 1075

Flota Aérea Mercante Argentina, 238, 239, 247
Food and Agricultural Organization, 316
Foreign Bondholders Protective Council, 534n–549 *passim*, 570–577 *passim*, 999–1009 *passim*
Foreign Liquidation Commission, 102, 115, 116, 518–519, 679, 681, 688, 738, 739, 740
Forrestal, James V., 103–104, 109–110, 113–115, 321, 322, 463, 772n, 965–966
Foster, William C., 476
Fournier, Ricardo, 583n, 583–584
Franczak, Wolf. *See* Utzinger, Gustav.
Freude, Ludwig, 190, 210, 215

Gainza Paz, Dr. Alberto, 319–325 *passim*
Galbraith, Willard, 357–358, 361, 362–363, 374–378, 390
Gallegos, Romulo, 1061
García, Celso Raul, 407–408, 419, 449, 450
García Sayán, Enrique, 37–38, 51–52, 83–84, 999n, 1009–1014
General Agreement on Tariffs and Trade, 627, 773–786 *passim*
Gerberich, Albert H., 79n, 155, 564–567
Góes Monteiro, Lt. Gen. Pedro Aurelio de, 54–55, 463, 464, 473
Gomez, Raul Juliet, 497n
González Muñoz, Rafael P., 16, 133, 134, 142
Gonzalez Videla, Gabriel, 498, 499–500, 501, 502, 503, 512, 533–534, 541
Grace, W. R., Company, 556–557, 559, 560
Grau San Martin, Ramón, 613, 624, 644–648 *passim*, 657
Greco, Col. John, 860, 861, 862
Greenup, Julian C., 269–276 *passim*, 290–292, 293–295, 306
Guachalla, Luis Fernando, 39, 68–69, 80–81, 329, 350n, 351, 380
Guatemala, 700–719
  Airports, U.S., reversion to Guatemala, 112–113
  Ambassador to United States (Arévalo), 58
  Armaments, comparison with neighboring countries, 661
  Inter-American Highway section, 148–149, 152–154
  Labor Code, U.S. concern over apparently discriminatory provisions, 705–719
    Employment of aliens provision (*art. 13*), 708, 711, 716
    Investment of foreign capital, probable effect on, 709–710
    Right to strike against agricultural enterprises employing *500* or more workers (*art. 243*), 708–715 *passim*

Guatemala—Continued
  Lend-lease account, status of, 700–705
  Mutual aid agreement with Guatemala, settlement of remaining U.S. obligation, 700–705
  Political situation, 707–708, 710, 713, 718–719
  U.S. armed forces in Guatemala, agreement on, 700
Guerra, Alfonso, 824
Gurney, Chan, 962, 963
Gutiérrez, Francisco de P., 587–588, 597–598
Gutierrez Vea Murguia, Guillermo, 344n, 345, 350

Haiti, 720–737
  Armaments, situation and U.S. policy on supply of, 661, 726–727
  Artibonite Valley and Hinche Plateau project, 730–731, 732, 733
  Census project, 731–732
  Cryptostegia program, 722, 723–725, 734
  Executive Agreement of *1941* re payment of *1922–1923* bonds, request for immediate termination of, 720–721, 727
  Eximbank credit of *1938*, request for readjustment of interest rate, 721–722
  Financial and other problems, 720–737
  Haitian Special Good Will Mission, 720–726, 730
  IIAA food suppy mission, 730, 733–734, 735–736
  Lend-lease account, status of, 103, 128, 736–737
  Political situation, 657
  Sanitary Mission, question of termination, 735–736
  SHADA obligation, 722, 728–729, 734
Hale, Gen. Willis F., 942
Hall, Carlos C., 332, 926, 931–932, 944–947
Halle, Louis J., Jr., 17–18, 19–20
Harnisch, Juan, 167, 190–215 *passim*
Harriman, W. Averell, 470, 471, 478
Hauch, Charles C., 139, 654–657, 659–661, 726, 728–732, 733–735, 1057
Havemeyer, J. K., 157–159, 161, 564–567
Heath, Donald R., 189–192
Hertzog, Enrique, 329, 338–339, 346–361 *passim*, 382
Hibbert, Lucien, 728–732
Highby, Leo I., 468, 469–470, 471–472, 479, 1037
Hilldring, Gen. John H., 113, 114, 117–120
Hines, Frank T., 881–904 *passim*, 914–928 *passim*, 942–949 *passim*, 960–961, 963
Holbrook, Robert G., 358–359, 361–362
Holman, Eugene, 282n, 299

Honduras, 738–745
  Armaments and military assistance, U.S. policy with respect to provision of, 661, 738–745
  Cooperative health and sanitation program agreement of *1942*, amendment and extension of, 745
  Engineering equipment, proposed purchase, 738, 740
  Inter-American Highway, 151
  Lend-lease account, status of, 739
  Nicaraguan frontier, 75
  Nicaraguan government of Roman y Reyes, position on recognition of, 867, 875–876
  Political situation, 742–743, 744
  U.S. Ambassador, appointment of (Briggs), 741–742, 742*n*
Hoover, Herbert, Jr., 460, 462, 463–464
Hoyt, Henry A., 995–996
Huezo, Rafael, 869, 870, 870*n*, 871
Hull, Cordell, 324
Human rights, protection of, U.S. position on multilateral approach to, 629–631

Independent Offices Appropriation Act, *1946*, 145, 147, 149, 153
Inter-American Coffee Agreement, 155–161
  Brazilian interests, 155, 157, 159, 160–161
  Inter-American Coffee Board, minutes of meeting of, 157–159
  National Coffee Association, 160–161
  Quota provisions, 156–157
Inter-American Conference for the Maintenance of Continental Peace and Security, Rio de Janeiro, *Aug. 15–Sept. 2, 1947*, 1–93, 643
  Appraisals, 79–93
  Argentine delegation, 21
  Argentine participation, U.S. position on, 176, 177, 194, 196, 207–208
  Cuban delegation, 16, 617–618
  Date of convocation, 4, 6, 10
  Defense zone for Americas, Mexican proposal, 56, 60, 65, 70, 89, 235
  Deliberations and decisions, 35–79
  Economic questions, postponement to Bogotá Conference, 37, 41, 45, 52, 53, 59, 80, 81, 93
  Ecuador, question of credentials, 69, 665, 667, 668
  Inter-American Social and Economic Council, proposals for economic cooperation, 37–59 *passim*, 80
  Military agency, postponement of consideration of to Bogotá Conference, 2–29 *passim*, 54, 223
  Nicaragua, discussions on representation and decision to exclude, 10–14 *passim*, 21–42 *passim*, 863–872 *passim*
  Observers to, 19–24 *passim*
  Pacific settlement procedures, question of action on, 3

Inter-American Conference for the Maintenance of Continental Peace and Security—Continued
  Preparations, 1–34
  President, Torres Bodet, 35; Soviet comments, 85–86, 87–88
  Treaty of reciprocal assistance:
    Provisions, discussions and comments on, 2–93 *passim*
    Treaty area, 59–60, 62, 75, 91–92
Inter-American Highway and Rama Road, U.S. cooperation with other governments, 145–154, 862
  Completion authorized by Pres. Truman, 146–147
  Congressional authorization, 145–153 *passim*
  Guatemalan section, 148–149, 152–154
  Honduran section, 151
  National treatment, condition for U.S. appropriation, 145–146, 147, 150, 153
  Reciprocal recognition of vehicle registration and drivers' licenses, condition of, 150
Inter-American Military Cooperation Act. See *under* Armaments and military assistance.
Inter-Governmental Maritime Consultative Organization, establishment, 254–255
International Conference of American States, *9th*, Bogotá, 93, 94, 223, 224
International Court of Justice, arbitration of Soviet refusal of visa to daughter-in-law of Chilean Ambassador, question of, 517–518
International Emergency Food Council, 304–316 *passim*, 468–479 *passim*, 1035–1044 *passim*
International Monetary Fund, 426, 447, 454, 544–545, 548–549
International Railways of Central America, 705–706, 711
International Telephone and Telegraph Corporation, 764–768, 771–772
International Trade Organization, proposed, 159, 422, 423, 424, 436, 563–564, 569, 609*n*, 773–784 *passim*
Inverchapel, Lord, 171, 220, 224–225
Isle of Pines Steamship Co., claims against Cuba, 606
Ivanissevich, Oscar, 23, 42–44, 186–189, 194–195, 197, 292–293, 310–311

Jaramillo, Esteban, 570, 571, 572
Jiménez, Enrique A., 886–888, 903, 926, 942, 944, 945, 947
Johnkoski, Vincent, 691, 693, 694, 697, 698
Johnson, Hallett, 578–579, 594–595

Kask, John L., 599–601, 603
Kempter, Charles W., 407–408, 688, 701*n*, 704
Key, David McK., 89–90, 132–143 *passim*, 393–420 *passim*, 440–441, 464, 466

Kinnear, Edwin R., 346, 349, 351, 358–359, 361–362, 690, 693
Kirk, Alan G., 227–230
Kyle, Edwin J., 707, 708, 710–713

La Follette, Robert M., 707
Lacayo Sacasa, Benjamin, 858–860, 864, 865n
Landis, James H., 241, 242, 243, 246–247, 250, 762
Leahy, Adm. William D., 475, 650
Lechin, Juan, 330
Leeper, Sir Reginald, 296–297, 323
Lie, Trygve, 20, 36
Lieberth, Juan Antonio (Hans), 198, 202–203, 209, 210
Linares Aranda, Don Francisco, 704–705
Lindner, Milton J., 808, 810–811
Livesey, Frederick, 542–543, 998, 1001
Lleras Camargo, Alberto, 13–14, 18, 38–39, 72
Lleras Restrepo, Carlos, 570, 571, 572, 572n, 573, 574, 575
López, Contreras, Gen. Eléazar, 638, 639, 645, 1054, 1056
López-Herrate, Enrique, 531–533
Lovett, Robert A., 454, 772n; Argentina, 248, 249, 271, 292–293, 307–308, 316, 319, 320; armaments, U.S. policy on supply of, 120–122, 128–129, 130, 230, 684–685; Bolivia, 388–389; Brazil, 395, 397, 420, 435–436, 455–456, 479–480; Chile, 501, 526, 549; Colombia, 561–562; Costa Rica, 602–603; Cuba, 624, 627–628, 649–650; Dominican Republic, 649–650; Ecuador, 668, 675, 684–685, 698; Guatemala, 715; Haiti, 736–737; Inter-American Highway, 149–150, 154; Mexico, 759, 760, 763–764, 768–769, 770–771, 791–792, 808, 819, 829–830, 832–833; Nicaragua, 39–40, 867–880 passim; Panama, 914, 916–917, 931, 941–942, 943; Paraguay, 994; Peru, 1015; RFC liquidation, 485–486; Rio Treaty, 90–93; Uruguay, 1048, 1051–1052
Lutes, Col. R., 904–905, 906
Lyon, Cecil B., 543–544, 977, 1009, 1057

MacLean, William G., 814–815, 823, 824, 831, 832, 833
Maffry, August, 728–732, 998, 999, 1013–1014, 1015
Magloire, Paul, 657
Maleady, Thomas J., 86–87, 131, 1054–1055, 1061
Malik, R. A., 508
Manchengo Cajas, Col. Carlos, 664–670, 681, 682, 683, 684
Manigat, Edmé, 76–77, 82
Mann, Thomas C., 165n, 166–168, 200–201
Mariaca, Guillermo, 345, 349, 350
Marques Castro, Mateo, 14–15, 36, 71–72

Marshall, George C., 147n
Argentina: Air transport agreement with United States negotiations, 248–249; corn, U.S. option on, 307; *La Prensa's 78th* anniversary, proposed congratulatory statement, 319–320; Nazi influence on, 193, 198; port discrimination in, 266; sale of arms to, U.S. policy, 217–218, 225–226, 227, 232, 233, 234–235
Bolivia: Air Transport agreement with United States, negotiations, 365–368; La Paz-Beni railway, proposed, 356–357; lend-lease account, 384, 385, 387–388; tin mine strike, safety of Americans, 336
Brazil: Discriminatory legislation, 429, 432, 439–440; lend-lease account, 409–410; petroleum problems, 466–467; property of enemy nationals, law, 486–489
Canal Zone, labor-racial relations, 948–949, 961–962
Chile: Sale of U.S. arms to, 523, 524–525; U.S. trade agreement, importance, 551
Colombia, anti-American incidents, 556–557
Costa Rican fisheries legislation, 598–599
Cuba: Dominican Republic invasion based in, 643–645; U.S. sugar bill, 30–31, 59, 615–617, 622
Dominican Republic, U.S. arms policy, 642–643, 648
Ecuador, question of recognition of Suarez regime, 672
Guatemala: Disposition of lend-lease material, 702–704; Labor Code, 706
Honduras, aircraft licensed for export to, 741n
Inter-American Coffee Agreement, 159–161
Inter-American Military Cooperation Act, 113–115
Mexico: Air Transport agreement, negotiations, 756–757; eradication of foot and mouth disease, financing of, 769; recruitment of agricultural workers from, 827–828
Nicaraguan politics, U.S. policy of nonintervention, 842–854, 859, 860, 863
Panama defense site agreement negotiations, 890, 912–913, 919–923, 928–929
Paraguay, U.S. position on mediation in, and observance of elections, 984, 985–986, 988–989
Peru: Requests for credit, 1002, 1004–1005, 1009; U.S. wheat commitments, 1036, 1038–1040, 1042–1043

Marshall, George C.—Continued
  Rio Conference, 2n, 6, 7–11, 18, 20–21, 26–27, 75–76; memos of conversations with other delegates, 41–52, 54–59, 64–72, 76–77; questions of observers to and status of Nicaraguan delegation, 23–25, 27–28, 42; summaries of conference developments, 35–36, 38–39, 40–41, 52–54, 61–64, 73–74, 77–78
  Uruguay-Argentine relations, 1046
Marshall Plan. See European Recovery Program.
Martin, William McChesney, 344–345, 449, 455
Martínez Vargas, Ricardo, 331–332, 339, 344n, 352, 353, 384, 385
Martins Pereira e Sousa, Carlos, 4–5, 6, 449, 451, 453, 454, 476–477, 975–976, 980
McBride, Robert H., 82, 732–733
McCaskill, Joseph C., 342–344
McCloy, John J., 532, 533, 543
McDonald, Augusto Charnaud, 716n, 718
McGinnis, Edgar L., 78–79, 536–538, 564–567, 1036–1038
McGraw-Warren Company, 344–363 passim
McGurk, Joseph F., 1045n
McSherry, Brig. Gen. Frank J., 948–949, 950–953, 964, 967
Mehaffey, Maj. Gen. Joseph C., 951n, 953–957, 967
Merchant, Livingston T., 245, 763n
Messersmith, George S., 163–200 passim, 219–220, 239–265 passim, 279–283, 304–306; resignation of, 201–202, 205
Mexico, 746–840
  Agricultural and other workers, arrangements for temporary migration into United States, 823–836
    Agreements of Apr. 26, 1943 and Mar. 10, 1947, and agreement superseding, Feb. 20 and 21, 1948, 832–835, 835n
    Conference, proposed, 830–831, 832
    Protocol and exchange of notes, Mar. 10, 825–829 passim
    U.S.-Mexican exchange of notes, Mar. 25 and Apr. 2, 826n
  Air transport agreement, breakdown of negotiations, 751–764; personal intervention of Pres. Truman, 753, 754–756, 757, 761n, 762, 763
  Balance of payments problems, 758, 776–797 passim
  Breadth of territorial waters, U.S. position on, 805–806, 807
  Communist influence in, 765
  Export-Import Bank loans for purchase of U.S. equipment, 764–772
    Colomilla hydroelectric power plant, 767, 768–769
    IT&T purchase of Ericsson Company, 764–768, 771–772

Mexico—Continued
  Export-Import Bank loans for purchase of U.S. equipment—Con.
    Poza Rica–Mexico City gas line project, 766, 767
  Fisheries relations with United States and exchange of views on proposed fisheries treaty, 802–811
    Publicity, probable adverse effect of, 808, 810–811
    U.S. fishing vessels, detention of, 805, 806, 807, 809n
  Flour purchased by Brazilian Army, resale to, 479
  Foot and mouth disease, joint U.S.-Mexican campaign for eradication of, 758, 793, 811–823
    Agreements and Mexican law, 813n
    Anti-American sentiment, 815
    Expenses of, 769, 813n, 815n, 817, 818–819
    Mexican-American Aftosa Commission, recommendations, 821–822
  Import restrictions, relation to revision of trade agreement with United States, 775–786
  Lend-lease obligations, discussions on, 746–751
    Acquisition of diplomatic property, 750–751
    Claims against Italy and Germany, effects of, 746–747
  Narcotic drugs, U.S. efforts to eliminate illicit traffic in, 836–840
  Nicaraguan ex-president Argüello, refuge in Mexico, 42, 876–877, 878–879
  Oil industry, U.S. policy on participation of foreign oil companies, 787–802; question of emergency reserve, 798
  Trade agreement revision, discussions, 772–786
Military assistance. See Armaments and military assistance.
Miller, Edward G., 448, 450, 772n
Mills, Sheldon T., 136–137, 341–342, 516–518, 545–547, 564–567, 667–675 passim, 697n
Miranda, Miguel, 173, 174, 219, 257, 274–314 passim, 1041
Molotov, Vyacheslav Mikhailovich, 391n
Montes y Montes, Eduardo, 370, 371
Moore-McCormack Lines, 252, 259–278 passim, 425, 437, 439
Morales, Carlos, 39, 47–49, 86–87, 136–144 passim
Morales López, Col. Oscar, 701–702, 704–705
Morínigo, Gen. Higinio, 65, 972–988 passim, 996–997
Morse, David A., 950, 951, 952
Murphy, Robert D., 202–204, 209–215, 490

Napp, Juan (Hans), 191, 198, 209, 210
Narcotic Drugs, Commission on, 839–840
Negrão de Lima, Francisco, 983–990 *passim*
Ness, Norman T., 103, 127–128, 445n, 446n, 545, 546, 547, 748–749, 998–999, 1011, 1012
Newbegin, Robert, 147n, 701–711 *passim*, 741–744n *passim*, 843–846, 875–876, 926n, 931–932, 966–967
Nicaragua, 841–880
  Armaments and military assistance, U.S. policy on provision of, 103, 844, 845–846
  Financial situation and efforts to obtain U.S. loan, 849, 850–852, 869–871, 874; Bank of America advance delayed, 844–845, 851, 865–866, 868–871
  Lend-lease account, status of, 128, 844, 845–846, 851
  Political situation and U.S. policies of nonintervention and nonrecognition, 587–589, 668, 841–880
  Argüello, election, deposition, exile, and death, 12, 841–858 *passim*, 876–879
  Costa Rica, effect of Nicaraguan situation on, 578, 579, 587–589, 872–880 *passim*
  Lacayo Sacasa regime, 859–864 *passim*, 865n
  Rio Conference, effect on representation in, 10–14, 21–31 *passim*, 39–40, 42, 863–872 *passim*
  Roman y Reyes regime, 42, 588, 589, 864–880 *passim*
  Somoza, influence on and activities in, 40, 42, 847–880 *passim*
Rama Road. *See* Inter-American Highway.
U.S. Ambassador, question of designation, 637
U.S. armed intervention, question of, 588
U.S. Military Mission, and transfer of ammunition belonging to, 860–863, 865
Nieto del Rio, Felix, 508n, 525–526, 545
Norton, Garrison, 112–113, 241–242, 268–269, 771–772, 838–839
Norweb, R. Henry, 16, 134, 135, 142–143, 607n, 609n, 620–622, 624n, 646n, 646–648, 650–651, 657
Nuñez, Ernesto, 67–68

O'Donoghue, Sidney E., 15, 165n, 166, 169–171, 226
Orloski, John A. E., 338–349 *passim*, 359–371 *passim*, 381–385
Ortega Frier, Julio, 642–657 *passim*
Ospina Pérez, Mariano, 570, 574, 575
Ostria Gutierrez, Alberto, 328, 341, 342
O'Toole, Richard F., 441–443, 449–450, 465–485 *passim*
Owen, George H., 564–567, 667–668, 670–671, 675, 687–688, 697

Pan American Airways, 101n, 102n, 102, 241, 249, 363–378 *passim*, 751–753
Pan American Union, 1–93 *passim*, 310–311
Panama, 881–971
  Canal Zone:
    Alleged discriminatory treatment of certain labor classes, discussions, 885, 924, 948–967
    Civil service positions on Panama Canal and the Panama railroad opened to Panamanians, 949, 957–958
    Draft letter for signature of the President, 963–965
    Gold and silver rolls, pay and other differentials, 950–952, 956, 960
    Interdepartmental committee, proposed, 964–967
    McCarran amendment, questions of effect, 953–957, 961–963
    Oath of allegiance to United States, requirement for civil service positions, 959–960
  Permanent market for Panamanian produce, 885, 924, 930
  Communist inspired anti-American demonstrations, 943–944, 945–946
  Defense sites agreement, negotiations, and rejection by the Panamanian Assembly, 49–51, 881–948
  Economic aid, U.S., Panamanian position on conditions of approval, 882, 884, 886, 922, 930, 932, 942–943
  Executive agreement form, questions of, 889, 890, 915
  Failure of Panamanian Assembly to ratify, 942–948
  Joint control, proposed, 881–908 *passim*, 933–934
  Rio Hato site, rental and length of lease, 883, 891–946 *passim*
  Symbolic return, proposal, 881–888 *passim*
  Text of agreement, signed *Dec. 10*, but not subsequently ratified, 932–941
  U.S. announcement, 941–942
  U.S. draft "G", 906–912
  Political situation, 891–892, 926, 944–947
  Radio communications in Panama and the Canal Zone, regulation of, and summary of proposed revised convention, 886, 967–971
  Sovereignty, U.S. recognition of and support for, 884
Paraguay, 972–997
  Air transport agreement with United States, 997
  Armaments supply, U.S. position on, 972–973, 979–980, 981–982
  Elections, provisions for observance of, 982–984, 985–986

1080 INDEX

Paraguay—Continued
  Insurrection in, U.S. position, 31, 65–66, 972–997
    Communist influence, 973–974, 985, 993, 995–996
    Inter-American mediation, questions of, 35, 42, 975–991 *passim*
    Seige of Asunción, 991–995
    U.S. military missions, effect on, 974–975, 995
  Lend-lease payment, 103, 128
  Military training in United States, 66
  Reciprocal trade agreement with United States, 997
  U.S. military aviation mission agreement renewing agreement of *Oct. 27, 1943*, 997
  U.S. military mission, agreement renewing agreement of *Dec. 10, 1943*, 997
  U.S. relations, improvement, 996–997
Patterson, Robert P., 101n–102n, 106–109, 110–112, 113–116
Pawley, William D., 28–30, 32–34, 54, 57, 167, 391–393, 406–407, 431–447 *passim*, 461–479 *passim*, 484–485, 486, 489, 491, 492
Pedregal, Guillermo del, 531, 533–535, 536–538, 538n, 539–541
Perón, Eva, 41, 52, 318, 320
Perón, Col. Juan, 21, 230–231, 257, 318; air transit agreement, position on, 239–250 *passim;* Argentine grains, availability of, 15, 307–315 *passim;* Government of, 196, 205–209; *La Prensa* anniversary, question of effect on Perón of U.S. congratulatory messages, 319–324 *passim;* Nazi connections, 187–215 *passim;* petroleum industry, protective legislation and views, 282–310 *passim*
Peru, 998–1044
  Boundary dispute with Ecuador, 38, 46–47, 84, 162
  Colombian boundary treaty, question of revision, 56
  Debt settlement conversations and Peru's need for loans, 998–1015
    Eximbank refusal of additional credit, 998–999, 1002, 1012–1015
    Montero Bernales mission of *1945*, 998–999, 1002
    Resumption of service on foreign bonds and FBAC objections, 1006–1008, 1009
  Economic and political situation, 37, 1005–1012 *passim*, 1032–1033
  Trade regulations, conflict of with U.S.-Peru trade agreement, 1015–1031
    GATT and ITO conferences, question of effect, 1024–1025
    Import, export, and foreign exchange controls, decree of *June 19*, 1013, 1025–1030

Peru—Continued
  Trade regulations—Continued
    Most-favored-nation duty rates, nonapplication by Peru to U.S. products, 1016–1017, 1021
    Taxes and charges authorized by laws antedating the trade agreement, 1017–1018, 1020–1022, 1023, 1030, 1031
    Tobacco tax law, 1018–1019, 1022–1023, 1031
  Wheat requirements, U.S. efforts to meet, 1027, 1031–1044
    Argentine wheat, attempts to obtain, 1032–1043
    Export of anthracite coal to United States, questions of, 1035
Petersen, Howard C., 113, 912
Picado, Teodoro, 586–587, 602, 872–873
Pol, Capt. German, 363–378 *passim*
Ponce, L. Neftalí, 22, 667–675 *passim*
Post, Richard H., 139–140, 564–567, 1060–1061, 1062, 1063
Prado, Jorge, 22, 1009, 1010–1011
Proclaimed List of Certain Blocked Nationals (U.S.), 378, 492, 493
Puerto Rico, alleged base for Dominican Republic invasion, 644–645

Rama Road, Nicaragua. *See* Inter-American Highway and Rama Road.
Ramsey, Adm. DeWitt C., 649–650
Ray, Guy W., 21, 31–32, 205–209, 247–248, 276–277, 283–284, 286–290, 311–312
Reconstruction Finance Corporation (U.S.), 326–342 *passim*, 485–486
Reynolds and Company, 456–457
Ridgway, Lt. Gen., M. B., 59–60
Rio Conference. *See* Inter-American Conference for the Maintenance of Continental Peace and Security.
Roberts, F. K., 234–235
Rocha, Antonio, 13–14
Rodríguez, Mario, 516–518
Rogers, James Grafton, 536–537, 541, 542–543, 549, 570, 573, 1004–1005
Román y Reyes, Victor Manuel, 42, 588n, 589, 864–880 *passim*
Royall, Kenneth C., 116n, 122n, 704n

Salazar, Joaquin E., 653–654
Sánchez Ganito, Vicente, 809, 814
Santa Cruz, Victor, 531, 536, 540–541, 542
Saugstad, J. E., 251–254, 256, 258
Schröll, Joseph (alias Alfonso Chantrain), 198, 210, 212
Scotten, Robert, 676
Seatrain Lines, Inc., 606–613 *passim*
Sevilla Sacasa, Guillermo, 588, 842–845, 865, 871–872, 879–880
Shaw, George P., 12–13, 677, 681–683, 693–695
Shields, Paul, 794, 795, 799, 800
Silva Peña, Eugenio, 707n, 708–710, 711

INDEX 1081

Simmons, John F., 25–26, 664–698 passim
Smith, H. Gerald, 105, 331, 443n
Smith, Walter Bedell, 85–86, 395, 405–406
Snyder, John W., 747n
Sohm, Earl D., 116, 122, 129
Somoza, Gen. Anastasio, 40, 42, 588, 841–880 passim
Souza Costa, Arthur de, 451, 452, 453, 454, 455
Soviet Union:
  Breach of relations with Brazil, 55, 391–406; with Chile, 512, 514, 515–516
  Influence and interests, question of, 31–32, 85–88, 206–207, 208–209
  Refusal to allow departure of Soviet daughter-in-law of Chilean Ambassador, 499, 512, 515–518
Sparks, Edward J., 14–15, 1045, 1046–1047
Spencer, George O., 139, 661–662, 704
Stafford, Maurice L., 823–826, 833
Stambaugh, Lynn, 690
Standard Fruit Company, 734–735
Standard Oil Company, 279–302 passim
Steinhardt, Laurence A., 514–515
Stenger, Jerome J., 444–447, 449, 456–458, 696, 697
Suarez Veintimilla, Mariano, 665, 666, 670–674
Sucre, Carlos, 881, 882, 890–891, 926
Sullivan, John L., 113
Symington, W. Stuart, 122–124

Taboga incident, *1920*, 50
Taillon, W. L., 712, 716, 719
Tello, Manuel, 809–810, 824
Tewksbury, Howard, 292–293, 310, 311, 313–316, 564–567
Thomen, Luis F., 660–661
Thompson, Cmdr. Edgar G., 1059
Thorp, Willard L., 101–102, 179–180, 277–278, 452, 453, 454, 455, 536–538, 554–555, 775–776, 804–807, 1011, 1012, 1013, 1014–1015, 1029
Thurston, Walter, 597n, 746–748, 750–751, 756, 757–759, 760n, 761–762, 784–791, 792–795, 798–802, 809n, 808–813, 815–819, 820–823, 829, 830–831, 839–840
Tittmann, Harold H., 726–727, 733–736
Torres Bodet, Jaime, 35, 41–42, 746–756 passim, 772n, 788, 800–801, 812, 830n, 839
Trueblood, Edward G., 66, 972–973, 974, 975, 977, 978–980, 983, 985, 986–988, 989–995
Treusch, Alberto, 198, 203–204, 209, 210
Trujillo, José Vicente, 26, 46–47, 53, 69, 665, 668, 673, 676, 686
Trujillo, Rafael Leonidas, 88–89, 131–145 passim, 633–645 passim, 652, 662, 663

Truman, Harry S.:
  Actions and position on: Air transport agreement with Mexico, personal intervention, 753, 754–756, 757, 761n, 762, 763; armaments and military assistance to Argentina, 187–189, 226n, to Mexico, 104; Dominican Republic, 634; economic problems of Europe and Latin America (address, *Sept. 2*, at Inter-American Conference), 78–79, 84; Inter-American Highway and Rama Road, authorization to resume work, 146–147; joint Brazilian-U.S. Technical Commission, approval, 455–456; Mexican-U.S. campaign against foot and mouth disease, approval of policy, 820n; resignation of Ambassador Messersmith, acceptance, 202n; Panama, 921–922
  Ambassador Ivanissevich, meetings with, 186–189, 193, 195–196, 197
  Brazil, visit to, 4–5; meeting with Pres. Dutra, 475
  Foreign press attacks, 320; Soviet press, 395
  Messages from Pres. Hertzog on Bolivian tin price, 338–339; Pres. Perón, 315

Ulate, Otillo, 578n, 589, 590–591
Ultramar Oil Company, 280–302 passim
United Fruit Company, 705–719 passim
United Kingdom:
  Argentina, relations with:
    La Prensa's 78th anniversary, congratulatory message to, 320, 323, 325
    Sale of arms to Argentina, policy on, 171, 225, 227–230, 233, 235; question of demilitarization of surplus armaments, 228–229, 230, 237
  Trade, 271, 275–276
  Axis influences in the American Republics, discussions with United States regarding, 382, 383
United Nations:
  Comparison with Inter-American system, 38–39
  General Assembly, question of consideration of problem of Soviet refusal of visa to daughter-in-law of Chilean Ambassador, 517–518
  Observer (Trygve Lie) at Rio Conference, 20, 23, 24
United States Immigration and Naturalization Service, 830, 835
Uruguay, 1045–1053
  Argentina, relations with, 1046, 1047n, 1048–1049
  Axis influence, end of campaign against, 1051–1053
  Compulsory military training, consideration of, 1047, 1049

Uruguay—Continued
  Defense needs, 1045–1050
  Human rights, *1945* proposal regarding, 630
  Lend-lease account, summary of status of, 1050–1051
  U.S. naval attaché at Montevideo, question of, 72
Utzinger, Gustav (Wolf Franczok), 189–215 *passim*

Vallarino, J. J., 892, 929–931
Vallarino, Octavio A., 881, 886, 902, 904, 926, 945
Vandenburg, Arthur H., 36, 40–41, 56, 60, 72, 75, 77, 164, 187, 914–915
Vaquero Davila, Col. Angel, 689–690
Vargas, Col. Julio Cesar, 1054, 1056
Vasconsellos, César, 997
Velasco Ibarra, José Maria, 26, 664–673 *passim*
Venezuela, 1054–1063
  Argentine foodstuffs, exchange of for Venezuelan oil, 303
  Armament levels, U.S. position, 661, 662
  Brazilian sale of arms to Dominican Republic, concern over, and proposed embargo of oil shipments to Brazil, 131–144 *passim*
  Colombian boundary treaty, question of revision, 56
  Communism in, 1060–1061
  Dominican Republic's intervention in Venezuelan affairs, 638–639, 662–663, 1054, 1055, 1056
  Election campaign, 132
  Revolutionary activity in, U.S. position on, 1054–1063; inadvisability of charging persons allegedly involved in plot, 1057–1060, 1062

Venezuela—Continued
  U.S. technical advisors (Curtice-Hoover commission), 460
Vergara, Roberto, 530, 536, 545–547, 549
Vergara Donoso, Germán, 36, 45, 505–506, 513, 550–551, 552–553
Vieira Machado, 454, 475, 476, 477, 478

Walker, William W., 606–619 *passim*, 653–654
Walters, Maj. Vernon A., 54–76 *passim*
Warner, Carlos J., 555–556, 557–558, 559–560, 573–577
Warren, Fletcher, 66n, 637, 841, 842n, 843n, 846–848, 996–997
Webb, James H., 516–518, 546–547
Wells, Milton K., 22, 152–153, 331–332, 538n, 716–719, 1002–1004, 1009, 1057
White, Wallace H., Jr., 969
Wiley, John C., 570–572
Wilson, Robert E., 704, 714–715
Wise, Murray M., 580–581, 582–586, 883–906 *passim*, 919–923, 950, 962–963
Wolf, Joseph J., 250–251, 751–753, 757, 760
Wood, C. Tyler, 768
Woodward, Robert F., 501–503, 531–533, 729–732, 1057
Woodward, Stanley, 5
Wooldridge, Rear Adm. E. T., 113
Wright, James H., 13, 166, 331, 332, 581, 617–619, 646, 653–654, 655–657, 914–915, 1000–1001, 1009, 1011, 1057

Yllescas Barreiro, Francisco, 676, 690
Yugoslavia, severance of relations with Chile, 502, 503–504, 507, 512–513

Zeller, Mozer y Cia, 379, 380
Zhukov, Dmitri Aleksandrovich, 499, 507
Zuleta Angel, Eduardo, 53–54